CIS 100 Introduction to Computers

for Pima Community College

Deborah Morley | Charles S. Parker
Gary B. Shelly | Misty E. Vermaat

CENGAGE
Learning™

Australia • Brazil • Japan • Korea • Mexico • Singapore • Spain • United Kingdom • United States

CENGAGE
Learning™

CIS 100 Introduction to Computers: for Pima Community College

Understanding Computers, Thirteenth Edition
Deborah Morley | Charles S. Parker

© 2011 Cengage Learning. All rights reserved.

Microsoft Office 2010
Gary B. Shelly | Misty E. Vermaat

© 2011 Cengage Learning. All rights reserved.

Executive Editors:
 Maureen Staudt
 Michael Stranz

Senior Project Development Manager:
 Linda deStefano

Marketing Specialist:
 Courtney Sheldon

Senior Production/Manufacturing Manager:
 Donna M. Brown

PreMedia Manager:
 Joel Brennecke

Sr. Rights Acquisition Account Manager:
 Todd Osborne

Cover Image:
 Getty Images*

*Unless otherwise noted, all cover images used by Custom
Solutions, a part of Cengage Learning, have been supplied
courtesy of Getty Images with the exception of the Earthview
cover image, which has been supplied by the National
Aeronautics and Space Administration (NASA).

For product information and technology assistance, contact us at
Cengage Learning Customer & Sales Support, 1-800-354-9706

For permission to use material from this text or product,
submit all requests online at **cengage.com/permissions**
Further permissions questions can be emailed to
permissionrequest@cengage.com

This book contains select works from existing Cengage Learning resources and
was produced by Cengage Learning Custom Solutions for collegiate use. As such,
those adopting and/or contributing to this work are responsible for editorial
content accuracy, continuity and completeness.

Compilation © 2011 Cengage Learning
ISBN-13: 978-1-133-44373-5

ISBN-10: 1-133-44373-7

Cengage Learning
5191 Natorp Boulevard
Mason, Ohio 45040
USA
Cengage Learning is a leading provider of customized learning solutions with
office locations around the globe, including Singapore, the United Kingdom,
Australia, Mexico, Brazil, and Japan. Locate your local office at:
international.cengage.com/region.

Cengage Learning products are represented in Canada by Nelson Education, Ltd.
For your lifelong learning solutions, visit **www.cengage.com/custom.**
Visit our corporate website at **www.cengage.com.**

Printed in the United States of America

Table of Contents

SAM 2010 Set-up

"Understanding Computers: Today and Tomorrow, 13e"

Chapter 1   Introduction to the World of Computers 4

Chapter 2   The System Unit: Processing and Memory 50

Chapter 3   Storage 92

Chapter 4   Input and Output 128

Chapter 5   System Software: Operating Systems and Utility Programs 176

Chapter 6   Application Software 212

Chapter 7   Computer Networks 256

Chapter 8   The Internet and the World Wide Web 298

Chapter 9   Network and Internet Security 346

Chapter 10   Multimedia and the Web 394

Chapter 11   E-Commerce 430

Chapter 12   Information Systems and System Development 466

Chapter 13   Program Development and Programming Languages 506

Chapter 14   Databases and Database Management Systems 548

Chapter 15   Computer Security and Privacy 590

Chapter 16   Intellectual Property Rights, Ethics, Health, Access and the
             Environment 632

             References and Resources Guide R-1

             Credits C-1

             Glossary/Index I-1

Microsoft OFFICE 2010 - Essential

Office 2010 and Windows 7

Chapter 1   Office 2010 and Windows 7: Essential Concepts and Skills .. OFF 1

Word 2010

Chapter 1   Creating, Formatting, and Editing and Word Document with
             Pictures .... WD 1

PowerPoint 2010

Chapter 1   Creating and Editing a Presentation with Clip Art .... PPT 1

Excel 2010

Chapter 1   Creating a Worksheet and an Embedded Chart .... EX 1

Access 2010

Chapter 1   Databases and Database Objects: An Introduction

Appendices

Appendix A   Project Planning Guidelines...................................... APP 1

Appendix B   Publishing Office 2010 Web Pages Online...................... APP 3

Appendix C   Saving to the Web Using Windows Live SkyDrive.............. APP 5

Index .... IND 1

Quick Reference Summary .... QR 1

SAM 2010

I. Initial Set Up

1. Ensure that you are connected to the Internet.

2. Launch your web browser (Internet Explorer 7 or 8, Firefox, Safari).

3. Enter http://sam2010.course.com to visit the SAM 2010 login page.

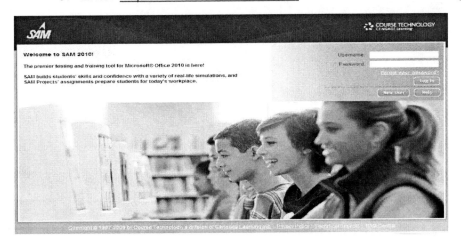

If you have a username/password: Enter your username and password in the appropriate fields, and click the **Login** button.

No username/password: Click the **New User** button; you will follow the on-screen prompts to create your SAM 2010 account

II. Pima Community College SAM Institution Key. T2031326.

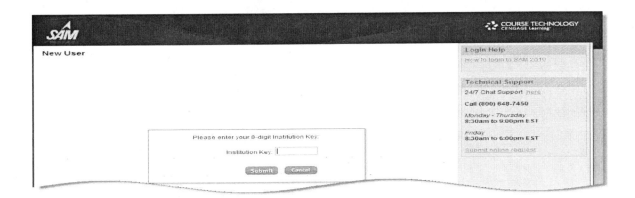

III. SAM 2010 Access code

You will enter your key code here. *This will be found inside the flap of the SAM 2010 package (card) you purchased with your textbooks.*

Click Save to go to the next screen.

NOTE: This 18-digit code is case–sensitive

IV. Create your user profile

You need to create your SAM User Profile. Enter your information in all of the required (*) fields, including a secret question and answer that will be used for security purposes should you ever forget your password. Click Save when you're done.

V. Terms and Conditions

VI. Home Screen

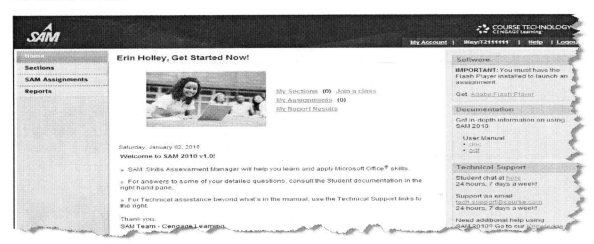

You should now see the SAM Home screen, where you will begin each SAM session. If the necessary Flash Player (v10) is not yet installed on your computer, click the links under Software to install it.

(Check with your instructor first; this may already be done for you.)

VII.   Join a Section

In order to see your SAM Assignments, you need to be enrolled in a Section (class). From the Home screen, click the Join a Class link. You can also click the Sections button (left navigation bar), then the Join a Section button.

To Join a Section, click the name of the section in the "All Sections" list on the left. Click the right arrow button to move it into "My Sections" and click **Save**.

PREFACE

In today's computer-oriented society, computers and technology impact virtually everyone's life. *Understanding Computers: Today and Tomorrow, 13th Edition* is designed to ensure that students are current and informed in order to thrive in our technologically oriented, global society. With this new edition, students not only learn about relevant cutting-edge technology trends, but they also gain a better understanding of technology in general and the important issues surrounding technology today. This information gives students the knowledge they need to succeed in today's world.

This nontechnical, introductory text explains in straightforward terms the importance of learning about computers, the various types of computer systems and their components, the principles by which computer systems work, the practical applications of computers and related technologies, the ways in which the world is being changed by these technologies, and the associated risks and other potential implications of computers and related technologies. The goal of this text is to provide readers with a solid knowledge of computer fundamentals, an understanding of the impact of our computer-oriented society, and a framework for using this knowledge effectively in their lives.

KEY FEATURES

Just like its previous editions, *Understanding Computers: Today and Tomorrow, 13th Edition* provides current and comprehensive coverage of important topics. Flexible organization and an engaging presentation, combined with a variety of learning tools associated with each chapter, help students master important concepts. Numerous marginal notations direct students to the Understanding Computers Web site where they can access **Online Videos**, **Podcasts**, **Video Podcasts**, and **Further Exploration** links, as well as other **Interactive Activities**, **Testing Activities**, **Study Tools**, and **Additional Resources**.

Currency and Accuracy

The state-of-the-art content of this book and its Web site reflect the latest technologies, trends, and classroom needs. To ensure the content is as accurate and up to date as possible, numerous **Industry Expert Reviewers** provided feedback and suggestions for improvements to the content in their areas of expertise. Throughout the writing and production stages, enhancements were continually made to ensure that the final product is as current and accurate as possible.

Comprehensiveness and Depth

Accommodating a wide range of teaching styles, *Understanding Computers: Today and Tomorrow, 13th Edition* provides comprehensive coverage of traditional topics while also covering relevant, up-to-the-minute new technologies and important societal issues, such as netbooks, graphene chips, UMPCs, 3D mice, USB monitors, Wi-Fi SD cards, and other new and emerging types of hardware; wireless power, one-time password (OTP) cards, TransferJet, Digital Copy DVDs, thin-film solar panels, portable fuel cell chargers, gesture input, and other hardware technologies; cloud computing, thumb drive PCs, and other computing concepts; new software products and technologies, such as Windows 7, Google Chrome, cloudware, Microsoft Office 2010, Android, cloud databases, column databases, and browser-based operating systems; new communications technologies, such as 4G cellular standards, emerging Wi-Fi standards, G.hn, personal mobile hotspots, and unified communications (UC); new and growing Internet applications, such as mobile voice search, Web notebooks, Twittering, social network management services, online financial alerts, business 3D worlds, lifestreaming, lifecasting, private browsing, mobile phone check deposits, user-generated content, and geobrowsing; new security threats (such as real-time credit card data theft, rogue antivirus programs, and drive-by pharming) and new security trends (such as social engineering tests, people-driven security, and two-factor authentication); new Web development technologies, such as Silverlight, HTML 5, Cascading Style Sheets (CSSs), rich Internet applications (RIAs), and Google Gears; search site optimization (SSO), Semantic Web, custom top-level domains (TLDs), crowdsourcing, and other growing systems topics; and important new societal issues, such as typosquatting, cyberbullying, and sexting.

Readability

We remember more about a subject if it is presented in a straightforward way and made interesting and exciting. This book is written in a conversational, down-to-earth style—one designed to be accurate without being intimidating. Concepts are explained clearly and simply, without the use of overly technical terminology. More complex concepts are explained in an understandable manner and with realistic examples from everyday life.

Chapter Learning Tools

1. **Outline**, **Learning Objectives**, **and Overview**: For each chapter, an **Outline** of the major topics covered, a list of student **Learning Objectives**, and a **Chapter Overview** help instructors put the subject matter of the chapter in perspective and let students know what they will be reading about.

2. **Boldfaced Key Terms and Running Glossary**: Important terms appear in boldface type as they are introduced in the chapter. These terms are defined at the bottom of the page on which they appear and in the end-of-text glossary.

3. **Chapter Boxes**: In each chapter, a **Trend** box provides students with a look at current and upcoming developments in the world of computers; an **Inside the Industry** box provides insight into some of the practices that have made the computer industry unique and fascinating; a **How It Works** box explains in detail how a technology or product works; and a **Technology and You** box takes a look at how computers and technology are used in everyday life.

4. **Ask the Expert Boxes**: In each chapter, three **Ask the Expert** boxes feature a question about a computing concept, a trend, or how computers are used on the job or otherwise in the real world along with the response from an expert. Experts for this edition include a former Navy pilot, a guitarist from a rock band, a software engineer from Walt Disney Imagineering, and executives from notable companies like McDonald's, Jack in the Box, Google, SanDisk, Kingston, Seagate, The Linux Foundation, ACM, RealNetworks, The Computer Ethics Institute, and Symantec.

5. **Marginal Tips and Caution Elements**: **Tip** marginal elements feature time-saving tips or ways to avoid a common problem or terminology mistake, or present students with interesting additional information related to the chapter content. New **Caution** elements warn of a possible problem students should avoid.

6. **Illustrations and Photographs**: Instructive, current, full-color illustrations and photographs are used to illustrate important concepts. Figures and screenshots show the latest hardware and software and are annotated to convey important information.

TIP

If your Internet connection slows down, try *power cycling* your modem and router: Unplug the modem and router for 30 seconds, then plug in the modem and wait for 30 seconds, then plug in the router.

 NEW

CAUTION CAUTION CAUTIC

When upgrading your mobile phone, be c phone to others. Before disposing of or re settings to clear all personal data from the

7. **Online Video Marginal Element**: **Online Video** marginal elements direct students to the Understanding Computers Web site to watch a short video (provided by Google, IBM, Symantec, and other companies) related to the topic in that section of the text.

8. **Video Podcast Marginal Elements**: **Video Podcast** marginal elements direct students to the Understanding Computers Web site to download and watch a practical "How To" video podcast related to the chapter content. Audio podcasts of the Expert Insight features are also available via this book's Web site.

9. **Summary and Key Terms**: The end-of-chapter material includes a concise, section-by-section **Summary** of the main points in the chapter. The chapter's Learning Objectives appear in the margin next to the relevant section of the summary so that students are better able to relate the Learning Objectives to the chapter material. Every boldfaced key term in the chapter also appears in boldface type in the summary.

10. **Review Activities**: End-of-chapter **Review Activities** allow students to test themselves on what they have just read. A matching exercise of selected **Key Terms** helps students test their retention of the chapter material. A **Self-Quiz** (with the answers listed at the end of the book) consists of ten true-false and completion questions. Five additional easily graded matching and short-answer **Exercises** are included for instructors who would like to assign graded homework. Two short **Discussion Questions** for each chapter provide a springboard to jump-start classroom discussions.

11. **Projects**: End-of-chapter **Projects** require students to extend their knowledge by doing research and activities beyond merely reading the book. Organized into six types of projects (**Hot Topics**, **Short Answer/Research**, **Hands On**, **Presentation/ Demonstration**, **Web Activities**, and a new **Ethics in Action** project), the projects feature explicit instructions so that students can work through them without additional directions from instructors. A special marginal icon denotes projects that require Internet access.

12. **Understanding Computers Web Site**: Throughout each chapter, **Further Exploration** marginal elements direct students to the Understanding Computers Web site where they can access collections of links to Web sites containing more in-depth information on a given topic from the text, as well as streaming videos and downloadable podcasts. At the end of every chapter, students are directed to the Understanding Computers Web site to access a variety of other **Interactive Activities**, as well as **Testing Activities**, **Study Tools**, and **Additional Resources**.

References and Resources Guide

A **References and Resources Guide** at the end of the book brings together in one convenient location a collection of computer-related references and resources, including a **Computer History Timeline**, a **Guide to Buying a PC**, **A Closer Look at Numbering Systems** feature, and a **Coding Charts** feature.

NEW and Updated Expert Insight Features

In this exciting feature located at the end of each module, industry experts provide students with personal insights on topics presented in the book, including their personal experiences with technology, key points to remember, and advice for the future. The experts, professionals from these major companies— **D-Link**, **Acer**, **Microsoft**, **Symantec**, **eBay**, **ACM/Google**, and **Dell**—provide a unique perspective on the module content and how the topics discussed in the module impact their lives and their industry, what it means for the future, and more!

ONLINE VIDEO

Go to the Chapter 1 page at **www.cengage.com/ computerconcepts/np/uc13** to watch the "Searching the Web on Your iPhone" video clip.

VIDEO PODCAST

Go to the Chapter 1 page at **www.cengage.com/ computerconcepts/np/uc13** to download or listen to the "How To: Control Your Computer with Twitter" video podcast.

FURTHER EXPLORATION

Go to the Chapter 1 page at **www.cengage.com/ computerconcepts/np/uc13** for links to information about computer certification programs.

Expanded Web Site Content

The **Understanding Computers Web site** includes a wealth of information at your fingertips to help enhance the classroom experience and to help students master the material covered in the book. Some of the content featured on the site includes new and updated **Key Term Matching, Self-Quizzes, Exercises,** and **Practice Tests**; interactive activities, such as **Student Edition Labs, Crossword Puzzles, Video Podcasts, Podcasts, Online Videos,** and **Further Exploration** links; and many other resources, including **Online Study Guides, Online Summaries, Online Glossaries, Expert Insights,** and **Online References and Resources Guide** content.

Student and Instructor Support Materials

Understanding Computers: Today and Tomorrow, 13ᵗʰ Edition is available with a complete package of support materials for instructors and students. Included in the package are the Understanding Computers Web site, Instructor Resources (available on CD and online), and SAM Computer Concepts.

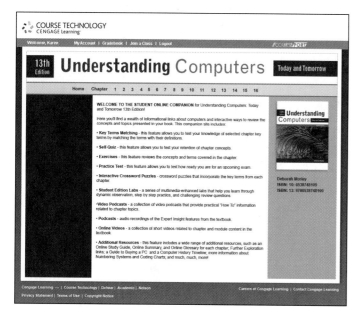

The Understanding Computers Web Site

The Understanding Computers Web site, which is located at **www.cengage.com/computerconcepts/np/uc13**, provides media-rich support for each chapter of the book. The Web site includes the following:

> **Key Term Matching**—this feature allows students to test their knowledge of selected chapter key terms.

> **Self-Quiz**—this feature allows students to test their retention of chapter concepts.

> **Exercises**—this feature reviews the concepts and terms covered in the chapter.

> **Practice Test**—this feature allows students to test how ready they are for upcoming exams.

> **Crossword Puzzles**—this feature incorporates the key terms from each chapter into an online interactive crossword puzzle.

> **Student Edition Labs**—this interactive feature reinforces and expands the concepts covered in the chapters.

> **Video Podcasts**—this feature includes several downloadable video podcasts per chapter that provide practical "How To" information related to chapter topics.

> **Podcasts**—this feature includes downloadable audio podcasts of the Expert Insight features.

> **Online Videos**—this feature includes several streaming videos per chapter related to the topics in that chapter.

> **Further Exploration**—this feature includes links to additional information about content covered in each chapter.

> **Additional Resources**—this feature includes a wide range of additional resources, such as **Expert Insights**; an **Online Study Guide, Online Summary,** and **Online Glossary** for each chapter; a **Guide to Buying a PC** and a **Computer History Timeline**; and more information about **Numbering Systems** and **Coding Charts**.

Instructor Resources

Course Technology instructional resources and technology tools provide instructors with a wide range of tools that enhance teaching and learning. These tools can be accessed from the Instructor Resources CD or at **www.cengage.com/coursetechnology**.

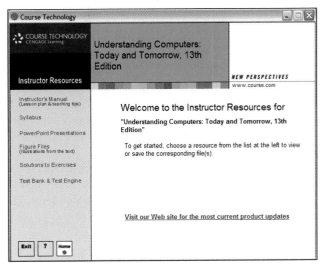

Electronic Instructor's Manual

The Instructor's Manual is written to provide instructors with practical suggestions for enhancing classroom presentations. For each of the 9 chapters in the Introductory book and 16 chapters in the Comprehensive book, the Instructor's Manual provides: **Lecture Notes**, **Teacher Tips**, **Quick Quizzes**, **Classroom Activities**, **Discussion Questions**, **Key Terms**, a **Chapter Quiz**, and more!

ExamView Test Bank

This textbook is accompanied by ExamView, a powerful testing software package that allows instructors to create and administer printed, computer (LAN-based), and Internet exams. ExamView includes 1,600 questions that correspond to the topics covered in this text, enabling instructors to create exams mapping exactly to the content they cover. The computer-based and Internet testing components allow instructors to administer exams over the computer and also save time by grading each exam automatically.

PowerPoint Presentations

This book comes with **Microsoft PowerPoint presentations** for each chapter. These are included as a teaching aid for classroom presentation, to make available to students on a network for chapter review, or to be printed for classroom distribution. Instructors can customize these presentations to cover any additional topics they introduce to the class. **Figure Files** for all figures in the textbook are also on the Instructor Resource CD.

Online Learning:

Course Technology has partnered with the leading distance learning solution providers and class-management platforms today. To access this material, Instructors can go to **www.cengage.com/coursetechnology** to visit our password-protected instructor resources. Instructor resources include the following: additional case projects, sample syllabi, PowerPoint presentations per chapter, and more. For additional information or for an instructor username and password, please contact your sales representative. For students to access this material, they must have purchased a WebTutor PIN-code specific to this title and your campus platform. The resources for students may include (based on instructor preferences) but are not limited to topic review, review questions, and practice tests.

SAM: Skills Assessment Manager

SAM 2007 is designed to help bring students from the classroom to the real world. It allows students to train and test on important computer skills in an active, hands-on environment. SAM's easy-to-use system includes powerful interactive exams, training and projects on the most commonly used Microsoft Office applications. SAM simulates the Office 2007 application environment, allowing students to demonstrate their knowledge and think through the skills by performing real-world tasks such as bolding text in Word or setting up slide transitions in PowerPoint. Add in live-in-the-application projects and students are on their way to truly learning and applying skills to business-centric documents.

Designed to be used with the New Perspectives Series, SAM includes handy page references, so students can print helpful study guides that match the New Perspectives Series textbooks used in class. For instructors, SAM also includes robust scheduling and reporting features.

ACKNOWLEDGEMENTS

We would like to extend a special thank you to all of the industry professionals who reviewed module content and provided their expertise for the **Expert Insight** features:

Introduction Module: Joe Melfi, Associate Director of Business Solutions, D-Link Systems
Hardware Module: Sumit Agnihotry, Vice President, Product Marketing, Acer Pan America
Software Module: Graham Watson, Senior Community Lead, Technical Audience Global Marketing, Microsoft
Networks and the Internet Module: Collin Davis, Senior Development Manager, Consumer Product Solutions, Symantec Corporation
Business on the Web Module: Jim Griffith, Dean of eBay Education, eBay
Systems Module: Stuart Feldman, Past President of ACM and Vice President, Engineering, Google
Computers and Society Module: Frank Molsberry, Technologist, Dell Inc.

In addition, we are very grateful to the numerous Industry Expert Reviewers that performed technical reviews and provided helpful suggestions to ensure this book is as accurate and current as possible. We would also like to thank the Educational Reviewers, who have helped to define and improve the quality of this text over the years. In particular, we would like to thank the following individuals:

Industry Expert Reviewers—13th Edition
Mike Hall, Corporate Communications, Seagate Technology
Kevin Curtis, CTO, InPhase Technologies
Sriram K. Peruvemba, Vice President, Marketing, E Ink Corporation
Jim Sherhart, Senior Director of Marketing, Data Robotics
Jack Dollard, Marketing, Mitek Systems
Joe Melfi, Associate Director of Business Solutions, D-Link Systems
Dave Gelvin, President, Tranzeo Wireless USA
Kevin Raineri, Director, Sales and Marketing, Innovative Card Technologies
Bill Shribman, Executive Producer, WGBH Interactive
Mike Markham, Vice President of Sales, Cadre Technologies
Renee Cassata, Marketing Manager, iDashboards
Russell T. Cross, Vice President of AAC Products, Prentke Romich Company
Dr. Kimberly Young, Director, The Center for Internet Addiction Recovery

Industry Expert Reviewers–Previous Editions
Jason Taylor, Worldwide Director of Corporate Communications, MobiTV; Nicole Rodrigues, Public Relations Manager, MobiTV; Stephen Yeo, Worldwide Strategic Marketing Director, IGEL Technology; Bob Hirschfeld, Public Information Officer, Lawrence Livermore National Lab; Bryan Crum, Vice President of Communication, Omnilert, LLC; David Bondurant, MRAM Product Manager, Freescale Semiconductor, Inc.; Rick McGowan, Vice President & Senior Software Engineer, Unicode, Inc.; Margaret Lewis, Director of Commercial Solutions, AMD; Mark Tekunoff, Senior Technology Manager, Kingston Technology; Billy Rudock, Customer Service Staff Engineer, Seagate Technology; James M. DePuydt, Ph.D., Technology Director, Imation Corporation; Dan Bloom, Sr. PR Manager, SanDisk; Kevin Curtis, CTO, InPhase Technologies; Gail Levy, Director of Marketing, TabletKiosk; Novell Marketing; John McCreesh, Marketing Project Lead, OpenOffice.org; Jackson Dunlap, ESP Systems; Laura Abram, Director of Corporate Marketing, Dust Networks; Kevin Schader, Communications Director, ZigBee Alliance; Mauro Dresti, Linksys Product Marketing Manager; Lianne Caetano, Executive Director, WirelessHD, LLC; Brad Booth; Howard Frazier; Bob Grow; Michael McCormack; George Cravens, Technical Marketing, D-Link; Christiaan Stoudt, Founder, HomeNetworkHelp.Info; Douglas M. Winneg, President, Software Secure, Inc.; Frank Archambeault, Director of Network Services, Dartmouth College; Adam Goldstein, IT Security Engineer, Dartmouth College; Ellen Young, Manager of Consulting Services, Dartmouth College; Becky Waring, Executive Editor, JiWire.com; Ellen Craw, General Manager, Ilium Software; Michael Behr, Senior Architect, TIBCO; Joe McGlynn, Director of Product Management, CodeGear; John Nash, Vice President of Marketing, Visible Systems; Josh Shaul, Director of Technology Strategy, Application Security, Inc.; Jodi Florence, Marketing Director, IDology, Inc.; Dr. Maressa Hecht Orzack, Director, Computer Addiction Services; Janice K. Mahon, Vice President of Technology Commercialization, Universal Display Corporation; Dr. Nhon Quach, Next Generation Processor Architect, AMD; Jos van Haaren, Department Head Storage Physics, Philips Research Laboratories; Terry O'Kelly, Technical Communications Manager, Memorex;

Randy Culpepper, Texas Instruments RFID Systems; Aaron Newman, CTO and Co-Founder, Application Security Inc.; Alan Charlesworth, Staff Engineer, Sun Microsystems; Khaled A. Elamrawi, Senior Marketing Engineer, Intel Corporation; Timothy D. O'Brien, Senior Systems Engineer, Fujitsu Software; John Paulson, Manager, Product Communications, Seagate Technology; Omid Rahmat, Editor in Chief, Tom's Hardware Guide; Jeremy Bates, Multimedia Developer, R & L Multimedia Developers; Charles Hayes, Product Marketing Manager, SimpleTech, Inc.; Rick McGowan, Vice President & Senior Software Engineer, Unicode, Inc.; Russell Reynolds, Chief Operating Officer & Web Designer, R & L Multimedia Developers; Rob Stephens, Director, Technology Strategies, SAS; Dave Stow, Database Specialist, OSE Systems, Inc.

Educational Reviewers

Marc Forestiere, Fresno City College; Beverly Amer, Northern Arizona University; James Ambroise Jr., Southern University, Louisiana; Virginia Anderson, University of North Dakota; Robert Andree, Indiana University Northwest; Linda Armbruster, Rancho Santiago College; Michael Atherton, Mankato State University; Gary E. Baker, Marshalltown Community College; Richard Batt, Saint Louis Community College at Meremec; Luverne Bierle, Iowa Central Community College; Fariba Bolandhemat, Santa Monica College; Jerry Booher, Scottsdale Community College; Frederick W. Bounds, Georgia Perimeter College; James Bradley, University of Calgary; Curtis Bring, Moorhead State University; Brenda K. Britt, Fayetteville Technical Community College; Cathy Brotherton, Riverside Community College; Chris Brown, Bemidji State University; Janice Burke, South Suburban College; James Buxton, Tidewater Community College, Virginia; Gena Casas, Florida Community College, Jacksonville; Thomas Case, Georgia Southern University; John E. Castek, University of Wisconsin-La Crosse; Mario E. Cecchetti, Westmoreland County Community College; Jack W. Chandler, San Joaquin Delta College; Alan Charlesworth, Staff Engineer, Sun Microsystems; Jerry M. Chin, Southwest Missouri State University; Edward W. Christensen, Monmouth University; Carl Clavadetscher, California State Polytechnic University; Vernon Clodfelter, Rowan Technical College, North Carolina; Joann C. Cook, College of DuPage; Laura Cooper, College of the Mainland, Texas; Cynthia Corritore, University of Nebraska at Omaha; Sandra Cunningham, Ranger College; Marvin Daugherty, Indiana Vocational Technical College; Donald L. Davis, University of Mississippi; Garrace De Groot, University of Wyoming; Jackie Dennis, Prairie State College; Donald Dershem, Mountain View College; John DiElsi, Marcy College, New York; Mark Dishaw, Boston University; Eugene T. Dolan, University of the District of Columbia; Bennie Allen Dooley, Pasadena City College; Robert H. Dependahl Jr.; Santa Barbara City College; William Dorin, Indiana University Northwest; Mike Doroshow, Eastfield College; Jackie O. Duncan, Hopkinsville Community College; John Dunn, Palo Alto College; John W. Durham, Fort Hays State University; Hyun B. Eom, Middle Tennessee State University; Michael Feiler, Merritt College; Terry Felke, WR Harper College; J. Patrick Fenton, West Valley Community College; James H. Finger, University of South Carolina at Columbia; William C. Fink, Lewis and Clark Community College, Illinois; Ronald W. Fordonski, College of Du Page; Connie Morris Fox, West Virginia Institute of Technology; Paula S. Funkhouser, Truckee Meadows Community College; Janos T. Fustos, Metropolitan State; Gene Garza, University of Montevallo; Timothy Gottleber, North Lake College; Dwight Graham, Prairie State College; Wade Graves, Grayson County College; Kay H. Gray, Jacksonville State University; David W. Green, Nashville State Technical Institute, Tennessee; George P. Grill, University of North Carolina, Greensboro; John Groh, San Joaquin Delta College; Rosemary C. Gross, Creighton University; Dennis Guster, Saint Louis Community College at Meremec; Joe Hagarty, Raritan Valley Community College; Donald Hall, Manatee Community College; Jim Hanson, Austin Community College; Sallyann Z. Hanson, Mercer County Community College; L. D. Harber, Volunteer State Community College, Tennessee; Hank Hartman, Iowa State University; Richard Hatch, San Diego State University; Mary Lou Hawkins, Del Mar College; Ricci L. Heishman, Northern Virginia Community College; William Hightower, Elon College, North Carolina; Sharon A. Hill, Prince George's Community College, Maryland; Alyse Hollingsworth, Brevard College; Fred C. Homeyer, Angelo State University; Stanley P. Honacki, Moraine Valley Community College; L. Wayne Horn, Pensacola Junior College; J. William Howorth, Seneca College, Ontario, Canada; Mark W. Huber, East Carolina University; Peter L. Irwin, Richland College, Texas; John Jasma, Palo Alto College; Elizabeth Swoope Johnson, Louisiana State University; Jim Johnson, Valencia Community College; Mary T. Johnson, Mt. San Antonio College; Susan M. Jones, Southwest State University; Amardeep K. Kahlon, Austin Community College; Robert T. Keim, Arizona State University; Mary Louise Kelly, Palm Beach Community College; William R. Kenney, San Diego Mesa College; Richard Kerns, East Carolina University, North Carolina; Glenn Kersnick, Sinclair Community College, Ohio; Richard Kiger, Dallas Baptist University; Gordon C. Kimbell, Everett Community College, Washington; Robert Kirklin, Los Angeles Harbor Community College; Judith A. Knapp, Indiana University Northwest; Mary Veronica Kolesar, Utah State University; James G. Kriz, Cuyahoga Community College, Ohio; Joan Krone, Denison University; Fran Kubicek, Kalamazoo Valley Community College; Rose M. Laird, Northern Virginia Community College; Robert Landrum, Jones Junior College; Shelly Langman, Bellevue Community College; James F. LaSalle, The University of Arizona; Chang-Yang Lin, Eastern Kentucky University; Linda J. Lindaman, Black Hawk College; Alden Lorents,

Northern Arizona University; Paul M. Lou, Diablo Valley College; Deborah R. Ludford, Glendale Community College; Kent Lundin, Brigham Young University-Idaho; Barbara J. Maccarone, North Shore Community College; Wayne Madison, Clemson University, South Carolina; Donna L. Madsen, Kirkwood Community College; Randy Marak, Hill College; Gary Marks, Austin Community College, Texas; Kathryn A. Marold, Ph.D., Metropolitan State College of Denver; Cesar Marron, University of Wyoming; Ed Martin, Kingsborough Community College; Vickie McCullough, Palomar College; James W. McGuffee, Austin Community College; James McMahon, Community College of Rhode Island; William A. McMillan, Madonna University; Don B. Medley, California State Polytechnic University; John Melrose, University of Wisconsin—Eau Claire; Dixie Mercer, Kirkwood Community College; Mary Meredith, University of Southwestern Louisiana; Marilyn Meyer, Fresno City College; Carolyn H. Monroe, Baylor University; William J. Moon, Palm Beach Community College; Marilyn Moore, Purdue University; Marty Murray, Portland Community College; Don Nielsen, Golden West College; George Novotny, Ferris State University; Richard Okezie, Mesa Community College; Joseph D. Oldham, University of Kentucky; Dennis J. Olsen, Pikes Peak Community College; Bob Palank, Florissant Community College; James Payne, Kellogg Community College; Lisa B. Perez, San Joaquin Delta College; Savitha Pinnepalli, Louisiana State University; Delores Pusins, Hillsborough CC; Mike Rabaut, Hillsborough CC; Robert Ralph, Fayetteville Technical Institute, North Carolina; Herbert F. Rebhun, University of Houston-Downtown; Nicholas John Robak, Saint Joseph's University; Arthur E. Rowland, Shasta College; Kenneth R. Ruhrup, St. Petersburg Junior College; John F. Sanford, Philadelphia College of Textiles and Science; Kammy Sanghera, George Mason University; Carol A. Schwab, Webster University; Larry Schwartzman, Trident Technical College; Benito R. Serenil, South Seattle Community College; Allanagh Sewell, Southeastern Louisiana University; Tom Seymour, Minot State University; John J. Shuler, San Antonio College, Texas; Gayla Jo Slauson, Mesa State College; Harold Smith, Brigham Young University; Willard A. Smith, Tennessee State University; David Spaisman, Katherine Gibbs; Elizabeth Spooner, Holmes Community College; Timothy M. Stanford, City University; Alfred C. St. Onge, Springfield Technical Community College, Massachusetts; Michael L. Stratford, Charles County Community College, Maryland; Karen Studniarz, Kishwaukee College; Sandra Swanson, Lewis & Clark Community College; Tim Sylvester, Glendale Community College; Semih Tahaoglu, Southeastern Louisiana University; Jane J. Thompson, Solano Community College; Sue Traynor, Clarion University of Pennsylvania; William H. Trueheart, New Hampshire College; James D. Van Tassel, Mission College; James R. Walters, Pikes Peak Community College; Joyce V. Walton, Seneca College, Ontario, Canada; Diane B. Walz, University of Texas at San Antonio; Joseph Waters, Santa Rosa Junior College, California; Liang Chee Wee, University of Arizona; Merrill Wells, Red Rocks Community College; Fred J. Wilke, Saint Louis Community College; Charles M. Williams, Georgia State University; Roseanne Witkowski, Orange County Community College; David Womack, University of Texas, San Antonio; George Woodbury, College of the Sequoias; Nan Woodsome, Araphoe Community College; James D. Woolever, Cerritos College; Patricia Joann Wykoff, Western Michigan University; A. James Wynne, Virginia Commonwealth University; Robert D. Yearout, University of North Carolina at Asheville; Israel Yost, University of New Hampshire; and Vic Zamora, Mt. San Antonio College.

We would also like to thank the people on the Course team—their professionalism, attention to detail, and enormous enthusiasm make working with them a pleasure. In particular, we'd like to thank Marie Lee, Kate Russillo, Heather Hopkins, Brandi Shailer, Leigh Hefferon, and Pam Conrad for all their ideas, support, and tireless efforts during the design, writing, rewriting, and production of this book. Thanks to Julia Leroux-Lindsey for managing the instructor resources and Ryan DeGrote and Kristen Panciocco for their efforts on marketing this text. We would also like to thank Marissa Falco for the new interior and cover design, and Tintu Thomas for all her help managing the production of the book. Thanks also to Nicole Jones Pinard.

We are also very appreciative of the numerous individuals and organizations that were kind enough to supply information and photographs for this text, the many organizations that generously allowed us to use their videos in conjunction with this text to continue to include the Online Video feature, and Daniel Davis of Tinkernut.com who kindly permitted us to incorporate his video podcasts into this edition of the text to create the new Video Podcast feature.

We sincerely hope you find this book interesting, informative, and enjoyable to read. If you have any suggestions for improvement, or corrections that you'd like to be considered for future editions, please send them to deborah.morley@cengage.com.

Deborah Morley
Charles S. Parker

BRIEF CONTENTS

Preface iii

MODULE Introduction 2
Chapter 1
Introduction to the World of Computers 4
Expert Insight on Personal Computers 46

MODULE Hardware 48
Chapter 2
The System Unit: Processing and Memory 50
Chapter 3
Storage 92
Chapter 4
Input and Output 128
Expert Insight on Hardware 172

MODULE Software 174
Chapter 5
System Software: Operating Systems and Utility Programs 176
Chapter 6
Application Software 212
Expert Insight on Software 252

MODULE Networks and the Internet 254
Chapter 7
Computer Networks 256
Chapter 8
The Internet and the World Wide Web 298
Chapter 9
Network and Internet Security 346
Expert Insight on Networks and the Internet 390

MODULE Business on the Web 392
Chapter 10
Multimedia and the Web 394
Chapter 11
E-Commerce 430
Expert Insight on Web-Based Multimedia and E-Commerce 462

MODULE Systems 464
Chapter 12
Information Systems and System Development 466
Chapter 13
Program Development and Programming Languages 506
Chapter 14
Databases and Database Management Systems 548
Expert Insight on Systems 586

MODULE Computers and Society 588
Chapter 15
Computer Security and Privacy 590
Chapter 16
Intellectual Property Rights, Ethics, Health, Access, and the Environment 632
Expert Insight on Computers and Society 678

References and Resources Guide R-1
Credits C-1
Glossary/Index I-1

CONTENTS

Preface iii

MODULE Introduction 2
Chapter 1 Introduction to the World of Computers 4

Overview 5

Computers in Your Life 5
> Why Learn About Computers? 5
> Computers in the Home 7
> Computers in Education 7
> Computers on the Job 8
> Computers on the Go 9

What Is a Computer and What Does It Do? 10
> Data vs. Information 11
> Computers Then and Now 12
> Hardware 14
> Software 16
> Computer Users and Professionals 17

Computers to Fit Every Need 19
> Embedded Computers 20
> Mobile Devices 20
> Personal Computers (PCs) 21
> Midrange Servers 25
> Mainframe Computers 26
> Supercomputers 26

Computer Networks and the Internet 27
> What Are the Internet and the World Wide Web? 27
> Accessing a Network or the Internet 29
> Surfing the Web 33
> Searching the Web 34
> E-Mail 34

Computers and Society 36
> Benefits of a Computer-Oriented Society 36
> Risks of a Computer-Oriented Society 36
> Differences in Online Communications 38
> The Anonymity Factor 39
> Information Integrity 39

Summary 40

Review Activities 42

Projects 44

TECHNOLOGY AND YOU M-Learning on Campus 9

TREND Cloud Computing 19

INSIDE THE INDUSTRY Mobile Phone Use on the Job? 22

HOW IT WORKS Campus Emergency Notification Systems 32

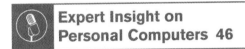

Expert Insight on Personal Computers 46

MODULE Hardware 48
Chapter 2 The System Unit: Processing and Memory 50

Overview 51

Data and Program Representation 51
> Digital Data Representation 51
> Representing Numerical Data: The Binary Numbering System 52
> Coding Systems for Text-Based Data 53
> Coding Systems for Other Types of Data 54
> Representing Software Programs: Machine Language 56

Inside the System Unit 56
> The Motherboard 56
> The Power Supply and Drive Bays 57
> The CPU 58
> Memory 62
> Fans, Heat Sinks, and Other Cooling Components 65
> Expansion Slots, Expansion Cards, and ExpressCard Modules 66
> Buses 68
> Ports and Connectors 70

How the CPU Works 72
> Typical CPU Components 72
> The System Clock and the Machine Cycle 75

Making Computers Faster and Better Now and in the Future 76
> Improving the Performance of Your System Today 77
> Strategies for Making Faster and Better Computers 79
> Future Trends 81

Summary 86
Review Activities 88
Projects 90

HOW IT WORKS Watson, the Ultimate Future *Jeopardy!* Contestant 59
INSIDE THE INDUSTRY Moore's Law 74
TREND High-Tech Investigators 75
TECHNOLOGY AND YOU The "Morph" Concept 82

Chapter 3 Storage 92
Overview 93
Storage Systems Characteristics 93
> Storage Media and Storage Devices 93
> Volatility 94
> Random vs. Sequential Access 94

> Logical vs. Physical Representation 95
> Type of Storage Technology Used 96

Hard Drives 96
> Magnetic Hard Drives and Solid-State Drives (SSDs) 96
> Internal and External Hard Drives 102
> Hard Drive Speed, Disk Caching, and Hybrid Hard Drives 103
> Hard Drive Partitioning and File Systems 104
> Hard Drive Interface Standards 105

Optical Discs 105
> Optical Disc Characteristics 105
> Read-Only Optical Discs: CD-ROM, DVD-ROM, and BD-ROM Discs 108
> Recordable Optical Discs: CD-R, DVD-R, DVD+R, and BD-R Discs 108
> Rewritable Optical Discs: CD-RW, DVD-RW, DVD+RW, and BD-RE Discs 109

Flash Memory 110
> Flash Memory Cards 110
> USB Flash Drives 112

Other Types of Storage Systems 114
> Network Storage and Online/Cloud Storage Systems 114
> Smart Cards 116
> Holographic Storage 117
> Storage Systems for Large Computer Systems 118

Evaluating Your Storage Alternatives 121
Summary 122
Review Activities 124
Projects 126

HOW IT WORKS Flash Memory 98
INSIDE THE INDUSTRY Data Recovery Experts 101
TREND IronKey: The World's Most Secure USB Flash Drive 110
TECHNOLOGY AND YOU Thumb Drive PCs 113

Chapter 4 Input and Output 128
Overview 129
Keyboards 129
Pointing and Touch Devices 131
> Mice 131
> Pens/Styluses 132
> Touch Screens 135
> Other Pointing Devices 136
Scanners, Readers, and Digital
   Cameras 138
> Scanners 139
> Readers 140
> Digital Cameras 146
Audio Input 148
> Voice Input and Speech Recognition
   Systems 148
> Music Input Systems 150
Display Devices 150
> Display Device Characteristics 150
> Flat-Panel Display Technologies 155
> Data and Multimedia Projectors 158
Printers 159
> Printer Characteristics 159
> Laser Printers 161
> Ink-Jet Printers 162
> Special-Purpose Printers 163
Audio Output 165
Summary 166
Review Activities 168
Projects 170

TREND Gesture Input 133
HOW IT WORKS Touch Screens 138
TECHNOLOGY AND YOU Mobile Phone
   Check Deposits 145
INSIDE THE INDUSTRY E-Paper 156

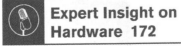

**Expert Insight on
Hardware 172**

MODULE Software 174
Chapter 5 System Software: Operating
Systems and Utility Programs 176
Overview 177
System Software vs. Application
   Software 177
The Operating System 178
> Functions of an Operating System 178
> Processing Techniques for Increased
   Efficiency 182
> Differences Among Operating
   Systems 185
Operating Systems for Personal Computers
   and Servers 188
> DOS 188
> Windows 188
> Mac OS 192
> UNIX 193
> Linux 193
Operating Systems for Mobile Phones
   and Other Devices 194
> Mobile and Embedded Versions
   of Windows 194
> Android 196
> iPhone OS 197
> BlackBerry OS 197
> Palm OS and Palm webOS 197
> Symbian OS 197
> Embedded Linux 198
Operating Systems for Larger
   Computers 198
Utility Programs 198
> File Management Programs 198
> Search Tools 201
> Diagnostic and Disk Management
   Programs 202
> Uninstall and Cleanup Utilities 202
> File Compression Programs 203
> Backup and Recovery Utilities 203
> Antivirus, Antispyware, Firewalls,
   and Other Security Programs 204

The Future of Operating Systems 205
Summary 206
Review Activities 208
Projects 210

TREND SideShow and Smart Notebook Covers 187
INSIDE THE INDUSTRY Smart Cars 195
HOW IT WORKS Downloading and Installing Programs 199
TECHNOLOGY AND YOU The Browser OS 205

Chapter 6 Application Software 212
Overview 213
The Basics of Application Software 213
> Software Ownership Rights 213
> Desktop vs. Mobile Software 217
> Installed vs. Web-Based Software 217
> Software Suites 220
> Common Software Commands 221
Word Processing Concepts 225
> What Is Word Processing? 225
> Creating a Word Processing Document 227
> Tables, Graphics, and Templates 229
> Word Processing and the Web 229
Spreadsheet Concepts 230
> What Is a Spreadsheet? 230
> Creating a Spreadsheet 230
> Charts and What-If Analysis 233
> Spreadsheets and the Web 233
Database Concepts 234
> What Is a Database? 234
> Creating a Database 235
> Queries and Reports 236
> Databases and the Web 237
Presentation Graphics Concepts 237
> What Is a Presentation Graphic? 237
> Creating a Presentation 238
> Finishing a Presentation 239
> Presentation Graphics and the Web 239
Graphics and Multimedia Concepts 240
> Graphics Software 240
> Audio Capture and Editing Software 241
> Video Editing and DVD Authoring Software 242
> Media Players 243
> Graphics, Multimedia, and the Web 243
Other Types of Application Software 243
> Desktop and Personal Publishing Software 243
> Educational, Entertainment, and Reference Software 244
> Note Taking Software and Web Notebooks 244
> CAD and Other Types of Design Software 244
> Accounting and Personal Finance Software 245
> Project Management, Collaboration, and Remote Access Software 245
Summary 246
Review Activities 248
Projects 250

INSIDE THE INDUSTRY Open Source Software 215
TECHNOLOGY AND YOU Mobile Voice Search 220
TREND Microsoft Office 2010 223
HOW IT WORKS Windows Vista Speech Recognition with Microsoft Word 226

 Expert Insight on Software 252

MODULE Networks and the Internet 254

Chapter 7 Computer Networks 256

Overview 257

What Is a Network? 257

Networking Applications 258
> The Internet 258
> Telephone Service 259
> Television and Radio Broadcasting 260
> Global Positioning System (GPS) Applications 260
> Monitoring Systems 261
> Multimedia Networking 262
> Videoconferencing, Collaborative Computing, and Telecommuting 263
> Telemedicine 264

Network Characteristics 265
> Wired vs. Wireless Networks 265
> Network Topologies 266
> Network Architectures 267
> Network Size and Coverage Area 268

Data Transmission Characteristics 270
> Bandwidth 270
> Analog vs. Digital Signals 271
> Transmission Type and Timing 271
> Delivery Method 272

Networking Media 273
> Wired Networking Media 273
> Wireless Networking Media 275

Communications Protocols and Networking Standards 278
> TCP/IP and Other Communications Protocols 278
> Ethernet (802.3) 279
> Phoneline, Powerline, G.hn, and Broadband over Powerline (BPL) 280
> Wi-Fi (802.11) 281
> WiMAX and Mobile WiMAX 283
> Cellular Standards 283
> Bluetooth, Ultra Wideband (UWB), and Other Short-Range Wireless Standards 284

Networking Hardware 287
> Network Adapters and Modems 287
> Switches, Routers, and Other Hardware for Connecting Devices and Networks 288
> Other Networking Hardware 289

Summary 292

Review Activities 294

Projects 296

INSIDE THE INDUSTRY Wireless Power 258

HOW IT WORKS Connecting to a Wi-Fi Hotspot 266

TECHNOLOGY AND YOU Wi-Fi SD Cards 282

TREND Personal Mobile Hotspots 291

Chapter 8 The Internet and the World Wide Web 298

Overview 299

Evolution of the Internet 299
> From ARPANET to Internet2 299
> The Internet Community Today 302
> Myths About the Internet 304

Getting Set Up to Use the Internet 305
> Type of Device 305
> Type of Connection and Internet Access 307
> Selecting an ISP and Setting Up Your Computer 311

Searching the Internet 312
> Search Sites 312
> Search Strategies 314
> Evaluating Search Results 316
> Citing Internet Resources 317

Beyond Browsing and E-Mail 317
> Other Types of Online Communications 317
> Social Networking 321
> Online Shopping and Investing 324
> Online Entertainment 325

> Online News, Reference, and
Information 328
> Online Education and Writing 331
Censorship and Privacy Issues 334
> Censorship 335
> Web Browsing Privacy 336
> E-Mail Privacy 339
Summary 340
Review Activities 342
Projects 344

INSIDE THE INDUSTRY ISP Bandwidth
Limits 306
TREND Geobrowsing 319
TECHNOLOGY AND YOU Social
Networking Management Services 323
HOW IT WORKS Podcasting 330

Chapter 9 Network and Internet
Security 346

Overview 347
Why Be Concerned About Network
and Internet Security? 347
Unauthorized Access and Unauthorized
Use 348
> Hacking 348
> War Driving and Wi-Fi Piggybacking 350
> Interception of Communications 351
Protecting Against Unauthorized Access
and Unauthorized Use 351
> Access Control Systems 351
> Firewalls, Encryption, and Virtual Private
6
spot Precautions 361
recautions 361
64

d Other
4
S) Attacks 367
eb Site Alteration 368

Protecting Against Computer
Sabotage 369
> Security Software 369
> Other Security Precautions 370
Online Theft, Online Fraud, and Other Dot
Cons 370
> Theft of Data, Information, and Other
Resources 371
> Identity Theft, Phishing, and
Pharming 372
> Online Auction Fraud 375
> Other Internet Scams 376
Protecting Against Online Theft, Online
Fraud, and Other Dot Cons 377
> Protecting Against Data and Information
Theft 377
> Protecting Against Identity Theft, Phishing,
and Pharming 377
> Protecting Against Online Auction Fraud
and Other Internet Scams 380
Personal Safety Issues 381
> Cyberbullying and Cyberstalking 381
> Online Pornography 382
Protecting Against Cyberbullying,
Cyberstalking, and Other Personal Safety
Concerns 382
> Safety Tips for Adults 382
> Safety Tips for Children and Teens 382
Network and Internet Security
Legislation 383
Summary 384
Review Activities 386
Projects 388

HOW IT WORKS Securing a Wireless
Home Router 357
TREND Evil Twins 362
INSIDE THE INDUSTRY New Tools
to Fight Malware 371
TECHNOLOGY AND YOU Online
Financial Alerts 379

**Expert Insight on Networks
and the Internet 390**

MODULE Business on the Web 392

Chapter 10 Multimedia and the Web 394

Overview 395

What Is Web-Based Multimedia? 395
> Why Learn About Web-Based Multimedia? 395
> Web-Based Multimedia Applications 396
> Advantages and Disadvantages of Using Web-Based Multimedia 398

Multimedia Elements 399
> Text 400
> Images 400
> Animation 404
> Audio 404
> Video 405

Multimedia Web Site Design 407
> Basic Design Principles 408
> Determining the Objectives and Intended Audience of the Site 409
> Using Flowcharts, Page Layouts, and Storyboards 410
> Navigational Design Considerations 411
> Access Considerations 412

Multimedia Web Site Development 414
> Creating the Multimedia Elements 414
> Creating the Web Site 414
> Testing, Publishing, and Maintaining the Site 422

The Future of Web-Based Multimedia 423

Summary 424
Review Activities 426
Projects 428

INSIDE THE INDUSTRY Business 3D Worlds 399
HOW IT WORKS MP3 Compression 406
TECHNOLOGY AND YOU Lifestreaming and Lifecasting 407
TREND Mashup Sites 420

Chapter 11 E-Commerce 430

Overview 431

What Is E-Commerce? 431
> Advantages of E-Commerce 432
> Disadvantages of E-Commerce 435

E-Commerce Business Models 436
> Business-to-Consumer (B2C) Business Model 437
> Business-to-Business (B2B) Business Model 437
> Consumer-to-Consumer (C2C) Business Model 437
> Business-to-Government (B2G) Business Model 437

Types of E-Commerce Web Sites 438
> Manufacturer and E-Tailer Sites 438
> Subscription Sites 438
> Brokerage Sites 438

Implementing Web-Based E-Commerce 440
> Step 1: Select Appropriate Business Models and Types of Web Sites 441
> Step 2: Select the Desired E-Commerce Applications 441
> Step 3: Develop Procedures for Handling Electronic Financial Transactions 441
> Step 4: Design and Develop an Effective E-Commerce Web Site 447
> Step 5: Implement Appropriate Sales and Marketing Strategies 449

Security Issues 455

Summary 456
Review Activities 458
Projects 460

HOW IT WORKS Buying Customized Products Online 434
TREND Mobile Coupons 446
TECHNOLOGY AND YOU Creating and Sharing an Online Store with Cartfly 450
INSIDE THE INDUSTRY Click Fraud 455

 Expert Insight on Web-Based Multimedia and E-Commerce 462

MODULE Systems 464

Chapter 12 Information Systems and System Development 466

Overview 467

What Is an Information System? 467
> The Need for System Development 468
> Enterprise Architecture 468
> Business Intelligence (BI) 469
> Information Systems Users 469

Types of Information Systems 471
> Office and User Productivity Support Systems 471
> Transaction Processing Systems (TPSs) 472
> Decision Making Support Systems 473
> Integrated Enterprise Systems 475
> Design and Manufacturing Systems 477
> Artificial Intelligence Systems 478

Responsibility for System Development 484
> The Information Systems (IS) Department 484
> Outsourcing 485

The System Development Life Cycle (SDLC) 488
> Preliminary Investigation 488
> System Analysis 489
> System Design 492
> System Acquisition 493
> System Implementation 495
> System Maintenance 497

Approaches to System Development 498
> The Traditional Approach 498
> The Iterative Approach 499
> The End-User Development Approach 499

Summary 500

Review Activities 502

Projects 504

HOW IT WORKS Digital Dashboards 470
INSIDE THE INDUSTRY The Turing Test and the Loebner Prize 478
TECHNOLOGY AND YOU Avoiding Common Job Hunting Mistakes 486
TREND Crowdsourcing 487

Chapter 13 Program Development and Programming Languages 506

Overview 507

Approaches to Program Design and Development 507
> Procedural Programming 507
> Object-Oriented Programming (OOP) 509
> Aspect-Oriented Programming (AOP) 510
> Adaptive Software Development 510

The Program Development Life Cycle (PDLC) 511
> Problem Analysis 511
> Program Design 512
> Program Coding 520
> Program Debugging and Testing 523
> Program Implementation and Maintenance 528

Tools for Facilitating Program Development 528
> Application Lifecycle Management (ALM) Tools 528
> Application Generators 529
> Device Software Development Tools 530
> Software Development Kits (SDKs) and Application Program Interfaces (APIs) 530
> Rich Internet Application (RIA) Tools 531

Programming Languages 531
> What Is a Programming Language? 531
> Categories of Programming Languages 532
> Common Programming Languages 535

Summary 542
Review Activities 544
Projects 546

TECHNOLOGY AND YOU Programming
Contests 521
INSIDE THE INDUSTRY The Original
Program "Bug" 523
TREND Google Gears 532
HOW IT WORKS Visual Basic 539

Chapter 14 Databases and Database
Management Systems 548
   Overview 549
   What Is a Database? 549
      > A Simple Relational Database
        Example 550
      > Individuals Involved with a Database
        Management System 551
      > The Evolution of Databases 553
      > Advantages and Disadvantages of the
        DBMS Approach 553
   Data Concepts and Characteristics 555
      > Data Hierarchy 555
      > Entities and Entity Relationships 555
      > Data Definition 556
      > The Data Dictionary 557
      > Data Integrity, Security, and Privacy 558
      > Data Organization 562
   Database Classifications 564
      > Single-User vs. Multiuser Database
        Systems 564
      > Client-Server and N-Tier Database
        Systems 564
      > Centralized vs. Distributed Database
        Systems 565
      > Disk-Based vs. In-Memory Database
        Systems 566
   Database Models 566
      > The Hierarchical and Network Database
        Models 566
      > The Relational Database Model 567

      > The Object-Oriented Database Model 574
      > Hybrid Database Models 575
      > Multidimensional Databases 576
   Databases and the Web 576
      > Examples of Web Databases in Use 576
      > How Web Databases Work 578
Summary 580
Review Activities 582
Projects 584

INSIDE THE INDUSTRY File
Management Systems 554
HOW IT WORKS Column
Databases 563
TREND Cancer Research
Databases 575
TECHNOLOGY AND YOU
Microtargeting 577

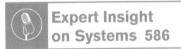

Expert Insight
on Systems 586

MODULE Computers and Society 588

Chapter 15 Computer Security
and Privacy 590
   Overview 591
   Why Be Concerned about Computer
      Security? 591
   Hardware Loss, Hardware Damage,
      and System Failure 591
      > Hardware Loss 592
      > Hardware Damage 592
      > System Failure and Other Disasters 592
      > Protecting Against Hardware Loss,
        Hardware Damage, and System
        Failure 593

Software Piracy and Digital
Counterfeiting 602
> Software Piracy 602
> Digital Counterfeiting 603
> Protecting Against Software Piracy
and Digital Counterfeiting 604
Why Be Concerned About Information
Privacy? 606
Databases, Electronic Profiling, Spam, and
Other Marketing Activities 607
> Databases and Electronic Profiling 607
> Spam and Other Marketing Activities 610
> Protecting the Privacy of Personal
Information 611
Electronic Surveillance and Monitoring 616
> Computer Monitoring Software 617
> Video Surveillance 619
> Employee Monitoring 621
> Presence Technology 622
> Protecting Personal and Workplace
Privacy 623
Computer Security and Privacy
Legislation 624
Summary 626
Review Activities 628
Projects 630

TREND Social Engineering Tests 594
HOW IT WORKS Self-Destructing
Devices 596
TECHNOLOGY AND YOU Protecting
Your PC 600
INSIDE THE INDUSTRY Data Killers 617

Chapter 16 Intellectual
Property Rights, Ethics, Health,
Access, and the Environment 632
Overview 633
Intellectual Property Rights 633
> Copyrights 634
> Trademarks 635
> Patents 637

Ethics 638
> Ethical Use of Copyrighted
Material 640
> Ethical Use of Resources and
Information 643
> Computer Hoaxes and Digital
Manipulation 647
> Ethical Business Practices and Decision
Making 649
Computers and Health 652
> Physical Health 652
> Emotional Health 658
Access to Technology 661
> The Digital Divide 661
> Assistive Technology 664
Environmental Concerns 666
> Green Computing 666
> Recycling and Disposal of
Computing Equipment 668
Related Legislation 671
Summary 672
Review Activities 674
Projects 676

INSIDE THE INDUSTRY High-Tech
Anticounterfeiting Systems 636
TECHNOLOGY AND YOU Virtual Gold
and Income Taxes 639
HOW IT WORKS Digital Copy
Movies 644
TREND Portable Fuel Cell
Chargers 670

 **Expert Insight on Computers
and Society 678**

References and Resources Guide R-1

Computer History Timeline R-2
  Guide to Buying a PC R-8
    > Analyzing Needs R-8
    > Listing Alternatives R-9
  A Look at Numbering Systems R-11
    > The Decimal and Binary Numbering System R-11
    > The Hexadecimal Numbering System R-11
    > Converting Between Numbering Systems R-12
    > Computer Arithmetic R-13
    > Using a Scientific Calculator R-14
  Coding Charts R-15
    > ASCII and EBCDIC R-15
    > Unicode R-16
  Answers to Self-Quiz R-17

Credits C-1
Glossary/Index I-1

UNDERSTANDING COMPUTERS:
TODAY AND TOMORROW

⏻ module

Introduction

Today, computers are virtually everywhere in our society. People encounter and use computers and computing technology many times during the average day. Individuals use personal computers and mobile devices both at home and while on the go to perform a variety of important daily tasks, such as to pay bills, shop, manage investments, communicate with others, research products, make travel arrangements, check current news and weather, look up phone numbers, and view maps of locations. Individuals also increasingly use these devices for a growing number of entertainment purposes, such as playing games, downloading and listening to music, and watching TV shows. Businesses, schools, government agencies, and other organizations use computers and related technologies to facilitate day-to-day transactions, provide better services to customers, communicate with others, retrieve and disseminate information, and assist managers in making good decisions. Because they are so embedded in our society today, it is essential for everyone to know something about computers and what they can do.

This module introduces you to computers and some of their uses. Chapter 1 helps you to understand what computers are, how they work, and how people use them today. Chapter 1 also provides an overview of common computer terms and concepts that you will encounter throughout this text, as well as gives you a brief look at how to use a computer to perform basic tasks and to access resources on the Internet and the World Wide Web.

Chapter 1
Introduction to the World of Computers 4

Overview 5

Computers in Your Life 5

What Is a Computer and What Does It Do? 10

Computers to Fit Every Need 19

Computer Networks and the Internet 27

Computers and Society 36

"Embrace computers as productivity tools and entertainment appliances, in whatever form they take."

For more comments from Guest Expert **Joe Melfi** of D-Link Systems, see the **Expert Insight on . . . Personal Computers** feature at the end of the module.

chapter 1

Introduction to the World of Computers

After completing this chapter, you will be able to do the following:

1. Explain why it is essential to learn about computers today and discuss several ways computers are integrated into our business and personal lives.

2. Define a computer and describe its primary operations.

3. List some important milestones in computer evolution.

4. Identify the major parts of a personal computer, including input, processing, output, storage, and communications hardware.

5. Define software and understand how it is used to instruct the computer what to do.

6. List the six basic types of computers, giving at least one example of each type of computer and stating what that computer might be used for.

7. Explain what a network, the Internet, and the World Wide Web are, as well as how computers, people, and Web pages are identified on the Internet.

8. Describe how to access a Web page and navigate through a Web site.

9. Discuss the societal impact of computers, including some benefits and risks related to their prominence in our society.

outline

Overview

Computers in Your Life
Why Learn About Computers?
Computers in the Home
Computers in Education
Computers on the Job
Computers on the Go

What Is a Computer and What Does It Do?
Data vs. Information
Computers Then and Now
Hardware
Software
Computer Users and Professionals

Computers to Fit Every Need
Embedded Computers
Mobile Devices
Personal Computers (PCs)
Midrange Servers
Mainframe Computers
Supercomputers

Computer Networks and the Internet
What Are the Internet and the World Wide Web?
Accessing a Network or the Internet
Surfing the Web
Searching the Web
E-Mail

Computers and Society
Benefits of a Computer-Oriented Society
Risks of a Computer-Oriented Society
Differences in Online Communications
The Anonymity Factor
Information Integrity

OVERVIEW

Computers and other forms of technology impact our daily lives in a multitude of ways. We encounter computers in stores, restaurants, and other retail establishments. We use computers and the Internet regularly to obtain information, experience online entertainment, buy products and services, and communicate with others. Many of us carry a mobile phone or other mobile device with us at all times so we can remain in touch with others on a continual basis and can access Internet information as we need it. It is even possible to use these portable devices to pay for purchases, play online games with others, watch TV and movies, and much, much more.

Businesses also use computers extensively, such as to maintain employee and customer records, manage inventories, maintain online stores and other Web sites, process sales, control robots and other machines in factories, and provide business executives with the up-to-date information they need to make decisions. The government uses computers to support our nation's defense systems, for space exploration, for storing and organizing vital information about citizens, for law enforcement and military purposes, and other important tasks. In short, computers and computing technology are used in an endless number of ways.

Understanding Computers: Today and Tomorrow is a guide to computers and related technology and how they are being used in the world today. It will provide you with a comprehensive introduction to computer concepts and terminology and give you a solid foundation for any future courses you may take that are related to computers or their use in the world today. It will also provide you with the basic knowledge you need to understand and use computers in school, on the job, and in your personal life, as well as give you an overview of the various societal issues related to technology, such as security and privacy issues, ethical considerations, and environmental concerns.

Chapter 1 is designed to help you understand what computers are, how they work, and how people use them. It introduces the important terms and concepts that you will encounter throughout this text and in discussions about computers with others, as well as includes an overview of the history of computers. It also takes a brief look at how to use a computer to perform basic tasks and to access resources on the Internet and the World Wide Web, in order to provide you with the knowledge, skills, and tools you need to complete the projects and online activities that accompany this textbook. The chapter closes with an overview of the societal impact of computers. ■

COMPUTERS IN YOUR LIFE

Computers today are used in virtually every aspect of most individuals' lives—at home, at school, at work, and while on the go. The next few sections provide an overview of the importance of computers and some of the most common computer-related activities that individuals may encounter every day.

Why Learn About Computers?

Fifty years ago, computers were used primarily by researchers and scientists. Today, computers are an integral part of our lives. Experts call this trend *pervasive computing*, in which few aspects of daily life remain untouched by computers and computing technology. With pervasive computing—also referred to as *ubiquitous computing*—computers are found virtually everywhere and computing technology is integrated into an ever-increasing number of devices to give those devices additional functionality, such as enabling them to communicate with other devices on an on-going basis. Because of the prominence of computers in our society, it is important to understand what a computer is, a little about how a computer works, and the implications of living in a computer-oriented society.

Prior to about 1980, computers were large and expensive, and few people had access to them. Most computers used in organizations were equipped to do little more than carry out high-volume processing tasks, such as issuing bills and keeping track of product inventories. The average person did not need to know how to use a computer for his or her job, and it was uncommon to have a computer at home. Furthermore, the use of computers generally required a lot of technical knowledge and the use of the *Internet* was reserved primarily for researchers and educational institutions. Because there were few good reasons or opportunities for learning how to use computers, the average person was unfamiliar with them.

Beginning in the early 1980s, things began to change. *Microcomputers*—inexpensive *personal computers* that you will read about later in this chapter—were invented and computer use increased dramatically. The creation of the *World Wide Web* (*WWW*) in the late 1980s and the graphical *Web browser* in the 1990s brought personal computing to a whole new level and began the trend of individuals buying and using computers for personal use. Today, more than 80% of all U.S. households include a personal computer, and most individuals use some type of computer on the job. Whether you become a teacher, attorney, doctor, engineer, restaurant manager, salesperson, professional athlete, musician, executive, or skilled tradesperson, you will likely use a computer to obtain and evaluate information, to facilitate necessary on-the-job tasks, and to communicate with others. Today's computers are very useful tools for these purposes; they are also taking on new roles in our society, such as delivering entertainment on demand. In fact, computers and the traditional communication and entertainment devices that we use every day—such as telephones, televisions, and home entertainment systems—are *converging* into single units with multiple capabilities. For instance, you can check your *e-mail* (electronic messages), watch videos, and view other Internet content on your living room TV; you can make telephone calls via your personal computer; and you can view Internet content and watch TV on your *mobile phone*. As a result of this *convergence* trend (see Figure 1-1), the personal computer has moved beyond an isolated productivity tool to become an integral part of our daily lives.

Just as you can learn to drive a car without knowing much about car engines, you can learn to use a computer without understanding the technical details of how a computer works.

FIGURE 1-1

Convergence.

Today's computers typically take on the role of multiple devices.

However, a little knowledge gives you a big advantage. Knowing something about cars can help you make wise purchasing decisions and save money on repairs. Likewise, knowing something about computers can help you buy the right one for your needs, get the most efficient use out of it, be able to properly *upgrade* it as your needs change, and have a much higher level of comfort and confidence along the way. Therefore, basic **computer literacy**—knowing about and understanding computers and their uses—is an essential skill today for everyone.

MOBILE DEVICES
Typically include the functions of a telephone, organizer, digital media player, gaming device, Web browser, and digital camera.

HOME COMPUTERS
Can often be used as a telephone, television, and stereo system, in addition to their regular computing functions.

>**Computer literacy.** The knowledge and understanding of basic computer fundamentals.

Computers in the Home

Home computing has increased dramatically over the last few years as computers and Internet access have become less expensive and as an increasing number of computer-related consumer activities have become available. Use of the Internet at home to look up information, exchange e-mail, shop, watch TV and videos, download music and movies, research products, pay bills and manage bank accounts, check news and weather, store and organize *digital photos*, play games, make vacation plans, and so forth is now the norm for many individuals (see Figure 1-2). Many individuals also use a computer at home for work-related tasks, such as to review work-related documents or check work e-mail from home.

As computers, the Internet, television, *digital video recorders* (*DVRs*), and *gaming consoles* continue to converge, the computer is also becoming a central part of home entertainment. *Wireless networking* has added to the convenience of home computing, allowing the use of computers in virtually any location and the ability to stream content wirelessly from one device to another. You can also use a computer to make telephone calls (referred to as *Voice over IP* or *VoIP*) via a personal computer, a special telephone adapter connected to your *landline phone*, or a *dual-mode mobile phone* (a mobile phone that can make phone calls over the Internet via a *Wi-Fi network*, in addition to making phone calls via a *cellular network*, as described in more detail in Chapter 7).

Computing technologies also make it possible to have *smart appliances*—traditional appliances (such as refrigerators or ovens) with some type of built-in computer or communications technology that allows them to be controlled by the user via a telephone or the Internet, to access and display Internet information, or to perform other computer-related functions. *Smart homes*—homes in which household tasks (such as watering the lawn, turning the air conditioning on or off, making coffee, monitoring the security of the home and grounds, and managing home entertainment content) are controlled by a main computer in the home or by the homeowner remotely via a mobile phone—have arrived, and they are expected to be the norm in less than a decade. Some believe that one primary focus of smart appliances and smart homes will be energy conservation—for instance, the ability to perform tasks (such as running the dishwasher and watering the lawn) during non-peak energy periods and to potentially transfer waste heat from one appliance (such as an oven) to another appliance (such as a dishwasher) as needed.

Computers in Education

Today's youth can definitely be called the *computing generation*. From *handheld gaming devices* to mobile phones to computers at school and home, most children and teens today have been exposed to computers and related technology all their lives. Although the amount of computer use varies from school to school and from grade level to grade level, most students today have access to computers either in a classroom or in a computer lab. Many schools (particularly college campuses) today also have *wireless hotspots* that allow students to use their personal computers to connect wirelessly to the college network and the Internet from anywhere on campus (see Figure 1-3). Today, students at all levels are typically required to use a computer to some extent as part of their normal coursework—such as for preparing papers, practicing skills, doing Internet research, accessing Internet content (for instance, class *Web pages* or their campus *YouTube* channel), or delivering presentations—and some colleges require a computer for enrollment. For a look at how mobile phones are beginning to be used as a teaching tool at some colleges, see the Technology and You box.

Computers are also used to facilitate *distance learning*—an alternative to traditional classroom learning in which students participate, typically at their own pace, from their

REFERENCE AND COMMUNICATIONS
Many individuals today have access to the Internet at home; retrieving information, obtaining news, viewing recipes, shopping online, and exchanging e-mail are popular home computer activities.

PRODUCTIVITY
Home computers are frequently used for editing and managing digital photos and home videos, creating and editing work-related documents, and other productivity tasks.

ENTERTAINMENT
Home computers and gaming consoles are becoming a central hub for entertainment, such as the delivery of photos, videos, music, games, and recorded TV.

 FIGURE 1-2
Computer use at home.

COMPUTER LABS AND CLASSROOMS
Many schools today have computers available in a lab or the library, as well as computers or Internet connections in classrooms, for student use.

CAMPUS WIRELESS HOTSPOTS
Many college students can access the Internet from anywhere on campus to do research, check e-mail, and more, via a campus hotspot.

DISTANCE LEARNING
With distance learning, students—such as these U.S. Army soldiers—can take classes from home or wherever they happen to be at the moment.

 FIGURE 1-3
Computer use in education.

 FIGURE 1-4
Computer use on the job.

current location (via their computers and Internet connections) instead of physically going to class. Consequently, distance learning gives students greater flexibility to schedule class time around their personal, family, and work commitments, as well as allows individuals located in very rural areas or stationed at military posts overseas to take courses when they are not able to attend classes physically.

DECISION MAKING
Many individuals today use a computer to help them make on-the-job decisions.

PRODUCTIVITY
Many individuals today use a computer to perform on-the-job tasks efficiently and accurately.

Computers on the Job

Although computers have been used on the job for years, their role is continually evolving. Computers were originally used as research tools for computer experts and scientists and then as productivity tools for office workers. Today, computers are used by all types of employees in all types of businesses—including corporate executives, retail store clerks, traveling sales professionals, artists and musicians, engineers, police officers, insurance adjusters, delivery workers, doctors and nurses, auto mechanics and repair personnel, and professional athletes. In essence, the computer has become a universal tool for on-the-job decision making, productivity, and communications (see Figure 1-4). Computers are also used extensively for access control at many businesses and organizations, such as *authentication systems* that allow only authorized individuals to enter an office building, punch in or out of work, or access the company network via an access card or a fingerprint or hand scan, as shown in Figure 1-4 and discussed in detail in Chapter 9. In addition to jobs that require the use of computers by employees, many new jobs have been created simply because computers

OFFSITE COMMUNICATIONS
Many individuals use portable computers or mobile devices to record data, access data, or communicate with others when they are out of the office.

AUTHENTICATION
Many individuals use authentication systems to punch in and out of work, access facilities, log on to company computers, or perform other security-related tasks.

TECHNOLOGY AND YOU

M-Learning on Campus

While mobile phones have been banned from many classrooms in past years, the tide may be turning. Despite concerns about cheating and distractions, some educators are now viewing mobile phones as a tool to enhance learning. One such school is Abilene Christian University (ACU) in Texas where entering freshman receive either an *iPhone 3G* or an *iPod Touch.* The devices are being used to facilitate *m-learning* (*mobile learning*) by providing the means for students to access class schedules, podcasts, flashcards, Google Apps, campus directories, news, and other student tools, as well as to facilitate real-time class polls, live assessments, and other in-class activities. These in-class activities can provide both instructors and students with immediate feedback, as well as keep students engaged and interested in the content being presented and discussed in class. ACU has a special mobile learning Web site (see the accompanying figure) to help students access available resources, which are expected to grow as the program evolves.

While notebook and tablet computers are used more often than mobile phones for m-learning activities on college campuses today, the time for mobile phone-based learning may have arrived. ACU considered notebook computers as their m-learning platform, but determined that the screens created a barrier between the teacher and the students and so selected the mobile phone as their m-learning platform instead. With the vast majority of college students already owning a mobile phone, and with Web-enabled mobile phones becoming the norm, m-learning could be the next logical step for education.

exist, such as jobs in electronics manufacturing, online retailing, and technology-related computer support.

Computers are also used extensively by military personnel for communications and navigational purposes, as well as to control missiles and other weapons, identify terrorists and other potential enemies, and perform other necessary national security tasks. To update their computer skills, many employees in all lines of work periodically take computer training classes or enroll in computer certification programs.

FURTHER EXPLORATION   Go

Go to the Chapter 1 page at **www.cengage.com/ computerconcepts/np/uc13** for links to information about computer certification programs.

Computers on the Go

In addition to using computers in the home, at school, and on the job, most people encounter and use all types of computers in other aspects of day-to-day life. For example, it is common for consumers to use *consumer kiosks* (small self-service computer-based stations that provide information or other services to the public, including those used for ATM transactions, bridal registries, ticketing systems, and more), *point-of-sale (POS) systems* (such as

PORTABLE COMPUTERS
Many people today carry a portable computer or mobile device with them at all times or when they travel in order to remain in touch with others and Internet resources.

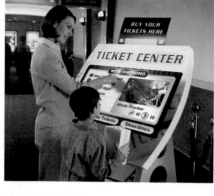

CONSUMER KIOSKS
Electronic kiosks are widely available to view conference or gift registry information, print photographs, order products or services, and more.

M-COMMERCE SYSTEMS
Allow individuals to pay for purchases using a mobile phone or other device.

CONSUMER AUTHENTICATION SYSTEMS
Allow access to facilities for authorized members only, such as for theme park annual pass holders, as shown here.

 FIGURE 1-5
Computer use while on the go.

those found at most retail stores to check customers out), and *self-checkout systems* (which allow retail store customers to scan their purchases and pay for them without a salesclerk) while in retail stores and other public locations. Individuals may also need to use a computer-based consumer authentication system to gain access to a local health club, theme park, or other membership-based facility (see Figure 1-5).

In addition, many individuals carry a *portable computer* or Web-enabled *mobile device* with them on a regular basis to remain electronically in touch with others and to access information (such as stock quotes, driving directions, airline flight updates, movie times, news headlines, and more) as needed while on the go. These portable devices are also increasingly being used to watch TV, download and listen to music, access *Facebook* and other *social networking sites*, and perform other mobile entertainment options, as well as to pay for products and services via *m-commerce systems* (refer again to Figure 1-5). GPS (*global positioning system*) capabilities are also frequently built into mobile phones, cars, and other devices to provide individuals with driving directions and other navigational aids while traveling or hiking.

WHAT IS A COMPUTER AND WHAT DOES IT DO?

A **computer** can be defined as a programmable, electronic device that accepts data, performs operations on that data, presents the results, and stores the data or results as needed. The fact that a computer is *programmable* means that a computer will do whatever the instructions—called the *program*—tell it to do. The programs used with a computer determine the tasks the computer is able to perform.

The four operations described in this definition are more technically referred to as *input*, *processing*, *output*, and *storage*. These four primary operations of a computer can be defined as follows:

> **Input**—entering data into the computer.

> **Processing**—performing operations on the data.

>**Computer.** A programmable, electronic device that accepts data input, performs processing operations on that data, and outputs and stores the results. >**Input.** The process of entering data into a computer; can also refer to the data itself. >**Processing.** Performing operations on data that has been input into a computer to convert that input to output.

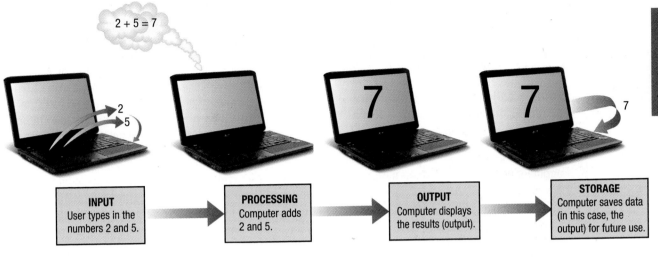

FIGURE 1-6
The information
processing cycle.

➤ **Output**—presenting the results.

➤ **Storage**—saving data, programs, or output for future use.

For example, assume that you have a computer that has been programmed to add two numbers. As shown in Figure 1-6, input occurs when data (in this example, the numbers 2 and 5) is entered into the computer, processing takes place when the computer program adds those two numbers, and output happens when the sum of 7 is displayed on the computer screen. The storage operation occurs any time the data, a change to a program, or some output is saved for future use.

For an additional example, look at a supermarket *barcode reader* to see how it fits this definition of a computer. First, the grocery item being purchased is passed over the barcode reader—input. Next, the description and price of the item are looked up—processing. Finally, the item description and price are displayed on the cash register and printed on the receipt—output—and the inventory, ordering, and sales records are updated—storage.

This progression of input, processing, output, and storage is sometimes referred to as the *IPOS cycle* or the *information processing cycle.* In addition to these four primary computer operations, today's computers also typically perform **communications** functions, such as sending or retrieving data via the Internet, accessing information located in a shared company database, or exchanging e-mail messages. Therefore, communications—technically an input or output operation, depending on which direction the information is going—is increasingly considered the fifth primary computer operation.

Data vs. Information

As just discussed, a user inputs **data** into a computer, and then the computer processes it. Almost any kind of fact or set of facts can become computer data, such as the words in a letter to a friend, the numbers in a monthly budget, the images in a photograph, the notes in a song, or the facts stored in an employee record. When data is processed into a meaningful form, it becomes **information**.

ASK THE EXPERT

Paul Baker, Senior Principal Software Engineer, Walt Disney Imagineering.

Would a college student graduating with a computer degree qualify for a job at Walt Disney Imagineering?

Computers play a large role at Walt Disney Imagineering, so a degree based on computers could be a great match if the course load includes science, math, and engineering courses. Every Disney ride is run by a computer and in many cases by several computers. In fact, some of the rides have computers on each and every vehicle. Unlike typical desktop computers, these "ride computers" are specialized for performing specific, distinct tasks and interfacing to the electronic devices that control and monitor mechanical equipment. Consequently, the algorithms used to run these rides—and ensure they operate in a dependable, predictable manner—are heavily based on engineering and physics. Two types of computer-related jobs that exist at Imagineering are Ride Engineering and Pre-Visualization—both require computer skills, as well as strong math, science, and engineering skills.

Information is frequently generated to answer some type of question, such as how many of a restaurant's employees work less than 20 hours per week, how many seats are available on a particular flight from Los Angeles to San Francisco, or what is Hank Aaron's lifetime home run total. Of course, you don't need a computer system to process data into information; for example, anyone can go through time cards or employee files and make a list of people who work a certain number of hours. If this work is done by hand, however, it could take a lot of time, especially for a company with a large number of employees. Computers, however, can perform such tasks almost instantly, with accurate results. *Information processing* (the conversion of data into information) is a vital activity today for all computer users, as well as for businesses and other organizations.

Computers Then and Now

The basic ideas of computing and calculating are very old, going back thousands of years. However, the computer in the form in which it is recognized today is a fairly recent invention. In fact, personal computers have only been around since the late 1970s. The history of computers is often referred to in terms of *generations*, with each new generation characterized by a major technological development. The next sections summarize some early calculating devices and the different computer generations.

Precomputers and Early Computers (before approximately 1946)

Based on archeological finds, such as notched bones, knotted twine, and hieroglyphics, experts have concluded that ancient civilizations had the ability to count and compute. The *abacus* is considered by many to be the earliest recorded calculating device; it was used primarily as an aid for basic arithmetic calculations. Other early computing devices include the *slide rule*, the *mechanical calculator*, and Dr. Herman Hollerith's *Punch Card Tabulating Machine and Sorter*. This latter device (see Figure 1-7) was the first electromechanical machine that could read *punch cards*—special cards with holes punched in them to represent data. Hollerith's machine was used to process the 1890 U.S. Census data and it was able to complete the task in two and one half years, instead of the decade it usually took to process the data manually. Consequently, this is considered to be the first successful case of an information processing system replacing a paper-and-pen-based system. Hollerith's company eventually became *International Business Machines (IBM)*.

First-Generation Computers (approximately 1946—1957)

The first computers were enormous, often taking up entire rooms. They were powered by thousands of *vacuum tubes*—glass tubes that look similar to large, cylindrical light bulbs—which needed replacing constantly, required a great deal of electricity, and generated a lot of heat. *First-generation computers* could solve only one problem at a time since they needed to be physically rewired with cables to be reprogrammed (see Figure 1-7), which typically took several days (sometimes even weeks) to complete and several more days to check before the computer could be used. Usually paper punch cards and paper tape were used for input, and output was printed on paper.

Two of the most significant examples of first-generation computers were *ENIAC* and *UNIVAC*. ENIAC, shown in Figure 1-7, was the world's first large-scale, general-purpose computer. Although it was not completed until 1946, ENIAC was developed during World War II to compute artillery-firing tables for the U.S. Army. Instead of the 40 hours required for a person to compute the optimal settings for a single weapon under a single set of conditions using manual calculations, ENIAC could complete the same calculations in less than two minutes. UNIVAC, released in 1951, was initially built for the U.S. Census Bureau and was used to analyze votes in the 1952 U.S. presidential election. Interestingly, its correct prediction of an Eisenhower victory only 45 minutes after the polls closed was not publicly aired because the results were not trusted. Despite this initial mistrust of its capabilities, UNIVAC did go on to become the first computer to be mass produced for general commercial use.

Second-Generation Computers (approximately 1958–1963)

The second generation of computers began when the *transistor*—a small device made of *semiconductor* material that acts like a switch to open or close *electronic circuits*—started to replace the vacuum tube. Transistors allowed *second-generation computers* to be physically smaller, less expensive, more powerful, more energy-efficient, and more reliable than first-generation computers. Typically, programs and data were input on punch cards and *magnetic tape*, output was on punch cards and paper printouts, and magnetic tape was used for storage (see Figure 1-7). *Magnetic hard drives* and *programming languages* (such as *FORTRAN* and *COBOL*) were developed and implemented during this generation.

Third-Generation Computers (approximately 1964–1970)

The replacement of the transistor with *integrated circuits* (*ICs*) marked the beginning of the third generation of computers. Integrated circuits incorporate many transistors and electronic circuits on a single tiny silicon *chip*, allowing *third-generation computers* to be even smaller and more reliable than computers in the earlier computer generations. Instead of punch cards and paper printouts, *keyboards* and *monitors* were introduced for input and output; magnetic hard drives were typically used for storage. An example of a widely used third-generation computer is shown in Figure 1-7.

PRECOMPUTERS AND EARLY COMPUTERS
Dr. Herman Hollerith's Punch Card Tabulating Machine and Sorter is an example of an early computing device. It was used to process the 1890 U.S. Census data.

FIRST-GENERATION COMPUTERS
First-generation computers, such as ENIAC shown here, were large and bulky, used vacuum tubes, and had to be physically wired and reset to run programs.

SECOND-GENERATION COMPUTERS
Second-generation computers, such as the IBM 1401 mainframe shown here, used transistors instead of vacuum tubes so they were smaller, faster, and more reliable than first-generation computers.

THIRD-GENERATION COMPUTERS
Third-generation computers used integrated circuits which allowed the introduction of smaller computers, such as the IBM System/360 mainframe shown here.

FOURTH-GENERATION COMPUTERS
Fourth-generation computers, such as the original IBM PC shown here, are based on microprocessors. Most of today's computers fall into this category.

FIGURE 1-7
A brief look at computer generations.

✓ **TIP**

For a more detailed timeline regarding the development of computers, see the "Computer History Timeline" located in the References and Resources Guide at the end of this book.

Go **FURTHER EXPLORATION**

Go to the Chapter 1 page at **www.cengage.com/ computerconcepts/np/uc13** for links to information about the history of computers.

Fourth-Generation Computers (approximately 1971–present)

A technological breakthrough in the early 1970s made it possible to place an increasing number of transistors on a single chip. This led to the invention of the *microprocessor* in 1971, which ushered in the fourth generation of computers. In essence, a microprocessor contains the core processing capabilities of an entire computer on one single chip. The original *IBM PC* (see Figure 1-7) and *Apple Macintosh* computers, and most of today's modern computers, fall into this category. *Fourth-generation computers* typically use a keyboard and *mouse* for input, a monitor and *printer* for output, and magnetic *hard drives*, *flash memory media*, and *optical discs* for storage. This generation also witnessed the development of *computer networks*, *wireless technologies*, and the Internet.

Fifth-Generation Computers (now and the future)

Although some people believe that the fifth generation of computers has not yet begun, most think it is in its infancy stage. *Fifth-generation computers* have no precise classification, since experts tend to disagree about the definition for this generation of computers. However, one common opinion is that fifth-generation computers will be based on *artificial intelligence*, allowing them to think, reason, and learn. Voice and touch are expected to be a primary means of input, and computers may be constructed differently than they are today, such as in the form of *optical computers* that process data using light instead of electrons, tiny computers that utilize *nanotechnology*, or as entire general-purpose computers built into desks, home appliances, and other everyday devices.

FIGURE 1-8
Common hardware listed by operation.

Hardware

The physical parts of a computer (the parts you can touch and discussed next) are called **hardware**. The instructions or programs used with a computer—called *software*—are discussed shortly. Hardware components can be *internal* (located inside the main box or *system unit* of the computer) or *external* (located outside the system unit and connected to the system unit via a wired or wireless connection). There are hardware devices associated with each of the five computer operations previously discussed (input, processing, output, storage, and communications), as summarized in Figure 1-8 and illustrated in Figure 1-9.

INPUT	PROCESSING
Keyboard	CPU
Mouse	**OUTPUT**
Microphone	Monitor
Scanner	Printer
Digital camera	Speakers
Digital pen/stylus	Headphones/headsets
Touch pad/touch screen	Data projector
Joystick	**STORAGE**
Fingerprint reader	Hard drive
COMMUNICATIONS	CD/DVD disc
Modem	CD/DVD drive
Network adapter	Flash memory card
	Flash memory card reader
	USB flash drive

Input Devices

An *input device* is any piece of equipment that is used to input data into the computer. The input devices shown in Figure 1-9 are the *keyboard*, *mouse*, and *microphone*. Other common input devices include *scanners*, *digital cameras*, *digital pens* and *styluses*, *touch pads* and *touch screens*, *fingerprint readers*, and *joysticks*. Input devices are discussed in more detail in Chapter 4.

Processing Devices

The main *processing device* for a computer is the *central processing unit* (*CPU*). The CPU is a *computer chip* located inside the system unit that performs the calculations and comparisons

> **Hardware.** The physical parts of a computer system, such as the keyboard, monitor, printer, and so forth.

FLASH MEMORY CARD READER
Reads and writes flash memory cards.

DVD DRIVE
Reads and writes CD and DVD discs.

HARD DRIVE
Located inside the system unit; stores programs and most data.

SYSTEM UNIT
Case that contains the CPU, memory, power supply, disk drives, and all other internal hardware.

MONITOR
Lets you see your work as you go; a primary output device.

PRINTER
Produces printed copies of computer output.

MICROPHONE
Captures spoken input.

SPEAKERS
Produce audio output.

KEYBOARD
Used to type instructions into the computer; a primary input device.

USB PORTS
Connect external devices that use the USB interface.

CD AND DVD DISCS
Deliver programs and store large multimedia files.

MOUSE
Used to make on-screen selections; a primary pointing device.

MODEM
Connects the computer to the Internet.

USB FLASH DRIVE
Used to store documents, digital photos, music files, and other content to be moved from one PC to another.

FLASH MEMORY CARDS
Used to store digital photos, music files, and other content.

FIGURE 1-9
Typical computer hardware.

needed for processing; it also controls the computer's operations. For these reasons, the CPU is often considered the "brain" of the computer. Also involved in processing are various types of *memory*—additional chips located inside the system unit that the computer uses to store data and instructions while it is working with them. The CPU, memory, and processing are discussed in detail in Chapter 2.

Output Devices

An *output device* accepts processed data from the computer and presents the results to the user, most of the time on the computer screen (*monitor*), on paper (via a *printer*), or through a *speaker*. Other common output devices include *headphones* and *headsets* (used to deliver audio output to a single user) and *data projectors* (used to project computer images onto a projection screen). Output devices are covered in more detail in Chapter 4.

Storage Devices

Storage devices (such as *CD/DVD drives* and *flash memory card readers*) are used to store data on or access data from *storage media* (such as *CD discs*, *DVD discs*, or *flash memory cards*). Some storage hardware (such as a *hard drive* or a *USB flash drive*) includes both a storage device and storage medium in a single piece of hardware. Storage devices are used to save data, program settings, or output for future use; they can be installed inside the computer, attached to the computer as an external device, or accessed remotely through a network or wireless connection. Storage is discussed in more detail in Chapter 3.

Communications Devices

Communications devices allow users to communicate electronically with others and to access remote information via the Internet or a home, school, or company computer network. Communications hardware includes *modems* (used to connect a computer to the Internet) and *network adapters* (used to connect a computer to a computer network). A variety of modems and network adapters are available because there are different types of Internet and network connections—a modem used to connect to the Internet via a cable connection is shown in Figure 1-9. Communications hardware and computer networks are discussed in more detail in Chapter 7; connecting to the Internet is covered in Chapter 8.

Software

The term **software** refers to the programs or instructions used to tell the computer hardware what to do. Software is traditionally purchased on a CD or DVD or is downloaded from the Internet; in either case, the software needs to be *installed* on a computer before it can be used. A rapidly growing alternative is running programs directly from the Internet (via Web pages) without installing them on your computer—referred to as *Web-based software*, *Software as a Service (SaaS)*, and *cloud computing* (see the Trend box) and discussed in more detail in Chapter 6.

Computers use two basic types of software: *system software* and *application software*. The differences between these types of software are discussed next.

VIDEO PODCAST

Go to the Chapter 1 page at **www.cengage.com/ computerconcepts/np/uc13** to download or listen to the "How To: Control Your Computer with Twitter" video podcast.

System Software

The programs that allow a computer to operate are collectively referred to as *system software*. The main system software is the **operating system**, which starts up the computer and controls its operation. Common operating system tasks include setting up new hardware, allowing users to run other software, and allowing users to manage the documents stored on their computers. Without an operating system, a computer cannot function. Common operating systems for personal computers are *Windows*, *Mac OS*, and *Linux*; these and other operating systems are discussed in detail in Chapter 5.

To use a computer, first turn on the power to the computer by pressing the power button, and then the computer begins to **boot**. During the *boot process*, part of the computer's operating system is loaded into memory, the computer does a quick diagnostic of itself, and then it launches any programs—such as an *antivirus* or *instant messaging (IM)* program—designated to run each time the computer starts up. You may need to *log on* to your computer or the appropriate computer network to finish the boot process.

Once a computer has booted, it is ready to be used and waits for input from the user. Most software today uses a variety of graphical objects (such as *icons* and *buttons*) that are selected with the mouse (or with a finger or stylus for a computer that supports touch or pen input) to tell the computer what to do. For instance, the **Windows desktop** (the basic workspace for computers running the Windows operating system; that is, the place where documents, folders, programs, and other objects are displayed when they are being used), along with some common graphical objects used in Windows and many other software programs, are shown in Figure 1-10.

>**Software.** The instructions, also called computer programs, that are used to tell a computer what it should do. >**Operating system.** A type of system software that enables a computer to operate and manage its resources and activities. >**Boot.** To start up a computer. >**Windows desktop.** The background work area displayed on the screen in Microsoft Windows.

WINDOWS DESKTOP
Provides the backdrop for icons, windows, and other objects.

ICONS
Represent folders, documents, or other items that can be opened.

WINDOWS
Rectangular areas containing programs, documents, or other data.

DIALOG BOX
Displayed when needed to request information from the user.

MENU BAR
Opens menus that can be used to issue commands.

TOOLBAR
Contains buttons or icons that can be used to issue commands.

START BUTTON
Opens the Start menu that is used to launch programs.

RIBBON
Replaces menus and toolbars in some programs.

SIZING BUTTONS
Minimize, maximize, or close a window.

HYPERLINK
Issues a command to the computer when clicked.

TASKBAR
Usually located at the bottom of the desktop.

TASKBAR TOOLBAR
Contains icons that can start programs.

TASKBAR BUTTONS
Correspond to open windows; can be used to change the active window.

SYSTEM TRAY
Shows the clock and other indicators.

FIGURE 1-10
The Windows desktop.

Application Software

Application software (see Figure 1-11) consists of programs designed to allow people to perform specific tasks using a computer, such as creating letters, preparing budgets, managing inventory and customer databases, playing games, watching videos, listening to music, scheduling appointments, editing digital photographs, designing homes, viewing Web pages, burning DVDs, and exchanging e-mail. Application software is launched via the operating system (such as by using the *Windows Start* menu shown in Figure 1-10 for Windows computers) and is discussed in greater detail in Chapter 6.

There are also application programs that help users write their own programs in a form the computer can understand using a *programming language* like *BASIC*, *Visual Basic*, *COBOL*, *C++*, *Java*, or *Python*. Some languages are traditional programming languages for developing applications; others are designed for use with Web pages or multimedia programming. *Markup* and *scripting* languages (such as *HTML*, *XHTML*, and *JavaScript*) used to create Web pages are covered in Chapter 10; traditional programming languages are discussed in detail in Chapter 13.

Computer Users and Professionals

In addition to hardware, software, data, and *procedures* (the predetermined steps to be carried out in particular situations), a computer system includes people. *Computer users*, or *end users*, are the people who use computers to perform tasks or obtain information.

TIP

To launch a program on a Windows computer quickly, begin to type the name of the desired program in the Search box at the bottom of the Start menu and then click the link to the desired program when it is displayed (or press Enter when the proper program name is highlighted).

> **Application software.** Programs that enable users to perform specific tasks on a computer, such as writing letters or playing games.

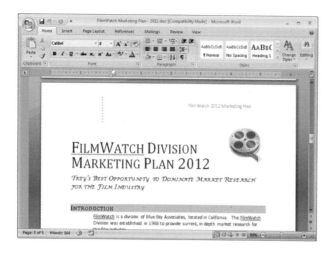

WORD PROCESSING PROGRAMS
Allow users to create written documents,
such as reports, letters, and memos.

MULTIMEDIA PROGRAMS
Allow users to perform tasks, such as playing music or videos
and transferring content to CDs and DVDs.

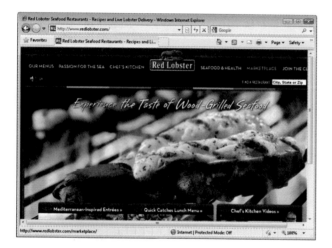

WEB BROWSERS
Allow users to view Web pages and
other information located on the Internet.

E-MAIL PROGRAMS
Allow users to compose, send, receive, and manage
electronic messages sent over the Internet or a private
network.

FIGURE 1-11
Examples of
application
software.

Anyone who uses a computer is a computer user, including an accountant electronically preparing a client's taxes, an office worker using a word processing program to create a letter, a supervisor using a computer to check and see whether or not manufacturing workers have met the day's quotas, a parent e-mailing his or her child's teacher, a college student analyzing science lab data, a child playing a computer game, and a person bidding at an *online auction* over the Internet.

Programmers, on the other hand, are computer professionals who write the programs that computers use. Other *computer professionals* include *systems analysts* (who design computer systems to be used within their companies as discussed in Chapter 12), *computer operations personnel* (who are responsible for the day-to-day computer operations at a company, such as maintaining systems or troubleshooting user-related problems), and *security specialists* (who are responsible for securing the company computers and networks against *hackers* and other intruders who are discussed in more detail in Chapter 9). Computer professionals are discussed in more detail in Chapter 12.

TREND

Cloud Computing

In general, the term *cloud computing* refers to computing in which tasks are performed by a "cloud" of servers, typically via the Internet. This type of network has been used for several years to create the supercomputer-level power needed for research and other power-hungry applications, but it was more typically referred to as *grid computing* in this context. Today, *cloud computing* typically refers to accessing Web-based applications and data using a personal computer, mobile phone, or any other Internet-enabled device (see the accompanying illustration). While many of today's cloud applications (such as Google Apps, Windows Live, Facebook, and YouTube) are consumer-oriented, business applications are also available and are expected to grow in the near future. Consequently, the term is also used to refer to businesses purchasing computing capabilities as they need them, such as through the *Amazon Elastic Compute Cloud* (*Amazon EC2*) service or other *cloud providers* that provide Web-based applications, computing power, *cloud storage*, and other cloud services.

Advantages of cloud computing include easy scalability, lower capital expenditure, and access to data from anywhere. It is also beneficial to business travelers and other individuals whose computers, mobile phones, or other devices may be lost or otherwise compromised while the individual is on the go—if no personal or business data is stored on the device, none can be compromised. Disadvantages include a possible reduction in performance of applications if they run more slowly via the cloud than they would run if installed locally, and the potentially high expense related to data transfer for companies with high bandwidth applications. In addition, numerous security concerns exist, such as how the data is protected against unauthorized access and data loss.

Despite the potential risks, many believe that cloud computing is the wave of the future and will consist of millions of computers located in data centers around the world that are connected together via the Internet. They also view cloud computing as a way to enable all of an individual's devices to stay synchronized and, and as a result, allow an individual to work with his or her data and applications on a continual basis.

THE INTERNET

END USERS **CLOUD PROVIDERS**

Cloud providers provide services via the Internet.

COMPUTERS TO FIT EVERY NEED

The types of computers available today vary widely—from the tiny computers embedded in consumer devices and appliances, to the pocket-sized computers and mobile phones that do a limited number of computing tasks, to the powerful and versatile *desktop computers* and *portable computers* found in homes and businesses, to the superpowerful computers used to control the country's defense systems. Computers are generally classified in one of six categories, based on size, capability, and price.

- ➤ *Embedded computers*—tiny computers embedded into products to perform specific functions or tasks for that product.

- ➤ *Mobile devices*—mobile phones and other small personal devices that contain built-in computing or Internet capabilities.

- ➤ *Personal computers*—fully-functioning portable or desktop computers that are designed to be used by a single individual at a time.

> *Midrange servers*—computers that host data and programs available to a small group of users.

> *Mainframe computers*—powerful computers used to host a large amount of data and programs available to a wide group of users.

> *Supercomputers*—extremely powerful computers used for complex computations and processing.

In practice, classifying a computer into one of these six categories is not always easy or straightforward. For example, some high-end personal computers today are as powerful as midrange servers, and some personal computers today are nearly as small as a mobile phone. In addition, technology changes too fast to have precisely defined categories and the computer of the future may not look anything like today's computers. In fact, future predictions envision personal computers built into a variety of useful objects to best fit a person's lifestyle—such as a ring or watch for an older person, eyeglasses for a technical worker, and a flexible mobile device that can physically change its shape as needed (as discussed in the Chapter 2 Technology and You box) for general consumer use. Future devices are also expected to use voice, touch, or gesture input instead of a keyboard and mouse, and to project output on any appropriate surface instead of using a monitor. Nevertheless, these six categories are commonly used today to refer to groups of computers designed for similar purposes.

ⓥ **FIGURE 1-12**
Embedded computers. This car's embedded computers control numerous features, such as notifying the driver when a car enters his or her blind spot.

A light indicates that a moving vehicle is in the driver's blind spot.

A camera located under the mirror detects moving vehicles in the driver's blind spot.

Embedded Computers

An **embedded computer** is a tiny computer embedded into a product designed to perform specific tasks or functions for that product. For example, computers are often embedded into household appliances (such as dishwashers, microwaves, ovens, coffee makers, and so forth), as well as into other everyday objects (such as thermostats, answering machines, treadmills, sewing machines, DVD players, and televisions), to help those appliances and objects perform their designated tasks. Typically, cars also use many embedded computers to assist with diagnostics, to notify the user of important conditions (such as an underinflated tire or an oil filter that needs changing), to control the use of the airbag and other safety devices (such as cameras that alert a driver that a vehicle is in his or her blind spot—see Figure 1-12—or auto braking systems that engage when a front collision is imminent, as discussed in the Chapter 5 Inside the Industry box), to facilitate the car's navigational or entertainment systems, and to help the driver perform tasks. Embedded computers are designed for specific tasks and specific products and so cannot be used as general-purpose computers.

ONLINE VIDEO

Go to the Chapter 1 page at **www.cengage.com/ computerconcepts/np/uc13** to watch the "Wireless O ROKR Sunglasses" video clip.

Mobile Devices

A **mobile device** is loosely defined as a very small communications device (such as a mobile phone) that has built-in computing or Internet capability. Mobile devices can typically be used to make telephone calls, send *text messages* (short text-based messages), view Web pages, take digital photos, play games, download and play music, watch TV shows, and access calendars and other personal productivity features. Most (but not all) mobile phones today include computing and Internet capabilities; these phones (such as the one in Figure 1-13) are sometimes referred to as **smartphones**; an older term is *PDA*

>**Embedded computer.** A tiny computer embedded in a product and designed to perform specific tasks or functions for that product. >**Mobile device.** A very small communications device that has built-in computing or Internet capability. >**Smartphone.** A mobile device based on a mobile phone.

(*personal digital assistant*), though some devices referred to as PDAs do not include telephone capabilities. Handheld gaming devices (such as the *Sony PSP* and the *Nintendo DSi*) and *portable digital media players* (such as the *iPod Touch* and *Zune*) that include Internet capabilities can also be referred to as mobile devices, though they have less overall capabilities than conventional mobile devices.

Today's mobile devices typically have small screens and keyboards. Because of this, mobile devices are most appropriate for individuals wanting continual access to e-mail, timely Web content (such as breaking news, weather forecasts, driving directions, and updates from Web sites like Facebook), and music collections rather than for those individuals wanting general Web browsing and computing capabilities. This is beginning to change, however, as mobile devices continue to grow in capabilities, as wireless communications continue to become faster, and as mobile input options (such as voice input) continue to improve. For instance, some mobile devices can perform Internet searches and other tasks via voice commands (as discussed in Chapter 6), some can be used to pay for purchases while you are on the go (as discussed in Chapter 11), and many can view and edit documents stored in a common format, such as *Microsoft Office* documents. For a look at some recent issues surrounding the use of mobile devices on the job, see the Inside the Industry box.

Personal Computers (PCs)

A **personal computer** (**PC**) or **microcomputer** is a small computer designed to be used by one person at a time. Personal computers are widely used by individuals and businesses today and range in size from *desktop computers* to *ultra-mobile PCs* (*UMPCs*), as discussed next. Because many personal computers today are continually connected to the Internet, securing those computers—such as protecting them against *computer viruses* and *hackers* as discussed more later in this chapter and in Chapter 9—is an essential concern for both individuals and businesses.

Desktop Computers

Conventional personal computers that are designed to fit on or next to a desk (see Figure 1-14) are often referred to as **desktop computers**. The most common style of desktop computer today uses a *tower case*; that is, a system unit that is designed to sit vertically, typically on the floor. Desktop computers can also have a *desktop case* that is designed to be placed horizontally on a desk's surface, or an *all-in-one case* that incorporates the monitor and system unit into a single piece of hardware (a tower case and all-in-one case are shown in Figure 1-14).

Desktop computers typically cost between $350 and $1,000 and usually conform to one of two standards or *platforms*: *PC-compatible* or *Macintosh*. PC-compatible computers (sometimes referred to as *Windows PCs* or *IBM-compatible PCs*) evolved from the original IBM PC—the first personal computer widely accepted for business

FIGURE 1-13
Smartphones. Most mobile devices today are based on the mobile phone.

FIGURE 1-14
Desktop computers.

TOWER CASES

ALL-IN-ONE CASES

> **Personal computer (PC).** A type of computer based on a microprocessor and designed to be used by one person at a time; also called a **microcomputer.** > **Desktop computer.** A personal computer designed to fit on or next to a desk.

INSIDE THE INDUSTRY

Mobile Phone Use on the Job?

While there are numerous jobs for which having access to a mobile phone and the Internet are needed and extremely useful, there are times when this isn't necessarily the case. One of the most well-known recent issues surrounding mobile phone use on the job was the decision involving President Obama's desire to continue to use his Blackberry after taking office. While the President was eventually allowed to keep his device to stay in touch with senior staff and a small group of personal friends—a first for any U.S. president—the decision brought the issue of mobile phone use on the job to the forefront, especially as it relates to security issues. Security experts stress the importance of protecting the content on mobile phones by using tools such as logon passwords, encryption, remote wiping features, and other security tools discussed in detail in Chapter 9.

In addition to security concerns, the issue of the appropriateness of mobile phone use on the job is also under scrutiny. While the ability to stay in touch with others and post information on a regular basis is often a useful business and personal tool, it can also violate company policy, laws, and even social norms. For instance, one professional basketball player was recently reprimanded for posting a Twitter update during half-time from the locker room and judges across the country are having to deal with the issue of mobile phone use by jurors to obtain and disseminate information about cases during trials.

From researching defendants online, to using Google Maps to determine walking or driving time between locations discussed in the trial, to Twittering about upcoming verdicts, juror mobile phone use is resulting in numerous mistrials and is raising many questions about jury instructions and juror access to technology during trials. Another issue is discretion and taste, as in the case of a newspaper reporter who recently posted Twitter updates during the funeral of a three-year-old boy. Mobile phone use is already prohibited in some public locations (see the accompanying illustration), such as theaters (for courtesy reasons) and airplanes and hospitals (for safety reasons). With mobile phones becoming ubiquitous, it is increasingly important for individuals to ensure that they use their mobile phones only in an appropriate and secure manner, both on the job and off.

ASK THE EXPERT

Debra Jensen, Vice President and Chief Information Officer, Jack in the Box Inc.

How long will it be until paying for fast-food purchases by mobile phone is the norm?

The technology exists today to allow for the payment of fast-food purchases by mobile phone and it's being used in Europe and Japan. Though it's also being tested in the United States, there are still some hurdles, primarily the adoption of the technology by cell phone providers and retailers, and consumers' willingness to use it. Another hurdle is consumer concerns about the technology being secure. It will likely be 2011 before there is widespread use.

use—and are the most common type of personal computer used today. In general, PC-compatible hardware and software are compatible with all brands of PC-compatible computers—such as those made by Dell, Hewlett-Packard, NEC, Acer, Lenovo, Fujitsu, and Gateway—and these computers typically run the Microsoft Windows operating system. Macintosh (*Mac*) computers are made by Apple, use the Mac OS operating system, and often use different hardware and software than PC-compatible computers. Although PC-compatible computers are by far the most widely used in the United States, the Mac is traditionally the computer of choice for artists, designers, and others who require advanced graphics capabilities. Extra powerful desktop computers designed for computer users running graphics, music, film, architecture, science, and other powerful applications are sometimes referred to as *workstations*.

Portable Computers

Portable computers are computers that are designed to be carried around easily, such as in a briefcase or pocket, depending on their size. Like mobile devices, portable computers are designed to be powered by rechargeable batteries so they can be used while on the go, though many can also be powered by electricity. Portable computers now outsell desktop computers and are often the computer of choice for students and for individuals buying a new home computer, as well as for many businesses. In fact, portable computers are essential for many workers, such as salespeople who need to make presentations or take orders from clients off-site, agents who need to collect data at remote locations, and managers who need computing and communications resources as they travel. Portable computers are available in a variety of configurations, as discussed next and shown in Figure 1-15.

NOTEBOOKS

SLATE TABLETS

NETBOOKS

ULTRA-MOBILE PCS (UMPCs)

FIGURE 1-15
Portable computers.

> ➤ **Notebook computers** (also called **laptop computers**)—computers that are about the size of a paper notebook and open to reveal a screen on the top half of the computer and a keyboard on the bottom. They are typically comparable to desktop computers in features and capabilities.

> ➤ **Tablet computers**—notebook-sized computers that are designed to be used with a digital pen or stylus. They can be either *slate tablets* (which are one-piece computers with just a screen on top and no keyboard, such as the one shown in Figure 1-15) or *convertible tablets* (which use the same *clamshell* design as notebook computers but the top half of the computer can be rotated and folded shut so it can also be used as a slate tablet.

> ➤ **Netbooks** (also called *mini-notebooks*, *mini-laptops*, and *ultraportable computers*)—notebook computers that are smaller (a 10-inch-wide screen is common), lighter (typically less than three pounds), and less expensive than conventional notebooks, so they are especially appropriate for students and business travelers. They typically don't include a CD or DVD drive and they have a smaller keyboard than a notebook computer. The market for this new category of portable computer is growing rapidly and it is expected to reach 50 million by 2012, according to the research firm Gartner.

> ➤ **Ultra-mobile PCs (UMPCs)** (also sometimes called **handheld computers**)—computers that are small enough to fit in one hand. UMPCs are smaller (with a typical screen size of seven inches or smaller) and lighter (usually less than two pounds) than netbooks. They can support keyboard, touch, and/or pen input, depending on the particular design being used.

It is important to realize that while a portable computer offers the convenience of mobility, it typically isn't as comfortable to use for a primary home or work computer as a desktop computer is, without additional hardware. For instance, many individuals find it more convenient to connect and use a conventional monitor, keyboard, and mouse when using a notebook

>**Portable computer.** A small personal computer, such as a notebook, tablet, netbook, or ultra-mobile PC (UMPC), designed to be carried around easily. >**Notebook computer.** A fully functioning portable computer that opens to reveal a screen and keyboard; also called a **laptop computer**. >**Tablet computer.** A portable computer about the size of a notebook that is designed to be used with an electronic pen. >**Netbook.** A very small notebook computer. >**Ultra-mobile PC (UMPC).** A portable personal computer that is small enough to fit in one hand; also called a **handheld computer**.

ASK THE EXPERT

Martin Smekal, President and Founder, TabletKiosk

How will personal computers five years from now be different than today?

I believe that five years from now people will rely even more on their computers than they do today. They will likely create a personal computing ecosystem that combines the stability of a desktop system with the portability of a mobile computer and that has full wireless access to key files and applications. Hopefully, this will evolve to one single adaptable computing device that is capable of meeting all of these needs by incorporating "always-on" wireless connectivity and a touch screen interface.

In general, the computers of the future will be smaller, lighter, and have a much longer battery life than today's models. Traditional modes of input like the keyboard and mouse could become obsolete as we begin to rely more on touch input, speech recognition, and improved handwriting recognition.

computer at a desk for a long computer session. This hardware can be connected individually to many portable computers via a wired or wireless connection; there are also special *docking stations* that can be used to connect a portable computer easily to the hardware devices that are attached to the docking station. Docking stations and other *ergonomic*-related topics are discussed in more detail in Chapter 16.

Thin Clients and Internet Appliances

Most personal computers today are sold as stand-alone, self-sufficient units that are equipped with all the necessary hardware and software needed to operate independently. In other words, they can perform input, processing, output, and storage without being connected to a network, although they can be networked if desired. In contrast, a device that must be connected to a network to perform processing or storage tasks is referred to as a *dumb terminal.* Two types of personal computers that may be able to perform a limited amount of independent processing (like a desktop or notebook computer) but are designed to be used with a network (like a dumb terminal) are *thin clients* and *Internet appliances.*

A **thin client**—also called a *network computer* (*NC*)—is a device that is designed to be used in conjunction with a company network. Instead of using local hard drives for storage, programs are typically accessed from and data is stored on a *network server.* The main advantage of thin clients over desktop computers is lower cost (such as for overall hardware and software, computer maintenance, and power and cooling costs), increased security (since data is not stored locally), and easier maintenance (since all software is located on a central server). Disadvantages include having limited or no local storage (although this is an advantage for companies with highly secure data that need to prevent data from leaving the facility) and not being able to function as a stand-alone computer when the network is not working. Thin clients are used by businesses to provide employees with access to network applications; they are also sometimes used to provide Internet access to the public. For instance, the thin client shown in Figure 1-16 is installed in a hotel in Boston, Massachusetts, and is used to provide guests with Internet access, hotel and conference information, room-to-room calling, and free phone calls via the Internet.

Network computers or other devices designed primarily for accessing Web pages and/or exchanging e-mail are called **Internet appliances** (sometimes referred to as *Internet devices*). Typically, Internet appliances are designed to be located in the home and can be built into another product (such as a refrigerator or telephone console) or can be stand-alone Internet devices (such as the *Chumby* device shown in Figure 1-16 that is designed to deliver news, sports scores, weather, and other personalized Web-based information). Gaming consoles (such as the *Nintendo Wii* shown in Figure 1-16 and the *Sony*

>**Thin client.** A personal computer designed to access a network for processing and data storage, instead of performing those tasks locally; also called a network computer (NC). >**Internet appliance.** A specialized network computer designed primarily for Internet access and/or e-mail exchange.

THIN CLIENTS

STAND-ALONE INTERNET DEVICES

INTERNET-ENABLED GAMING CONSOLES

FIGURE 1-16
Thin clients and
Internet appliances.

PlayStation 3) that can be used to view Internet content, in addition to their gaming abilities, can also be classified as Internet appliances when they are used to access the Internet. There are also Internet capabilities beginning to be built into television sets, which make these TVs Internet appliances, as well.

Midrange Servers

A **midrange server**—also sometimes called a *minicomputer* or *midrange computer*—is a medium-sized computer used to host programs and data for a small network. Typically larger, more powerful, and more expensive than a desktop computer, a midrange server is usually located in a closet or other out-of-the-way place and can serve many users at one time. Users connect to the server through a network, using their desktop computer, portable computer, thin client, or a dumb terminal consisting of just a monitor and keyboard (see Figure 1-17). Midrange servers are often used in small- to medium-sized businesses (such as medical or dental offices), as well as in school computer labs. There are also special *home servers* designed for home use, which are often used to *back up* (make duplicate copies of) the content located on all the computers in the home automatically and to host music, photos, movies, and other media to be shared via a *home network*.

Some midrange servers consist of a collection of individual *circuit boards* called *blades*; each blade contains the hardware necessary to provide the complete processing power of one personal computer. These servers—called *blade servers*—are much easier to expand and upgrade than traditional servers, have lower overall power and cooling costs, and are more secure. With some blade servers, the processing power of the blades is shared among users. With others, each user has an individual blade, which functions as that individual's personal computer, but the blades are locked in a secure location instead of having that hardware located on each employee's desk. In either case, the thin client designed specifically to access a blade server is sometimes called a *blade workstation*.

One trend involving midrange servers (as well as the *mainframe computers* discussed next) today is **virtualization**—creating *virtual* (rather than actual) versions of a computing resource; in this case, separate server environments that, although physically located on the same computer, function

FIGURE 1-17
Midrange servers.
Midrange servers are
used to host data and
programs on a small
network, such as a
school computer lab or
medical office network.

Users connect to the
server using computers, thin
clients, or dumb terminals.

The server is typically
stored in a nearby closet or
other out-of-the way place.

as separate servers and do not interact with each other. For instance, all applications for an organization can be installed in virtual environments on one or more physical servers instead of using a separate server for each application. Using a separate server for each application often wastes resources since the servers are typically not used to full capacity—one estimate is that about only 10% of server capability is frequently utilized. With virtualization, companies can fulfill their computing needs with fewer servers, which translates into reduced costs for hardware and server management, as well as lower power and cooling costs. Consequently, one of the most significant appeals of *server virtualization* today is increased efficiency. The concepts of virtualization are also beginning to be applied to other computing areas, such as networking and storage.

Mainframe Computers

▼ FIGURE 1-18
Mainframe computers.

A **mainframe computer** is a powerful computer used by many large organizations—such as hospitals, universities, large businesses, banks, and government offices—that need to manage large amounts of centralized data. Larger, more expensive, and more powerful than midrange servers, mainframes can serve thousands of users connected to the mainframe via personal computers, thin clients, or dumb terminals, in a manner similar to the way users connect to midrange servers. Mainframe computers are typically located in climate-controlled *data centers* and connect to the rest of the company computers via a computer network. During regular business hours, a mainframe typically runs the programs needed to meet the different needs of its wide variety of users. At night, it commonly performs large processing tasks, such as payroll and billing. Today's mainframes are sometimes referred to as *high-end servers* or *enterprise-class servers* and they usually cost at least several hundred thousand dollars each.

One issue facing businesses today is the high cost of electricity to power and cool the mainframes, servers, and personal computers used in an organization. Consequently, making the computers located in a business—particularly mainframes and servers—more energy efficient is a high priority today. For example, IBM recently consolidated approximately 4,000 servers located in its data centers into just 30 mainframes (one of the new mainframes is shown in Figure 1-18). This new environment is expected to consume approximately 80 percent less energy and result in significant savings in energy, software, and system support costs. Energy efficiency and other *green computing* topics are discussed in more detail in Chapter 16.

Supercomputers

Some applications require extraordinary speed, accuracy, and processing capabilities—for example, sending astronauts into space, controlling missile guidance systems and satellites, forecasting the weather, exploring for oil, and assisting with some kinds of scientific research. **Supercomputers**—the most powerful and most expensive type of computer available—were developed to fill this need. Some relatively new supercomputing applications include hosting extremely complex Web sites and *decision support systems* for corporate executives, as well as *three-dimensional applications* (such as 3D medical imaging, 3D image projections, and 3D architectural modeling). Unlike mainframe computers, which typically run multiple applications simultaneously to serve a wide variety of users, supercomputers generally run one program at a time, as fast as possible.

Conventional supercomputers can cost several million dollars each. To reduce the cost, supercomputers today are often built by connecting hundreds of smaller and less

>**Mainframe computer.** A computer used in large organizations (such as hospitals, large businesses, and colleges) that need to manage large amounts of centralized data and run multiple programs simultaneously. >**Supercomputer.** The fastest, most expensive, and most powerful type of computer.

expensive computers (increasingly midrange servers) into a **supercomputing cluster** that acts as a single supercomputer. The computers in the cluster usually contain multiple CPUs each and are dedicated to processing cluster applications. For example, IBM's *Roadrunner* supercomputer (shown in Figure 1-19)— currently the fastest computer in the world—contains approximately 19,000 CPUs. This supercomputing cluster, built for the U.S. Department of Energy, is installed at Los Alamos National Lab in California and is used primarily to ensure the safety and reliability of the nation's nuclear weapons stockpile. Roadrunner, which cost about $100 million and occupies about 5,200 square feet, is the first supercomputer to reach *petaflop* (quadrillions of *floating point operations per second*) speeds. This supercomputer is also one of the most energy efficient computers in the *TOP500* list of the 500 fastest computers in the world. A new IBM supercomputer named *Sequoia* that is currently under development for the Lawrence Livermore National Laboratory is expected to use approximately 1.6 million CPUs and perform at 20 petaflops.

FIGURE 1-19
The Roadrunner supercomputer. Supercomputers are used for specialized situations in which immense processing speed is required.

COMPUTER NETWORKS AND THE INTERNET

A **computer network** is a collection of computers and other devices that are connected together to enable users to share hardware, software, and data, as well as to communicate electronically with each other. Computer networks exist in many sizes and types. For instance, home networks are commonly used to allow home computers to share a single printer and Internet connection, as well as to exchange files. Small office networks enable workers to access company records stored on a *network server*, communicate with other employees, share a high-speed printer, and access the Internet (see Figure 1-20). School networks allow students and teachers to access the Internet and school resources, and large corporate networks often connect all of the offices or retail stores in the corporation, creating a network that spans several cities or states. Public wireless networks—such as those available at some coffeehouses, restaurants, public libraries, and parks—provide Internet access to individuals via their portable computers and mobile devices. Most computers today connect to a computer network. Chapter 7 discusses networks in greater detail.

What Are the Internet and the World Wide Web?

The **Internet** is the largest and most well-known computer network in the world. It is technically a network of networks, since it consists of thousands of networks that can all access each other via the main *backbone* infrastructure of the Internet. Individual users connect to the Internet by connecting their computers to servers belonging to an **Internet service provider** **(ISP)**—a company that provides Internet access, usually for a fee. ISPs (which include conventional and mobile telephone companies like AT&T, Verizon, and Sprint; cable providers like Comcast and Time Warner; and stand-alone ISPs like NetZero and EarthLink) function as gateways or onramps to the Internet, providing Internet access to their subscribers. ISP servers are continually connected to a larger network, called a *regional network*, which, in turn, is connected to one of the major high-speed networks within a country, called a *backbone network*. Backbone networks within a country are connected to each other and to backbone networks in other countries. Together they form one enormous network of networks—the Internet. Tips for selecting an ISP are included in Chapter 8.

TIP

Although some people use the terms *Internet* and *Web* interchangeably, technically the Web—the collection of Web pages available over the Internet—is only one resource available via the Internet.

> **Supercomputing cluster.** A supercomputer comprised of numerous smaller computers connected together to act as a single computer.
> **Computer network.** A collection of computers and other hardware devices that are connected together to share hardware, software, and data, as well as to communicate electronically with one another. > **Internet.** The largest and most well-known computer network, linking millions of computers all over the world. > **Internet service provider (ISP).** A business or other organization that provides Internet access to others, typically for a fee.

BETTY'S PC

WEB PAGE
(for Mary)

THE INTERNET

FILES
(for Tom)

INTERNET CONNECTION

WEB PAGE
(for Mary)

E-MAIL
(to a customer)

MARY'S PC

NETWORK SERVER

SHARED PRINTER

TOM'S PC

FILES
(for Tom)

E-MAIL
(to a customer)

FIGURE 1-20
Example of a
computer network.

Millions of people and organizations all over the world are connected to the Internet. Some of the most common Internet activities today are exchanging e-mail and instant messages (IMs), and accessing content located on *Web pages*. While the term *Internet* refers to the physical structure of that network, the **World Wide Web** (**WWW**) refers to one resource—a collection of documents called **Web pages**—available through the Internet. A group of Web pages belonging to one individual or company is called a **Web site**. Web pages are stored on computers (called **Web servers**) that are continually connected to the Internet; they can be accessed at any time by anyone with a computer (or other Web-enabled device) and an Internet connection. A wide variety of information is available via Web pages, such as company and product information, government forms and publications, maps, telephone directories, news, weather, sports results, airline schedules, and much, much more. You can also use Web pages to shop, bank, trade stock, and perform other types of online financial transactions; access *social networks* like *Facebook* and *MySpace*; and listen to music, play games, watch television shows, and perform other entertainment-oriented activities (see Figure 1-21). Web pages are viewed using a **Web browser**, such as *Internet Explorer* (*IE*), *Chrome*, *Safari*, *Opera*, or *Firefox*.

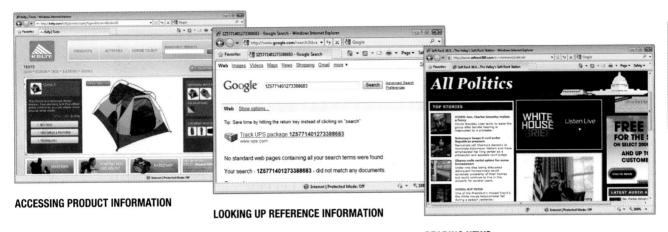

ACCESSING PRODUCT INFORMATION

LOOKING UP REFERENCE INFORMATION

READING NEWS

SHOPPING

ACCESSING SOCIAL NETWORKS

WATCHING TV SHOWS AND MOVIES

Accessing a Network or the Internet

To access a local computer network (such as a home network, a school or company network, or a public wireless hotspot), you need to use a network adapter (either built into your computer or attached to it) to connect your computer to the network. With some computer networks you need to supply logon information (such as a *username* and a password) to *log on* to a network. Once you are connected to the network, you can access network resources, including the network's Internet connection. If you are connecting to the Internet without going through a computer network, your computer needs to use a modem to connect to the communications media (such as a telephone line or cable connection) used by your ISP. Network adapters and modems are discussed in more detail in Chapter 7.

    Most Internet connections today are *direct* (or *always-on*) *connections*, which means the computer or other device being used to access the Internet is continually connected to the ISP's computer. With a direct connection, you only need to open your Web browser to begin using the Internet. With a dial-up connection, you must start the program that instructs your computer to dial and connect to the ISP's server via a telephone line, and then open a Web browser, each time you want to access the Internet.

    To request a Web page or other resource located on the Internet, its **Internet address**—a unique numeric or text-based address—is used. The most common types of Internet addresses are *IP addresses* and *domain names* (to identify computers), *URLs* (to identify Web pages), and *e-mail addresses* (to identify people).

FIGURE 1-21
Some common Web activities.

> **Internet address.** An address that identifies a computer, person, or Web page on the Internet, such as an IP address, domain name, or e-mail address.

IP Addresses and Domain Names

IP addresses and their corresponding **domain names** are used to identify computers available through the Internet. IP (short for *Internet Protocol*) addresses are numeric, such as *207.46.197.32*, and are commonly used by computers to refer to other computers. A computer that hosts information available through the Internet (such as a Web server hosting Web pages) usually has a unique text-based domain name (such as *microsoft.com*) that corresponds to that computer's IP address in order to make it easier for people to request Web pages located on that computer. IP addresses and domain names are unique; that is, there cannot be two computers on the Internet using the exact same IP address or exact same domain name. To ensure this, specific IP addresses are allocated to each network (such as a company network or an ISP) to be used with the computers on that network, and there is a worldwide registration system for domain name registration. When a domain name is registered, the IP address of the computer that will be hosting the Web site associated with that domain name is also registered; the Web site can be accessed using either its domain name or corresponding IP address. When a Web site is requested using its domain name, the corresponding IP address is looked up using one of the Internet's *domain name system* (*DNS*) *servers* and then the appropriate Web page is displayed.

Domain names typically reflect the name of the individual or organization associated with that Web site and the different parts of a domain name are separated by a period. The far right part of the domain name (beginning with the rightmost period) is called the *top-level domain* (*TLD*) and traditionally identifies the type of organization or its location (such as *.com* for businesses, *.edu* for educational institutions, *.jp* for Web sites located in Japan, or *.fr* for Web sites located in France). There were seven original TLDs used in the United States; additional TLDs and numerous two-letter *country code TLDs* have since been created (see some examples in Figure 1-22). A new proposal allows for the creation of new TLDs that can be virtually any combination of up to 64 characters and that can use non-Latin characters. While custom TLDs are possible (such as to better represent a company name or personal name), they are also expected to be expensive to register (one estimate is about $100,000 each). Consequently, the initial interest in custom TLDs is by countries (such as Russia) whose native languages use non-Latin characters, groups of businesses and organizations that are interested in new activity-oriented TLDs like *.sports* and *.shop*, and community organizations interested in city-based TLDs like *.nyc* and *.paris* (for New York City and Paris businesses, respectively). Assuming the new plan is implemented, the new TLDs are expected to become available in 2010.

ORIGINAL TLDS	INTENDED USE
.com	Commercial businesses
.edu	Educational institutions
.gov	Government organizations
.int	International treaty organizations
.mil	Military organizations
.net	Network providers and ISPs
.org	Noncommercial organizations

NEWER TLDS	INTENDED USE
.aero	Aviation industry
.biz	Businesses
.fr	French businesses
.info	Resource sites
.jobs	Employment sites
.mobi	Sites optimized for mobile devices
.name	Individuals
.pro	Licensed professionals
.uk	United Kingdom businesses

FIGURE 1-22
Sample top-level domains (TLDs).

TIP

Only the legitimate holder of a trademarked name (such as Microsoft) can use that trademarked name as a domain name (such as microsoft.com); trademarks are discussed in detail in Chapter 16.

Uniform Resource Locators (URLs)

Similar to the way an IP address or domain name uniquely identifies a computer on the Internet, a **uniform resource locator** (**URL**) uniquely identifies a specific Web page

>**IP address.** A numeric Internet address used to uniquely identify a computer on the Internet. >**Domain name.** A text-based Internet address used to uniquely identify a computer on the Internet. >**Uniform resource locator (URL).** An Internet address (usually beginning with http://) that uniquely identifies a Web page.

(including the *protocol* or standard being used to display the Web page, the Web server hosting the Web page, the name of any folders on the Web server in which the Web page file is stored, and the Web page's filename, if needed).

The most common Web page protocols are *Hypertext Transfer Protocol* (*http://*) for regular Web pages or *Secure Hypertext Transfer Protocol* (*https://*) for *secure Web pages* that can safely be used to transmit sensitive information, such as credit card numbers. *File Transfer Protocol* (*ftp://*) is sometimes used to upload and download files. The *file extension* used for the Web page file indicates the type of Web page that will be displayed (such as *.html* and *.htm* for standard Web pages created using *Hypertext Markup Language*, as discussed in Chapter 10). For example, looking at the URL for the Web page shown in Figure 1-23 from right to left, we can see that the Web page is called *index.html*, is stored in a folder called *jobs* on the Web server associated with the *twitter.com* domain, and is a regular (nonsecure) Web page since the standard *http://* protocol is being used.

Web page URLs usually begin with the standard protocol identifier http://.

This part of the URL identifies the Web server hosting the Web page.

Next comes the folder(s) in which the Web page is stored, if necessary.

This is the Web page document that is to be retrieved and displayed.

FIGURE 1-23
A Web page URL.

TIP

Be sure that any Web page used to send sensitive data (such as your social security number or credit card information) is secure. Look for a URL that starts with *https* instead of *http* and a locked padlock icon on the Address bar.

E-Mail Addresses

To contact people using the Internet, you most often use their **e-mail addresses**. An e-mail address consists of a **username** (an identifying name), followed by the @ symbol, followed by the domain name for the computer that will be handling that person's e-mail (called a *mail server*). For example,

jsmith@cengage.com
maria_s@cengage.com
sam.peterson@cengage.com

are the e-mail addresses assigned respectively to jsmith (John Smith), maria_s (Maria Sanchez), and sam.peterson (Sam Peterson), three hypothetical employees at Cengage Learning, the publisher of this textbook. Usernames are typically a combination of the person's first and last names and sometimes include periods, underscores, and numbers, but cannot include blank spaces. To ensure a unique e-mail address for everyone in the world, usernames must be unique within each domain name. So, even though there could be a *jsmith* at Cengage Learning using the e-mail address *jsmith@cengage.com* and a *jsmith* at Stanford University using the e-mail address *jsmith@stanford.edu*, the two e-mail addresses are unique. It is up to each organization with a registered domain name to ensure that one—and only one—exact same username is assigned to its domain. Using e-mail addresses to send e-mail messages is discussed later in this chapter; other forms of online communications—such as instant messaging (IM)—are covered in Chapter 8. For a look at how online communications are being used to help keep college students safe, see the How It Works box.

> **E-mail address.** An Internet address consisting of a username and computer domain name that uniquely identifies a person on the Internet.
> **Username.** A name that uniquely identifies a user on a specific computer network.

HOW IT WORKS

Campus Emergency Notification Systems

Recent on-campus tragedies, such as the Virginia Tech shootings in 2007, have increased attention on ways organizations can quickly and effectively notify a large number of individuals. Following the Virginia Tech tragedy, which involved a shooting rampage lasting about two hours and killing more than 30 individuals, the *Higher Education Opportunity Act* was signed into law. The law provides grants and other assistance to colleges and universities to create an emergency communications system that can be used to contact students when a significant emergency or dangerous situation emerges. In response, colleges across the U.S. are implementing emergency notification systems to notify students, faculty, staff, and campus visitors of an emergency, severe weather condition, campus closure, or other critical event.

Since nearly all college students in the U.S. today have mobile phones, sending emergency alerts via text message is a natural option for many colleges. To be able to send a text message to an entire campus typically requires the use of a company who specializes in this type of mass communications. One such company is *Omnilert*, which has systems installed in more than 600 colleges and universities around the country. With the Omnilert campus notification system—called *e2Campus*—the contact information of the students, faculty, and staff to be notified is entered into the system and then the individuals can be divided into groups, depending on the types of messages each individual should receive. When an alert needs to be sent, an administrator sends the message (via a mobile phone or computer) and it is distributed to the appropriate individuals (see the accompanying illustration). In addition to text messages, alerts can also be sent simultaneously and automatically via virtually any voice or text communications medium, such as voice messages, e-mail messages, RSS feeds, instant messages, Twitter feeds, Facebook pages, school Web pages, personal portal pages, desktop pop-up alerts, digital signage systems (such as signs located inside dorms and the student union), indoor and outdoor campus public address (PA) systems, and more.

To facilitate campus emergency notification systems, some colleges now require all undergraduate students to have a mobile phone. Some campuses also implement other useful mobile services, such as tracking campus shuttle buses, participating in class polls, and accessing class assignments and grades. An additional safety feature available at some schools is the ability to use the phones to activate an alert whenever a student feels unsafe on campus; these alerts automatically send the student's physical location (determined via the phone's GPS coordinates) to the campus police so the student can be quickly located.

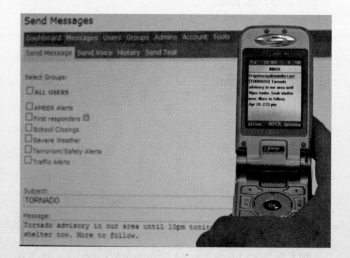

Pronouncing Internet Addresses

Because Internet addresses are frequently given verbally, it is important to know how to pronounce them. A few guidelines are listed next, and Figure 1-24 shows some examples of Internet addresses and their proper pronunciations.

➤ If a portion of the address forms a recognizable word or name, it is spoken; otherwise, it is spelled out.

➤ The @ sign is pronounced *at*.

➤ The period (.) is pronounced *dot*.

➤ The forward slash (/) is pronounced *slash*.

TYPE OF ADDRESS	SAMPLE ADDRESS	PRONUNCIATION
Domain name	berkeley.edu	berkeley dot e d u
URL	microsoft.com/windows/ie/default.asp	microsoft dot com slash windows slash i e slash default dot a s p
E-mail address	president@whitehouse.gov	president at whitehouse dot gov

FIGURE 1-24
Pronouncing
Internet addresses.

Surfing the Web

Once you have an Internet connection, you are ready to begin *surfing the Web*—that is, using a Web browser to view Web pages. The first page that your Web browser displays when it is opened is your browser's starting page or *home page.* Often this is the home page for the Web site belonging to your browser, school, or ISP. However, you can use your browser's customization options to change the current home page to any page that you plan to visit regularly. From your browser's home page, you can move to any Web page you desire, as discussed next.

Using URLs and Hyperlinks

To navigate to a new Web page for which you know the URL, type that URL in the appropriate location for your Web browser (such as Internet Explorer's *Address bar*, as shown in Figure 1-25) and press Enter. Once that page is displayed, you can use the *hyperlinks*—graphics or text linked to other Web pages—located on that page to display other Web pages. In addition to Web pages, hyperlinks can also be linked to other types of files, such as to enable Web visitors to view or download images, listen to or download music files, view video clips, or download software programs.

The most commonly used Web browsers include Internet Explorer (shown in Figure 1-25), Chrome (shown in Figure 1-26), and Firefox. The newest versions of these browsers include *tabbed browsing* (which allows you to have multiple Web pages open at the same time), improved *crash recovery* and security, and improved ability to search for and *bookmark* Web pages, as discussed shortly. *Internet Explorer 8 (IE 8)* also includes the ability to subscribe to *Web Slices*—small pieces of a Web site, such as a particular online

TIP

If you get an error message when typing a URL, first check to make sure you typed it correctly. If it is correct, edit the URL to remove any folder or filenames and press Enter to try to load the home page of that site.

FIGURE 1-25
Surfing the Web with IE 8. URLs, hyperlinks, and favorites can be used to display Web pages.

TOOLBARS
Include Back, Home, and Print buttons, and the Favorites bar.

USING URLS
Type a URL in the Address bar and press Enter to display the corresponding Web page.

USING HYPERLINKS
Point to a hyperlink to see the corresponding URL on the status bar; click the hyperlink to display that page.

STATUS BAR
Includes zoom options and security indicators.

TABS
Click the rightmost tab to open a new tab.

USING FAVORITES
Click a page name to display that Web page.

WEB SLICES
Click a Web Slice to see its current status.

auction or a particular Facebook page—and see the current status of that Web Slice without leaving your current page (refer again to Figure 1-25). In any browser, you can use the Back button on the browser's toolbar to return to a previous page. To print the current Web page, click the browser's Print button or select *Print* from the browser's menu or toolbar.

Using Favorites and the History List

All Web browsers have a feature (usually called *Favorites* or *Bookmarks* and accessed via a Favorites or Bookmarks menu or button) that you can use to save Web page URLs. Once a Web page is saved as a favorite or a bookmark, you can redisplay that page without typing its URL—you simply select its link from the Favorites or Bookmarks list. You can also use this feature to save a group of tabbed Web pages to open the entire group again at a later time. Web browsers also maintain a *History list*, which is a record of all Web pages visited during a period of time specified in the browser settings; you can revisit a Web page located on the History list by displaying the History list and selecting that page.

Most Web browsers today allow you to delete, move into folders, and otherwise organize your favorites/bookmarks, as well as to search your favorites/bookmarks or History list to help you find pages more easily. Chrome goes one step further by displaying thumbnails of your most visited sites, a list of your most recent bookmarks, and a history search box each time you open a new browser tab.

OTHER SEARCHES
Use these options to search for images, news, video, and more instead of for Web pages.

ADVANCED SEARCHES
Click to display a fill-in form to perform a more specific search.

KEYWORD SEARCHES
Since the Web option is selected, type keywords here and press Enter to see a list of Web pages matching your search criteria.

 FIGURE 1-26
The Google search site displayed in the Chrome browser.

Searching the Web

People typically turn to the Web to find specific types of information. There are a number of special Web pages, called *search sites*, available to help you locate what you are looking for on the Internet. One of the most popular search sites— *Google*—is shown in Figure 1-26. To conduct a search, you typically type one or more *keywords* into the search box on a search site, and a list of links to Web pages matching your search criteria is displayed (many browsers also allow you to type search terms in the Address bar instead of a URL and an Internet search will be performed). There are also numerous *reference sites* available on the Web to look up addresses, phone numbers, ZIP codes, maps, and other information. To find a reference site, type the information you are looking for (such as "ZIP code lookup" or "topographical maps") in a search site's search box to see links to sites with that information. Searching the Web is discussed in more detail in Chapter 8.

E-Mail

Electronic mail (more commonly called **e-mail**) is the process of exchanging electronic messages between computers over a network—usually the Internet. E-mail is one of the

> **Electronic mail (e-mail).** Electronic messages sent from one user to another over the Internet or other network.

most widely used Internet applications—Americans alone send billions of e-mail messages daily and worldwide e-mail traffic is expected to exceed one-half trillion messages per day by 2013, according to the Radicati Group. You can send an e-mail message from any Internet-enabled device (such as a desktop computer, portable computer, or mobile device) to anyone who has an Internet e-mail address. As illustrated in Figure 1-27, e-mail messages travel from the sender's computer to his or her ISP's *mail server*, and then through the Internet to the mail server being used by the recipient's ISP. When the recipient logs on to the Internet and requests his or her e-mail, it is displayed on the computer he or she is using. In addition to text, e-mail messages can include attached files, such as photos and other documents.

E-mail can be sent and received via an *e-mail program*, such as *Microsoft Outlook*, installed on the computer being used (sometimes referred to as *conventional e-mail*) or via a Web page belonging to a Web mail provider such as *Gmail* or *Windows Live Mail* (referred to as *Web-based e-mail* or just *Web mail*). Using an installed e-mail program is convenient for individuals who use e-mail often and want to have copies of sent and received e-mail messages stored on their computer. To use an installed e-mail program, however, it must first be set up with the user's name, e-mail address, incoming mail server, and outgoing mail server information. Web-based e-mail does not require this set up and a user's e-mail can be accessed from any computer with an Internet connection by just displaying the appropriate Web mail page and logging on. Consequently, Web-based e-mail is more flexible than conventional e-mail since it can be accessed easily from any computer with an Internet connection. However, Web-based e-mail is typically slower than conventional e-mail and messages can only be viewed when the user is online and logged on to his or her Web mail account, unless the Web-based e-mail provider offers *offline e-mail* service. Despite these limitations, use of Web-based e-mail for both personal and business use is growing and, according to a Gartner estimate, as much as 20% of business e-mail accounts are expected to be Web-based by 2012—up from only 2% in 2007.

Web-based e-mail is typically free and virtually all ISPs used with personal computers include e-mail service in their monthly fee. Some plans from mobile phone providers that provide Internet service for mobile phones include a limit on the number and/or size of e-mail messages that can be sent or received during a billing period; messages after that point result in additional fees. Other types of mobile communications, such as text messages that typically use the *Short Message Service (SMS)* protocol when sent between mobile phones, may also incur a fee. Messaging and other types of online communications that can be used in addition to e-mail are discussed in Chapter 8.

FIGURE 1-27
How e-mail works.

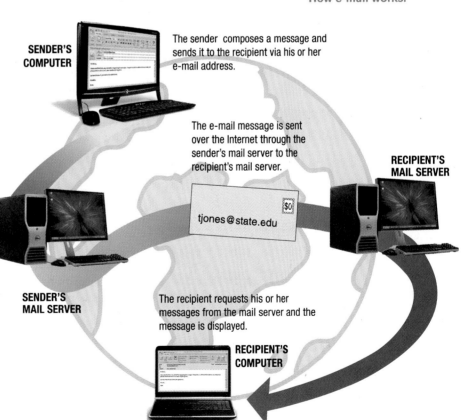

SENDER'S COMPUTER

The sender composes a message and sends it to the recipient via his or her e-mail address.

The e-mail message is sent over the Internet through the sender's mail server to the recipient's mail server.

RECIPIENT'S MAIL SERVER

tjones@state.edu

SENDER'S MAIL SERVER

The recipient requests his or her messages from the mail server and the message is displayed.

RECIPIENT'S COMPUTER

COMPUTERS AND SOCIETY

The vast improvements in technology over the past decade have had a distinct impact on daily life, both at home and at work. Computers have become indispensable tools in our personal and professional lives, and related technological advancements have changed the way our everyday items—cars, microwaves, coffee pots, toys, exercise bikes, telephones, televisions, and more—look and function. As computers and everyday devices become smarter, they tend to do their intended jobs faster, better, and more reliably than before, as well as take on additional capabilities. In addition to affecting individuals, computerization and technological advances have changed society as a whole. Without computers, banks would be overwhelmed by the job of tracking all the transactions they process, moon exploration and the space shuttle would still belong to science fiction, and some scientific advances—such as DNA analysis and gene mapping—would be nonexistent. In addition, we as individuals are getting accustomed to the increased automation of everyday activities, such as shopping and banking, and we depend on having fast and easy access to information via the Internet and rapid communications via e-mail and instant messaging. In addition, many of us would not think about making a major purchase without first researching it online. In fact, it is surprising how fast the Internet and its resources have become an integral part of our society. But despite all its benefits, *cyberspace* has some risks. Some of the most important societal implications related to computers and the Internet are introduced next; many of these issues are covered in more detail in later chapters of this text.

Benefits of a Computer-Oriented Society

The benefits of having such a computer-oriented society are numerous, as touched on throughout this chapter. The capability to virtually design, build, and test new buildings, cars, and airplanes before the actual construction begins helps professionals create safer end products. Technological advances in medicine allow for earlier diagnosis and more effective treatment of diseases than ever before. The benefit of beginning medical students performing virtual surgery using a computer instead of performing actual surgery on a patient is obvious. The ability to shop, pay bills, research products, participate in online courses, and look up vast amounts of information 24 hours a day, 7 days a week, 365 days a year via the Internet is a huge convenience. In addition, a computer-oriented society generates new opportunities. For example, technologies—such as *speech recognition software* and Braille input and output devices—enable physically- or visually-challenged individuals to perform necessary job tasks and to communicate with others more easily.

In general, technology has also made a huge number of tasks in our lives go much faster. Instead of experiencing a long delay for a credit check, an applicant can get approved for a purchase, loan, or credit card almost immediately. Documents and photographs can be e-mailed or faxed in mere moments, instead of taking at least a day to be mailed physically. We can watch many of our favorite TVs shows online (see Figure 1-28) and access up-to-minute news at our convenience. And we can download information, programs, music files, movies, and more on demand when we want or need them, instead of having to order them and then wait for delivery or physically go to a store to purchase the desired items.

FIGURE 1-28

Episodes of many televisions shows are available online to be viewed at the user's convenience.

Risks of a Computer-Oriented Society

Although there are a great number of benefits from having a computer-oriented society and a *networked economy*, there are risks as well. A variety of problems have emerged from our extensive computer use, ranging from stress and health concerns, to the proliferation of *spam* (unsolicited e-mails) and *malware* (harmful programs that can be installed on our computers without our knowledge), to security and privacy issues, to legal and ethical dilemmas. Many of the security and privacy concerns stem from the fact that so much of our personal business takes place online—or at least ends up as data in a computer database somewhere—and the potential for misuse of this data is enormous. Another concern is the repercussions of collecting such vast amounts of information electronically. Some people worry about creating a "Big Brother" situation, in which the government or another organization is watching everything that we do. Although the accumulation and distribution of information is a necessary factor of our networked economy, it is one area of great concern to many individuals. And some Internet behavior, such as downloading music or movies from an unauthorized source or viewing pornography on an office computer, can get you arrested or fired.

Security Issues

One of the most common online security risks today is your computer becoming infected with a malware program, such as a *computer virus*—a malicious software program designed to change the way a computer operates. Malware often causes damage to the infected computer, such as erasing data or bogging down the computer so it does not function well; it can also be used to try to locate sensitive data on your computer (such as Web site passwords or credit card numbers) and send that data to the malware creator. Malware can be attached to a program (such as one downloaded from a Web page), as well as attached to, or contained within, an e-mail message. To help protect your computer, never open an e-mail attachment from someone you do not know or that has an executable *file extension* (the last three letters in the filename preceded by a period), such as *.exe*, *.com*, or *.vbs*, without checking with the sender first to make sure the attachment is legitimate. You should also be careful about what files you download from the Internet. In addition, it is crucial to install *security software* on your computer and to set up the program to monitor your computer on a continual basis (see Figure 1-29). If a virus or other type of malware attempts to install itself on your computer (such as through an e-mail message attachment or a downloaded file), the antivirus program will block it. If malware does find its way onto your computer, the antivirus program will detect it during a regular scan, notify you, and attempt to remove it.

 FIGURE 1-29

Antivirus software.

Antivirus software is crucial for protecting your computer from viruses and other types of malware.

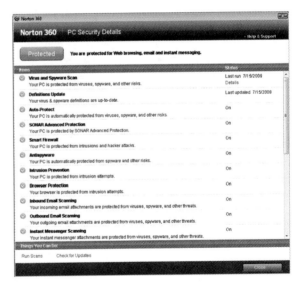

Another ongoing security problem is *identity theft*—in which someone else uses your identity, typically to purchase goods or services. Identity theft can stem from personal information discovered from offline means—like discarded papers or stolen mail—or from information found online, stolen from an online database, or obtained via a malware program. *Phishing*—in which identity thieves send fraudulent e-mails to people masquerading as legitimate businesses to obtain social security numbers or other information needed for identity theft—is also a major security issue today. Common security concerns and precautions, such as protecting your computer from malware and protecting yourself against identity theft and phishing schemes, are discussed in detail in Chapter 9.

Privacy Issues

Some individuals view the potential risk to personal privacy as one of the most important issues regarding our networked society. As more and more data about our everyday activities is collected and stored on computers accessible via the Internet, our privacy is at risk because the potential for privacy violations increases. Today, data is collected about practically anything we buy online or offline, although offline purchases may not be associated with our identity unless we use a credit card or a membership or loyalty card. At issue is not that data is collected—with virtually all organizations using computers for recordkeeping, that is unavoidable—but rather how the collected data is used and how secure it is. Data collected by businesses may be used only by that company or, depending on the businesses' *privacy policy*, may be shared with others. Data shared with others often results in *spam*—unsolicited e-mails. Spam is an enormous problem for individuals and businesses today, and it is considered by many to be a violation of personal privacy. Privacy concerns and precautions are discussed in detail in Chapter 15.

CAUTION CAUTION CAUTION CAUTION CAUTION CAUTION CAUT

Using your primary e-mail address when shopping online or signing up for a sweepstake or other online activity will undoubtedly result in spam being sent to that e-mail address. Use a *throw-away e-mail address* (a free e-mail address from Gmail or another free e-mail provider that you can change easily) for these activities instead to help protect your privacy and cut back on the amount of spam delivered to your regular e-mail account.

Differences in Online Communications

There is no doubt that e-mail, instant messaging, and other online communications methods have helped speed up both personal and business communications and have made them more efficient (such as avoiding the telephone tag problem). As you spend more and more time communicating online, you will probably notice some differences between online communications methods (such as e-mail and instant messaging) and traditional communications methods (such as telephone calls and written letters). In general, online communications tend to be much less formal. This may be because people usually compose e-mail messages quickly and just send them off, without taking the time to reread the message content or check the spelling or grammar. However, you need to be careful not to be so casual—particularly in business—that your communications appear unprofessional or become too personal with people you do not know.

To help in that regard, a special etiquette—referred to as *netiquette*—has evolved to guide online behavior. A good rule of thumb is always to be polite and considerate of others and to refrain from offensive remarks. This holds true whether you are asking a question via a company's e-mail address, posting a message on someone's *Facebook Wall*, or IMing a friend. When the communication involves business, you should also be very careful with your grammar and spelling, to avoid embarrassing yourself. Some specific guidelines for what is considered to be proper online behavior are listed in Figure 1-30.

FIGURE 1-30

Netiquette. Use these netiquette guidelines and common sense when communicating online.

RULE	EXPLANATION
Use descriptive subject lines	Use short, descriptive subject lines for e-mail messages and discussion group posts. For example, "Question regarding MP3 downloads" is much better than a vague title, such as "Question".
Don't shout	SHOUTING REFERS TO TYPING YOUR ENTIRE E-MAIL MESSAGE OR DISCUSSION GROUP POST USING CAPITAL LETTERS. Use capital letters only when it is grammatically correct to do so or for emphasizing a few words.
Watch what you say	Things that you say or write online can be interpreted as being sexist, racist, ethnocentric, xenophobic, or in just general bad taste. Also check spelling and grammar—typos look unprofessional and nobody likes wading through poorly written materials.
Avoid e-mail overload	Don't send spam mail, which is unsolicated bulk e-mail and the Internet equivalent of junk mail. The same goes for forwarding e-mail chain letters or every joke you run across to everyone in your address book.
Be cautious	Don't give out personal information—such as your real name, telephone number, or credit card information—to people you meet in a chat room or other online meeting place.
Think before you send	Once you send an e-mail or text message or post something online, you lose control of it. Don't send messages that include content (such as compromising photos) that you would not want shared with others.

Another trend in online communications is the use of abbreviations and *emoticons*. Abbreviations or *acronyms*, such as BTW for "by the way," are commonly used to save time in all types of communications today. They are being used with increased frequency in text messaging and e-mail exchanged via mobile phones to speed up the text entry process. Emoticons are illustrations of faces showing smiles, frowns, and other expressions that are created with keyboard symbols—such as the popular :-) smile emoticon—and allow people to add an emotional tone to written online communications. Without these symbols, it is sometimes difficult to tell if the person who sent the online communication is serious or joking, since you cannot see the individual's face or hear his or her tone of voice. While most people would agree that using abbreviations and emoticons with personal communications is fine, they are not usually viewed as appropriate for formal business communications.

The Anonymity Factor

By their very nature, online communications lend themselves to *anonymity*. Since recipients usually do not hear senders' voices or see their handwriting, it is difficult to know for sure who the sender is. Particularly on *message boards* (online discussions in which users post messages and respond to other posts), in *virtual worlds* (online worlds that users can explore), and other online activities where individuals use made-up names instead of real names, there is an anonymous feel to being online.

Being anonymous gives many individuals a sense of freedom, which makes them feel able to say or do anything online. This sense of true freedom of speech can be beneficial. For example, a reserved individual who might never complain about a poor product or service in person may feel comfortable lodging a complaint by e-mail. In political discussion groups, many people feel they can be completely honest about what they think and can introduce new ideas and points of view without inhibition. Anonymous e-mail is also a safe way for an employee to blow the whistle on a questionable business practice, or for an individual to tip off police to a crime or potential terrorist attack.

But, like all good things, online anonymity can be abused. Using the Internet as their shield, some people use rude comments, ridicule, profanity, and even slander to attack people, places, and things they do not like or agree with. Others may use multiple online identities (such as multiple usernames on a message board) to give the appearance of increased support for their points of view. Still others may use multiple identities to try to manipulate stock prices (by posting false information about a company to drive the price down, for instance), to get buyers to trust an online auction seller (by posting fictitious positive feedback about themselves), or to commit other illegal or unethical acts.

It is possible to hide your true identity while browsing or sending e-mail by removing personal information from your browser and e-mail program or by using privacy software that acts as a middleman between you and Web sites and hides your identity, as discussed in more detail in Chapter 15. But, in fact, even when personal information is removed, ISPs and the government may still be able to trace communications back to a particular computer when a crime has occurred, so it is difficult—perhaps impossible—to be completely anonymous online.

Information Integrity

The Web contains a vast amount of information on a wide variety of topics. While much of the information is factual, other information may be misleading, biased, or just plain wrong. As more and more people turn to the Web for information, it is crucial that they take the time to determine if the information they obtain and pass on to others is accurate. There have been numerous cases of information intended as a joke being restated on a Web site as fact, statements being quoted out of context (which changed the meaning from the original intent), and hoaxes circulated via e-mail. Consequently, use common sense when evaluating what you read online, and double-check information before passing it on to others.

One way to evaluate online content is by its source. If you obtain information from a news source that you trust, you should feel confident that the accuracy of its online information is close to that of its offline counterpart. For information about a particular product, go to the originating company. For government information, government Web sites are your best source for fact checking. There are also independent Web sites (such as the *Snopes* Web site shown in Figure 1-31) that report on the validity of current online rumors and stories.

FIGURE 1-31

Snopes.com. This Web site can be used to check out online rumors.

SUMMARY

COMPUTERS IN YOUR LIFE

Chapter Objective 1:
Explain why it is essential to learn about computers today and discuss several ways computers are integrated into our business and personal lives.

Computers appear almost everywhere in today's world, and most people need to use a computer or a computerized device frequently on the job, at home, at school, or while on the go. **Computer literacy**, which is being familiar with basic computer concepts, helps individuals feel comfortable using computers and is a necessary skill for everyone today.

Computers abound in today's homes, schools, workplaces, and other locations. Most students and employees need to use a computer for productivity, research, or other important tasks. Individuals often use computers at home and/or carry portable computers or devices with them to remain in touch with others or to use Internet resources on a continual basis. Individuals also frequently encounter computers while on the go, such as *consumer kiosks* and *point-of-sale (POS)* systems.

WHAT IS A COMPUTER AND WHAT DOES IT DO?

Chapter Objective 2:
Define a computer and describe its primary operations.

A **computer** is a *programmable* electronic device that accepts **input**; performs **processing** operations; **outputs** the results; and provides **storage** for data, programs, or output when needed. Most computers today also have **communications** capabilities. This progression of input, processing, output, and storage is sometimes called the *information processing cycle.*

Data is the raw, unorganized facts that are input into the computer to be processed. Data that the computer has processed into a useful form is called **information**. Data can exist in many forms, representing *text*, *graphics*, *audio*, and *video.*

Chapter Objective 3:
List some important milestones in computer evolution.

One of the first calculating devices was the *abacus*. Early computing devices that predate today's computers include the *slide rule*, the *mechanical calculator*, and Dr. Herman Hollerith's *Punch Card Tabulating Machine and Sorter. First-generation computers*, such as *ENIAC* and *UNIVAC*, were powered by *vacuum tubes*; *second-generation computers* used *transistors*; and *third-generation computers* were possible because of the invention of the *integrated circuit (IC)*. Today's *fourth-generation computers* use *microprocessors* and are frequently connected to the *Internet* and other *networks*. Some people believe that *fifth-generation computers* will likely be based on *artificial intelligence.*

Chapter Objective 4:
Identify the major parts of a personal computer, including input, processing, output, storage, and communications hardware.

A computer is made up of **hardware** (the actual physical equipment that makes up the computer system) and **software** (the computer's programs). Common hardware components include the *keyboard* and *mouse* (*input devices*), the *CPU* (a *processing device*), *monitors* and *printers* (*output devices*), and *storage devices* and *storage media* (such as *CDs*, *DVD drives, hard drives, USB flash drives*, and *flash memory cards*). Most computers today also include a *modem, network adapter*, or other type of *communications device* to allow users to connect to the Internet or other network.

All computers need *system software*, namely an **operating system** (usually *Windows, Mac OS*, or *Linux*), to function. The operating system assists with the **boot** process, and then controls the operation of the computer, such as to allow users to run other types of software and to manage their files. Most software programs today use a variety of graphical objects that are selected to tell the computer what to do. The basic workspace for a Windows' users is the **Windows desktop**.

Chapter Objective 5:
Define software and understand how it is used to instruct the computer what to do.

Application software consists of programs designed to allow people to perform specific tasks or applications, such as word processing, Web browsing, photo touch-up, and so on. Software programs are written using a *programming language*. Programs are written by *programmers*; *computer users* are the people who use computers to perform tasks or obtain information.

INT ⏻

COMPUTERS TO FIT EVERY NEED

Embedded computers are built into products (such as cars and household appliances) to give them added functionality. **Mobile devices** are small devices with computing or Internet capabilities; a mobile device based on a mobile phone is called a **smartphone**.

Small computers used by individuals at home or work are called **personal computers** (**PCs**) or **microcomputers**. Most personal computers today are either **desktop computers** or **portable computers** (**notebook computers**, **laptop computers**, **tablet computers**, **netbooks**, or **ultra-mobile PCs** (**UMPC**)—also called **handheld computers**) and typically conform to either the *PC-compatible* or *Macintosh* standard. Tablet computers come in both *slate tablet* and *convertible tablet* formats. **Thin clients** are designed solely to access a network; **Internet appliances** are designed specifically for accessing the Internet and e-mail.

Medium-sized computers, or **midrange servers**, are used in many businesses to host data and programs to be accessed via the company network. A growing trend is **virtualization**—creating separate virtual environments on a single server that act as separate servers. The powerful computers used by most large businesses and organizations to perform the information processing necessary for day-to-day operations are called **mainframe computers**. The very largest, most powerful computers, which typically run one application at a time, are **supercomputers**. A supercomputer comprised of numerous smaller computers connected together to act as a single computer is a **supercomputing cluster**.

Chapter Objective 6:
List the six basic types of computers, giving at least one example of each type of computer and stating what that computer might be used for.

COMPUTER NETWORKS AND THE INTERNET

Computer networks are used to connect individual computers and related devices so that users can share hardware, software, and data as well as communicate with one another. The **Internet** is a worldwide collection of networks. Typically, individual users connect to the Internet by connecting to computers belonging to an **Internet service provider** (**ISP**)—a company that provides Internet access, usually for a fee. One resource available through the Internet is the **World Wide Web** (**WWW**)—an enormous collection of **Web pages** located on **Web servers**. The starting page for a **Web site** (a related group of Web pages) is called the *home page* for that site. Web pages are viewed with a **Web browser**, are connected with *hyperlinks*, and can be used for many helpful activities.

To access a computer network, you need some type of *modem* or *network adapter*. To access the Internet, an Internet service provider (ISP) is also used. **Internet addresses** are used to identify resources on the Internet and include numerical **IP addresses** and text-based **domain names** (used to identify computers), **uniform resource locators** or **URLs** (used to identify Web pages), and **e-mail addresses** (a combination of a **username** and domain name that is used to send an individual e-mail messages).

Web pages are displayed by clicking hyperlinks or by typing appropriate URLs in the browser's *Address bar. Favorites/Bookmarks* and the *History list* can be used to redisplay a previously-visited Web page and *search sites* can be used to locate Web pages matching specified criteria. **Electronic mail** (**e-mail**) is used to send electronic messages over the Internet.

Chapter Objective 7:
Explain what a network, the Internet, and the World Wide Web are, as well as how computers, people, and Web pages are identified on the Internet.

Chapter Objective 8:
Describe how to access a Web page and navigate through a Web site.

COMPUTERS AND SOCIETY

Computers and devices based on related technology have become indispensable tools for modern life, making ordinary tasks easier and quicker than ever before and helping make today's worker more productive than ever before. In addition to the benefits, however, there are many risks and societal implications related to our heavy use of the Internet and the vast amount of information available through the Internet. Issues include privacy and security risks and concerns (such as *malware*, *identity theft*, *phishing*, and *spam*), the differences in online and offline communications, the anonymity factor, and the amount of unreliable information that can be found on the Internet.

Chapter Objective 9:
Discuss the societal impact of computers, including some benefits and risks related to their prominence in our society.

REVIEW ACTIVITIES

KEY TERM MATCHING

a. computer

b. hardware

c. Internet

d. netbook

e. processing

f. software

g. storage

h. supercomputer

i. uniform resource locator (URL)

j. Web site

Instructions: Match each key term on the left with the definition on the right that best describes it.

1. _____ A collection of related Web pages usually belonging to an organization or individual.

2. _____ An Internet address, usually beginning with http://, that uniquely identifies a Web page.

3. _____ A programmable, electronic device that accepts data input, performs processing operations on that data, and outputs and stores the results.

4. _____ A very small notebook computer.

5. _____ Performing operations on data that have been input into a computer to convert that input to output.

6. _____ The operation of saving data, programs, or output for future use.

7. _____ The fastest, most expensive, and most powerful type of computer.

8. _____ The instructions, also called computer programs, that are used to tell a computer what it should do.

9. _____ The largest and most well-known computer network, linking millions of computers all over the world.

10. _____ The physical parts of a computer system, such as the keyboard, monitor, printer, and so forth.

SELF-QUIZ

Instructions: Circle **T** if the statement is true, **F** if the statement is false, or write the best answer in the space provided. **Answers for the self-quiz are located in the References and Resources Guide at the end of the book.**

1. **T F** A mouse is one common input device.

2. **T F** Software includes all the physical equipment in a computer system.

3. **T F** A computer can run without an operating system if it has good application software.

4. **T F** One of the most common types of home computers is the midrange server.

5. **T F** An example of a domain name is *microsoft.com*.

6. _____ is the operation in which data is entered into the computer.

7. A(n) _____ computer can come in convertible or slate form.

8. _____ is frequently used with servers today to create several separate environments on a single server that act as separate servers.

9. Electronic messages sent over the Internet that can be retrieved by the recipient at his or her convenience are called _____.

10. Write the number of the term that best matches each of the following descriptions in the blank to the left of its description.

   a. _____ Allows access to resources located on the Internet.

   b. _____ Supervises the running of all other programs on the computer.

   c. _____ Enables users to perform specific tasks on a computer.

   d. _____ Allows the creation of application programs.

1. Application software
2. Operating system
3. Programming language
4. Web browser

---

1. For the following list of computer hardware devices, indicate the principal function of each device by writing the appropriate letter—I (input device), O (output device), S (storage device), P (processing device), or C (communications device)—in the space provided.

   a. CPU _____   d. Keyboard _____   g. Speakers _____

   b. Monitor _____   e. Hard drive _____   h. DVD drive _____

   c. Mouse _____   f. Modem _____   i. Microphone _____

2. Supply the missing words to complete the following statements.

   a. The Internet is an example of a(n) _____, a collection of computers and other devices connected together to share resources and communicate with each other.

   b. The starting page for a Web site is called the site's _____.

   c. For the e-mail address *jsmith@cengage.com*, *jsmith* is the _____ and *cengage.com* is the _____ name.

   d. The e-mail address pronounced *bill gee at microsoft dot com* is written _____.

3. What are three differences between a desktop computer and an ultra-mobile PC (UMPC)?

4. List two reasons why a business may choose to network its employees' computers.

5. If a computer manufacturer called Apex created a home page for the Web, what would its URL likely be? Also, supply an appropriate e-mail address for yourself, assuming that you are employed by that company.

---

1. There is usually a positive side and a negative side to each new technological improvement. Select a technology you use every day and consider its benefits and risks. What benefits does the technology provide? Are there any risks involved and, if so, how can they be minimized? If you chose not to use this technology because of the possible risks associated with it, how would your life be affected? Who should determine if the benefits of a new technology outweigh the potential risks? Consumers? The government?

2. The ubiquitous nature of mobile phones today brings tremendous convenience to our lives, but will misuse of new improvements to this technology result in the loss of that convenience? For instance, camera phones are now banned in many fitness centers, park restrooms, and other similar facilities because some people have used them inappropriately to take compromising photos, and mobile phones are banned in many classrooms because of the disruption of constant text messaging and the use of the phone by dishonest students to cheat on exams. Do you think these reactions to mobile phone misuse are justified? Is there another way to ensure the appropriate use of mobile phones without banning their use for all individuals? Should there be more stringent consequences for those who use technology for illegal or unethical purposes?

PROJECTS

1. **Mobile TV** As discussed in this chapter, TV is one of the newest entertainment options available for mobile phones. From live TV to video clips and movies, mobile TV is taking off.

   For this project, investigate the mobile TV options available today. Find at least two services and compare features, such as cost, compatibility, channels, and programming. Do your selected services offer live TV, video-on-demand, or both? If you have a mobile phone, are any of the services available through your mobile provider? Are there currently Web sites where mobile users can view episodes of TV shows for free, like personal computer users can? What is the current status of the push by the *Open Mobile Video Coalition* to have a free mobile TV standard across the United States? Have you ever watched TV on a mobile phone? If so, how do you rate your experience and would you do it again? If not, would you want to watch TV on a mobile phone? Do you think mobile TV is the wave of the future? Why or why not? At the conclusion of your research, prepare a one-page summary of your findings and opinions and submit it to your instructor.

2. **Buying a New PC** New personal computers are widely available directly from manufacturers, as well as in retail, computer, electronic, and warehouse stores. Some stores carry only standard configurations as set up by the manufacturers; others allow you to customize a system.

   For this project, assume that you are in the market for a new personal computer. Give some thought to the type of computer (such as desktop, notebook, or netbook computer) that best fits your lifestyle and the tasks you wish to perform (such as the application programs you wish to use, how many programs you wish to use at one time, and how fast you desire the response time to be). Make a list of your hardware and software requirements (refer to the "Guide for Buying a PC" in the References and Resources Guide at the end of this book, if needed), being as specific as possible. By researching newspaper ads, manufacturer Web sites, and/or systems for sale at local stores, find three systems that meet your minimum requirements. Prepare a one-page comparison chart, listing each requirement and how each system meets or exceeds it. Also include any additional features each system has, and information regarding the brand, price, delivery time, shipping, sales tax, and warranty for each system. On your comparison sheet, mark the system that you would prefer to buy and write one paragraph explaining why. Turn in your comparison sheet and summary to your instructor, stapled to copies of the printed ads, specifications printed from Web sites, or other written documentation that you collected during this project.

3. **The Internet** The Internet and World Wide Web are handy tools that can help you research topics covered in this textbook, complete many of the projects, and perform the online activities available via the textbook's Web site that are designed to enhance your learning and help you prepare for exams on the content covered in this textbook.

   For this project, find an Internet-enabled computer on your campus, at home, or at your public library and access the Understanding Computers Web site located at **www.cengage.com/ computerconcepts/np/uc13**. Once you are at the site, note the types of information and activities that are available to you as a student and select a few of them by using your mouse to click the hyperlinks corresponding to the options you want to explore. At the conclusion of this task, prepare a one-page summary describing the resources available through this textbook's Web site, and your opinion about their usefulness in enhancing your learning experience and/or preparing for exams related to this text, and submit it to your instructor.

4. **Gossip Sites** A recent trend on college campuses today is the use of campus gossip sites, where students can post campus related news, rumors, and basic gossip. These sites were originally set up to promote free speech and to allow participants to publish comments anonymously without repercussions from school administrators, professors, and other officials. However, they are now being used to post vicious comments about others. What do you think of campus gossip sites? Is it ethical to post a rumor about another individual on these sites? How would you feel if you read a posting about yourself on a gossip site? School administrators cannot regulate the content since the sites are not sponsored or run by the college, and federal law prohibits Web hosts from being liable for the content posted by its users. Is this ethical? What if a posting leads to a criminal act, such as a rape, murder, or suicide? Who, if anyone, should be held responsible?

    For this project, form an opinion about the ethical ramifications of gossip Web sites and be prepared to discuss your position (in class, via an online class discussion group, in a class chat room, or via a class blog, depending on your instructor's directions). You may also be asked to write a short paper expressing your opinion.

ETHICS IN ACTION

5. **Online Education** The amount of distance learning available through the Internet and World Wide Web has exploded in the last couple of years. A few years ago, it was possible to take an occasional course online—now, an entire college degree can be earned online.

    For this project, look into the online education options available at your school and two other colleges or universities. Compare and contrast the programs in general, including whether or not the institution is accredited, the types of courses available online, whether or not an entire certificate or degree can be earned online, and the required fees. Next, select one online course and research it more closely. Find out how the course works in an online format—including whether or not any face-to-face class time is required, whether assignments and exams are submitted online, which software programs are required, and other course requirements—and determine if you would be interested in taking that course. Share your findings with the class in the form of a short presentation. The presentation should not exceed 10 minutes and should make use of one or more presentation aids, such as the chalkboard, handouts, overhead transparencies, or a computer-based slide presentation (your instructor may provide additional requirements). You may also be asked to submit a summary of the presentation to your instructor.

**PRESENTATION/
DEMONSTRATION**

Instructions: Go to the Chapter 1 page at **www.cengage.com/computerconcepts/np/uc13** to work the following Web Activities.

WEB ACTIVITIES

6. **Interactive Activities** Work the interactive **Crossword Puzzle**, watch the **Video Podcasts** and **Online Videos**, and explore the **Further Exploration** links associated with this chapter.

    If you have a SAM user profile, you may have access to hands-on instruction, practice, and assessment of the skills covered in this chapter. Check with your instructor for instructions and the correct URL/Web site to access those assignments.

7. **Student Edition Labs** Work the following interactive **Student Edition Labs.**
    ➤ **Using Windows**   ➤ **E-Mail**

8. **Test Yourself** Review the **Online Study Guide** for this chapter, then test your knowledge of the terms and concepts covered in this chapter by completing the **Key Term Matching** exercise, the **Self-Quiz**, the **Exercises**, and the **Practice Test**.

SAM

Student Edition Labs

expert insight on...

Personal Computers

D-Link ®
Building Networks for People

Joe Melfi is the
Associate Director of
Business Solutions for
D-Link Systems. He has
worked in the area of
communications and
electronics technologies
for more than 25 years,
including as a Systems
Engineer, Software
Engineer, Application
Engineer, and Technical
Marketing Engineer,
before accepting his cur-
rent position at D-Link.
Joe holds a Bachelor
of Science degree in
Electrical Engineering,
as well as several tech-
nical certificates. He
has also been a college
instructor, teaching
courses in microproces-
sor systems, data com-
munications, and digital
electronics.

A conversation with JOE MELFI

Associate Director of Business Solutions, D-Link Systems

" *. . . it is important to be cautious about what information is shared online because, once it is out there, it can't be taken back.* "

My Background . . .

In my youth, I had an endless curiosity about how things worked. I took everything apart to see what was inside, which led me down the path to become an electrical engineer. Eventually, I found my calling in computer communications. All in all, I have more than 25 years of applied experience in a wide range of communications and electronics technologies. Currently, I serve as Associate Director of Business Solutions for D-Link, a leading company in the area of business and consumer networking hardware. My primary responsibilities include driving marketing programs, creating sales materials, and overseeing technical aspects of the marketing department.

Throughout my career, I've found I favor roles that merge technology with marketing. I credit my engineering education and experience; my hands-on experience as a technician and hobbyist; my teaching experience; and my experience as a techie working with sales teams and making pre-sentations with giving me the experience and skills needed to succeed in my chosen career.

It's Important to Know . . .

Computers are everywhere, and take many forms. Computers are more than the PC on your desk. They are in your cars, your televisions, your phones, and so many other places. The smartphone is one current technology that may end up having the biggest impact on our lives. Today's mobile phones typically can be used for much more than placing phone calls. They often include a camera, GPS capabilities, a voice recorder, Internet connectivity, multimedia functions, and access to e-mail, calendars, contact information, and more. It will be interesting to see how far this technology goes.

Computers are ubiquitous on the job. They are an integral part of almost any job today. Therefore, you can never know enough about computers and how to utilize them effectively.

Computers have also affected social behavior. While computers increase productivity and enhance functionality, we should not forget that sometimes human interaction is needed. And, when dealing with people, we should remember that people are not computers and shouldn't be treated as such—they require patience and emotional consideration.

How I Use this Technology . . .

I use computers in almost every aspect of my life, both professional and personal. My home is completely networked with computers on every floor, cameras for surveillance, servers and storage devices for managing all my data, and centralized printers and scanners accessible throughout the network. I also have networked media players that deliver video and audio from my home comput-ers, storage devices, or the Internet to my big screen TV and entertainment systems. In addition, I have wireless home control, which is something that I expect to become more popular in the near future. My mobile phone also syncs data from my network so I can take essential information with me wherever I go.

What the Future Holds . . .

There was a time when individuals and businesses hesitated to embrace the Internet, but that has clearly changed in recent years. We are surely becoming a connected society and computers, computer communications, and the Internet have changed the way businesses operate in so many ways. Mobile phones are quickly replacing landline phones, and they are becoming handheld computers that bring us amazing capabilities, including allowing us to be more mobile than ever before. And, with Internet usage becoming such an integral part of our business and personal lives, high-speed networking is changing from optional to commonplace.

But there is more change to come. The new wireless standards that are on the horizon will continue to improve communication performance and functionality in the near future. We will have Internet access everywhere, anytime, via handheld devices, and entertainment will use the Internet as a significant method of delivery. This continued evolution of computers and communications will provide us with easier access to goods and services, instant accomplishment of tasks, and an endless assortment of entertainment and productivity options at our disposal.

It is important to remember, however, that while our increasingly connected society has many benefits, it also brings additional security and privacy risks. Computers and the Internet allow more ways for the curious and the deviant to peek into our lives and access data that has traditionally been private. In addition, many individuals today voluntarily provide personal data without hesitation, and social networking has made it so easy for a person's voice to be heard that many people spend a great deal of time posting their opinions online. But it is important to be cautious about what information is shared online because, once it is out there, it can't be taken back.

"Computers are an integral part of almost any job today. Therefore, you can never know enough about computers and how to utilize them effectively."

My Advice to Students . . .

Embrace computers as productivity tools and entertainment appliances, in whatever form they take. Overcome the fear that keeps many people from taking full advantage of computers. I highly recommend learning how computers function by learning what hardware is located inside. In fact, I build computers for fun and learning; there is no better way to learn than with a hands-on experience.

Discussion Question

Joe Melfi views the mobile phone as one current technology that may end up having the biggest impact on our lives in the future. Think about which tasks you use your mobile phone for and which ones you cannot. What changes need to be made in the future in order to perform all of these tasks on a mobile phone? Will they be primarily hardware or software changes? Is the mobile phone the computer of the future? Be prepared to discuss your position (in class, via an online class discussion group, in a class chat room, or via a class blog, depending on your instructor's directions). You may also be asked to write a short paper expressing your opinion.

> **For more information on D-Link Systems, visit www.dlink.com.**

Hardware

When most people think of computers, images of hardware usually fill their minds. Hardware includes the system unit, keyboard, mouse, monitor, and all the other interesting pieces of equipment that make up a computer system. This module explores the rich variety of computer hardware available today. But, as you already know, hardware needs instructions from software in order to function. Hardware without software is like a car without a driver or a canvas and paintbrush without an artist. Software is discussed in detail in the next module.

This module divides coverage of hardware into three parts. Chapter 2 describes the hardware located inside the system unit, which is the main box of the computer and where most of the work of a computer is performed. Chapter 3 discusses the different types of devices that can be used for data storage. Chapter 4 covers the wide variety of hardware that can be used for input and output.

Chapter 2
The System Unit: Processing and Memory 50

Overview 51

Data and Program Representation 51

Inside the System Unit 56

How the CPU Works 72

Making Computers Faster and Better Now and in the Future 76

Chapter 3
Storage 92

Overview 93

Storage Systems Characteristics 93

Hard Drives 96

Optical Discs 105

Flash Memory 110

Other Types of Storage Systems 114

Evaluating Your Storage Alternatives 121

Chapter 4
Input and Output 128

Overview 129

Keyboards 129

Pointing and Touch Devices 131

Scanners, Readers, and Digital Cameras 138

Audio Input 148

Display Devices 150

Printers 159

Audio Output 165

"Technology has to adapt to market needs, not the other way around."

For more comments from Guest Expert **Sumit Agnihotry** of Acer Pan America, see the **Expert Insight on . . . Hardware** feature at the end of the module.

chapter 2

The System Unit: Processing and Memory

After completing this chapter, you will be able to do the following:

1. Understand how data and programs are represented to a computer and be able to identify a few of the coding systems used to accomplish this.

2. Explain the functions of the hardware components commonly found inside the system unit, such as the CPU, memory, buses, and expansion cards.

3. Describe how peripheral devices or other hardware can be added to a computer.

4. Understand how a computer's CPU and memory components process program instructions and data.

5. Name and evaluate several strategies that can be used today for speeding up the operations of a computer.

6. List some processing technologies that may be used in future computers.

outline

Overview

Data and Program Representation
Digital Data Representation
Representing Numerical Data: The Binary Numbering System
Coding Systems for Text-Based Data
Coding Systems for Other Types of Data
Representing Software Programs: Machine Language

Inside the System Unit
The Motherboard
The Power Supply and Drive Bays
The CPU
Memory
Fans, Heat Sinks, and Other Cooling Components
Expansion Slots, Expansion Cards, and ExpressCard Modules
Buses
Ports and Connectors

How the CPU Works
Typical CPU Components
The System Clock and the Machine Cycle

Making Computers Faster and Better Now and in the Future
Improving the Performance of Your System Today
Strategies for Making Faster and Better Computers
Future Trends

OVERVIEW

The system unit of a computer is sometimes thought of as a mysterious "black box" and often the user does not have much understanding of what happens inside it. In this chapter, we demystify the system unit by looking inside the box and closely examining the functions of the parts. Consequently, the chapter gives you a feel for what the CPU, memory, and other devices commonly found inside the system unit do and how they work together to perform the tasks that the user requests.

To start, we discuss how a computer system represents data and program instructions. Here we talk about the codes that computers use to translate data back and forth from the symbols that computers can manipulate, to the symbols that people are accustomed to using. These topics lead to a discussion of how the CPU and memory are arranged with other components inside the system unit, the characteristics of those components, and how a CPU performs processing tasks. Finally, we look at strategies that can be used today to speed up a computer, plus some strategies that may be used to create faster and better computers in the future.

Many of you will apply this chapter's content to conventional personal computers—such as desktop and notebook computers. However, it is important to realize that the principles and procedures discussed in this chapter apply to other types of computers as well, such as those embedded in toys, consumer devices, household appliances, cars, and other devices, and those used with mobile devices, powerful servers, mainframes, and supercomputers. ∎

DATA AND PROGRAM REPRESENTATION

In order to be understood by a computer, data and software programs need to be represented appropriately. Consequently, *coding systems* are used to represent data and programs in a manner that can be understood by the computer. These concepts are discussed in the next few sections.

Digital Data Representation

Virtually all computers today—such as the embedded computers, mobile devices, personal computers, midrange servers, mainframes, and supercomputers discussed in Chapter 1—are *digital computers*. Most digital computers are *binary computers*, which can understand only two states, usually thought of as *off* and *on* and represented by the digits 0 and 1. Consequently, all data processed by a binary computer must be in binary form (0s and 1s). The 0s and 1s used to represent data can be represented in a variety of ways, such as with an open or closed circuit, the absence or presence of electronic current, two different types of magnetic alignment on a storage medium, and so on (see Figure 2-1).

Regardless of their physical representations, these 0s and 1s are commonly referred to as *bits*, a computing term derived

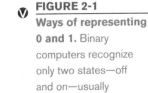

FIGURE 2-1

Ways of representing 0 and 1. Binary computers recognize only two states—off and on—usually represented by 0 and 1.

Open = 0 (off)

Closed = 1 (on)

CIRCUIT

Negative = 0 (off)

Positive = 1 (on)

MAGNETIZATION

from the phrase *binary digits*. A **bit** is the smallest unit of data that a binary computer can recognize. Therefore, the input you enter via a keyboard, the software program you use to play your music collection, the term paper stored on your computer, and the digital photos located on your mobile phone are all just groups of bits. Representing data in a form that can be understood by a digital computer is called *digital data representation.*

Because most computers can only understand data and instructions in binary form, binary can be thought of as the computer's *natural language.* People, of course, do not speak in binary. For example, you are not likely to go up to a friend and say,

$$0100100001001001$$

which translates into the word "HI" using one binary coding system. People communicate with one another in their natural languages, such as English, Chinese, Spanish, and French. For example, this book is written in English, which uses a 26-character alphabet. In addition, most countries use a numbering system with 10 possible symbols—0 through 9. As already mentioned, however, binary computers understand only 0s and 1s. For us to interact with a computer, a translation process from our natural language to 0s and 1s and then back again to our natural language is required. When we enter data into a computer system, the computer translates the natural-language symbols we input into binary 0s and 1s. After processing the data, the computer translates and outputs the resulting information in a form that we can understand.

A bit by itself typically represents only a fraction of a piece of data. Consequently, large numbers of bits are needed to represent a written document, computer program, digital photo, music file, or virtually any other type of data. Eight bits grouped together are collectively referred to as a **byte**. It is important to be familiar with this concept because *byte* terminology is frequently used in a variety of computer contexts, such as to indicate the size of a document or digital photo, the amount of memory a computer has, or the amount of room left on a storage medium. Since these quantities often involve thousands or millions of bytes, prefixes are commonly used in conjunction with the term *byte* to represent larger amounts of data (see Figure 2-2). For instance, a **kilobyte (KB)** is equal to 1,024 bytes, but is usually thought of as approximately 1,000 bytes; a **megabyte (MB)** is about 1 million bytes; a **gigabyte (GB)** is about 1 billion bytes; a **terabyte (TB)** is about 1 trillion bytes; a **petabyte (PB)** is about 1,000 terabytes (2^{50} bytes); an **exabyte (EB)** is about 1,000 petabytes (2^{60} bytes); a **zettabyte (ZB)** is about 1,000 exabytes (2^{70} bytes); and a **yottabyte (YB)** is about 1,000 zettabytes (2^{80} bytes). Using these definitions, 5 KB is about 5,000 bytes, 10 MB is about 10 million bytes, and 2 TB is about 2 trillion bytes.

Computers represent programs and data through a variety of binary-based coding systems. The coding system used depends primarily on the type of data that needs to be represented; the most common coding systems are discussed in the next few sections.

Representing Numerical Data: The Binary Numbering System

A *numbering system* is a way of representing numbers. The numbering system we commonly use is called the **decimal numbering system** because it uses 10 symbols—the digits 0, 1, 2, 3, 4, 5, 6, 7, 8, and 9—to represent all possible numbers. Numbers greater than nine, such as 21 and 683, are represented using combinations of these 10 symbols. The **binary numbering system** uses only two symbols—the digits 0 and 1—to represent all

FIGURE 2-2

Bits and bytes.
Document size, storage capacity, and memory capacity are all measured in bytes.

	Abbreviation	Approximate Size
	KB	1 thousand bytes
	MB	1 million bytes
	GB	1 billion bytes
	TB	1 trillion bytes
	PB	1,000 terabytes

DECIMAL NUMBERING SYSTEM
Each place value in a decimal number represents 10 raised to the appropriate power.

The decimal number **7216**

10 raised to different powers

means 6 x 1   =   6
means 1 x 10   =   10
means 2 x 100   =   200
means 7 x 1,000   = 7,000
                    7,216

BINARY NUMBERING SYSTEM
Each place value in a binary number represents 2 raised to the appropriate power.

The binary number **1001**

2 raised to different powers

means 1 x 1 = 1
means 0 x 2 = 0
means 0 x 4 = 0
means 1 x 8 = 8
            9

Decimal equivalent

FIGURE 2-3
Examples of using the decimal and binary numbering systems.

possible numbers. Consequently, binary computers use the binary numbering system to represent numbers and to perform math computations.

In both numbering systems, the position of each digit determines the power, or exponent, to which the *base number* (10 for decimal or 2 for binary) is raised. In the decimal numbering system, going from right to left, the first position or column (the ones column) represents 10^0 or 1; the second column (the tens column) represents 10^1 or 10; the third column (the hundreds column) represents 10^2 or 100; and so forth. Therefore, as Figure 2-3 shows, the decimal number 7,216 is understood as $7 \times 10^3 + 2 \times 10^2 + 1 \times 10^1 + 6 \times 10^0$ or $7,000 + 200 + 10 + 6$ or 7,216. In binary, the concept is the same but the columns have different place values. For example, the far-right column is the ones column (for 2^0), the second column is the twos column (2^1), the third column is the fours column (2^2), and so on. Therefore, although 1001 represents "one thousand one" in decimal notation, 1001 represents "nine" ($1 \times 2^3 + 0 \times 2^2 + 0 \times 2^1 + 1 \times 2^0$ or $8 + 0 + 0 + 1$ or 9) in the binary numbering system, as illustrated in the bottom half of Figure 2-3.

Coding Systems for Text-Based Data

While numeric data is represented by the binary numbering system, text-based data is represented by binary coding systems specifically developed for text-based data—namely, *ASCII*, *EBCDIC*, and *Unicode*. These codes are used to represent all characters that can appear in text data—such as numbers, letters, and special characters and symbols like the dollar sign, comma, percent symbol and many mathematical characters.

TIP

For more information about and examples of converting between numbering systems, see the "A Guide to Numbering Systems" section in the References and Resources Guide at the end of this book.

CHARACTER	ACSII
0	00110000
1	00110001
2	00110010
3	00110011
4	00110100
5	00110101
A	01000001
B	01000010
C	01000011
D	01000100
E	01000101
F	01000110
+	00101011
!	00100001
#	00100011

FIGURE 2-4

Some extended ASCII code examples.

ASCII and EBCDIC

ASCII (**American Standard Code for Information Interchange**) is the coding system traditionally used with personal computers. *EBCDIC* (*Extended Binary-Coded Decimal Interchange Code*) was developed by IBM, primarily for use with mainframes. ASCII is a 7-digit (7-bit) code, although there are several different 8-bit *extended versions* of ASCII that contain additional symbols not included in the 7-bit ASCII code. The extended ASCII character sets (see some examples of 8-bit ASCII codes in Figure 2-4) and EBCDIC represent each character as a unique combination of 8 bits. One group of 8 bits (1 byte) allows 256 (2^8) unique combinations. Therefore, an 8-bit code can represent up to 256 characters (twice as many as a 7-bit code)—enough to include the characters used in the English alphabet, as well as some non-English characters, the 10 decimal digits, the other characters usually found on a keyboard, and many special characters not included on a keyboard such as mathematical symbols, graphic symbols, additional punctuation marks, and other symbols.

Unicode

Unlike ASCII and EBCDIC, which are limited to only the Latin alphabet used with the English language, **Unicode** is a universal international coding standard designed to represent text-based data written in any ancient or modern language, including those with different alphabets, such as Chinese, Greek, Hebrew, Amharic, Tibetan, and Russian (see Figure 2-5). Unicode uniquely identifies each character using 0s and 1s, no matter which language, program, or computer platform is being used. It is a longer code, consisting of 1 to 4 bytes (8 to 32 bits) per character, and can represent over one million characters, which is more than enough unique combinations to represent the standard characters in all the world's written languages, as well as thousands of mathematical and technical symbols, punctuation marks, and other symbols and signs. The biggest advantage of Unicode is that it can be used worldwide with consistent and unambiguous results.

Unicode is quickly replacing ASCII as the primary text-coding system. In fact, Unicode includes the ASCII character set so ASCII data can be converted easily to Unicode when needed. Unicode is used by most Web browsers and is widely used for Web pages and Web applications (Google data, for instance, is stored exclusively in Unicode). Most recent software programs, including the latest versions of Microsoft Windows, Mac OS, and Microsoft Office, also use Unicode, as do modern programming languages, such as Java and Python. Unicode is updated regularly to add new characters and new languages not originally encoded—the most recent version is *Unicode 5.2*.

CHINESE   GREEK   HEBREW

AMHARIC   TIBETAN   RUSSIAN

FIGURE 2-5

Unicode. Many characters, such as these, can be represented by Unicode but not by ASCII or EBCDIC.

Coding Systems for Other Types of Data

So far, our discussion of data coding schemes has focused on numeric and text-based data, which consists of alphanumeric characters and special symbols, such as the comma and dollar sign. Multimedia data, such as graphics, audio, and video data, must also be represented in binary form in order to be used with a computer, as discussed next.

Graphics Data

Graphics data consists of still images, such as photographs or drawings. One of the most common methods for storing graphics data is in the form of a *bitmap image*—an image comprised of a grid of small dots, called *pixels* (short for *picture elements*), that are colored appropriately to represent an image. The color to be displayed at each pixel is represented by some combination of 0s and 1s, and the number of bits required to store the color for each pixel ranges from 1 to 24 bits. For example, each pixel in a *monochrome graphic* can be only one of two possible colors (such as black or white). These monochrome images require only one bit of storage space per pixel (for instance, the bit would contain a 1 when representing a pixel that should display as white, and the bit would contain a 0 for a pixel that should display as black). Images with more than two colors can use 4, 8, or 24 bits to store the color data for each pixel—this allows for 16 (2^4), 256 (2^8), or 16,777,216 (2^{24}) colors respectively, as shown in Figure 2-6.

The number of bits used per pixel depends on the type of image being stored; for instance, the *JPEG* images taken by most digital cameras today use 24-bit *true color images*. While this can result in large file sizes, some images (like JPEGs) can be *compressed* when needed, such as to reduce the amount of storage space required to store that image or to allow faster transmission over the Internet.

One sample pixel: 1110

16-COLOR IMAGE
The color of each pixel is represented using one half byte (4 bits).

One sample pixel: 01110110

256-COLOR IMAGE
The color of each pixel is represented using one byte (8 bits).

One sample pixel: 101001100100110111001011

PHOTOGRAPHIC-QUALITY (TRUE COLOR) IMAGE (16.8 million colors)
The color of each pixel is represented using three bytes (24 bits).

FIGURE 2-6
Representing graphics data. With bitmapped images, the color of each pixel is represented by bits; the more bits used, the better the image quality.

Audio Data

Like graphics data, *audio data*—such as a song or the sound of someone speaking—must be in digital form in order to be stored on a storage medium or processed by a computer. To convert analog sound to digital sound, several thousand *samples*—digital representations of the sound at particular moments—are taken every second. When the samples are played back in the proper order, they recreate the sound of the voice or music. For example, audio CDs record sound using 2-byte samples, which are sampled at a rate of 44,100 times per second. When these samples are played back at a rate of 44,100 samples per second, they sound like continuous voice or music. With so many samples, however, sound files take up a great deal of storage space—about 32 MB for a 3-minute stereo song (44,100 times × 2 bytes × 180 seconds × 2 channels).

Because of its large size, audio data is usually compressed to reduce its file size when it is transmitted over the Internet or stored on an iPod or other portable digital media player. For example, files that are *MP3-encoded*—that is, compressed with the *MP3 compression algorithm* developed by the *Motion Pictures Expert Group* (*MPEG*)—are about 10 times smaller than their uncompressed digital versions, so they download 10 times faster and take up one-tenth of the storage space. The actual storage size required depends on the *bit rate*—the number of bits to be transferred per second when the file is played—used when the file is initially created; audio files using the common bit rate of 128 *Kbps* (thousands of bits per second) are about one-tenth the size of the original CD-quality recording.

TIP

For more examples of ASCII, EBCDIC, and Unicode, see the "Coding Charts" section in the References and Resources Guide at the end of this book.

ASK THE EXPERT

Mark Davis, President, The Unicode Consortium

What should the average computer user know about Unicode?

Whenever you read or write anything on a computer, you're using Unicode. Whenever you search on Google, Yahoo!, MSN, Wikipedia, or other Web sites, you're using Unicode. It's the way that text in all the world's languages can be stored and processed on computers.

HW

✓ **TIP**

Graphics, audio, video, and file compression are discussed in detail in Chapter 10.

Video Data

Video data—such as home movies, feature films, video clips, and television shows—is displayed using a collection of frames; each frame contains a still image. When the frames are projected one after the other (typically at a rate of 24 frames per second), the illusion of movement is created. With so many frames, the amount of data involved in showing a two-hour feature film can be substantial. Fortunately, like audio data, video data can be compressed to reduce it to a manageable size. For example, a two-hour movie can be compressed to fit on a single DVD disc; it can be compressed even further to be delivered over the Web.

Representing Software Programs: Machine Language

Just as numbers, text, and multimedia data must be represented by 0s and 1s, software programs must also be represented by 0s and 1s. Before a computer can execute any program instruction, such as requesting input from the user, moving a file from one storage device to another, or opening a new window on the screen, it must convert the instruction into a binary code known as **machine language**. An example of a typical machine language instruction is as follows:

01011000011100000000000100000010

A machine language instruction might look like a meaningless string of 0s and 1s, but it actually represents specific operations and storage locations. The 32-bit instruction shown here, for instance, moves data between two specific memory locations on one type of computer system. Early computers required programs to be written in machine language, but today's computers allow programs to be written in a programming language, which is then translated by the computer into machine language in order to be understood by the computer. Programming languages and *language translators* are discussed in detail in Chapter 13.

INSIDE THE SYSTEM UNIT

The **system unit** is the main case of a computer. It houses the processing hardware for that computer, as well as a few other devices, such as storage devices, the power supply, and cooling fans. The system unit for a desktop computer often looks like a rectangular box, although other shapes and sizes are available, such as the all-in-one computer illustrated in Figure 1-14. The inside of a system unit for a typical desktop computer system is shown in Figure 2-7. In general, the system unit contains a *CPU*, several types of *memory*, interfaces to connect external *peripheral devices* (such as printers), and other components all interconnected through sets of wires called *buses* on the *motherboard*. These components are discussed in detail in the next few sections. Portable computers (like notebook computers and ultra-mobile PCs (UMPCs)) and mobile devices have similar components, but the system unit and components are usually smaller and the system unit is usually combined with the computer screen to form a single piece of hardware. The components typically found inside a system unit are discussed next.

The Motherboard

A *circuit board* is a thin board containing *computer chips* and other electronic components. Computer chips are very small pieces of silicon or other semiconducting material that contain *integrated circuits* (*ICs*)—collections of electronic circuits containing microscopic

CPU
Performs the calculations and does the comparisons needed for processing, as well as controls the other parts of the computer system.

POWER SUPPLY
Converts standard electrical power into a form the computer can use.

FAN
Cools the CPU.

HARD DRIVE
Stores data and programs; the principal storage device for most computers.

EXPANSION CARD
Connects peripheral devices or adds new capabilities to a computer.

DRIVE BAYS
Hold storage devices, such as the DVD and hard drives shown here.

EXPANSION SLOTS
Connect expansion cards to the motherboard to add additional capabilities.

DVD DRIVE
Accesses data stored on CDs or DVDs.

MOTHERBOARD
Connects all components of the computer system; the computer's main circuit board.

FLASH MEMORY CARD READER
Accesses data stored on flash memory cards.

MEMORY (RAM) MODULES
Store data temporarily while you are working with it.

USB PORTS
Connect USB devices to the computer.

MEMORY SLOTS
Connect memory modules to the motherboard.

FIGURE 2-7

Inside a typical system unit. The system unit houses the CPU, memory, and other important pieces of hardware.

pathways along which electrical current can travel—and *transistors*—switches controlling the flow of electrons along the pathways. The main circuit board inside the system unit is called the **motherboard**.

As shown in Figure 2-7, the motherboard has a variety of chips, boards, and connectors attached to it. All devices used with a computer need to be connected via a wired or wireless connection to the motherboard. Typically, *external devices* (such as monitors, keyboards, mice, and printers) connect to the motherboard by plugging into a *port*—a special connector exposed through the exterior of the system unit case. The port is either built directly into the motherboard or created via an *expansion card* inserted into an *expansion slot* on the motherboard. Wireless external devices typically use a *transceiver* that plugs into a port on the computer to transmit data between the wireless device and the motherboard or they use wireless networking technology (such as *Bluetooth*) built into the motherboard. Ports and system expansion are discussed in more detail later in this chapter; wireless networking is covered in Chapter 7.

The Power Supply and Drive Bays

Most personal computers plug into a standard electrical outlet. The *power supply* inside a desktop computer connects to the motherboard to deliver electricity to the computer. Portable computers almost always contain a *rechargeable battery pack* to power the computer when it is not connected to a power outlet, as well as an external power supply adapter that connects the computer to a power outlet to recharge the battery when needed. One issue with newer portable computers and mobile devices is the growing use

>**Motherboard.** The main circuit board of a computer, located inside the system unit, to which all computer system components connect.

of nonremovable batteries. Although these batteries allow the devices to be lighter and are supposed to last for the typical life of the device, they are more difficult and expensive to replace if they fail—and often it is not worth the trouble and expense to replace them in some mobile devices like mobile phones and portable digital media players. The ramifications of the growing amount of *electronic trash* (*e-trash*), such as discarded mobile phones and other electronics, that is being generated worldwide is discussed in Chapter 16.

Most conventional computers (such as desktop computers) also contain *drive bays* (rectangular metal racks) inside the system unit into which storage devices (a *hard drive*, *DVD drive*, and *flash memory card reader*, for instance) can be inserted and secured. Storage devices inside the system unit are connected via a cable to the motherboard, as well as to the internal power supply, if necessary. Storage devices with removable media that need to be inserted into and removed from the drive (such as a DVD drive), are accessible through the front of the system unit (refer again to Figure 2-7). Storage devices that are not used in conjunction with removable storage media (such as an internal hard drive) are not visible outside the system unit. Many desktop computers come with empty drive bays so users can add additional storage devices as needed.

The CPU

The **central processing unit** (**CPU**) consists of a variety of circuitry and components that are packaged together and connected directly to the motherboard. The CPU—also called the **microprocessor** (when talking about personal computers) or just the **processor** (when speaking in general terms for any computer)—does the vast majority of the processing for a computer. Most personal computers today use CPUs manufactured by Intel or Advanced Micro Devices (AMD); some examples of their processors are shown in Figure 2-8. For a look inside a computer that may one day be able to compete with human contestants on the *Jeopardy!* TV show, see the How It Works box.

As shown in Figure 2-8, there are processors designed for desktop computers, servers and workstations, conventional portable computers (like notebook and tablet computers), and very small portable computers (like netbooks and UMPCs). In addition, there are also processors designed for mobile phones and embedded computers. Many CPUs today are **multi-core CPUs**; that is, CPUs that contain the processing components or *cores* of multiple independent processors on a single CPU. For example, **dual-core CPUs** contain two cores and **quad-core CPUs** contain four cores. Up until just a few years ago, most CPUs designed for desktop computers had only a

Ⓥ FIGURE 2-8

CPUs. CPUs today typically have multiple cores.

Four cores

Shared Level 3 cache memory

DESKTOP PROCESSORS
Typically have 2 to 4 cores and are designed for performance.

SERVER AND WORKSTATION PROCESSORS
Typically have at least 4 cores and are designed for very high performance.

NOTEBOOK PROCESSORS
Typically have 2 to 4 cores and are designed for performance and increased battery life.

NETBOOK PROCESSORS
Typically have 1 to 2 cores, are small in size, and are designed for extended battery life.

> **Central processing unit (CPU).** The chip located on the motherboard of a computer that performs the processing for a computer. Also called the **processor**. >**Microprocessor.** A central processing unit (CPU) for a personal computer. >**Multi-core CPU.** A CPU that contains the processing components or core of more than one processor in a single CPU. >**Dual-core CPU.** A CPU that contains two separate processing cores. >**Quad-core CPU.** A CPU that contains four separate processing cores.

HOW IT WORKS

Watson, the Ultimate Future *Jeopardy!* Contestant

While game shows traditionally have human contestants, IBM is working on an advanced computing system that will be capable of competing with humans on the popular quiz show, *Jeopardy!* (see the accompanying illustration). This system, codenamed *Watson*, uses software called *Question Answering* (QA) and is designed to understand complex questions and answer them with enough precision and speed to make it a viable *Jeopardy!* contestant. Like human contestants, Watson will not have access to the Internet or any other outside assistance. However, it will have access to its self-contained data, and researchers are teaching it how to go beyond basic data retrieval and analyze its data deeply. For example, they are teaching Watson to use context to "understand" how words relate to each other, to consider factors such as keywords and statistical paraphrasing, and to deal with puns and wordplay in order to come up with a proper response to a question (or to come up with a question to match an answer, as is the case with *Jeopardy!*). To achieve this with the speed and accuracy required for *Jeopardy!*, Watson will need to be based on a supercomputer platform, such as the IBM Blue Gene/P platform, which can contain over one million CPU cores to obtain close to petaflop performance.

While creating a computer that can play *Jeopardy!* is entertaining and newsworthy, IBM plans to make the same technology available for other, perhaps more practical, applications, such as in medical systems used to diagnose patients and in business intelligence systems used for making business decisions. IBM also envisions the technology being used with consumer applications—most likely via cloud computing on a fee per question or fee per minute basis. But, before that happens, we can enjoy Watson's *Jeopardy!* debut—currently targeted for late 2010.

single core; as a result, a common way to increase the amount of processing performed by the CPU was to increase the speed of the CPU. However, heat constraints are making it progressively more difficult to continue to increase CPU speed, so CPU manufacturers today are focusing on multi-core CPUs to increase the amount of processing that a CPU can do in a given time period.

Multi-core CPUs allow computers to work simultaneously on more than one task at a time, such as burning a DVD while surfing the Web, as well as to work faster within a single application if the software is designed to take advantage of multiple cores. Another benefit of multi-core CPUs is that they typically experience fewer heat problems than *single-core CPUs* because each core typically runs slower than a single-core CPU, although the total processing power of the multi-core CPU is greater. In addition to heat reduction, goals of CPU manufacturers today include creating CPUs that are as energy-efficient as possible (in order to reduce power consumption and increase battery life) and that use materials that are not toxic when disposed of (in order to lessen the e-trash impact of computers, as discussed in detail in Chapter 16).

CPUs commonly used with desktop computers include the Intel *Core i7* (quad-core) and AMD *Phenom II* (available in dual-core, *triple-core*, and quad-core versions). Lower-end home computers may use a dual-core CPU, such as the Intel *Core 2 Duo* or the AMD *Athlon X2*. Workstations and servers use more powerful processors, such as the Intel *Xeon* or the AMD *Opteron* processors. Notebook computers can use the same CPUs as desktop computers (more common with notebooks designed as *desktop replacements* than those

ONLINE VIDEO

Go to the Chapter 2 page at **www.cengage.com/ computerconcepts/np/uc13** to watch the "A Look at Watson, the Ultimate Future *Jeopardy!* Contestant" video clip.

TYPE OF PROCESSOR	NAME	NUMBER OF CORES	CLOCK SPEED	TOTAL CACHE MEMORY		
				LEVEL 1	LEVEL 2	LEVEL 3
DESKTOP	Intel Core i7	4	2.66–3.33 GHz	64 KB*	256 KB*	8 MB
	AMD Phenom II	2–4	2.4–3.2 GHz	128 KB*	512 KB*	4–6 MB
SERVER/ WORKSTATION	Intel Xeon (5500 series)					
	AMD Opteron (3rd generation)	2 or 4 4 or 6	1.86–3.2 GHz 2.0–3.1 GHz	64 KB* 128 KB*	256 KB* 512 KB*	4–8 MB 6 MB
NOTEBOOK	Intel Core 2 Mobile	1, 2, or 4	1.06–3.06 GHz	64 KB*	1–12 MB	none
	AMD Turion X2 Mobile	2	2.0–2.5 GHz	128 KB*	1–2 MB*	none
NETBOOK			800 MHz–2 GHz			
	Intel Atom	1–2	GHz	56 KB*	512 KB*	none
	AMD Athlon Neo	1	1.6 MHz	128 KB*	512 KB*	none

* Per core

FIGURE 2-9

Some examples of current Intel and AMD CPUs.

designed for lightweight traveling notebooks), or a CPU designed specifically for portable computers. CPUs designed specifically for notebook and tablet computers (such as the Intel *Core 2* mobile processors and the AMD *Turion X2* mobile processors) typically run a little slower than comparable desktop CPUs, but run cooler and consume less power to allow the portable computers to run longer on battery power without a recharge. CPUs designed specifically for netbooks (such as the Intel *Atom* processor shown in Figure 2-8 and the AMD *Athlon Neo*) are typically much lower in power, performance, and price than other CPUs. Some examples of current CPUs and their characteristics (which are defined and discussed shortly) are shown in Figure 2-9.

In addition to computers, CPUs are incorporated into a number of other devices, such as mobile phones, portable digital media players, consumer appliances, cars, gaming consoles, exercise machines, and more. The CPUs for these devices (such as the *Cell* processor used in the Sony PlayStation 3 gaming console) are typically different from the ones used in personal computers.

ONLINE VIDEO

Go to the Chapter 2 page at www.cengage.com/ computerconcepts/np/uc13 to watch the "The Computing Power of the IBM Roadrunner Supercomputer" video clip.

Processing Speed

One measurement of the *processing speed* of a CPU is the *CPU clock speed*, which is typically rated in *megahertz (MHz)* or *gigahertz (GHz)*. A higher CPU clock speed means that more instructions can be processed per second than the same CPU with a lower CPU clock speed. For instance, a Core i7 processor running at 3.2 GHz would be faster than a Core i7 processor running at 2.66 GHz if all other components remain the same. CPUs for the earliest personal computers ran at less than 5 MHz; today's fastest CPUs have a clock speed of more than 3 GHz. Although CPU clock speed is an important factor in computer performance, other factors (such as the number of cores, the amount of *RAM* and *cache memory*, the speed of external storage devices, and the *bus width* and *bus speed*) greatly affect the overall processing speed of the computer. As a result, computers today are beginning to be classified less by CPU clock speed and more by the computer's overall processing speed or performance.

One measurement of overall processing speed is the maximum number of instructions the CPU can process per second—such as *megaflops*, *gigaflops*, and *teraflops* (millions, billions, and trillions of floating-point operations per second, respectively). It is also common for experts associated with computer journals, technical Web sites, and other organizations to test the performance of CPUs. These tests—called *benchmark tests*—typically run the same series of programs on several computer systems that are identical except for one component (such as the CPU) and measure how long each task takes in order to determine the overall relative performance of the component being tested. Because the large number of factors affecting computer performance today makes it increasingly difficult for consumers to evaluate the performance of CPUs and computers, benchmark tests are becoming an extremely important resource for computer shoppers.

Word Size

A computer word is the amount of data (measured in bits or bytes) that a CPU can manipulate at one time. While CPUs just a few years ago used 32-bit words (referred to as *32-bit processors*), most CPUs today are *64-bit processors* (that is, they are capable of using 64-bit words, in addition to 32-bit words). Usually, a larger word size allows for faster processing and the use of more RAM, provided the software being used is written to take advantage of 64-bit processing. For instance, a computer with a 64-bit processor running the 64-bit version of the Windows operating system can use more RAM and has a higher performance than the same computer running the regular 32-bit version of Windows. However, much of today's software is still 32-bit software.

Cache Memory

Cache memory is a special group of very fast memory circuitry located on or close to the CPU. Cache memory is used to speed up processing by storing the data and instructions that may be needed next by the CPU in handy locations. In theory, it works the same way you might work at your desk; that is, with the file folders or documents you need most often placed within an arm's length and with other useful materials placed farther away but still within easy reach. The computer works in a similar manner. Although it can access materials (data, instructions, and programs, for instance) in RAM relatively quickly, it can work much faster if it places the most urgently needed materials into areas—cache memory—that allow even faster access. When cache memory is full and the CPU calls for additional data or a new instruction, the system overwrites as much data in cache memory as needed to make room for the new data or instruction. This allows the data and instructions that are most likely still needed to remain in cache memory.

Cache memory today is usually *internal cache* (built right into the CPU chip). In the past, some cache memory was *external cache* (located close to, but not inside, the CPU), but that is less common today because the continued miniaturization of CPU components

FURTHER EXPLORATION Go

Go to the Chapter 2 page at **www.cengage.com/ computerconcepts/np/uc13** for links to information about CPUs.

> **Cache memory.** A group of fast memory circuitry located on or near the CPU to help speed up processing.

allows for more room inside the CPU. Cache memory level numbers indicate the order in which the various caches are accessed by the CPU when it requires new data or instructions. *Level 1 (L1) cache* (which is the fastest type of cache but typically holds less data than other levels of cache) is checked first, followed by *Level 2 (L2) cache*, followed by *Level 3 (L3) cache* if it exists. If the data or instructions are not found in cache memory, the computer looks for them in RAM, which is slower than cache memory. If the data or instructions cannot be found in RAM, then they are retrieved from the hard drive—an even slower operation. Typically, more cache memory results in faster processing. Most multi-core CPUs today have some cache memory (such as a L1 and L2 cache) dedicated to each core; they may also use a larger shared cache memory (such as L3 cache) that can be accessed by any core as needed.

8-BIT BUS

16-BIT BUS

FIGURE 2-10

Bus width. A wider bus can transfer more data at one time than a narrower bus.

Bus Width, Bus Speed, and Bandwidth

A *bus* is an electronic path over which data can travel. There are buses inside the CPU, as well as on the motherboard. You can picture a bus as a highway with several lanes; each wire in the bus acts as a separate lane, transmitting one bit at a time. The number of bits being transmitted at one time is dependent on the *bus width*—the number of wires in the bus over which data can travel. Just as a wider highway allows more cars to travel at one time, a wider bus allows more data to be transferred at one time (see Figure 2-10). The *bus speed* is also a very important factor, since the bus width and bus speed together determine the bus's **throughput** or **bandwidth**; that is, the amount of data that can be transferred via the bus in a given time period.

Memory

Memory refers to chip-based storage. When the term *memory* is used alone, it refers to chip-based storage used by the computer—usually the amount of the computer's main memory (called *random access memory* or *RAM*, as discussed next), which is located inside the system unit. In contrast, the term *storage* refers to the amount of long-term storage available to a computer—usually in the form of the computer's hard drive or removable storage media, such as CDs, DVDs, flash memory cards, and USB flash drives, all discussed in the next chapter.

In addition to RAM, computer users should be familiar with four other types of computer memory. Two of these—*cache memory* and *registers*—are **volatile** like RAM, which means that their content is erased when power to the memory ceases; the other two—*read-only memory (ROM)* and *flash memory*—are **nonvolatile**. Cache memory has already been discussed; the other four types of memory are explained next.

Random Access Memory (RAM)

RAM (random access memory), also called *main memory*, is used to store the essential parts of the operating system while the computer is running, as well as the programs and data that the computer is currently using. When someone uses the term *memory* in reference to computers, that person is usually referring to RAM. Since RAM is volatile, its content is lost when the computer is shut off. Data in RAM is also deleted when it is no

---

> **Bandwidth.** The amount of data that can be transferred in a given period of time; also referred to as **throughput**. > **Memory.** Chip-based storage. > **Volatile.** A characteristic of memory or storage in which data is not retained when the power to the computer is turned off.
> **Nonvolatile.** A characteristic of memory or storage in which data is retained even when the power to the computer is turned off.
> **RAM (random access memory).** Chips connected to the motherboard that provide a temporary location for the computer to hold data and program instructions while they are needed.

longer needed, such as when the program using that data is closed. If you want to retrieve a document later, you need to save the document on a storage medium before closing it, as discussed in more detail in Chapter 3. After the document is saved to a storage medium, it can be retrieved from the storage medium when it is needed, even though the document is erased from RAM when the document or the program being used to create that document is closed.

Like the CPU, RAM consists of electronic circuits etched onto chips. These chips are arranged onto circuit boards called *memory modules* (see Figure 2-11), which, in turn, are plugged into the motherboard. Most desktop and server memory modules today are *dual in-line memory modules* or *DIMMs*; notebook computers typically use a smaller type of memory module referred to as a *small outline DIMM* or *SO-DIMM* (an example of each is shown in Figure 2-11). Most personal computers sold today have slots for two to four memory modules and at least one slot will be filled. For example, in the motherboard shown in Figure 2-7, there are two memory modules already installed and room to add an additional two modules, if needed. If you want to add more RAM to a computer and no empty slots are available, you must replace at least one of the existing memory modules with higher capacity modules in order to increase the amount of RAM in that computer.

RAM capacity is measured in bytes. The amount of RAM that can be installed in a computer system depends on both the CPU in that computer and the operating system being used. For instance, while computers using 64-bit CPUs today can utilize a virtually unlimited amount of RAM (older 32-bit CPUs can use up to only 4 GB of RAM), a 64-bit operating system is needed in order to use more than 4 GB of RAM. In addition, different versions of a 64-bit operating system may support different amounts of RAM; for instance, the 64-bit versions of Windows Vista can use up to 8 GB, up to 16 GB, or more than 128 GB of RAM, depending on the edition of Windows Vista being used. Consequently, when you are considering adding more RAM to a computer, it is important to determine that your computer can support it. More RAM allows more applications to run at one time and the computer to respond more quickly when a user switches from task to task. Most notebook and desktop computers sold today have at least 1 GB of RAM and 2 to 8 GB of RAM is generally considered a normal amount for home computers.

In addition to knowing the type of memory module and the amount of memory your computer can support, it is also important to select the proper type and speed of RAM when adding new memory. Most personal computers today use *SDRAM* (*synchronous dynamic RAM*). SDRAM is commonly available in *DDR* (*double-data rate*), *DDR2*, and *DDR3* versions. DDR memory sends data twice as often as ordinary SDRAM to increase throughput, DDR2 transmits twice as much data in the same time period as DDR, and DDR3 is about twice as fast as the highest-speed DDR2 memory available today. Each type of SDRAM is typically available in a variety of speeds (measured in MHz)—for optimal performance, you should use the type and speed of RAM your computer was designed to use.

To further improve memory performance, memory today typically uses a *dual-channel memory architecture*, which has two paths that go to and from memory and so it can transfer twice as much data at one time as *single-channel memory architecture* of the same speed. *Tri-channel* (three paths) and *quad-channel* (four paths) *memory architecture* are also beginning to be used for higher performance. In order to take advantage of the improved performance of using multiple paths, multi-channel RAM typically needs to be installed in matched sets, such as two 1 GB dual-channel memory modules instead of a single 2 GB dual-channel memory module. As the number of cores used with CPUs grows,

DESKTOP RAM (DIMM)

The memory module contains memory chips.

This part of the memory module is plugged into a memory slot on the motherboard.

NOTEBOOK RAM (SO-DIMM)

FIGURE 2-11
RAM memory modules.

ASK THE EXPERT

Kingston **Mark Tekunoff,** Senior Technology Manager,
Kingston Technology

What's the best way to find out if more memory can be added to a particular computer and the type of memory that is needed?

The best way to upgrade is to go to a Web site that has a list of PCs and other products along with a list of the memory options available to support those PCs and products. A good example is Kingston's Web site at www.kingston.com, where Kingston supports over 20,000 products with a variety of memory solutions.

In general, Windows Vista and basic Windows 7 users typically will want at least 2 GB of memory for good functionality. For advanced 32-bit Windows 7 users, we recommend 3 to 4 GB of RAM; power users with 64-bit Windows 7 are better off with 4 to 8 GB of RAM.

RAM performance is becoming increasingly important to ensure that data can be delivered to the CPU fast enough to match its processing capabilities.

While RAM as we know it today is volatile, there are several forms of *nonvolatile RAM* (*NVRAM*)—that is, memory that retains its data when the power to the device is off—becoming available or under development. Two of the most promising types of nonvolatile RAM are *magnetic RAM* (or more precisely, *magnetoresistive RAM*), and *memristor-based RAM*. Magnetoresistive RAM (commonly referred to as *MRAM*) uses *magnetic polarization* rather than an electrical charge to store data; memristor-based RAM uses *memristors* (short for *memory resistors*) that change their resistance in response to current flowing through them. Two other emerging types of nonvolatile memory are *PRAM* (*phase change random access memory*), which has a special coating that changes its physical state when heat is applied (similar to the recordable CDs and DVDs discussed in Chapter 4), and *NRAM*, which uses *carbon nanotubes* (which are discussed later in this chapter).

The most common applications for nonvolatile RAM today include storing critical data for enterprise systems as they operate to guard against data loss and saving the data necessary to help industrial automation and robotics systems recover quickly from a power loss. Future applications include "instant-on" computers and mobile devices that can be turned on and off like an electric light, without any loss of data. It is possible that a form of nonvolatile RAM (such as one of the types discussed in this section or *flash memory*, discussed shortly) will eventually replace SDRAM as the main memory for a computer.

Regardless of the type of RAM used, the CPU must be able to find data and programs located in memory when they are needed. To accomplish this, each location in memory has an address. Whenever a block of data, instruction, program, or result of a calculation is stored in memory, it is usually stored in one or more consecutive addresses, depending on its size (each address typically holds only one byte). The computer system sets up and maintains directory tables that keep track of where data is stored in memory, in order to facilitate the retrieval of that data. When the computer has finished using a program or set of data, it frees up that memory space to hold other programs and data. Therefore, the content of each memory location constantly changes. This process can be roughly compared with the handling of the mailboxes in your local post office: the number on each P.O. box (memory location) remains the same, but the mail (data) stored inside changes as patrons remove their mail and as new mail arrives (see Figure 2-12).

FIGURE 2-12
Memory addressing.

Each location in memory has a unique address, just like mailboxes at the post office.

Programs and blocks of data are almost always too big to fit in a single address. A directory keeps track of the first address used to store each program and data block and the number of addresses each block spans.

Registers

A **register** is high-speed memory built into the CPU. Registers are used by the CPU to store data and intermediary results temporarily during processing. Registers are the fastest type of memory used by the CPU, even faster than Level 1 cache. Generally, more registers and larger registers result in increased CPU performance. Most CPUs contain multiple registers; registers are discussed in more detail later in this chapter.

Read-Only Memory (ROM)

ROM (**read-only memory**) consists of nonvolatile chips that permanently store data or programs. Like RAM, these chips are attached to the motherboard inside the system unit, and the data or programs are retrieved by the computer when they are needed. An important difference, however, is that you can neither write over the data or programs in ROM chips (which is the reason ROM chips are called *read-only*), nor erase their content when you shut off the computer's power. ROM is used for storing permanent instructions used by a computer (referred to as *firmware*). However, ROM is increasingly being replaced with *flash memory*, as discussed next, for any data that may need to be updated during the life of the computer.

Flash Memory

Flash memory consists of nonvolatile memory chips that can be used for storage by the computer or the user. Flash memory chips have begun to replace ROM for storing system information, such as a computer's *BIOS* or *basic input/output system*—the sequence of instructions the computer follows during the boot process. For instance, one of the computer's first activities when you turn on the power is to perform a *power-on self-test* or *POST*. The POST takes an inventory of system components, checks each component for proper functioning, and initializes system settings, which produces the beeps you may hear as your computer boots. Traditionally, the instructions for the POST have been stored in ROM. By storing this information in flash memory instead of ROM, however, the BIOS information can be updated as needed. Similarly, firmware for personal computers and other devices (such as mobile phones and networking hardware) are now typically stored in flash memory that is embedded in the device so the firmware can be updated over the life of the product.

Flash memory chips are also built into many types of devices (such as portable computers, mobile phones, digital cameras, and portable digital media players) for user storage, as well as built into storage media and devices (such as flash memory cards and USB flash drives). Flash memory media and devices used for storage purposes are discussed in more detail in Chapter 3.

FURTHER EXPLORATION Go

Go to the Chapter 2 page at **www.cengage.com/ computerconcepts/np/uc13** for links to information about memory.

Fans, Heat Sinks, and Other Cooling Components

One byproduct of packing an increasing amount of technology in a smaller system unit is heat, an ongoing problem for CPU and computer manufacturers. Since heat can damage components and cooler chips can run faster, virtually all computers today employ *fans*, *heat sinks* (small components typically made out of aluminum with fins that help to dissipate heat), or other methods to cool the CPU and system unit. For instance, desktop computers today typically include several fans, such as one fan on the power supply that can be seen on the back of the computer and one fan and a heat sink on top of the CPU, and notebook computers typically include at least one fan. One of the newest cooling methods

---

>**Register.** High-speed memory built into the CPU that temporarily stores data during processing. >**ROM (read-only memory).** Nonvolatile chips located on the motherboard into which data or programs have been permanently stored. >**Flash memory.** Nonvolatile memory chips that can be used for storage by the computer or user; can be built into a computer or a storage medium.

Built-in fan is powered by a USB cable on the bottom of the stand.

Fans on the back of the system unit

Fan on top of the CPU

Water cooling tubes

FANS AND WATER COOLING SYSTEMS
These cooling methods and heat sinks are used with computers today to cool the inside of the computer.

NOTEBOOK COOLING STANDS
These stands cool the underside of a notebook computer by allowing for better air circulation; some stands also include a fan.

FIGURE 2-13
Computer cooling methods.

being used with desktop computers consists of liquid-filled tubes that draw heat away from processors. Although initially expensive, difficult to install, and complicated to use, these *water cooling systems* are now available in simpler and less expensive formats. An added bonus of water-cooled computers is that they are quieter than conventional systems. As shown in Figure 2-13, some desktop computers use a combination of fans and water cooling systems. When a notebook's built-in fan isn't sufficient to cool the underside of the computer—one of the problem areas with many notebook computers—a *notebook cooling stand* (such as the one shown in Figure 2-13) can be used to help cool this part of the computer.

Because heat is an ongoing problem with computers, new cooling technologies are continually being developed. One possibility for the future is the *ion pump cooling system* that strips electrons from molecules of oxygen and nitrogen in the air, resulting in positively charged ions; the positively charged ions then flow to a negatively charged collector electrode, resulting in a flow of air that cools nearby components. Ion pump cooling systems have no moving parts, use minimal energy consumption, and could potentially be integrated into CPUs and other computer components during manufacturing because they can be made of silicon.

Expansion Slots, Expansion Cards, and ExpressCard Modules

Expansion slots are locations on the motherboard into which **expansion cards** (also called *interface cards*) can be inserted to connect those cards to the motherboard. Expansion cards are used to give desktop computers additional capabilities, such as to connect the computer to a network, to add a TV tuner to allow television shows to be watched and

> **Expansion slot.** A location on the motherboard into which expansion cards are inserted. > **Expansion card.** A circuit board that can be inserted into an expansion slot location on a computer's motherboard to add additional functionality or to connect a peripheral device to that computer.

recorded on the computer, or to connect a monitor to the computer. Today, some basic capabilities (such as the necessary connectors for speakers and monitors) are being integrated directly into the motherboard instead of requiring the use of an expansion card. However, an expansion card can be added and used instead, if needed. For instance, a *video graphics card* can be added to a computer to add additional capabilities not allowed by the computer's *integrated graphics* feature. Most new desktop computers come with a few empty expansion slots on the motherboard so that new expansion cards can be added when new capabilities are needed. There are several different types of expansion cards, such as *PCI* and *PCIe*—each corresponds to a specific type of expansion slot, as discussed in the next section, and they are not interchangeable.

Traditionally, *PC Cards* were used for notebook expansion. Today, however, most notebook and netbook computers use the newer **ExpressCard modules** instead. ExpressCard modules are inserted into the computer's *ExpressCard slot* in order to be used; they can also be used with any desktop computer that has an ExpressCard slot. ExpressCard modules and ExpressCard slots are available in two widths: 34 mm and 54 mm, referred to as *ExpressCard/34* and *ExpressCard/54*, respectively. While ExpressCard/34 modules can be used in both sized slots, ExpressCard/54 modules can only be used with ExpressCard/54 slots.

Figure 2-14 shows a typical expansion card and ExpressCard module, and lists some examples of common uses for expansion cards and ExpressCard modules. Expansion cards or ExpressCard modules designed to connect external devices (such as a monitor or piece of networking hardware) have a port accessible to connect that device; cards that do not need to connect to additional hardware (such as wireless networking cards) do not have an exposed port. Expansion for UMPCs and mobile devices is usually much more limited and is often restricted to devices that can plug into a *USB port* or *flash memory card slot*; desktop and portable computers can connect some peripherals using these ports as well. Ports are discussed in more detail shortly.

HW

FIGURE 2-14
Expansion cards and ExpressCard modules. These are most often used with desktop and notebook computers, respectively.

EXPANSION CARD
This part of the card plugs into an empty PCI Express slot on the motherboard.

The port on this network interface card is accessible through the exterior of the system unit's case.

EXPRESSCARD MODULE
This end of the card is inserted into an ExpressCard/34 slot. There is no external port because this is a wireless networking card.

COMMON EXPANSION CARDS/MODULES	
CARD TYPE	**PURPOSE**
Disk controller card	Enables a particular type of disk drive to interface with the computer.
Modem	Provides communications capabilities to connect to a network or the Internet.
Network adapter	Enables a computer to connect to a network.
Sound card	Enables users to attach speakers to a computer and provides sound capabilities.
TV tuner card	Allows a computer to pick up television signals.
USB/FireWire card	Adds one or both of these ports to a computer.
Video graphics card	Enables the connection of a monitor; can provide additional graphics capabilities not available with graphics integrated into the motherboard.

> **ExpressCard module.** A module that can be inserted into a computer's ExpressCard slot to add additional functionality or to connect a peripheral device to that computer; commonly used with notebook computers.

Buses

As already discussed, a **bus** in a computer is an electronic path over which data travels. There are buses located within the CPU to move data between CPU components; there are also a variety of buses etched onto the motherboard to tie the CPU to memory and to peripheral devices (one possible design is shown in Figure 2-15). The buses that connect peripheral (typically input and output) devices to the motherboard are often called **expansion buses**. Expansion buses connect directly to ports on the system unit case or

FIGURE 2-15

Buses and expansion slots.

Buses transport bits and bytes from one component to another, including the CPU, RAM, and peripheral devices.

CPU CHIP
Fetches data from cache or RAM when needed.

INTERNAL CPU BUSES
Used to move data around inside the CPU.

MEMORY BUS
Connects the CPU and RAM.

FRONTSIDE BUS (FSB)
Connects the CPU to the I/O chipset.

MEMORY SLOTS
Hold RAM memory modules.

PCI EXPRESS x16
A PCIe x16 bus and expansion slot are commonly used to connect a monitor to the computer.

INTERNAL CACHE MEMORY
Built right into the CPU chip. The CPU looks here first to find the data it needs.

I/O AND SOUTHBRIDGE CHIPSETS
Most CPUs use a two-piece chipset as a hub or bridge to tie the various buses to the CPU. The top chipset is sometimes called the *I/O chipset*; the bottom is called the *Southbridge*.

PCI EXPRESS x1
Each PCIe x1 bus connects to a separate PCIe x1 expansion slot. These slots are expected to eventually replace standard PCI expansion slots.

PCI BUS
The PCI bus and expansion slots are an older way to connect peripheral devices to the computer.

USB BUS
The USB bus and port can be used to connect USB-compatible devices to the computer without using an expansion card. A FireWire (IEEE 1394) bus works in a similar fashion.

>**Bus.** An electronic path on the motherboard or within the CPU or other computer component along which data is transferred. >**Expansion bus.** A bus on the motherboard used to connects peripheral devices.

to expansion slots on the motherboard (some of the most common expansion buses and expansion slots are illustrated in Figure 2-15). It is important to realize that expansion slots are not interchangeable—that is, each type of expansion slot is designed for a specific type of expansion card, such as *PCI* or *PCI Express (PCIe)*. The specific buses shown in Figure 2-15 are discussed next.

Memory Bus

One recent change in the bus architecture used with most new personal computers today is connecting the CPU directly to RAM, as shown in Figure 2-15. This change allows for increased performance; the bus used to connect the CPU to RAM is typically called the **memory bus**.

Frontside Bus (FSB)

The **frontside bus** (**FSB**) connects the CPU to the chipset (most often called the *I/O bridge* today, though sometimes the older term *Northbridge* is still used) that connects the CPU to the rest of the *bus architecture*. Because of the importance of this connection, CPU manufacturers typically use special high-speed technologies: Intel uses its *QuickPath Interconnect (QPI)* technology; AMD uses its *HyperTransport Technology*.

PCI and PCI Express Bus

The *PCI (Peripheral Component Interconnect) bus* has been one of the most common types of expansion buses in past years. In new computers, the PCI bus has essentially been replaced with the **PCI Express (PCIe) bus**. The PCIe bus is available in several different widths. The 16-bit version of PCIe (referred to as *PCIe x16*) is commonly used with video graphics cards to connect a monitor to a computer; expansion cards for other peripherals often connect via the 1-bit PCIe bus (referred to as *PCIe x1*). PCIe is extremely fast—the 1-bit PCIe bus, at 5 *Gbps* (billions of bits per second), is approximately four times faster than the standard PCI bus; PCIe x16 is significantly faster at 80 Gbps. The emerging *PCI 2.0* standard essentially doubles the speed of each PCIe bus. PCIe buses are also increasingly being used with *mini cards* (such as *PCIe Mini*) that are smaller than conventional expansion cards and that are used in UMPCs and other small portable computers.

USB Bus

One of the more versatile bus architectures is the **Universal Serial Bus** (**USB**). The USB standard allows 127 different devices to connect to a computer via a single USB port on the computer's system unit. At 12 *Mbps* (millions of bits per second), the original *USB 1.0* standard is slow. However, the newer *USB 2.0* standard supports data transfer rates of 480 Mbps and the emerging 4.8 Gbps *USB 3.0* standard (also called *SuperSpeed USB*) is about 10 times as fast as USB 2.0. The convenience and universal support of USB have made it one of the most widely used standards for connecting peripherals today.

FireWire/IEEE 1394 Bus

FireWire (also known as *IEEE 1394*) is a high-speed bus standard developed by Apple for connecting devices—particularly multimedia devices like digital video cameras—to a computer. Like USB, FireWire can connect multiple external devices via a single port. FireWire is relatively fast—the original FireWire standard supports data transfer rates of up to 320 Mbps, the newer FireWire standard (called *FireWire 800*) standard supports data

---

> **Memory bus.** The connection between the CPU and RAM. > **Frontside bus (FSB).** The bus that connects the CPU (via the I/O bridge) to the rest of the bus architecture. > **PCI Express (PCIe) bus.** One of the buses most commonly used to connect peripheral devices. > **Universal Serial Bus (USB).** A universal bus used to connect up to 127 peripheral devices to a computer without requiring the use of additional expansion cards. > **FireWire.** A high-speed bus standard often used to connect digital video cameras and other multimedia hardware to a computer.

transfer rates up to 800 Mbps, and the emerging *FireWire 3200* standard offers 3.2 Gbps transfer rates.

Ports and Connectors

As already mentioned, **ports** are the connectors located on the exterior of the system unit that are used to connect external hardware devices. Each port is attached to the appropriate bus on the motherboard so that when a device is plugged into a port, the device can communicate with the CPU and other computer components. Several of the original ports used with desktop computers—such as the *parallel ports* traditionally used to connect printers—are now considered *legacy ports* and so are not typically included on newer computers. Typical ports for a desktop computer and the connectors used with those ports are shown in Figure 2-16; these and additional ports you might find on your computer are discussed next.

➤ *Monitor ports* are used to connect a monitor to a computer. Traditionally, monitors connect via a *VGA connector*; today's *flat-panel monitors* typically connect via a *Digital Video Interface* (*DVI*) connector and *high-definition monitors* connect via an *HDMI* (*High-Definition Multimedia Interface*). Monitors and emerging options for connecting them to a computer are discussed in Chapter 4.

➤ *Network ports* are used to connect a computer to a computer network via a networking cable—typically a cable using an *RJ-45 connector*, which looks similar to a telephone connector but is larger. Networks and networking hardware are discussed in detail in Chapter 7.

FIGURE 2-16

Typical ports for desktop computers and examples of connectors.

POWER CONNECTOR
Connects the computer to a power outlet.

VGA MONITOR PORT
Connects a VGA monitor.

USB PORTS
Connect a keyboard, mouse, scanner, flash memory drive, printer, digital camera, or other USB devices.

HDMI PORT
Connects a high-definition monitor.

FIREWIRE PORT
Connects FireWire devices.

NETWORK PORT
Connects the computer to a network.

AUDIO PORTS
Connect speakers, headphones, and a microphone.

EMPTY SLOTS
Ports located on new expansion cards added to the computer will be accessible here.

CONNECTORS

Monitor (VGA)

USB

Monitor (HDMI)

FireWire

Network (RJ-45)

Audio (3.5mm)

>**Port.** A connector on the exterior of a computer to which a device may be attached.

> *Modem ports* are used to connect a computer to a phone outlet via telephone connectors, as discussed in Chapter 7.

> *USB ports* are used to connect USB devices (such as keyboards, mice, printers, hard drives, and digital cameras) to a computer via a USB connector. Multiple USB devices can connect to a single USB port via a *USB hub*. USB hubs can either be wired or wireless; a wireless USB hub is shown in Figure 2-17.

> *FireWire (IEEE 1394) ports* are used to connect FireWire devices to the computer via a FireWire connector. Similar to USB, a *FireWire hub* can be used to connect multiple devices to a single port. FireWire connections are most often used with digital video cameras and other multimedia peripherals.

> *Keyboard ports* and *mouse ports* (also called *PS/2 ports*) are used to connect a keyboard and mouse with a *PS/2 connector* to the system unit. Many computers today do not include PS/2 ports; instead, they are designed to be used with USB keyboards and mice.

> *SCSI (Small Computer System Interface) ports* are high-speed parallel ports sometimes used to attach printers, scanners, and hard drives.

> *MIDI ports* are used to connect *MIDI (musical instrument digital interface)* devices (such as a musical keyboard) to the computer.

> *IrDA (Infrared Data Association) ports* and *Bluetooth ports* are used to receive wireless transmissions from devices; since the transmissions are wireless, these ports do not use a plug. IrDA ports are commonly used to "beam" data from a portable computer or mobile device to a computer; Bluetooth ports are most often used with wireless keyboards, mice, and headsets. Wireless data transmission is discussed in more detail in Chapter 7.

> *Flash memory card slots* are used to connect flash media cards or other hardware using a flash media interface. As discussed shortly, some hardware for portable computers is designed to connect using these slots.

> *Game ports* are used to connect a joystick, game pad, steering wheel, or other device commonly used with computer gaming programs.

> *Audio ports* are used to connect speakers or a microphone to the computer.

> *eSATA (external SATA) ports* are used to connect external SATA devices (most commonly, an external hard drive). External hard drives that connect via eSATA are much faster than external hard drives that connect via a USB or FireWire connection. Hard drives are discussed in detail in Chapter 3.

Plug this adapter into the computer's USB port to connect the wireless USB hub to the computer.

Plug up to four USB devices to this hub to connect them wirelessly to the computer.

FIGURE 2-17
USB hubs. A USB hub can be used to connect multiple USB devices to a single USB port.

Most computers today support the *Plug and Play* standard, which means the computer automatically configures new devices as soon as they are installed and the computer is powered up. If you want to add a new device to your desktop computer and there is an available port for the device you want to add, then you just need to plug it in (shut down the computer first, unless the device uses a USB or FireWire port). If the appropriate port is not available, you need to either install the appropriate expansion card to create the necessary port or use a USB or FireWire version of the device, if you have one of those two ports available on your computer. USB and FireWire devices are *hot-swappable*, meaning they can be plugged into their respective ports while the computer is powered up. Hot-swappable devices—along with some removable storage media, such as flash memory

Right panel ports
(not shown):
SD card slot
eSATA port

HDMI
monitor port

VGA
monitor port

USB
ports

FireWire
port

Network
port

ExpressCard
slot

PC Card
slot

NOTEBOOK COMPUTERS

SDIO
barcode
reader

SD slot

SD flash
memory
card

MOBILE DEVICES

FIGURE 2-18

Typical ports for
portable computers.

cards—are recognized by the computer as soon as they are connected to it and can be used right away. Other devices are recognized by the computer when the computer is first powered up after the device has been added.

Notebook and netbook computers have ports similar to desktop computers (see Figure 2-18), but sometimes have less of them. UMPCs and mobile devices have a more limited amount of expandability. However, they usually come with at least one built-in expansion slot—typically a USB port or an *SD slot*, which can be used with both the postage-stamp-sized *Secure Digital (SD)* flash memory cards, as well as with peripheral devices adhering to the *Secure Digital Input/Output (SDIO) standard* (see Figure 2-18).

HOW THE CPU WORKS

As already discussed, a CPU consists of a variety of circuitry and components packaged together into a single component. The key element of the processor is the *transistor*—a device made of semiconductor material that controls the flow of electrons inside a chip. Today's CPUs contain hundreds of millions of transistors, and the number doubles approximately every 18 months. This phenomenon is known as *Moore's Law* and is explained in the Inside the Industry box. The primary components of a typical CPU are discussed next.

Typical CPU Components

To begin to understand how a CPU works, you need to know how the CPU is organized and what components it includes. This information will help you understand how electronic impulses move from one part of the CPU to another to process data. The architecture and components included in a CPU (referred to as *microarchitecture*) vary from processor to processor. A simplified example of the principal components that might be included in a single core of a typical CPU is shown in Figure 2-19 and discussed next. There are also additional components that are typically located inside the CPU, but not within each core. For instance, there are buses to connect the CPU cores to each other (typically via QuickPath Interconnect (QPI) or HyperTransport Technology connections), buses to connect each core to the CPU's *memory controller* (which controls the communication between the CPU cores and RAM), and buses to connect each core to any cache memory that is shared between the cores. For a look at the companies that are used to examine the parts of the CPU or other computer components to gather evidence for patent lawsuits and other official actions, see the Trend box.

CONTROL UNIT
Is in charge of the entire process, making sure everything happens at the right time. It instructs the ALU, FPU, and registers what to do, based on instructions from the decode unit.

PREFETCH UNIT
Requests instructions and data from cache or RAM and makes sure they are in the proper order for processing; it attempts to fetch instructions and data ahead of time so that the other components don't have to wait.

ARITHMETIC/LOGIC UNIT AND FLOATING POINT UNIT
Performs the arithmetic and logical operations, as directed by the control unit.

REGISTERS
Hold the results of processing.

DECODE UNIT
Takes instructions from the prefetch unit and translates them into a form that the control unit can understand.

BUS INTERFACE UNIT
The place where data and instructions enter or leave the core.

INTERNAL CACHE MEMORY
Stores data and instructions before and during processing.

FIGURE 2-19
Inside a CPU core.

HW

Arithmetic/Logic Unit (ALU) and Floating Point Unit (FPU)

The **arithmetic/logic unit** (**ALU**) is the section of a CPU core that performs arithmetic (addition, subtraction, multiplication, and division) involving integers and logical operations (such as comparing two pieces of data to see if they are equal or determining if a specific condition is true or false). Arithmetic requiring decimals is usually performed by the **floating point unit** (**FPU**). Arithmetic operations are performed when mathematical calculations are requested by the user, as well as when many other common computing tasks are performed. For example, editing a digital photograph in an image editing program, running the spell checker in a word processing program, and burning a music CD are all performed by the ALU, with help from the FPU when needed, using only arithmetic and logical operations. Most CPUs today have multiple ALUs and FPUs that work together to perform the necessary operations.

Control Unit

The **control unit** coordinates and controls the operations and activities taking place within a CPU core, such as retrieving data and instructions and passing them on to the ALU or FPU for execution. In other words, it directs the flow of electronic traffic within the core, much like a traffic cop controls the flow of vehicles on a roadway. Essentially, the control unit tells the ALU and FPU what to do and makes sure that everything happens at the right time in order for the appropriate processing to take place.

Prefetch Unit

The **prefetch unit** orders data and instructions from cache or RAM based on the current task. The prefetch unit tries to predict what data and instructions will be needed and retrieves them ahead of time, in order to help avoid delays in processing.

>**Arithmetic/logic unit (ALU).** The part of a CPU core that performs logical operations and integer arithmetic. >**Floating point unit (FPU).** The part of a CPU core that performs decimal arithmetic. >**Control unit.** The part of a CPU core that coordinates its operations. >**Prefetch unit.** The part of a CPU core that attempts to retrieve data and instructions before they are needed for processing in order to avoid delays.

INSIDE THE INDUSTRY

Moore's Law

In 1965, Gordon Moore, the cofounder of Intel and shown in the accompanying photograph, observed that the number of transistors per square inch on chips had doubled every two years since the integrated circuit was invented. He then made a now-famous prediction—that this doubling trend would continue for at least 10 more years. Here we are, about 45 years later, and transistor density still doubles about every 18 months. Due to technological breakthroughs, *Moore's Law* has been maintained for far longer than the original prediction and most experts, including Moore himself, expect the doubling trend to continue for at least another decade. In fact, Intel states that the mission of its technology development team is to continue to break barriers to Moore's Law.

Interestingly, other computer components also follow Moore's Law. For example, storage capacity doubles approximately every 20 months, and chip speed doubles about every 24 months. Consequently, the term *Moore's Law* has been expanded and is now used to describe the amount of time it takes components to double in capacity or speed. Many experts predict that, eventually, a physical limit to the number of transistors that can be crammed onto a chip will end Moore's Law. But the end is not yet in sight.

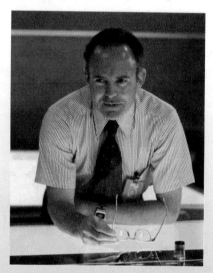

Gordon Moore (1970).

ONLINE VIDEO

Go to the Chapter 2 page at **www.cengage.com/ computerconcepts/np/uc13** to watch the "The Impact of Moore's Law" video clip.

Decode Unit

The **decode unit** takes the instructions fetched by the prefetch unit and translates them into a form that can be understood by the control unit, ALU, and FPU. The decoded instructions go to the control unit for processing.

Registers and Internal Cache Memory

As mentioned earlier, registers and cache memory are both types of memory used by the CPU. Registers are groups of high-speed memory located within the CPU that are used during processing. The ALU and FPU use registers to store data, intermediary calculations, and the results of processing temporarily. CPUs today typically have a variety of other registers used for specific purposes. Internal cache memory (such as the Level 1 and Level 2 cache typically built into each core of a CPU and the Level 3 cache that is often shared by all cores of the CPU) is used to store instructions and data for the CPU, to avoid retrieving them from RAM or the hard drive.

Bus Interface Unit

The **bus interface unit** allows the core to communicate with other CPU components, such as the memory controller and other cores. As previously mentioned, the memory controller controls the flow of instructions and data going between the CPU cores and RAM.

> **Decode unit.** The part of a CPU core that translates instructions into a form that can be processed by the ALU and FPU. > **Bus interface unit.** The part of a CPU core that allows it to communicate with other CPU components.

TREND

High-Tech Investigators

With the high value of technology today and claims of stolen technology and patent infringements happening all the time, what can companies in the computer industry do to find out the truth? Increasingly, they turn to reverse engineering companies, such as TAEUS International. Short for "Tear Apart Everything Under the Stars," TAEUS is a leader in the area of applying engineering skills and industry knowledge in order to analyze products and evaluate patent claims. In a nutshell, companies like TAEUS tear products apart to hunt for patented technologies that should not be there. Just as with criminal investigations, patent infringement claims require physical proof, and TAEUS engineers inspect and photograph critical elements of a product (see the accompanying photo) to compare that product to existing patents.

In just the past few years, TAEUS has helped to settle numerous patent infringement claims. For instance, it helped Intel avoid litigation when it was sued by Digital Equipment Corporation (DEC) for a share of Intel's Pentium CPU profits. After TAEUS found patented Intel technology inside DEC's servers, the case was settled with no money changing hands. TAEUS also does preemptive work helping tech companies avoid patent liabilities by searching through existing patents to determine which technology patents are enforceable before a problem arises. At a rate of $100,000 to reverse engineer one computer chip,

services such as the ones TAEUS provide are not cheap, but with patent lawsuits often exceeding $100 million, for tech companies that avoid litigation by using TAEUS services, it is money well spent.

Other companies in the area of *computer forensics* specialize in finding other types of digital evidence needed for legal proceedings, such as recovering files deleted from a computer or storage medium, determining activities previously performed on a computer, unlocking encrypted files, and so forth. Computer forensics experts are often hired by individual companies, as well as by law enforcement agencies.

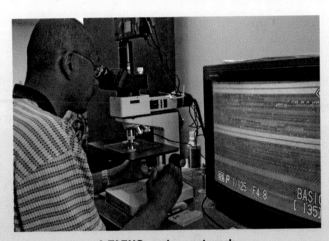

A TAEUS engineer at work.

The System Clock and the Machine Cycle

As mentioned at the beginning of this chapter, every instruction that you issue to a computer—by either typing a command or clicking something with the mouse—is converted into machine language. In turn, each machine language instruction in a CPU's *instruction set* (the collection of basic machine language commands that the CPU can understand) is broken down into several smaller, machine-level instructions called *microcode*. Microcode instructions, such as moving a single piece of data from one part of the computer system to another or adding the numbers located in two specific registers, are built into the CPU and are the basic instructions used by the CPU.

In order to synchronize all of a computer's operations, a **system clock**—a small quartz crystal located on the motherboard—is used. The system clock sends out a signal on a regular basis to all other computer components, similar to a musician's metronome or a person's heartbeat. Each signal is referred to as a *cycle*. The number of cycles per second is measured in *hertz (Hz)*. One megahertz (MHz) is equal to one million ticks of the system clock.

>**System clock.** The timing mechanism within the computer system that synchronizes the computer's operations.

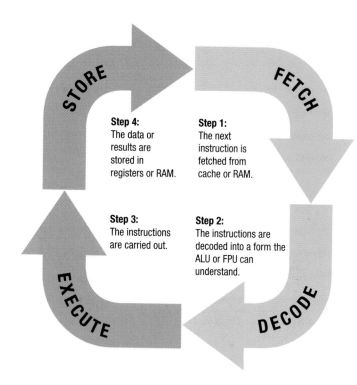

Step 4:
The data or results are stored in registers or RAM.

Step 1:
The next instruction is fetched from cache or RAM.

Step 3:
The instructions are carried out.

Step 2:
The instructions are decoded into a form the ALU or FPU can understand.

FIGURE 2-20

A machine cycle.
A machine cycle is typically accomplished in four steps.

Many personal computers today have system clocks that run at 200 MHz, and all devices (such as CPUs) that are synchronized with these system clocks run at either the system clock speed or at a multiple of or a fraction of the system clock speed. For example, a CPU with a *CPU clock speed* of 2 GHz uses a multiplier of 10, meaning that the CPU clock essentially "ticks" 10 times during each system clock tick. During each CPU clock tick, the CPU can execute one or more pieces of microcode. Most computers today can process more than one piece of microcode at one time—a characteristic known as *superscalar*, which is the ability to process multiple *instructions per cycle* (*IPC*). A CPU with a higher CPU clock speed processes more instructions per second than the same CPU with a lower CPU clock speed.

Whenever the CPU processes a single piece of microcode, it is referred to as a **machine cycle**. Each machine cycle consists of the four general operations illustrated in Figure 2-20 and discussed next.

1. *Fetch*—the program instruction is fetched.
2. *Decode*—the instructions are decoded so the control unit, ALU, and FPU can understand them.
3. *Execute*—the instructions are carried out.
4. *Store*—the original data or the result from the ALU or FPU execution is stored in the CPU's registers.

Because each machine cycle processes only a single microcode instruction, many seemingly simple commands (such as multiplying two numbers) might require more than one machine cycle, and a computer might need to go through thousands, millions, or even billions of machine cycles to complete a user command or program instruction. For instance, a CPU processing the command 2 + 3 would typically require at least four machine cycles, such as to:

1. Fetch the number 2 from RAM, decode it, and store it in register X.
2. Fetch the number 3 from RAM, decode it, and store it in a register Y.
3. Fetch and decode the addition instruction, then add the two numbers (currently stored in registers X and Y) and store the sum in register Z.
4. Fetch and decode the instruction to display the sum, and then output the sum (currently stored in register Z) to RAM.

MAKING COMPUTERS FASTER AND BETTER NOW AND IN THE FUTURE

Over the years, computer designers have developed a number of strategies to achieve faster, more powerful, and more reliable computing performance. Researchers are also constantly working on ways to improve the performance of computers of the future. There are several ways computer users can speed up their existing computers today, and a number of

>**Machine cycle.** The series of operations involved in the execution of a single machine level instruction.

technologies are being developed by manufacturers to improve computers both today and in the future.

Improving the Performance of Your System Today

Several strategies you can use to try to improve the performance of your current computer are discussed next.

Add More Memory

With today's graphic-intensive interfaces and applications, much more memory is required than was necessary even a couple of years ago. If your computer is just a few years old, slows down significantly when you have multiple programs open, and has less than 2 GB of RAM installed, you should consider adding more memory to your system. To accomplish this, first check to see if there is room inside your computer for additional memory modules (either by looking inside the computer or by using a scanning utility like the one shown in Figure 2-21 that is available on some memory manufacturers' Web sites). You can then determine (either by the scan information or by checking with your computer's manufacturer) how much memory can be added to your computer and what type and speed of RAM your computer requires. If you do not have enough empty memory slots in your computer, you will need to remove some of the old memory modules and replace them with newer, higher capacity ones in order to add more memory to your system. Remember that some memory modules must be added in sets (such as pairs or triplets) for optimal performance.

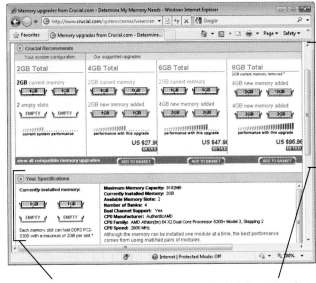

Details the quantity and type of RAM that is currently installed.

Lists the options for memory expansion.

FIGURE 2-21

Online memory scanners can help you determine what memory can be added to your computer.

> **CAUTION CAUTION CAUTION CAUTION CAUTION CAUTION CAUT**
>
> Never open the case of your computer when it is powered up or plugged into an electrical outlet. To avoid damaging your computer with the static electricity stored in your body, consider wearing an *antistatic wristband*.

Perform System Maintenance

As you work and use your hard drive to store and retrieve data, and as you install and uninstall programs, most computers tend to become less efficient. One reason for this is because as large documents are stored, retrieved, and then stored again, they often become *fragmented*—that is, not stored in contiguous (adjacent) storage areas. Because the different pieces of the document are physically located in different places, it takes longer for the computer to retrieve or store them. Another reason a computer might become inefficient is that when programs are uninstalled, pieces of the program are sometimes left behind or references to these programs are left in operating system files, such as the *Windows registry*. Yet another reason is that as a hard drive begins to get full, it takes longer to locate and manipulate the data stored on the hard drive. All of these factors can result in a system performing more slowly than it should.

To avoid some of these problems, regular system maintenance should be performed. Some system maintenance tips every computer user should be aware of are:

> ➤ Uninstall any programs that you no longer want on your computer in order to free up space on your hard drive. Be sure to use the proper removal process, such as the *Uninstall a program* option in the Windows Control Panel or an Uninstall option for that program located on the Start menu. Windows users can also periodically use a

VIDEO PODCAST

Go to the Chapter 2 page at **www.cengage.com/ computerconcepts/np/uc13** to download or listen to the "How To: Deal with a Blue Screen of Death" video podcast.

FIGURE 2-22
Windows Disk Cleanup. Running the Disk Cleanup program can help free up room on your hard drive.

FURTHER EXPLORATION

Go to the Chapter 2 page at **www.cengage.com/ computerconcepts/np/uc13** for links to information about system maintenance.

TIP

Using an external USB or FireWire hard drive to store your data makes it very fast and easy to move your data to a different computer, when needed. It also protects your data from being lost if the main hard drive on your computer stops working or if you need to restore your computer's main hard drive back to its original state.

registry cleaner (a number of free registry cleaners are available online) to clean the Windows registry to remove references to nonexistent programs.

➤ If you have large files (such as digital photos or videos) stored on your computer that you do not need on a regular basis but want to keep, consider moving them to a removable storage medium, such as a DVD disc or an external hard drive. Once copied onto the new medium, the files can be deleted from your hard drive to free up space. Be sure to open the files from the storage medium to confirm that the transfer was successful before deleting the files from your hard drive, and consider copying important files to two different storage mediums. Backing up files, deleting files, and types of storage media are discussed in more detail in later chapters.

➤ Delete the temporary files (such as installation files, Web browsing history, and files in the Recycle Bin) stored by your computer and Web browser to free up room on your hard drive. You can delete these files manually, if desired, but the *Windows Disk Cleanup* program shown in Figure 2-22 can locate and delete these temporary files for you.

➤ *Error-check* and *defragment* your hard drive periodically to make it work more efficiently. Windows users can right-click a hard drive icon in Windows Explorer, select *Properties*, and then select the *Check Now* option on the Tools tab to check that hard drive for errors, or select *Defragment Now* to defragment that hard drive.

➤ Scan for *computer viruses* and *spyware* continually. A computer that suddenly slows down might be the result of a computer virus, spyware program, or other threat. *Antivirus* and *antispyware programs* can help detect and correct these problems and are discussed in more detail in Chapter 9.

➤ Clean out the dust from inside the system unit of desktop computers once or twice a year using a can of compressed air or a small vacuum cleaner. Although the dust may not slow down your system by itself, it can slow down the fans that cool your computer as well cause the components inside your computer to run hotter than they should, which can cause problems with your computer such as overheating, burned out components, and periodic shutting down without warning. Notebook users should check the bottom of their computers to see if there is a removable dust filter—if there is one, it should be cleaned periodically.

Buy a Larger or Second Hard Drive

As already mentioned, hard drives become less efficient as they fill up. If your hard drive is almost full and you do not have any data or programs that you can remove, consider buying and installing a second hard drive. The new hard drive can be an internal hard drive if you have an empty drive bay inside your computer. It can also be an external hard drive that connects via an available (typically USB) port. Alternatively, you can replace your existing hard drive with a larger one, although the data transfer process will be a little more complicated. Hard drives are discussed in detail in Chapter 3.

Upgrade Your Internet Connection

If your system seems slow primarily when you are using the Internet, the culprit might be your Internet connection. If you are using a *conventional dial-up connection* (the relatively slow Internet access available via your telephone line), you may wish to upgrade to a faster type of connection. Switching to *cable, satellite, DSL, fixed wireless*, or another type of *broadband Internet service* is more expensive than dial-up, but is significantly faster. The differences between these and other types of Internet connections are described in Chapters 7 and 8.

Upgrade Your Video Graphics Card

If programs, documents, and other items seem sluggish as they are displayed on your monitor, you can check to see if a video upgrade might help. First, determine if your computer uses *shared video memory* (in which some of your computer's RAM is used for video memory instead of separate dedicated memory located on a video graphics card). If so, then installing a separate video card containing adequate video memory may speed up your system since it will free up the RAM currently being used for video memory. You may also want to buy and install a new video card (assuming your computer has an available appropriate expansion slot) if it is necessary to connect a second monitor to your computer, or if you are a gamer, computer artist, graphical engineer, or otherwise use 3D-graphic-intensive applications.

Strategies for Making Faster and Better Computers

Researchers and manufacturers are using several strategies today to continue to build faster and better personal computers. Some relate to technology in general (such as the *virtualization* trend discussed in Chapter 1); others are techniques used specifically to speed up the CPU. Some of these strategies are described in the next few sections.

Improved Architecture

Computer manufacturers are continually working to improve the basic architecture of computers, such as to make them faster, cooler, quieter, more energy efficient, and more reliable. For example, new designs for motherboards and CPUs are always under development, and computer components are continually being built smaller, so more power and capabilities can be contained in the same size package. In fact, today's CPUs—which are formed using a process called *lithography* that imprints patterns on semiconductor materials—typically contain transistors that are 45 *nanometers* (*nm*) in size (one nanometer is a billionth of a meter); 32 nm chips are becoming available, and transistors as small as 10 nm have been created in lab settings. As lithography techniques continue to improve, transistors will likely continue to shrink, allowing more transistors to fit on the same-sized CPU. Creating components smaller than 100 nm fits the definition of *nanotechnology*, which is discussed in more detail shortly.

Other improvements include faster memory and faster bus speeds to help speed up processing and to help reduce or eliminate bottlenecks, and creating CPUs with multiple cores. CPUs are also increasingly including additional technology to meet new needs, such as support for virtualization and increased 3D graphics processing. Improvements to CPU instruction set designs are made as needed to expand the instruction set design for new applications—particularly the growing use of multimedia applications, such as editing digital movies and photos, and burning music CDs. For example, *MMX (Multimedia Extensions)* is a set of 57 multimedia instructions for handling many common multimedia operations. In addition, new *streaming SIMD extensions (SSEs)* are implemented on a regular basis to help CPUs perform floating-point-intensive applications (such as video and audio handling, 3D modeling, and physical simulations) much more quickly than before, provided the software being used supports the SSEs being used.

Improved Materials

Traditionally, CPU chips used aluminum circuitry etched onto a silicon chip. As the number of aluminum circuits that can be packed onto a silicon chip without heat damage or interference approached its limit, chipmakers began to look for alternate materials. Copper was one of the next choices since it is a far better electrical conductor, and it can produce chips containing more circuitry at a lower price. As transistors have continued to shrink (which results in an increased leakage of current), CPU manufacturers have looked to new materials that reduce current leakage to allow more reliable high-speed operation. For instance, Intel switched to a new material called *high-k* for some of the silicon components in its 45 nm and 32 nm CPUs.

A possibility for an entirely new material is the *graphene chip*, which uses *graphene*—flat sheets of carbon, such as those used to create *carbon nanotubes* (which are discussed shortly)—instead of silicon. However, instead of rolling up graphene, which is the process used when making carbon nanotubes, the graphene for chips is cut into strips. According to Georgia Tech physics professor Walter de Heer, one of the leading researchers in this area, silicon can't keep up with the current growth in chip technology and graphene may be the answer. Since electrons move through graphene with almost no resistance, they generate little heat; graphene also allows any heat that is generated to dissipate quickly. As a result, graphene-based chips can operate at much higher speeds than silicon. While de Heer estimates that graphene chips are likely at least 10 years away, he estimates that graphene can be 100 times faster than silicon—in the *terahertz* (*THz*) range.

For integrating computer components into clothing and other flexible materials (such as to create clothing, backpacks, and other objects that can control your electronic devices or display content on demand), a number of companies are developing flexible electronic components, such as the flexible processor shown in Figure 2-23. In addition to the ability to be bent without damaging the circuitry, flexible processors are thinner, lighter, generate little heat, and consume significantly less energy than conventional processors. In addition, if the processors are made from plastic (which some researchers believe is a viable alternative to silicon), it means that future CPUs could be printed on plastic sheets and be much faster than, but cost about the same as, today's silicon chips.

FIGURE 2-23
Flexible processors.

Pipelining

In older computer systems, the CPU had to finish processing one instruction completely before starting another. Today's computers, however, can process multiple instructions at one time. One way to accomplish this is through **pipelining**. With pipelining, a new instruction begins executing as soon as the previous one reaches the next stage of the pipeline. Figure 2-24 illustrates this process with a 4-stage pipeline. Notice that while the pipelined CPU is executing one instruction, it is simultaneously fetching and getting the next instruction ready for execution. Without a pipeline, the ALU and FPU would be idle while an instruction is being fetched and decoded.

Pipelines for CPUs today usually have between 10 and 20 stages, and the machine cycle is broken down in as many parts as needed to match the number of stages used. For example, with a 10-stage pipeline, the 4 steps of the machine cycle would be broken down into a total of 10 steps so that all stages of the pipeline can be used at one time. Pipelining increases the number of machine cycles completed per second, which increases the number of instructions performed per second, which improves performance.

Multiprocessing and Parallel Processing

The use of more than one processor or processing core in a computer (such as using multiple CPUs in a server, mainframe, or supercomputer, or using a multi-core CPU in a personal computer) is common today. When two or more processors or processing cores are located within a single computer, techniques that perform operations simultaneously—such

> **Pipelining.** The capability of a CPU to begin processing a new instruction as soon as the previous instruction completes the first stage of the machine cycle.

Stages

Fetch Instruction 1	Decode Instruction 1	Execute Instruction 1	Store Result Instruction 1	Fetch Instruction 2	Decode Instruction 2	Execute Instruction 2

Stages

Fetch Instruction 1	Fetch Instruction 2	Fetch Instruction 3	Fetch Instruction 4	Fetch Instruction 5	Fetch Instruction 6	Fetch Instruction 7
	Decode Instruction 1	Decode Instruction 2	Decode Instruction 3	Decode Instruction 4	Decode Instruction 5	Decode Instruction 6
		Execute Instruction 1	Execute Instruction 2	Execute Instruction 3	Execute Instruction 4	Execute Instruction 5
			Store Result Instruction 1	Store Result Instruction 2	Store Result Instruction 3	Store Result Instruction 4

WITHOUT PIPELINING
Without pipelining, an instruction finishes an entire machine cycle before another instruction is started.

WITH PIPELINING
With pipelining, a new instruction is started when the preceding instruction moves to the next stage of the pipeline.

FIGURE 2-24
Pipelining. Pipelining streamlines the machine cycle by executing different stages of multiple instructions at the same time so that the different parts of the CPU are idle less often.

HW

as **multiprocessing** (where each processor or core typically works on a different job) and **parallel processing** (where multiple processors or cores work together to make one single job finish sooner) are possible.

The use of multiprocessing and parallel processing can increase astronomically the number of calculations performed in any given time period. For example, IBM's Roadrunner supercomputer (shown in Figure 1-19 in Chapter 1) uses approximately 19,000 processors and operates at more than 1 petaflop; that is, it is able to process more than one quadrillion operations per second. To increase efficiency in multiprocessing systems, CPUs specifically designed to work with a particular number of processors (such as two or eight) can be used. These CPUs include technology (such as direct links between the processors) to improve communications and increase efficiency.

A concept related to multiprocessing is *Hyper-Threading Technology*—a technology developed by Intel to enable software to treat a single processing core as two cores. Since it utilizes processing power in the chip that would otherwise go unused, this technology lets the chip operate more efficiently, resulting in faster processing, provided the software being used supports Hyper-Threading Technology.

Future Trends

Some of the strategies discussed in the prior sections are currently being used, but some ideas are further from being implemented on a wide-scale basis. Selected trends we will likely see more of in the near future are discussed next.

Nanotechnology

Although there are varying definitions, most agree that **nanotechnology** involves creating computer components, machines, and other structures that are less than 100 nanometers in size. As already discussed, today's CPUs contain components that fit the definition of nanotechnology. However, some experts believe that, eventually, current technology

> **Multiprocessing.** The capability to use multiple processors or multiple processing cores in a single computer, usually to process multiple jobs at one time faster than could be performed with a single processor. > **Parallel processing.** A processing technique that uses multiple processors or multiple processing cores simultaneously, usually to process a single job as fast as possible. > **Nanotechnology.** The science of creating tiny computers and components by working at the individual atomic and molecular levels.

TECHNOLOGY AND YOU

The "Morph" Concept

While still a concept device, the *Morph* concept (developed by researchers at Nokia and the University of Cambridge Nanoscience Centre) demonstrates how nanotechnology may allow future mobile devices to be stretchable and flexible, allowing users to transform their mobile devices into radically different shapes. For instance, the Morph concept can be worn on the wrist, folded into a phone, or opened into a larger handheld device that features a touch pad or keyboard (see the accompanying illustration). Nanotechnology enables the material to repel water, dirt, and fingerprints and to be self-cleaning. Integrated sensors can monitor pollution and chemicals and notify the user as needed of any possible risks. The device is solar-powered via a covering of *Nanograss* that harvests solar power. According to Dr. Bob Iannucci, Chief Technology Officer, Nokia, "Nokia Research Center is looking at ways to reinvent the form and function of mobile devices; the Morph concept shows what might be possible."

Possible configurations for the Morph concept device.

ONLINE VIDEO

Go to the Chapter 2 page at **www.cengage.com/ computerconcepts/np/uc13** to watch the "Introducing the Morph Concept" video clip.

will reach its limits. At that point, transistors and other computer components may need to be built at the atomic and molecular level—starting with single atoms or molecules to construct the components. Prototypes of computer products built in this fashion include a single switch that can be turned on and off like a transistor but is made from a single organic molecule, as well as tiny nickel-based *nanodots* that would, theoretically, allow about 5 TB of data to be stored on a hard drive roughly the size of a postage stamp. In other nanotechnology developments, researchers at the University of Arizona recently discovered how to turn single molecules into working transistors and they created transistors as small as a single nanometer. In addition, prototypes of tiny *nanogenerators* have been developed that may someday power mobile devices with low-frequency vibrations, such as a heartbeat or simple body movements like walking. For a look at a concept mobile device that nanotechnology may make possible in the future, see the Technology and You box.

One nanotechnology development that is already being used in a variety of products available today is **carbon nanotubes**—tiny, hollow tubes made up of carbon atoms. The wall of a single-walled carbon nanotube is only one carbon atom thick and the tube diameter is approximately 10,000 times smaller than a human hair. Carbon nanotubes have great potential for future computing products since they can conduct electricity better than copper, are stronger than steel, conduct heat better than diamonds, and can transmit electronic impulses faster than silicon. Lithium ion batteries that use nanotubes are currently on the

>**Carbon nanotubes.** Tiny, hollow tubes made of carbon atoms.

market and several nanotube-based computing products—like nanotube-based display screens and memory—are currently under development. Since carbon nanotubes can transmit electricity and are transparent, they are also being used for product development in the areas of TVs, solar cells, light bulbs, and other similar non-computing applications. In addition, because of their strength and lightness for their size, carbon nanotubes are being integrated into products that benefit from those characteristics, such as automobile panels, airplanes, tennis rackets, and racing bikes. In fact, the frame of a bike model that several professional cyclists ride is built with carbon nanotubes (see Figure 2-25)—the entire bike frame weighs less than one kilogram (2.2 pounds). Carbon nanotubes are also beginning to be combined with other materials, such as plastic, to increase the durability of materials used to produce other consumer items, such as surfboards.

FIGURE 2-25
Carbon nanotubes make this bike frame very strong, but light.

Two other recent developments are *nanoparticles* that can remove contaminants from water sources and *nanosensors* that can detect small amounts of cancer-causing toxins or cancer drugs inside single living cells. Possible future applications of nanotechnology include disposing of e-trash by rearranging dangerous components at the atomic level into inert substances, microscopic devices that can enter the bloodstream and perform tests or irradiate cancerous tumors, improved military uniforms that protect against bullets and germ warfare, and computers and sensors that are small enough to be woven into the fibers of clothing or embedded into paint and other materials. Some of the devices generated by nanotechnology research may contain or be constructed out of organic material. Complete *organic computers* (discussed shortly) are a long way off, but researchers have already created biological computing devices—such as the *MAYA-II* computer that uses strands of DNA to perform computations. Although very slow and only programmed to play tic-tac-toe, the computer has never lost at that game.

FIGURE 2-26
Quantum computers.
The vial of liquid shown here contains the 7-qubit computer used by IBM researchers in 2001 to perform the most complicated computation by a quantum computer to date—factoring the number 15.

Quantum Computing

The idea of **quantum computing** emerged in the 1970s, but it has received renewed interest lately. Quantum computing applies the principles of quantum physics and quantum mechanics to computers, going beyond traditional physics to work at the subatomic level. Quantum computers differ from conventional computers in that they utilize atoms or nuclei working together as *quantum bits* or *qubits*. Qubits function simultaneously as both the computer's processor and memory, and each qubit can represent more than just the two states (one and zero) available to today's electronic bits; a qubit can even represent many states at one time. Quantum computers can perform computations on many numbers at one time, making them, theoretically, exponentially faster than conventional computers. Physically, quantum computers in the future might consist of a thimbleful of liquid whose atoms are used to perform calculations as instructed by an external device.

While quantum computers are still in the pioneering stage, working quantum computers do exist. For instance, in 2001 the researchers at IBM's Almaden Research Center created a 7-qubit quantum computer (see Figure 2-26) composed of the nuclei of seven atoms that can interact with each other and be programmed by radio frequency pulses. This quantum computer successfully factored the number 15—not a complicated computation for a conventional computer, but the fact that a quantum computer was able to understand the problem and compute the correct answer is viewed as a highly significant event in the area of quantum computer research.

>**Quantum computing.** A technology that applies the principles of quantum physics and quantum mechanics to computers to direct atoms or nuclei to work together as quantum bits (qubits), which function simultaneously as the computer's processor and memory.

More recently, Canadian scientists developed a 16-qubit quantum computer that can solve Sudoku puzzles, and Yale University researchers developed the first rudimentary electronic quantum processor (based on a 2-qubit chip) that can successfully perform a few simple tasks. In addition, Hewlett-Packard scientists have developed a *crossbar latch*—a switch just a single molecule thick that can store binary data and might one day function as a transistor in a quantum computer. One of the obstacles to creating a fully functional quantum computer has been the inability of researchers to control the actions of a single qubit inside a matrix of other qubits. In 2009, researchers successfully accomplished this in an experiment; this breakthrough is viewed as a significant step toward the ability to create more sophisticated working quantum computers in the future.

Quantum computing is not well suited for general computing tasks but is ideal for, and expected to be widely used in, the areas of *encryption* (discussed in Chapter 9) and code breaking.

Optical Computing

Optical chips, which use light waves to transmit data, are also currently in development. A possibility for the future is the **optical computer**—a computer that uses light, such as from laser beams or infrared beams—to perform digital computations. Because light beams do not interfere with each other, optical computers can be much smaller and faster than electronic computers. For instance, according to one NASA senior research scientist, an optical computer could solve a problem in one hour that would take an electronic computer 11 years to solve. While some researchers are working on developing an all-optical computer, others believe that a mix of optical and electronic components—or an *opto-electronic computer*—may be the best bet for the future. Opto-electronic technology is already being used to improve long-distance fiber-optic communications. Initial opto-electronic computer applications are expected to be applied to the area of speeding up communications between computers and other devices, as well as between computer components. In fact, prototypes of chips that have both optical and electrical functions combined on a single silicon chip—a feat that was thought to be impossible until recently—already exist. One recent breakthrough in optical computing is the development by researchers of ways to make lasers smaller than was originally thought possible. These *nanolasers* could conceivably be incorporated into small electronic components in order to speed up communications inside a computer, such as within a CPU or between a CPU and other computer components.

▼ FIGURE 2-27

Avalanche Photodetector (APD) silicon light sensor.

Silicon Photonics

Silicon photonics refers to the process of sending optical information among computers and other electronic devices using standard silicon manufacturing techniques—essentially converging *photonics* (the control and manipulation of light) and electronics. This technology is viewed as one possible low-cost solution to future data-intensive computing applications, such as *telemedicine* and lifelike *3D virtual worlds* (which are both discussed in later chapters). According to Patrick Gelsinger, a senior vice president at Intel, "Today, optics is a niche technology. Tomorrow, it's the mainstream of every chip that we build."

One recent development in this area from Intel Labs researchers is the creation of a silicon-based light sensor (called an *Avalanche Photodetector* or *APD* and shown in Figure 2-27) that achieved world-record performance in a recent test. This test showed that a silicon photonics device could exceed the performance of a device

> **Optical computer.** A computer that uses light, such as from laser beams or infrared beams, to perform digital computations.

made with more expensive optical materials, such as indium phosphide. Silicon photonics technology has great potential in the area of transferring large amounts of data very quickly between chips inside computers, in addition to between computers; it is expected to begin being incorporated in some personal computer components by 2011.

Terascale Computing

As demand by consumers and businesses for online software, services, and media-rich experiences continues to increase, some experts predict that *terascale computing*—the ability of a CPU to process one trillion floating-point operations per second (teraflops) will eventually be needed. While supercomputers currently reach teraflop and petaflop speeds, much of today's terascale research is focusing on creating multi-core processors with tens to hundreds of cores used in conjunction with multithreaded hardware and software to achieve teraflop performance. The research also includes working on developing higher-speed communications between computers, such as between Web servers and high-performance mobile devices or computers, to help facilitate high-performance cloud computing.

Intel, one of the leaders in terascale research, has created a *teraflop processor* that contains 80 cores to test strategies for moving terabytes of data rapidly from core to core and between cores and memory. It has also developed a 20-megabyte SRAM memory chip that is attached directly to the processor in order to speed up communication between processors and memory. This design allows thousands of interconnections, which enable data to travel at more than one *terabyte per second* (*TBps*) between memory and the processor cores. It is expected that this speed will be needed to handle the terabytes of data used by applications in the near future.

3D Chips

Three-dimensional (*3D*) *chips* are another technique for packing an increasing number of components onto small chips. With 3D chips, the transistors are layered, which cuts down on the surface area required. Typically, 3D chips are created by layering individual silicon wafers on top of one another. The layering is typically accomplished via a special machine that uses cameras to align the wafers properly. However, researchers at the University of Southampton, UK, have recently developed wafers that contain matching sets of pegs and holes, similar to the way Lego bricks fit together. In preliminary tests, the researchers lined up the edges of two chips by hand and pressed them together— images taken with an electron microscope show that the two chips aligned roughly five times better than with the camera-based technique. While still in the research stage, the researchers believe that this new design could aid the development of 3D chips and other 3D electronic components.

3D chips are now available for some applications (such as video) and are expected to be used for other applications (such as stacking up chips and memory controllers in some CPU architectures) in the near future. One hurdle in 3D chips is the amount of heat generated. Some new cooling methods (such as the ion pump method discussed earlier in this chapter) can't be used with 3D chips so other alternatives—such as IBM's prototype water cooling systems that can cool between the layers of a chip (see Figure 2-28)—are in development.

FIGURE 2-28

3D chips. IBM's interlayer water cooling system cools between the layers in the chip.

SUMMARY

DATA AND PROGRAM REPRESENTATION

Chapter Objective 1:
Understand how data and programs are represented to a computer and be able to identify a few of the coding systems used to accomplish this.

Most *digital computers* work in a two-state, or *binary*, fashion. It is convenient to think of these binary states in terms of 0s and 1s. Computer people refer to these 0s and 1s as bits. Converting data to these 0s and 1s is called *digital data representation*.

While most individuals use the **decimal number system** to represent numbers and perform numeric computations, computers use the **binary numbering system**. Text-based data can be represented with one of several fixed-length binary codes (such as **ASCII** (**American Standard Code for Information Interchange**) or **Unicode**) that represent single characters of data—a numeric digit, alphabetic character, or special symbol—as strings of **bits**. Each string of eight bits is called a **byte**. Use of Unicode is growing since it can represent text in all written languages, including those that use alphabets different from English, such as Chinese, Greek, and Russian.

The storage capacity of computers is often expressed using prefixes in conjunction with the term *byte* to convey the approximate quantity being represented, such as using **kilobyte** (**KB**), about one thousand bytes; **megabyte** (**MB**), about one million bytes; **gigabyte** (**GB**), about one billion bytes; or **terabyte** (**TB**), about one trillion bytes. Other possibilities are **petabyte** (**PB**), about 1,000 terabytes; **exabyte** (**EB**), about 1,000 petabytes; **zettabyte** (**ZB**), about 1,000 exabytes; and **yottabyte** (**YB**), about 1,000 zettabytes.

The binary system can represent not only text but also graphics, audio, and video data. **Machine language** is the binary-based code through which computers represent program instructions. A program must be translated into machine language before the computer can execute it.

INSIDE THE SYSTEM UNIT

Chapter Objective 2:
Explain the functions of the hardware components commonly found inside the system unit, such as the CPU, memory, buses, and expansion cards.

Personal computers typically contain a variety of hardware components located inside the **system unit**. For instance, *chips* are mounted onto *circuit boards*, and those boards are positioned in slots on the **motherboard**—the main circuit board for a computer. Every computer has a **central processing unit** (**CPU**) or **processor**—also called a **microprocessor** when referring to personal computers—attached to its motherboard that performs the processing for the computer. CPU chips differ in many respects, such as what types of computer the CPU is designed for, its *clock speed*, and *word size*. They can also be **multi-core CPUs**, such as the **dual-core** (two cores) and **quad-core** (four cores) **CPUs** now available. Another difference is the amount of **cache memory**—memory located on or very close to the CPU chip to help speed up processing. Other important differences are the general architecture of the CPU and the bus speed and width being used. The overall *processing speed* of the computer determines its performance. One of the most consistent measurements of overall performance is a *benchmark test*.

Memory refers to chip-based storage. The main memory for a personal computer is **RAM** (**random access memory**). Traditional RAM is **volatile** and used to hold programs and data temporarily while they are needed; **nonvolatile** RAM is under development. RAM is available in different types and speeds, and is measured in bytes. **ROM** (**read-only memory**) is a type of nonvolative memory that stores nonerasable programs. **Flash memory** is a type of nonvolatile memory that can be used for storage by the computer or the user. Flash memory chips can be found in many personal computers and mobile devices; flash memory chips are also integrated into storage media and devices. **Registers** are memory built into the CPU chip to hold data before or during processing. *Fans*, *heat sinks*, and other techniques are used to compensate for the heat that CPUs and other components generate.

Most desktop computers contain internal **expansion slots**, into which users can insert **expansion cards** to give the computer added functionality. **ExpressCard modules** can be used to add additional capabilities to computers containing an *ExpressCard slot.*

A computer **bus** is an electronic path along which bits are transmitted. The **memory bus** moves data between the CPU and RAM. The **frontside bus (FSB)** connects the CPU to the *I/O bridge*, which connects the CPU and memory to the rest of the *bus architecture.* Common **expansion buses** include *PCI*, **PCI Express (PCIe) bus**, **Universal Serial Bus (USB)**, and **FireWire**. The performance of a bus can be measured by the the bus's **throughput** or **bandwidth**; that is, the amount of data that can be transferred via the bus in a given time period.

System units typically have external **ports** that are used to connect peripheral devices to the computer. Notebook, tablet, and netbook computers may have fewer ports than desktop computers. Ultra-mobile PCs and mobile device users often add new capabilities via USB ports or *Secure Digital (SD) cards* or other types of flash memory cards.

Chapter Objective 3:
Describe how peripheral devices or other hardware can be added to a computer.

HOW THE CPU WORKS

CPUs today include at least one **arithmetic/logic unit (ALU)**, which performs integer arithmetic and logical operations on data, and most include at least one **floating point unit (FPU)**, which performs decimal arithmetic. The **control unit** directs the flow of electronic traffic between memory and the ALU/FPU and also between the CPU and input and output devices. Registers—high-speed temporary holding places within the CPU that hold program instructions and data immediately before and during processing—are used to enhance the computer's performance. The **prefetch unit** requests data and instructions before or as they are needed, the **decode unit** decodes the instructions input into the CPU, internal cache stores frequently used instructions and data, and the **bus interface unit** allows the various parts of the CPU to communicate with each other.

The CPU processes instructions in a sequence called a **machine cycle**, consisting of four basic steps. Each machine language instruction is broken down into several smaller instructions called *microcode*, and each piece of microcode corresponds to an operation (such as adding two numbers located in the CPU's registers) that can be performed inside the CPU. The computer system has a built-in **system clock** that synchronizes all of the computer's activities.

Chapter Objective 4:
Understand how the computer's CPU and memory components process program instructions and data.

MAKING COMPUTERS FASTER AND BETTER NOW AND IN THE FUTURE

There are several possible remedies for a computer that is performing too slowly, including adding more memory, performing system maintenance to clean up the computer's hard drive, buying a larger or additional hard drive, and upgrading the computer's Internet connection or video card, depending on the primary role of the computer and where the processing bottleneck appears to be. To make computers work faster overall, computer designers have developed a number of strategies over the years, and researchers are continually working on new strategies. Some of the strategies already being implemented include improved architecture, **pipelining**, **multiprocessing**, **parallel processing**, and the use of new or improved materials.

One possibility for future computers is **nanotechnology** research, which focuses on building computer components at the individual atomic and molecular levels. Some computer and consumer products (such as NRAM, solar cells, tennis rackets, and bikes) using **carbon nanotubes** (tiny hollow tubes made of carbon atoms) are currently on the market. **Quantum computing** and **optical computers** are other possibilities being researched, along with *silicon photonics*, *terascale computing*, and *three-dimensional (3D) chips.*

Chapter Objective 5:
Name and evaluate several strategies that can be used today for speeding up the operations of a computer.

Chapter Objective 6:
List some processing technologies that may be used in future computers.

REVIEW ACTIVITIES

KEY TERM MATCHING

a. ASCII

b. binary numbering system

c. byte

d. central processing unit (CPU)

e. control unit

f. motherboard

g. nanotechnology

h. parallel processing

i. RAM (random access memory)

j. Universal Serial Bus (USB)

Instructions: Match each key term on the left with the definition on the right that best describes it.

1. _____ A processing technique that uses multiple processors or processing cores simultaneously, usually to process a single job as fast as possible.

2. _____ A fixed-length, binary coding system used to represent text-based data for computer processing on many types of computers.

3. _____ A group of 8 bits.

4. _____ A universal bus used to connect up to 127 peripheral devices to a computer without requiring the use of additional expansion cards.

5. _____ Chips connected to the motherboard that provide a temporary location for the computer to hold data and program instructions while they are needed.

6. _____ The chip located on the motherboard of a computer that performs the processing for a computer.

7. _____ The main circuit board of a computer, located inside the system unit, to which all computer system components connect.

8. _____ The numbering system that represents all numbers using just two symbols (0 and 1).

9. _____ The part of the CPU that coordinates its operations.

10. _____ The science of creating tiny computers and components by working at the individual atomic and molecular levels.

SELF-QUIZ

Instructions: Circle **T** if the statement is true, **F** if the statement is false, or write the best answer in the space provided. **Answers for the self-quiz are located in the References and Resources Guide at the end of the book.**

1. **T F** A storage medium that can hold 256 GB can hold about 256 billion characters.

2. **T F** The amount of data that can be transferred over a bus in a given time period determines the bus's volatility.

3. **T F** Cache memory is typically built into a CPU.

4. **T F** A bus is a pathway, such as on the motherboard or inside the CPU, along which bits can be transferred.

5. **T F** Computers that process data with light are referred to as quantum computers.

6. The binary number 1101 is equivalent to the decimal number _____.

7. A CPU with four separate processing cores is referred to as a(n) _____ CPU.

8. A(n) _____ is a connector on the exterior of a computer into which a peripheral device may be plugged.

9. Multi-core CPUs allow _____, in which the CPU is able to work on multiple jobs at one time.

10. Number the following terms from 1 to 9 to indicate their size from smallest to largest.

a. _____ Petabyte   d. _____ Yottabyte   g. _____ Zettabyte

b. _____ Kilobyte   e. _____ Exabyte   h. _____ Terabyte

c. _____ Gigabyte   f. _____ Byte   i. _____ Megabyte

---

1. What do each of the following acronyms stand for?

a. KB _____   c. ROM _____   e. PCIe _____

b. RAM _____   d. USB _____   f. CPU _____

2. Using the ASCII code chart in this chapter or in the References and Resources Guide at the end of the book, decode the following word. What does it say?

01000011   01000001   01000110   01000101
_____   _____   _____   _____

3. Supply the missing words to complete the following statements.

a. The smallest piece of data that can be represented by a computer (a 0 or 1) is called a(n) _____.

b. _____ is an international coding system for text-based data using any written language.

c. L1 is a type of _____.

d. The part of the CPU that performs logical operations and integer arithmetic is the _____.

4. Assume you have a USB mouse, USB keyboard, and USB printer to connect to a computer, but you have only two USB ports. Explain one solution to this problem that does not involve buying a new mouse, keyboard, or printer.

5. If your computer seems sluggish, list two things you could do to try to speed it up without resorting to purchasing an entirely new system.

---

1. As discussed in the chapter, one push by computer manufacturers is making computers run as efficiently as possible to save battery power and electricity. What do you think is the motivation behind this trend? Is it social responsibility or a response to consumer demands? Should the energy consumption of electronic devices be regulated and controlled by the government or another organization? Why or why not? How responsible should consumers be for energy conservation in relation to electronic use? In your opinion, what, if anything, should all computer users do to practice *green computing*?

2. In addition to being used with computers and consumer products, there are also processors and other components designed to be implanted inside the human body, such as the *VeriChip* (discussed in Project 4), implantable wafers containing medication and a processor that delivers the medication at the appropriate time and dosage, *camera pills* that are swallowed to transmit images of an individual's digestive system to a receiving unit, and pacemakers designed to regulate an individual's heart rate. One step further is *brain-to-computer interfacing* (*BCI*), which involves implanting electrodes directly into the human brain to restore lost functionality or to facilitate the communication ability of severely disabled individuals, such as by enabling them to control a mouse using only their thoughts. What do you think about these implantable chip applications? Are the benefits worth the risk of something going wrong with the chips implanted inside your body? Are there any privacy risks? Would you consider using an implanted device? Why or why not?

PROJECTS

1. **Wearable PCs** There are some computers available today that are designed to be worn on a belt or wrist. As mentioned in the Technology and You box, computers in the future may be able to morph into different configurations, such as a wristband, upon demand. Today's wearable computers are primarily designed for mobile workers, surgeons, military personnel, and other individuals who need hands-free access to a computer.

   For this project, locate one wearable computer on the market and determine its purpose, cost, and capabilities. What tasks can it perform? Who would use this computer? Is it geared for consumer use? If so, would you wear this computer in public? Why or why not? If not, what would need to change in order for you to be willing to wear it? Think about your chosen profession—would a wearable computer be needed or be useful? At the conclusion of your research, prepare a one-page summary of your findings and opinions and submit it to your instructor.

2. **Adding Memory** Adding additional RAM to a computer is one of the most common computer upgrades. Before purchasing additional memory, however, it is important to make sure that the memory about to be purchased is compatible with the computer.

   For this project, select a computer (such as your own computer, a school computer, or a computer at a local store) and then determine (by looking at the computer or asking an appropriate individual—such as a lab aide in the school computer lab or a salesperson at the local store) the following: manufacturer and model number, CPU, current amount of memory, total memory slots, and the number of available memory slots. (If you look inside the computer, be sure to unplug the power cord first and do not touch any components inside the system unit.) Once you have the necessary information, call a local store or use your information and a memory supplier's Web site to determine the appropriate type of memory needed for your selected computer. What choices do you have in terms of capacity and configuration? Can you add just one memory module, or do you have to add memory in pairs? Can you keep the old memory modules, or do they have to be removed? At the conclusion of your research, prepare a one-page summary of your findings and recommendations and submit it to your instructor.

3. **Intel Museum Tour** Intel Corporation has a great deal of interesting information about processors on its Web site, including information available through its online museum.

   For this project, go to the Intel Museum at **www.intel.com/museum/index.htm** (if this URL no longer works, go to the Intel home page at www.intel.com and search for "Intel Museum"). Once you are at the Intel Museum home page, select either the *Online Exhibits* option or the *Intel Corporate Archives* option to locate an exhibit or documents related to processors or memory, such as *From Sand to Circuits*, *Memory Technology*, or *Moore's Law*, and then tour the exhibit or read through the available information, making a note of at least three interesting facts you didn't know before. At the conclusion of this task, prepare a short summary listing the tour you took and the interesting facts you recorded and submit it to your instructor.

4. **People Chips** The *VeriChip* is a tiny chip that is designed to be implanted under a person's skin, such as on the forearm. Currently, VeriChips are used primarily for identification purposes—the unique number contained in a VeriChip can be read by a proprietary scanner and can be used in conjunction with a database, such as to provide hospital emergency room personnel with health information about an unconscious patient. However, implanted chips can also be used to control access to secure areas and for electronic payment purposes. What do you think of implanted devices, such as the VeriChip, being used for access control (such as for government buildings or highly-secure facilities), for expediting passage through security check points (such as at airports), or for making electronic payments (such as at a grocery store)? Would you be willing to be "chipped" if it made some tasks (such as unlocking your home or car) easier or some types of transactions (such as ATM withdrawals) more secure? Is it ethical for a government to require its citizens to be chipped, similar to a national ID card? Is it ethical for a business to request that its employees be chipped for security purposes? Should businesses be allowed to require chipping as a condition of employment?

For this project, form an opinion about the ethical use and ramifications of human-implantable chips and be prepared to discuss your position (in class, via an online class discussion group, in a class chat room, or via a class blog, depending on your instructor's directions). You may also be asked to write a short paper expressing your opinion.

PRESENTATION/ DEMONSTRATION

5. **Binary Conversions** As discussed in the chapter, all numbers processed by the CPU must be represented in a binary format. Binary (base 2) represents all numbers using 2 digits, decimal uses 10 digits, and hexadecimal uses 16 digits.

For this project, research how to convert a three-digit decimal number to both binary and hexadecimal and back again, without the use of a calculator (refer to the "A Look at Numbering Systems" feature located in the References and Resources Guide at the end of this book if needed). Next, determine how to represent the decimal number 10 in base 3 (the numbering system that uses only the digits 0, 1, and 2). Share your findings with the class in the form of a short presentation, including a demonstration of the conversions between binary and hexadecimal and the representation of the decimal number 10 in base 3. The presentation should not exceed 10 minutes and should make use of one or more presentation aids such as the chalkboard, handouts, overhead transparencies, or a computer-based slide presentation (your instructor may provide additional requirements). You may also be asked to submit a summary of the presentation to your instructor.

Instructions: Go to the Chapter 2 page at **www.cengage.com/computerconcepts/np/uc13** to work the following Web Activities.

6. **Interactive Activities** Work the interactive **Crossword Puzzle**, watch the **Video Podcasts** and **Online Videos**, and explore the **Further Exploration** links associated with this chapter.

If you have a SAM user profile, you may have access to hands-on instruction, practice, and assessment of the skills covered in this chapter. Check with your instructor for instructions and the correct URL/Web site to access those assignments.

7. **Student Edition Labs** Work the following interactive **Student Edition Labs**.
   ➢ **Binary Numbers**   ➢ **Understanding the Motherboard**

8. **Test Yourself** Review the **Online Study Guide** for this chapter, then test your knowledge of the terms and concepts covered in this chapter by completing the **Key Term Matching** exercise, the **Self-Quiz**, the **Exercises**, and the **Practice Test**.

WEB ACTIVITIES

chapter 3

Storage

After completing this chapter, you will be able to do the following:

1. Name several general characteristics of storage systems.

2. Describe the two most common types of hard drives and what they are used for today.

3. Discuss the various types of optical discs available today and how they differ from each other.

4. Identify some flash memory storage devices and media and explain how they are used today.

5. List at least three other types of storage systems.

6. Summarize the storage alternatives for a typical personal computer.

outline

Overview

Storage Systems Characteristics
Storage Media and Storage Devices
Volatility
Random vs. Sequential Access
Logical vs. Physical Representation
Type of Storage Technology Used

Hard Drives
Magnetic Hard Drives and Solid-State Drives (SSDs)
Internal and External Hard Drives
Hard Drive Speed, Disk Caching, and Hybrid Hard Drives
Hard Drive Partitioning and File Systems
Hard Drive Interface Standards

Optical Discs
Optical Disc Characteristics
Read-Only Optical Discs: CD-ROM, DVD-ROM, and BD-ROM Discs
Recordable Optical Discs: CD-R, DVD-R, DVD+R, and BD-R Discs
Rewritable Optical Discs: CD-RW, DVD-RW, DVD+RW, and BD-RE Discs

Flash Memory
Flash Memory Cards
USB Flash Drives

Other Types of Storage Systems
Network Storage and Online/Cloud Storage Systems
Smart Cards
Holographic Storage
Storage Systems for Large Computer Systems

Evaluating Your Storage Alternatives

OVERVIEW

In Chapter 2, we discussed the role of RAM, the computer's main memory. RAM temporarily holds program instructions, data, and output while they are needed by the computer. For instance, when you first create a letter or other word processing document on your computer, both the word processing program and the document are temporarily stored in RAM. But when the word processing program is closed, the computer no longer needs to work with the program or the document, and so they are both erased from RAM. Consequently, anything (such as your word processing document) that needs to be preserved for future use needs to be stored on a more permanent medium. Storage systems fill this role.

We begin this chapter with a look at the characteristics common among all storage systems. Then, we discuss the primary storage for most personal computers—the hard drive. From there, we turn our attention to optical discs, including how they work and the various types of CDs and DVDs available today. Next, we discuss flash memory storage systems, followed by a look at a few other types of storage systems, including network and online/cloud storage, smart cards, holographic storage, and the storage systems used with large computer systems. The chapter concludes with a summary of the storage alternatives for a typical personal computer. ■

STORAGE SYSTEMS CHARACTERISTICS

All *storage systems* have specific characteristics, including having a *storage medium* and a *storage device*, *portability*, *volatility*, how data is accessed and represented, the type of storage technology used, and so on. These characteristics are discussed in the next few sections.

Storage Media and Storage Devices

There are two parts to any storage system: the **storage medium** and the **storage device**. A storage medium is the hardware where data is actually stored (for example, a *CD* or a *flash memory card*); a storage medium is inserted into its corresponding storage device (such as a *CD drive* or a *flash memory card reader*) in order to be read from or written to. Often the storage device and storage medium are two separate pieces of hardware (that is, the storage medium is *removable*), although with some systems—such as a *hard drive* or most *USB flash drives*—the two parts are permanently sealed together to form one piece of hardware.

Storage devices can be *internal* (located inside the system unit), *external* (plugged into an external port on the system unit), or *remote* (located on another computer, such as a network server). Internal devices have the advantage of requiring no additional desk space and

---

> **Storage medium.** The part of a storage system where data is stored, such as a DVD disc. > **Storage device.** A piece of hardware, such as a DVD drive, into which a storage medium is inserted to be read from or written to.

CD/DVD drives are usually assigned letters after the hard drives, such as D and E in this example.

The various slots in a built-in flash memory card reader are typically assigned next, such as the letters F, G, H and I, in this example.

Other letters, beginning with J in this example, are used for any other storage devices attached to the computer, such as via these USB ports.

The letter C is usually assigned to the first hard drive.

FIGURE 3-1

Storage device identifiers. To keep track of storage devices in an unambiguous way, the computer system assigns letters of the alphabet or names to each of them.

are usually faster than their external counterparts. External devices, however, can be easily transported from one location to another (such as to share data with others, to transfer data between a work computer and a home computer, or to take digital photos to a photo store). They can also be removed from the computer and stored in a secure area, when needed (such as for backup purposes or to protect sensitive data). Remote devices are accessed over a network. Some remote storage devices, such as those accessed via the Internet, have the additional advantage of being able to be accessible from any computer with an Internet connection.

Regardless of how storage devices are connected to a computer, letters of the alphabet and/or names are typically assigned to each storage device so that the user can identify each device easily when it needs to be used (see Figure 3-1). Some drive letters, such as the letter *C* typically used with the primary hard drive, are usually consistent from computer to computer and do not change even if more storage devices are added to a computer. The rest of the drive letters on a computer may change as new devices are added either permanently (such as when an additional hard drive is installed inside the computer) or temporarily (such as when a USB flash drive, digital camera, or portable digital media player is connected to the computer). When a new storage device is detected, the computer just assigns and reassigns drive letters, as needed.

Volatility

As discussed in Chapter 2, conventional RAM is volatile so programs and documents held in RAM are erased when they are no longer needed by the computer or when the power to the computer is turned off. Storage media, however, are nonvolatile, so the data remains on the media even when the power to the computer or storage device is off. Consequently, storage media are used for anything that needs to be saved for future use.

Random vs. Sequential Access

When the computer receives an instruction that requires data located on a storage medium, it must go to the designated location on the appropriate storage medium and retrieve the requested data. This procedure is referred to as access. Two basic access methods are available: *random* and *sequential*.

Random access, also called *direct access*, means that data can be retrieved directly from any location on the storage medium, in any order. A random access device works in a manner similar to a CD or DVD player used to play music or movies; that is, it can jump directly to a particular location on the medium when data located at that location is needed. Most storage devices used with computers today—including hard drives, CD/DVD drives, and USB flash drives—are random access devices.

Media that allow random access are sometimes referred to as *addressable* media. This means that the storage system can locate each piece of stored data at a unique *address*, which is determined by the computer system. With *sequential access*, however, the data can only be retrieved in the order in which it is physically stored on the medium. One type of storage device that is sometimes used with computers and that uses sequential access is a *magnetic tape drive*. Computer tapes work like audiocassette tapes or videotapes—to get to a specific location on the tape, you must play or fast forward through all of the tape before it.

Logical vs. Physical Representation

Anything (such as a program, letter, digital photograph, or song) stored on a storage medium is referred to as a **file**. Data files are also often called *documents*. When a document that was just created (such as a memo or letter in a word processing program) is saved, it is stored as a new file on the storage medium that the user designates. During the storage process, the user is required to give the file a name, called a **filename**; that filename is used to retrieve the file when it is needed at a later time.

To keep files organized, related documents are often stored in **folders** (also called *directories*) located on the storage medium. For example, one folder might contain memos to business associates while another might hold a set of budgets (see Figure 3-2). To organize files further, you can create *subfolders* (*subdirectories*) within a folder. For instance, you might create a subfolder within the *Budgets* subfolder for each fiscal year. In Figure 3-2, both *Budgets* and *Memos* are subfolders inside the *Documents* folder; the *Budgets* subfolder contains two additional subfolders (*2010* and *2011*).

Although both the user and the computer use drive letters, folder names, and filenames to save and retrieve documents, they perceive them differently. The user typically views how data is stored (what has been discussed so far in this section and what appears in the *Windows Explorer file management program* screen shown in Figure 3-2) using *logical file representation*. That is, individuals view a document stored as one complete unit in a particular folder on a particular drive. Computers, however, use *physical file representation*; that is, they access a particular document stored on a storage medium using its physical location or locations. For example, the *ABC Industries Proposal Memo* file shown in Figure 3-2 is *logically* located in the *Memos* folders in the *Documents* and *Debbie* folders on the hard drive C, but the content of this file could be *physically* stored in many different pieces scattered across that hard drive. When this occurs, the computer keeps track of the various physical locations used to store that file, as well as the logical representations (filename, folder names, and drive letter) used to identify that file, in order to retrieve the entire file when needed. Fortunately, users do not have to be concerned with how files are physically stored on a storage medium because the computer keeps track of that information and uses it to retrieve files whenever they are requested.

FIGURE 3-2

Organizing data.
Folders are used to organize related items on a storage medium.

Folders

2010
2011
BUDGETS
MEMOS
DOCUMENTS

Files

Folders; the Memos folder is selected.

Files in the Memos folder.

> **File.** Something stored on a storage medium, such as a program, a document, or an image. > **Filename.** A name given to a file by the user; it is used to retrieve the file at a later time. > **Folder.** A named place on a storage medium into which files can be stored to keep the files stored on that medium organized.

Type of Storage Technology Used

Data is stored *magnetically* or *optically* on many types of storage media. With magnetic storage systems, such as conventional hard drives, data is stored magnetically on the storage medium, which means the data (0s and 1s) is represented using different magnetic alignments. The storage device can change the magnetic alignment when needed, so data can be written to the medium, deleted from the medium, or rewritten to the medium. Optical storage media (such as CDs and DVDs) store data optically using laser beams. On some optical media, the laser burns permanent marks to represent 0s and 1s into the surface of the medium so the data cannot be erased or rewritten. With *rewritable* optical media, the laser changes the reflectivity of the medium to represent 0s and 1s but it does not permanently alter the disc surface so the reflectivity of the medium can be changed back again as needed. Consequently, the data stored on a rewritable optical disc can be changed.

Some storage systems use a combination of magnetic and optical technology. Others use a different technology altogether, such as *flash memory storage systems* that represent data using *electrons* (electrons are either trapped or not trapped inside *flash memory cells* to represent 0s and 1s). Some of the most widely used storage systems are discussed next.

HARD DRIVES

With the exception of computers designed to use only network storage devices (such as network computers and some Internet appliances), virtually all personal computers come with a **hard drive** that is used to store most programs and data. *Internal hard drives* (those located inside the system unit) are not designed to be removed, unless they need to be repaired or replaced. *External hard drives* typically connect to a computer via a USB or FireWire port and are frequently used for additional storage (such as for digital photos, videos, and other large multimedia files), to move files between computers, and for backup purposes. In addition to being used with computers, hard drives are also increasingly being incorporated into other consumer products, such as mobile phones, portable digital media players, digital video recorders (DVRs), gaming consoles, digital camcorders, and more.

For security purposes, both internal and external hard drives today are increasingly coming with built-in *encryption* that automatically encrypts all data stored on the hard drive and protects access to the hard drive with a *secure password*; external hard drives may use a built-in *fingerprint reader* to grant only authorized users access to the hard drive. Encryption, secure passwords, and fingerprint readers are discussed in detail in Chapter 9.

Magnetic Hard Drives and Solid-State Drives (SSDs)

Traditional hard drives are *magnetic hard drives* that contain *magnetic hard disks*, *read/write heads*, and an *access mechanism*. Data is written to the magnetic hard disks by read/write heads, which magnetize particles a certain way on the surface of the disks to represent the data's 0s and 1s. The particles retain their magnetic orientation until the orientation is changed again, so files can be stored, retrieved, rewritten, and deleted as needed. Storing data on a magnetic disk is illustrated in Figure 3-3.

A newer type of hard drive is the *solid-state drive* (*SSD*) that uses flash memory technology instead of magnetic technology to store data (for a look at how flash memory technology works, see the How It Works box). While magnetic hard drives are currently less expensive and are currently available in larger capacities than SSDs, the use of SSDs is growing rapidly—especially with portable computers like notebook and netbook computers. This is because the flash memory technology that SSDs are based on allows for faster operation

---

>**Hard drive.** The primary storage system for most computers; used to store most programs and data used with a computer.

(one study showed a nine-fold increase in performance over conventional magnetic hard drives), reduced power consumption (SSDs use at least 50% less power than magnetic hard drives use), and increased shock-resistance.

Magnetic Hard Drives

A **magnetic hard drive** (usually what individuals are referring to when they use the term *hard drive*) contains one or more round pieces of metal (called *hard disks* or *platters*) that are coated with a magnetizable substance. These hard disks are permanently sealed inside the hard drive case, along with the *read/write heads* used to store (*write*) and retrieve (*read*) data and an *access mechanism* used to move the read/write heads in and out over the surface of the hard disks (see Figure 3-4). Hard drives designed for desktop computers (sometimes referred to as *desktop hard drives*) typically use 2.5-inch or 3.5-inch hard disks and notebook hard drives typically use 2.5-inch hard disks. Portable digital media players, mobile phones, and other mobile devices that include a magnetic hard drive typically use tiny 1.5-inch or smaller hard drives instead. Regardless of the size, one hard drive usually contains a stack of several hard disks; if so, there is a read/write head for each hard disk surface (top and bottom), as illustrated in Figure 3-4, and these heads move in and out over the disk surfaces simultaneously.

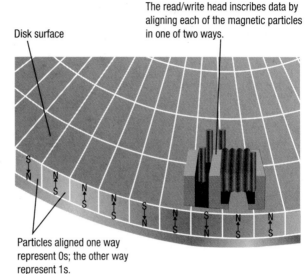

Disk surface

The read/write head inscribes data by aligning each of the magnetic particles in one of two ways.

Particles aligned one way represent 0s; the other way represent 1s.

 FIGURE 3-3
Storing data on magnetic disks.

MOUNTING SHAFT
The mounting shaft spins the hard disks at a speed of several thousand revolutions per minute while the computer is turned on.

SEALED DRIVE
The hard disks and the drive mechanism are hermetically sealed inside a case to keep them free from contamination.

READ/WRITE HEADS
There is a read/write head for each hard disk surface, and they move in and out over the disks together.

HARD DISKS
There are usually several hard disk surfaces on which to store data. Most hard drives store data on both sides of each disk.

INSIDE A 3.5-INCH HARD DRIVE

ACCESS MECHANISM
The access mechanism moves the read/write heads in and out together between the hard disk surfaces to access required data.

2.5-INCH HARD DRIVE LOCATED INSIDE A NOTEBOOK COMPUTER

 FIGURE 3-4
Magnetic hard drives.

> **Magnetic hard drive.** A hard drive consisting of one or more metal magnetic disks permanently sealed, with an access mechanism and read/write heads, inside its drive.

HOW IT WORKS

Flash Memory

Instead of representing data magnetically or optically, flash memory devices represent data with electrical charges stored within *flash memory cells*. Flash memory cells are arranged in grids of rows and columns with two *gates* (the parts of a transistor that can allow electrical current to flow through the transistor's circuits) within each cell and two *lines* or wires connecting the flash memory cell to the circuitry surrounding the flash memory cell. One of the gates (the *control gate*) is connected to one of the wires (typically called the *control line* or *word line*). The other gate (the *floating gate*) is completely surrounded by an *oxide* layer and is not connected electrically to the other flash memory cell components. Since the floating gate is isolated electrically from the rest of the cell components, any electrical charge placed on the floating gate remains there until it is removed, even when the power to the flash memory device is off. The cell also has a *source* and *drain* that are connected via a wire (usually called the *bit line*) to the circuitry surrounding the flash memory cell. Under certain conditions, as described shortly, electrical current can flow from the source to the drain; this current is controlled by the voltage applied to the control gate.

To store data in a flash memory cell, a large amount of voltage is applied to the control gate. When the appropriate amount of voltage is applied, electrons are able to tunnel through the oxide layer surrounding the floating gate and become trapped on the floating gate. To remove those electrons, voltage of the opposite polarity is applied to the control gate and the electrons tunnel off the floating gate back through the oxide.

To read data stored in a flash memory cell, a smaller amount of voltage is applied to the control gate. When this occurs, it causes current to flow from the source to the drain if there are no electrons trapped on the floating gate. If electrons are trapped on the floating gate, they will prevent the current from flowing. Whether or not the current flows from the source to the drain (and therefore, whether or not there are electrons on the floating gate) determines the value of the data (0 or 1) stored in that cell, as shown in the accompanying illustration.

Flash memory originally held a single bit per memory cell, called *single-level cell* (*SLC*) *flash*. To increase storage capacity and reduce its cost, manufacturers are increasingly using multiple bits per cell, called *multilevel cell* (*MLC*) *flash*. To increase speed, *NAND flash memory* (the type of memory used in flash memory cards, USB flash drives, and most other types of flash memory-based storage media and devices) reads and writes data in small blocks called pages, instead of in single bytes.

1. The appropriate voltage is applied to the control gate via the control line to read the contents of the cell.

No electrons are trapped on the floating gate.

2. The current flows from the source to the drain, so the value of the cell is 1.

1 STATE

1. The appropriate voltage is applied to the control gate via the control line to read the contents of the cell.

Electrons are trapped on the floating gate.

2. The current does not flow from the source to the drain, so the value of the cell is 0.

0 STATE

How flash memory reads data.

SECTORS
Each disk is divided into pie-shaped groups of sectors.

TRACKS
Data is stored on circular tracks; the 0s and 1s are represented magnetically.

Track 13 of Disk 1, top surface
Track 13 of Disk 1, bottom surface

Track 13 of Disk 2, top surface
Track 13 of Disk 2, bottom surface

Track 13 of Disk 3, top surface
Track 13 of Disk 3, bottom surface

Track 13 of Disk 4, top surface
Track 13 of Disk 4, bottom surface

CYLINDER
A cylinder consists of a vertical stack of tracks, the same relative track on each disk surface.

CLUSTERS
One or more sectors form a cluster, the smallest storage area on a disk.

FIGURE 3-5

Magnetic hard disks are organized into sectors, tracks, clusters, and cylinders.

The surface of a hard disk is organized into **tracks** (concentric rings) and pie-shaped groups of **sectors** (small pieces of tracks), as shown in Figure 3-5. On most computer systems, the smallest storage area on a hard drive is a **cluster**—one or more sectors. The computer numbers the tracks, sectors, and clusters so it can keep track of where data is stored. The computer uses a *file system* to record where each file is physically stored on the hard drive and what filename the user has assigned to it. When the user requests a document (always by filename), the computer uses its file system to retrieve it. Since a cluster is the smallest area on a hard drive that a computer can access, everything stored on a hard drive always takes up at least one cluster of storage space.

In addition to tracks, sectors, and clusters, hard drives are also organized into **cylinders** (refer again to Figure 3-5). A cylinder is the collection of one particular track, such as the first track or the tenth track, on each hard disk surface. In other words, it is the area on all of the hard disks inside a hard drive that can be accessed without moving the read/write access mechanism, once it has been moved to the proper position. For example, the hard drive shown in Figure 3-5 contains four hard disks, which means there are eight possible recording surfaces (using both sides of each hard disk). A cylinder for that hard drive would consist of eight tracks, such as track 13 on all eight surfaces. Because all of the read/write heads move together, all of the tracks in a cylinder are accessible at the same time.

Traditionally, the magnetic particles on a hard disk have been aligned horizontally, parallel to the hard disk's surface (referred to as *longitudinal magnetic recording*). To increase capacity and reliability, most new hard drives today use *perpendicular magnetic recording* (*PMR*), in which the bits are placed upright (as in Figure 3-3) to allow them to be closer together than is possible with a horizontal layout. For instance, PMR currently allows a recording density up to 400 *gigabits per square inch* (*Gb/inch²*), which results in internal hard drives with capacities up to 2 TB. Researchers believe that the theoretical limit for

>**Track.** A concentric path on a disk where data is recorded. >**Sector.** A small piece of a track. >**Cluster.** One or more sectors; the smallest addressable area of a disk. >**Cylinder.** The collection of tracks located in the same location on a set of hard disk surfaces.

recording density with today's hard drive technology will be 1 *terabit per square inch* (*Tb/inch^2*), which translates into about 4 TB of storage for a 3.5-inch hard drive, 1 TB for a 2.5-inch hard drive, and 100 GB for a 1-inch hard drive.

To allow for higher capacities in the future, new hard drive technologies are under development. For instance, *Heat-Assisted Magnetic Recording* (*HAMR*), which uses lasers to temporarily heat the surface of the hard disks when storing data in order to pack more data onto the surface than is normally possible, may eventually boost the storage capacity of a hard drive to 50 Tb/inch^2. Another emerging possibility for high-capacity storage—*holographic storage*—is discussed later in this chapter.

It is important to realize that a magnetic hard drive's read/write heads never touch the surface of the hard disks at any time, even during reading and writing. If the read/write heads do touch the surface—for example, if a desktop computer is bumped while the hard drive is spinning or if a foreign object gets onto the surface of a hard disk, a *head crash* occurs, which may do permanent damage to the hard drive. Because the read/write heads are located extremely close to the surface of the hard disks (less than one-half millionth of an inch above the surface), the presence of a foreign object the width of a human hair or even a smoke particle on the surface of a hard disk is like placing a huge boulder on a road and then trying to drive over it with your car. When hard drives containing critical data become damaged, *data recovery firms* may be able to help out, as discussed in the Inside the Industry box.

> **CAUTION** CAUTION CAUTION CAUTION CAUTION CAUTION CAUT
>
> Because you never know when a head crash or other hard drive failure will occur—there may be no warning whatsoever—be sure to *back up* the data on your hard drive on a regular basis. Backing up data—that is, creating a second copy of important files—is critical not only for businesses but also for individuals and is discussed in detail in Chapter 5 and Chapter 15.

Solid-State Drives (SSDs)

Solid-state drives (SSDs) are hard drives that use flash memory technology instead of spinning hard disk platters and magnetic technology; consequently, data is stored as electrical charges on flash memory media and SSDs have no moving parts. These characteristics mean that SSDs (along with the other types of flash memory storage systems discussed later in this chapter) are not subject to mechanical failures like magnetic hard drives, and are, therefore, more resistant to shock and vibration. They also consume less power, make no noise, and boot faster. Consequently, SSDs are an especially attractive option for portable computers and mobile devices. Although previously too expensive for all but specialty applications, prices of SSDs (also sometimes called *flash memory hard drives*) have fallen significantly over the past few years and they are becoming the norm for netbooks and other very portable computers.

> **Solid-state drive (SSD).** A hard drive that uses flash memory media instead of metal magnetic hard disks.

INSIDE THE INDUSTRY

Data Recovery Experts

It happens far more often than most people imagine. A computer's hard drive quits working the day before a big report is due, a notebook computer is dropped in the parking lot and then run over by a car, a mobile phone falls into a lake or fountain, or a business burns down taking the computer containing the only copy of the company records with it. If the data on a device was recently backed up, the data can be installed on a new hard drive or device with just a little expense and a short delay. When critical data located on a potentially destroyed hard drive or device is not backed up, it is time to seek help from a professional data recovery expert.

Data recovery firms, such as DriveSavers in California, specialize in recovering data from severely damaged storage media (see the accompanying photos). The damaged storage media (such as a computer's hard drive or the storage media integrated into a mobile phone) are taken apart in a *clean room* (a sealed room similar to the ones in which computer chips are manufactured) and temporarily repaired in order to copy all of the data (bit by bit) from the media onto a server. The copied data is then used to reconstruct the information located on the damaged drive or device. If the file directory is not recovered, engineers try to match the jumbled data to file types in order to reconstruct the original files. DriveSavers' celebrity clients have included Bruce Willis, Harrison Ford, and Sean Connery; the executive producer of *The Simpsons*, whose computer crashed taking scripts for 12 episodes of the show with it; an individual whose notebook computer was trapped for two days beneath a sunken cruise ship in the Amazon River; a MacWorld attendee whose notebook computer containing a sales presentation due in two days was run over and crushed by a shuttle bus; and a Fortune 500 company, which lost all its financial data and stockholder information when its server went down. In all of these cases, DriveSavers was able to recover all of the lost data.

In addition to these dramatic examples, data recovery firms are also frequently used when hard drives and other storage media just stop functioning. In fact, DriveSavers estimates that 75% of its business is due to malfunctioning devices. And with the vast amounts of digital data (such as digital photos, music, home videos, personal documents, and school papers) that the average person stores today, data recovery firms are increasingly being used by individuals to recover personal data, in addition to being used by businesses to recover important business data.

Data recovery firms stress the importance of backing up data to avoid data loss when a malfunction occurs. According to Scott Gaidano, president of DriveSavers, "The first thing we tell people is back up, back up, back up. It's amazing how many people don't back up." It is also important to make sure the backup procedure is working. For instance, the Fortune 500 company mentioned previously performed regular backups and kept the backup media in a fire-resistant safe, but when they went to use the backup after their server crashed, they discovered that the backup media were all blank.

Because potentially losing all the data on a storage medium can be so stressful and traumatic, DriveSavers has its own data-crisis counselor, a former suicide hotline worker. Fortunately for its clients, DriveSavers has a 90% recovery rate. The services of data recovery experts are not cheap, but when the lost data is irreplaceable, they are a bargain.

Data recovery. All the data located on the hard drive of this computer (left) that was virtually destroyed in a fire was recovered by data recovery experts in less than 24 hours. Recovery takes place in a clean room (right).

Data is stored in flash memory chips located inside the drive; there are no moving parts like in magnetic hard drives.

🅐 **FIGURE 3-6**
Solid-state drives (SSDs).

🅥 **FIGURE 3-7**
External hard drives.

SSDs are available in the same dimensions as a conventional magnetic 2.5-inch hard drive (see Figure 3-6) so they can easily be used instead of conventional magnetic hard drives in notebooks, netbooks, and other personal computers. There are also smaller 1.8-inch SSDs available that can be used when a smaller physical size is needed, such as for a portable digital media player or mobile phone. SSDs are currently available in capacities up to 512 GB.

Internal and External Hard Drives

Internal hard drives are permanently located inside a computer's system unit and typically are not removed unless there is a problem with them. Virtually all computers have at least one internal hard drive (either a magnetic hard drive or an SSD) that is used to store programs and data. In addition, a variety of *external hard drives* are available (see Figure 3-7). External hard drives are commonly used to transport a large amount of data from one computer to another (by moving the entire hard drive to another computer), for backup purposes, and for additional storage.

Today, because of their large capacity, full-sized external hard drives (which typically are magnetic hard drives and hold between 500 GB and 4 TB) are often used by individuals to store their digital photos, digital music, home movies, recorded TV shows, and other multimedia content to be distributed to the computers and entertainment devices located in the home. In fact, special hard drive products (typically called *home servers* or *media servers*) are available that are designed to be connected to a home network to serve as a centralized storage device for all the computers in the home, as well as to back up the data on those computers automatically. There are also *DVR extender* hard drives designed to add additional storage to an individual's digital video recorder (DVR).

While full-sized external hard drives can be moved from computer to computer when needed, *portable hard drives* are smaller external hard drives specifically designed for that purpose. Unlike full-sized hard drives (which typically need to be plugged into a power outlet to be used), portable hard drives are often powered via the computer they are being used with instead. Portable magnetic hard drives typically hold up to 500 GB; the capacity of portable SSD hard drives at the present time is smaller—up to 128 GB. Most external desktop and portable hard drives connect to the computer via a USB connection. However, some can connect via a wired or wireless networking connection instead, and *ExpressCard hard drives* connect via an ExpressCard slot (refer again to Figure 3-7).

FULL-SIZED EXTERNAL HARD DRIVES
Are about the size of a 5 by 7-inch picture frame, but thicker; this drive holds 1.5 TB.

PORTABLE HARD DRIVES (MAGNETIC)
Are about the size of a 3 by 5-inch index card, but thicker; this drive holds 500 GB.

PORTABLE HARD DRIVES (SSD)
Are about the size of a credit card, but thicker; this drive holds 18 MB.

EXPRESSCARD HARD DRIVES
Fit into an ExpressCard slot; this drive holds 32 GB.

Hard Drive Speed, Disk Caching, and Hybrid Hard Drives

The hard disks inside a magnetic hard drive typically spin continually at a rate of between 7,200 and 15,000 revolutions per minute. The total time that it takes for a hard drive to read or write data is called the **disk access time** and requires the following three steps:

1. Move the read/write heads to the cylinder that contains (or will contain) the desired data—called *seek time*.

2. Rotate the hard disks into the proper position so that the read/write heads are located over the part of the cylinder to be used—called *rotational delay*.

3. Move the data, such as reading the data from the hard disk and transferring it to memory, or transferring the data from memory and storing it on the hard disk—called *data movement time*.

A typical disk access time is around 8.5 milliseconds (ms). To minimize disk access time, magnetic hard drives usually store related data on the same cylinder. This strategy reduces seek time and, therefore, improves the overall access time. Because SSDs do not have to move any parts to store or retrieve data, they don't require seek time or rotational delay and their access time is much faster than magnetic hard drives—essentially instantaneous at about 0.1 ms on some benchmark tests. To speed up magnetic hard drive performance, *disk caching* is often used.

A *cache* (pronounced "cash") is a place to store something temporarily. For instance, in Chapter 2 we learned that cache memory is very fast memory used by the CPU to store data and instructions that might be needed in order to speed up processing. A **disk cache** is similar in concept—it stores copies of data or programs that are located on the hard drive and that might be needed soon in memory chips in order to avoid having to retrieve the data or programs from the hard drive when they are requested. Since the hard disks do not have to be accessed if the requested data is located in the disk cache and since retrieving data from memory is much faster than from a magnetic hard disk, disk caching can speed up performance. Disk caching also saves wear and tear on the hard drive and, in portable computers, can also extend battery life.

While the memory used for disk caching can be a designated portion of RAM, today's hard drives typically use a disk cache consisting of memory chips located on a circuit board inside the hard drive case. When a magnetic hard drive uses disk caching (as most do today), any time the hard drive is accessed the computer copies the requested data, as well as extra data located in neighboring areas of the hard drive (such as all of the data located on the cylinder being accessed), to the disk cache. When the next data is requested, the computer checks the disk cache first to see if the data it needs is already there. If it is, the data is retrieved for processing; if not, the computer retrieves the requested data from the hard disks.

Most conventional magnetic hard drives today include a flash memory-based disk cache ranging in size from 2 MB to 16 MB built into the hard drive case. However, **hybrid hard drives**—essentially a combination flash memory/magnetic hard drive (see Figure 3-8)—use a much larger amount of flash memory (up to 1 GB today). In addition to using the flash

FIGURE 3-8

Hybrid hard drives. Hybrid hard drives contain both magnetic hard disks and a large quantity of flash memory for increased performance.

MAGNETIC HARD DRIVE
This drive contains 2 hard disks and 4 read/write heads that operate in a manner similar to a conventional hard drive.

FLASH MEMORY DISK CACHE
This drive uses 256 MB of flash memory disk cache to duplicate data as it is stored on the hard disks so the data can be accessed when hard disks are not spinning.

>**Disk access time.** The time it takes to locate and read data from (or position and write data to) a storage medium. >**Disk cache.** Memory used in conjunction with a magnetic hard drive to improve system performance. >**Hybrid hard drive.** A hard drive that contains both a large amount of flash memory and magnetic hard disks.

memory to reduce the number of times the hard disks in a hybrid hard drive need to be read, hybrid hard drives can also use the flash memory to temporarily store (cache) data to be written to the hard disks, which can further extend the battery life of portable computers and mobile devices. The additional flash memory in a hybrid hard drive can also allow encryption or other security measures to be built into the drive (encryption is discussed in Chapter 9).

Hard Drive Partitioning and File Systems

Partitioning a hard drive enables you to divide the physical capacity of a single hard drive logically into separate areas, called *partitions* or *volumes*. Partitions function as independent hard drives and are sometimes referred to as *logical drives* because each partition is labeled and treated separately (such as C drive and D drive) when viewed in a file management program such as Windows Explorer, but they are still physically one hard drive. One or more partitions are created when a hard drive is first *formatted* (prepared for data storage). For instance, many new personal computers come with a C drive partition ready to use for programs and data and another logical drive (such as a D drive) set up as a *recovery partition*. A recovery partition (see Figure 3-9) contains the data necessary to restore a hard drive back to its state at the time the computer was purchased and is designed to be used only if the computer malfunctions.

FIGURE 3-9

Hard drive partitions. New personal computers today often come with the primary hard drive divided into two partitions.

In the past, operating systems could only use hard drives up to 512 MB, so hard drives larger than that limit had to use multiple partitions. While today's operating systems can use much larger hard drives and, therefore, do not require the use of multiple partitions, partitioning a large hard drive can make it function more efficiently. This is because operating systems typically use a larger cluster size with a larger hard drive. Since even tiny files have to use up one entire cluster of storage space, disk space is often wasted when a large cluster size is used. When a hard drive is partitioned, each logical drive can use a smaller cluster size, since each logical drive is smaller than the original hard drive.

Users can create additional partitions on a hard drive, if desired, but should be careful when partitioning a computer's primary hard drive, since deleting a partition erases all data contained on that partition. One reason advanced users may partition a primary hard drive is to be able to use two different operating systems on the same hard drive—such as Windows and Linux (these and other operating systems are discussed in detail in Chapter 5). With a *dual-boot system* such as this, the user specifies the operating system to be run each time the computer boots. Another reason for partitioning a hard drive is to create the appearance of having separate hard drives for file management, multiple users, or other purposes. For instance, some users choose to partition a new second or external hard drive into multiple logical drives to organize their data before storing data on that hard drive. Storing data files on a separate physical hard drive or logical partition makes it easier for the user to locate data files. It also enables users to back up all data files simply by backing up the entire hard drive or partition containing the data.

The partition size, cluster size (on magnetic hard drives), maximum drive size, and maximum file size that can be used with a hard drive are determined by the *file system* being used. For instance, Windows users have three file system options to choose from: the original *FAT* file system (not commonly used with hard drives today, though it is used with some removable storage devices like USB flash drives), the newer *FAT32* file system, and the newest *NTFS* file system. The recommended file system for computers running current versions of Windows is NTFS because it supports much larger hard drives and files than either FAT or FAT32 and it includes better security and error-recovery capabilities. Computers with older versions of Windows have to use FAT32, which has a maximum partition size of 32 GB and a maximum file size of 4 GB.

Hard Drive Interface Standards

Hard drives connect, or interface, with a computer using one of several different standards. The most common internal *hard drive interface standard* for desktop computers today is *serial ATA* (*SATA*). The SATA standard was designed to replace the older, slower *parallel ATA* (*PATA*) standard, which is also referred to as *Fast ATA* and *EIDE* (*Enhanced Integrated Drive Electronics*). SATA is faster (up to 6 Gbps) than PATA and uses thinner cables, which means SATA hard drives take up less room inside the system unit. External hard drives most often connect to the computer via a USB or FireWire port, though an *eSATA* (*External SATA*) interface can be used to connect to the computer via an eSATA expansion card if faster speeds are desired.

The most common hard drive interfaces used with servers are *serial attached SCSI* (*SAS*), which is a newer version of the SCSI interface, and *Fibre Channel*, which is a reliable, flexible, and very fast standard geared for long-distance, high-bandwidth applications. For network storage, new standards, such as *Internet SCSI* (*iSCSI*) and *Fibre Channel over Ethernet* (*FCoE*), have evolved that communicate over the Internet or another network using the *TCP/IP* networking standard.

OPTICAL DISCS

Data on **optical discs** (such as *CDs* and *DVDs*) is stored and read *optically*; that is, using laser beams. General characteristics of optical discs are discussed next, followed by a look at the various types of optical discs available today.

Optical Disc Characteristics

Optical discs are thin circular discs made out of *polycarbonate substrate*—essentially a type of very strong plastic—that are topped with layers of other materials and coatings used to store data and protect the disc. Data can be stored on one or both sides of an optical disc, depending on the disc design, and some types of discs use multiple recording layers on each side of the disc to increase capacity. An optical disc contains a single spiral track (instead of multiple tracks like magnetic disks), and the track is divided into sectors to keep data organized. As shown in Figure 3-10, this track (sometimes referred to as a *groove* in order to avoid confusion with the

FIGURE 3-10
How recorded optical discs work.

TRACK
A single track spirals from the center of the disc outward; recorded data is stored on the track.

SECTORS
The track is divided into sectors for data organization.

LAND

PIT

WRITING DATA
When data is written to the disc, a laser beam creates pits, represented by dark, nonreflective areas on the disc.

READING DATA
A low intensity laser beam reads the disc. A transition between a pit and a land is interpreted as a 1; a set period of time between transitions is interpreted as a 0.

> **Optical disc.** A type of storage medium read from and written to using a laser beam.

term *tracks* used to refer to songs on an audio CD) begins at the center of the disc and spirals out to the edge of the disc.

Advantages of optical discs include relatively large capacity for their size (as discussed shortly) and durability (they are more durable than magnetic media and don't degrade with use, like some magnetic media does). However, the discs should be handled carefully and stored in their cases when they are not in use, in order to protect the recorded surfaces of the discs from scratches, fingerprints, and other marks that can interfere with the usability of the discs. Optical discs are the standard today for software delivery; they are also commonly used for backup purposes, and for storing and/or transporting music, photo, video, and other large files.

Representing Data on an Optical Disc

Data is written to an optical disc in one of two ways. With *read-only optical discs* like movie, music, and software CDs and DVDs, the surface of the disc is molded or stamped appropriately to represent the data. With *recordable* or *rewritable optical discs* that can be written to using an *optical drive* such as a *CD drive* or *DVD drive*, as discussed shortly, the reflectivity of the disc is changed using a laser to represent the data. In either case, the disc is read with a laser and the computer interprets the reflection of the laser off the disc surface as 1s and 0s.

To accomplish this with molded or stamped optical discs, tiny depressions (when viewed from the top side of the disc) or bumps (when viewed from the bottom) are created on the disc's surface. These bumps are called *pits*; the areas on the disc that are not changed are called *lands*. Although many people think that each individual pit and land represents a 1 or 0 that is not completely accurate—it is the transition between a pit and land that represents a 1. When the disc is read, the amount of laser light reflected back from the disc changes when the laser reaches a transition between a pit and a land. When the optical drive detects a transition, it is interpreted as a 1; no transition for a specific period of time indicates a 0.

With a CD or DVD that is recorded using a CD or DVD drive, the recording laser beam changes the reflectivity of the appropriate areas on the disc to represent the data stored there—dark, nonreflective areas are pits; reflective areas are lands, as illustrated in Figure 3-10. The transition between a pit and a land still represents a 1 and no transition for a specific distance along the track represents a 0. Different types of optical discs use different types of laser beams. Conventional **CD discs** use *infrared* lasers; conventional **DVD discs** use *red* lasers, which allow data to be stored more compactly on the same size disc; and high-definition **Blu-ray Discs (BD)** use *blue-violet lasers*, which can store data even more compactly on a disc.

Optical Drives

Optical discs in each of the three categories (CD, DVD, and BD) can be read-only, recordable, or rewritable; they can use the + or − standard; and they can be either *single-layer* or *dual-layer (DL) discs*. Optical discs are designed to be read by **optical drives**, such as *CD*, *DVD*, and *BD drives*, and the type of optical drive being used must support the type of optical disc being used. Most optical drives today support multiple types of optical discs—some support all possible types. Optical drives are almost always *downward-compatible*, meaning they can be used with lower (older) types of discs but not higher (newer) ones. So, while a DVD drive would likely support all types of CD and DVD discs, it cannot be used with BD discs, but most BD drives today support all types of CD, DVD, and Blu-ray Discs.

>**CD disc.** A low capacity (typically 650 MB) optical disc that is often used to deliver music and software, as well as to store user data.
>**DVD disc.** A medium capacity (typically 4.7 MB or 8.5 MB) optical disc that is often used to deliver software and movies, as well as to store user data. >**Blu-ray Disc (BD).** A high-capacity (typically 25 MB or 50 MB) that is often used to deliver high-definition movies, as well as to store user data. >**Optical drive.** A drive used with optical discs, such as CD or DVD discs.

To use an optical disc, it is inserted into an appropriate optical drive. Purchased optical discs often have a title and other text printed on one side; if so, they are inserted into the optical drive with the printed side facing up. Two-sided commercial discs typically identify each side of a disc by printing that information on the disc close to the inner circle.

The process of recording data onto an optical disc is called *burning*. To burn an optical disc (such as a *CD-R* or a *DVD-R disc*), the optical drive being used must support burning and the type of disc being used. In addition, *CD-burning* or *DVD-burning* software is required. Many burning programs are available commercially, and recent versions of operating systems (including Windows and Mac OS) include CD and DVD burning capabilities. In addition, most CD and DVD drives come bundled with burning software. Some optical drives—such as *LightScribe-enabled drives*—are even capable of burning label information on the surface of a disc after the content has been recorded. (To do this, you first burn the data to the disc, and then you flip the disc over and burn the desired label information on the other side of the disc.) Most personal computers today come with an internal optical drive; one exception is netbooks, which typically do not include an optical drive. An *external optical drive* that connects via a USB port (see Figure 3-11) can be used with these computers whenever an optical drive is temporarily needed.

HW

FIGURE 3-11
External optical drives. Can be connected as needed, typically via a USB port, such as to the netbook shown here.

Optical Disc Shapes, Sizes, and Capacities

Standard-sized optical discs are 120-mm (approximately 4½-inch) discs. There are also smaller 80-mm (approximately 3-inch) *mini discs*, most often used in conjunction with *digital video cameras*. In addition, optical discs can be made into a variety of sizes and shapes—such as a heart, triangle, irregular shape, or the hockey-rink shape commonly used with *business card CDs*—because the track starts at the center of the disc and the track just stops when it reaches an outer edge of the disc. Standard shapes are molded and less expensive; custom shapes—such as those that match a service or product being sold (a soda can, musical instrument, saw blade, candy bar, or house, as in Figure 3-12)—are custom cut and are more costly. The practice of using optical discs to replace ordinary objects, such as business cards and mailed advertisements, is becoming more common. For marketing purposes, *flexible DVDs* and *scented discs* are also available. Flexible DVDs can be bent or rolled so they can be attached to the cover of a magazine or wrapped around a product, for example. Scented discs have a specific scent (such as a particular perfume, popcorn, pine trees, or a specific fruit) added to the label side of the disc; the scent is released when the surface of the disc is rubbed.

FIGURE 3-12
Optical discs are available in a variety of sizes, appearances, and capacities.

STANDARD 120 MM (4.7 INCH) SIZED DISC

MINI 80 MM (3.1 INCH) SIZED DISC

CUSTOM-SHAPED BUSINESS CARD DISC

Go **FURTHER EXPLORATION**

Go to the Chapter 3 page at
**www.cengage.com/
computerconcepts/np/uc13**
for links to information about
DVD technology.

One of the biggest advantages of optical discs is their large capacity. To further increase capacity, many discs are available as *dual-layer discs* (also called *double-layer discs*) that store data in two layers on a single side of the disc, so the capacity is approximately doubled. For an even larger capacity, discs with more than two layers are in development. Standard-sized CD discs are normally single-layer and hold either 650 MB or 700 MB, standard-sized DVD discs hold 4.7 GB (single-layer discs) or 8.5 GB (dual-layer discs), and standard-sized BD discs hold either 25 GB (single-layer discs) or 50 GB (dual-layer discs). Discs can also be *double sided*, which doubles the capacity; however, the disc must be turned over to access the second side. Double-sided discs are most often used with movies and other prerecorded content, such as to store a *widescreen version* of a movie on one side of a DVD disc and a *standard version* on the other side. Small optical discs have a smaller storage capacity than their larger counterparts: typically, single-layer, single-sided 3-inch mini CD, DVD, and BD discs hold about 200 MB, 1.4 GB, and 7.5 GB, respectively, and business card-sized CD and DVD discs hold about 50 MB and 325 MB, respectively.

As with magnetic disks, researchers are continually working to increase the capacity of optical discs without increasing their physical size. One promising recent development is a discovery by a Harvard research team that narrows the width of the laser beam used to record data on an optical disc. This is significant because a narrower beam means that more data can be stored on a disc. Instead of using a lens to focus the laser light (which results in a laser beam width of 405 billionths of a meter when recording DVDs), the researchers used two tiny gold rods as antennas at the end of the laser and they were able to narrow the laser beam width to just 40 billionths of a meter. Although products based on this technology may be 10 years away, researchers predict that this new technique could eventually result in regular-sized optical discs that hold 3 TB—roughly 600 times more than a standard DVD today.

FIGURE 3-13

High-definition movies are available on Blu-ray Discs (BDs).

Read-Only Optical Discs: CD-ROM, DVD-ROM, and BD-ROM Discs

CD-ROM (*compact disc read-only memory*) **discs** and **DVD-ROM** (*digital versatile disc read-only memory*) **discs** are *read-only optical discs* that come prerecorded with commercial products, such as software programs, clip art and other types of graphics collections, music, and movies. For high-definition content (such as feature films—see Figure 3-13), **BD-ROM** (*Blu-ray Disc read-only memory*) **discs** are available. There are also additional read-only disc formats for specific gaming devices, such as the *UMD* (*Universal Media Disc*) format used with the Sony PSP handheld gaming device and the proprietary discs used with the Wii, Xbox, and Playstation gaming consoles. The data on a read-only disc cannot be erased, changed, or added to because the pits that are molded into the surface of the disc when the disc is produced are permanent.

Recordable Optical Discs: CD-R, DVD-R, DVD+R, and BD-R Discs

Recordable optical discs (also sometimes called *write-once discs*) can be written to, but the discs cannot be erased and reused. Recordable CDs are referred to as **CD-R discs**. Single-layer recordable DVDs are called either

>**CD-ROM disc.** A CD that can be read from, but not written to, by the user. >**DVD-ROM disc.** A DVD that can be read from, but not written to, by the user. >**BD-ROM disc.** A Blu-ray Disc that can be read from, but not written to, by the user. >**CD-R disc.** A recordable CD.

DVD-R discs or **DVD+R discs**, depending on the standard being used, and dual-layer recordable DVDs are called *DVD+R DL* or *DVD-R DL discs*. Recordable BD discs are also available in both single-layer and dual-layer (**BD-R discs** and *BD-R DL discs*, respectively). The capacities of recordable optical discs are the same as the read-only formats (see Figure 3-14).

Instead of having physically molded pits, most recordable optical discs have a recording layer containing organic light-sensitive dye embedded between the disc's plastic and reflective layers. One exception to this is the BD-R disc, which has a recording layer consisting of inorganic material. When data is written to a recordable disc, the recording laser inside the recordable optical drive burns the dye (for CD and DVD discs) or melts and combines the inorganic material (for BD-R discs), creating nonreflective areas that function as pits. In either case, the marks are permanent, so data on the disc cannot be erased or rewritten.

Recordable CDs are commonly used for backing up files, sending large files to others, and creating custom music CDs (for example, from MP3 files legally downloaded from the Internet or from songs located on a music album purchased on CD). DVD-Rs can be used for similar purposes when more storage space is needed, such as for backing up large files and for storing home movies, digital photos, and other multimedia files. BD-R discs can be used when an even greater amount of storage is needed, such as very large backups or high-definition multimedia files.

Rewritable Optical Discs: CD-RW, DVD-RW, DVD+RW, and BD-RE Discs

Rewritable optical discs can be written to, erased, and overwritten just like magnetic hard disks. The most common types of rewritable optical discs are **CD-RW**, **DVD-RW**, **DVD+RW**, and **BD-RE discs**; BD-RE discs are also available as dual-layer discs (*BD-RE DL discs*). The capacities of rewritable discs are the same as their read-only and recordable counterparts. An additional, but not widely used, rewritable DVD format is *DVD-RAM*. DVD-RAM and DVD-RAM DL discs are supported by *DVD-RAM drives*, as well as by some DVD and BD drives.

To write to, erase, or overwrite rewritable optical discs, *phase change* technology is used. With this technology, the rewritable CD or DVD disc is coated with layers of a special metal alloy compound that can have two different appearances after it has been heated and then cooled, depending on the heating and cooling process used. With one process, the material *crystallizes* and that area of the disc is reflective. With another process, the area cools to a nonreflective *amorphous* state. Before any data is written to a rewritable optical disc, the disc is completely reflective. To write data to the disc, the recording laser heats the metal alloy in the appropriate locations on the spiral track and then uses the appropriate cooling process to create either the nonreflective areas (pits) or the reflective areas (lands). To erase the disc, the appropriate heating and cooling process is used to change the areas to be erased back to their original reflective state.

Rewritable optical discs are used for many of the same purposes as recordable optical discs. However, they are particularly appropriate for situations in which data written to the optical disc can be erased at a later time so the disc to be reused (such as transferring large files from one computer to another or temporarily storing TV shows recorded on your computer that you will later watch using your living room TV and DVD player).

FIGURE 3-14
Recordable CDs and DVDs.

CD-R DISCS
Hold 650 MB.

DVD+R DL DISCS
Hold 8.5 GB.

BD-R DL DISCS
Hold 50 GB.

>**DVD-R/DVD+R discs.** Recordable DVDs. >**BD-R disc.** A recordable Blu-ray Disc. >**CD-RW disc.** A rewritable CD. >**DVD-RW/DVD+RW discs.** Rewritable DVDs. >**BD-RE disc.** A rewritable Blu-ray Disc.

TREND

IronKey: The World's Most Secure USB Flash Drive

Today, the security of data being carried on portable devices, such as USB flash drives, is extremely important and the use of encrypted portable devices is a growing trend. For individuals, business employees, or government employees that need today's most secure USB flash drive, *IronKey* (see the accompanying illustration) might just be the answer.

Available in three versions (Basic, Personal, and Enterprise) in capacities ranging from 1 GB to 8 GB, IronKey uses always-on, hardware-based encryption to protect all data written to the device. The encryption is enabled by an onboard *Cryptochip* that securely stores the encryption keys generated when the device is initialized and the user password is selected. There is also an internal counter to protect against password guessing attacks by an unauthorized individual trying to access the device. After 10 incorrect password attempts, the device self-destructs and erases all data and encryption keys stored on the device. The Personal and Enterprise versions contain additional features, such as a secure version of the Firefox browser that can be used for anonymous Web browsing (so no browsing data is stored on the local computer—just on the

IronKey drive) and the ability to store and use other portable applications on the device.

IronKey has received security validation for use by the U.S. and Canadian governments and is approved to carry classified government data. Overkill for personal use? Perhaps. But for anyone carrying sensitive data from computer to computer, highly secure USB flash drives like the IronKey can't be beat for security and convenience.

FLASH MEMORY

As previously discussed, **flash memory** is a chip-based storage medium that represents data using electrons. It is used in a variety of storage systems, such as the SSDs and hybrid hard drives already discussed and the additional storage systems shown in Figure 3-15. Because flash memory media is physically very small, it is increasingly being embedded directly into a variety of consumer products—such as portable digital media players, digital cameras, handheld gaming devices, GPS devices, mobile phones, and even sunglasses and wristwatches—to provide built-in data storage. In addition, a variety of types of *flash memory cards* and *USB flash drives* are available to use with computers and other devices for data storage and data transfer, as discussed next. For a look at what is billed as the world's most secure USB flash drive—*IronKey*—see the Trend box.

Flash Memory Cards

One of the most common types of flash memory media is the **flash memory card**—a small card containing one or more flash memory chips, a controller chip, other electrical components, and metal contacts to connect the card to the device or reader with which it is being used. Flash memory cards are available in a variety of formats, such as

---

>**Flash memory.** A chip-based storage medium that stores data using electrons; used in a variety of storage systems. >**Flash memory card.** A small, rectangular flash memory medium, such as a CompactFlash (CF) or Secure Digital (SD) card; often used with digital cameras and other portable devices.

Flash memory card

EMBEDDED FLASH MEMORY
Flash memory is often embedded into consumer products, such as this digital media player, for storage purposes.

FLASH MEMORY CARDS AND READERS
Flash memory cards are often used to store data for digital cameras and other devices; the data can be transferred to a computer via a flash memory card reader, as needed.

USB FLASH DRIVES
USB flash drives are often used to store data and transfer files from one computer to another.

 FIGURE 3-15
Flash memory systems. Flash memory is used in a variety of storage systems today.

TIP

Flash memory cards can be inserted into a reader only one way and must go in the proper slot, so be sure to check the slot type and look for the directional tips often printed on the card before inserting a card into a flash memory reader.

CompactFlash (*CF*), *Secure Digital* (*SD*), *Secure Digital High Capacity* (*SDHC*), *Secure Digital Extended Capacity* (*SDXC*), *MultiMedia Card* (*MMC*), *xD Picture Card* (*xD*), and *Memory Stick* (*MS*) (see Figure 3-16). These formats are not interchangeable, so the type of flash memory card used with a device is determined by the type of flash media card that device can accept. Flash memory cards are the most common type of storage media for digital cameras, portable digital media players, mobile phones, and other portable devices. They can also be used to store data for a personal computer, as needed, as well as to transfer data from a portable device to a computer. Consequently, most desktop and notebook computers today come with a *flash memory card reader* capable of reading flash memory cards; an external flash memory card reader (that typically connects via a USB port and is shown in Figure 3-16) can be used if a built-in reader is not available. The capacity of flash memory cards is continually growing and is up to about 4 GB for standard cards and 32 GB for high-capacity cards; the even higher capacity extended capacity cards are just beginning to become available and are expected to reach capacities of 2 TB by 2014.

FIGURE 3-16
Flash memory cards. Shown here are some of the most widely used types of flash memory cards and a multicard reader.

FLASH MEMORY CARD READERS
Can be built-in or external and usually support several different types of flash memory media; external readers such as this one typically connect to a computer via a USB port.

COMPACTFLASH (CF) CARDS

MEMORY STICKS

SECURE DIGITAL (SD) CARDS

XD PICTURE CARDS

One of the most widely used types of flash memory media—Secure Digital (SD)—is available in different physical sizes, as well as in different capacities. For instance, standard-sized SD cards are often used in digital cameras and computers; the smaller *miniSD* and *microSD* (about one-half and one-quarter the size of a standard SD card, respectively, as shown in Figure 3-16) are designed to be used with mobile phones and other mobile devices. When more storage space is needed, higher capacity *miniSDHC* and *microSDHC* cards can be used. MMC cards and memory sticks are also available in mobile sizes; adapters can be used with mobile-sized flash memory cards in order to use them in a full-sized memory card reader.

While general purpose flash memory cards can be used for most applications, there are also flash memory cards designed for specific uses. For instance, *professional flash memory cards* designed for professional photographers are faster and more durable than consumer cards; *gaming flash memory cards* are specifically designed for gaming consoles and devices, such as the Nintendo Wii or Sony PSP; and *netbook flash memory cards* are designed to be used to expand the storage capabilities of a netbook computer. There are even Wi-Fi-enabled flash memory cards that can wirelessly upload digital photos taken with a camera using that card for storage, as discussed in the Technology and You box in Chapter 7.

Typically, flash memory media is purchased blank, but some flash-memory-based software (such as games, encyclopedias, and language translators) is available. A new option for portable music is *slotMusic*—music albums that come stored on microSD cards. These cards can be used with any phone or portable digital media player that has a microSD slot and they typically contain extra storage space to add additional files as desired. Movies are also beginning to be delivered via flash memory media. In fact, Panasonic and Disney have announced plans to begin releasing movies on microSD cards by 2010 and Sonic Solutions has announced movies stored on USB flash drives should begin to become available at about the same time. These new options for portable multimedia are geared toward individuals who would like access to this content via a mobile phone, car navigation system, netbook, or other device often used while on the go that has a flash memory card slot or a USB port.

FURTHER EXPLORATION

Go to the Chapter 3 page at **www.cengage.com/computerconcepts/np/uc13** for links to information about flash memory media and storage systems.

USB Flash Drives

USB flash drives (sometimes called *USB flash memory drives*, *thumb drives*, or *jump drives*) consist of flash memory media integrated into a self-contained unit that connects to a computer or other device via a standard USB port and is powered via the USB port. USB flash drives are designed to be very small and very portable. In order to appeal to a wide variety of users, USB flash drives are available in a range of sizes, colors, and appearances—including those designed to be attached to backpacks or worn on a lanyard around the neck; those built into necklaces, wristbands, or wristwatches; those thin enough to fit easily into a wallet; and those made into custom shapes for promotional or novelty purposes (see Figure 3-17). When

FIGURE 3-17
USB flash drives.

CONVENTIONAL USB FLASH DRIVES

USB FLASH DRIVE WRISTBANDS

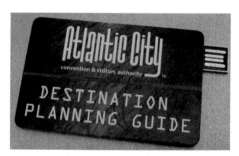

USB FLASH DRIVE WALLET CARDS

>**USB flash drive.** A small storage device that plugs into a USB port and contains flash memory media.

TECHNOLOGY AND YOU

Thumb Drive PCs

We all know that USB flash drives are a great way to transport documents from one location to another, but what about using one to take a personalized computer with you wherever you go? It's possible and easy to do with the use of *portable applications* (also called *portable apps*)—computer programs that are designed to be used with portable devices like USB flash drives. When the device is plugged into the USB port of any computer, you have access to the software and personal data (including your browser bookmarks, calendar, e-mail and instant messaging contacts, and more) stored on that device, just as you would on your own computer. And when you unplug the device, none of your personal data is left behind because all programs are run directly from the USB flash drive. Many portable applications (such as the PortableApps suite shown in the accompanying illustration) are free and include all the basics you might want in a single package. For instance, PortableApps includes a menu structure, antivirus program, Web browser, e-mail program, calendar program, the OpenOffice.org office suite, and more. To set up a USB flash drive as a portable computer, you need to perform the following steps:

1. Download your desired portable applications (such as the PortableApps suite) to your desktop or notebook computer.

2. Plug in your USB flash drive and run the portable apps installation program, using your USB flash drive as the destination folder.

3. Open a file management program such as Windows Explorer, double-click your USB flash drive, and then launch your portable apps software to test it.

4. Download and install any additional portable apps you would like to use (it is a good idea to include an antivirus program to try to prevent the USB flash drive from becoming infected with a computer virus).

To use your thumb drive computer, plug it into the USB port of any computer—many portable apps will launch automatically and display a main menu, such as the one shown in the accompanying illustration. Portable apps can also be installed on an iPod or other portable digital media player (instead of a USB flash drive) if you prefer to use that device as your portable computer.

1. USB flash drive is plugged into a computer.

2. This menu is displayed; all programs run off the USB flash drive.

the USB flash drive is built into a consumer product (such as a watch, sunglasses, or a Swiss Army knife), a retractable cord is used to connect the device to a computer when needed. Because they are becoming so widely used, additional hardware related to USB flash drives are becoming available, such as *USB duplicator systems* used by educators to copy assignments or other materials to and from a large collection of USB flash drives at one time.

To read from or write to a USB flash drive, you just plug it into a USB port. If the USB flash drive is being used with a computer, it is assigned a drive letter by the computer, just like any other type of attached drive, and files can be read from or written to the USB flash drive until it is unplugged from the USB port. The capacity of most USB flash drives today ranges from 1 GB to 64 GB. USB flash drive use has become commonplace for individuals, students, and employees to transport files from one computer to another, as well as to quickly back up important files. For a look at how you can carry your personal computer with you on a USB flash drive, see the Technology and You box.

VIDEO PODCAST

Go to the Chapter 3 page at **www.cengage.com/ computerconcepts/np/uc13** to download or listen to the "How To: Use Portable Applications with a USB Flash Drive" video podcast.

In addition to providing basic data storage and data portability, USB flash drives can provide additional capabilities. For instance, they can be used to lock a computer and to issue Web site passwords; they can also include *biometric features*—such as a built-in fingerprint reader—to allow only authorized individuals access to the data stored on the USB flash drive or to the computer with which the USB flash drive is being used.

OTHER TYPES OF STORAGE SYSTEMS

Other types of storage systems used with personal and business computers today include *remote storage*, *smart cards*, and *holographic storage*. There are also storage systems and technologies designed for large computer systems. These systems are discussed next.

Network Storage and Online/Cloud Storage Systems

Remote storage refers to using a storage device that is not connected directly to the user's computer; instead, the device is accessed through a local network or through the Internet. Using a remote storage device via a local network (referred to as *network storage*) works in much the same way as using *local storage* (the storage devices and media that are directly attached to the user's computer). To read data from or write data to a remote storage device (such as a hard drive in another computer being accessed via a network), the user just selects it (see Figure 3-18) and then performs the necessary tasks in the normal fashion. Network storage is common in businesses; it is also used by individuals with home networks for backup purposes or to share files with another computer in the home.

Because of the vast amount of data shared and made available over networks today, network storage has become increasingly important. Two common types of network storage used today are **network attached storage (NAS)** devices and **storage area networks (SANs)**. NAS devices are high-performance storage servers that are connected individually to a network to provide storage for the computers connected to that network. They can be large storage servers designed for a large business, or smaller NAS devices designed for a home or small business (such as the one in Figure 3-18). A growing trend, in fact, is home NAS devices designed to store multimedia data (such as downloaded music, recorded TV shows, and downloaded movies) to be distributed over a home entertainment network. NAS devices typically connect to the network via a wired networking connection, although some (like the one shown in Figure 3-18) use a wireless networking connection; networking is explained in detail in Chapter 7.

A storage area network (SAN) also provides storage for a network, but it consists of a separate network of hard drives or other storage devices, which is attached to the main network. The primary difference between network attached storage and a storage area network

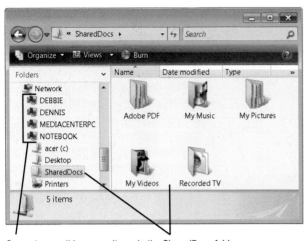

Computers on this network.

Items in the SharedDocs folder on the computer called NOTEBOOK.

SHARED FOLDERS
Shared folders on network computers appear and are accessed in a manner similar to local folders.

NETWORK ATTACHED STORAGE (NAS) DEVICES
This wireless NAS device holds 1 TB of data and provides storage for all computers on the network.

FIGURE 3-18
Network storage.

is how the storage devices interface with the network—that is, whether the storage devices act as individual network nodes, just like computers, printers, and other devices on the network (NAS), or whether they are located in a completely separate network of storage devices that is accessible to the main network (SAN). However, in terms of functionality, the distinction between NAS and SANs is blurring, since they both provide storage services to the network. Typically, both NAS and SAN systems are scalable, so new devices can be added as more storage is needed, and devices can be added or removed without disrupting the network.

Remote storage devices accessed via the Internet are often referred to as **online storage** or **cloud storage**. While these terms are often used interchangeably, some view cloud storage as a specific type of online storage that can be accessed on demand by various Web applications. Most online applications (such as Google Docs, the Flickr photo sharing service, and social networking sites like Facebook, for instance) provide online storage for these services. There are also sites whose primary

ASK THE EXPERT

Bill Hansen, Global Product Manager, Network Storage Products, Iomega Corporation

Do home networks today need network hard drives?

Definitely! Just as the Internet has changed the way we communicate, network hard drives are changing the way we share information in the home. By plugging a network hard drive into your home network, you can share files and folders easily with anyone on that network—no more walking a CD or USB flash drive around to every computer like in the past. Today's network hard drives are simple to set up and use, and they are designed to allow you to access and share your music, pictures, videos, or other files easily with the other devices on your home network. You can also use a network hard drive as a backup target for all of your computers. In a nutshell, network hard drives greatly enhance the ability to share and store your valuable digital files at home.

> **Online storage.** Remote storage devices accessed via the Internet; also called **cloud storage**.

LOGGING ON
Users log on to see their personal files stored on the site's server.

FOLDERS AND FILES
Folders can be private, public, or shared with selected individuals.

FIGURE 3-19
Online storage. This site provides 25 GB of free storage.

VIDEO PODCAST

Go to the Chapter 3 page at **www.cengage.com/ computerconcepts/np/uc13** to download or listen to the "How To: Create a Gmail Drive" video podcast.

objective is to allow users to store documents online, such as *Box.net* or Microsoft *SkyDrive*. Typically, online/cloud storage sites are password-protected (see Figure 3-19) and allow users to specify uploaded files as private files or as shared files that designated individuals can access.

The ability to store documents online (or "in the cloud") is growing in importance as more and more applications are becoming Web based and as individuals increasingly want access to their files from anywhere with any Internet-enabled device, such as a portable computer or mobile phone. Online storage is also increasingly being used for backup purposes—some online storage sites have an automatic backup option that uploads the files in designated folders on your computer to your online account at regular specified intervals, as long as your computer is connected to the Internet. Many Web sites providing online storage to individuals offer the service for free (for instance, SkyDrive gives each individual 25 GB of free storage space); others charge a small fee, such as $10 per month for 50 GB of storage space.

Business cloud storage services are also available, such as those offered in conjunction with the cloud computing services discussed in Chapter 1, which allow subscribers to access a flexible amount of both storage and computing power as needed on demand. For instance, *Amazon Simple Storage Service* (*Amazon S3*)—one of the leaders in *enterprise cloud storage*—charges a monthly fee per GB of storage used plus a fee based on the amount of data transferred that month. This service can be used alone or in conjunction with Amazon's cloud computing service, Amazon Elastic Compute Cloud (Amazon EC2). In addition to these *public cloud storage services*, businesses can also create *private clouds* designed to service just that particular business.

Smart Cards

A **smart card** is a credit card-sized piece of plastic that contains computer circuitry and components—typically a processor, memory, and storage (see Figure 3-20). Smart cards today store a relatively small amount of data (typically 64 KB or less) that can be used for payment or identification purposes. For example, a smart card can store a prepaid amount of *digital cash*, which can be used for purchases at a smart card-enabled vending machine or computer—the amount of cash available on the card is reduced each time the card is used. Smart cards are also commonly used worldwide for national and student ID cards, credit and debit cards, and cards that store identification data for accessing facilities or computer networks.

>**Smart card.** A credit card-sized piece of plastic containing a chip and other circuitry that can store data.

Although these applications have used conventional *magnetic stripe* technology in the past, the processor integrated into a smart card can perform computations—such as to authenticate the card and encrypt the data on the card to protect its integrity and secure it against unauthorized access—and data can be added to the card or modified on the card as needed. The increased capabilities of smart cards has also allowed for new applications, such as storing biometric data (such as the characteristics of a fingerprint) and other identifying data needed to accelerate airport security and to link patients to the *electronic health records* increasingly being used by hospitals.

To use a smart card, it must either be inserted into a *smart card reader* (if it is the type of card that requires contact) or placed close to a smart card reader (if it is a *contactless* card) built into or attached to a computer, keyboard, vending machine, or other device (refer again to Figure 3-20). Once a smart card has been verified by the card reader, the transaction—such as making a purchase or unlocking a door—can be completed. For an even higher level of security, some smart cards today store biometric data in the card and use that data to ensure the authenticity of the card's user before authorizing the smart card transaction (biometrics, encryption, and other security procedures are discussed in more detail in Chapter 9). An emerging trend is the use of *mobile smart cards*—smart microSD cards that are designed to add smart card capabilities to any computer or mobile device that contains a microSD slot.

USING A SMART CARD TO LOG ON TO A COMPUTER

Smart card circuitry

A SMART CARD

USING A SMART CARD TO ACCESS A SECURE FACILITY

USING A SMART CARD TO PAY FOR A VENDING MACHINE PURCHASE

 FIGURE 3-20
Smart cards. Smart cards can be used to log on to computers and networks, access facilities, pay for goods and services, and so forth.

Holographic Storage

Holographic storage is a type of three dimensional (3D) storage system that, after many years of research and development, is now a reality. *Holographic drives* typically connect to a computer via a serial attached SCSI (SAS) or Fibre Channel interface. To record data

> **Holographic storage.** An emerging type of storage technology that uses multiple blue laser beams to store data in three dimensions.

HOW HOLOGRAPHIC STORAGE WORKS

Detector

Storage medium

Reference beam

4. When data needs to be read, it is projected onto a detector to be reconstructed.

3. Data is converted into a hologram, which is stored where the beams intersect in the storage medium.

Holographic drive

Holographic cartridge

Spatial light modulator (SLM)

Signal beam

2. The beam is split into two beams (a reference beam and a signal beam) here, which intersect again at the storage medium.

Laser

1. A laser beam is used to write or read data.

HOLOGRAPHIC DRIVES AND CARTRIDGES

FIGURE 3-21

Holographic storage. Holographic drives store up to one million bits of data in a single flash of light.

ONLINE VIDEO

Go to the Chapter 3 page at **www.cengage.com/ computerconcepts/np/uc13** to watch the "Holographic Storage: Data at the Speed of Light" video clip.

onto a *holographic disc* or *holographic cartridge*, the holographic drive splits the light from a blue laser beam into two beams (a *reference beam* whose angle determines the address used to store data at that particular location on the storage medium and a *signal beam* that contains the data). The signal beam passes through a device called a *spatial light modulator* (*SLM*), which translates the data's 0s and 1s into a *hologram*—a three-dimensional representation of data in the form of a checkerboard pattern of light and dark pixels. The two beams intersect within the recording medium to store the hologram at that location (see Figure 3-21) by changing the optical density of the medium.

Over one million bits of data can be stored at one time in a single flash of light, so holographic storage systems are very fast. And, because the hologram goes through the entire thickness of the medium, much more data can be stored on a holographic disc or cartridge than on a CD, DVD, or BD of the same physical size. In fact, hundreds of holograms can be stored in an overlapping manner in the same area of the medium—a different reference beam angle or position is used for each hologram so it can be uniquely stored and retrieved when needed. To read data, the reference beam projects the hologram containing the requested data onto a *detector* that reads the entire data page at one time. Today's holographic storage systems typically use removable recordable holographic cartridges that hold 300 GB per cartridge; 1.6 TB cartridges are expected by 2011.

Holographic data storage systems are particularly suited to applications in which large amounts of data need to be stored or retrieved quickly, but rarely changed, such as for business data archiving, high-speed digital video delivery, and image processing for medical, video, and military purposes. Rewritable holographic drives and media are currently in the development stage and are expected to be available by 2010.

Storage Systems for Large Computer Systems

Businesses and other organizations have tremendous storage needs. In addition to regular business data storage (such as employee files, customer and order data, business documents, and Web site content), new regulations are continually increasing the types of and amounts of data that many businesses need to archive. For instance, the *Health Insurance Portability and Accountability Act* (*HIPAA*) requires healthcare providers to archive huge amounts of medical data, and the *Sarbanes-Oxley Act* requires certain accounting records and work papers to be archived for five years. In addition, a recent *e-discovery* federal mandate requires businesses to locate and provide to the courts in a timely manner any document stored electronically (such as e-mail messages, IM logs, and text documents) that is needed for evidence in civil litigation involving their companies. All of these requirements mean that business storage needs are growing exponentially—one forecast predicts that digital storage needs will increase by eight times in the next six years—and the documents must be stored in a manner in which they can be readily retrieved as needed.

Storage systems for large computer systems (such as those containing mainframe computers and midrange servers) utilize much of the same storage hardware, standards, and principles as those used with personal computers, but on a much larger scale. Instead of finding a single hard drive installed within the system unit, you are most likely to find a **storage server**—a separate piece of hardware containing multiple high-speed hard drives—connected to the computer system or network. Large storage servers typically contain racks (also called *chassis*) of hard drives for a large total capacity. For instance, the storage system shown in Figure 3-22 can include up to 1,280 hard drives for a total capacity of 600 TB. These types of storage systems—also referred to as *enterprise storage systems*—typically use fast Fibre Channel or iSCSI connections and are *scalable*, meaning that more racks of hard drives can be added as needed up to the maximum capacity. In addition to being used as stand-alone storage for large computer systems, storage servers may also be used in network attached storage (NAS), storage area network (SAN), and *RAID* (*redundant arrays of independent disks*) storage systems. Most storage servers are based on magnetic hard disks, although *magnetic tape storage systems* are also possible. RAID and magnetic tape systems are discussed next.

HARD DRIVES
Each drive chassis holds up to 40 individual hard drives that can store up to 1 TB each.

STORAGE SERVER
This server can manage up to 1,280 hard drives located in up to 5 cabinets like the one shown here, for a total capacity of 600 TB in a single system.

FIGURE 3-22
Storage servers.
Storage servers are usually scalable so additional hard drives can be added as needed.

RAID

RAID (redundant arrays of independent disks) is a method of storing data on two or more hard drives that work together. Although RAID can be used to increase performance, it is most often used to protect critical data on a storage server. Because RAID usually involves recording redundant (duplicate) copies of stored data, the copies can be used, when necessary, to reconstruct lost data. This helps to increase the *fault tolerance*—the ability to recover from an unexpected hardware or software failure, such as a system crash—of a storage system.

There are several different RAID designs or levels that use different combinations of RAID techniques. For example, *RAID 0* uses *disk striping*, which spreads files over two or more hard drives (see the leftmost part of Figure 3-23). Although striping improves performance since multiple hard drives can be accessed at one time to store or retrieve data, it does not provide fault tolerance. Another common RAID technique is *disk mirroring*, in which data is written to two duplicate hard drives simultaneously (see the rightmost part of Figure 3-23). The objective of disk mirroring is to increase fault tolerance—if one of the hard drives fails, the system can instantly switch to the other hard drive without any loss of

ONLINE VIDEO
Go to the Chapter 3 page at **www.cengage.com/ computerconcepts/np/uc13** to watch the "Understanding RAID" video clip.

>**Storage server.** A storage device designed for large computer systems and that typically contains multiple high-speed hard drives. >**RAID (redundant arrays of independent disks).** A storage method that uses several hard drives working together, typically to increase performance and/or fault-tolerance.

STRIPING
When a file is written to a RAID system using striping, it is split among two or more drives.

MIRRORING
When a file is written to a RAID system using mirroring, an identical copy of the file is sent to another drive in the system.

FIGURE 3-23
RAID. Two primary RAID techniques are striping and mirroring.

data or service. *RAID 1* uses disk mirroring. Levels beyond RAID 1 use some combination of disk striping and disk mirroring, with different types of error correction provisions.

One disadvantage of RAID in the past is the difficulty traditionally involved with setting up and maintaining the system. A new storage system—*Drobo*, shown in Figure 3-24—eliminates this concern. Drobo connects to an individual computer similar to an external hard drive (such as via a USB or FireWire connection) and has four empty drive bays into which hard drives with a capacity of up to 2 terabytes each can be inserted. An even newer *DroboPro* version has eight empty drive bays and can be connected directly to a network, in addition to being connected to a computer.

Like many RAID systems, Drobo and DroboPro offer continuous data redundancy, but they are much easier to use than conventional RAID systems and no special skills are needed to manage, repair, or upgrade them. For instance, hard drives just slide in and out of the Drobo devices and drives can be swapped while the devices are being used, in order to replace a bad hard drive or to increase capacity. When a drive is replaced, the system automatically copies data as needed to the new hard drive to restore the system back to its configuration before the hard drive failed or was removed. This ease of use makes the Drobo systems particularly appropriate for individuals and small businesses that need the security of data redundancy but have no IT personnel to assign to a RAID system.

FIGURE 3-24
The Drobo storage system.

Magnetic Tape Systems

Magnetic tape consists of plastic tape coated with a magnetizable substance that represents the bits and bytes of digital data, similar to magnetic hard disks. Although magnetic tape is no longer used for everyday storage applications because of its sequential-access property, it is still used today for business data archiving and backup. One advantage of magnetic tape is its low cost per megabyte.

>**Magnetic tape.** Storage media consisting of plastic tape with a magnetizable surface that stores data as a series of magnetic spots; typically comes as a cartridge.

Most computer tapes today are in the form of *cartridge tapes*, such as the one shown in Figure 3-25. Computer tapes are read by *tape drives*, which can be either an internal or an external piece of hardware. Tape drives contain one or more read/write heads over which the tape passes to allow the tape drive to read or write data. Cartridge tapes are available in a variety of sizes and formats; tape sizes and formats generally are not interchangeable. Tape cartridge capacity varies widely, from 500 MB to more than 1 TB per cartridge. When an even larger capacity is required, *tape libraries*—devices that contain multiple tape drives—can be used to boost storage capacity up to 10 PB.

FIGURE 3-25
A magnetic tape cartridge.

EVALUATING YOUR STORAGE ALTERNATIVES

Storage alternatives are often compared by weighing a number of product characteristics and cost factors. Some of these product characteristics include speed, compatibility, storage capacity, convenience, and the portability of the media. Keep in mind that each storage alternative normally involves trade-offs. For instance, most systems with removable media are slower than those with fixed media, and external drives are typically slower than internal ones. Although cost is a factor when comparing similar devices, it is often not the most compelling reason to choose a particular technology. For instance, although USB flash drives are relatively expensive per GB compared to optical discs and external hard drives, many users find them essential for transferring files between work and home or for taking presentations or other files with them as they travel. For drives that use a USB interface, the type of USB port is also significant. For example, storage devices that connect via a USB port adhering to the original USB 1.0 standard transfer data at up to 12 Mbps—USB 2.0 devices are about 40 times faster and the emerging USB 3.0 devices will be about 10 times as fast as USB 2.0 devices.

With so many different storage alternatives available, it is a good idea to research which devices and media are most appropriate for your personal situation. In general, most users today need a hard drive (for storing programs and data), some type of recordable or rewritable optical drive (for installing programs, backing up files, and sharing files with others), and a flash memory card reader (for transferring photos, music, and other content between portable devices and the computer). Users who plan to transfer music, digital photos, and other multimedia data on a regular basis between devices—such as a computer, digital camera, mobile phone, and printer—will want to select and use the flash memory media that are compatible with the devices they are using. They will also need to obtain the necessary adapter for their computer if it does not include a compatible built-in flash memory reader. Virtually all computer users today will also need at least one convenient free USB port to be used to connect external hard drives, USB flash drives, and other USB-based storage hardware, as well as USB devices that contain storage media, such as digital cameras and portable digital media players.

SUMMARY

STORAGE SYSTEM CHARACTERISTICS

Chapter Objective 1:
Name several general characteristics of storage systems.

Storage systems make it possible to save programs, data, and processing results for later use. They provide nonvolatile storage, so when the power is shut off, the data stored on the storage medium remains intact. All storage systems involve two physical parts: A **storage device** (such as a DVD drive) and a **storage medium** (such as a DVD disc). Data is often stored *magnetically* or *optically* on storage media, and storage media are read by the appropriate types of drive. Drives can be *internal*, *external*, or *remote*. Drives are typically assigned letters by the computer; these letters are used to identify the drive.

Sequential access allows a computer system to retrieve the records in a file only in the same order in which they are physically stored. *Random access* (also called *direct access*) allows the system to retrieve records in any order. In either case, **files** (sometimes called *documents*) stored on a storage medium are given a **filename** and can be organized into **folders**. This is referred to as *logical file representation*. *Physical file representation* refers to how the files are physically stored on the storage medium by the computer.

HARD DRIVES

Chapter Objective 2:
Describe the two most common types of hard drives and what they are used for today.

Hard drives are used in most computers to store programs and data. Conventional hard drives are **magnetic hard drives**; a newer type of hard drive that uses flash memory instead of magnetic disks is the **solid-state drive** (**SSD**). Hard drives can be *internal* or *external*; external hard drives can be full-sized or portable. **Hybrid hard drives** are a combination of a magnetic hard drive and an SSD, containing a large amount of flash memory that is used in conjunction with magnetic hard disks to provide increased performance while reducing power consumption.

Magnetic hard drives contain metal hard disks that are organized into concentric **tracks** encoded with magnetized spots representing 0s and 1s. **Sector** boundaries divide a magnetic disk surface into pie-shaped pieces. A **cluster**, which is the smallest amount of disk space that can be allocated to hold a file, is comprised of one or more sectors. All tracks in the same position on all surfaces of all disks in a hard drive form a **cylinder**. A separate *read/write head* that corresponds to each disk surface is used to read and write data. Hard drives can be divided into multiple *partitions* (logical drives) for efficiency or to facilitate multiple users or operating systems. Solid-state drives (SSDs) are increasingly used for portable computers because they are more shock-resistant and energy-efficient.

The total time it takes for a magnetic hard drive to read from or write to disks is called **disk access time**. A **disk cache** strategy, in which the computer transfers additional data to memory whenever disk content is retrieved, can help to speed up access time. Hard drives can connect to a computer using one of several standards, such as *serial ATA (SATA)*, *parallel ATA (PATA)*, *serial attached SCSI (SAS)*, *eSATA*, *Fibre Channel*, FireWire, or USB.

OPTICAL DISCS

Chapter Objective 3:
Discuss the various types of optical discs available today and how they differ from each other.

Optical discs, such as **CD discs**, **DVD discs**, and **Blu-ray Discs** (**BDs**), store data *optically* using laser beams, and they can store data much more densely than magnetic disks. They are divided into tracks and sectors like magnetic disks, but they use a single spiral track instead of concentric tracks. Data is represented by *pits* and *lands* permanently formed on the surface of the disk. Optical discs are available in a wide variety of sizes, shapes, and capacities and are read by **optical drives**, such as *CD* or *DVD drives*. **CD-ROM discs** come with data already stored on the disc. CD-ROM discs cannot be erased or overwritten—they are *read-only*. **DVD-ROM discs** are similar to CD-ROM discs, but they hold much more data (at least 4.7 GB instead of 650 MB). High-capacity read-only optical discs designed for high-definition content are **BD-ROM discs**. *Recordable discs* (**CD-R**, **DVD-R/DVD+R**, and **BD-R discs**, for example) and *rewritable disks* (**CD-RW**, **DVD-RW/DVD+RW**, and **BD-RE discs**, for instance) can all be written to, but only rewritable discs can be erased and rewritten to, similar to a hard drive. Recordable CDs and DVDs store data by burning permanent marks onto the disc, similar to CD-ROM and DVD-ROM discs; rewritable discs typically use *phase change* technology to temporarily change the reflectivity of the disc to represent 1s and 0s.

FLASH MEMORY

Flash memory is used in a variety of storage systems. **Flash memory cards**, one of the most common types of *flash memory media*, are commonly used with digital cameras, portable computers, and other portable devices, as well as with desktop computers. Flash memory cards come in a variety of formats—the most common are *CompactFlash* (*CF*) and *Secure Digital* (*SD*) *cards*. **USB flash drives** connect to a computer or other device via a USB port and are a convenient method of transferring files between computers. They can also provide other capabilities, such as to lock a computer or control access to the data stored on the USB flash drive.

Chapter Objective 4:
Identify some flash memory storage devices and media and explain how they are used today.

OTHER TYPES OF STORAGE SYSTEMS

Remote storage involves using a storage device that is not directly connected to your computer. One example is using a *network storage* device, such as a **network attached storage** (**NAS**) or **storage area network** (**SAN**). Another is **online storage** or **cloud storage**; that is, storage available via the Internet. **Smart cards** contain a chip or other circuitry usually used to store data or a monetary value. **Holographic storage**, which uses multiple blue laser beams to store data in three dimensions, is now available for high-speed data retrieval applications.

Storage systems for larger computers implement many of the same standards as the hard drives used with personal computers. Instead of finding a single set of hard disks inside a hard drive permanently installed within a system unit, however, a **storage server** is often used. **RAID** (**redundant arrays of independent disks**) technology can be used to increase *fault tolerance* and performance. **Magnetic tape** systems store data on plastic tape coated with a magnetizable substance. Magnetic tapes are usually enclosed in cartridges and are inserted into a *tape drive* in order to be accessed.

Chapter Objective 5:
List at least three other types of storage systems.

EVALUATING YOUR STORAGE ALTERNATIVES

Most personal computers today include a hard drive, some type of optical drive, a flash memory card reader, and multiple USB ports that can be used to connect USB-based storage devices, such as external hard drives and USB flash drives, as well as other USB hardware. The type of optical drive and any additional storage devices are often determined by weighing a number of factors, such as cost, speed, compatibility, storage capacity, removability, and convenience.

Chapter Objective 6:
Summarize the storage alternatives for a typical personal computer.

REVIEW ACTIVITIES

KEY TERM MATCHING

a. disk cache

b. file

c. flash memory card

d. folder

e. hard drive

f. holographic storage

g. RAID

h. remote storage

i. solid-state drive (SSD)

j. storage server

Instructions: Match each key term on the left with the definition on the right that best describes it.

1. _____ A named place on a storage medium into which files can be stored to keep the files stored on that medium organized.

2. _____ A hard drive that uses flash memory media instead of metal magnetic hard disks.

3. _____ An emerging type of storage technology that uses multiple blue laser beams to store data in three dimensions.

4. _____ A small, rectangular flash memory medium, such as a CompactFlash (CF) or Secure Digital (SD) card; often used with digital cameras and other portable devices.

5. _____ A storage device designed for large computer systems and that typically contains multiple high-speed hard drives.

6. _____ A storage device that is not directly connected to the computer being used, such as one accessed through a local network or the Internet.

7. _____ A storage method that uses several hard drives working together, typically to increase performance and/or fault-tolerance.

8. _____ Memory used in conjunction with a magnetic hard drive to improve system performance.

9. _____ Something stored on a storage medium, such as a program, a document, or an image.

10. _____ The primary storage system for most computers; used to store most programs and data used with that computer.

SELF-QUIZ

Instructions: Circle **T** if the statement is true, **F** if the statement is false, or write the best answer in the space provided. **Answers for the self-quiz are located in the References and Resources Guide at the end of the book.**

1. **T F** A computer system with a C drive and a D drive must have two physical hard drives.

2. **T F** The smallest amount of space a file on a disk can take up is one cluster.

3. **T F** External hard drives typically connect via a flash memory reader.

4. **T F** A CD-R disc can be written to by the user.

5. **T F** A hybrid hard drive contains both magnetic hard disks and optical discs.

6. The drive letter that would most likely be assigned to the primary hard drive on a typical personal computer is _____.

7. Storage media are not _____, meaning they do not lose their contents when the power is shut off.

8. A single-sided, single-layer CD disc typically holds _____.

9. A(n) _____ looks similar to a credit card but contains a chip and other circuitry that can store data.

10. Secure Digital (SD) cards are one type of _____ medium.

1. Assume, for simplicity's sake, that a kilobyte is 1,000 bytes, a megabyte is 1,000,000 bytes, and a gigabyte is 1,000,000,000 bytes. You have a 500-gigabyte hard drive with the following content:

ITEM	STORAGE SPACE USED
Operating system	65 MB
Other software	1,350 MB
Digital photos and videos	1,000 MB
Other documents	85 MB

How much storage space is currently being used? _____ How much is left? _____

2. Supply the missing words to complete the following statements.

   a. A(n) _____ disc can hold either 25 GB or 50 GB and is designed for high-definition content, such as movies.

   b. *Thumb drive* is another name for a(n) _____.

   c. Memory used in conjunction with a magnetic hard drive to improve system performance is called a(n) disk _____.

3. Explain why CD-ROM discs are not erasable, but CD+RW discs are.

4. List two possible advantages and two possible disadvantages for using online storage.

5. Which types of storage media would be appropriate for someone who needed to exchange large (5 MB to 75 MB) files with another person? List at least three different types, stating why each might be the most appropriate under specific conditions.

1. There are a number of types of flash memory cards available, such as SD, CF, XD, and memory stick. Is there an advantage to having multiple standards or would it be beneficial to consumers if there was only one flash memory standard, such as just the various sizes of SD cards? Would having a single standard be less expensive and more convenient for consumers? If so, will a single standard naturally evolve or should it be mandated by the storage industry or the government? If you use multiple types of flash memory cards with your devices, would you prefer they all used the same type? Why or why not?

2. People send their digital photos over the Internet in different ways. For instance, digital photos are often e-mailed to others, posted on Facebook pages and other social networking sites, and uploaded to a server (such as one belonging to Snapfish, Wal-Mart, or Costco) in order to order prints, enlargements, or other photo-based items. If you have ever sent photos over the Internet, were you concerned about someone other than the intended recipient intercepting or viewing your photo files? If you have ever uploaded files to a processing service for printing, did you check to see if the Web server being used was secure? Should individuals be concerned about sending their personal photos over the Internet? There are a number of advantages, but are there privacy risks, as well?

PROJECTS

HOT TOPICS

1. **Thumb Drive PCs** As discussed in the chapter Technology and You box, USB flash drives can be used to bring your personal software and settings with you to any computer with which you use that drive. In addition, USB flash drives can be used to securely store files, grant access to a computer, and more.

   For this project, research two features that USB flash drives can provide, in addition to just data storage. For your selected features, determine what the feature does, how it works, what benefits it provides, and some examples of USB flash drives that are currently being sold that include that feature. Is there an additional cost for drives that contain this feature? If so, do you think it is worth the extra cost? Do you think the feature is beneficial? Why or why not? At the conclusion of your research, prepare a one- to two-page summary of your findings and opinions and submit it to your instructor.

SHORT ANSWER/ RESEARCH

2. **Big Brother?** Some of the storage technology used today, such as smart cards, can help facilitate fast and secure access to locked facilities, can protect against the use of stolen credit card numbers, and, when used in conjunction with a biometric characteristic, can unequivocally identify an individual. They can also be used for employee monitoring, such as to identify the location of an employee carrying or wearing his or her smart card at any time. While some people find benefits to the applications just discussed, others worry that smart cards and other devices will be used to track our movements.

   For this project, write a short essay expressing your opinion about the use of smart cards and similar technology to identify individuals for various applications. Is the convenience of smart card technology worth the possible loss of privacy? Do you think employers or the government have the right to track individuals' movements? If so, under what conditions? What are some advantages and disadvantages for the government and your employer always knowing where you are? Have you ever used a smart card or been identified with a biometric system? If so, how do you rate the experience? Submit your opinion on this issue to your instructor in the form of a one-page paper.

HANDS ON

3. **Online/Cloud Storage** There are a number of online or cloud storage services (such as ADrive, SkyDrive, and Box.net) designed to allow individuals to back up files online and share specific files with others; specialty online storage services designed for digital photo sharing include Flickr, Photobucket, and SnapFish.

   For this project, visit at least one online/cloud storage site designed for backup and file exchange, and at least one site designed for digital photo sharing. You can try the sites listed above or use a search site to find alternative sites. Tour your selected sites to determine the features each service offers, the cost, the amount of storage space available, and the options for sending uploaded files to others. Do the sites password protect your files, or are they available for anyone with an Internet connection to see? What are the benefits for using these types of storage services? Can you think of any drawbacks? Would you want to use any of the storage sites you visited? Why or why not? At the conclusion of this task, prepare a short summary of your findings and submit it to your instructor.

4. **Lost and Found** Portable computers, mobile phones, USB flash drives, and other portable devices are lost all the time today. They can be dropped out of a pocket or bag, inadvertently left on a table, and so forth. If the owner has identifying information (name, phone number, or e-mail address, for instance) printed on the device, the individual who finds the device can attempt to return it to the owner. But what if there is no identifying information clearly visible on the device? Should the finder look at the contents of the device to try to determine the owner? If the device is lost in a location where there is a responsible party (such as an airplane or a restaurant) the finder can turn over the device to that authority (such as a flight attendant or manager), but is it ethical for the responsible party to look at the contents in order to identify the owner? If you lost a device, would you want someone to look at the contents to try to determine your identity? Why or why not? Is looking at the contents on a found device ever ethical? Should it be illegal?

For this project, form an opinion about the ethical ramifications of lost devices and be prepared to discuss your position (in class, via an online class discussion group, in a class chat room, or via a class blog, depending on your instructor's directions). You may also be asked to write a short paper expressing your opinion.

5. **Flash Cards** There are a wide variety of flash memory card products available today and they can be used with a variety of devices.

For this project, find at least two different examples of flash memory card products in each of the following three categories: user storage; software, music, or movie delivery; and an interface for a peripheral device. Share your findings with the class in the form of a short presentation, including the products that you found, their purpose, what devices they are intended to be used with, and their cost. Be sure to also mention any additional categories or applications using flash cards (in addition to the three categories listed here) that you found doing your research. The presentation should not exceed 10 minutes and should make use of one or more presentation aids, such as the chalkboard, handouts, overhead transparencies, or a computer-based slide presentation (your instructor may provide additional requirements). You may also be asked to submit a summary of the presentation to your instructor.

Instructions: Go to the Chapter 3 page at **www.cengage.com/computerconcepts/np/uc13** to work the following Web Activities.

6. **Interactive Activities** Work the interactive **Crossword Puzzle**, watch the **Video Podcasts** and **Online Videos**, and explore the **Further Exploration** links associated with this chapter.

If you have a SAM user profile, you may have access to hands-on instruction, practice, and assessment of the skills covered in this chapter. Check with your instructor for instructions and the correct URL/Web site to access those assignments.

7. **Student Edition Labs** Work the following interactive **Student Edition Lab**.
   ➤ **Managing Files and Folders**

8. **Test Yourself** Review the **Online Study Guide** for this chapter, then test your knowledge of the terms and concepts covered in this chapter by completing the **Key Term Matching** exercise, the **Self-Quiz**, the **Exercises**, and the **Practice Test**.

chapter 4

Input and Output

After completing this chapter, you will be able to do the following:

1. Explain the purpose of a computer keyboard and the types of keyboards widely used today.

2. List several different pointing devices and describe their functions.

3. Describe the purposes of scanners and readers and list some types of scanners and readers in use today.

4. Explain what digital cameras are and how they are used today.

5. Understand the devices that can be used for audio input.

6. Describe the characteristics of a display device and explain some of the technologies used to display images.

7. List several types of printers and explain their functions.

8. Identify the hardware devices typically used for audio output.

outline

Overview

Keyboards

Pointing and Touch Devices
Mice
Pens/Styluses
Touch Screens
Other Pointing Devices

Scanners, Readers, and Digital Cameras
Scanners
Readers
Digital Cameras

Audio Input
Voice Input and Speech Recognition Systems
Music Input Systems

Display Devices
Display Device Characteristics
Flat-Panel Display Technologies
Data and Multimedia Projectors

Printers
Printer Characteristics
Laser Printers
Ink-Jet Printers
Special-Purpose Printers

Audio Output

OVERVIEW

In Chapter 2, we learned how data is processed by a computer. The focus of this chapter is on the hardware designed for inputting data into the computer, and then outputting results to the user after the data has been processed. We begin with a look at input. First we discuss the most common input devices used with personal computers—mainly, keyboards and pointing devices (such as a mouse or pen). Next, we discuss hardware designed for capturing data in electronic form (such as scanners, barcode readers, and digital cameras), followed by an overview of the devices that are used to input audio data.

The second part of this chapter explores output devices. Most output today occurs on a screen (via a display device) or on paper (via a printer). Display devices are covered first, including their basic properties and the various types of display devices that are in use today. Next, we discuss printers and then devices used for audio output. Due to the vast number of different types of input and output devices that can be used for various needs, this chapter focuses on the most common types of input and output devices in use today. ■

PODCAST

Go to **www.cengage.com/ computerconcepts/np/uc13** to download or listen to the "Expert Insight on Hardware" podcast.

KEYBOARDS

Most computers today are designed to be used with a **keyboard**—a device used to enter characters at the location on the screen marked by the *insertion point* or *cursor* (typically a blinking vertical line). Keyboards can be built into a device, attached using a wired cable (such as via a USB or keyboard port), or connected via a wireless connection (such as via a *Bluetooth* wireless networking connection, which is discussed in more detail in Chapter 7). A typical desktop computer keyboard is shown in Figure 4-1. Like most keyboards, this keyboard contains standard *alphanumeric keys* to input text and numbers, as well as additional keys used for various purposes. For instance, this keyboard contains a *numeric keypad* (for entering numbers), *function keys* (for issuing commands in some programs), *Delete* and *Backspace keys* (for deleting characters), *Control* and *Alternate keys* (for issuing commands in conjunction with other keys on the keyboard, such as Ctrl+S to save the current document in some programs), and *arrow keys* (for moving around within a document). Some keyboards also contain special keys that are used for a specific purpose, such as to control the speaker volume or DVD playback, or to launch an e-mail program or favorite Web site. To allow individuals to work under a variety of lighting conditions (such as in a dark living room or in an airplane), keyboards today (such as the one in Figure 4-1) are increasingly using *illuminated keys* to light up the characters on the keyboard.

Many computer keyboards today include *touch pads*, *scroll wheels*, and other components for easier control over some functions, such as scrolling through documents. Some keyboards also include a *fingerprint reader* or other *biometric reader* that can be used for

>**Keyboard.** An input device containing numerous keys that can be used to input letters, numbers, and other symbols.

FUNCTION KEYS
Perform a different command or function in each program designed to use them.

KEYBOARD DISPLAY
Displays images, videos, communication and gaming data, etc.

ENTER KEY
Used to enter commands into the computer, end paragraphs, and insert blank lines in documents.

BACKSPACE KEY
Erases one character to the left of the insertion point.

ALPHANUMERIC KEYS
Usually arranged in the same order as the keys on a standard typewriter.

TAB KEY
Moves to the next tab location.

MEDIA KEYS
Control music, videos, and images.

CAPS LOCK KEY
Turns all caps on or off.

SCROLL WHEEL
Scrolls through documents.

WINDOWS KEY
Opens the Windows Start menu.

INSERT KEY
Toggles between inserting text and typing over text in many programs.

USER PROGRAMMABLE KEYS
Perform functions as defined by the user.

NUMERIC KEYPAD
Used to efficiently enter numerical data.

CONTROL AND ALTERNATE KEYS
Used in combination with other keys to enter commands into the computer.

SPACE BAR
Enters a blank space.

SHIFT KEY
Produces uppercase letters and symbols on the upper part of certain keys when the Caps Lock key is not on.

DELETE KEY
Deletes one character to the right of the insertion point.

ARROW KEYS
Move the cursor around a document without disturbing existing text.

PAGE UP AND PAGE DOWN KEYS
Move up or down one page or screen in most programs.

FIGURE 4-1
A typical desktop keyboard.

TIP

If the specifications for a computer or device state that it uses a *QWERTY keyboard*, that means the alphanumeric keys are laid out in the same position as they are on a standard computer keyboard (with QWERTY as the first six letters in the top row).

TIP

If your mobile device includes an *automatic orientation sensor* (*accelerometer*), an on-screen keyboard (as well as Web pages and other displayed content) will rotate as you rotate the device, as shown in Figure 4-2.

identification purposes, as discussed in more detail later in this chapter and in Chapter 9. In addition, some keyboards are made for languages other than English, and some keyboards are designed for special purposes, such as to allow easy input for specific systems (a library electronic card catalog or a company database, for instance), to input music into a computer (such as a *MIDI keyboard* used for piano compositions), or to be regularly and easily sterilized (such as keyboards used in hospitals).

Notebook and netbook computers usually have a keyboard that is similar to a desktop keyboard, but it is typically smaller, contains fewer keys (it often has no numeric keypad, for instance), and the keys are typically placed somewhat closer together. Notebook and netbook computer users can also connect and use a conventional keyboard to make inputting data easier if their computer contains an appropriate port (such as a USB port).

Increasingly, ultra-mobile PCs (UMPCs) and mobile devices today have a built-in keyboard; often these are *slide-out keyboards* that can be revealed when needed and hidden when not in use. Many UMPCs and mobile devices also support *pen input* and/ or *touch input* (discussed shortly) and can use an *on-screen keyboard* instead of, or in addition to, a physical keyboard (see Figure 4-2). The order and layout of the keys on a mobile device may be different from the order and layout on a conventional keyboard, and the keyboard layout may vary from device to device. If a mobile device does not have a built-in keyboard, a *portable keyboard* (that folds or rolls up and connects to the device via a wired or wireless connection when needed) can often be used with the device for easier data entry. One possibility for the future is printing keyboards directly on clothing and other products that can connect wirelessly to the devices being used. For example, keyboards might be printed on jackets to allow consumers to wirelessly input data or otherwise control their mobile phones while on the go, or keyboards might be printed on soldiers' uniforms to be used with UMPCs or other small computers while in the field.

On-screen keyboard rotates as the device is rotated.

BUILT-IN KEYBOARDS   **SLIDE-OUT KEYBOARDS**   **ON-SCREEN KEYBOARDS**

⚫ **FIGURE 4-2**
Keyboards for mobile devices.

POINTING AND TOUCH DEVICES

In addition to a keyboard, most computers today are used in conjunction with some type of **pointing device**. Pointing devices are used to select and manipulate objects, to input certain types of data (such as handwritten data), and to issue commands to the computer. Two of the most common pointing devices are the *mouse* and the *pen/stylus*, which are used to *click* screen objects and perform *pen input*, respectively; a common pointing device that uses *touch input* is the *touch screen*. For a look at an emerging input option—*gestures*—see the Trend box.

ONLINE VIDEO ▷

Go to the Chapter 4 page at **www.cengage.com/ computerconcepts/np/uc13** to watch the "What Is a 3D Mouse" video clip.

Mice

The **mouse** (see Figure 4-3) is the most common pointing device for a desktop computer. It typically rests on the desk or other flat surface close to the user's computer, and it is moved across the surface with the user's hand in the appropriate direction to point to and select objects on the screen. As it moves, an on-screen *mouse pointer*—usually an arrow—moves accordingly. Once the mouse pointer is pointing to the desired object on the screen, the buttons on the mouse are used to perform actions on that object (such as to open a hyperlink or to resize an image). Similar to keyboards, mice today typically connect via a USB or mouse port, or via a wireless connection.

Older *mechanical mice* have a ball exposed on the bottom surface of the mouse to control the pointer movement. Most mice today are *optical*

▼ **FIGURE 4-3**
Examples of mice.

A LASER MOUSE

A 3D MOUSE

>**Pointing device.** An input device that moves an on-screen pointer, such as an arrow, to allow the user to select objects on the screen.
>**Mouse.** A common pointing device that the user slides along a flat surface to move a pointer around the screen and clicks its buttons to make selections.

POINT
Move the mouse until the mouse pointer is at the desired location on the screen.

CLICK
Press and release the left mouse button.

RIGHT-CLICK
Press and release the right mouse button.

DOUBLE-CLICK
Press and release the left mouse button twice, in rapid succession.

DRAG-AND-DROP
When the mouse pointer is over the appropriate object, press and hold down the left mouse button, drag the object to the proper location on the screen by moving the mouse, and then drop the object by releasing the mouse button.

SCROLL WHEEL/BUTTON
If your mouse has a wheel or button on top, use it to scroll through the displayed document.

FIGURE 4-4
Common mouse operations.

mice or *laser mice* that track movements with light. For use with *virtual worlds, animation programs,* and other *3D* applications, *3D mice* are available that are designed to make navigation through a 3D environment easier. For example, the *3Dconnexion SpaceNavigator 3D mouse* shown in Figure 4-3 has a *controller cap,* which can be lifted up to move an object up, rotated to "fly" around objects, or tilted to "look" up. In addition to being used with desktop computers, mice can also be used with portable computers (such as notebook and netbook computers), as long as an appropriate port (such as a USB port) is available. There are also special *cordless presenter* mice that can be used by presenters to control on-screen slide shows.

Mice are used to start programs; open, move around, and edit documents; draw or edit images; and more. Some of the most common mouse commands are described in Figure 4-4.

Pens/Styluses

Many devices today, including some desktop computers and many tablet computers and mobile devices, can accept *pen input;* that is, input by writing, drawing, or tapping on the screen with a pen-like device called a **stylus**. Sometimes, the stylus (also called a *digital pen, electronic pen,* or *tablet pen*) is simply a plastic device with no additional functionality; more commonly, it is a pressure-sensitive device that transmits the pressure applied by the user to the device that the stylus is being used with in order to allow more precise input. These more sophisticated styluses also are typically powered by the device that it is being used with, have a smooth rounded tip so they don't scratch the screen, and contain buttons or switches to perform actions such as erasing content or right-clicking.

The idea behind pen input and *digital writing* in general is to make using a computer or other device as convenient as writing with a pen, while adding the functionality that pen input can provide (such as converting pen input to editable typed text). Pen input is being used increasingly for photography, graphic design, animation, industrial design, document processing, and healthcare applications. In addition to supporting handwritten input (referred to as *inking*), digital pens can also be used to navigate through a document and issue commands to the computer (such as to print, delete, copy, and more) via specific gestures with the pen, known as *pen flicks* in Microsoft Windows. Pen input is also a useful alternative to touch input for mobile device users who have long fingernails, who wear gloves in the winter, or who have a device with a screen that is too small to have accurate touch input via a finger. Some of the most common devices that use pen input are discussed next.

Pen-Based Computers

Although their capabilities depend on the type of computer and software being used, pen input can be used with a variety of computer types (see Figure 4-5). Most often, pens are used with mobile devices, UMPCs, and tablet computers to both input handwritten text and sketches, and to manipulate objects (such as to select an option from a menu, select text, or resize an image). They can also be used with a desktop computer if the

---

>Stylus. An input device that is used to write electronically on the display screen.

TREND

Gesture Input

We already have some devices that support gestures—such as the Nintendo Wii and the Apple iPhone—but some view gesture input as the next step toward making computer input easier and more natural to use. While devices like the Wii and iPhone use special hardware (such as an *accelerometer*) to detect gestures, gesture-based input systems used with computers typically use cameras to detect input based solely on a user's movements. For instance, hand gestures can be used to select and manipulate objects on the screen, similar to the system used by Tom Cruise's character in the movie *Minority Report* to change the images on his display by gesturing with his hands. Gesture input is noncontact, which avoids the fingerprint and germ issues related to public keyboard and touch screen use; it also enables input to be performed from a slight distance (such as through a glass storefront window). In addition, gesture input allows for full body input and, because cameras are used, it can enable the user's image to be imported into the application, such as to have the user's image displayed in a game or virtual world, showing his or her current movements in real time.

Currently, gesture input devices are being used primarily with consumer gaming applications and large screen interactive displays used for advertising purposes (see the accompanying photo) or to convey information in public locations. However, they are also beginning to be used with mobile phones and personal computers and, according to the president and co-founder of Gesturetek (one of the leading companies in gesture input), 3D gesture input is expected to make its way to televisions by 2010.

Gesture input enables the user to control a computer with noncontact hand movements.

monitor supports pen input. Depending on the software being used, handwritten input can be stored as an image, stored as handwritten characters that can be recognized by the computer, or converted to editable, typed text. For the latter two options, software with **handwriting recognition** capabilities must be used.

FIGURE 4-5
Pen-based computers.

Stylus
MOBILE DEVICES

TABLET COMPUTERS

DESKTOP COMPUTERS

> **Handwriting recognition.** The ability of a device to identify handwritten characters.

With handwriting recognition, the computer interprets handwritten pen input as individual characters. For instance, handwritten notes can be converted by the computer to typed notes and data written on a *digital form* (such as the patient assessment form shown in Figure 4-6) can be handwritten and then automatically converted into typed text. The use of handwriting recognition technology in conjunction with digital forms saves time, reduces paper waste, and increases data accuracy. The use of digital forms is growing rapidly and is expected to continue to grow as companies increasingly move toward digital records and digital documents, such as *electronic health records*. In addition, the U.S. government is converting many paper forms to electronic forms. For example, the United States Department of Defense (DoD) has announced a new forms management system that allows nearly 1,000 electronic forms used by DoD entities (including the Army, Navy, Air Force, Marines, Coast Guard, Joint Chiefs of Staff, and the Office of the Secretary of Defense) to be filled out, saved, digitally signed, and submitted electronically. This new system is expected to save time and minimize the need for printed copies.

FIGURE 4-6

Digital forms. If the software supports it, the text handwritten on a digital form can be converted by the computer to typed text.

Digital Writing Systems

Digital writing systems are pen-based systems (such as the one shown in Figure 4-7, which is designed to facilitate student note taking) that capture handwritten input as it is being written. Typically, digital writing systems require the use of special paper that contains a grid of dots so the pen (which contains a camera) can determine what is being written or drawn on the paper and where that data was written on the paper. The handwritten input can be transferred to a computer, typically via a wireless connection when a Send button on the paper is selected or by docking the pen in its cradle attached to a computer. If the pen being used supports handwriting recognition capabilities and the necessary software is installed on the computer, the handwritten text can be converted to typed text.

FIGURE 4-7

Other uses for digital pens.

DIGITAL WRITING SYSTEMS
Record all input written on the paper and transfer it wirelessly to a computer upon demand.

GRAPHICS/PEN TABLETS
Transfer all input written or drawn on the tablet to the computer in real time and allow the use of pen flicks and other pen navigation tools.

SIGNATURE CAPTURE DEVICES
Record signatures for purchases, deliveries, and other applications that require recorded authorization.

Graphics Tablets

A **graphics tablet**—also called a *pen tablet* or *digitizing tablet*—is a flat, touch-sensitive tablet used in conjunction with a digital pen (see Figure 4-7). The graphics tablet is typically connected to a computer via a USB port and anything drawn or written on the graphics tablet is automatically transferred to the connected computer. The graphics tablet can also be used to issue commands to the computer. Graphic artists, photographers, and other graphics professionals often use graphics tablets in conjunction with *image editing software* to create original images or to modify digital photographs. Graphics tablets can also be used to add overall pen capabilities to a computer.

Signature Capture Devices

Another type of pen-based input device is the *signature capture device* (see Figure 4-7). These devices are found most often at checkout counters to record signatures used to authorize credit card purchases electronically. Delivery companies, restaurants, retail stores, and other service businesses may also use a signature capture device—or a portable computer with a stylus and appropriate software—to record authorizing signatures.

Touch Screens

Touch screens allow the user to touch the screen with his or her finger to select commands or otherwise provide input to the computer associated with the touch screen. Their use is becoming common with devices such as personal computers, mobile phones, mobile devices, and consumer kiosks (see Figure 4-8) in order to provide easy input. Some touch screens (such as the one used on the Apple iPhone 3G) are *multi-touch*; that is, they can recognize input from more than one finger at a time. Similar multi-touch products are used for large wall displays, such as for use in

ASK THE EXPERT

Martin Smekal, President and Founder, TabletKiosk

What do you expect to be the optimal input device of the future?

Right now, touch screens are gaining major momentum in enterprise business communities. Companies are recognizing that touch screen applications can increase productivity and that the mode of input is extremely intuitive. Ideally, the optimal device for mobile computing will incorporate both touch screen and digital ink capabilities. The touch function will be used for menu-driven applications like restaurant point-of-sale systems and multiple choice survey questionnaires, and the inking capabilities will be used for handwriting recognition.

FIGURE 4-8
Touch screens.

DESKTOP COMPUTERS

MOBILE DEVICES

SURFACE COMPUTING DEVICES

CONSUMER KIOSKS

> **Graphics tablet.** A flat, rectangular input device that is used in conjunction with a stylus to transfer drawings, sketches, and anything written on the device to a computer. > **Touch screen.** A display device that is touched with the finger to issue commands or otherwise provide input to the connected device.

ONLINE VIDEO

Go to the Chapter 4 page at **www.cengage.com/ computerconcepts/np/uc13** to watch the "A Look at Gesture and Multi-Touch Displays" video clip.

museums, government command centers, and newsrooms. For instance, CNN's multi-touch *Magic Wall* was used extensively during the 2008 elections to display maps, photos, videos, charts, and other data during broadcasts, and a similar *Weather Wall* is used by Al Roker on his new *Wake Up with Al* show on The Weather Channel.

One new trend in touch screens is referred to as *surface computing*—using a combination of multi-touch input from multiple users and object recognition to interact with computers that are typically built into tabletops and other surfaces. One example is *Microsoft Surface*. This product (shown in Figure 4-8) uses touch and gestures performed via the screen, as well as objects placed on the screen, as input. It can recognize input from multiple users and multiple objects placed on the table simultaneously. According to Panos Panay, the general manager of Microsoft Surface, Microsoft Surface breaks down the barriers between people and technology—moving beyond the traditional mouse and keyboard experience to blend the physical and virtual worlds—and allows for effortless interaction with digital information in a simple, intuitive way.

Touch screens are also used in consumer kiosks and other point-of-sale (POS) systems, and they are useful for on-the-job applications (such as factory work) where it might be impractical to use a keyboard or mouse. A growing trend is to use touch screens that provide *tactile feedback*—a slight movement or other physical sensation in response to the users' touch so they know their input has been received by the computer. For a closer look at how touch screens work, see the How It Works box. While touch screens make many devices today (computers, mobile phones, televisions, and many other consumer electronics) more convenient for the majority of individuals to use, there is also concern that these devices and their applications are not accessible to blind individuals, users with limited mobility, and other individuals with a disability; accessibility is discussed in detail in Chapter 16.

Other Pointing Devices

A few other common pointing devices are described next and shown in Figure 4-9. In addition to these and the other pointing devices discussed in this chapter, pointing devices specifically designed for users with limited mobility are available. These pointing devices—along with *ergonomic keyboards*, *Braille keyboards*, and other types of input devices designed for users with special needs—are discussed in Chapter 16.

Gaming Devices

A variety of gaming devices today (such as the ones shown in Figure 4-9) can be used as controllers to supply input to a computer. For instance, the stick of a *joystick* can be moved with the hand to move an on-screen object (such as a player or vehicle in a game) and the buttons pressed to perform their assigned functions (such as jumping or firing a weapon). *Gamepads* perform similar functions but are held in the hand instead; *steering wheels* are also available for driving games. There are also input devices designed to be used with gaming consoles, such as the Wii, Xbox 360, and Playstation 3. These include gamepads and steering wheels; guitars, drums, and other musical instruments; dance pads and balance boards, and other motion sensitive controllers; and proprietary controllers such as the *Wii Remote* used with the Nintendo Wii gaming system.

Guitar controller

Joystick

Gamepad

Steering wheel

GAMING DEVICES
Most often used for gaming applications.

Trackballs

Similar to an upside-down mechanical mouse, a *trackball* has the ball mechanism on top, instead of on the bottom. The ball is rotated with the thumb, hand, or finger to move the on-screen pointer. Because the device itself does not need to be moved, trackballs take up less space on the desktop than mice; they also are easier to use for individuals with limited hand or finger mobility.

Thumb wheel

Select button

BUTTONS AND WHEELS
Commonly found on portable digital media players and other consumer devices.

TOUCH PADS
Commonly found on notebook and netbook computers.

FIGURE 4-9
Other common pointing devices.

Buttons and Wheels

Many consumer devices today, such as portable digital media players, GPS devices, and handheld gaming devices, use special buttons and wheels to select items and issue commands to the device. For instance, the portable digital media player shown in Figure 4-9 contains a *thumb wheel* that is rotated to navigate through menus and a *select button* that is used to select items in order to access music and other content stored on the device.

Touch Pads

A **touch pad** is a rectangular pad across which a fingertip or thumb slides to move the on-screen pointer; tapping the touch pad typically performs clicks and other mouse actions. Although most often found on notebook and netbook computers (see Figure 4-9), touch pads are also available as stand-alone devices to be used with desktop computers and are built into some keyboards.

> **Touch pad.** A small rectangular-shaped input device, often found on notebook computers, that is touched with the finger or thumb to control an on-screen pointer and make selections.

HOW IT WORKS

Touch Screens

A touch screen typically has three main components. First, a *touch responsive surface* is needed. Typically, touch screens today use clear (often glass) touch sensitive panels that have an electrical current or charge passing over them whenever the touch screen is on. While there are various methods that can be used to detect the touch input, usually touching the screen causes a voltage or signal change that is registered by the touch screen. Next, a *touch screen controller* uses this data to determine the physical location on the screen that the user touched and passes that information on to the computer being used with the touch screen. Finally, special software determines how to interpret the touch information sent from the controller; for example, to identify the option on the screen that the user selected (such as an item to be purchased) and what action to take as the result of the input (such as adding that item to the individual's order).

One type of touch screen (a *capacitive touch screen*) is shown in the accompanying illustration. Using this method of touch input, a small amount of voltage is present in the four corners of the touch screen at all times when the screen is on. Touching the screen draws a small amount of current from the corners of the screen to the point of contact, allowing the touch screen controller to determine the location on the screen that the user touched and then pass that information on to the computer to determine the appropriate action to be taken.

1. A small amount of voltage is applied to the four corners of the touch screen while it is on.

2. The user's finger draws a tiny amount of current from the corners to the point of contact.

3. The circuitry inside the touch screen uses the voltage change to determine the exact location on the screen that the user touched.

SCANNERS, READERS, AND DIGITAL CAMERAS

There are a variety of input devices designed to capture data in digital form so a computer can manipulate it. Some of these devices (such as *scanners* and *readers*) are designed to convert data that already exists in physical form (such as on *source documents* like order forms, photographs, invoices, checks, ID cards, or shipping labels); others (such as *digital cameras* and the digital writing systems already discussed) capture data initially in digital form. Automating the data entry process is referred to as *source data automation* and can refer to capturing data electronically from a source document or entering data directly into a computer at the time and place the data is generated (see Figure 4-10).

Source data automation can save a great deal of time and is much more accurate than recording the data on paper and then later entering it into a computer via a keyboard. It also allows the people who know the most about the events that the data represents to be the ones who input the data, which helps increase accuracy during the data-entry process. For instance, an insurance adjuster or auto mechanic entering data directly into a computer about the condition of a car involved in an accident will likely have fewer input errors than if he or she records that data on paper, and then an assistant keys the data into a computer later.

Many devices used in source data automation are *scanning* or *reading devices*, that is, devices that scan or read printed text, codes, or graphics, and then translate the results into digital form. The next few sections discuss several different types of scanning and reading devices, followed by a look at *digital cameras*, which capture images in digital form.

Scanners

A **scanner**, more officially called an *optical scanner*, captures an image of an object (usually a flat object, such as a printed document, photograph, or drawing) in digital form, and then transfers that data to a computer. Typically, the entire document (including both text and images) is input as a single graphical image that can be resized, inserted into other documents, posted on a Web page, e-mailed to someone, printed, or otherwise treated like any other graphical image. The text in the scanned image, however, cannot be edited unless *optical character recognition (OCR)* software is used in conjunction with the scanner to input the scanned text as individual text characters.

Individuals frequently use scanners to input printed photographs and other personal documents into a computer. Businesses are increasingly using scanners to convert paper documents into electronic format for archival or document processing purposes. Most scanners scan in color and some are *duplex scanners*—that is, they can scan both sides of a document at one time. The most common types of scanners are discussed next.

RECORDING DATA DIRECTLY INTO A COMPUTER

CAPTURING DATA FROM ITS SOURCE DOCUMENT

FIGURE 4-10
Source data automation. Recording data initially in digital form or capturing data directly from a source document can help reduce data input errors and save time.

Types of Scanners

Flatbed scanners are designed to scan flat objects one page at a time, and they are the most common type of scanner. Flatbed scanners work in much the same way that photocopiers do—whatever is being scanned remains stationary while the scanning mechanism moves underneath it to capture the image (see Figure 4-11). Some scanners can scan slides and

FIGURE 4-11
Optical scanners.

FLATBED SCANNERS
Used to input photos, sketches, slides, book pages, and other relatively flat documents into the computer.

PORTABLE SCANNERS
Used to capture small amounts of text; the text is typically transferred to a computer at a later time.

INTEGRATED SCANNERS
Built into other devices, such as into the ATM machine shown here to capture images of deposited checks.

>**Scanner.** An input device that reads printed text and graphics and transfers them to a computer in digital form. >**Flatbed scanner.** An input device that scans flat objects one at a time.

film negatives, in addition to printed documents. Scanners designed for high-volume business processing come with automatic document feeders so that large quantities of paper documents can be scanned (one page after the other) with a single command.

Portable scanners are designed to capture text and other data while on the go. Some are *full-page portable scanners* that can capture images of an entire document (such as a printed document or receipt) encountered while on the go; others are *handheld scanners* designed to capture text one line at a time (such as the one shown in Figure 4-11). In either case, the scanner is typically powered by batteries, the scanned content is stored in the scanner, and the content is transferred to a computer (via a cable or a wireless connection) when needed. Some handheld scanners can also be used to translate scanned text from one language to another.

Multimedia, medical, and some business applications may require the use of a *three-dimensional (3D) scanner*, which can scan an item or person in 3D. Task-specific scanners, such as *receipt scanners* and *business card scanners*, are also available. In addition, scanning hardware is being incorporated into a growing number of products, such as ATM machines to scan the images of checks deposited into the machine (refer again to Figure 4-11); typically, the check images are printed on the deposit receipt and can be viewed online via online banking services.

FIGURE 4-12

Scanning resolution.

96 dpi
(833 KB)

300 dpi
(1,818 KB)

600 dpi
(5,374 KB)

RESOLUTION

Most scanners let you specify the resolution (in dpi) to use for the scan. High-resolution images look sharper but result in larger file sizes.

Scanning Quality and Resolution

The quality of scanned images is indicated by *optical resolution*, usually measured in the number of *dots per inch* (*dpi*). When a document is scanned (typically using scanning software, though some application programs allow you to scan images directly into that program), the resolution of the scanned image can often be specified. The resolution of a scanned image can also be specified when the image is saved or if it is modified at a later time using an image editing program. Scanners today usually scan at between 2,400 × 2,400 dpi and 4,800 × 9,600 dpi. A higher resolution results in a better image but also results in a larger file size, as illustrated in Figure 4-12. A higher resolution is needed, however, if the image is to be enlarged significantly or if only one part of the image is to be extracted and enlarged. The file size of a scanned image is also determined in part by the physical size of the image. Once an image has been scanned, it can usually be resized and then saved in the appropriate file format and resolution for the application with which the image is to be used. Scanners can cost anywhere from less than one hundred dollars to several thousand dollars.

Readers

A variety of *readers* are available to read the different types of codes and marks used today, as well as to read an individual's *biometric* characteristics. Some of the most common readers are discussed next.

Barcode Readers

A **barcode** is an *optical code* that represents data with bars of varying widths or heights. Two of the most familiar barcodes are *UPC* (*Universal Product Code*), the barcode found on packaged goods in supermarkets and other retail stores, and *ISBN* (*International Standard Book Number*), the type of barcode used with printed books (see Figure 4-13). A new barcode for small consumer goods like fresh foods and jewelry is the *DataBar*,

---

> **Portable scanner.** A scanner designed to capture input while on the go. > **Barcode.** A machine-readable code that represents data as a set of bars.

also shown in Figure 4-13. Businesses and organizations can also create and use custom barcodes to fulfill their unique needs. For instance, shipping organizations (such as FedEx and UPS) use custom barcodes to mark and track packages, retailers (such as Target and Wal-Mart) use custom barcodes added to customer receipts to facilitate returns, hospitals use custom barcodes to match patients with their charts and medicines, libraries and video stores use custom barcodes for checking out and checking in books and movies, and law enforcement agencies use custom barcodes to mark evidence. In fact, any business with a *barcode printer* and appropriate software can create custom barcodes for use with its products or to classify items (such as paper files or equipment) used within its organization. The most popular barcode for these types of nonfood use is *Code 39*, which can encode both letters and numbers. Examples of the Code 39 barcode and the *Intelligent Mail barcode* (used by the U.S. Postal Service to represent destination ZIP codes, as well as shipper IDs and other identifying data specified by the shipper) are shown in Figure 4-13.

These conventional types of barcodes are referred to as *one-dimension (1D) barcodes* because they contain data only horizontally, in one direction. Newer *two-dimensional (2D) barcodes* store information both horizontally and vertically and can hold significantly more data—up to several hundred times more. One of the most common 2D barcodes—the *QR (Quick Response) code* that represents data with a matrix of small bars—is also shown in Figure 4-13. Today, 2D barcodes are beginning to be used by consumers with mobile phones for activities such as viewing a video clip or photo (stored either in the code or online) or downloading a coupon or ticket when the barcode is captured with the phone's camera. In Japan, 2D barcodes are even beginning to appear on tombstones to enable graveside visitors to access information about the deceased via their mobile phones.

Barcodes are read with **barcode readers**. Barcode readers use either light reflected from the barcode or imaging technology to interpret the bars contained in the barcode as the numbers or letters they represent. Then, data associated with that barcode—typically identifying data, such as data used to uniquely identify a product, shipped package, or other item—can be retrieved. *Fixed* barcode readers are frequently used in point-of-sale (POS) systems (see Figure 4-14); *portable* barcode readers are also available for individuals who

ISBN CODES

UPC (UNIVERSAL PRODUCT CODE) CODES

DATABAR CODES

INTELLIGENT MAIL CODES

123ABC

CODE 39 CODES

QR CODES

FIGURE 4-13
Common types of barcodes.

FIGURE 4-14
Barcode readers.

FIXED BARCODE READERS
Used most often in retail point-of-sale applications.

PORTABLE BARCODE READERS
Used when portability is needed.

INTEGRATED BARCODE READERS
Used most often for consumer applications.

>**Barcode reader.** An input device that reads barcodes.

need to scan barcodes while on the go, such as while walking through a warehouse, retail store, hospital, or other facility. In addition, barcode reading capabilities can be integrated into portable computers and mobile devices, such as by adding a barcode reader attachment (like the one shown in Figure 2-18 in Chapter 2) or by downloading a barcode reading software program to a camera phone (such as the one shown in Figure 4-14).

Radio Frequency Identification (RFID) Readers

Radio frequency identification (RFID) is a technology that can store, read, and transmit data located in **RFID tags**. RFID tags contain tiny chips and radio antennas (see Figure 4-15); they can be attached to objects, such as products, price tags, shipping labels, ID cards, assets (such as livestock, vehicles, computers, and other expensive equipment), and more. The data in RFID tag is read by **RFID readers**. Whenever an RFID-tagged item is within range of an RFID reader (from two inches to up to 300 feet or more, depending on the type of tag and the frequency being used), the tag's built-in antenna allows the information located within the RFID tag to be sent to the reader. Unlike barcodes, RFID tags only need to be within range (not within line of sight) of a reader. This enables RFID readers to read the data stored in many RFID tags at the same time and read them through cardboard and other materials—a definite advantage for shipping and inventory applications. Another advantage over barcodes is that the RFID tag attached to each item is unique (unlike UPC codes, for instance, that have the same code on all instances of a single product), so each tag can be identified individually and the data can be updated as needed. RFID technology is cost-prohibitive for low-cost items at the present time; however, the many advantages RFID has over barcodes make it possible that RFID may eventually replace barcodes on product labels and price tags—especially as the costs associated with RFID technology go down and its usage becomes even more commonplace. Because RFID technology can read numerous items at one time, it is also possible that, someday, RFID will allow a consumer to perform self-checkout at a retail store by just pushing a shopping cart past an RFID reader, which will ring up all items in the cart at one time.

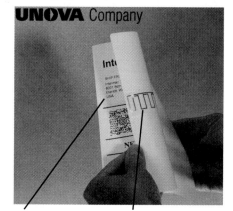

Label for
shipping carton

RFID circuitry
(chip and antenna)

FIGURE 4-15
RFID tags.

RFID is used today for many different applications (see Figure 4-16 for some examples). Some of the initial RFID applications were tracking the movement of products and shipping containers during transit, managing inventory in retail stores, tagging pets and livestock, and tracking tractors and other large assets. Many of these applications use GPS technology in conjunction with the RFID tags to provide location information for the objects to which the tags are attached. For several years now, RFID has also been used for *electronic toll collection* (automatically deducting highway tolls from a payment account when an RFID-tagged car drives past the tollbooth). More recent RFID applications include tracking patients at hospitals, increasing efficiency in ticketing applications (such as train passes, concert tickets, and ski lift tickets), and speeding up the identification process of travelers at border crossings. In the United States, for instance, several states are issuing *enhanced driver's licenses* that contain RFID chips, and all *U.S. Passports* and *U.S. Passport Cards* issued today contain RFID chips. RFID is also used to facilitate *electronic payments* via RFID-enabled credit cards or mobile phones that support *Near Field Communications* (*NFC*)—a short-range wireless communication standard used in conjunction with RFID and mobile phones. For security purposes, *high-frequency RFID chips* (which requires the item containing the RFID chip to be within an inch or so of the reader) are used in electronic payment applications. Electronic payments, NFC, and *mobile commerce* are discussed in more detail in Chapter 11.

In addition, because RFID chips can be updated during the life of a product (such as to record information about a product's origin, shipping history, and the temperature range the item has been exposed to), and because that information can be read when needed (such as at a product's final destination), RFID is being used by prescription drug manufacturers to comply with government mandates, which require that the drugs be tracked throughout their life cycles. While not mandated yet (though some believe it is just a matter of time), RFID is also beginning to be used to implement life cycle tracking of food products in response to the recent food poisoning outbreaks. For instance, Hawaii recently implemented a three-year pilot RFID initiative to track all fresh produce throughout the state in order to obtain information about the grower, pesticides used, time in cold storage, and other factors when needed, as well as to facilitate recalls. RFID is also used extensively by the military, primarily for asset tracking.

INVENTORY TRACKING
This portal RFID reader reads all of the RFID tags attached to all of the items on the palette at one time.

TICKETING APPLICATIONS
This stationary RFID reader is used to automatically open ski lift entry gates for valid lift ticket holders at a ski resort in Utah.

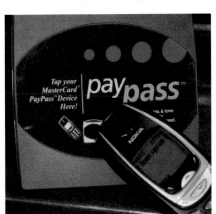

MOBILE PAYMENTS
This stationary RFID reader is used at checkout locations to quickly process payments via RFID-enabled credit cards or mobile phones.

BORDER SECURITY
This stationary RFID reader is used at the U.S.-Mexico border crossing located in San Diego to reduce wait time.

FIGURE 4-16
RFID applications.

A variety of RFID readers—including *handheld*, *portal*, and *stationery RFID readers*—are available to fit the various RFID applications in use today. Handheld RFID readers are used by workers to read RFID tags on the go or to read RFID-enabled tickets at a venue entrance. Portal RFID readers are used to read all the RFID tags located on all the products located inside sealed shipping boxes on a palette at one time when the palette passes through the portal. Stationary RFID readers are used at checkstands, border crossings, and other locations where RFID tags need to be read on a continual basis. A portal reader and a few stationary readers are shown in Figure 4-16.

Despite all its advantages, a number of privacy and security issues need to be resolved before RFID gains widespread use at the consumer level. Precautions against fraudulent use—such as using high-frequency tags that need to be within a few inches of the reader, and requiring a *PIN code*, signature, or other type of authorization when an RFID payment system is used—are being developed. Currently, a price limit (such as $25) for completely automated purchases (without a signature or other authorization) is being debated as a compromise between convenience and security. Privacy advocates are concerned about linking RFID tag data with personally-identifiable data contained in corporate databases, such as to track consumer movements or shopping habits. As of now, no long-term solution to this issue has been reached.

CAUTION CAUTION CAUTION CAUTION CAUTION CAUTION CAUT

Keep your enhanced driver's license and passport in the supplied protective sleeve when not in use to protect against unauthorized reading or tracking. While currently no personal data is stored in the RFID chips used in these documents, hackers have demonstrated the ability to read these documents if they are not properly shielded. Because of this, privacy advocates recommend taking this precaution with any RFID-enabled identity document.

FIGURE 4-17

Optical mark readers (OMRs).

OMRs are commonly used to score tests and tally questionnaires.

Optical Mark Readers (OMRs)

Optical mark readers (OMRs) input data from special forms to score or tally exams, questionnaires, ballots, and so forth. Typically, you use a pencil to fill in small circles or other shapes on the form to indicate your selections, and then the form is inserted into an optical mark reader (such as the one shown in Figure 4-17) to be scored or tallied. The results can be input into a computer system if the optical mark reader is connected to a computer.

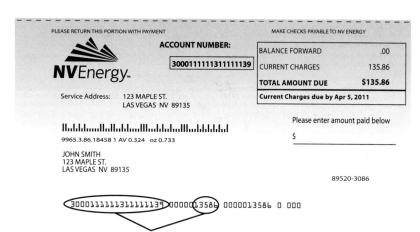

OPTICAL CHARACTERS

These OCR characters indicate the customer account number and amount due and can be read by both computers and humans.

FIGURE 4-18

Optical characters.

The most common use of optical characters is in turnaround documents, such as on the utility bill shown here.

Optical Character Recognition (OCR) Devices

Optical character recognition (OCR) refers to the ability of a computer to recognize text characters. The characters are read by a compatible scanning device, such as a flatbed scanner, barcode reader, or dedicated *OCR reader*, and then *OCR software* is used to identify each character and convert it to editable text. While OCR systems can recognize many typed fonts, *optical characters*—which are characters specifically designed to be identifiable by humans as well as by an OCR device—are often used on documents intended to be processed by an OCR system. For example, optical characters are widely used in processing *turnaround documents*, such as the monthly bills for credit card and utility companies (see Figure 4-18). These documents contain optical characters in certain places on the bill to aid processing when consumers send it back with payment—or "turn it around."

Magnetic Ink Character Recognition (MICR) Readers

Magnetic ink character recognition (MICR) is a technology used primarily by the banking industry to facilitate check processing. MICR characters (such as those located on the bottom of a check that represent the bank routing number, check number, and account number) are inscribed on checks with magnetic ink when the checks are first printed.

>**Optical character recognition (OCR).** The ability of a computer to recognize scanned text characters and convert them to electronic form as text, not images.

TECHNOLOGY AND YOU

Mobile Phone Check Deposits

You use your mobile phone today for a wide number of functions—such as phone calls, texting, accessing Web information, and storing music and photos—but depositing your paychecks? Yes, now you can, thanks to a new technology developed by Mitek Systems.

While the use of remote deposit by businesses is growing, this new technology opens the door to remote deposit by individuals. In order to make a remote deposit via your mobile phone, you need to have the mobile deposit application on your mobile phone (if it is not included in your mobile banking software, you can typically download it). To make a remote deposit, you simply need to log on to your mobile banking service, and then you can enter the amount of the check and use your phone's built-in camera to take a photo of the front and back of the check (see the accompanying photo) in order to deposit that check into your bank account. After the software optimizes the image and verifies it meets the Check 21 Law image standards, the check images and deposit data are transmitted to your bank and you receive a confirmation text message. The software can be used with virtually any mobile banking system and a secure connection is used to protect the data as it is being transmitted.

Mobile phone cameras can be used to submit check images for remote deposit.

These characters can be read and new characters (such as to reflect the check's amount) can be added by an *MICR reader* (also called a *check scanner*) when needed. High-volume MICR readers are used by banks to process checks deposited at the bank. Smaller units (such as the one shown in Figure 4-19) are used by many businesses to deposit paper checks remotely (referred to as *remote deposit* and permitted by the *Check 21 Law*, which allows financial institutions to exchange digital check images and process checks electronically). To make a remote deposit using an MICR reader, the check is scanned and then the check data is transmitted to the bank electronically for payment. There are also MICR readers incorporated in most new ATM machines today to enable the MICR information located on checks inserted into the ATM machine to be read at the time of the deposit.

Remote deposit and electronic check processing is a growing trend. It is faster and more convenient for businesses and individuals. It also helps the environment since, according to one estimate, a typical check travels 48 miles during processing, which results in an annual cost to the environment for check processing of more than 80,000 tons of paper used and more than 160 million gallons of fuel consumed. In addition to MICR readers, remote deposit can be performed by using a flat-bed scanner or, as discussed in the Technology and You box, even by using your mobile phone.

FIGURE 4-19

Magnetic ink character recognition (MICR) readers are used primarily to process checks.

STAND-ALONE FINGERPRINT READERS
Often used to control access to facilities or computer systems, such as to the notebook computer shown here.

BUILT-IN FINGERPRINT READERS
Typically used to control access to the device into which the reader is built, such as to the external hard drive shown here.

FIGURE 4-20
Biometric readers.

Biometric Readers

Biometrics is the science of identifying individuals based on measurable biological characteristics. **Biometric readers** are used to read biometric data about a person so that the individual's identity can be verified based on a particular unique physiological characteristic (such as a fingerprint or a face) or personal trait (such as a voice or a signature). As shown in Figure 4-20, a biometric reader can be stand-alone or built into another piece of hardware, such as a keyboard, a portable computer, an external hard drive, or a USB flash drive. Biometric readers can be used to allow only authorized users access to a computer or facility or to the data stored on a storage device, as well as to authorize electronic payments, log on to secure Web sites, or punch in and out of work. Biometrics used for access control is covered in more detail in Chapter 9.

ONLINE VIDEO

Go to the Chapter 4 page at **www.cengage.com/ computerconcepts/np/uc13** to watch the "How Mobile Deposit Works" video clip.

TIP

When comparing the zoom capabilities of a digital camera, look for *optical zoom*, not *digital zoom*, specifications. Optical zoom specifications reflect how much the camera can zoom without losing image quality.

Digital Cameras

Digital cameras work much like conventional film cameras, but instead of recording images on film they record them on a digital storage medium, such as a flash memory card, digital tape cartridge, built-in hard drive, or DVD disc. Digital cameras are usually designated either as *still* cameras (which take individual still photos) or *video* cameras (which capture moving video images), although many cameras today take both still images and video. In addition to stand-alone still and video cameras, digital camera capabilities are integrated into many portable computers and mobile phones today.

Digital Still Cameras

Digital still cameras are available in a wide variety of sizes and capabilities, such as inexpensive point-and-shoot digital cameras designed for consumers, professional digital cameras, and digital cameras integrated into mobile phones and other mobile devices (see Figure 4-21). Consumer digital cameras start at about $50; professional digital cameras can cost several thousand dollars each.

The primary appeal of digital still cameras is that the images are immediately available for viewing or printing, instead of having to have the film developed first. One disadvantage of digital cameras is the slight delay between when the user presses the button and when the camera takes the photo, which is especially important when taking action shots. Although not yet as quick as conventional film cameras, the delay typically associated with digital cameras is continually being made shorter. Digital still cameras most often use flash memory cards for storage; the number of digital photos that can be stored at one

---

>**Biometric reader.** A device used to input biometric data, such as an individual's fingerprint or voice. >**Digital camera.** An input device that takes pictures and records them as digital images.

time depends on the capacity of the card being used, as well as the photo resolution being used.

Photos taken with a digital camera are typically transferred to a computer or printer via the flash memory card containing the images or by connecting the camera to the computer or printer using a wired or wireless connection. Some digital cameras and flash memory cards can even connect directly to photo sharing Web sites via a *Wi-Fi* connection, as discussed in the Chapter 7 Trend box, to upload your photos automatically as they are taken. Once the photos have been transferred to a computer, they can be retouched with image editing software, saved, printed, posted to a Web page, or burned onto a CD or DVD disc, just like any other digital image. The images on the storage medium can be deleted at any time to make room for more photos.

One factor affecting digital camera quality is the number of pixels (measured in *megapixels* or millions of pixels) used to store the data for each image. Today's cameras are typically between 6 and 20 megapixels. Although other factors—such as the quality of the lens and the technology used inside the camera to capture and process images—also affect the quality of digital photographs, the number of pixels does impact how large the digital photos can be printed. For instance, to print high-quality 8 by 10-inch or larger prints, at least a 5-megapixel camera is needed.

The integration of digital cameras into most mobile phones today has many advantages, such as the ability to keep your friends up to date about your current activities; to take photos of car accidents and other incidents for authorities; and to read barcodes, remotely deposit checks, and facilitate gesture input, as discussed earlier in this chapter. However, they have also created new ethical problems in our society, such as the ability to take and distribute compromising photos. For instance, there have been many cases of individuals using camera phones to take and distribute compromising photos of others, as well as cases of teenagers using camera phones to send compromising photos of themselves to others (a form of *sexting*, as discussed in more detail in Chapter 9).

PREVIEWS
Virtually all digital cameras let you display and erase images.

STORAGE MEDIA
Most cameras use removable storage media in addition to, or instead of, built-in storage.

TYPICAL CONSUMER DIGITAL CAMERAS

PROFESSIONAL DIGITAL CAMERAS

DIGITAL CAMERAS INTEGRATED INTO MOBILE PHONES

FIGURE 4-21
Digital cameras.
Digital cameras, which record images on digital media instead of on film, are available in many shapes and sizes.

ASK THE EXPERT

SanDisk **Tanya Chuang,** Director of Worldwide Retail Product Marketing, High Performance Imaging, SanDisk

Does the speed of the flash memory card in a digital camera affect the delay factor when taking a digital photo?

The performance is important for both the camera and card. If you have a fast camera but a slow card, or vice versa, you can miss some great shots. If you've ever pressed the shutter button and have had to wait for 5 seconds to take a picture, you'll understand the frustration. At one point, up to early 2000, the cards were too slow. Now, the memory cards are much faster than the cameras so it's important to have the right card for your camera.

HW

DIGITAL CAMCORDERS
Typically store video on a built-in hard drive (as in this camera) or on DVD discs.

FIGURE 4-22
Digital video cameras.

Stand-alone video camera

PC VIDEO CAMERAS
Commonly used to deliver video over the Internet, such as in the video chat session shown here.

Digital Video Cameras

Digital video cameras (see Figure 4-22) include *digital camcorders* and small digital video cameras used in conjunction with computers and other devices. Digital video cameras are often built into portable computers and mobile devices, but they are also available as stand-alone devices that typically connect via a USB port. Digital camcorders are similar to conventional *analog* camcorders, but they store images on digital media—typically on built-in hard drives or rewritable DVDs for conventional-sized camcorders or on flash memory for pocket-sized camcorders. Many mobile phones also include digital video capabilities. Once a video is recorded, it can be transferred to a computer, edited with software as needed, and saved to a DVD or other type of storage medium. It can also be *compressed* (made smaller), if needed, and then uploaded to video-sharing sites, such as YouTube. Some digital video cameras today can take high-definition (HD) video. Video cameras used with personal computers—commonly called *PC cams* or *Web cams*—are typically used to transmit still or video images over the Internet (such as during a *Web conference* or *video phone call*) or to broadcast images continually to a Web page.

Both individuals and businesses commonly use digital video cameras today. Typical personal applications include recording home movies with a digital camcorder and making video phone calls with a PC cam. An emerging personal application is using special *home surveillance video cameras* for security purposes—such as to monitor an empty house or keep an eye on a sleeping baby. Typically, these systems either transmit the video via the Internet to a computer or mobile device, or via a wireless connection to a special display device located in the home. Their use is growing and has had some initial success. In 2009, for instance, a woman checked her home surveillance video via the Internet while at work, saw her house being robbed, and notified the police, who were able to catch the individuals in her house and charge them with burglary. Businesses also often use digital video cameras for security applications, as well as to create videos for marketing purposes and to perform *videoconferences* and *Webinars* (seminars that take place via the Web). Digital video cameras can also be used for identification purposes, such as with the *face recognition technology* used to authorize access to a secure facility or computer resource via an individual's face, as discussed in more detail in Chapter 9.

AUDIO INPUT

Audio input is the process of entering audio data into the computer. The most common types of audio input are voice and music.

Voice Input and Speech Recognition Systems

Voice input—inputting spoken words and converting them to digital form—is typically performed via a *microphone* or *headset* (a set of *headphones* with a built-in microphone). It can be used in conjunction with *sound recorder software* to store the voice in an audio file, such as to create a *podcast*—a recorded audio file that is distributed via the Internet, as discussed in Chapter 8, as well as with *Voice over IP systems* that allow individuals to place telephone calls from a computer over the Internet. It can also be used in conjunction with *speech recognition software* to provide spoken instructions to a computer.

Speech recognition systems enable the computer to recognize voice input as spoken words and require appropriate software, such as *Dragon NaturallySpeaking* or *Windows Speech Recognition*. With speech recognition, voice input can be used to control the computer, such as opening and closing programs, selecting options from a menu or list, and moving the insertion point. It can also be used to input and edit text, including dictating text to be typed, selecting text to be formatted or edited, deleting text, correcting errors, and so forth. Voice input systems are used by individuals who cannot use a keyboard, as well as by individuals who prefer not to use a keyboard or who can generate input faster via a voice input system. For instance, medical and legal transcription is the most frequently used voice input application at the present time.

To enable hands-free operation, speech recognition capabilities are increasingly incorporated into mobile phones, GPS systems, and other mobile devices. They are also commonly built into cars to enable hands-free control of navigation systems and sound systems, as well as to allow hands-free mobile phone calls to take place via the car's voice interface. Specialty speech recognition systems are frequently used to control machines, robots, and other electronic equipment, such as by surgeons during surgical procedures.

With a typical speech recognition system (see Figure 4-23), a microphone is used to input the spoken words into the computer, and then the sounds are broken into digital representations of *phonemes*—the basic elements of speech, such as *duh*, *aw*, and *guh* for the word *dog*. Next, the speech recognition software analyzes the content of the speech to convert the phonemes to words. Once words are identified, they are displayed on the screen. If a match is questionable or a homonym is encountered (such as the choice between *two*, *too*, and *to*), the program analyzes the context in which the word is used in an attempt to identify the correct word. If the program inserts an inappropriate word while converting the user's voice input to text, the user can correct it. To increase accuracy, most speech recognition software can be trained by individual users to allow the program to become accustomed to the user's speech patterns, voice, accent, and pronunciation.

The basic concept of speech recognition is also being applied to other audio input applications that enable computers and devices to recognize sounds other than voice. For instance, one type of *sound recognition* system located inside a computer could monitor the sound a hard drive is making to detect a possible malfunction before it happens, and another type could be used in conjunction with security systems to "listen" for the sound of a door opening or other suspicious sounds in order to alert security personnel.

FIGURE 4-23

Speech recognition systems.

2. An analog-to-digital converter on the sound card located inside the computer converts the spoken words to phonemes, the fundamental sounds in the language being used, and digitizes them.

The patient exhibits signs of...

The patient exhibits signs of|

1. The user speaks into a microphone that cancels out background noise and inputs the speech into the computer.

4. The spoken words appear on the screen in the application program (such as a word processor or an e-mail program) being used.

3. Voice recognition software determines the words that were spoken.

> **Speech recognition system.** A system, consisting of appropriate hardware and software, used to recognize voice input, such as dictation or audio computer commands.

Music Input Systems

Music input systems are used to input music into a computer, such as to create an original music composition or arrangement, or to create a custom music CD. Existing music can be input into a computer via a music CD or a Web download. For original compositions, microphones and *keyboard controllers*—essentially piano keyboards connected to a computer—can be used (see Figure 4-24). Original music compositions can also be created using a conventional computer keyboard with appropriate software or a special device (such as a microphone or digital pen) designed to input music and convert it to a printed musical score. Once the music is input into the computer, it can be saved, modified, played, inserted into other programs, or burned to a CD or DVD.

FIGURE 4-24

Music input systems. Musicians can input original compositions into a computer via microphones, MIDI keyboards, and other devices.

DISPLAY DEVICES

A **display device**—the most common form of output device—presents output visually on some type of screen. Because the output appears temporarily on a display device, it is sometimes referred to as *soft copy*. The display device for a desktop computer is more formally called a **monitor**; the display device for a notebook computer, netbook computer, UMPC, mobile phone, or other device for which the screen is built into the device is typically called a **display screen**. In addition to being used with computers and mobile devices, display screens are also built into handheld gaming devices, home entertainment devices (like remote controls, televisions, and portable DVD players) and kitchen appliances. They are also an important component in *digital photo frames* (stand-alone or wall mounted photo frames, which display digital photos that are typically transferred to the frame via a flash memory card or a wireless networking connection), *e-book readers* (which display electronic versions of books), portable digital media players, and other consumer products (see Figure 4-25).

Display screens also appear in public locations on *digital signage systems*—digital signs whose content can be changed throughout the day as needed. The content displayed on a digital sign can be graphics or video sent from a computer, video streamed via a camera, live Internet content, and more. For instance, the digital signage system shown in Figure 4-25 is located in Times Square in New York and displays advertising clips, live broadcasts, public service announcements, and video of special events taking place at Times Square in the main screen at the top of the display, and real-time CNN.com news feeds and weather forecasts in the bottom screen. In addition to these types of *digital billboard* applications, digital signage systems are also frequently used in office buildings and convention centers (such as for directories and other information), in retail stores and restaurants (to advertise specials and to display menus, for instance), on consumer kiosks, in lecture halls, and in sporting arenas. They are even found in displays used to target advertising to consumers when they are waiting in a checkout line, riding in an elevator or taxi, stopped at a traffic light, or some other location where they are captive for a few minutes—a trend referred to as *captive marketing*.

Display Device Characteristics

Several characteristics and features differentiate one type of display device from another. The following sections discuss a few of the most significant characteristics.

ONLINE VIDEO

Go to the Chapter 4 page at **www.cengage.com/ computerconcepts/np/uc13** to watch the "An Introduction to Digital Signage" video clip.

>**Display device.** An output device that contains a viewing screen. >**Monitor.** A display device for a desktop computer. >**Display screen.** A display device built into a notebook computer, netbook, UMPC, or other device.

PORTABLE COMPUTERS

HANDHELD GAMING DEVICES

DIGITAL PHOTO FRAMES

MOBILE DEVICES

DIGITAL SIGNAGE SYSTEMS

FIGURE 4-25
Uses for display devices.

Color vs. Monochrome Displays

Display devices form images by lighting up the proper configurations of **pixels** (the smallest colorable areas on a display device—essentially tiny dots on a display screen). A variety of technologies can be used to light up the appropriate pixels needed to display a particular image, as discussed shortly. Display devices can be *monochrome displays* (in which each pixel can only be one of two colors, such as black or white) or *color displays* (in which each pixel can display a combination of three colors—red, green, and blue—in order to display a large range of colors). Most monitors and display devices today are color displays.

CRT Monitors vs. Flat-Panel Displays

The **CRT monitor** used to be the norm for desktop computers. CRT monitors use the same *cathode-ray tube* technology used in conventional televisions in which an electron gun sealed inside a large glass tube projects an electron beam at a screen coated with red, green, and blue phosphor dots; the beam lights up the appropriate colors in each pixel to display the necessary image. As a result, CRTs are large, bulky, and heavy.

>**Pixel.** The smallest colorable area in an electronic image, such as a scanned image, a digital photograph, or an image displayed on a display screen. >**CRT monitor.** A type of display device that projects images onto a display screen using a technology similar to the one used with conventional TVs.

Four flat-panel monitors.

⚠ **FIGURE 4-26**

Flat-panel displays.
The smaller footprint of a flat-panel display makes it possible to use multiple monitors together with a single computer to increase productivity.

While CRT monitors are still in use, most computers today (as well as most television sets) use the thinner and lighter **flat-panel displays**. Flat-panel display technology is also used in the display screens integrated into mobile phones and consumer electronics. As discussed in more detail shortly, flat-panel displays form images by manipulating electronically charged chemicals or gases sandwiched between thin panes of glass or other transparent material. Flat-panel displays take up less desk space, which makes it possible to use multiple monitors working together to increase the amount of data the user can view at one time (see Figure 4-26), increasing productivity. Flat-panel displays also consume less power than CRTs and most use digital signals to display images (instead of the analog signals used with CRT monitors), which allows for sharper images. To use multiple monitors, you must have the necessary hardware to support it, such as a monitor port on a notebook computer or an appropriate video adapter, as discussed shortly. One disadvantage to a flat-panel display is that the images displayed on a flat-panel display sometimes cannot be seen clearly when viewed from certain angles.

Size and Aspect Ratio

Display device size is measured diagonally from corner to corner, in a manner similar to the way TV screens are measured. Most desktop computer monitors today are between 17 inches and 27 inches (though larger screens—up to 60 inches and more—are becoming increasingly common); notebook and tablet displays are usually between 15 inches and 20 inches; and netbooks typically have displays that are 10 inches or smaller. To better view DVDs and other multimedia content, many monitors today are *widescreen displays*, which conform to the *16:9 aspect ratio* of widescreen televisions, instead of the conventional *4:3 aspect ratio*.

⚥ **FIGURE 4-27**

Screen resolution.
A higher screen resolution (measured in pixels) displays more content than a lower screen resolution, but everything is displayed smaller.

Screen Resolution

Regardless of the technology used, the screen of a display device is divided into a fine grid of tiny pixels, as previously discussed. The number of pixels used on a display screen determines the *screen resolution*, which affects the amount of information that can be displayed on the screen at one time. When a higher resolution is selected, such as 1,280 pixels horizontally by 1,024 pixels vertically for a standard computer monitor (written as 1,280 × 1,024 and read as *1280 by 1024*), more information can fit on the screen, but everything will be displayed smaller than with a lower resolution, such as 1,024 × 768 (see Figure 4-27). The screen resolution on many computers today can be changed by users to match their preferences and the software being used. On Windows computers,

1,024 × 768   1,280 × 1,024

>**Flat-panel display.** A slim type of display device that uses electronically charged chemicals or gases instead of an electron gun to display images.

display options are changed using the Control Panel. When multiple monitors are used, typically the screen resolution of each display can be set independently of the others. Very high-resolution monitors are available for special applications, such as viewing digital X-rays.

Video Adapters, Interfaces, and Ports

The *video card* installed inside a computer or the integrated graphics component built directly into the motherboard of the computer houses the *graphics processing unit (GPU)*—the chip devoted to rendering images on a display device. The video card or the integrated graphics component determines the graphics capabilities of the computer, including the screen resolutions available, the number of bits used to store color information about each pixel (called the *bit depth*), the total number of colors that can be used to display images, the number of monitors that can be connected to the computer via that video card or component, and the types of connectors that can be used to connect a monitor to the computer. Video cards typically contain a fan and other cooling components to cool the card. Most video cards also contain memory chips (typically called *video RAM or VRAM*) to support graphics display, although some do not and are designed to use a portion of the computer's regular RAM as video RAM instead. To support higher resolutions, higher bit depths, and a greater number of colors, a sufficient amount of video RAM is required. Most video cards today contain between 256 MB and 1 GB of video RAM. A typically video card is shown in Figure 4-28.

The three most common types of interfaces used to connect a monitor to a computer are *VGA (Video Graphics Array)*, *DVI (Digital Visual Interface)*, and *HDMI (High-Definition Multimedia Interface)*. VGA uses a 15-pin D-shaped connector and it is commonly used with CRT monitors and many flat-panel monitors to transfer analog images to the monitor. DVI uses a more rectangular connector and it is frequently used with flat-panel displays to allow the monitor to receive clearer, more reliable digital signals than is possible with a VGA interface. HDMI uses a smaller connector and can be used with display devices that support high-definition content. A newer type of connector is *DisplayPort*, which is designed to eventually replace VGA and DVI ports on computers, video cards, and monitors. In fact, Apple already includes a smaller version—referred to as a *Mini DisplayPort*—on its newest MacBooks. The ports used with each of these possible connections are illustrated in Figure 4-28.

A video card or integrated video component in a desktop computer will have at least one port exposed through the system unit case to connect a monitor. Notebook computers and other computers with a built-in display typically contain a monitor port to connect a second monitor to the computer. An emerging option is connecting monitors to a computer via a USB port. *USB monitors* (monitors designed to connect via a USB port) can be added to a computer without requiring a video card that supports multiple monitors. Conventional monitors can also connect to a computer via a USB port if a *USB display adapter* (such

VGA **DVI** **TV-OUT** **HDMI**

DISPLAYPORT

FAN
Cools the components on the video card.

GPU
Renders images on the display screen (is located beneath the fan on this card for cooling purposes).

PORTS
Determine how a monitor can connect.

PCI EXPRESS x16 CONNECTOR
Plugs into the PCIe x16 slot on the motherboard.

VIDEO RAM CHIPS
Provide memory for video display (are located beneath the heat sinks on this card for cooling purposes).

FIGURE 4-28
Video cards. Provide a connection to a monitor, as well as determine video capabilities.

ONLINE VIDEO

Go to the Chapter 4 page at **www.cengage.com/ computerconcepts/np/uc13** to watch the "Connecting and Using Three DisplayLink USB Monitors" video clip.

A USB port on this side of the adapter connects the adapter to the computer.

A DVI cable connects the display device to the adapter.

FIGURE 4-29
A USB display adapter.

as the one shown in Figure 4-29) or a peripheral device (such as a docking station) that includes USB display capabilities is used. A USB connection allows multiple monitors to be connected easily to a device. For instance, many USB monitors are designed to be *daisy-chained* together so they all connect via a single USB port, and multiple USB display adapters (such as the one shown in Figure 4-29) can typically be used to connect multiple conventional monitors to a single computer.

Wired vs. Wireless Displays

Most computer monitors today are *wired displays*; that is, monitors that are physically connected to the system unit via a cable. Some display devices—such as digital photo frames, e-book readers, and some computer monitors and television sets, however—are designed to be wireless. *Wireless displays* connect to a computer using a wireless networking connection such as *Wi-Fi* or *Bluetooth* (discussed in more detail in Chapter 7), typically display content from a computer located within range of the monitor, and may support touch or pen input for when the display is used away from the computer.

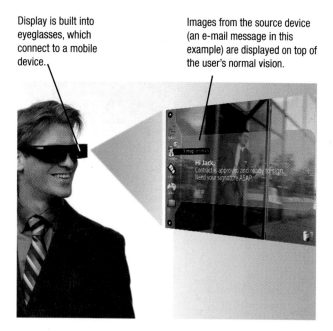

Display is built into eyeglasses, which connect to a mobile device.

Images from the source device (an e-mail message in this example) are displayed on top of the user's normal vision.

FIGURE 4-30
3D wearable displays.

2D vs. 3D Displays

Recent improvements in flat-panel display technology and graphics processing have led to several emerging *three-dimensional (3D) output devices*, including *3D display screens* for computers. While traditional 3D displays require special 3D glasses, the newest 3D products use filters, prisms, multiple lenses, and other technologies built into the display screen to create the 3D effect and, as a result, do not require 3D glasses. Some 3D displays resemble conventional monitors; others are shaped differently, such as the dome-shaped *Perspecta* 3D display. Perspecta is used primarily for medical imaging; scientists, architects, and other professionals who routinely view detailed graphics or diagrams in the course of their work also frequently use 3D displays.

Other 3D displays are designed to be wearable. A *3D wearable display* (such as the eyeglasses-based display shown in Figure 4-30) projects the image from a mobile device (typically a mobile phone or portable digital media player) to a display screen built into the glasses. Typically, the technology allows the user to see the image as if it is on a distant large screen display, and many 3D wearable displays overlay the projected image on top of what the user is seeing in real time in order to provide situational awareness while the display is being used. While 3D wearable displays have entertainment applications, there are also wearable 3D displays designed for soldiers and other mobile workers.

Touch and Gesture Capabilities

As discussed earlier in this chapter, it is increasingly common for monitors and display screens to support touch input. Touch screen displays are commonly used with personal computers, as well as with consumer kiosks, portable gaming devices, mobile phones, portable digital media players, and other consumer devices. Gesture input is beginning to become available with these products as well. According to Francis MacDougall, Co-Founder and Chief Technology Officer of GestureTek, that company is working with major telecom companies and electronics manufacturers to enable gesture control for their set top boxes, consoles, and other consumer electronics devices.

Flat-Panel Display Technologies

The most common flat-panel technologies include *liquid crystal display* (*LCD*), various types of *light emitting diode* (*LED*), and *gas plasma*. Emerging flat-panel technologies include *interferometric modulator display* (*IMOD*) and *surface-conduction electron-emitter display* (*SED*). These display technologies are discussed next. Another technology used by some flat-panel displays (including e-book readers, some digital signage systems, and the display on some wristwatches and USB flash drives) is *e-paper* technology, discussed in the Inside the Industry box.

Liquid Crystal Displays (LCDs)

A **liquid crystal display (LCD)** uses charged liquid crystals located between two sheets of clear material (usually glass or plastic) to light up the appropriate pixels to form the image on the screen. Several layers of liquid crystals are used, and, in their normal state, the liquid crystals are aligned so that light passes through the display. When an electrical charge is applied to the liquid crystals (via an electrode grid layer contained within the LCD panel), the liquid crystals change their orientation or "twist" so that light cannot pass through the display, and the liquid crystals at the charged intersections of the electrode grid appear dark. Color LCD displays use a color filter that consists of a pattern of red, green, and blue *subpixels* for each pixel. The voltage used controls the orientation (twisting) of the liquid crystals and the amount of light that gets through, affecting the color and shade of that pixel—the three different colors blend to make the pixel the appropriate color.

LCD displays can be viewed only with reflective light, unless light is built into the display. Consequently, LCD panels used with computer monitors typically include a light inside the panel, usually at the rear of the display—a technique referred to as *backlighting*. LCDs are currently the most common type of flat-panel technology used for small- to medium-sized computer monitors (the monitors shown in Figure 4-26 are LCD monitors). However, it is expected that, someday, LCD monitors may be completely replaced by newer technologies, such as the *LED technologies* discussed next.

Light Emitting Diode (LED) and Organic Light Emitting Diode (OLED) Displays

LED (*light emitting diode*) *technology* is also commonly used with consumer products, such as alarm clocks, Christmas lights, car headlights, and more. LEDs are also beginning to be used to backlight LCD panels, although another form of LED—*OLED*—may eventually replace LCD technology entirely.

Organic light emitting diode (OLED) displays use layers of organic material, which emit a visible light when electric current is applied. Because they emit a visible light, OLED displays do not use backlighting. This characteristic makes OLEDs more energy efficient than LCDs and lengthens the battery life of portable devices using OLED displays. Other advantages of OLEDs are that OLEDs are thinner than LCDs, that they have a wider viewing angle than LCDs and so displayed content is visible from virtually all directions, and that their images are brighter and sharper than LCDs. OLED displays are incorporated into many digital cameras, mobile phones, portable digital media

---

> **Liquid crystal display (LCD).** A type of flat-panel display that uses charged liquid crystals to display images.   > **Organic light emitting diode (OLED) display.** A type of flat-panel display that uses emissive organic material to display brighter and sharper images.

INSIDE THE INDUSTRY

E-Paper

Electronic paper (*e-paper*) is a type of flat panel display device that attempts to mimic the look of ordinary printed paper. The purpose of an *Electronic Paper Display* (*EPD*) is to give the user the experience of reading from paper, while providing them with the ability to update the information shown on the device electronically. EPDs display content in high-contrast, so they can be viewed in direct sunlight. They also require much less electricity than other types of displays, since they don't require a backlight and they don't require power to maintain the content shown on the display—they only require power to change the content. Because the content stored in an EPD can be erased when it is no longer needed and then replaced with new content, EPDs are more environmentally friendly than conventional paper documents. An additional benefit is portability; an *e-book reader* (such as the *Amazon Kindle* and the *Sony Reader* shown in the accompanying photograph), for instance, can hold over a thousand books stored in electronic format in a device about the size of a paperback novel. In fact, with an e-book reader, you could carry a small library in your backpack.

E-paper is also widely used for *e-signs*, which look like ordinary paper signs, but their text can be changed wirelessly. Their low power consumption means that e-signs can run off battery power for an extended period of time, even with moving data. Some e-signs don't even require a battery; instead, the wireless signal used to transmit data to the display is strong enough to update the sign content by itself. Other retail applications currently on the market include e-paper shelf price tags that can communicate electronically with the store's database so the current price is always displayed, e-paper displays on wristwatches and USB flash drives, destination displays on trains, and e-paper newspapers that can be updated periodically during the day to reflect the latest news. For instance, in late 2007, the French newspaper *Les Echos* announced an electronic paper edition. This e-newspaper is delivered automatically to subscribers via a Wi-Fi connection and it is updated every hour during the day on weekdays. The Amazon Kindle e-book reader can also receive newspaper content (in addition to e-book content)—and thanks to its proprietary high-speed wireless connection, it can download 1,000 pages in less than one minute. E-paper technology used with fabric, plastic, metal, and other materials is in development and is expected to be used to enable keyboards to be printed onto military uniform sleeves, light switches to be printed onto wallpaper, and radio

circuitry and controls to be printed onto clothing and other everyday objects. It may also allow e-paper to be used on billboards, T-shirts, and even paint for easy redecorating, as well as regular-sized e-paper that can be inserted into a special computer printer to be printed electronically and then reused over and over. One improvement that has already occurred is the incorporation of touch and pen input with e-paper displays. For instance, both touch and pen input can be used in conjunction with the Sony e-book reader shown in the accompany photograph to flip the "pages" of the book and otherwise control the device.

So how does e-paper work? It is based on a display technology called *electrophoretic*, which was invented and is now manufactured and marketed by E Ink® Corporation. An electrophoretic display contains *electronic ink*—essentially charged ink that consists of millions of tiny beads or *microcapsules* about half the diameter of a human hair. These beads contain positively charged white particles and negatively charged black particles suspended in a clear fluid. When voltage is applied to the beads (through the circuitry contained within the display), either the white or the black particles rise to the top and the opposite colored particles are pulled to the bottom of the bead, depending on the polarity of the charge applied. Consequently, the beads in each pixel appears to be either white or black (see the accompanying illustration) and remain in that state until another transmission changes the pattern.

The white particles are at the top, so this pixel appears white.

AN E-BOOK   **AN E-INK MICROCAPSULE**

players, and other consumer devices (see Figure 4-31). They are also beginning to appear in television and computer displays.

There are also a few special types of OLEDs that support applications not possible with CRT or LCD technology. For instance, *flexible OLED* (*FOLED*) displays—a technology developed by Universal Display Corporation—are OLED displays built on flexible surfaces, such as plastic or metallic foil. Flexible displays using FOLED technology—such as displays for portable computers and mobile devices that can roll up when not in use (see Figure 4-32)—are being developed by several companies. Other possible uses for flexible screens include making lighter desktop and portable computer monitors, integrating displays on military uniform sleeves, and allowing retractable wall-mounted big screen televi-

FIGURE 4-31
How OLED displays work. Each pixel on an OLED display emits light in the necessary color.

sions and monitors. The flexibility of FOLED displays also adds to their durability, and their thinness makes FOLED technology extremely suitable for mobile devices.

Another form of OLED developed by Universal Display Corporation is *transparent OLED* (*TOLED*). TOLED displays are transparent and can emit light toward the top and bottom of the display surface. The portion of the display that does not currently have an image displayed (and the entire display device when it is off) is nearly as transparent as glass, so the user can see through the screen (see Figure 4-32). TOLEDs open up the pos-

sibility of displays on home windows, car windshields, helmet face shields, and other transparent items. A third type of OLED is *Phosphorescent OLED* or *PHOLED*. The term *phosphorescence* refers to a process that results in much more conversion of electrical energy into light instead of heat; with phosphorescence, OLEDs can be up to four times more efficient than without it. Consequently, PHOLED technology is especially appropriate for use on mobile devices, consumer electronics, and other devices where power consumption is an important concern.

FOLEDS
Used to create flexible displays on plastic or another type of flexible material.

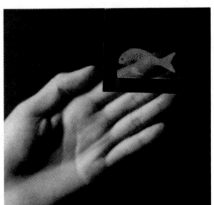

TOLEDS
Used to create transparent displays.

FIGURE 4-32
Special types of OLEDs.

Interferometric Modulator (IMOD) Displays

Another emerging flat-panel display technology is *interferometric modulator (IMOD) displays*. Designed initially for mobile phones and other portable devices, an IMOD display is essentially a complex mirror that uses external light—such as from the sun or artificial light inside a building—to display images. Because IMOD displays are utilizing light instead of fighting it the way LCD displays do, images are bright and clear even in direct sunlight (see Figure 4-33). And, because backlighting isn't used, power consumption is much less than what is needed for LCD displays. In fact, similar to e-paper, devices using IMOD displays use no power unless the image changes so they can remain on at all times without draining the device battery. Beginning to be used initially with mobile devices, IMODs could eventually be used for outdoor television screens, large digital signs, and other outdoor display devices that normally consume a great deal of power.

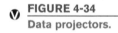

FIGURE 4-33
An IMOD display is bright and readable, even in direct sunlight.

Plasma Displays and Surface-Conduction Electron-Emitter Displays (SEDs)

Plasma displays use a layered technology like LCD and OLEDs and look similar to LCD displays, but they use a layer of gas between two plates of glass, instead of liquid crystals or organic material. A phosphor-coated screen (with red, green, and blue phosphors for each pixel) is used, and an electron grid layer and electronic charges are used to make the gas atoms light up the appropriate phosphors to create the image on the screen. The very large displays used by businesses, as well as many large screen televisions, are typically plasma displays.

A display technology in development for high-definition displays is *surface-conduction electron-emitter display* (*SED*). SED is being developed by Toshiba and Canon. It uses millions of tiny electron guns (similar to those used in CRTs but much smaller and millions of them instead of one) to power the pixels on a flat-panel display. SED displays are thin and bright, and they have less flicker than LCD and plasma screens. Televisions based on SED technology are beginning to become available.

Data and Multimedia Projectors

A **data projector** is used to display output from a computer to a wall or projection screen. Conventional data projectors are often found in classrooms, conference rooms, and similar locations and can be freestanding units or permanently mounted onto the ceiling. While most data projectors connect via cable to a computer, *wireless projectors* that use a Wi-Fi connection are available. Some projectors (such as the one shown in Figure 4-34) also include an *iPod dock* to connect a video iPod in order to project videos stored on that device.

FIGURE 4-34
Data projectors.

CONVENTIONAL DATA PROJECTORS
Frequently used for both business and classroom presentations.

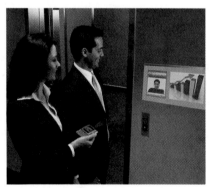

INTEGRATED AND PORTABLE PROJECTORS
Images displayed on the device (such as the mobile phone shown here) are projected onto any surface.

HOLOGRAPHIC PROJECTORS
Project 3D images of objects or individuals.

>**Plasma display.** A type of flat-panel display that uses layers of gas to display images; most often used on large displays. >**Data projector.** A display device that projects all computer output to a wall or projection screen.

Another type of data projector is the *integrated projector*—tiny projectors that are beginning to be built into mobile phones, portable computers, portable digital media players, and other portable devices to enable the device to project an image (such as a document, presentation, or movie) onto a wall or other flat surface from up to 12 feet away (refer again to Figure 4-34). These integrated projectors typically create a display up to 10 feet wide in order to easily share information on the device with others on the go without having to crowd around a tiny screen. This same technology is also incorporated into very small stand-alone *portable projectors* that can be used for making presentations while on the go. Another type of data projector shown in Figure 4-34 is designed to project actual 3D projections or *holograms*. For instance, holograms of individuals and objects can be projected onto a stage for a presentation and hologram display devices can be used in retail stores, exhibitions, and other locations to showcase products or other items in 3D.

PRINTERS

Instead of the temporary, ever-changing soft copy output that a monitor produces, **printers** produce *hard copy*; that is, a permanent copy of the output on paper. Most desktop computers are connected to a printer; portable computers can use printers as well.

Printer Characteristics

Printers differ in a number of important respects, such as the technology used, size, speed, and print quality. Some general printer characteristics are discussed next, followed by a look at the most common types of printers.

Printing Technology

Printers produce images through either impact or nonimpact technologies. *Impact printers*, like old ribbon typewriters, have a print mechanism that actually strikes the paper to transfer ink to the paper. For example, a *dot-matrix printer* (see Figure 4-35) uses a *print head* consisting of pins that strike an inked ribbon to transfer the ink to the paper—the appropriate pins are extended (and, consequently, strike the ribbon) as the print head moves across the paper in order to form the appropriate words or images. Impact printers are used today primarily for producing multipart forms, such as invoices, packing slips, and credit card receipts.

Most printers today are *nonimpact printers*, meaning they form images without the print mechanism actually touching the paper. Nonimpact printers usually produce higher-quality images and are much quieter than impact printers are. The two most common types of printers today—*laser printers* and *ink-jet printers*—are both nonimpact printers. As discussed in more detail shortly, laser printers form images with *toner powder* (essentially ink powder) and ink-jet printers form images with liquid ink. Both impact and nonimpact printers form images with dots, in a manner similar to the way monitors display images with pixels. Because of this, printers are very versatile and can print text in virtually any size, as well as print photos and other graphical images. In addition to paper, both impact and nonimpact printers can print on transparencies, envelopes, mailing labels, and more.

FIGURE 4-35

Dot-matrix printers.
Dot-matrix printers are impact printers; today they are typically high-speed printers used in manufacturing, shipping, or similar applications.

>**Printer.** An output device that produces output on paper.

Color vs. Black and White

Both *color printers* and *black-and-white printers* are available. Color printers work similarly to black-and-white printers, except that, instead of using just black ink, they also use cyan (blue), magenta (red), and yellow ink (see Figure 4-36). Either color printers apply all of the colors in one pass, or they go through the entire printing process multiple times, applying one color during each pass. Color printers are often used in homes (to print photographs, greeting cards, flyers, and more). Businesses may use black-and-white printers for output that does not need to be in color (since it is less expensive and faster to print in black and white) and color printers for output that needs to be in color (such as product brochures and other colorful marketing materials).

FIGURE 4-36

Color printing.
Color printers require multiple color cartridges or cartridges that contain multiple colors.

Personal vs. Network Printers

Printers today can be designated as *personal printers* (printers designed to be connected directly to a single computer) or *network printers* (printers designed to be connected directly to a home or an office network). Personal printers can be shared over a home network if the computer to which the printer is connected is powered up and the printer is designated as a shared device and some personal printers today include Wi-Fi capabilities to enable individuals to print from any Wi-Fi-enabled device via a home Wi-Fi network. However, network printers are designed to connect directly to a network (instead of to a single computer) so they can be used by anyone connected to the network via a wired or wireless connection. In addition, many network printers today are designed for high-volume office printing and often include other capabilities, such as to collate, staple, hole-punch, and print on both sides of the page (referred to as *duplex printing*). Networking is discussed in detail in Chapter 7.

Print Resolution

Most printing technologies today form images with dots of liquid ink or flecks of toner powder. The number of dots per inch (dpi)—called the *print resolution*—affects the quality of the printed output. Printers with a higher print resolution tend to produce sharper text and images than printers with a lower resolution tend to produce, although other factors (such as the technology and number of colors used) also affect the quality of a printout. Guidelines for acceptable print resolution are typically 300 dpi for general-purpose printouts, 600 dpi for higher-quality documents, 1,200 dpi for photographs, and 2,400 dpi for professional applications.

Print Speed

Print speed is typically measured in *pages per minute* (*ppm*). How long it takes a document to print depends on the actual printer being used, the selected print resolution, and the content being printed. For instance, pages containing photographs or other images typically take longer to print than pages containing only text, and full-color pages take longer to print than black-and-white pages. Common speeds for personal printers today range from about 15 to 35 ppm; network printers typically print from 40 to 100 ppm.

Connection Options

Most personal printers today connect to a computer via a USB connection; some have the option of connecting via a Wi-Fi wireless connection as well. In addition, many personal printers can receive data to be printed via a flash memory card, a cable connected to a digital camera (such as for printers and cameras adhering to the *PictBridge standard*), or a *camera docking station* (a device connected to a printer into which a digital camera is placed so images stored in the camera can be printed). Most network printers connect via a wired *Ethernet* networking connection or a wireless Wi-Fi connection. Networking connections are discussed in detail in Chapter 7.

Multifunction Capabilities

Some printers today offer more than just printing capabilities. These units—referred to as **multifunction devices (MFDs)** or *all-in-ones*—typically copy, scan, fax, and print documents. MFDs (see Figure 4-37) can be based on ink-jet printer or laser printer technology, and they are available as both color and black-and-white devices. Although multifunction devices have traditionally been desktop units used in small offices and home offices, larger workgroup multifunction devices are now available that are designed for multiple users, either as stand-alone stations or as networked units.

FIGURE 4-37
A multifunction device (MFD).

Laser Printers

Laser printers are the standard for business documents and come in both personal and network versions; they are also available as both color and black-and-white printers. To print a document, the laser printer first uses a laser beam to charge the appropriate locations on a drum to form the page's image, and then *toner powder* (powdered ink) is released from a *toner cartridge* and sticks to the drum. The toner is then transferred to a piece of paper when the paper is rolled over the drum, and a heating unit fuses the toner powder to the paper to permanently form the image (see Figure 4-38). Laser printers print one entire

FIGURE 4-38
How black-and-white laser printers work.

1. The paper enters the printer, and then it is given an electrical charge so the toner can stick to the paper, as explained in step 5.

2. The printer's microprocessor decodes page data sent from the computer.

3. Instructions from the printer's microprocessor control a laser beam that charges the appropriate locations on the drum so the toner will stick to the drum, as explained in step 4.

4. Toner powder is applied to the drum and sticks only to the charged areas on the drum.

5. The paper rolls over the drum and the toner is transferred to the paper, forming the image for the entire page.

6. The paper goes through the fusing unit, at which point the toner is permanently affixed to the paper through heat and pressure.

7. The paper exits the printer.

>**Multifunction device (MFD).** A device that offers multiple functions (such as printing, scanning, and faxing) in a single unit. >**Laser printer.** An output device that uses toner powder and technology similar to that of a photocopier to produce images on paper.

page at a time and are typically faster and have better quality output than *ink-jet printers*, discussed next. Common print resolutions for laser printers are between 600 and 2,400 dpi; speeds for personal laser printers range from about 15 to 30 ppm. Black-and-white laser printers start at about $100; color laser printers start at about $300.

Ink-Jet Printers

Ink-jet printers form images by spraying tiny drops of liquid ink from one or more *ink cartridges* onto the page, one printed line at a time (see Figure 4-39). Some printers print with one single-sized ink droplet; others print using different-sized ink droplets and using multiple nozzles or varying electrical charges for more precise printing. The print head for an ink-jet printer typically travels back and forth across the page, which is one reason why ink-jet printers are slower than laser printers. However, an emerging type of ink-jet printer uses a printhead that is the full width of the paper, which allows the printhead to remain stationary while the paper feeds past it. These printers are very fast, printing up to 60 ppm for letter-sized paper.

Because they are relatively inexpensive, have good-quality output, and can print in color, ink-jet printers are usually the printer of choice for home use. With the use of special photo paper, *photo-quality ink-jet printers* can also print photograph-quality digital photos. Starting at less than $50 for a simple home printer, ink-jet printers are affordable, although the cost of the replaceable ink cartridges can add up, especially if you do a lot of color printing.

FIGURE 4-39

How ink-jet printers work.

Each ink cartridge is made up of multiple tiny ink-filled firing chambers; to print images, the appropriate color ink is ejected through the appropriate firing chamber.

Ink-jet printer

Heating element

Steam bubble

Firing chamber

Paper

Steam bubble

Ink droplet

Steam bubble

Ink droplet

1. A heating element makes the ink boil, which causes a steam bubble to form.

2. As the steam bubble expands, it pushes ink through the firing chamber.

3. The ink droplet is ejected onto the paper and the steam bubble collapses, pulling more ink into the firing chamber.

>**Ink-jet printer.** An output device that sprays droplets of ink to produce images on paper.

In addition to being used in computer printers, ink-jet technology is being applied to a number of other applications. For instance, ink-jet technology may eventually be used for dispensing liquid metals, aromas, computer chips and other circuitry, and even "printing" human tissue and other organic materials for medical purposes.

Special-Purpose Printers

Although both laser and ink-jet printers can typically print on a variety of media—including sheets of labels, envelopes, transparencies, photo paper, and even fabric, in addition to various sizes of paper—some printers are designed for a particular purpose. Some of the most common *special-purpose printers* are discussed next and illustrated in Figure 4-40.

Photo Printers

Photo printers are color printers designed to print photographs. Although many photo printers are connected to a computer to print photos stored on the hard drive, most photo printers also can print photos directly from a digital camera or a storage medium (such as a flash memory card) without transferring the photos to a computer first. Often, photo

FIGURE 4-40
Special-purpose printers.

Photos can be previewed and edited here.

Flash memory media can be inserted here.

PHOTO PRINTERS
Used to print digital photographs in a variety of sizes.

BARCODE PRINTERS
Used to print barcoded labels. This printer can also program RFID tags, when they are embedded inside the barcoded labels.

PORTABLE AND INTEGRATED PRINTERS
This printer uses no ink and is integrated into the digital camera to print digital photographs.

WIDE-FORMAT PRINTERS
Used for printouts that are too big for a standard-sized printer.

3D PRINTERS
Used to print items (such as plastic parts or models) in 3D.

> **Photo printer.** An output device designed for printing digital photographs.

printers have a preview screen (see Figure 4-40) to allow for minor editing and cropping before printing, but it is usually more efficient to do extensive editing on a computer. Some photo printers can print a variety of photo paper sizes; others—sometimes called *snapshot printers*—print only on standard 4 by 6-inch photo paper. Although photo printers offer the convenience of printing digital photos at home and whenever the need arises, the cost per photo is typically higher than using a photo printing service at a retail store or an Internet photo printing service.

Barcode, Label, and Postage Printers

Barcode printers enable businesses and other organizations to print custom barcodes on price tags, shipping labels, and other documents for identification or pricing purposes. Most barcode printers can print labels in a variety of barcode standards; some (such as the one shown in Figure 4-40) can also encode RFID tags embedded in labels. For other types of labels, such as for envelopes, packages, and file folders, regular *label printers* may come in handy. Some special-purpose label printers referred to as *postage printers* can print *electronic postage* (also called *e-stamps*). E-stamps are valid postage stamps that can be printed once a postage allotment has been purchased via the Internet or from an e-stamp vendor; postage values are deducted from your allotment as you print the e-stamps. Some e-stamp services also allow stamps to be printed directly onto shipping labels and envelopes using laser or ink-jet printers, as well.

Portable and Integrated Printers

Portable printers are small, lightweight printers that can be used on the go, such as with a notebook computer or mobile device, and connect via either a wired or wireless connection. Portable printers that can print on regular-sized (8.5 by 11-inch) paper are used by businesspeople while traveling; portable receipt and barcode printers are used in some service professions. Printers can also be integrated into other devices. For instance, the digital camera shown in Figure 4-40 contains an *integrated printer* that is based on a new technology developed by *ZINK* (for "zero ink") *Imaging*. This printer uses no ink; instead, it uses special paper that is coated with special color dye crystals. Before printing, the embedded dye crystals are clear, so *ZINK Paper* looks like regular white photo paper. The ZINK printer uses heat to activate and colorize these dye crystal when a photo is printed, creating a full color image. In addition to being integrated into a variety of consumer electronics devices, including digital cameras and digital picture frames, stand-alone *ZINK printers* are also available.

Wide-Format Ink-Jet Printers

To print charts, drawings, maps, blueprints, posters, signs, advertising banners, and other large documents in one piece, a larger printer (such as the one shown in Figure 4-40) is needed. Today, most large format printers (sometimes called *plotters*) are *wide-format ink-jet printers*, which are designed to print documents from around 24 inches to 60 inches in width. Although typically used to print on paper, some wide-format ink-jet printers can print directly on fabric and other types of materials.

3D Printers

When 3D output is required, such as to print a 3D model of a new building or prototype of a new product, **3D printers** (see Figure 4-40) can be used. Instead of printing on paper,

---

>**Barcode printer.** An output device that prints barcoded documents. >**Portable printer.** A small, lightweight printer designed to be used while on the go. >**3D printer.** An output device designed to print three-dimensional objects, such as product prototypes.

these printers typically form output in layers using molten plastic during a series of passes to build a 3D version of the desired output—a process called *fused deposition modeling (FDM)*. Some printers can produce multicolor output; others print in only one color and need to be painted by hand, if color output is desired.

AUDIO OUTPUT

Audio output includes voice, music, and other audible sounds. **Computer speakers**, the most common type of audio output device, connect to a computer and provide audio output for computer games, music, video clips and TV shows, Web conferencing, and other applications. Computer speaker systems resemble their stereo system counterparts and are available in a wide range of prices. Some speaker systems (such as the one shown in Figure 4-41) consist of only a pair of speakers. Others include additional speakers and a subwoofer to create better sound (such as surround sound) for multimedia content. Instead of being stand-alone units, the speakers for some desktop computers are built directly into, or permanently attached to, the monitor. Portable computers and mobile devices typically have speakers integrated into the device; mobile devices can also be connected to a stereo system or other consumer device (such as the treadmill shown in Figure 4-41) that contains an *iPod/MP3 dock* and integrated speakers designed to be used to play music stored on a portable digital media player. In addition, many cars can connect a portable digital media player to the car's stereo system; typically devices are connected via the device's headphone jack or USB port.

Headphones can be used instead of speakers so the audio output does not disturb others (such as in a school computer lab or public library). **Headsets** (see Figure 4-41) are headphones with a built-in microphone and are often used when dictating to a computer and when making telephone calls or participating in Web conferences using a computer; wireless headsets are commonly used in conjunction with mobile phones. Even smaller than headphones are the *earphones* and *earbuds* often used with portable digital media players, handheld gaming devices, and other mobile devices.

FIGURE 4-41
Audio output devices.

COMPUTER SPEAKERS
Used to output sound from a computer.

IPOD/MP3 DOCK
Used to output sound from a portable digital media player.

HEADSETS
Used when both voice input and audio output are required.

>**Computer speakers.** Output devices connected to computers that provide audio output. >**Headphones.** A personal audio output device used by an individual so only he or she can hear the sound; headphones with a built-in microphone are typically referred to as **headsets**.

SUMMARY

KEYBOARDS

Most people use a **keyboard** to input data into a personal computer. Keyboards typically include the standard alphanumeric keys, plus other keys for special purposes. Many mobile phones and other mobile devices include a keyboard today—if not, a *portable keyboard* can often be used. *Wireless keyboards* are also available.

POINTING AND TOUCH DEVICES

Pointing devices are hardware devices that move an on-screen *mouse pointer* or similar indicator. The most widely used pointing device is the **mouse**. Another common pointing device is the **stylus**, which is used with pen-based computers, many mobile devices, and *digital writing systems* to input handwritten data and to select options; with **handwriting recognition** technology, the input can be converted to typed text. Use of *digital forms* in conjunction with handwriting recognition is a growing trend. **Touch screens** are monitors that are touched with the finger to select commands or provide input. Touch screens are commonly used in consumer kiosks, as well as with personal computers, mobile phones, mobile devices, and other consumer devices. Other pointing devices include **graphics tablets**, gaming devices, and **touch pads**.

SCANNERS, READERS, AND DIGITAL CAMERAS

There are many different input devices that can be used to convert data that already exists (such as *source documents*) to digital form or to initially capture data in digital form. A **scanner** allows users to input data that exists in physical form, such as photographs, drawings, and printed documents, into a computer. Most scanners are **flatbed scanners** or **portable scanners**. *Receipt*, *3D*, and *business card scanners* are also available. When used with **optical character recognition** (**OCR**) software, the computer can recognize scanned text characters as editable text; if not, the scanned page is input as a single image.

Barcode readers read **barcodes**, such as the *UPC codes* used to identify products in many retail stores. **Radio frequency identification** (**RFID**) is a technology used to store and transmit data located in **RFID tags**, which contain tiny chips and antennas and which are attached to items. RFID tags are read by **RFID readers** and are most often used in conjunction with shipping containers and other large assets. RFID technology can also be used to track individuals, assets, and other items, as well as be used for electronic payment systems.

Optical mark readers (*OMRs*) read specific types of marks on certain forms, such as on testing forms and voter ballots. *OCR readers* read characters, such as the specially printed *optical characters* used on bills and other *turnaround documents*. *Magnetic ink character recognition* (*MICR*) is used by the banking industry to rapidly sort, process, and route checks to the proper banks. **Biometric readers** read *biometric* characteristics (such as a fingerprint, hand geometry, or a face) in order to identify individuals.

Digital cameras work much like conventional film cameras, but they record digital images on a digital storage medium (such as a flash memory card, digital tape cartridge, built-in hard drive, or DVD disc), instead of on conventional film or videotape. The images are immediately available without processing and can be transferred to a computer for manipulation or printing, or sent directly to some printers for printing. *Digital still cameras* take still photos; *digital video cameras* are either *digital camcorders* or *PC cam/Web cam* digital video cameras that are used in conjunction with personal computers.

AUDIO INPUT

Speech recognition systems, which enable computer systems to recognize spoken words, are one means of *audio input*. Speech recognition can be used for data input, as well as for controlling a computer or other device (such as a mobile phone, car navigation system, or surgical robot). *Music input systems* are used to input music, such as original music compositions, into a computer. Music can also be input via a CD, DVD, or Web download.

Chapter Objective 5:
Understand the devices that can be used for audio input.

DISPLAY DEVICES

Display devices (also called **monitors** and **display screens**) are the most common type of output device for a computer; they are also incorporated into a wide variety of other electronic devices. Display devices are available in a wide variety of sizes and are generally either **CRT monitors** or **flat-panel displays**. Flat-panel displays are most often **liquid crystal displays** (**LCDs**) or **plasma displays**, but these technologies are expected to be replaced by **organic light emitting diode** (**OLED**) **displays** and other new display technologies, such as *interferometric modulator* (*IMOD*) displays and *surface-conduction electron-emitter displays* (*SEDs*). Special types of OLEDs (such as *flexible*, *transparent*, and *Phosphorescent OLEDs*) are emerging for special applications. Regardless of the technology used, the screen of a display device is divided into a fine grid of small areas or dots called **pixels**. Monitors can be *color* or *monochrome*, *wired* or *wireless*, and are available in a wide variety of sizes. Some monitors support 3D images, and some include touch screen capabilities. The *video card* or integrated graphics component being used determines many of the graphics capabilities of the computer. **Data projectors** connect to a computer and project any output sent to the computer's monitor through the projector onto a wall or projection screen. Some projectors are integrated into mobile devices; others project *holograms*.

Chapter Objective 6:
Describe the characteristics of a display device and explain some of the technologies used to display images.

PRINTERS

Printers produce *hard copy* output through either *impact* or *nonimpact* printing technology. Most printers today form images as matrices of dots, although with many technologies, the dots are too small to be visible. Printer quality is usually measured in *dots per inch* (*dpi*); speed is typically measured in *pages per minute* (*ppm*). Both *personal* and *network printers* are available and there are a number of options for connecting a printer to a network, computer, or other device. Some printers print in color and others print in just black and white. **Multifunction devices** (**MFDs**) incorporate the functions of multiple devices—typically a printer, scanner, and fax machine—into a single unit.

The most common printers are **laser printers** (which use *toner powder*) and **ink-jet printers** (which use liquid ink). Special-purpose printers include **photo printers**, **barcode printers**, **portable printers**, *wide-format ink-jet printers*, and **3D printers**. Some printers are integrated into other devices, such as digital cameras.

Chapter Objective 7:
List several types of printers and explain their functions.

AUDIO OUTPUT

The most common *audio output* device is **computer speakers**, which output music or spoken voice. **Headphones** or **headsets** can be used to prevent the sound from disturbing other people; speakers are also integrated into some consumer devices (such as treadmills) to play music stored on portable digital media players.

Chapter Objective 8:
Identify the hardware devices used for audio output.

HW

REVIEW ACTIVITIES

KEY TERM MATCHING

a. digital camera

b. ink-jet printer

c. laser printer

d. mouse

e. OLED display

f. optical character recognition (OCR)

g. RFID tag

h. scanner

i. stylus

j. touch screen

Instructions: Match each key term on the left with the definition on the right that best describes it.

1. _____ A common pointing device that the user slides along a flat surface to move a pointer around the screen and clicks its buttons to make selections.

2. _____ A device containing a tiny chip and a radio antenna that is attached to an object so it can be identified using radio frequency identification technology.

3. _____ A display device that is touched with the finger to issue commands or otherwise provide input to the connected device.

4. _____ An input device that reads printed text and graphics and transfers them to a computer in digital form.

5. _____ An input device that is used to write electronically on the display screen.

6. _____ An input device that takes pictures and records them as digital images.

7. _____ An output device that uses toner powder and technology similar to that of a photocopier to produce images on paper.

8. _____ A type of flat-panel display that uses emissive organic material to display brighter and sharper images.

9. _____ An output device that sprays droplets of ink to produce images on paper.

10. _____ The ability of a scanning device to recognize scanned text characters and convert them to electronic form as text, not images.

SELF-QUIZ

Instructions: Circle **T** if the statement is true, **F** if the statement is false, or write the best answer in the space provided. **Answers for the self-quiz are located in the References and Resources Guide at the end of the book.**

1. **T F** A keyboard is an example of a pointing device.

2. **T F** Most digital still cameras store photos on flash memory media.

3. **T F** UPC is a type of barcode.

4. **T F** Consumer kiosks located in retail stores commonly use touch screens for input.

5. **T F** An ink-jet printer normally produces a better image than a laser printer.

6. With _____ software, pen-based computers can convert handwritten text into editable, typed text.

7. A(n) _____ can be used to convert flat printed documents, such as a drawing or photograph, into digital form.

8. The smallest colorable area in an electronic image (such as a scanned document, digital hotograph, or image displayed on a display screen) is called a(n) _____.

9. Portable computers and mobile devices virtually always use _____ displays, while some desktop computers may use the larger, more bulky _____ monitors.

10. Match each input device to its input application, and write the corresponding number in the blank to the left of the input application.

a. _____ Pen-based computing   **1.** Keyboard

b. _____ Consumer kiosk   **2.** Stylus

c. _____ Text-based data entry   **3.** RFID tag

d. _____ Secure facility access   **4.** Biometric reader

e. _____ Tracking goods   **5.** Touch screen

1. For the following list of computer input and output devices, write the appropriate abbreviation (I or O) in the space provided to indicate whether each device is used for input (I) or output (O).

a. _____ Biometric reader   f. _____ Digital camera

b. _____ Graphics tablet   g. _____ Data projector

c. _____ Speaker   h. _____ Microphone

d. _____ Photo printer   i. _____ OLED monitor

e. _____ Flat-panel display   j. _____ Joystick

2. Write the number of the type of printer that best matches each of the printing applications in the blank to the left of each printing application.

a. _____ To print inexpensive color printouts for a wide variety of documents.

b. _____ To print all output for an entire office.

c. _____ To print receipts for jet-ski rentals at the beach.

d. _____ To print high-quality black-and-white business letters and reports at home.

1. Personal laser printer

2. Network laser printer

3. Ink-jet printer

4. Portable printer

3. List three advantages of RFID technology over barcode technology.

4. Would an OLED display or an LCD display use more battery power? Explain why.

5. List one personal or business application that you believe is more appropriate for a dot-matrix printer, instead of another type of printer, and explain why.

1. While gaming and texting are both popular pastimes, it is possible to become injured by performing these activities. For instance, some Wii users have developed tennis elbow and other ailments from some Wii Sports games and heavy texters have developed problems with their thumbs. Think of the devices you use regularly. Have you ever become sore or injured from their use? If so, was it the design of the input device being used, overuse, or both? What responsibilities do hardware manufacturers have in respect to creating safe input devices? If a user becomes injured due to overuse of a device, whose fault it is? Should input devices come with warning labels?

2. The choice of an appropriate input device for a product is often based on both the type of device being used and the target market for that device. For instance, a device targeted to college students and one targeted to older individuals may use different input methods. Suppose that you are developing a device to be used primarily for Internet access that will be marketed to senior citizens. What type of hardware would you select as the primary input device? Why? What are the advantages and disadvantages of your selected input device? How could the disadvantages be minimized?

PROJECTS

HOT TOPICS

1. **Biometrics and Personal Privacy** Biometric input devices, such as fingerprint readers and iris scanners, are increasingly being used for security purposes, such as to clock in and out of work, or to obtain access to locked facilities, a computer, or a computer network. Other uses of biometric technology are more voluntary, such as expedited airport-screening programs used by some frequent travelers and the fingerprint payment systems used at some retail stores. While viewed as a time-saving tool by some, other individuals may object to their biometric characteristics being stored in a database for this purpose. Is convenience worth compromising some personal privacy? What about national security? Would you be willing to sign up for a voluntary program, such as an airport-screening system or a fingerprint payment system, that relies on biometric data? Would you work at a job that required you to use a biometric input device on a regular basis? Do you think a national ID card containing hard-to-forge biometric data could help prevent terrorist attacks, such as the September 11, 2001 attacks? If so, do you think most Americans would support its use?

    For this project, research the use of biometric input devices today and form an opinion about their use and any potential impact their use may have on personal privacy. At the conclusion of your research, prepare a one-page summary of your findings and opinions and submit it to your instructor.

SHORT ANSWER/ RESEARCH

2. **Printer Shopping** Printers today have many more features than a few years ago. These features may include improved quality, more memory, photo printing capabilities, digital camera connectivity, built-in flash memory card readers, wireless connectivity, and faster speed.

    For this project, suppose you are in the market for a new personal printer. Make a list of the most important features needed to meet your needs, and then research printers to identify the best printer for your needs. Be sure to consider both the price of the printer and the price of consumables (such as paper and ink/toner) in your evaluation process. At the conclusion of your research, prepare a one-page summary of your findings and best options and submit it to your instructor.

HANDS ON

3. **Keyboarding Speed Test** Although voice and other alternative means of input are emerging, most data input today is still performed via the keyboard. Proper keyboarding technique can help increase speed and accuracy. Online keyboarding tests can help to evaluate your keyboarding ability.

    For this project, find a site (such as Typingtest.com) that offers a free online typing test and test your keyboarding speed and accuracy. At the conclusion of the test, rate your keyboarding ability and determine whether a keyboarding course or tutor program, or just keyboarding practice, will help you improve if your score is not at least 20 correct words per minute (cwpm). Take the test one more time to see if your speed improves now that you are familiar with how the test works. If your speed is fast, but accuracy is low, take the test once more, concentrating on accuracy. If you still test less than 20 cwpm, locate a free typing tutor program or Web site and evaluate it to see if it would help you to increase your speed and accuracy. At the conclusion of this task, prepare a short summary of your experience, including the typing test site used and your best score.

4. **Green Technology Mandates** The chapter Inside the Industry box discusses e-paper—an erasable, reusable alternative to traditional paper and ink. While e-paper has many societal benefits (such as reducing the use of traditional paper and ink and the resources needed to create and dispose of them), it has been slow to catch on. When a new technology, such as e-paper, that has obvious benefits to society is developed, who (if anyone) should be responsible for making sure it gets implemented in a timely fashion? Do we, as a society, have an ethical responsibility to ensure the new product succeeds? Should the government mandate the use of beneficial technology? Will businesses or individuals choose to use e-paper products if the only incentive is a cleaner environment? Would you be willing to switch to a new technology (such as e-paper) that is beneficial to society if it costs more than the existing technology? Is it ethical for an industry or the government to mandate the use of new technologies if they create an additional cost or inconvenience to individuals?

    For this project, form an opinion about the ethical obligations individuals, businesses, and the government have in regards to the development and implementation of beneficial new technologies and be prepared to discuss your position (in class, via an online class discussion group, in a class chat room, or via a class blog, depending on your instructor's directions). You may also be asked to write a short paper expressing your opinion.

5. **Assistive Computing** In addition to the conventional input and output hardware mentioned in the chapter, there are a variety of assistive input and output devices that physically challenged individuals can use to make computing easier and more efficient.

    For this project, select one type of disability, such as being blind, deaf, paraplegic, quadriplegic, or having the use of only one arm or hand. Research the hardware and software options that could be used with a new computer for someone with the selected disability. Make a list of potential limitations of any standard computer hardware and the assistive hardware and software that would be appropriate for this individual. Research each assistive option, comparing the ease of use, cost, and availability, and then prepare a recommendation for the best computer system for your selected hypothetical situation. Share your findings with the class in the form of a short presentation. The presentation should not exceed 10 minutes and should make use of one or more presentation aids, such as the chalkboard, handouts, overhead transparencies, or a computer-based slide presentation (your instructor may provide additional requirements). You may also be asked to submit a summary of the presentation to your instructor.

Instructions: Go to the Chapter 4 page at **www.cengage.com/computerconcepts/np/uc13** to work the following Web Activities.

6. **Interactive Activities** Work the interactive **Crossword Puzzle**, watch the **Video Podcasts** and **Online Videos**, and explore the **Further Exploration** links associated with this chapter.

    If you have a SAM user profile, you may have access to hands-on instruction, practice, and assessment of the skills covered in this chapter. Check with your instructor for instructions and the correct URL/Web site to access those assignments.

7. **Student Edition Labs** Work the following interactive **Student Edition Labs**.
   - **Using Input Devices**
   - **Peripheral Devices**

8. **Test Yourself** Review the **Online Study Guide** for this chapter, then test your knowledge of the terms and concepts covered in this chapter by completing the **Key Term Matching** exercise, the **Self-Quiz**, the **Exercises**, and the **Practice Test**.

Hardware

ac̄er

Sumit Agnihotry is the
Vice President of Product
Marketing for Acer Pan
America. In his 15+
years in the computer
field, he has held various
positions in computer
product marketing. He
started at the Acer Group
in 1998 as a product
manager, and has suc-
cessfully helped launch
numerous Acer products
through U.S. consumer
channels. Sumit holds
a Bachelor of Science
Degree in Marketing and
has attended Executive
Education programs in
Leadership Development
and Cross-Cultural
Negotiation at the John
Hopkins University.

A conversation with **SUMIT AGNIHOTRY**

Vice President, Product Marketing, Acer Pan America

" . . . storage technology will need to continue to evolve to improve accessibility, performance, and capacity, and to support new high-definition and content-on-the-go applications. "

My Background . . .

I started in the computer industry when I got my first job as a manufacturer's representative while still in school, marketing computer peripherals and accessories to retailers. I began my career at the Acer Group in 1998 as a product manager for mobile products. I'm now the Vice President of product marketing for the Americas region and my responsibilities include working with engineers to develop the latest cutting-edge products, and then launching those products through various chan-nels in North, Central, and South America. I also oversee the marketing of Acer notebooks, net-books, desktop computers, and monitors. I believe that my ability to understand consumer needs and pain points, coupled with my knowledge of this industry and technology, has helped me succeed in this field and in my current position.

It's Important to Know . . .

Moore's Law is still valid. The trend of improvements in the area of computing hardware is well described by Moore's Law, which basically says that the number of transistors that can be placed inexpensively on an integrated circuit has increased exponentially since the invention of the integrated circuit in 1958 and will continue to do so. But, in addition to the density of components and transis-tors, many other measures of digital technology are improving at exponential rates as well, including computing performance, power consumption, battery life, and network capacity. This growth trend is expected to continue for at least another decade.

The world is becoming wireless. Consumers today want access to information anytime and any-where. The desire of consumers to access digital and voice information on the go dictates that emerg-ing devices will need to have wireless connectivity and high performance, as well as be able to support popular applications such as social networking. In addition, devices will need to be ultra thin and light, and have an all-day battery life. They must also be designed to appeal to the mass market, but still be affordable.

Storage technology will continue to evolve. Optical storage media (such as DVDs and CDs) and flash storage media (such as flash memory cards and USB flash drives) are widely used today. However, storage technology will need to continue to evolve to improve accessibility, performance, and capacity, and to support new high-definition and content-on-the-go applications. The potential impact of current and future technologies on the environment will need to be taken into consider-ation as well.

How I Use this Technology . . .

I spend a lot of time on the road visiting suppliers and customers so I use my BlackBerry and laptop throughout the day—basically anytime I am not sleeping or flying. When I don't have access to my laptop or it's not convenient to use it, I am still able to respond to e-mail messages and perform other mission-critical tasks in a timely manner using my BlackBerry. These devices also allow me to connect with my family easily when I am away from home. Of course, another personal favorite use of technology is entertainment and I frequently download movies and TV shows to watch while I'm on the go; for instance, I watched an episode of "The Office" that I downloaded from iTunes on a recent flight from San Francisco to Taipei.

What the Future Holds . . .

Over the past few decades, computing has evolved from mainframes, to desktop computers, to luggable so-called "portable" computers, to today's laptops and mobile devices. I believe that as consumers continue to embrace digital information consumption on the go, the vision of a "laptop for every lap" will come true. However, the device may not look like today's laptop. As the cost of creating wireless and mobile devices continue to drop, we will see huge improvements in portable computing products in the near future that will enable us to provide consumers with portable, yet affordable, devices that can be used to access the types of information that are important to them, whenever they want to do so.

My Advice to Students . . .

Technology has to adapt to market needs, not the other way around. So when you think about innovative technology, it has to be centered on improving consumer experience and pain points.

> *The desire of consumers to access digital and voice information on the go dictates that emerging devices will need to have wireless connectivity and high performance . . .*

Discussion Question

Sumit Agnihotry believes the vision of a "laptop for every lap" will become a reality in the near future. Think about the computing and communications tasks you wish to do on a daily basis, which tasks you prefer to do on the go, and the size and connectivity requirements for the optimal device to accomplish these tasks. What capabilities would the device need to have? Would your optimal device be based on today's mobile phone, notebook computer, netbook computer, or something entirely different? What other hardware characteristics would your optimal device need? Is the future of personal computing a mobile device? Be prepared to discuss your position (in class, via an online class discussion group, in a class chat room, or via a class blog, depending on your instructor's directions). You may also be asked to write a short paper expressing your opinion.

>**For more information on Acer and Acer products, visit us.acer.com. For news about hot technology products, trends, and ideas, visit www.engadet.com and www.ted.com.**

Software

In Chapter 1, we looked at the basic software concepts involved with starting up and using a computer. We continue that focus in this module, discussing in more depth both system software—the software used to run a computer—and application software—the software that performs the specific tasks users want to accomplish using a computer.

Chapter 5 focuses on system software and how it enables the hardware of a computer system to operate and to run application software. Chapter 6 discusses application software, including some important basic concepts and characteristics, as well as an overview of some of the most common types of application software used today—namely, word processing, spreadsheet, database, presentation graphics, and multimedia software.

Chapter 5
System Software: Operating Systems and Utility Programs 176

Overview 177

System Software vs. Application Software 177

The Operating System 178

Operating Systems for Personal Computers and Servers 188

Operating Systems for Mobile Phones and Other Devices 194

Operating Systems for Larger Computers 198

Utility Programs 198

The Future of Operating Systems 205

Chapter 6
Application Software 212

Overview 213

The Basics of Application Software 213

Word Processing Concepts 225

Spreadsheet Concepts 230

Database Concepts 234

Presentation Graphics Concepts 237

Graphics and Multimedia Concepts 240

Other Types of Application Software 243

"Technology should be used as an enabler to achieve your goals, improve your life, and improve the lives of others."

For more comments from Guest Expert **Graham Watson** of Microsoft, see the **Expert Insight on . . . Software** feature at the end of the module.

chapter 5

System Software: Operating Systems and Utility Programs

After completing this chapter, you will be able to do the following:

1. Understand the difference between system software and application software.

2. Explain the different functions of an operating system and discuss some ways that operating systems enhance processing efficiency.

3. List several ways in which operating systems differ from one another.

4. Name today's most widely used operating systems for personal computers and servers.

5. State several devices other than personal computers and servers that require an operating system and list one possible operating system for each type of device.

6. Discuss the role of utility programs and outline several tasks that these programs perform.

7. Describe what the operating systems of the future might be like.

outline

Overview

System Software vs. Application Software

The Operating System
Functions of an Operating System
Processing Techniques for Increased Efficiency
Differences Among Operating Systems

Operating Systems for Personal Computers and Servers
DOS
Windows
Mac OS
UNIX
Linux

Operating Systems for Mobile Phones and Other Devices
Mobile and Embedded Versions of Windows
Android
iPhone OS
BlackBerry OS
Palm OS and Palm webOS
Symbian OS
Embedded Linux

Operating Systems for Larger Computers

Utility Programs
File Management Programs
Search Tools
Diagnostic and Disk Management Programs
Uninstall and Cleanup Utilities
File Compression Programs
Backup and Recovery Utilities
Antivirus, Antispyware, Firewalls, and Other Security Programs

The Future of Operating Systems

OVERVIEW

As you already know, all computers require software in order to operate and perform basic tasks. For instance, software is needed to translate your commands into a form the computer can understand, to open and close other software programs, to manage your stored files, and to locate and set up new hardware as it is added to a computer. The type of software used to perform these tasks is system software—the focus of this chapter. System software runs in the background at all times, launching other software when needed and making it possible for you to use your computer.

We begin this chapter by looking at the difference between system software and application software. System software, the primary topic of this chapter, is usually divided into two categories: operating systems and utility programs. First we examine the operating system—the primary component of system software. We discuss the functions of and general differences between operating systems, and then we explore the specific operating systems most widely used today. Next, we look at utility programs. Utility programs typically perform support functions for the operating system, such as allowing you to manage your files, perform maintenance on your computer, check your computer for viruses, or uninstall a program you no longer want on your computer. Chapter 5 closes with a look at what the future of operating systems may hold. ■

SYSTEM SOFTWARE VS. APPLICATION SOFTWARE

Computers run two types of software: system software and application software.

➤ **System software** consists of the operating system and utility programs that control a computer system and allow you to use your computer. These programs enable the computer to boot, to launch application programs, and to facilitate important jobs, such as transferring files from one storage medium to another, configuring your computer to work with the hardware connected to it, managing files on your hard drive, and protecting your computer system from unauthorized use.

➤ **Application software** includes all the programs that allow you to perform specific tasks on your computer, such as writing a letter, preparing an invoice, viewing a Web page, listening to a music file, checking the inventory of a particular product, playing a game, preparing financial statements, designing a home, and so forth. Application software is discussed in detail in Chapter 6.

In practice, the difference between system and application software is not always straightforward. Some programs, such as those used to burn DVDs, were originally viewed as utility programs. Today, these programs typically contain a variety of additional features,

---

> **System software.** Programs, such as the operating system, that control the operation of a computer and its devices, as well as enable application software to run on the computer. > **Application software.** Programs that enable users to perform specific tasks on a computer, such as writing a letter or playing a game.

such as the ability to organize and play music and other media files, transfer videos and digital photos to a computer, edit videos and photos, create DVD movies, copy CDs and DVDs, and create slide shows. Consequently, these programs now fit the definition of application programs more closely. On the other hand, system software today typically contains several application software components. For example, the *Microsoft Windows* operating system includes a variety of application programs including a Web browser, a calculator, a calendar program, a painting program, a media player, a movie making program, an instant messaging program, and a text editing program. A program's classification as system or application software usually depends on the principal function of the program, and the distinction between the two categories is not always clear cut.

THE OPERATING SYSTEM

A computer's **operating system** is a collection of programs that manage and coordinate the activities taking place within the computer and it is the most critical piece of software installed on the computer. The operating system boots the computer, launches application software, and ensures that all actions requested by a user are valid and processed in an orderly fashion. For example, when you issue the command for your computer to store a document on your hard drive, the operating system must perform the following steps: 1) make sure that the specified hard drive exists, 2) verify that there is adequate space on the hard drive to store the document and then store the document in that location, and 3) update the hard drive's directory with the filename and disk location for that file so that the document can be retrieved again when needed. In addition to managing all of the resources associated with your local computer, the operating system also facilitates connections to the Internet and other networks.

In general, the operating system serves as an intermediary between the user and the computer, as well as between application programs and the computer system's hardware (see Figure 5-1). Without an operating system, no other program can run, and the computer cannot function. Many tasks performed by the operating system, however, go unnoticed by the user because the operating system works in the background much of the time.

FIGURE 5-1
The intermediary role of the operating system.

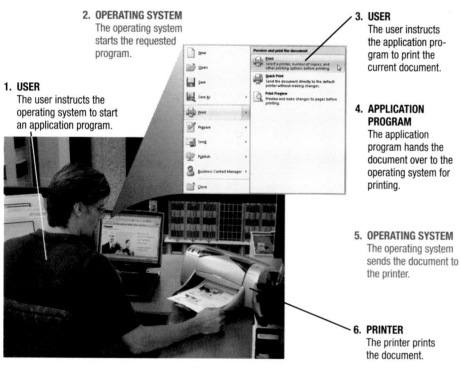

2. OPERATING SYSTEM
The operating system starts the requested program.

1. USER
The user instructs the operating system to start an application program.

3. USER
The user instructs the application program to print the current document.

4. APPLICATION PROGRAM
The application program hands the document over to the operating system for printing.

5. OPERATING SYSTEM
The operating system sends the document to the printer.

6. PRINTER
The printer prints the document.

Functions of an Operating System

Operating systems have a wide range of functions—some of the most important are discussed next.

> **Operating system.** The main component of system software that enables the computer to manage its activities and the resources under its control, run application programs, and interface with the user.

Interfacing with Users

As Figure 5-1 illustrates, one of the principal roles of every operating system is to translate user instructions into a form the computer can understand. It also translates any feedback from hardware—such as a signal that the printer has run out of paper or that a new hardware device has been connected to the computer—into a form that the user can understand. The means by which an operating system or any other program interacts with the user is called the *user interface*; user interfaces can be *text-based* or *graphics-based*, as discussed in more detail shortly. Most, but not all, operating systems today use a *graphical user interface* (*GUI*).

Booting the Computer

As discussed in Chapter 1, the first task your operating system performs when you power up your computer is to *boot* the computer. During the boot process, the essential portion, or core, of the operating system (called the **kernel**) is loaded into memory. The kernel remains in memory the entire time the computer is on so that it is always available; other parts of the operating system are retrieved from the hard drive and loaded into memory when they are needed. Before the boot process ends, the operating system determines the hardware devices that are connected to the computer and configured properly, and it reads an opening batch of instructions. These startup instructions (which the user can customize to some extent when necessary) assign tasks for the operating system to carry out each time the computer boots, such as prompting the user to sign in to an instant messaging program or launching a security program to run continually in the background to detect possible threats.

Typically, many programs are running in the background at any one time, even before the user launches any application software (Figure 5-2 lists all the programs running on one computer immediately after it boots). These programs are launched automatically by the operating system, and they all consume memory and processing power. In Windows, users can see some of the application programs that are running in the background by looking at the icons in the system tray. To close a program, right-click the icon and select the appropriate option. To view the programs that will run each time the computer boots or to remove a program from this *startup list*, Windows users can use the *Startup* tab on the *Microsoft System Configuration Utility*. To open this utility, type *msconfig* in the search box at the bottom of the Start menu and then click the *msconfig* program name when it is displayed. To avoid creating a problem with your computer, however, be sure not to disable a program from the startup list without knowing absolutely what the program does and that it can be safely disabled. Other system configuration information is stored in the *Windows registry* files, which should be modified only by the Windows program itself or by advanced Windows users.

TIP

Press Ctrl+Alt+Delete to open the Task Manager window shown in Figure 5-2.

TIP

Run the msconfig program on a new Windows computer to remove the many *bloatware* programs that are typically preinstalled on a new computer and set to run at start up.

SW

FIGURE 5-2
Running programs.
Many programs are launched by the operating system when the computer boots.

TASK MANAGER
These programs are running, even before any application programs are launched by the user.

SYSTEM TRAY ICONS
These programs were launched during the boot process and will show up in the system tray unless they are closed by the user (right-click an icon to see if you can close that program).

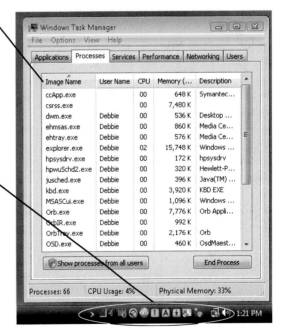

>**Kernel.** The essential portion, or core, of an operating system.

FIGURE 5-3

**Finding new
hardware.** Most
operating systems are
designed to detect
new hardware and
to try to configure it
automatically.

VIDEO PODCAST

Go to the Chapter 5 page at
**www.cengage.com/
computerconcepts/np/uc13**
to download or listen to the "How
To: Find Out What's Running on
Your PC" video podcast.

FIGURE 5-4

**Program
malfunctions.** Most
operating systems
attempt to close only
the program causing
the problem, rather than
requiring a full reboot.

Configuring Devices

The operating system also configures all devices connected to a computer. Small programs called **device drivers** (or simply **drivers**) are used to communicate with peripheral devices, such as monitors, printers, and keyboards. Most operating systems today include the drivers needed for the most common peripheral devices. In addition, drivers often come on a CD packaged with the peripheral device, or they can be downloaded from the manufacturer's Web site. Most operating systems today look for and recognize new devices each time the computer boots. If a new device is found, the operating system typically tries to install the appropriate driver automatically in order to get the new hardware ready to use (see Figure 5-3)—a feature called *Plug and Play*. Because USB and FireWire devices can be connected to a computer when the computer is running, those devices are recognized and configured, as needed, each time they are plugged in to the computer.

Once a device and its driver have been installed properly, they usually work fine. If the device driver file is deleted, becomes *corrupted*, or has a conflict with another piece of software, then the device will no longer work. Usually, the operating system detects problems like this during the boot process and notifies the user, and then tries to reinstall the driver automatically. If the operating system is unable to correct the problem, the user can reinstall the driver manually. You may also need to update or reinstall some device drivers if you *upgrade* your operating system to a newer version. To keep your system up-to-date, many operating systems have an option to check for operating system updates automatically—including updated driver files—on a regular basis. Enabling these *automatic updates* is a good idea to keep your system running smoothly and protected from new threats (like the *computer viruses* discussed in Chapter 9).

Managing and Monitoring Resources and Jobs

As you work on your computer, the operating system continuously manages your computer's resources (such as software, disk space, and memory) and makes them available to devices and programs when they are needed. If a problem occurs—such as a program stops functioning or too many programs are open for the amount of memory installed in the computer—the operating system notifies the user and tries to correct the problem, often by closing the offending program (see Figure 5-4). If the problem cannot be corrected by the operating system, then the user typically needs to reboot the computer.

As part of managing system resources, the operating system schedules jobs (such as documents to be printed or files to be retrieved from a hard drive) to be performed using those resources. *Scheduling routines* in the operating system determine the order in which jobs are carried out, as well as which commands get executed first if the user is working with more than one program at one time or if the computer (such as a server or mainframe) supports multiple users.

File Management

Another important task that the operating system performs is *file management*—keeping track of the files stored on a computer so that they can be retrieved when needed. As discussed in Chapter 3, you can organize the files on a storage medium into folders to simplify file management. Usually the operating system files are stored inside one folder (such as a

---

>**Device driver.** A program that enables an operating system to communicate with a specific hardware device; often referred to simply as a **driver**.

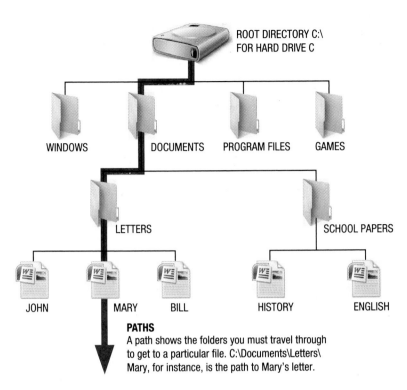

ROOT DIRECTORY C:\
FOR HARD DRIVE C

WINDOWS   DOCUMENTS   PROGRAM FILES   GAMES

LETTERS   SCHOOL PAPERS

JOHN   MARY   BILL   HISTORY   ENGLISH

PATHS
A path shows the folders you must travel through
to get to a particular file. C:\Documents\Letters\
Mary, for instance, is the path to Mary's letter.

FOLDERS AND FILES

FOLDERS
A folder (directory) stores related
information and can contain both
files and other folders. Folders are
designated by a file folder icon.

Word
(word processing)

FILES
A file (document) can contain such
things as a letter, budget, or
Web page. Application programs
typically use unique icons so the
user can quickly identify the
program associated with each file.

Excel
(spreadsheet)

WinZip
(compressed file)

Internet Explorer
(Web page)

FIGURE 5-5
A sample hard drive organization.

FIGURE 5-6
Common file extensions.

Windows folder), and each application program is stored in its own separate folder inside a main programs folder (such as *Program Files*). Other folders designed for storing data files are typically created by the operating system (such as the *Documents* (or *My Documents*) and *Music* (or *My Music*) folders in Windows, depending on the version of Windows being used); individuals may create additional folders, as desired, to keep their files organized. Folders can contain both files and other folders (called *subfolders*).

Files and folders are usually viewed in a hierarchical format; the top of the hierarchy for any storage medium is called the *root directory* (such as C: for the root directory of the hard drive C shown in Figure 5-5). The root directory typically contains both files and folders. To access a file, you generally navigate to the folder containing that file by opening the appropriate drive, folder, and subfolders. Alternatively, you can specify the *path* to a file's exact location. For example, as Figure 5-5 shows, the path

C:\Documents\Letters\Mary

leads through the root directory of the C drive and the *Documents* and *Letters* folders to a file named *Mary*. A similar path can also be used to access the files *John* and *Bill*. As discussed in Chapter 3, you specify a filename for each file when you initially save the file on a storage medium; there can be only one file with the exact same filename in any particular folder on a storage medium.

Filename rules vary with each operating system. For instance, current versions of Windows support filenames that are from 1 to 260 characters long (the length includes the entire path to the file's location) and may include numbers, letters, spaces, and any special characters except / : * ? " < > and |. Filenames typically include a *file extension* at the end of the filename. File extensions are usually three or four characters preceded by a period and are automatically added to a filename by the program in which that file was created, although sometimes the user may have a choice of file extensions supported by a program. Some common file extensions are listed in Figure 5-6 (graphics, audio, and video file formats are explained in more detail in Chapter 10).

File extensions should not be changed by the user because the operating system uses them to identify the program that should be used to open the file. For instance, if you issue a command to open a file named *Letter to Mom.docx*, the file will open using the Microsoft Word program (assuming a recent version of that program is

DOCUMENTS

.doc .docx .txt .rtf .htm .html
.mhtml .xml .xls .xlsx .mdb. .accdb
.ppt .pptx .pdf .sxc .sxi .odf

PROGRAMS

.com .exe

GRAPHICS

.bmp .tif .tiff .jpg .jpe .jpeg .eps
.gif .png .pcx .svg .dib

AUDIO

.wav .au .mp3 .snd .aiff .midi
.aac .wma .ra .m4a

VIDEO

.mpg .mp2 .mp4 .mpe .mov .avi
.rm .wmv .wm .asf

COMPRESSED FILES

.zip .sit .sitx .tar

installed on the computer) because the *.docx* file extension is associated with the Microsoft Word program. Files can be opened, as well as moved, copied, renamed, and deleted, using a *file management program* such as *Windows Explorer*. You may not be able to see file extensions in your file management program, however, since they are typically hidden by default. The Windows Explorer file management program and other utilities typically included in an operating system are discussed near the end of this chapter.

Security

A computer's operating system can use *passwords*, *biometric characteristics* (such as fingerprints), and other security procedures to prevent outsiders from accessing system resources that they are not authorized to access. Most operating systems have other security features available, such as an integrated *firewall* to protect against unauthorized access via the Internet or an option to download and install *security patches* (small program updates that correct known security problems) automatically from the operating system's manufacturer on a regular basis. Operating system passwords can also be used to ensure that *administrative level* operating system tasks (such as installing programs or changing system settings) are performed only by authorized users. Passwords, biometrics, and other security issues related to networks and the Internet are discussed in detail in Chapter 9.

Processing Techniques for Increased Efficiency

Operating systems often utilize various processing techniques in order to operate more efficiently and increase the amount of processing the computer system can perform in any given time period. Some of the techniques most commonly used by operating systems to increase efficiency are discussed in the next few sections.

Multitasking

Multitasking refers to the ability of an operating system to have more than one program (also called a *task*) open at one time. For example, multitasking allows a user to edit a spreadsheet file in one window while loading a Web page in another window or to retrieve new e-mail messages in one window while a word processing document is open in another window. Without the ability to multitask, an operating system would require the user to close one program before opening another program. Virtually all of today's operating systems support multitasking.

Although multitasking enables a user to work with multiple programs at one time, a single CPU core cannot execute more than one task at one time (unless Intel's Hyper-Threading Technology or another technology that allows a single core to function as two cores is used, as discussed in Chapter 2). Consequently, the CPU rotates between processing tasks, but it works so quickly that to the user it appears as though all programs are executing at the same time.

Multithreading

A *thread* is a sequence of instructions within a program that is independent of other threads. Examples might include spell checking, printing, and opening documents in a word processing program. Operating systems that support *multithreading* have the ability to rotate between multiple threads (similar to the way multitasking can rotate between multiple programs) so that processing is completed faster and more efficiently, even though only one thread is executed by a single core at one time. An exception to this is computers using Intel's Hyper-Threading Technology, which allows more than one thread to be executed by a single CPU core at one time. Most current operating systems support multithreading.

>**Multitasking.** The capability of an operating system to run more than one program at one time.

SEQUENTIAL PROCESSING
Tasks are performed one right after the other.

(multitasking and multithreading)

SIMULTANEOUS PROCESSING
Multiple tasks are performed at the exact same time.

(multiprocessing)

(parallel processing)

⚫ **FIGURE 5-7**
Sequential vs. simultaneous processing.

Multiprocessing and Parallel Processing

As discussed in Chapter 2, both multiprocessing and parallel processing involve using two or more CPUs (or multiple cores in a single CPU) in one computer system to perform work more efficiently. The primary difference between these two techniques is that, with multiprocessing, each CPU typically works on a different job; with parallel processing, the processors usually work together to complete one job more quickly. In either case, the CPUs can perform tasks *simultaneously* (at the exactly the same time), in contrast with multitasking and multithreading which use a single CPU and process tasks *sequentially* (by rotating through tasks, as discussed previously). Figure 5-7 illustrates the difference between simultaneous and sequential processing, using tasks typical of a desktop computer.

Multiprocessing is supported by most operating systems and is used with personal computers that have multi-core CPUs (as discussed in Chapter 2), as well as with servers and mainframe computers that have multi-core CPUs and/or multiple CPUs. Parallel processing is used most often with supercomputers and supercomputing clusters.

Memory Management

Another key function of the operating system is *memory management*, which involves optimizing the use of main memory (RAM). The operating system allocates RAM to programs as needed and then reclaims that memory when the program is closed. With today's memory-intensive programs, good memory management can help speed up processing. Since each additional running program or open window consumes memory, users can also help with memory management by limiting the number of programs running in the background (as discussed in an earlier section) to only the ones that are absolutely necessary, as well as by closing windows when they are no longer needed.

One memory management technique frequently used by operating systems is **virtual memory**, which uses a portion of the computer's hard drive as additional RAM. All programs and data located in RAM are divided into fixed-length *pages* or variable-length *segments*, depending on the operating system being used. When the amount of RAM

TIP

Although memory used by a program or process is supposed to be released when it is no longer needed, this does not always happen. Referred to as *memory leaking*, this problem can cause your computer to run out of memory temporarily. When this occurs, reboot your computer to refresh its RAM.

> **Virtual memory.** A memory-management technique that uses hard drive space as additional RAM.

1. Pages of programs or data are copied from RAM to the virtual memory area of the hard drive.

2. Pages are copied back to RAM as they are needed for processing.

3. As more room in RAM is needed, pages are copied to virtual memory and then deleted from RAM.

4. The swapping process continues until the program finishes executing.

FIGURE 5-8
How virtual memory works.

required exceeds the amount of RAM available, the operating system moves pages from RAM to the virtual memory area of the hard drive (this area is called the *page file* or *swap file*). Consequently, as a program is executed, some of the program may be stored in RAM and some in virtual memory. As RAM gets full, pages are moved to virtual memory, and as pages stored in virtual memory are required, they are retrieved from virtual memory and moved to RAM (see Figure 5-8). This *paging* or *swapping* process continues until the program finishes executing. Virtual memory allows you to use more memory than is physically available on your computer, but using virtual memory is slower than just using RAM. Most operating systems today allow the user to specify the total amount of hard drive space to be used for virtual memory. For additional memory to speed up operations, users with computers running recent versions of Windows can also use flash memory media (such as a USB flash drive) in conjunction with Windows' *ReadyBoost* feature.

Buffering and Spooling

Some input and output devices are exceedingly slow, compared to today's CPUs. If the CPU had to wait for these slower devices to finish their work, the computer system would experience a horrendous bottleneck. For example, suppose a user sends a 100-page document to the printer. Assuming the printer can output 20 pages per minute, it would take 5 minutes for the document to finish printing. If the CPU had to wait for the print job to be completed before performing other tasks, the computer would be tied up for 5 minutes.

To avoid this problem, most operating systems use two techniques—*buffering* and *spooling*. A **buffer** is an area in RAM or on the hard drive designated to hold input and output on their way in or out of the system. For instance, a *keyboard buffer* stores characters as they are entered via the keyboard, and a *print buffer* stores documents that are waiting to be printed. The process of placing items in a buffer so they can be retrieved by the appropriate device when needed is called **spooling**. The most common use of buffering and spooling is *print spooling*. Print spooling allows multiple documents to be sent to the printer at one time and to print, one after the other, in the background while the computer and user are performing other tasks. The documents waiting to be printed are said to be in a *print queue*, which designates the order the documents will be printed. While in the print queue, most operating systems allow the user to cancel print jobs and pause the printer (see Figure 5-9); some also allow the user to prioritize the documents in the print queue.

FIGURE 5-9
A print queue.

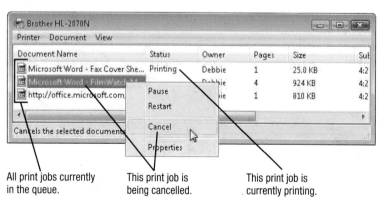

All print jobs currently in the queue.

This print job is being cancelled.

This print job is currently printing.

>**Buffer.** An area in RAM or on the hard drive designated to hold input and output on their way in and out of the system. >**Spooling.** The process of placing items in a buffer so the appropriate device (such as a printer) can retrieve them when needed.

Although originally used primarily for keyboard input and print jobs, most computers and operating systems today use several other buffers to speed up operations. For instance, it is common today for computers to use buffers to assist in redisplaying images on the screen and to temporarily store data that is in the process of being burned onto a CD or DVD.

Differences Among Operating Systems

There are different types of operating systems available to meet different needs. Some of the major distinctions among operating systems include the type of user interface utilized, whether the operating system is targeted for personal or network use, and what type of processing the operating system is designed for.

FIGURE 5-10

Command line
vs. graphical user
interfaces.

Command Line vs. Graphical User Interface

As mentioned earlier in this chapter, a user interface is the manner in which an operating system interacts with its users. Most operating systems today use a **graphical user interface** (**GUI**). The older *DOS* operating system and some versions of the *UNIX* and *Linux* operating systems use a **command line interface** (see Figure 5-10), although graphical versions of UNIX and Linux are available. Command line interfaces require users to input commands using the keyboard; graphical user interfaces allow the user to issue commands by selecting icons, buttons, menu items, and other graphical objects with a mouse or other pointing device.

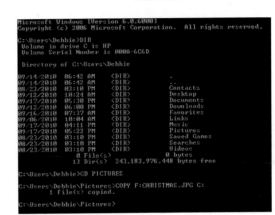

COMMAND LINE INTERFACE
Commands are entered using the keyboard.

Types of Operating Systems

Operating systems used with personal computers are typically referred to as **personal operating systems** (also called *desktop operating systems*) and they are designed to be installed on a single computer. In contrast, **server operating systems** (also called *network operating systems*) are designed to be installed on a network server to grant multiple users access to a network and its resources. Each computer on a network has its own personal operating system installed (just as with a standalone computer) and that operating system controls the activity on that computer, while the server operating system controls access to network resources. Computers on a network may also need special *client* software to access the network and issue requests to the server.

For instance, when you boot a computer connected to a network, the personal operating system installed on your computer boots that computer; the server operating system then asks for your username and password or whatever other data is required to log on to the network, and then allows you to access to the network resources you are authorized to access. To the computers on a network, network resources (such as a shared network hard drive or printer) generally look like *local* (non-network) resources. For instance, you will see a network hard drive listed with its own identifying letter (such as F or G) along with the drives located on your computer, and you will see a network printer included in your list of available printers whenever you open a Print dialog box. If you do not log on to the network or if the network

GRAPHICAL USER INTERFACE
Icons, buttons, menus, and other objects are selected with the mouse to issue commands to the computer.

> **Graphical user interface (GUI).** A graphically based interface that allows a user to communicate instructions to the computer easily.
> **Command line interface.** A user interface that requires the user to communicate instructions to the computer via typed commands.
> **Personal operating system.** A type of operating system designed to be installed on a single personal computer. > **Server operating system.**
A type of operating system designed to be installed on a network server.

1. The client software provides a shell around your desktop operating system. The shell program enables your computer to communicate with the server operating system, which is located on the network server.

Client shell

Desktop operating system

Application software

Your print job

2. When you request a network activity, such as printing a document using a network printer, your application program passes the job to your desktop operating system, which sends it to the client shell, which sends it on to the server operating system, which is located on the network server.

Network server running a server operating system

Your print job

Your print job

Desktop computer running Windows and client software for the server operating system being used.

3. The server operating system then lines up your job in its print queue and prints the job when its turn comes.

Your print job

4. Your print job

3. Job C

2. Job B

1. Job A

Network printer   **PRINT QUEUE**

FIGURE 5-11
How operating systems are used in a network environment.

is down, you cannot access network resources, such as to launch a program located on the network server, save a document to a network hard drive, print using a shared printer, or access the Internet via a shared Internet connection. However, the personal operating system installed on your computer will allow you to work locally on that computer, just as you would on a stand-alone computer. An overview of how a typical personal operating system and a server operating system interact on a computer network is illustrated in Figure 5-11.

In addition to personal operating systems and server operating systems, there are **mobile operating systems** that are designed to be used with mobile phones and other mobile devices, and **embedded operating systems** that are built into consumer kiosks, cash registers, some consumer electronics, and other devices. Specific examples of personal, server, mobile, and embedded operating systems are covered later in this chapter.

The Types of Processors Supported

Most operating systems today are designed to be used with specific types of processors, such as mobile, desktop, or server processors, as well as specific numbers of processors. For instance, some personal operating systems (such as Microsoft Vista) can be used with only one or two processors. In addition, most operating systems are designed for either 32-bit or 64-bit CPUs. Because their word size is twice as large, 64-bit processors can process up to twice as much data per clock cycle as 32-bit processors (depending on the extent to which the application being used supports 64-bit processing), and they can address more than 4 GB of RAM. Both of these factors help to speed up processing in some applications if a 64-bit operating system is being used. Operating systems that support 64-bit CPUs often include other architectural improvements that together may result in a more efficient operating system and, consequently, faster operations. Windows, Mac OS, Linux,

TREND

SideShow and Smart Notebook Covers

Ever want to change the cover of your portable computer to reflect your mood or to check your e-mail when your computer is closed? Well, the solution is just about here. Because of the progress being made in the area of flexible electronics, experts predict that soon a variety of images and information will be able to be displayed on the cover of a portable computer, even if the computer is turned off. Possibilities include changing the color or displaying images on the entire computer for decorative purposes, as well as displaying useful content from the computer. While this feature has yet to materialize on the entire cover of a portable computer, recent versions of Windows include support for a secondary display device—such as a small display located on the cover of a portable computer, on a keyboard, or on other hardware. The technology, called *SideShow*, allows users to access content—such as e-mail messages, news updates, schedules, maps, flight information, stock quotes, address books, Wi-Fi connectivity information, digital music, and more—from the computer the SideShow display is being used with and display that information on the secondary display. The SideShow device can be a part of the computer itself or built into devices such as keyboards, monitors, laptop bags, remote controls, digital picture frames, or stand-alone displays (see the accompanying photos). In any case, the SideShow device displays information received from the associated computer. For example, a SideShow-enabled remote control can be used to retrieve TV listings or information about recorded TV shows from a Windows Media Center computer, and a SideShow-enabled digital picture frame can be used to display e-mail messages, flight information, and other information, in addition to displaying digital photos.

Because it uses minimal power, a SideShow device can be left on continually; in fact, it can be set up to access information on the computer it is being used with and refresh the content displayed on the SideShow device on a regular basis. SideShow devices typically connect to their respective computers via a wireless networking connection, and users can determine the information they would like displayed on the SideShow device by installing and configuring *gadgets*—small programs—on the SideShow device.

SECONDARY DISPLAY BUILT INTO A NOTEBOOK COVER

Each display has its own directional and selection controls.

Content, such as new e-mail messages, maps, stock quotes, or schedule information, is displayed here.

STAND-ALONE SECONDARY DISPLAY

and most other widely used operating systems are all available in 64-bit versions. Details about these and other operating systems are discussed shortly.

Support for Virtualization and Other Technologies

As new technologies or trends (such as new types of buses, virtualization, power consumption concerns, touch and gesture input, and the move to Web-based software, for example) emerge, operating systems must be updated in order to support those new technologies or trends. On the other hand, as technologies become obsolete, operating system manufacturers need to decide when support for those technologies will cease. Alternatively, hardware manufacturers also need to respond to new technologies introduced by operating systems. For instance, the latest versions of Windows support a new *SideShow* feature that requires the incorporation of a secondary display device built into hardware, such as into the cover of a notebook computer. When a new operating system feature (such as SideShow) is introduced, hardware manufacturers must decide if they want to adapt their hardware to support the new feature. For a look at SideShow and how it can be used to provide you with updates of the information you want to see on a regular basis, see the Trend box.

OPERATING SYSTEMS FOR PERSONAL COMPUTERS AND SERVERS

As previously discussed, many operating systems today are designed either for personal computers (such as desktop and notebook computers) or for network servers. The most widely used personal and server operating systems are discussed next. Mobile and embedded versions of these operating systems are discussed later in this chapter.

DOS

During the 1980s and early 1990s, **DOS (Disk Operating System)** was the dominant operating system for microcomputers. DOS traditionally used a command line interface, although newer versions of DOS support a menu-driven interface. There are two primary forms of DOS: *PC-DOS* and *MS-DOS*. PC-DOS was created originally for IBM PCs (and is owned by IBM), whereas MS-DOS was created for use with IBM-compatible PCs. Both versions were originally developed by Microsoft Corporation, but neither version is updated any longer. DOS is not widely used with personal computers today because it does not utilize a graphical user interface and does not support modern processors and processing techniques. Some computers (such as computers running the Windows operating system), however, can still understand DOS commands and users can issue these commands using the *Command Prompt* window, as shown in Figure 5-12.

CHANGE DIRECTORY (CD) COMMAND
Changes to a new location on the current drive.

DRIVE COMMAND
Changes to a new drive.

COPY COMMAND
Copies files from one location to another.

DIRECTORY (DIR) COMMAND
Displays the files and folders in the current location.

FIGURE 5-12
DOS. Even though DOS has become technologically obsolete, Windows users can still issue DOS commands via the Command Prompt.

Windows

Microsoft Windows has been the predominant personal operating system for many years and still holds about 90% of the market. There have been many different versions of **Windows** over the years; the next few sections chronicle the main developments of this operating system.

Windows 1.0 Through Windows XP

Microsoft created the original version of Windows—*Windows 1.0*—in 1985 in an effort to meet the needs of users frustrated by having to learn and use DOS commands. Windows 1.0 through *Windows 3.x* (*x* stands for the version number of the software, such as Windows 3.0, 3.1, or 3.11) were not, however, full-fledged operating systems. Instead, they were *operating environments* for the DOS operating system; that is, graphical shells that operated around the DOS operating system and were designed to make DOS easier to use.

> **DOS (Disk Operating System).** The operating system designed for and widely used on early IBM and IBM-compatible PCs. > **Windows.** The primary personal computer operating system developed by Microsoft Corporation; the most recent version is Windows 7.

In 1994, Microsoft announced that all versions of Windows after 3.11 would be full-fledged operating systems instead of just operating environments. The next several versions of Windows are as follows:

➤ *Windows 95* (released in 1995) and *Windows 98* (released in 1998)—both used a GUI similar to the one used with Windows 3.x but were easier to use than earlier versions of Windows. Both Windows 95 and Windows 98 supported multitasking, long filenames, a higher degree of Internet integration, more options for customizing the desktop user interface, larger hard drives, DVD drives, and USB devices.

➤ *Windows NT* (*New Technology*)—the first 32-bit version of Windows designed for high-end workstations and servers. Windows NT was built from the ground up using a different kernel than the other versions of Windows.

➤ *Windows Me* (*Millennium Edition*)—the replacement for Windows 98. Designed for home computers, Windows Me supported improved home networking and a shared Internet connection; it also featured improved multimedia capabilities, better system protection, a faster boot process, and more Internet-ready activities and games.

➤ *Windows 2000*—released in 2000 to replace Windows NT. Windows 2000 was geared toward high-end business workstations and servers, and it included support for wireless devices and other types of new hardware.

➤ *Windows XP*—replaced both Windows 2000 (for business use) and Windows Me (for home use) and included improved photo, video, and music editing and sharing; improved networking capabilities; and support for handwriting and voice input. While Microsoft is phasing out Windows XP and only netbooks can be purchased with that version of Windows today, there is still a large installed base of Windows XP users and Microsoft plans to support Windows XP until 2014.

Windows Vista

Windows Vista replaced Windows XP and was the current version of Windows until *Windows 7* was released in late 2009. However, Windows Vista is still widely used today. It comes in four basic editions (*Home Basic*, *Home Premium*, *Business*, and *Ultimate*) and in both 32-bit and 64-bit versions. One of the most obvious initial changes in Windows Vista is the *Aero* interface. Aero is a new visual graphical user interface that uses glass-like transparency, vibrant colors, and dynamic elements like *Live Thumbnails* of taskbar buttons and a *Flip 3D* feature to view all open windows in 3D to make the Vista experience more productive and enjoyable

ASK THE EXPERT

Tony Onorati, Former Naval Aviator and Former Commanding Officer, Strike Fighter Weapons School Pacific, NAS Lemoore

What computer experience is needed to be a U.S. Navy pilot?

While no computer experience is necessarily required to enter flight school, failure to have a solid knowledge of the Windows operating system will put the candidate well behind his/her contemporaries when they finally do reach the fleet as a pilot. All the tactical planning tools for preflight preparation, navigation, ordnance delivery, and mission planning, as well as all aircraft-specific publications, manuals, and training, are all computer based. For the FA-18 Hornet, all mission data is created on the computer, copied to a mission computer card, and plugged into the jet where it is downloaded into the aircraft's computer for use in flight. Becoming a naval aviator without computer skills is like entering flight school without ever having flown before—it can be done but it places you well behind the power curve.

AERO INTERFACE
Features translucent, glass-like windows and 3D effects.

ICONS
Represent programs, folders, documents, and other items that can be opened with the mouse.

SIDEBAR
Contains the user's selected gadgets.

WINDOWS
Contain programs, icons, documents, and so forth.

SEARCHES
Can be saved for later use.

QUICK LAUNCH TOOLBAR
Used to launch programs.

START MENU
Includes a search box to search for and open documents, programs, and Web sites.

FIGURE 5-13
Windows Vista.

(see Figure 5-13). Windows Vista also introduced the *Sidebar* feature that contains *gadgets*—small applications that are used to perform a variety of tasks, such as displaying weather information, a clock, a calendar, a calculator, sticky notes, news headlines, personal photos, e-mail messages, stock tickers, and more.

The Vista Start menu is more streamlined than in Windows XP. It also contains an *Instant Search* feature located at the bottom of the Start menu to allow users to easily search for and open programs and documents stored on their computers. Searches can be saved in *Search Folders* so that updated search results based on that search criteria can be viewed at any time just by opening the appropriate Search Folder, as discussed in more detail later in this chapter.

Vista also contains several built-in security features and much improved networking, collaboration, and synchronization tools. Improved multimedia capabilities include a new *Windows Photo Gallery*, *Windows DVD Maker*, and a *Windows Media Center* used to access digital entertainment, such as recorded TV shows and downloaded music. *Windows Speech Recognition* allows users to interact with their computers using their voice; with this program, users can control the operating system, dictate documents, and fill out Web-based forms verbally, as discussed in the Chapter 6 How It Works box.

One issue surrounding Vista is its higher level of hardware requirements when compared to earlier versions of Windows and other operating systems. Windows Vista requires a significant amount of memory in order to function at an acceptable speed; it also has specific graphics requirements that must be met in order to use the Aero interface. These limitations are one reason many individuals and businesses decided to stay with Windows XP instead of upgrading to Vista.

Windows 7

Windows 7, released in late 2009, is the newest version of Windows. Windows 7 is available in both 32-bit and 64-bit versions and in four main editions, including *Home Premium* (the primary version for home users) and *Professional* (the primary version for businesses). While the minimum suggested system requirements for Windows 7 are essentially the same as for Vista, Windows 7 is designed to start up and respond faster than Vista. In addition, Microsoft states that all versions of Windows 7 will run well on netbooks—something Vista could not do and a very important feature since netbooks are one of the fastest growing areas of the personal computer market today.

>**Windows 7.** The current version of Windows.

AERO INTERFACE
Windows are still transparent and 3D options
(such as Live Thumbnails) are active.

PROGRAM ICONS
Can be pinned to
the taskbar.

TASKBAR BUTTONS
Can be rearranged by the user; pointing
to a button displays a Live Thumbnail.

DESKTOP GADGETS
Gadgets are now located on the desktop.

JUMP LISTS
Right-click an icon to display the most
recent documents for that program.

SHOW DESKTOP
Point to the Show Desktop button
to make all windows temporarily
transparent.

FIGURE 5-14
Windows 7.

The appearance of Windows 7 is similar to Windows Vista—many of the improvements in Windows 7 focus on making it faster and easier to use. For instance, you can now drag taskbar buttons to rearrange them in the order you prefer, and you can *pin* (lock) a program to the taskbar so it can be launched with a single click (this feature replaces the *Quick Launch toolbar* in Windows Vista). In addition, you can view a larger version of a window by pointing to its taskbar thumbnail, and you can right-click a taskbar button (and some Start menu items) to bring up a *jump list* to show your most recent documents for that program (see Figure 5-14). To quickly arrange two windows side by side, you can drag a window to the left or right edge of the desktop to have it automatically resize and snap into place to fill half of the screen. Gadgets have moved from the Sidebar (as in Windows Vista) to the desktop in Windows 7 to free up the entire screen for documents and other content. Gadgets (and other items located on the desktop) can be viewed easily by pointing to the *Show Desktop* button in the bottom far right corner of the taskbar. This option temporarily makes all open windows transparent so items on the desktop are visible (as in the right image in Figure 5-14).

To make it easier to use and manage all of your connected devices (such as printers, portable digital media players, USB flash drives, and so forth), Windows 7 includes a new *Device Stage*. To easily stream media content stored on your computer to any networked device (such as another computer, a stereo, or an Xbox 360), Windows 7 includes a *Play To* option. In addition, Windows 7 includes a *HomeGroup* feature for improved home networking, one-click Wi-Fi connections, support for both touch and pen input, and improved accessory programs (such as a more versatile Calculator and a Paint program that uses the *Ribbon* interface found in recent versions of Microsoft Office).

TIP

With Windows 7, some programs
(such as Messenger, Mail, Photo
Gallery, and Movie Maker) are no
longer included in the operating
system but are available for free
as *Windows Live Essentials*
downloads from the Windows Live
Web site.

Windows Server and Windows Home Server

Windows Server is the version of Windows designed for server use. *Windows Server 2008* includes *Internet Information Services 7.0*, which is a powerful Web platform for Web applications and Web services; built-in virtualization technologies; a variety of new security tools and enhancements; and streamlined configuration and management tools. The latest version of Windows Server 2008 is called *Windows Server 2008 R2* and includes features that are designed specifically to work with client computers running Windows 7.

A related operating system designed for home use is *Windows Home Server*, which is preinstalled on home server devices and designed to provide services for a home network. For instance, a home server can serve as a central storage location for all devices (computers, gaming consoles, portable digital media players, and so forth) in the home. Home servers also can be set up to back up all devices in the home on a regular basis, as well as to give users access to the data on the home server and to control the home network from any computer via the Internet.

Mac OS

Mac OS (see Figure 5-15) is the proprietary operating system for computers made by Apple Corporation. It is based on the UNIX operating system (discussed shortly) and originally set the standard for graphical user interfaces. Many of today's operating systems follow the trend that Mac OS started and, in fact, use GUIs that highly resemble the one used with Mac OS.

The latest versions of Mac OS (such as *Mac OS X Leopard* and *Mac OS X Snow Leopard*) are part of the **Mac OS X** family. Mac OS X allows multithreading and multitasking, supports dual 64-bit processors, and has a high level of multimedia functions and connectivity. In addition, it includes the *Safari* Web browser, a *Spaces* feature that allows you to organize groups of applications and windows into Spaces that can be displayed or hidden as desired, a *Stacks* feature that allows you to store files (documents, programs, and so on) in a Stack on the *Dock*, and a *Quick Look* feature that shows you previews of files without opening them. The main improvement provided by the most recent version of Mac OS X (Snow Leopard) over the previous version (Leopard) is responsiveness. For instance, the *Time Machine* automatic backup and restore system is 50% faster, *Mail* loads messages 85% faster and conducts

Ⓥ **FIGURE 5-15**
Mac OS X Leopard.

QUICK LOOK
Shows previews of files without opening them.

WINDOWS
Contain programs, icons, documents, and so forth.

STACK
Contains a collection of documents stored on the dock by the user.

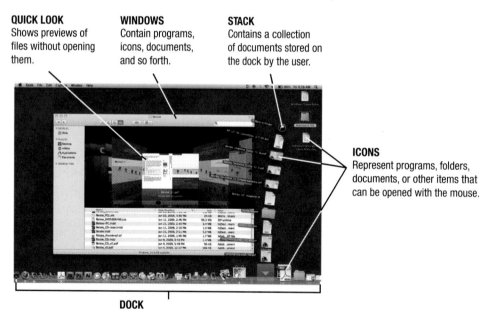

ICONS
Represent programs, folders, documents, or other items that can be opened with the mouse.

DOCK
Contains the user's Stacks and commonly used icons.

searches up to 90% faster, and the new 64-bit Safari browser is faster and more resistant to crashes. Snow Leopard is also more efficient, requiring only about one-half the hard drive space as previous versions.

Mac OS X Server is the server version of Mac OS X. The latest version, *Mac OS X Server Snow Leopard*, is a full 64-bit operating system that is up to twice as fast as earlier server versions. New capabilities built into Snow Leopard Server include *Podcast Producer 2* for creating and publishing podcasts, and *Mobile Access Server* for providing authorized users secure remote access to firewall protected servers via Macs, iPhones, and other Apple devices.

UNIX

UNIX was originally developed in the late 1960s at AT&T Bell Laboratories as an operating system for midrange servers. UNIX is a multiuser, multitasking operating system. Computer systems ranging from microcomputers to mainframes can run UNIX, and it can support a variety of devices from different manufacturers. This flexibility gives UNIX an advantage over competing operating systems in some situations. However, UNIX is more expensive, requires a higher level of technical knowledge, and tends to be harder to install, maintain, and upgrade than most other commonly used operating systems.

There are many versions of UNIX available, as well as many other operating systems that are based on UNIX. These operating systems—such as Mac OS—are sometimes referred to as *UNIX flavors*. In fact, the term *UNIX*, which initially referred to the original UNIX operating system, has evolved to refer today to a group of similar operating systems based on UNIX. Many UNIX flavors are not compatible with each other, which creates some problems when a program written for one UNIX computer system is moved to another computer system running a different flavor of UNIX. To avoid this incompatibility problem, the *Open Group* open source consortium is dedicated to the development and evolution of the *Single UNIX Specification*—a standardized programming environment for UNIX applications. Both personal and server versions of UNIX-based operating systems are available.

FIGURE 5-16
Linux. This version of Linux includes a 3D graphical interface to increase the user's workspace.

Linux

Linux is an operating system developed by *Linus Torvalds* in 1991 when he was a student at the University of Helsinki in Finland. The operating system resembles UNIX but was developed independently from it. Linux was released to the public as *open source software*; that is, a program whose *source code* is available to the public and can be modified to improve it or to customize it to a particular application, as discussed in more detail in Chapter 6. Over the years, the number of Linux users has grown, and volunteer programmers from all over the world have collaborated to improve it, sharing their modified code with others over the Internet. Although Linux originally used a command line interface, most recent versions of Linux programs use a graphical user interface (see Figure 5-16). Linux is widely available as a free download via

ASK THE EXPERT

 Jim Zemlin, Executive Director, The Linux Foundation

Is there a downside to installing Linux on a personal computer?

No, I don't think so. More consumers than ever are using Linux on their PCs. Recently, Microsoft introduced a new operating system that won't run well on PCs more than just a few years old. Many people are finding that Linux is well suited for these older computers. This is good for users who don't want to throw away a perfectly good computer, and it's good for the environment and our landfills. Desktop Linux is easy to install and use. In fact, the Russian government recently installed Linux on all computers in their schools. The upsides of running Linux on a personal computer are flexibility, customization, and choice, among others. It's also free and comes with all the software you need! A computer is your personal property and you should have the freedom to customize it as you see fit—both inside and out. Linux allows you this freedom.

the Internet; companies are also permitted to customize Linux and sell it as a retail product. Commercial Linux distributions (such as those available from Red Hat and Novell) come with maintenance and support materials (something that many of the free versions do not offer) making the commercial versions more attractive for corporate users.

Over the years, Linux has grown from an operating system used primarily by computer techies who disliked Microsoft to a widely accepted operating system with strong support from mainstream companies, such as IBM, HP, Dell, and Novell. Linux is available in both personal and server versions; it is also widely used with mobile phones, as discussed shortly. The use of Linux with inexpensive personal computers is growing. In fact, one Linux-based operating system (*Android*) developed for mobile phones may be extended to netbooks and other very portable personal computers in the near future.

One reason individuals and organizations are switching to Linux and other open source software is cost. Typically, using the Linux operating system and a free or low-cost office suite, Web browser program, and e-mail program can save several hundreds of dollars per computer.

OPERATING SYSTEMS FOR MOBILE PHONES AND OTHER DEVICES

ONLINE VIDEO

Go to the Chapter 5 page at www.cengage.com/ computerconcepts/np/uc13 to watch the "Smart Car Technologies" video clip.

While notebook, netbook, UMPCs, and other portable personal computers typically use the same operating systems as desktop computers, mobile phones and other mobile devices usually use mobile operating systems—either mobile versions of personal operating systems (such as Windows or Linux) or special operating systems (such as *Apple iPhone OS* or *Blackberry OS*) that are designed solely for mobile devices. There are also embedded operating systems designed to be used with everyday objects, such as home appliances, gaming consoles, digital cameras, toys, watches, GPS systems, home medical devices, voting terminals, and cars (for a look at some of the features now available in *smart cars*, see the Inside the Industry box). Most users select a mobile phone by considering the mobile provider, hardware, and features associated with the phone, instead of considering the operating system used. However, users should understand that the operating system used with a phone or other device determines some of the capabilities of the phone (such as whether it can accept touch input or whether its display can rotate automatically as the phone is moved from portrait to landscape orientation), the interface used, and the applications that can run on that device. The most widely used mobile and embedded operating systems are discussed next.

Mobile and Embedded Versions of Windows
The mobile and embedded versions of Windows are called *Windows Mobile* and *Windows Embedded*, respectively.

INSIDE THE INDUSTRY

Smart Cars

Computers have been integrated into cars for years to perform specific tasks, such as assisting with gear shifting and braking. Lately, however, the use of computers in cars has skyrocketed and they are also being used to add additional convenience and safety to the driving experience. Some features, such as GPS navigation systems and smart air bag systems that adjust the deployment of an air bag based on the weight of the occupant, are fairly standard today. Integrated *infotainment systems* that use Bluetooth and USB ports to tie mobile phones and portable digital media players to the car stereo system, as well as to steering wheel and voice control systems, are also now available. Some other new and emerging trends in smart cars are discussed next.

> *Self-parking systems*—use cameras and/or sensors to assist in parallel parking; the onboard computer completely controls the car's steering wheel during the parking process and instructs the driver when any action (such as changing gears) is needed in order to park the car correctly.

> *Lane departure systems*—use cameras to view the markings on the road and vibrate the steering wheel if the car begins to veer out of its lane.

> *Drowsiness detection systems*—use cameras to evaluate the driver's blinking pattern and eyelid movements and vibrate the seat or otherwise alert the driver if the driver becomes drowsy.

> *Blind spot detection systems*—use cameras mounted on the car's side mirrors to detect vehicles in the driver's blind spot and display a warning light near the mirror to notify the driver that something is in the blind spot (shown in Figure 1-12 in Chapter 1).

> *Adaptive cruise control and distance alert systems*—use a radar system installed on the front of the car to detect the speed and distance of the vehicle ahead of it, and then automatically decrease or increase the speed of the car to maintain a safe distance from the vehicle ahead of it.

> *Collision warning and auto brake systems*—use radar and camera systems installed on the front of the car to warn the driver when they are too close to the car in front of them; if a collision is imminent, the brakes are automatically activated at that point (see the accompanying illustration).

> *Electronic traffic sign recognition systems*—use cameras to read speed limit, one-way, and other important traffic signs and notify the driver of any potential problems (such as exceeding the speed limit or driving the wrong way on a one-way street). When used with adaptive cruise control systems, the car can be set to adjust the speed to the correct speed limit automatically.

> *Keyless entry and ignition systems*—use the owner's fingerprint to unlock and start the car; future applications will likely include mobile phone applications that perform these tasks.

One of the biggest challenges for smart car technologies is the safe use of all the smart gadgets being incorporated into cars. The concern stems from studies consistently showing that distracted drivers are the cause of a vast majority of crashes. Voice-controlled dashboard components, mobile phones, and other devices help because they are hands-free, although studies have found that your risk of an accident requiring a trip to the hospital quadruples when you are talking on a mobile phone—hands-free or not.

Volvo's collision warning and auto brake system.

WINDOWS MOBILE

ANDROID

IPHONE OS

BLACKBERRY OS

FIGURE 5-17
Examples of mobile operating systems.

Windows Mobile

Windows Mobile is the version of Windows designed for mobile phones. It has some of the look and feel of the larger desktop versions of Windows (see the Start button shown in Figure 5-17), but it also has features useful to mobile users. For instance, Windows Mobile supports multitasking; includes an improved mobile Web browser; supports a free *My Phone* service that automatically syncs and backs up contacts, text messages, and other information to the Web; and supports a variety of software, including Facebook applications, mobile versions of Microsoft Word, Excel, and PowerPoint; and more. The current version of Microsoft Mobile is *Microsoft Mobile 6.1*. The next version—*Windows Mobile 6.5*, also called *Microsoft Phone*—features a new honeycomb Home screen interface that allows users to view the information most important to them at a glance and accurately select the desired item by touch, and a new *Windows Marketplace for Mobile* application store to help users locate and purchase additional mobile applications. Windows Mobile 6.5 is expected to be available in 2010.

Windows Embedded

Windows Embedded is a family of operating systems based on Windows that is designed primarily for consumer and industrial devices that are not personal computers, such as cash registers, digital photo frames, GPS devices, ATM machines, medical devices, and robots. There are multiple versions of Windows Embedded based on different versions of Windows (including Windows XP, Windows Vista, and Windows Mobile) to match the type of device the operating system is to be used with and the computers with which the devices may need to interact. There are also versions of Windows specifically designed to be embedded into cars, such as *Microsoft Auto*—an embedded version of Windows that is designed specifically for integrated in-vehicle communication, entertainment, and navigation systems. For instance, Microsoft Auto powers the *Ford SYNC* system, which enables calls from mobile phones and music from portable digital media players to be controlled by voice or with buttons on the steering wheel.

Android

Android (refer again to Figure 5-17) is a Linux-based operating system developed by the Open Handset Alliance, a group that includes Google and more than 30 technology and mobile companies. Android supports multitasking and, as a relatively new operating system, it was able to built from the ground up with current mobile device capabilities in mind, which enables developers to create mobile applications that take full advantage of all the features a mobile device has to offer. It is an open platform, so users can connect to any mobile network and mobile phone provider they choose and they can customize their mobile phones (including the home screen, dialer, and applications used) as much as desired. A large number of applications have already been developed for Android and more applications and more Android-based phones (and, potentially, Android-based personal computers) are expected to be released soon.

iPhone OS

The mobile operating system designed for Apple mobile phones and mobile devices, such as the *iPhone 3G* and the *iPod Touch*, is **iPhone OS** (see Figure 5-17). This operating system is based on Apple's OS X operating system, supports multi-touch input, and has thousands of applications available via the *App Store*. While earlier versions of iPhone OS do not allow multitasking of third-party software (reportedly to increase battery life and stability), the newest version—*iPhone 3.0*—supports limited multitasking. It also includes an improved version of the Safari Web browser; a new media player; the ability to copy, cut, and paste text; the ability to send photos via text messaging; and improved search capabilities.

BlackBerry OS

BlackBerry OS is the operating system designed for BlackBerry devices (see Figure 5-17). It supports multitasking and, like other mobile operating systems, it includes e-mail and Web browsing support, music management, video recording, calendar tools, and more. In addition, BlackBerry OS includes a *voice note* feature that allows you to send a voice note via e-mail or text message and has an integrated maps feature. The latest version is *Blackberry OS 5.0*.

Palm OS and Palm webOS

Palm OS is the original operating system designed for Palm devices. In 2009, Palm released **Palm webOS**—a new Linux-based mobile operating system developed for next-generation Palm mobile phones, such as the *Palm Pre*. Unlike Palm OS, Palm webOS supports full multitasking; it also includes *Palm Synergy* to synchronize contacts and calendars from multiple locations, an improved Web browser, and a Web-based application suite.

Symbian OS

Symbian OS is a mobile operating system that supports multithreading and multitasking; it also includes support for Web browsing, e-mail, handwriting recognition, synchronization, and a range of other applications designed for mobile communications and computing. It has a flexible user interface framework that enables mobile phone manufacturers to develop and customize user interfaces to meet the needs of their customers. While not as widely used in North America as in other locations, Symbian OS is the most widely used mobile operating system worldwide, running on nearly half of the world's mobile phones, and is used on most Nokia mobile phones. The current version is *Symbian OS 9.5*.

ONLINE VIDEO

Go to the Chapter 5 page at **www.cengage.com/ computerconcepts/np/uc13** to watch the "A Tour of the Ford SYNC System" video clip.

ONLINE VIDEO

Go to the Chapter 5 page at **www.cengage.com/ computerconcepts/np/uc13** to watch the "A Tour of the T-Mobile G1 Android Mobile Phone" video clip.

SW

FURTHER EXPLORATION Go

Go to the Chapter 5 page at **www.cengage.com/ computerconcepts/np/uc13** for links to information about operating systems.

Embedded Linux

Embedded Linux is another operating system alternative for mobile phones, GPS devices, portable digital media players, and other mobile devices. Just as with desktop and server versions of Linux, embedded Linux is available in a variety of flavors from different companies. Linux is also the basis for several other mobile operating systems, such as Android, iPhone OS, and Palm webOS.

OPERATING SYSTEMS FOR LARGER COMPUTERS

Larger computer systems—such as high-end servers, mainframes, and supercomputers—sometimes use operating systems designed solely for that type of system. For instance, IBM's *i5/OS* and *z/OS* are designed for IBM servers and mainframes, respectively. In addition, many servers and mainframes today run conventional operating systems, such as Windows, UNIX, and Linux. Linux in particular is increasingly being used with both mainframes and supercomputers; often a group of Linux computers are linked together to form a Linux supercomputing cluster, as discussed in Chapter 1. Larger computer systems may also use a customized operating system based on a conventional operating system; for instance, many IBM mainframes and Cray supercomputers use versions of UNIX developed specifically for those computers (*AIX* and *UNICOS*, respectively).

UTILITY PROGRAMS

A **utility program** is a software program that performs a specific task, usually related to managing or maintaining the computer system. Many utility programs—such as programs for finding files, diagnosing and repairing system problems, cleaning up a hard drive, viewing images, playing multimedia files, and backing up files—are built into operating systems. There are also many stand-alone utility programs available as an alternative to the operating system's utility programs (such as a *search* or a *backup program*) or to provide additional utility features not usually built into operating systems (such as an *antivirus* or a *file compression program*). Stand-alone utility programs are often available in a *suite* of related programs (such as a collection of *maintenance programs* or *security programs*, as shown in Figure 5-18). Some of the most commonly used integrated and stand-alone utility programs are discussed next. For a look at how to download and install a new utility program from the Internet, see the How It Works box.

FIGURE 5-18
Utility suites. Utility suites contain a number of related utility programs.

File Management Programs

File management programs allow you to perform file management tasks such as looking to see which files are stored on a storage medium, and copying, moving, deleting, and renaming folders and files. The file management program incorporated into Windows is **Windows Explorer**; some common file management tasks using this program are summarized next.

HOW IT WORKS

Downloading and Installing Programs

Many software programs—including utility programs—are available for download via the Web. To download a program, generally a hyperlink is clicked and then the file is downloaded to your computer. With some installations, you can specify the location where the downloaded program should be stored on your computer—a good location for Windows users is the desktop for the installation files that you want to store only temporarily or the Downloads folder for the installation files that you want to retain. To start the installation process once the installation file is downloaded, open the installation file (navigate to the folder in which the installation is located, if needed, and then double-click the file). Many programs require that you accept the terms of a license agreement at the beginning of the installation process in order for the program to install. If the product was purchased, you may also be required to type in a *registration code* or *product key* at some point during the installation process;

these codes are typically e-mailed to you (or otherwise provided to you) after your payment for the product is processed. You may also be asked to specify or verify the installation location or other settings during the installation process; once the installation process has been completed, the program can be launched. This procedure is illustrated in the accompanying illustrations.

DOWNLOADING THE PROGRAM

1. Click the download link, then click Save to start the download process.

2. Specify the download location, then click Save to download the installation file.

INSTALLING THE PROGRAM

1. Launch the installation program, click the Run button, and then follow the prompts to launch the installation program.

2. You will often have to agree to the terms of a license agreement before installation will take place.

3. Specify or verify the desired location, click Next, and then follow the prompts to install the program.

USING THE INSTALLED PROGRAM

Click the program name on the Start menu to launch the installed program.

Use the Organize button to create new folders and copy files and folders.

Use the Back button to go to the previous location.

Use the Views button to specify how the items in the right pane are displayed.

The Address bar shows the current location.

Enter keywords to search for a folder or file meeting the criteria you supply.

Click a drive or folder icon in the left pane to display its contents in the right pane.

Click a dark arrow to close a folder and hide its contents.

Click a clear arrow to open a folder and display its contents.

The Navigation pane contains Favorite Links and the Folders list.

Double-click a folder to open it.

Double-click a document to open it in its associated program.

FIGURE 5-19
Using Windows Explorer to look at the contents of a computer.

Looking at the Folders and Files Stored on a Computer

Once a file management program is open, you can look at the folders and files stored on your computer. For instance, you can do the following in Windows Explorer (see Figure 5-19):

> To see the folders and files stored on your hard drive, USB flash drive, or any other storage medium, click the appropriate letter or name for that medium in the left pane (called the *Navigation pane*).

> To look inside a folder, click it (in the left pane) or double-click it (in the right pane). To go back to the previous location, click the Back toolbar button.

> To open a file in its associated program, double-click it.

> To create a new folder in the current location, click the *Organize* button, select *New Folder*, and then type the name for the new folder.

Copying and Moving Files and Folders

To copy or move a file or folder using a file management program, you first need to navigate to the drive and folder where the item is located and then select the desired file or folder. Next, issue either the *Copy command* (to copy the item) or the *Cut command* (to move the item), such as by using Windows Explorer's Organize button as shown in Figure 5-20, to copy or move that item to the *Clipboard* (a temporary location used for copying items). You then need to navigate to the drive and folder where you want the file to go, and use the *Paste command* to copy or move the item to that location.

Renaming Files and Folders

You can also change the name of a file and folder using a file management program. To rename an item in Windows Explorer, select the item to be renamed, use the Organize button to issue the *Rename command* (or click a second time on the filename once the item is selected), and then retype or edit the filename.

TIP

Hold the Control key down while clicking files to select multiple files at one time; hold the Shift key down to select a group of adjacent files.

TIP

You can also copy, move, rename, or delete a file or folder in Windows Explorer by right-clicking the item and selecting the desired action from the shortcut menu that is displayed.

VIDEO PODCAST

Go to the Chapter 5 page at **www.cengage.com/ computerconcepts/np/uc13** to download or listen to the "How To: Restore Deleted Files" video podcast.

2. Click the Organize button and select *Copy* to copy the file to the Clipboard.

3. Navigate to the drive and folder where you want the file to go.

1. Navigate to the drive and folder containing the file you want to copy or move, and then select the file.

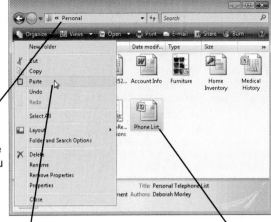

4. Click the Organize button and select *Paste* to copy the file to the current location.

5. The file is copied.

Deleting Files and Folders

To delete a file or folder using a file management program, navigate to the drive and folder that contains the file or folder you want to delete, select the desired item, and then press the Delete key on the keyboard. You will need to select *Yes* when the Confirm File/Folder Delete dialog box opens to finish the deletion process. Deleting a folder deletes all of the contents located inside that folder.

Search Tools

As the amount of e-mail, photos, documents, and other important data individuals store on their computers continues to grow, **search tools**—utility programs that search for documents and other files on a user's hard drives—are becoming more important. Search tools are often integrated into file management programs and they are highly improved in recent versions of some operating systems, such as Mac OS and Windows. There are also a number of third-party search tools available.

Search tools typically are used to find files located somewhere on the specified storage medium that meet specific criteria, such as being in a certain folder, including certain characters in the filename, being of a particular type (a song, digital photo, or spreadsheet, for instance), and/or having a particular date associated with the file. If a document has been manually or automatically assigned *metadata tags* (information about the file, such as author, artist, or keywords), some search programs can search by those tags as well.

In Windows, for instance, users can use the *Search box* located at the top right corner of the Windows Explorer window (refer again to Figure 5-19) to search for files and folders in the current location that match the keywords entered into the Search box. Searches can be saved by clicking the Save Search button that appears on the toolbar at the top of the Windows Explorer window after a search is performed; saved searches can be run again by opening the user's *Searches folder* in the Navigation pane. For a quick search, users can also search for programs, documents, and Web pages by typing keywords in the Search box at the bottom of the Start menu.

A variety of Internet search companies—such as Google, Microsoft, and Yahoo!—have also developed *desktop search tools* that apply the technology used in their Internet search tools to an individual's computer. Typically these programs search through files,

FIGURE 5-20
Using Windows Explorer to copy files.

TIP

To *restore* a file or folder deleted from your computer's hard drive, open your computer's *Recycle Bin* and restore the file to its original location. Files and folders deleted from removable media cannot be restored in this manner, but there are special utility programs available to help you recover deleted files from flash memory cards and USB flash drives, as long as you have not written anything to the card or drive since the files were deleted.

TIP

To help you better organize and locate your files, Windows 7 uses *Libraries*—special folders designed to provide access to common types of files (such as photos, documents, music, or videos), regardless of where those items are physically stored on your computer; you just specify which folders on your computer each Library should include.

>**Search tool.** A utility program designed to search for files on the user's hard drive.

ASK THE EXPERT

John Christopher, Senior Data Recovery Engineer, DriveSavers, Inc.

How important are disk-maintenance procedures—such as defragmenting a hard drive—in preventing a hard drive failure?

It's important to run a disk maintenance program occasionally to fix minor directory corruption and repair incorrect disk or file permissions. In addition, defragmenting files—or optimizing as it is sometimes called—can help improve the performance of a hard drive.

During regular use, a computer system will always try to write data files to consecutive sectors on the hard drive. When that's not possible because the hard drive is nearing capacity or files are exceptionally large, files are fragmented—broken into logical pieces and recorded in different locations on the drive. Defragmenting reassembles the file pieces so the access time (the time needed to read all the file pieces and load them into the computer's memory) is reduced, thus improving performance.

Computer users who create large high-resolution graphics, professional audio recording, and video production files should defragment regularly; these users will see the most benefit from a regular defragmenting routine.

e-mail and chat messages, cached Web pages, and other content stored on the user's hard drive to find the items that match the user's supplied search terms. To speed up searching, most of these search tools create an index of the computer content on an ongoing basis.

Diagnostic and Disk Management Programs

Diagnostic programs evaluate your system, looking for problems and making recommendations for fixing any errors that are discovered. *Disk management programs* diagnose and repair problems related to your hard drive. Diagnostic and disk management utilities built into the Windows operating system include programs to check your hard drive for errors and programs to optimize your hard drive (by rearranging the data on the hard drive so all files are stored in contiguous locations—called *disk defragmentation*) so it works more efficiently. Third-party utility programs can perform these and other related tasks, as well.

Uninstall and Cleanup Utilities

As programs are used, temporary data is often created. When programs are *uninstalled* (removed from the hard drive), this data and other remnants of that program can be left behind on the hard drive or in system files unless an *uninstall utility* is used. If a user removes programs by deleting the program's folder (which is not the recommended method for removing programs), the extraneous data is left behind, using up valuable disk space and, sometimes, slowing down the computer. Uninstall utilities remove the programs along with related extraneous data, such as references to those programs in your system files. Some uninstall capabilities are built into most operating systems; often an uninstall option is also included in a program's folder or under that program's Start menu item when that program is originally installed.

Cleanup utilities (such as Windows *Disk Cleanup* shown in Figure 2-22 in Chapter 2) are designed to delete temporary files (such as deleted files still in the Recycle Bin, temporary Internet files, temporary installation files, and so forth) in order to free up disk space. Some specialty cleanup programs (called *registry cleaners*) are designed to locate unnecessary information in the Windows registry and other system files (such as from uninstalled programs) and delete it, making your computer run more efficiently.

CAUTION CAUTION CAUTION CAUTION CAUTION CAUTION CAUTION CAU

To avoid deleting any system files used by other programs when uninstalling a program, be sure to keep all files (such as *.dll* files) that an uninstall utility asks you about and says might be needed by another program. As an extra precaution, you can create a *System Restore point* (using the *System Restore* tools) before uninstalling a program (if you are using a Windows computer), so you can roll the computer's settings back to that point if a problem occurs after the program is uninstalled.

File Compression Programs

File compression programs reduce the size of files so they take up less storage space on a storage medium or can be transmitted faster over the Internet. The most common format for user-compressed files in the Windows environment is the *.zip* format, which is created by file compression programs such as the *WinZip* program shown in Figure 5-21. Mac users typically use *StuffIt* (which creates files in the *.sit* or *.sitx* format) or a similar program instead, although many file compression programs can open files compressed with other programs.

A file compression program is required to both compress (*zip*) and decompress (*unzip*) files, unless the zipped file is made *executable*. Executable zipped files have the extension *.exe* and decompress automatically when they are opened, even if the appropriate file compression program is not installed on the recipient's computer. File compression programs can compress either a single file or a group of files into a single compressed file. When multiple files are compressed, they are separated back into individual files when the file is decompressed. Some file compression programs can also *encrypt* your zipped files so that a password is needed to unzip them. Encryption is discussed in detail in Chapter 9.

FILE SIZE
The 27 files, totalling nearly 17 MB, are zipped into a single 5 MB *.zip* file.

COMPRESSION RATIOS
Certain image file formats (such as .tif) compress more than others (such as .jpg, which is already in a compressed format). Documents containing text fall somewhere in between.

FIGURE 5-21
File compression.
File compression can be used with both image and text files, although image files generally compress more efficiently.

Backup and Recovery Utilities

Virtually every computer veteran will warn you that, sooner or later, you will lose some critical files. This could happen due to a power outage (if the file you are working on has not yet been saved), a hardware failure (such as if your computer or hard drive stops functioning), a major disaster (such as a fire that destroys your computer), or a user error (such as accidentally deleting or overwriting a file).

Creating a **backup** means making a duplicate copy of important files so that when a problem occurs, you can restore those files using the backup copy to avoid data loss. Performing a backup can include backing up an entire computer (so it can be restored at a later date, if needed), backing up all data files (in order to restore them in case the computer is lost or damaged), or backing up only selected files (to make sure you have a clean copy of each file if the original is accidentally lost or destroyed). Depending on their size, backup data can be placed on a recordable or rewritable CD or DVD disc, an external hard drive, a USB flash drive, or virtually any other storage medium. To protect against fires and other natural disasters, backup media should be stored in a different physical location than your computer or inside a fire-resistant safe.

It is critical for a business to have backup procedures in place that back up all data on a frequent, regular basis—such as every night. A rotating collection of backup media should be used so it is possible to go back beyond the previous day's backup, if needed. While individuals tend to back up in a less formal manner, personal backups are becoming increasingly necessary as the amount of important information that users store digitally (such as home movies, music, digital photos, and tax returns) grows. Personal backups can

TIP

Be sure to save your documents frequently as you work, in case the power goes out. Creating a copy of a document with a different filename (by using the *Save As* option of the File menu, for example) before editing a document is another good idea, so you can return to the original version, if needed.

>**File compression program.** A program that reduces the size of files, typically to be stored or transmitted more efficiently. >**Backup.** A duplicate copy of data or other computer content in case the original version is destroyed.

WINDOWS BACKUP PROGRAM
Allows you to back up files to the desired backup medium manually or on a regular basis automatically.

WEB-BASED BACKUP SERVICE
Allows you to back up files to a secure Web site.

FIGURE 5-22
Backup utilities.

VIDEO PODCAST

Go to the Chapter 5 page at
**www.cengage.com/
computerconcepts/np/uc13**
to download or listen to the
"How To: Back Up Your Files
Automatically" video podcast.

be as simple as copying important documents to a USB flash drive or uploading them to an online storage service Web site, or as comprehensive as backing up the entire contents of your computer.

You can perform backups by manually copying files using your file management program, but there are *backup utility* programs (both stand-alone and built-into operating systems) that make the backup process easier, such as the *Windows Backup* program shown in Figure 5-22. For convenience, many backup programs can be scheduled to back up specified files, folders, or drives on a regular basis (such as every night or every Friday night, depending on how important the contents of your computer are and how often you modify files). There are also online backup services (such as the *MozyHome* service shown in Figure 5-22) that can back up your specified files automatically to a secure Web server on a regular basis, provided you have a broadband Internet connection. Backups and *disaster recovery* are discussed in more detail in Chapter 15.

Antivirus, Antispyware, Firewalls, and Other Security Programs

As discussed in detail in Chapter 9, a *computer virus* is a software program that is designed to cause damage to the computer system or perform some other malicious act, and *spyware* is a software program installed without the user's knowledge that secretly collects information and sends it to an outside party via the user's Internet connection. Other security concerns today include *phishing* schemes that try to trick users into supplying personal information that can be used for credit card fraud, *identity theft*, and other criminal acts. Because of these threats, it is critical that all computer users today protect themselves and their computers. There are many *security programs* available, such as *antivirus programs* and *antispyware programs* (that protect against malicious software being installed on your computer) and *firewall programs* (that protect against someone accessing your computer via the Internet or a wireless connection). Increasingly, operating systems are including security software integrated into the operating system. For instance, recent versions of Windows include *Windows Firewall* and *Windows Defender* (an antispyware program). Because network and Internet security is such an important topic today, Chapter 9 is dedicated to these topics.

Go **FURTHER EXPLORATION**

Go to the Chapter 5 page at
**www.cengage.com/
computerconcepts/np/uc13**
for links to information about utility
programs.

TECHNOLOGY AND YOU

The Browser OS

As the emphasis of personal computing moves from desktop applications to Web-based applications, it is expected that soon operating systems will be focused more on providing access to Web-based tools and applications than on running installed applications. Consequently, a Web browser could function as the operating system of the future. With the recent release of Google Chrome—Google's Web browser that was built with Web applications in mind—this prediction is becoming much closer to reality.

While Chrome is sometimes referred to as *a cloud operating system* by others, Google doesn't call Chrome an operating system, even though some features of Chrome are designed to make using Web-based applications easier. For instance, Chrome's application shortcut feature allows users to create shortcuts (such as on the desktop or Start menu, depending on their preference) to Web-based applications. Clicking an application shortcut loads the Web-based application in a streamlined Chrome window (with no browser tabs, search box, or navigation buttons, for instance) to give the user as much working room as possible while working with the application (see the accompanying illustration of how to create and use an application shortcut for the Google Docs Web-based program). This ability to launch Web-based applications as if they were installed applications is bringing us closer to the point where the browser might be an operating system that controls all your applications. And, in fact, Google has announced that they are now developing a Linux-based operating system built around Chrome. This new operating system, expected to be released in late 2010, is currently dubbed *Google Chrome OS* and is initially targeted to the netbook market, with desktop computers a possibility for the future.

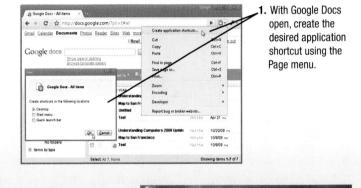

1. With Google Docs open, create the desired application shortcut using the Page menu.

2. Click the application shortcut to launch the application in a streamlined window.

3. The program can then be used in its normal fashion, such as opening and editing documents.

Creating a Google Docs application shortcut with Google Chrome.

THE FUTURE OF OPERATING SYSTEMS

The future configuration of operating systems is anyone's guess, but it is expected that they will continue to become more user-friendly and, eventually, may be driven primarily by a voice, touch, and/or gesture interface. Operating systems are also likely to continue to become more stable and self-healing, repairing or restoring system files as needed. In addition, they are expected to continue to include security and technological improvements as they become available.

Improvements will almost certainly continue to be made in the areas of synchronizing and coordinating data and activities among a person's various computing and communications devices, such as his or her personal computer and mobile phone. In addition, with the pervasiveness of the Internet, operating systems in the future may be used primarily to access software available through the Internet or other networks, instead of accessing software on the local computer. For a look at a possible operating system of the future—your Web browser—see the Technology and You box.

SUMMARY

SYSTEM SOFTWARE VS. APPLICATION SOFTWARE

System software consists of the programs that coordinate the activities of a computer system. The basic role of system software is to act as a mediator between **application software** (programs that allow a user to perform specific tasks on a computer, such as word processing, playing a game, preparing taxes, browsing the Web, and so forth) and the computer system's hardware, as well as between the computer and the user.

THE OPERATING SYSTEM

A computer's **operating system** is the primary system software program; it manages the computer system's resources and interfaces with the user. The essential portion, or core, of an operating system is called its **kernel**. The functions of the operating system include booting the computer, configuring devices and **device drivers** (often simply called **drivers**), communicating with the user, managing and monitoring computer resources, file management, and security. *File management programs* allow the user to manage the enormous collection of files typically found on a computer's hard drive by organizing files hierarchically into folders. To access a file in any directory, the user can specify the *path* to the file; the path identifies the drive and folders the user must navigate through in order to access the file.

A variety of processing techniques can be built into operating systems to help enhance processing efficiency. **Multitasking** allows more than one program to be open at one time; *multithreading* allows for rotation between program *threads*; and multiprocessing and parallel processing involve using two or more CPUs (or CPU cores) to perform work at the same time. Operating systems typically use **virtual memory** to extend conventional memory by using a portion of the hard drive as additional memory, and **spooling** frees up the CPU from time-consuming interaction with input and output devices, such as printers, by storing input and output on the way in or out of the system in a **buffer**.

Some of the differences among operating systems center around whether they use a **graphical user interface** (**GUI**) or **command line interface**, whether they are a **personal operating system** designed for individual users or a **server operating system** designed for multiple users, and the types and numbers of processors supported. Operating systems that are used with mobile devices or are embedded in other devices are called **mobile operating systems** or **embedded operating systems**, respectively.

OPERATING SYSTEMS FOR PERSONAL COMPUTERS AND SERVERS

One of the original operating systems for IBM and IBM-compatible personal computers was **DOS** (**Disk Operating System**), which is still in existence but not widely used. Most desktop computers today run a version of **Windows**. *Windows 3.x*, the first widely used version of Windows, was an *operating environment* that added a GUI shell to DOS, replacing the DOS command line interface with a system of menus, icons, and screen boxes called *windows*. *Windows 95*, *Windows 98*, *Windows 98 Second Edition* (*SE*), *Windows NT*, *Windows Me*, *Windows 2000*, *Windows XP*, and *Windows Vista*—all full-fledged operating systems and successors to Windows 3.*x*—each included an increasing number of enhancements, such as multitasking, a better user interface, and more Internet, multimedia, and communications functions. The current personal version of Windows is **Windows 7**; the current network version of Windows (**Windows Server**) is *Windows Server 2008 R2*.

Mac OS is the operating system used on Apple computers. The current personal version is **Mac OS X** (and includes *Mac OS X Leopard* and the newer *Mac OS X Snow Leopard*); **Mac OS X Server** is designed for server use. **UNIX** is a flexible operating system that was originally developed for use with midrange servers, but is now available for a variety of devices. UNIX comes in many versions or *UNIX flavors* and is the basis of several other operating systems, including Mac OS. The open source **Linux** operating system has gathered popularity because it is distributed free over the Internet and can be used as an alternative to Windows and Mac OS. Linux has earned support as a mainstream operating system in recent years and is being used in computer systems of all sizes, from netbooks to supercomputers.

OPERATING SYSTEMS FOR MOBILE PHONES AND OTHER DEVICES

Mobile phones and mobile devices usually require a different operating system than a desktop computer or server. Widely used mobile operating systems include **Windows Mobile**, **Android**, **iPhone OS**, **BlackBerry OS**, **Palm OS** and the newer **Palm webOS**, and **Symbian OS**. Other everyday devices that contain a computer—such as cars, cash registers, and consumer electronics devices—typically use an embedded operating system, such as **Windows Embedded** and **Embedded Linux**.

Chapter Objective 5: State several devices other than desktop computers and servers that require an operating system and list one possible operating system for each type of device.

OPERATING SYSTEMS FOR LARGER COMPUTERS

High-end servers, mainframes, and supercomputers may use an operating system designed specifically for that type of system, but are increasingly using customized versions of conventional operating systems, such as Windows, UNIX, and Linux.

UTILITY PROGRAMS

A **utility program** is a type of system software written to perform specific tasks usually related to maintaining or managing the computer system. **File management programs** enable users to perform file management tasks, such as copying, moving, and deleting files. The file management system built into Windows is **Windows Explorer**. **Search tools** are designed to help users find files on their hard drives; *diagnostic* and *disk management programs* are used mainly to diagnose and repair computer problems, such as hard drive errors and files deleted accidentally, as well as maintenance tasks, such as performing *disk defragmentation*. *Uninstall utilities* remove programs from a hard drive without leaving annoying remnants behind, **file compression programs** reduce the stored size of files so they can be more easily archived or sent over the Internet, and **backup** programs make it easier for users to back up the contents of their hard drive. There are also a number of security-oriented utility programs, such as *antivirus*, *antispyware*, and *firewall* programs.

Chapter Objective 6: Discuss the role of utility programs and outline several tasks that these programs perform.

THE FUTURE OF OPERATING SYSTEMS

In the future, operating systems will likely become even more user-friendly, voice-driven, and stable, repairing themselves when needed and causing errors and conflicts much less frequently. They will also likely continue to include improved security features, support for new technologies, and assistance for coordinating data and activities among a user's various computing and communications devices. They may also one day be designed primarily for accessing Web-based applications.

Chapter Objective 7: Describe what the operating systems of the future might be like.

REVIEW ACTIVITIES

KEY TERM MATCHING

a. Android

b. backup

c. device driver

d. kernel

e. multitasking

f. operating system

g. spooling

h. utility program

i. virtual memory

j. Windows

Instructions: Match each key term on the left with the definition on the right that best describes it.

1. _____ A duplicate copy of data or other computer content for use in the event that the original version is destroyed.

2. _____ A Linux-based operating system designed for mobile phones and developed by a group of companies that includes Google.

3. _____ A memory-management technique that uses hard drive space as additional RAM.

4. _____ A program that enables an operating system to communicate with a specific hardware device.

5. _____ A type of software that performs a specific task, usually related to managing or maintaining the computer system.

6. _____ The capability of an operating system to run more than one program at one time.

7. _____ The essential portion, or core, of an operating system.

8. _____ The main component of system software that enables the computer to manage its activities and the resources under its control, run application programs, and interface with the user.

9. _____ The primary personal computer operating system developed by Microsoft Corporation.

10. _____ The process of placing items in a buffer so the appropriate device (such as a printer) can retrieve them when needed.

SELF-QUIZ

Instructions: Circle **T** if the statement is true, **F** if the statement is false, or write the best answer in the space provided. **Answers for the self-quiz are located in the References and Resources Guide at the end of the book.**

1. **T** **F** Windows 7 is an example of an operating system.

2. **T** **F** Most operating systems today use a command line interface.

3. **T** **F** Mobile devices, such as portable digital media players and mobile phones, typically require an operating system.

4. **T** **F** Windows Explorer is an operating system designed for mobile phones.

5. **T** **F** Windows Mobile is a versatile operating system designed to be used on a variety of computer types, such as mainframes, servers, personal computers, and mobile phones.

6. _____ refers to the ability of an operating system to have more than one program open at one time.

7. _____ is an operating system that is available for free over the Internet.

8. To decrease the size of a file, a(n) _____ utility program can be used.

9. To guard against losing your data if a computer problem occurs, you should _____ your data files on a regular basis.

10. Match each device to the most appropriate operating system and write the corresponding number in the blank to the left of the device.

a. _____ Home office computer   **1.** Windows Embedded

b. _____ Mainframe computer   **2.** Palm webOS

c. _____ Mobile phone   **3.** Windows 7

d. _____ Car   **4.** UNIX

EXERCISES

1. For the following path, identify the drive the document is located on, the name of the file (including its file extension), and whether or not the document is stored inside a folder. If the file is stored inside one or more folders, list the folder name(s).

C:\Documents\Resume.docx

2. Match each program or processing technique with the appropriate term and write the corresponding number in the blank to the left of each term.

a. _____ Zipped file   **1.** Spooling

b. _____ Printer   **2.** File management program

c. _____ Swap file   **3.** File compression program

d. _____ Folder   **4.** Virtual memory

3. Would a new notebook computer typically have Windows XP, Windows 7, Windows Mobile, or Windows Server 2008 R2 installed as its operating system? Explain your answer.

4. What type of utility program is designed to make duplicate copies of your hard drive content?

5. Identify the purpose of each of the following types of utility programs.

a. File management program _____

b. Uninstall utility _____

c. File compression program _____

d. Antivirus program _____

DISCUSSION QUESTIONS

1. There are a few companies, such as Microsoft and Google, that have moved into many different areas of computing, such as operating systems, application software, Web-based software, search, and more, and both of these companies have been accused of monopolistic procedures. Is there a risk for the consumer or for businesses if one company is involved with so many different aspects of computing? Should this be prohibited or should the natural order of the free market be trusted to prevent areas of computing from being monopolized by one company?

2. As discussed in the chapter, many everyday devices—including cars and other vehicles—are controlled by operating systems. There are advantages, such as avoiding possible driver errors and the ability to change the speed of or reroute trains automatically to avoid collisions. But are there potential risks, as well? For example, Thailand's Finance Minister once had to be rescued from inside his limousine after the onboard computer malfunctioned, leaving the vehicle immobilized and the door locks, power windows, and air conditioning not functioning. Do you think the benefits of increased automation of devices that could put us in danger if they malfunction outweigh the risks? What types of safeguards should be incorporated into computer-controlled cars, subway trains, and other automated vehicles? What about medication dispensers and other automated medical devices?

SW

PROJECTS

1. **New OSs** There have been a number of new operating systems developed in the past few years, such as Android, Palm webOS, and the Google Chrome OS that was in development at the time of this writing.

   For this project, select one new or emerging operating system and research it. What is the purpose and targeted market for this operating system? What advantages does it have over any current competition for this market? If the operating system was developed to fulfill a new need, are there other operating systems that are being adapted or being developed as a result? Do you think your selected operating system will succeed? Why or why not? At the conclusion of your research, prepare a one- to two-page summary of your findings and opinions and submit it to your instructor.

2. **File Compression** As described in the chapter, compression programs can be used to reduce the size of files before they are stored or sent over the Internet. The most common compression programs create files with the file extensions *.zip*, *.sit*, *.sitx*, and *.exe*. Self-extracting compressed files decompress automatically when you download them, while compressed files must be decompressed with a version of the program that compressed them.

   For this project, identify compression programs associated with each of the file extensions listed above and determine which extensions represent a self-extracting format, as well as which extensions are associated with the Windows and Mac OS operating systems. For the type of computer you use most often, find at least two compression programs that you might use and compare their costs and capabilities. At the conclusion of your research, prepare a one-page summary of your findings and submit it to your instructor.

3. **File Practice** As discussed in the chapter, all operating systems have a file management-system, such as the Windows Explorer program illustrated in Figures 5-19 and 5-20.

   For this project, obtain a removable storage medium (such as a USB flash drive) appropriate for a computer you have access to, connect it to that computer, and perform the following tasks.

   a. Open the file management program and select the icon representing the removable storage medium being used to display its contents. Are there any files on the storage medium? How much room is available on the storage medium?

   b. Open any word processing program available on your computer (such as Word or Notepad for a Windows computer). Create a new document consisting of just your name, then save the document to your storage medium (be sure to change the save location to the appropriate drive and use an appropriate filename). In the file management program, view the content of your storage medium to see the new document. What is the file size and how much room is now left on your storage medium?

   c. Prepare a short summary of your work to submit to your instructor, listing the software programs and storage medium used, the name and size of the file, and the amount of space left on your storage medium once the file was stored on it.

   d. Return to your file management program and delete the file from your storage medium.

4. **Operating System Bugs** Most software, including operating systems, is not error-free when it is first released. Some programs, in fact, contain thousands of problems, called *bugs*. Software companies regularly release fixes (called *patches*) to correct known issues with released software. Is it ethical for software companies to release products that have known problems? Many hackers and other criminals target these bugs with computer viruses or other attacks, frequently on the day a new vulnerability is discovered—called a *zero-day attack*. Obviously, the acts by these criminals are not ethical, but what responsibility does a software company have to consumers if they are put at risk due to the company's carelessness or rush to market? What responsibility do consumers have to make sure they keep their computers patched against new vulnerabilities?

   For this project, form an opinion about the ethical ramifications of software bugs and be prepared to discuss your position (in class, via an online class discussion group, in a class chat room, or via a class blog, depending on your instructor's directions). You may also be asked to write a short paper expressing your opinion.

5. **OS Support** No matter which operating system you have, it's likely you will eventually need to get some help resolving a problem. Support options typically include the following: searchable knowledge bases, technical support phone numbers and e-mail addresses, online chat, FAQs, and user discussion groups.

   For this project, select one operating system and go to the manufacturer's Web site to determine which of the support options listed in the previous paragraph are available. Select one support option and find out how it is used and what type of information can be obtained. Share your findings with the class in the form of a short presentation. The presentation should not exceed 10 minutes and should make use of one or more presentation aids, such as the chalkboard, handouts, overhead transparencies, or a computer-based slide presentation (your instructor may provide additional requirements). You may also be asked to submit a summary of the presentation to your instructor.

Instructions: Go to the Chapter 5 page at **www.cengage.com/computerconcepts/np/uc13** to work the following Web Activities.

6. **Interactive Activities** Work the interactive **Crossword Puzzle**, watch the **Video Podcasts** and **Online Videos**, and explore the **Further Exploration** links associated with this chapter.

   If you have a SAM user profile, you may have access to hands-on instruction, practice, and assessment of the skills covered in this chapter. Check with your instructor for instructions and the correct URL/Web site to access those assignments.

7. **Student Edition Labs** Work the following interactive **Student Edition Labs**.
   - ➤ **Backing up Your Computer**   ➤ **Maintaining a Hard Drive**

8. **Test Yourself** Review the **Online Study Guide** for this chapter, then test your knowledge of the terms and concepts covered in this chapter by completing the **Key Term Matching** exercise, the **Self-Quiz**, the **Exercises**, and the **Practice Test**.

Student Edition Labs

chapter 6

Application Software

After completing this chapter, you will be able to do the following:

1. Describe what application software is, the different types of ownership rights, and the difference between installed and Web-based software.

2. Detail some concepts and commands that many software programs have in common.

3. Discuss word processing and explain what kinds of documents are created using this type of program.

4. Explain the purpose of spreadsheet software and the kinds of documents created using this type of program.

5. Identify some of the vocabulary used with database software and discuss the benefits of using this type of program.

6. Describe what presentation graphics and electronic slide shows are and when they might be used.

7. List some types of graphics and multimedia software that consumers use frequently.

8. Name several other types of application software programs and discuss what functions they perform.

outline

Overview

The Basics of Application Software
Software Ownership Rights
Desktop vs. Mobile Software
Installed vs. Web-Based Software
Software Suites
Common Software Commands

Word Processing Concepts
What Is Word Processing?
Creating a Word Processing Document
Tables, Graphics, and Templates
Word Processing and the Web

Spreadsheet Concepts
What Is a Spreadsheet?
Creating a Spreadsheet
Charts and What-If Analysis
Spreadsheets and the Web

Database Concepts
What Is a Database?
Creating a Database
Queries and Reports
Databases and the Web

Presentation Graphics Concepts
What Is a Presentation Graphic?
Creating a Presentation
Finishing a Presentation
Presentation Graphics and the Web

Graphics and Multimedia Concepts
Graphics Software
Audio Capture and Editing Software
Video Editing and DVD Authoring
Software
Media Players
Graphics, Multimedia, and the Web

Other Types of Application Software
Desktop and Personal Publishing
Software
Educational, Entertainment, and
Reference Software
Note Taking Software and Web
Notebooks
CAD and Other Types of Design Software
Accounting and Personal Finance
Software
Project Management, Collaboration,
and Remote Access Software

OVERVIEW

As discussed in previous chapters, application software consists of programs designed to perform specific tasks or applications. Today, a wide variety of application software is available to meet virtually any user need. Individuals and businesses use software to perform hundreds of tasks, including to write letters, keep track of their finances, participate in videoconferences, watch videos, learn a foreign language, entertain themselves or their children, create music CDs or home movie DVDs, manage a business's inventory, create greeting cards and flyers, make business presentations, process orders, prepare payrolls and tax returns, touch up digital photos, and teach their kids the ABCs.

This chapter begins with a discussion of some general characteristics of application software. Then we look at five of the most widely used types of application software: word processing, spreadsheet, database, presentation graphics, and graphics and multimedia software. The chapter concludes with an overview of some of the other types of application software you may encounter in your personal and professional life. ■

THE BASICS OF APPLICATION SOFTWARE

All computer users should be familiar with the basic characteristics and concepts related to **application software**; for instance, the different possible ownership rights and delivery methods used with application software, how software for personal computers and mobile devices differs, and the basic commands that are common to most types of application software. Although these topics are discussed next in the context of application software, they also apply to other types of software, such as system software (discussed in Chapter 5) and programming languages (discussed in Chapter 13).

PODCAST

Go to **www.cengage.com/computerconcepts/np/uc13** to download or listen to the "Expert Insight on Software" podcast.

Software Ownership Rights

The *ownership rights* of a software program specify the allowable use of that program. After a software program is developed, the developer (typically an individual or an organization) holds the ownership rights for that program and decides whether or not the program can be sold, shared with others, or otherwise distributed. When a software program is purchased, the buyer is not actually buying the software. Instead, the buyer is acquiring a **software license** that permits him or her to use the software. This license specifies the conditions under which a buyer can use the software, such as the number of computers on which it may be installed (many software licenses permit the software to be installed on just one computer). In addition to being included in printed form inside the packaging of most software programs, the licensing agreement is usually displayed and must be agreed to by the end user at the beginning of the software installation process (see Figure 6-1).

> **Application software.** Programs that enable users to perform specific tasks on a computer, such as writing a letter or playing a game.
> **Software license.** An agreement, either included in a software package or displayed on the screen during installation, that specifies the conditions under which a buyer of the program can use it.

This statement explains that you are accepting the terms of the license agreement by installing the software.

This statement explains that the program can be tried for 14 days and then it needs to be either registered or uninstalled.

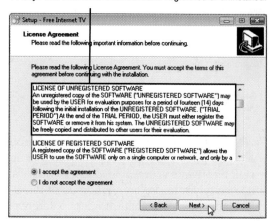

COMMERCIAL SOFTWARE PROGRAM

SHAREWARE PROGRAM

 FIGURE 6-1

Software licenses.
Most software programs display their licensing agreements at the beginning of the installation process.

There are four basic categories of software: *commercial software*, *shareware*, *freeware*, and *public domain software* (see Figure 6-2). Each of these types of software has different ownership rights, as discussed next. In addition, software that falls into any of these four categories can also be **open source software**—programs whose source code is available to the public. An open source program can be copyrighted, but individuals and businesses are allowed to modify the program and redistribute it—the only restrictions are that changes must be shared with the open source community and the original copyright notice must remain intact. For more information about open source software, see the Inside the Industry box.

FIGURE 6-2

Software ownership rights.

Commercial Software

Commercial software is software that is developed and sold for a profit. When you buy a commercial software program (such as *Microsoft Office*, *TurboTax*, or *GarageBand*), it typically comes with a *single-user license*, which means you cannot legally make copies of the installation CD to give to your friends and you cannot legally install the software on their computers using your CD. You cannot even install the software on a second computer that you own, unless allowed by the license. For example, some software licenses state that the program can be installed on one desktop computer and one portable computer belonging to the same individual. To determine which activities are allowable for a particular commercial software program, refer to its software license. Schools or businesses that need to install software on a large number of computers or need to have the software available to multiple users over a network can usually obtain a *site license* or *network license* for the number of users needed.

TYPE OF SOFTWARE	EXAMPLES
Commercial Software	Microsoft Office (office suite) Norton AntiVirus (antivirus program) Adobe Photoshop (image editing program) World of Warcraft (game)
Shareware	WinZip (file compression program) Ulead Video Toolbox (video editing/conversion program) Image Shrinker (image optimizer) Deluxe Ski Jump 3 (game)
Freeware	Internet Explorer (Web browser) OpenOffice.org (office suite) QuickTime Player (media player) Yahoo! Messenger (instant messaging program)
Public domain software	Lynx (text-based Web browser) Pine (e-mail program)

>**Open source software.** Software programs whose source code is made available to the public. >**Commercial software.** Copyrighted software that is developed, usually by a commercial company, for sale to others.

INSIDE THE INDUSTRY

Open Source Software

The use of open source software has grown over the past few years, primarily for cost reasons. One of the first widely known open source programs is the Linux operating system, which was discussed in Chapter 5. However, there are also low-cost or no-cost open source alternatives for a wide selection of application programs today. For instance, the free *OpenOffice.org* office suite (see the accompanying screen shot) can be used as an alternative to Microsoft Office, and the free *GIMP* program can be used to retouch photos instead of Adobe Photoshop or another pricey image editing program. In addition to saving you money, these alternative programs often require less disk space and memory than their commercial software counterparts require.

Other possible benefits of using open source software include increased stability and security (since they are tested and improved by a wide variety of programmers and users), and the ability to modify the application's source code. Perceived risks of using open source software include lack of support and compatibility issues. However, both Linux and open source application programs are continuing to gain acceptance and their use is growing. Some insiders feel that the open source movement is finally gathering the momentum it deserves.

An emerging trend is applying open source principles to hardware—some hardware designers are releasing designs for new hardware to the public in hopes that manufacturing companies will use the designs in new products and credit them as the original designer. Like open source software developers, open source hardware designers can possibly earn revenue from consulting work related to their designs.

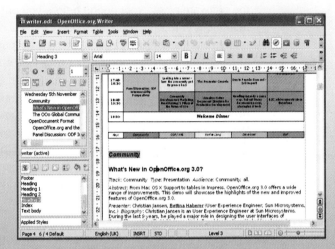

The OpenOffice.org Writer word processing program.

In addition to their full versions, some commercial software is available in a *demo* or *trial version*. Typically, these versions can be used free of charge and distributed to others, but often they are missing some key features (such as the ability to save or print a document) or they will not run after the trial period expires. Since these programs are not designed as replacements for the fee-based version, it is ethical to use them only to determine if you would like to buy the full program. If the decision is made against purchasing the product, the demo or trial version should be uninstalled from your computer.

Recent trends in computing—such as multiprocessing, virtualization, and cloud computing, all discussed in earlier chapters of this book—are leading to new software licensing issues for commercial software companies. For example, software companies must decide whether the number of installations allowed by the license is counted by the number of computers on which the software is installed or by the total number of processors or CPU cores used by those computers, as well as decide how to determine the number of users in a virtualized environment. Some Microsoft software, for instance, is licensed per processor, regardless of the number of cores each processor has. And, for some server software used within a virtual environment, Microsoft computes the number of users based on a *per running instance*—that is, the number of software instances (installed or virtual) being used at any given time—instead of how many virtual environments the software is actually available to. Another software vendor (Altair Engineering) uses *license tokens* that are drawn from a central license server when the application is running and returned to the server when the application is finished. This system allows the number of tokens used by an

---

TIP

Ownership rights for original creative works are referred to as *copyrights* and are discussed in more detail in Chapter 16.

TIP

Businesses should periodically audit their software licenses to ensure they are not paying for too many licenses or for licenses associated with software that is not being used. They should also consider negotiating new types of licensing agreements that best fit the company, such as concurrent-user pricing instead of per-computer pricing.

ASK THE EXPERT

Greg Weir, Webmaster, Tucows

Why should an individual or business pay for shareware?

In short, because it's the right thing to do. You are obligated to pay for shareware if you continue to use it past the end of the trial period. The fact that shareware publishers allow you to try their software on your computer at your leisure so you can be certain the software meets your needs before you pay for it is testament to their belief in the quality of their product.

There are a number of good reasons for paying for shareware beyond personal or business ethics. In some cases, the title will cease to function after its trial period or will display an annoying "nag" screen every time you start the program to remind you to pay. In addition, payment allows the publisher to enhance the product, fix bugs, and provide support. Continued use of a shareware product past its trial period without paying for it should rightly be considered theft.

individual computer to vary depending on the computing hardware (such as number of cores) being used, but still ensures that the number of users accessing the software at any one time does not exceed the limits specified in the software license. Software vendors are expected to continue to develop and implement new licensing models to address these and other trends in the future.

Shareware

Shareware programs are software programs that are distributed on the honor system. Most shareware programs are available to try free of charge, but typically require a small fee if you choose to use the program regularly (refer again to the shareware license in Figure 6-1). By paying the requested registration fee, you can use the program for as long as you want to use it and may be entitled to product support, updates, and other benefits. You can legally and ethically copy shareware programs to pass along to friends and colleagues for evaluation purposes, but those individuals are expected to pay the shareware fee if they decide to keep the product.

FIGURE 6-3

Shareware and freeware programs are typically downloaded via the Internet.

Many shareware programs have a specified trial period, such as one month. Although it is not illegal to use shareware past the specified trial period, it is unethical to do so. Ethical use of shareware dictates either paying for the program or uninstalling it from your computer at the end of the trial period. Shareware is typically much less expensive than commercial versions of similar software because it is often developed by a single programmer and because it uses the shareware marketing system to sell directly to consumers (typically via a variety of software download sites, such as the one shown in Figure 6-3) with little or no packaging or advertising expenses. Shareware authors stress that the ethical use of shareware helps to cultivate this type of software distribution. Legally, shareware and demo versions of commercial software are similar, but shareware is typically not missing key features.

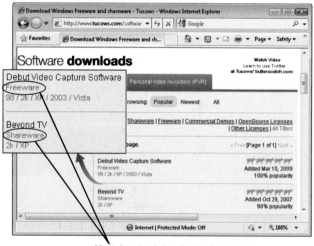

Most download sites list the license type for each program.

Freeware

Freeware programs are software programs that are given away by the author for others to use free of charge. Although freeware is available without charge and can be shared with others, the author retains the ownership rights to the program, so you cannot do anything with it—such as sell it or modify it—that is not expressly allowed by the author. Freeware programs are

---

> **Shareware.** Copyrighted software that is distributed on the honor system; consumers should either pay for it or uninstall it after the trial period.

> **Freeware.** Copyrighted software that may be used free of charge.

frequently developed by individuals; commercial software companies sometimes release freeware as well, such as Microsoft's *Internet Explorer* and Real's *RealPlayer*. Like shareware programs, freeware programs are widely available over the Internet.

Public Domain Software

Public domain software is not copyrighted; instead, the ownership rights to the program have been donated to the public domain. Consequently, it is free and can be used, copied, modified, and distributed to others without restrictions.

FURTHER EXPLORATION (Go)

Go to the Chapter 6 page at **www.cengage.com/ computerconcepts/np/uc13** for links to information about free and low-cost office suites.

Desktop vs. Mobile Software

Notebook computers, tablet computers, UMPCs, and other portable computers typically run the same application software as desktop computers. However, mobile phones and other mobile devices typically require *mobile software*; that is, software specifically designed for a specific type of mobile phone or other mobile device. A wide range of mobile software is available today. For instance, there are mobile versions of popular programs like Word or PowerPoint, games and media players, business tools that record inventory data or keep track of your business expenses, calendars and programs that allow you to organize notes and voice recordings, applications that allow you to broadcast your current location to friends, and Web browsers for accessing Web sites (see Figure 6-4). In fact, there are over 15,000 applications for the iPhone alone and that number is growing all the time. Many mobile applications are available free of charge.

FIGURE 6-4
Mobile software.
There is a wide variety of software available today for mobile phones and other mobile devices.

In addition to having a more compact, efficient appearance, many mobile applications include features for easier data input, such as an on-screen keyboard, a phrase list, or handwriting recognition capabilities. Some mobile software programs are designed to be compatible with popular *desktop software*, such as Microsoft Office, to facilitate sharing documents between the two platforms. The desktop versions of the most common Microsoft Office programs are illustrated later in this chapter. For a look at a new mobile application—*mobile voice search*—see the Technology and You box.

Installed vs. Web-Based Software

Software also differs in how it is accessed by the end user. It can be installed on and run from the end user's computer (or installed on and run from a network server in a network setting), or it can be Web-based and accessed by the end user over the Internet.

>**Public domain software.** Software that is not copyrighted and may be used without restriction.

Downloaded version will be downloaded to the buyer's computer.

Packaged version will be shipped to the buyer.

FIGURE 6-5

Installed software.

Installed software can be purchased in a physical package or downloaded via the Internet.

Installed Software

Installed software must be installed on a computer before it is run. Desktop software can be purchased in physical form (such as on a CD or DVD) or downloaded from the Internet (see Figure 6-5); mobile software is almost always downloaded. Many mobile phone manufacturers have download sites to facilitate this, such as Apple's *App Store*, Blackberry's *App World*, and the *Android Market*. In either case, the program is installed using its *installation program* (which typically runs automatically when the software CD or DVD is inserted into the drive or when the downloaded program is opened, as explained in the Chapter 5 How It Works box). Once the software is installed, it is ready to use. Whether or not installed software requires a fee depends on whether the program is a commercial, demo/trial, shareware, freeware, or public domain program.

Web-Based Software

Instead of being available in an installed format, some software is run directly from the Internet as **Web-based software**. A Web-based software program is delivered on demand via the Web to wherever the user is at the moment, provided he or she has an Internet connection (and has paid to use the software if a payment is required). Also referred to as **Software as a Service (SaaS)** and **cloudware**, the use of Web-based software is growing rapidly. In fact, research firm Gartner predicts that 25% of new business software will be delivered via the Web by 2011, up from 5% of new software purchases in 2006. Typically, documents created using Web-based software are stored online.

There is a wide range of both free and fee-based Web-based software available (see Figure 6-6). For instance, many free interactive games are available through Web sites and there are several free online *office suites* (such as *Google Docs*, *ThinkFree Online*, and the *Zoho* suite of programs) that can be used as an alternative to the Microsoft Office office suite (discussed in more detail shortly). In addition, Microsoft has been testing an online version of Microsoft Office 2007 (code-named *Albany*) and it is planning a Web-based version of the upcoming *Microsoft Office 2010* product (as discussed in the Trend box later in this chapter). In addition, many business software services are offered as SaaS, including applications geared for collaboration, scheduling, customer service, accounting, project management, and more. Typically, business SaaS applications use a subscription (often per user, per month) pricing scheme; companies that deliver SaaS are sometimes referred to as *application service providers (ASPs)*. As it evolves, Web-based software is beginning to move from single stand-alone applications to groups of products that can work together to fulfill a wide variety of needs. For instance, the Google Docs Home page provides access to the Google Docs applications, but it also allows easy access to other Google online services, such as Gmail, Calendar, Photos, and Web search.

One advantage of Web-based software over installed software is that the programs and your files can be accessed from any computer with an Internet connection regardless of the type of computer or operating system used; some can also be accessed via a mobile phone, portable digital media player, or other type of Internet-enabled mobile device. This makes Web-based software especially appropriate for applications like shared scheduling and collaboration applications that are time-critical because documents and other data can be shared regardless of an individual's location or device. Other advantages of Web-based

> **Installed software.** Software that must be installed on a computer in order to be used. > **Web-based software.** Software that is delivered on demand via the Web; also referred to as **Software as a Service (SaaS)** and **cloudware**.

ONLINE APPLICATIONS
This program allows you to create presentations online.

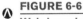

WEB DATABASE APPLICATIONS
This application allows you to retrieve property information, such as home values and homes for sale.

BUSINESS SAAS APPLICATIONS
This program allows you to share documents and collaborate on projects online.

FIGURE 6-6
Web-based software.

ONLINE VIDEO

Go to the Chapter 6 page at
**www.cengage.com/
computerconcepts/np/uc13**
to watch the "Zillow iPhone App"
video clip.

software include the ability of individuals and businesses to try out new applications for little or no out-of-pocket costs while they decide whether or not to continue subscribing to the software, the ability of small businesses to have access to complex (and normally expensive) powerful business applications at an affordable price, and the benefit of always working with the most current version of the software without having to perform software updates on company computers. In addition, Web-based applications can easily interface with existing online databases, such as online maps and property records (for instance, the real estate applications accessible via the Zillow Web site shown in Figure 6-6 utilize maps, property record information, and real estate listing information pulled from various online databases).

Some potential disadvantages of Web-based software are that online applications tend to run more slowly than applications stored on a local hard drive, that many online applications have a limit regarding the file size of the documents you create, and that the cost may eventually exceed the cost of buying a similar installed software program. In addition, you cannot access the Web-based program and your data if the server on which they reside goes down or if you are in a location with no Internet access, such as while traveling

TECHNOLOGY AND YOU

Mobile Voice Search

You know you can do many things with your mobile phone—including accessing and searching the Web on most of today's phones. Web searching has traditionally been text based, but *mobile voice search* is now available. Mobile voice search allows you to speak, rather than type, search terms into your mobile phone, and then see the results of that search. The newest systems—such as Yahoo!'s *oneSearch* service shown in the accompanying illustration—allow the user to just press a button on the phone and speak the search terms into the phone, and then the search results are immediately displayed, just as with a text-based Web page search. Commonly requested information includes movie show times, information about and directions to local businesses, stock quotes, sports scores, weather information, airline flight updates, and more. In addition to providing the requested information, Yahoo! oneSearch also supplies other relevant information (such as displaying weather information for the departure and arrival cities when flight information is requested), as shown in the accompanying illustration. Usually, search results are filtered by proximity to the user's geographical area (which is determined by the GPS information or nearby cell tower locations relayed by the mobile phone being used)—a feature called *geobrowsing*. Geobrowsing (discussed in more detail in the Chapter 8 Trend box) is based on the assumption that mobile users are likely searching for something nearby. When used in

conjunction with geobrowsing, mobile voice search essentially turns your mobile phone into your personal concierge.

1. Hold down the appropriate button on your mobile phone and speak your search request.

2. Your spoken request is translated into typed text and the search is performed.

3. The search results are displayed.

Getting a flight update with Yahoo! oneSearch.

or in a rural area. To eliminate this last concern, a growing trend is for online applications to also function, at least in part, offline. For instance, Google Docs added offline capabilities so that users can access the Google Docs applications and their documents locally on their computers, when needed. Edits are stored locally on the computer when a user is offline and, when the user reconnects to the Internet, the changes are synchronized with the documents stored on the Google Docs servers. The technology behind some offline Web applications—*Google Gears*—is discussed in the Chapter 13 Trend box.

Software Suites

Sometimes, related software programs (such as a group of graphics programs, utility programs, or office-related software) are sold bundled together as a **software suite**. Businesses and many individuals often use *office suites*, sometimes called *productivity software suites*, to produce written documents. Typically, office suites contain the following programs;

> **Software suite.** A collection of software programs bundled together and sold as a single software package.

many also contain additional productivity tools—such as a calendar, a messaging program, or collaboration tools.

> ➤ *Word processing software*—allows users to easily create and edit complex text-based documents that can also include images and other content.

> ➤ *Spreadsheet software*—provides users with a convenient means of creating documents containing complex mathematical calculations.

> ➤ *Database software*—allows users to store and organize vast amounts of data and retrieve specific information when needed.

> ➤ *Presentation graphics software*—allows users to create visual presentations to convey information more easily to others.

One of the most widely used office software suites is **Microsoft Office**. The latest version is Microsoft Office 2007, though Office 2010 is scheduled to be released in 2010. (For a look at this new version of Office, see the Trend box.) Similar suites are available from Corel (*WordPerfect Office*) and Apple (*iWork*) (see Figure 6-7); a free alternative office suite is *OpenOffice.org*. Many office suites are available in a variety of versions, such as a home or student version that contains fewer programs than a professional version. Not all software suites are available for all operating systems, however. For example, Microsoft Office is available for both Windows and Mac OS computers; iWork is available only for Mac OS computers; and OpenOffice.org is available for Windows, Linux, and Mac OS computers. OpenOffice.org is also available in more than 30 different languages.

The primary advantages of using a software suite include a common interface among programs in the suite and a total cost that is lower than buying the programs individually. Although most programs written for the same operating system (such as Windows or Mac OS) use similar interfaces and commands, the entire command interface for a software suite is usually very similar from program to program. This similarity is not just for basic commands (such as *Save* and *Print*), but for all commands (such as adding borders and shading or inserting a row or column) that appear in more than one program in the suite. The standardization of the user interface across all programs in a suite means that once you are familiar with how to use one program in a suite, you will probably find it easy to learn another program in that suite.

Common Software Commands

One of the greatest advantages of using software instead of paper and pencil to create a document is that you do not have to recreate the entire document when you want to make changes to it. This is because the document is created in RAM and then saved on a storage medium, instead of it being created directly on paper. Consequently, the document can be retrieved, modified, saved, and printed as many times as needed. The commands used to perform these tasks are similar in most application programs; the most common ways to issue commands to application programs are discussed next.

FIGURE 6-7
Office suites. Three of the most common commercial office suites are Microsoft Office, Corel WordPerfect Office, and Apple iWork.

Toolbars, Menus, Keyboard Shortcuts, and the Ribbon

Most commands in an application program are issued through *menus*, *keyboard shortcuts*, or *command buttons* located on a *toolbar* or *Ribbon*. As shown in Figure 1-10

> **Microsoft Office.** One of the most widely used office software suites.

COMMAND	COMMAND BUTTON	KEYBOARD SHORTCUT	DESCRIPTION
Open		Ctrl+O	Opens a saved document from a storage medium, usually for editing or printing.
Save		Ctrl+S	Saves the current version of the document to a storage medium.
Print		Ctrl+P	Prints the current version of the document onto paper.
Cut		Ctrl+X	Moves the selected item to the clipboard.
Copy		Ctrl+C	Copies the selected item to the clipboard.
Paste		Ctrl+V	Pastes the contents of the clipboard to the current location.
Undo		Ctrl+Z	Undoes the last change to the document.
Close		Alt+F4	Closes the document. Any changes made to the document are lost if the document wasn't saved first.

FIGURE 6-8
Common application software commands.

FIGURE 6-9
The Microsoft Office Ribbon.

in Chapter 1, the *menu bar* appears at the top of many windows and contains text-based lists (menus), which provide access to commands that can be selected to perform actions in that program. Many programs also have toolbars—sets of *icons* or command buttons that are clicked with the mouse to issue commands. **Keyboard shortcuts** are key combinations that correspond to specific commands, such as Ctrl+S for the Save command (this keyboard shortcut is issued by holding down the Ctrl key and pressing the S key). A list of common keyboard shortcuts used in Microsoft Office and many other programs is shown in Figure 6-8, along with examples of the command buttons typically used to perform these operations.

The **Ribbon** is a new feature in versions of Microsoft Office, starting with Office 2007. The Ribbon (see Figure 6-9) consists of *tabs*, which contain *groups* of related commands for the program being used. For convenience, most programs have a *Home tab* that contains the most frequently used commands in that program. In addition to the standard Ribbon tabs that are available whenever the program is open, additional *contextual tabs* are displayed as needed, depending on the action being taken. For instance, selecting a picture or other graphic

MICROSOFT OFFICE BUTTON
Contains common document commands, such as Save and Print.

QUICK ACCESS TOOLBAR
Contains command buttons for frequently used commands; can be modified by the user.

TABS
Organize related groups of commands; the Home tab is currently selected.

GALLERY
Displays sets of options that can be selected for a particular feature; this is the Styles gallery.

COMMAND BUTTONS
Issue a command or display a list of related commands.

GROUPS
Related commands on the Ribbon are organized into groups; these are the Font and Paragraph groups.

DIALOG BOX LAUNCHER
Opens a dialog box or task pane for that group.

MORE BUTTON
Opens a gallery to display more options.

HELP BUTTON
Launches the Office Help system.

> **Keyboard shortcut.** A combination of keyboard keys that are pressed in unison to issue a specific software command. > **Ribbon.** A feature found in recent versions of Microsoft Office that uses tabs to organize groups of related commands.

TREND

Microsoft Office 2010

The upcoming version of Microsoft Office—*Office 2010*—takes advantage of the trends of cloud computing and mobile computing and has specific versions of Office available for those users, in addition to the traditional installed version. The *Web version* of Office enables users to store, access, and collaborate on documents online, such as from the Windows Live *SkyDrive* online storage service. The *Mobile version* is designed for mobile phones and other mobile devices; desktop users can also create a portable version of Office to carry with them on a USB flash drive, when needed.

The overall appearance of Office 2010 is similar to Office 2007 (see the accompanying illustration). The Ribbon is still used for most commands, though the Office button now opens a full-screen menu containing more options and information than in Office 2007. New features include improved image editing tools, improved document protection features to better manage permissions and metadata associated with documents, extended printing capabilities from within Office applications, and the *jump lists* introduced in Microsoft Windows 7 to provide quick access to commonly used tasks.

Web version of Word   Installed version of Excel

Office 2010 comes in both installed and Web versions.

in Word displays the *Picture Tools tab* that contains commands related to a picture, such as to crop, resize, rotate, or recolor the picture. Clicking a command button on the Ribbon either carries out that command or displays a *gallery* of choices from which the user can select the desired action. The *Microsoft Office Button* replaces the File menu used in older versions of Office and contains commands commonly used with documents, such as to open, save, print, send, and publish them.

Editing a Document

Editing a document refers to changing the content of the document, such as adding or deleting text. Most application programs that allow text editing have an **insertion point** that looks like a blinking vertical line on the screen and shows where the next change will be made to the document currently displayed on the screen. To insert text, just start typing and the text will appear at the insertion point location. To delete text, press the Delete key to delete one character to the right of the insertion point or press the Backspace key to delete one character to the left of the insertion point. If the insertion point is not in the proper location for the edit, it must be moved to the appropriate location in the document by using the arrow keys on the keyboard or by pointing and clicking with the mouse. To select an object or block of text, click the object or drag the mouse over the text. Usually, once an object or some text is selected, it can be manipulated, such as to be moved, deleted, copied, or *formatted.*

> **TIP** ✓
>
> The *Quick Access Toolbar* (located to the right of the Microsoft Office Button in recent Microsoft Office programs) contains frequently used commands and can be customized by the user. Right-click a command button on the Ribbon and select *Add to Quick Access Toolbar* to add that command to your Quick Access Toolbar.

> **Editing.** Changing the content of a document, such as inserting or deleting words. > **Insertion point.** An on-screen character that looks like a blinking vertical line; indicates the current location in a document, which is where the next change will be made.

This is 10-point Arial.

This is 12-point Times New Roman.

This is 16-point Lucida Handwriting.

This is 20-point Calibri.

This 16-point Calibri text is bold and italic.

This 16-point Calibri text is red and underlined.

FIGURE 6-10

Fonts. The font face, size, style, and color used with text can be specified in many application programs.

Formatting a Document

While editing changes the actual content of a document, **formatting** changes the appearance of the document. One common type of formatting is changing the appearance of selected text in a document. You can change the *font face* or *typeface* (a named collection of text characters that share a common design, such as Calibri or Times New Roman), *font size* (which is measured in *points*), *font style* (such as bold, italic, or underline), and *font color* (see Figure 6-10). Other common types of formatting include changing the *line spacing* or *margins* of a document; adding *page numbers*; and adding *shading* or *borders* to a paragraph, image, or other item.

Getting Help

Most people have an occasional question or otherwise need some help as they work with a software program. There are various options for getting help when you need it. For instance, most application programs have a built-in help feature, typically available through a *Help button* or a *Help* option on a menu. The type and amount of built-in help available varies from program to program, but typically includes one or more of the following forms.

➤ *Table of Contents*—works much like the table of contents in a book; that is, with related help topics organized under main topics. With most help systems, selecting a main topic reveals the subtopics related to that main topic; subtopics can then be selected until the desired help topic is displayed. Selecting a help topic displays information related to that topic on the screen (see Figure 6-11).

➤ *Browsing*—allows you to click hyperlinks related to major help categories, similar to a Table of Contents but each time a topic is clicked, a new page containing links appears, similar to the way Web pages work. Clicking a link representing a help topic displays information related to that topic on the screen.

ASK THE EXPERT

OpenOffice.org

John McCreesh, Marketing Project Lead, OpenOffice.org

Can a student use the free OpenOffice.org suite at home and the Microsoft Office suite at school for the same documents? If so, would any content or formatting be lost in the translation process?

OpenOffice.org will read and write Microsoft Office file formats with a high degree of accuracy. There may be occasional slight differences in formatting—just as there are if you open old files in a newer version of Microsoft Office.

The best solution is to always store all office documents in OpenDocument Format (ODF), which is the ISO approved format for saving office files. OpenOffice.org uses this by default; Microsoft Office users can use a converter.

➤**Formatting.** Changing the appearance of a document, such as changing the margins or font size.

> *Search*—allows you to search for help topics by typing a keyword or phrase, and then the help system displays a list of links to possible matching help topics; clicking a help topic link displays information related to that topic on the screen.

Some help systems automatically search for online help from the manufacturer's Web site if the program detects an Internet connection. In addition, there is a vast amount of additional information about application software programs available via the Web, such as online articles, tutorials, and *message boards* for particular software programs, and e-mail support from software companies. Of course, online and offline books are also available for many software programs.

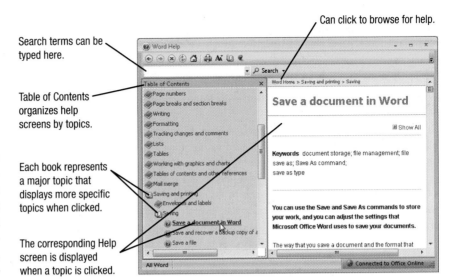

Search terms can be typed here.

Table of Contents organizes help screens by topics.

Each book represents a major topic that displays more specific topics when clicked.

The corresponding Help screen is displayed when a topic is clicked.

Can click to browse for help.

FIGURE 6-11
Getting help. Most application programs have built-in help systems.

SW

WORD PROCESSING CONCEPTS

Word processing is one of the most widely used application programs today. Although the actual commands and features vary somewhat from program to program, it is important to be familiar with the general concept of what word processing enables you to do, as well as the basic features of word processing. The following sections discuss these concepts and features.

What Is Word Processing?

Word processing refers to using a computer and **word processing software** to create, edit, save, and print written documents, such as letters, contracts, manuscripts, newsletters, invoices, marketing material, and reports. At its most basic level, word processing is used to do what was done on a typewriter before computers were commonplace. Many documents created with word processing software also include content that was not possible to create using a typewriter, such as photos, drawn objects, clip art images, hyperlinks, video clips, and text in a variety of sizes and appearances. Like any document created with software instead of paper and pencil, word processing documents can be retrieved, modified, and printed as many times as needed.

Word processing programs today typically include improved collaboration, security, and *rights-management tools* (tools used to protect original content from misuse by others). Rights management and intellectual property rights are discussed in more detail in Chapter 16; *digital signatures*, *encryption*, and other security tools that are now used to secure word processing documents are discussed in Chapter 9. Word processing programs today also typically include a variety of Web-related tools, as well as support for speech and pen input. For a look at how to use speech input with Microsoft Word on a Windows Vista computer, see the How It Works box.

> **Word processing.** Using a computer and word processing software to create, edit, save, and print written documents, such as letters, contracts, and manuscripts. > **Word processing software.** Application software used to create, edit, save, and print written documents.

HOW IT WORKS

Windows Vista Speech Recognition with Microsoft Word

Speech recognition has arrived. Surgeons use it to control surgical robotic equipment, individuals use it to dial their mobile phones, and now you can use it to control your computer.

The Speech Recognition feature built into recent versions of Windows allows you to use your voice to issue commands to your computer, such as to launch programs, switch to a different open program, close a window, and so forth. You can also use it in application programs—such as your e-mail program or Microsoft Word—to dictate text to the computer, as well as to edit and format already typed text.

To use Windows Speech Recognition, you need to have a microphone connected to your computer and then run through the setup process to test your microphone, adjust the volume, and so forth (choose *Ease of Access* and then *Speech Recognition Options* to start the setup process). Once Speech Recognition is set up and enabled, you will see the *Speech Recognition microphone bar* on your screen (see the accompanying

illustration). When the system is "sleeping," you need to say "Start Listening" to wake it up. After that point, until you say "Stop Listening," the system will respond to your voice commands. For instance, speaking text that is not an official command will cause that text to be typed in the program in the active window. Speaking a command (such as "Undo" to undo the last change, "Select *word*" to select that word in your document, or "Correct *word*" to correct the spelling of a particular word) will carry out that command. To see a list of possible commands, say "What can I say?" and the system will display a *Speech Reference Card* on your screen.

If there are multiple possibilities for a command or correction that you issue (refer again to the accompanying illustration), the system displays a numbered list of possibilities and waits for your selection. If the system doesn't understand a command, it will display a "What was that?" message.

While there are numerous speech recognition software programs on the market, for basic dictation and voice commands Windows Speech Recognition does the trick.

1. The system types your words as you talk.

2. The computer typed the wrong word; to correct this error, speak the command "Correct two".

3. Numbered icons are displayed next to each word that sounds like the word that needs to be corrected; say the appropriate number followed by "OK".

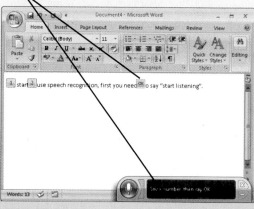

4. After the word "two" is selected for correction, possible replacement words are displayed; select the proper word by saying the number "3" and then "OK".

5. The correction is made.

Virtually all formal writing today is performed using a word processing program. Among today's most frequently used word processing programs are *Microsoft Word*, *Corel WordPerfect*, and *Apple Pages*—all part of the software suites mentioned earlier in this chapter. Most word processing programs offer hundreds of features, but virtually all support a core group of features used to create, edit, and format documents. Some of these basic features are described in the next few sections, using Microsoft Word 2007 as the example. Recent versions of Word save documents using the *.docx* extension by default, although other file formats (including the original *.doc* Word 97–2003 format for files that need to be opened in older versions of Word, the more universal *Rich Text Format* (*.rtf*), and several Web page formats) can be used instead when needed.

Creating a Word Processing Document

Every word processing program contains an assortment of operations for creating and editing documents, including commands to insert text, graphics, and other items, and then move, copy, delete, or otherwise edit the content, as needed. Some features in a typical word processing program are shown in Figure 6-12.

When entering text in a word processing document, it is important to know when to press the Enter key. Word processing programs use a feature called **word wrap**, which means the insertion point automatically moves to the beginning of the next line when the

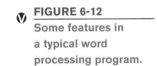

FIGURE 6-12
Some features in a typical word processing program.

FONT SIZE
Measured in points; the size of the selected text is 36 pts.

FILENAME
Appears on the title bar once a file has been saved one time.

ALIGNMENT
The selected text is centered.

CONTEXTUAL TAB
Provides access to additional commands when objects (such as the clip art image below) are selected.

FONT FACE
The font face of the selected text is currently being changed.

STYLES
Can be used to apply the same formatting to similar sections of the document.

RIBBON
Contains tabs of commands; the Home tab is selected.

HEADER
Text entered by the user that appears at the top of each page.

LIVE PREVIEW
Changes the appearance of selected items when a formatting command is pointed to.

CLIP ART
Clip art and other graphics can be inserted and resized or otherwise modified as necessary.

MINI TOOLBAR
Appears when text is selected with a mouse.

WORD WRAP
Wraps text to the next line automatically when the text being typed reaches the end of the screen line; the user should not press Enter until the end of the paragraph.

STATUS BAR
Indicates the number of pages and words currently in the document, the current document view and zoom level, and so on.

TABLE
Can be used to neatly organize data or lay out the text in a document.

FOOTER
Text entered by the user that appears at the bottom of each page. This footer contains the page number.

> **Word wrap.** The feature in a word processing program that automatically returns the insertion point to the next line when the end of the screen line is reached.

TIP

When typing text in a word processing program, you should only press Enter after a short line (like a title), at the end of a paragraph, and to leave a blank line between paragraphs.

TIP

To save paper, always preview your documents before printing and use Word's *Shrink One Page* option if the document has a mostly blank last page.

end of the screen line is reached. Consequently, the Enter key should not be pressed until it is time to begin a new paragraph or leave a blank line. With word wrap, when changes are made to the document—such as adding, modifying, or deleting text or changing the text size or page margins—the program will automatically adjust the amount of text on each screen line, as long as the Enter key was not pressed at the end of each line.

In most word processing programs, formatting can be applied at the character, paragraph, and document levels. *Character formatting* changes the appearance of individual characters, such as to change the font face, size, style, or color. To format characters, you usually select them with the mouse, and then apply the appropriate format. In recent versions of Word, for instance, you can use the command buttons on the Ribbon's Home tab or the *Mini toolbar* (which appears when text is selected and is designed to allow easy text formatting), or you can click the *Font Dialog Box Launcher* (a small arrow at the bottom right corner of the *Font group* of the Home tab) to open the *Font dialog box*. As shown in Figure 6-12, Word includes a *Live Preview* feature, which allows the user to see the results of many formatting commands before they are applied, such as watching selected text change as the user scrolls through a list of font faces or sizes.

Paragraph formatting changes an entire paragraph at one time, such as specifying the *line spacing* for a particular paragraph. To format paragraphs, you usually select the paragraph with the mouse, and then apply the appropriate format. In Word, for instance, you can use the command buttons in the *Paragraph group* on the Ribbon's Home tab or you can click the *Paragraph Dialog Box Launcher* to open the *Paragraph dialog box*. The most common types of paragraph formatting include *line spacing*, *indentation*, and *alignment*. Line spacing is the amount of blank space between lines of text—usually set to 1 for single spacing or 2 for double spacing. Indentation is the distance between the paragraph and the left or right margin. Alignment indicates how the paragraph is aligned in relation to the left and right margins of the document, such as *left*, *center*, *right*, or *justify* (flush with both the left and right edges of the document as in this textbook). *Tabs* are set locations to which the insertion point is moved when the Tab key on the keyboard is pressed. Usually the tab settings are preset to every one-half inch, but the tab settings can be changed by the user. *Styles*—named format specifications—can also be applied on a paragraph-by-paragraph basis. Styles are used to keep a uniform appearance for related parts of a document. Once a paragraph has been assigned a style (such as one of Word's predefined styles, like Heading 1, or a new style defined by the user), all other paragraphs formatted with that style will appear the same and any formatting changes made to the style will be applied to all paragraphs using that style.

Most word processing programs also have a variety of *page formatting* options, such as changing the *margins*, the *paper size* being used, and whether you want the page to use the traditional *portrait orientation* (8.5 inches wide by 11 inches tall on standard paper) or the wider *landscape orientation* (11 inches wide by 8.5 inches tall on standard paper). In recent versions of Word, most page formatting options are found on the *Page Layout tab* on the Ribbon. You can also use the *Insert tab* on the Ribbon to add page numbers at the top or bottom of the page, or to specify a *header* or *footer*. As shown in Figure 6-12, a header or a footer is specified text or images that print automatically on every page; a header appears at the top of every page and a footer appears at the bottom of every page. Many of these options can be applied to an individual page as page formatting or to the entire document (called *document formatting*). Other types of document formatting include generating *footnotes* and *end notes*, a *table of contents*, or an *index*, as well as applying a *background* or a *theme* to the entire document.

CAUTION CAUTION CAUTION CAUTION CAUTION CAUTION CAUT

To avoid the embarrassment of distributing a document with hidden text, internal comments, and other data you may not wish to pass onto others, click the Office button, then *Prepare*, and then *Inspect Document* to check for and remove this data before distribution.

INSERT TAB
Used to insert a table, picture, shape, or other object into the document.

TABLE TOOLS CONTEXTUAL TABS
Used to change the design or layout of a table; available only when a table is selected.

PICTURE TOOLS CONTEXTUAL TAB
Used to format a picture object, such as to crop it or change its size, color, or border; available only when an image is selected.

Tables, Graphics, and Templates

Most word processing programs today have advanced features to help users create documents or add special features to documents. For instance, a *table* feature allows content to be organized in a table consisting of *rows* and *columns*. Tables can be used as basic data tables, such as the one shown in Figure 6-12; they can also be used to lay out documents, such as when creating a newsletter, résumé, or Web page. Once a table has been created, shading, borders, and other formatting can be applied to the table and/or its contents, and rows and columns can be inserted or deleted, as needed. There are a number of Ribbon tabs that can be used in Word to help users insert and modify tables. For instance, the Insert tab (shown in Figure 6-13) is used to insert tables (as well as pictures, shapes, charts, text boxes, and other objects). Once a table is created and selected, the *Table Tools* contextual tabs (*Design* and *Layout*—Layout is the active tab in Figure 6-13) appear on the Ribbon and contain commands that can be used to modify the table.

Graphics or *drawing* features are also commonly found in word processing programs. Virtually all word processing programs allow images (such as a photograph, a drawing from another program, a geometric shape, or a *clip art image* like the one in Figure 6-12) to be inserted into a document. Once an image is inserted into a document, it can be modified (such as changing the brightness or contrast of a digital photo, cropping an image, converting a color image to grayscale, compressing an image to reduce the file size of the document, or adding borders). The *Picture Tools* contextual tab, which is used in Word for these purposes and is displayed on the Ribbon whenever an image is selected, is shown in Figure 6-13. Once images are inserted into a document, they can be copied, moved, deleted, or otherwise modified, just like any other object in the document.

To help users create new documents quickly, many word processing programs have a variety of *templates* available. A template is a document that is already created and formatted to fit a particular purpose, such as a fax cover sheet, résumé, memo, business card, calendar, business plan, newsletter, or Web page. Usually placeholder text is included for text that can be customized so that all the user needs to do is to replace the placeholder text with the appropriate content.

Word Processing and the Web

Most word processing programs today include Web-related features, such as the ability to send a document as an e-mail message via the word processing program, the inclusion of Web page hyperlinks in documents, and the ability to create or modify Web pages or blogs. The latest versions of Office also include the ability to collaborate with others online.

FIGURE 6-13
Ribbon tabs used to insert and modify tables and images.

SW

TIP
When using a table for layout purposes, change the table borders to *None* after the document is finished to make the table outline invisible.

TIP
Additional templates are often available free of charge through software manufacturer Web sites, such as Microsoft's *Office Online* Web site.

TIP
To open the Web page associated with a hyperlink included in a document (assuming you have an active Internet connection), hold down the Control key and then click the hyperlink.

SPREADSHEET CONCEPTS

Another widely used application program is *spreadsheet software*. Spreadsheet software is commonly used by a variety of businesses and employees, including CEOs, managers, assistants, analysts, and sales representatives. Basic spreadsheet concepts and features are described next.

What Is a Spreadsheet?

A **spreadsheet** is a group of values and other data organized into rows and columns, similar to the ruled paper worksheets traditionally used by bookkeepers and accountants. **Spreadsheet software** is the type of application software used to create computerized spreadsheets, which typically contain a great deal of numbers and mathematical calculations. Most spreadsheets include *formulas* that are used to compute calculations based on data entered into the spreadsheet. All formula results are updated automatically whenever any changes are made to the data. Consequently, no manual computations are required, which increases accuracy. In addition, the automatic recalculation of formulas allows individuals to modify spreadsheet data as often as necessary either to create new spreadsheets or to experiment with various possible scenarios (called *what-if analysis*, as discussed shortly) to help make business decisions. Spreadsheet software typically includes a variety of data analysis tools, as well as the ability to generate charts.

The most widely used spreadsheet programs today are *Microsoft Excel*, *Corel Quattro Pro*, and *Apple Numbers*—again, all are part of their respective software suites mentioned near the beginning of this chapter. Some of the basic features supported by all spreadsheet programs are described in the next few sections, using Microsoft Excel 2007 as the example. Recent versions of Excel save spreadsheet files with the *.xlsx* extension by default.

Creating a Spreadsheet

A single spreadsheet document is often called a **worksheet**. Most spreadsheet programs allow multiple worksheets to be saved together in a single spreadsheet file, called a **workbook**. Worksheets are divided into **rows** and **columns**. The intersection of a row and a column is called a **cell**. Each cell is identified by its *cell address*, which consists of the column letter followed by the row number, such as B4 or E22. The *cell pointer* is used to select a cell; the selected cell is called the *active cell* or *current cell* and has a border around it so it is easy to identify. You can enter content into the active cell, as well as apply formatting to content already in the active cell. The cell pointer can be used to select more than one cell; if so, the selected cells are called a *range* or *block*. Ranges are always rectangular and are identified by specifying two opposite corners of the range, such as D8 through E9 for the four cells in the range shown in Figure 6-14 (and usually typed as *D8:E9* or *D8..E9*, depending on the spreadsheet program being used). As with Word, the Excel interface uses the Ribbon, contextual tabs, the Mini toolbar, and Live Preview for editing and formatting.

Entering Data into a Spreadsheet Cell

Data is entered directly into worksheet cells by clicking a cell to make it the active cell and then typing the data to be contained in that cell. The contents of the active cell can be erased by pressing the Delete key or by typing new content, which replaces the old contents of that cell. The data entered into a cell is usually a *label*, a *constant value*, a *formula*,

>**Spreadsheet.** A document containing a group of values and other data organized into rows and columns; also called a worksheet in a spreadsheet program. >**Spreadsheet software.** Application software used to create spreadsheets, which typically contain a great deal of numbers and mathematical computations organized into rows and columns. >**Worksheet.** A single spreadsheet document in a spreadsheet program. >**Workbook.** A collection of worksheets saved in a single spreadsheet file. >**Row.** In a spreadsheet program, a horizontal group of cells on a worksheet. >**Column.** In a spreadsheet program, a vertical group of cells on a worksheet. >**Cell.** The location at the intersection of a row and column on a worksheet into which data can be typed.

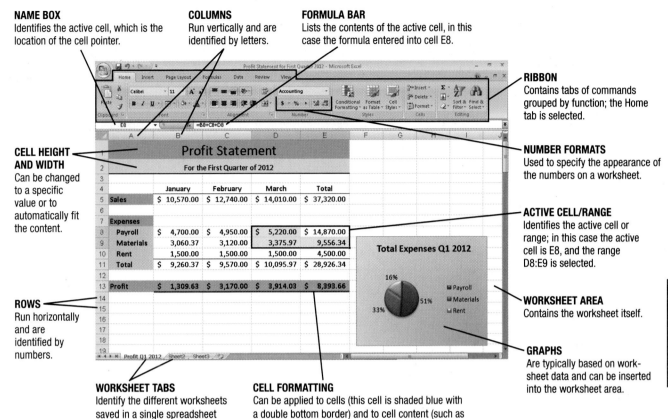

NAME BOX
Identifies the active cell, which is the location of the cell pointer.

COLUMNS
Run vertically and are identified by letters.

FORMULA BAR
Lists the contents of the active cell, in this case the formula entered into cell E8.

RIBBON
Contains tabs of commands grouped by function; the Home tab is selected.

CELL HEIGHT AND WIDTH
Can be changed to a specific value or to automatically fit the content.

NUMBER FORMATS
Used to specify the appearance of the numbers on a worksheet.

ACTIVE CELL/RANGE
Identifies the active cell or range; in this case the active cell is E8, and the range D8:E9 is selected.

ROWS
Run horizontally and are identified by numbers.

WORKSHEET AREA
Contains the worksheet itself.

GRAPHS
Are typically based on worksheet data and can be inserted into the worksheet area.

WORKSHEET TABS
Identify the different worksheets saved in a single spreadsheet (workbook) file.

CELL FORMATTING
Can be applied to cells (this cell is shaded blue with a double bottom border) and to cell content (such as currency with two decimal places).

FIGURE 6-14
Some features in a typical spreadsheet program.

FIGURE 6-15
Universal mathematical operators.

or a *function*. **Labels** are words, column headings, and other nonmathematical data, such as *Profit Statement* and *January* in Figure 6-14. **Constant values** are numbers (such as *105* or *12740.25*) and are entered into a cell without any additional characters (such as a dollar sign or comma). A **formula** performs mathematical operations using the content of other cells (such as adding or multiplying the values in the specified cells) and displays the result in the cell containing the formula. A **function** is a named, preprogrammed formula, such as to compute the average of a group of cells or to calculate a mortgage payment amount. There are literally hundreds of functions that can be used in spreadsheets for statistical, date and time, engineering, math, logical, and text-based computations. The standard mathematical operators used in formulas and functions are shown in Figure 6-15; some examples of commonly used spreadsheet functions are listed in Figure 6-16.

When entering a formula or function into a cell, most spreadsheet programs require that you begin with some type of mathematical symbol—usually the equal sign (=). You can then enter the cell addresses and mathematical operators to create the formula, or you can type the appropriate function name and *arguments* (such as a cell or range address). When creating formulas and functions, it is important to always use the cell addresses of the numbers you want to include in the calculation (such as =B8+C8+D8 for the formula used to calculate the value displayed in cell E8 in Figure 6-14), rather than the numbers themselves (such as =4700+4950+5220). If the actual numbers are used in the formula instead of the cell addresses, the result of that formula (such as the total in cell E8) will not be correctly updated if one of the numbers (such as January payroll expenses in cell B8) is changed. When a

SYMBOL	OPERATION
+	Addition
−	Subtraction
*	Multiplication
/	Division
∧	Exponentiation

>**Label.** A text-based entry in a worksheet cell that identifies data on the worksheet. >**Constant value.** A numerical entry in a worksheet cell.
>**Formula.** An entry in a worksheet cell that performs computations on worksheet data and displays the results. >**Function.** A named formula that can be entered into a worksheet cell to perform some type of calculation or to extract information from other cells in the worksheet.

EXAMPLES OF FUNCTIONS

= SUM (range)	Calculates the sum of all values in a range.
= MAX (range)	Finds the highest value in a range.
= MIN (range)	Finds the lowest value in a range.
= AVERAGE (range)	Calculates the average of values in a range.
= FV (rate, number of payments, payment amount)	Calculates the future value of an annuity at a specified interest rate.
= PMT (rate, number of payments, loan amount)	Calculates the periodic payment for a loan.
= IF (conditional expression, value if true, value if false)	Supplies the values to be displayed if the conditional expression is true or if it is false.
= NOW ( )	Inserts the current date and time.

FIGURE 6-16
Common spreadsheet functions.

FIGURE 6-17
Relative vs. absolute cell referencing.

proper formula (using the cell references instead of the actual numbers) is used, the formula will be recomputed automatically every time any data in any of the cells used in that formula is changed. The appearance of numeric content (such as constant values or the result of a formula or numeric function) in a cell is determined by the *number format* applied to a cell (such as *Currency*, *Comma*, or *Percent*).

Absolute vs. Relative Cell Referencing

The Copy command can be used to copy content from one cell to another, in order to create a spreadsheet more quickly. This is especially true for cells containing formulas because the cells in a column or row often contain similar formulas (such as to add the values in the cells in the three columns to the left of the Total cells in column E in the spreadsheet shown in Figure 6-14) and typing formulas can be time-consuming. Labels and constant values are always copied exactly to the new location; what happens to formulas when they are copied depends on whether they use *relative cell referencing* or *absolute cell referencing*.

Relative cell references are used in most spreadsheet programs by default. When a formula containing relative cell references is copied, the cell addresses in the copied formula are adjusted to reflect their new location, so the formula performs the same operation (such as adding the two cells to the left of the cell containing the formula) but in the new location. In other words, the formula in the new location does the same *relative* operation as it did in the original location. For example, in the left screen in Figure 6-17, the formula in cell D2 (which uses relative cell references to add the two cells to the left of the cell containing the formula) is copied to cells D3 and D4. Because the cell references are all relative, when the formula is copied to the new cells, the cell references are adjusted to continue to add the two cells to

COPYING WITH RELATIVE CELL REFERENCES
In most formulas, cell addresses are relative and will be adjusted as the formula is copied.

Formula in cell D2 =B2+C2

	A	B	C	D
1		Cones	Sundaes	Total
2	April	600	200	800
3	May	800	500	1300
4	June	1500	600	2100
5	Total			
6				

Formula in cell D4 is =B4+C4.

Results when the formula in cell D2 is copied to cells D3 and D4.

COPYING WITH ABSOLUTE CELL REFERENCES
A dollar sign ($) marks a cell reference as absolute; it will be copied exactly as it appears in the source cell.

Formula in cell D2 =$B$2+$C$2

	A	B	C	D
1		Cones	Sundaes	Total
2	April	600	200	800
3	May	800	500	800
4	June	1500	600	800
5	Total			
6				

Results when the formula in cell D2 is copied to cells D3 and D4.

Formula in cell D4 is =$B$2+$C$2.

IMPROPER USE

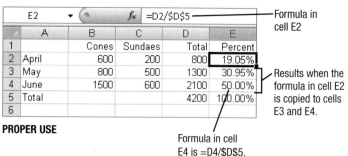

Formula in cell E2 =D2/$D$5

	A	B	C	D	E
1		Cones	Sundaes	Total	Percent
2	April	600	200	800	19.05%
3	May	800	500	1300	30.95%
4	June	1500	600	2100	50.00%
5	Total			4200	100.00%
6					

Results when the formula in cell E2 is copied to cells E3 and E4.

PROPER USE

Formula in cell E4 is =D4/$D$5.

the left of the formula cell. For instance, the formula in cell D3 is updated automatically to =B3+C3 and the formula in cell D4 is updated automatically to =B4+C4. Relative cell references are also adjusted automatically when a row or column is inserted or deleted.

In contrast, when *absolute cell references* are used, formulas are copied exactly as they are written (see the rightmost screens in Figure 6-17). It is appropriate to use an absolute cell reference when you want to use a specific cell address in all copies of the formula—such as always multiplying by a constant value (perhaps a sales tax rate or overtime rate located in a particular cell on the worksheet) or always dividing by a total in order to compute a percentage. In other words, whenever you do not want a cell address to be adjusted when the formula is copied, you must use an absolute cell reference in the formula. To make a cell reference in a formula absolute, a special symbol—usually a dollar sign ($)—is placed before each column letter and row number that should not change. For example, both of the cell references in the formula in cell D2 in the top right screen in Figure 6-17 are absolute, resulting in the formula =$B$2+$C$2 being placed in both cells (D3 and D4) when the formula is copied. Obviously, this is not the correct formula for these cells—the formulas in these cells need to use relative cell references in order to display the proper totals. In cells E2 through E4 in the bottom right screen, however, an absolute cell reference is correctly used for cell D5 (and written as $D$5) in order to divide the total sales for each month (located in cells D2, D3, and D4, respectively) by the total sales for all three months (located in cell D5) to compute the percent of total sales. An absolute reference for cell D5 is necessary if the formula in cell E2 is to be copied to cells E3 and E4, since the denominator in all three cells should be D5.

Charts and What-If Analysis

Most spreadsheet programs include some type of *charting* or *graphing* capability. Because the data to be included in many business charts is often already located on a spreadsheet, using that program's charting feature eliminates reentering that data into another program. Instead, the cells containing the data to be charted are selected, and then the type of chart—as well as titles and other customizations—can be specified. Charts are inserted into an Excel spreadsheet using the commands in the *Charts group* on the Insert tab on the Ribbon. Finished charts can be moved like other graphical objects to the desired located on the worksheet (refer again to Figure 6-14). Selecting an existing chart displays three *Chart Tools* contextual tabs on the Ribbon. These three tabs can be used to change the design, layout, or format of the chart.

Because spreadsheet programs automatically recalculate all formulas on a worksheet every time the content of a cell on the worksheet is edited, spreadsheet programs are particularly useful for *what-if analysis* (also called *sensitivity analysis*)—a tool frequently used to help make business decisions. For example, suppose you want to know *what* profit would have resulted for January in Figure 6-14 *if* sales had been $15,000 instead of $10,570. You can simply enter the new value (15000) into cell B5, and the spreadsheet program automatically recalculates all formulas, allowing you to determine (from looking at the new value in cell B13) that the profit would have been $5,739.63. This ability to enter new numbers and immediately see the result allows businesspeople to run through many more possibilities in a shorter period of time before making decisions than in the past when all such calculations had to be performed by hand. Another type of sensitivity analysis (called *goal seeking* in Microsoft Excel) involves having the spreadsheet compute the amount a constant value would need to be in order for the result of a particular formula to become a specified amount (such as the total sales required to obtain a January profit of $5,000 if all of the expenses stayed the same).

Spreadsheets and the Web

As with word processors, most spreadsheet programs have built-in Web capabilities. Although they are used less commonly to create Web pages, many spreadsheet programs include the option to save the current worksheet as a Web page, and hyperlinks can be inserted into worksheet cells. Microsoft Word includes the ability to send a document as an e-mail message and to collaborate online; ranges of cells can also be copied to a Web publishing or word processing program to insert spreadsheet data into a document as a table.

DATABASE CONCEPTS

People often need to retrieve specific data rapidly while on the job. For example, a customer service representative may need to locate a customer's order status quickly while the customer is on the telephone. The registrar at a university may have to look up a student's grade point average or rapidly determine if the student has any outstanding fees before processing his or her class registration. A clerk in a video store may need to determine if a particular DVD is available for rental and, if not, when it is scheduled to be returned. The type of software used for such tasks is a *database management system*. Computer-based database management systems are rapidly replacing the paper-based filing systems that people used in the past to find information. The most common type of database used with personal computers today is a *relational database*. The basic features and concepts of this type of database software are discussed next. Other types of database programs are discussed in Chapter 14.

What Is a Database?

A **database** is a collection of related data that is stored on a computer and organized in a manner that enables information to be retrieved as needed. A *database management system* (*DBMS*)—also called **database software**—is the type of program used to create, maintain, and organize data in a database, as well as to retrieve information from it. Typically data in a database is organized into *fields*, *records*, and *files*. A **field** (today more commonly called a **column**) is a single type of data, such as last name or telephone number, to be stored in a database. A **record** (today more commonly called a **row**) is a collection of related fields—for example, the ID number, name, address, and major of Phyllis Hoffman (see Figure 6-18).

⊽ **FIGURE 6-18**
Paper-based vs. computerized databases. Data is organized into fields (columns), records (rows), and tables.

One student's record stored in the Addresses file.

Data is organized into fields.

PAPER-BASED DATABASE

Student database

ID: 16231
Name: Hoffman, Phyllis
Street: 706 Elm Street
City: New Milford
State: NJ
Major: Business

16231

Addresses file

Grades file

Schedules file

COMPUTERIZED DATABASE

Fields (columns) Table

Record (row)

ID	Name	Street	City	Stat	Major
15265	Michaels, Jane	111 First Avenue	Boston	MA	Math
16231	Hoffman, Phyllis	706 Elm Street	New Milford	NJ	Business
48595	Adams, Jose	45 Center Street	New York	NY	Business
49658	Gomez, Maria	3699 Lincoln	Boston	MA	Nursing
78982	Rivera, Cynthia	122 Morton	Martinez	CA	Chemistry
79856	Jenkins, Paul	789 White Avenue	Hamilton	NJ	Pre-Med

Record: 2 of 919   No Filter   Search

> **Database.** A collection of related data that is stored in a manner enabling information to be retrieved as needed; in a relational database, a collection of related tables. > **Database software.** Application software that allows the creation and manipulation of an electronic database. > **Field.** A single category of data to be stored in a database, such as a person's last name or telephone number. Also called a column. > **Column.** In a database, a field. > **Record.** A collection of related fields in a database. Also called a row. > **Row.** In a database program, a record.

A **table** is a collection of related rows (such as all student address data, all student grade data, or all student schedule data). One or more related tables can be stored in a database file.

The most commonly used *relational database management systems* (*RDBMSs*) include *Microsoft Access* (part of the Microsoft Office software suite), as well as *Oracle Database* and IBM's *DB2*. Some of the basic features of relational database programs in general are described in the next few sections, using Microsoft Access 2007 as the example. Recent versions of Access save database files with the *.accdb* extension by default.

Creating a Database

An Access database can contain a variety of *objects*. *Tables* are the objects that contain the database data. Other types of objects (such as *forms*, *queries*, and *reports*, discussed shortly) can be created and used in conjunction with tables when needed. As shown in Figure 6-19, a list of the various objects stored in a database file is displayed when the file is opened. However, you do not see the content of a database object until you open that object.

To create a database, you create the database file first, and then you create the database objects you want the database to contain. Each time Access is launched, you have the option of creating a new blank database file, creating a database file from a template, or opening an existing database file. If you choose to create a new blank database file, a new blank table opens in *Datasheet view* (which displays the table in rows and columns similar to a spreadsheet—see the top screen in Figure 6-20).

DATABASE FILE
Contains the Inventory database objects.

RIBBON
Contains tabs of commands grouped by function; the Create tab, which is used to create new database objects, is selected.

DATABASE OBJECTS
Include Tables (for storing data), Forms (for viewing and editing table data), and Queries and Reports (for retrieving information from tables).

FIGURE 6-19
Typical database objects. Common database objects include tables, forms, queries, and reports. The first object to be created is the table.

FIGURE 6-20
Creating a database table.

SW

DATASHEET VIEW

As data is entered into a new table using Datasheet view, the structure of the table is created.

The table has been saved as "Product" and is in Design view.

This field was renamed "Product Name" and is a Text field.

Click to select Design View.

Properties of the Product Name field.

DESIGN VIEW

>**Table.** In a relational database, a collection of related records or rows.

As data is entered into a new table using Datasheet view, the *structure* of the table (the fields and their properties) is created. Each column becomes a new field and is given a temporary *field name* (an identifying name unique within the table, such as *Field1*) and is assigned an appropriate *data type* (which identifies the type of data to be contained in the field; for example, text, a number, or a date) based on the data initially entered into that field. These properties can be changed by selecting the field and using the commands on the *Datasheet tab* of the Ribbon (such as selecting the *Rename* option to rename the field or selecting a different data type in the *Data Type* box). Each field should be given a descriptive field name and the data type should be changed if the data type set by default is not correct. A field can also be declared a *required* field if the field should not be left blank. *Design view* (shown in the bottom screen in Figure 6-20) can be used to change other field properties, such as the *field size* (which is the maximum number of characters allowed for the content of that field), the *default value* (which is the initial content of that field that remains until it is changed), the field *description*, and the *format* (which describes how the field content should be displayed, such as including commas or dollar signs with numeric data). When the table is saved, it is given a name by the user and both the table data and table structure are saved in that table object.

To add new data to an existing table, to edit data, or to delete data, either a *form* or Datasheet view can be used. As shown in Figure 6-21, a form (which is created by the user for a particular table) typically displays one record at a time, while Datasheet view displays several records at one time. However, either Datasheet view or a form can be used to change the data in the table. Data can be edited by clicking inside the appropriate field and then making the necessary edits. A record can be deleted by clicking to the left of the first field in the appropriate Datasheet row or on the left edge of a form to select that record, and then pressing the Delete key. A field can be deleted in Datasheet view by selecting the appropriate field (column), and then pressing the Delete key. The *Record buttons* at the bottom of the form or Datasheet view window can be used to move through the records as needed.

FORM
Displays one record at a time.

DATASHEET VIEW
Displays multiple records at a time.

Click to the left of a form or table record to select that record.

Click the Record buttons to display other records.

Click in a field to edit it.

FIGURE 6-21
Table data can be modified using a form or the Datasheet view.

Queries and Reports

To retrieve information from a database, *queries* and *reports* are used. A *query* is a question, or, in database terms, a request for specific information from the database. Like other database objects, each query object is created and then saved using an appropriate name as a part of the database file. A query object is associated with a particular table and contains *criteria*—specific conditions that must be met in order for a record (row) to be included in the query results—as well as instructions regarding which fields (columns) should appear in the query results. For instance, the query shown in Figure 6-22 is designed to retrieve information from the Product table shown in Figure 6-21. The query retrieves all products in that table that have prices less than $25, and the query results display only the Product Name, Product Number, and Price fields. Whenever the query is opened, only the records meeting the specified criteria at the time the query is opened are displayed, and only the specified fields for those records are listed. For instance, the query results shown in Figure 6-22 contain only two records from the Product table in Figure 6-21 because only two records in that table contain products with prices less than $25. If a new product priced less than $25 is added to the database, three records will be displayed the next time the query is opened.

When a more formal output is required, *reports* are used. Reports can contain page and column headings, as well as a company logo or other graphics, and can be formatted and customized as desired. Reports are associated with a database table or query and can be easily created using the *Report button* or *Report Wizard button* on the *Create tab* on the Ribbon. Existing reports can be modified using the *Report Design button*. Whenever a report object is opened, the corresponding data is displayed in the specified location in the report. Consequently, just as with queries, reports always display the data contained in a table at the time the report is generated. Queries and reports are discussed in more detail in Chapter 14.

Databases and the Web

Databases are often used on the Web. Many Web sites use one or more databases to keep track of inventory; to allow searching for people, documents, or other information; to place real-time orders; and so forth. For instance, any time you type keywords in a search box on a search site or hunt for a product on a retail store's Web site using its search feature, you are using a Web database. Web databases are explained in more detail in Chapter 14.

PRESENTATION GRAPHICS CONCEPTS

If you try to explain to others what you look like, it may take several minutes. Show them a color photograph, on the other hand, and you can convey the same information within seconds. The saying "a picture is worth a thousand words" is the cornerstone of *presentation graphics*. The basic concepts and features of presentation graphics are discussed in the next few sections.

What Is a Presentation Graphic?

A **presentation graphic** (see Figure 6-23) is an image designed to enhance a presentation (such as an *electronic slide show* or a printed report) visually, typically to convey information more easily to people. A variety of software (including spreadsheet programs, *image editing programs*, and *presentation graphics software*) can be used to create presentation graphics. Presentation graphics often take the form of electronic **slides** containing images,

QUERY DESIGN SCREEN
This query will display only the records that meet the specified criteria each time the query is retrieved.

Only these three fields will be displayed in the query results.

Only the records in which the price is less than $25 will be displayed in the query results.

QUERY RESULTS
The two records meeting the specified criteria are displayed.

FIGURE 6-22
Creating and using a database query.

FIGURE 6-23
Examples of presentation graphics.

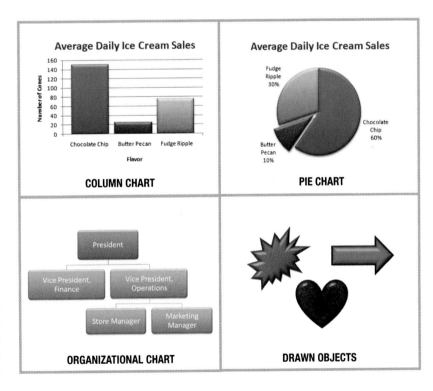

COLUMN CHART

PIE CHART

ORGANIZATIONAL CHART

DRAWN OBJECTS

> **Presentation graphic.** An image, such as a graph or text chart, designed to visually enhance a presentation. > **Slide.** A one-page presentation graphic that can be displayed in a group with others to form an electronic slide show.

text, video, and more that are displayed one after the other in an **electronic slide show**. Electronic slide shows are created with **presentation graphics software** and can be run on individual computers or presented to a large group using a computer projector; for instance, they are frequently used for business and educational presentations. Some of today's most common presentation graphics programs are *Microsoft PowerPoint*, *Corel Presentations*, and *Apple Keynote*—again, all part of their respective software suites. The next few sections discuss creating an electronic slide show, using Microsoft PowerPoint 2007 as the example. Recent versions of PowerPoint save files with the *.pptx* extension by default.

Creating a Presentation

A presentation graphics program, such as the one shown in Figure 6-24, contains an assortment of tools and operations for creating and editing slides. For instance, new slides can be added to a new or existing presentation (preformatted *slide layouts* containing placeholders for text and charts and other elements in a slide can be used, if desired). Text, photographs, tables, shapes, charts, and more can then be added to slides using the Insert tab and formatted as needed using the *Format tab*. To create more exciting and dynamic presentations, multimedia objects and animation effects can be used. For instance, video and audio clips

FIGURE 6-24
Some features in a typical presentation graphics program.

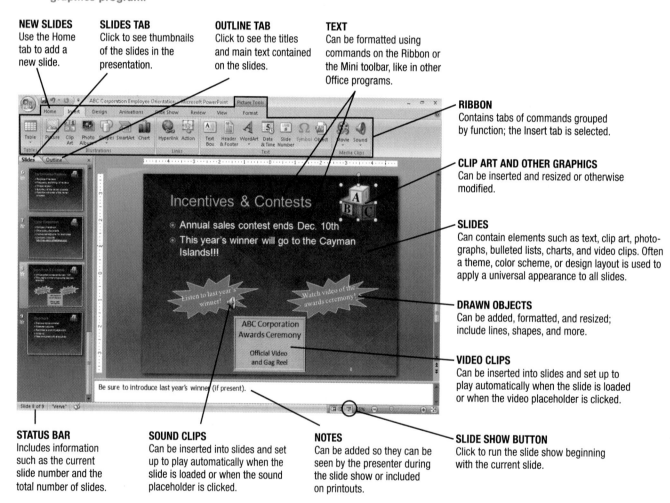

NEW SLIDES
Use the Home tab to add a new slide.

SLIDES TAB
Click to see thumbnails of the slides in the presentation.

OUTLINE TAB
Click to see the titles and main text contained on the slides.

TEXT
Can be formatted using commands on the Ribbon or the Mini toolbar, like in other Office programs.

RIBBON
Contains tabs of commands grouped by function; the Insert tab is selected.

CLIP ART AND OTHER GRAPHICS
Can be inserted and resized or otherwise modified.

SLIDES
Can contain elements such as text, clip art, photographs, bulleted lists, charts, and video clips. Often a theme, color scheme, or design layout is used to apply a universal appearance to all slides.

DRAWN OBJECTS
Can be added, formatted, and resized; include lines, shapes, and more.

VIDEO CLIPS
Can be inserted into slides and set up to play automatically when the slide is loaded or when the video placeholder is clicked.

STATUS BAR
Includes information such as the current slide number and the total number of slides.

SOUND CLIPS
Can be inserted into slides and set up to play automatically when the slide is loaded or when the sound placeholder is clicked.

NOTES
Can be added so they can be seen by the presenter during the slide show or included on printouts.

SLIDE SHOW BUTTON
Click to run the slide show beginning with the current slide.

> **Electronic slide show.** A group of electronic slides that are displayed one after the other on a computer monitor or other display device.
> **Presentation graphics software.** Application software used to create presentation graphics and electronic slide shows.

can be inserted into a slide and set up to play automatically each time the slide containing those elements is displayed, or, alternatively, to play when certain objects on the slide are clicked. Text or other objects can be *animated* so that a special effect (such as *flying* the text in from the edge of the screen or *dissolving* the text in or out on a slide) is used to display that text or object each time the slide is viewed. *Animation settings* can be specified to indicate the sequence in which objects are displayed (such as to build a bulleted list one item at a time), whether or not a video loops continuously, and more.

Once the basic slides in a presentation have been created, the overall appearance of the entire slide show can be changed by applying a *theme* (a combination of colors, fonts, and effects that can be applied to an entire slide show at one time) to the presentation using the *Design tab*. In addition, *transitions*—special effects used between slides—can be applied to specific slides, or random transitions can be selected for the entire slide show. In PowerPoint, animations and transitions are both specified using the *Animations tab*.

Finishing a Presentation

Once all of the slides in a slide show have been created and the desired animation and transition effects have been applied, the slide show is ready to be finalized. To preview the slides and rearrange them if needed, presentation graphics programs typically have a special view, such as PowerPoint's *slide sorter view*, that shows thumbnails of all the slides in a presentation. Using this view, slides can easily be rearranged by dragging them with the mouse to their new location in the presentation. When the slide show is run, the slides are displayed in the designated order. The slides advance either automatically or manually, depending on how the presentation is set up. For an *automatic slide show*, the amount of time each slide should be displayed is specified using the *Slide Show tab* on the Ribbon before the presentation is saved. For a *manual slide show*, the speaker (or person viewing the slide show, for a stand-alone presentation) moves to the next slide by pressing the spacebar or by clicking anywhere on the screen using the mouse. If desired, PowerPoint allows narration to be recorded and played back when the slide show is run, and *speaker notes* can be added to the slides, as needed.

PowerPoint, like many other presentation software programs, also has a variety of *speaker tools*. For instance, the speaker can choose a ballpoint pen, felt tip pen, or highlighter tool and "write" on the slides while the slide show is running, perhaps to circle a particular sentence for emphasis or to draw an arrow pointing to one part of the slide. Recent versions of PowerPoint also include a *Presenter View* (see Figure 6-25) that can be used when two display devices are available (such as when a data projector is connected to the notebook computer being used to run the presentation). The regular slide show is projected in full screen for the audience on one display device (such as projected onto a large screen via the data projector), while a special Presenter View version of the slide show (containing a smaller version of the current slide along with speaker notes, thumbnails of surrounding slides, a timer, and so forth) is displayed for the presenter on the second display device (such as the notebook computer's display screen). Most presentation software programs can also print the speaker notes, as well as the slides (either full-sized or miniature versions printed several to a page) to create overhead transparencies or audience handouts.

Presentation Graphics and the Web

As with the other application programs discussed so far, presentation graphics programs can be used to generate Web pages or Web page content, and slides can include hyperlinks. When a slide show is saved as a

Ⓥ **FIGURE 6-25**
Running an electronic slide show.

SLIDE SHOW VIEW
Displays the slide show for the audience in full screen with the software interface hidden. Slides can be advanced at predetermined intervals or by clicking the mouse or pressing the spacebar.

PRESENTER VIEW
Seen only by the presenter on a different display device; includes thumbnails, a timer, speaker notes, annotation tools, and so forth.

series of Web pages and displayed using a Web browser, generally forward and backward navigational buttons are displayed on the slides to allow the user to control the presentation.

GRAPHICS AND MULTIMEDIA CONCEPTS

Graphics are graphical images, such as digital photographs, clip art, scanned drawings, and original images created using a software program. *Multimedia* technically refers to any application that contains more than one type of media (as discussed in Chapter 10), but is often used to refer to audio and video content. There are a variety of software programs designed to help individuals create or modify graphics, edit digital audio or video files, play media files, burn CDs and DVDs, and so forth, as discussed next. Some programs focus on just one task; others are designed to perform multiple tasks, such as to import and edit images, audio, and video, and then create a finished DVD.

Graphics Software

Graphics software—also called *digital imaging software*—is used to create or modify images. Graphics software programs are commonly distinguished by whether they are primarily oriented toward painting, drawing, or image editing, although these are general categories, not strict classifications.

Painting programs traditionally create *bitmap images*, which are created by coloring the individual pixels in an image. One of the most common painting programs is *Microsoft Paint* (shown in Figure 6-26). Painting programs are often used to create and modify simple

FIGURE 6-26
Graphics software.

PAINTING PROGRAMS
Typically create images pixel by pixel so images cannot be layered or resized.

DRAWING PROGRAMS
Typically create images using mathematical formulas so images can consist of multiple objects that can be layered, and the images can be resized without distortion.

PHOTO EDITING PROGRAMS
Allow users to edit digital photos.

>**Graphics software.** Application software used to create or modify images.

images, but, unless the painting program supports *layers* and other tools discussed shortly, use for these programs is relatively limited. This is because when something is drawn or placed on top of a bitmap image, the pixels in the image are recolored to reflect the new content so whatever was beneath the new content is lost. In addition, bitmapped images cannot be enlarged and still maintain their quality, since the pixels in the images just get larger, which makes the edges of the images look jagged. Some painting programs today (such as *Corel Painter*) do support layers and so are more versatile. Painting tools are also increasingly included in other types of software, such as in office suites and the drawing programs discussed next.

Drawing programs (also referred to as *illustration programs*) typically create *vector graphics*, which use mathematical formulas to represent image content instead of pixels. Unlike bitmap images, vector images can be resized and otherwise manipulated without loss of quality. Objects in drawing programs can also typically be *layered* so, if you place one object on top of another, you can later separate the two images if desired. Drawing programs are often used by individuals and small business owners to create original art, logos, business cards, and more; they are also used by professionals to create corporate images, Web site graphics, and so forth. Popular drawing programs include *Adobe Illustrator* and *CorelDRAW* (shown in Figure 6-26).

Image editing or *photo editing programs* are drawing or painting programs that are specifically designed for touching up or modifying images, such as original digital images and digital photos. Editing options include correcting brightness or contrast, eliminating red eye, cropping, resizing, and applying filters or other special effects. Most programs also include options for *optimizing* images to reduce the file size. Optimization techniques include reducing the number of colors used in the image and converting the image to another file format. Some of the most widely used consumer image editing and photo editing programs are *Adobe Photoshop Elements*, *Ulead Photo Express*, *Apple iPhoto*, *Corel Paint Shop Pro Photo X2*, *Microsoft Office Picture Manager*, and the free *Picasa 3* program (shown in Figure 6-26). For professional image editing, *Adobe Photoshop* is the leading program.

ASK THE EXPERT

Ben Bardens, Creative Director, Bark Animation Co.

To prepare for a career in computer animation, which computer programs should an individual learn first and what other computer skills are important to master?

First and foremost is a solid understanding of how computers and the different operating systems function. In particular, it is important to understand how to navigate and manage files within different file systems. It is not uncommon for digital artists to be expected to work proficiently on both Mac and Windows platforms and sometimes switch between the two.

Beyond this, all digital artists (including graphic designers, motion graphics artists, animators, illustrators, and photographers) should aim to achieve an intermediate understanding of Adobe Photoshop. Photoshop is considered by many to be the fundamental computer graphics program, and has a broad range of uses and applications within several related fields. Any aspiring computer animator or digital artist should start by learning Photoshop. Once a student knows how to create and edit layered images within Photoshop, it is much easier to transition to learning other computer graphics and animation programs, such as Adobe Illustrator, After Effects, or Flash.

Audio Capture and Editing Software

For creating and editing audio files, *audio capture* and *audio editing* software is used. To capture sound from a microphone, *sound recorder* software is used; to capture sound from a CD, *ripping software* is used. In either case, once the audio is captured, it can then be modified, as needed. For instance, background noise or pauses can be removed, portions of the selection can be edited out, multiple segments can be spliced together, and special effects such as fade-ins and fade-outs can be applied. There are also specialized audio capture and editing programs designed for specific applications, such as creating podcasts or musical

ⓐ **FIGURE 6-27**
Audio editing
software.

compositions. Professional audio capture and editing software (such as *Sony Creative Software Sound Forge 9* and *Adobe Audition 3*) is used to create professional audio for end products, Web pages, commercial podcasts, presentations, and so forth. Common consumer audio capture and editing programs include *Windows Sound Recorder*, *Apple GarageBand*, and *Sony Creative Software Sound Forge Audio Studio* software (see Figure 6-27).

Video Editing and DVD Authoring Software

It is common today for individuals to want to create finished videos, such as to create a video to upload to YouTube or to edit home videos and transfer them to a DVD. Businesses also often find the need for *video editing*, such as to prepare video clips for presentations and Web sites. Most video capture today is in digital form; if so, the video can be imported directly into a video editing program by connecting the camera to the computer or by inserting the storage media containing the video (such as a DVD) into the computer. Once the video has been imported, video editing (such as deleting or rearranging scenes, adding voice-overs, and adding other special effects) can be performed (see Figure 6-28). Some video editing software today can edit video in high definition format.

DVD authoring refers to organizing content to be transferred to DVD, such as importing video clips and then creating the desired menu structure for the DVD to control the playback of those videos. *DVD burning* refers to recording data (such as a collection of songs or a finished video) on a recordable or rewritable DVD. DVD authoring and burning capabilities

ⓥ **FIGURE 6-28**

Video creation
software. Often
includes both video
editing and DVD
authoring capabilities.

VIDEO EDITING
Allows users to import and edit video; the finished video can be stored in a file or included in a DVD presentation.

Click to burn the
finished presentation
to a DVD.

The DVD includes the video clips
and uses the titles and appearance
designated by the user.

Video clips can be edited as needed; the timeline is used to crop out sections of the current video clip.

DVD AUTHORING
Allows users to import and organize photos, video, and music into a finished DVD presentation.

are commonly included with video editing capabilities in *video creation software*; there are also stand-alone *DVD authoring programs*, and DVD burning capabilities are preinstalled on computers containing a recordable or rewritable optical drive. Many file management programs (such as Windows Explorer) include CD and DVD burning capabilities, as well.

Consumer video creation software includes *Serif MoviePlus X3* (shown in Figure 6-28), *Roxio Creator 2009*, *Roxio MyDVD 10*, *Apple iMovie* and *iDVD*, *Windows Movie Maker*, *Ulead VideoStudio X2*, *Ulead DVD MovieFactory 6 Plus*, and *Sony Creative Software Vegas Movie Studio 9*. Professional products include *Adobe Premiere Pro*, *Sony Creative Software Vegas Pro*, and *Sonic CineVision*.

Media Players

Media players are programs designed to play audio and video files. They are used to play media available via your computer—such as music CDs, downloaded music, or video streamed from the Internet. Many media players are available for free, such as *RealPlayer* (see Figure 6-29), *Windows Media Player*, and *QuickTime Player*. Media players typically allow you to arrange your stored music and videos into *playlists*, and then transfer them to CDs or portable digital music players. Some also include the ability to download video from the Web and/or purchase and download music via an associated *music store*.

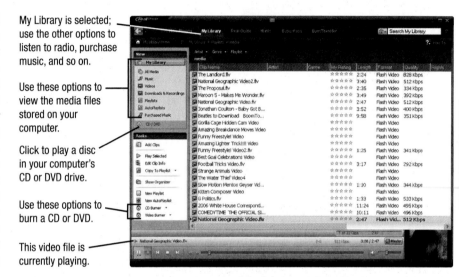

My Library is selected; use the other options to listen to radio, purchase music, and so on.

Use these options to view the media files stored on your computer.

Click to play a disc in your computer's CD or DVD drive.

Use these options to burn a CD or DVD.

This video file is currently playing.

FIGURE 6-29
A typical media player program.

It is important when using digital music to adhere to copyright laws, such as only transferring music from CDs that you have purchased and only downloading digital music files from sites that compensate the artists and record labels. While most music download sites today are legal and charge around $1 per title, illegal *peer-to-peer* (*P2P*) MP3 file exchanges do exist. Copyrights and P2P networks are discussed in more detail in later chapters.

Graphics, Multimedia, and the Web

Graphics and multimedia software are often used by individuals and businesses alike to create Web sites or content to be shared or distributed via the Web. In addition, games, tutorials, videos, demonstrations, and other multimedia content available on the Web are often created with multimedia software. Multimedia elements and creating multimedia Web sites are the focus of Chapter 10.

OTHER TYPES OF APPLICATION SOFTWARE

There are many other types of application software available today. Some are geared for business or personal productivity; others are designed for entertainment or educational purposes. Still others are intended to help users with a particular specialized application, such as preparing financial reports, issuing prescriptions electronically, designing buildings, controlling machinery, and so forth. A few of the most common types of application software not previously covered are discussed next.

Desktop and Personal Publishing Software

Desktop publishing refers to using a personal computer to combine and manipulate text and images to create attractive documents that look as if they were created by a

FIGURE 6-30

Desktop publishing software. Allows users to create publication-quality documents.

professional printer (see Figure 6-30). Although many desktop publishing effects can be produced using a word processing program, users who frequently create publication-style documents usually find a desktop publishing program a more efficient means of creating those types of documents. Some popular desktop publishing programs are *Adobe InDesign*, *Microsoft Publisher*, and *Serif PagePlus X3*. *Personal publishing* refers to creating desktop-publishing-type documents—such as greeting cards, invitations, flyers, calendars, certificates, and so forth—for personal use. There are also specialized personal publishing programs for particular purposes, such as to create scrapbook pages, cross stitch patterns, CD and DVD labels, and so forth.

Educational, Entertainment, and Reference Software

A wide variety of educational and entertainment application programs are available. *Educational software* is designed to teach one or more skills, such as reading, math, spelling, a foreign language, and world geography, or to help prepare for standardized tests. *Entertainment software* includes games, simulations, and other programs that provide amusement. A hybrid of these two categories is called *edutainment*—educational software that also entertains. *Reference software* includes encyclopedias, dictionaries, atlases, mapping/travel programs, cookbook programs, and other software designed to provide valuable information. Although still available as stand-alone software packages, reference information today is also obtained frequently via the Internet.

FIGURE 6-31

Note taking software. Allows individuals to record and organize important data.

Note Taking Software and Web Notebooks

Note taking software is used by both students and businesspeople to take notes during class lectures, meetings, and similar settings. It is used most often with tablet computers and other devices designed to accept pen input. Typically, note taking software (such as Microsoft *OneNote*, Agilix Labs *GoBinder*, or Circus Ponies *Notebook 3.0* program shown in Figure 6-31) supports both typed and handwritten input; handwritten input can usually be saved in its handwritten form as an image or converted to typed text. Note taking software contains features designed specifically to make note taking—and, particularly, retrieving information from the notes—easier. Like a paper notebook, tabbed sections can be created (such as one tab per course) and files, notes, Web links, and any other data are stored under the appropriate tabs. The built-in search tools allow you to find the information that you need quickly and easily. Online versions of these programs (such as *Google Notebook* and *Zoho Notebook*) are referred to as *Web notebooks* and are designed to help organize your online research, including text, images, Web links, search results, and other content located on Web pages.

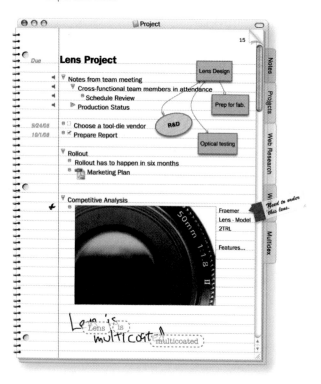

CAD and Other Types of Design Software

As discussed in more detail in Chapter 12, *computer-aided design (CAD) software* enables designers to design objects on the computer. For example, engineers or architects can create designs of buildings or other objects and modify the designs as often as needed. Increasingly, CAD programs are including capabilities to analyze designs in terms of how well they meet a number of design criteria, such as testing how a building design will hold up during an earthquake or how a car will perform under certain conditions. Besides playing an important role in the design of finished products, CAD is useful in fields such as art, advertising, law, architecture, and movie production. In addition to the powerful CAD programs used in business, there are also design programs designed for home and small business use, such as for designing new homes, and for making remodeling plans, interior designs, and landscape designs.

Accounting and Personal Finance Software

Accounting software is used to automate some of the accounting activities that need to be performed on a regular basis. Common tasks include recording purchases and payments, managing inventory, creating payroll documents and checks, preparing financial statements, and keeping track of business expenses (see Figure 6-32). *Personal finance software* is commonly used at home by individuals to write checks and balance checking accounts, track personal expenses, manage stock portfolios, and prepare income taxes. Increasingly, personal finance activities are becoming Web-based, such as the *online banking* and *online portfolio management* services available through many banks and brokerage firms and discussed in more detail in Chapter 8.

Project Management, Collaboration, and Remote Access Software

Project management software is used to plan, schedule, track, and analyze the tasks involved in a project, such as the construction of a building or the schedule for preparing a large advertising campaign for a client. Project management capabilities are often included in *collaboration software*—software that enables a group of individuals to work together on a project—and are increasingly available as Web-based software programs.

Remote access software enables individuals to access content on another computer they are authorized to access, via the Internet. Some programs allow you to control the remote computer directly; others allow you to access your media files (such as recorded TV shows or music) from any Web-enabled device while you are away from home. For instance, the *Slingbox* product gives you access to and control over your cable box and DVR via the Internet (as discussed in Chapter 7), and *Orb* software allows you to access the files on your computer (documents, as well as recorded TV shows and music) from any Web-enabled device while you are away from home. Other remote access software automatically backs up all data files on your main computer to a secure Web server so they can be accessed from any Web-enabled device (such as a portable computer or mobile phone, in some cases), as well as shared with others for collaboration purposes. To make it easier to share single large files with others, you can use Web-based *file sending applications* (such as *YouSendIt* shown in Figure 6-33).

FIGURE 6-32
Accounting software. This iPhone application helps individuals keep track of business expenses.

FIGURE 6-33
File sending applications. This Web-based application allows you to easily send large files to others via the Internet.

2. Recipient is notified via e-mail and downloads the files.

1. Sender selects files to be sent to the recipient.

SUMMARY

Chapter Objective 1:
Describe what application software is, the different types of ownership rights, and the difference between installed and Web-based software.

THE BASICS OF APPLICATION SOFTWARE

Application software is software designed to carry out a specific task. Common types of application software include games, Web browsers, word processing programs, multimedia software, and more. Many application software programs today are **commercial software** programs that are developed and sold for a profit. When a software program is purchased, individual users receive a **software license** authorizing them to use the software. Some commercial software is available in a *demo* or *trial version*. Other software is available as **shareware**, **freeware**, or **public domain software**. **Open source software** is the term for programs whose source code is available to the general public. Software is designed as either *desktop software* or *mobile software*. **Installed software** is installed on a local computer or network server; **Web-based software**, which is also called **Software as a Service** (**SaaS**) and **cloudware**, is run from the Internet instead. Organizations that provide Web-based software are referred to as *application service providers* (*ASPs*).

Chapter Objective 2:
Detail some concepts and commands that many software programs have in common.

Many office-oriented programs are sold bundled together as a **software suite**. One of the most widely used software suites is **Microsoft Office**. Although they are used for different purposes, most application software programs share some of the same concepts and functions, such as similar document-handling operations and help features. For instance, documents are commonly *opened*, *saved*, *printed*, *edited*, and *formatted* in a similar manner. **Editing** a document changes its content; **formatting** a document changes its appearance (such as by changing the *font face*, *font size*, or *font style* of text, or by changing the *line spacing* or *margins*. Commands can be issued via a variety of methods, such as by using *menus*, *toolbars*, **keyboard shortcuts**, or the Microsoft Office **Ribbon**— the **insertion point** typically looks like a blinking vertical line and identifies the current position in a document. Online help is available in many programs.

Chapter Objective 3:
Discuss word processing and explain what kinds of documents are created using this type of program.

WORD PROCESSING CONCEPTS

Word processing refers to using a computer and **word processing software** to create, manipulate, and print written documents, such as letters, contracts, and so forth. When creating or editing a word processing document, the **word wrap** feature automatically moves the insertion point to the next line when the end of the screen line is reached. Formatting can be applied at the character, paragraph, or document level. Other enhancements found in most word processing programs include the ability to include graphical images and *tables*, and to use *styles*, *templates*, or *wizards* for more efficient document creation. Documents can also include hyperlinks and be saved as Web pages in many programs. Most word processors also include a spelling and grammar check feature and other useful tools.

Chapter Objective 4:
Explain the purpose of spreadsheet software and the kinds of documents created using this type of program.

SPREADSHEET CONCEPTS

Spreadsheet software is used to create documents (**spreadsheets** or **worksheets**) that typically include a great deal of numbers and mathematical computations; a collection of worksheets stored in the same spreadsheet file is called a **workbook**. A worksheet is divided into **rows** and **columns** that intersect to form **cells**, each of which can be accessed through a *cell address*, such as B3. A rectangular group of cells is referred to as a *range*.

Content is entered into individual cells and may consist of **labels**, **constant values**, **formulas**, or **functions**. Formulas can be typed using *relative cell* or *absolute cell references*, depending on the type of computation required. Once created, the content of individual cells may be edited and formatted. *Numeric formats* are used to change the appearance of numbers, such as adding a dollar sign or displaying a specific number of decimal places. Spreadsheet programs commonly include a *charting* or *graphing* feature and the ability to perform *what-if analysis*. Some spreadsheet programs allow worksheets to be saved in the form of a Web page and the inclusion of hyperlinks in cells.

DATABASE CONCEPTS

A *database management system (DBMS)* or **database software** program enables the creation of a **database**—a collection of related data stored in a manner so that information can be retrieved as needed. In a relational DBMS (the most common type found on personal computers), a **field** or **column** is a collection of characters that make up a single piece of data, such as a name or phone number; a **record** or **row** is a collection of related fields; and a **table** is a collection of related records. One or more tables can be stored in a database file.

A relational database typically contains a variety of *objects*, such as tables, *forms* to input or view data, *queries* to retrieve specific information, and *reports* to print a formal listing of the data stored in a table or the results of a query. When a table is created, the table fields are specified along with their characteristics, such as *field name*, *field size*, and *data type*. This structure, as well as the data, are saved in the table and can be modified when needed. Databases are commonly integrated into the Web, such as to keep track of inventory and to facilitate online ordering.

Chapter Objective 5:
Identify some of the vocabulary used with database software and discuss the benefits of using this type of program.

PRESENTATION GRAPHICS CONCEPTS

Presentation graphics are images used to visually enhance the impact of information communicated to other people. **Presentation graphics software** can be used to create presentation graphics and **electronic slide shows** consisting of electronic **slides**. The individual slides in the slide show are created, and then they can be edited and formatted, as can the overall appearance of the presentation. Multimedia elements, such as images and video clips, can also be included. After all slides have been created for a presentation, the order of the slides can be rearranged and *transitions* between the slides can be specified. It is becoming increasingly common to find slide-based presentations available through the Web. Web-based slide shows can include multimedia elements, as well as hyperlinks and other navigational buttons.

Chapter Objective 6:
Describe what presentation graphics and electronic slide shows are and when they might be used.

GRAPHICS AND MULTIMEDIA CONCEPTS

Graphics are graphical images, such as digital photographs, clip art, and original art. *Multimedia* refers to applications that include more than one type of media, but often refers to audio and video content. To create graphics, **graphics software**—such as a *painting*, a *drawing*, or an *image editing program*—can be used. *Audio editing*, *video editing*, and *DVD authoring software* are common types of multimedia programs, as are the *media player* programs used to play audio and video files. *CD* and *DVD burning software* can be used to burn songs or other data on a CD or DVD disc.

Chapter Objective 7:
List some types of graphics and multimedia software that consumers use frequently.

OTHER TYPES OF APPLICATION SOFTWARE

Other types of application software include *desktop publishing* and *personal publishing* programs, *computer-aided design (CAD)* and other types of *design software*, *accounting software*, *personal finance software*, and *project management software*. The use of *collaboration*, *remote access*, and *note taking software* is growing. *Educational*, *entertainment*, and *reference software* are very popular with home users.

Chapter Objective 8:
Name several other types of application software programs and discuss what functions they perform.

REVIEW ACTIVITIES

KEY TERM MATCHING

a. cell

b. database

c. field

d. formula

e. label

f. public domain software

g. record

h. shareware

i. software license

j. workbook

Instructions: Match each key term on the left with the definition on the right that best describes it.

1. _____ A collection of related data that is stored in a manner enabling information to be retrieved as needed.

2. _____ A collection of related fields in a database. Also called a row.

3. _____ A collection of worksheets saved in a single spreadsheet file.

4. _____ An agreement, either included in a software package or displayed on the screen during installation, that specifies the conditions under which a buyer of the program can use it.

5. _____ An entry in a worksheet cell that performs computations on worksheet data and displays the results.

6. _____ A single category of data to be stored in a database, such as a person's name or telephone number. Also called a column.

7. _____ A text-based entry in a worksheet cell that identifies data on the worksheet.

8. _____ Copyrighted software that is distributed on the honor system; consumers should either pay for it or uninstall it after the trial period.

9. _____ Software that is not copyrighted and may be used without restriction.

10. _____ The location at the intersection of a row and column on a worksheet into which data can be typed.

SELF-QUIZ

Instructions: Circle **T** if the statement is true, **F** if the statement is false, or write the best answer in the space provided. **Answers for the self-quiz are located in the References and Resources Guide at the end of the book.**

1. **T F** Microsoft Office is one example of a software suite.

2. **T F** Changing the font size in a document is an example of a formatting operation.

3. **T F** In a word processing document, the Enter key is always pressed at the end of each screen line to move down to the next line.

4. **T F** The formula =A2+B2 located in cell C2 would multiply the two cells to the left of cell C2.

5. **T F** Software can be installed on both personal computers and servers.

6. With a(n) _____ program, the source code for the program is made available to the public and so can be modified by others.

7. The blinking vertical line displayed on the screen that indicates the current location in a document, such as where the next change will be made to the document in a word processing program, is called the _____.

8. A named formula (such as @SUM) in a spreadsheet program is called a(n) _____.

9. In a relational database, the database object that contains the actual data is the _____.

10. Match each application with its type of application program, and write the corresponding number in the blank to the left of each application.

   a. _____ Listening to a music CD.

   b. _____ Creating a child's birthday invitation.

   c. _____ Creating a home movie DVD.

   1. DVD authoring software

   2. Media player

   3. Personal publishing software

EXERCISES

1. List the programs included in the Microsoft Office software suite that fit in the following categories.

   a. Spreadsheet software _____

   b. Presentation graphics software _____

   c. Word processing software _____

   d. Database software _____

2. Match each spreadsheet element with its term and write the corresponding number in the blank to the left of each term.

   a. _____ An absolute cell address

   b. _____ A relative cell address

   c. _____ A function

   1. =SUM(A1:A2)

   2. $D$4

   3. B6

3. For a customer database containing 50 customers and recording data about the customer's number, last name, street, city, state, ZIP code, and current balance, answer the following questions.

   a. How many records are in the database? _____

   b. How many fields are in the database? _____

   c. To display a list of all customers who live in Texas and have a current balance of less than $10, what database tool should be used? _____

4. Write the number of the presentation graphic that best matches each of the following possible uses in the blank to the left of each use.

   a. _____ Adding an arrow to highlight a point located on a slide.

   b. _____ Illustrating the percent of sales coming from each sales territory.

   c. _____ Conveying the key points in an educational lecture.

   1. Pie chart

   2. Slide

   3. Drawn object

5. Would rearranging the paragraphs in a document using a word processing program be an editing operation or a formatting operation? Explain your answer.

DISCUSSION QUESTIONS

1. There are an increasing number of Web-based applications available and the new version of Office will be available in both installed and Web versions. What are the advantages and disadvantages of Web-based software? Which do you prefer to use for school-related documents? Why? If you prefer installed software, what would have to change about Web-based software in the future to change your opinion?

2. Open source software is usually reviewed and improved at no cost. Proponents of open source software believe that if programmers who are not concerned with financial gain work on an open source program, they will produce a more useful and error-free product much faster than the traditional commercial software development process. As open source use continues to grow, will it force existing commercial software companies to cut costs to better compete with open source products? Or will they strive to produce products that are better and more reliable than open source competitors? Or will commercial software companies simply go out of business? Will commercial software manufacturers be justified in raising their prices to make up for revenue lost to open source competitors? Do you think open source software will have an overall positive or negative impact on the quality of software?

PROJECTS

1. **Natural Input** As pen and voice input technologies continue to improve, these types of more natural input methods are increasingly being supported by software programs.

   For this project, research either pen input or voice input and its use in conjunction with application software. How frequently is it used today with desktop and portable computers? Select one office application (such as a word processor or spreadsheet program) and determine what hardware or software is needed to use your selected method of input. What are the advantages of your input method? The disadvantages? Would you prefer to use a keyboard and mouse or your selected method of input with this program? Explain. At the conclusion of your research, prepare a one- to two-page summary of your findings and opinions and submit it to your instructor.

SHORT ANSWER/ RESEARCH

2. **Software Search** Just as with toys, movies, and music, the price of a software program can vary tremendously, based on where you buy it, sales, rebates, and more. Although most packages claim a manufacturer's suggested retail price, it is almost always possible to beat that price—sometimes by a huge amount—with careful shopping.

   For this project, select one software program that you might be interested in buying and research it. By reading the program specifications either in a retail store or on a Web page, determine the program's minimum hardware and software requirements. By checking in person, over the phone, or via the Internet, locate three price quotes for the program, including any sales tax and shipping, and check availability and estimated delivery time. Do any of the vendors have the option to download the software? If so, do you have to register the program online or enter a code to activate the product after it is downloaded? At the conclusion of this task, prepare a one-page summary of your research and submit it to your instructor. Be sure to include a recommendation of where you think it would be best to buy your chosen product and why.

HANDS ON

3. **Online Tours** There are many online tours and tutorials for application programs. Some are available through the software company's Web site; others are located on third-party Web sites.

   For this project, select one common software program (such as Word, Excel, PowerPoint, Chrome, Google Docs, or Paint). Locate a free online tour or tutorial for the program you selected (go to the Further Exploration links at the Chapter 6 page at **www.cengage.com/ computerconcepts/np/uc13** for some suggestions) and work your way through one tour or tutorial. How useful is it? Is it easy to use and understand? Did you encounter any errors or other problems? Are there multiple versions for varying levels of difficulty? Would you recommend this tour or tutorial to others? At the conclusion of this task, prepare a one-page summary of your efforts and submit it to your instructor.

4. **Emotion Recognition Software** An emerging application is *emotion recognition software*, which uses camera input to try to read a person's current emotion. The first expected application of such a system is for ATM machines, since they already have cameras installed. Possibilities include changing the advertising display based on the customer's emotional response to displayed advertising, and enlarging the screen text if the customer appears to be squinting. Is it ethical for businesses using emotion recognition software to read the emotions of citizens without their consent? Proponents of the technology argue that it is no different than when human tellers or store clerks interpret customers' emotions and modify their treatment of the customer accordingly. Do you agree? Why or why not? Is this a worthy new technology or just a potential invasion of privacy? Would you object to using an ATM machine with emotion-recognition capabilities? Why or why not?

For this project, form an opinion about the ethical ramifications of emotion recognition systems and be prepared to discuss your position (in class, via an online class discussion group, in a class chat room, or via a class blog, depending on your instructor's directions). You may also be asked to write a short paper expressing your opinion.

ETHICS IN ACTION

5. **Compatibility** Files created by an application program are often upward-compatible, but not always downward-compatible. For example, a *.docx* file created in Microsoft Word 2007 cannot be opened in Word 2003, but a Word 2003 *.doc* file can be opened in Word 2007. Most application programs feature a "Save As" option that can be used to save a file in one of several formats.

For this project, select one widely used software program and determine in which file formats the program can save documents and which file formats the program can open. If there are older versions of the program, are documents upward-compatible? Downward compatible? Research *plain text* (*.txt*) and the *Rich Text Format* (*.rtf*) and determine their purposes, the programs in which documents saved in each of these formats can be opened, and any disadvantages for using these formats. Have you ever experienced a compatibility problem with a document? If so, how was the problem resolved? Share your findings with the class in the form of a short presentation. The presentation should not exceed 10 minutes and should make use of one or more presentation aids, such as the chalkboard, handouts, overhead transparencies, or a computer-based slide presentation (your instructor may provide additional requirements). You may also be asked to submit a summary of the presentation to your instructor.

PRESENTATION/ DEMONSTRATION

SW

Instructions: Go to the Chapter 6 page at **www.cengage.com/computerconcepts/np/uc13** to work the following Web Activities.

6. **Interactive Activities** Work the interactive **Crossword Puzzle**, watch the **Video Podcasts** and **Online Videos,** and explore the **Further Exploration** links associated with this chapter.

If you have a SAM user profile, you may have access to hands-on instruction, practice, and assessment of the skills covered in this chapter. Check with your instructor for instructions and the correct URL/Web site to access those assignments.

7. **Student Edition Labs** Work the following interactive **Student Edition Labs**.

- ➤ **Word Processing**   ➤ **Spreadsheets**
- ➤ **Databases**   ➤ **Presentation Software**

8. **Test Yourself** Review the **Online Study Guide** for this chapter, then test your knowledge of the terms and concepts covered in this chapter by completing the **Key Term Matching** exercise, the **Self-Quiz,** the **Exercises,** and the **Practice Test**.

WEB ACTIVITIES

SAM

Student Edition Labs

Software

A conversation with GRAHAM WATSON

Senior Community Lead, Technical Audience Global Marketing, Microsoft

" . . . as computers become smaller, more powerful, and more connected, additional opportunities open up. "

Microsoft

Graham Watson is a Senior Community Lead in the Technical Audience Group Marketing Team at Microsoft. He has worked for Microsoft for 16 years, initially as an enterprise infrastructure consultant. In all, he has over 30 years of experience working in the computer industry, beginning as a computer operator and then as a support engineer. Graham has a Bachelor of Arts degree in Computer Studies and runs a blog at blogs.technet.com/grahamtwatson.

My Background . . .

I actually got started with computers at school when I discovered I could either take a lesson where I played with a computer terminal or one involving cross-country running in winter! I quickly worked out that the computer was more fun! I'm now part of the Technical Audience Global Marketing Group at Microsoft. My specific responsibilities include making sure that the IT Professional and Developer User Groups around the world—representing over four million people—have the connection they need with Microsoft.

It's Important to Know . . .

About computer systems. No matter how directly you will be involved with computer systems in your career, everyone will need to know enough about systems to be able to make appropriate decisions as to how to use technology to help them in their work and daily lives in general. For example, everyone needs to know how to at least send an e-mail and create, edit, and print a document. Think about the business tasks you need to complete each day, and make sure you can efficiently use the right tools on your computer to help you work more effectively.

The impact of Windows 7. One of the biggest impacts on society that Windows 7 will have is enhanced security for users. One problem with the connectivity that computers provide is that it can also provide thieves and other miscreants with access to you. Each version of Windows improves on previous versions and, although Windows Vista was the most secure mass-marketed operating system when it was launched, Windows 7 continues this evolution and its use will further improve resilience against most forms of attack.

How IT affects your chosen career. It is important to understand the business impact and future trends within the IT space and how it can affect your chosen career. For example, think about the way the retail sales industry has changed over the past ten years. Depending on your chosen career, computer power, graphics, communications capabilities, or mobility may be particularly important to you. You will also need to keep abreast of the latest trends and understand the benefits, costs, risks, and details of how to implement solutions to business problems successfully, taking into account the needs of the customer and the user.

How I Use this Technology . . .

There are two main areas where computers affect me personally. The first one is the most obvious—it provides me with highly enjoyable employment! It's interesting, though, how my current role is more related to computers as a social tool, given my responsibilities toward technical communities. The second one is the same as for many people—my family and friends are all connected, and I often communicate with my wife and children via e-mail or IM. I also do most of my shopping via the Internet—I think I got most of my Christmas shopping done last year without leaving my desk. It's hard to imagine how I would live my life without Windows!

What the Future Holds . . .

Connectivity is probably the biggest thing—not just between people, but also between parts of computer applications. Web services will continue to grow in importance, and Windows 7, together with .NET 3.0 and Microsoft "Azure," will further enable the ability to develop applications quickly by "stitching together" services obtained from a variety of companies and building on them to fulfill specific needs. Mobility is another interesting area—as computers become smaller, more powerful, and more connected, additional opportunities open up. On one hand, we are finding some devices becoming more general purpose (for example, your cell phone may also take pictures and play music), but at the same time there is an opposite movement toward more dedicated devices which work better. Some people just want a simple-to-use cell phone.

    I expect that the software we know today will continue to evolve and get more sophisticated but be simpler to use—for example, Microsoft Office continues to improve on its ability to create professional documents very easily. There will probably be at least one "left field" innovation—something that will be obvious once it's taken off, but almost unnoticed until that time. Examples of this from the last few years include digital video recorders (such as TiVo or Windows Media Center Edition), Voice over IP, and social media tools (such as Twitter). One possibility for the future is intelligent search–something that Microsoft is making significant progress on with *Bing* (imagine being able to ask your computer almost any question in the same way you would ask a friend, and get a single, correct answer). Another possibility we'll likely see in the near future is improved connectivity between computers and devices (imagine phoning friends and arranging to meet them, and then automatically getting directions given to you by your car, meetings set up and moved, flights booked, etc.).

"Use technology to become a better informed and connected person and use the information and connections gained to move forward in your chosen career."

My Advice to Students . . .

Use technology to become a better informed and connected person and use the information and connections gained to move forward in your chosen career. Technology should be used as an enabler to achieve your goals, improve your life, and improve the lives of others.

Discussion Question

Graham Watson believes that every employee needs to know at least how to send an e-mail and how to create, edit, and print a document. Think about the jobs available today. Are there any that may not require computer skills? If so, would computer skills give that employee an advantage, even if it's not required? Should companies be required to teach any necessary computer skills or is it reasonable to require basic computer skills for any job today? Be prepared to discuss your position (in class, via an online class discussion group, in a class chat room, or via a class blog, depending on your instructor's directions). You may also be asked to write a short paper expressing your opinion.

> **For more information on Microsoft, visit www.microsoft.com. For interesting IT-related information, visit technet.microsoft.com and msdn.microsoft.com. To check if your PC is Windows 7 ready, go to www.microsoft.com/windows/windows-7/get/upgrade-advisor.aspx.**

module

Networks and the Internet

From telephone calls, to home and business networks, to Web surfing and online shopping, networking and the Internet are deeply embedded in our society today. Because of this, it is important for individuals to be familiar with basic networking concepts and terminology, as well as with the variety of activities that take place today via networks—including the Internet, the world's largest network. It is also important for all individuals to be aware of the potential problems and risks associated with networks and our networked society.

The purpose of Chapter 7 is to introduce basic networking principles, including what a computer network is, how it works, and what it can be used for. The Internet and World Wide Web are the topics of Chapter 8. Although they were introduced in Chapter 1, Chapter 8 explains in more detail how the Internet and World Wide Web originated, and looks more closely at common Internet activities, including how to search the Web effectively for information. This chapter also discusses the various options for connecting to the Internet, as well as how to select an Internet service provider (ISP). Chapter 9 takes a look at some of the risks related to network and Internet use, and explains measures computer users can take to lessen these risks.

Chapter 7
Computer Networks 256
Overview 257
What Is a Network? 257
Networking Applications 258
Network Characteristics 265
Data Transmission Characteristics 270
Networking Media 273
Communications Protocols and
  Networking Standards 278
Networking Hardware 287

Chapter 8
The Internet and the World
Wide Web 298
Overview 299
Evolution of the Internet 299
Getting Set Up to Use the Internet 305
Searching the Internet 312
Beyond Browsing and E-Mail 317
Censorship and Privacy Issues 334

Chapter 9
Network and Internet
Security 346
Overview 347
Why Be Concerned about Network
  and Internet Security? 347
Unauthorized Access and Unauthorized
  Use 348
Protecting Against Unauthorized Access
  and Unauthorized Use 351
Computer Sabotage 364
Protecting Against Computer
  Sabotage 369
Online Theft, Online Fraud, and Other
  Dot Cons 370
Protecting Against Online Theft, Online
  Fraud, and Other Dot Cons 377
Personal Safety Issues 381
Protecting Against Cyberbullying,
  Cyberstalking, and Other Personal
  Safety Concerns 382
Network and Internet Security
  Legislation 383

". . . the more
and more
"connected"
data and
applications
become,
the more
important it
becomes to
secure them."

For more comments from
Guest Expert **Collin Davis**
of Symantec Corporation,
see the **Expert Insight**
on . . . Networks and
the Internet feature at
the end of the module.

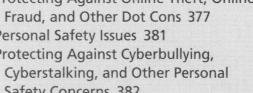

chapter 7

Computer Networks

After completing this chapter, you will be able to do the following:

1. Define a network and its purpose.

2. Describe several uses for networks.

3. Understand the various characteristics of a network, such as topology, architecture, and size.

4. Understand characteristics about data and how it travels over a network.

5. Name specific types of wired and wireless networking media and explain how they transmit data.

6. Identify the most common communications protocols and networking standards used with networks today.

7. List several types of networking hardware and explain the purpose of each.

outline

Overview

What Is a Network?

Networking Applications
The Internet
Telephone Service
Television and Radio Broadcasting
Global Positioning System (GPS) Applications
Monitoring Systems
Multimedia Networking
Videoconferencing, Collaborative Computing, and Telecommuting
Telemedicine

Network Characteristics
Wired vs. Wireless Networks
Network Topologies
Network Architectures
Network Size and Coverage Area

Data Transmission Characteristics
Bandwidth
Analog vs. Digital Signals
Transmission Type and Timing
Delivery Method

Networking Media
Wired Networking Media
Wireless Networking Media

Communications Protocols and Networking Standards
TCP/IP and Other Communications Protocols
Ethernet (802.3)
Phoneline, Powerline, G.hn, and Broadband over Powerline (BPL)
Wi-Fi (802.11)
WiMAX and Mobile WiMAX
Cellular Standards
Bluetooth, Ultra Wideband (UWB), and Other Short-Range Wireless Standards

Networking Hardware
Network Adapters and Modems
Switches, Routers, and Other Hardware for Connecting Devices and Networks
Other Networking Hardware

OVERVIEW

The term *communications*, when used in a computer context, refers to *telecommunications*; that is, data sent from one device to another using communications media, such as telephone lines, privately owned cables, and the airwaves. Communication usually takes place over a private (such as a home or business) network, the Internet, or a telephone network and it is an integral part of our personal and professional lives today.

The purpose of Chapter 7 is to introduce you to the concepts and terminology associated with computer networks. First, a computer network is defined, followed by a look at some common networking applications. Next, a number of technical issues related to networks are discussed, including general characteristics of data and data transmission, and the types of transmission media in use today. We then proceed to an explanation of the various communications protocols and networking standards, which help explain the ways networked devices communicate with one another. The chapter closes with a look at the various types of hardware used with a computer network. ■

VIDEO PODCAST

Go to the Chapter 7 page at **www.cengage.com/ computerconcepts/np/uc13** to download or listen to the "How To: Share a Printer over a Network" video podcast.

NET

WHAT IS A NETWORK?

A *network*, in general, is a connected system of objects or people. As discussed in Chapter 1, a **computer network** is a collection of computers and other hardware devices connected together so that network users can share hardware, software, and data, as well as communicate with each other electronically. Today, computer networks are converging with *telephone networks* and other *communications networks*, with both data and voice being sent over these networks. Computer networks range from small private networks to the Internet and are widely used by individuals and businesses today (see Figure 7-1).

In most businesses, computer networks are essential. They enable employees to share expensive resources, access the Internet, and communicate with each other, as well as with business partners and customers. They facilitate the exchange and collaboration of documents and they are often a key component of the ordering, inventory, and fulfillment systems used to process customer orders. In homes, computer networks enable individuals to share resources, access the Internet, and communicate with others. In addition, they allow individuals to access a wide variety of information, services, and entertainment, as well as share data (such as digital photos, downloaded movies, and music) among the networked

FIGURE 7-1
Common uses for computer networks.

USES FOR COMPUTER NETWORKS

Sharing an Internet connection among several users.

Sharing application software, printers, and other resources.

Facilitating Voice over IP (VoIP), e-mail, video-conferencing, IM, and other communications applications.

Working collaboratively, such as sharing a company database or using collaboration tools to create or review documents.

Exchanging files among network users and over the Internet.

Connecting the computers and the entertainment devices (such as TVs, gaming consoles, and stereo systems) located within a home.

>**Computer network.** A collection of computers and other hardware devices that are connected together to share hardware, software, and data, as well as to communicate electronically with one another.

INSIDE THE INDUSTRY

Wireless Power

Imagine recharging your notebook computer or mobile phone automatically, without plugging it into an electrical outlet. That scenario may soon be possible with *wireless power.* Researchers have been working on the concept of wireless power transmission for decades, but recent developments indicate that the concept may be feasible in the relatively near future. For instance, researchers recently demonstrated making a 60-watt light bulb glow with 75% efficiency from an energy source 3 feet away—an important development because one of the biggest challenges in transmitting power wirelessly is preventing too much power from escaping during transit. Other challenges are ensuring that wireless power is safe for humans and other living things in the areas where power will be broadcast, as well as creating a standard for wireless power so that multiple devices from different manufacturers can be charged at the same time using the same technology.

One company working toward this standard is Fulton Innovation. This company, along with other members of the *Wireless Power Consortium* (such as Olympus, Philips, and Texas Instruments), supports wireless power technology that uses *magnetic induction* to transfer power wirelessly from a charging power supply device to a target device containing the appropriate receiving technology. Ideally, wireless power systems will power devices without any direct physical contact, will automatically adjust the power transmitted to each device being charged to meet the needs of that device, and will deactivate the charging process when the device is fully charged.

Initial consumer applications for wireless power will likely be wireless charging bases that recharge devices (such as mobile phones, digital media players, remote controls, notebook computers, and small kitchen appliances) located on or near them—called *near-field wireless power transfer.* These charging bases could be stand-alone devices or they could be built into car consoles (see the accompanying illustration), desks, kitchen countertops, and other objects. As the technology matures and if the safety issues can be resolved, future wireless power applications could even include charging transmitters built into walls and furniture to power all of the devices located in the home on a continual basis.

ONLINE VIDEO

Go to the Chapter 7 page at **www.cengage.com/ computerconcepts/np/uc13** to watch the "Wireless Power: eCoupled Overview" video clip.

devices in a home. On the go, networks enable individuals to work from remote locations, locate information whenever and wherever it is needed, and stay in touch with others.

NETWORKING APPLICATIONS

Today, there are a wide variety of important networking applications used by businesses and individuals for communications, information retrieval, and other applications. Some of the most common networking applications are described next. For a look at an emerging networking application—*wireless power*—see the Inside the Industry box.

The Internet

As previously discussed, the Internet is the largest computer network in the world. Many networking applications today (such as information retrieval, shopping, entertainment, and e-mail) take place via the Internet. Accessing Web pages and exchanging e-mail were discussed in Chapter 1; additional Internet-based activities are covered in Chapter 8.

Telephone Service

The original telephone network, sometimes called the *plain old telephone service* (*POTS*), was one of the first communications networks. This network is still used today to provide telephone service to conventional and cordless *landline phones*, and is used for some types of Internet connections.

Mobile phones (also called *wireless phones*) are phones that use a wireless network for communications instead of the regular telephone network. Billions of mobile phones are in use worldwide and approximately 75% of Americans and close to half of the world's population use mobile phones. In fact, there are over twice as many mobile phones in use worldwide than landline phones, according to one estimate, and mobile phones may be the only telephone alternative in developing countries and other locations with a poor landline telephone infrastructure. Even in developed countries, however, many individuals—nearly 20% of all Americans, according to a recent Nielsen Mobile report—are dropping their conventional landline telephone service in favor of using their mobile phones as their primary telephones.

In addition to making telephone calls, most mobile phones today can be used for a wide variety of other purposes, such as exchanging e-mail and text messages, viewing Web information, taking digital photos, and watching TV shows. Some mobile phones can also be used to pay for goods or services and to unlock doors. These types of applications are more prominent in countries like Asia and Europe that have a longer history of mobile phone use than the United States, but they are beginning to become available in the U.S. as well.

The most common type of mobile phone is the **cellular (cell) phone** (see Figure 7-2), which communicates via *cellular technology*. Cell phone service is available in most populated areas of the U.S., but coverage varies depending on location because cell phones need to be within range of a *cell tower* to function, as described later in this chapter. Some cell phones today are **dual-mode phones**—phones that allows users to make telephone calls using more than one communications network, such as via both a *cellular* and a *Wi-Fi network*. This allows users to carry a single device (such as the one shown in Figure 7-2) and, at any given time, use the network that is available, least expensive, or has the needed capabilities. For example, as an individual using a *cellular/Wi-Fi dual-mode phone* moves in and out of range of a Wi-Fi network, the phone is able to switch seamlessly between the Wi-Fi network and a cellular network, such as using a home or office Wi-Fi network (and that network's

CELLULAR PHONES
Can be used wherever cellular phone coverage is available.

DUAL-MODE PHONES
Can be used with both cellular and Wi-Fi networks.

SATELLITE PHONES
Can be used virtually anywhere.

FIGURE 7-2
Types of mobile phones.

NET

Internet connection) when the caller is indoors and then switching to a cellular network when the individual leaves the building. Cellular/Wi-Fi dual-mode phones are expected to experience rapid growth in the near future. In fact, Juniper Research predicts that cellular/Wi-Fi dual-mode phones will eventually dominate the mobile phone market worldwide.

Another, but less common, type of mobile phone is the **satellite phone** (refer again to Figure 7-2), which communicates via *satellite technology*, also described in detail later in this chapter. Although more expensive than cellular service, satellite phone coverage is typically much broader, often on a country-by-country basis, and some satellite phone services cover the entire earth. Consequently, satellite phones are most often used by individuals—such as soldiers, journalists, wilderness guides, and researchers—traveling in remote areas where continuous cellular service might not be available. They are also useful during times when cellular service might be interrupted, such as during a hurricane or other emergency. An emerging option is the *cellular/satellite dual-mode phone* that can be used with cellular service when it is available and then switches to satellite service when cellular service is not available.

Television and Radio Broadcasting

Two other original communications networks are *broadcast television networks* and *radio networks*. These networks are still used to deliver TV and radio content to the public, though some of this content is also available via the Internet today. Other networks involved with television content delivery are *cable TV networks*, *satellite TV networks*, and the private *closed-circuit television* (*CCTV*) systems used by businesses for surveillance and security purposes. Cable and satellite TV networks are also used today to provide access to the Internet.

Global Positioning System (GPS) Applications

The **global positioning system** (**GPS**) network consists of 24 Department of Defense *GPS satellites* (in orbit approximately 12,000 miles above the earth) that are used for location and navigation purposes. A *GPS receiver* measures the distance between the receiver and four GPS satellites simultaneously to determine the receiver's exact geographic location; these receivers are accurate to within 3 meters (less than 10 feet).

GPS receivers (see some examples in Figure 7-3) are commonly used by individuals to determine their geographic location while hiking and to obtain driving directions while traveling. GPS receivers are also commonly used on the job, such as by surveyors, farmers, and fishermen. In addition to just relaying location information, GPS can be used to guide vehicles and equipment (for example, to locate and dispatch ambulances, police cars, and other emergency vehicles, or to guide bulldozers and other construction equipment automatically according to a project's preprogrammed instructions) and GPS is used by the military to guide munitions. GPS capabilities are also built into consumer devices that are designed for specific purposes, such as fitness devices that use GPS technology to record workout data for runners or bicyclists. In addition to their practical uses, GPS receivers can also be used for entertainment. For example, *geocaching*, in which individuals use GPS receivers to locate secret caches hidden by others, is growing in popularity, particularly among families. To find the secret caches, participants follow the coordinates posted on a geocaching Web site.

> **Satellite phone.** A mobile phone that communicates via satellite technology. > **Global positioning system (GPS).** A system that uses satellites and a receiver to determine the exact geographic location of the receiver.

HANDHELD GPS RECEIVERS

CAR-MOUNTED GPS RECEIVERS

GPS RECEIVERS INTEGRATED INTO MOBILE PHONES

FIGURE 7-3
GPS receivers.
Allow people to determine their exact geographical location, usually for safety or navigational purposes.

One recent concern regarding GPS technology is the possibility that the aging GPS satellites might fail (and, consequently, interrupt GPS services) before new replacement satellites can be launched. A recent General Accountability Office (GAO) report concluded that there is an 80% chance that full GPS service will be operational until 2014. Currently, there are 30 GPS satellites in orbit—six more than the 24 GPS satellites needed to ensure continuous coverage of the entire earth.

Monitoring Systems

Monitoring systems use networking technology to determine the current location or status of an object. Some monitoring systems in use today use the RFID tags and RFID readers discussed in Chapter 4 to monitor the status of the objects (such as shipping boxes, livestock, or expensive equipment) to which the RFID tags are attached. Other monitoring systems use GPS technology. For instance, the *OnStar* system built into many GM cars uses GPS to locate vehicles when the occupant activates the service or when sensors indicate that the car was involved in an accident. There are also *vehicle monitoring systems* that are installed in cars by parents and employers to monitor the use of the vehicles (by children or employees, respectively) using networking technology. These monitoring systems typically record factors such as where the vehicle was driven and how fast it was driven; some also allow the location of a vehicle to be tracked in real time via a Web site (see Figure 7-4). Some vehicle monitoring systems can even be used to set up a "virtual fence" for the car or a maximum allowable speed; the parent or employer is notified (usually via a text message) anytime the vehicle leaves the prescribed geographical area or exceeds the maximum designated speed. Monitoring systems are also available for GPS-enabled mobile phones to allow parents to track their child's location or be notified if their child's mobile phone leaves a designated area.

FIGURE 7-4
GPS-based vehicle monitoring systems.
Allow parents or employers to track a vehicle in real time.

1. A GPS monitor like this is installed inside the car.

2. The location and speed of the car is available online.

⊘ **FIGURE 7-5**
Home medical
monitoring systems.

Go **FURTHER EXPLORATION**

Go to the Chapter 7 page at
www.cengage.com/
computerconcepts/np/uc13
for links to information about
GPS, RFID, and monitoring
systems.

⊘ **FIGURE 7-6**
Placeshifting.
Products like the
Slingbox are used to
placeshift multimedia
content to the user's
current location.

Another area in which monitoring systems are frequently used is home healthcare. With the U.S. population aging, a variety of home medical monitoring systems are available to monitor elderly or infirm individuals and notify someone if a possible problem is detected. For instance, *electronic medical monitors* (see Figure 7-5) take the vital signs of an individual (such as weight, blood-sugar readings, or blood pressure) or prompt an individual to answer questions (such as if he or she ate yet that day, took prescribed medication, or feels well). These monitors then transfer readings or the individual's responses to a healthcare provider via the Internet or a telephone network for evaluation and feedback and to detect potential problems as early as possible.

Other monitoring systems use *sensors*—devices that respond to a stimulus (such as heat, light, or pressure) and generate an electrical signal that can be measured or interpreted. The sensors (sometimes called *motes*) are usually small and lightweight; contain the necessary hardware and software to sense and record the appropriate data, as well as transmit the data to a central computer and/or the other motes in the network; and include a power source (typically a battery). Sensors can be included in a network anytime there is a situation with measurable criteria that needs precise, automatic, and continual monitoring. For example, *sensor networks* can be used during transport to monitor the temperature inside cargo containers to ensure that products stay within the allowable temperature range, in pharmaceutical plants to monitor temperature and relative humidity in the drug development process, and in homes to manage and control smart devices such as smart appliances and home automation systems.

Multimedia Networking

A growing use of home networks is to deliver digital multimedia content (such as digital photos, digital music, home movies, downloaded movies, and recorded TV shows) to devices (such as computers, televisions, and home entertainment systems) on that network. A number of *multimedia networking* devices (such as *digital media receivers*) can be used to share and deliver digital content throughout the home via a multimedia network. Some are also able to connect to the Internet to deliver Internet content via the network. Two alternatives to a digital media receiver are *Windows Media Center Extenders*, which allow Windows Media Center computer users to access content from their computers and display it on their TVs via their home network, and *Apple TVs*, which stream content from the iTunes libraries of up to five computers to one TV set.

Other multimedia networking devices (such as the *Slingbox* shown in Figure 7-6) are designed to *placeshift* multimedia content—that is, to allow individuals to view their multimedia content at a more convenient location. For instance, an individual with a Slingbox installed at home can use a portable computer or mobile phone (along with software and his or her Slingbox ID code) to remotely control his or her cable box, satellite receiver, or digital video recorder (DVR) and transfer that content to his or her current location via the Internet. For instance, he or she can watch local news while out of town, watch a recorded TV show while at the beach, or start recording a TV show from the office.

1. Slingbox device is connected to the user's home TV system.

2. SlingPlayer Mobile software allows the user to watch and control his or her home TV and DVR.

Videoconferencing, Collaborative Computing, and Telecommuting

Videoconferencing is the use of networking technology to conduct real-time, face-to-face meetings between individuals physically located in different places. While videoconferencing can take place via a personal computer and the Internet (sometimes called *online conferencing* and discussed in more detail in Chapter 8), it can also take place via a dedicated videoconferencing setup, such as the one in Figure 7-7. As shown in this figure, videoconferencing technology is continuing to improve to more closely mimic a real-time meeting environment—a trend referred to as *telepresence videoconferencing*. Although telepresence videoconferencing setups are expensive, with travel becoming increasingly more expensive and time-consuming, many businesses view videoconferencing as a viable replacement for face-to-face meetings involving individuals in different locations. Videoconferencing is also used in educational settings and to provide language translation services (particularly for nonverbal languages such as American Sign Language that cannot be translated via a telephone) in locations such as airports and hospitals.

Life-size video images of remote participants appear on the display screen.

FIGURE 7-7
Telepresence videoconferencing.

Networking technology is also widely used today with collaborative software tools to enable individuals to work together on documents and other project components. This trend toward online collaboration is usually called *workgroup computing* or *collaborative computing*. For many industries, collaboration is a very important business tool. For example, engineers and architects commonly collaborate on designs; advertising firms and other businesses often route proposals and other important documents to several individuals for comments before preparing the final version of a client presentation; and newspaper, magazine, and book editors must read and edit drafts of articles and books before they are published. Instead of these types of collaborations taking place on paper, as in the not-too-distant past, collaboration tools (such as the Microsoft Office *markup tools* and specialized *collaboration software*) are used in conjunction with networking technology (typically a company network or the Internet) to allow multiple individuals to edit and make comments in a document without destroying the original content. Once a document has been reviewed by all individuals and is returned to the original author, he or she can

---

ASK THE EXPERT

Google **Rajen Sheth,** Senior Product Manager, Google Enterprise

How will Web 2.0 impact the daily life of the average individual?

Web 2.0 means that users can create and share content easily using blogs, social networks, and collaborative tools online. Compare that with the Web a decade ago: at that time, it was difficult to publish information; you needed to know HTML just to push things onto the Web. Now we're starting to see user-driven content and collaboration taking off across multiple communities, starting with consumers, but also extending into work environments.

Technologies driving this trend include (1) user tools such as blogs, wikis, and social networking sites and (2) Web technology itself, including AJAX and JavaScript.

It used to be that the interface of Web applications was inferior to the interface of desktop client applications. Now it's arguably superior on the Web in terms of how rich and dynamic the functionality is.

NET

>**Videoconferencing.** The use of computers, video cameras, microphones, and networking technologies to conduct face-to-face meetings over a network.

read the comments and accept or reject changes that others have made. Some collaboration software incorporates shared calendars, project scheduling, and videoconferencing tools in addition to document sharing.

The increased availability of videoconferencing, collaborative computing, and other tools (such as the Internet, e-mail, and mobile phones) has made **telecommuting** a viable option for many individuals. With telecommuting, individuals work from a remote location (typically their homes) and communicate with their places of business and clients via networking technologies. Telecommuting allows the employee to be flexible, such as working nontraditional hours or remaining with the company after a relocation. It also enables a company to save on office and parking space, as well as office-related expenses such as utilities. As an environmental plus, telecommuting helps cut down on the traffic and pollution caused by traditional work commuting. In addition, it gives a business the possibility to continue operations during situations that may affect an employee's ability to get to the office, such as during hurricanes, during a bridge or highway closure, or during a flu outbreak. As a result, many experts suggest businesses include telecommuting procedures in their *business continuity plans*, even if they don't intend to use telecommuting on a regular basis. Business continuity plans and disaster recovery are discussed in detail in Chapter 15.

◉ FIGURE 7-8
Examples of telemedicine applications.

REMOTE CONSULTATIONS
Using remote-controlled teleconferencing robots, physicians can "virtually" consult with patients or other physicians in a different physical location (left); the robot transmits video images and audio to and from the doctor (via his or her computer) in real time (right).

REMOTE DIAGNOSIS
At remote locations, such as the New York childcare center shown here, trained employees provide physicians with the real-time data (sent via the Internet) they need to make a diagnosis.

TELESURGERY
Using voice or computer commands, surgeons can now perform operations via the Internet; a robotic system uses the surgeon's commands to operate on the patient.

Telemedicine

Telemedicine is the use of networking technology to provide medical information and services and is most often used to provide care to individuals who may not otherwise have access to that care, such as allowing individuals living in remote areas to consult with a specialist. For instance, physicians can use videoconferencing to communicate remotely with other physicians or with hospitalized patients (see Figure 7-8). Physicians can also use telemedicine to perform remote diagnosis of patients (for example, healthcare workers at rural locations, childcare facilities, and other locations can use video cameras, electronic stethoscopes, and other devices to send images and vital statistics of a patient to a physician located at a medical facility).

Another example of telemedicine is **telesurgery**—a form of *robot-assisted surgery* (where a robot controlled by a physician operates on the patient) in which at least one of the surgeons performs the operation by controlling the robot remotely over the Internet or another network (refer again to Figure 7-8). Robot-assisted surgery systems typically use cameras to give the human surgeon an extremely close view of the surgical area. As a result, robot-assisted surgery is typically more precise and results in smaller incisions than those made by a human surgeon, allowing for less invasive surgery (for example, not having to crack through the rib cage to access the heart) and resulting in less pain for the patient, a faster recovery time, and fewer potential complications.

Telemedicine has enormous potential for providing quality medical care to individuals who live in rural or underdeveloped areas and who do not have access to sufficient medical care. Telemedicine will also be necessary for future long-term space explorations—such as a trip to Mars and back that may take three years or more—since astronauts will undoubtedly need medical care while on the journey. In fact, NASA astronauts and physicians recently performed telesurgery experiments in the Aquarius Undersea Laboratory 50 feet below the ocean surface to help in the development of a robotic unit that will eventually allow physicians to perform surgery remotely on patients who are in outer space. Some individuals envision the eventual use of portable robot-assisted telesurgery units in space, war zones, and other environments where access to surgeons is extremely limited.

NETWORK CHARACTERISTICS

Networks can be identified by a variety of characteristics, including whether they are designed for wired or wireless access, their *topology*, their *architecture*, and their *size* or *coverage area*. These topics are described in the next few sections.

Wired vs. Wireless Networks

Networks can be designed for access via *wired* and/or *wireless* connections. With a **wired network** connection, the computers and other devices on the network are physically connected (via cabling) to the network. With a **wireless network** connection, wireless (usually radio) signals are used to send data through the air between devices, instead of using physical cables. Wired networks include the conventional telephone network, cable TV networks, and the wired networks commonly found in schools, businesses, and government facilities. Wireless networks include conventional television and radio networks, cellular telephone networks, satellite TV networks, and the wireless networks commonly found in homes, schools, and businesses. Wireless networks are also found in many public locations (such as coffeehouses, businesses, airports, hotels, and libraries) to provide Internet access to users while they are on the go via public *wireless hotspots*. For a look at how to connect a Windows computer to a public *Wi-Fi hotspot*, see the How It Works box.

Many networks today are accessible via both wired and wireless connections. For instance, a business may have a wired main company network to which the computers in employee offices are always connected, as well as provide wireless access to the network for visitors and employees to use while in waiting rooms, conference rooms, and other locations. A home network may have a wired connection between one computer and the devices needed to connect that computer to the Internet (such as a *router*), plus wireless access for other devices (such as computers, printers, and portable gaming devices) that may need to access the home network wirelessly.

Wired networks tend to be faster and more secure than wireless networks, but wireless networks have the advantage of allowing easy connections in locations where physical wiring is impractical or inconvenient (such as inside an existing home or outdoors), as well

NET

>**Wired network.** A network in which computers and other devices are connected to the network via physical cables. >**Wireless network.** A network in which computers and other devices are connected to the network without physical cables; data is typically sent via radio waves.

HOW IT WORKS

Connecting to a Wi-Fi Hotspot

To connect to a Wi-Fi hotspot, all you need is a device (such as a mobile phone or a notebook computer) with a Wi-Fi adapter installed and enabled. (Note: Some notebook computers have a switch located on the case to turn off wireless networking and some power settings disable it—check these things if you can't connect using the following steps.) On a Windows computer that has a Wi-Fi adapter installed, there should be an icon in the system tray representing your wireless network connection. When you are within range of a Wi-Fi hotspot, click this icon and choose "View Available Wireless Networks" or "Connect to a Network" (depending on which version of Windows you are using) to see all of the Wi-Fi access points in the area (see the accompanying illustration). If there is more than one hotspot listed, select the appropriate one and then click the Connect button. For free hotspots that are in range, you should be connected shortly and can then open your browser and perform Internet activities. For secured networks, you will be asked to supply the appropriate passphrase before you can connect to the Internet via that hotspot, as discussed in more detail in Chapter 9. For most fee-based hotspots (and some free ones, as well, such as networks at a hotel or conference center designed for registered guests only), you will see a logon screen and will need to obtain an appropriate username and password from a hotspot representative and enter that information via the logon screen before being connected. Security issues related to public hotspot use are discussed in more detail in Chapter 9.

2. Select the desired network and click Connect.

3. When selecting an unsecured network, you may see a warning notice.

1. Click the wireless network icon and select the Connect option to view the available wireless networks in range.

4. The connection is established.

as giving users much more freedom regarding where they can use their computers. With wireless networking, for example, you can surf the Web on your notebook computer from anywhere in your house, access the Internet with your portable computer or mobile phone while you are on the go, and create a home network without having to run wires among the rooms in your house.

Network Topologies

The physical *topology* of a computer network indicates how the devices in the network are arranged. Three of the most common physical topologies are *star*, *bus*, and *mesh* (see Figure 7-9).

> ➤ **Star network**—used in traditional mainframe environments, as well as in small office, home, and wireless networks. All the networked devices connect to a central device (such as a server or a *switch*, discussed later in this chapter) through which all network transmissions are sent. If the central device fails, then the network cannot function.

>**Star network.** A network that uses a host device connected directly to several other devices.

> **Bus network**—uses a central cable to which all network devices connect. All data is transmitted down the bus line from one device to another so, if the bus line fails, then the network cannot function.

> **Mesh network**—uses a number of different connections between network devices so that data can take any of several possible paths from source to destination. With a *full mesh topology* (such as the one shown in Figure 7-9), each device on the network is connected to every other device on the network. With a *partial mesh topology*, some devices are connected to all other devices, but some are connected only to those devices with which they exchange the most data. Consequently, if one device on a mesh network fails, the network can still function, assuming there is an alternate path available. Mesh networks are used most often with wireless networks.

Many networks, however, don't conform to a standard topology. Some networks combine topologies and connect multiple smaller networks, in effect turning several smaller networks into one larger one. For example, two star networks may be joined together using a bus line.

Network Architectures

Networks also vary by their *architecture*; that is, the way they are designed to communicate. The two most common network architectures are *client-server* and *peer-to-peer* (*P2P*).

Client-Server Networks

Client-server networks include both *clients* (computers and other devices on the network that request and utilize network resources) and *servers* (computers that are dedicated to processing client requests). Network servers are typically powerful computers with lots of memory and a very large hard drive. They provide access to software, files, and other resources that are being shared via the network. Servers typically perform a variety of tasks. For example, a single server can act as a *network server* to manage network traffic, a *file server* to manage shared files, a *print server* to handle printing-related activities, and/or a *mail server* or *Web server* to manage e-mail and Web page requests, respectively. For instance, there is only one server in the network illustrated in Figure 7-10, and it is capable of performing all server tasks for that network. When a client retrieves files from a server, it is called *downloading*; transferring data from a client to a server is called *uploading*.

Peer-to-Peer (P2P) Networks

With a *peer-to-peer* (*P2P*) *network*, a central server is not used (see Figure 7-11). Instead, all the computers on the network work at the same functional level, and users have direct access to the computers and other devices attached to the network. For instance, users can access files stored on a peer computer's hard drive and print using a peer computer's printer, provided those devices have been designated as *shared devices*. Peer-to-peer networks are less expensive and less complicated to implement than client-server networks because there are no dedicated servers, but they may not have the same performance as client-server

STAR NETWORKS
Use a central device to connect each device directly to the network.

BUS NETWORKS
Use a single central cable to connect each device in a linear fashion.

MESH NETWORKS
Each computer or device is connected to multiple (sometimes all of the other) devices on the network.

FIGURE 7-9
Basic network topologies.

NET

CLIENT

CLIENT

THE INTERNET

NETWORK SERVER
(provides client devices
with network services,
such as file, print, e-mail,
and Internet access)

**SHARED NETWORK
PRINTER**

CLIENT

FIGURE 7-10

Client-server networks.
With this type of network,
client computers
communicate through one
or more servers.

FIGURE 7-11

Peer-to-peer networks.
With this type of network,
computers communicate
directly with one another.

P2P HOME NETWORKS
Devices connect and communicate via the home
network.

THE INTERNET

INTERNET P2P NETWORKS
Devices connect and communicate
via the Internet.

networks under heavy use. Peer-to-peer capabilities are built into many personal operating systems and are often used in conjunction with small office or home networks.

Another type of peer-to-peer networking—sometimes called *Internet peer-to-peer* (*Internet P2P*) *computing*—is performed via the Internet. Instead of placing content on a Web server for others to view via the Internet, content is exchanged over the Internet directly between individual users via a peer-to-peer network. For instance, one user can copy a file from another user's hard drive to his or her own computer via the Internet. Internet P2P networking is commonly used for exchanging music and video files with others over the Internet—an illegal act if the content is copyright-protected and the exchange is unauthorized, although legal Internet P2P networks exist. Copyright law, ethics, and other topics related to peer-to-peer file exchanges are covered in Chapter 16.

CAUTION CAUTION CAUTION CAUTION CAUTION CAUTION CAUT

Do not enable sharing for folders that you do not want others on your network to see. And, if you choose to use a P2P network, be sure to designate the files in your shared folder as *read-only* to prevent your original files from being overwritten by another P2P user.

Network Size and Coverage Area

One additional way networks are classified is by the size of their coverage area. This also impacts the types of users the network is designed to service. The most common categories of networks are discussed next; these networks can use both wired and wireless connections.

Personal Area Networks (PANs)

A **personal area network** (**PAN**) is a network of personal devices for one individual (such as his or her portable computer,

>**Personal area network (PAN).** A network that connects an individual's personal devices that are located close together.

mobile phone, headset, digital camera, portable digital media player, and printer) that is designed to enable those devices to communicate and share data. PANs can be set up to work together automatically as soon as the devices get within a certain physical distance of each other. For instance, a PAN can be used to synchronize portable devices automatically with a desktop computer as soon as the individual returns home or to the office. The range of a PAN is very limited, so devices in a PAN must be physically located close together. Wireless PANs (see Figure 7-12), sometimes called *wireless personal area networks* (*WPANs*), are more common today than wired PANs.

Local Area Networks (LANs)

A **local area network** (**LAN**) is a network that covers a relatively small geographical area, such as a home, office building, or school. LANs allow users on the network to exchange files and e-mail, share printers and other hardware, and access the Internet. The client-server network shown in Figure 7-10 is an example of a LAN.

FIGURE 7-12
WPANs. Wireless PANs connect and synchronize an individual's devices wirelessly.

Metropolitan Area Networks (MANs)

A **metropolitan area network** (**MAN**) is a network designed to service a metropolitan area, typically a city or county. Most MANs are owned and operated by a city or by a network provider in order to provide individuals in that location access to the MAN. Some wireless MANs (often referred to as *municipal Wi-Fi* projects—see Figure 7-13) are created by cities or large organizations (including Microsoft and Google) to provide free or low-cost Internet access to area residents; these projects are typically supported by local taxes. In addition, some Internet service providers (such as Comcast) are experimenting with setting up free wireless MANs in select metropolitan areas for their subscribers to use when they are on the go.

Wide Area Networks (WANs)

A **wide area network** (**WAN**) is a network that covers a large geographical area. Typically, a WAN consists of two or more LANs that are connected together using communications technology. The Internet, by this definition, is the world's largest WAN. WANs may be publicly accessible, like the Internet, or they may be privately owned and operated. For instance, a company may have a private WAN to transfer data from one location to another, such as from each retail store to the corporate headquarters. Large WANs, like the Internet, typically use a mesh topology.

FIGURE 7-13
Municipal Wi-Fi. This MAN covers downtown Riverside, California.

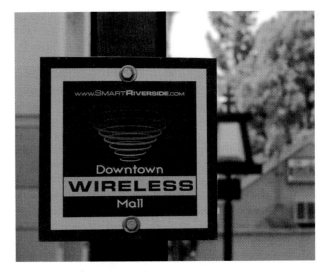

Intranets and Extranets

An **intranet** is a private network (such as a company LAN) that is designed to be used by an organization's employees and is set up like the Internet (with data posted on Web pages that are accessed with a Web browser). Consequently, little or no employee training is required to use an intranet, and intranet content can be accessed using a variety of devices. Intranets today are used for many purposes, such as coordinating internal e-mail and communications, making company publications (such as contact information, manuals, forms,

NET

---

job announcements, and so forth) available to employees, facilitating collaborative computing, and providing access to shared calendars and schedules.

A company network that is accessible to authorized outsiders is called an **extranet**. Extranets are usually accessed via the Internet, and they can be used to provide customers and business partners with access to the data they need. Access to intranets and extranets is typically restricted to employees and other authorized users, similar to other company networks.

Virtual Private Networks (VPNs)

A **virtual private network (VPN)** is a private, secure path across a public network (usually the Internet) that is set up to allow authorized users private, secure access to the company network. For instance, a VPN can allow a traveling employee, business partner, or employee located at a satellite office or public wireless hotspot to connect securely to the company network via the Internet. A process called *tunneling* is typically used to carry the data over the Internet; special *encryption* technology is used to protect the data so it cannot be understood if it is intercepted during transit (encryption is explained in Chapter 9). Essentially, VPNs allow an organization to provide secure, remote access to the company network without the cost of physically extending the private network.

DATA TRANSMISSION CHARACTERISTICS

Data transmitted over a network has specific characteristics, and it can travel over a network in various ways. These and some other characteristics related to data transmission are discussed next.

Bandwidth

As discussed in Chapter 2, the term *bandwidth* (also called *throughput*) refers to the amount of data that can be transferred (such as over a certain type of networking medium) in a given time period. Text data requires the least amount of bandwidth; video data requires the most. Just as a wide fire hose allows more water to pass through it per unit of time than a narrow garden hose allows, a networking medium with a high bandwidth allows more data to pass through it per unit of time than a networking medium with a low bandwidth. Bandwidth is usually measured in the number of *bits per second (bps)*, *Kbps* (thousands of bits per second), *Mbps* (millions of bits per second), or *Gbps* (billions of bits per second).

> **Extranet.** An intranet that is at least partially accessible to authorized outsiders. > **Virtual private network (VPN).** A private, secure path over the Internet that provides authorized users a secure means of accessing a private network via the Internet.

Analog vs. Digital Signals

Data can be represented as either *analog* or *digital* signals. Voice and music data in its natural form, for instance, is analog, and data stored on a computer is digital. Most networking media send data using **digital signals**, in which data is represented by only two *discrete states*: 0s and 1s (see Figure 7-14). **Analog signals**, such as those used by the conventional telephone system, represent data with *continuous waves*. The data to be transmitted over a networking medium must match the type of signal (analog or digital) that the medium supports; if it doesn't originally, then it must be converted before the data is transmitted. For instance, analog data that is to be sent using digital signals (such as analog music broadcast by a digital radio station) must first be converted into digital form, and digital data to be sent using analog signals (such as computer data sent over a conventional analog telephone network) must be converted into analog form before it can be transmitted. The conversion of data between analog and digital form is performed by networking hardware.

ANALOG SIGNALS

DIGITAL SIGNALS

FIGURE 7-14
Analog vs. digital signals.

Transmission Type and Timing

Networking media can also use either *serial transmission* or *parallel transmission*. With **serial transmission**, data is sent one bit at a time, one after the other along a single path (see Figure 7-15). When **parallel transmission** is used, the message is sent at least one byte at a time, with each bit in the byte taking a separate path (refer again to Figure 7-15). While parallel transmission is frequently used within computer components (such as for buses) and is used for some wireless networking applications, networking media typically use serial transmission.

When data is sent using serial transmission, a technique must be used to organize the bits being transferred so the data can be reconstructed after it is received. Three ways of timing serial transmissions are by using *synchronous*, *asynchronous*, and *isochronous* connections (see Figure 7-16). Although all three of these methods send data one bit at a time, the methods vary with respect to how the bits are organized for transfer.

FIGURE 7-15
Serial vs. parallel transmissions.

SERIAL TRANSMISSIONS
All the bits in one byte follow one another over a single path.

PARALLEL TRANSMISSIONS
The eight bits in each byte are transmitted over separate paths at the same time.

> *Synchronous transmission*—data is organized into groups or blocks of data, which are transferred at regular, specified intervals. Since the transmissions are synchronized, both devices know when data can be sent and when it should arrive. Most data transmissions within a computer and over a network are synchronous transmissions.

> *Asynchronous transmission*—data is sent when it is ready to be sent, without being synchronized. To identify the bits that belong in each byte, a *start bit* and *stop bit* are used at the beginning and end of the byte, respectively. This overhead makes asynchronous transmission less efficient than synchronous transmission and so it is not as widely used as synchronous transmission.

> *Isochronous transmission*—data is sent at the same time as other related data to support certain types of real-time applications that require the different types of data to be delivered at the proper speed for that application. For example, when transmitting a video file, the audio data must be received at the proper time in order for it to be played with its corresponding video data. To accomplish this with isochronous transmission, the sending and receiving devices first communicate to determine the bandwidth and other factors needed for the transmission, and then the necessary bandwidth is reserved just for that transmission.

SYNCHRONOUS TRANSMISSIONS
Data is sent in blocks and the blocks are timed so that the receiving device knows when they will arrive.

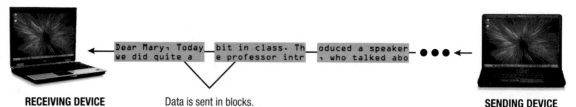

RECEIVING DEVICE   Data is sent in blocks.   SENDING DEVICE

ASYNCHRONOUS TRANSMISSIONS
Data is sent one byte at a time, along with a start bit and a stop bit.

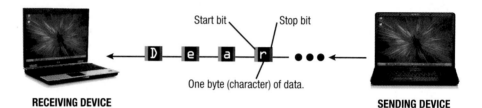

RECEIVING DEVICE   SENDING DEVICE

ISOCHRONOUS TRANSMISSIONS
The entire transmission is sent together after requesting and being assigned the bandwidth necessary for all the data to arrive at the correct time.

RECEIVING DEVICE   Entire transmission is sent together.   SENDING DEVICE

FIGURE 7-16

Transmission timing. Most network transmissions use synchronous transmission.

Another distinction between types of transmissions is the direction in which transmitted data can move.

> *Simplex transmission*—data travels in a single direction only (like a doorbell). Simplex transmission is relatively uncommon in data transmissions since most devices that are mainly one-directional, such as a printer, can still transmit error messages and other data back to the computer.

> *Half-duplex transmission*—data can travel in either direction, but only in one direction at a time (like a walkie-talkie where only one person can talk at a time). Some network transmissions are half-duplex.

> *Full-duplex transmission*—data can move in both directions at the same time (like a telephone). Many network and most Internet connections are full-duplex; sometimes two connections between the sending device and receiving device are needed to support full-duplex transmissions.

Delivery Method

When data needs to travel across a large network (such as a WAN), typically one of three methods is used (see Figure 7-17). With *circuit switching*, a dedicated path over a network is established between the sender and receiver and all data follows that path from the sender to the receiver. Once the connection is established, the physical path or circuit is dedicated to that connection and cannot be used by any other device until the transmission is finished. The most common example of a circuit-switched network is the conventional telephone system.

The technique used for data sent over the Internet is *packet switching*. With packet switching, messages are separated into small units called *packets*. Packets contain information about the sender and the receiver, the actual data being sent, and information about how to reassemble the packets to reconstruct the original message. Packets travel along the network separately, based on their final destination, network traffic, and other network conditions. When the packets reach their destination, they are reassembled in the proper order (refer again to Figure 7-17). Another alternative is *broadcasting*, in which data is sent out (typically in packets) to all nodes on a network and is retrieved only by the intended recipient. Broadcasting is used primarily with LANs.

◀ **FIGURE 7-17**

Circuit-switched,
packet-switched,
and broadcast
networks.

CIRCUIT-SWITCHED NETWORKS
Data uses a dedicated path from the sender to the recipient.

PACKET-SWITCHED NETWORKS
Data is sent as individual packets, which are assembled at the recipient's destination.

BROADCAST NETWORKS
Data is broadcast to all nodes within range; the designated recipient retrieves the data.

NETWORKING MEDIA

To connect the devices in a network, either *wired media* (physical cables) or *wireless media* (typically radio signals) can be used. The most common wired and wireless networking media are discussed next.

Wired Networking Media

The most common types of wired networking media are *twisted-pair*, *coaxial*, and *fiber-optic cable*.

Twisted-Pair Cable

A **twisted-pair cable** is made up of pairs of thin strands of insulated wire twisted together (see Figure 7-18). Twisted-pair is the least expensive type of networking cable and has been in use the longest. In fact, it is the same type of cabling used inside most homes for telephone communications. Twisted-pair cabling can be used with both analog and digital data transmission and is commonly used for LANs. Twisted-pair cable is rated by *category*, which indicates the type of data, speed, distance, and other factors that the cable supports. *Category 3 (Cat 3)* twisted-pair cabling is regular telephone cable; higher speed and quality cabling—such as *Category 5 (Cat 5)*, *Category 6 (Cat 6)*, and *Category 7 (Cat 7)*—is frequently used for home or business networks. The pairs of wires in twisted-pair wire are twisted together to reduce interference and improve performance. To further improve performance it can be *shielded* with a metal lining. Twisted-pair cables used for networks have different connectors than those used for telephones. Networking connectors are typically *RJ-45* connectors, which look similar to but are larger than telephone *RJ-11* connectors.

Coaxial Cable

Coaxial cable (also known as *coax*) was originally developed to carry a large number of high-speed video transmissions at one time, such as to deliver cable TV service. A coaxial cable (see Figure 7-18) consists of a relatively thick center wire surrounded by insulation and then covered with a shield of braided wire to block electromagnetic signals from entering the cable. Coaxial cable is commonly used today in computer networks, for short-run

>**Twisted-pair cable.** A networking cable consisting of wire strands twisted in sets of two and bound into a cable. >**Coaxial cable.** A networking cable consisting of a center wire inside a grounded, cylindrical shield, capable of sending data at high speeds.

The entire cable is covered by a plastic covering.

Pairs of copper wires are insulated with a plastic coating and twisted together; most cables contain at least two pairs.

TWISTED-PAIR CABLES

The entire cable is covered by a plastic covering.

Outer conductor is made out of woven or braided metal.

White insulating material surrounds the copper wire.

The innermost part of the cable is a single copper wire.

COAXIAL CABLES

The entire cable is surrounded by strengthening material and covered by a plastic covering.

The core of each fiber is a single glass or plastic tube, which is surrounded by a reflective cladding.

A protective plastic coating protects each fiber; a cable contains multiple fibers.

FIBER-OPTIC CABLES

FIGURE 7-18
Wired network transmission media.

telephone transmissions outside of the home, and for cable television delivery. Although more expensive than twisted-pair cabling, it is much less susceptible to interference and can carry more data more quickly. While not used extensively for networking home computers at the moment, that may change with the relatively new option of networking via the existing coax in a home. Coax is also growing in popularity for home multimedia networks. The most common types of connectors used with coaxial cable are the slotted *BNC connectors* that are turned once to lock or unlock them into place (and are on the cable shown in Figure 7-18) and the threaded *F connectors* frequently used with cable TV and antenna applications.

Fiber-Optic Cable

Fiber-optic cable is the newest and fastest of these three types of wired transmission media. It contains multiple (sometime several hundred) clear glass or plastic fiber strands, each about the thickness of a human hair (refer again to Figure 7-18). Fiber-optic cable transfers data represented by light pulses at speeds of billions of bits per second. Each strand has the capacity to carry data for several television stations or thousands of voice conversations, but each strand can only send data in one direction so two strands are needed for full-duplex data transmissions.

Fiber-optic cable is commonly used for the high-speed backbone lines of a network, such as to connect networks housed in separate buildings or for the Internet infrastructure. It is also used for telephone backbone lines and, increasingly, is being installed by telephone companies all the way to the home or business to provide super-fast connections directly to

>**Fiber-optic cable.** A networking cable that utilizes hundreds of thin transparent fibers over which lasers transmit data as light.

the end user. The biggest advantage of fiber-optic cabling is speed; the main disadvantage of fiber-optic cabling is the initial expense of both the cable and the installation. Fiber-optic connectors are less standardized than connectors for other types of wired media, so it is important to use cables with the connectors that match the hardware with which the cable will be used. Common connectors include the push-pull *SC connector* (shown in Figure 7-18) and the slotted *ST connector* that works similarly to a BNC connector.

Wireless Networking Media

Wireless networks usually use *radio signals* to send data through the airwaves. Depending on the networking application, radio signals can be short range (such as to connect a wireless keyboard or mouse to a computer), medium range (such as to connect a computer to a wireless LAN or public hotspot), or long range (such as to provide Internet access or cell phone coverage to a relatively large geographic area or to broadcast TV or radio shows). The radio signals used in wireless networks and the types of technologies used to transmit them are discussed next.

The Electromagnetic and Wireless Spectrums

All wireless applications in the United States—such as wireless networks, mobile phones, radio and TV broadcasts, sonar and radar applications, and GPS systems—use specific *frequencies* as assigned by the Federal Communications Commission (FCC). Frequencies are measured in *hertz (Hz)* and the frequencies that comprise the *electromagnetic spectrum*—the range of common *electromagnetic radiation* (energy)—are shown in Figure 7-19. Different parts of the spectrum have different properties (such as the distance a signal can travel, the amount of data a signal can transmit in a given period of time, and the types of objects a signal can pass through), which make certain frequencies more appropriate for certain applications. As illustrated in this figure, most wireless networking applications use frequencies located in the *radio frequency (RF)* band at the low end (up to 300 GHz) of the electromagnetic spectrum—this range is sometimes referred to as the *wireless spectrum*.

The frequencies assigned to an application, such as FM radio or cell phone service, typically consist of a range of frequencies to be used as needed for that application. For instance, FM radio stations broadcast on frequencies from 88 MHz to 108 MHz and each radio station in a particular geographic area is assigned its own frequency. Most radio frequencies in the U.S. are licensed by the FCC and can only be used for that specific application by the licensed individuals in their specified geographic areas. However, the 900 MHz, 2.4 GHz, 5 GHz, and 5.8 GHz frequencies used by many cordless landline phones, garage door openers, and other consumer devices—as well as for *Wi-Fi*, *WiMAX*, and *Bluetooth* wireless networking—fall within an unlicensed part of the spectrum and, therefore, can be used by any product or individual. A frequency range can be further broken down into multiple *channels*, each of which can be used simultaneously by different users. There are also ways to combine multiple signals to send them over a transmission medium at one time to allow more users than would otherwise be possible.

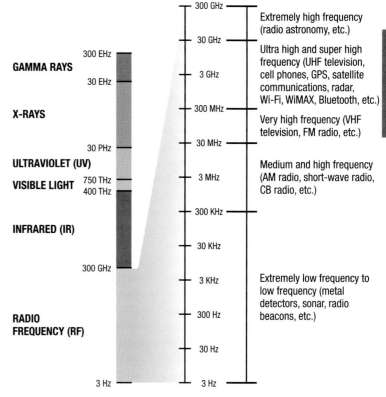

NET

FIGURE 7-19
The electromagnetic spectrum. Each type of communication is assigned specific frequencies within which to operate.

Because the number of wireless applications is growing all the time and there is a limited amount of the parts of the spectrum appropriate for today's wireless networking applications, the wireless spectrum is relatively crowded and frequencies are in high demand. One benefit of the 2009 switch from analog to digital television broadcasts is that it freed up some of the VHF and UHF frequencies for other applications. While some of these frequencies were allocated to public safety communications applications, a large portion were auctioned off in 2008 and are expected to be used for new wireless networks and applications—particularly for mobile users.

Cellular Radio Transmissions

Cellular radio transmissions are used with cell phones and are sent and received via *cellular (cell) towers*—tall metal poles with antennas on top. Cellular service areas are divided into honeycomb-shaped zones called *cells*; each cell contains one cell tower (see Figure 7-20). When a cell phone user begins to make a call, it is picked up by the appropriate cell tower (the one that is located in the cell in which the cell phone is located and that belongs to the user's mobile phone provider). That cell tower then forwards the call to the mobile phone company's *Mobile Telephone Switching Office (MTSO)*, which routes the call to the recipient's telephone via his or her mobile or conventional telephone service provider (depending on the type of phone being used by the recipient). When a cell phone

FIGURE 7-20

How cellular phones work.

1. The sender (in this example, the passenger in the car) makes a call using a cell phone.

2. The call is transmitted as radio waves to the tower located in the same cell as the sender.

3. The tower transmits the call to the switching office.

4. When the sender travels out of the current cell, the next tower takes over.

Cell tower

CELL B

CELL C

CELL A

Mobile Telephone Switching Office (MTSO)

Regular telephone network

5. The Mobile Telephone Switching Office (MTSO) routes the call to the appropriate telephone network; in this example, the regular telephone network.

6. The recipient answers the phone (in this example, using a conventional phone at home).

>**Cellular radio.** A form of broadcast radio designed for use with cellular telephones that broadcasts using antennas located inside honeycomb-shaped cells.

user moves out of the current cell into a new cell, the call is passed automatically to the appropriate cell tower in the cell that the user is entering. Data (such as e-mail and Web page requests) sent via cell phones works in a similar manner. The speed of cellular radio transmissions depends on the type of *cellular standard* being used, as discussed later in this chapter.

Microwave and Satellite Transmissions

Microwaves are high-frequency radio signals that can send large quantities of data at high speeds over long distances. Microwave signals can be sent or received using *microwave stations* or *communications satellites*, but must travel in a straight line from one station or satellite to another without encountering any obstacles, since microwave signals are *line of sight*. **Microwave stations** are earth-based stations that can transmit microwave signals directly to each other over distances of up to about 30 miles. To avoid buildings, mountains, and the curvature of the earth obstructing the signal, microwave stations are usually placed on tall buildings, towers, and mountaintops. Microwave stations typically contain both a dish-shaped *microwave antenna* and a transceiver. When one station receives a transmission from another, it amplifies it and passes it on to the next station. Microwave stations can exchange data transmissions with *communications satellites*, discussed next, as well as with other microwave stations. Microwave stations designed specifically to communicate with satellites (such as for satellite TV and satellite Internet services) are typically called *satellite dishes*. Satellite dishes are usually installed permanently where they are needed, but they can also be mounted on trucks, boats, RVs, and other types of transportation devices when portable transmission capabilities are necessary or desirable, such as for military or recreational applications.

Communications satellites are space-based devices launched into orbit around the earth to receive and transmit microwave signals to and from earth (see the satellite Internet example in Figure 7-21). Communications satellites were originally used to facilitate microwave transmission when microwave stations were not economically viable (such as over large, sparsely populated areas) or were physically impractical (such as over large bodies of water). Today, communications satellites are used to send and receive transmissions to and from a variety of other devices, such as personal satellite dishes used for satellite television and Internet service, GPS receivers, satellite radio receivers, and satellite phones.

FIGURE 7-21
How satellite Internet works.

3. An orbiting satellite receives the request and beams it down to the satellite dish at the ISP's operations center.

2. The request is sent up to a satellite from the individual's satellite dish.

4. The ISP's operations center receives the request (via its satellite dish) and transfers it to the Internet.

THE INTERNET

1. Data, such as a Web page request, is sent from the individual's computer to the satellite dish via a satellite modem.

5. The request travels over the Internet as usual. The requested information takes a reverse route back to the individual.

> **Microwave station.** An earth-based device that sends and receives high-frequency, high-speed radio signals. > **Communications satellite.** An earth-orbiting device that relays communications signals over long distances.

FURTHER EXPLORATION

Go to the Chapter 7 page at
**www.cengage.com/
computerconcepts/np/uc13**
for links to information
about wired and wireless
communications media.

Traditional communications satellites maintain a *geosynchronous* orbit 22,300 miles above the earth; since they travel at a speed and direction that keeps pace with the earth's rotation, they appear (from earth) to remain stationary over any given spot. Because these satellites are so far above the surface of the earth, there is a slight delay while the signals travel from earth, to the satellite, and back to earth again. This delay—less than one half-second—is not normally noticed by most users (such as individuals who receive Internet or TV service via satellite), but it does make geosynchronous satellite transmissions less practical for voice, gaming, and other real-time communications. Because of this delay factor, *low earth orbit* (*LEO*) satellite systems were developed for use with satellite telephone systems. LEO satellites typically are located anywhere from 100 to 1,000 miles above the earth and, consequently, provide faster transmission than traditional satellites. *Medium earth orbit* (*MEO*) systems typically use satellites located about 1,000 to 12,000 miles above the earth and are used most often for GPS.

Infrared (IR) Transmissions

One type of wireless networking that does not use signals in the RF band of the electromagnetic spectrum is **infrared (IR) transmission**, which sends data as infrared light rays over relatively short distances. Like an infrared television remote control, infrared technology requires line-of-sight transmission. Because of this limitation, many formerly infrared devices (such as wireless mice and keyboards) now use RF radio signals instead. Infrared transmissions are still used with remote controls (such as for computers that contain TV tuners). They are also used to beam data between some mobile devices, as well as between some game consoles, handheld gaming devices, and other home entertainment devices.

COMMUNICATIONS PROTOCOLS AND NETWORKING STANDARDS

A *protocol* is a set of rules to be followed in a specific situation; in networking, for instance, there are *communications protocols* that determine how devices on a network communicate. The term *standard* refers to a set of criteria or requirements that has been approved by a recognized standards organization (such as the *American National Standards Institute* (*ANSI*), which helps to develop standards used in business and industry, or *IEEE*, which develops networking standards) or is accepted as a de facto standard by the industry. Standards are extremely important in the computer industry because they help hardware and software manufacturers ensure that the products they develop can work with other computing products. *Networking standards* typically address both how the devices in a network physically connect (such as the types of cabling that can be used) and how the devices communicate (such as the communications protocols that can be used). Communications protocols and the most common wired and wireless networking standards are discussed in the next several sections.

TCP/IP and Other Communications Protocols

The most widely used communications protocol today is **TCP/IP**. TCP/IP is the protocol used for transferring data over the Internet and actually consists of two protocols: *Transmission Control Protocol* (*TCP*), which is responsible for the delivery of data, and *Internet Protocol* (*IP*), which provides addresses and routing information. TCP/IP uses packet switching to transmit data over the Internet; when the packets reach their destination, they are reassembled

---

>**Infrared (IR) transmissions.** A wireless networking medium that sends data as infrared light rays. >**TCP/IP.** A networking protocol that uses packet switching to facilitate the transmission of messages; the protocol used with the Internet.

in the proper order (see Figure 7-22). Support for TCP/IP is built into virtually all operating systems, and IP addresses are commonly used to identify the various computers and devices on networks such as LANs.

The first widely used version of IP—*Internet Protocol Version 4 (IPv4)*—was standardized in the early 1980s. IPv4 uses 32-bit addresses and so allows for 2^{32} possible unique addresses. While still widely used today, IPv4 was never designed to be used with the billions of devices that access the Internet today and, consequently, a newer version of IP (*IPv6*) was developed. IPv6 uses 128-bit addresses (and so allows for 2^{128} possible unique addresses) and adds many improvements to IPv4 in areas such as routing, data security, and network autoconfiguration. While IPv4 and IPv6 are expected to coexist for several years until IPv6 eventually replaces IPv4, the U.S. government has mandated that all federal agencies be capable of switching to IPv6. Experts suggest that businesses perform a network audit to determine what hardware and software changes will be needed to switch to IPv6 so that the business is prepared when the change is deemed necessary.

While TCP/IP is used to connect to and communicate with the Internet, other protocols are used for specific Internet applications. For instance, as discussed in Chapter 1, *HTTP (Hypertext Transfer Protocol)* and *HTTPS (Secure Hypertext Transfer Protocol)* are protocols used to display Web pages, and *FTP (File Transfer Protocol)* is a protocol used to transfer files over the Internet. Protocols used to deliver e-mail over the Internet include *SMTP (Simple Mail Transfer Protocol)* and *POP3 (Post Office Protocol)*.

1. Each message is split into packets.

Dear Jim,
Blah! Blah! Blah! Blah! Blah! Blah! Blah! Blah! Blah! Blah! Blah! Blah!
Blah! Blah! Blah! Blah! Blah! Blah! Blah! Blah! Blah! Blah! Blah! Blah!
Blah! Blah! Blah! Blah! Blah! Blah!
From, Sue

SUE'S PC

2. The packets are addressed to the same destination.

From: SueG@usc.edu   0¢
To: JimS@cu.edu

From: SueG@usc.edu   0¢
To: JimS@cu.edu

From: SueG@usc.edu   0¢
To: JimS@cu.edu

4. The packets are reassembled into the message at the destination.

Dear Jim,
Blah! Blah! Blah! Blah! Blah! Blah! Blah! Blah! Blah! Blah! Blah! Blah!
Blah! Blah! Blah! Blah! Blah! Blah! Blah! Blah! Blah! Blah! Blah! Blah!
Blah! Blah! Blah! Blah! Blah! Blah!
From, Sue

JIM'S PC

3. The packets may travel the same or different routes to the destination.

University of Colorado (CU)

University of Southern California (USC)

FIGURE 7-22
How TCP/IP works.
TCP/IP networks (like the Internet) use packet switching.

NET

Ethernet (802.3)

Ethernet (802.3) is the most widely used standard for wired networks. It is typically used with LANs that have a star topology (though it can also be used with WANs and MANs) and can be used in conjunction with twisted-pair, coaxial, or fiber-optic cabling. Ethernet

>**Ethernet (802.3).** A widely used wired LAN networking standard.

STANDARD	MAXIMUM SPEED
10BASE-T	10 Mbps
Fast Ethernet (100BASE-T or 100BASE-TX)	100 Mbps
Gigabit Ethernet (1000BASE-T)	1,000 Mbps (1 Gbps)
10 Gigabit Ethernet (10GBASE-T)	10 Gbps
40 Gigabit Ethernet*	40 Gbps
100 Gigabit Ethernet*	100 Gbps
Terabit Ethernet**	1,000 Gbps (1 Tbps)

* Expected by 2010
** Expected by 2015

FIGURE 7-23
Ethernet standards.

PoE SWITCH

PoE CAMERA

PoE ADAPTER

POWER CABLE
ETHERNET CABLE

NON-PoE OUTDOOR WIRELESS ACCESS POINT

FIGURE 7-24
With Power over Ethernet (PoE), devices are powered through the Ethernet connection.

was invented in the mid-1970s and has continued to evolve over the years; about every three years the new approved amendments are incorporated into the existing IEEE 802.3 Ethernet standard to keep it up to date. Figure 7-23 summarizes the various Ethernet standards; of these, the most common today are *Fast Ethernet*, *Gigabit Ethernet*, and *10 Gigabit Ethernet*. The even faster standards shown in Figure 7-23 are currently under development and are expected to be used for connections between servers, as well as for delivering video, digital X-rays and other digital medical images, and other high-speed, bandwidth-intensive networking applications.

Early Ethernet networks were half-duplex and used a set of procedures collectively called *CSMA/CD (Carrier Sense Multiple Access/Collision Detection)* to avoid multiple messages from being sent at one time and to detect any collisions of messages as they occur. Beginning in 1997, Ethernet became full-duplex and so collisions no longer occur.

A recent Ethernet development is *Power over Ethernet (PoE)*, which allows electrical power to be sent along the cables in an Ethernet network (often referred to as *Ethernet cables*) along with data (see Figure 7-24). Consequently, in addition to sending data, the Ethernet cable can be used to supply power to the devices on the network. PoE is most often used in business networks with remote wired devices (such as outdoor networking hardware, security cameras, and other devices) that are not located near a power outlet. It can also be used to place networked devices near ceilings or other locations where a nearby power outlet may not be available. Using PoE requires special hardware and devices designed for PoE but it eliminates the need for access to power outlets for that portion of the network. Regular Ethernet-enabled devices can be powered via PoE if a special *PoE adapter*, such as the one shown in Figure 7-24, is used.

Phoneline, Powerline, G.hn, and Broadband over Powerline (BPL)

Two alternatives to the Ethernet standard for wired home networks are the *Phoneline* and *Powerline standards*. Phoneline (also called the *Home Phoneline Networking Association* or *HomePNA standard*) allows computers to be networked through ordinary telephone wiring and telephone jacks (without interfering with voice telephone calls), as well as over existing home coaxial cable wiring. The newest version of this standard—*HomePNA 3.0*—supports speeds up to 320 Mbps and is designed to network both the computers and the home entertainment devices within a home. The Powerline (also called *HomePlug*) standard allows computers to be networked over existing power lines using conventional electrical outlets. Similar to Phoneline networks, Powerline networks are quick and easy to set up and are relatively fast (up to 200 Mbps). In addition, they have the advantage that houses usually have many more power outlets than phone outlets. Similar to the newest Phoneline standard, the newest Powerline standard—named *HomePlug AV*—can be used to network home entertainment devices in addition to computers.

The *G.hn* standard is an emerging standard designed as a unified worldwide standard for creating home networks over phone lines, power lines, and coaxial cable. It is being promoted by the HomeGrid Forum and is supported by the Home Phoneline Networking Association. Once the standard is finalized (expected by 2010), products that support all three types of home networking connections discussed in this section (via phone lines, power lines, and coaxial cable) can be developed.

An emerging technology based on the Powerline standard that is under development and that is designed to deliver broadband Internet to homes via the existing outdoor power lines (with the addition of some new hardware at the power poles) is *broadband over powerline* (*BPL*). BPL service is only available in limited areas at the moment (available through the area's power company), but BPL has great potential for delivering broadband Internet access to virtually any home or business that has access to electricity.

ONLINE VIDEO

Go to the Chapter 7 page at **www.cengage.com/computerconcepts/np/uc13** to watch the "How to Create a Powerline Network" video clip.

Wi-Fi (802.11)

One of the most common networking standards used with wireless LANs is **Wi-Fi (802.11)**—a family of wireless networking standards that use the IEEE 802.11 standard. Wi-Fi (sometimes called *wireless Ethernet* because it is designed to easily connect to a wired Ethernet network) is the current standard for wireless networks in the home or office, as well as for public Wi-Fi hotspots. Wi-Fi hardware is built into virtually all portable computers sold today; it is also built into many mobile phones to allow faster Web browsing via Wi-Fi when the user is within range of a Wi-Fi network. In addition to portable computers and mobile phones, Wi-Fi capabilities are becoming increasingly integrated into everyday products, such as printers, digital cameras, portable digital media players, handheld gaming devices, and gaming consoles (see Figure 7-25), to allow those devices to wirelessly network with other devices or to access the Internet. For a look at a new Wi-Fi-enabled consumer product you can use to automatically upload digital photos to your favorite photo-sharing sites—Wi-Fi flash memory cards—see the Technology and You box.

The speed of a Wi-Fi network and the area it can cover depend on a variety of factors, including the *Wi-Fi standard* and hardware being used, the number of solid objects (such as walls, trees, or buildings) between the access point and the computer or other device being used, and the amount of interference from cordless phones, baby monitors, microwave ovens, and other devices that also operate on the same radio frequency as Wi-Fi (usually 2.4 GHz). In general, Wi-Fi is designed for medium-range data transfers—typically between 100 and 300 feet indoors and 300 to 900 feet outdoors. Usually both speed and distance degrade with interference. The distance of a Wi-Fi network can be extended using additional *antennas* and other hardware designed for that purpose.

FIGURE 7-25
Wi-Fi enabled products. Many consumer products today contain built-in Wi-Fi connectivity.

PORTABLE COMPUTERS

MOBILE PHONES

DIGITAL CAMERAS

PORTABLE DIGITAL MEDIA PLAYERS

GAMING CONSOLES

>**Wi-Fi (802.11).** A widely used networking standard for medium-range wireless networks.

TECHNOLOGY AND YOU

Wi-Fi SD Cards

One interesting new Wi-Fi product that became available recently is the *Wi-Fi SD card*. These cards (such as the *Eye-Fi cards* shown in the accompanying illustration) are designed to upload photos wirelessly and automatically from your camera to your computer via a Wi-Fi network. Some cards can also *geotag* your photos with location information (based on geographic coordinates) as you take them to show where the photos were taken; others can automatically upload your photos to photo sharing Web sites like Flickr, Facebook, or Picasa.

For instance, all three Eye-Fi cards in the accompanying photo wirelessly transfer your photos from your digital camera to your home computer as soon as the camera is within range of your home Wi-Fi network. The *Eye-Fi Share* and the *Eye-Fi Pro* cards can also wirelessly upload photos to your favorite photo sharing Web site, and the Eye-Fi Pro card automatically geotags your photos. In addition, the Eye-Fi Pro card can upload videos and uncompressed *RAW* files in addition to photos, send images to photo sharing Web sites and your home computer via a wireless hotspot when you are away from home, and upload photos directly to your computer while on the go (without a wireless router via a

peer-to-peer connection) whenever the camera is in range of your computer.

In addition to allowing you to share your photos immediately with others (such as while on a vacation or at a special event), using a Wi-Fi SD card for your digital photos can also give you the peace of mind that your photos are backed up on your home computer and/or online. This is especially beneficial if your camera is stolen or the card becomes damaged. In fact, using an Eye-Fi card enabled one woman to catch the individual who stole her camera gear while she was on vacation—her photos, along with images of the thief with the camera gear, were uploaded to her home computer and the police were able to apprehend the thief and recover the stolen gear.

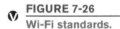
FIGURE 7-26
Wi-Fi standards.

WI-FI STANDARD	DESCRIPTION
802.11b	An early Wi-Fi standard; supports data transfer rates of 11 Mbps.
802.11a	Supports data transfer rates of 54 Mbps, but uses a different radio frequency (5 GHz) than 802.11g/b (2.4 GHz), making the standards incompatible.
802.11g	A current Wi-Fi standard; supports data transfer rates of 54 Mbps and uses the same 2.4 GHz frequency as 802.11b, so their products are compatible.
802.11n	The newest Wi-Fi standard; supports speeds up to about 300 Mbps and has twice the range of 802.11g. It can use either the 2.4 GHz or 5 GHz frequency.
802.11s*	Designed for Wi-Fi mesh networks.
802.11u*	Includes additional security features.
802.11z*	Designed for direct (ad hoc) networking between advices.
802.11ac and 802.11ad**	Designed to increase throughput.

* Expected by 2010
** Expected no earlier than 2012

A summary of the different Wi-Fi standards in use and under development is shown in Figure 7-26; of these, the most widely used today are *802.11g* and *802.11n*. The 802.11n standard is currently the fastest Wi-Fi standard today. Its use of *MIMO* (*multiple in, multiple out*) *antennas* to transfer multiple streams of data at one time, in addition to other improvements, allows for data transmissions typically about five times as fast as 802.11g and about twice the range.

Typically, 802.11g and 802.11n products can be used on the same network and the products are backward-compatible (so computers using older 802.11g hardware can connect to 802.11n networks, for instance, though they will only connect at 802.11g speeds). To ensure that hardware from various vendors will work together, consumers can look for products that are certified by the *Wi-Fi Alliance* (see Figure 7-27).

While Wi-Fi is very widely used today, it does have some limitations—particularly its relatively limited range. For instance, an individual using a Wi-Fi hotspot inside a Starbucks coffeehouse will lose that Internet connection when he or she moves out of range of that network and will need to locate another hotspot at his or her next location. In addition, many businesses may be physically too large for a Wi-Fi network to span the entire organization. While hardware can be used to extend a Wi-Fi network, an emerging possibility for creating larger wireless networks is *WiMAX*, discussed next.

FIGURE 7-27
Wi-Fi CERTIFIED
logo.

WiMAX and Mobile WiMAX

WiMAX (*Worldwide Interoperability for Microwave Access*) is a series of standards designed for longer range wireless networking connections. Similar to Wi-Fi, WiMAX (also known as *802.16a*) is designed to provide Internet access to fixed locations (sometimes called *hotzones*), but the coverage is significantly larger (a typical hotzone radius is close to 2 miles, though WiMAX can transmit data as far as 6 miles or so without line of sight). With WiMAX, it is feasible to provide coverage to an entire city or other geographical area by using multiple WiMAX towers (see Figure 7-28), similar to the way cell phone cells overlap to provide continuous cell phone service. WiMAX can use licensed radio frequencies, in addition to unlicensed frequencies like Wi-Fi, to avoid interference issues.

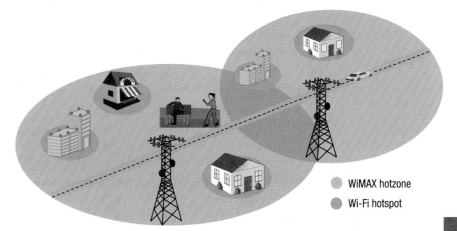

● WiMAX hotzone
● Wi-Fi hotspot

FIGURE 7-28
WiMAX vs. Wi-Fi.
WiMAX hotzones can provide service to anyone in the hotzone, including mobile users, while the range of Wi-Fi hotspots is fairly limited.

Mobile WiMAX (*802.16e*) is the mobile version of the WiMAX wireless networking standard. It is designed to deliver broadband wireless networking to mobile users via a mobile phone, portable computer, or other WiMAX-enabled device. WiMAX capabilities are beginning to be built into portable computers and other devices, and WiMAX is currently being used to provide Internet access to selected geographical areas by a number of companies in over 135 countries. In the U.S., for instance, Sprint Nextel's WiMAX division and WiMAX leader Clearwire have merged and are in the process of building a new WiMAX-based nationwide high-speed network designed to deliver both fixed and mobile WiMAX-based Internet service to businesses and individuals. This new network is expected to be able to provide service to at least 140 million users by 2010.

Cellular Standards

Cellular standards have evolved over the years to better fulfill the demand for mobile Internet, mobile multimedia delivery, and other relatively recent mobile trends. The original *first-generation phones* were analog and designed for voice data only. Newer cell phones, starting with *second-generation (2G) phones*, are digital, support both data and voice, and are faster. Common *2G wireless standards* include *GSM* (*Global System for Mobile*

ONLINE VIDEO

Go to the Chapter 7 page at **www.cengage.com/ computerconcepts/np/uc13** to watch the "WiMAX vs. Wi-Fi" video clip.

NET

>**WiMAX.** An emerging wireless networking standard that is faster and has a greater range than Wi-Fi. >**Mobile WiMAX.** A version of WiMAX designed to be used with mobile phones.

i'm lovin' it

Dave Weick, Senior Vice President, Chief Information Officer, McDonald's Corporation

How has the emergence of Wi-Fi affected companies such as McDonalds?

The emergence of Wi-Fi has fueled our customers' expectations of having immediate access to information. Our customers and employees love the convenience and relevance of McDonald's "hotspots." Through wireless connectivity, Wi-Fi is creating a more modern and relevant experience for our customers. The ability to conveniently check e-mail or download music or games can be a deciding factor in choosing a place to eat—a trend we don't see ending anytime soon.

communications) and *CDMA* (*Code Division Multiple Access*). Both of these standards are designed for voice traffic and both support speeds up to 14.4 Kbps, though some wireless providers have developed technologies such as *EDGE* (*Enhanced Data Rates for GSM Evolution*) that can be used with 2G networks to provide faster service (for instance, EDGE supports speeds up to 135 Kbps). These interim developments are sometimes referred to as *2.5G cellular standards*. Both GSM and CDMA are used in the United States (but are not compatible with each other, although some phones are available that can be used with both standards). GSM is also widely used overseas, though with different frequencies so international travelers will need to ensure their 2G phone supports the frequencies used in their destination location— some 2G phones support multiple frequencies to permit international roaming.

The current standard for cellular networks today in the U.S. and many other countries is *3G* (*third generation*). *3G cellular standards* use packet-switching (like TCP/IP) instead of circuit-switching (like conventional telephones and earlier mobile phones) and are designed to support both data and voice. Users of 3G mobile phones and other 3G mobile devices can access broadband Internet content (such as online maps, music, games, TV, videos and more—see Figure 7-29) at relatively fast speeds—up to about 1.7 Mbps at the present time, with speeds expected to reach 3 Mbps in the near future. These speeds are equivalent to the speeds many home broadband Internet users experience; consequently, Internet access via a 3G network is often referred to as *mobile broadband*. In addition to mobile phones, computers can access the Internet via a 3G network with appropriate hardware.

Virtually all mobile phone providers today have, or are in the process of building, a 3G network. The 3G standard used with a network depends on the type of cellular network. For instance, GSM mobile networks (like AT&T Wireless and T-Mobile) typically use the *HSDPA* (*High Speed Downlink Packet Access*)/*UMTS* (*Universal Mobile Telecommunications System*) 3G standards for their 3G networks; CDMA networks (like *Verizon Wireless* and *Cricket Wireless*) typically use the *EV-DO* (*Evolution Data Optimized*) 3G standard instead. To get 3G speeds, mobile users need to be in range of their providers' 3G network; typically, users outside the coverage area can still get service, but only at 2G speeds.

The next generation for mobile networks—*4G* (*fourth generation*)—is under development and two standards have emerged at the present time: the mobile WiMAX standard already discussed and *Long Term Evolution* (*LTE*). LTE (supported by AT&T Wireless, Verizon Wireless, and T-Mobile) is a cellular standard and is based on UMTS. LTE networks are expected to arrive in the U.S. by 2011. While mobile WiMAX is not a cellular standard, the new national WiMAX network being built in the U.S. by Sprint Nextel and Clearwire will be used to provide 4G mobile phone service to subscribers, in addition to Internet service.

FIGURE 7-29

Mobile broadband.
3G networks provide mobile phone users with broadband access to multimedia content.

Bluetooth, Ultra Wideband (UWB), and Other Short-Range Wireless Standards

There are several wireless networking standards in existence or being developed that are designed for short-range wireless networking connections. Most of these are used to facilitate PANs or very small, special-purpose home networks, such as connecting home entertainment devices or appliances within a home. The most common of these standards are discussed next.

Bluetooth and Wireless USB

Bluetooth is a wireless standard that is designed for very short-range (10 meters, approximately 33 feet, or less) connections. It is designed to replace cables between devices, such as to connect a wireless keyboard or mouse to a desktop computer, to send print jobs wirelessly from a portable computer to a printer, or to connect a mobile phone to a wireless headset (see Figure 7-30). Bluetooth devices automatically recognize and network with each other when they get within transmission range. For instance, Bluetooth enables a portable computer or mobile phone to be synchronized with a desktop computer automatically on entering the home or office, or a wireless keyboard to be connected to a computer automatically as soon as the computer is powered up. Bluetooth signals can transmit through clothing and other nonmetallic objects, so a mobile phone or other device in a pocket or briefcase can connect with Bluetooth hardware (such as a headset) without having to be removed from the pocket or briefcase. In addition, some industry experts predict that major household appliances will be Bluetooth-enabled in the future, resulting in an automatic, always connected, smart home.

Bluetooth works using radio signals in the frequency band of 2.4 GHz, the same as Wi-Fi, and traditionally supports data transfer rates up to 3 Mbps, though the newest *Bluetooth 3.0* standard incorporates 802.11 technology to support transfers up to 24 Mbps. Once two Bluetooth-enabled devices come within range of each other, their software identifies each other (using their unique identification numbers) and establishes a link. Because there may be many Bluetooth devices within range, up to 10 individual Bluetooth networks (called *piconets*) can be in place within the same physical area at one time. Each piconet can connect up to eight devices, for a maximum of 80 devices within any 10-meter radius. To facilitate this, Bluetooth divides its allocated radio spectrum into multiple channels of 1 MHz each. Each Bluetooth device can use the entire range of frequencies, jumping randomly (in unison with the other devices in that piconet) on a regular basis to minimize interference between piconets, as well as from other devices (such as garage-door openers, Wi-Fi networks, and some cordless phones and baby monitors) that use the same frequencies. Since Bluetooth transmitters change frequencies 1,600 times every second automatically, it is unlikely that any two transmitting devices will be on the same frequency at the same time.

As the use of Bluetooth grows, the standard is evolving to meet new needs. For instance, *Bluetooth 2.1* includes support for *Near Field Communications* (*NFC*), a standard for making payments via mobile phone, as discussed in more detail in Chapter 11, and the newest Bluetooth 3.0 standard is fast enough to support multimedia applications, such as transferring music, photos, and videos between computers, mobile phones, and other devices. One interesting emerging Bluetooth application is intended to protect teenagers from texting or talking on their mobile phones while driving—a special Bluetooth-enabled car key prevents the driver's mobile phone from being used while the car is on.

The desktop computer, keyboard, printer, and mouse form a piconet to communicate with each other. The headset and cell phone (not shown in this photo) belong to another piconet.

The headset and cell phone form a piconet when they are within range to communicate with each other.

FIGURE 7-30

Bluetooth. Bluetooth is designed for short-range wireless communications between computers or mobile devices and other hardware.

NET

ONLINE VIDEO

Go to the Chapter 7 page at **www.cengage.com/ computerconcepts/np/uc13** to watch the "What Is Bluetooth?" video clip.

>**Bluetooth.** A networking standard for very short-range wireless connections; the devices are automatically connected once they get within the allowable range.

A new standard that is designed to connect peripheral devices, similar to Bluetooth, but that transfers data more quickly is **wireless USB**. The speed of wireless USB depends on the distance between the devices being used, but is approximately 100 Mbps at 10 meters (about 33 feet) or 480 Mbps at 2 meters (about 6.5 feet). While Bluetooth and wireless USB can be used for similar applications, it is possible they might coexist. For example, wireless USB might be used to connect computer hardware in more permanent setups, while Bluetooth might be used in short-range mobile situations with portable computers and mobile devices. One of the first wireless USB devices to come on the market was the wireless USB hub, shown in Figure 2-17 in Chapter 2.

Ultra Wideband (UWB), WirelessHD (WiHD), and TransferJet

There are several wireless technologies being developed to transfer multimedia content quickly between nearby devices. One example is **Ultra Wideband (UWB)**. Similar to wireless USB (since wireless USB is based on UWB), UWB speeds vary from 100 Mbps at 10 meters (about 33 feet) to 480 Mbps at 2 meters (about 6.5 feet). UWB is especially appropriate for applications that require high-speed transfers over short distances, such as wirelessly delivering multimedia content—such as video, music, and photos—between computers, TVs, digital cameras, DVD players, and more.

Another possibility is **wirelessHD (WiHD)**. Similar to UWB, WiHD is designed for fast transfers of high-definition video between home consumer electronic devices (such as high-definition TVs, set-top boxes, gaming consoles, and DVD players) but it is faster. Backed by seven major electronics companies, WiHD is designed to transfer full-quality uncompressed high-definition audio, video, and data within a single room at speeds up to 25 Gbps, though those speeds have not been obtained yet. WiHD operates at 60 GHz and incorporates a smart antenna system that allows the system to steer the transmission, allowing for non-line-of-sight communications. WiHD aims to help users create an easy to manage wireless video network. Devices that include WiHD capabilities began to become available in 2009.

A new wireless standard designed for very fast transfers between devices that are extremely close together (essentially touching each other) is **TransferJet**. Developed by Sony, TransferJet is designed to quickly transfer large files (such as digital photos, music, and video) between devices as soon as they come in contact with each other, such as to transfer data between mobile phones or between digital cameras, to download music or video from a consumer kiosk or digital signage system to a mobile phone or other mobile device, or to transfer images or video from a digital camera to a TV set or printer. At a maximum speed of 560 Mbps, TransferJet is fast enough to support the transfer of video files. TransferJet-compatible devices are expected to be available by 2010.

FURTHER EXPLORATION

Go to the Chapter 7 page at
**www.cengage.com/
computerconcepts/np/uc13**
for links to information about wireless networking standards.

ZigBee

An emerging networking standard designed for inexpensive and simple short-range networking (particular sensor networks) is *ZigBee (802.15)*. ZigBee is intended for applications that require low data transfer rates and several years of battery life. For instance, ZigBee can be used for home and commercial automation systems to connect a wide variety of devices (such as appliances and lighting, heating, cooling, water, filtration, and security systems), and allows for their control from anywhere in the world. ZigBee is also used in industrial plant manufacturing, personal home healthcare, device tracking, telecommunications, and wireless sensor networks.

ZigBee is designed to accommodate more than 65,000 devices on a single network and supports speeds from 20 Kbps to 250 Kbps, depending on the frequency being used

---

>**Wireless USB.** A wireless version of USB designed to connect peripheral devices. >**Ultra Wideband (UWB).** A networking standard for very short-range wireless connections among multimedia devices. >**WirelessHD (WiHD).** An emerging wireless networking specification designed for connecting home consumer devices. >**TransferJet.** A networking standard for very short-range wireless connections between devices; devices need to touch in order to communicate.

CATEGORY	EXAMPLES	INTENDED PURPOSE	APPROXIMATE RANGE
Short range	Bluetooth Wireless USB	To connect peripheral devices to a mobile phone or computer.	33 feet
	Ultra Wideband (UWB) WirelessHD (WiHD) TransferJet	To connect and transfer multimedia content between home consumer electronic devices (computers, TVs, DVD players, etc.).	1 inch–33 feet
	ZigBee	To connect a variety of home, personal, and commercial automation devices.	33 feet–328 feet
Medium range	Wi-Fi (802.11)	To connect computers and other devices to a local area network.	100–300 feet indoors; 300–900 feet outdoors
Long range	WiMAX Mobile WiMAX	To provide Internet access to a large geographic area for fixed and/or mobile users.	6 miles non-line of sight; 30 miles line of sight
	Cellular standards (2G and 3G)	To connect mobile phones and mobile devices to a cellular network for telephone and Internet service.	10 miles

(several different frequencies are available for ZigBee networks). ZigBee has a range of 10 to 100 meters (about 33 to 328 feet) between devices, depending on power output and environmental characteristics; a wireless mesh configuration can be used to greatly extend the range of the network.

For a summary of the wireless networking standards just discussed, see Figure 7-31.

FIGURE 7-31
Summary of common wireless networking standards.

NETWORKING HARDWARE

Various types of hardware are necessary to create a computer network, to connect multiple networks together, or to connect a computer or network to the Internet. The most common types of networking hardware used in home and small office networks are discussed next.

Network Adapters and Modems

A **network adapter**, also called a **network interface card** (**NIC**) when it is in the form of an expansion card, is used to connect a computer to a network (such as a home or business network). A **modem** (derived from the terms *modulate* and *demodulate*) is used to connect a computer to a network over telephone lines. Technically, to be called a *modem*, a device must convert digital signals (such as those used by a computer) to modulated analog signals (such as those used by conventional telephone lines) and vice versa. However, in everyday use, the term *modem* is also used to refer to any device that connects a computer to a broadband Internet connection, such as a *cable modem* used for cable Internet service. In addition, the term *modem* is often used interchangeably with *network adapter* when describing devices used to obtain Internet access via certain networks, such as cellular or WiMAX networks.

Most computers and mobile devices today come with a network adapter and/or modem built in; the type of network adapter and modem used depends on the type of network (such as Ethernet, Wi-Fi, or 3G) and Internet access being used. For instance, to connect a computer to an Ethernet network, an Ethernet network adapter is used. To connect a

TIP

If your Internet connection slows down, try *power cycling* your modem and router: Unplug the modem and router for 30 seconds, then plug in the modem and wait for 30 seconds, then plug in the router.

> **Network adapter.** A network interface, such as an expansion card or external network adapter. > **Network interface card (NIC).** An expansion card through which a computer can connect to a network. > **Modem.** A device that enables a computer to communicate over analog networking media, such as connecting to the Internet via telephone lines.

Port for twisted-pair Ethernet cable

PCI EXPRESS GIGABIT ETHERNET ADAPTERS FOR DESKTOP COMPUTERS

Connects to USB port

USB WI-FI ADAPTERS FOR DESKTOP OR NOTEBOOK COMPUTERS

Connects via a cable to USB port   Connects to a power outlet

USB POWERLINE ADAPTERS FOR DESKTOP OR NOTEBOOK COMPUTERS

Slides into ExpressCard slot

EXPRESSCARD WI-FI ADAPTERS FOR NOTEBOOK COMPUTERS

Connects to USB port

USB 3G EV-DO MODEMS FOR DESKTOP OR NOTEBOOK COMPUTERS

Incoming coaxial cable from cable provider and either a USB or Ethernet cable coming from the computer or router connect to the back of the modem.

USB/ETHERNET CABLE MODEMS

FIGURE 7-32

Network adapters and modems.

computer to a cable Internet connection, typically both a cable modem and an Ethernet network adapter are used. To connect a computer to a Wi-Fi or WiMAX network or public hotspot, a Wi-Fi or WiMAX network adapter, respectively, is used.

When selecting a network adapter or modem, the type of device being used and the expansion slots and ports available on that device need to be considered as well. For example, network adapters and modems for desktop computers typically come in PCI, PCI Express (PCIe), or USB format, and network adapters and modems for portable computers usually connect via USB or an ExpressCard slot. In addition, the network adapter or modem needs to support the type of networking media (such as twisted-pair cabling, coaxial cabling, or wireless signal) being used. Some examples of network adapters and modems are shown in Figure 7-32.

Switches, Routers, and Other Hardware for Connecting Devices and Networks

A variety of networking hardware is used to connect the devices on a network, as well as to connect multiple networks together. For instance, as mentioned earlier in this chapter, networks using the star topology need a central device to connect all of the devices on the network. In a wired network, this device was originally a *hub*. A hub transmits all data received to all network devices connected to the hub, regardless of which device the data is being sent to, so the bandwidth of the network is shared and the network is not extremely efficient. Today, the central device in a wired network is usually a **switch**. A switch contains ports to which the devices on the network connect (typically via networking cables) and facilitates communications between the devices, similar to a hub. But, unlike hubs, switches identify which device connected to the switch is the one the data is intended

TIP

You can often update the *firmware*—embedded instructions—for a router and other networking hardware to improve performance or obtain new capabilities. Firmware updates are usually downloaded from the manufacturer's site; often router updates need to be installed with a computer connected to the device via a wired, not wireless, connection.

>**Switch.** A device used to connect multiple devices on a single (typically wired) network; forwards packets to only the intended recipient.

for and send the data only to that device, rather than sending data out to all connected devices. Consequently, switches are more efficient than hubs.

To connect multiple networks (such as two LANs, two WANs, or a LAN and the Internet), a **router** is used. Routers pass data on to the intended recipient only and can plan a path through the network to ensure the data reaches its destination in the most efficient manner possible, and are used to route traffic over the Internet.

A **wireless access point** is a device used to grant network access to wireless client devices. In home and small business networks, typically the capabilities of a switch, router, and wireless access point are integrated into a single **wireless router** device. A wireless router (such as the one shown in Figure 7-33) is commonly used to connect both wireless (via Wi-Fi) and wired (via Ethernet cables) devices to a network and to connect that network to an Internet connection. Some broadband modems today include wireless router capabilities to create a wireless network and to provide Internet access using a single piece of hardware. To connect just two LANs together, a **bridge** can be used. The most common use for a bridge in a home network is to wirelessly connect a wired device (such as a home audio/video system, DVR, or gaming console) to a home network via a wireless connection.

There are also routers and other devices used to connect multiple devices to a cellular network. For instance, *3G mobile broadband routers* are used to share a 3G mobile wireless Internet connection with multiple devices (such as your cell phone, personal computer, and handheld gaming device)—essentially creating a Wi-Fi hotpot that connects to your 3G Internet connection. For a closer look at one possibility for wirelessly creating a personal mobile hotspot wherever you are—see the Trend box. Other devices (sometimes called *femtocells*) can be used to route cell phone calls over a broadband network in order to provide better cellular coverage while indoors.

An example of how the devices discussed in this section, as well as the other networking hardware discussed in the next section, might be used in a network is shown in Figure 7-34.

Other Networking Hardware

Additional networking hardware is often needed to extend the range of a network and to share networking media, as discussed next.

Repeaters, Range Extenders, and Antennas

Repeaters are devices that amplify signals along a network. They are necessary whenever signals have to travel farther than would be otherwise possible over the networking medium being used. Repeaters are available for both wired and wireless networks; repeaters for a wireless network are often called **range extenders**. Range extenders usually connect wirelessly to the network and repeat the wireless signal to extend coverage of that network outside or to an additional floor of a building, or to eliminate *dead spots*—areas within the

Wireless devices connect wirelessly

A shared USB printer or external hard drive can connect here

Wired devices connect here

Modem connects here

FIGURE 7-33
Wireless routers.
Typically allow both wired and wireless users access to each other and an Internet connection.

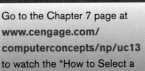

ONLINE VIDEO

Go to the Chapter 7 page at **www.cengage.com/ computerconcepts/np/uc13** to watch the "How to Select a Wireless Router" video clip.

VIDEO PODCAST

Go to the Chapter 7 page at **www.cengage.com/ computerconcepts/np/uc13** to download or listen to the "How To: Set Up a Wireless Network" video podcast.

TIP

When using any type of wireless router, it is very important to secure it against unauthorized access. This and other security precautions are discussed in Chapter 9.

>**Router.** A device that connects multiple networks together; routes packets to their next location in order to efficiently reach their destination.
>**Wireless access point.** A device on a wireless network that connects wireless devices to that network. >**Wireless router.** A router with a built-in wireless access point; most often used to connect wireless devices to a network and an Internet connection and often contains a built-in switch. >**Bridge.** A device used to bridge or connect two LANs; most often used to connect wired devices wirelessly to a network. >**Repeater.** A device on a network that amplifies signals. >**Range extender.** A repeater for a wireless network.

DIAL-UP CUSTOMER

DIAL-UP CUSTOMER

DIAL-UP CUSTOMER

ISP'S CONCENTRATOR

GAMING DEVICES

COMPUTER

COMPUTER

WIRELESS ROUTER
(with built-in 4-port switch)

CABLE MODEM

COMPUTER

HOME NETWORKS
(containing both wired and wireless devices)

ISP

ROUTER

ROUTER

THE INTERNET

ROUTER

ROUTER

ISP

OUTDOOR WIRELESS ACCESS POINT

WIRELESS BRIDGE

SWITCH

SWITCH

WIRELESS ROUTER

MODEM

WIRELESS BRIDGE

SCHOOLS OR BUSINESSES WITH MULTIPLE LANS

FIGURE 7-34

Networking hardware.

As shown in this example, many different types of hardware are used to connect networking devices.

normal network range that don't have coverage. Some *WDS* (*Wireless Distribution System*) wireless access points can be used as range extenders by extending the network coverage from one access point to another.

Another alternative for increasing the range of a Wi-Fi network is using a *higher-gain* (stronger) **antenna**. The MIMO antennas used by many 802.11n routers allow for faster connections and a greater range than typically experienced by 802.11g wireless networks, but sometimes this still isn't enough. Using a network adapter designed for the router being used typically helps the network range to some extent; so does replacing the antenna on the router with a higher-gain antenna or adding an *external antenna* to a networking adapter, if the adapter contains an antenna connector.

> **Antenna.** A device used for receiving or sending radio signals; often used to increase the range of a network.

TREND

Personal Mobile Hotspots

You know you can access Wi-Fi hotspots in many locations, but how about creating your own hotspot whenever you need it? That's now possible with several emerging products designed to create personal mobile hotspots that can be used with any Wi-Fi device, such as notebook computers, mobile phones, and portable gaming devices.

One such product is Verizon Wireless's *MiFi Intelligent Mobile Hotspot*, shown in the accompanying illustration. After its initial setup, this product (about the size of several stacked credit cards) creates a mobile hotspot by just powering up the device. The MiFi device connects to Verizon Wireless's 3G mobile network and provides access to that network for up to five Wi-Fi devices. To those devices, the MiFi hotspot appears as any other Wi-Fi hotspot, so users connect as they normally would. While the cost per MB is relatively expensive and there is currently no unlimited data plan, this device is useful for many situations—such as iPhone users who need to quickly download files larger than the limit allowed via a cellular connection

and so need to use a Wi-Fi connection instead, and families who want to all access the Internet while traveling in a car. With a recent poll indicating that 90% of consumers surveyed prefer Internet access to DVD video players in their cars, it appears that mobile personal hotspots are hot.

Antennas come in a variety of formats and are classified as either *directional antennas* (antennas that concentrate the signal in a particular area) or *omnidirectional antennas* (antennas that are equally effective in all directions). Directional antennas have a farther range than omnidirectional antennas, but have a more limited delivery area. The strength of an antenna is measured in *decibels* (*dB*). For applications where a large Wi-Fi coverage area is needed (such as in a large business or a hotel), high-gain outdoor antennas can be used (in conjunction with outdoor range extenders and access points, if needed) to enable the network to span a larger area than the hardware would normally allow.

> **TIP**
> When buying an external antenna for a device, be sure they are compatible. For instance, 802.11n MIMO routers with three antennas cannot use a single antenna designed for 802.11g devices.

Multiplexers and Concentrators

High-speed communications lines are expensive and almost always have far greater capacity than a single device can use. Because of this, signals from multiple devices are often combined and sent together to share a single communications medium. A *multiplexer* combines the transmissions from several different devices and sends them as one message. For instance, multiple analog signals can be sent at one time by using multiple frequencies, and multiple optical signals can be sent at one time by using multiple wavelengths. Regardless of how the signals are sent, when the combined signal reaches its destination, the individual messages are separated from one another. Multiplexing is frequently used with fiber-optic cables and other high-capacity media to increase data throughput. For instance, if eight signals are multiplexed and sent together over each fiber in one fiber-optic cable, then the throughput of that cable is increased by a factor of eight.

A *concentrator* is a type of multiplexer that combines multiple messages and sends them via a single transmission medium in such a way that all the individual messages are simultaneously active, instead of being sent as a single combined message. For example, ISPs often use concentrators to combine the signals from their conventional dial-up modem customers to be sent over faster communications connections to their Internet destinations.

> **TIP**
> There are also range extenders and antennas designed to extend the range of a cellular network, such as to boost reception inside a home in order to use a cell phone as a primary home telephone.

SUMMARY

WHAT IS A NETWORK?

Communications refers to data being sent from one device to another over a distance—such as over long-distance phone lines, via privately owned cables, or by satellite. A **computer network** is a collection of computers and other hardware devices that are connected together to share hardware, software, and data, as well as to facilitate electronic communications. Computer networks include home networks, business networks, and the Internet.

NETWORKING APPLICATIONS

Some of the oldest networking applications are conventional telephone service and television and radio broadcasting. Many of today's networking applications take place via the Internet. There are, however, a variety of other important business and personal applications that utilize networks. For making phone calls while on the go, **mobile phones**—namely, **cellular** (**cell**) and **satellite phones**—are used; **dual-mode phones** can utilize more than one network, such as placing calls via both a cellular and Wi-Fi network. There are a variety of **global positioning system** (**GPS**) and monitoring system applications used by individuals and businesses; many homes today also have a *multimedia network*. To communicate and work with others remotely, **videoconferencing**, *collaborative computing*, and **telecommuting** applications are used; **telesurgery** and other **telemedicine** applications can be used to provide remote medical care.

NETWORK CHARACTERISTICS

Networks can be either **wired networks** (where devices are physically connected) or **wireless networks** (where devices are connected with wireless signals). Wired networks are found in businesses and some homes; wireless networks are becoming very common in both businesses and homes, and are frequently found in public locations to provide a wireless connection to the Internet. Networks can be classified in terms of their *topology* or physical arrangement (such as a **star network**, **bus network**, or **mesh network**). They can also be classified according to their *architecture* (such as *client-server* networks, which consist of *server* devices that provide network services to *client* computers, or *peer-to-peer* (*P2P*) networks, in which the users' computers and the shared peripherals in the network communicate directly with one another instead of through a server). With *Internet peer-to-peer* (*P2P*) *computing*, files are exchanged directly with other peers via the Internet.

Networks can also be classified by size. **Personal area networks** (**PANs**) connect the devices immediately around an individual; **local area networks** (**LANs**) connect geographically close devices, such as within a single building; **metropolitan area networks** (**MANs**) provide Internet access to cities; and **wide area networks** (**WANs**) span relatively wide geographical areas. Networks classified as **intranets** are private networks that implement the infrastructure and standards of the Internet and the World Wide Web, **extranets** are private networks accessible to authorized outsiders, and **virtual private networks** (**VPNs**) are used to transfer private information over a public communications system.

DATA TRANSMISSION CHARACTERISTICS

Data that travels over a network can use **analog signals** (where data is sent as continuous waves) or **digital signals** (where data is coded as 0s and 1s). Data transmissions can also be characterized by their *bandwidth* (the amount of data that can be transferred at one time), whether it uses **serial transmission** or **parallel transmission**, how serial transmissions are timed (namely, *synchronous*, *asynchronous*, or *isochronous transmission*), and whether it transmits in *simplex*, *half-duplex*, or *full-duplex* directions. Data can also be transferred using *circuit switching*, *packet switching*, or *broadcasting*.

NETWORKING MEDIA

Networking media used with wired networks include **twisted-pair**, **coaxial**, and **fiber-optic cable**. Wireless networks typically send messages through the air in the form of *radio signals* and typically use the frequencies in the *radio frequency* (*RF*) band of the *electromagnetic spectrum*. Wireless signals can be sent using **cellular radio** transmissions (which send and receive data via *cell towers* located within designated areas or *cells*), using **microwave stations** and/or **communications satellites** (which send and receive data to and from microwave stations and satellites), or using **infrared** (**IR**) **transmissions** (which send data over short distances as infrared light rays).

Chapter Objective 5:
Name specific types of wired and wireless networking media and explain how they transmit data.

COMMUNICATIONS PROTOCOLS AND NETWORKING STANDARDS

A *communications protocol* determines how the devices on a network communicate; a networking standard typically addresses both how the devices connect and the communications protocols used. The most common communications protocol is **TCP/IP**—the protocol used with the Internet. The most common networking standard for wired networks is **Ethernet** (**802.3**), which is available in a variety of speeds, as well as the *Power over Ethernet* (*PoE*) standard, which allows both power and data to be transferred via an Ethernet network. Alternatives for wired networks increasingly being used within the home include the *Phoneline* and *Powerline* standards and the emerging universal *G.hn* standard. *Broadband over powerline* (*BPL*) can be used to deliver Internet via the existing power pole infrastructure.

The most common networking standard for home and business wireless LANs is **Wi-Fi** (**802.11**). Wi-Fi is designed for medium-range wireless transmissions, and there are various versions of the standard that support different speeds and distances. When a network with a greater range is needed, **WiMAX** and **mobile WiMAX** can be used. There are a variety of *cellular standards* used with mobile phones; the newest and fastest are *3G* and *4G standards*. For very short-range applications (such as wirelessly connecting a keyboard to a computer), **Bluetooth** can be used. Other standards used to connect devices wirelessly include **Ultra Wideband** (**UWB**) and **WirelessHD** (**WiHD**), which are most often used to connect home electronic devices; **wireless USB**, which is a wireless version of USB used to connect peripheral devices to a computer; and **TransferJet**, which is used to transfer data between devices as they are touched together.

Chapter Objective 6:
Identify the most common communications protocols and networking standards used with networks today.

NETWORKING HARDWARE

Computer networks require a variety of hardware. Computers usually connect to a network through either a **network adapter** (called a **network interface card** (**NIC**) when it is in the form of an expansion card); a **modem** is used to connect to a network via telephone lines, though many devices that connect a computer to the Internet today are commonly referred to as *modems*. The type of network adapter or modem used depends on the type of computer, connection, and networking media being used.

A **switch** is used to connect multiple (typically wired) devices to a network. **Routers** connect multiple devices together; **wireless routers** typically include a router, switch, and **wireless access point** to connect both wireless and wired devices to a network and the Internet. A **bridge** can be used to connect two LANs or a wired device to a wireless network. **Repeaters**, **range extenders**, and **antennas** can be used to extend the range of a network; *multiplexers* and *concentrators* are most commonly used with larger networks.

Chapter Objective 7:
List several types of networking hardware and explain the purpose of each.

NET

REVIEW ACTIVITIES

KEY TERM MATCHING

a. antenna

b. Bluetooth

c. computer network

d. digital transmission

e. Ethernet

f. global positioning system (GPS)

g. mesh network

h. switch

i. TCP/IP

j. WiMAX

Instructions: Match each key term on the left with the definition on the right that best describes it.

1. _____ A collection of computers and other hardware devices that are connected together to share hardware, software, and data, as well as to communicate electronically with one another.

2. _____ A device used for receiving or sending radio signals; often used to increase the range of a network.

3. _____ A device used to connect multiple devices on a single (typically wired) network; forwards packets to only the intended recipient.

4. _____ A networking standard for very short-range wireless connections; the devices are automatically connected once they get within the allowable range.

5. _____ A network in which there are multiple connections between the devices on the network so that messages can take any of several possible paths.

6. _____ An emerging wireless networking standard that is faster and has a greater range than Wi-Fi.

7. _____ A networking protocol that uses packet switching to facilitate the transmission of messages; the protocol used with the Internet.

8. _____ A system that uses satellites and a receiver to determine the exact geographic location of the receiver.

9. _____ A type of data transmission where the data is represented by 0s and 1s.

10. _____ A widely used wired LAN networking standard.

SELF-QUIZ

Instructions: Circle **T** if the statement is true, **F** if the statement is false, or write the best answer in the space provided. **Answers for the self-quiz are located in the References and Resources Guide at the end of the book.**

1. **T F** GPS systems are used only by the government.

2. **T F** With serial transmissions, each bit of data is sent individually.

3. **T F** The Internet is an example of a LAN.

4. **T F** The type of cable used inside most homes for telephone service is twisted-pair wire.

5. **T F** A router is a type of modem.

6. With a(n) _____ network topology, all devices are connected in a line to a central cable.

7. A(n) _____ phone can be used with more than one communications network, such as with both a cellular and Wi-Fi network.

8. A small network designed to connect the personal devices for an individual (such as via Bluetooth) is called a(n) _____.

9. A(n) _____ is a network that transfers private information securely over the Internet or other public network.

10. Match each description to its networking application, and write the corresponding number in the blank to the left of the description.

   a. _____ To diagnose a patient from a distance.

   b. _____ To work for a company in New York when you live in California.

   c. _____ To watch a TV show in the living room that is recorded on your computer.

   d. _____ To receive telephone calls while you are out shopping.

   e. _____ To determine your physical location while hiking in the mountains.

1. Multimedia networking
2. GPS
3. Telemedicine
4. Telecommuting
5. Cellular phone

EXERCISES

1. Match each description to its networking hardware, and write the corresponding number in the blank to the left of each description.

   a. _____ A device used to connect network devices via cabling.

   b. _____ A device that enables a computer to communicate over telephone lines.

   c. _____ A device used to connect wireless devices to a wired network.

   d. _____ A device used to amplify signals on a network.

1. Repeater
2. Modem
3. Switch
4. Wireless access point

2. Match each description to the networking standard most suited for this purpose, and write the corresponding number in the blank to the left of each description.

   a. _____ To connect a portable computer to a wireless hotspot.

   b. _____ To connect a wireless keyboard to a computer.

   c. _____ To create a wired home or business network.

   d. _____ To wirelessly connect home entertainment devices.

1. Bluetooth
2. Wi-Fi
3. Ultra Wideband (UWB)
4. Ethernet

3. If you need to transfer a 35 MB file from one computer to another over a Fast Ethernet network that supports data transfer rates of 100 Mbps, how long should it take to download the file? What real-world conditions might affect this download time?

4. What is the most common use of the TCP/IP networking standard?

5. Explain the difference between Wi-Fi and Bluetooth, including speed, range, and the purpose of each networking standard.

DISCUSSION QUESTIONS

1. As discussed in the chapter, Internet peer-to-peer (P2P) networking involves sharing files and other resources directly with other computers via the Internet. While some content is legally exchanged via an Internet P2P network, some content (such as movies and music) is exchanged illegally. Should Internet P2P networks be regulated to ensure they are used for only legal activities? Why or why not? If a P2P network set up for legitimate use is used for illegal purposes, should the organization or person who set up the P2P network be responsible? Would you want to use an Internet P2P network?

2. Interference with wireless devices is happening much more often than in the past. For instance, unlicensed walkie-talkies used on TV sets have interfered with police radios, and British air traffic control transmissions have been interrupted by transmissions from nearby baby monitors. If devices that use unlicensed radio frequencies interfere with each other, whose fault is it? The individual for buying multiple products that use the same radio frequency? The manufacturers for not ensuring their products can switch channels as needed to use a free channel? The government for allowing unregulated airwaves? Is there a solution to this problem? Who, if anyone, should be responsible for fixing this problem?

NET

PROJECTS

HOT TOPICS

1. **WiMAX vs. Wi-Fi** As discussed in the chapter, WiMAX and Wi-Fi are both wireless networking standards.

   For this project, research WiMAX and Wi-Fi to determine their current status and the differences between the two standards. Are they designed for the same or different purposes? Explain. How are they being used today? Do you think the standards will coexist in the future, or will one eventually replace the other? At the conclusion of your research, prepare a one-page summary of your findings and opinions and submit it to your instructor.

SHORT ANSWER/ RESEARCH

2. **Unwired** As discussed in the chapter, home networks—particularly wireless home networks—are becoming very common today.

   For this project, suppose that you have a home desktop computer and you are planning to buy a notebook computer to use at home, as well as on the go. You would like to network the two computers wirelessly. Determine the hardware you will need to accomplish this. Create a labeled sketch of the network and a list of the hardware you would need to acquire. Next, research the approximate cost of the hardware to determine the overall cost of the network. Does the cost seem reasonable for the benefits? Would you want to network your home computers in this manner? If you also wanted to use a printer with both computers, would you need any additional hardware? Why or why not? At the conclusion of your research, prepare a one-page summary of your findings and submit it to your instructor, along with your sketch and list of hardware.

HANDS ON

3. **Geocaching** Geocaching is a GPS application that is essentially a form of high-tech hide and seek—someone hides a water-tight container filled with a "treasure" (usually toys or cheap collectors' goodies) and posts the location of the cache (in GPS coordinates) on a geocaching Web site. Other individuals use their GPS equipment to find the cache and then sign a log (if one is included in the cache), take an item from the cache, and put another object into the cache as a replacement.

   For this project, find out how to geocache, including the required equipment and any "rules" or courtesies common among geocachers regarding listing or finding a cache, by searching online or visiting a geocaching Web site (such as **www.geocaching.com**). Next, use a geocaching site to find information about a cache currently hidden close to your city and determine what you would need to do in order to find it. At the conclusion of your research, prepare a one-page summary of your findings and submit it to your instructor.

4. **Net Neutrality and Your ISP** The term *net neutrality* refers to the equality of data as it is transferred over the Internet. For instance, the data from an individual and the data from Microsoft are treated the same. A recent controversy surrounding the cable giant Comcast brought up the possibility of ISPs interfering with the delivery of Internet data. According to complaints by customers, Comcast has been blocking the use of P2P sites like BitTorrent to download movies, music, and other large files. Comcast, like most ISPs, includes a statement in its terms of service that allows it to use tools to "efficiently manage its networks", in order to prevent those customers using a higher than normal level of bandwidth from interfering with the access of other customers. However, the Comcast issue was considered by many to be a blatant net neutrality issue—blocking access to multimedia from sources other than its own cable sources. Do you think the actions taken by Comcast were ethical? Does an ISP have a right to block selected Internet traffic? Why or why not? Was there a more ethical way Comcast could have handled the problem of some users consuming a higher than normal level of bandwidth?

For this project, form an opinion about the ethical ramifications of ISPs blocking selected Internet traffic and be prepared to discuss your position (in class, via an online class discussion group, in a class chat room, or via a class blog, depending on your instructor's directions). You may also be asked to write a short paper expressing your opinion.

ETHICS IN ACTION

5. **Wired Home Network** If you have two or more computers at home and want to share files, an Internet connection, or a printer, you will need to set up a home network. Although a wireless network is an option, wired networks still exist and new options for wired networks are emerging.

For this project, suppose that you want to set up a wired home network. Create a scenario (real or fictitious) that describes the number of computers and other devices involved, where each item is located, and the tasks for which the network will be used. Select a wired networking option (such as Ethernet, Powerline, or Phoneline) and determine the steps and equipment necessary to implement that network for your scenario. Be sure to include the cost of the necessary hardware and how the network would be physically installed. Share your findings (including a diagram of your proposed network) with your class in the form of a presentation. The presentation should not exceed 10 minutes and should make use of one or more presentation aids, such as the chalkboard, handouts, overhead transparencies, or a computer-based slide presentation (your instructor may provide additional requirements). You may also be asked to submit a summary of the presentation to your instructor.

PRESENTATION/ DEMONSTRATION

Instructions: Go to the Chapter 7 page at **www.cengage.com/computerconcepts/np/uc13** to work the following Web Activities.

6. **Interactive Activities** Work the interactive **Crossword Puzzle**, watch the **Video Podcasts** and **Online Videos**, and explore the **Further Exploration** links associated with this chapter.

If you have a SAM user profile, you may have access to hands-on instruction, practice, and assessment of the skills covered in this chapter. Check with your instructor for instructions and the correct URL/Web site to access those assignments.

7. **Student Edition Labs** Work the following interactive **Student Edition Labs.**
   - ➤ **Networking Basics**   ➤ **Wireless Networking**

8. **Test Yourself** Review the **Online Study Guide** for this chapter, then test your knowledge of the terms and concepts covered in this chapter by completing the **Key Term Matching** exercise, the **Self-Quiz**, the **Exercises**, and the **Practice Test.**

WEB ACTIVITIES

Student Edition Labs

chapter 8

The Internet and the World Wide Web

After completing this chapter, you will be able to do the following:

1. Discuss how the Internet evolved and what it is like today.

2. Identify the various types of individuals, companies, and organizations involved in the Internet community and explain their purposes.

3. Describe device and connection options for connecting to the Internet, as well as some considerations to keep in mind when selecting an ISP.

4. Understand how to search effectively for information on the Internet and how to cite Internet resources properly.

5. List several ways to communicate over the Internet, in addition to e-mail.

6. List several useful activities that can be performed via the Web.

7. Discuss censorship and privacy, and how they are related to Internet use.

http:

outline

Overview

Evolution of the Internet
From ARPANET to Internet2
The Internet Community Today
Myths About the Internet

Getting Set Up to Use the Internet
Type of Device
Type of Connection and Internet Access
Selecting an ISP and Setting Up Your Computer

Searching the Internet
Search Sites
Search Strategies
Evaluating Search Results
Citing Internet Resources

Beyond Browsing and E-Mail
Other Types of Online Communications
Social Networking
Online Shopping and Investing
Online Entertainment
Online News, Reference, and Information
Online Education and Writing

Censorship and Privacy Issues
Censorship
Web Browsing Privacy
E-Mail Privacy

OVERVIEW

With the prominence of the Internet in our personal and professional lives today, it is hard to believe that there was a time not too long ago that few people had even heard of the Internet, let alone used it. But technology is continually evolving and, in fact, it is only relatively recently that it has evolved enough to allow the use of multimedia applications—such as downloading music and movies, watching TV and videos, and playing multimedia interactive games—over the Internet to become everyday activities. Today, the Internet and the World Wide Web are household words, and, in many ways, they have redefined how people think about computers, communications, and the availability of news and information.

Despite the popularity of the Internet, however, many users cannot answer some important basic questions about it. What makes up the Internet? Is it the same thing as the World Wide Web? How did the Internet begin, and where is it heading? How can the Internet be used to find specific information? This chapter addresses these types of questions and more.

Chapter 8 begins with a discussion of the evolution of the Internet, followed by a look at the many individuals, companies, and organizations that make up the Internet community. Next, the chapter covers different options for connecting to the Internet, including the types of devices, Internet connections, and ISPs that are available today. Then, one of the most important Internet skills you should acquire—efficient Internet searching—is discussed. To help you appreciate the wide spectrum of resources and activities available over the Internet, we also take a brief look at some of the most common applications available via the Internet. The chapter closes with a discussion of a few of the important societal issues that apply to Internet use. ■

EVOLUTION OF THE INTERNET

The **Internet** is a worldwide collection of separate, but interconnected, networks accessed daily by millions of people using a variety of devices to obtain information, disseminate information, access entertainment, or communicate with others. While *Internet* has become a household word only during the past two decades or so, it has actually operated in one form or another for much longer than that.

From ARPANET to Internet2

The roots of the Internet began with an experimental project called *ARPANET*. The Internet we know today is the result of the evolution of ARPANET and the creation of the *World Wide Web* (WWW).

>**Internet.** The largest and most well-known computer network, linking millions of computers all over the world.

ARPANET

The U.S. Department of Defense *Advanced Research Projects Agency* (*ARPA*) created **ARPANET** in 1969. One objective of the ARPANET project was to create a computer network that would allow researchers located in different places to communicate with each other. Another objective was to build a computer network capable of sending or receiving data over a variety of paths to ensure that network communications could continue even if part of the network was destroyed, such as in a nuclear attack or by a natural disaster.

Initially, ARPANET connected four supercomputers and enabled researchers at a few dozen academic institutions to communicate with each other and with government agencies. As the project grew during the next decade, students were granted access to ARPANET as hundreds of college and university networks were connected to it. These networks consisted of a mixture of different computers so, over the years, protocols were developed for tying this mix of computers and networks together, for transferring data over the network, and for ensuring that data was transferred intact. Additional networks soon connected to ARPANET, and this *internet*—or network of networks—eventually evolved into the present day Internet.

The Internet infrastructure today can be used for a variety of purposes, such as researching topics of interest; exchanging e-mail and instant messages; participating in videoconferences and making telephone calls; downloading software, music, and movies; purchasing goods and services; watching TV and video online; accessing computers remotely; and sharing files with others. Most of these activities are available through the primary Internet resource—the *World Wide Web* (*WWW*).

The World Wide Web

In its early years, the Internet was used primarily by the government, scientists, and educational institutions. Despite its popularity in academia and with government researchers, the Internet went virtually unnoticed by the public and the business community for over two decades because 1) it required a computer and 2) it was hard to use (see the left image in Figure 8-1). As always, however, computer and networking technology improved and new applications quickly followed. Then, in 1989, a researcher named *Tim Berners-Lee* proposed the idea of the **World Wide Web** (**WWW**). He envisioned the World Wide Web as a way to organize information in the form of pages linked together through selectable text or images (today's hyperlinks) on the screen. Although the introduction of Web pages did not replace all other Internet resources (such as e-mail and collections of downloadable files), it became a popular way for researchers to provide written information to others.

In 1993, a group of professors and students at the University of Illinois *National Center for Supercomputing Applications* (*NCSA*) released the *Mosaic* Web browser. Soon after, use

Ⓥ FIGURE 8-1

Using the Internet: Back in the "old days" versus now.

EARLY 1990s
Even at the beginning of the 1990s, using the Internet for most people meant learning how to work with a cryptic sequence of commands. Virtually all information was text-based.

TODAY
Today's Web organizes much of the Internet's content into easy-to-read pages that can contain text, graphics, animation, video, and interactive content that users access via hyperlinks.

> **ARPANET.** The predecessor of the Internet, named after the Advanced Research Projects Agency (ARPA), which sponsored its development.
> **World Wide Web (WWW).** The collection of Web pages available through the Internet.

of the World Wide Web began to increase dramatically because Mosaic's graphical user interface (GUI) and its ability to display images on Web pages made using the World Wide Web both easier and more fun than in the past. Today's Web pages are a true multimedia, interactive, experience (see the right image in Figure 8-1). They can contain text, graphics, animation, sound, video, and three-dimensional virtual reality objects.

A growing number of today's Web-based applications and services are referred to as *Web 2.0* applications. Although there is no precise definition, Web 2.0 generally refers to applications and services that use the Web as a platform to deliver rich applications that enable people to collaborate, socialize, and share information online. Some Web 2.0 applications (such as cloud computing) have been discussed in previous chapters; others (such as *social networking sites, RSS feeds, podcasts, blogs*, and *wikis*) are covered later in this chapter.

Although the Web is only part of the Internet, it is by far the most widely used part. Today, most companies regard their use of the Internet and their World Wide Web presence as indispensable competitive business tools, and many individuals view the Internet—and especially the Web—as a vital research, communications, and entertainment medium.

One remarkable characteristic of both the Internet and World Wide Web is that they are not owned by any person or business, and no single person, business, or organization is in charge. Web pages are developed by individuals and organizations, and are hosted on Web servers owned by individuals, schools, businesses, or other entities. Each network connected to the Internet is privately owned and managed individually by that network's administrator, and the primary infrastructure that makes up the *Internet backbone* is typically owned by communications companies, such as telephone and cable companies. In addition, the computers and other devices used to access the Internet belong to individuals or organizations. So, while individual components of the Internet are owned by individuals and organizations, the Internet as a whole has no owner or network administrator. The closest the Internet comes to having a governing body is a group of organizations that are involved with issues such as establishing the protocols used on the Internet, making recommendations for changes, and encouraging cooperation between and coordinating communications among the networks connected to the Internet.

ASK THE EXPERT

i'm lovin' it

Dave Weick, Senior Vice President, Chief Information Officer, McDonald's Corporation

How important is it for a business to have a Web site today if it doesn't sell products and services online?

For McDonald's, our online presence is about extending the McDonald's experience to our customers. Mcdonalds.com allows our customers another channel to engage with our brand without ever entering a restaurant. Through our Web site, customers can find promotions and nutritional information on all of our products. On the Open for Discussion blog, customers are talking about McDonald's corporate sustainability efforts. Happymeal.com is connecting kids across the globe in fun, interactive, and uniquely McDonald's ways. Finally, customers can download podcasts about food safety.

For McDonald's, our Web site allows us the opportunity to connect with our customers on topics that are important to them and in the way that they want to connect. In addition, in some parts of the world you can order off the menu located on our Web site and have it delivered to your door. As our customers demand even more convenience and control over the "ordering process," this may become even more prevalent in the future.

Internet2

Internet2 is a consortium of researchers, educators, and technology leaders from industry, government, and the international community that is dedicated to the development of revolutionary Internet technologies. Internet2 uses high-performance networks linking over 200 member institutions to deploy and test new network applications and capabilities. It is important to realize, however, that the Internet2 network is not a new network designed to eventually replace the Internet—it is simply a research and development tool to help develop technologies that ensure the Internet in the future can handle tomorrow's applications. Much of Internet2 research is focused on speed. For instance, the *Internet2 Land Speed Record* is an ongoing contest for the highest-bandwidth end-to-end network. The current record is an average speed of 9.08 Gbps while transferring 20.42 TB of data across about 30,000 miles of network.

The Internet Community Today

The Internet community today consists of individuals, businesses, and a variety of organizations located throughout the world. Virtually anyone with a computer or other Web-enabled device can be part of the Internet, either as a user or as a supplier of information or services. Most members of the Internet community fall into one or more of the following groups.

Users

Users are people who use the Internet to retrieve content or perform online activities, such as to look up a telephone number, read the day's news headlines or top stories, browse through an online catalog, make an online purchase, download a music file, watch an online video, make a phone call, or send an e-mail message. According to the Pew Internet & American Life Project, approximately 75% of the United States population are Internet users, using the Internet at work, home, school, or another location. The availability of low-cost computers, low-cost or free Internet access (such as at libraries, school, and other public locations), and bundled pricing for obtaining Internet service in conjunction with telephone and/or television service has helped Internet use begin to approach the popularity and widespread use of telephones and TVs.

Internet Service Providers (ISPs)

Internet service providers (**ISPs**) are businesses or other organizations (see some examples in Figure 8-2) that provide Internet access to others, typically for a fee. ISPs (sometimes called *wireless ISPs* or *WISPs* when referring to ISPs that offer service via a wireless network) include most communications and media companies, such as conventional and mobile phone companies, cable providers, and satellite providers. Some ISPs (such as cable and cellular phone companies) offer Internet service over their private networks; other ISPs provide Internet service over the regular telephone lines or the airwaves. While many ISPs (such as Road Runner and EarthLink) provide service nationwide, others provide service to a more limited geographical area. Regardless of their delivery method and geographical coverage, ISPs are the onramp to the Internet, providing their subscribers with access to the World Wide Web, e-mail, and other Internet resources. In addition to Internet access, some ISPs provide proprietary online services available only to their subscribers. A later section of this chapter covers ISPs in more detail, including factors to consider when selecting an ISP.

Ⓥ FIGURE 8-2

Companies that provide Internet access today include telephone, cable, and satellite companies.

wireless broadband

Internet Content Providers

Internet content providers supply the information that is available through the Internet. Internet content providers can be commercial businesses, nonprofit organizations, educational institutions, individuals, and more. Some examples of Internet content providers are listed next.

> ➤ A photographer who posts samples of her best work on a Web page.

> ➤ An individual who publishes his opinion on various subjects to an online journal or *blog*.

>**Internet service provider (ISP).** A business or other organization that provides Internet access to others, typically for a fee. >**Internet content provider.** A person or an organization that provides Internet content.

> ➤ A software company that creates a Web site to provide product information and software downloads.

> ➤ A national news organization that maintains an online site to provide up-to-the-minute news, feature stories, and video clips.

> ➤ A television network that develops a site for its TV shows, including episode summaries, cast information, and links to watch past episodes online.

Application Service Providers (ASPs) and Web Services

Application service providers (ASPs) are companies that manage and distribute Web-based software services to customers over the Internet. Instead of providing access to the Internet like ISPs do, ASPs provide access to software applications via the Internet. In essence, ASPs rent access to software programs to companies or individuals—typically, customers pay a monthly or yearly fee to use each application. As discussed in Chapter 6, this software can be called *Web-based software, Software as a Service (SaaS)*, and *cloud-ware*. Common ASP applications for businesses include office suites, collaboration and communications software, accounting programs, and e-commerce software.

One type of self-contained business application designed to work over the Internet or a company network is a **Web service**. A Web service can be added to Web pages to provide a service that would otherwise not be feasible (such as the inclusion of mapping information on a Web site or in a Web application using Microsoft's *MapPoint .NET Web service*). A Web service can also be used to provide a service via a user's computer and the Internet. For instance, the *FedEx QuickShip Web service* allows users to create a shipment to any Microsoft Outlook contact from within Microsoft Outlook (by right-clicking the contact's name, as shown in Figure 8-3, or using the FedEx QuickShip toolbar displayed in Microsoft Outlook); the toolbar can also be used to track packages, order pickups, check rates, and more. It is important to realize that Web services are not stand-alone applications and, therefore, do not have a user interface—they are simply a standardized way of allowing different applications and computers to share data and processes via a network so they can work together with other Web services and be used with many different computer systems. A company that provides Web services is sometimes referred to as a *Web services provider*.

FIGURE 8-3

Web services. Once downloaded and installed, this Web service allows users to create and manage FedEx shipments from within Microsoft Outlook.

The QuickShip toolbar can be used for a variety of shipping tasks.

Right-click a contact to create a shipment to that individual.

Infrastructure Companies

Infrastructure companies are the enterprises that own or operate the paths or "roadways" along which Internet data travels, such as the Internet backbone and the communications networks connected to it. Examples of infrastructure companies include conventional and mobile phone companies, cable companies, and satellite Internet providers.

Hardware and Software Companies

A wide variety of hardware and software companies make and distribute the products used with the Internet and Internet activities. For example, companies that create or sell the software used in conjunction with the Internet (such as Web browsers, e-mail programs, e-commerce and multimedia software, and Web development tools) fall into this category. So, too, do the companies that make the hardware (network adapters, modems, cables, routers, servers, computers, and mobile phones, for instance) that is used with the Internet.

The Government and Other Organizations

Many organizations influence the Internet and its uses. Governments have the most visible impact; their laws can limit both the information made available via Web servers located in a particular country and the access individuals residing in that country have to the Internet. For example, in France, it is illegal to sell items or post online content related to racist groups or activities; in China there are tight controls imposed on what information is published on Web servers located in China, as well as on the information available to its citizens. And in the United States, anything illegal offline (illegal drugs, child pornography, and so forth) is illegal online.

Legal rulings also can have a large impact on the communications industry in general. For example, the 1968 *Carterfone Decision* allowed companies other than AT&T to utilize the AT&T infrastructure and the 1996 *Telecommunications Act* deregulated the entire communications industry so that telephone companies, cable TV and satellite operators, and firms in other segments of the industry were free to enter each other's markets. A petition to apply the Carterfone Decision to wireless networks in order to allow open access to wireless networks so that any phone can be used with any network is under consideration now by the Federal Communications Commission (FCC). In addition to making these types of decisions, the FCC also greatly influences the communications industry through its ability to allocate radio frequencies (as discussed in Chapter 7) and to implement policies and regulations related to interstate and international communications via radio, television, wire, satellite, and cable. The ability of the government to approve or block potential mergers between communications companies and to break apart companies based on antitrust law to prevent new monopolies also impacts the Internet and communications industry.

Key Internet organizations are responsible for many aspects of the Internet. For example, the *Internet Society* (*ISOC*) provides leadership in addressing issues that may impact the future of the Internet. It also oversees the groups responsible for Internet infrastructure standards, such as determining the protocols that can be used and how Internet addresses are constructed. *ICANN* (*Internet Corporation for Assigned Names and Numbers*) coordinates activities related to the Internet's naming system, such as IP address allocation and domain name management. The *World Wide Web Consortium* (*W3C*) is a group of over 450 organizations dedicated to developing new protocols and specifications to promote the evolution of the Web and to ensure its interoperability. In addition, many colleges and universities support Internet research and manage blocks of the Internet's resources.

Myths About the Internet

Because the Internet is so unique in the history of the world—and its content and applications keep evolving—several widespread myths about it have surfaced.

Myth 1: The Internet Is Free

This myth stems from the fact that there has traditionally been no cost associated with accessing online content—such as news and product information—or with e-mail exchange, other than what the Internet users pay their ISPs for Internet access. And many people—such as students, employees, and consumers who opt for free Internet service or use free access available at public libraries or other public locations—pay nothing for Internet access. Yet it should also be obvious that someone, somewhere, has to pay to keep the Internet up and running.

Businesses, schools, public libraries, and most home users pay Internet service providers flat monthly fees to connect to the Internet. In addition, businesses, schools, libraries, and other large organizations might have to lease high-capacity communications lines (such as from a telephone company) to support their high level of Internet traffic.

Mobile users that want Internet access while on the go typically pay hotspot providers or mobile phone providers for this access. ISPs, phone companies, cable companies, and other organizations that own part of the Internet infrastructure pay to keep their parts of the Internet running smoothly. ISPs also pay software and hardware companies for the resources they need to support their subscribers. Eventually, most of these costs are passed along to end users through ISP fees. ISPs that offer free Internet access typically obtain revenue by selling on-screen ads that display on the screen when the service is being used.

Another reason that the idea the Internet is free is a myth is the growing trend of subscription or per-use fees to access Web-based resources. For instance, downloadable music and movies are very common today (see Figure 8-4) and some journal or newspaper articles require a fee to view them online. In fact, some newspapers and magazines have moved entirely online and most charge a subscription fee to view the level of content that was previously published in a print version. In lieu of a mandatory fee, some Web sites request a donation for use of the site. Many experts expect the use of fee-based Internet content to continue to grow at a rapid pace.

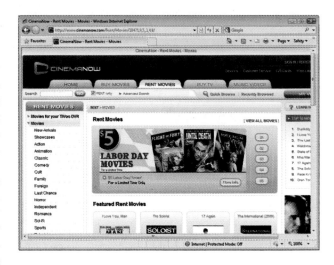

FIGURE 8-4
Fee-based Web content. The use of fee-based Web content, such as downloadable movies and music, is growing.

Myth 2: Someone Controls the Internet

As already discussed, no single group or organization controls the Internet. Governments in each country have the power to regulate the content and use of the Internet within their borders, as allowed by their laws. However, legislators often face serious obstacles getting legislation passed into law—let alone getting it enforced. Making governmental control even harder is the "bombproof" design of the Internet itself. If a government tries to block access to or from a specific country or Web site, for example, users can use a third party (such as an individual located in another country or a different Web site) to circumvent the block. This occurred recently in Iran when the Iranian government blocked access to social networking sites after the 2009 elections—some Iranian citizens were able to send and read Twitter updates via third-party sites.

Myth 3: The Internet and the World Wide Web Are Identical

Since you can now use a Web browser to access most of the Internet's resources, many people think the Internet and the Web are the same thing. Even though in everyday use many people use the terms *Internet* and *Web* interchangeably, they are not the same thing. Technically, the Internet is the physical network, and the Web is the collection of Web pages accessible over the Internet. A majority of Internet activities today take place via Web pages, but there are Internet resources other than the Web that are not accessed via a Web browser. For instance, files can be uploaded and downloaded using an *FTP (File Transfer Protocol) program* and conventional e-mail can be accessed using an e-mail program.

GETTING SET UP TO USE THE INTERNET

Getting set up to use the Internet typically involves three decisions—determining the type of device you will use to access the Internet, deciding which type of connection is desired, and selecting the Internet service provider to be used. Once these determinations have been made, your computer can be set up to access the Internet.

Type of Device

The Internet today can be accessed using a variety of devices. The type of device used depends on a combination of factors, such as the devices available to you, if you need

NET

INSIDE THE INDUSTRY

ISP Bandwidth Limits

Internet traffic has increased tremendously recently as individuals are watching TV and videos online, downloading music and movies, playing online multiplayer gaming, using online backup services, and otherwise performing high-bandwidth activities (see the accompanying illustration). This has created the issue of ISPs potentially running out of bandwidth available for customers, resulting in outages or delays. In response, some ISPs have, at times, blocked selected traffic to and from their customers, such as cable giant Comcast blocking the use of P2P sites like BitTorrent that is often used to download movies, music, and other large files. Other ISPs are slowing down traffic to and from heavy users during peak Internet usage periods or experimenting with *bandwidth caps* as Internet usage management tools. For instance, Comcast is currently testing slowing down traffic to and from heavy users during peak periods, Time Warner Cable is testing tiered pricing based on usage in certain areas, and AT&T is testing bandwidth caps for new customers in certain areas. With a bandwidth cap, customers either temporarily lose Internet access or are charged an additional fee if they exceed their download limit (often 5 GB to 150 GB per month).

Comcast, like most ISPs, includes a statement in its terms of service agreement that allows it to use tools to "efficiently manage its networks" in order to prevent customers from using a higher than normal level of bandwidth. However, many considered Comcast's blocking of P2P content to be a blatant *net neutrality* issue since Comcast was blocking access to multimedia from a source other than its own cable source and the Internet is designed for all content to be treated equally. There are also concerns about bandwidth caps and that overcharges will grow to an unreasonable level—particularly by cable companies and other providers who may want to stifle Internet multimedia to protect their TV advertising revenues. To protect against this, the *Broadband Internet Fairness Act* has been introduced in the U.S. to require broadband providers to submit tiered pricing plans to the FTC to ensure they are not unreasonable or discriminatory. While it is unclear at this time as to the outcome of this bill, as well as whether or not bandwidth caps will be part of the future of home Internet service, it is clear that, as Internet usage by the average consumer continues to grow, the issue of a finite amount of Internet bandwidth versus an increasing demand for online multimedia content will remain.

Online TV, videos, and other multimedia content require a great deal of bandwidth.

access just at home or while on the go, and what types of Internet content you want to access. Some possible devices are shown in Figure 8-5 and discussed next.

Personal Computers

Most users who have access to a personal computer (such as a desktop or notebook computer) at home, work, or school will use it to access the Internet. One advantage of using personal computers for Internet access is that they have relatively large screens for viewing Internet content, and they typically have a full keyboard for easier data entry. They can also be used to view or otherwise access virtually any Web page content, such as graphics, animation, music files, games, and video clips. In addition, they typically have a large hard drive and are connected to a printer so Web pages, e-mail messages, and downloaded files can be saved and/or printed easily.

Mobile Phones

Mobile phones are increasingly being used to view Web page content, exchange e-mail and instant messages, and download music and other online content. In fact, mobile Web

PERSONAL COMPUTERS

MOBILE PHONES

TELEVISIONS

FIGURE 8-5
A variety of devices can be used to access the Internet.

use—or *wireless Web*, as it is sometimes called—is one of the fastest growing uses of the Internet today. While mobile phones are convenient to use on the go, they typically have a relatively small display screen. Some devices include a built-in or sliding keyboard for easier data entry; others utilize pen or touch input instead.

Gaming Devices and Televisions

Another option is using a gaming device (such as a gaming console or handheld gaming device) to access Web content, in addition to using that device to play games. For instance, the Sony PlayStation 3, Sony PSP, Nintendo Wii, and Nintendo DSi all have Web browsers that can be used to access Web content. In addition to gaming consoles that can connect to television sets to display Internet content, an emerging option is *broadband-enabled TVs* that have Internet capabilities built-in in order to display Web pages and other Web content (such as the weather, stock quote, and other information displayed at the bottom of the TV screen shown in Figure 8-5) without any additional hardware.

Type of Connection and Internet Access

In order to use the Internet, your computer needs to be connected to it. Typically, this occurs by connecting the computer or other device you are using to a computer or a network (usually belonging to your ISP, school, or employer) that is connected continually to the Internet.

As discussed in Chapter 7, there are a variety of wired and wireless ways to connect to another device. Most types of connections today are *broadband* or high-speed connections. In fact, more than 60% of all home Internet connections in the U.S. are broadband connections, and that percentage is expected to climb to 77% by 2012, according to a recent Gartner study. As applications requiring high-speed connections continue to grow in popularity, access to broadband Internet speeds are needed in order to take full advantage of these applications. For instance, high-definition television, video-on-demand (VOD), and other multimedia applications all benefit from fast broadband connections (see Figure 8-6). For a look at a topic related to the increased use of multimedia Internet content—*ISP bandwidth limits*—see the Inside the Industry box.

FIGURE 8-6
Length of time to download a 1.5 GB movie using different home Internet options.

The difference between *dial-up* and *direct* Internet connections are discussed next, followed by an overview of the most common types of Internet connections used for personal use today; these types of Internet connections are also summarized in Figure 8-7. Many providers today offer bundles (such as cable TV, telephone, and Internet service) to lower an individual's overall total cost for the services. Additional home Internet alternatives—such

TYPE OF INTERNET CONNECTION	AVAILABILITY	APPROXIMATE MAXIMUM SPEED*	APPROXIMATE MONTHLY PRICE
Conventional dial-up	Anywhere there is telephone service	56 Kbps	Free–$20
Cable	Virtually anywhere cable TV service is available	5–20 Mbps	$40–60
DSL	Within 3 miles of a switching station that supports DSL	1–7 Mbps	$20–40
Satellite	Anywhere there is a clear view to the southern sky and where a satellite dish can be mounted and receive a signal	1–1.5 Mbps	$60–80
Fixed wireless	Selected areas where service is available	1–2 Mbps	$40–60
Broadband over fiber (BoF)	Anywhere fiber has been installed to the building	10–50 Mbps	$50–145
Mobile wireless (3G)	Virtually anywhere cellular phone service is available	700 Kbps–1.7 Mbps	Varies greatly; often bundled with mobile phone service

* Download speed; most connections have slower upload speeds.

FIGURE 8-7
Typical home Internet connection options.

TIP

Sign up for and set up your computer to use a free dial-up Internet account (such as from NetZero) to have a backup Internet service if your regular Internet service ever goes down.

as the emerging *broadband over power lines* (*BPL*) standard discussed in Chapter 7, which allows people to connect to the Internet through their power outlets—will likely be available in the future.

Dial-Up vs. Direct Connections

While some Internet connections are *dial-up connections* (in which your computer dials up and connects to your ISP's computer only when needed), most are *direct* (or *always-on*) *connections* (in which you have a continuous connection to your ISP).

Dial-up connections usually work over standard telephone lines. To connect to the Internet, your computer dials its modem and then connects to a modem attached to a computer belonging to your ISP via the telephone lines. While you are connected to your ISP, your computer can access Internet resources. To end your Internet session, you disconnect from your ISP. One advantage of a dial-up connection is security. Since you are not continually connected to the Internet, it is much less likely that anyone (such as a *hacker*, as discussed in Chapter 9) will gain access to your computer via the Internet, either to access the data located on your computer or, more commonly, to use your computer in some type of illegal or unethical manner. However, dial-up connections are much slower than other types of connections; they are also inconvenient, since you have to instruct your computer to dial up your ISP every time you want to connect to the Internet. Also, your telephone line will be tied up while you are accessing the Internet, unless you have a second phone line. The most common type of dial-up Internet service is *conventional dial-up*.

Direct connections keep you continually connected to your provider and, therefore, continually connected to the Internet. With a direct connection (such as *cable, DSL, satellite,* or *fixed wireless*), you access the Internet simply by opening a Web browser, such as Internet Explorer, Chrome, or Firefox. Direct Internet connections are typically broadband connections, are commonly used in homes and businesses, and are often connected to a LAN to share the Internet connection with multiple devices within the home or business. Because direct connections keep your computer connected to the Internet at all times (as long as your computer is powered up), it is important to protect your computer from unauthorized access or hackers. Consequently, all computers with a direct Internet connection should use a *firewall* program. Firewall programs block access to a computer from outside computers and enable each user to specify which programs on his or her computer are allowed to have access to the Internet. Firewalls, as well as other network and Internet security precautions, are discussed in more detail in Chapter 9.

>**Dial-up connection.** A type of Internet connection in which the computer or other device must dial up and connect to a service provider's computer via telephone lines before being connected to the Internet. >**Direct connection.** A type of Internet connection in which the computer or other device is connected to the Internet continually.

Conventional Dial-Up

Conventional dial-up Internet access uses a conventional dial-up modem connected to a standard telephone jack with regular twisted-pair telephone cabling. Conventional dial-up Internet service is most often used with home computers for users who don't need, or do not want to pay for, broadband Internet service. Advantages include inexpensive hardware, ease of setup and use, and widespread availability. The primary disadvantage is slow connection speed, since conventional dial-up modems connect to the Internet at a maximum of 56 Kbps.

Cable

Cable Internet access uses a direct connection and is the most widely used type of home broadband connection, with over half of the home broadband market. Cable connections are very fast (typically between 5 and 20 Mbps, though some faster services are available for a premium fee) and are available wherever cable TV access is available, provided the local cable provider supports Internet access. Consequently, cable Internet is not widely available in rural areas. Cable Internet service requires a cable modem.

DSL

DSL (Digital Subscriber Line) Internet access is a type of direct connection that transmits via standard telephone lines, but it does not tie up your telephone line. DSL requires a DSL modem and is available only to users who are relatively close (within three miles) to a telephone switching station and who have telephone lines capable of handling DSL. DSL speeds are about one-half of cable speeds and the speed of the connection degrades as the distance between the modem and the switching station gets closer and closer to the three-mile limit. Consequently, DSL is usually only available in urban areas. Download speeds are typically between 1 and 7 Mbps.

Satellite

Satellite Internet access uses a direct connection, but is slower and more expensive than cable or DSL access (typically up to around 1.5 Mbps). However, it is often the only broadband option for rural areas. In addition to a satellite modem, it requires a *transceiver* satellite dish mounted outside the home or building to receive and transmit data to and from the satellites being used. Installation requires an unobstructed view of the southern sky (to have a clear line of sight between the transceiver and appropriate satellite), and performance might degrade or stop altogether during very heavy rain or snowstorms.

Fixed Wireless

Fixed wireless Internet access uses a direct connection and is similar to satellite Internet in that it uses wireless signals, but it uses radio transmission towers (either stand-alone towers like the one shown in Figure 8-8 or transmitters placed on existing cell phone towers) instead of satellites. Fixed wireless Internet access requires a modem and, sometimes, an outside-mounted transceiver. Fixed wireless companies typically use Wi-Fi and/or WiMAX technology to broadcast the wireless signals to customers. Speeds are typically up to about 2 Mbps, though the speed depends somewhat on the distance between

> **TIP**
>
> Before using a dial-up access number to connect to the Internet, verify that it is a local telephone number; if it is not, you will incur long-distance charges.

> **TIP**
>
> If you have a direct Internet connection, leave your e-mail program open to retrieve your e-mail on a continual basis.

FIGURE 8-8
WiMAX towers. This tower is installed at the peak of Whistler Mountain in British Columbia.

> **Conventional dial-up Internet access.** Dial-up Internet access via standard telephone lines. >**Cable Internet access.** Fast, direct Internet access via cable TV lines. >**DSL (Digital Subscriber Line) Internet access.** Fast, direct Internet access via standard telephone lines. >**Satellite Internet access.** Fast, direct Internet access via the airwaves and a satellite dish. >**Fixed wireless Internet access.** Fast, direct Internet access available in some areas via the airwaves.

the tower and the customer, the types and number of obstacles in the path, and the type and speed of the connection between the wireless transmitter and the Internet.

Broadband over Fiber (BoF)

A new type of direct connection available to homes and businesses in areas where there is fiber-optic cabling available all the way to the building is generically called **broadband over fiber (BoF)** or **fiber-to-the-premises (FTTP) Internet access**, with other names being used by individual providers, such as Verizon's *fiber-optic service (FiOS)*. These fiber-optic networks are most often installed by telephone companies in order to upgrade their overall infrastructures and, where installed, are used to deliver telephone and TV service, in addition to Internet service. However, some cities are creating fiber-optic MANs that include connections to businesses and homes to provide very fast broadband Internet services. Where available, download speeds for BoF service typically range between 10 Mbps and 50 Mbps and the cost varies accordingly. BoF requires a special networking terminal installed at the building to convert the optical signals into electrical signals that can be sent to a computer or over a LAN.

Mobile Wireless

Mobile wireless Internet access is the type of direct connection most commonly used with mobile phones and other mobile devices to keep them connected to the Internet via a mobile phone network, even as they are carried from place to place. Some mobile wireless services can be used with notebook computers and other computers as well. For instance, AT&T's DataConnect service allows you to access the Internet on your notebook or netbook computer via the AT&T wireless network, and some mobile phones can be connected to a notebook computer to act as a modem to connect that computer to the mobile phone's wireless network. As discussed in Chapter 7, the speed of mobile wireless depends on the cellular standard being used—3G networks typically have speeds between 1 and 1.7 Mbps. Costs for mobile wireless Internet access vary widely, with some packages including unlimited Internet, some charging by the number of minutes of Internet use, and some charging by the amount of data transferred.

Wi-Fi Hotspots

While not typically used for primary Internet access, another option for Internet access is a **Wi-Fi hotspot**—a location with a direct Internet connection and a wireless access point that allows users to connect wirelessly (via Wi-Fi) to the hotspot to use its Internet connection (see Figure 8-9). Public Wi-Fi hotpots are widely available

FIGURE 8-9

Wi-Fi hotspots.

Hotspots are used to wirelessly connect to the Internet via the Internet connection belonging to a business, city, school, or other organization.

COFFEEHOUSES AND OTHER PUBLIC LOCATIONS
Often fee-based, though some are available for free.

HOSPITALS, BUSINESSES, AND OTHER ORGANIZATIONS
Usually designed for employees but are sometimes also available free to visitors.

COLLEGE CAMPUSES
Usually designed for students and faculty; sometimes used directly in class for student assignments, as shown here.

>**Broadband over fiber (BoF) Internet access.** Very fast, direct Internet access via fiber-optic networks; also referred to as **fiber-to-the-premises (FTTP) Internet access.** >**Mobile wireless Internet access.** Internet access via a mobile phone network. >**Wi-Fi hotspot.** A location that provides wireless Internet access to the public.

today, such as at many coffeehouses and restaurants; at hotels, airports, and other locations frequented by business travelers; and in or nearby public areas such as libraries, subway stations, and parks. Some public Wi-Fi hotspots are free; others charge per hour, per day, or on a subscription basis. College campuses also typically have Wi-Fi hotspots to provide Internet access to students; many businesses and other organizations have Wi-Fi hotspots for use by employees in their offices, as well as by employees and guests in conference rooms, waiting rooms, lunchrooms, and other onsite locations.

FURTHER EXPLORATION Go

Go to the Chapter 8 page at **www.cengage.com/ computerconcepts/np/uc13** for links to information about types of Internet access and ISPs.

Selecting an ISP and Setting Up Your Computer

Once the type of Internet access to be used is determined, the final steps to getting connected to the Internet are selecting an ISP and setting up your system. While this discussion is geared primarily toward a home Internet connection used with a personal computer, some of the concepts apply to business or mobile users as well.

Selecting an ISP

The type of device used (such as a personal computer or mobile phone), the type of Internet connection and service desired (such as cable Internet or mobile wireless), and your geographical location (such as metropolitan or rural) will likely determine your ISP options. The pricing and services available through any two ISPs will probably differ somewhat, based on the speed of the service, as well as other services available. The questions listed in Figure 8-10 can help you narrow your ISP choices and determine the questions you want answered before you decide on an ISP. A growing trend is for ISPs to offer a number of *tiers*; that is, different levels (speeds) of service for different prices so users requiring faster service can get it, but at a higher price.

FIGURE 8-10 Choosing an ISP. Some questions to ask before making your final selection.

Setting Up Your Computer

The specific steps for setting up your computer to use your selected type of Internet connection depend on the type of device, the type of connection, and the ISP you have chosen to use. Some types of Internet connections, such as satellite and broadband over fiber, require professional installation, after which you will be online; with other types, you can install the necessary hardware (typically a modem that connects to your computer or wireless router via an Ethernet cable) yourself. You will usually need to select a username and your desired payment method at some point during the ordering or setup process. This username is needed to log on to some types of Internet connections; it is also used in your e-mail address that will be associated with that Internet service.

After one computer is successfully connected to the Internet, you may need to add additional hardware to connect other computers and devices that you want to be able to access the Internet. For instance, to

AREA	QUESTIONS TO ASK
Services	Is the service compatible with my device?
	Is there a monthly bandwidth limit?
	How many e-mail addresses can I have?
	What is the size limit on incoming and outgoing e-mail messages and attachments?
	Do I have a choice between conventional and Web-based e-mail?
	Is there dial-up service that I can use when I'm away from home?
	Are there any special member features or benefits?
	Does the service include Web site hosting?
Speed	How fast are the maximum and usual downstream (ISP to my PC) speeds?
	How fast are the maximum and usual upstream (my PC to ISP) speeds?
	How much does the service slow down under adverse conditions, such as high traffic or poor weather?
Support	Is 24/7 telephone technical support available?
	Is Web-based technical support (such as via e-mail) available?
	Is there ever a charge for technical support?
Cost	What is the monthly cost for the service? Is it lower if I prepay a few months in advance? Are different tiers available?
	Is there a set-up fee? If so, can it be waived with a 6-month or 12-month agreement?
	What is the cost of any additional hardware needed, such as modem or transceiver? Can the fee be waived with a long-term service agreement?
	Are there any other services (telephone service, or cable or satellite TV, for instance) available from this provider that I have or want and that can be combined with Internet access for a lower total cost?

NET

share a broadband connection, you can connect other computers directly to the modem (via an Ethernet cable or Wi-Fi connection) if the modem contains a built-in switch or wireless router. If the modem does not include switching or wireless routing capabilities, you will need to connect a switch or wireless router to the modem (typically via an Ethernet cable), and then connect your devices to the switch or router, in order to share the Internet connection with those devices.

SEARCHING THE INTERNET

Most people who use the Internet turn to it to find specific information. For instance, you might want to find out the lowest price of the latest *Pirates of the Caribbean* DVD, the flights available from Los Angeles to New York on a particular day, a recipe for clam chowder, the weather forecast for the upcoming weekend, a video of President Obama's inaugural address, or a map of hiking trails in the Grand Tetons. The Internet provides access to a vast array of interesting and useful information, but that information is useless if you cannot find it when you need it. Consequently, one of the most important skills an Internet user can acquire today is how to search for and locate information on the Internet successfully. Basic Internet searching was introduced in Chapter 1, but understanding the various types of search sites available and how they work, as well as some key searching strategies, can help you perform more successful and efficient Internet searches. These topics are discussed next.

Search Sites

Search sites (such as *Google, Bing, Yahoo! Search, Microsoft Live Search, Ask.com, Cuil*, and so forth) are Web sites designed specifically to help you find information on the Web. Most search sites use a **search engine**—a software program—in conjunction with a huge database of information about Web pages to help visitors find Web pages that contain the information they are seeking. Search site databases are updated on a regular basis; for example, Google estimates that its entire index is updated about once per month. Typically, this occurs using small, automated programs (often called *spiders* or *webcrawlers*) that use the hyperlinks located on Web pages to jump continually from page to page. At each Web page, the spider program records important data about the page into the search site's database, such as the page's URL, its title, the keywords that appear frequently on the page, and the keywords and descriptive information added to the page's code by the Web page author when the page was created. Spider programs can be tremendously fast, visiting millions of pages per day. In addition to spider programs, search site databases also obtain information from Web page authors who submit Web page URLs and keywords associated with their Web sites to the search site, as discussed more in Chapter 11. The size of the database used varies with each particular search site, but typically includes information collected from several billion Web pages; at the time of this writing, for instance, the spider used with the Cuil search site had crawled a total of 186 billion Web pages.

To begin a search using a search site, type the URL for the desired search site in the Address bar of your browser. Most search sites today are designed for *keyword searches*; some sites allow *directory searches* as well. These two types of searches are discussed next. In addition, as the ability to search becomes more and more important, new types of searching are being developed. One emerging possibility is *real-time search engines* that search the Web

---

> **Search site.** A Web site designed to help users search for Web pages that match specified keywords or selected categories. > **Search engine.** A software program used by a search site to retrieve matching Web pages from a search database.

live, instead of relying on a search site database (one such service—called *MyLiveSearch*—was in development at the time of this writing). Another emerging search site—*ChaCha Search*—uses human guides that you can chat with via the ChaCha Search page if you can't find the information you are looking for. Searching by mobile phone is another growing area, including *mobile voice search*, which is discussed in the Chapter 6 Technology and You box.

Keyword Search

The most common type of Internet search is the **keyword search**—that is, when you type appropriate **keywords** (one or more key terms) describing what you are looking for into a search box. The site's search engine then uses those keywords to return a list of Web pages (called *hits*) that match your search criteria; you can view any one of these Web pages by clicking its corresponding hyperlink (see Figure 8-11). Search sites differ in determining how close a match must be between the specified search criteria and a Web page before a link to that page is displayed, so the number of hits from one search site to another may vary. To reduce the number of hits displayed, good search strategies (discussed shortly) can be used. Search sites also differ with respect to the order in which the hits are displayed. Some sites list the most popular sites (usually judged by the number of Web pages that link to it) first; others list Web pages belonging to organizations that pay a fee to receive a higher rank (typically called *sponsored links*) first.

The keyword search is the most commonly used search type. It is used not only on conventional search sites like the Google search site shown in Figure 8-11, but also on many other Web sites. For instance, Web pages like the one shown in Figure 8-12 often include a keyword search box so visitors can search that Web site to find information (such as items for sale via the site or specific documents or Web pages located on that site). Many of these Web site searches are powered by search engine technology, such as by *Google Site Search*.

Directory Search

An alternate type of Internet search available on some search sites is the **directory search**, which uses lists of categories instead of a search box. To perform a directory search, click the category that best matches what you are looking for in order to display a list of more specific subcategories within the main category. You can then click specific subcategories to drill down to more specific topics until you see hyperlinks to Web pages matching the information you are looking for.

1. Type appropriate keywords in the search box to display the search results.

2. Click the hyperlink for a Web page in the search results to display that page.

FIGURE 8-11
Using a search site.

FIGURE 8-12
Web page keyword searches. Allow users to search the Web site for the desired content.

Search box

NET

>**Keyword search.** A type of Internet search in which keywords are typed in a search box to locate information on the Internet. >**Keyword.** A word typed in a search box on a search site or other Web page to locate information related to that keyword. >**Directory search.** A type of Internet search in which categories are selected to locate information on the Internet.

FUNCTION	EXPLANATION
Calculator	Enter a mathematical expression or a conversion to see the result.
Currency converter	Enter an amount and currency type to see the corresponding value.
Dictionary	Enter the term *define* followed by a term to view definitions for that term from online sources.
Flight information	Enter an airline and a flight number to see status information.
Movie showtimes	Enter the term *movie* followed by a ZIP code to view movies showing in that area.
Number search	Enter a UPS, FedEx, or USPS tracking number; an area code; or a UPC code to view the associated information.
Phonebook	Enter a name followed by a city and a state, a ZIP code, or an area code to look up that person's address and phone number.
Reverse phonebook	Enter a telephone number to look up the person or business associated with that number.
Stock quotes	Enter one or more stock ticker symbols to retrieve stock quotes.
Street maps	Enter an address to find a map to that location.
Time	Enter the term *time* followed by a city name to see the current time in that city.
Travel conditions	Enter an airport code followed by the term *airport* to view current conditions at that airport.
Weather	Enter the term *weather* followed by a city name or ZIP code to view the weather for that location.
Yellow pages	Enter a type of business and city name or ZIP code to view businesses in that local area.

EXAMPLES:

| 10 miles in feet | Search |

10 miles = 52 800 feet

| time paris | Search |

10:10pm Wednesday (CEST)
Time in **Paris**, France

| weather san francisco | Search |

Weather for **San Francisco, CA**
68°F
Mostly Cloudy
Wind: NW at 1 mph
Humidity: 76%

	Wed	Thu	Fri
	65°F | 50°F	68°F | 52°F	70°F | 52°F

FIGURE 8-13
Google search tools.

Search Site Tools

Many search sites contain a variety of tools that can be used to find specific types of information. For instance, many search sites include links next to the search box that allow you to search for items other than Web pages, such as music files, videos, images, maps, news articles, products for sale—even files on your computer. Google is one of the most versatile search sites at the present time and is continually adding new search options. In addition to the options just listed, Google allows a variety of special searches to be conducted by typing specific search criteria in its search box to find other useful information, such as to quickly track a shipped package, look up a telephone number, check on the status of an airline flight, or make a calculation or conversion. Some examples of search tools that can be performed using the Google search box are listed in Figure 8-13.

Search Strategies

There are a variety of strategies that can be used to help whittle down a list of hits to a more manageable number (some searches can return billions of Web pages). Some search strategies can be employed regardless of the search site being used; others are available only on certain sites. Some of the most useful search strategies are discussed next.

Using Phrases

One of the most straightforward ways to improve the quality of the hits returned is to use *phrase searching*—essentially typing more than one keyword in a keyword search. Most search engines automatically list the hits that include all the keywords first, followed by hits matching most of the keywords, continuing down to hits that fit only one of the keywords. To force this type of sorting, virtually all search engines allow you to use some type of character—often quotation marks—to indicate that you want to search for the entire phrase together. Because search options vary from site to site, it is best to look for a search tips link on the search site you are using; the search tips should explain all of the search options available for that site. Examples of the results based on different search phrases to find Web pages about hand signals used with dogs and conducted at two search sites are listed in Figure 8-14. Notice that while the last two search phrases shown in Figure 8-14

SEARCH PHRASE USED	SEARCH SITE	NUMBER OF PAGES FOUND	TITLE OF FIRST TWO NONSPONSORED PAGES FOUND*
dogs	Google	48,600,000	Dogs & Puppies – Next Day Pets Dogs – Dog Information, Pictures and Reviews for over 350 Dogs
	Yahoo!	633,000,000	American Kennel Club (AKC) Animal Planet's Dog Guide
hand signals	Google	58,600,000	Hand Signals Bicycle Safety – Hand Signals
	Yahoo!	45,100,000	Hand Signals – Wikipedia, the free encyclopedia Bicycle Safety – Hand Signals
dog hand signals	Google	1,010,000	DDEAF Training Hand Signals How to Teach a Dog Hand Signals | eHow.com
	Yahoo!	7,660,000	How to Train a Dog Using Hand Signals | eHow.com Dog Training – Hand Signals – Amazingdogtrainingman.com
"dog hand signals"	Google	713	How to Teach a Dog Hand Signals | eHow.com D for Dog – Deaf dog hand signals sign language
	Yahoo!	213	How to Train a Dog Using Hand Signals | eHow.com Dog Training – Hand Signals – Amazingdogtrainingman.com

* Highlighted entries indicate Web pages about dog hand signals.

both returned relevant (and similar) Web pages, the number of Web pages found varied dramatically (hundreds of pages versus millions).

Using Boolean Operators

To further specify exactly what you want a search engine to find, *Boolean operators*—most commonly AND, OR, and NOT—can often be used in keyword searches. For example, if you want a search engine to find all documents that cover *both* the Intel and AMD microprocessor manufacturers, you can use the search phrase *Intel AND AMD* if the search engine supports Boolean operators. If, instead, you want documents that discuss *either* of these companies, the search phrase *Intel OR AMD* can be used. On the other hand, if you want documents about microprocessors that are cataloged with no mention of Intel, *microprocessors NOT Intel* can be used. Just as with other operators, the rules for using Boolean operators might vary from search site to search site (for instance, Google automatically assumes the AND operator as the default operator any time more than one search term is listed and uses a minus sign (−) instead of the word *NOT*). Be sure to check the search tips for the search site that you are using to see what operators can be used on that site. Some search sites also include an *Advanced Search* option that helps you specify Boolean conditions and other advanced search techniques using a fill-in-the-blank form.

Using Multiple Search Sites

Most users have a favorite search site that they are most comfortable using. However, as illustrated in Figure 8-14, different search sites can return different results. It is important to realize that sometimes a different search site might perform better than the one you use regularly. If you are searching for something and are not making any progress with one search site, then try another search site.

Using Appropriate Keywords, Synonyms, Variant Word Forms, and Wildcards

When choosing the keywords to be used with a search site, it is important to select words that represent the key concept you are searching for. For example, if you want to find out about bed and breakfasts located in the town of Leavenworth, Washington, a keyword

FIGURE 8-14
Examples of phrase searching. Using different search phrases and different search sites can dramatically change the search results.

NET

TIP

When searching, be efficient—if an appropriate Web page is not included among the first page or two of hits, redo the search using more specific criteria or a different search strategy.

FIELD TYPE	EXAMPLE	EXPLANATION
Title	title:"tax tips"	Searches for Web pages containing the words "tax tips" in the page title.
URL	url:taxtips	Searches for Web pages containing "taxtips" in the page URL.
Text	text:"tax tips"	Searches for Web pages containing "tax tips" in the text of the page.
Site	forms site:irs.gov	Searches for Web pages associated with the keyword "forms" that are located only on the irs.gov Web site.
Domain	tax tips site:*.gov	Searches for Web pages associated with the keywords "tax tips" that are located on government Web sites (they can have anything for the first part of the domain name, but must have a .gov TLD).

FIGURE 8-15

Field searching.
Field searches limit search results to just those pages that match specific field criteria, in addition to any specified search criteria.

phrase (such as *Leavenworth Washington bed and breakfast*) should return appropriate results. If your initial search does not produce the results you are hoping for, you can try *synonyms*—words that have meanings similar to other words. For example, you could replace *bed and breakfast* with *hotel* or *lodging*. To use synonyms in addition to the original keywords, Boolean operators can be used, such as the search phrase *"bed and breakfast" OR hotel OR lodging AND Leavenworth AND Washington.*

Variant—or alternate—word forms are another possibility. Try to think of a different spelling or form of your keywords, if your search still does not work as desired. For example, *bed and breakfast* could be replaced or supplemented with the variants *bed & breakfast* and *B&B*, and the *hand signals* keywords used in Figure 8-14 could be replaced with the variants *hand signal* and *hand signaling*. Using alternative spellings is a form of this strategy, as well. Another strategy that is sometimes used with keywords is the *wildcard* approach. A wildcard is a special symbol that is used in conjunction with a part of a word to specify the pattern of the terms you want to search for. For instance, the asterisk wildcard (*) is used to represent one or more letters at the asterisk location, so on many sites searching for *hand sign** would search for *hand sign, hand signal, hand signals, hand signaling*, and any other keywords that fit this specific pattern.

Using Field Searches

Another strategy that can be used when basic searching is not producing the desired results is *field searching*. A field search limits the search to a particular search characteristic (or *field*), such as the page title, URL, page text, top-level domain, or Web site (see Figure 8-15). When a field search is performed, only the hits associated with the Web pages that match the specified criteria in the specified field are displayed. You can also use field searching in conjunction with regular search terms, such as to search for a particular keyword on just Web sites that use a specific domain. Many, but not all, search engines support some type of field searching. Check the search tips for the particular search site you are using to see if it has that option.

FURTHER EXPLORATION

Go to the Chapter 8 page at **www.cengage.com/ computerconcepts/np/uc13** for links to information about citing online references.

Evaluating Search Results

Once a list of Web sites is returned as the result of a search, it is time to evaluate the sites to determine their quality and potential for meeting your needs. Two questions to ask yourself before clicking a link in the search results are as follows:

> Does the title and listed description sound appropriate for the information you are seeking?

> Is the URL from an appropriate company or organization? For example, if you want technical specifications about a particular product, you might want to start with information on the manufacturer's Web site. If you are looking for government publications, stick with government Web sites.

After an appropriate Web page is found, the evaluation process is still not complete. To determine if the information can be trusted, you should evaluate both the author and the

TYPE OF RESOURCE	CITATION EXAMPLE
Web page article (magazine)	Dvorak, John (2009, May 5). Data Mining and the Death of Privacy. *PC Magazine*. Retrieved February 14, 2010, from http://www.pcmag.com/article2/0,1895,2346287,00.asp
Web page article (journal)	Sensmeier, Joyce (2009, March). Advancing the EHR (Electronic Health Record): Are We There Yet? *Nursing Management*, 40 no. 3. Retrieved June 21, 2010, from http://www.nursingcenter.com/library/JournalArticle.asp?Article_ID=850211
Web page article (not appearing in a periodical)	Baldor, Lolita (2009, May 6). Air Traffic Systems Vulnerable to Cyber Attack. MSNBC. Retrieved March15, 2010, from http://www.msnbc.msn.com/id/30602242
Web page content (not an article)	*Browse the Web Safely*. (n.d.) Retrieved April 11, 2010 from http://www.symantec.com/norton/security_response/browsewebsafely.jsp
E-mail (cited in text, not reference list)	Maria Rodriquez (personal communication, March 28, 2010).

source to decide if the information can be considered reliable and whether or not it is biased. Be sure to also check for a date to see how up-to-date the information is—many online articles are years old. If you will be using the information in a report, paper, or other document in which accuracy is important, try to verify the information with a second source.

Citing Internet Resources

According to the online version of the Merriam-Webster Dictionary, the term *plagiarize* means "to steal and pass off the ideas or words of another as one's own" or to "use another's production without crediting the source." To avoid plagiarizing Web page content, you need to credit Web page sources—as well as any other Internet resources—when you use them in papers, on Web pages, or in other documents.

The guidelines for citing Web page content are similar to those for written sources. In general, the author, date of publication, and article or Web page title are listed along with a "Retrieved" statement listing the date the article was retrieved from the Internet and the URL of the Web page used to retrieve the article. Some citation examples based on the guidelines obtained from the *American Psychological Association (APA)* Web site are shown in Figure 8-16. If in doubt when preparing a research paper, check with your instructor as to the style manual (such as APA, *Modern Language Association (MLA)*, or *Chicago Manual of Style*) he or she prefers you to follow and refer to that guide for direction.

BEYOND BROWSING AND E-MAIL

In addition to basic browsing and e-mail (discussed in Chapter 1), there are a host of other activities that can take place via the Internet. Some of the most common of these Web-based applications are discussed next.

Other Types of Online Communications

Many types of online communications methods exist. E-mail, discussed in Chapter 1, is one of the most common; other types of online communications are discussed in the next few sections. While originally the programs that supported the various types of online communications discussed next were dedicated to a single task, today's programs often can be used for a variety of types of online communications. For instance, many *instant messaging (IM) programs* today (such as the one shown in Figure 8-17) can also be used to exchange *text messages*,

FIGURE 8-16
Citing Web sources.
It is important to properly credit your Web sources. These examples follow the American Psychological Association (APA) citation guidelines.

FIGURE 8-17
Online messaging programs can often be used to perform a variety of communications tasks.

1. After signing in to your messaging program, select a contact in order to start an IM or initiate a voice call, video call, game, or other activity with that individual.

2. IMs show up on both the sender's and the recipient's computers.

NET

make voice calls via *Voice over Internet Protocol* (*VoIP*), and make *video phone calls*, and many *VoIP programs* today can be used to exchange instant messages and text messages, in addition to making voice phone calls. This online communications convergence trend is found in both personal and business applications; in business, it is referred to as *unified communications* (*UC*). With UC, the various channels of business communications (such as e-mail, instant messaging, and telephone calls) are tied together and work with a single unified mailbox and interface. For instance, UC enables you to receive voice mail messages and faxes in your e-mail Inbox, listen to e-mail messages and calendar items over the phone, call a contact by clicking that person's name in your online contact list, view the availability status of co-workers before initiating a phone call, and so forth. UC is expected to be nearly a $50 billion business by 2012, according to Wainhouse Research.

Instant Messaging (IM) and Text Messaging

Instant messaging (**IM**) allows you to exchange real-time typed messages with people on your *buddy list*—a list of individuals (such as family, friends, and business associates) that you specify. *Instant messages* (*IMs*) can be sent via computers and mobile phones using installed *messaging programs* (such as *AIM, Windows Live Messenger, Yahoo! Messenger*, or *Google Talk*), Web-based messaging services (such as *Meebo.com* or Web versions of AIM, Yahoo! Messenger, or Google Talk), or other online communications programs that support instant messaging. Originally a popular communications method among friends, IM has also become a valuable business tool.

In order to send an IM, you must be signed in to your IM service. You can then select an online buddy and send an IM, which then appears immediately on your buddy's computer (refer again to Figure 8-17). You can also typically engage in other types of activities with an online buddy via the IM program, such as sending a photo or file, starting a voice or video conversation, or playing an online game. Instant messaging capabilities are also sometimes integrated into Web pages, such as to ask questions of a customer service representative or to start a conversation with one of your friends via a social networking site; this type of messaging is sometimes referred to as *chat*.

Because IM applications display the status of your buddies (such as if they are online, or if they have set their status to "Busy" or "In a meeting"), IM is an example of an application that uses *presence technology*—technology that enables one computing device to identify the current status of another device. Presence technology is increasingly being integrated into devices and applications and is discussed in more detail in Chapter 15. For a look at a growing presence application—*geobrowsing*—that you may use to keep track of your friends and family while they are on the go, see the Trend box.

Text messaging is a form of messaging frequently used by mobile phone users. Also called *Short Message Service* or *SMS*, text messaging is used to send short (less than 160 character) text-based messages via a cellular network. The messages are typically sent to the recipient via his or her mobile phone number (though some mobile phones can receive text messages sent via an e-mail address). Individuals may incur a fee for exchanging IMs and text messages, if these services are not included in their mobile phone plan.

Twittering and Other Types of Status Updates

Twittering is a relatively new way of staying in touch and connected with your friends' current activities. Sometimes referred to as *microblogging*, this free service allows

---

>**Instant messaging (IM).** A way of exchanging real-time typed messages with other individuals. >**Text messaging.** A way of exchanging real-time typed messages with other individuals via a cellular network and, typically, cell phones. >**Twittering.** Sending short status updates about your current activities via the Twitter service.

TREND

Geobrowsing

One of the biggest trends in mobile Web services today is geobrowsing—that is, information that is displayed based on the physical location of your phone (typically determined by the phone's GPS coordinates). Because most mobile phones today can be tied to location information and because most individuals carry a mobile phone with them at all times, geo-browsing services are becoming available at a record pace. Some geobrowsing applications and services (such as *GyPSii* and *Buddy Beacon*—see the accompanying illustration) allow you to broadcast your current location to friends and view the names and mapped locations of your friends that are near your current location. Others (such as *Eventful*) are designed to find businesses and events that are close to your current location.

Using the mobile phone to deliver location-based, real-time information seems like a natural evolution to many. And the trend shows no signs of slowing down. In fact, the Gartner Group predicts that location-based services will soon become mainstream and the market will grow to 300 million users worldwide (and more than $8 billion annually) by 2011.

members (both individuals and businesses) to post short (up to 140 character) updates (called *tweets*) about what they are doing at any moment (see Figure 8-18). The updates can be sent via text message, IM, or e-mail and are posted to the member's Twitter.com page. Tweet updates can also be sent to your friends' mobile phones if they have set up their accounts to follow you via text updates (standard text messaging rates apply when a mobile phone is used to send or receive tweets). Members can also search the Twitter Web site to find tweets of interest.

Features similar to Twitter tweets (generally referred to as *status updates*) are available on some social networking sites to keep your friends up to date on your current activi-ties, as discussed shortly. The use of status updates is growing—a recent report by the Pew Internet & American Life Project found that 11% of online adults use Twitter or another online service to post status updates—and it is changing the way some people communicate online. Twitter is used today to get updates on the weather, to ask for assistance with problems or to conduct information searches—even for personal safety purposes. For instance, the U.S. State Department recently began using Twitter to issue traveling advisories and one Berkeley graduate student used Twitter to send the tweet "Arrested" as he was being arrested in Egypt for photographing an antigovernment protest. After being notified by the student's Twitter friends, the U.S. embassy was able to secure his release.

 FIGURE 8-18
Twitter. Allows individuals to post tweets via computer, mobile phone, or Xbox (as shown here).

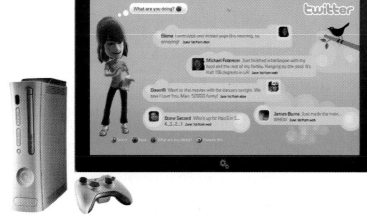

Message Boards

For asking questions of, making comments to, or initiating discussions with a large group of individuals, **message boards** (also called *discussion groups, newsgroups,* and *online forums*) can be used. Message boards are Web pages designed to facilitate written discussions between people on specific subjects, such as TV shows, computers, movies, investing, gardening, music, photography, or politics. When a participant posts a message, it is displayed for anyone accessing the message board to read and respond to. Messages are usually organized by topics (called *threads*); participants can post new messages in response to an existing message and stay within that thread, or they can post discussion group messages that start new threads. Participants in discussion groups do not have to be online at the same time because participants can post and respond to messages at their convenience.

Voice over Internet Protocol (VoIP)

Internet telephony is the original industry term for the process of placing telephone calls over the Internet. Today, the standard term for placing telephone calls over the Internet or any other type of data network is **Voice over Internet Protocol** (**VoIP**) and it can take many forms. At its simplest level, VoIP calls can take place from computer to computer, such as by starting a voice conversation with an online buddy using an IM program and a headset or microphone connected to the computer. Computer to computer calls (such as via the popular *Skype* service, as well as via messaging programs that support voice calls) are generally free. Often calls can be received from or made to conventional or mobile phones for a small fee, such as two cents per minute for domestic calls.

More permanent VoIP setups (sometimes referred to as *digital voice, broadband phone,* or *Internet phone service*) are designed to replace conventional landline phones in homes and businesses. VoIP is offered through some ISPs, such as cable, telephone, and mobile phone companies; it is also offered through dedicated VoIP providers, such as *Vonage.* Permanent VoIP setups require a broadband Internet connection and a *VoIP phone adapter* (also called an *Internet phone adapter*) that goes between a conventional phone and a broadband router, as shown in Figure 8-19. Once your phone calls are routed through your phone adapter and router to the Internet, they travel to the recipient's phone, which can be another VoIP phone, a mobile phone, or a landline phone. VoIP phone adapters are typically designed for a specific VoIP provider. With these more permanent VoIP setups, most users switching from landline phone service can keep their existing telephone number.

The biggest advantage of VoIP is cost savings, such as unlimited local and long-distance calls for as little as $25 per month, or cable and VoIP services bundled together for about $50 per month. One of the biggest disadvantages of VoIP at the present time is that it does not function during a power outage or if your Internet connection (such as your cable connection for cable Internet users) goes down.

Web Conferences and Webinars

As discussed in Chapter 7, the term *videoconferencing* refers to the use of computers, video cameras, microphones, and other communications technologies to

Ⓥ FIGURE 8-19
Voice over IP (VoIP).
Permanent VoIP setups allow telephone calls to be placed via a broadband Internet connection using a conventional telephone.

THE INTERNET

1. A conventional phone is plugged into a VoIP adapter, which is connected to a broadband modem.

2. Calls coming from the VoIP phone travel over the Internet to the recipient's phone.

>**Message board.** A Web page that enables individuals to post messages on a particular topic for others to read and respond to; also called a discussion group or online forum. >**Voice over Internet Protocol (VoIP).** The process of placing telephone calls via the Internet.

conduct face-to-face interactive meetings between people in different locations. Videoconferencing that takes place via the Internet is often called *Web conferencing* or *online conferencing*. **Web conferences** typically take place via a personal computer or mobile phone and are used by businesses and individuals. Basic Web conferences (such as a video call between individuals as in Figure 8-20) can be performed via any online communications program (such as an instant messaging program) that supports video phone calls. Business Web conferences that require multiple participants or other communication tools (such as a shared whiteboard or the ability for attendees to share the content on their computer screens) may need to use *Web conferencing software* or services instead. Business Web conferencing is often used for meetings between individuals located in different geographical locations, as well as for employee training, sales presentations, customer support, and other business applications.

FIGURE 8-20
Web conferencing.
Allows individuals to talk with and see each other in real time, such as this student talking to her family from her dorm room.

Webinars (Web seminars) are similar to Web conferences, but typically have a designated presenter and an audience. Although interaction with the audience is usually included (such as question and answer sessions), a Webinar is typically more one-way communication than a Web conference.

Social Networking

A **social networking site** can be loosely defined as any site that creates a community of individuals who can communicate with and/or share information with one another. Some examples are *MySpace* and *Facebook* that allow users to post information about themselves for others to read, *Meetup.com* that connects people with common hobbies and interests, video sharing sites like *YouTube*, and photo sharing sites like *Flickr* and *Fotki*. Social networking can be performed via personal computers, though the use of *mobile social networking*—social networks accessed with a mobile phone or other mobile device—is growing rapidly. In fact, Jupiter Research predicts the number of active mobile social networking users will rise from 54 million today to 730 million in five years, and MySpace expects half of its traffic to come from mobile devices within a few years. Some reasons for this include that most individuals carry a mobile phone with them all the time, many individuals like to communicate with others via the Web while they are on the go, and the use of a mobile phones enables location applications to be integrated into the social networking experience.

Social networking sites are used most often to communicate with existing friends.

THROW THE FIGHT

Ryan Baustert, Guitarist, Throw the Fight

What impact has the Internet and social networking sites had on your band's success?

The Internet has had a major impact on us. The best marketing is when the distance between artist and audience is short and direct. Due to sites like MySpace, Purevolume, and Facebook, we are able to stay better connected and interact with our fans on a more personal level. We can also gauge how our music is received by peoples' reactions and comments online.

It's much easier to promote shows, tours, and album releases, as well. More recently, with the explosion of Twitter, we can go one step further and give fans more insight into what is going on in our lives behind the scenes. This, in turn, helps us build brand loyalty.

NET

>**Web conference.** A face-to-face meeting taking place via the Web; typically uses video cameras and microphones to enable participants to see and hear each other. >**Webinar.** A seminar presented via the Web. >**Social networking site.** A site that enables a community of individuals to communicate and share information.

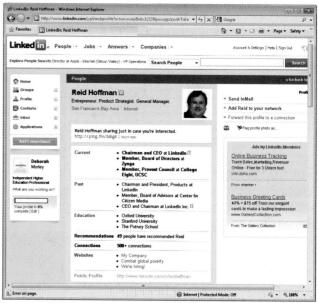

PERSONAL PROFILING SITES
Allow individuals to post information about themselves, link pages with friends, exchange messages, and so forth.

BUSINESS NETWORKING SITES
Help businesspeople find business contacts, potential new employees and clients, dinner and traveling partners during business trips, and so forth.

⚠ **FIGURE 8-21**
Social networking sites. A variety of social networking sites are available to meet different needs.

Facebook, for instance (shown in Figure 8-21), allows you to post photos, videos, music, and other content for your *Facebook friends* (individuals you have chosen to communicate with via Facebook) to view. You can also chat with your Facebook friends who are currently online, and publish notes and status updates (similar to Twitter tweets) on your *Facebook wall*, as well as the walls of your friends' Facebook pages. For privacy purposes, you can limit access to your Facebook page to the individuals you identify (such as just to your Facebook friends). To help keep track of all your friends' social networking activities, *social networking management services* can help, as discussed in the Technology and You box.

In addition to being used to communicate with existing friends, social networking sites are also used to learn about individuals you currently don't know. For instance, one new application for social networks like Facebook is their use by college-bound students to meet other incoming freshmen before the school year starts. Class pages for many colleges in the United States emerge prior to the fall semester so that incoming freshmen can "facestalk" (view the profiles of) other students in their graduating class, look up the profiles of their dorm roommates, find fellow students with common interests, and more—all before actually setting foot on campus.

In addition to being used for personal use, social networking sites today are also viewed as a business marketing tool. For instance, MySpace, Facebook, and YouTube are often used by businesses, political candidates, emerging musicians, and other professionals or professional organizations to increase their online presence. There are also business social networking sites designed for business networking. These sites (such as LinkedIn shown in Figure 8-21) are used for recruiting new employees, finding new jobs, building professional contacts, and other business activities. Other specialized social networking sites include sites designed for children (these usually work in a manner similar to

TECHNOLOGY AND YOU

Social Networking Management Services

With the popularity of social networking sites comes the problem of trying to keep up with the seemingly endless stream of input (such as Flickr photos, Twitter tweets, MySpace messages, Facebook posts, and so forth) generated by friends and contacts. There are a number of different *social networking management tools* available now that can help. These tools typically display new content from your friends and contacts (such as from your Facebook friends and/or people in your IM or e-mail contact list) in a central location to make it easier to follow all of your friends' activities at one time.

Some social networking management capabilities are built into portal pages and IM programs. For instance, the *What's New* area at the bottom of the *Windows Live Messenger* screens displays updates about activities the people you have specified as being in your Live network have performed recently, such as new blog posts or new uploaded photos. Other services are more universal, such as the *Yoono* browser plug-in that contains various widgets located on the left side of your browser to conveniently display different types of information aggregated from the Web. The *Friends Widget* (shown in the accompanying illustration) displays your friend's social networking activities continuously, and the updates can be displayed in chronological order, by social network, or by friend. The Friends Widget also provides one-click access to e-mail and IM, and allows you to upload media to your favorite social networks.

With the popularity and use of social networks still growing at an astounding rate, expect to see many more types of social management services in the future.

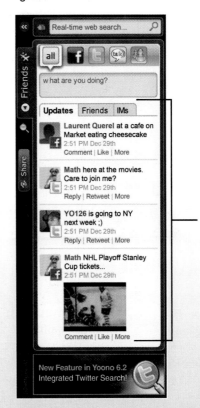

Most recent activity (Facebook posts and Twitter tweets in this example) by friends.

MySpace, but they have safeguards in place to prevent personal information from being posted, to monitor language, and so forth) and families (such as to exchange messages, view online tasks lists, and access a shared family calendar).

When using a social networking site, adults and children should be cautious about revealing too much personal information via these sites, both for personal safety reasons and to prevent the information from being used in personalized, targeted *spear phishing* attacks, discussed in Chapter 9. In addition, social networking content is increasingly being monitored by colleges (to find inappropriate behavior by students and to research college applicants) and employers (to find unprofessional behavior by current employees and to research potential job candidates). Because of this, all individuals should be careful about the types of photos and other content they post online. There have been numerous cases over the past few years of students being disciplined or not admitted to a college, and individuals being fired or not hired, due to content posted to a social networking site. Consequently, it is a good idea for individuals to take a close look at their online posts and photos and remove anything that might be potentially embarrassing if viewed by current or future employers, a future partner, or other people important to them now or in the future.

Another emerging issue is what happens to social networking content when someone dies unexpectedly, since family members and heirs cannot access the sites without logon information or access to the deceased's e-mail for password recovery purposes. In response, some special services have emerged to help individuals store information about their online assets and to designate a beneficiary—the person designated to receive that information upon the individual's death. These services can be used to store logon information for Web sites and e-mail accounts and to leave e-mail messages to be distributed to designated individuals when the individual dies, such as to loved ones, online and offline friends, online gaming companions, and other individuals. An alternative is for individuals to leave the necessary online contact and access information, as well as instructions regarding how to notify online friends and sites, with a trusted friend or relative who is instructed to use the information only in the event of the individual's death.

✓ **TIP**

The data on online auction pages is typically not updated automatically once it is displayed on your screen. To get updated information—such as the current bid for an auction and auction time remaining—use your browser's Refresh or Reload button to redisplay the page.

Online Shopping and Investing

Online shopping and *online investing* are examples of *e-commerce*—online financial transactions. It is very common today to order products, buy and sell stock, pay bills, and manage financial accounts online. However, since *online fraud, credit card fraud*, and *identity theft* (a situation in which someone gains enough personal information to pose as another person) are continuing to grow at a rapid pace, it is important to be cautious when participating in online financial activities. To protect yourself, use a credit card or *online payment service* such as *PayPal* (discussed in Chapter 11) whenever possible when purchasing goods or services online so that any fraudulent activities can be disputed. Also, be sure to enter your payment information only on a *secure Web page* (look for a URL that begins with *https* instead of *http*). Online financial accounts should also be protected with *strong user passwords* that are changed frequently. Internet security and strong passwords are discussed in detail in Chapter 9, and e-commerce is the topic of Chapter 11.

Ⓥ **FIGURE 8-22**

Online shopping.
Allows you to purchase goods and services online.

Online Shopping and Online Auctions

Online shopping is commonly used to purchase both physical products (such as clothing, books, DVDs, shoes, furniture, and more) and downloadable products (such as software, movies, music, and e-books) via Web pages. Typically, shoppers locate the items they would like to purchase using an online shopping site (one example is shown in Figure 8-22), and then they add those items to their online *shopping carts* or *shopping bags*. The site's *checkout* process—including supplying the necessary billing and shipping information—is then used to complete the sale. After the payment is processed, the item is either shipped to the customer (if it is a physical product), or the customer is given instructions on how to download it (if it is a downloadable product). Forrester Research predicts that U.S. online sales will reach approximately $335 billion by 2012.

Online auctions are the most common way to purchase items online from other individuals. Sellers list items for sale on an auction site (such as *eBay* or *Yahoo! Auctions*) and pay a small listing fee (and a commission to the auction site if the item is sold). Individuals can visit the auction site and enter bids on auction items until the end of the auction. At that time, the person with the highest bid is declared the successful bidder (provided the minimum selling price, if one was established, was met) and arranges payment for and delivery of the item directly with the

---

>**Online shopping.** Buying products or services over the Internet. >**Online auction.** An online activity for which bids are placed for items, and the highest bidder purchases the item.

seller. Online auctions are described in more detail in Chapter 11. Another common way to purchase items from other individuals is via online classified ads, such as those posted on the popular *Craigslist* site.

Online Banking and Online Investing

Many banks today offer **online banking** as a free service to their customers to enable customers to check balances on all their accounts (such as checking, credit cards, mortgage, and investment accounts), view cashed checks and other transactions, transfer funds between accounts, pay bills electronically, and perform other activities related to their bank accounts. Online banking is continually growing—according to the Pew Internet & American Life Project, close to one-half of all U.S. adults now bank online.

Buying and selling of stocks, bonds, mutual funds, and other types of securities is referred to as **online investing**. Although it is common to see stock quote capabilities on many search and news sites, trading stocks and other securities requires an *online broker*. The biggest advantages of online investing include lower transaction fees and the ability to quickly buy or sell stock when desired—a convenience for those investors who do a lot of trading. Common online investing services include the ability to order sales and purchases; access performance histories, corporate news, and other useful investment information; and set up an *online portfolio* that displays the status of the stocks you specify. On some Web sites, stock price data is delayed 20 minutes; on other sites, real-time quotes are available. Like other Web page data, most stock price data is current at the time it is retrieved via a Web page, but it will not be updated (and you will not see current quotes, for instance) until you reload the Web page using your browser's Refresh or Reload toolbar button. An exception to this rule is if the Web page is designed to refresh the content automatically on a regular basis. For example, the portfolio shown in Figure 8-23 uses a *Java applet*—a small program built into a Web page—to redisplay updated data continuously.

FIGURE 8-23
Online investing.
Allows you to buy and sell stock, view your portfolio, get real-time quotes, and more.

Online Entertainment

There are an ever-growing number of ways to use the Web for entertainment purposes, such as listening to music, watching TV and videos, and playing online games. Some applications can be accessed with virtually any type of Internet connection; others are only practical with a broadband connection. Many online entertainment applications require the use of a *media player program* or *plug-in* (such as *QuickTime Player* or *Silverlight*) to deliver multimedia content.

Online Music

There are a number of options available today for **online music**, such as listening to live radio broadcasts via an *online radio station*, watching music videos on *MTV.com* or *Yahoo! Music*, or downloading music from *online music stores*, such as the *iTunes Music Store*, *Rhapsody MP3 Store*, or *Wal-Mart MP3 Music Downloads*. Online radio

---

>**Online banking.** Performing banking activities via the Web. >**Online investing.** Buying and selling stocks or other types of investments via the Web. >**Online music.** Music played or obtained via the Web.

stations typically allow you to listen to music free of charge on your computer; online music stores allow you to purchase and then download music singles and albums to your computer, mobile phone, or portable digital media player. Music files downloaded to your computer can be played from your computer's hard drive; they can also be copied to a CD to create a custom music CD or transferred to a portable digital media player or mobile phone provided the download agreement does not preclude it. *Mobile music downloads* is a rapidly growing market, and Juniper Research predicts it will exceed $17.5 billion business by 2012.

VIDEO PODCAST

Go to the Chapter 8 page at **www.cengage.com/ computerconcepts/np/uc13** to download or listen to the "How To: Watch Free TV and Movies Online" video podcast.

Online TV, Videos, and Movies

Watching TV shows, videos, and movies online is another very popular type of online entertainment. **Online videos** (such as news videos and movie trailers, videos posted to Web sites belonging to businesses and other organizations, personal videos posted to blogs and social networking pages, and videos shared via YouTube and Google Video) have been available to watch online for a number of years. Today, however, you also have the option of **online TV** and **online movies**. The availability of live online TV has been fairly limited in the past, but is growing. Some Web sites (such as *CNN.com Live*) offer live news coverage, and some TV shows and sporting events can be delivered in real time to mobile phones (referred to as *mobile TV* and shown in Figure 8-24). As demand for live TV keeps rising (for instance, it is estimated that more than 70 million people watched the 2009 Presidential Inauguration live coverage online), its availability is expected to grow.

There is also a wide variety of recorded TV content (such as episodes of current TV shows after they have been aired) available through the respective television network Web sites for viewing online. There are also a number of Web sites, such as *Hulu, TV.com, Fancast*, and *CastTV* (see Figure 8-24), that provide free access to many prime time TV

FIGURE 8-24

Online TV and movies.

MOBILE TV
Both live and recorded TV shows can be delivered directly to a mobile phone.

ONLINE TV AND MOVIES
TV shows and movies can be watched online for free via a variety of Web sites.

VIDEO-ON-DEMAND (VOD)
Fee-based feature films and other content can be delivered to a computer or TV.

> **Online video.** Video watched or downloaded via the Web. > **Online TV.** Live or recorded TV shows available via the Web. > **Online movies.** Feature films available via the Web.

shows, a wide variety of older TV shows, and many full-length feature films. In addition, YouTube and the *Internet Movie Database* (*IMDb*) recently added full-length TV shows and movies that visitors can watch for free, and Comcast is currently testing a new *On Demand Online* service designed to provide TV subscribers with free online TV content. A new trend is the development of original TV series, sometimes referred to as *telewebs*, that are only available online. Typically, online TV and online movies are streaming media, in which the video plays from the server when it is requested. Consequently, you need an Internet connection in order to view the video.

Another entertainment option is renting video via the Internet—typically referred to as **video-on-demand** (**VOD**). With VOD, individuals order movies and television shows via a VOD provider (such as the individuals' cable company or a Web site such as *CinemaNow, iTunes, BLOCKBUSTER OnDemand, Netflixs,* or *Amazon Video On Demand*). Rentals typically cost $3.99 or less; purchasing a movie costs around $15. In either case, the movies are downloaded to a computer, to a DVR or other device (such as the *Roku* digital media player shown in Figure 8-24) that is connected to your TV, or to a mobile phone or mobile device to be watched while on the go. Rented movies can usually be viewed only for a limited time; some services allow movies downloaded to a computer to be transferred to a portable digital media player or other mobile device during the allowable viewable period.

Many believe the future of delivering TV content over the Internet (sometimes referred to as *Internet Protocol Television* or *IPTV*) will be the delivery of content via the Internet directly to your television. Digital media players that can download VOD movies, gaming consoles that can be used to access Internet content, and multimedia networks that allow Internet content to be streamed from your computer to your TV are a step in that direction. A new option just becoming available—*broadband-enabled TVs* that connect to your Internet connection without any additional hardware—go one step farther. These TVs can be used to view Web pages, watch online TV and videos, and display *widgets* or *gadgets*—small pieces of current information such as sport scores, news headlines, or product information (as shown in Figure 8-5 earlier in this chapter). The demand for Web-to-TV content is expected to grow at an astounding pace with 24 million U.S. households expected to be viewing Internet content on their TVs by 2013, according to a report by In-Stat.

Online Gaming

Online gaming refers to games played over the Internet. Many sites—especially children's Web sites—include games for visitors to play. There are also sites whose sole purpose is hosting games that can be played online. Some of the games are designed to be played alone or with just one other person. Others, called *online multiplayer games*, are designed to be played online against many other online gamers. Online multiplayer games (such as *Doom, EverQuest, Final Fantasy,* and *City of Heroes*) are especially popular in countries, such as South Korea, that have readily available high-speed Internet connections and high levels of Internet use in general. Internet-enabled gaming consoles (such as the PlayStation 3, Xbox 360, and Wii) and portable gaming devices (such as the Sony PSP and Nintendo DSi) that have built-in Internet connectivity can also be used for multiplayer online gaming. Online gaming is also associated quite often with *Internet addiction*— the inability to stop using the Internet or to prevent extensive use of the Internet from interfering with other aspects of one's life. Internet addiction is a growing concern and is discussed in more detail in Chapter 16.

NET

> **Video-on-demand (VOD).** The process of downloading movies and television shows, on demand, via the Web.   > **Online gaming.** Playing games via the Web.

Online News, Reference, and Information

There is an abundance of news and other important information available through the Internet. The following sections discuss some of the most widely used news, reference, and information resources.

News and Reference Sites

News organizations, such as television networks, newspapers, and magazines, nearly always have Web sites that are updated on a continual basis to provide access to current local and world news, as well as sports, entertainment, health, travel, politics, weather, and other news topics (see Figure 8-25). Many news sites also have searchable archives to look for past articles, although some require a fee to view back articles. Once articles are displayed, they can typically be saved, printed, or sent to other individuals via e-mail. A growing trend is for newspapers and magazines to abandon print subscriptions and to provide Web-only service—primarily for cost reasons. Although some subscribers miss the print versions, there are some advantages to digital versions, such as the ability to easily search through content in some digital publications. Other online news resources include news radio programs that are broadcast over the Internet, as well as the wide variety of news video clips available through many Web sites.

News can also be delivered via gadgets displayed on computer desktops, TVs, dashboards, and other objects. News gadgets typically display headlines, and clicking a headline displays that news story. Recent versions of Windows include a number of gadgets that can be added to the Windows desktop, as discussed in Chapter 5.

Reference sites are designed to provide users access to specific types of useful information. For example, reference sites can be used to generate maps (see Figure 8-25), check the weather forecast, look up the value of a home, or provide access to encyclopedias, dictionaries, ZIP code directories, and telephone directories. One potential downside to the increased availability of online reference sites is use by criminals. For instance, one California lawmaker has introduced a bill requiring mapping sites to blur out details of schools, churches, and government buildings after being informed that some terrorists have used these maps to plan bombings and other attacks.

FIGURE 8-25

Online news and reference.

NEWS SITES
News organizations typically update their sites several times per day to provide access to the most current news and information.

REFERENCE SITES
Reference Web sites provide access to specific types of useful information, such as the maps and driving directions available via this Web site.

Portal Pages, RSS Feeds, and Podcasts

Portal Web pages are Web pages designed to be selected as a browser's home page and visited on a regular basis. Portal pages typically include search capabilities, news headlines, weather, and other useful content, and can usually be customized by users to display their requested content (see Figure 8-26). Once the portal page is customized, each time the user visits the portal page, the specified information is displayed. Popular portals include *My Yahoo!, iGoogle, My MSN,* and *AOL.com.*

RSS (Really Simple Syndication) is an online news tool designed for facilitating the delivery of news articles and other content regularly published to a Web site. Provided the content has an associated *RSS feed*, individuals can *subscribe* (usually for free) to that feed. You typically subscribe to an RSS feed by clicking a *subscribe* link

Content is customized for each user

Search capabilities

Access to Web mail

RSS feed subscriptions

Social networking updates

Selected news headlines

Selected weather

Other gadgets

on the associated Web page to add the feed content to your browser feed list or by copying the URL for the RSS feed to your portal page. To view the feed content, you can select that feed from your browser's feed list (such as the *Favorites Feeds* list in Internet Explorer) or you can click the appropriate link on your portal page, such as the links shown on the portal page in Figure 8-26. In either case, as new content for the subscribed feed becomes available, it will be accessible via the feed links. In addition to computers, RSS feeds today can also be delivered to mobile phones and other mobile devices. In the future, we will likely see RSS feeds delivered directly to televisions—and perhaps even to watches, refrigerators, and other consumer devices that have a display screen.

Another Web resource that can provide you with useful information is a **podcast**—a recorded audio or video file that can be downloaded via the Internet, such as the audio and video podcasts available for download via the Web site that accompanies this text. The term *podcast* is derived from the iPod portable digital media player (the first widely used device for playing digital audio files), although podcasts today can also be listened to using a computer or mobile phone.

Podcasting (creating a podcast) enables individuals to create self-published, inexpensive Internet radio broadcasts, such as to share their knowledge, express their opinions on particular subjects, or share original poems, songs, or short stories with interested individuals. Originally created and distributed by individuals, podcasts are now also being created and distributed by businesses. Some commercial radio stations are making portions of their broadcasts available via podcasts, and a growing number of news sites and corporate sites now have regular podcasts available. In fact, some view podcasts as the new and improved radio since it is an easy way to listen to your favorite radio broadcasts on your own schedule. Podcasts are typically uploaded to the Web on a regular basis, and RSS feeds can be used to notify subscribers when a new podcast is available. For a look at how to create an audio podcast, see the How It Works box.

FIGURE 8-26

Portal pages. Portal pages can contain a wide variety of customized news and information.

VIDEO PODCAST

Go to the Chapter 8 page at **www.cengage.com/ computerconcepts/np/uc13** to download or listen to the "How To: Create an RSS Feed" video podcast.

VIDEO PODCAST

Go to the Chapter 8 page at **www.cengage.com/ computerconcepts/np/uc13** to download or listen to the "How To: Create a Podcast" video podcast.

> **Portal Web page.** A Web page designed to be designated as a browser home page; typically can be customized to display personalized content.
> **RSS (Really Simple Syndication).** A tool used to deliver selected Web content to subscribers as the content is published to a Web site.
> **Podcast.** A recorded audio or video file that can be played or downloaded via the Web.

HOW IT WORKS

Podcasting

To create an audio podcast, you need a microphone or headset connected to your computer and audio capture software, such as the free *Audacity* program shown in the accompanying illustration. You can then record your podcast content and save it. You can also import additional audio files to mix in with your recorded content and otherwise edit the podcast as needed, such as arranging the order of the tracks, transition opening or closing segments by fading in or out, editing out sneezes or long stretches of silence, adding sound effects, and so forth.

Once the podcast is finished, it is typically saved in the MP3 format (the Audacity program requires you to download the free *LAME* MP3 encoder in order to save files in the MP3 format). During the save process, you should add *ID3 tags*, which include important details about your show, such as the title of the show, your name, your URL, a copyright notice, and other relevant information. The ID3 information is displayed when the podcast is played; it is also used to help your podcast be located easily by podcasting search sites and directories.

Finished podcasts can be uploaded to a podcast hosting site or your own Web site. If you use a podcast hosting site (such as the free hosting site shown in the accompanying illustration), you typically just upload the file and the site creates the download link for you automatically. If you are hosting the podcast on your own site, you will need to upload the file to your site and create the download link on the appropriate Web page yourself. If you would like individuals to be able to subscribe to your podcast via an RSS feed, you also need to create a *podcast feed*—an RSS file that contains the information needed for users to subscribe to your podcast. RSS files can be created in a text editing program like Windows Notepad and saved with an *.rss* file extension. There are also Web sites that can generate a podcast feed for you, and some podcast editing programs include the ability to create a podcast feed. To be safe, you should test your download link and/or podcast feed to make sure they work properly. Once your podcast is ready to go, you can submit it to podcast directories, such as Podcast Alley, so people can find and download it.

ID3 tags are added during the save process.

1. Record the podcast, then import additional audio tracks and edit as needed.

The introductory segment plays first and then fades out.

The podcast track was moved to start when the opening segment is fading out.

2. Save the podcast file as an MP3 file.

3. Upload the files to the appropriate Web site, such as the free podcasting hosting site shown here.

4. The podcast is available for download

Product, Corporate, Government, and Other Information

The Web is a very useful tool for locating product and corporate information. Manufacturer and retailer Web sites often include product specifications, instruction manuals, and other information that is useful to consumers before or after they purchase a product. There are also numerous consumer review sites (such as *Epinions.com*) to help purchasers evaluate their options before buying a product online or in a physical store. For investors and consumers, a variety of corporate information is available online, from both company Web sites and sites (such as *Hoovers.com*) that offer free or fee-based corporate information.

Government information is also widely available on the Internet. Most state and federal agencies have Web sites to provide information to citizens, such as government publications, archived documents, forms, and legislative bills. You can also perform a variety of tasks, such as downloading tax forms and filing your tax returns online. In addition, many cities, counties, and states allow you to pay your car registration fees, register to vote, view property tax information, or update your driver's license online.

There is also a wide variety of information available from various organizations, such as non-profit organizations, conservation groups, political parties, and more. For instance, many sites dedicated to energy conservation and saving the environment have emerged over the past few years to bring awareness to this issue, and the 2008 presidential race brought numerous online resources for learning the positions of political candidates and other information important to voters. For example, the nonpartisan *FactCheck.org* Web site shown in Figure 8-27 is dedicated to monitoring the factual accuracy of what is being said by major U.S. political candidates and elected officials and reporting it, in an attempt to reduce the level of deception and confusion in U.S. politics. According to a study by the Pew Internet & American Life Project, more than one-half of U.S. adults used the Internet in conjunction with the 2008 Election, such as to share political content with others, research issues, or watch political videos.

FIGURE 8-27

FactCheck.org. This Web site can be used to check the accuracy of political statements.

Online Education and Writing

Online education—using the Internet to facilitate learning—is a rapidly growing Internet application. The Internet can be used to deliver part or all of any educational class or program; it can also be used to supplement or support traditional education. In addition, many high school and college courses use Web content—such as online syllabi, schedules, discussion boards, podcasts, and tutorials—as required or suggested supplements. For example, the Web site that supplements this book contains an online study guide, online quizzes, online hands-on labs,

NET

ASK THE EXPERT

INSTITUTE FOR POLITICS
DEMOCRACY & THE INTERNET
www.ipdi.org

Julie Barko Germany, Director, Institute for Politics, Democracy, & the Internet

What is the most significant way that the Internet affects politics today?

The Internet and its applications—from Twitter to social networking sites to blogs to videos—have a significant impact on the invisible primary in American politics, as well on the elections. Today, technologically-savvy candidates and politicians use the Internet to push information out to voters, to fundraise, to solicit opinions from constituents, and to gain media coverage. One of the most valuable ways that politicians can use the Internet today, but that I believe is underutilized, is to listen to voters and each other. Really listening to the issues and concerns important to their constituents helps elected officials create better public policy and gain trust. When our leaders don't listen, we can then use the Internet (from blogs to Twitter to video to email) to get their attention—and to mobilize to vote them out of office, if necessary.

FIGURE 8-28

Web-based learning.

The Understanding Computers Web site provides a variety of Web-based learning opportunities for readers of this textbook.

Web links, downloadable audio and video podcasts, streaming videos, and other online resources for students taking a course that uses this textbook (see Figure 8-28). There are also Web-based *learning management systems* (such as *Blackboard*) that can be used to deliver course content, manage assignments and grades, and more; and the use of *student response systems*—where students use a special device or their mobile phone to respond to surveys or review questions during in-class lectures is growing. The next few sections take a look at some of the most widely used online education applications.

Web-Based Training and Distance Learning

The term **Web-based training** (**WBT**) refers to any instruction delivered via the Web. It is commonly used for employee training, as well as for delivering instruction in an educational setting. **Distance learning** occurs whenever students take classes from a location—often home or work—which is different from the one where the delivery of instruction takes place. Distance learning today typically includes Web-based training or other online learning tools (and so is also called *online learning* and *e-learning*) and is available through many high schools, colleges, and universities, as well as organizations that provide professional certifications. Distance learning can be used to learn just one task or new skill; it can also be used to complete a college course or an entire degree program. Typically the majority of distance learning coursework is completed over the Internet via class Web pages, YouTube videos, Webinars, podcasts, discussion groups, and e-mail, although schools might require some in-person contact, such as sessions for orientation and testing.

The biggest advantage of Web-based training and distance learning is that they are typically experienced individually and at the user's own pace. Online content for Web-based training components is frequently customized to match the pace of each individual user and can be completed at the user's convenience. Web-based content can be updated as needed and online content and activities (such as exercises, exams, and animations) typically provide immediate feedback to the student. One disadvantage is the possibility of technological problems—since students need a working computer and Internet connection to access the material, they cannot participate if they have no access to a computer or if their computer, their Internet connection, or the Web server hosting the material goes down. Another concern among educators is the lack of face-to-face contact, and security issues—such as the difficulty in ensuring that the appropriate student is completing assignments or taking exams. Some possible solutions for this later concern are discussed in the next section.

Online Testing

In both distance learning and traditional classes, *online testing*—which allows students to take tests via the Internet—is a growing trend. Both objective tests (such as those containing multiple choice or true/false questions) and performance-based exams (such as those given in computer classes to test student mastery of software applications) can be administered and taken online. For instance, there are SAM (*Skills Assessment Manager*) tests available for use in conjunction with this textbook to test both Microsoft Office software skills and computer concepts. Typically online tests are graded automatically, freeing up the instructor's time for other activities, as well as providing fast feedback to the students.

One challenge for online testing is ensuring that an online test is taken by the appropriate individual and in an authorized manner, in order to avoid cheating. Some distance learning programs require students to go physically to a testing center to take the test or to find an acceptable test proctor (such as an educator at a nearby school or a commanding officer for military personnel). Other options are using smart cards, fingerprint scans, and other means to authenticate students taking an online exam from a remote location. For instance, one secure testing solution being used at a number of schools nationwide to enable students to take online tests from their remote locations while still ensuring the integrity of the exams is the *Securexam Remote Proctor* system shown in Figure 8-29. This system uses a device that first authenticates the individual taking the test via a fingerprint scan, and then captures real-time audio and video during the exam. The device's camera points to a reflective ball, which allows it to capture a full 360-degree image of the room, and the recording is uploaded to a server so it can be viewed by the instructor from his or her location. The Securexam software locks down the computer so that it cannot be used for any purpose not allowed during the test (such as performing an Internet search). It also flags suspicious behavior (such as significant noises or movements) in the recording so that the instructor can review those portions of the recording to see if any unauthorized behavior (such as leaving the room or making a telephone call) occurred during the testing period.

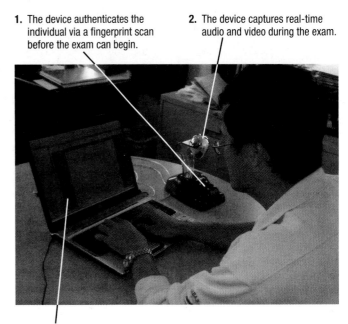

1. The device authenticates the individual via a fingerprint scan before the exam can begin.

2. The device captures real-time audio and video during the exam.

3. The computer is locked down during the exam so it can only be used for authorized activities.

FIGURE 8-29
Secure online testing.

FIGURE 8-30
Blogs. Allow individuals to post entries to an online personal journal.

Blogs, Wikis, and Other Types of Online Writing

A **blog**—also called a *Web log*—is a Web page that contains short, frequently updated entries in chronological order, typically as a means of expression or communication (see Figure 8-30). In essence, a blog is an online personal journal accessible to the public that is usually created and updated by one individual. Blogs are written by a wide variety of individuals—including ordinary people, as well as celebrities, writers, students, and experts on particular subjects—and can be used to post personal commentary, research updates, comments on current events, political opinions, celebrity gossip, travel diaries, television show recaps, and more.

Blogging software, which is available via blogging sites such as Blogger.com, is usually used to easily create and publish blogs and blog updates to the Web. Blogs are also frequently published on school, business, and personal Web sites. Blogs

>**Blog.** A Web page that contains short, frequently updated entries in chronological order, typically by just one individual.

are usually updated frequently, and entries can be posted via computers, e-mail, and mobile phones. Blogs often contain text, photos, and video clips. With their increased use and audiences, bloggers and the *blogosphere* (the complete collection of blogs on the Internet) are beginning to have increasing influence on businesses, politicians, and individuals today. One new ethical issue surrounding blogging relates to bloggers who are paid to blog about certain products. Although some Web sites that match up bloggers with advertisers require that the blogger reveal that he or she receives payment for "sponsored" posts, some believe that commercializing blogging will corrupt the blogosphere. Others, however, view it as a natural evolution of word-of-mouth advertising.

Another form of online writing sometimes used for educational purposes is the **wiki**. Wikis, named for the Hawaiian phrase *wiki wiki* meaning *quick*, are a way of creating and editing collaborative Web pages quickly and easily. Similar to a blog, the content on a wiki page can be edited and republished to the Web just by pressing a Save or Submit button. However, wikis are intended to be modified by others and so are especially appropriate for collaboration, such as for class Web pages or group projects. To protect the content of a wiki from sabotage, the entire wiki or editing privileges for a wiki can be password protected.

One of the largest wikis is *Wikipedia* (shown in Figure 8-31), a free online encyclopedia that contains over eight million articles written in 250 languages, is updated by more than 75,000 active contributors, and is visited by hundreds of thousands of individuals each day. While most Wikipedia contributors edit articles in a responsible manner, there are instances of erroneous information being added to Wikipedia pages intentionally. As with any resource, visitors should carefully evaluate the content of a Wikipedia article before referencing it in a report, Web page, or other document, as discussed earlier in this chapter.

FIGURE 8-31

Wikis. Wikis, such as the Wikipedia collaborative online encyclopedia shown here, can be edited by any authorized individual.

An **e-portfolio**, also called an *electronic portfolio* or *digital portfolio*, is a collection of an individual's work accessible through a Web site. Today's e-portfolios are typically linked to a collection of student-related information, such as résumés, papers, projects, and other original works. Some e-portfolios are used for a single course; others are designed to be used and updated throughout a student's educational career, culminating in a comprehensive collection of information that can be used as a job-hunting tool.

CENSORSHIP AND PRIVACY ISSUES

There are many important societal issues related to the Internet. One important issue—network and Internet security—is covered in Chapter 9. Two other important issues—*censorship* and *privacy*—are discussed next, in the context of Internet use. Other societal issues—including computer security, ethics, health, and the environment—related to computer use are discussed in further detail in Chapters 15 and 16.

>**Wiki.** A collaborative Web page that is designed to be edited and republished by a variety of individuals. >**E-portfolio.** A collection of an individual's work accessible via the Web.

Censorship

The issue of Internet censorship affects all countries that have Internet access. In some countries, Internet content is filtered by the government, typically to hinder the spread of information from political opposition groups, to filter out subjects deemed offensive, or to block information from sites that could endanger national security. Increasingly, some countries are also blocking information (such as blogs and personal Web pages) from leaving the country, and have occasionally completely shut down Internet access to and from the country during political protests to stop the flow of information in and out of that country.

In the United States, the First Amendment to the U.S. Constitution guarantees a citizen's right to free speech. This protection allows people to say things to others without fear of arrest. But how does the right to free speech relate to potentially offensive or indecent materials available over the Internet where they might be observed by children or by people who do not wish to see them? There have been some attempts in the United States and other countries to regulate Internet content—what some would view as *censorship*—in recent years, but the courts have had difficulty defining what is "patently offensive" and "indecent" as well as finding a fair balance between protection and censorship. For example, the *Communications Decency Act* was signed into law in 1996 and made it a criminal offense to distribute patently indecent or offensive material online in order to protect children from being exposed to inappropriate Web content. In 1997, however, the Supreme Court overturned the portion of this law pertaining to indecent material on the basis of free speech, making this content legal to distribute via the Internet and protecting Web sites that host third-party content from being liable for that content.

Another example of legislation designed to protect children from inappropriate Web content is the *Children's Internet Protection Act* (*CIPA*). CIPA requires public libraries and schools to implement Internet safety policies and technologies to block children's access to inappropriate Web content in order to receive certain public funds. While this law was intended to protect children, it was fought strenuously by free speech advocacy groups and some library associations on the basis that limiting access to some Internet content violates an individual's First Amendment rights to free speech. While CIPA was ruled unconstitutional by a federal court in 2002, the Supreme Court reversed the lower court decision in 2003 and ruled that the law is constitutional because the need for libraries to prevent minors from accessing obscene materials outweighs the free speech rights of library patrons and Web site publishers. However, the Court also modified the law to require the library to remove the technologies for an adult library patron at the patron's request.

One technology commonly used to conform to CIPA regulations, as well as by parents and employees, is **Internet filtering**—the act of blocking access to particular Web pages or types of Web pages. It can be used on home computers (for instance, by individuals to protect themselves from material they would view as offensive or by parents to protect their children from material they feel is inappropriate). It is also commonly used by employers to keep employees from accessing non-work-related sites, by some ISPs and search sites to block access to potentially objectionable materials, and by many schools and libraries to control the Web content that children are able to view. Internet filtering typically restricts access to Web pages that contain offensive language, sex/pornography, racism, drugs, or violence (based on either the keywords contained

---

>**Internet filtering.** Using a software program or browser option to block access to particular Web pages or types of Web pages.

PARENTAL CONTROLS
Affect a particular user
account, such as "Kids"
in this example.

CONTENT ADVISOR
Affects all users on
this computer.

Ⓐ **FIGURE 8-32**

Internet filtering.
Browser settings can
be changed to deny
access to Web pages
with objectionable
content.

on each site or a database of URLs containing restricted content). It can also be used
to block access to specific sites (such as social networking sites, YouTube, or eBay), as
well as to restrict the total number of hours or the time of day that the Internet can be
used.

Most browsers include some Internet filtering options. For instance, Internet Explorer's
Content Advisor (see Figure 8-32) can be used to filter the Web sites displayed for all users
of a particular computer (although blocked Web sites can be viewed if the user knows the
appropriate password); and *Parental Controls* can be used to set restrictions for individual
users, such as the Web sites that can be viewed, whether or not the user can download files,
and so forth. More comprehensive Internet filtering can be obtained with stand-alone filtering programs, such as *NetNanny* or *Safe Eyes*.

Web Browsing Privacy

Privacy, as it relates to the Internet, encompasses what information about individuals is
available, how it is used, and by whom. As more and more transactions and daily activities
are being performed online, there is the potential for vast amounts of private information to
be collected and distributed without the individual's knowledge or permission. Therefore,
it is understandable that public concern regarding privacy and the Internet is on the rise.
Although personal privacy will be discussed in more detail in Chapter 15, a few issues that
are of special concern to Internet users regarding Web browsing privacy and e-mail privacy
are discussed in the next few sections.

Cookies

Many Web pages today use **cookies**—small text files that are stored on your hard drive by a Web server—to identify return visitors and their preferences. While some individuals view all cookies as a potential invasion of privacy, Web sites can read only their own cookie files and the use of cookies can provide some benefits to consumers. For example, cookies can enable a Web site to remember preferences for customized Web site content (for instance, displaying customized content on a portal page, such as the one shown in Figure 8-26), as well as to retrieve a shopping cart containing items selected during a previous session. Some Web sites also use cookies to keep track of which pages on their Web sites each person has visited, in order to recommend products on return visits that match that person's interests. A use of cookies that is more objectionable to some is the use of *third-party cookies* (cookies placed on your hard drive by a company other than the one associated with the Web page that you are viewing—typically a Web advertising company). Third-party cookies target advertisements to Web site visitors based on their activities on the site (such as products viewed or advertisements clicked).

The information stored in a cookie file typically includes the name of the cookie, its expiration date, and the domain that the cookie belongs to. In addition, a cookie contains either personal information that you have entered while visiting the Web site or an ID number assigned by the Web site that allows the Web site's server to retrieve your personal information from its database. Such a database can contain two types of information: *personally identifiable information* (*PII*) and *non-personally identifiable information* (*Non-PII*). Personally identifiable information is connected with a specific user's identity—such as his or her name and address—and is typically given during the process of ordering goods or services. Non-personally identifiable information is anonymous data—such as which product pages were viewed or which advertisements located on the site were clicked—that is not directly associated with the visitor's name or another personally identifiable characteristic.

Cookies stored on your computer's hard drive can be looked at, if desired, although sometimes deciphering the information contained in a cookie file is difficult. Internet Explorer users can view and/or delete cookies and other temporary files by using Internet Explorer's Tools menu to open the Internet Options dialog box and selecting the appropriate options in the *Browsing history* section on the General tab. The Privacy tab in this dialog box (shown in Figure 8-33) can be

FIGURE 8-33

Browser cookie management. The desired cookies settings can be specified in the browser settings.

COOKIE SETTINGS
Click the Advanced button on the Internet Options Privacy tab to specify your cookie settings.

COOKIE PROMPTS
After selecting the "Prompt" option, you will be prompted to accept or reject cookies as they are encountered.

Web sites requesting cookie use

> **Cookie.** A small file stored on a user's hard drive by a Web server; commonly used to identify personal preferences and settings for that user.

used to specify which type of cookies (if any) are allowed to be used, such as permitting the use of regular cookies, but not third-party cookies or cookies using personally identifiable information.

Turning off cookies entirely might make some features—such as a shopping cart—on some Web sites inoperable. The *Medium High* privacy option in Internet Explorer is a widely used setting since it allows the use of regular cookies but blocks third-party cookies that use personally identifiable information without explicit permission. Users who want more control over their cookies can choose to accept or decline cookies as they are encountered in most browsers. Although this option interrupts your Web surfing frequently, it is interesting to see the cookies generated from each individual Web site. For example, the two cookie prompts shown in the bottom of Figure 8-33 were generated while visiting the BestBuy.com Web site. Although one cookie request is from the BestBuy.com Web site directly, the other is a third-party cookie from an online marketing company.

Another alternative is the *private browsing* option available with many Web browsers, including Internet Explorer, Chrome, and Safari. As discussed more in Chapter 15, this option allows you to browse the Web without leaving any history (including browsing history, form data, cookies, usernames, and passwords) on the computer you are using. Private browsing is useful for individuals using school, library, or other public computers to visit password-protected sites, research medical information, or perform other tasks that the user may prefer to keep private. Individuals using a computer to shop for presents or other surprises for family members who share the same computer may find the feature useful, as well.

CAUTION CAUTION CAUTION CAUTION CAUTION CAUTION CAUT

Cookies (typically placed by advertising companies) that attempt to track your activities across a Web site or the Web sites belonging to an advertising network are referred to as *tracking cookies*. If your security software includes tracking cookie protection, be sure it is enabled to avoid these cookies from being stored on your computer. Setting your browser's privacy settings to block third-party cookies can offer you some additional protection against tracking cookies.

Spyware and Adware

Spyware is the term used for any software program that is installed without the user's knowledge and that secretly gathers information about the user and transmits it through his or her Internet connection. Spyware is sometimes used to provide advertisers with information used for marketing purposes, such as to help select advertisements to display on each person's computer. The information gathered by the spyware software is usually not associated with a person's identity. But spyware is a concern for privacy advocates because it is typically installed without a user's direct knowledge (such as at the same time another program is installed, often when a program is downloaded from a Web site or a P2P service) and conveys information about a user's Internet activities. Spyware can also be used by criminals to retrieve personal data stored on your computer for use in criminal activities, as discussed in more detail in Chapter 9.

> **Spyware.** A software program that is installed without the user's permission and that secretly gathers information to be sent to others.

Unfortunately, spyware use is on the rise and can affect the performance of a computer (such as slowing it down or causing it to work improperly), in addition to its potential security risks. And the problem will likely become worse before it gets any better. Some spyware programs—sometimes referred to as *stealthware*—are getting more aggressive, such as delivering ads regardless of the activity you are doing on your computer, changing your browser home page or otherwise altering your browser settings (referred to as *browser hijacking*), and performing other annoying actions. The worst spyware programs rewrite your computer's main instructions—such as the Windows registry—to change your browser settings back to the hijacked settings each time you reboot your computer, undoing any changes you may have made to your browser settings.

A related type of software is *adware*, which is free or low-cost software that is supported by on-screen advertising. Many free programs that can be downloaded from the Internet, such as the free version of the *NetZero* e-mail program, include some type of adware, which results in on-screen advertising. The difference between spyware and adware is that adware typically does not gather information and relay it to others via the Internet (although it can), and it is not installed without the user's consent. Adware might, however, be installed without the user's direct knowledge, since many users do not read licensing agreements before clicking OK to install a new program. When this occurs with a program that contains adware, the adware components are installed without the user's direct knowledge.

Both spyware and adware can be annoying and use up valuable system resources, in addition to revealing data about individuals. As discussed in detail in Chapter 9, *firewalls* and *antispyware programs* can be used to protect against spyware.

E-Mail Privacy

Many people mistakenly believe that the e-mail they send and receive is private and will never be read by anyone other than the intended recipient. Since it is transmitted over public media, however, only *encrypted* (electronically scrambled) e-mail can be transmitted safely, as discussed in Chapter 9. Although unlikely to happen to your personal e-mail, *nonencrypted* e-mail can be intercepted and read by someone else. Consequently, from a privacy standpoint, a nonencrypted e-mail message should be viewed more like a postcard than a letter (see Figure 8-34).

It is also important to realize that your employer and your ISP have access to the e-mail you send through those organizations. Businesses and ISPs typically archive (keep copies of) e-mail messages that travel through their servers and are required to comply with subpoenas from law enforcement agencies for archived e-mail messages.

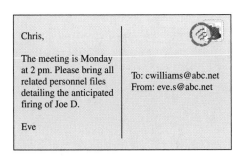

REGULAR (NONENCRYPTED E-MAIL) = POSTCARD

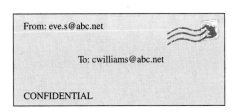

ENCRYPTED E-MAIL = SEALED LETTER

FIGURE 8-34
You cannot assume e-mail messages are private, unless they are encrypted.

SUMMARY

EVOLUTION OF THE INTERNET

Chapter Objective 1:
Discuss how the Internet evolved and what it is like today.

The origin of the **Internet**—a worldwide collection of interconnected networks that is accessed by millions of people daily—dates back to the late 1960s. At its start and throughout its early years, the Internet was called **ARPANET**. It was not until the development of the **World Wide Web** (**WWW**) that public interest in the Internet began to soar. Most companies have Web sites today and consider the Web to be an indispensable business tool. While the Web is a very important and widely used Internet resource, it is not the only one. Over the years, *protocols* have been developed to download files, send e-mail messages, and perform other tasks, in addition to using Web pages. Today, the term *Internet* has become a household word and, in many ways, has redefined how people think about computers and communications. The next significant improvement to the Internet infrastructure may be the result of projects such as *Internet2*.

Chapter Objective 2:
Identify the various types of individuals, companies, and organizations involved in the Internet community and explain their purposes.

The Internet community is made up of individual *users*; companies, such as **Internet service providers** (**ISPs**), **Internet content providers**, **application service providers** (**ASPs**), *infrastructure companies*, and a variety of software and hardware companies; the government; and other organizations. Virtually anyone with a computer with communications capability can be part of the Internet, either as a user or supplier of information or services. **Web services** are self-contained business functions that operate over the Internet.

Because the Internet is so unique in the history of the world—and it remains a relatively new and ever-changing phenomenon—several widespread myths about it have surfaced. Three such myths are that the Internet is free, that it is controlled by some central body, and that it is synonymous with the World Wide Web.

GETTING SET UP TO USE THE INTERNET

Chapter Objective 3:
Describe device and connection options for connecting to the Internet, as well as some considerations to keep in mind when selecting an ISP.

Most Internet connections today are **direct connections** (always connected to the Internet), though some are **dial-up connections** (which need to dial up and connect to the Internet to provide access). Dial-up connections are typically **conventional dial-up Internet access**; common types of direct Internet connections include **cable**, **DSL** (**Digital Subscriber Line**), **satellite**, **fixed wireless**, **mobile wireless**, and **broadband over fiber** (**BoF**)—also called **fiber-to-the-premises** (**FTTP**)—**Internet access**. Individuals can also connect to the Internet via a **Wi-Fi hotspot**. When preparing to become connected to the Internet, you need to decide which type of device (personal computer or mobile phone, for instance), which type of Internet connection, and which specific Internet service provider to use. Once all these decisions are made, you can acquire the proper hardware and software and set up your system for Internet access.

SEARCHING THE INTERNET

Chapter Objective 4:
Understand how to search effectively for information on the Internet and how to cite Internet resources properly.

Search sites are Web sites that enable users to search for and find information on the Internet. They typically locate pages using a **keyword search** (in which the user specifies **keywords** for the desired information)—a **search engine** retrieves the list of matching Web pages from a database. A **directory search** (in which the user selects categories corresponding to the desired information) is another possibility. Search site databases are generally maintained by automated *spider* programs.

There are a variety of search strategies that can be used, including typing phrases instead of single keywords; using *Boolean operators*; trying the search at multiple search sites; and using *synonyms, variant word forms, wildcards*, and *field searches*. Once a list of links to Web pages matching the search criteria is displayed, the hits need to be evaluated for their relevancy. If the information found on a Web page is used in a paper, report, or other original document, the source should be credited appropriately.

BEYOND BROWSING AND E-MAIL

The Internet can be used for many different types of activities in addition to basic Web browsing and e-mail exchange. Common types of online communications include **instant messaging** (**IM**) and **text messaging** (sending real-time typed messages via a computer or mobile phone, respectively), **Twittering** (sending short status updates via Twitter), **message boards** (online locations where people post messages on a particular topic for others to read and respond to), **Web conferencing** (real-time meetings taking place via the Web that typically use video cameras and microphones to enable participants to see and hear each other), and **Webinars** (seminars presented over the Web). **Social networking sites** also allow the members of an online community to communicate and exchange information. **Voice over Internet Protocol** (**VoIP**) refers to making voice telephone calls over the Internet.

Common Web activities for individuals include a variety of consumer *e-commerce* activities, such as **online shopping**, **online auctions**, **online banking**, and **online investing**. When performing any type of financial transaction over the Internet, it is very important to use only *secure* Web pages.

Online entertainment applications include **online gaming**, downloading music files and other types of **online music**, and **online TV**, **online movies**, and other types of **online video**. Selecting and receiving TV shows and movies via the Web is called **video-on-demand** (**VOD**). A wide variety of news, reference, government, product, and corporate information is available via the Web as well. News, reference, and search tools are commonly found on **portal Web pages**; **RSS** (**Really Simple Syndication**) feeds can be used to deliver current news, **podcasts**, and other Web content to individuals as it becomes available.

Online education options include **Web-based training** (**WBT**) and **distance learning**. *Online testing* can be used for both objective and performance-based exams and can be secured by a variety of means. Online writing includes **blogs** (Web pages that contain frequently updated entries by individuals), **wikis** (Web pages designed to be created and edited by multiple individuals), and **e-portfolios** (collections of an individual's work).

CENSORSHIP AND PRIVACY ISSUES

Among the most important societal issues relating to the Internet are *censorship* and *privacy*. Web content is not censored as a whole, but **Internet filtering** can be used by parents, employers, educators, and anyone wishing to prevent access to sites they deem objectionable on computers for which they have control. *Privacy* is a big concern for individuals, particularly as it relates to their Web activity. **Cookies** are typically used by Web sites to save customized settings for that site and can also be used for advertising purposes. Another item of possible concern is **spyware** (software installed without the user's permission that sends information to others). Unless an e-mail message is *encrypted*, it should not be assumed to be completely private.

Chapter Objective 5:
List several ways to communicate over the Internet, in addition to e-mail.

Chapter Objective 6:
List several useful activities that can be performed via the Web.

NET

Chapter Objective 7:
Discuss censorship and privacy, and how they are related to Internet use.

REVIEW ACTIVITIES

KEY TERM MATCHING

a. cookie

b. dial-up connection

c. direct connection

d. distance learning

e. Internet

f. keyword

g. podcast

h. search engine

i. video-on-demand (VOD)

j. World Wide Web (WWW)

Instructions: Match each key term on the left with the definition on the right that best describes it.

1. _____ A learning environment in which the student is physically located away from the instructor and other students; commonly, instruction and communications take place via the Web.

2. _____ A type of Internet connection in which the computer or other device is connected to the Internet continually.

3. _____ A small file stored on a user's hard drive by a Web server; commonly used to identify personal preferences and settings for that user.

4. _____ A software program used by a search site to retrieve matching Web pages from a search database.

5. _____ A type of Internet connection in which the computer or other device must dial up and connect to a service provider's computer via telephone lines before being connected to the Internet.

6. _____ A recorded audio or video file that can be played or downloaded via the Web.

7. _____ A word typed in a search box on a search site to locate information on the Internet.

8. _____ The collection of Web pages available through the Internet.

9. _____ The largest and most well-known computer network, linking millions of computers all over the world.

10. _____ The process of downloading movies and television shows, on demand, via the Web.

SELF-QUIZ

Instructions: Circle **T** if the statement is true, **F** if the statement is false, or write the best answer in the space provided. **Answers for the self-quiz are located in the References and Resources Guide at the end of the book**.

1. **T F** When the Internet was first developed, it was called Mosaic.

2. **T F** On the Internet, an *access provider* and a *content provider* are essentially the same thing.

3. **T F** With a direct connection, you need only open your browser to start your Internet session.

4. **T F** A Wi-Fi hotspot is used to provide Internet access to individuals via a wireless connection.

5. **T F** A Webinar is a Web site designed to allow individuals to easily create and publish blogs.

6. _____ is a type of always-on broadband Internet service that transmits data over standard telephone lines but does not tie up your phone line.

7. With a(n) _____ search, keywords are typed into the search box; with a(n) _____ search, users select categories to find matching Web pages.

8. A(n) _____ is a Web site (such as Facebook) designed to enable a community of individuals to communicate and exchange information.

9. With a(n) _____ , people bid on products over the Internet, and the highest bidder purchases the item.

10. Match each Internet application to its possible situation, and write the corresponding number in the blank to the left of each situation.

a. _____ To communicate with a friend in a different state.

b. _____ To pay only as much as you specify for an item purchased through the Internet.

c. _____ To pay a bill without writing a check.

d. _____ To find Web pages containing information about growing your own Bonsai trees.

1. Online banking

2. E-mail

3. Internet searching

4. Online auction

---

1. Match each type of Internet access to its description, and write the corresponding number in the blank to the left of each description.

a. _____ A common type of home broadband connection; does not use standard phone lines.

b. _____ Provides access to the Internet via a very fast fiber-optic network.

c. _____ Accesses the Internet via standard phone lines and ties up your phone; the maximum speed is 56 Kbps.

1. Conventional dial-up

2. BoF

3. Cable

2. What would each of the following searches look for?

a. hot AND dogs _____

b. snorkel* _____

c. text:"Internet privacy" domain:*.gov _____

3. List three different sets of keywords that could be used to search for information on how to maintain a trumpet.

4. Explain the difference between a blog, a wiki, and a podcast.

5. List one advantage and one disadvantage of the use of Web site cookies.

---

1. Twittering became virtually an overnight sensation, but some question its usefulness. Do you want to know the routine activities your friends (or other individuals you choose to follow) are doing during the day? Is it useful information to tweet that you are stuck in traffic or having a bad day? Do you follow anyone on Twitter or tweet regularly? Why or why not? Since Twitter updates have to be very short, some may think that twittering on the job does not take up enough time to be a concern, but what about the distraction factor? Should employers allow employees to use Twitter, Facebook, and other popular online activities during work hours? Why or why not?

2. Some courtrooms today are becoming high-tech, such as using videoconferencing systems to allow defendants and witnesses to participate in proceedings from remote locations. Allowing defendants to participate remotely from the jail facility saves travel time and expense, as well as eliminates any risk of flight. Remote testimony from witnesses can save both time and money. But, could having defendants and witnesses participate remotely affect the jury's perspective? If the videoconference takes place via the Internet, can it be assured that proceedings are confidential? Do you think the benefits of these systems outweigh any potential disadvantages?

NET

PROJECTS

HOT TOPICS

1. **Social Network Addiction** As discussed in the chapter, social networks (such as Facebook and MySpace) are very popular with individuals. However, it has become apparent recently that some individuals are moving from casual social networking use to compulsive or addictive behavior.

   For this project, investigate either Facebook addiction or Internet addiction. How common is it? What are some of the warning signs? Is there an actual medical disorder associated with it? If so, what is it and how is it treated? Find one example in a news or journal article of a person who was "addicted" to using a social networking site or other online activity—why was their behavior considered addictive? Were they able to modify their behavior? Have you ever been concerned about becoming addicted to any Internet activities? At the conclusion of your research, prepare a one-page summary of your findings and opinions and submit it to your instructor.

**SHORT ANSWER/
RESEARCH**

2. **Online Travel Planning** Planning and booking travel arrangements online is a very popular Internet activity today and there are a number of sites that can be used.

   For this project, review two popular travel sites, such as Expedia.com and Travelocity.com, to see what services they offer and how easy it is to locate the information needed to plan and book a flight via those sites. Select a destination and use one of the sites to obtain a quote for a particular flight on a particular day. Next, go to the Web site for the airline of the flight and use the site to obtain a quote for the same flight. Is there a difference in price or flight availability? Could you make a reservation online through both sites? Would you feel comfortable booking an entire vacation yourself online, or are there services that a travel agent could provide that you feel would be beneficial? Do you think these sites are most appropriate for making business travel plans or vacation plans, or are they suited to both? At the conclusion of your research, prepare a one-page summary of your findings and submit it to your instructor.

HANDS ON

3. **Web Searching** Search sites can be used to find Web pages containing specific information, and there are strategies that can be used to make Web searching an efficient and useful experience.

   For this project, go to the Google search site and perform the following searches, then submit your results and printouts to your instructor. (Note: Some of the answers will vary from student to student.)

   a. Search for *rules*. How many pages were found? What is the name of the first page in the list of hits? Next, search for *backgammon rules*. How many pages were found? Use the hits to find a picture of how a backgammon board is initially set up, then, print that page.

   b. Search to find a recipe for Buffalo Chicken Wings; a map of where your house, apartment, or dorm is located; and the ZIP code for 200 N. Elm Street, Hinsdale, IL and print the pages containing this information.

   c. Go to the Advanced Search option. Use the form fields to perform a search for Web pages that contain all of the words *hiking trails Sierras*, do not contain the word *horse*, and have the domain *.gov*. After the hits are displayed, record the actual search phrase that is listed in the search box along with the name and URL of the first page displayed in the list of hits.

4. **Paid Bloggers** Blogs are traditionally online personal journals where the blogger expresses his or her opinion on desired topics. Unlike professional journalists, bloggers typically post because they want to, not because they have been hired to do so. However, as discussed in the chapter, bloggers are increasingly being paid or "sponsored" to blog. Is this ethical? If a blogger is paid to post his or her honest opinion about a product or service, does that lessen the credibility of that post? Does it change your opinion if the blogger reveals that it is a sponsored blog? If you based a purchase on a review posted in a blog that you later found out was sponsored, would you feel misled? How, if at all, do sponsored posts affect the blogosphere as a whole?

   For this project, form an opinion about the ethical ramifications of paid blogging and be prepared to discuss your position (in class, via an online class discussion group, in a class chat room, or via a class blog, depending on your instructor's directions). You may also be asked to write a short paper expressing your opinion.

5. **Wi-Fi Hotspots** There are an increasing number of public locations offering Wi-Fi hotspots available for public use.

   For this project, find one location in your local area that offers public Wi-Fi access and either visit the location or call the provider on the phone to find out the how the hotspot works, in terms of fees and access. Is there a fee to use the hotspot? If so, do you have to subscribe on a regular basis, or can you pay only when you want to use the hotspot? Where and how is payment made? Do you need any special software to access the hotspot? Do you need to be assigned a username or key (such as a *WEP, WPA,* or *WPA 2* key) before you can use the service? Share your findings and opinions with the class in the form of a short presentation. The presentation should not exceed 10 minutes and should make use of one or more presentation aids, such as the chalkboard, handouts, overhead transparencies, or a computer-based slide presentation (your instructor may provide additional requirements). You may also be asked to submit a summary of the presentation to your instructor.

Instructions: Go to the Chapter 8 page at **www.cengage.com/computerconcepts/np/uc13** to work the following Web Activities.

6. **Interactive Activities** Work the interactive **Crossword Puzzle**, watch the **Video Podcasts** and **Online Videos**, and explore the **Further Exploration** links associated with this chapter.

   If you have a SAM user profile, you may have access to hands-on instruction, practice, and assessment of the skills covered in this chapter. Check with your instructor for instructions and the correct URL/Web site to access those assignments.

7. **Student Edition Labs** Work the following interactive **Student Edition Labs**.
   - **Connecting to the Internet**
   - **Getting the Most Out of the Internet**

8. **Test Yourself** Review the **Online Study Guide** for this chapter, then test your knowledge of the terms and concepts covered in this chapter by completing the **Key Term Matching** exercise, the **Self-Quiz**, the **Exercises**, and the **Practice Test**.

chapter 9

Network and Internet Security

After completing this chapter, you will be able to do the following:

1. Explain why computer users should be concerned about network and Internet security.

2. List several examples of unauthorized access and unauthorized use.

3. Explain several ways to protect against unauthorized access and unauthorized use, including access control systems, firewalls, and encryption.

4. Provide several examples of computer sabotage.

5. List how individuals and businesses can protect against computer sabotage.

6. Discuss online theft, identity theft, spoofing, phishing, and other types of dot cons.

7. Detail steps an individual can take to protect against online theft, identity theft, spoofing, phishing, and other types of dot cons.

8. Identify personal safety risks associated with Internet use.

9. List steps individuals can take to safeguard their personal safety when using the Internet.

10. Discuss the current state of network and Internet security legislation.

outline

Overview

Why Be Concerned about Network and Internet Security?

Unauthorized Access and Unauthorized Use
Hacking
War Driving and Wi-Fi Piggybacking
Interception of Communications

Protecting Against Unauthorized Access and Unauthorized Use
Access Control Systems
Firewalls, Encryption, and Virtual Private Networks (VPNs)
Additional Public Hotspot Precautions
Sensible Employee Precautions

Computer Sabotage
Botnets
Computer Viruses and Other Types of Malware
Denial of Service (DoS) Attacks
Data, Program, or Web Site Alteration

Protecting Against Computer Sabotage
Security Software
Other Security Precautions

Online Theft, Online Fraud, and Other Dot Cons
Theft of Data, Information, and Other Resources
Identity Theft, Phishing, and Pharming
Online Auction Fraud
Other Internet Scams

Protecting Against Online Theft, Online Fraud, and Other Dot Cons
Protecting Against Data and Information Theft
Protecting Against Identity Theft, Phishing, and Pharming
Protecting Against Online Auction Fraud and Other Internet Scams

Personal Safety Issues
Cyberbullying and Cyberstalking
Online Pornography

Protecting Against Cyberbullying, Cyberstalking, and Other Personal Safety Concerns
Safety Tips for Adults
Safety Tips for Children and Teens

Network and Internet Security Legislation

OVERVIEW

As discussed in the last few chapters, networks and the Internet help many of us be more efficient and effective workers, as well as add convenience and enjoyment to our personal lives. However, there is a downside, as well. The wide-spread use of home and business networks and the Internet increases the risk of unauthorized computer access, theft, fraud, and other types of computer crime. In addition, the vast amount of business and personal data stored on computers acces-sible via company networks and the Internet increases the chances of data loss due to crime or employee errors. Some online activities can even put your personal safety at risk, if you are not careful.

This chapter looks at a variety of security concerns stemming from the use of computer networks and the Internet in our society, including unauthorized access and use, computer viruses and other types of sabotage, and online theft and fraud. Safe-guards for each of these concerns are also covered, with an explanation of precautions that can be taken to reduce the chance that these security problems will happen to you. Personal safety issues related to the Internet are also discussed, and the chapter closes with a look at legislation related to network and Internet security. ■

PODCAST

Go to **www.cengage.com/ computerconcepts/np/uc13** to download or listen to the "Expert Insight on Networks and the Internet" podcast.

NET

WHY BE CONCERNED ABOUT NETWORK AND INTERNET SECURITY?

From a *computer virus* making your computer function abnormally, to a *hacker* using your personal information to make fraudulent purchases, to someone harassing you online in a discussion group, a variety of security concerns related to computer networks and the Internet exist. Many Internet security concerns today can be categorized as **computer crimes**. Computer crime—sometimes referred to as *cybercrime*—includes any illegal act involving a computer. Many computer crimes today are committed using the Internet or another computer network and include theft of financial assets or information, manipulating data (such as grades or account information), and acts of sabotage (such as releasing a computer virus or shutting down a Web server). Cybercrime is an important security concern today. It is a multibillion-dollar business that is often performed by seasoned criminals. In fact, according to the FBI, organized crime organizations in many countries are increasingly turning to computer crime to target millions of potential victims easily, and *phishing attacks* and other *Internet scams* (discussed shortly) are expected to increase in reaction to the recent troubled economy. These and other computer crimes that are carried out via the Internet or another computer network are discussed in this chapter. Other types of computer crime (such as using a computer to create counterfeit currency or make illegal copies of a DVD) are covered in Chapter 15.

> **Computer crime.** Any illegal act involving a computer.

With some security concerns, such as when a spyware program changes your browser's home page, the consequence may be just an annoyance. In other cases, such as when someone steals your identity and purchases items using your name and credit card number, the consequences are much more serious. And, with the growing use of wireless networks, Web 2.0 applications (such as social networking sites), and individuals accessing company networks remotely, paired with an increasing number of security and privacy regulations that businesses need to comply with, network and Internet security has never been more important. Consequently, all computer users should be aware of the security concerns surrounding computer network and Internet use, and they should take appropriate precautions. The most common types of security risks related to network and Internet use, along with some corresponding precautions, are discussed throughout this chapter.

UNAUTHORIZED ACCESS AND UNAUTHORIZED USE

Unauthorized access occurs whenever an individual gains access to a computer, network, file, or other resource without permission—typically by *hacking* into the resource. **Unauthorized use** involves using a computer resource for unauthorized activities. Often, they happen at the same time, but unauthorized use can occur when a user is authorized to access a particular computer or network but is not authorized for the particular activity the user performs. For instance, while a student may be authorized to access the Internet via a campus computer lab, some use—such as viewing pornography—would likely be deemed off-limits. If so, viewing that content from a school computer would be considered unauthorized use. For employees of some companies, checking personal e-mail or visiting personal Facebook pages at work might be classified as unauthorized use.

Unauthorized access and many types of unauthorized use are criminal offenses in the United States and many other countries. They can be committed by both *insiders* (people who work for the company whose computers are being accessed) and *outsiders* (people who do not work for that company). Whether or not a specific act constitutes unauthorized use or is illegal depends on the circumstances, as well as the specific company or institution involved. To explain acceptable computer use to their employees, students, or other users, many organizations and educational institutions publish guidelines for behavior, often called *codes of conduct* (see Figure 9-1). Codes of conduct typically address prohibited activities, such as playing games, installing personal software, violating copyright laws, causing harm to computers or the network, and snooping in other people's files.

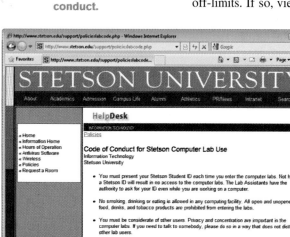

FIGURE 9-1
A sample code of conduct.

Hacking

Hacking refers to the act of breaking into a computer or network. It can be performed in person by hacking into a computer the *hacker* has physical access to, but it is more often performed via the Internet or another network. Unless authorized (such as when a company hires a *professional hacker* to test the security of its system), hacking in the United States and many other countries is a crime.

Typically, the motivation for hacking is to steal data, sabotage a computer system, or perform some other type of illegal act. In particular, the theft of consumer data (such as credit card numbers and cardholder information) has increased dramatically over the past several years—one breach, discovered in 2009, compromised the data of millions of debit and credit cards. Another growing trend is to hack into a computer and "hijack" it for use in an illegal or unethical act, such as generating spam or hosting pornographic Web sites. Hackers are also increasingly aiming attacks at very specific individuals, such as product designers and other individuals who have access to valuable corporate data.

In addition to being a threat to individuals and businesses, hacking is also considered a very serious threat to national security in the United States. The increased number of systems that are controlled by computers and are connected to the Internet, along with the continually improving abilities of hackers and the increasing availability of sets of tools (sometimes called *rootkits*) that allow hackers to access a system, has led to an increased risk of *cyberterrorism*—where terrorists launch attacks via the Internet. Current concerns include attacks against the computers controlling vital systems (such as the nation's power grids, banks, and water filtration facilities), as well as computers related to national defense, the airlines, and the stock market. In fact, outsiders attempt to access U.S. Pentagon computers millions of times each day, and military leaders are concerned about the potential of cybersecurity threats from other countries. As a result, President Obama has made cybersecurity a priority, including setting up a cybersecurity task force and czar, and stating, "It's now clear this cyber threat is one of the most serious economic and national security challenges we face as a nation."

Today, hackers often gain access via a wireless network. This is because wireless networks are becoming increasingly common and it is easier to hack into a wireless network than a wired network. In fact, as discussed in Chapter 7, it is possible to gain access to a wireless network just by being within range (about 100 to 300 feet, depending on the Wi-Fi standard being used) of a wireless access point, unless the access point is sufficiently protected. Although security features are built into wireless routers and other networking hardware, they are typically not enabled by default. As a result, many wireless networks belonging to businesses and individuals—some estimates put the number as high as 70% of all Wi-Fi networks—are left unsecured. Securing a Wi-Fi network is discussed shortly.

ASK THE EXPERT

Moshe Vardi, Rice University, Co-Chair of the ACM Globalization and Offshoring of Software Taskforce

Is there a national security risk to outsourcing/offshoring software development?

Offshoring magnifies existing risks and creates new and often poorly understood threats. When businesses offshore work, they increase not only their own business-related risks (e.g., intellectual property theft) but also risks to national security and to individuals' privacy. While it is unlikely these risks will deter the growth of offshoring, businesses and nations should employ strategies to mitigate the risks. Businesses have a clear incentive to manage these new risks to suit their own interests, but nations and individuals often have little awareness of the exposures created. For example, many commercial off-the-shelf (COTS) systems are developed offshore, making it extremely difficult for buyers to understand all of the source and application code in the systems. This creates the possibility that a hostile nation or nongovernmental hostile agent (such as a terrorist or criminal) could compromise these systems. Individuals are also often exposed to loss of privacy or identity theft due to the number of business processes being offshored today and managed under laws that are much less restrictive than in most developed countries.

NET

War Driving and Wi-Fi Piggybacking

Unauthorized use of a Wi-Fi network is called **war driving** or **Wi-Fi piggybacking**, depending on the location of the hacker at the time. War driving typically involves driving in a car with a portable computer looking for unsecured Wi-Fi networks to connect to. Wi-Fi piggybacking refers to accessing someone else's unsecured Wi-Fi network from the hacker's current location (such as inside his or her home, outside a Wi-Fi hotspot location, or near a local business). Both war driving and Wi-Fi piggybacking are ethically—if not legally—questionable acts. They can also lead to illegal behavior, such as individuals deciding to use data (credit card numbers, for instance) they run across while war driving for fraudulent purposes, as was the case with two men who illegally accessed a Lowe's wireless network during a war drive and later decided to steal credit card numbers via that network. War driving and Wi-Fi piggybacking can also have security risks, both for the hacker and the owner of the Wi-Fi network that is being used. For instance, they both risk the introduction of computer viruses (either intentionally or unintentionally) and unauthorized access of the data located on their computers. In addition, the owner may experience reduced performance or even the cancellation of his or her Internet service if the ISP limits bandwidth or the number of computers allowed to use a single Internet connection.

While there are products and services available to help mobile users locate legitimate public Wi-Fi hotspots (see Figure 9-2), laws in some countries, such as the U.K., are clear that unauthorized access of a Wi-Fi connection is illegal. In the United States, federal law is not as clear, although some states (such as Michigan) have made using a Wi-Fi connection without permission illegal. In fact, a Michigan man was found guilty, fined, and sentenced to community service in 2007 for using the free Wi-Fi service offered to customers at a local café because he was using the service from his parked car located on the street outside the café to check his e-mail on a regular basis.

Advocates of war driving and Wi-Fi piggybacking state that, unless individuals or businesses protect their access points, they are welcoming others to use them. Critics compare that logic to that of an unlocked front door—you cannot legally enter a home just because the front door is unlocked. Some wireless network owners do leave their access points unsecured on purpose and some communities are creating a collection of wireless access points to provide wireless Internet access to everyone in that community. However, it is difficult—if not impossible—to tell if an unsecured network is that way intentionally, unless connecting to the wireless network displays a welcome screen stating that it is a free public Wi-Fi hotspot.

Some feel the ethical distinction of using an unsecured wireless network is determined by the amount of use, believing that it is acceptable to borrow someone's Internet connection to do a quick e-mail check or Google search, but that continually using a neighbor's Internet connection to avoid paying for your own is crossing over the line. Others feel that allowing outsiders to share an Internet connection is acceptable use, as long as the subscriber does not charge the outsider for that access. Still others believe that an Internet connection is intended for use only by the subscriber and that sharing it with others is unfair to the subscriber's ISP. This issue is beginning to be addressed by the courts and

FIGURE 9-2

Wi-Fi finders. Some online mapping services list the Wi-Fi hotspots for a particular geographic area.

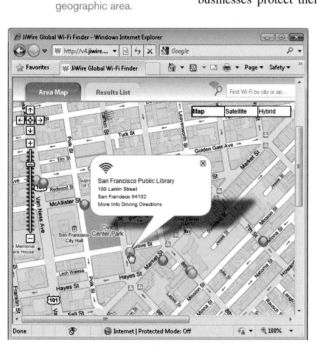

>**War driving.** Driving around an area with a Wi-Fi-enabled computer or mobile device to find a Wi-Fi network to access and use without authorization. >**Wi-Fi piggybacking.** Accessing an unsecured Wi-Fi network from your current location without authorization.

ISPs, and some answers regarding the legality of "Wi-Fi borrowing" and Internet connection sharing will likely be forthcoming in the near future. However, the ethical questions surrounding this issue may take longer to resolve.

Interception of Communications

Instead of accessing data stored on a computer via hacking, some criminals gain unauthorized access to data, files, e-mail messages, VoIP calls, and other content as it is being sent over the Internet. For instance, *unencrypted* (unsecured) messages, files, logon information, and more sent over a wireless network (such as while using a public Wi-Fi hotspot or over an unsecured home or business Wi-Fi network) can be captured and read by anyone within range using software designed for that purpose. Once intercepted, the data can be used for unintended or fraudulent purposes.

Although it is unlikely that anyone would be interested in intercepting personal e-mail sent to friends and relatives, proprietary corporate information and sensitive personal information (such as credit card numbers and Web site logon information) is at risk if it is sent unsecured over the Internet or over a wireless home or corporate network. The widespread use of wireless networks, as well as the increased use of wireless connections to transmit data via mobile phones and other portable devices, has opened up new opportunities for data interception. For instance, the data on mobile devices with Bluetooth capabilities enabled can be accessed by other Bluetooth devices that are within range.

A new trend is criminals intercepting credit and debit card information during the card verification process; that is, intercepting the data from a card in real time as a purchase is being authorized. In several recent cases, this occurred via *packetsniffing* software installed at payment terminals (such as restaurant cash registers or gas station credit/debit card readers) by hackers—the packetsniffing software gathered the data during transactions and then sent it to the hackers. The increased occurrence of real-time attacks may be partly because of the new *Payment Card Industry Data Security Standard* (*PCI DSS*) rules that require companies to limit the credit card data stored on company servers and to *encrypt* the data that is allowed to be stored. Consequently, hackers may be moving away from targeting data stored on company servers and focusing on stealing data in real time during credit card and debit card transactions.

PROTECTING AGAINST UNAUTHORIZED ACCESS AND UNAUTHORIZED USE

The first step in protecting against unauthorized access and unauthorized use is controlling access to an organization's facilities and computer networks to ensure that only authorized individuals are granted access. In addition, steps need to be taken to ensure that authorized individuals access only the resources that they are supposed to access.

Access Control Systems

Access control systems are used to control access to facilities, computer networks, company databases, individual Web site accounts, and other assets. They can be *identification systems*, which verify that the person trying to access the facility or system is listed as an authorized user, and/or *authentication systems*, which determine whether or not the person attempting access is actually who he or she claims to be. In businesses, access control systems are often integrated into a comprehensive *identity management (IDM) system* designed to manage users' access to enterprise systems, such as to grant them secure and appropriate access to the systems they are allowed to access in as convenient a manner as possible to the end user. The three most common types of access control systems are discussed next, followed by a discussion of additional considerations for controlling access to wireless networks.

I'm A Current Online Customer

Email Address: janedoe@aol.com

Password: ••••••••
(Password is case sensitive.)

[log in]

 FIGURE 9-3

Passwords.

Passwords are used to log on to computers, networks, Web sites, and other computing resources.

FIGURE 9-4

Strategies for creating good passwords.

PASSWORD STRATEGIES

Make the password at least eight characters, if possible. A five-character password can be cracked by a computer program in less than one minute. A ten-character password, in contrast, has about 3,700 trillion possible character permutations and is considerably safer.

Choose passwords that are not in a dictionary—for instance, mix numbers and special characters with abbreviations or unusual words you will remember, but that do not conform to a pattern a computer can readily figure out.

Do not use your name, your kids' or pets' names, your address, your birthdate, or any other public information as your password.

Determine a *passphrase* that you can remember and use corresponding letters and symbols (such as the first letter of each word) for your password. For instance, the passphrase "My son John is five years older than my daughter Abby" could be used to remember the corresponding strong password "Msji5yotMd@".

Do not keep a written copy of the password in your desk or taped to your monitor. If you need to write down your password, create a password-protected file on your computer that contains all your passwords so you can look them up as needed.

Use a different password for your highly sensitive activities (such as online banking or stock trading) than for Web sites that remember your settings or profile (such as online news, auction, shopping, or bookstore sites). If a hacker determines your password on a low-security site (which is easier to break into than a site located on a secure Web server), he or she can use it on an account containing sensitive data if you use the same password on both accounts.

Change your passwords frequently.

Possessed Knowledge Access Systems

A **possessed knowledge access system** is an identification system that requires the individual requesting access to provide information that only the authorized user is supposed to know. *Passwords* and *cognitive authentication systems* fall into this category.

Passwords, the most common type of possessed knowledge, are secret words or character combinations associated with an individual. They are typically used in conjunction with a *username* (often a variation of the person's first and/or last names or the individual's e-mail address). Username/password combinations are often used to restrict access to networks, computers, Web sites, routers, and other computing resources—the user is granted access to the requested resource only after supplying the correct information. While usernames and e-mail addresses are not secret, passwords are and, for security purposes, typically appear as asterisks or dots as they are being entered so they cannot be viewed (see Figure 9-3). For some applications (such as ATM machines), a *PIN* or *personal identification number*—a secret combination of numeric digits selected by the user—is used instead of a password. Numeric passwords are also referred to as *passcodes*.

One of the biggest disadvantages of password-based systems is that passwords can be forgotten. Another disadvantage is that any individual possessing the proper password will be granted access to the system because the system recognizes the password, regardless of whether or not the person using the password is the authorized user, and passwords can be guessed or deciphered by a hacker or a hacker's computer easily if secure password selection strategies are not applied. For example, many hackers are able to access networking hardware and databases because the system administrator passwords for those resources are still the default passwords (the ones assigned during manufacturing) and so are commonly known; some insiders gain unauthorized access to systems using passwords written down on sticky notes attached to a user's monitor. Consequently, it is important to select passwords that are *strong passwords* but are also easy to remember without writing them down. Strong passwords are passwords that are at least eight characters long; use a combination of letters, numbers, and symbols; and do not form words found in the dictionary or that match the username that the password is associated with. Some strategies for selecting good passwords are listed in Figure 9-4.

A growing trend in possessed knowledge access systems is the use of *cognitive authentication systems* instead of, or in conjunction with, usernames and passwords. Cognitive authentication systems use information that an individual should know or can remember easily.

> **Possessed knowledge access system.** An access control system that uses information only the individual should know to identify that individual.
> **Password.** A secret combination of characters used to gain access to a computer, computer network, or other resource.

Some systems use personal information about the individual (such as his or her city of birth, first elementary school attended, or amount of home mortgage) that was pulled from public databases or the company database and the individual must supply the correct answer in order to be granted access. Other systems (such as the password recovery systems used by many secure Web sites to verify individuals when they forget their password) allow the individual to supply answers to questions when the account is created and then the individual can supply those answers again for authentication purposes when needed.

Possessed knowledge systems are often used in conjunction with the *possessed object access systems* and *biometric access systems* that are discussed next. Using two different methods to authenticate a user is called **two-factor authentication**. Typically, the methods used are some type of possessed knowledge (something you know) along with either a *possessed object* (something you have) or a *biometric feature* (something you are). Two-factor authentication adds an additional level of security to an access control system, since hackers are much less likely to be able to gain access to two different required factors. One emerging type of two-factor authentication used to protect access to sensitive online accounts (such as online banking accounts) uses a conventional username/ password combination in conjunction with an access card (such as the one shown in Figure 9-5) that displays a *one-time password (OTP)* when the button on the card is pressed. The OTP changes each time the button is pressed and the current OTP must be entered on the logon screen along with the username/password in order to log on to the account. Two-factor authentication systems are common in many countries and use is growing in the United States. In fact, a federal guideline that went into effect in 2007 instructs banks, credit unions, and other financial institutions to replace single-factor authentication systems (typically username/password systems) with systems using two-factor authentication, and some banks (such as Bank of America) offer two-factor authentication protection via an OTP access card or an OTP sent on demand to your mobile phone. Many other countries are considering or implementing similar guidelines or mandates.

FIGURE 9-5

Two-factor authentication. With this system, the user must have both the access card (to obtain the OTP) and his or her conventional username/ password combination, in order to log on to his or her online account.

1. Press the button to display the OTP passphrase.

2. The displayed OTP passphrase is used in the PayPal logon process.

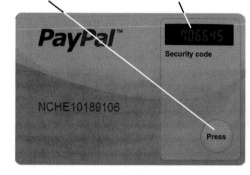

NET

> **CAUTION** CAUTION CAUTION CAUTION CAUTION CAUTION CAUT

> Don't supply answers to the cognitive authentication questions (like your high school or your pet's name) used in the password recovery process of many Web sites that a hacker may be able to guess based on information found on your Facebook page, an online database, or another online source. Instead, supply answers that you can remember but that also follow secure password rules. For instance, if your dog's name is Spot, you could enter *MDN1s$pOT* as the answer to a question about your pet's name and remember it as "My dog's name is Spot."

Possessed Object Access Systems

Possessed object access systems use physical objects for identification purposes and they are frequently used to control access to facilities and computer systems. Common types of possessed objects are smart cards, RFID-encoded badges, and magnetic cards that are swiped through or placed close to a reader to be read (see Figure 9-6). Increasingly, *USB security keys* (also called *USB security tokens*)—USB flash drives that are inserted into a computer to grant access to a network, to supply Web site usernames and passwords, or

---

>**Two-factor authentication.** Using two different methods to authenticate a user. >**Possessed object access system.** An access control system that uses a physical object an individual has in his or her possession to identify that individual.

SMART CARDS
Are read by a smart card reader to provide access to a facility or computer system.

USB SECURITY TOKENS
Are inserted into one of the computer's USB ports to provide access to that computer system.

FIGURE 9-6

Possessed objects. Help protect against unauthorized access; some can also store additional security credentials.

to provide other security features—are also being used. Access cards (like the one shown in Figure 9-5) and other devices used to supply the OTPs used to log on to Web sites and other resources are another type of *security token* possessed object.

One disadvantage of using possessed objects is that the object can be lost or, like passwords, can be used by an unauthorized individual if that individual has possession of the object. This latter disadvantage can be overcome by using a second factor, such as requiring the user to supply a username/password combination or be authenticated by a fingerprint or other type of *biometric* data in order to use the possessed object.

Biometric Access Systems

Biometrics is the study of identifying individuals using measurable, unique physiological or behavioral characteristics. **Biometric access systems** typically identify users by a particular unique biological characteristic (such as a fingerprint, a hand, a face, or an iris), although personal traits are used in some systems. For instance, some systems today use *keystroke dynamics* to recognize an individual's unique typing pattern to authenticate the user as he or she types in his or her username and password; other systems identify an individual via his or her voice, signature, or gait. Because the means of access (usually a part of the body) cannot typically be used by anyone other than the authorized individual, biometric access systems can perform both identification and authentication.

To identify and authenticate an individual, biometric access systems typically use a biometric reader (such as a *fingerprint reader* or *hand geometry reader* to identify an individual based on his or her fingerprint or hand image) or a digital camera (to identify an individual based on his or her face or iris), in conjunction with software and a database. The system matches the supplied biometric data with the biometric data that was stored in the database when the individual was enrolled in the system and authenticates the individual if the data matches. To speed up the process, many biometric access systems require users to identify themselves first (such as by entering a username or swiping a smart card), and then the system uses that identifying information to verify that the supplied biometric data matches the identified person.

Biometric access systems are used to control access to secure facilities (such as corporate headquarters and prisons); to log users on to computers, networks, and secure Web sites (by using an external reader or one built into the computer); to punch employees in and out of work; and to confirm consumers' identities at ATM machines and check-cashing services. Biometric readers are also increasingly being built into notebook computers, external hard drives (like the one shown in Figure 4-20 in Chapter 4), USB flash drives, and other hardware to prevent unauthorized use of those devices.

> **Biometric access system.** An access control system that uses one unique physical characteristic of an individual (such as a fingerprint, face, or voice) to authenticate that individual.

In addition to being used to control access to computers, networks, and other resources, biometrics are an important part of the systems used by law enforcement agencies and the military to identify individuals. For instance, the border control systems in many countries use biometrics to identify citizens, travelers, criminal suspects, and potential terrorists, and biometric identification systems are used extensively by law enforcement agencies and the military in areas of conflict. For example, biometric identification systems are being used in Iraq to identify members of the Iraqi police and military, prisoners, prison guards, authorized gun owners, citizens, contract employees, known criminals, and criminal suspects. In addition, *face recognition systems* (biometric systems that use cameras and a database of photos to attempt to identify individuals as they walk by the cameras) are used in many airports and other public locations to help identify known terrorists and criminal suspects.

Biometric access systems are very accurate. In fact, the odds of two different individuals having identical irises is 1 in 10^{78} and the statistical probability of two different irises being declared a match are 1 in 1.2 million—even identical twins (who have the same DNA structure) have different fingerprints and irises. Systems based on biological characteristics (such as a person's iris, hand geometry, face, or fingerprint) tend to be more accurate than those based on a personal trait (such as a person's voice or written signature) because biological traits do not change, but physical traits might change (such as an individual's voice, which might be affected by a cold, or a written signature, which might be affected by a broken wrist). In addition, biometric characteristics cannot be lost (like an access card), cannot be forgotten (like a password), and do not have to be pulled out of a briefcase or pocket (like an access card or other type of possessed object).

The primary disadvantages of biometric access systems are that much of the necessary hardware and software is expensive, and the data used for authentication (such as a fingerprint or an iris image) cannot be reset if it is compromised. In addition, fingerprint and hand geometry systems typically require contact with the reader device, though some systems under development (such as one that identifies individuals based on the veins in their hands) are contactless systems.

Some examples of the most commonly used types of biometric access and identification systems are shown in Figure 9-7.

FINGERPRINT RECOGNITION SYSTEMS
Typically used to protect access to office computers, to automatically supply Web site passwords on home computers, and to pay for products or services.

HAND GEOMETRY SYSTEMS
Typically used to control access to facilities (such as government offices, prisons, and military facilities) and to punch in and out of work.

FACE RECOGNITION SYSTEMS
Typically used to control access to highly secure areas, as well as to identify individuals for law enforcement purposes.

IRIS RECOGNITION SYSTEMS
Typically used to control access to highly secure areas and by the military; also beginning to be used to authenticate ATM users and other consumers.

NET

FIGURE 9-7
Types of biometric access and identification systems.

VIDEO PODCAST

Go to the Chapter 9 page at **www.cengage.com/ computerconcepts/np/uc13** to download or listen to the "How To: Use Face Recognition with Your Computer" video podcast.

Controlling Access to Wireless Networks

As already discussed, wireless networks—such as Wi-Fi networks—are less secure, in general, than wired networks. There are Wi-Fi security procedures, however, that can be used to protect against unauthorized use of a wireless network and to *encrypt* data sent over the network so that it is unreadable if it is intercepted. The original Wi-Fi security standard was

Because the SSID is being broadcast, the user can select the network from the list.

The user must supply the appropriate network key or passphrase in order to connect to the network.

If the SSID isn't broadcast, the user must add the network manually, using its SSID, in order to log on.

FIGURE 9-8

Accessing a Wi-Fi network. To access a secure network, the appropriate passphrase must be supplied.

WEP (*Wired Equivalent Privacy*). WEP is now considered insecure and has been replaced with the more secure *WPA* (*Wi-Fi Protected Access*) and the even more secure *WPA2* standards. However, Wi-Fi security features only work if they are enabled. Most Wi-Fi hardware today is shipped with the security features switched off, and many network owners never enable them, leaving those networks unsecured.

To protect against unauthorized access, Wi-Fi network owners should secure their networks by changing the router or access point settings to enable one of the encryption standards and to assign a *network key* or *passphrase* (essentially a password) that must be supplied in order to access the secured network. In addition, the name of the network (called the *SSID*) can be hidden from view by switching off the SSID broadcast feature. While hiding the network name will not deter serious hackers, it may reduce the number of casual war drivers or neighbors accessing the network. Once a network is secured, users who want to connect to that network need to either select or supply the network SSID name (depending on whether or not the SSID is being broadcast) and then enter the network key assigned to that network (see Figure 9-8). For an overview of how you can secure your wireless home router, see the How It Works box.

Firewalls, Encryption, and Virtual Private Networks (VPNs)

In addition to the access control systems just discussed, there are a number of other tools that can be used to prevent access to an individual computer or to prevent data from being intercepted in an understandable form during transit. These tools are discussed next.

Firewalls

A **firewall** is a security system that essentially creates a barrier between a computer or network and the Internet in order to protect against unauthorized access. Firewalls are typically two-way, so they check all incoming (from the Internet to the computer or the network) and outgoing (from the computer or the network to the Internet) traffic and allow only authorized traffic to pass through the firewall. *Personal firewalls* are typically software-based systems that are geared toward protecting home computers from hackers attempting to access those computers through their Internet connections. All computers with direct Internet connections (such as DSL, cable, satellite, or fixed wireless Internet access) should use a firewall (computers using dial-up Internet access only are relatively safe from hackers). Personal firewalls can be stand-alone programs (such as the free *ZoneAlarm* program); they are also built into many operating systems (such as the *Windows Firewall* program shown in Figure 9-9). Many routers, modems, and other pieces of networking hardware also include built-in firewall capabilities to help secure the networks these devices are used with. Firewalls designed to protect business networks may be software-based, hardware-based, or a combination of the two. They can typically be used both to prevent network access by hackers and other outsiders, as well as to control employee Internet access.

TIP

If a legitimate application installed on your computer needs to access the Internet but cannot, check your firewall settings—you may need to unblock that program.

>**Firewall.** A collection of hardware and/or software intended to protect a computer or computer network from unauthorized access.

HOW IT WORKS

Securing a Wireless Home Router

If you have a home wireless network, it is important to secure it properly so it cannot be used by unauthorized individuals. Security settings are specified in the router's configuration screen, such as the one shown in the accompanying illustration. To open your router's configuration screen to check or modify the settings, type the IP address assigned to that device (such as 192.168.0.1—check for a sticker on the bottom of your router or your router's documentation for its default IP address and username) in your browser's Address bar. Use the default password listed in your router documentation to log on the first time, and then change the password using the configuration screen to prevent unauthorized individuals from changing your router settings. To secure the router, enter the network name (SSID) you want to have associated with the router, select the appropriate security mode (such as WEP, WPA, or WPA2) to be used, and then type a secure passphrase to be used in order to log on to the network.

For additional security, *MAC (Media Access Control) address filtering* can be used to allow only the devices whose network adapter MAC addresses you enter into your router's settings access to the network. Because hackers can "spoof" MAC addresses by changing the MAC addresses of their devices to match an authorized MAC address (once the hacker determines those addresses), MAC address filtering should not be considered an alternative to using WPA or WPA2 encryption. However, it does add another layer of protection. Other precautions include designating specific times (such as when you are away from home) that the router will deny access to any device, and reducing the strength of the wireless signal if its current strength reaches farther than you need.

Use the router's IP address to display the router's configuration screen.

Use this tab to enable MAC address filtering.

Use this tab to change the administrator password used to access this configuration screen.

Type your desired SSID here.

Enable SSID broadcast here.

Select the desired security mode here.

Type your desired network key here.

Firewalls work by closing down all external *communications port addresses* (the electronic connections that allow a computer to communicate with other computers) to unauthorized computers and programs. While business firewalls are set up by the network administrator and those settings typically cannot be changed by end users, individuals may choose to change the settings for their personal firewall. For example, the user can choose to be notified when any application program on the computer is trying to access the Internet, to specify the programs that are allowed to access the Internet, or to block all incoming connections temporarily. In addition to protecting your computer from outside access, firewall programs also protect against

ONLINE VIDEO

Go to the Chapter 9 page at **www.cengage.com/computerconcepts/np/uc13** to watch the "Securing Your Wireless Router" video clip.

FIGURE 9-9
A personal firewall program. The firewall is on, so only authorized traffic can access the computer.

1. Click to run the security scan.

2. No threats were found.

FIGURE 9-10
Online security scans can check your system for vulnerabilities.

any spyware, computer viruses, or other malicious programs located on your computer that are designed to send data from your computer (such as credit card numbers, Web site passwords, and other sensitive data stored on your hard drive) to a hacker at the hacker's request.

A related type of security system increasingly being used by businesses today is an *intrusion prevention system (IPS)*. Whereas a firewall tries to block unauthorized traffic, an IPS continuously monitors and analyzes the traffic allowed by the firewall to try to detect possible attacks as they are occurring. If an attack is in progress, IPS software can immediately block it.

After installing and setting up a firewall (and an IPS if needed), individuals and businesses should test their systems to determine if vulnerabilities still exist. Individuals can use online security tests—such as the *Symantec Security Check* shown in Figure 9-10 or the tests at Gibson Research's *Shields Up* site—to check their computers; businesses may wish to hire an outside consultant to perform a comprehensive security assessment.

Encryption

Encryption is a way of temporarily converting data into a form, known as a *cipher*, which is unreadable until it is *decrypted* (unscrambled) in order to protect that data from being viewed by unauthorized individuals. As previously discussed, secure Wi-Fi networks use encryption to secure data that is transferred over the network. **Secure Web pages** use encryption so that sensitive data (such as credit card numbers) sent via the Web page is protected as it travels over the Internet. The most common security protocols used with secure Web pages are *Secure Sockets Layer (SSL)* and *Extended Validation Secure Sockets Layer (EV SSL)*. The URL for Web pages using either form of SSL begins with *https:* instead of *http:*.

Some Internet services (such as *Skype VoIP* calls and *HushMail* Web-based e-mails) use built-in encryption. Encryption can also be added manually to a file or an e-mail message before it is sent over the Internet to ensure that the content is unreadable if the file or message is intercepted during transit. In addition to securing files during transit, encryption can be used to protect the files stored on a hard drive so they will be unreadable if opened by an unauthorized person (such as if a hacker accesses a file containing sensitive data or if a computer containing sensitive files is lost or stolen). Increasingly, computers and hard drives (particularly those used with portable computers) are *self-encrypting*; that is, encrypting all data automatically and invisibly to the user. Windows, Mac OS, and other current operating systems support encryption and businesses are increasingly turning to encryption to prevent data loss, if a data breach should occur.

TIP

Sensitive information (such as credit card numbers, account numbers, and Web site passwords) should only be entered on secure Web pages to prevent that data from being intercepted by a criminal.

TIP

An emerging encryption standard thay may eventually replace SSL is *Transport Layer Security* (*TLS*).

> **Encryption.** A method of scrambling the contents of an e-mail message or a file to make it unreadable if an unauthorized user intercepts it.
> **Secure Web page.** A Web page that uses encryption to protect information transmitted via that Web page.

The two most common types of encryption in use today are *public key encryption* (often used with content being transmitted over the Internet, such as secure Web pages and encrypted e-mail) and *private key encryption* (most often used to encrypt files or the content of a hard drive or other device). **Private key encryption**, also called *symmetric key encryption*, uses a single secret *private key* (essentially a password) to both encrypt and decrypt the file or message. It is often used to encrypt files stored on an individual's computer, since the individual who selects the private key is likely the only one who will need to access those files. Private key encryption can also be used to send files securely to others, provided both the sender and recipient agree on the private key that will be used to access the file. Private key encryption capabilities are incorporated into a variety of programs today, including Microsoft Office, the WinZip file compression program, and Adobe Acrobat (the program used to create PDF files). To encrypt a document in Microsoft Word, for instance, you use the *Prepare* option on the Office menu, choose *Encrypt Document*, type the desired password (private key), and then save the file. To open that document again (or any copies of the file, such as those sent via e-mail), the password assigned to that file must be entered correctly.

Public key encryption, also called *asymmetric key encryption*, utilizes two encryption keys to encrypt and decrypt documents. Specifically, public key encryption uses a pair of keys (a private key and a *public key*) that are related mathematically to each other and have been assigned to a particular individual. An individual's public key is not secret and is available for anyone to use, but the corresponding private key is used only by the individual to whom it was assigned. Documents or messages encrypted with a public key can only be decrypted with the matching private key.

Public/private key pairs are generated by the program being used to perform the encryption or they are obtained via the Internet through a *Certificate Authority*, such as VeriSign or Thawte. Once obtained, encryption keys are stored in your browser, e-mail program, and any other program with which they will be used—this is typically done automatically for you when you obtain your key pairs. Obtaining a business public/private key pair usually requires a fee, but free key pairs for personal use are available through some Certificate Authorities. If a third-party encryption program is used (such as *Pretty Good Privacy* or *PGP*), the program typically takes care of obtaining and managing your keys for you.

To send someone an encrypted e-mail message or file using public key encryption, you need his or her public key. If that person has previously sent you his or her public key (such as via an e-mail message), it was likely stored by your e-mail program in your address book or contacts list, or by your encryption program in a central key directory used by that program. In either case, that public key is available whenever you want to send that person an encrypted document. If you do not already have the public key belonging to the individual to whom you wish to send an encrypted e-mail or file, you will need to request it from that individual. Once the recipient's public key has been used to encrypt the file or e-mail message and that document is received, the recipient uses his or her private key to decrypt the encrypted contents (see Figure 9-11).

To avoid the need to obtain the recipient's public key before sending that person an encrypted e-mail, *Web-based encrypted e-mail* can be used. Web-based encrypted e-mail works similarly to regular Web-based e-mail (in which e-mail is composed and viewed on a Web page belonging to a Web-based e-mail provider), but Web-based encrypted e-mail systems use secure Web servers to host the Web pages that are used to compose and read e-mail messages. Some Web-based encrypted e-mail systems—such as the popular free *HushMail* service that automatically encrypts all e-mail sent through the

VIDEO PODCAST

Go to the Chapter 9 page at **www.cengage.com/ computerconcepts/np/uc13** to download or listen to the "How To: Create an Encrypted Partition On Your Hard Drive" video podcast.

NET

FURTHER EXPLORATION Go

Go to the Chapter 9 page at **www.cengage.com/ computerconcepts/np/uc13** for links to information about encryption.

>**Public key encryption.** A type of encryption that uses key pairs to encrypt and decrypt the file or message. >**Private key encryption.** A type of encryption that uses a single key to encrypt and decrypt the file or message.

1. The e-mail message (including any attached files) is created by the sender, who then uses the recipient's public key to encrypt the e-mail (including any attached files) using the Message Options dialog box.

Joe's public key

2. The e-mail (including any attached files) is transmitted over the Internet in its encrypted form.

||START
GjTw4rbwFGeyqiLR77MBiBapKS0Ka0:3ss5CyASSEzw3lXj8V
khzIAFfLylqyiuwo:uZKx4ECQNq5kLnQ;lwa81bhckhXNgHAj
YUPO,6TTJozHMvYU7rEBlXfZcU7GoIYXDd7h8XjERAmP9r
yi:th30MeZr7QdcVwXfdAo7Ey3eUEX19nmxjTul;qqxwGows9
OwWZcJ0Y:euiQEDbgVGdWTjSan3UjpVCyXcXEODNhnNP
wYCdjMeG1dFOrsuFc4CUniQ1UVR0ML51N2LJ8uXsYwsrzP
psn3f2zJCCEiGun59VEc4dUBMF1he1UFC7IE0RkSZ22gAAQ
UEsgWB5pWYUsuWLc1kmQ:AHzejiWRRLDkG3LwqB6qaQJ
AGmu2Pap8uW8PgQ0J74G5BNEjgy0O3wceuYeApaNE
END||

Joe's private key

3. The recipient receives the encrypted message and opens it using an e-mail program. When prompted by the program, the recipient enters his or her private key to decrypt the e-mail (including any attached files) so it becomes readable again.

FIGURE 9-11
Using public key encryption to secure an e-mail message.

service—require both the sender and recipient to have accounts. Others require only the sender to have an account and the recipient is sent an e-mail containing instructions regarding how to view the message on a secure Web page.

There are various strengths of encryption available; the stronger the encryption, the more difficult it is to crack. Older 40-bit encryption (which can only use keys that are 40 bits or 5 characters long) is considered *weak encryption*. Stronger encryption is available today, such as *strong 128-bit encryption* (which uses 16-character keys) and *military-strength 2,048-bit encryption* (which uses 256-character keys), although not without some objections from law enforcement agencies and the government because they state that terrorists routinely use encryption methods to communicate.

Virtual Private Networks (VPNs)

While e-mail and file encryption can be used to transfer individual messages and files securely over the Internet, a **virtual private network (VPN)** is designed to be used when a continuous secure channel over the Internet is needed. A VPN provides a secure private tunnel from the user's computer through the Internet to another destination and is most often used to provide remote employees with secure access to a company network. VPNs use encryption and other security mechanisms to ensure that only authorized users can access the remote network and that the data cannot be intercepted during transit. Since it uses the Internet instead of an expensive private physical network, a VPN can provide a secure environment over a large geographical area at a manageable cost. Once a VPN is set up, the user just needs to log on (such as with a username/password combination or a security token) in order to use the VPN.

VPNs are often used by both businesses and individuals at public Wi-Fi hotspots to prevent data interception when connecting to the Internet via the hotspot. While businesspeople will typically use a VPN set up by their companies, individuals can create *personal VPNs* using software designed for that purpose. This software automatically encrypts all inbound and outbound Internet traffic, including Web pages, e-mail messages, IMs, VoIP calls, and

TIP

Unless it is absolutely necessary and you are using a VPN, do not perform sensitive transactions (such as shopping or banking) at a public hotspot.

>**Virtual private network (VPN).** A private, secure path over the Internet that provides authorized users a secure means of accessing a private network via the Internet.

so forth, and also acts as a personal firewall. Using a personal VPN at a public hotspot can help individuals from becoming the victim of a growing trend—*evil twin* Wi-Fi access points, discussed in the Trend box.

Additional Public Hotspot Precautions

The precautions already discussed (such as using firewall software, secure Web pages, VPNs, and encryption) are a good start for protecting against unauthorized access and unauthorized use at a public Wi-Fi hotspot. However, there are additional precautions individuals can use to avoid data (both that which is on their computers and that which is being sent over the Internet) from being compromised. These precautions are listed in Figure 9-12.

Sensible Employee Precautions

A significant number of business security breaches—over 60%, according to a recent University of Washington study—are the responsibility of insiders. Sometimes the employee deliberately performs the act; other times the employee makes a mistake, such as losing a portable computer or removable storage medium, or inadvertently providing access to sensitive data. Consequently, it pays for employers to be cautious with their employees. Some suggestions to avoid security breaches by employees are listed next.

Screen Potential New Hires Carefully

Employers should carefully investigate the background of all potential employees. Some people falsify résumés to get jobs. Others may have criminal records or currently be charged with a crime. One embarrassing mistake made by Rutgers University was to hire David Smith, the author of the *Melissa* computer virus, as a computer technician when he was out on bail following the arrest for that crime.

Watch for Disgruntled Employees and Ex-Employees

The type of employee who is most likely to commit a computer crime is one who has recently been terminated or passed over for a promotion, or one who has some reason to want to "get even" with the organization. Limiting access for each employee to only the resources needed for his or her job (referred to as the *Principle of Least Privilege*) and monitoring any attempts to access off-limit resources can help prevent some types of problems, such as unauthorized access of sensitive files, unintentional damage like deleting or changing files inadvertently, or sabotage like deleting or changing company files intentionally. In addition, it is vital that whenever an employee leaves the company for any reason, all access to the system for that individual (username, password, e-mail address, and so forth) should be removed immediately. For employees with high levels of system access, simultaneously removing access while the termination is taking place is even better. Waiting even a few minutes can be too late, since just-fired employees have been known to barricade themselves in their office immediately after being terminated in order to change passwords, sabotage records, and perform other malicious acts. Some wait slightly longer, such as one computer administrator at a Houston organ and tissue donation center who recently pled guilty to accessing the company computer system the evening of and day after being fired and intentionally deleting numerous software applications and important files, such as organ donation records, accounting files, and backup files. She was charged with one

---

PUBLIC HOTSPOT PRECAUTIONS

Turn off automatic connections and pay attention to the list of available hotspots to try to make sure you connect to a legitimate access point (not an evil twin).

Use a personal firewall to control the traffic going to and from your computer and temporarily use it to block all incoming connections.

Use a virtual private network (VPN) to secure all activity between your computer and the Internet.

Only enter passwords, credit card numbers, and other data on secure Web pages using a VPN.

If you're not using a VPN, encrypt all sensitive files before transferring or e-mailing them.

If you're not using a VPN, avoid online shopping, banking, and other sensitive transactions.

Turn off file sharing so others can't access the files on your hard drive.

Turn off Bluetooth and Wi-Fi when you are not using them.

Disable *ad hoc* capabilities to prevent another computer from connecting to your computer directly without using an access point.

Use antivirus software and make sure your operating system is up to date.

FIGURE 9-12
Sensible precautions for public Wi-Fi hotspot users.

NET

TREND

Evil Twins

An *evil twin* is a fake Wi-Fi hotspot set up by a thief to masquerade as a legitimate Wi-Fi hotspot in order to gather personal or corporate information from individuals who connect to that hotspot thinking it is the legitimate one. Typically, the thief selects a legitimate hotspot and moves within range of that hotspot, uses software to discover the network name (SSID) and radio frequency being used by the legitimate hotspot, and then broadcasts his or her hotspot using the same SSID as the legitimate one. To the end user, the evil twin looks like the legitimate hotspot because it uses the same SSID and settings as the "good twin" it is impersonating. If an end user connects to the evil twin to access the Internet, the thief can intercept sensitive data sent to the Internet, such as passwords or credit card information. That information can then be used for *identity theft* and other fraudulent activities.

Because of the increased use of Wi-Fi hotspots and the availability of software enabling a would-be thief to set up an evil twin hotspot, evil twins are an increasing threat. To make matters worse, some evil twins are able to disconnect users from the legitimate hotspot in hopes the users will be reconnected automatically to the evil twin instead of the legitimate hotspot. To protect yourself, set up your portable computer to only connect manually to hotspots so you cannot be connected to an evil

twin hotspot inadvertently. In addition, refrain from performing sensitive transactions (such as shopping and banking) at public hotspots. Businesspeople should use a VPN when connecting to the company server via a Wi-Fi hotspot; individuals needing to perform sensitive transactions should use a personal VPN, such as the one shown in the accompanying figure.

count of unauthorized computer access, sentenced to two years in prison, and ordered to pay more than $94,000 in restitution.

Develop Policies and Controls

All companies should develop policies and controls regarding security matters. As already mentioned, employees should be granted the least amount of access to the company network that they need to perform their job. Employees should be educated about the seriousness and consequences of hacking, data theft, and other computer crimes, and they should be taught what to do when they suspect a computer crime has been committed. Employees should also be instructed about proper computer and e-mail usage policies—such as whether or not downloading and installing software on company computers is allowed, whether or not employees are responsible for updating their computers, and the types of removable storage mediums (such as USB flash drives or portable digital media players) that may be used with company computers—in order to avoid inadvertently creating a security problem. Policies for removing computers and storage media containing sensitive data from the premises should also be implemented and enforced, and sensitive documents should be shredded when they are no longer needed. In addition, policies should be updated as needed to respond to new types of threats. For instance, the Pentagon banned USB flash drives in late 2008 due to a computer virus threat; it is unknown at this time when or if their use will be allowed again.

Employees who work from home or otherwise access the company network via the Internet also need to be educated about security policies for remote access and the proper precautions that need to be taken. These precautions include keeping their operating system and security software up to date, and using only encrypted storage devices (such as self-encrypting USB flash drives) when transporting documents between work and home. In addition, telecommuting workers and outside contractors should not be allowed to have peer-to-peer (P2P) software on computers containing company documents, since data is increasingly being exposed through the use of P2P networks. For instance, classified data about the U.S. presidential helicopter was discovered recently on a computer in Iran and traced back to a P2P network and the computer of a military contractor in Maryland, and the Social Security numbers and other personal data belonging to about 17,000 current and former Pfizer workers were leaked onto a P2P network in 2007 after an employee installed unauthorized P2P software on a company notebook computer provided for use at her home.

Use Data-Leakage Prevention and Enterprise Rights-Management Software

As employees are increasingly bringing portable devices (such as mobile phones, portable digital media players, and USB flash drives) that can interact with business networks to the office, the challenge of securing these devices (and the company network against these devices) has grown. Some companies now prohibit all portable devices; others allow only company-issued devices so they can ensure appropriate security measures, such as encryption, password protection, and the ability to wipe the device clean remotely if it is lost or stolen, are implemented.

To protect against employees copying or sending confidential data to others either intentionally or accidentally, *data-leakage prevention systems* can be used. Data-leakage prevention systems are available as software and/or hardware systems, and have a range of capabilities, but the overall goal is to prevent sensitive data from exposure. For instance, some systems control which devices (such as USB flash drives and portable digital media players) can be connected to an employee's computer (see Figure 9-13) in order to prevent sensitive data from being taken home inadvertently or intentionally. Other data-leakage prevention systems—sometimes also called *outbound-content monitoring systems*—scan all outgoing communications (e-mail, transferred files, instant messages, and so forth) for documents containing Social Security numbers, intellectual property, and other confidential information. Some can also continually scan network devices to locate sensitive data in documents stored on computers to ensure that sensitive files are not on the computer of an employee who should not have access to them. For even stronger protection of confidential company documents, *enterprise rights-management software*, which encrypts confidential documents and limits functions such as printing, editing, and copying the data to only authorized users with the appropriate password, can be used.

Ask Business Partners to Review their Security

In this networked economy, many organizations provide some access to internal resources for business partners. If those external companies are lax with their security measures, however, attacks through the business partners' computers (such as via an employee or hacker) are possible. Consequently, businesses should make sure that their business partners maintain adequate security policies and controls. Regulations—such as the *Sarbanes-Oxley Act of 2002*—increasingly require businesses to ensure that adequate controls are in place to preserve the integrity of financial reports. This includes outside companies—such as business partners and *outsourcing companies* (outside vendors for specific business tasks, as discussed in Chapter 12)—if they have access to sensitive corporate data. Companies that utilize cloud computing also need to ensure that the cloud vendor's policies (such as for protecting access to stored data, using adequate encryption techniques and backup procedures, submitting to necessary audits, and storing data in locations with the desired security and privacy laws) match the company's requirements.

FIGURE 9-13

Data-leakage prevention software can control which devices can be connected to an employee's computer.

COMPUTER SABOTAGE

Computer sabotage—acts of malicious destruction to a computer or computer resource—is another common type of computer crime today. Computer sabotage can take several forms, including launching a *computer virus* or a *denial of service (DoS) attack*, altering the content of a Web site, or changing data or programs located on a computer. A common tool used to perform computer sabotage is a *botnet*, discussed next. Computer sabotage is illegal in the United States, and acts of sabotage are estimated to cost individuals and organizations billions of dollars per year, primarily for labor costs related to correcting the problems caused by the sabotage, lost productivity, and lost sales.

Botnets

A computer that is controlled by a hacker or other computer criminal is referred to as a **bot** or *zombie computer*; a group of bots that are controlled by one individual and can work together in a coordinated fashion is called a **botnet**. According to the FBI, an estimated one million U.S. computers are currently part of a botnet; consequently, botnets are a major security threat. Criminals (called *botherders*) are increasingly creating botnets to use for computer sabotage, such as to spread *malware* and to launch *denial of service (DoS) attacks*, discussed shortly. Botherders also often sell their botnet services to send spam and launch Internet attacks on their clients' behalf, as well as use them to steal identity information, credit card numbers, passwords, corporate secrets, and other sensitive data, which are then sold to other criminals or otherwise used in an illegal manner.

Computer Viruses and Other Types of Malware

Malware is a generic term that refers to any type of malicious software. Malware programs are intentionally written to perform destructive acts, such as damaging programs, deleting files, erasing an entire hard drive, or slowing down the performance of a computer. This damage can take place immediately after a computer is *infected* (that is, the malware software is installed) or it can begin when a particular condition is met. A malware program that activates when it detects a certain condition, such as when a particular keystroke is pressed or an employee's name is deleted from an employee file, is called a *logic bomb*. A logic bomb that is triggered by a particular date or time is called a *time bomb*.

Writing a computer virus or other type of malware or even posting the malware code on the Internet is not illegal, but it is considered highly unethical and irresponsible behavior. Distributing malware, on the other hand, is illegal, and virus writers who release their malware are being vigorously prosecuted. Malware can be very costly in terms of the labor costs associated with removing the viruses and correcting any resulting damage, as well as the cost of lost productivity of employees. One type of malware often used by computer criminals to send sensitive data secretly from

ASK THE EXPERT

symantec. **Marian Merritt,** Internet Safety Advocate, Symantec Corporation

How can individuals tell if their computers are part of a botnet?

Bots were created to steal your personal information or take control of your computer without you knowing. Because of that, they are silent in nature. The only way computer users can tell their computers are infected by a bot is by using a security solution with bot detection capabilities.

>**Computer sabotage.** An act of malicious destruction to a computer or computer resource. >**Bot.** A computer that is controlled by a hacker or other computer criminal. >**Botnet.** A group of bots that are controlled by one individual. >**Malware.** Any type of malicious software.

infected computers to the criminal—spyware—was discussed in Chapter 8. The most common other types of malware are discussed next.

Computer Viruses

One type of malware is the **computer virus**—a software program that is installed without the permission or knowledge of the computer user, that is designed to alter the way a computer operates, and that can replicate itself to infect any new media it has access to. Computer viruses are often embedded into program or data files (often games, videos, and music files downloaded from Web pages or shared via a P2P service). They are spread whenever the infected file is downloaded, is transferred to a new computer via an infected removable storage medium, or is e-mailed to another computer (see Figure 9-14). Viruses can also be installed when a recipient clicks a link in an e-mail message (often in an unsolicited e-mail message that resembles a legitimate e-mail message that normally contains a link, such as an electronic greeting card e-mail that contains a link to view the card), as well as through links in instant messages. Regardless of how it is obtained, once a copy of the infected file reaches a new computer it typically embeds itself into program, data, or system files on the new computer and remains there, affecting that computer according to its programmed instructions, until it is discovered and removed.

FIGURE 9-14

How a computer virus or other type of malicious software might spread.

1. A computer virus originates when an unscrupulous programmer intentionally creates it and embeds it in a file. The infected file is then posted to a Web page where it will be downloaded via the Internet or is sent as an e-mail attachment to a large group of people.

THE INTERNET

COMPANY NETWORK

3. A virus can spread very quickly because every computer that comes in contact with the virus—whether through an infected removable storage medium, infected downloaded file, or infected e-mail attachment—becomes infected, unless virus-protection software is used to prevent it.

2. When the infected file is opened on a computer, the virus copies itself to that computer's hard drive and the computer becomes infected. The virus may then e-mail itself to people in the newly infected computer's e-mail address book or copy itself to any removable storage medium inserted into the that computer.

>**Computer virus.** A software program installed without the user's knowledge and designed to alter the way a computer operates or to cause harm to the computer system.

Computer Worms

Another common form of malware is the **computer worm**. Like a computer virus, a computer worm is a malicious program that is typically designed to cause damage. Unlike a computer virus, however, a computer worm does not infect other computer files on the infected computer in order to replicate itself; instead, it spreads by creating copies of its code and sending those copies to other computers via a network. Often, the worm is sent to other computers as an e-mail attachment. Usually after the infected e-mail attachment is opened by an individual, the worm inflicts its damage and then automatically sends copies of itself to other computers via the Internet or a private network, typically using addresses in the e-mail address book located on the newly infected computer. When those e-mail messages and their attachments are opened, the new computers become infected and the cycle continues. Because of its distribution method, a worm can spread very rapidly. For instance, the *Mydoom* worm (which was released in 2004 and is considered one of the fastest spreading worms ever) spread so rapidly that, at one point, one out of every 10 e-mails contained the worm.

Some newer worms do not require any action by the users (such as opening an e-mail attachment) to infect their computers. Instead, the worm scans the Internet looking for computers that are vulnerable to that particular worm and sends a copy of itself to those computers to infect them. Other worms just require the user to view an infected e-mail message or insert an infected removable storage medium (such as a USB flash drive) into the computer, in order to infect the computer. Still other worms are specifically written to take advantage of newly discovered *security holes* (vulnerabilities) in operating systems and e-mail programs. Worms and other types of malware that are designed to take advantage of a security hole and are released at a time when no security patch to correct the problem is available are referred to as *zero-day attacks*. Unfortunately, as malware writing tools become more sophisticated, zero-day attacks are becoming more common.

FIGURE 9-15

Rogue antivirus programs. These programs try to trick victims into purchasing subscriptions to remove nonexistent malware supposedly installed on their computers.

Trojan Horses

A **Trojan horse** is a type of malware that masquerades as something else—usually an application program (such as what appears to be a game or utility program). When the seemingly legitimate program is downloaded or installed, the malware part of the Trojan horse infects the computer. Many recent Trojan horses masquerade as normal ongoing activities (such as the Windows Update service or an *antivirus* or *antispyware program* telling you to download a file containing program updates) when they are installed to try to trick unsuspecting users into downloading another malware program or buying a useless program. For instance, after a *rogue antivirus program* like the one shown in Figure 9-15 is installed (usually without the user's direct knowledge or permission), the malware takes over the computer displaying warning messages or scan results (see Figure 9-15) indicating the computer is infected with malware. In addition, the rogue antivirus program typically prevents access to any Web sites other than its own and prompts the user to buy a fake antimalware program to get rid of the "malware." Usually the only malware on the computer is the rogue program,

> **Computer worm.** A malicious program designed to spread rapidly to a large number of computers by sending copies of itself to other computers.
> **Trojan horse.** A malicious program that masquerades as something else.

but it is often very intrusive (such as displaying constant messages on the desktop and in pop-up windows and hiding the options needed to change the hijacked settings back to normal), and it is extremely hard to remove.

Unlike viruses and worms, Trojan horses cannot replicate themselves. Trojan horses are usually spread by being downloaded from the Internet, though they may also be sent as an e-mail attachment, either from the Trojan horse author or from individuals who forward it, not realizing the program is a Trojan horse. Some Trojan horses today act as spyware and are designed to find sensitive information about an individual (such as a Social Security number or a bank account number) or about a company (such as corporate intellectual property like mechanical designs, electronic schematics, and other valuable proprietary information) located on infected computers and then send that information to the malware creator to be used in illegal activities. One emerging type of Trojan horse is called a *RAT* (*Remote-Access Trojan*). RATs are typically installed via small files obtained from an Internet download, such as free software, games, or electronic greeting cards. Once installed, RATs are designed to record every keystroke made on the infected computer and then send the sensitive information they recorded (such as account numbers and passwords) to criminals.

Mobile Malware

In addition to computers, malware also can infect mobile phones, portable digital media players, printers, and other devices that contain computing hardware and software. In fact, some GPS devices and portable digital media players (including some video iPods) shipped recently had malware already installed on them. Mobile phones with Bluetooth capabilities in particular are vulnerable since they can be infected via a Bluetooth connection just by being within range (about 30 feet) of a carrier. Some *mobile malware* is designed to crash the phone's operating system; others are designed to be a nuisance by changing icons or otherwise making the device more difficult to use. Still others are money-oriented, such as malware designed to steal credit card data located on the mobile phone. According to IBM, more malware directed to mobile phones and other devices—such as cars—that contain embedded computers is expected in the near future as those devices continue to incorporate more software components and, consequently, become more vulnerable to malware. However, the lack of a universal operating system for mobile devices (compared with the relatively few operating systems used with personal computers) at the present time limits the amount of mobile malware currently in circulation.

Denial of Service (DoS) Attacks

A **denial of service (DoS) attack** is an act of sabotage that attempts to flood a network server or Web server with so many requests for action that it shuts down or simply cannot handle legitimate requests any longer, causing legitimate users to be denied service. For example, a hacker might set up one or more computers to *ping* (contact) a server continually with a request to send a responding ping back to a false return address, or to request nonexistent information continually. If enough useless traffic is generated, the server has no resources left to deal with legitimate requests (see Figure 9-16). An emerging trend is DoS attacks aimed at mobile wireless networks. These attacks typically involve repeatedly establishing and releasing connections with the goal of overloading the network to disrupt service.

NET

>**Denial of service (DoS) attack.** An act of sabotage that attempts to flood a network server or a Web server with so much activity that it is unable to function.

1. Hacker's computer sends several simultaneous requests; each request asks to establish a connection to the server but supplies false return information. In a distributed DoS attack, multiple computers send multiple requests at one time.

Hello? I'd like some info...

Hello? I'd like some info...

2. The server tries to respond to each request but can't locate the computer because false return information was provided. The server waits for a short period of time before closing the connection, which ties up the server and keeps others from connecting.

I can't find you, I'll wait and try again...

I'm busy, I can't help you right now.

HACKER'S COMPUTER

3. The hacker's computer continues to send new requests, so as a connection is closed by the server, a new request is waiting. This cycle continues, which ties up the server indefinitely.

Hello? I'd like some info...

LEGITIMATE COMPUTER

4. The server becomes so overwhelmed that legitimate requests cannot get through and, eventually, the server usually crashes.

WEB SERVER

FIGURE 9-16
How a denial of service (DoS) attack might work.

DoS attacks today are often directed toward popular sites (for example, Twitter was recently shut down for two hours due to a DoS attack) and typically are carried out via multiple computers (referred to as a *distributed denial of service attack* or *DDoS attack*). DDoS attacks are typically performed by botnets created by hackers; the computers in the botnet participate in the attacks without the owners' knowledge. Because home computers are increasingly using direct Internet connections but tend to be less protected than school and business computers, hackers are increasingly targeting home computers for botnets used in DDoS attacks and other forms of computer sabotage.

Denial of service attacks can be very costly in terms of business lost (such as when an e-commerce site is shut down), as well as the time and expense required to bring the site back online. Networks that use VoIP are particularly vulnerable to DoS attacks since the real-time nature of VoIP calls means their quality is immediately affected when a DoS attack slows down the network.

Data, Program, or Web Site Alteration

Another type of computer sabotage occurs when a hacker breaches a computer system in order to delete data, change data, modify programs, or otherwise alter the data and programs located there. For example, a student might try to hack into the school database to change his or her grade; a hacker might change a program located on a company server in order to steal money or information; or a disgruntled or former employee might perform a vengeful act, such as altering programs so they work incorrectly, deleting customer records or other critical data, or randomly changing data in a company's database. Like other forms of computer sabotage, data and program alteration is illegal.

Data on Web sites can also be altered by hackers. For instance, individuals sometimes hack into and alter other people's social networking accounts. In early 2009, for instance, the Twitter accounts of over 30 high-profile individuals (including then President-elect Obama) were accessed by an unauthorized individual who sent out fake (and sometimes embarrassing) tweets posing as those individuals. It is also becoming more common for hackers to compromise legitimate Web sites and then use those sites to perform malware attacks. Typically, a hacker alters a legitimate site to display an official-looking message that informs the user that a particular software program must be downloaded, or the hacker posts a rogue banner ad on a legitimate site that redirects the user to a malware site instead of the site for the product featured in the banner ad. According to a report released this year by security company Websense, more than half of the Web sites classified as malicious are actually legitimate Web sites that have been compromised.

PROTECTING AGAINST COMPUTER SABOTAGE

One of the most important protections against computer sabotage is using *security software*, and ensuring that it is kept current.

Security Software

To protect against becoming infected with a computer virus or other type of malware, all computers and other devices used to access the Internet or a company network in both homes and offices should have **security software** installed. Security software typically includes a variety of security features, including a firewall, protection against spyware and bots, and protection against some types of *online fraud*, discussed shortly. One of the most important components is **antivirus software**, which protects against computer viruses and other types of malware.

Antivirus software typically runs continuously whenever the computer is on to perform real-time monitoring of the computer and incoming e-mail messages, instant messages, Web page content, and downloaded files, in order to prevent malicious software from executing. Many antivirus programs also automatically scan any devices as soon as they are connected to a USB port in order to guard against infections from a USB flash drive, a portable digital media player, or other USB device. Antivirus software helps prevent malware from being installed on your computer since it deletes or *quarantines* (safely isolates) any suspicious content (such as e-mail attachments or downloaded files) as they arrive; regular full system scans can detect and remove any viruses or worms that find their way onto your computer (see Figure 9-17).

According to McAfee Security, a manufacturer of antivirus and security software, there are millions of threats in existence today, and research firm IDC estimates that 450 new viruses and other types of malware are released each day. Consequently, it is vital to keep your antivirus program up to date. Antivirus software is usually set up to download new *virus definitions* automatically from its associated Web site on a regular basis, as often as several times per day—a very important precaution. Most fee-based antivirus programs come with a year of access to free updates; users should purchase additional years after that to continue to be protected or they should switch to a free antivirus program, such as *AVG Free*, that can be updated regularly at no cost. Schools and businesses should also ensure

FIGURE 9-17
Security software.
Most security software is set up to monitor your system on a continual basis, removing threats as they are discovered.

NET

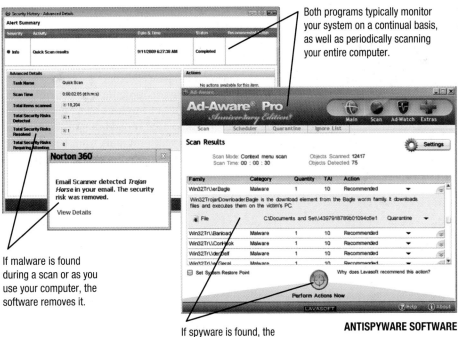

ANTIVIRUS SOFTWARE

Both programs typically monitor your system on a continual basis, as well as periodically scanning your entire computer.

If malware is found during a scan or as you use your computer, the software removes it.

If spyware is found, the software recommends quarantining or removing it.

ANTISPYWARE SOFTWARE

VIRUS PREVENTION STRATEGIES

Use antivirus software to check incoming e-mail messages and files, and download updated virus definitions on a regular basis.

Limit the sharing of flash memory cards, USB flash drives, and other removable storage media with others.

Only download files from reputable sites.

Only open e-mail attachments that come from people you know and that do not have an executable file extension (such as .exe, .com, .bat, or .vbs); double-check with the sender before opening an unexpected, but seemingly legitimate, attachment.

For any downloaded file you are unsure of, upload it to a Web site (such as VirusTotal.com) that tests files for viruses before you open them.

Keep the preview window of your e-mail program closed so you will not view messages until you determine that they are safe to view.

Regularly download and install the latest security patches available for your operating system, browser, and e-mail programs.

Avoid downloading files from P2P sites.

FIGURE 9-18
Sensible precautions can help protect against computer virus infections.

TIP

If you suspect you are infected with a malware program that your antivirus software cannot detect or remove, try a software program that specializes in removing hard-to-remove malware, such as the free *MalwareBytes Anti-Malware* program.

that students and employees connecting to the campus or company network with personal computers are using up-to-date antivirus software so they will not infect the network with malware inadvertently. Some colleges now require new students to go through a *quarantine process*, in which students are not granted access to the college network until they complete a security process that checks their computers for security threats, updates their operating systems, and installs antivirus software. Some additional virus-prevention strategies are listed in Figure 9-18.

Many ISPs today also offer some malware protection to their subscribers. Typically, ISP antivirus software scans all incoming e-mail messages at the mail server level to filter out messages containing a virus. If a message containing a virus is detected, it is usually deleted and the recipient is notified that the message contained a virus and was deleted. Another type of program, which is currently in development and which is designed to protect against viruses sent via e-mail, is an *e-mail authentication system*. E-mail authentication systems are designed to tell recipients exactly where e-mail messages come from to help them determine which messages are safe to open and which might contain malware. For a look at an emerging tool in the fight against malware—*people-driven security* and *whitelisting*—see the Inside the Industry box.

Other Security Precautions

Individuals and businesses can protect against some types of computer sabotage (such as program, data, or Web site alteration) by controlling access to their computers and networks, as discussed earlier in this chapter. Intrusion protection systems can help businesses detect and protect against denial of service (DoS) attacks. For extra protection against spyware, rogue antivirus programs, and other specialized malware, specialized security programs (such as the antispyware program shown in Figure 9-17 for detecting and removing spyware) can be used. In addition, most Web browsers have security settings that can be used to help prevent programs from being installed on a computer without the user's permission, such as prompting the user for permission whenever a download is initiated. Enabling these security settings is a wise additional precaution.

ONLINE THEFT, ONLINE FRAUD, AND OTHER DOT CONS

A booming area of computer crime involves online fraud, theft, scams, and related activities designed to steal money or other resources from individuals or businesses—these are collectively referred to as **dot cons**. According to a report by the *Internet Crime Complaint Center (IC3)*, a joint venture of the FBI and the National White Collar Crime Center that receives cybercrime complaints from consumers and reports them to the appropriate law enforcement agency, online crime hit a record high in 2008. In all, more than

>**Dot con.** A fraud or scam carried out through the Internet.

INSIDE THE INDUSTRY

New Tools to Fight Malware

People-driven security refers to using the judgments of individuals to identify new threats. For instance, Google has a page where users can submit URLs of Web sites they believe are malicious (see the accompanying illustration), and antivirus companies like Symantec and McAfee rely on malware samples that they receive from users to help keep their virus lists and programs current. Many security experts believe that user involvement is crucial today in the fight against malware and phishing. People-driven security is also being used today to identify spammers.

The idea behind *whitelisting* is the opposite of blocking potentially dangerous applications from running on your computer; with whitelisting, only known good programs are allowed to run. While some users believe that whitelisting is annoying (because trying to run a program not on the whitelist requires responding to a pop-up alert message), many security companies believe that keeping track of known good software might be easier than trying to keep track of all the malware in existence today. Both Symantec and Kaspersky Lab are advocates of whitelisting and Kaspersky recently integrated the database

of Bit9, a company that maintains a list of over six billion known good applications, into its antivirus programs. While antivirus companies are currently working on maintaining their own whitelists to use in conjunction with their products, some view a central whitelist maintained by a neutral group and available to everyone as the most efficient solution for consumers.

275,000 reports were received with an average individual loss of $931. Some of the most common types of dot cons are discussed next.

Theft of Data, Information, and Other Resources

Data theft or *information theft* is the theft of data or information located on or being sent from a computer. It can be committed by stealing an actual computer (as discussed in more detail in Chapter 15); it can also take place over the Internet or a network by an individual gaining unauthorized access to that data by hacking into the computer or by intercepting the data in transit. Common types of data and information stolen via the Internet or another network include customer data (such as Web site passwords or credit card information) and proprietary corporate information. Over the past years, there have been numerous examples of hackers stealing information from company databases. For instance, one hacker obtained the contact information of more than 1.6 million users of the Monster.com online job search service; another breached the systems of the Heartland credit and debit card processor and several retail stores, stealing more than 130 million credit and debit card numbers, according to the charges filed against the hacker. Stolen consumer data is often used in fraudulent activities, such as *identity theft*, as discussed shortly.

Money is another resource that can be stolen via a computer. Company insiders sometimes steal money by altering company programs to transfer small amounts of money—for example, a few cents' worth of bank account interest—from a very large number of transactions to an account controlled by the thieves. This type of crime is sometimes called *salami shaving*. Victims of salami-shaving schemes generally are unaware that their funds have been accessed because the amount taken from each individual is very small. However, added together, the amounts can be substantial. Another example of monetary theft performed via computers involves hackers electronically transferring money illegally from online bank accounts, traditional bank accounts, credit card accounts, or accounts at online payment services (such as *PayPal*, which is discussed more in Chapter 11).

Identity Theft, Phishing, and Pharming

A growing dot con trend is obtaining enough information about an individual to perform fraudulent financial transactions. Often, this is carried out in conjunction with *identity theft*; techniques frequently used to obtain the necessary personal information to commit identity theft are *phishing*, *spear phishing*, and *pharming*. These topics are discussed next.

Identity Theft

Identity theft occurs when someone obtains enough information about a person to be able to masquerade as that person—usually to buy products or services in that person's name (see Figure 9-19). Typically, identity theft begins with obtaining a person's name, address, and Social Security number, often from a discarded or stolen document (such as a preapproved credit card application that was sent in the mail), from information obtained via the Internet (such as from a résumé posted online), or from information located on a computer (such as on a stolen computer or hacked server, or information sent from a computer via a computer virus or spyware program installed on that computer). The thief may then order a copy of the individual's birth certificate, obtain a "replacement" driver's license, make purchases and charge them to the victim, and/or open credit or bank accounts in the victim's name. Identity theft is illegal and, in 1998, the federal government passed the *Identity Theft and Assumption Deterrence Act*, which made identity theft a federal crime.

Assuming the thief requests a change of address for these new accounts after they are opened, it may take quite some time—often until a company or collections agency contacts the victim about overdue bills—for the victim to become aware that his or her identity has been stolen. Although identity theft often takes place via a computer today, information used in identity theft can also be gathered from trash dumpsters, mailboxes, and other locations. Other commonly used techniques are *skimming* and *social engineering*. Skimming involves stealing credit card or debit card numbers by using an illegal device attached to an ATM machine or credit card reader that reads and stores the card numbers to be retrieved by the thief

FIGURE 9-19

How identity theft works.

1. The thief obtains information about an individual from discarded mail, employee records, credit card transactions, Web server files, or some other method.

2. The thief uses the information to make purchases, open new credit card accounts, and more in the victim's name. Often, the thief changes the address on the account to delay the victim's discovery of the theft.

3. The victim usually finds out by being denied credit or by being contacted about overdue bills generated by the thief. Clearing one's name after identity theft is time-consuming and can be very difficult and frustrating for the victim.

>**Identity theft.** Using someone else's identity to purchase goods or services, obtain new credit cards or bank loans, or otherwise illegally masquerade as that individual.

at a later time. Social engineering involves pretending—typically via phone or e-mail—to be a bank officer, potential employer, or other trusted individual in order to get the potential victim to supply personal information. One recent social engineering scheme placed phony parking tickets on cars instructing the owners to go to a particular Web site; going to that site installed software on the users' computers to capture their keystrokes.

Unfortunately, identity theft is a very real danger to individuals today. According to the Federal Trade Commission (FTC), millions of Americans have their identity stolen each year. Identity theft can be extremely distressing for victims, can take years to straighten out, and can be very expensive. Some identity theft victims, such as Michelle Brown, believe that they will always be dealing with their "alter reality" to some extent. For a year and a half, an identity thief used Brown's identity to obtain over $50,000 in goods and services, to rent properties—even to engage in drug trafficking. Although the culprit was eventually arrested and convicted for other criminal acts, she continued to use Brown's identity and was even booked into jail using Brown's stolen identity. As a final insult after the culprit was in prison, U.S. customs agents detained the real Michelle Brown when she was returning from a trip to Mexico because of the criminal record of the identity thief. Brown states that she has not traveled out of the country since, fearing an arrest or some other serious problem resulting from the theft of her identity, and estimates she has spent over 500 hours trying to correct all the problems related to the identity theft.

ASK THE EXPERT

symantec. Marian Merritt, Internet Safety Advocate, Symantec Corporation

What is the single most important thing computer users should do to protect themselves from online threats?

The single most important step to protect computer users from online threats is to make sure their Internet security solution is current and up to date. There are several all-in-one security solutions available, such as Symantec's Norton 360, which combine PC security, antiphishing capabilities, backup, and tuneup technologies.

It's also pivotal to maintain a healthy wariness when receiving online communications. Do not click on links in suspicious e-mails or instant messages (IMs). These links will often direct you to sites that will ask you to reveal passwords, PINs, or other confidential data. Genuine organizations or institutions do not send such e-mails, nor do they ask for confidential data (like your Social Security number) for ordinary business transactions. If you're unsure whether or not an e-mail is legitimate, type the URL directly in your browser or call the institution to confirm they sent you that e-mail. Finally, do not open attachments in e-mails of questionable origin, since they may contain viruses.

Phishing and Spear Phishing

Phishing (pronounced "fishing") is the use of a *spoofed* e-mail message (an e-mail appearing to come from eBay, PayPal, Bank of America, or another well-known legitimate organization, but is actually sent from a phisher) to trick the recipient into revealing sensitive personal information (such as Web site logon information or credit card numbers). Once obtained, this information is used in identity theft and other fraudulent activities. A phishing e-mail typically looks legitimate and it contains links in the e-mail that appear to go to the Web site of the legitimate business, but these links go to the phisher's Web site that is set up to look like the legitimate site instead—an act called *Web site spoofing*. Phishing e-mails are typically sent to a wide group of individuals and usually include an urgent message stating that the individual's credit card or account information needs to be updated and instructing the recipient of the e-mail to click the link provided in the e-mail in order

>**Phishing.** The use of spoofed e-mail messages to gain credit card numbers and other personal data to be used for fraudulent purposes.

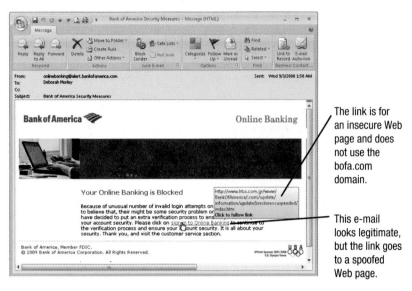

The link is for an insecure Web page and does not use the bofa.com domain.

This e-mail looks legitimate, but the link goes to a spoofed Web page.

FIGURE 9-20

Phishing. Phishing schemes use legitimate-looking e-mails to trick users into providing private information.

to keep the account active (see Figure 9-20). If the victim clicks the link and supplies the requested information via the spoofed site, the criminal gains access to all information provided by the victim, such as account numbers, credit card numbers, and Web site passwords. Phishing attempts can occur today via IM, text messages (called *smishing*), fake messages sent via eBay or MySpace, Twitter tweets, and pop-up security alert windows, in addition to via e-mail. Phishers also frequently utilize spyware; typically, clicking the link in the phishing e-mail installs the spyware on the victim's computer, and it will remain there (transmitting passwords and other sensitive data to a phisher) until it is detected and removed.

To fool victims into using the spoofed Web site, phishing e-mails and the spoofed Web sites often look legitimate. To accomplish this, phishers typically use copies of the spoofed organization's logo and other Web site content from the legitimate Web site. For spoofed banking Web pages and other pages where the victim would expect to see a secure Web page, some criminals use a secure connection between the victim and the criminal's server so the Web page looks secure with an *https:* in the Address bar. The domain name of the legitimate company (such as *ebay* for an eBay phishing page) is also often used as part of the URL of the phishing link (such as a URL starting with the text *ebay* even though the URL's domain is not ebay.com) to make it appear more legitimate. Other phishing schemes use a technique called *typosquatting*, which is setting up spoofed Web sites with addresses slightly different from legitimate sites. For example, a spoofed Web site using the URL www.amazon.com might be used to catch shoppers intending to reach the Amazon.com Web site located at www.amazon.com in hopes that customers making this error when typing the URL will not notice it and will supply logon information via the spoofed site when they arrive at it.

Another recent trend is the use of more targeted, personalized phishing schemes, known as **spear phishing**. Spear phishing e-mails are directly targeted to a specific individual and typically appear to come from an organization or person that the targeted individual has an association with. They also often include personalized information (such as the potential victim's name) to make the spear phishing e-mails seem even more legitimate. Several recent spear phishing attacks were targeted at users of social networking sites like MySpace since the personal information (name, age, hobbies, friends list, favorite music, and so forth) typically included on these sites makes them a good resource for spear phishers. Some of these attacks used spoofed logon pages for the social networking sites to obtain an individual's logon information and password. Since many individuals use the same logon information for a variety of sites, once a scammer has a valid username/password combination, he or she can try it on a variety of common e-commerce sites, such as shopping sites, online banking sites, and online payment services like PayPal. If the scammer is able to log on successfully to one of these sites, he or she can buy products, transfer money, and perform other types of financial transactions posing as the victim. Another recent tactic is to use the victim's social networking site logon information to log on to the victim's account and then post comments or send messages containing phishing links (posing as the victim) to the victim's friends, who are much more likely to click on the links because they appear to come from a friend.

>**Spear phishing.** A personalized phishing scheme targeted at an individual.

Spear phishers also target employees of selected organizations by posing as someone within the company, such as a human resources or technical support employee. These spear phishing e-mails often request confidential information (such as logon IDs and passwords) or direct the employee to click a link to supposedly reset his or her password. The goal for corporate spear phishing attacks is usually to steal intellectual property, such as software source code, design documents, or schematics. It can also be used to steal money. For instance, in one recent case, a grocery store received fraudulent e-mails that appeared to come from two approved suppliers. The e-mails instructed the grocery store chain to send future payments to new bank accounts listed in the e-mail—the grocery store chain deposited more than $10 million into two fraudulent bank accounts before the scam was discovered.

Pharming and Drive-By Pharming

Pharming is another type of scam that uses spoofing—specifically spoofed domain names used to obtain personal information for use in fraudulent activities. With pharming, the criminal reroutes traffic intended for a commonly used Web site to a spoofed Web site set up by the pharmer. Sometimes pharming takes place via malicious code sent to a computer via an e-mail message or other distribution method. More often however, it takes place via changes made to a *DNS server*—a computer that translates URLs into the appropriate IP addresses needed to display the Web page corresponding to a URL. This type of pharming can take place at one of the 13 *root DNS servers* (the DNS servers used in conjunction with the Internet), but it more often takes place at a *company DNS server* (the DNS server for that company used to route Web page requests received via company Web site URLs to the appropriate company server). After hacking into a company DNS server (typically for a company with a commonly used Web site), the pharmer changes the IP addresses used in conjunction with a particular company URL (called *DNS poisoning*) so any Web page requests made via the legitimate company URL is routed (via the company's poisoned DNS server) to a phony spoofed Web page located on the pharmer's Web server. So, even though a user types the proper URL to display the legitimate company Web page in his or her browser, the spoofed page is displayed instead.

Since spoofed sites are set up to look like the legitimate sites, the user typically does not notice any difference, and any information sent via that site is captured by the pharmer. To avoid suspicion, some pharming schemes capture the user's account name and password as it is entered the first time on the spoofed site, and then display a password error message. The spoofed site then redirects the user back to the legitimate site where he or she is able to log on to the legitimate site, leaving the user to think that he or she must have just mistyped the password the first time. But, by then, the pharmer has already captured the victim's username and password and can use that information to gain access to the victim's account.

A recent variation of pharming is *drive-by pharming*. The goal is still to redirect victims to spoofed sites; however, the pharmer accomplishes this by changing the victim's designated DNS server (which is specified in the victim's router settings) to the pharmer's DNS server in order to direct the victim to spoofed versions of legitimate Web sites when the victim enters the URLs for those sites. Typically, the pharmer uses malicious JavaScript code placed on a Web page to changes the victim's DNS settings to use the pharmer's DNS server; this change can only occur on a router in which the default administrator password was not changed.

Online Auction Fraud

Online auction fraud (sometimes called *Internet auction fraud*) occurs when an online auction buyer pays for merchandise that is never delivered, or that is delivered but it is not as represented. Online auction fraud is an increasing risk for online auction bidders. According to the Internet Crime Complaint Center (IC3), online auction fraud accounted for about 25% of all reported online fraud cases in 2008 for an average loss of around $600. Like other types of fraud, online auction fraud is illegal, but similar to many types of Internet cons, prosecution is difficult for online auction fraud because multiple jurisdictions are usually involved. Although most online auction sites have policies that suspend sellers with a certain number of complaints lodged against them, it is very easy for those sellers to come back using a new e-mail address and identity.

Other Internet Scams

There is a wide range of other scams that can occur via Web sites or unsolicited e-mails. The anonymity of the Internet makes it very easy for con artists to appear to be almost anyone they want to be, including a charitable organization or a reputable-looking business. Common types of scams include loan scams, work-at-home cons, pyramid schemes, bogus credit card offers and prize promotions, and fraudulent business opportunities and franchises. These offers typically try to sell potential victims nonexistent services or worthless information, or they try to convince potential victims to voluntarily supply their credit card details and other personal information, which are then used for fraudulent purposes. Some scammers use hacking as a means of obtaining a list of e-mail addresses for potential targets for a scam (such as stealing contact information from sites related to investing for a stock market scam) to increase the odds of a potential victim falling for the scam. A recent trend involves scammers who hack into Web mail and social networking accounts and send messages (posing as the victim) to the victim's entire contact list requesting money or urging recipients to buy specific products.

One ongoing Internet scam is the *Nigerian letter fraud* scheme. This scheme involves an e-mail message that appears to come from the Nigerian government and that promises the potential victim a share of a substantial amount of money in exchange for the use of the victim's bank account. Supposedly the victim's bank account information is needed to facilitate a wire transfer (but the victim's account is emptied instead) and/or up-front cash is needed to pay for nonexistent fees (that is kept by the con artist with nothing given in return). The theme of these scams often changes to fit current events, such as the war in Iraq or the Katrina hurricane. However, the scams always involve a so-called fortune that is inaccessible to the con artist without the potential victims' help (see Figure 9-21) and the victims always lose money when they pay fees or provide bank account information in the hope of sharing in the wealth. Despite the fact that this con is well known, people are still falling for it and with heavy losses—at $1,650, the Nigerian letter fraud scam had the third highest average dollar loss per individual for 2008 complaints, according to a report issued by the Internet Crime Complaint Center (IC3).

Other schemes involve con artists who solicit donations after disasters and other tragic events, but who keep the donations instead of giving them to any charitable organization. Another common scam involves setting up a pornographic site that requires a valid credit card, supposedly to prove that the visitor is of the required age (such as over 18), but which is then used for credit card fraud. A relatively new type of scam involves posting fake job listings on job search sites to elicit personal information (such as Social Security numbers) from job seekers. An even more recent twist is to hire individuals through online job sites for seemingly legitimate positions involving money handling (such as bookkeeping or accounting positions), but then use those individuals—often without their knowledge—as illegitimate go-betweens to facilitate Internet auction scams and other monetary scams.

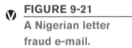

FIGURE 9-21
A Nigerian letter fraud e-mail.

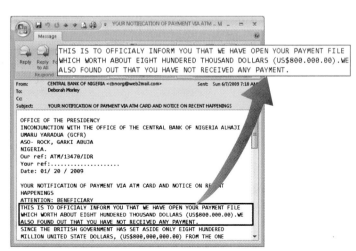

PROTECTING AGAINST ONLINE THEFT, ONLINE FRAUD, AND OTHER DOT CONS

In a nutshell, the best protection against many dot cons is protecting your identity; that is, protecting any identifying information about you that could be used in fraudulent activities. There are also specific precautions that can help protect against online theft, identity theft, online auction fraud, and other types of dot cons, as discussed next. With any dot con, it is important to act quickly if you think you have been a victim. For instance, you should work with your local law enforcement agency, credit card companies, and the three major consumer credit bureaus (*Equifax*, *Experian*, and *TransUnion*) to close any accessed or fraudulent accounts, place fraud alerts on your credit report, and take other actions to prevent additional fraudulent activity while the fraud is being investigated.

Arrests and prosecutions by law enforcement agencies may also help cut down on cybercrimes. Prosecution of online scammers has been increasing and sentences are not light. For instance, one man—the first person convicted by a jury under the *CAN-SPAM Act of 2003* for operating a phishing scheme—was sentenced in mid-2007 to 70 months in federal prison and ordered to pay over one million dollars to his victims.

Protecting Against Data and Information Theft

Businesses and individuals can both help to prevent some types of data and information theft. For instance, businesses should use good security measures to protect the data stored on their computers. Individuals should be vigilant about protecting their private information by sending sensitive information via secure Web servers only and not disclosing personal information—especially a Social Security number or a mother's maiden name—unless it is absolutely necessary and they know how the information will be used and that it will not be shared with others. In addition, individuals should never give out sensitive personal information to anyone who requests it over the phone or by e-mail—businesses that legitimately need bank account information, passwords, or credit card numbers will not request that information via phone or e-mail. Encrypting computers and other hardware containing sensitive information, so it will not be readable if the hardware is lost or stolen, is another important precaution.

Protecting Against Identity Theft, Phishing, and Pharming

Some of the precautions used for other types of online theft (such as being careful to disclose your personal information only when it is necessary and only via secure Web pages) can help reduce the chance that identity theft will happen to you. So can using security software (and keeping it up to date) to guard against computer viruses, spyware, and other malware that can be used to send information from your computer or about your activities (the Web site passwords that you type, for example) to a criminal. In addition, to prevent someone from using the preapproved credit card offers and other documents containing personal information that frequently arrive in the mail, shred them before throwing them in the trash. To prevent the theft of outgoing mail containing sensitive information, don't place it in your mailbox—mail it at the post office or in a USPS drop box.

To avoid phishing schemes, never click a link in an e-mail message to go to a secure Web site—always type the URL for that site in your browser (not necessarily the URL shown in the e-mail message) instead. Phishing e-mails typically sound urgent and often contain spelling and grammatical errors—see Figure 9-22 for some tips to help you recognize phishing e-mails. Remember that

FIGURE 9-22

Tips for identifying phishing e-mail messages.

A PHISHING E-MAIL OFTEN . . .
Tries to scare you into responding by sounding urgent, including a warning that your account will be cancelled if you do not respond, or telling you that you have been a victim of fraud.
Asks you to provide personal information, such as your bank account number, an account password, credit card number, PIN number, mother's maiden name, or Social Security number.
Contains links that do not go where the link text says it will go (point to a hyperlink in the e-mail message to view the URL for that link).
Uses legitimate logos from the company the phisher is posing as.
Appears to come from a known organization, but one you may not have an association with.
Appears to be text or text and images but is actually a single image; it has been created that way to avoid being caught in a spam filter (a program that sorts e-mail based on legitimate e-mail and suspected spam) since spam filters cannot read text that is part of an image in an e-mail message.
Contains spelling or grammatical errors.

TIPS FOR AVOIDING IDENTITY THEFT

Protect your Social Security number—give it out only when necessary.

Be careful with your physical mail and trash—shred all documents containing sensitive data.

Secure your computer—update your operating system and use up-to-date security (antivirus, antispyware, firewall, etc.) software.

Be cautious—never click on a link in an e-mail message or respond to a too-good-to-be-true offer.

Use strong passwords for your computer and online accounts.

Verify sources before sharing sensitive information—never respond to e-mail or phone requests for sensitive information.

Be vigilant while on the go—safeguard your wallet, mobile phone, and portable computer.

Watch your bills and monitor your credit reports—react immediately if you suspect fraudulent activity.

Use security software or browser features that warn you if you try to view a known phishing site.

FIGURE 9-23

Tips to reduce your risk of identity theft.

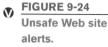

TIP

You can order your free credit reports online quickly and easily via Web sites like *AnnualCreditReport.com*.

FIGURE 9-24

Unsafe Web site alerts.

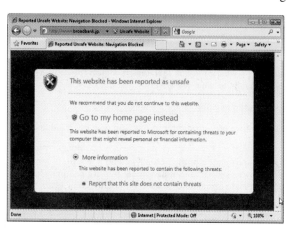

spear phishing schemes may include personalized information (such as your name)—do not let that fool you into thinking the phishing e-mail is legitimate. If you think an unsolicited e-mail message requesting information from you may be legitimate (for instance, if the credit card you use to make an automatic payment for an ongoing service is about to expire and you receive an e-mail message asking you to update your credit card information), type the URL for that site in your browser to load the legitimate site and then update your account information. To prevent a drive-by pharming attack, all businesses and individuals should change the administrator password for routers, access points, and other networking hardware from the default password to a strong password.

Keeping a close eye on your credit card bills and credit history is also important to make sure you catch any fraudulent charges or accounts opened by an identity thief as soon as possible. Make sure your bills come in every month (some thieves will change your mailing address to delay detection), and read credit card statements carefully to look for unauthorized charges. Be sure to follow up on any calls you get from creditors, instead of assuming it is just a mistake. Most security experts also recommend ordering a full credit history on yourself a few times a year to check for accounts listed in your name that you did not open and any other problems. The *Fair and Accurate Credit Transactions Act (FACTA)* enables all Americans to get a free copy of their credit report, upon request, each year from the three major consumer credit bureaus. Ideally, you should request a report from one of these bureaus every four months to monitor your credit on a regular basis. These reports contain information about inquiries related to new accounts requested in your name, as well as any delinquent balances or other negative reports. For another tool that you can use to help detect identity theft—*online financial alerts*—see the Technology and You box. You can also use browser-based *antiphishing* tools and *digital certificates* to help guard against identity theft and the phishing and pharming schemes used in conjunction with identity theft, as discussed next. Some additional tips for minimizing your risk of identity theft are listed in Figure 9-23.

Antiphishing Tools

Antiphishing tools are built into many e-mail programs and Web browsers to help notify users of possible phishing Web sites. For instance, some e-mail programs will disable links in e-mail messages identified as questionable, unless the user overrides it; many recent browsers warn users when a Web page associated with a possible phishing URL is requested (see Figure 9-24); and antiphishing capabilities are included in many recent security suites.

In addition, some secure Web sites are adding additional layers in security to protect against identity thieves. For example, some online banking sites analyze users' habits to look for patterns that vary from the norm, such as accessing accounts online at an hour unusual for that individual or a higher than normal level of online purchases. If a bank suspects the account may be compromised, it contacts the owner for verification. Bank of America and some other financial institutions have also added an additional step in their logon process—displaying an image or word preselected by the user and stored on the bank's server—to prove to the user that the site being viewed is the legitimate (not a phishing) site. In addition, if the system does not recognize the

TECHNOLOGY AND YOU

Online Financial Alerts

Want to know as soon as possible when a transaction that might be fraudulent is charged to your credit card? Well, *online financial alerts* might be the answer.

Many online banking services today allow users to set up e-mail alerts for credit card activity over a certain amount, low balances, and so forth. For individuals wishing to monitor multiple accounts, however, online money management aggregator services (such as *Mint.com*) make it easier. Once you have set up a free Mint.com account with your financial accounts (including credit cards and checking, savings, and PayPal accounts) and their respective passwords, you can see the status of all your accounts through the Mint.com interface. You can also set up alerts for any of the accounts based on your desired criteria, such as any transaction over a specified amount (see the accompanying illustration). The alerts are sent to you via e-mail or text message, depending on your preference, to help notify you as soon as possible if a suspicious activity occurs. And timeliness is of the essence, because the sooner identity theft is discovered, the less time the thief has to make additional fraudulent transactions. For security purposes, Mint.com doesn't store online banking usernames and passwords;

instead, a secure online financial services provider is used to connect Mint.com to the appropriate financial institutions as needed to update your activity. In addition, the Mint.com Web site cannot be used to move money out of or between financial accounts—it can be used only to view information.

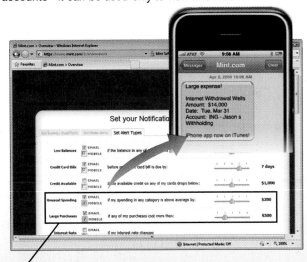

Unusual Spending and Large Purchases alerts can help you detect fraudulent charges to your financial accounts.

computer that the user is using to log on to the system, the user is required to go through an authentication process (typically by correctly answering cognitive authentication questions) before being allowed to access the system via that computer. The questions used are specifically designed to be "out of wallet" questions—easy for the individual to answer but difficult for hackers to guess the correct answer or find in a stolen wallet. Bank of America is also one bank offering customers the option of adding the use of one-time passwords (autogenerated by a security token like the one shown in Figure 9-5 or sent via text message to the individual's mobile phone) to their online banking logon procedure.

Digital Certificates and Digital Signatures

The purpose of a **digital certificate** is to authenticate the identity of an individual or organization. Digital certificates are granted by Certificate Authorities and typically contain the name of the person, organization, or Web site being certified along with a certificate serial number and an expiration date. Digital certificates also include a public/private key pair. In addition to being used by the certificate holder to encrypt files and e-mail messages (as discussed earlier in this chapter), these keys and the digital certificate are used with secure Web pages to guarantee the Web pages are secure and actually belong to the stated organization (so users can know for sure who their credit card number or other sensitive data is really being sent to, in order to protect against some online scams).

> **Digital certificate.** A group of electronic data that can be used to verify the identity of a person or organization; includes a key pair that can be used for encryption and digital signatures.

Red indicates a problem with the site's digital certificate.

Green indicates a valid EV SSL digital certificate.

Click to view certificate information.

FIGURE 9-25
EV SSL certificates.
The browser's Address bar reflects information about the digital certificate being used.

TIP

According to the Electronic Signatures in Global and National Commerce Act, any form of electronic signature is as legally binding as a handwritten signature.

Secure Web sites can obtain either a normal *SSL digital certificate* or a newer *Extended Validation (EV) SSL digital certificate* that was developed to provide consumers with a higher level of trust while online. While both digital certificates require an application process, the verification process to obtain an EV SSL digital certificate is more thorough, requiring the use of reputable third-party sources to verify that the company has the right to use the Web site domain name in question and that the business requesting the certificate is authorized to do so. With both types of certificates, individuals can click the secure Web page icon in their browser window to view that site's digital certificate in order to ensure that the certificate is valid and issued to the company associated with the Web site being viewed. If an EV SSL certificate is used, however, additional information is displayed when the Web site is viewed in an EV-compliant browser, such as recoloring the Address bar green to indicate a site using a valid EV SSL certificate and displaying certificate information in the *Security Status bar* to the right of the Address bar, as shown in Figure 9-25.

The keys included in a digital certificate can also be used to authenticate the identity of a person sending an e-mail message or other document via a **digital signature**. To digitally sign an e-mail message or other document, the sender's private key is used and that key, along with the contents of the document, generates a unique digital signature; consequently, a digital signature is different with each signed document. When a digitally signed document is received, the recipient's computer uses the sender's public key to verify the digital signature. Since the document is signed with the sender's private key (that only the sender should know) and the digital signature will be deemed invalid if even one character of the document is changed after it is signed, digital signatures guarantee that the document was sent by a specific individual and that it was not tampered with after it was signed.

Digital signatures are an important component of the emerging *e-mail authentication systems* (such as the *DomainKeys* system used by Yahoo!, eBay, Google, PayPal, and other companies) that may help prevent some types of online fraud in the future as these systems become more widely used. These systems are designed to authenticate e-mail messages via digital signatures and so can help ISPs block phishing e-mails because messages coming from a participating company must be digitally signed by that company in order to be deemed authentic.

Protecting Against Online Auction Fraud and Other Internet Scams

The best protection against many dot cons is common sense. Be extremely cautious of any unsolicited e-mail messages you receive and realize that if an offer sounds too good to be true, it probably is. You should also be cautious when dealing with individuals online through auctions and other person-to-person activities. Before bidding on an auction item, check out the feedback rating of the seller to see comments written by other auction sellers and buyers. Always pay for auctions and other online purchases using a credit card or an online payment service (such as PayPal) that accepts credit card payments so you can dispute the transaction through your credit card company, if needed. Using an online payment service that bills the charge to your credit card, instead of allowing the seller to charge your credit card, has the extra advantage of keeping your credit card information private.

>**Digital signature.** A unique digital code that can be attached to a file or an e-mail message to verify the identity of the sender and guarantee the file or message has not been changed since it was signed.

In addition, some auction sites and online payment services offer free buyer protection against undelivered items or auction items that are significantly different from the description provided in the auction information. For instance, most eBay purchases paid for via PayPal have at least $200 of buyer protection coverage at no additional cost. For expensive items, consider using an *escrow service*, which allows you to ensure that the merchandise is as specified before your payment is released to the seller.

PERSONAL SAFETY ISSUES

In addition to being expensive and inconvenient, cybercrime can also be physically dangerous. Although most of us may not ordinarily view using the Internet as a potentially dangerous activity, cases of physical harm due to Internet activity do happen. For example, children and teenagers have become the victims of pedophiles who arranged face-to-face meetings by using information gathered via e-mail, message boards, social networking sites, or other online sources. There are also a growing number of incidents in which children are threatened by classmates via e-mail, Web site posts, or text messages. Adults may fall victim to unscrupulous or dangerous individuals who misrepresent themselves online, and the availability of personal information online has made it more difficult for individuals to hide from people who may want to do them harm, such as abused women trying to hide from their abusive husbands. Two of the most common ways individuals are harassed online—*cyberbullying* and *cyberstalking*—are discussed next.

Cyberbullying and Cyberstalking

Children and teenagers bullying other children or teenagers via the Internet—such as through e-mail, a text message, a social networking site, a blog, or other online communications method—is referred to as **cyberbullying**. Unfortunately, cyberbullying is common today—by some estimates, it affects as many as one-half of all U.S. teenagers. Cyberbullying can take place via direct online communication (such as with an e-mail or instant message), as well as via more subtle means. For instance, there have been cases of students posting videos on YouTube of other students being bullied and cases of individuals hacking into a student's MySpace or Facebook account and changing the content on the student's pages to harass that student. In one tragic instance, a 13-year-old girl hanged herself after the mother of one of the girl's classmates arranged to have a MySpace profile created for a nonexistent teenage boy in order to determine what the victim was saying about her daughter, and then cruelly ended the friendship. While the mother was convicted of three misdemeanor charges of unauthorized access to computers in conjunction with the case, her conviction was dismissed in 2009. However, the case prompted many states and schools to look at harassment statutes and bullying policies and resulted in several states implementing new laws or amending existing harassment laws to address cyberbullying.

Repeated threats or other harassment carried out online between adults is referred to as **cyberstalking**. Cyberstalkers sometimes find their victims online; for instance, someone in a discussion group who makes a comment or has a screen name that the cyberstalker does not like, or bloggers who are harassed and threatened with violence or murder because of their blogging activities. Other times, the attack is more personal, such as employers who are stalked online by ex-employees who were fired or otherwise left their position under adverse conditions, and celebrities who are stalked online by fans.

Cyberstalking typically begins with online harassment—such as sending harassing or threatening e-mail messages or unwanted files to the victim, posing as the victim in order to

FURTHER EXPLORATION Go

Go to the Chapter 9 page at **www.cengage.com/ computerconcepts/np/uc13** for links to information about how to prevent and deal with identity theft and online auction fraud.

NET

> **Cyberbullying.** Children or teenagers bullying other children or teenagers via the Internet. > **Cyberstalking.** Repeated threats or harassing behavior between adults carried out via e-mail or another Internet communications method.

sign the victim up for pornographic or otherwise offensive e-mail newsletters, publicizing the victim's home address and telephone number, or hacking into the victim's social networking pages to alter the content. Cyberstalking can also lead to offline stalking and possibly physical harm—in at least one case, it led to the death of the victim. While there are as yet no specific federal laws against cyberstalking, all states have made it illegal (and it is being increasingly prosecuted), and some federal laws do apply if the online actions include computer fraud or another type of computer crime, suggest a threat of personal injury, or involve sending obscene e-mail messages. Many cyberstalkers are not caught, however, due in part to the anonymity of the Internet, which assists cyberstalkers in concealing their true identities.

Online Pornography

A variety of controversial and potentially objectionable material is available on the Internet. Although there have been attempts to ban this type of material from the Internet, they have not been successful. For example, the *Communications Decency Act*, signed into law in 1996—which made it a criminal offense to distribute patently indecent or offensive material online—was ruled unconstitutional in 1997 by the U.S. Supreme Court. However, like its printed counterpart, online pornography involving minors is illegal. Because of the strong link they believe exists between child pornography and child molestation, many experts are very concerned about the amount of child pornography that can be found and distributed via the Internet. They also believe that the Internet makes it easier for sexual predators to act out, such as by striking up "friendships" with children online and convincing these children to meet them in real life. And this can have devastating consequences, as it did for a 13-year-old girl from Connecticut who was strangled to death in 2002 by a 25-year-old man she met originally online and eventually in person. Although the man confessed, he maintains that the strangling was accidental. The man was sentenced in late 2003 to a total of 40 years in prison for state and federal charges relating to the crime.

PROTECTING AGAINST CYBERBULLYING, CYBERSTALKING, AND OTHER PERSONAL SAFETY CONCERNS

The growing increase in attention to cyberbullying and cyberstalking is leading to more efforts to improve safeguards for children. For instance, social networking sites have privacy features that can be used to protect the private information of their members. In addition, numerous states in the U.S. have implemented cyberbullying and cyberstalking laws. While there is no surefire way to protect against cyberbullying, cyberstalking, and other online dangers completely, some common-sense precautions can reduce the chance of a serious personal safety problem occurring due to online activities.

Safety Tips for Adults

It is wise to be cautious and discreet online—especially in online profiles, message boards, and other online locations where individuals communicate with strangers. To protect yourself against cyberstalking and other types of online harassment, use gender-neutral, nonprovocative identifying names, such as *jsmith*, instead of *janesmith* or *iamcute*. Be careful about the types of photos you post of yourself online and do not reveal personal information—such as your real name, address, or telephone number—to people you meet online. In addition, do not respond to any insults or other harassing comments you may receive online. You may also wish to request that your personal information be removed from online directories—especially those associated with your e-mail address or other online identifiers.

Safety Tips for Children and Teens

Most experts agree that the best way to protect children from online dangers is to stay in close touch with them as they explore the Internet. In order for parents to be able to monitor their children's online activities, children and teenagers should use a computer in a family room or other public location, instead of their bedroom, and they should be told which activities are allowed, which types of Web sites are off-limits, and why. In addition, it should be made clear that they are never to reveal personal information about themselves online without a parent's permission. They should also be instructed to tell a parent (or teacher if at school) if an individual ever requests personal information or a personal meeting, or threatens or otherwise harasses the child, via any type of online communications medium. Older children should also be cautioned about sending compromising photos of themselves to others. This practice—referred to as *sexting*—is a growing problem. In one recent study, for instance, more than 20% of teens reported sending nude or seminude photos of them-

FIGURE 9-26

Computer network and Internet security legislation.

selves to others. Part of the problem is that many young people don't realize they lose control of photos and other compromising content once that information has been sent to others and, in one case, a teenage girl committed suicide after the nude photos she had sent her boyfriend were sent to other students once the couple broke up. Sexting has also resulted in child pornography charges being filed against teens for sending their own photos to others or having compromising photos of other children on their mobile phones.

NETWORK AND INTERNET SECURITY LEGISLATION

Although new legislation is passed periodically to address new types of computer crimes, it is difficult for the legal system to keep pace with the rate at which technology changes. In addition, there are both domestic and international jurisdictional issues because many computer crimes affect businesses and individuals located in geographic areas other than the one in which the computer criminal is located, and hackers can make it appear that activity is coming from a different location than it really is. Nevertheless, computer crime legislation continues to be proposed and computer crimes are being prosecuted. A list of selected federal laws concerning network and Internet security is shown in Figure 9-26.

DATE	LAW AND DESCRIPTION
2004	**Identity Theft Penalty Enhancement Act** Adds extra years to prison sentences for criminals who use identity theft (including the use of stolen credit card numbers) to commit other crimes, including credit card fraud and terrorism.
2003	**CAN-SPAM Act** Implements regulations for unsolicited e-mail messages.
2003	**Fair and Accurate Credit Transactions Act (FACTA)** Amends the Fair Credit Reporting Act (FCRA) to require, among other things, that the three nationwide consumer reporting agencies (Equifax, Experian, and TransUnion) provide to consumers, upon request, a free copy of their credit report once every 12 months.
2003	**PROTECT Act** Includes provisions to prohibit virtual child pornography.
2003	**Health Insurance Portability and Accountability Act (HIPAA)** Includes a Security Rule that sets minimum security standards to protect health information stored electronically.
2002	**Homeland Security Act** Includes provisions to combat cyberterrorism, including protecting ISPs against lawsuits from customers for revealing private information to law enforcement agencies.
2002	**Sarbanes-Oxley Act** Requires archiving a variety of electronic records and protecting the integrity of corporate financial data.
2001	**USA PATRIOT Act** Grants federal authorities expanded surveillance and intelligence-gathering powers, such as broadening the ability of federal agents to obtain the real identity of Internet users, intercept e-mail and other types of Internet communications, follow online activity of suspects, expand their wiretapping authority, and more.
1998	**Identity Theft and Assumption Deterrence Act of 1998** Makes it a federal crime to knowingly use someone else's means of identification, such as name, Social Security number, or credit card, to commit any unlawful activity.
1997	**No Electronic Theft (NET) Act** Expands computer piracy laws to include distribution of copyrighted materials over the Internet.
1996	**National Information Infrastructure Protection Act** Amends the Computer Fraud and Abuse Act of 1984 to punish information theft crossing state lines and to crack down on network trespassing.
1994	**Computer Abuse Amendments Act** Amends the Computer Fraud and Abuse Act of 1984 to include computer viruses and other harmful code.
1986	**Computer Fraud and Abuse Act of 1986** Amends the 1984 law to include federally regulated financial institutions.
1984	**Computer Fraud and Abuse Act of 1984** Makes it a crime to break into computers owned by the federal government. This act has been regularly amended over the years as technology has changed.

NET

SUMMARY

WHY BE CONCERNED ABOUT NETWORK AND INTERNET SECURITY?

Chapter Objective 1:
Explain why computer users should be concerned about network and Internet security.

There are a number of important security concerns related to computers and the Internet. Many of these are **computer crimes**. Because computers and networks are so widespread and many opportunities for criminals exist, all computer users should be aware of the risks of using networks and the Internet so they can take appropriate precautions.

UNAUTHORIZED ACCESS AND UNAUTHORIZED USE

Chapter Objective 2:
List several examples of unauthorized access and unauthorized use.

Two risks related to networks and the Internet are **unauthorized access** and **unauthorized use**. **Hacking** is using a computer to break into a computer. **War driving** and **Wi-Fi piggybacking** refer to the unauthorized use of unsecured Wi-Fi network. Data can be intercepted as it is transmitted over the Internet or a wireless network.

PROTECTING AGAINST UNAUTHORIZED ACCESS AND UNAUTHORIZED USE

Chapter Objective 3:
Explain several ways to protect against unauthorized access and unauthorized use, including access control systems, firewalls, and encryption.

Access control systems are used to control access to a computer, network, or other resource. These include **possessed knowledge access systems** that use **passwords** or other types of possessed knowledge; **possessed object access systems** that use physical objects; and **biometric access systems** that identify users by a particular unique biological characteristic, such as a fingerprint. Passwords should be *strong passwords*; **two-factor authentication systems** that use multiple factors are more effective than single-factor systems.

To protect wireless networks, they should be secured; **firewalls** protect against unauthorized access. Sensitive transactions should be performed only on **secure Web pages**; sensitive files and e-mails should be secured with **encryption**. **Public key encryption** uses a private key and matching public key; **private key encryption** uses only a private key. A **virtual private network (VPN)** can be used to provide a secure remote connection to a company network, as well as to protect individuals at public Wi-Fi hotspots. Employers should take appropriate precautions with current and former employees to limit the risk of unauthorized access and use, as well as accidental exposure of sensitive information.

COMPUTER SABOTAGE

Chapter Objective 4:
Provide several examples of computer sabotage.

Computer sabotage includes **malware** (**computer viruses**, **computer worms**, and **Trojan horses** designed to cause harm to computer systems), **denial of service (DoS) attacks** (designed to shut down a Web server), and data and program alteration. Computer sabotage is often performed via the Internet, increasingly by the **bots** in a **botnet**.

PROTECTING AGAINST COMPUTER SABOTAGE

Chapter Objective 5:
List how individuals and businesses can protect against computer sabotage.

Protection against computer sabotage includes using appropriate access control systems to keep unauthorized individuals from accessing computers and networks, as well as using **security software**. In particular, **antivirus software** protects against computer viruses and other types of malware. It is important to keep your security software up to date.

ONLINE THEFT, ONLINE FRAUD, AND OTHER DOT CONS

There are a variety of types of theft, fraud, and scams related to the Internet—collectively referred to as **dot cons**—that all Internet users should be aware of. Data, information, or money can be stolen from individuals and businesses. A common crime today is **identity theft**, in which an individual poses as another individual—typically to steal money or make purchases posing as the victim. The information used in identity theft is often gathered via **phishing**, **spear phishing**, and **pharming**. **Online auction fraud** is another common dot con.

Chapter Objective 6:
Discuss online theft, identity theft, spoofing, phishing, and other types of dot cons.

PROTECTING AGAINST ONLINE THEFT, ONLINE FRAUD, AND OTHER DOT CONS

To protect against identity theft, individuals should guard their personal information carefully. To check for identity theft, watch your bills and credit history. When interacting with other individuals online or buying from an online auction, it is wise to be conservative and use a credit card whenever possible. To avoid other types of dot cons, be very wary of responding to unsolicited offers and e-mails, and steer clear of offers that seem too good to be true. Never click a link in an e-mail message to update your personal information. To verify a Web site, a **digital certificate** can be used. To verity the sender of a document, a **digital signature** can be used. Digital certificates include key pairs that can be used to both digitally sign documents and to encrypt files.

Chapter Objective 7:
Detail steps an individual can take to protect against online theft, identity theft, spoofing, phishing, and other types of dot cons.

PERSONAL SAFETY ISSUES

There are also personal safety risks for both adults and children stemming from Internet use. **Cyberbullying** and **cyberstalking**—online harassment that frightens or threatens the victim—is more common in recent years, even though most states have passed laws against it. Cyberbully is a growing risk for children, as is the potential exposure to online pornography and other materials inappropriate for children, and the growing *sexting* trend.

Chapter Objective 8:
Identify personal safety risks associated with Internet use.

PROTECTING AGAINST CYBERBULLING, CYBERSTALKING, AND OTHER PERSONAL SAFETY CONCERNS

To protect their personal safety, adults and children should be cautious in online communications. They should be wary of revealing any personal information or meeting online acquaintances in person. To protect children, parents should keep a close watch on their children's online activities, and children should be taught never to reveal personal information to others online without a parent's consent.

Chapter Objective 9:
List steps individuals can take to safeguard their personal safety when using the Internet.

NETWORK AND INTERNET SECURITY LEGISLATION

The rapid growth of the Internet and jurisdictional issues have contributed to the lack of network and Internet security legislation. However, computer crime legislation continues to be proposed and computer crimes are actively prosecuted.

Chapter Objective 10:
Discuss the current state of network and Internet security legislation.

REVIEW ACTIVITIES

KEY TERM MATCHING

a. computer virus

b. denial of service (DoS) attack

c. dot con

d. encryption

e. firewall

f. hacking

g. identity theft

h. password

i. phishing

j. Trojan horse

Instructions: Match each key term on the left with the definition on the right that best describes it.

1. _____ A collection of hardware and/or software intended to protect a computer or computer network from unauthorized access.

2. _____ A fraud or scam carried out through the Internet.

3. _____ A malicious program that masquerades as something else.

4. _____ A method of scrambling the contents of an e-mail message or a file to make it unreadable if it is intercepted by an unauthorized user.

5. _____ A secret combination of characters used to gain access to a computer, computer network, or other resource.

6. _____ A software program installed without the user's knowledge and designed to alter the way a computer operates or to cause harm to the computer system.

7. _____ An act of sabotage that attempts to flood a network server or a Web server with so much activity that it is unable to function.

8. _____ The use of spoofed e-mail messages to gain credit card numbers and other personal data to be used for fraudulent purposes.

9. _____ Using a computer to break into another computer system.

10. _____ Using someone else's identity to purchase goods or services, obtain new credit cards or bank loans, or otherwise illegally masquerade as that individual.

SELF-QUIZ

Instructions: Circle **T** if the statement is true, **F** if the statement is false, or write the best answer in the space provided. **Answers for the self-quiz are located in the References and Resources Guide at the end of the book.**

1. **T   F**   A computer virus can only be transferred to another computer via a storage medium.

2. **T   F**   An access control system that uses passwords is a possessed knowledge access system.

3. **T   F**   Using a password that is two characters long is an example of two-factor authentication.

4. **T   F**   Secure Web pages use encryption to securely transfer data sent via those pages.

5. **T   F**   Cyberstalking is the use of spoofed e-mail messages to gain credit card numbers and other personal data to be used for fraudulent purposes.

6. Driving around looking for a Wi-Fi network to access is referred to as _____.

7. _____ access control systems use some type of unique physical characteristic of a person to authenticate that individual.

8. A(n) _____ can be used at a Wi-Fi hotspot to create a secure path over the Internet.

9. A(n) _____ can be added to a file or an e-mail message to verify the identity of the sender and guarantee the file or message has not been changed.

10. Match each computer crime to its description, and write the corresponding number in the blank to the left of the description.

   a. _____ A person working for the Motor Vehicle Division deletes a friend's speeding ticket from a database.

   b. _____ An individual does not like someone's comment on a message board and begins to send that individual harassing e-mail messages.

   c. _____ An individual sells the same item to 10 individuals via an online auction site.

   d. _____ A person accesses a computer belonging to the IRS without authorization.

1. Online auction fraud

2. Hacking

3. Data or program alteration

4. Cyberstalking

---

1. Write the appropriate letter in the blank to the left of each term to indicate whether it is related to unauthorized access (U) or computer sabotage (C).

   a. _____ Time bomb   c. _____ Malware   e. _____ War driving

   b. _____ DoS attack   d. _____ Wi-Fi piggybacking

2. Is the password *john1* a good password? Why or why not? If not, suggest a better password.

3. Supply the missing words to complete the following statements regarding public/private key pairs.

   a. With an encrypted e-mail message, the recipient's _____ key is used to encrypt the message, and the recipient's _____ key is used to decrypt the message.

   b. With a digital signature, the sender's _____ key is used to sign the document, and the sender's _____ key is used to validate the signature.

4. To secure files on your computer so they are unreadable to a hacker who might gain access to your computer, what type of encryption (public key or private key) would be the most appropriate? Explain.

5. List two precautions that individuals can take to secure a wireless router against unauthorized access.

---

1. The term *hacktivism* is sometimes used to refer to the act of hacking into a computer system for a politically or socially motivated purpose. While some view hacktivists no differently than they view other hackers, hacktivists contend that they break into systems in order to bring attention to political or social causes. Is hacktivism a valid method of bringing attention to specific causes? Why or why not? Should hacktivists be treated differently than other types of hackers when caught?

2. According to security experts, several worms released in past years contain more than just the virus code—they contain code to remove competing malware from the computers they infect and messages taunting other virus writers. The goal seems to be not only to gain control of an increasing number of infected machines—a type of "bot war" to build the biggest botnet—but also to one-up rivals. If this trend continues, do you think it will affect how hackers and other computer criminals will be viewed? Will they become cult heroes or be viewed as dangerous criminals? Will continuing to increase prosecution of these individuals help or hurt the situation?

PROJECTS

1. **Wi-Fi Hotspot Safety** As discussed in the chapter, it is possible to inadvertently connect to an evil twin instead of the legitimate Wi-Fi hotspot you intended to connect to and, even if you are connected to a legitimate hotspot, any data you send unsecured via the hotspot can be intercepted by a criminal. In either case, if the thief intercepts your credit card number, Web site passwords, or other sensitive data, it can be used for identity theft and other criminal activities.

   For this project, research these and any other possible risks you can think of related to using a Wi-Fi hotspot. For each risk, identify a possible precaution that can be taken to guard against that risk. If you have ever used a Wi-Fi hotspot, were you at risk? Knowing what you do now, would you take any new precautions the next time you use one? Is it possible to surf safely using a Wi-Fi hotspot? At the conclusion of your research, prepare a one-page summary of your findings and opinions and submit it to your instructor.

2. **New Viruses** Unfortunately, new computer viruses and other types of malware are released all the time.

   For this project, identify a current virus or worm (most security companies, such as Symantec and McAfee, list the most recent security threats on their Web sites) and answer the following questions: When was it introduced? What does it do? How is it spread? How many computers have been affected so far? Is there an estimated cost associated with it? Is it still in existence? At the conclusion of your research, prepare a one-page summary of your findings and submit it to your instructor.

3. **Virus Check** There are several Web sites that include a free virus check, as well as other types of diagnostic software.

   For this project, find a free virus check available on the Web site of a company that makes antivirus software (such as the Symantec Security Scan at **security.symantec.com**) and run the free virus check. NOTE: The programs may require temporarily downloading a small program or an ActiveX component. If you are unable to perform this task on a school computer, ask your instructor for alternate instructions. If the check takes more than 10 minutes and there is an option to limit the check to a particular drive and folder, redo the check but scan only part of the hard drive (such as the Documents folder) to save time. After the virus scan is completed, print the page displaying the result. Did the program find any viruses or other security threats? At the conclusion of this task, submit your printout with any additional comments about your experience to your instructor.

4. **Teaching Computer Viruses** Some college computer classes include instruction on writing computer viruses. At one university, precautions for containing code created during this course include only allowing fourth year students to take the course, not having a network connection in the classroom, and prohibiting the removal of storage media from the classroom. Do you think these precautions are sufficient? Should writing virus code be allowed as part of a computer degree curriculum? Some believe that students need to know how viruses work in order to be able to develop antivirus software; however, the antivirus industry disagrees, and most antivirus professionals were never virus writers. Is it ethical for colleges to teach computer virus writing? Is it ethical for students to take such a course? Will teaching illegal and unethical acts (such as writing virus code) in college classes help to legitimize the behavior in society? Would you feel comfortable taking such a course? Why or why not?

   For this project, form an opinion about the ethical implications of including the instruction of writing virus code in college classes and be prepared to discuss your position (in class, via an online class discussion group, in a class chat room, or via a class blog, depending on your instructor's directions). You may also be asked to write a short paper expressing your opinion.

ETHICS IN ACTION

5. **Virus Hoaxes** In addition to the valid reports about new viruses found in the news and on antivirus software Web sites, reports of viruses that turn out to be hoaxes abound on the Internet. In addition to being an annoyance, virus hoaxes waste time and computing resources. In addition, they may eventually lead some users to routinely ignore all virus warning messages, leaving them vulnerable to a genuine, destructive virus.

   For this project, visit at least two Web sites that identify virus hoaxes, such as the Symantec or McAfee Web sites and Snopes.com. Explore the sites to find information about recent virus hoaxes, as well as general guidelines for identifying virus hoaxes and other types of online hoaxes. Share your findings with the class in the form of a short presentation. The presentation should not exceed 10 minutes and should make use of one or more presentation aids, such as the chalkboard, handouts, overhead transparencies, or a computer-based slide presentation (your instructor may provide additional requirements). You may also be asked to submit a summary of the presentation to your instructor.

PRESENTATION/ DEMONSTRATION

(((o))) NET

Instructions: Go to the Chapter 9 page at **www.cengage.com/computerconcepts/np/uc13** to work the following Web Activities.

6. **Interactive Activities** Work the interactive **Crossword Puzzle**, watch the **Video Podcasts** and **Online Videos**, and explore the **Further Exploration** links associated with this chapter.

   If you have a SAM user profile, you may have access to hands-on instruction, practice, and assessment of the skills covered in this chapter. Check with your instructor for instructions and the correct URL/Web site to access those assignments.

7. **Student Edition Labs** Work the following interactive **Student Edition Lab**.

   ➤ **Keeping Your Computer Virus Free**

8. **Test Yourself** Review the **Online Study Guide** for this chapter, then test your knowledge of the terms and concepts covered in this chapter by completing the **Key Term Matching** exercise, the **Self-Quiz**, the **Exercises**, and the **Practice Test**.

WEB ACTIVITIES

SAM

Student Edition Labs

expert insight on . . .
Networks and the Internet

Collin Davis is a Senior Development Manager in the Consumer Product Solutions Group at Symantec Corporation. He has worked for Symantec for nine years, initially as a Software Development Intern while in college. He has over 12 years of experience working with computer systems, networks, and other computer-related areas. Collin has a Bachelor of Science degree in Computer Science from the UCLA Henry Samueli School of Engineering.

A conversation with **COLLIN DAVIS**

Senior Development Manager, Consumer Product Solutions, Symantec Corporation

"Cyber criminals aren't in it for just notoriety anymore; they want your money—or worse, your identity."

My Background . . .

I have been working in the computer security industry for nine years. I started in 2001 as a Software Development Intern while studying at UCLA. After earning my Bachelor's degree in computer science from the University of California, Los Angeles, Henry Samueli School of Engineering, I joined Symantec as an engineer on the Norton AntiVirus product team and helped develop and ship six iterations of that product. I then joined the team responsible for the creation of Symantec's all-in-one security solution, Norton 360. Most recently, I lead the development of OnlineFamily. Norton, a new, unique family safety solution that helps parents protect their kids online and fosters communication about their online activities.

It's Important to Know . . .

To use a layered security system. A layered security system consists of multiple layers of protection to guard against intrusions and other threats. You should use a secure wireless router and advanced firewall and antivirus technologies. You should also ensure that all your passwords are secure and change them often.

That you need to stay up to date. The threat landscape is constantly changing. There are actually more "bad" files today than "good" ones. This has led some security software makers to rely less on signature-based detection. Instead, they use a combination of whitelisting and advanced reputation engines to trust only the good files and block everything else. Use software with this type of technology if possible. Regardless, it is critical that you keep your security products up to date to stay protected from the latest threats. It's fairly easy for computer users to do this since most products download updates automatically or notify you when you need to download a new version. Don't ignore these notifications.

To think before you act. The online world is no different from the real one. If a link seems suspicious, proceed with caution before clicking it or seek information and services elsewhere.

How I Use this Technology . . .

I use this technology every day in my personal life. I also realize that the more and more "connected" data and applications become, the more important it becomes to secure them. Every time I connect to the Internet to send an e-mail, bank online, or view family photos, I am using the networking and Internet technologies discussed in this module to make the connection, and I am using the security technologies listed in this module to ensure my private data is protected. I don't always see these technologies as they do their job (this is a good thing!), but the fact that they are there gives me the confidence to take advantage of all the other great technologies being offered today.

What the Future Holds . . .

Our lives are becoming increasingly more and more dependent on technology. We store our documents and photos online. We work online and even date and form social networks online. All of this introduces increased privacy and security concerns that we must be aware of. It's important to be aware of what data is stored online and to use appropriate protection measures to secure it.

One of the biggest Internet-related risks today is that threats have evolved to exploit people for financial gain. Cyber criminals aren't in it for just notoriety anymore; they want your money—or worse, your identity. People need to be particularly cautious about whom they give their personal information (like credit card and Social Security numbers) to online. Everyone should check their bank and credit card statements often to monitor for fraudulent charges and change their passwords frequently.

In the future, we can expect to see businesses moving toward delivering an even more connected online experience. Personal computers are moving back toward their past role as simple "terminals" that provide a connection to the Internet where a wide array of data and applications are hosted. The line between what is stored and run from your local computer and what is "online" is being blurred. One impact of our online and local content becoming more interconnected is that we will be able to access our own personalized application experience from anywhere in the world, with many different types of devices. Wherever we are, our experience will remain consistent, according to our preferences and our content. However, security will remain essential. If people cannot trust that their information is secure and protected, they will be unable to take advantage of all the exciting services and benefits being offered today.

My Advice to Students . . .

Be curious—explore every facet of a technology that interests you. Try to learn everything about its inner workings but don't lose sight of the big picture. If you're interested in a career in a particular field, get an internship. There is no better way to learn something than to do it.

> *" The online world is no different from the real one. If a link seems suspicious, proceed with caution before clicking it or seek information and services elsewhere. "*

NET

Discussion Question

Collin Davis stresses the importance of people trusting that their information is secure and protected. Think about the systems that contain personal data about you. How would you feel if those systems were breached and your information was stolen? Does your viewpoint change if the information was monetary (such as credit card information) versus private information (such as grades or health information)? What security precautions, if any, do you think should be imposed by laws? Are organizations that hold your personal data morally responsible for going beyond the minimum requirements? What types of security measures would you implement to protect these systems? Be prepared to discuss your position (in class, via an online class discussion group, in a class chat room, or via a class blog, depending on your instructor's directions). You may also be asked to write a short paper expressing your opinion.

>**For more information on Symantec, visit www.symantec.com. To view the latest Symantec Internet Security Threat Report results, go to www.symantec.com/business/ theme.jsp?themeid=threatreport.**

Business on the Web

In the previous module, we took a look at how the Internet and World Wide Web work and at some of the most common online activities. Two applications found on the Web that have not yet been discussed in detail are multimedia and e-commerce. This module introduces you to these two important Web-related topics, their use and significance in today's networked economy, and their impact on businesses today.

Chapter 10 delves into multimedia, looking at what it is, advantages and disadvantages of using multimedia, common types of multimedia elements, and how to design and develop a multimedia Web site. The focus of this chapter is on Web-based multimedia—that is, multimedia found on Web sites today. Chapter 11 explains in detail what e-commerce is and how it can be implemented via a Web site.

Chapter 10
Multimedia and the Web 394

Overview 395

What Is Web-Based Multimedia? 395

Multimedia Elements 399

Multimedia Web Site Design 407

Multimedia Web Site Development 414

The Future of Web-Based Multimedia 423

Chapter 11
E-Commerce 430

Overview 431

What Is E-Commerce? 431

E-Commerce Business Models 436

Types of E-Commerce Web Sites 438

Implementing Web-Based E-Commerce 440

Security Issues 455

" . . . the most valuable asset for any business, online or offline, is the customer."

For more comments from Guest Expert **Jim Griffith** of eBay, see the **Expert Insight on . . . Web-Based Multimedia and E-Commerce** feature at the end of the module.

chapter 10

Multimedia and the Web

After completing this chapter, you will be able to do the following:

1. Define Web-based multimedia and list some advantages and disadvantages of using multimedia.

2. Describe each of the following multimedia elements—text, images, animation, audio, and video—and tell how they differ.

3. Briefly describe the basic steps and principles involved with designing a multimedia Web site.

4. List the various tasks involved with developing a multimedia Web site.

5. Explain how markup languages, scripting languages, and other tools are used today to create multimedia Web pages.

6. Discuss the possible use of Web-based multimedia in the future.

outline

Overview

What Is Web-Based Multimedia?
Why Learn about Web-Based Multimedia?
Web-Based Multimedia Applications
Advantages and Disadvantages of Using Web-Based Multimedia

Multimedia Elements
Text
Images
Animation
Audio
Video

Multimedia Web Site Design
Basic Design Principles
Determining the Objectives and Intended Audience of the Site
Using Flowcharts, Page Layouts, and Storyboards
Navigational Design Considerations
Access Considerations

Multimedia Web Site Development
Creating the Multimedia Elements
Creating the Web Site
Testing, Publishing, and Maintaining the Site

The Future of Web-Based Multimedia

OVERVIEW

The term *multimedia* refers to any type of application that involves more than one type of media, such as text, images, video, animation, and sound. Multimedia is used in a wide variety of applications, both on and off the Web. This chapter focuses on the multimedia found on Web sites, although the concepts and techniques discussed in this chapter can be applied to non-Web-based multimedia, as well. In this chapter, we look first at what Web-based multimedia is and how it used today, including some of the most common types of Web-based multimedia applications and the advantages and disadvantages of using multimedia in general. Next, we discuss the basic multimedia elements commonly found on Web pages, such as text, images, animation, audio, and video. We then turn to the fundamental steps and principles involved in designing a multimedia Web site, followed by a discussion of how a multimedia Web site is developed and the software that can be used during this process. The chapter closes with a brief look at the future of Web-based multimedia. ■

WHAT IS WEB-BASED MULTIMEDIA?

While **multimedia** refers to the integration of a variety of media, **Web-based multimedia** (also called *rich media*) refers to multimedia—typically sound, video, or animation, in addition to text and images—located on Web pages. Like other Web pages, multimedia Web pages are *interactive*, displaying information as requested by the Web page visitor via hyperlinks. In addition, multimedia Web sites often contain other interactive elements that the user interacts with directly, such as playing or pausing a video clip, controlling a 3D object, or playing a game.

In the past, Web-based multimedia was very limited because computers and Internet connections were too slow to support it. Today's fast computers and broadband Internet connections, however, make Web-based multimedia very feasible and the use of Web-based multimedia is growing rapidly. In fact, the vast majority of Web sites today include multimedia—for instance, it is often used in Web-page advertisements, as regular Web site content (such as TV shows and photos posted on TV network Web sites or podcasts available via company Web sites), or as *user-generated content* uploaded to Web sites (such as videos uploaded to YouTube or photos uploaded to Flickr).

Why Learn About Web-Based Multimedia?

Because multimedia is such an integral component of the Web today, it is important for businesses and individuals to understand the characterstics of the various types of multimedia elements and the impact of adding them to a Web site—both for the business or individual creating the Web site and for the visitors accessing the content. For instance, video is widely used on Web sites today. Before adding video to a Web site, however, the

---

>**Multimedia.** The integration of a variety of media, such as text, images, video, animation, and sound. >**Web-based multimedia.** Multimedia located on Web pages.

business or individual associated with the Web site needs to consider the cost of creating or obtaining the video, the cost associated with the bandwidth required to enable visitors to access the video, whether or not their intended audience is technically able to view the video with their access device of choice, and the file format the video should be made available in. Individuals uploading video to YouTube or sending video clips to others via their mobile phones also need to understand file format and bandwidth limitations to ensure the video will be able to be viewed by the recipient and will not create a bandwidth issue for the receipient. Individuals choosing to view movie trailers, TV shows, and other video content via a Web site need to ensure the bandwidth required to access that content will not create problems for themselves, such as an unexpected expense for mobile users with a limited data plan or interruption of service for home broadband users with a bandwidth cap.

Some examples of the multimedia applications commonly found on the Web today are discussed next, followed by advantages and disadvantages of using multimedia on a Web site.

Web-Based Multimedia Applications

There are a vast number of multimedia applications that can be found on the Web. Some of the most common Web-based multimedia applications are discussed next; some examples are shown in Figure 10-1. Because multimedia applications (particularly video) are bandwidth-intensive, your Internet connection may limit the multimedia applications that you can access. For instance, most streaming video sites require a minimum broadband connection speed of 500 Kbps for standard-definition video; a faster connection is typically necessary for high-definition (HD) content. In addition, if your ISP has a bandwidth cap, you can go through your allotment quickly viewing or downloading Web-based video. For instance, a 1-hour standard-definition TV show is about 200 MB—the daily maximum bandwidth allowed by at least one Internet provider. Consequently, being familiar with any bandwidth caps or additional charges for large downloads imposed by your ISP is important if you access Web-based multimedia content.

FIGURE 10-1

Web-based multi-media applications.

INFORMATION DELIVERY
Images, video, audio, and animation are often used to convey information, such as via this Web-based training activity.

E-COMMERCE
Images and video are often used for e-commerce purposes, such as this virtual model home tour located on a home builder's Web site.

ENTERTAINMENT
Video and audio are often used in entertainment applications, such as this site that offers TV shows for online viewing.

3D VIRTUAL WORLDS
Images, animation, and sound are integral components of many 3D virtual worlds, such as Second Life shown here.

Information Delivery

Multimedia is commonly used to deliver a wide variety of information via Web sites. For instance, manufacturers use photos and online versions of users' manuals to convey information about their products to visitors, news Web sites use video clips and podcasts to bring news updates to visitors, restaurants use photos to illustrate their menu selections and maps to help visitors find the restaurant, and politicians use photos and video clips to convey their political positions and garner support. Multimedia is also an important component of Web-based training (WBT)—delivering instruction via the Web, as discussed in Chapter 8. For instance, one of the Web-based training activities available through this textbook's Web site is shown in Figure 10-1.

E-Commerce

Multimedia is also often used on e-commerce Web sites to portray the products that can be purchased via the site. For instance, Web sites selling multimedia products (such as music and movies) often use multimedia elements (such as samples of songs or movie trailers) that customers can listen to or view before making a final selection. Web sites selling other types of products typically use online product catalogs containing photos that visitors can use to find products on the site. These online product catalogs almost always contain photos of the products and often the photos can be manipulated (such as zoomed or rotated) for a better view of the product.

Many e-commerce sites also enable visitors to recolor the product images to show the desired finished product (such as a car or article of clothing); some clothing retail sites (such as Lands' End) allow shoppers to view their selected clothes on a *virtual model* that the user customizes (by selecting body shape, height, weight, hair cut, hair color, and so forth) to better visualize how the clothes will look on the shopper. Still other e-commerce sites utilize **virtual reality (VR)** to display environments or show what products (such as a car or a home) look like in the real world. For instance, the Web-based VR e-commerce application shown in Figure 10-1 allows potential home buyers to take a virtual tour of model homes, in order to better evaluate the various available models.

An emerging VR possibility for mobile users is *augmented VR* (also known as *augmented reality*)—overlaying computer generated images on top of real-time images. These applications typically use GPS information, the video feed from the mobile phone's camera, a digital compass, and other data obtained from the phone, and overlay appropriate data (based on the data obtained via the phone and the specific application being used) on top of the video images displayed on the phone. For instance, the *Wimbleton Seer App* that is designed to be used by Wimbleton attendees overlays data about the tennis matches (such as the match being played, current score, information about subsequent matches, relevant Twitter tweets, and more when the phone's camera is pointed toward a tennis court), as well as data about Wimbleton facilities (such as the current wait time and menu specials when the phone's camera is pointed toward a restaurant).

ASK THE EXPERT

Ryan Baustert, Guitarist, Throw the Fight

How has the Internet changed the music industry today and what impact do you expect it to have in the future?

The Internet makes it much easier to reach a larger audience around the world. People that might not ever have a chance to see us play can still be exposed to our music online—which, in turn, can help generate more CD, merchandise, and MP3 sales for us. A lot of the music industry is all about numbers, so the more people that know about you, the better off you're going to be all around.

The Internet also makes it easier for bands to sell their music on their own without having a traditional record or distribution deal. Due to the explosion of digital stores like iTunes, Napster, and Rhapsody, any musician can make his or her music available to people around the world.

TIP

E-commerce is discussed in detail in Chapter 11.

ONLINE VIDEO

Go to the Chapter 10 page at **www.cengage.com/ computerconcepts/np/uc13** to watch the "A Look at Mobile Augmented Reality" video clip.

>**Virtual reality (VR).** The use of a computer to create three-dimensional environments that look like they do in the real world.

Entertainment

Entertainment is perhaps the most widely-used Web-based multimedia application. As discussed in Chapter 8, a wide variety of TV shows and movies are available online through TV network Web sites, as well as through online videos sites like Hulu, Fancast, and CastTV (see Figure 10-1). Many Web sites also feature online games, which typically utilize background music, sound effects, images, animated effects, narration, talking characters, video clips, and other types of multimedia. In addition, many individuals regularly visit YouTube for entertaining video clips, and many individuals include music and video clips on their Facebook and MySpace pages.

Another popular multimedia-based online entertainment option is the *3D virtual world*. These online worlds (such as Second Life shown in Figure 10-1) are locations where individuals can go (via their *avatar*) to meet other individuals (via their avatars), join in discussions, play games, shop, visit exotic virtual locations, buy clothing and other items for their avatars, and build and sell virtual products to other avatars. Membership is typically free, though the online currency (*Linden Dollars* in Second Life, for instance) must be purchased with real money. For a look at how the use of 3D virtual worlds is extending to business applications, see the Inside the Industry box.

FIGURE 10-2

Multimedia-based applications are often more effective than their single-medium counterparts.

MULTIMEDIA INSTRUCTIONS

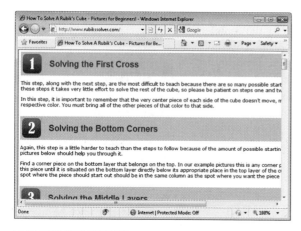

TEXT-ONLY INSTRUCTIONS

Advantages and Disadvantages of Using Web-Based Multimedia

There are advantages and disadvantages of using Web-based multimedia for the business or individual creating a Web site, as well as for the Web site visitors. Perhaps one of the biggest advantages of using multimedia is that it makes it possible to deliver some content (such as online TV and online music) via Web pages that it would not be possible to deliver otherwise. Another important advantage is that multimedia can address a variety of learning styles. For instance, some people are *visual learners* who learn best by seeing, others are *auditory learners* who learn best by hearing, and still others are *kinesthetic learners* who learn best by doing. While a concept presented using a single medium might be appropriate for some users, other users might be missing out on the full experience simply because the presentation does not match their learning styles. However, multimedia has the advantage of presenting the material in multiple learning styles. For example, an interactive Web-based exercise using printed text, images, spoken narration, and hands-on activities that the user completes utilizes all three types of learning styles just discussed, which increases the chance that the information will be understood and remembered by a wider range of individuals.

Another advantage of using multimedia is that it often makes the presented material more interesting and enjoyable. In addition, many ideas are easier to convey in multimedia format than in a single format. For example, compare the multimedia (text, video, and audio) instructions for solving a Rubik's cube shown in the top image in Figure 10-2 to the text-based instructions shown in the bottom image—the multimedia version should be much more effective in teaching individuals how to solve a Rubik's cube than the text-only version.

One disadvantage of a business or individual adding multimedia to a Web site is development time and cost. Multimedia Web sites

INSIDE THE INDUSTRY

Business 3D Worlds

The increased familiarity by a growing number of individuals with social networks and virtual worlds, combined with an increasingly distributed workforce and the growing cost of travel, has led to the use of 3D virtual worlds for business meetings and other business applications. For instance, IBM and Linden Lab recently demonstrated the first private corporate region of the Second Life Grid that is secured behind IBM's corporate firewall and that enables IBM employees to access both public and private regions of Second Life via a single interface. Another example is Palomar Pomerado Health, which opened a virtual hospital in Second Life to give current and potential clients a virtual tour of its real-world state-of-the-art medical center that is currently under construction. In addition, services that provide 3D meeting space to businesses are now available. For example, 3D virtual conferences, trade shows, job shows, and more can be held online via virtual events-hosting services such as *Unisfair*, and the new *Qwaq* service enables businesses to set up secure virtual meeting rooms where team members can meet in real time and view and exchange documents. A free option for 3D virtual business meetings is available from Crowne Plaza via its three *Place to Meet* conference rooms (see the accompanying figure) located on its Second Life private island. Individuals

and businesses can reserve any of the three available rooms; all rooms allow for streaming audio, video, and PowerPoint viewing and can accommodate up to 30 people. A recent 3D virtual world development that opens up even more possibilities for the future is an experiment by IBM and Linden Lab in which research teams from these companies successfully teleported avatars from the Second Life Preview Grid to an OpenSim virtual world—the first time an avatar has moved from one virtual world to another.

are usually much more time-consuming and expensive to create than simple text-based Web sites. Although multimedia elements for a Web site can be created in-house (if an employee has the necessary skills and experience and the appropriate multimedia software), many businesses opt to *outsource* the development of their multimedia Web site to a professional development firm, which tends to add to the expense. In addition, the cost for hosting and delivering the multimedia needs to be considered. If a video you put on your Web site goes *viral* (gains widespread popularity as the link to the video is passed on from one individual to another) and the number of visitors viewing the video clip via your site doubles or triples, there is potentially a huge increase in costs due to the increased traffic. Other possible limitations of multimedia include the impact on visitors that have slow Internet connections or low bandwidth caps—these users may not be able to access the multimedia content placed on a site at all. These factors all need to be considered when a multimedia Web site is designed and created, as discussed in more detail later in this chapter.

2.0 WEB

> **TIP**
>
> Outsourcing and other system development options are discussed in more detail in Chapter 12.

MULTIMEDIA ELEMENTS

Web sites can contain a variety of multimedia elements. The most common are discussed next.

Serif

Times New Roman

No serif

ABC
DEFGHIJKLM
NOPQRSTUV
WXYZ
0123456789

Cooper Black

SERIF TYPEFACES

ABC
DEFGHIJKLM
NOPQRSTUV
WXYZ
0123456789

Arial

A B C
DEFGHIJKLM
NOPQRSTUV
WXYZ
0123456789

Dom Casual

SANS SERIF TYPEFACES

 FIGURE 10-3

Typefaces. Typefaces are collections of text characters that share a common design and can be either serif or sans serif.

Text

Text is an important part of virtually all Web sites. It is used to supply basic content, as well as for text-based menus and hyperlinks. It is also frequently added to buttons, logos, banners, and other Web page images as they are being created. As discussed in Chapter 6, text can be displayed in a variety of font faces, colors, sizes, and appearances; a font face or typeface is a collection of text characters that share a common design, such as the Times New Roman, Cooper Black, Arial, and Dom Casual typefaces illustrated in Figure 10-3. *Serif typefaces*—typefaces (such as Times New Roman) that have small lines called *serifs* on the edges of the letters—are often used for large quantities of text since they tend to be more readable. *Sans serif typefaces*, such as Arial, do not have serifs and are frequently used for titles, headings, Web page banners, and other text elements that usually are displayed larger than body text or that otherwise need a more distinctive appearance.

A wide variety of typefaces are available, and one typeface may convey an entirely different feeling than another typeface. For example, Times New Roman is a traditional, business-like typeface, whereas Dom Casual is more whimsical and fun. Consequently, when selecting a typeface to be used on a Web page or in a multimedia element that contains text, it is important to select a typeface that matches the style of the Web site. In addition to selecting an appropriate typeface, it is also important to use an appropriate font size. A normal text size is around 11 or 12 points—it is not a good idea to use smaller text because it can be difficult to read. On the other hand, don't make your text too large because it will take up too much space on the screen. You want to make sure enough information fits on the screen at one time to avoid making visitors scroll needlessly to see the content—an action that may annoy them. Also, be sure to watch your color combinations. A high degree of contrast between the text color and the Web page's background color results in the most readable text—do not use dark text on a dark background or light text on a light background, for instance. For the same readability reason, do not use a busy image as a background image for a Web page.

When selecting the typeface and font size to be used with Web page text, there is one additional important consideration: the computer and Web browser used to display the Web page ultimately determine the size and appearance of Web page text. Only the typefaces installed on a user's computer can be used to display Web page text unless the typeface is embedded in the Web page when the Web page is created. In addition, the size of the monitor and the screen resolution the user has selected impact the size of the text. So it is important to remember that when text is used on a Web page, there is a chance that it will not be displayed exactly as intended. For these reasons, when a consistent text appearance is needed—such as for a company logo or navigation buttons—an *image* containing the text is used instead. Unlike regular text, text that is part of an image is displayed the same on all computers, regardless of the user's browser settings because the text is part of the image's file. Images are discussed next.

Images

Images or **graphics** refer to digital representations of photographs, drawings, charts, and other visual objects. Unlike *animation* or *video* (discussed shortly), images are static. Images can be created by scanning a photograph or document, taking a picture with a digital camera, or creating or modifying an image in an image editing program, such as the ones discussed in Chapter 6. They can also be obtained as *clip art images* (predrawn images) or *stock photographs* (professional photographs). Clip art is often included with

ONLINE VIDEO

Go to the Chapter 10 page at **www.cengage.com/ computerconcepts/np/uc13** to watch the "IBM, the Mayo Clinic, and Medical Imaging" video clip.

>**Text.** Alphanumeric characters kept in a text, not graphic, format. >**Image.** A digital representation of a photograph, drawing, chart, or other visual image; also called a **graphic**.

CLIP ART IMAGES
Typically use the GIF format and can be downloaded from a variety of Web sites. The images on this site are free for both personal and commercial use.

STOCK PHOTOGRAPHS
Typically use the JPEG format and are available through stock photograph agencies. The agency shown here has a variety of images organized by topics; all images require a fee for use, but all are royalty free.

office suite programs and image editing programs; it is also available in collections on CDs and DVDs. Both clip art and stock photographs can be downloaded from the Web (see Figure 10-4). While downloadable images typically require a fee, some free clip art images are available. In addition, many clip art images and stock photographs are *royalty-free*, which means they can be used as often as desired and in as many different documents as needed (such as in several newsletters and on multiple Web pages) without further payment or permission.

Images are available in many formats, such as *TIF*, *BMP*, *GIF*, *JPEG*, and *PNG*. Scanned images, images used for medical imaging, and images used for desktop publishing are generally saved in the TIF format. Images created using Windows Paint and similar painting programs are usually saved in the BMP format. Images created for use on Web pages are usually saved in the GIF, JPEG, or PNG format—all of which can be displayed in virtually all Web browsers without a special *plug-in* (a free small program that adds additional capabilities to your browser). The file format and file size of an image can be changed using an image editing program, which allows the image to be *optimized* for use on a Web page. For instance, a high-resolution JPEG photograph could be saved with a higher level of compression (as discussed shortly) to decrease the file size of the image so it will load faster when it is placed on a Web page; it could also be saved as a lower-resolution GIF image to be used as part of a navigation button or Web page banner. Image file formats and resolution are explained in more detail next.

FIGURE 10-4
Both clip art and stock photographs are plentiful on the Web.

ASK THE EXPERT

Bill Shribman, Executive Producer, WGBH Interactive

How important is it today to include multimedia on a Web site?

Multimedia is the overarching way to connect people to online content—especially for content directed toward young people. While reading text is necessary for all kids of reading age, the hunger online for young kids is for games and video. Even for older kids, the ability to devour a Harry Potter book in a weekend doesn't necessarily translate to the desire to read text online. And so, the core activities for the Web sites that my team produces at WGBH, such as the Web sites for the PBS TV shows *Arthur* and *Curious George*, are multimedia-based educational (and fun) activities. Today, the focus is primarily on activities that visitors can play or watch. But as multimedia tools and digital media continue to evolve, we expect other, more social activities like those that involve the user in creating, publishing, and sharing content to incorporate more multimedia in the coming years.

2.0 WEB

NONTRANSPARENT VS. TRANSPARENT GIFS

Nontransparent (the image's white background is visible on top of the page's yellow background).

Transparent with white specified as the transparent color (the page's yellow background is visible through the transparent areas of the image, so the image appears to be nonrectangular).

NONINTERLACED VS. INTERLACED GIFS

Noninterlaced GIF (the image is displayed top to bottom).

Interlaced GIF (the complete image is displayed initially, but the quality is progressively increased).

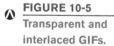
FIGURE 10-5
Transparent and interlaced GIFs.

GIF

The **GIF** format (short for *Graphics Interchange Format* and using the file extension *.gif*) is a standard format for Web page images and is used most often with logos, banners, and other nonphotographic images. It is an efficient, compressed format that uses *lossless file compression*, so the quality of the image is not decreased when it is saved in the GIF format. GIF images can contain no more than 256 colors; using the smallest color palette size possible helps reduce the file size of the saved image.

GIF images are always rectangular, but they can use a *transparent* background color to make the images appear to be nonrectangular (see Figure 10-5). GIF images can also be *interlaced*, which means that the image is displayed initially at low resolution, and its quality is progressively increased until it is displayed at full quality; noninterlaced GIFs are displayed top to bottom at full quality. Even though an interlaced image does not actually load faster, interlacing enables the viewer to more quickly perceive what the image looks like, and so, to the viewer, the image appears to load faster. Transparency is usually set by the Web page developer when the image is created; interlacing is typically designated by the Web page developer when the image is inserted into a Web page.

PNG

The **PNG** format (short for *Portable Network Graphics* and using the file extension *.png*) is a format that was specifically created in 1996 for Web page images in response to patent issues surrounding the GIF format (image editing programs that use the GIF compression algorithm to output GIF images are subject to licensing fees). The PNG format uses lossless compression, similar to GIF, but it can compress more efficiently than the GIF format for many nonphotographic images, which results in slightly smaller file sizes. PNG images can use a specific color palette of 256 colors or less (like GIF images) or they can use *true color* (more than 16 million colors, like JPEG images, discussed next). PNG images can also be interlaced and transparent.

JPEG

The **JPEG** format (short for *Joint Photographic Experts Group* and using the file extension *.jpg*) is the standard format for Web page photographs. JPEG images are compressed using *lossy file compression*, so image quality is lost during the compression process. A compression amount from 0% to 100% is selected when an image is saved in the JPEG

>**GIF.** An image format that supports 256 colors and is commonly used for Web page line art images. >**PNG.** An image format designed specifically for use with Web page images. >**JPEG.** An image format that supports true color and is commonly used for Web page photographs.

| No compression (37 KB) | 40% compression (13 KB) | 80% compression (7 KB) | 100% compression (3 KB) |

format. When a higher compression rate is selected, the file size is smaller but the image quality is reduced, as illustrated in Figure 10-6. JPEGs can be designated as *progressive*, which means that the image is displayed initially in low resolution and the image quality is progressively improved, similar to interlaced GIFs. JPEG images can use true color, and so the JPEG format is typically used for photographs and other images that may require more than 256 colors.

FIGURE 10-6
The amount of compression in a JPEG file affects both the file size and the display quality.

Choosing a Graphic Format

When creating an image for use on a Web page, it is important to use the most appropriate graphic format and choose the appropriate settings to have as small a file size as possible (while retaining an acceptable level of quality), in order to reduce loading time. The GIF or PNG format is usually selected for *line art*, such as clip art, logos, navigation buttons, and so forth because using these formats with line art images typically results in better quality images with smaller file sizes than using the JPEG format. With photographs, however, the JPEG format usually results in a higher-quality image at a smaller file size than if the GIF or PNG format was used.

It is also important to realize that the physical size of the image can greatly affect file size. Therefore, Web page images should be sized to their appropriate display size in an image editing program and saved before being inserted into a Web page. When a Web page requires a very large image (such as to better show a product, home for sale, or featured piece of art), a **thumbnail image** can be used. Thumbnail images are small versions of images that are linked to a corresponding full-sized image; when a thumbnail image is clicked, the full-sized image is displayed (see Figure 10-7). Because the file size of a thumbnail image is very small, the use of thumbnail images doesn't significantly increase the page loading time for all users, but still allows the users who wish to view the full-sized image to do so.

FIGURE 10-7
Thumbnail images.

Clicking a thumbnail image displays the full-sized image.

> **Thumbnail image.** A small image on a Web page that is linked to a larger, higher-resolution image.

⊘ **FIGURE 10-8**
Animated GIFs.

When the animated GIF containing the images shown above are displayed one after the other, it appears that the leopard is running.

 VIDEO PODCAST

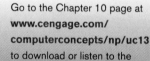 Go to the Chapter 10 page at **www.cengage.com/ computerconcepts/np/uc13** to download or listen to the "How To: Create an Animated GIF" video podcast.

Animation

Animation is the term used to describe a series of images that are displayed one after the other to simulate movement. To add simple animation to a Web page, *Java applets* and *animated GIFs* are frequently used. A **Java applet** is a small program inserted into a Web page that performs a specific task, such as changing the values in a stock portfolio or scrolling text and/or images across the screen. An **animated GIF** is a group of GIF images stored in a special animated GIF file that is inserted in a Web page, similar to any other image. The individual images contained in the animated GIF file (such as the ones shown in Figure 10-8) display one after another to simulate movement. Animated GIFs are often used to change the images displayed in an on-screen advertising banner.

Web pages can also have more complex animations or interactivity, such as having text or an image change as a button on a menu or *navigation bar* is pointed to, as in Figure 10-9. These animations are often created using *JavaScript* or another *scripting language*, or they are created using animation development tools such as **Flash** or **Silverlight**. Many animations found on Web pages require a browser plug-in to be viewed. For instance, the Flash-based game in Figure 10-9 requires the *Adobe Flash Player*. Other widely used plug-ins include *Java* and *Adobe Shockwave Player*. Animation and interactivity can also be achieved using *programming languages*, as discussed in Chapter 13.

Audio

Audio includes all types of sound, such as music, spoken voice, and sound effects. Sound is commonly found on Web sites in the form of background music and downloadable music and podcasts, and as part of games, tutorials, videos, and other multimedia elements. Audio can be recorded using a microphone or MIDI instrument; it can also be captured from CDs or downloaded from the Internet (some music and sound effect files are available for free; others require a fee to download and use). Audio files can be very large, so compression methods—such as the *MP3 format*—are frequently used to reduce their file size. For more information about MP3 compression, see the How It Works box.

Audio is often played automatically when a particular event occurs, such as narration or music starting when a Flash or Shockwave activity is loaded or a sound effect playing when the mouse points to a navigation button. Web pages can also contain hyperlinks to audio files so they will not play unless the user clicks that link. To speed up delivery, audio files on Web pages are often in the form of *streaming audio*. With a streaming audio file, only a small portion of the audio file is initially downloaded and *buffered* (placed in memory or temporarily stored on the hard drive); this allows the audio file to begin playing while the remainder of the file downloads simultaneously.

Some of the most widely used audio file formats are listed next; audio files on Web pages are commonly played using an appropriate media player (such as *Windows Media Player*, *Apple QuickTime Player*, or *RealPlayer*) installed on the user's computer.

> ➤ *Waveform (.wav)*—used for most music CDs; not compressed, so usually results in large file sizes.

> ➤ *Moving Picture Experts Group Audio Layer 3 (.mp3)*—used to create very efficient, high-quality compressed audio files. Waveform files can be converted to MP3 files to reduce their size.

> ➤ *Musical Instrument Digital Interface (.midi)*—used for files created with a MIDI device.

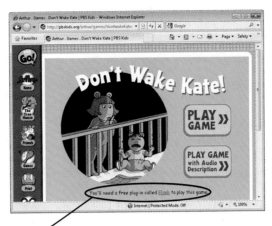

JAVASCRIPT
JavaScript is used in conjunction with Flash to light up the menu buttons as they are pointed to, to animate the characters, and to randomly change the images displayed in the two TV screens.

FLASH
Many games and other animated or interactive activities found on Web sites are created with Flash or Shockwave, so a plug-in is required to view the content.

FIGURE 10-9
JavaScript and Flash are commonly used on Web pages.

> *Audio Interchange Format File (.aiff)*—used for files created with Apple Mac computers; a compressed version is *AIFF-Compressed*.

> *Advanced Audio Coding (.aac or .m4a)*—used to encode audio data using the *Moving Picture Experts Group 4 (.mp4)* standard; a newer alternative to MP3 for both fixed and mobile Web applications.

Video

While animation consists of individual images that are displayed one after another to look like they occur in that sequence, **video** begins as a continuous stream of visual information that is broken into separate images or *frames* when the video is recorded. When the frames are projected—typically at a rate of 30 frames per second—they look like the original continuous stream of information. As you might imagine, at 30 images per second, video files can become extremely large. Consequently, video data—like audio data—is often compressed. A variety of compression standards exist. Some of the most common video file formats are listed next; like audio files, most can be played using a standard media player.

> *Audio-Video Interleave (.avi)*—a standard video file format developed by Microsoft.

> *Moving Picture Experts Group 2 (.mp2)*—a high-quality, compressed video file format.

> *Moving Picture Experts Group 4 (.mp4)*—a versatile format designed for media delivered via the Web; can include still and audio data, but frequently used for video as well.

> *QuickTime (.mov)*—a versatile video format developed by Apple and widely used to distribute video over the Web.

> *Windows Media Video (.wmv)*—a video format developed by Microsoft for use with Windows Media Player.

>**Video.** A continuous stream of visual information broken into separate images or frames to be displayed one after the other to simulate the original visual event.

HOW IT WORKS

MP3 Compression

The *MP3 format* is a type of compression used with music. It is used to reduce the number of bytes in a song without sacrificing musical quality. MP3 is officially *MPEG Audio Layer 3,* an *MPEG (Moving Pictures Experts Group)* compression standard. Each MPEG layer uses a different sampling rate to obtain different compression results. MP3 (Layer 3)–the norm for digital music today–typically compresses a CD-quality song to about one-tenth of its original size. For example, the 21 MB Queen song shown in the accompanying illustration compresses to less than 2 MB after it is converted to an MP3 file. Because of its efficiency, the MP3 format is widely used for music downloaded from the Internet, as well as when music is copied from a CD to a computer or a portable digital media player. Because of their smaller file sizes, MP3 files can be downloaded much more rapidly, and hundreds of MP3 files can be stored on a single CD or portable digital media player.

The MP3 standard utilizes two compression techniques. The first technique uses the principle of *perceptual coding;* that is, removing the parts of the song that the human ear would not hear anyway, such as sounds that occur in frequencies too high or too low to be perceived by the human ear or soft sounds that are played at the same time as louder sounds. Although data is lost by using this compression technique, the lost data is considered superfluous, so the size of the song is reduced without significantly altering the quality of the song. The second compression technique, called *Huffman coding,* substitutes shorter strings of bits for frequently used larger strings. Since the bits are reconstructed when the song is played, no information is lost during this process. The resulting MP3 file—saved with the file extension *.mp3*—can then be played on a computer using media player software, burned onto a CD, or copied to a portable digital media player.

1. CD (WAV format) version of song: 21 MB.
2. Software removes the unnecessary parts of the song and codes the song in the MP3 format.
3. MP3 version of song: 1.9 MB.

VIDEO PODCAST

Go to the Chapter 10 page at **www.cengage.com/ computerconcepts/np/uc13** to download or listen to the "How To: Convert Videos to High Definition (HD) for YouTube" video podcast.

Video to be included on a Web site is typically recorded with a digital video camera and then edited as needed to create the final video file. Web page video applications include delivering video clips of television shows, news broadcasts, and corporate speeches; facilitating panoramic video tours of facilities or products; explaining the benefits of a product or service; displaying live video feeds from specific locations; and so forth. Businesses and individuals can include video clips on their Web sites; like audio files, *streaming video* is recommended to speed up delivery, so the video file begins playing once a portion of the video has been downloaded. Videos can also be posted to video-sharing sites like YouTube, as well as to Facebook pages. For a look at how video can be used to keep others informed of the events in your life, see the Technology and You box.

TECHNOLOGY AND YOU

Lifestreaming and Lifecasting

Lifestreaming refers to creating an online record of your daily activities—typically via your frequently updated online content, such as blog posts, MySpace updates, Flickr photos, Twitter tweets, and so forth. Lifestreaming can be performed by aggregating the online content of a person using a social network management tool (as discussed in the Chapter 8 Technology and You box) or via that person's Facebook page (such as by using the Facebook *Mini-Feed tool*). A video version of lifestreaming is *lifecasting*; that is, broadcasting live video feeds of your daily activities via your mobile phone. The video feeds can be sent directly to your friends' mobile phones or sent to a Web page (such as a lifecasting Web site or your MySpace or Facebook page) that others can view when desired. Some consider lifecasting the new replacement for text messaging—why write to your friends about something when you can show them using a video instead? And, in fact, some lifecasting services allow recipients to type messages while the video is playing (see the accompanying illustration) that are sent to and displayed on the sender's device, allowing for real-time feedback from your viewers. Lifecasting can

also have a professional purpose. For instance, some entertainment professionals use lifecasting to deliver behind-the-scenes content to fans.

In order to lifecast, a lifecasting service (such as *Kyte, JuiceCaster,* or *Qik*) is typically used. You should make sure that the service you select is compatible with your mobile phone and includes the features you desire (such as phone-to-phone transfers, phone-to-Web transfers, messaging capabilities, and so forth). You should also make sure you have unlimited data streaming for your mobile phone service to avoid surprise charges.

CAUTION CAUTION CAUTION CAUTION CAUTION CAUTION CAUT

When including video and other high-bandwidth content on your Web site, be sure to consider the bandwidth cost of delivering that content to your visitors. Unlike TV distribution (which has no marginal cost per additional viewer), many Web hosting services charge fees based on the amount of traffic and data transferred via the site. As a result, if twice as many people visit your site as you expected, your could incur surprise expenses. To be safe, plan and budget accordingly; you can also upload your video to YouTube or another file-sharing site and just embed the link to that video on your Web site, instead of hosting the video yourself.

MULTIMEDIA WEB SITE DESIGN

Web site design refers to the process of planning what your Web site will look like and how it will work. Although this chapter focuses on designing and developing multimedia Web sites, the process of designing multimedia applications that are not run via the Web (such as those delivered via a DVD or kiosk) and Web sites that do not contain multimedia are similar in many respects. In all instances, the importance of careful planning cannot be

---

>**Web site design.** The process of planning what a Web site will look like and how it will function.

overemphasized. Time spent planning and designing a site on paper before jumping into the development process pays off in the long run. Some of the most important design considerations and guidelines are discussed next.

Basic Design Principles

When designing a multimedia Web site, two of the most important things to keep in mind are what you want to say via your site and how to get people to visit your site to access your content. Two basic principles for attracting visitors to your site and keeping them there are that individuals like interesting and exciting applications and Web-site visitors typically have little patience with slow-to-load or hard-to-use applications.

A site is *interesting* if it provides information of value or interest to its target audience; users find it *exciting* if it rewards them with a stimulating experience. Unfortunately, interest and excitement wear off over time. If visitors see the same information on your site day after day, boredom sets in and they will likely stop visiting. Therefore, it is important to refresh the content of your site regularly with new information.

In general, Web site visitors also do not have much patience with poorly designed sites, so ease of use is an important factor in determining whether or not individuals will choose to visit a Web site regularly. For example, if visitors have a hard time figuring out how to navigate a site to get the information they want or if pages on the site take too long to load, they will often move on to another site and may never return. To facilitate navigation and reduce user frustration, you should design an intuitive Web site with clear, consistent navigational tools and you should present information in a manner that makes sense. Web pages should also load quickly—to accomplish this, you need to select your multimedia elements carefully and modify them as necessary (such as optimizing images) to be as efficient as possible.

Another factor that impacts the design of a Web site is the device that your target audience will use to access the site. If your audience includes individuals using devices that range from large desktop computer monitors to mobile phones, a one-size-fits-all Web site is obviously not the most desirable option. At a minimum, you should decide early on whether the site will be designed for individuals using conventional desktop or portable computers, those using netbooks and other small computers, or mobile users, or whether content will be optimized for multiple delivery methods. Some development programs allow you to test your Web site by viewing it as it will appear on various devices and screen sizes (such as certain computer monitor sizes or specific mobile devices). For instance, the *Adobe Device Central* program that can be used in conjunction with Adobe Development programs, such as Flash and *Dreamweaver* (discussed shortly), is shown in Figure 10-10. With this program, the content can be viewed as it will appear on hundreds of different devices. This program also includes a profile on each device that contains important information for developers, such as the display size of the device and what types of content are supported by the device.

FIGURE 10-10

Testing on multiple platforms. Emulators (stand-alone or built into Web development programs) allow you to test your multimedia content on a variety of devices.

Even if a single delivery method is assumed (such as a conventional computer), you still need to consider the wide variety of platforms, Web browsers, and settings that can be used by Web page visitors. Because of this, it is important to set up the site so it can be used with as many different configurations as possible. Consequently, careful consideration should be given to the following:

> *Features that require a specific browser.* The capabilities and features of browsers (such as Internet Explorer, Firefox, Opera, Chrome, and Safari) are growing more closely together, but there are still features not supported by all browsers. While it is safer to stick with the features that will work on all common browsers, you can use *browser sniffing* (identifying the browser used by each visitor, typically via

JavaScript code) to display a version of your site that matches the visitor's browser, if you choose to use browser-specific features.

> *Features that require little used plug-ins.* Although it is annoying to have to download a plug-in before being able to use a Web page feature, most users tolerate downloading a few of the most widely used plug-ins the first time they are needed. Do not annoy your visitors by requiring unusual plug-ins that they may not have or have no other reason to obtain.

> *The size of the page content.* Keep in mind that different browsers and screen resolutions allow different amounts of room to display Web page content. This affects how wide your images and columns of text should be. To ensure that the content is visible on virtually all desktop and notebook computers with a maximized browser, without the user having to scroll down unnecessarily, keep *banner images*, *image maps*, and other full-width items to 710 pixels or less. Full-height items (such as an image map) should be less than 420 pixels tall. Content designed for mobile users needs to be smaller, typically no more than 300 pixels wide.

> *High-bandwidth items.* Although broadband Internet is becoming the norm, there are still individuals using conventional dial-up Internet connections and not all mobile users have broadband service. If the intended audience of your site includes a large number of dial-up or mobile users, pay extra close attention to the file size of the images on the site, and use techniques to allow the user to decide whether to take the time to access certain features of the site. For example, instead of automatically playing an audio or a video file, have a link to it (with a file size and an estimated download time listed). When large images are needed, use thumbnail images, and use streaming audio and video files whenever possible. Finally, be sure that all multimedia elements are consistent with the purpose of your site and add something significant. Do not add extra elements—particularly audio and video files—without a good reason. They just slow down your site and potentially annoy your visitors.

Determining the Objectives and Intended Audience of the Site

One of the first steps in designing a multimedia Web site should be determining the site's primary objectives and the intended audience of the site. The objectives of the site affect the content of the site because you will want to make sure that the site includes the information needed to meet those objectives. For instance, you need to determine the main purpose of the site (such as to market or sell a product or service), as well as any supplementary objectives or activities the site should support (such as a gaming feature or blog to entice visitors to return regularly, an online community for customer support, or a medium for visitors to communicate with one another or to post user-generated content). If your site will support mobile users, you also need to decide if you will include features geared toward those visitors, such as content tied to the visitor's location or other popular mobile applications. In addition, you need to decide if you want to utilize other Web sites (such as creating a Facebook page to reach out to current and potential customers, using a LinkedIn page for creating business contacts, uploading videos to YouTube to increase their potential audience, or using a Twitter feed for relaying timely information to customers), in order to boost your online presence. If so, you should also decide if you will include links to that content (such as to your Facebook page or Twitter feed) on your Web site.

The physical design (such as the style, graphics, fonts, and colors) of the site is typically selected to match the intended audience of the site. For example, three types of sites designed to appeal to distinctly different audiences are shown in Figure 10-11. The intended audience also impacts the types of multimedia elements that can be included on a site. If you are designing a site to be accessed through an intranet, for example, you do not have to be as concerned about file size and file format as someone designing a Web

TIP

Whenever you include content on a Web page that requires a plug-in (such as the Flash Player plug-in or a specific media player program), include an obvious link on that Web page to a location where visitors can download a free version of that plug-in, if needed.

TIP

Topics related to generating revenue via a Web site (selling products, subscriptions, banner ads, and so forth) are discussed in Chapter 11.

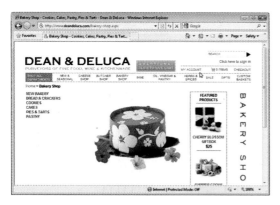

BOLD AND CLEAN
Shopping sites often use bold colors and crisp typefaces to give the site a contemporary, but rich and uncluttered, feel.

CONSERVATIVE
Many business sites use a conservative appearance to match their conservative business image.

WHIMSICAL AND FUN
Sites catering to young people often have an especially friendly look, sporting bright graphics and large fanciful typefaces.

 FIGURE 10-11
The intended audience affects Web site design.

site to be accessed by the public. When determining your target audience, also give some thought to how users will access the site and how technologically-savvy they are. Will they be using up-to-date browsers and have a variety of multimedia plug-ins installed? If your answer is "no," that may impact the types of multimedia elements you include on the site.

Once the objectives and audience have been identified, you should have a good idea of the main topics that need to be included in the site. If the needed content is unclear to you, however, do not go any further into the design process until you understand what the content should be. Rethink your objectives and audience, explore other sites on the Web, and talk to potential users until you determine what the Web site's content should include. Once the main topics for your site are finalized, you can finalize what specific content (images, text, video files, audio files, animations, navigational tools, and so forth) will be needed.

Using Flowcharts, Page Layouts, and Storyboards

After the objectives, intended audience, and basic content to be included in a Web site have been determined, the structure and layout of the site can be designed. To this end, design tools—such as *flowcharts*, *page layouts*, and *storyboards*—are often used. All of these can be created either by hand or on a computer using appropriate software.

A **flowchart**, when used to design a Web site, describes how the pages in the site relate to one another. For example, the top part of Figure 10-12 shows a flowchart for a bed and breakfast Web site. A Web site flowchart is essentially a map of the structure of the Web site. It uses a single box to represent each Web page, and the lines between boxes show the logical organization of the site. Remember, however, that you can link pages in any way you like, and visitors may visit the pages of the site in any order. Although the lines between the flowchart boxes indicate necessary hyperlinks, typically there are additional links between the pages. For instance, it is a good idea to place links to the main pages of the site (such as Home, Rooms, Maps, About Three Rivers, and Reservations for the bed and breakfast flowchart shown in Figure 10-12) in a navigation bar on all pages of the site. More complex flowcharts that illustrate the logical steps and sequence of a multimedia component (similar to the *program flowcharts* used when designing computer programs, as discussed in detail in Chapter 13) can be used when designing multimedia content.

For illustrating the layout and navigational structure of a Web site, **page layouts** are typically used. Usually, two page layouts are created: one for the home page (see the home page layout in Figure 10-12) and one to be used for all other pages on the site. When designing a page layout, carefully consider where each component of the Web page belongs. For instance, studies show that most people look at the upper left corner of a Web page first, so that's the location where most logos are placed on Web sites.

>**Flowchart.** A tool that can be used during the Web design process to illustrate how the pages in a Web site relate to one another. >**Page layout.** A sketch of a Web page often developed during the Web design process to illustrate the basic layouts of the home page and the rest of the pages on a Web site.

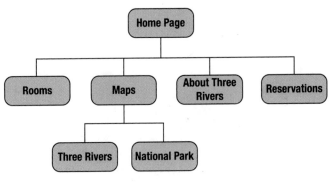

FLOWCHARTS
Describe the logical organization of the site. Each box represents a separate Web page.

PAGE LAYOUTS
Illustrate the basic design and navigational structure of a Web site. There are typically two layouts—one for the home page (shown here) and one for all other pages on the site.

FIGURE 10-12

Web site flowcharts and page layouts.

A sample flowchart and page layout for a bed and breakfast Web site are shown here.

A **storyboard** is an ordered series of sketches depicting each page or screen in an animation sequence. Storyboards are commonly used when designing animated components that will be located on a multimedia Web site, such as for an animated *splash page* (an introductory page that appears before the home page of a Web site is displayed).

Navigational Design Considerations

As already mentioned, it is extremely important that you carefully design your navigational structure. After drawing a preliminary flowchart of a Web site, take a look at its balance. You want enough main topics to keep the information organized, but not so many that users have difficulty finding what they are looking for. As a rule of thumb, users should be able to get to most pages on a Web site within three mouse clicks. For large sites, navigational tools—such as drop-down menus, *site maps* (table of contents pages that contain links to all main pages on the sites), and search boxes—can help accomplish this. Other options include text-based hyperlinks, navigation bars, and menu tabs; image-based navigation bars; *image maps* (single images with separate areas linked to different locations); and hyperlinks that display more options or a description of the link when pointed to. Examples of some of these navigational elements are shown in Figure 10-13.

When designing your navigational structure, be sure to place the same navigation buttons or links in the same location on every page so that users can find them easily. Also be sure that any icons or other graphics used on your navigation buttons are easily understood. Whenever possible, add a text name to the image, such as adding the text "Shopping Bag" next to a shopping bag icon. In addition, users have come to expect underlined text to be a hyperlink; for that reason, do not underline text that is not a link.

For long Web pages, consider separating the content into several pages to reduce scrolling and loading time; the pages are typically viewed using "Back" and "Next" buttons or with a linked table of contents. When you break a large document apart, consider including a link to view or download the entire document intact either as a Web page or in a common format (such as Word or PDF) so that users can read or print the entire document at one time if they prefer. You can also include a table of contents at the top of a long

TIP

The design for a Web site is also sometimes called the *wireframe*.

TIP

Place the company or Web site logo in the same location on each page of a Web site and link the logo to the home page of the site to give users a consistent means of displaying the home page from any page on the site.

WEB 2.0

> **Storyboard.** An ordered series of sketches that can be developed during the design process of an animated sequence or other multimedia component of a Web site that illustrates what each page or screen will look like.

HOME PAGE LINK
Gives users a quick link to the site's home page from any page on the site; link is often a company logo.

SITE MAP
A Web page that contains links to all of the main pages on a site.

MENU TABS
Provide access to the main pages of a site, as well as indicate the currently displayed page.

ICONS
Help users identify navigational links.

NAVIGATION BAR
A group of text- or image-based links; should be in the same location on every page of the site.

SEARCH BOX
Allows users to find pages on the site containing specific information.

FIGURE 10-13
Navigational tools.
A wide variety of navigational tools exists to help make Web sites easy to use.

Web page or for a series of Web pages that each contain one part of a single article, to allow users to jump to a particular section of the document. For long Web pages, be sure to periodically include a link that jumps users back to the top of the page.

One final navigational tip: Be sure to include identifying information on each page of the site to indicate which page is currently displayed because not all users will enter your site at the home page. This information can be text-based or reflected on your navigational structure, such as with a pushed-in navigation button, a different colored tab, or an unlinked or bolded hyperlink on a text-based navigation bar. You should also include the name of the organization and a link to the Web site home page on all pages of the site.

Access Considerations

When designing a multimedia Web site, two types of access considerations should be kept in mind: compatibility with the various types of devices that may be used to access the site and functionality for users with physical disabilities.

FIGURE 10-14
Web pages display differently on different devices.

DESKTOP COMPUTERS

MOBILE PHONES

Device Compatibility

As already discussed, the device being used to access a Web site affects how the site will appear on the site, as well as how functional it will be. For example, while many mobile phones today can display Web pages, they typically display a smaller amount at one time than a desktop or notebook computer (see Figure 10-14). If you anticipate your intended audience will access your site with mobile devices, you need to plan on modifying the content into a mobile format. For instance, some Web sites have mobile versions of the site that are designed for mobile users and, consequently, display less content on a page or display the content in a more streamlined manner; the URLs for these sites typically begin with *m* such as *m.myspace.com* or *m.google.com*.

Assistive Technology

A second access consideration involves the site's ability to be accessed by users of *assistive technology*—hardware and software specially designed for use by individuals with physical disabilities. For example, as discussed in more detail in Chapter 16, visually impaired users may use a *screen reader* that reads aloud the content displayed on the user's screen or a *Braille display* that converts all screen content into Braille form. Assistive technology affects Web page design because certain features are easier for visitors using assistive input devices to access than other features and some content

ALTERNATIVE TEXT
Images have alternative text descriptions.

COLORS AND CONTRAST
There is a high degree of contrast between the text and the background colors to make the text as readable as possible.

DESCRIPTIVE HYPERLINKS
Hyperlinks make sense when read aloud because they are descriptive.

is not accessible using these devices. For instance, screen reading software and Braille displays typically can read only text-based data. Consequently, in order for navigational images or other images to be understandable to visitors using these systems, the images must be identified with an **alternative text** description. Alternative text can easily be added to an image when the Web page is developed, but it is not always done. In addition to being accessed by screen readers, alternative text descriptions are displayed when the graphic is pointed to with a mouse or other pointing device (see Figure 10-15), as well as when the option to display pictures is disabled in a Web browser. Other features that make a Web page accessible to a broader audience include meaningful text-based hyperlinks (such as *How to Contact Us* instead of *Click Here*) and alternative content for Flash, JavaScript, or other animated components that may be incompatible with some assistive technologies. When a great deal of incompatible content is included on a Web page, an alternate text-based page can be developed and made available for those users. Some characteristics of an accessible Web page are shown in Figure 10-15.

Several organizations have released guidelines for creating accessible Web sites, such as the *Web Content Accessibility Guidelines* by the World Wide Web Consortium (W3C). There are also Web sites that can be used to test Web accessibility and some *Web site development software* can test for accessibility, as well as for browser and device compatibility. These topics are discussed later is this chapter. In addition, the *Rehabilitation Act* requires U.S. federal agencies to make their Web site content accessible to people with disabilities, specifically to make it able to be used as effectively by people with disabilities as by those without. While this law only applies to federal Web sites, it was hoped that passing this requirement would lead other organizations to make their Web content more accessible to people with disabilities. Recent legal actions—such as the recently settled class action suit against Target.com that contends the company violated the *Americans with Disabilities Act* (*ADA*) by failing to make its Web site accessible to blind patrons—may eventually extend state and federal disabilities statues to Internet content. As Tim Berners-Lee, the inventor of the World Wide Web, once said, "The power of the Web is in its universality. Access by everyone regardless of disability."

One additional accessibility concern for Web sites in the United States is usability by individuals with low literacy levels or whose native language is not English. Recent studies indicate that about one-half of Americans read at an 8th-grade level or below, and 25 million primarily speak a non-English language. However, the average readability level of American state and federal Web sites is at the 11th-grade level. Consequently, Web site developers should keep readability in mind when they evaluate the accessibility of their Web sites.

FIGURE 10-15
Some Web page characteristics that are compatible with assistive technology.

ONLINE VIDEO

Go to the Chapter 10 page at **www.cengage.com/computerconcepts/np/uc13** to watch the "The Importance of Alt Tags" video clip.

FURTHER EXPLORATION

Go to the Chapter 10 page at **www.cengage.com/computerconcepts/np/uc13** for links to information about Web site design.

>**Alternative text.** A text description for a Web page image; is displayed when the image is pointed to and can be read by assistive technology.

MULTIMEDIA WEB SITE DEVELOPMENT

Once a Web site has been carefully designed, it is time to create it. This process is called **Web site development**. The development of a Web site can be performed in-house (if employees with the appropriate skills and appropriate software are available), or it can be outsourced to a professional Web developer. In either case, the development process of a multimedia Web site includes three basic steps:

> Creating the multimedia elements.

> Creating the Web site.

> Testing, publishing, and maintaining the site.

These three steps, along with the various types of software that can be used during each step, are discussed next.

FIGURE 10-16

Web page banner being created in Adobe Flash.

Creating the Multimedia Elements

Before the actual Web pages are created, it is a good idea to create all of the individual multimedia elements (such as images, animated components, video files, and audio files) that will be used on the site. To accomplish this, typically several different programs are used, such as the image editing, audio editing, and video editing software discussed in Chapter 6. For creating animated or interactive components—such as games, tutorials, advertisements, and animated splash pages—to be inserted into a Web page, *Adobe Flash*, *Adobe After Effects*, or another *Web animation program* can be used. Flash in particular is widely used today; creating an animated banner for a Web site using Flash is shown in Figure 10-16.

Silverlight is a technology that is used for displaying animated or interactive Web applications, similar to Flash. It is considered a competitor to Flash since they are used for similar purposes, but, unlike Flash, Silverlight applications are not created using a specific software program. Instead, Silverlight applications are written using JavaScript, *VisualStudio*, or another development tool and the Silverlight plug-in is used to display the content. An alternative to Flash and Silverlight for creating large multimedia applications (such as complex games and training simulations) is using *multimedia authoring software*, such as *Adobe Director*. Director is frequently used to create Shockwave content to be incorporated into multimedia Web sites and played with the Shockwave Player. Regardless of the program used to create each individual element, as the elements are finished they should be saved in the appropriate size, resolution, and file format so that they are ready to be inserted into Web pages or animation sequences.

Creating the Web Site

Most Web pages today are written using a **markup language**—a coding system used to define the structure, layout, and general appearance of the content of a Web page. When a markup language is used, *markup tags* are inserted around the Web page content to identify where elements are to be displayed and how they should look when displayed. JavaScript

---

>**Web site development.** The process of creating, testing, publishing, and maintaining a Web site. >**Markup language.** A language that uses symbols or tags to describe what a document should look like when it is displayed in a Web browser.

and other *scripting languages* can be used to add dynamic content to a Web page; *Web site authoring software* is frequently used to create an entire site, tying together all the Web pages, scripts, and multimedia elements contained within a site.

Hypertext Markup Language (HTML)

The original markup language designed for creating Web pages is **HTML (Hypertext Markup Language)**. HTML files have the file extension *.htm* or *.html* and use *HTML tags*—text-based codes embedded into a Web page's *source code* (the code used to create the Web page)—to indicate where an effect (such as enlarged, bolded, or centered text) should begin and where the effect should end. HTML tags are also used to specify where images, hyperlinks, video clips, animation sequences, and other elements are to be located on the page. Other uses for HTML tags include assigning a title to a page, marking the ends of paragraphs, specifying the layout of tables, and identifying *keywords* and other *meta tags* to be associated with the page (used by search sites and discussed in Chapter 11). Some common HTML tags are shown in Figure 10-17.

When a Web page is created—using a word processor, text editor, or Web site authoring program—the HTML tags are inserted in the appropriate locations in the Web page's source code. HTML tags are not case sensitive, so it does not matter if they are typed in uppercase or lowercase. Some tags are used alone; others are used in pairs. For example, the HTML tag ** turns bolding on for the text that follows the tag until the ** tag is reached, so the HTML statement

<b> This text is bold. </b>

would have the following appearance

This text is bold.

when viewed with most Web browsers. A Web page and its corresponding HTML source code are shown in Figure 10-18.

It is important to realize that with a markup language like HTML, the Web browser, Web browser settings, and computer used to display the Web page ultimately determine what the Web page will look like. For instance, if you use common font faces—such as Times New Roman and Arial—for your Web page text, those font faces will likely be installed on the user's computer and, if so, will be used to display the text of your Web page. But if you use a font face that is not installed on the user's computer, an alternate installed font face will be used. And, although you can specify font size when developing a Web page, the user can control the size of the text displayed in his or her browser, as well as the screen resolution being used. As a result, the appearance of your Web pages may vary somewhat from user to user.

TAG	PURPOSE
`<html></html>`	Marks the beginning and end of an HTML document.
`<head></head>`	Marks the head section which contains the page title and meta tags.
`<title></title>`	Marks the title of the Web page.
`<body></body>`	Defines attributes of an HTML Web document, such as background color, background image, text color, margins, etc.
`<h1></h1>` to `<h6></h6>`	Formats headings larger or smaller than the regular text in the document; H1 is the largest text.
`<img>`	Indicates an image file to be inserted; attributes included within this tag specify the image filename, display size, alternative text, border, etc.
`<a></a>`	Creates a hyperlink.
`<b></b>`	Bolds text.
`<i></i>`	Italicizes text.
`<center></center>`	Centers text.
`<hr>`	Inserts a horizontal rule.
` `	Inserts a line break (new line within the same paragraph).
`<p>`	Inserts a paragraph break (starts a new paragraph).

FIGURE 10-17
Sample HTML tags.

VIDEO PODCAST

Go to the Chapter 10 page at **www.cengage.com/ computerconcepts/np/uc13** to download or listen to the "How To: Create a Web Site Using HTML" video podcast.

>**HTML (Hypertext Markup Language).** A markup language widely used for creating Web pages.

Web page as displayed in browser. | Click to view the Web page's source code. | HTML version of the Web page. | Specifies the title displayed on the browser's title bar. | Defines the table used to lay out the page content.

The page's text begins here with a bold HTML tag.

Creates the navigation button links at the top of the page.

FIGURE 10-18

An HTML Web page and its corresponding source code.

Extensible Markup Language (XML) and Extensible Hypertext Markup Language (XHTML)

XML (**Extensible Markup Language**) is a set of rules for exchanging data over the Web. It is called "extensible" because the data contained in XML documents can be extracted when needed and used in a variety of ways, such as combined to create new documents or used to display a single Web page on a variety of types of computers or mobile devices—the device being used to view the document displays it in a format appropriate for that device. This is possible because XML focuses on identifying the data itself—not the format of that data. To accomplish this, *XML tags* are assigned to pieces of data (such as surrounding the name of a client or an employee with the tag pair <name> </name>). There are no standard XML tags; instead, each organization using XML to create documents determines the XML tags to be used with that organization's documents. Once the data is tagged, it can be used with any XML document created for that organization. XML is increasingly being used with ordinary business documents and company databases to allow easy retrieval and updating of data by applications.

XHTML (**Extensible Hypertext Markup Language**) is a version of HTML that is based on XML. Like HTML, XHTML is used to create Web pages, but it also supports XML, so XML-tagged data can be incorporated easily into XHTML Web pages. When this occurs, XML controls the content displayed, and XHTML controls the appearance and format of the Web page. XHTML tags are similar to HTML tags, but there are stricter rules about how the markup tags are written. For instance, all attribute values (such as filenames, numeric values, colors, and so forth) must be enclosed in quotation marks. In addition, XHTML is case-sensitive, so all tags are written in lowercase; all tags must be *closed* (have an ending tag); and the tags must be in the proper order around elements. For example, the statement

This text should be bold and italic.

must be used instead of

This text should be bold and italic.

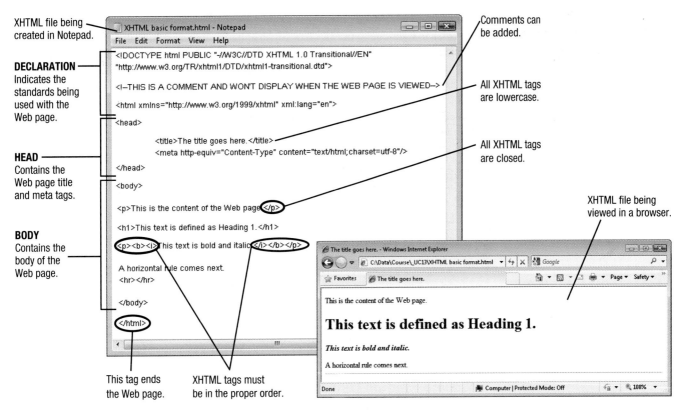

XHTML file being created in Notepad.

DECLARATION Indicates the standards being used with the Web page.

HEAD Contains the Web page title and meta tags.

BODY Contains the body of the Web page.

Comments can be added.

All XHTML tags are lowercase.

All XHTML tags are closed.

XHTML file being viewed in a browser.

This tag ends the Web page.

XHTML tags must be in the proper order.

FIGURE 10-19 A sample XHTML Web page source code and corresponding Web page.

While the latter sequence will work in HTML, it will not work properly in XHTML. As long as the stricter rules are followed, however, basic HTML tags—such as the ones shown in Figure 10-17—can be used in XHTML Web pages. For instance, to follow the rule regarding closed tags, a tag that is not closed in HTML (such as <p> to indicate a paragraph break) must have a matching ending tag (such as </p>) in XHTML. Alternately, you can *self-close* an open tag in XHTML by including a space and the forward slash in the opening tag (such as <p />); with self-closing tags, a separate ending tag is not used. An example of an XHTML Web page is shown in Figure 10-19. This example also illustrates the following three main sections of an XHTML Web page:

➤ A *declaration* statement at the top of the page that indicates the XHTML standard (*Document Type Definition* or *DTD*) being used (the *XHTML 1.0 Transitional* option used in Figure 10-19 supports the older HTML tags and the newer XHTML elements), as well other general information about the page. Notice the <html> tag in the last line of the declaration section is closed at the end of the Web page using the </html> tag.

➤ A *head* statement that contains the title to be displayed on the browser's title bar when the Web page is viewed and any desired *meta* tags (such as to indicate the type of Unicode character set being used with the Web page, as in Figure 10-19, or the keywords to be associated with the Web page, as discussed in more detail in Chapter 11).

➤ The *body* (content) of the Web page.

HTML 5

The specifications for HTML and XHTML are developed by the World Wide Web Consortium (W3C) and are continually evolving. The newest version of HTML under development is *HTML 5* and is designed to replace the current versions of both HTML and XHTML. HTML 5 includes new tags and features that support the creation of more complex Web pages and applications, including those that involve animation and

2.0 WEB

multimedia. While developers creating exceptionally complex and interactive applications may wish to continue to use Flash or Silverlight or another multimedia or animation development tool, HTML 5 opens up the possibility of more Web pages using browser-based animation instead. The advantage of using HTML 5, in conjunction with other non-proprietary tools like JavaScript and *Cascading Style Sheets* (discussed next), is that they are open standards. Consequently, no proprietary software is required (Web pages can be created using just a text editor) and the features will be supported by Web browsers as the standard becomes closer to finalization, so no plug-ins are required.

Cascading Style Sheets (CSSs)

While markup languages like HTML and XHTML can be used to describe the formatting of text (such as font, size, and color) and the layout of a Web page (such as how bulleted lists appear or how tables are arranged), **Cascading Style Sheets** (**CSSs**) can be used instead to specify the styles used with a Web page or an entire Web site. While the actual CSS styles can be specified directly in the head section of an individual Web page (called an *internal style sheet*), they are normally saved in a separate file (called an *external style sheet* and using the file extension *.css*). The CSS file is linked to the Web pages of a site using a *link* statement in the head section of those pages and the CSS styles specified in the CSS file are applied to all of the linked Web pages at one time. Using an external CSS file improves consistency and efficiency because any changes made to the styles in the CSS file are automatically applied to all Web pages associated with that CSS file.

Wireless Markup Language (WML)

Wireless Markup Language (**WML**) is a language used to create Web pages to be displayed on WAP-enabled wireless devices, such as some older mobile phones and those used in some developing countries. To display Web content, a WAP-enabled browser—sometimes called a *microbrowser*—is used. Many mobile phones today (like the one shown in Figure 10-14) are designed to display HTML Web pages instead of WML pages.

Scripting Languages

For Web pages with a great deal of dynamic content (content that will be changed based on user actions), a *scripting language* is typically used. Such languages enable Web developers to build program instructions, or *scripts*, directly into a Web page's code to add dynamic content or database integration. Three of the most popular scripting languages are *JavaScript*, *VBScript*, and *Perl*. When using a scripting language, it is important to realize that not all commands work with all browsers and users can disable the use of scripted commands in their browser. Consequently, if you use a scripting language, it is a good idea to preview your Web pages with the scripting functionality disabled to evaluate the effectiveness of your site without the scripted commands, and then make any edits (such as adding non-scripted content to convey the same information), if needed.

JavaScript

JavaScript was developed to enable Web authors to implement interactive Web sites (for instance, JavaScript is used to animate the Cyberchase Web site shown in Figure 10-19). It is commonly used to add interactive content to Web pages, such as pop-up windows, text, or other objects that are displayed when the mouse points to a particular object, button, or menu item on a Web page.

>**Cascading Style Sheet (CSS).** A tool used to specify and apply the styles used for a Web site. >**Wireless Markup Language (WML).** A language used to display Web pages on WAP-enabled devices, such as some mobile phones. >**JavaScript.** A scripting language widely used to add dynamic content to Web pages.

VBScript

Another scripting language in use today is *VBScript* (*Visual Basic Scripting Edition*), a scripting language developed by Microsoft that is based on the *Visual Basic* programming language. VBScript is used for purposes similar to what JavaScript is used for—it enables Web developers to include interactive elements, such as pop-up content, on their Web pages viewed with the Internet Explorer or other compatible browsers. Individuals who are already familiar with Visual Basic can easily incorporate VBScript content into their Web pages.

Perl

Short for *Practical Extraction and Report Language*, *Perl* was originally developed as a programming language designed for processing text. Because of its strong text-processing abilities, Perl has become one of the most popular languages for writing *CGI scripts*—scripts that are often used to process data entered into Web page forms tied to databases, as discussed in more detail in Chapter 14.

AJAX

To better handle Web page interactivity, a new set of Web standards—called **AJAX** (*Asynchronous JavaScript and XML*)—has been developed. AJAX is used today on numerous Web sites—including Windows Live Mail, Google Maps, Gmail, Flickr, and numerous other popular Web applications—and uses a combination of HTML (or XHTML), JavaScript, and XML to create faster and more efficient interactive Web applications.

Chandra Krintz, University of California, Santa Barbara; Vice Chair of the ACM Special Interest Group on Programming Languages

ASK THE EXPERT

Are programming skills necessary to be a Web site developer today?

Yes, more than ever. Web sites today are dynamic, interactive, complex, and highly adaptive to appeal to the specific and changing needs of the individual users that constitute today's competitive commercial markets and popular Web communities. Programming languages have evolved to support existing and emerging Web technologies. Developers today must be able to use a wide range of high-level programming language technologies effectively, such as Java, AJAX, Ruby/Rails, Python, ASP.NET, and PHP, and to adapt quickly to new languages, frameworks, and practices. Programming expertise enables developers to implement dynamic Web page content efficiently, as well as the distributed and layered systems through which Web pages interact with databases and other back-end applications. In addition, strong and marketable programming skills today include team-based work styles and pair programming, test-driven program deployment, agile workplaces, and use of visual and interactive development environments. Programming skills are key to the success, productivity, and satisfaction of today's Web developers.

Traditional interactive Web applications submit data from the user (such as via a form or search box) to a Web server, and then the Web server responds back by displaying a new Web page containing the appropriate information. Because the Web server must send a new Web page each time the user provides new input, traditional Web applications run relatively slowly. AJAX applications, on the other hand, request only new data and add just that data to the existing Web page when it is refreshed so much less content needs to be downloaded each time the Web page changes. To speed things up even more, any actions that do not require new data from the server—such as validating the input a user enters into a form—are handled within the AJAX application, instead of by the Web server. Consequently, interactive Web pages built with AJAX run faster and have a responsiveness closer to the one users associate with desktop applications. And, if done correctly, AJAX applications require less bandwidth than conventional Web applications since page layout and structure data is

2.0 WEB

> **AJAX.** A set of Web standards designed to better handle Web page interactivity by downloading only new data from the Web server, instead of redownloading the entire Web page.

TREND

Mashup Sites

A *mashup site* is a Web site that combines content from more than one source. While technically a mashup can be any sort of composite Web application, mashups are most often used today to pull data from one Web site (such as Google Maps) into another site. For instance, hundreds of mashup sites overlay customized data (such as homes for sale or rent in a particular area, the distance for a specified walking route, the best fishing areas, New York subway routes, or vacation photos tagged with GPS location information) on top of the Google Maps interface. These applications are possible using the Google Maps API (*application programming interface*)—the published specifications that describe to developers how they can access the Google Maps service (see the accompanying illustration). With the Google Maps API, developers can use JavaScript commands to display maps of specified locations and then overlay customized information on top of them. Other popular sites frequently used in mashups include Flickr, Amazon, Virtual Earth, YouTube, and eBay.

In addition to being used to create Web applications, mashup tools are also used to integrate data from multiple sources (often both internal data, such as Excel spreadsheets and company databases, and external Web-based data, such as maps, social networking site data, news, and competitor data) to create new enterprise

applications—referred to as *enterprise mashups*. Mashups are currently a hot technology trend and are rapidly gaining acceptance in businesses. In fact, Forrester Research predicts that the enterprise mashup market will reach nearly $700 million by 2013. While mashups can save time and money, businesses do need to make sure that the data collected by mashup tools is appropriate, is accurate, and meets corporate governance guidelines.

APIs, available via numerous Web sites, make mashups possible.

---

downloaded only once, and then only the data on the page that needs updating is downloaded when it is needed. To implement AJAX more easily, a variety of *AJAX toolkits*—AJAX application development programs—are available.

Other Content Development Tools

Two content development tools not yet discussed are *ActiveX* and *VRML* (*Virtual Reality Modeling Language*). Another useful Web development tool is the ability to create a *Web archive* in order to transmit an entire Web site at one time, such as via e-mail. Today, this is usually accomplished with *MHTML*. For a look at a Web site development trend—the use of *mashup tools*—see the Trend box.

ActiveX

ActiveX, developed by Microsoft Corporation but compatible with most browsers today, is a set of specifications for reusing software components that can be used to integrate multimedia and other interactive elements into Web pages. Essentially, ActiveX extends *object linking and embedding* (*OLE*)—also developed by Microsoft and adopted widely as a standard by the software industry—to work on the Web. OLE makes it possible to integrate content from two or more programs, such as including spreadsheet objects (a chart or group of cells, for instance) in a word processing document. ActiveX, when used to implement OLE on the Web, allows you to view all types of files from within your Web browser. For instance, you can add word processing or spreadsheet documents to a Web page, and the appropriate program or viewer plug-in will be launched from within the Web browser to display that content when that page is viewed. It also enables your Web browser to play special content on Web pages; for instance, the Shockwave ActiveX control can play interactive multimedia presentations that are created in the Shockwave format. Essentially, ActiveX allows Web publishers to take files from their hard drives that are suitable for the Web and drop them directly into their Web pages. Such a capability is especially useful for office intranets because a great deal of potential Web page content may already exist in the form of office documents. To view ActiveX content, your browser must either directly support it or have the appropriate ActiveX plug-in.

Virtual Reality Modeling Language (VRML) and X3D

Short for *Virtual Reality Modeling Language*, *VRML* is the original specification for displaying three-dimensional objects on Web pages. It is essentially the 3D equivalent of HTML. Files written in VRML have the extension *.wrl* (short for "world") and viewing VRML files in your browser requires a VRML plug-in. VRML objects—cars, homes, and other photo-realistic 3D objects, for instance—can be rotated and viewed from any angle. The successor to VRML is *X3D*. X3D includes support for the latest developments in professional graphics, as well as support for XML and other more recent technologies. Virtual reality can also be implemented using software that supports 3D technologies, such as *QuickTime VR*.

Web Site Authoring Software

Web pages can be created by typing the page's text, HTML tags, JavaScript code, and other needed content in any word processor or text editor. For instance, the XHTML Web page shown in Figure 10-19 was created in the Windows Notepad program. However, creating complex Web pages (such as those containing tables, animation, or input forms that are linked to a database) in this manner is a very difficult task. **Web site authoring software** (also called *Web site development software*) makes the job of creating Web pages and complete Web sites much easier. Instead of entering the HTML tags by hand, most Web site authoring programs automatically generate the appropriate HTML or XHTML statements and Cascading Style Sheets when options are selected from menus, toolbar buttons are clicked, or the developer otherwise specifies what content the Web page should contain and what it should look like. Similarly, as menu options are selected, the appropriate JavaScript or other code used to add animation or interactivity is generated. In addition, Web site authoring programs virtually always have the capability to include a wide variety of other multimedia elements, such as Shockwave and Flash animations, animated GIFs, video clips, and audio clips. Some of the most popular Web site authoring programs are *Adobe Dreamweaver* (shown in Figure 10-20) and *Microsoft Expression Web*.

Another benefit of using a Web site authoring program is that it allows you to create an entire cohesive Web site more easily. For instance, effects, styles, backgrounds, and navigational tools can be applied to an entire site at one time, saving time and increasing consistency at the same time. In addition, many Web site authoring programs allow you to include forms and database connectivity easily for more dynamic interactions with your visitors. These programs also include other helpful development tools—such as tests for *broken links* (links to nonexistent Web pages), browser compatibility, and accessibility—and the ability to *publish* the entire site easily and at one time, as discussed next.

> **Web site authoring software.** A type of application program used to create Web pages and entire Web sites.

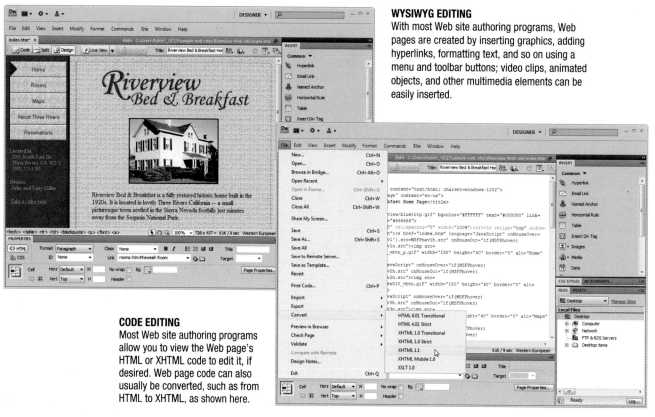

WYSIWYG EDITING
With most Web site authoring programs, Web pages are created by inserting graphics, adding hyperlinks, formatting text, and so on using a menu and toolbar buttons; video clips, animated objects, and other multimedia elements can be easily inserted.

CODE EDITING
Most Web site authoring programs allow you to view the Web page's HTML or XHTML code to edit it, if desired. Web page code can also usually be converted, such as from HTML to XHTML, as shown here.

FIGURE 10-20
The Dreamweaver Web site authoring program.

Testing, Publishing, and Maintaining the Site

Once a multimedia Web site has been created, it must be thoroughly tested before allowing it to go "live" by publishing it to a Web server. Each and every hyperlink needs to be clicked to ensure it takes the user to the proper location, and every possible action (such as clicking or pointing to) that could take place with an animated element should be tested. Complex animations (such as games and tutorials) should be tested individually before they are inserted into the Web page; after inserting the animation into a Web page, that page should be tested to ensure the animation works correctly. Web page code can be tested in some Web site authoring programs, as well as via some Web page validators, such as the XHTML validator shown in Figure 10-21.

Ideally, Web site testing should take place on a variety of computers using different operating systems, browsers, and screen resolutions, and with a diverse selection of users. The testers should be a variety of ages and have a wide range of computer abilities. If possible, an observer should discreetly watch the testers and take note of any point during the testing that users seem confused or end up somewhere they did not intend to go. Finished Web pages should also be proofread carefully to locate and correct any spelling or grammatical errors. Many Web site authoring programs include spelling and hyperlink checkers to assist you with testing, but these electronic tools should not replace careful proofreading and testing.

After the mechanics of a Web site are tested, some companies choose to subject their site to a "stress test." These tests are frequently performed by an outside agency and examine the capacity of the site and how many visitors and activities it can handle at one time. Some stress testing software is also available, and there are also software programs an organization can use to continuously monitor its site for problems and bottlenecks, as well as chart usage (such as which hyperlinks are clicked most often and how long each Web page is viewed—a statistic referred to as *time on page*) to evaluate the effectiveness of the Web site and help determine any changes or updates that should be made.

Once a site is thoroughly tested, it is ready to be *published*; that is, uploaded to the appropriate Web server (such as a company or a school Web server, or a Web server

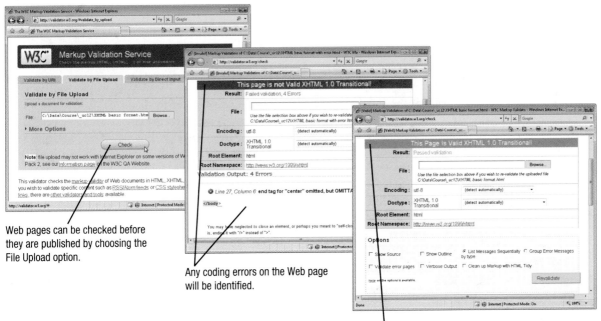

Web pages can be checked before they are published by choosing the File Upload option.

Any coding errors on the Web page will be identified.

Once any coding errors have been corrected, the page will be declared valid.

belonging to an ISP or a Web hosting site). Once the Web server to be used has been identified, all of the content for the Web site (including the HTML files, all image files, any animation files, and so forth) need to be published to the Web server. Depending on the program used to create the Web site and the particular Web server being used, the site may be able to be published from within the Web site authoring program, published via *File Transfer Protocol* (*FTP*), or published via online tools located on the host's Web site. To view the site once it has been published, the URL associated with the site—including the domain name being used (often the domain name for the hosting site, unless the user has purchased a domain name to use with the site), the proper folder name (if applicable), and the filename of the home page of the site—needs to be typed in the Address bar of a browser. To avoid having to type the home page filename, most Web servers are set up to have a default filename for the home page, such as index.html. If so and the home page is given that filename, the home page of the site can be viewed by just typing the domain name (and folder name, if appropriate)—the Web page filename is not needed.

After a site is up and running, the maintenance phase begins. As mentioned earlier, Web sites should be updated regularly to keep them current and interesting. Web sites should also be evaluated on a regular basis to locate areas needing improvement, new problems that have become apparent, and so forth. Hyperlinks to external Web sites need to be checked on a regular basis because the pages could be moved or become inappropriate for that link. If, at some point, it appears that the site needs a major overhaul, the design and development process should start over.

THE FUTURE OF WEB-BASED MULTIMEDIA

Although no one knows exactly what types of multimedia will be available in the future, it is a safe bet that they will be even more exciting and more embedded into everyday events than at present. Web-based multimedia and home entertainment devices will likely continue to converge to allow seamless access to the desired content on the user's device of choice (TV, computer, mobile phone, and so forth), regardless of where that content is located. Technology will continue to evolve to support the growing desire for mobile multimedia; the use of multimedia applications that are tied to a geographical location or current status and that involve user-generated content will also likely continue to grow.

FIGURE 10-21
Validating an XHMTL Web page. This Web site (validator.w3.org) can be used to validate XHTML Web pages.

SUMMARY

WHAT IS WEB-BASED MULTIMEDIA?

Multimedia is the integrated use of more than one type of media, such as text, graphics, video, animation, and sound. **Web-based multimedia** refers to multimedia located on Web pages. Multimedia applications are usually *interactive*. With today's fast computers and Internet connections, multimedia applications are frequently used on Web pages, such as for information delivery, e-commerce, and entertainment purposes. Some Web pages today use **virtual reality** (**VR**) to create environments that look like they do in the real world. Because multimedia is such an integral component of the Web today, it is important for both businesses and individuals to understand the characteristics of the various types of multimedia elements and the impact of adding them to a Web site.

One major advantage of using multimedia is that it appeals to a wide variety of people and complements different learning styles. Multimedia tends to hold users' interest more than single media applications, and it makes some ideas easier to convey. Disadvantages include issues related to cost, development, and delivery of multimedia.

MULTIMEDIA ELEMENTS

Multimedia applications typically contain **text** in a variety of typefaces and appearances. Text is used to deliver content, as well as for instructions, menus, and hyperlinks. *Serif typefaces* are commonly used for large sections of text; *sans serif typefaces* are more frequently used with titles and headings. When a consistent text appearance is important, the text is often rendered as part of an **image** (also called a **graphic**), so it will look the same for all users. Types of images include photographs, drawings, company logos, and other static images. Already created *clip art* and *stock photographs* are widely available for purchase or for free, and many are available for downloading via the Internet.

Common graphic formats include **GIF** (*Graphics Interchange Format*) and **PNG** (*Portable Network Graphics*) for line art images, and **JPEG** (*Joint Photographic Experts Group*) for photographs. Other possible formats include *TIF* for scanned images and *BMP* for Paint images. When creating images for Web pages, the most appropriate format—as well as the needed physical size and the smallest file size—should be used. For Web pages that include large images, **thumbnail images**—small images that are linked to the full-quality larger images—can be used.

Animation consists of a series of graphical images displayed one after the other to simulate movement—**Java applets**, **animated GIFs**, *JavaScript* Web applications, and **Flash** and **Silverlight** animations are common on Web pages today. Some animated elements require a *plug-in* to be viewed. **Audio** includes all types of sound (such as music, spoken voice, and sound effects), and **video** is a continuous stream of visual information captured as a series of separate images or frames. Audio, video, and images are frequently compressed to reduce the finished file size. Web-based audio and video can be delivered as *streaming* in order to reduce the amount of time required before the content begins to play.

MULTIMEDIA WEB SITE DESIGN

When designing a multimedia Web site, careful planning (called **Web site design**) is essential to ensure an interesting and intuitive site that is attractive and easy to use. Web pages should also be efficient and versatile enough to be used with multiple browsers and platform configurations. Early steps in the design process include determining the primary objectives, intended audience, basic layout, and navigational structure for the site or application. The types of devices that will be used to access the site are another important consideration. Tools, such as **flowcharts**, **page layouts**, and **storyboards**, can be used during the design process. Features that require a specific browser or infrequently used plug-ins should be avoided whenever possible; high-bandwidth items should be used only when needed and should be user-controlled (such as providing a hyperlink for users to click if they wish to view a video file), if possible.

There are a number of navigational tools, such as drop-down menus, *site maps*, search boxes, *image maps*, *frames*, and navigation bars, that can be used when creating the navigational structure of the site. In addition, you should consider breaking long Web pages up into multiple pages and using a linked table of contents to enable the user to easily access any of the document. Compatibility with the various devices that might be used to access the site, as well as with assistive hardware, should be considered. For instance, **alternative text** descriptions should be used with all Web page images.

MULTIMEDIA WEB SITE DEVELOPMENT

Once a multimedia Web site is designed, the **Web site development** process can begin. Necessary tasks include creating the multimedia elements to be used on the site, creating the site itself, and testing and publishing the finished product. To create multimedia elements, graphics software, animation software, and audio and video editing software can be used. Once the individual elements have been created, they can be inserted into Web pages.

Web sites can be created with a **markup language**, such as **HTML** (**Hypertext Markup Language**), which uses *HTML tags* to indicate text characteristics, page layout, hyperlinks, and more. The **XML** (**Extensible Markup Language**) version of HTML is **XHTML** (**Extensible Hypertext Markup Language**). The emerging *HTML 5* is expected to replace current versions of both HTML and XHTML. **Cascading Style Sheets (CSSs)** can be used to apply a set of styles to a Web site easily and consistently. **Wireless Markup Language** (**WML**) is a markup language used to create Web pages for some older mobile devices. Additional tools for creating Web pages include *scripting languages* such as **JavaScript**, *VBScript*, and *Perl*, as well as development tools like **AJAX**, *ActiveX*, and *VRML*. **Web site authoring software** (such as *Dreamweaver*) can also be used to create the site more easily. In addition to enabling Web page developers to create Web pages more easily using menus and buttons instead of typing the code directly, Web site authoring software allows developers to apply effects, styles, backgrounds, navigational tools, and other elements to an entire site.

After the site has been completed, it must be thoroughly tested to ensure all features and links work, and that it is compatible with as many different types of computers, platforms, operating systems, and browsers as possible. Proofreading the pages on the site is also very important. When it is ready to go live, it is *published* on a Web server typically by using a Web authoring program, an *FTP* program, or the online tools on the Web hosting site being used. The site then needs to be maintained on a regular basis.

THE FUTURE OF WEB-BASED MULTIMEDIA

Multimedia will likely continue to be integrated into our everyday lives. Trends, such as the convergence of Web-based multimedia and home entertainment devices, are helping to lead us in that direction. The use of mobile multimedia will continue to grow, along with mobile multimedia applications that are tied to geographical locations or that allow user-generated content.

Chapter Objective 4:
List the various tasks involved with developing a multimedia Web site.

Chapter Objective 5:
Explain how markup languages, scripting languages, and other tools are used today to create multimedia Web pages.

2.0 WEB

Chapter Objective 6:
Discuss the possible use of Web-based multimedia in the future.

REVIEW ACTIVITIES

KEY TERM MATCHING

a. alternative text

b. animation

c. GIF

d. JPEG

e. markup language

f. multimedia

g. Silverlight

h. video

i. XHTML (Extensible Hypertext Markup Language)

j. Web site authoring software

Instructions: Match each key term on the left with the definition on the right that best describes it.

1. _____ A continuous stream of visual information broken into separate images or frames to be displayed one after the other to simulate the original visual event.

2. _____ An image format that supports 256 colors and is commonly used for Web page line art images.

3. _____ An image format that supports true color and is commonly used for Web page photographs.

4. _____ A language that uses symbols or tags to describe what a document should look like when it is displayed in a Web browser.

5. _____ A newer, stricter version of HTML that is based on XML.

6. _____ A technology used to create and display Web animations and interactive Web-based multimedia applications.

7. _____ A text description for a Web page image; is displayed when the image is pointed to and can be read by assistive technology.

8. _____ A type of application program used to create Web pages and entire Web sites.

9. _____ The integration of a variety of media, such as text, images, video, animation, and sound.

10. _____ The process by which a series of graphical images are displayed one after the other to simulate movement.

SELF-QUIZ

Instructions: Circle **T** if the statement is true, **F** if the statement is false, or write the best answer in the space provided. **Answers for the self-quiz are located in the References and Resources Guide at the end of the book.**

1. **T F** One advantage of multimedia Web pages is that they are visual, and this is an advantage because all people are visual learners.

2. **T F** Clip art images are predrawn images that can be inserted into Web pages.

3. **T F** A stock photograph can be used to add animation to a Web page.

4. **T F** A flowchart of a Web site illustrates the pages on the site and their relationships to one another.

5. **T F** A markup language is typically used to create the animated elements of a Web page.

6. _____ audio and video files, in which the file begins playing before it has been completely downloaded, are frequently used on Web pages to make their delivery more efficient.

7. When beginning to design a multimedia Web site, it is important to determine the _____ and the _____ of the site.

8. _____ software is commonly used to create an entire multimedia Web site, tying all of the components together into a finished site.

9. A(n) _____ is a sketch that illustrates the basic layouts of the home page and the rest of the pages on a Web site.

10. Match each phrase to its descripton, and write the corresponding number in the blank to the left of the description.

a. _____ A type of animation where a series of images are displayed one after the other to simulate movement, and the entire set of images is saved together in one file.

b. _____ A small program used in conjunction with a Web browser that enables a multimedia element on the page to work.

c. _____ A tool used to design an animated sequence.

1. animated GIF

2. storyboard

3. plug-in

1. Match each acronym to its descripton, and write the corresponding number in the blank to the left of the description.

a. _____ The original markup language used to create Web pages.

b. _____ An image format designed for use on Web pages.

c. _____ A set of rules for exchanging data over the Web.

d. _____ A set of standards for handling Web page interactivity.

1. AJAX

2. PNG

3. HTML

4. XML

2. Supply the missing words to complete the following statements.

a. _____ is used on Web sites to enable visitors to view content in a 3D environment that looks like it does in real life.

b. _____ are used on Web sites to enable only those visitors who wish to view full-sized images to do so.

3. The Web site for XZY Corporation should include information about Products, Orders, Corporate Information, and Contact Us. Sketch a brief flowchart and one possible page layout for the home page of the site.

4. List three types of software programs that might be used when creating a multimedia Web site. Explain what each program would be used for and list one example (program name and publisher) of each.

5. Name one situation in which a hyperlink would not be identified as a broken link by a Web site authoring program testing feature, but would still be wrong and could only be detected by a human tester.

2.0 WEB

1. As discussed in the chapter, lifecasting involves sending video from your mobile phone to others to share various events taking place during your day. While some friends may enjoy this type of status update, could it be an imposition to others? Should lifecasters get permission from recipients before sending video feeds? What if the recpient is charged for the video download—is the sender ethically responsible for the fee related to his or her video transmission? Have you or would you choose to lifecast? Why or why not?

2. *Neuromarketing*—the study of the brain's responses to advertising—is a somewhat controversial, but growing, new marketing trend. Neuromarketing companies can help businesses analyze their marketing materials by wiring the scalps of volunteers with electrodes and studying their responses as they view commercials, view print ads, experience new products, and so forth. Do you think neuromarketing is a viable business tool? Should there be any regulations governing its use? If a company decided to use this technology to better market a product to you, would you object? How about using it for political purposes?

PROJECTS

HOT TOPICS

1. **Online News** Online news sites typically contain a wide variety of multimedia and are a common means of obtaining the news today.

   For this project, visit at least two news Web sites (such as **MSNBC.com**, **CNN.com**, or **CBSNews.com**), investigate the types of multimedia features they offer, and evaluate their usefulness. What multimedia components are available? Do the components work smoothly and add value to your experience? Are there any multimedia components missing that you think would be useful? What are the advantages to using an online news site compared to radio or television news broadcasts? Are there any disadvantages? Do you use an online news site as your primary source of news? Why or why not? At the end of your research, prepare a one-page summary of your findings and opinions and submit it to your instructor.

SHORT ANSWER/ RESEARCH

2. **Section 508** Section 508 is a section of the Rehabilitation Act that refers to requirements for making electronic and information technology accessible to people with disabilities.

   For this project, research Section 508 and the Rehabilitation Act in general to see how the law applies to Web site design and to whom the law applies. If you were to set up a personal or small business Web site, would you be legally obligated to conform to Section 508 regulations? What types of features or modifications does a Web site need to include to be Section 508 compliant? How would one go about testing to see if a Web site was Section 508 compliant? Prepare a one-page summary of your findings and submit it to your instructor.

HANDS ON

3. **Using XHTML** As discussed in the chapter, all that is needed to create a basic Web page is a text editor or word processing program and a basic knowledge of HTML or XHTML coding. For this project, locate a Windows-based computer that you are allowed to use and perform the following tasks.

   a. Open Notepad and type the XHTML code shown to the left exactly as shown (substituting your name for the (*your name*) placeholder). Save your file as *My Web page.html* in an appropriate location.

   b. Use Windows Explorer to locate your saved file, and then double-click the file to open it in your browser. Compare your Web page to the one shown to the left to make sure it is correct, then, if you are connected to the Internet, click on the Google hyperlink to make sure it works. If you find any errors, return to Notepad, make the corrections, save the file again, and redisplay the page in your browser.

   c. Once your Web page is correct, use Notepad to edit the code so the second sentence in the Web page ("This Web page...") is bold, in addition to being italic (refer to the HTML tags in Figure 10-17, if needed). Save the file and redisplay it in your browser, then print the finished Web page to turn in to your instructor.

```
<!DOCTYPE html PUBLIC "-//W3C//DTD XHTML 1.0 Transitional//EN"
"http://www.w3.org/TR/xhtml1/DTD/xhtml1-transitional.dtd">

<html xmlns="http://www.w3.org/1999/xhtml" xml:lang="en">

<head>
        <title>Sample Web Page</title>
        <meta http-equiv="Content-Type" content="text/html;charset=utf-8"/>
</head>

<body>
<h1>(your name)'s Sample Web Page</h1>
<i>This Web page shows some introductory XHTML tags.</i>
<hr/>
My favorite search site is <a href="http://google.com">Google</a>.
</body>

</html>
```

4. **Domain Tasting** When you register a domain name, there is a five-day grace period during which time you can receive a full refund. Though originally designed to protect purchasers who might make a typo and mistakenly register the wrong name, this grace period policy has led to "domain tasting"—in which millions of domain names at any given time are held for the grace period. The domain names are usually registered for the purpose of testing their marketability and/or generating income via pay-per-click ads. At the end of the grace period, the domain names that do not generate enough revenue are returned for a full refund. Do you think testing domain names in this manner is ethical? Can you think of an ethical reason for registering multiple domain names with the intention of keeping only some? Should the grace period be eliminated? In response to the increase in domain tasting, ICANN (which supervises domain name registration) implemented a new policy allowing a set number of free returns per company. Do you think this is a good solution? One twist is the practice by Network Solutions to register instantly all available domain names that match domain name searches conducted via its Web site and hold them for four days. A lawsuit was filed in 2008 to stop Network Solutions from this practice, but the suit has not yet been resolved. Is this practice ethical? Is domain tasting ever ethical? Like cybersquatting, should domain tasting be illegal?

For this project, form an opinion about the ethical ramifications of domain tasting and be prepared to discuss your position (in class, via an online class discussion group, in a class chat room, or via a class blog, depending on your instructor's directions). You may also be asked to write a short paper expressing your opinion.

5. **Free Multimedia** Many Web sites have free clip art, animated GIFs. stock photographs, video clips, or audio clips available for download and use on Web sites.

For this project, use a search site to find a Web site (such as Clip-Art.com or The Free Graphics Store) that offers free multimedia for use on personal Web sites. Determine the types of multimedia available, what file formats are used, and how the multimedia is downloaded. Is there a sufficient amount of free multimedia available online to create a Web site? What additional custom multimedia might an individual need to create to supplement the free resources available online? Share your findings and opinions with the class in the form of a short presentation, including a demonstration of using one of the Web sites to download a multimedia file, if possible. The presentation should not exceed 10 minutes and should make use of one or more presentation aids, such as the chalkboard, handouts, overhead transparencies, or a computer-based slide presentation (your instructor may provide additional requirements). You may also be asked to submit a summary of the presentation to your instructor.

Instructions: Go to the Chapter 10 page at **www.cengage.com/computerconcepts/np/uc13** to work the following Web Activities.

6. **Interactive Activities** Work the interactive **Crossword Puzzle**, watch the **Video Podcasts** and **Online Videos**, and explore the **Further Exploration** links associated with this chapter.

If you have a SAM user profile, you may have access to hands-on instruction, practice, and assessment of the skills covered in this chapter. Check with your instructor for instructions and the correct URL/Web site to access those assignments.

7. **Student Edition Labs** Work the following interactive **Student Edition Labs.**

   ➤ **Working with Graphics**   ➤ **Working with Audio**   ➤ **Working with Video**

8. **Test Yourself** Review the **Online Study Guide** for this chapter, then test your knowledge of the terms and concepts covered in this chapter by completing the **Key Term Matching** exercise, the **Self-Quiz**, the **Exercises**, and the **Practice Test.**

chapter 11

E-Commerce

After completing this chapter, you will be able to do the following:

1. Explain what e-commerce is and describe some of the advantages and disadvantages involved with implementing e-commerce.

2. Identify a variety of e-commerce business models and discuss their differences.

3. Discuss the types of Web sites that can be used to implement e-commerce.

4. List several strategies for implementing e-commerce using the Web, including some of the decisions that need to be made, the options available for accepting payments, and the process of designing and developing an effective Web site.

5. Outline some sales and marketing strategies that can be used in conjunction with an e-commerce Web site.

6. Discuss some security issues related to e-commerce sites.

outline

Overview

What Is E-Commerce?
  Advantages of E-Commerce
  Disadvantages of E-Commerce

E-Commerce Business Models
  Business-to-Consumer (B2C)
    Business Model
  Business-to-Business (B2B) Business
    Model
  Consumer-to-Consumer (C2C)
    Business Model
  Business-to-Government (B2G)
    Business Model

Types of E-Commerce Web Sites
  Manufacturer and E-Tailer
    Web Sites
  Subscription Sites
  Brokerage Sites

**Implementing Web-Based
E-Commerce**
  Step 1: Select Appropriate Business
    Models and Types of Web Sites
  Step 2: Select the Desired
    E-Commerce Applications
  Step 3: Develop Procedures for
    Handling Electronic Financial
    Transactions
  Step 4: Design and Develop an
    Effective E-Commerce Web Site
  Step 5: Implement Appropriate
    Sales and Marketing Strategies

Security Issues

OVERVIEW

The Internet and World Wide Web have greatly affected the way most of us live and do business. In addition to using the Web to look up information, communicate with others, and be entertained, many consumers like to use the Web today to purchase goods and services. Consequently, it is common today for businesses to offer goods and services online. In fact, Web-based e-commerce (electronic commerce)—the act of doing business transactions over the Internet via Web pages—is redefining the way businesses operate and compete in the 21st century. E-commerce spending in the United States has been steadily rising over the past years and it is expected to exceed $1 trillion annually by 2012. In addition, the Web influences offline sales, such as the scores of consumers who use the Web to research purchases they eventually make offline.

This chapter begins by defining e-commerce and discussing some of the potential advantages and disadvantages of e-commerce for both businesses and consumers. It then covers the various types of e-commerce business models in use today and the types of Web sites used to implement e-commerce. Then, you will learn about the issues a business needs to consider when implementing an e-commerce Web site. These issues include which types of business models and e-commerce applications to use, how to handle the financial transactions generated via the Web site, and how to design and develop an effective e-commerce Web site. The chapter closes with a look at sales and marketing strategies for e-commerce Web sites and a discussion of e-commerce security issues. ■

PODCAST

Go to **www.cengage.com/ computerconcepts/np/uc13** to download or listen to the "Expert Insight on Web-Based Multimedia and E-Commerce" podcast.

2.0 WEB

WHAT IS E-COMMERCE?

E-commerce is the term used to describe conducting business transactions—generally financial transactions—via communications technology. It was originally performed via private networks; for instance, the banking industry has carried out *electronic funds transfers (EFT)* via private networks for many years. Today, however, e-commerce is most often performed via Web sites. Businesses that sell goods and services via only the Web are often called **dot-coms** because they typically have a *.com* top-level domain in the URLs used to access their Web sites. Many businesses today have both an *online store* and a **brick-and-mortar store** (a physical store); these businesses are sometimes referred to as *click-and-mortar stores* or *bricks and clicks*.

In addition to being carried out via personal computers and conventional Web sites, e-commerce can also be carried out via mobile phones or mobile devices, such as to buy fast food, pay for a cab or parking, buy theater tickets, or send money to other individuals while you are on the go (see Figure 11-1). E-commerce performed via a mobile phone or other mobile device is referred to as **m-commerce**. M-commerce transactions typically

> **E-commerce.** The act of doing business transactions over the Internet or similar technology. > **Dot-com.** An Internet-only store with no physical presence. > **Brick-and-mortar store.** A conventional store with a physical presence. > **M-commerce.** E-commerce carried out via mobile phones and other mobile devices.

take place via a mobile Web page or text message; if a proof of purchase is needed for the transaction (such as a movie or plane ticket that must be presented for admittance), it usually appears on the mobile phone screen as a barcode that can be scanned by a barcode reader when it is needed. An emerging m-commerce option is *Near Field Communications* (*NFC*) technology, which uses RFID to facilitate communication between devices, including transferring payment information, receipts, boarding passes, and other information wirelessly between payment terminals and mobile phones. Worldwide, vending machines are increasingly going cashless—supporting only NFC, credit cards, and other electronic payment methods, instead of cash—particularly in locations where theft is an issue.

The collection of hardware, software, people, policies, and strategies used to perform and support e-commerce is referred to as an *e-commerce system*. There are both advantages and disadvantages involved with implementing an e-commerce system; some of the more prominent ones are listed in Figure 11-2 and discussed in the next few sections. Because of the prominence of e-commerce in our society today, it is important for both businesses and individuals to understand the advantages and potential disadvantages of using e-commerce.

Advantages of E-Commerce

E-commerce offers many advantages to both businesses and consumers. Most of these advantages center on convenience and efficiency. A few of the most significant advantages are discussed next.

For Businesses

The primary advantages for businesses include reduced costs, increased customer satisfaction, a broader customer base, and potentially higher sales.

Many of the cost reductions result from the need for smaller facilities and fewer staff. In particular, stores with only an online (not a physical) presence experience lower costs because they do not have the expenses associated with maintaining a physical storefront, like conventional brick-and-mortar stores do. Even though a dot-com store may need a company headquarters and possibly one or more inventory warehouses, these types of facilities are much less expensive to operate than a retail store that may need to have a physical presence in multiple prime locations in order to reach potential customers. Other potential areas of cost reductions associated with e-commerce include the ability to sell directly to customers (and, therefore, save the cost associated with using retailers or other middlemen), using electronic marketing resources (such as e-mail announcements and Web site ads) instead of printed materials to save on marketing and advertising costs, and increased accuracy in order processing and pricing.

Higher customer satisfaction is another potential advantage of e-commerce for businesses. Convenience is a big factor in determining if a customer is satisfied and, when an e-commerce Web site is set up properly, the customer should find the process of shopping very easy and convenient. Online stores are open *24/7/365* (24 hours a day/7 days a week/365 days a year) so customers can shop at their convenience. They also do not have to

FIGURE 11-1
M-commerce allows you to pay for goods and services via mobile phone.

FIGURE 11-2
Potential advantages and disadvantages of e-commerce.

ADVANTAGES	DISADVANTAGES
For businesses	*For businesses*
• Reduced costs	• Must have an effective, always-working Web site
• Increased customer satisfaction	• Lost business, since some people will never perform online transactions
• Broader customer base	• Higher rate of fraudulent transactions
• Potentially higher sales	• Recurring threat of new competitors offering lower prices
For customers	*For customers*
• Convenience	• Potential for fraud
• Easier comparison shopping	• Buying goods without seeing them in person
• Higher degree of selection	• Possible expensive returns
• Potential cost savings	
• Customized products	

drive to a physical location to pick up their purchases since purchases are typically shipped directly to the customers' homes or businesses, and gifts can often be shipped directly to the recipient—an added convenience for the buyer.

Another possibility for increased customer satisfaction is the ability of businesses to send customers personalized information, such as special offers for products the customer might be interested in and notification when a previously out-of-stock product becomes available. Using data obtained from customers' activities on their e-commerce site, businesses can also make suggestions for relevant products while customers are shopping, as well as identify general trends and patterns to be used for future marketing activities. Increased customer satisfaction can also result from the ability of customers to access order information online, to print duplicate receipts, to track shipments, and more. These types of *electronic customer relationship management* (*eCRM*) activities are discussed later in this chapter.

There is also enormous potential for increased sales when an e-commerce site is used since online stores have a much broader customer base. Instead of serving a specific geographical area like a brick-and-mortar store, for instance, e-commerce businesses can offer their goods or services worldwide. There are fewer physical restraints to growth, as well. As the business grows, e-commerce businesses can just add the necessary resources (such as a more powerful server or more support staff) to their online presence, instead of having to build new physical stores or other expensive, time-consuming solutions.

For Customers

Advantages for customers include convenience, easier comparison shopping, a higher degree of selection, potential cost savings, and the ability to customize products easily.

As already mentioned, e-commerce is a tremendous convenience for those customers who take advantage of it. They can shop via their computers at any time of the day or night and have the products delivered to the appropriate locations, usually within just a few days. If the appropriate online customer support tools are in place, they can also check on the status of their orders, track the delivery of shipped items, look up their past purchases, and so forth. E-commerce is especially convenient when individuals are ill or when they would prefer not to go to a retail establishment, such as during inclement weather or busy shopping times.

Another big advantage for customers is the ability to comparison shop easily (see Figure 11-3). Many customers like to comparison shop before purchasing products or signing up for certain services.

> **TIP**
>
> If you have a question about a product you bought online or offline, go to the manufacturer's Web site and see what types of eCRM features—such as online manuals, online chat, or e-mail tech support—are available.

FIGURE 11-3

Comparison shopping. Web sites, such as the PriceGrabber.com site shown here, can help consumers find the lowest online prices for specific items.

1. User searches for a product using the search options.

2. User selects a product to view a list of vendors that sell that product.

3. User enters a ZIP code to find the lowest overall cost for that product, including product cost, shipping cost, and any taxes.

2.0 WEB

HOW IT WORKS

Buying Customized Products Online

Over the past few years, digital cameras have made customized products—such as photo mugs, T-shirts, calendars, and more—much more common and easier to obtain than in the past. *FedEx Kinko's* has offered photo products in the store and online for several years, and *Snapfish* is a popular source for online photo gifts. As more and more content is available in digital form and as people are growing more accustomed to personalized online experiences, the market for customized products is growing. Today, individuals can order a wide variety of professional-looking, customized products online on demand.

One company specializing in customized online products is *Zazzle*. Via the Zazzle Web site, customers can create their choice of custom products (such as T-shirts, neckties, bags, aprons, greeting cards, postage stamps, calendars, mouse pads, and posters) using their personal photos, licensed popular images (such as from Disney, Star Wars, Barbie, Looney Tunes, Marvel Comics, The Family Guy, Scooby Doo, and more), or historical images. First, the customer selects the item to be customized and chooses the appropriate options, such as size and color. Next, he or she adds images and text as desired (see the accompanying illustration). As the customer edits the item, a preview image is updated immediately to reflect the new design. Customers can save their designs to change or reuse later, if

desired. Once the product design is finished, the customer adds the item to his or her shopping cart and completes the checkout procedure. There is no minimum order or setup fee, and most items ship within 24 hours. If the business at Zazzle is any indication—the company ships tens of thousands of customized products each day—the demand for fast and affordable custom products will only increase in the future.

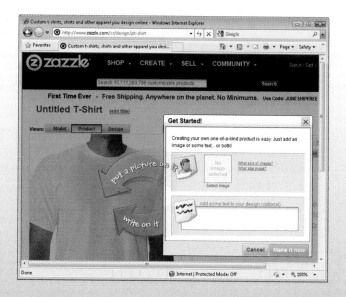

With a brick-and-mortar business, this requires physically going to the store to look at the selections available, or at least calling and gathering information over the telephone. With e-commerce, however, shoppers can view and read reviews of products online, find online merchants with the desired products in stock, and search for the lowest price at numerous online stores, in order to determine the products they would like to buy and the online merchant they would like to use. Since shoppers typically have access to more stores online than in person, online shoppers also have a greater product selection than brick-and-mortar shoppers. In addition to giving shoppers a wider variety of products, the ability to comparison shop with a larger number of potential online vendors can save the shopper money, although not all products purchased via online stores are less expensive than those products purchased in their brick-and-mortar counterparts, especially once shipping charges are added.

To help with comparison shopping, a variety of *comparison shopping Web sites*—sometimes called *shopping bots*—are available to gather prices and shipping information from multiple sites for a particular product and summarize the results to help locate the best buys from potential vendors. Some portal pages offer this service; others sites, such as mySimon.com and PriceGrabber.com (shown in Figure 11-3), are dedicated to this purpose. Another potential cost savings is the lack of sales tax on some online purchases, although that may change in the future if a mandatory Internet sales tax is implemented. A final advantage of e-commerce for customers is the ability to order a variety of customized products online, as discussed in the How It Works box.

Disadvantages of E-Commerce

While e-commerce has many advantages for both businesses and consumers, there are potential disadvantages, as well. A few of the most significant disadvantages are discussed next.

For Businesses

One disadvantage of doing a significant amount of your business via an e-commerce Web sites is that sales can only take place when the Web site is up and running. The "always open" nature of e-commerce puts enormous pressure on online stores to have solid, well designed, and reliable Web sites and Web hosting setups. A Web site that is offline, is not working properly, or that is simply too slow or disorganized can drive potential customers away in a hurry. Another disadvantage is the possibility of lost business because some individuals will choose to never shop online. Without a brick-and-mortar store or some other acceptable alternative, those individuals' business can never be obtained. A third disadvantage is the risk of fraudulent credit card transactions. Since credit cards do not have to be physically presented for online purchases, e-commerce credit card transactions are much more likely to be fraudulent than conventional credit card transactions. Recent improvements in credit card security (such as *virtual credit card numbers* and credit cards with one-time password (OTP) displays, as discussed later in this chapter) will likely help to reduce fraudulent charges.

Another disadvantage for e-commerce companies is the ease of entry into the marketplace for competitors. While large brick-and-mortar businesses may not be threatened by a new "mom and pop" business opening in the area, large or well-known e-commerce sites may lose business to small online stores. Because of the low overhead costs associated with online stores, new e-commerce businesses can enter the marketplace relatively inexpensively and they can attract business away from other established e-commerce sites—especially if they undercut prices or otherwise offer additional incentives to attract customers, and have a professional-looking, well-designed Web site. Of course, from the perspective of the new e-commerce business, this is an advantage, not a disadvantage.

For Customers

Perhaps the biggest disadvantage from a customer standpoint is the risk (or perceived risk) of fraud and other potential security problems. From placing an order with a nonexistent company that never delivers the ordered merchandise to having credit card information stolen from a legitimate company's Web server, the opportunity for fraud exists when transactions take place online or through a brick-and-mortar store that stores purchase information on a computer that is potentially accessible to a hacker. In addition to the actual risk of fraud and other problems, the fear of a problem resulting from an e-commerce transaction may put a damper on the online shopping experience for some consumers. The recent improvements in credit card security that are becoming available, as well as reassurance features offered by online merchants and credit card companies, will likely help to increase confidence in reluctant online shoppers. For instance, many online auction sites today offer free *buyer protection* for items up to a certain dollar amount if the items do not arrive or are not as advertised, and most credit card companies today offer 100% protection against fraudulent online purchases charged to a credit card.

Another potential disadvantage for consumers is not being able to see and touch goods in person before purchasing them. This limitation may be somewhat overcome as Web site and Internet technology improves—enabling customers to more easily view products and view them more like they would in person (such as by using high-resolution photos that can be rotated and viewed in three dimensions). The expense of returning merchandise the consumer finds unacceptable is another potential disadvantage. Some click-and-mortar stores, such as Old Navy, Best Buy, and Barnes & Noble, eliminate this concern by allowing consumers to return merchandise they ordered online to a local store in order to avoid return shipping charges.

FURTHER EXPLORATION   Go

Go to the Chapter 11 page at **www.cengage.com/ computerconcepts/np/uc13** for links to information about online shopping precautions.

WEB 2.0

E-COMMERCE BUSINESS MODELS

The policies, operations, and technologies used by a business help to define its *business model*. In essence, a company's business model describes how the company generates revenue. One way **e-commerce business models** can be defined is by the types of entities (such as businesses, consumers, or the government) selling and buying the goods or services. The four main e-commerce business models are illustrated in Figure 11-4 and discussed next; an e-commerce site typically fits one or more of these models.

FIGURE 11-4
E-commerce business models.

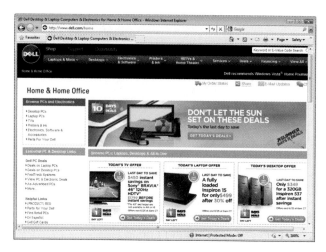

BUSINESS TO CONSUMER (B2C)
Transactions are between businesses and consumers; this site sells computers and related equipment to individuals.

BUSINESS TO BUSINESS (B2B)
Transactions are between businesses and other businesses; this site sells printers to businesses.

CONSUMER TO CONSUMER (C2C)
Transactions are between consumers and other consumers; this site helps individuals find items for sale by other individuals in their geographic area.

BUSINESS TO GOVERNMENT (B2G)
Transactions are between businesses and the government; this site allows businesses to pay government fees and taxes online.

> **E-commerce business model.** A description of how an e-commerce company does business, such as the types of buyers and sellers involved.

Business-to-Consumer (B2C) Business Model

With the **business-to-consumer** (**B2C**) **model**, businesses sell goods or services to individual consumers. The B2C model was one of the first major types of e-commerce business models found on the Web. Product-oriented B2C sites (such as Amazon.com, Walmart.com, Overstock.com, and BestBuy.com) sell a wide variety of goods including clothing, electronics, medicine, flowers, books, sports equipment, toys, movies, and office supplies. Service-oriented B2C sites include tax preparation, video-on-demand (VOD), travel agency, distance learning, and music subscription services.

Business-to-Business (B2B) Business Model

The **business-to-business** (**B2B**) **model** includes any type of e-commerce transaction taking place between two businesses. Possibilities include businesses buying goods and services needed for their operations, as well as purchasing manufacturing supplies and raw goods. Initially, B2C was expected to be the most prominent type of e-commerce business model; however, revenues from the B2B model are now expected to far surpass the B2C marketplace.

In addition to B2B businesses that sell products and services directly to other businesses (such as the one shown in Figure 11-4), there are businesses that bring buyers and sellers together instead. While they can be considered B2B businesses since they do receive revenue from the participating (buying and selling) businesses, they are often called *intermediary hubs* instead. Some intermediary hubs help connect a single business looking for products or services with a business selling those products or services; others combine a number of individual buyers (such as multiple small businesses) so they can buy as a group and receive volume discount pricing to better compete with large organizations. In either case, intermediary hubs usually receive a transaction fee from the selling organization, frequently based on the dollar amount of the sale, although some intermediaries charge a monthly or an annual fee to use their services instead. When intermediary hubs specialize in a specific industry (such as healthcare), they are sometimes called *vertical hubs*; when they specialize in a specific type of products or services used by a number of different industries (such as office equipment), they are sometimes called *horizontal hubs*.

Consumer-to-Consumer (C2C) Business Model

The **consumer-to-consumer** (**C2C**)—sometimes referred to as the *person-to-person* (*P2P*)—**model** involves individuals selling directly to other individuals. Typically, C2C transactions are carried out via intermediary Web sites set up to facilitate this, such as *online auction sites* like *eBay* (discussed in more detail shortly) and *online classified ad sites* like *Craigslist* (shown in Figure 11-4). In fact, with millions of products up for auction at any time, eBay is one of the largest C2C e-commerce sites today.

Business-to-Government (B2G) Business Model

The **business-to-government** (**B2G**) **model** includes transactions between businesses and local, state, and federal governments. For instance, many B2G e-commerce sites specialize in selling products and services to government agencies. Other B2G activities (which can be thought of as *G2B* activities because the government is providing services to businesses) involve businesses paying government taxes and fees online, such as via the state portal page shown in Figure 11-4. Individual citizens can also often pay a variety of government fees online, such as vehicle and boat registration fees; state, property, and federal income taxes; parking fees; and so forth. These activities can be thought of as *G2C* activities, since the government is supplying goods or services to consumers.

TYPES OF E-COMMERCE WEB SITES

In addition to the type of entities buying and selling the goods or services, another way an e-commerce business can be described is by the type of Web site being used for the e-commerce activities. Three of the most common types of Web sites (manufacturer and e-tailer sites, subscription sites, and brokerage sites) are described next. Other types of Web sites (such as personal Web sites, free social networking sites, and online forums) may generate revenue via the Web (such as via online ads), but are not included in the following discussion because they typically do not have direct online financial transactions with customers.

Manufacturer and E-Tailer Sites

Both manufacturers and online retailers—often called **e-tailers** or *e-retailers*—can sell directly to customers via their Web sites (a manufacturer Web site was shown in Figure 11-4 and an e-tailer Web site is shown in Figure 11-5). In either case, these sites (often called online stores) typically feature an online catalog of goods and/or services from which the buyer can select items and then purchase those items via the site. After the purchase is completed, the items are usually either shipped to the buyer (for physical goods) or downloaded by the buyer (for electronic products, such as software, music, video rentals, and e-books). However, some physical goods (most often electronics, furniture, cars, and other heavy items) may be picked up the buyer instead to avoid shipping costs, if permitted by the site.

FIGURE 11-5

Online retailers (e-tailers) sell products and services via their Web sites.

Subscription Sites

Instead of selling an actual physical or electronic product to customers, **subscription sites** sell access to online services. For instance, some online newspapers and journals charge a subscription fee to access online versions of these publications. In addition, some Web-based software requires a monthly or annual subscription fee, and some video-on-demand (VOD) services (like Netflix) offer monthly subscriptions for unlimited movie rental downloads. Instead of requiring a subscription to view any content located on the site, some sites choose to offer some free content to all visitors, but restrict some features to those who subscribe to their *premium content*. For instance, some online communities (such as the Classmates.com site designed to help individuals connect with friends from school that was shown in Figure 1-21 in Chapter 1) require visitors to subscribe before they can receive full access to the services.

Brokerage Sites

Brokerage sites bring buyers and sellers together to facilitate transactions between the two parties and earn revenue in the form of commissions on sales made via the site. Some examples of brokerage sites are discussed next.

>**E-tailer.** An online retailer. >**Subscription site.** A site that sells access to its online content. >**Brokerage site.** A type of Web site that brings buyers and sellers together to facilitate transactions between them; the site earns revenue in the form of commissions on sales made via the site.

Online Auctions

Online auction sites are designed to facilitate the sale of goods and services between individuals or between businesses. *Consumer online auction sites* (such as eBay, shown in Figure 11-6) provide individuals with a structured medium for selling goods and services to other individuals. While designed for C2C transactions, small businesses may use consumer online auction sites to sell their products, in addition to, or instead of, maintaining an e-commerce Web site. And some individuals make a business of selling products entirely via eBay. Online auction sites that are designed for transactions between businesses are referred to as *business online auction sites*.

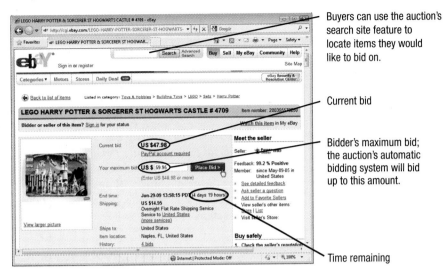

Buyers can use the auction's search site feature to locate items they would like to bid on.

Current bid

Bidder's maximum bid; the auction's automatic bidding system will bid up to this amount.

Time remaining

FIGURE 11-6
How online auctions work.

Both consumer and business online auction sites provide standardized rules so that all bidders are treated equally. To put an item up for auction, the seller provides information about the item, such as a detailed description and a photo. Potential buyers then use the auction site to find items they would like to bid on. To help potential buyers evaluate the trustworthiness of a potential seller before they decide to bid on a particular item, many online auction sites collect comments about transactions (typically called *feedback*) after the transaction has been completed. For instance, a buyer may choose to only bid on items from sellers with a high positive feedback score, such as 98% or higher. Once a prospective buyer decides to bid on an item, he or she places a bid. If a bidder is outbid before the auction closes, he or she can place a higher bid, if desired. To assist with this, some online auction sites (such as eBay, shown in Figure 11-6) have an *automatic bidding system*. To use this option, the bidder specifies a maximum bid and the system automatically keeps bidding (using the minimum bid increment, such as $1) whenever the bidder is outbid until his or her specified maximum bid limit is reached. Bidders are notified (via e-mail or text message, depending on their preference) when they are outbid so they have the opportunity to increase their maximum bid, if desired. Once the online auction closes, the highest bidder finalizes the purchase by arranging payment and delivery directly with the seller.

An online auction site usually obtains revenue from the seller when items are initially listed for sale, as well as when the successful bidder purchases the item. For example, at the time of this writing, the fee for listing an item on eBay ranged from 10 cents to $4, depending on the starting bid specified by the seller; special features, such as specifying the minimum bid amount, adding more than one photo, or having a bolded listing, cost extra. When the online auction closes, the seller also pays the online auction site a percentage of the selling price—usually from 6% on up, depending on the final selling price.

A type of site related to online auctions is the *dynamic pricing site*. Instead of a formal auction with a specific ending time and an automatic winner, these sites—such as Priceline.com—allow buyers to bid on items or services listed for sale, and then the seller decides whether to accept each offer on an individual basis.

> **Online auction site.** A Web site where potential buyers bid on an item and, at the end of a set time period, the highest bidder buys the item as long as all bidding criteria (such as minimum selling price) have been met.

CAUTION CAUTION CAUTION CAUTION CAUTION CAUTION CAUT

A bid on an online auction site like eBay is considered a contract and, if you win the item, you are obligated to buy it. Consequently, do not bid on an auction item unless you are willing to buy it if you are the winning bidder.

Financial Brokerages

Financial brokerage sites facilitate the exchange of financial items (such as stocks, bonds, futures, and options) between buyers and sellers. One example of a financial brokerage site is the online broker (discussed in Chapter 8 and illustrated in Figure 8-23). Financial brokerage sites generate revenue by charging commissions or transaction fees for each transaction.

Real Estate, Travel, and Other Consumer Brokerages

Online real estate brokers and online travel agencies (see Figure 11-7) are two examples of *consumer brokerage sites* that assist consumers in finding the resources they desire, such as a house, airline tickets, hotel reservations, and more. Some brokerage sites (such as real estate sites) may negotiate deals directly with individual buyers and sellers. Others (like travel sites) may choose to broker deals between individuals and businesses only.

Market and Commodity Exchanges

A *market exchange* site is designed to help match organizations with goods or services to sell with potential buyers and to help match buyers looking for specific items with suppliers who can provide those resources. Like online auctions and other brokerage sites, a market exchange site—sometimes referred to as an *e-marketplace*—acts only as an intermediary between the buyer and seller, creating a community in which buyers and suppliers can easily find one another and do business with. However, items are not auctioned; instead, the buyers and suppliers decide which companies they would like to do business with. For instance, buyers may supply specifications of needed products that are sent to qualified suppliers. The suppliers who wish to compete for the business submit a proposal and quote, and then the buyer selects the desired supplier. Products sold via a market exchange site can range from computers to manufacturing parts to specialty equipment and more. When commodities, such as natural resources and raw goods, are being sold, the terms *commodity exchange* and *commodity broker* are sometimes used. Common commodities sold in this manner include energy, cattle, chemicals, and metals. Some market exchange sites earn a fee for each transaction they facilitate; others charge sellers an annual membership fee to participate.

IMPLEMENTING WEB-BASED E-COMMERCE

Several factors should be considered when an organization decides to implement Web-based e-commerce. These include the type of Web site and software to be used, the means of handling financial transactions, strategies for sales and marketing, and security precautions. The process of implementing Web-based e-commerce typically involves the five steps listed in Figure 11-8; these steps and the decisions made during the implementation process are discussed throughout the remainder of this chapter. Some companies perform some or all of these steps themselves; others hire a firm specializing in e-commerce implementation to carry out these tasks for them. Because the in-depth details involved with developing a Web-based e-commerce system are beyond the scope of this book, this discussion focuses on the general tasks involved in this process.

Step 1: Select Appropriate Business Models and Types of Web Sites

The first step for a company planning to implement an e-commerce Web site is to evaluate its business plan and determine which business models are currently being used and which should be used with the new e-commerce system. E-commerce business models are not necessarily mutually exclusive; for example, an e-commerce Web site can sell both to consumers (the B2C model) and to businesses (the B2B model). The company should also decide the type of Web site that best corresponds to the activities to be held via that site, such as selling products or services via an e-tailer site or selling subscriptions to online content. Just as with business models, companies can choose to implement more than one type of site.

TYPICAL STEPS

1. Select appropriate business models and types of Web sites.

2. Select the desired e-commerce applications.

3. Develop procedures for handling electronic financial transactions.

4. Design and develop an effective e-commerce Web site.

5. Implement appropriate sales and marketing strategies.

FIGURE 11-8
Implementing Web-based e-commerce.

Step 2: Select the Desired E-Commerce Applications

In addition to determining the desired business models and types of Web sites to be used, a company should decide which e-commerce applications will be performed. Although most e-commerce Web sites involve online selling, other activities can be implemented, as well. For instance, many e-commerce sites include *electronic customer relationship management* (*eCRM*) activities, which are used to support customers and build relationships with them in order to increase their satisfaction and loyalty. Common eCRM activities include providing product information, online order status information, and links for tracking delivery of shipments; notifying customers about product upgrades and special offers; and providing online technical support, such as via e-mail or live chat (see Figure 11-9). Other factors to be decided include whether an ordering system will be linked in real time to an inventory database, as well as what type of system will be used to process and fulfill customer orders.

Link to open live chat window

Quick links to order status and online help

Account information and preferences options

Order and return information options

FIGURE 11-9
Common eCRM features include order status, return information, and live chat.

Step 3: Develop Procedures for Handling Electronic Financial Transactions

Successfully performing electronic financial transactions is the cornerstone of any e-commerce site. Therefore, a business should give careful thought to which payment options it will offer and how it will process payments securely and accurately. The payment options used with an e-commerce site typically depend on the type of site it is and the types of customers involved. For B2C sites, for instance, the options include standard credit cards and debit cards, and online payment services and other forms of *digital cash*, as discussed next. B2B sites may need to consider additional payment options, such as purchase orders.

Typically, a B2C e-commerce site will use multiple payment options. The available payment options are usually displayed on an e-commerce site's order form or *checkout page* (see Figure 11-10), along with the necessary options to enable customers to enter the appropriate information during the checkout process. As discussed in earlier chapters, order forms should always be set up as secure Web pages. Specific payment options are discussed next.

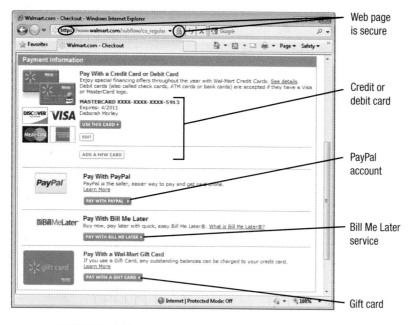

Web page is secure

Credit or debit card

PayPal account

Bill Me Later service

Gift card

FIGURE 11-10

E-commerce payment options.

Each e-commerce site must decide the payment options to be supported.

Credit and Debit Card Processing

Credit card processing is the first thing that comes to mind when considering online payments. Although some people are hesitant to submit their credit card information via a Web page, credit cards are by far the most common payment method used for online purchases. And, though it is possible to run an online business without accepting credit cards, it is essential for most B2C e-commerce sites.

In order to accept credit cards, a business typically opens an *e-commerce merchant account*, also called an *Internet merchant account*—usually from a U.S. bank. The bank that issues this account handles all the credit and debit transactions. Each time an online credit card transaction is made, the bank obtains the money from the issuing credit card company and transfers it to the merchant account. When an online purchase is made using a debit card, the bank deducts the amount from the buyer's checking account and transfers it to the merchant account. For providing these services, the bank usually is paid a monthly fee, plus a transaction fee and a commission (a percentage of the transaction amount) for each credit card or debit card sale. To reduce these fees, one new area of interest is the use of low-cost card-swipe devices by consumers making online purchases with a debit or credit card. Using these devices allows online merchants to use the lower "card-present" processing rates brick-and-mortar stores can use, instead of the more expensive "card-not-present" rates required when the card is not physically used in the transaction. Whether this idea will catch on with online shoppers remains to be seen, but a few e-commerce businesses (such as some airlines and travel sites) have already set up their Web sites to allow card-swipe authorization.

To help alleviate shoppers' concerns about supplying credit card information that might then be used for fraudulent transactions if the information is obtained by a hacker, many credit card companies offer *virtual account numbers* to their cardholders. Virtual account numbers are essentially disposable credit card numbers that can be used to buy goods and services that will be charged to the customer's regular credit card. While some virtual account numbers can be used until the cardholder cancels them, many are good for a single transaction only. Since these *single-use virtual credit card numbers* can be used only one time, they are useless if they are intercepted during transmission or stolen from a Web server's database. In either case, virtual account numbers are usually requested by the cardholder by logging on to his or her credit card online account and clicking a link to generate a new virtual account number. That virtual credit card number is then entered on the e-commerce checkout page, just like a conventional credit card number. Virtual credit card numbers, however, should not be used for transactions (such as airline ticket purchases, hotel stays, BestBuy.com online orders that are picked up at the store, and so forth) that require you to eventually present the physical credit card used in the transaction. Virtual account numbers are also available for many debit cards.

Smart cards (typically credit, debit, or ID cards with embedded computer chips to hold data such as digital cash values or identifying data for authentication purposes, as discussed in Chapter 3) are another option. When used with a smart card reader, e-commerce transactions can be authorized with a password, biometric characteristic, or other access control feature. A newer technology introduced to fight credit card fraud is the use of one-time passwords (OTPs) in conjunction with credit cards. Similar to the OTPs used with access cards (as discussed in Chapter 9), OTPs displayed on credit cards prove that the credit card is in the authorized cardholder's possession at the time the e-commerce purchase is made. This is accomplished by requiring the cardholder to enter his or her PIN number using the keypad built into the card (see Figure 11-11) to generate a temporary

ONLINE VIDEO

Go to the Chapter 11 page at **www.cengage.com/ computerconcepts/np/uc13** to watch the "Secure Shopping with Emue OTP Credit Cards" video clip.

security code that is displayed on the card and that needs to be entered along with the credit card number to authorize the purchase.

For individuals who wish to reduce the liability in the event a credit or debit card is used by an unauthorized individual, *prepaid credit cards* (credit cards that are preloaded with a specific amount of money, which becomes the total liability of the card) can be used. Reloadable prepaid credit cards are available from some credit card companies; disposable cards for a fixed amount can be purchased in some countries, such as in New Zealand where the cards are available at any postal outlet in that country. For the online merchant, the procedure for processing smart credit cards, credit cards that use virtual numbers or OTPs, and prepaid credit cards is the same as the procedure for processing regular credit cards.

Online Payment Services and Other Types of Digital Cash

Online payment methods that electronically transfer money from a buyer to the seller have become increasingly popular—especially for online auction payments. These payment options are sometimes referred to as *digital cash*. The most common way of exchanging digital cash is via an *online payment service*; other forms of digital cash include *digital gift certificates*, *digital gift cards*, and *digital coupons*.

Online Payment Services

There are a number of services available online to help shoppers electronically pay for purchases. One of the most widely used is *PayPal*—an **online payment service** that allows individuals to transfer money easily from their *online payment account* to someone else's. Online payment services are often used to pay for online auction purchases (in fact, PayPal is owned by eBay), but other e-commerce sites can accept PayPal payments as well. To accept PayPal payments, many e-commerce sites simply add a PayPal payment button to their order form; this button brings the buyer to the PayPal site, where the buyer can sign in to his or her account and then enter the necessary data to finalize the transaction. Other e-commerce sites collect the necessary PayPal data on their order forms and the data is processed directly on their e-commerce sites. To pay for an e-commerce purchase via PayPal, you must have a PayPal account (opening an account is free). You can deposit funds from your bank account into that PayPal account before making purchases, set up the account to charge payments to your credit card, or set up the account to transfer the appropriate amount of funds from your bank account as purchases are made.

Individuals can view their PayPal activity, as well as transfer money in and out of their PayPal accounts and request payments from others, via the PayPal Web site (shown in Figure 11-12) or a mobile phone. Payment recipients receive an e-mail message (or text message if

1. Cardholder types his or her PIN number using the keypad.

2. A one-time security code is then displayed to be used to authorize the credit card transaction.

FIGURE 11-11
An OTP credit card.

FIGURE 11-12
How PayPal works.

ADDING/WITHDRAWING MONEY
This tab can be used to add or withdraw money, as well as view your recent transactions.

REQUESTING MONEY
This tab can be used to send a money request or an invoice to others.

SENDING MONEY
Money can be sent to anyone via an e-mail address or mobile phone number; the money is either deducted from the account's balance or charged to a credit card, depending on how the account is set up.

2.0 WEB

> **Online payment service.** A type of payment service accessed via the Internet and used to make electronic payments to others, such as via deposited funds, a bank account, or a credit card.

FIGURE 11-13
The PayPal browser plug-in.

Go **FURTHER EXPLORATION**

Go to the Chapter 11 page at
**www.cengage.com/
computerconcepts/np/uc13**
for links to information about
e-commerce payment options.

the funds were sent to a mobile phone number) when they receive a PayPal payment and can access the money via their PayPal account. For security purposes, PayPal users have the option of using a *PayPal Security Key* during the logon process. Similar to other OTP authentication systems discussed in Chapter 9, the PayPal Security Key generates a random temporary security code (which is displayed on a card like the one shown in Figure 9-5 or is sent via a text message, depending on the user's preference) that must be used in conjunction with the account holder's username and password to sign in to PayPal.

Online payment accounts appeal to many online shoppers because they enable the shopper to pay for purchases via a credit card (and, therefore, be able to dispute charges via the credit card company if a problem arises with a transaction) without revealing the credit card number to the merchant. Merchants using PayPal pay a transaction fee to PayPal, but the fee is typically lower than the fee for processing conventional credit and debit card purchases.

One recent PayPal development is the *PayPal Plug-In* that allows online shoppers to make PayPal payments on any site that accepts MasterCard. Through a partnership with MasterCard, the plug-in generates a unique MasterCard virtual debit card number that is linked to the shopper's PayPal account. The PayPal Plug-In (see Figure 11-13) is displayed on the browser toolbar so the user can generate a secure virtual debit card number whenever it is needed; he or she can choose between a single-use virtual debit card or a virtual debit card that can be used for multiple transactions. The plug-in also has additional useful features, such as the ability to fill in online forms automatically and quick access to the user's PayPal account.

Two additional online payment services are *Bill Me Later* and *eBillme*, which can be selected during the checkout process at participating online stores (see the Bill Me Later option on the Wal-Mart checkout page in Figure 11-10). When either service is selected, the shopper's payment is deferred until after the checkout process is completed. These services pay the online store and bill the shopper separately. The shopper then pays the bill (usually online via the customer's regular online banking account, though some offline payment options are available with both services). Similar to other online payment services, these services provide the consumer the advantage of not having to reveal his or her real credit card number to the online merchant.

Digital Gift Certificates, Gift Cards, and Coupons

Digital gift certificates and *gift cards* are convenient methods of allowing a gift recipient to select his or her own items to buy at an online store. They work similarly to conventional gift certificates and gift cards, but a serial number or other identifying number is entered during the checkout process to use and verify the certificate or card. Some gift certificates and gift cards that are redeemed electronically are purchased in physical form; others are entirely electronic. *Digital coupons* consist of codes—typically called *coupon codes*—that are entered into the appropriate location on a checkout page to deduct the coupon amount from a purchase total. Many sites specialize in gathering and summarizing coupon codes for a variety of online merchants. If an invalid coupon code is entered or if a coupon code has expired, the coupon discount will not be applied. An emerging trend is the use of digital coupons with mobile phones, as discussed in the Trend box.

Digital Wallets

Digital wallets (sometimes referred to as *e-wallets*) offer customers a convenient way of storing information (such as online payment account information, credit card information,

---

>**Digital wallet.** A program or online service that holds a buyer's information (such as electronic payment, billing, and shipping information) that can be used to speed up online purchase transactions.

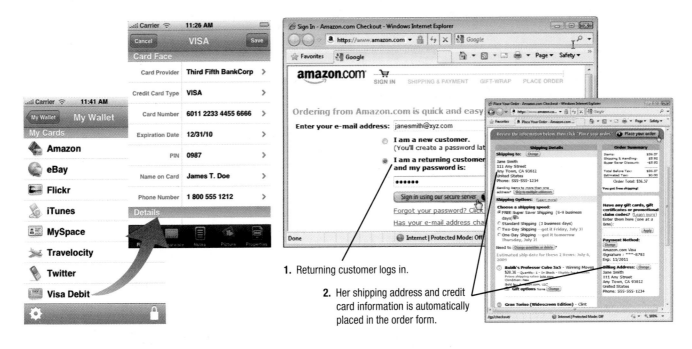

1. Returning customer logs in.

2. Her shipping address and credit card information is automatically placed in the order form.

DIGITAL WALLET PROGRAMS
Allow credit card numbers, Web site passwords, and other important information to be stored; content can be copied to an on-screen order form.

SITE-SPECIFIC DIGITAL WALLETS
Store shipping, billing, and credit card information so that returning customers can place orders quickly and easily.

FIGURE 11-14
Digital wallets.
Digital wallets store billing, payment, and shipping information for faster online shopping transactions.

Web site passwords, and shipping and billing information) that is needed regularly for e-commerce purchases. Digital wallets are available as both stand-alone programs and online services. In either case, the information in the digital wallet is encrypted and protected by a password and the necessary checkout information is transferred (either manually or automatically) to the online order form, as it is needed.

Digital wallet programs are available for both conventional personal computers and mobile phones; an iPhone digital wallet is shown in Figure 11-14. Some digital wallets include a feature that automatically supplies information (such as a username and password) whenever that information is needed for sites that the user specifies in the digital wallet program. Other digital wallets include a menu option to copy the appropriate information (such as a credit card number or shipping address) to the appropriate location on a Web form as needed.

An *online digital wallet* stores the same types of information as a digital wallet program, but the information is accessed online during the checkout procedure instead of by launching the digital wallet program. An example of an online digital wallet that can be used with a variety of e-commerce sites is *Google Checkout*. To use Google Checkout, individuals need to sign up at the Google Checkout site, supplying their shipping, billing, and e-mail address, as well as their credit card information. To make a purchase at a Web site offering Google Checkout, the shopper just selects that option on the checkout page, signs in to Google Checkout, and the transaction is completed using his or her registered information. There are also *site-specific digital wallets* that store checkout information in the customer's account for use with purchases on that site only; for example, see the Amazon.com site shown in Figure 11-14. These digital wallets facilitate purchases on return visits.

E-commerce sites wanting to offer their customers digital wallet services need to decide which types of digital wallets they will support (such as stand-alone digital wallet programs and/or online digital wallets like Google Checkout), as well as whether they wish to offer a custom digital wallet service just for their site.

TREND

Mobile Coupons

For years we have had coupons in the Sunday newspaper, and then digital coupons became available via the Internet. The newest trend in digital coupons is delivery to your mobile phone.

Although common in Asia and Europe for several years, digital coupons delivered to mobile phones is relatively new to the United States. But with businesses and consumers alike now viewing the mobile phone as an essential productivity and communications tool, mobile phone coupon use is growing rapidly. Digital coupons typically are delivered to mobile phones via e-mail or text message, and they can be redeemed by showing the coupon code or having the coupon's barcode scanned at the store or restaurant issuing the coupon, similar to using a paper coupon (and like other mobile phone applications, standard text messaging or data charges apply). To increase effectiveness and prevent unwanted intrusions—particularly because of the potential fees involved with receiving text messages—many mobile coupon companies require consumers to sign up or *opt-in* to coupon delivery. Some include software that can be downloaded to the phone to locate coupons for desired products and services in the user's geographical area, as well as to organize stored coupons and automatically delete expired coupons. Redemption rates for mobile coupons are much higher than for paper coupons—in part, because the coupons aren't forgotten at home.

What is the next step for electronic coupons expected to be? One likely possibility is sending electronic coupons to a mobile phone based on an individual's current geographical location (determined via the GPS capabilities built into most mobile phones today). For instance, an individual who walks by a Starbucks might get an electronic coupon via his or her mobile phone for 50 cents off a mocha Frappuccino. Now that's effective impulse marketing!

Special Considerations for B2B Financial Transactions

Although some of the payment methods already discussed can be used with B2B financial transactions, the large volume of many B2B purchases often requires other considerations.

B2B Transaction Processing

Larger B2B businesses may benefit from using an electronic payment company specializing in *business-to-business transaction processing*. These companies usually allow merchants to customize their payment processing plans to fit their needs. They commonly offer many of the following services:

- Credit card, debit card, check, and digital cash settlement.
- Credit checking for new customers.
- Expense tracking.
- Electronic billing.
- Payment settlement services compatible with other widely used systems (such as *ERP* (*enterprise resource planning*) systems, which are discussed in Chapter 12).
- Consolidation and reconciliation of business transactions, such as order processing, invoicing, and settlement.

➤ *Escrow services* (acting as an intermediary in the payment/delivery process so that the seller does not receive payment until the buyer receives and accepts the merchandise).

Order-Fulfillment Companies

Order-fulfillment companies (also called *e-fulfillment companies*) are companies that provide a distribution network for merchants who cannot or who choose not to process their own orders. Order-fulfillment companies can be used with all e-commerce models, including B2C, B2B, and B2G transactions, and are most commonly used with businesses that have a high transaction volume and that do not already have a warehousing and order processing operation in place to meet their needs. Some of the services that may be offered by an order-fulfillment company include the following:

➤ Order management—real-time online ordering, ideally integrated with purchasing and inventory services.

➤ Distribution services—services such as shipping, inventory, and returns processing.

➤ *Customer relationship management* (*CRM*) services—a professional customer response system that is integrated with the distribution process to provide services, such as order tracking, and designed to help build effective customer relations.

➤ Marketing tools—reports and other tools to assist in strategic planning.

➤ E-fulfillment strategic planning—consulting and development services for areas such as a business's supply chain, database, and e-commerce Web site.

➤ Integration with existing systems—seamless integration of a business's e-commerce site with its other system, such as its ERP system.

Step 4: Design and Develop an Effective E-Commerce Web Site

As discussed in Chapter 10, *Web site design* is the process of planning what a Web site will look like and how it will work, and *Web site development* is the process of building the Web site, including developing all of the components to be used on the Web site, creating the actual Web pages, testing the site, and publishing the site. Additional considerations for e-commerce sites include ensuring order forms and checkout pages are located on a secure Web server, diligently maintaining the Web site, and continually evaluating the security of the Web site and any collected sensitive data. E-commerce Web sites can be designed and developed in-house, although it is common for a business to *outsource* these tasks to a professional Web development company that specializes in e-commerce Web sites. One Web site development tool that is used only when creating an e-commerce Web site (and so was not discussed in Chapter 10) is *storefront software*.

2.0 WEB

Storefront software is a type of software that can be used to create an online store. Storefront software varies widely in capabilities and some programs have multiple versions available in order to create different types of e-commerce businesses. For instance, some programs are most appropriate for a small business owner who wants to begin selling a limited number of products online; others are designed for large businesses that require real-time inventory capabilities, multiple pricing structures, the ability for salespeople to place orders from the field, and other more complex features. Virtually all storefront software programs support credit card sales and secure checkout pages; some have wizards and other tools to help create the storefront quickly and easily.

Storefront software is available in both installed and Web-based versions. If installed storefront software is used, the e-commerce site is usually published to the business's Web server or to a third-party Web hosting service, depending on the preference of the business. Web-based storefront software, however, typically creates the e-commerce site directly on the server where it will be hosted so the site is ready to use as soon as it is finished. An example of creating an online store using Web-based storefront software is shown in Figure 11-15. In addition to creating and hosting a site, Web-based storefront software companies frequently also offer a variety of other services related to creating an

FIGURE 11-15

Web-based storefront services can be used to quickly and easily create an e-commerce site.

CREATING THE SITE
Menu options and wizards are used to input the necessary information, such as the site colors and appearance, products to be sold, checkout options, and more.

THE FINISHED SITE
Uses the content and appearance specified when the site was created.

>**Storefront software.** E-commerce software that facilitates the creation of an online store.

e-commerce Web site, such as domain name registration, Web hosting, SSL and EV SSL certificates for secure Web pages, integration with widely-used accounting software programs, and more.

For businesses that already have an existing Web site and just need to add ordering capabilities and checkout procedures to that site, **shopping cart software** can be used. Some Web hosting services offer free shopping cart software that can be used with Web sites hosted on their servers. However, a large organization may wish to create a customized shopping cart experience for its Web site, in order to better integrate with the existing Web site, company databases, and other company resources.

Whatever method is used to create an e-commerce Web site and storefront, there are a few guidelines to keep in mind to help lower the rate of *shopping cart abandonment* (when a customer places items in his or her cart but never actually purchases them). Shopping cart abandonment is a growing problem for e-commerce sites and, in fact, a recent PayPal study revealed that nearly half of the online shoppers surveyed had abandoned at least one shopping cart within the past three weeks. To improve the chance that online shoppers will actually end up purchasing the items in their carts, make sure the "Add to Cart" button is obvious on all product pages (so users can find it easily when they want to add items to their cart) and the checkout option is located on all pages of the site (so users can start the checkout process whenever they want to). In addition, make sure your product catalog is attractive and organized in an intuitive manner, and make sure the checkout process is as fast and easy as possible for your customers. For instance, only request needed information, fill out as much of the needed information as possible for the customer (such as entering the address of a return customer, having a checkbox to copy the entered shipping address to the billing address section, and preselecting the most common type of shipping option). It is also help-

ful to include a progress indicator (such as "Step 1 of 4") on each checkout page so the customer can anticipate how much more time is needed to finalize the order (see the Wal-Mart example shown in Figure 11-16). On the final checkout page where the customer completes the purchase, keep it simple and consider adding statements to encourage customer trust, such as money back guarantee information, if appropriate, or *privacy* or *security trust certifications* (discussed shortly). For a look at a new easy way to add an online store to your MySpace or Facebook page, see the Technology and You box.

VIDEO PODCAST

Go to the Chapter 11 page at **www.cengage.com/ computerconcepts/np/uc13** to download or listen to the "How To: Create a Free Online Store" video podcast.

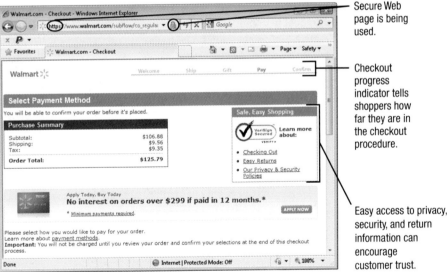

Secure Web page is being used.

Checkout progress indicator tells shoppers how far they are in the checkout procedure.

Easy access to privacy, security, and return information can encourage customer trust.

FIGURE 11-16
Good checkout design.

Step 5: Implement Appropriate Sales and Marketing Strategies

Once an e-commerce Web site has been properly designed, created, and published, there are a variety of strategies to help the business increase traffic to that Web site and increase sales. A few of these strategies are discussed next.

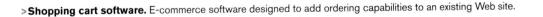

> **Shopping cart software.** E-commerce software designed to add ordering capabilities to an existing Web site.

TECHNOLOGY AND YOU

Creating and Sharing an Online Store with Cartfly

Need a fast and easy way to create an online store? Perhaps *Cartfly* can help. Cartfly is a new e-commerce tool that allows you to create a basic online store quickly and easily and then embed that store into social networking pages, blogs, personal Web pages, and other Web locations. To create a store, you just need an e-mail address and a PayPal account; you can then build the initial store (including the name, price, photo, description, and shipping cost for each product that you wish to sell). The initial store is created on the Cartfly site and can be accessed with a URL such as yoursite.cartfly.com. What is unique about Cartfly is that after the initial store is created, you can easily embed that store into your MySpace or Facebook page, your personal Web site, and/or your blog. In fact, you can add your Cartfly store to any Web site that allows you to add custom code (just a few lines of "share code" need to be copied and pasted to a site to display your storefront on that site). In addition, each embedded Cartfly store contains a "Share Store" button so your friends and any other individuals viewing your store on a Web page can easily add your store to their Web pages. There is no cost to create or share a Cartfly store; instead, Cartfly collects a 3% commission on all transactions generated through a Cartfly store so you only pay when

your store generates sales. While the commission might add up for stores with a high level of sales, for individuals and small businesses that want to get an e-commerce site up and running quickly without a lot of upfront fees, Cartfly might be just the ticket.

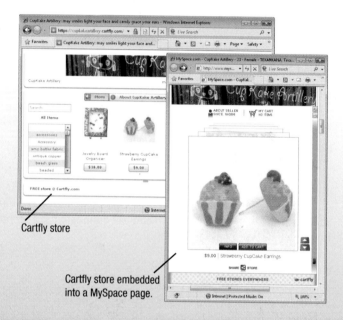

Cartfly store

Cartfly store embedded into a MySpace page.

Use an Appropriate Domain Name and URL

Because many customers will type the URL of an e-commerce site when they want to access that site to make a purchase or to access customer service features, it is important that the URL is easy to remember and easy to type. When selecting and registering a domain name for an e-commerce site, be sure it is an intuitive domain name (such as your business's name or the name of your key product). When setting up the site to use that URL, be sure to use your Web server's default home page name for the home page of your site (as discussed in Chapter 10) so that customers do not need to type anything other than the domain name to access the home page of your Web site. For instance, the home page for Wal-Mart uses the URL walmart.com—visitors do not need to type a Web page name or a folder path in addition to the domain name (such as walmart.com/index.html) to view the home page of that site.

As discussed in Chapter 1, domain names are unique and are registered with an official domain name registrar. You can visit a domain name registrar Web site, such as NetworkSolutions.com or Register.com, to see if a domain name that matches your business's name is available. If your business name is not available, you can try variations of the name—many registration sites automatically help by displaying available names that are similar to the one typed if the name you originally requested is unavailable. Keep in mind, however, that if you own the trademark to your business name, the *Anticybersquatting Consumer Protection Act* protects your trademark in cyberspace. According to the law, domain names similar to a trademarked name cannot be registered, unless the person has a legitimate claim to that name (for example, the domain name is the same as his or her last name) or if the domain name was registered prior to the use of the registered trademark. Registering a domain name in order to cause confusion, to dilute the established trademark, or with the intent of reselling the trademark (called *cybersquatting*) has been ruled illegal and is discussed in more detail in Chapter 16.

Include Adequate Customer Service Features

Every e-commerce Web site should include adequate customer service features to increase customer satisfaction and loyalty. Widely used eCRM services include online order tracking, online versions of product instruction manuals, and customer service via e-mail or live chat. If e-mail support it used, a very short turn-around time—definitely within 24 hours—is essential. Including enough self-service eCRM services (such as links to display FAQs, order status, warranty information, product specs, or product manuals) so that customers can find the information they need on their own can be very cost effective since one cost estimate for a customer speaking with a live customer service agent is $6.85 to $15 per call. However, including a toll-free number that customers can call and speak to a customer service agent, when needed, to place orders or ask questions is also an important service.

ASK THE EXPERT

Sean Kaine, Director of Domain Services, Network Solutions

How will the ability to use custom TLDs in domain names impact businesses?

Custom TLDs will offer businesses new online branding and revenue generation tools, allowing them to create branded ecosystems that go beyond the traditional .com or .net online presence. For example, custom TLDs can be used to deliver consumers intuitively to the appropriate Web site based on the product or service desired, such as producta.xyz or usa.xyz. If a city acquires a custom TLD representing its name, local businesses can use that TLD in their domain to enable customers to locate their businesses easily. In addition, generic new TLDs (such as .auto or .shop) allow businesses to create intuitive domain names (such as domesticdealership.auto or newyork.shop) to improve branding, increase Web site traffic, and improve search rankings. As with current domains, these new domains will be protected from fraud due to the controllable and trusted seal of approval branded TLDs offer.

Collect Taxes from Customers Only If Required by Law

Similar to mail order purchases, purchases made in the U.S. via the Internet have not been universally subject to sales tax. This is the result of a 1992 Supreme Court decision that says states can only collect sales tax on online and catalog sales when the buyer lives in the same state where the merchant maintains a physical presence, such as a brick-and-mortar store or distribution center. However, the increasing percentage of state sales tax revenue lost as the result of online shopping (one study estimates the total annual sales tax losses due to e-commerce will total approximately $12 billion in 2012) has prompted many state and local governments to want the law to change. Currently, Congress is considering legislation to permit states to require out-of-state online and mail-order retailers to collect sales taxes on purchases made to residents of those states. No federal legislation has passed at the time of this writing, although New York recently passed a law to that effect that has been upheld despite the fact that it contradicts the U.S. Supreme Court ruling. To facilitate mandatory online sales tax collection, the *Streamlined Sales Tax Project* (*SSTP*) has been in development since 2000. The goal of this project is to simplify the sales tax collection process enough to make it feasible to collect sales tax on all online purchases; currently, 23 states have adopted the streamlined tax rules. While U.S. consumers located in states with sales taxes are supposed to keep track of non-taxed purchases and pay a *use tax* when they file their income taxes, they do not have to do this at the time of purchase so collecting sales taxes only when you are required to might be a draw for your Web site.

Display a Privacy Policy and Security Statement

Many online consumers are very concerned about their online privacy and security when purchasing items over the Internet. To reassure these customers, all e-commerce sites should develop and display a privacy policy stating how collected information will be used; e-commerce sites should also consider being certified by an organization that offers a

TRUSTE TRUSTMARK

VERISIGN SECURED SEAL

FIGURE 11-17

Web site privacy
and security seals.

FIGURE 11-18

Keyword meta tags.
Keywords added to a
Web page by the Web
page author are used
by search sites when
classifying that page in
their search databases.

privacy seal. One of the most recognized privacy seals is the *TRUSTe trustmark* shown in Figure 11-17. Web sites displaying the TRUSTe trustmark must adhere to established privacy principles and agree to comply with ongoing TRUSTe oversight and consumer resolution procedures.

As mentioned earlier in this chapter, all exchanges of financial information should take place on a secure Web page. A security statement or a link to a security policy (such as the one on the Walmart.com checkout Web page in Figure 11-16) should be used to reassure customers that their transactions are secure and their information cannot be intercepted by a third party when it is transferred over the Internet. *Security seals* (such as the *VeriSign Secured Seal* shown in Figure 11-17) can also be used. Security seals are issued by the Certificate Authority issuing the site's SSL or EV SSL certificate and are designed to remind shoppers that the site is protected by that certificate (as with any secure Web site, shoppers can click the appropriate security icon in the Address bar of their browser to view and verify the site's certificate).

Promote Your Web Site Sufficiently

Promotion of your site—that is, advertising its existence, purpose, and URL—is critical to ensure that customers are aware of your site and can find it when they want to shop online. Since the typical Web site gets more than 60% of its traffic from search engine results, one of the best ways to promote your site is by getting it listed with as many search sites—such as Google, Yahoo!, Bing, Cuil, Excite, AltaVista, and Ask.com—as fast and accurately as you can. Usually this process involves two steps. First, be sure to include appropriate **meta tags** on the pages of your site. Meta tags are special HTML or XHTML codes that provide information about a Web page and that are inserted into a Web page's code at the time the page is created. The *keywords meta tag* is used to specify keywords that should be associated with that page (see Figure 11-18); that is, the search terms you expect people to enter when searching for your Web page. These meta tags are then used by many (but not all) search engines to classify the Web page when it is added to a search database. The *description meta tag* is also used by some search sites to classify the page, as are the page titles and major headings. Consequently, these items should contain appropriate keywords as well.

Since it may take some time until your Web page is classified automatically by a search site's spider program traveling the Web, the second step is to submit your site directly to search sites. Some search sites may not take submissions and others may only take suggestions for additions to their search databases—check each search site for a link to more information about that site's policy. To submit a site to a search site, typically a form is filled out specifying the title, URL, description, keywords, and other information needed to classify the page appropriately. Businesses can also use *site submission services*, which submit the site's keywords and other data

L.L.Bean
home page

The description and
keywords associated
with the L.L. Bean
home page.

>**Meta tag.** A special HTML or XHTML tag containing information about a Web page that is added by the person creating the Web page and is used primarily by search sites.

to several search sites at one time, usually for a fee of about $200 or less. Many businesses find that using a submission service is the most efficient means of promoting a new site.

Another option for promoting an e-commerce Web site is to become a *sponsored link* or *sponsored listing* on a search site's results page. Sponsored links are associated with a specific search term and are the links displayed first or in a special sponsored links area whenever that term is searched for. To become a sponsored link, companies bid against other companies interested in the same keyword or phrase by specifying the maximum amount they are willing to pay each time someone viewing the search results clicks on the sponsored link. Often, the search site will allow more than one Web site to be associated with a keyword or phrase—the company paying the highest amount per click (called the *cost per click* or *CPC*) is listed first in the sponsored link list. To avoid unexpected charges, some search sites allow companies to specify a maximum budget per billing period—after that amount is reached, that company's Web site will not be a sponsored link until the next billing period begins. Typical CPCs range from a few cents to about $15 per click, depending on the search term (*Google AdWords* allows CPCs from 1 cent to $100). For a look at one new controversial topic related to sponsored listings—*click fraud*—see the Inside the Industry box.

An important tool that Web site developers can use to evaluate the effectiveness of their search site strategy is **search site optimization (SSO)**. Search site optimization is the process of making changes to Web pages, as needed, to increase their visibility in search site results. The goal of SSO is for your Web site to be listed as close as possible to the top of the search result hits that are displayed when an individual performs a Web search using keywords related to your site or business. In addition to evaluating the use of keywords and the other strategies already discussed, the SSO process can identify other possible areas for improved site promotion, such as links to your site from other sites. For instance, you can consider negotiating link exchanges with other well-known, but noncompeting, Web sites. In addition, since many search results today include links to content other than traditional Web pages (such as links to videos and blogs), you may be able to create additional hits to search results by utilizing that content. For instance, you can add properly tagged nontraditional content to your Web site, as well as upload that content to other sites that will be classified by search site spiders (such as uploading company video clips to YouTube and press releases to online news sites). If desired, companies can hire an SSO company to audit its Web site and make recommendations for improvement.

Another promotional option that should be considered is the placement of *banner ads* (ads like the ones shown in Figure 11-19 that are linked to the advertised company's Web site) on other Web sites. While banner ads originally were static ads, it is more common today to use dynamic banner ads that play a short video or animation sequence when the page hosting the banner ad is displayed. Use of these dynamic multimedia ads—called *rich media ads*—is growing. In fact, they accounted for nearly 40% of total online display ads in 2007 and they are expected to grow to about two-thirds of the display ad market by 2011, according to JupiterResearch. To place banner ads on appropriate Web sites, typically an online advertising firm is used and the company pays a fee to each Web site on which its banner ad is displayed, as well as a fee to the advertising company. An alternative that is especially appropriate for small businesses with limited advertising budgets is free banner ad placement, such as via *banner ad exchanges* that facilitate displaying banner ads for your site on other Web sites, in return for you displaying other banner ads on your site.

Several strategies can be used in conjunction with banner ads to make them more effective. One strategy is using software and *Web analytic tools* to analyze the performance of online ads and modify them as needed—a procedure referred to as *optimizing ads*. According to one estimate, optimized ads perform 15 to 30% better than their standard counterparts.

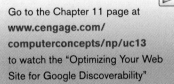
> **Search site optimization (SSO).** The process of evaluating a Web site and making changes as needed to improve search site results.

STATIC BANNER ADS
These ads are linked to their corresponding Web sites; the ads are not animated.

RICH MEDIA BANNER ADS
These ads contain animated components that play when viewed on a Web page; the ads are also linked to their corresponding Web sites.

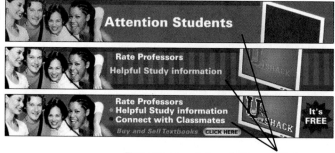

These ads are part of a set of banners that are displayed one after the other until the completed ad (the bottom image) is displayed.

FIGURE 11-19
Banner ads. Banner ads, in a variety of shapes and sizes, are used on Web sites for marketing purposes.

Another strategy is the use of *behavioral ads*—that is, ads that are targeted to individuals based on their preferences, buying habits, or interests. These preferences are usually determined by cookies placed on participating Web sites by advertising networks; the cookies keep track of the Web pages visited on each site belonging to the network, the ads that were clicked, and if that individual bought anything, and appropriate ads are then displayed based on the determined interests.

Another technique is using *ad retargeting* services. With ad retargeting, an e-commerce site notes any visitors who visit the site but don't make a purchase and then passes the visitor's information to an ad retargeting company. When the visitor visits another Web site that is part of the same retargeting network within a specified time frame (such as one month), the retargeting firm displays ads containing special offers or discounts related to the original e-commerce site that the visitor viewed. Typically, the visitor receives one to five retargeted ads during a period of about 30 days and the value of the special offers often increase with each ad.

While some individuals view any type of targeted ad as a potential privacy risk, marketers stress that they are careful to protect the privacy of individuals. For instance, most targeted ads today are based on the individual's interest (determined by the Web pages visited), but they are not linked to that individual's identity. Google's *AdWords* keyword ads (banner ads displayed on the search results page based on the keywords that the user entered in the search box) are one of the first successes of behavioral targeting and part of the reason for its recent growth.

Behavioral targeting can also be used to generate additional revenue within a single site. For instance, Amazon.com lists product recommendations for signed-in customers that are based on products purchased in the past from Amazon.com, as well as products recently viewed on that Web site. Personalized shopping experiences are a powerful way to satisfy customers and keep them coming back to a Web site.

A final important promotional strategy is regularly updating your site with new content. Visitors are more likely to visit your Web site on a regular basis if you consistently refresh it with interesting or exciting information or with offers to win free products or services. Sweepstakes and contests are especially popular, as are blogs, podcasts, videos, special offers from Web site sponsors, and other regularly updated content. If you require an e-mail address to register for a prize, contest, or other special service, these promotional strategies can help you build your

INSIDE THE INDUSTRY

Click Fraud

Click fraud occurs when sponsored links (see the accompanying image)—such as on a search site results page—are clicked when there is no interest in the product or service associated with the sponsored link. The links can be clicked by a person or by an automated clicking program (sometimes referred to as a *click-bot* and often performed by botnets). The motive for click fraud is usually financial. For instance, although viewed as unethical in the business world, a company might click on a competitor's sponsored links in order to deplete that company's advertising budget. In addition, some companies or individuals create Web pages consisting primarily of sponsored links (usually sponsored links from Google, Yahoo!, or other search sites that are placed on other sites via ad networks) for the purpose of click fraud. Web sites hosting a sponsored link get a fee each time the link on that page is clicked, so these companies or individuals manually or automatically (via software or botnets) click the ads on their sites to fraudulently generate revenue. In fact, the independent click fraud monitoring and reporting service Click Forensics estimates that more than 60% of all ad traffic coming from these types of sites is fraudulent.

Click fraud is growing (Click Forensics estimates that approximately 13% of all online ad clicks are attributed to click fraud), and so it is the subject of some controversy and increasing litigation. For instance, Google recently agreed to pay $90 million to settle a class action lawsuit alleging the search site was charging companies for clicks not generated by legitimate users. To try to prevent overcharging companies due to click fraud, both Google and Yahoo! try to identify clicks associated with click fraud and credit the advertiser's account accordingly; however, many advertisers feel that the search sites could do a better job combating click fraud. The problem is compounded by the fact that, as search sites improve their ability to detect click fraud, the fraudsters continue to develop ways to disguise click fraud. Pay-per-click advertising is currently one of the fastest-growing types of advertising, but some fear that click fraud may inhibit further growth of Web-based advertising unless a solution is reached.

> Sponsored Links
>
> **Nintendo Wii**
> Save on **Nintendo Wii** & Other Video
> Games at MSN Shopping - Shop Now!
> Shopping.MSN.com

customer database to target promotions and marketing materials to potential customers. Some marketing activities that can be performed via e-mail include offers of free shipping to return customers and notifications of new products or specials on products in which those customers might be interested. According to experts, all e-mail marketing campaigns should be free of errors and attractive to read. They should also include an easy way for the customer to respond to the message or forward it to a friend, provide links to more information about products or services mentioned in the e-mail, and provide a way for the recipient to unsubscribe to future e-mail messages if they want to opt out.

SECURITY ISSUES

Many security topics related to an e-commerce site (such as securing a network against hackers, encryption, and digital certificates) were discussed in Chapter 9, but security is such an important topic for e-commerce that some of the key points are emphasized here. An e-commerce Web site must provide the following:

> ➤ *Secure transactions*—All financial transactions should take place on a secure Web server; secure Web sites use encryption to safely transfer sensitive data over the Internet.

> ➤ *Secure sensitive documents and files*—Sensitive business documents should also be encrypted when sent to protect their contents while in transit; encrypted documents can be decrypted by the authorized party when they are received.

> ➤ *Authenticate online business partners*—Tools such as digital certificates and digital signatures can be used to verify and authenticate the validity of each party involved in an Internet transaction. This is especially important when contracts and other important documents are signed and exchanged electronically.

WEB 2.0

SUMMARY

WHAT IS E-COMMERCE?

Chapter Objective 1:
Explain what e-commerce is and describe some of the advantages and disadvantages involved with implementing e-commerce.

The term **e-commerce** is used to describe the process of performing financial transactions online. Although implemented today most commonly via the Internet, e-commerce has been performed for years via private networks, such as *electronic funds transfers* (*EFT*) by banks. E-commerce is growing at a rapid pace. One rapidly growing type of e-commerce is **m-commerce** (*mobile commerce* performed via mobile phones or other mobile devices). A **brick-and-mortar store** is a traditional store with a physical presence; online stores that also have a physical presence are sometimes called *click-and-mortar stores*. Internet-only stores are sometimes referred to as **dot-coms**.

The benefits of e-commerce to businesses include reduced cost (as the result of needing smaller facilities and lower staff requirements, among other things), increased customer satisfaction (due to the convenience factor of online shopping and the ability to implement a variety of *electronic customer relationship management* (*eCRM*) services via the Web), a broader customer base (since there are no geographical boundaries for online stores), and potentially higher sales. For consumers, the benefits include convenience, easier comparison-shopping, a higher degree of selection, possible lower cost, and the ability to order customized products. The disadvantages of e-commerce for businesses include losing sales when their Web sites are down, loss of sales to customers who are not comfortable performing transactions online, a higher rate of fraudulent transactions, and the recurring threat of new competition from dot-coms offering lower prices. Possible disadvantages for consumers include the potential for fraud, not being able to see and touch items before purchasing them, and the cost of returning items.

E-COMMERCE BUSINESS MODELS

Chapter Objective 2:
Identify a variety of e-commerce business models and discuss their differences.

A company's *business model* defines its policies, operations, and technology in generating revenue. **E-commerce business models** typically define the types of buyers and sellers involved. Some of the most common e-commerce business models include the **business-to-consumer** (**B2C**), **business-to-business** (**B2B**), **consumer-to-consumer** (**C2C**), and **business-to-government** (**B2G**) **models**. With B2C, businesses sell products and services directly to consumers; with B2B, businesses sell products and services to other businesses; C2C transactions are between consumers; and B2G transactions are between businesses and government agencies.

TYPES OF E-COMMERCE WEB SITES

Chapter Objective 3:
Discuss the types of Web sites that can be used to implement e-commerce.

An e-commerce business model can also be described by the types of Web sites used for e-commerce activities. Some of the most common are manufacturer sites and **e-tailer** (online retailer) Web sites (which sell goods or services online), **subscription sites** (which charge a fee for online content), and **brokerage sites** (which bring buyers and sellers together and facilitate transactions between them). **Online auction sites** are brokerage sites that allow individuals and/or companies to bid on merchandise and the winning bidder purchases the item. Other brokerage sites that facilitate transactions include *financial brokerages* (such as those used to buy and sell stocks online), *consumer brokerages* (used to assist consumers in finding the resources they desire, such as a house or an airline ticket), and *market exchanges* (used to allow buyers to more easily find the suppliers of the goods they need). Brokerage sites typically obtain revenue by charging commissions, fees for each brokered transaction, or annual fees.

IMPLEMENTING WEB-BASED E-COMMERCE

When implementing Web-based e-commerce, five basic steps are usually followed. First, the types of business models and Web sites to be used are selected (a site may select one or more than one of each type). Then, the desired e-commerce applications are determined. The business must also decide how to handle the electronic financial transactions that occur via the site. Most B2C sites accept credit card and debit card payments; for increased security, customers can use *virtual credit cards* or credit cards that are secured with a PIN and one-time password (OTP). Other possibilities include accepting *smart cards*; payments via **online payment services** (such as *PayPal*); and *digital gift certificates*, *digital gift cards*, and/or *digital coupons*. Some customers may want to use a **digital wallet** to supply shipping and billing information; e-commerce sites can also choose to implement a *site-specific digital wallet* to remember this information for return customers. In general, each online business must decide which payment possibility it wants to support.

B2B sites may want to consider using a *B2B transaction processing service* or *order-fulfillment company* to assist with their transactions. These businesses can help with payment processing, billing, customer relationship services, escrow services, and other services.

The design and development of an e-commerce Web site are extremely important. An intuitive, easy-to-use site is a must. In addition, the site must be secure so that potential customers feel confident performing financial transactions online. **Storefront software** is commonly used to create an e-commerce site; **shopping cart software** can be used to add shopping cart capabilities to an existing Web site. Storefront software is available both in packaged form and as a Web-based service. Good design of the site and checkout procedure can help avoid *shopping cart abandonment*.

After an e-commerce site has been completed, some of the strategies the site can use to increase traffic and sales include adequate customer service features, collecting sales tax only if required by law, displaying privacy and security statements prominently on the site, using an appropriate domain name and URL so customers can find and access the site easily, and promoting the Web site sufficiently. Using appropriate **meta tags** (special HTML or XHTML codes that provide information about a Web page and are inserted into a Web page's code by the person creating the Web page), submitting the site to search sites, and using *banner ads* on other sites are all ways of promoting the site. *Sponsored links* are another possibility, although *click fraud* is a growing concern. Some growing online marketing trends are *rich media ads*, *behavioral targeting*, and *ad retargeting*. To encourage visitors to return, sites should be updated on a regular basis. Interesting content, such as blogs, videos, and sweepstakes, can help generate return visits. **Search site optimization (SSO)** can help a business evaluate its Web site and improve search site results.

SECURITY ISSUES

Some of the key security issues that all businesses conducting e-commerce activity should be concerned with are using a secure Web server for all financial transactions to ensure credit card numbers and other sensitive data are transferred securely over the Internet, encrypting sensitive documents and files sent over the Internet, and authenticating online business partners.

Chapter Objective 4:
List several strategies for implementing e-commerce using the Web, including some of the decisions that need to be made, the options available for accepting payments, and the process of designing and developing an effective Web site.

Chapter Objective 5:
Outline some sales and marketing strategies that can be used in conjunction with an e-commerce Web site.

Chapter Objective 6:
Discuss some security issues related to e-commerce sites.

2.0 WEB

REVIEW ACTIVITIES

KEY TERM MATCHING

a. brick-and-mortar store

b. business-to-business (B2B) model

c. business-to-consumer (B2C) model

d. digital wallet

e. e-commerce

f. e-tailer

g. m-commerce

h. meta tag

i. online payment service

j. storefront software

Instructions: Match each key term on the left with the definition on the right that best describes it.

1. _____ A conventional store with a physical presence.

2. _____ A type of payment service accessed via the Internet and used to make electronic payments to others, such as via deposited funds, a bank account, or a credit card.

3. _____ An e-commerce model in which a business provides goods or services to other businesses.

4. _____ An e-commerce model in which a business provides goods or services to consumers.

5. _____ A program or online service that holds a buyer's information (such as electronic payment, billing, and shipping information) that can be used to speed up online purchase transactions.

6. _____ An online retailer.

7. _____ E-commerce carried out via mobile phones and other mobile devices.

8. _____ E-commerce software that facilitates the creation of an online store.

9. _____ A special HTML or XHTML tag containing information about the Web page that is added by the person creating a Web page and is used primarily by search sites.

10. _____ The act of doing business transactions over the Internet or similar technology.

SELF-QUIZ

Instructions: Circle **T** if the statement is true, **F** if the statement is false, or write the best answer in the space provided. **Answers for the self-quiz are located in the References and Resources Guide at the end of the book.**

1. **T F** E-commerce typically takes place via the Internet.

2. **T F** Because most users shop online during the daytime, e-commerce sites can shut down for maintenance during the middle of the night without losing sales.

3. **T F** An e-commerce business model describes how the company generates revenue, such as the types of buyers and sellers involved.

4. **T F** A business can only use one type of e-commerce business model.

5. **T F** An example of an online payment service is PayPal.

6. A(n) _____ site brings together buyers and sellers to facilitate transactions between them and earns revenue in the form of commissions on sales made via the site.

7. A(n) _____ can help speed up online purchases by storing a buyer's payment, shipping, and billing information so it can be supplied electronically.

8. A(n) _____ is an advertisement, usually image-based, that is placed on one site and that is linked to the advertised site; can be static or dynamic.

9. _____ is the process of evaluating a Web site and making changes to improve search site results.

10. Match each e-commerce business model with its description, and write the corresponding number in the blank to the left of each description.

   a. _____ Online bookstore, such as BarnesandNoble.com.

   b. _____ Consumer auction site, such as eBay.

   c. _____ Office supply storefront selling primarily to businesses.

   1. B2C
   2. B2B
   3. C2C

EXERCISES

1. List two potential advantages of e-commerce for a business.

2. List two potential disadvantages of e-commerce for a business.

3. Match each description with its best payment method, and write the corresponding number in the blank to the left of each description.

   a. _____ A person buying a book from Amazon.com who does not have an online payment account.

   b. _____ A person who wants to type in a code found on a Web site to reduce the cost of a purchase.

   c. _____ A person purchasing an inexpensive item from an individual via an online auction.

   1. Credit card
   2. Online payment account
   3. Digital coupon

4. Answer the following questions regarding e-commerce Web site marketing strategies.

   a. Which of the following three URLs would be the best to use for the home page of an online store called "Johnson Music Supply" that sells sheet music, instrument supplies, and so forth? Explain your answer.

      www.johnson.com   www.johnson.net   www.johnsonmusic.com

   b. For the Johnson Music Supply online store described in the previous question, list five possible keywords that should be included as meta tags in the site's home page HTML code.

5. A(n) _____ ad includes video, animation, or other dynamic content; a(n) _____ ad is displayed for an individual based on his or her preferences, buying habits, or interests.

DISCUSSION QUESTIONS

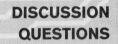

1. A luxury can be defined as something that is an indulgence, rather than a necessity. Most people in the world would view items such as food, shelter, and water as necessities. In the United States, many would likely add electricity and indoor plumbing to that list. Today, many individuals are beginning to view Internet access as a necessity. But is it really a necessity—that is, essential for existence? If so, what about the individuals who do not have Internet access or those who choose not to use it? How might the perception of Internet access being or not being a necessity affect the growth of e-commerce?

2. An increasing amount of state sales tax revenue is being lost due to online shopping; as a result, many states want that law to change and plans are underway for a national online sales tax plan that would apply a simplified, standardized sales tax on all online, mail-order, and telephone purchases. Do you think an online sales tax plan should be enacted? If so, do you think online sales will decline? If you do not think online sales should be taxed, will other taxes need to be increased if state tax revenues continue to decline as more and more purchases are made online? What is the best solution to this issue?

PROJECTS

1. **M-Commerce** As discussed in the chapter, mobile commerce (m-commerce) is becoming available in the U.S. and other countries.

    For this project, research the current status of m-commerce in the United States. What types of m-commerce services are available via mobile phone today? If you have a mobile phone, what types of m-commerce transactions do you have access to? Have you used them? Can you use an RFID-based system, such as the service offered to MasterCard holders, with your phone? Are there any locations in your area in which you could purchase goods or services using a mobile phone RFID payment system? At the conclusion of your research, prepare a one-page summary of your findings and opinions and submit it to your instructor.

2. **Click Fraud** As discussed in the Inside the Industry box, click fraud occurs when sponsored links are clicked with the goal of costing the sponsor money.

    For this project, research click fraud and determine how big the problem is and the form it most commonly takes today. What are search sites doing to detect or prevent click fraud? What actions can a company take if it believes it is a victim of click fraud? Is click fraud illegal? At the conclusion of your research, prepare a one-page summary of your findings and submit it to your instructor.

3. **Storefront Options** As discussed in the chapter, there are several options for adding storefront capabilities to an existing Web site.

    For this project, suppose you have a small business with a basic Web site and you want to add online shopping capabilities. Select one of the options discussed next and investigate it thoroughly to determine the steps and costs involved. In addition to the questions listed below, answer the following for your selected option: Will the storefront be tied into a database that you will update? How will items be added and deleted from the storefront as your business evolves? Is there a maximum number of items the system will handle? At the conclusion of your research, submit a short summary of your findings to your instructor.

    a. **Web developer option:** Contact one possible firm, explain your hypothetical situation, and request a rough quotation in both cost and time to get the storefront up and running.

    b. **Software option:** Locate and choose one particular product and find out more about it to form an opinion about the software and how easy it is to use. Determine the approximate pricing of the product and what types of Web sites it is compatible with. Can the software be used in conjunction with a Web development program, such as Dreamweaver or Microsoft Expression Web?

    c. **Web host option:** Contact one possible firm, explain your hypothetical situation, and request a rough quotation in both cost and time to get the storefront up and running. Is the software compatible with any types of Web sites or are there restrictions?

4. **Internet Sales Tax** Based on a 1992 Supreme Court decision regarding mail order sales tax collection, online purchases in the U.S. have not been subject to sales tax, unless the buyer lives in the same state where the merchant maintains a physical presence. However, some online merchants now voluntarily collect sales tax and mandatory sales tax collection on online purchases is a possibility for the future. This issue brings up ethical decisions for both businesses and individuals. Should a business collect sales tax, even if it isn't required to by law? Why or why not? Consumers who live in a state that collects sales tax are technically required to pay a "use" tax to the state when an Internet retailer doesn't collect sales tax. Do you think individuals that are required to pay a use tax will do so ? Why or why not? Is it unethical for a person not to pay this tax? If so, how careful should individuals be with respect to keeping track of online purchases for tax purposes?

   For this project, form an opinion about Internet sales tax collection and the ethical implications for businesses and consumers. Be prepared to discuss your position (in class, via an online class discussion group, in a class chat room, or via a class blog, depending on your instructor's directions). You may also be asked to write a short paper expressing your opinion.

5. **Your Domain** As mentioned in the chapter, e-commerce Web sites should select domain names that are easy for customers to remember.

   For this project, select a domain name you would like to use for a fictitious e-commerce site. Visit at least two domain name registration Web sites (such as NetworkSolutions.com and Register.com) to determine how you would register your domain name and the cost. Which top-level domains would you be able to use for your Web site? For each, determine any requirements, such as length and allowable characters. Think of an appropriate domain name for your site and use a lookup feature available on a registration site to see if that domain name is available. If not, keep trying variations of that name until you find an appropriate available domain name. Would the available name be easy for customers to remember? Share your findings with the class in the form of a short presentation. The presentation should not exceed 10 minutes and should make use of one or more presentation aids, such as the chalkboard, handouts, overhead transparencies, or a computer-based slide presentation (your instructor may provide additional requirements). You may also be asked to submit a summary of the presentation to your instructor.

Instructions: Go to the Chapter 11 page at **www.cengage.com/computerconcepts/np/uc13** to work the following Web Activities.

6. **Interactive Activities** Work the interactive **Crossword Puzzle**, watch the **Video Podcasts** and **Online Videos**, and explore the **Further Exploration** links associated with this chapter.

   If you have a SAM user profile, you may have access to hands-on instruction, practice, and assessment of the skills covered in this chapter. Check with your instructor for instructions and the correct URL/Web site to access those assignments.

7. **Student Edition Labs** Work the following interactive **Student Edition Labs**.

   ➤ **E-Commerce**   ➤ **Web Design Principles**   ➤ **Creating Web Pages**

8. **Test Yourself** Review the **Online Study Guide** for this chapter, then test your knowledge of the terms and concepts covered in this chapter by completing the **Key Term Matching** exercise, the **Self-Quiz**, the **Exercises**, and the **Practice Test**.

Web-Based Multimedia and E-Commerce

Jim Griffith, aka "Griff," is the Dean of eBay Education, a roving eBay ambassador, an eBay spokesperson, the host of eBay Radio, and the author of *The Official eBay Bible*. An enthusiastic eBay buyer and seller since 1996, Griff spends nearly all his waking hours teaching others how to use eBay effectively, safely, and profitably, and spreading the word about eBay across print, radio, and TV. Griff has worked for eBay for 13 years.

A Conversation with JIM GRIFFITH
Dean of eBay Education, eBay

"In the future, more brick-and-mortar business owners will adopt the Internet as a primary or secondary channel for their businesses."

My Background ...

Although I have many roles at eBay, my most public role—Dean of eBay Education—is unique, slightly unorthodox, and best understood in the context of my history with the company. I was originally a user on eBay in the very early days (1996) and spent a lot of time assisting other buyers and sellers on eBay's one chat board. My posts came to the attention of eBay founder Pierre Omidyar who offered me a job as eBay's first customer support rep. I continued to be an active member of the eBay community along with my new duties at the time, which included assisting and teaching buyers, sellers, and eBay employees how to use eBay. Over time, I also became an eBay spokesperson, lead instructor of our eBay University program, author of *The Official eBay Bible* (now in its third edition), and host of eBay Radio.

In addition to the obvious knowledge of the eBay Web site, our policies, and the basics of business, the skills that proved to be most critical during my thirteen-year tenure at eBay (and I should say I am still refining them) would be diplomacy, empathy, civility, and a strong sense of self-deprecating humor.

It's Important to Know ...

The basic principles behind successful e-commerce are no different than those behind traditional offline commerce. For example, the most valuable asset for any business, online or offline, is the customer. This is especially true for e-commerce where the competition for customers is fierce. Although the technologies and transaction experience for the Web and for traditional retail are markedly different, the standard, tried-and-true business basics (such as business planning, inventory procurement and management, and marketing) are as crucial to e-commerce as they are to traditional business.

The importance of an easy-to-use, well-designed, and appealing Web site. All of the inventory in the world is for naught if the buyer cannot search through it and purchase it with ease.

Online commerce technologies are constantly changing. What is cutting edge today will soon be passé. Anyone who makes his or her living online absolutely must stay on top of all online marketplace technology advances and adopt and implement them as necessary. Consumers in general—and online consumers in particular—are much more business and technology savvy than they were a mere 5 years ago. Demanding consumers will have little or no patience for online businesses that do not provide the best possible shopping experience.

How I Use this Technology ...

Besides working for eBay, I am an avid consumer and seller online. I make at least one online purchase a day and I always have a selection of items up for sale (on eBay). My online e-commerce activity along with my job of instructing and assisting buyers and sellers to navigate and utilize eBay and PayPal requires an extensive working knowledge of and familiarity with our own Web sites (eBay and PayPal).

What the Future Holds . . .

The Internet revolution has in many ways changed the nature of human commerce forever. The most important impact of the Internet revolution has been the empowerment of the consumer. Never before has the buyer had so much control over the direction of the marketplace. This will only increase as time goes on, and the businesses that acknowledge this new reality and plan accordingly are the ones that will survive and thrive.

In the future, more brick-and-mortar business owners will adopt the Internet as a primary or secondary channel for their businesses. In addition, more small businesses will start up solely on the Internet as the cost of entry into the online marketplace continues to drop and the gap in the costs of starting an online and offline business continues to grow. This will lead to even more choices for the online consumer, who will continue to exert increasing service demands and pricing pressure on online sellers.

However, as the Internet becomes more a part of our day to day lives, the idea of the Internet as a unique environment will start to disappear, especially as access to the Internet becomes cheaper and more widespread (for example, embedded in appliances, cell phones, media devices, and even the walls of our homes!). Just like technologies before it (such as telegraph, telephone, radio, and television), we will soon take the Internet for granted as it matures and eventually becomes completely entwined within the matrix of our daily lives.

"Anyone who makes his or her living online absolutely must stay on top of all online marketplace technology advances and adopt and implement them as necessary."

My Advice to Students . . .

Unless you're interested in pursuing a career in computer science, engineering, or programming, an academic study of the inner workings of the Internet or computers will not be a requirement for a career in an Internet-based industry. However, Internet companies will have an ever-increasing demand for inventive product marketing personnel, product designers, and intellectual property attorneys.

That said, whatever career you pursue, never forget that the direction of online commerce (and the world in general) is toward more control in the hands of the individual. Adjust your career path accordingly!

Discussion Question

Jim Griffith views the online buyer as an extremely influential part of the e-commerce marketplace. Think of online purchases you have made. How did your buying decision differ from shopping locally? What factors influenced your final decision? How does the increased number of online sources for products impact the online marketplace? Do consumers have more influence over online stores than over brick-and-mortar stores? Why or why not? If you were starting a business, would you have an e-commerce presence? A brick-and-mortar presence? Both? Be prepared to discuss your position (in class, via an online class discussion group, in a class chat room, or via a class blog, depending on your instructor's directions). You may also be asked to write a short paper expressing your opinion.

> For more information on eBay, visit www.ebay.com. For more information about e-commerce, read *FutureShop* by Daniel Nissanoff, and for more information about effective, safe, and successful buying or selling on eBay, refer to *The Official eBay Bible* by Jim "Griff" Griffith.

module

Systems

The hardware and software discussed in earlier chapters in this book, along with data, people, and procedures, all work together to form a variety of systems. These systems are the topic of this module.

Chapter 12 focuses on information systems. It first discusses the types of information systems found in organizations, and then looks at the activities performed during the system development process. Chapter 13 covers the program development process—one important step in the system development process—and the various tools and programming languages developers may choose from when creating new programs. Database management systems are the subject of Chapter 14. This chapter discusses database concepts in much more detail than in previous chapters, including more specific database vocabulary, wider coverage of possible database models, and how databases are used in conjunction with the World Wide Web.

in this module

Chapter 12
Information Systems and System Development 466

Overview 467

What Is an Information System? 467

Types of Information Systems 471

Responsibility for System Development 484

The System Development Life Cycle (SDLC) 488

Approaches to System Development 498

Chapter 13
Program Development and Programming Languages 506

Overview 507

Approaches to Program Design
  and Development 507

The Program Development Life Cycle (PDLC) 511

Tools for Facilitating Program Development 528

Programming Languages 531

"System capabilities have made enormous increases in efficiency possible, and have also opened up new types of business and social activities."

Chapter 14
Databases and Database Management Systems 548

Overview 549

What Is a Database? 549

Data Concepts and Characteristics 555

Database Classifications 564

Database Models 566

Databases and the Web 576

For more comments from Guest Expert **Stuart Feldman** of ACM (Association for Computing Machinery) and Google, see the **Expert Insight on . . . Systems** feature at the end of the module.

chapter 12

Information Systems and System Development

After completing this chapter, you will be able to do the following:

1. Understand what information systems are and why they are needed.

2. Discuss who uses information systems in a typical organization.

3. Identify several types of information systems commonly found in organizations and describe the purpose of each.

4. Explain the individuals responsible for system development.

5. Identify and describe the different steps of the system development life cycle (SDLC).

6. Discuss several approaches used to develop systems.

outline

Overview

What Is an Information System?
The Need for System Development
Enterprise Architecture
Business Intelligence (BI)
Information Systems Users

Types of Information Systems
Office and User Productivity
   Support Systems
Transaction Processing Systems (TPSs)
Decision Making Support Systems
Integrated Enterprise Systems
Design and Manufacturing Systems
Artificial Intelligence Systems

Responsibility for System Development
The Information Systems (IS)
   Department
Outsourcing

The System Development Life Cycle (SDLC)
Preliminary Investigation
System Analysis
System Design
System Acquisition
System Implementation
System Maintenance

Approaches to System Development
The Traditional Approach
The Iterative Approach
The End-User Development
   Approach

OVERVIEW

So far in this textbook we have looked at a wide variety of hardware and software. In this chapter, we turn to the process of putting these elements together with people, procedures, and data to form complete systems.

A variety of systems are found in all organizations including systems to facilitate accounting activities, such as issuing bills and processing payrolls; systems to provide information to help managers make decisions; systems to help run factories efficiently; and systems to enable workers to exchange information and collaborate on projects. Systems typically require considerable effort to design, build, and maintain and, while no two system development projects are exactly alike, there is a set of general principles and procedures that can be used during system development to enhance the likelihood of the project's success. Those principles and procedures are the primary subject of this chapter.

The chapter opens with a discussion of information systems—systems that support the information needs of companies. We discuss how information systems are used by different levels of employees in an organization, and we look at the most common types of information systems. From there we turn to the process of system development, beginning with the computer professionals who develop systems and their primary responsibilities. We then look at the system development life cycle—the set of activities that is typically followed when developing a new system. The chapter closes with a discussion of the different system development approaches that can be taken. ■

WHAT IS AN INFORMATION SYSTEM?

A **system** is a collection of *elements* and *procedures* that interact to accomplish a goal. A football game, for example, is played according to a system. It consists of elements (two teams, a playing field, referees, and so on) and procedures (the rules of the game) that interact to determine which team is the winner. A transit system is a collection of elements and procedures (people, buses or trains, fares, and schedules, for instance) designed to get people from one place to another. An **information system (IS)** is a collection of elements (people, hardware, software, and data) and procedures that interact to generate information needed by the users in an organization (see Figure 12-1). Information systems manage and process data from the time it is generated (such as data resulting from orders, documents, and other business transactions) through its conversion into information. Typically, information systems are computerized, although they don't have to be. The information that information systems provide is used to support a wide variety of activities, from day-to-day transactions to long-term strategic planning.

FIGURE 12-1
Components of an information system.

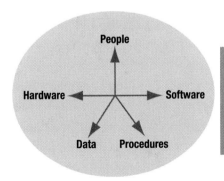

People

Hardware ← → Software

Data   Procedures

>**System.** A collection of elements and procedures that interact to accomplish a goal. >**Information system (IS).** A system used to generate information to support users in an organization.

Although the majority of information systems within organizations serve employees, information systems are increasingly supporting the needs of customers and suppliers, as well. In addition, some information systems need to be accessed by employees while on the go. Consequently, information systems are increasingly being made accessible via the Internet.

The Need for System Development

Businesses typically use a variety of information systems. These systems are created and modified in response to changing needs within an organization and shifting conditions within its surrounding environment. When problems arise in an existing system or when a new system is needed, *system development* comes into play. In general terms, **system development** is the process of analyzing a work environment, designing a new system or making modifications to the current system to fit the current needs of that work environment, acquiring any needed hardware and software, training users, and getting the new or modified system to work.

System development may be required for many reasons. For instance, new laws may call for the collection of data that was not collected in the past. A government may require additional reports regarding financial data, internal controls, or procedures, like those required in the United States by the *Sarbanes-Oxley Act*. A government may also require new security or privacy procedures to be used with collected data (such as the procedures regulated in the U.S. by the *Health Insurance Portability and Accountability Act* (*HIPAA*) *Privacy Rule*), or it may change the legal requirements for retaining business data (such as the recent update in the U.S. to the *Federal Rules of Civil Procedure*). In addition, the introduction of new technology may prompt the revision of a system. For instance, it is common today for a business to provide customers and suppliers with access to some information systems via the Internet, and the growing use of RFID, NFC, and other technologies may require changes to some systems to accommodate that technology. An organization may also make a change to its information systems to gain a competitive edge.

In the early days of commercial computing, businesses used computers almost exclusively to perform routine processing tasks related to business transactions, such as to process orders and payments. As time passed, however, it became apparent that computers could do much more than just *transaction processing*—they could also provide a variety of information to assist managers and other employees with decision making. In addition, computers could be used to better understand the structure and operations of a company, in order to make better strategic decisions. Two general concepts related to systems—*enterprise architecture* and *business intelligence* (*BI*)—are discussed next, followed by a look at the users of information systems.

Enterprise Architecture

Enterprise architecture is a conceptual blueprint that defines the structure and operations of an *enterprise* (a business, organization, government agency, or other entity). The goal of enterprise architecture is to provide a detailed picture of an organization, its functions, and its systems, and the relationships among these items—it is essentially a map of an organization's business functions and systems. Enterprise architecture has existed in theory for some time, but businesses have only recently focused on applying these principles on a practical level. With the complexity of today's systems, enterprise architecture allows managers to better organize and maximize the use of *information technology* (*IT*) resources, as well as make informed decisions with fewer mistakes. Experts agree that developing an enterprise architecture is not easy and requires a great deal of time and effort. The first step

---

>**System development.** The process of designing and implementing a new or modified system. >**Enterprise architecture.** A comprehensive framework used to describe and manage an organization's business functions and systems.

is usually to examine the existing systems and functions to identify gaps, overlaps, and other possible issues with the existing setup. Enterprise architecture development is usually viewed as a long-term process, but, after it is in place, it is a valuable tool.

Business Intelligence (BI)

While enterprise architecture provides an overall picture of an organization, **business intelligence** (**BI**) is the process of gathering, storing, accessing, and analyzing data about a company in order to make better business decisions. For instance, BI can help a business identify its most profitable customers and offer them products at the right prices to increase sales, or BI can be used to optimize inventory systems in order to decrease costs while ensuring products are available as needed. Typically, information systems are used to support BI, often in conjunction with sophisticated analysis and modeling tools—referred to as *business analytic tool*s—that are used to analyze data. While in the past BI tools were difficult to work with, today's BI tools—including the *digital dashboards* discussed in the How It Works box—are more user-friendly. Many of the information systems discussed in the next few sections can be classified as *business intelligence systems*.

Business intelligence systems often are used in conjunction with data stored in a *data warehouse* or *data mart*. Both contain a comprehensive collection of data about a company, but a **data mart** is usually smaller and stores data related to a particular subject or department, whereas a **data warehouse** typically stores data for an entire enterprise. Data warehouses and data marts typically contain data from a variety of sources, including data from product sales and other business transactions, activities performed via the company Web site (called *clickstream* data), customer surveys, marketing data, and so on. **Data mining**—the use of intelligent software to find subtle patterns that may not be evident otherwise—is often used with data warehouses and data marts to identify patterns and relationships between data (see Figure 12-2). Data mining can be used to identify processes that need improvement; it can also be used for *customer profiling*—a useful sales and marketing tool to help companies match customers with products they would be likely to purchase. Wal-Mart is one company that uses extensive data mining and markets specific types of merchandise in its local stores based on the characteristics of the people who live in that geographical area. Data mining used in conjunction with Web site data (typically usage data that indicates the navigational patterns of visitors) is referred to as *Web mining*. Data mining and Web mining can be used to generate information useful for decision making that would otherwise be too time-consuming and expensive, or even impossible, to generate manually.

FIGURE 12-2

Data mining. The goal of data mining is to find patterns and relationships in data.

Information Systems Users

Some information systems are very specialized and are used by just one individual or department in an organization; others are more general purpose and may be used by nearly all employees. Systems that are used by an entire enterprise are referred to as **enterprise systems**. Systems that link and are used by multiple enterprises—such as a business and its suppliers and other business partners—are often called **inter-enterprise systems**.

>**Business intelligence (BI).** The process of gathering, storing, accessing, and analyzing data about a company in order to make better business decisions. >**Data mart.** A collection of data related to a particular subject or department in a company. >**Data warehouse.** A comprehensive collection of data about a company and its customers. >**Data mining.** The process of using intelligent software to analyze data warehouses for patterns and relationships. >**Enterprise system.** A system that is used throughout an entire enterprise (business, organization, government agency, and so on). >**Inter-enterprise system.** A system that links multiple enterprises, such as a business and its suppliers and strategic partners.

HOW IT WORKS

Digital Dashboards

A *digital dashboard*, also known as an *enterprise dashboard* or *executive dashboard*, is a business intelligence (BI) tool used to provide a visual, at-a-glance display of key business data. Referred to as a "dashboard" because the user interface somewhat resembles an automobile's dashboard, a digital dashboard can pull data from a variety of sources (such as from information systems, databases, and spreadsheets and other documents) and display it in a central location. In a nutshell, a digital dashboard provides a decision maker with the summaries, charts, warnings, and other information needed to make decisions in a single, easy-to-view location. Some digital dashboards can also send alerts to a specified e-mail address

when a particular *key performance indicator* (*KPI*) falls outside of an acceptable range. Such automated alerts ensure that the proper individuals are notified of the change as soon as possible.

Digital dashboards are created using special software designed for that purpose, such as the *iDashboards* software shown in the accompanying illustration. Typically, the first step in creating a digital dashboard is to identify the overall layout of the dashboard, including the number of charts and other indicators to appear on the dashboard. Next, the appearance and data source for each indicator is selected, and then the dashboard is complete. Once the dashboard is up and running, the indicators change as the data sources they are linked to change; usually, the indicators can be clicked with the mouse to "drill-down" to more detailed information.

1. The overall layout of the dashboard is selected.

2. The appearance and data source for each indicator is then specified.

3. The dashboard is complete. Many indicators can be clicked to reveal more detailed information.

Creating a digital dashboard.

While some information systems may be used by all levels of employees, others are designed for management decision making. Information systems can provide managers with efficient access to the information they need when making decisions. However, in order to do this, information systems must be set up to deliver the correct information to the manager at the right time.

Managers are usually classified into three categories (*executive, middle*, and *operational*), based on the job functions they perform and the types of decisions they make. These positions are often pictured as a *management pyramid* (see Figure 12-3) to illustrate their usual ratio and hierarchical ranking—executive managers are fewer in number and at the top of the pyramid, and operational managers are greater in number and near the bottom of the pyramid. Figure 12-3 also includes the other users of information systems; namely, nonmanagement workers and *external users*, such as customers, suppliers, and strategic partners.

Managers most often manage the employees who are one level below them on the pyramid. For example, executive managers are typically in charge of middle managers, and operational managers supervise nonmanagement workers. Each group of users and the types of decisions those users typically make are summarized next.

> **✓ TIP**
>
> The disappearance of middle management in some companies is referred to as the *flattening* of the organizational structure.

➤ *Executive managers*—include the highest management positions in an organization, such as the president and chief executive officer (CEO); they use information systems to make relatively unstructured, long-term strategic decisions.

➤ *Middle managers*—include managers who fall between executive managers and operational managers; they use information systems to make moderately structured, tactical decisions.

➤ *Operational managers*—include supervisors, office managers, foremen, and other managers who supervise nonmanagement workers; they use information systems to make highly structured, operational decisions geared toward meeting short-term objectives.

➤ *Nonmanagement workers*—include office workers, accountants, engineers, and other workers; they use information systems to make the on-the-job decisions necessary to perform their jobs.

➤ *External users*—include individuals outside an organization, such as customers, suppliers, and other types of strategic partners; they use the organization's information systems to obtain the information needed in the context of their relationship with that organization.

FIGURE 12-3
Information system users. Users include managers, nonmanagement employees, and external users.

TYPES OF INFORMATION SYSTEMS

There are many different types of information systems in use today. While some information systems are unique and others vary somewhat from company to company, they can usually be grouped by their basic functions into one of six categories summarized in Figure 12-4 and discussed next.

FIGURE 12-4
Types of information systems.

Office and User Productivity Support Systems

Computers are widely used to increase productivity and facilitate communications in the office. The combination of hardware, software, and other resources used for this purpose is collectively referred to as an **office system** or an *office information system*. Office systems are used by virtually all employees. Some examples of office systems are described next.

Document Processing Systems

The cornerstone of most organizations is the document—memos, letters, reports, manuals, forms, invoices, and so forth. Consequently, a major focus of office systems relates to the electronic creation, distribution, and storage

TYPE OF SYSTEM	DESCRIPTION
Office and user productivity systems	Facilitate communications and enhanced productivity in office tasks
Transaction processing systems	Process and record business transactions
Decision making support systems	Provide needed information to decision makers
Integrated enterprise systems	Integrate activities throughout an entire enterprise
Design and manufacturing systems	Help with the design and/or manufacturing of products
Artificial intelligence systems	Perform actions based on characteristics of human intelligence

>**Office system.** A type of system in which hardware, software, and other resources are used to facilitate communications and enhance productivity.

of documents—sometimes referred to as *document processing*. Although the predicted *paperless office* has yet to materialize, and some in the industry are not sure it will anytime soon, most business documents today are stored digitally. **Document processing systems** include the hardware and software needed to create electronic documents (such as the ones created using the office suites discussed in Chapter 6 and the digital forms discussed in Chapter 4), as well as to convert printed documents into electronic form so they can be processed or *archived* electronically.

Document Management Systems (DMSs) and Content Management Systems (CMSs)

To help store, organize, and retrieve documents once they have been created in or converted to digital form, a **document management system** (**DMS**) can be used. A DMS can store documents that may be needed on a regular basis, as well as documents stored for archival purposes. Document management systems that can include images, multimedia files, and other content in addition to conventional documents are typically called **content management systems** (**CMSs**). For instance, a DMS can be used for normal office documents (such as letters, forms, reports, and spreadsheets), while a CMS can be used for the electronic medical records and digital X-rays (see Figure 12-5) increasingly used by medical offices and hospitals. Using digital versions of documents has many advantages, including increased efficiency, better service, and a reduction of errors. For instance, hospital information systems can enable physicians to remotely access patient records and X-rays; they can also reduce medication errors because medication bottles and patient wristbands can be scanned to confirm a drug and its dosage match that patient before the drug is administered. The use of these *e-health* systems, including the use of *electronic health records* (*EHRs*), is expected to increase tremendously in the near future.

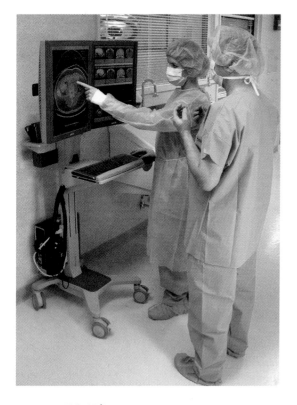

FIGURE 12-5

Digital x-rays. X-rays are one type of unconventional document now being created and stored in digital form.

Communication Systems

The various types of **communication systems** in place in many organizations include e-mail, messaging, videoconferencing, collaborative (workgroup) computing, and telecommuting. These systems, discussed in detail in Chapter 7, allow employees to communicate with each other, as well as with business partners and customers.

Transaction Processing Systems (TPSs)

Virtually every organization carries out a number of routine, structured business transactions, most of which involve some form of tedious recordkeeping. These operations, such as payroll and accounts receivable, inspired some of the earliest commercial applications for computers. Because these systems involve processing business transactions—paying employees and recording customer purchases and payments, for instance—they are called **transaction processing systems** (**TPSs**). TPS transactions are typically processed in *real time*; that is, data in the system is updated as the transactions are entered. This contrasts with *batch processing*, in which a set (or *batch*) of transactions are collected over a period of time and then processed all together (such as each evening) without any interaction with the user. While batch processing is still sometimes used for large routine tasks, such as printing payroll checks and invoices, most TPSs today use real-time processing.

Some of the most common types of transaction processing systems are discussed next. In addition to these normal business transaction processing systems, there are also specialty transaction processing systems used by law enforcement, the military, financial institutions, and other organizations. For instance, city, state, and federal governments need systems to process tax payments, fines, and other transactions, and law enforcement and judicial organizations need systems to issue citations and judgments. Like other transaction processing systems, these systems are increasingly being automated (see Figure 12-6).

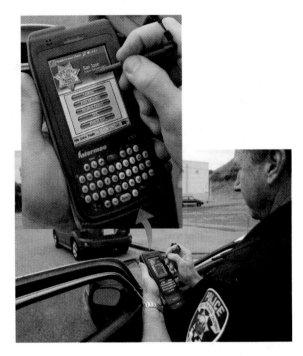

Order Entry Systems

Whether by phone, by mail, via the Internet, or in person, many organizations handle some type of order processing on a daily basis. The systems used to help employees record order data are called **order entry systems**. Two specific types of order entry systems are *e-commerce systems* (used for financial transactions performed over the Internet) and *point-of-sale* (*POS*) *systems* (used to record purchases at the point where the customer physically purchases a product or service, such as at a checkout counter).

FIGURE 12-6
Electronic citation systems. This type of transaction processing system allows officers to issue citations electronically.

Payroll Systems

Payroll systems compute employee taxes, deductions, and pay, and then use this information to issue paychecks. These systems also typically prepare payroll reports for management and for tax purposes for federal, state, and local governments.

Accounting Systems

Accounting systems refer to the variety of systems in place to record the details of a company's financial transactions (such as payments and purchases) for accounting purposes. For instance, *accounts receivable systems* keep track of customers' purchases, payments, and account balances and produce invoices and monthly account statements; *accounts payable systems* keep track of purchases made and bills to be paid, and then issue checks when needed. Many accounting systems feed into a *general ledger system*, which keeps track of all financial transactions and produces income statements, balance sheets, and other accounting documents.

Decision Making Support Systems

Many information systems are designed to help individuals make decisions. Some of these systems assist with routine operating decisions; others are designed for less structured decisions. Three of the most common types of decision support systems are discussed next.

Management Information Systems (MISs)

A **management information system** (**MIS**) is an information system that provides decision makers with regular, routine, and timely information that is used to make decisions.

> **Order entry system.** A type of transaction system that records and manages order processing. > **Payroll system.** A type of transaction system that generates employee payroll amounts and reports. > **Accounting system.** A type of transaction system that deals with the financial transactions and financial recordkeeping for an organization. > **Management information system (MIS).** A type of information system that provides decision makers with preselected information that can be used to make middle-management decisions.

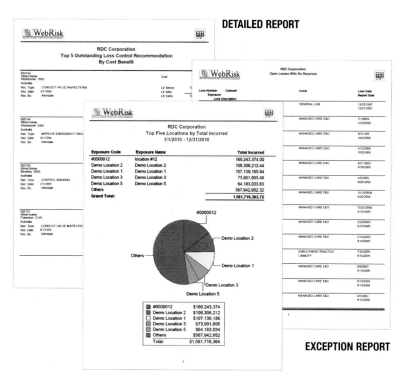

DETAILED REPORT

SUMMARY REPORT

EXCEPTION REPORT

⊘ **FIGURE 12-7**
MISs typically generate a variety of reports.

⊙ **FIGURE 12-8**
Decision support systems (DSSs).
This transportation DSS is used to create optimal routes for delivery vehicles.

In other words, the goal of an MIS is to provide managers and other decision makers with the information they need to perform their jobs. Often, the data used by an MIS is obtained during transaction processing. For example, a sales manager might receive reports on a regular basis detailing the sales orders received during a certain time period, an inventory supervisor might receive reports summarizing the current status of inventory, and a manager in the accounts receivable department might receive a report on a regular basis that lists customers with overdue balances. These three types of reports are called *detailed, summary,* and *exception reports,* respectively, and are the three primary types of reports that an MIS generates (see Figure 12-7). The information generated from an MIS is most frequently used to make moderately structured, middle-management decisions.

Decision Support Systems (DSSs)

A **decision support system** (**DSS**) is an information system that is also used to help make decisions. Unlike the more structured transaction processing and management information systems, however, decision support systems are typically interactive and provide information on demand whenever a decision needs to be made. Consequently, DSSs are most often used by middle and executive managers when unstructured, unpredictable, on-demand information is needed for decisions. DSSs may incorporate data from internal (within a particular enterprise) and external (outside of that enterprise) sources. External data used in a DSS might include interest rates, current construction costs, consumer confidence index numbers, the Dow Jones Industrial Average, and other economic indicators. A DSS specifically targeted to upper management is called an *executive information system* (*EIS*).

Decision support systems are often designed to help with specific types of decisions. For instance, a *Sales Support DSS* is aimed at the special decision making needs of sales or marketing personnel, and a *Transportation DSS* (see Figure 12-8) helps create routes for trucks, planes, and other transportation vehicles and modify those routes to react to real-time changing events (such as new pickups or deliveries for a delivery vehicle).

Geographic Information Systems (GISs)

A **geographic information system** (**GIS**) is an information system that combines geographic information (such as maps and terrain data) with other types of data (such as information about customers, sales, population, income, and so forth) in order to provide a better understanding of the relationships between the data. GIS output is often in the form of data superimposed on maps, which allows decision makers to see relationships, patterns, or trends that they may not see otherwise. GISs are commonly used to make a variety of decisions that involve locations, such as finding the best location for a new store, analyzing the flood or tornado risk for a particular home or neighborhood, developing regional marketing plans, or detecting crime patterns for specific geographic locations (see Figure 12-9). For example, visualizing potential locations for a new store on a map, along with data representing other factors—such as traffic, population, weather, housing prices, household income, crime statistics, and possible environmental concerns like wetlands or protected species that might hamper construction—can help a manager select the optimal location.

GISs are also an essential component of emergency response and disaster relief systems. For instance, in the first two weeks after Hurricane Katrina hit the Gulf Coast in late 2005, about 60 volunteer GIS experts used GISs to assist in the rescue and disaster relief efforts. They used GISs to build search maps for rescue workers, to translate street addresses of survivors requiring helicopter rescues into map coordinates for the helicopter pilots, and to create maps illustrating various issues, such as where electrical power had and had not been restored.

FIGURE 12-9

Geographic information systems (GISs). This GIS shows the locations of crime incidents based on the selected crime type, location, and date range.

Integrated Enterprise Systems

Some types of systems in a business or other enterprise are designed to be *integrated systems*; that is, separate systems that are designed to work in conjunction with other systems. Some specific examples are discussed next.

ONLINE VIDEO

Go to the Chapter 12 page at **www.cengage.com/ computerconcepts/np/uc13** to watch the "UNICEF's Bee System: Emergency Connectivity in Developing Countries" video clip.

Electronic Data Interchange (EDI)

Electronic data interchange (**EDI**) refers to the transfer of data electronically between different companies using networks, such as the Internet. With EDI, the computers located at one company are linked to the computers of key customers or suppliers so that business data and information (such as purchase orders and invoices) can be exchanged electronically as needed. EDI can speed up *business processes* (sets of tasks and activities used to accomplish a specific organizational goal) tremendously, such as enabling a company to order the appropriate materials automatically from the appropriate supplier when the stocks of those materials have reached the designated reorder point.

Enterprise Resource Planning (ERP)

Enterprise resource planning (**ERP**) is a special type of large, integrated system that ties together all types of a company's activities, such as planning, manufacturing, sales, marketing, distribution, customer service, and finance. Instead of each department having its own separate system, as in the past, an ERP system combines them all into a single, integrated application. Data is usually stored in a central database and the ERP system provides a standard access medium to all employees who need to access that data. For example, when an order is placed, the employee who takes the order from a customer has

SYS

>**Electronic data interchange (EDI).** The transfer of data between different companies using the Internet or another network. >**Enterprise resource planning (ERP).** A large integrated system that ties together all of a business's activities.

ASK THE EXPERT

i'm lovin' it

Dave Weick, Senior Vice President, Chief
Information Officer, McDonald's Corporation

What role does technology play in the day-to-day operations at McDonald's?

Technology is inherent in many of McDonald's day-to-day restaurant operations. From the moment a customer places his or her food order, technology has a significant role. For example, a customer's order is routed over a network to the kitchen for preparation, video screens provide instructions for our kitchens and drive-thrus, and cashless payments are processed. Furthermore, McDonald's restaurants depend on technology to keep track of inventory, to know how much product is required at different times of the day, and to determine the number of crew members required. Technology is also creating innovations in how we enhance the customer experience, such as self-ordering via kiosks or mobile phones. Providing consumers in over 31,000 restaurants worldwide an experience that is modern and relevant, as well as based on a secure and flexible foundation, is central to McDonald's success, and technology powers this experience as never before.

all the information necessary to complete the order (such as the customer's credit information and shipping address, the company's inventory levels, and the shipping schedule). Throughout the order fulfillment and billing process, everyone in the company who deals with the order has access to the same information related to that customer's order, without having to reenter the data. When one department finishes with the order, the ERP system may automatically route it to the next department. At any point in the process, the order status can be determined by anyone in the company authorized to access the system.

Today's ERP applications are commonly available via the Web so authorized users both inside and outside the company can get easy access to ERP-generated data. When information from an ERP or other type of internal system is exchanged between different applications (either within an organization or between organizations), it is called *enterprise application integration* (*EAI*).

Inventory and Product Management Systems

Inventory management systems (sometimes called *inventory control systems*) are systems designed to help track and manage inventory. They can help optimize ordering to reduce

FIGURE 12-10

Inventory management systems.

costs and manage inventory during the manufacturing process (for instance, an inventory management system used to create an *optimized replenishment order*—the optimal point in time products should be reordered—is shown in Figure 12-10). The process of overseeing materials, and the information and finances related to those materials, as they move from the original supplier to the consumer (through the entire *supply chain*) is often referred to as *supply chain management* (*SCM*). The goal of SCM is to reduce operating and inventory costs while meeting delivery objectives and increasing profits; that is, to be able to deliver the right product to the right place, at the right time, and at the right price. One ordering strategy sometimes used in manufacturing to eliminate wasted resources (such as materials, money, and warehouse space) is *just-in-time* (*JIT*). With a JIT system, inventory, production resources, and finished products are limited to the right number at the right time as required to fill orders. Some inventory management systems go beyond just inventory to act as a complete distribution system (including inventory, order, shipping, and

>**Inventory management system.** A system used to track and manage inventory.

transportation management among other features)—this type of system is often referred to as a *warehouse management system* (*WMS*). Increasingly, inventory management and warehouse management systems use RFID technology (as discussed in Chapter 4) to track inventory.

Product lifecycle management (**PLM**) **systems** are designed to manage a product as it moves through the various stages of its life cycle, from design to manufacturing to retirement. PLM systems organize and correlate all information about a product (such as specifications, quality history, customer feedback, research and testing results, and sales history) to help companies improve products, more efficiently create and manage the production of products, get more products on the market faster, and increase product profitability.

Both inventory and product management systems are often designed to work together with other systems, such as a company's ERP system.

Design and Manufacturing Systems

The systems used to improve productivity at the product design stage and at the manufacturing stage are typically referred to as *design and manufacturing systems*. Two of the most common design and manufacturing systems are discussed next.

Computer-Aided Design (CAD)

The purpose of **computer-aided design** (**CAD**) is to reduce the time designers spend developing products. CAD software, such as *AutoCAD*, is available to help design buildings, bridges, and other structures; design new products; design mechanical and electrical systems; create landscape and interior designs; and so forth. Advantages of using CAD include the ability to make modifications to a design more easily and quickly, as well as to test it under simulated conditions (such as testing the design of a new building for earthquake stability to determine if the design is compliant with current regulations or if it needs revision). In addition, the ability of most CAD programs today to create realistic 3D renderings of designs allows individuals to more easily picture what a finished product will look like, including "walking through" a new building or landscape design virtually (see Figure 12-11). These features allow accurate decisions to be made early in the design process to save both time and money.

FIGURE 12-11
Computer-aided design (CAD). CAD programs can be used for a wide variety of design applications.

Computer-Aided Manufacturing (CAM)

Computer-aided manufacturing (**CAM**) is used to help manage manufacturing operations and control the machinery used in those processes. For instance, computers can open and shut valves as directed by their programs, shape and assemble parts to create products, and control the *robots* (discussed shortly) used to carry out many manufacturing processes. CAM is widely used today to build cars, ships, and other products; monitor power plants; manufacture food and chemicals; and perform a number of other functions. Advantages of using CAM include consistency, human safety, and reduced manufacturing time. CAD

SYS

> **Product lifecycle management (PLM) system.** A system designed to manage a product as it moves through the various stages of its life cycle, from design to retirement. > **Computer-aided design (CAD).** A general term applied to the use of computer technology to automate design functions. > **Computer-aided manufacturing (CAM).** A general term applied to the use of computer technology to automate manufacturing functions.

INSIDE THE INDUSTRY

The Turing Test and the Loebner Prize

According to John McCarthy, who coined the term *artificial intelligence* (*AI*) in 1956 and is considered by many to be one of its fathers, AI is "the science and engineering of making intelligent machines." In other words, AI researchers are working to create intelligent devices controlled by intelligent software programs; in essence, machines that think and act like people. In 1950, Alan Turing—one of the first AI researchers—argued that if a machine could successfully appear to be human to a knowledgeable observer, then it should be considered intelligent. To illustrate this idea, Turing developed a test—later called the *Turing Test*—in which one observer interacts electronically with both a computer and a person. During the test, the observer submits written questions electronically to both the computer and the person, evaluates the typed responses, and tries to identify which answers came from the computer and which came from the person. Turing argued that if the computer could repeatedly fool the observer into thinking it was human, then it should be viewed as intelligent.

Many Turing Test contests have been held over the years, and, in 1990, Dr. Hugh Loebner initiated the *Loebner Prize*, pledging a grand prize of $100,000 and a solid gold medal (see the accompanying photo) for the first computer whose responses to a Turing Test were indistinguishable from that of a human's responses. A contest is held every year, awarding a prize of $2,000 and a bronze medal to the most human computer, but so far, the gold medal has not been awarded.

The Loebner Prize gold medal.

and CAM are commonly used in conjunction with each other (referred to as *CAD/CAM systems*) to speed up both the design and manufacturing of products. For instance, the introduction of a CAD/CAM system used to design and produce custom-made sockets used in prosthetic limbs for injured U.S. soldiers has greatly reduced the time needed to fit the soldiers with new limbs. Using this system, a mold for the socket can be created in 20 minutes or less, which is significantly faster than a plaster cast mold that might take a day or two to create. Since soldiers require new sockets as their limbs heal (up to eight before leaving the hospital), this system is a significant improvement in the treatment of this type of injury.

VIDEO PODCAST

Go to the Chapter 12 page at **www.cengage.com/computerconcepts/np/uc13** to download or listen to the "How To: Add a Text-to-Speech System to Your Browser" video podcast.

Artificial Intelligence Systems

Although they cannot yet think completely on their own, computers and software programs have become more sophisticated, and computers are being programmed to act in an increasingly intelligent manner. When computer systems perform in ways that would be considered intelligent if observed in humans, it is referred to as *artificial intelligence* (*AI*). For a look at two activities related to AI—the *Turing Test* and the *Loebner Prize*—see the Inside the Industry box.

Some of the initial advances in AI were made in the area of game playing—namely, chess. Early chess-playing programs were easily defeated by amateur chess players. But, as computers became more powerful and AI software became more sophisticated, chess-playing programs improved significantly. In 1996, IBM's Deep Blue computer won two of six games in a chess match against then world chess champion Garry Kasparov. A landmark moment in AI history occurred in 1997 when Deep Blue beat Kasparov in a rematch, winning the match 3½ to 2½ (three of the six games ended in a draw). And in late 2006, world chess champion Vladimir Kramnik lost a match to the chess program *Deep Fritz* (see Figure 12-12)—the beginning of the end of humans being able to beat chess programs, in the opinion of some AI researchers. One reason for this is because once the human player makes a mistake, there is no hope (as there would be with a human opponent) that the computer opponent will make its own mistake at a later time to level the playing field in that game.

KRAMNIK VS. DEEP FRITZ
Shown here are images from the match in 2006 during which the Deep Fritz chess program beat world champion Vladimir Kramnik 4 games to 2.

FIGURE 12-12
AI and chess playing.

Today's AI applications contain some aspect of artificial intelligence, although they tend to mimic human intelligence rather than display pure intelligence. Technological advances will undoubtedly help AI applications continue to evolve and become more intelligent and sophisticated in the future. For instance, one recent advancement—IBM's new Watson supercomputer that has the ability to analyze complex questions and form answers well enough to compete with humans on the *Jeopardy!* game show, as discussed in the Chapter 2 How It Works box—is considered a significant step forward in the area of artificial intelligence. While many welcome the idea of more intelligent computers to help people, some foresee a future in which people and computers may eventually merge. Not surprisingly, that scenario is frightening and objectionable to some. Just as the debate about what constitutes intelligence in nonhumans will continue, so will the debate about how far we as a society should delve into the area of artificial intelligence.

Systems that use artificial intelligence are called **artificial intelligence (AI) systems**. Some examples of AI systems are discussed next.

Intelligent Agents

Intelligent agents are programs that perform specific tasks to help make a user's work environment more efficient or entertaining. Typically, the agent program runs in the background until it is time for the agent to perform a task, and it usually modifies its behavior based on the user's actions or instructions. Intelligent agents are found on Web sites, as well as incorporated into software programs. Some specific types of intelligent agents include the following:

> *Application assistants*—provide help or assistance for a particular application program. Some can detect when the user might be having trouble with the program and automatically offer appropriate advice.

> *Shopping bots*—search online stores to find the best overall prices for specified products.

> *Entertainment bots*—provide entertainment, such as a virtual pet to take care of or an animated character to play games with.

> *Chatterbots*—carry on written "conversations" with people in a *natural language* (such as English, Spanish, French, or Japanese). Chatterbots are often represented

SYS

by an animated character and typically respond both verbally and with appropriate physical gestures to create the illusion that the exchange is taking place between two thinking, living entities (see Figure 12-13).

Intelligent agents are expected to be an important part of the *Semantic Web*—a predicted evolution of the current Web in which all Web content is stored as if it were data in a database so that it can be retrieved easily when needed to fulfill user requests. To accomplish this, the *semantics* (structure) of the data is defined in a standard manner (using tags and other identifying data), similar to the way XML is used to mark documents and data today in a universal manner. It is also anticipated that many new types of intelligent agents and applications will be developed specifically to take advantage of the Semantic Web. Whether or not the Semantic Web—viewed as part of the next generation *Web 3.0* by some—actually arrives, and arrives in the format in which it is now envisioned, remains to be seen. If it does, however, it is expected to have a huge impact on how Web services and AI are deployed in the future.

Expert Systems

Expert systems are software programs that can make decisions and draw conclusions, similar to a human expert. Expert systems have two main components: a *knowledge base* (a database that contains facts provided by a human expert and rules that the expert system should use to make decisions based on those facts) and an *inference engine* (a software program that applies the rules to the data stored in the knowledge base in order to reach decisions). For instance, as shown in Figure 12-14, an expert system used to authorize credit card purchases would have a knowledge base with facts about customers and rules about credit authorization, such as "Do not automatically authorize purchase if the customer has exceeded his or her credit limit."

Expert systems are widely used for tasks such as diagnosing illnesses, making financial forecasts, scheduling routes for delivery vehicles, diagnosing mechanical problems, and performing credit authorizations. Some expert systems are designed to take the place of human experts, while others are designed to assist them. For instance, medical expert systems are often used to assist physicians with patient diagnoses, suggesting possible diagnoses based on the patient's symptoms and other data supplied to the expert system. Because it has access to an extensive knowledge

FIGURE 12-13

A Web page chatterbot.

FIGURE 12-14

An expert system at work.

QUERY: Should we approve a $700 purchase for Mr. Jones?

RESPONSE: Yes

INFERENCE ENGINE

The inference engine is the computer program that runs the expert system. It processes queries by checking rules in the knowledge base against the customer database.

Jones is customer account 0000-9999.

Jones has a $5,000 credit limit.

Jones has spent $1,529 in the current period.

Jones has made two transactions today.

KNOWLEDGE BASE

RULES

Authorize purchase only if the customer has an active account.

Authorize purchase only if the customer has not exceeded his or her credit limit.

Authorize purchase automatically if the customer has made less than three purchases today.

CUSTOMER DATABASE

>**Expert system.** A computer system that provides the type of advice that would be expected from a human expert.

base, the expert system may provide more possible diagnoses to the attending physician than he or she may have thought of otherwise.

When using an expert system, it is important to realize that its conclusions are based on the data and rules stored in its knowledge base, as well as the information provided by the users. If the expert knowledge is correct, the inference engine program is written correctly, and the user supplies accurate information in response to the questions posed by the expert system, the system will draw correct conclusions; if the knowledge base is wrong, the inference engine is faulty, or the user provides inaccurate input, the system will not work correctly.

Neural Networks

Artificial intelligence systems that attempt to imitate the way a human brain works are called **neural networks**. Neural networks (also called *neural nets*) are networks of processors that are connected together in a manner similar to the way the neurons in a human brain are connected. They are designed to emulate the brain's pattern-recognition process in order to recognize patterns in data and make more progressive leaps in associations and predictions than conventional computer systems. Neural networks are used in areas such as handwriting, speech, and image recognition; medical imaging; crime analysis; biometric identification (see Figure 12-15); and *vision systems* that use cameras to inspect objects and make determinations—for example, the systems that check products for defects at manufacturing plants or that recognize stamps during postal processing.

Robotics

Robotics is the field devoted to the study of **robots**—devices, controlled by a person or a computer, that can move and react to sensory input. Robots are widely used by the military and businesses to perform high-precision but monotonous jobs, as well as to perform tasks that are dangerous or impossible for people to perform. There are also robots designed to perform personal tasks for individuals. The appearance of robots varies depending on their purpose, such as robot arms permanently connected to an assembly line, robots built on sturdy mobile platforms designed to travel over rough terrain, robots with fins for water tasks, robots shaped like animals (such as snakes or spiders) to give them special climbing abilities, and robots that resemble pets or humans for consumer applications. Some examples of how robots are used in the military, in business, and for personal use are discussed next.

Military Robots

Robots are used extensively by the U.S. military. For instance, they are used in areas of conflict to investigate caves, buildings, trails, and other locations before soldiers enter them to make sure the locations are safe (see Figure 12-16), and to help soldiers locate and

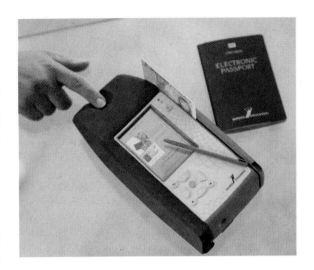

FIGURE 12-15
Neural network systems. Neural networks are often used in biometric identification systems, such as analyzing fingerprints in the fingerprint identification system shown here.

FIGURE 12-16
Military robotic applications.

PACKBOT EXPLORER ROBOT
Designed to investigate hostile and inaccessible areas prior to human entry.

HULC EXOSKELETON
Designed to give soldiers enhanced mobility and endurance while carrying heavy loads.

SYS

>**Neural network.** An expert system in which the human brain's pattern-recognition process is emulated by the computer system. >**Robotics.** The study of robot technology. >**Robot.** A device, controlled by a human operator or a computer, that can move and react to sensory input.

dispose of bombs, landmines, and other explosive devices. In addition to land-based robots, there are also military robots designed for underwater use, such as to detect mines or perform underwater surveillance and reconnaissance. Currently, military robots are controlled remotely by soldiers, though researchers are working on more *autonomous robots* that can navigate on their own, perceiving obstacles and determining their course without continuous directions from a human operator, to accompany soldiers into combat. According to national security expert John Pike, autonomous armed robotic soldiers may become a reality as soon as 2020.

An emerging military robotic application is the *exoskeleton suit*, whose name refers to a hard protective or supportive outer structure. Currently being researched and developed by several organizations under grants from the Defense Advanced Research Projects Agency (DARPA), exoskeleton suits are wearable robotic systems designed to give an individual additional physical capabilities and protection. For instance, an exoskeleton suit can give a soldier the ability to run faster and carry heavier items than he or she could without the suit—up to 200 pounds at a top speed of 10 mph for the *Human Universal Load Carrier* (*HULC*) exoskeleton suit shown in Figure 12-16. While lower-body exoskeleton suits like the HULC are in development and are expected to be field tested by soldiers in 2010, full exoskeleton suits are expected to be available in the future and may include additional capabilities, such as being made of bulletproof material that is able to solidify on demand to form a shield or turn into a medical cast if a soldier is injured. Other possible features include changing its color automatically for camouflage purposes; relaying information via sensors about a soldier's health, injuries, and location to field headquarters; and administering painkillers or applying pressure to a wound when directed by a physician. DARPA is also involved with the development of robotic prosthetic arms that feel, look, and perform like natural arms—these robotic arms will be used by military personnel who are injured in the line of duty.

Business and Industrial Robots

Robots are used in business for a variety of purposes, such as for looking for intruders, gas leaks, and other hazards, working on factory assembly lines, and other monotonous tasks (see Figure 12-17). Robots are also used for mining coal, repairing oil rigs, locating survivors in collapsed mines and buildings, and other dangerous tasks. They can also be used to facilitate videoconferencing by sitting in for a remote participant and relaying video and audio images to and from that participant. For instance, the videoconferencing robot shown in

ONLINE VIDEO

Go to the Chapter 12 page at **www.cengage.com/ computerconcepts/np/uc13** to watch the "A Look at the HULC Exoskeleton" video clip.

FIGURE 12-17
Business robots.

ASSEMBLY LINE ROBOTS

VIDEOCONFERENCING ROBOTS

Figure 12-17 is designed to be controlled by a remote physician to enable him or her to conduct "virtual rounds" from his or her office or another remote location. In addition, robots are used for *robot-assisted surgery* (as discussed in Chapter 7) and in search and rescue missions, firefighting, and other service tasks.

Personal Robots

There are also a number of *personal robots* (also called *service robots*) available or in development to assist with personal tasks. Some are primarily entertainment robots. They typically use sensors, cameras, microphones, and other technologies to input data about their current surroundings, and then interact with people (such as by reciting phrases, delivering messages, taking photos or video, or singing and dancing). Others, such as the toy robot shown in Figure 12-18, are designed to be toys or companions for children. Still other personal robots are designed for household tasks, such as to mow the lawn, clean the floor (refer again to Figure 12-18), or clean the pool.

Household robots that can assist individuals with more complex tasks, such as putting away the dishes or picking up toys before vacuuming the living room, are a little further in the future, when robot technology improves to allow for better navigation and improved physical manipulation, and as prices come down. Expected to have a more *humanoid* form than the household robots currently on the market, these future robots could be used to assist the elderly and wheelchair-bound individuals, in addition to helping with household tasks. In fact, it has been reported that the South Korean government expects to have at least one robot in every South Korean household by 2020. There are also personal exoskeleton suits in development that are designed to be used to give the elderly back their youthful physical abilities, or provide paralyzed people with a means of mobility.

Societal Implications of Robots

Many would agree that the use of robots has numerous benefits to society—such as adding convenience to our lives, replacing humans for dangerous tasks, and, potentially, monitoring and assisting the disabled and the elderly. But some individuals are concerned that, as true artificial intelligence becomes closer to reality, a class of robots with the potential for great harm could be created. In response, several organizations—including the South Korean government and the European Robotics Research Network—are in the process of developing standards for robots, users, and manufacturers concerning the appropriate use and development of robots. The U.S. military is also studying ways to ensure robotic soldiers can be programmed to recognize and obey international laws of war and the U.S. military's rules of engagement, in order to prevent them from performing acts such as firing on a hospital or crowd of civilians, even if enemy forces are nearby. Regardless of the progress in the area of implementing controls on robots, the issue of the role robots should take in our society is likely to continue to be debated for quite some time.

TOY ROBOTS
This talking robot is designed to be a companion for children.

HELPER ROBOTS
This vacuum robot is designed to clean workshop, garage, and patio floors.

FIGURE 12-18
Personal robots.

FURTHER EXPLORATION Go

Go to the Chapter 12 page at **www.cengage.com/ computerconcepts/np/uc13** for links to information about robots.

SYS

CAUTION   CAUTION   CAUTION   CAUTION   CAUTION   CAUTION   CAUT

While some robots are designed to be durable and used in adverse conditions, remember that robotic devices are electronic. To avoid the risk of electric shock and damage to robotic devices, do not use them in the water or in other adverse conditions unless the instructions specifically state that the action is safe.

ONLINE VIDEO

Go to the Chapter 12 page at **www.cengage.com/ computerconcepts/np/uc13** to watch the "The Google Interview Process" video clip.

FURTHER EXPLORATION

Go to the Chapter 12 page at **www.cengage.com/ computerconcepts/np/uc13** for links to information about computer careers.

RESPONSIBILITY FOR SYSTEM DEVELOPMENT

As mentioned earlier, *system development* is the process that includes planning, building, and maintaining systems. When a need arises for a new system or a system no longer meets the needs of the organization and needs to be modified, the job of system development begins. System development can take place in-house (usually by the organization's *information systems (IS) department*) or it can be *outsourced* to external companies.

The Information Systems (IS) Department

The **information systems (IS)** department—also called the **information technology (IT)** department—is responsible for developing, running, and maintaining the computers and information systems in an organization, as well as processing the vast amount of data that passes through the organization to keep its critical systems (such as transaction processing systems) running smoothly. The IS department varies in structure from one company to another, but includes most, if not all, of the computer and networking personnel for that organization. For instance, an IS department may include the people who design and implement information systems, the people who provide support services to computer users, the people who create and manage networks and databases, and the people who secure the company systems and networks from unauthorized access.

According to the Bureau of Labor Statistics, two of the top five projected fastest growing careers in the United States through 2016 are IT jobs. The job classified as *network systems and data communications analyst* is number one, with a projected growth of 54% by 2016; the other computer-related job in the top five is *computer software engineers*. These jobs typically require a bachelor's degree and have a current average salary of $67,000 and $82,000, respectively. Figure 12-19 describes these and a number of other typical IT jobs. For some tips regarding common mistakes while job hunting that you may wish to avoid, see the Technology and You box.

The IT person most involved with system development is the **systems analyst**. When a new system or a system modification is needed, the systems analyst manages the necessary activities related to designing and implementing the new or modified system throughout all stages of the system development process. Another individual critical to system development is the *business analyst*, who is charged with making sure that new systems meet the business requirements of the organization. Other key individuals include the *application programmers* (who code computer programs to perform the tasks specified in the design specifications), the *operations personnel* (who manage day-to-day processing once a system has become operational), and the *security specialist* (who is responsible for securing the organization's hardware, software, and data). In some organizations, the systems analyst takes on the roles of some of these other individuals, in additional to the traditional systems analyst responsibilities.

>**Information systems (IS) department.** The department in an organization responsible for that organization's computers, systems, and other technology; also called the **information technology (IT) department**. >**Systems analyst.** A person who studies systems in an organization in order to determine what work needs to be done and how this work may best be achieved.

Application programmer
Codes application software.

Business analyst
Identifies the business needs of a system and makes sure systems meet those needs.

Communications analyst
Analyzes, maintains, and troubleshoots data communications networks and assists with connectivity.

Computer operations manager
Oversees the computer operations staff and facility.

Computer operator
Responsible for the operation of mainframe computers and their support.

Computer software engineer
Designs and builds complex software applications. Can be an *application software engineer* or a *systems software engineer*.

Database administrator
Responsible for setting up and managing large databases within an organization.

Database analyst
Responsible for designing and developing an organization's data flow models and database architecture.

Data center architect
Manages the whole data center environment including servers, virtualization, power, cooling, security, and so on.

Data entry operator
Responsible for keying data into a computer system.

Help desk technician
Assists users in solving software and hardware problems.

Information engineer
Analyzes an organization's data to locate trends, problems, and other useful information for management.

Knowledge engineer
Responsible for setting up and maintaining the base of expert knowledge used in expert system applications.

Multimedia developer
Develops the multimedia content needed for Web sites and other applications.

Network and computer system administrator
Responsible for planning and implementing computers and networks within an organization.

Network operator/troubleshooter
Responsible for overseeing the day-to-day activities for a network, such as troubleshooting problems, documenting network events, and performing necessary duties to keep the network operating smoothly.

Network systems and data communications analyst
Manages the networks in an organization and determines what changes, if any, are needed; also known as a **network architect**.

Network technician
Installs, maintains, and upgrades networking hardware and software.

Operations personnel
Manage the day-to-day processing for a system.

Security specialist
Responsible for seeing that an organization's hardware, software, and data are protected from hackers, malware, natural disasters, accidents, and the like. Also known as the **chief security officer (CSO)**.

System administrator
Responsible for maintaining a large, multiuser system.

System programmer
Codes system software, fine-tunes operating system performance, and performs other system software-related tasks.

Systems analyst
Studies systems in an organization to determine what changes need to be made and how to best accomplish these changes.

Trainer
Provides education to users about a particular program, system, or technology.

Vice president of information systems
Oversees routing transaction processing and information systems activities, as well as other computer-related areas. Also known as the **chief information officer (CIO)**.

Webmaster
Responsible for all technical aspects of a Web site.

Web designer/developer
Designs and develops Web sites.

Web programmer
Writes the program code necessary for a Web site, such as to provide animation and database connectivity.

FIGURE 12-19
Computer and networking jobs. Many of these positions are found in an organization's information systems (IS) department.

Outsourcing

When an organization hires an outside firm to perform specific tasks, it is referred to as **outsourcing**. System development can be outsourced, but it is typically just specific development tasks (such as creating a new software program or Web application) instead of the

>**Outsourcing.** Turning over specific business tasks to an outside vendor; increasingly, the vendor is located in a different country with lower labor costs.

TECHNOLOGY AND YOU

Avoiding Common Job Hunting Mistakes

In addition to creating a great number of jobs—both in and out of the IT field—computers, in conjunction with the Internet and social networking sites, have changed the job hunting process. For instance, Web sites like *CareerBuilder.com* and *Monster.com* (see the accompanying illustration) can help you find positions you may wish to apply for; with the ability to work remotely via the Internet, you can even apply for some jobs that are out of your immediate geographical area. However, the Internet also provides you with the opportunity to post content that may reappear at inopportune times, and provides employers with the ability to research job applicants more quickly, easily, and thoroughly and, perhaps, find that inappropriate content.

When posting pictures and other personal information online, many individuals forget that it may be available to be viewed by current or potential employers. According to a recent CareerBuilder study, however, 45% of employers use social networking sites like Facebook to research prospective employees and an additional 11% were planning on implementing social networking screening in the near future. In addition, 35% of employers surveyed reported rejecting candidates based on the data found on social networking sites. Reasons cited included provocative or inappropriate photos or information, drinking or drug use, poor communications skills, discriminatory comments, and bad-mouthing a previous employer, coworker, or client. While some may not view poor grammar on your Facebook page as a valid reason to lose a job opportunity, this study is a good reminder that you should be cautious about the information you post online. Some tips to help you avoid the most common job-hunting mistakes are discussed next.

When applying for a job, avoid common mistakes like submitting a resume or job application that contains spelling or grammatical errors, including outdated skills or misusing industry jargon, or presenting a vague or dishonest picture of your experience and education. Be sure to emphasize your

soft skills—skills like effective writing, teamwork, and the ability to speak clearly and concisely in a group setting—which are increasingly of interest to employers today. In general, it is important to remember that your goal in your application package is to explain why you would be a valuable asset to the company and convince them that you are worthy of a face-to-face interview.

To avoid potential problems during a preliminary background check and to increase your chances of getting an interview, self-censor your online content. Make sure no personal content publicly viewable on your Facebook page or other social networking site could be viewed as objectionable by potential employers, and carefully edit your social networking pages, blogs, or other online content to ensure they are well written. Once you land your job, continue to be cautious about your online activities. There have been numerous cases of individuals losing their jobs because of content posted on social networking sites. A good rule of thumb is not to post anything online that you wouldn't want an employer (or a parent, spouse, or other significant other, for that matter) to view. Be careless and you could join the rising number of people who are "Facebook fired."

entire system development process. Many companies also outsource a variety of ongoing system tasks, such as customer service, technical support, credit card processing, and payroll accounting. Much of outsourcing today is *offshore*; that is, outsourced to another country. In fact, the world outsourcing market today is estimated to be worth $373 billion and India alone has an annual revenue from outsourcing of nearly $50 billion per year. In the United States, business tasks are often sent to India, China, and the Philippines. The use of *nearshoring* (outsourcing to nearby countries, such as Canada and Latin America for U.S. companies) is also growing—Latin America is especially attractive to many U.S. companies today for customer service and other tasks that involve direct communication with customers because of America's large Hispanic market.

TREND

Crowdsourcing

Crowdsourcing is the act of taking a job traditionally performed by an employee and outsourcing it to a large—typically undefined—group of people. Crowdsourcing nearly always takes place via the Internet and is sometimes used by businesses to solicit free feedback on a product or service; it is also used to locate individuals who will be paid to perform a service. For instance, the *crowdSPRING* crowdsourcing marketplace (shown in the accompanying illustration) allows individuals and businesses to post projects for graphic design, Web design, industrial design, photography, and other creative services. The projects include specifications, a set price, and a deadline and designers can choose to submit an entry for consideration—the individual or business then chooses a winning design from the entries received. Other crowdsourcing services are available for other types of projects, such as *TopCoder* for programming projects.

While crowdsourcing has taken off recently (fueled, in part, by the recent economic turmoil), some believe that it is the trend for the future, combining a huge potential pool of participants with extremely fast turnaround time. For instance, the crowd-SPRING network contains more than 40,000 designers located in over 150 countries and the average project receives 77 submissions—most in just days. And it works. LG, for instance, recently used crowdSPRING to solicit designs for a new mobile phone for their "Design of the Future" competition—paying just over $80,000 in awards for the selected designs, instead of the millions typically required by a design firm. LendingTree is an example of a company that uses crowdsourcing as a competitive tool in the area of software development. For instance, it holds Conceptualization contests to locate the best ideas for new products and services, Wireframe contests to develop the best models of those ideas, and otherwise leverages the TopCoder community to help its business grow quickly and efficiently.

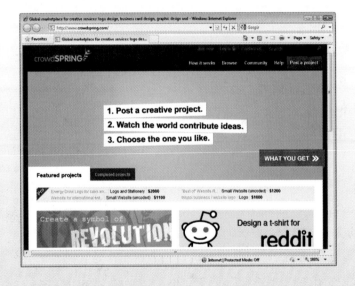

Many outsourcing firms have a fixed location from which workers operate, but a growing trend is *homesourcing* (also called *homeshoring*); that is, outsourcing work to home-based workers (see Figure 12-20). Originally, *call-center* type work (such as customer service) was the most common type of work homesourced, but today homesourcing has evolved to include professionals such as architects, accountants, editors, and more. The home-based workers can be employees of the company that telecommute from home, but are more often temporary workers (either self-employed individuals or individuals working for a homesourcing company). In either case, advantages for the worker include convenience and no commuting time or expense; employers benefit since they may be able to get more experienced and qualified workers (such as experienced retired workers or educated stay-at-home moms). For a look at a growing trend—*crowdsourcing*—see the Trend box.

One of the primary reasons companies outsource is cost. Because the pay rate is much lower in other countries, the cost savings for offshore outsourcing can be enormous. Outsourcing also allows companies to be flexible with their staffing, using additional workers only when they are needed and hiring the best employees regardless of their physical locations. In fact, the terms

FIGURE 12-20
Homesourcing is a growing trend in outsourcing.

global sourcing and *strategic sourcing* are now being used in some companies instead of outsourcing to describe the process of hiring employees as needed, regardless of where they are located or if they are employees of the company. Some companies are also committed to practicing *socially responsible outsourcing*—looking at factors such as how an outsourcing company treats its employees, interacts with its community, adheres to high ethical standards, and minimizes its impact on the environment when selecting an outsourcing company. This new focus on socially responsible outsourcing stems from a variety of factors, including the emergence of outsourcing as a critical process at many companies, the increased attention on ethical standards within a company's own operations, and the recent concerns about poor treatment or working conditions of employees at outsourcing companies.

While outsourcing has its advantages, it is not without drawbacks. Personnel changes at the outsourcing company, conflicts between in-house and outsourcing personnel, communication problems, and cultural differences may all create problems. In addition, quality control and security are very important factors. Some outsourcing companies try to reassure their clients by utilizing very strict security measures, such as conducting employee searches, providing no opportunities for employees to copy files, allowing no outside telephone access, and so forth. At other outsourcing companies, however, security measures are lax. And when a problem—such as data or proprietary information being stolen—occurs, prosecution and data recovery are much more complicated since they must be pursued via law enforcement agencies in the outsourcing company's country. Another concern is the possibility of offshore outsourcing being used to sabotage software or otherwise launch a cyberattack on the United States or U.S. companies. To minimize these risks, some companies are creating *captive offshoring sites* in countries where it is less expensive to do business; that is, organizing their own facilities and hiring employees in a foreign country instead of using a third-party outsourcing company. Although more expensive than conventional outsourcing, captive offshoring does give a company much more control over the employees and procedures used than with conventional outsourcing.

THE SYSTEM DEVELOPMENT LIFE CYCLE (SDLC)

There are many specific tasks involved with system development. Although the arrangement and order of these tasks may vary from organization to organization and project to project, system development typically involves six steps or phases, which make up the **system development life cycle** (**SDLC**) as illustrated in Figure 12-21. The SDLC describes the development of a system from the time it is first studied until the time it is it updated or replaced. As shown in Figure 12-21, each step results in some type of *documentation* that carries forward to the next step in the cycle. The activities that may occur during each step of the SDLC are discussed next.

Preliminary Investigation

When a proposal for a new system or system modification is submitted, one of the first steps is to conduct a **preliminary investigation**. The purpose of this investigation is to define and evaluate the situation relatively quickly, to see if it is worthy of further study. The preliminary investigation typically examines the nature of the problem, possible solutions, and the approximate costs and benefits of each proposed solution. In this phase, like all of the

---

>**System development life cycle (SDLC).** The process consisting of the six phases of system development: preliminary investigation, system analysis, system design, system acquisition, system implementation, and system maintenance. >**Preliminary investigation.** The phase of the system development life cycle in which a brief feasibility study is performed to assess whether or not a full-scale project should be undertaken.

Completed project folder

1. Preliminary investigation

Feasibility report

6. System maintenance

Implementation schedule, test data, and training materials

2. System analysis

Diagrams, tables, trees, and models that describe the current system

5. System implementation

3. System design

RFPs, RFQs, and vendor evaluation materials

4. System acquisition

Specifications of the new system and cost-benefit analysis

FIGURE 12-21

The system development life cycle (SDLC). Each phase of the system development life cycle produces some type of documentation to pass on to the next phase.

phases of the SDLC, the systems analyst plays an important role—see Figure 12-22 for a description of the duties of the systems analyst during each step of the SDLC.

Documentation: Feasibility Report

The main output of the preliminary investigation is the *feasibility report*, which includes the systems analyst's findings on the status of the existing system, as well as the benefits and feasibility of changing to a new system. Feasibility is commonly measured using a few different perspectives, such as whether the organization has (or can acquire) the hardware, software, and personnel needed to implement the new system; whether the new system would fit well with the other systems in the organization; and whether the estimated benefits of the new system outweigh the estimated costs. The feasibility report also contains the systems analyst's recommendations about whether or not the project should move on to the next stage in the SDLC: *system analysis*.

System Analysis

System analysis is the phase of system development in which the problem area is studied in depth and the needs of system users are assessed. The principal purpose of this stage is

---

>**System analysis.** The phase of the system development life cycle in which a problem area is thoroughly examined to determine what should be done.

FIGURE 12-22

The role of the systems analyst in the six phases of system development.

to help the systems analyst study the current system and then organize his or her findings in order to draw conclusions about the adequacy of the current system and to determine whether or not the project should move on to the *system design* stage. The main activities conducted during system analysis are *data collection* and *data analysis*.

Data Collection

The objective of *data collection* is to gather useful data about the system being studied. Some data-gathering tools that can be used include reviewing documents that show how the system is intended to work, reviewing *organizational charts* to determine the people and areas of responsibility in the part of the organization that the system is or will be located, sending questionnaires to users, and interviewing and observing those who use the system or the information produced by it.

Data Analysis

Once data about the system is gathered, it then needs to be analyzed to determine the effectiveness and efficiency of the current system and/or the requirements for a new or modified system. The tools used in *data analysis* vary depending on the type of system being studied and the preferences of the systems analyst; some of the most widely used data analysis tools are discussed next.

Entity-Relationship Diagrams (ERDs) and Data Flow Diagrams (DFDs)

Entity-relationship diagrams (*ERDs*) and *data flow diagrams* (*DFDs*) are used to model the *entities* (something, such as a person, object, or event, for which data is collected, as discussed in more detail in Chapter 14) in a system and the flow of data within a system, respectively. An ERD shows the logical relationships and interaction among system entities, such as customers, employees, and orders. A DFD illustrates the activities that are part of a system, as well as the data or information flowing into and out of each activity. In essence, it provides a visual representation of data movement in an organization. Figure 12-23 shows a data flow diagram for the order processing operation of a B2B e-commerce company.

Decision Tables and Decision Trees

Decision tables are useful for identifying procedures and summarizing the decision making process for one step of a system. For example, the decision table in Figure 12-23 summarizes the "Verify order is valid" decision process on the data flow diagram in that same figure along with the correct action to take based on all possible conditions. For instance, according to the information in the first column in the decision table shown in Figure 12-23, a new customer with incomplete information will result in an invalid order. The process of creating the table helps to ensure that all possible conditions have been considered. When the data in a decision table is expressed in a tree format, it is called a *decision tree*.

Business Process Modeling Notation (BPMN)

Business Process Modeling Notation (*BPMN*) is a graphical, standardized notation used to model a business process. It is often used to model the business processes used within systems and is designed to be readily understood by all individuals (including executives, managers, system developers, and end users) involved in analyzing, designing, managing, or using a system. BPMN expresses business processes graphically using *Business Process Diagrams* (*BPDs*)–which look similar to the *flowcharts* used to illustrate programs, as discussed in detail in Chapter 13.

RULES	POSSIBLE ORDER SCENARIOS							
CONDITIONS New customer?	Y	Y	Y	Y	N	N	N	N
New customer information complete?	N	Y	Y	Y	–	–	–	–
30+ day balance>0?	–	–	–	–	N	Y	N	N
Valid quantity and product number?	–	Y	N	Y	Y	–	N	Y
Quantity in stock?	–	Y	–	N	Y	–	–	N
ACTIONS Valid order–proceed to assembly stage		X			X			
Valid backorder–send backorder notices to customer and assembly stage				X				X
Invalid order	X		X			X	X	

DECISION TABLES

This decision table describes the actions taking place in the "Verify order is valid" process. Each column represents one scenario; N = No, Y = Yes, and X indicates the resulting action for each scenario. The rules in this decision table determine whether or not an order moves on to the order assembly stage.

DATA FLOW DIAGRAMS

In this data flow diagram for a B2B e-commerce company, an order triggers the processes of verification, assembly of the goods ordered, and billing.

FIGURE 12-23

Data flow diagrams and decision tables. These tools are frequently used to analyze a system during the system analysis phase of the SDLC.

SYS

CLASS DIAGRAM
Lists the attributes and methods that all instances in the class (in this case the Customer class) possess.

USE CASE DIAGRAM
Lists a user of the system (in this case a real customer) and its use cases (the actions the user may take).

 FIGURE 12-24

Class and use case diagrams. These tools are frequently used to model object-oriented systems.

Class Diagrams and Use Case Diagrams

Class diagrams and *use case diagrams* are used to illustrate systems that are based on the concept of *objects*. Unlike more traditional systems that treat processes and data as separate components, object-oriented systems contain objects consisting of data (called *attributes* or *variables*) that describe the object and the processes (called *methods*) that can be used with that data. A group of objects that share some common properties is called a *class*; an object *inherits*—or automatically possesses—all characteristics of the class to which it belongs. Many programs and databases today are object-oriented. Objects and *object-oriented programming* are discussed in more detail in Chapter 13; *object-oriented databases* are defined in Chapter 14. As shown in Figure 12-24, class diagrams are used to describe the types of objects in a system (specifically, the attributes and methods used with a particular class) and use case diagrams are used to illustrate the users (people or other systems) who interact with the system.

Documentation: Diagrams, Tables, Trees, and Models

The documentation resulting from the system analysis phase includes any instruments (such as questionnaires or interview questions) used in the data-gathering stage, as well as the resulting diagrams, tables, trees, models, and other tools used to summarize and analyze the gathered data.

System Design

System design focuses on specifying what the new system will look like and how it will work. This phase primarily consists of developing the design and specifications for the new system and performing a detailed analysis of the expected benefits and costs.

Developing the Design and Specifications for the New System

When designing a system, the systems analyst must take into account a variety of factors. One important factor is input. The systems analyst needs to determine the data that will be input into the new system and then usually creates a *data dictionary* (which describes the characteristics of all data used in a system) for the new system. The data dictionary typically includes the type of each piece of data in a system and its allowable size, any restrictions on its format (such as having to be within a certain numerical range or consisting of only certain letters of the alphabet), and who has the authority to update that piece of data. Data dictionaries and designing a database are discussed in detail in Chapter 14.

In addition to a data dictionary, the systems analyst will also create the diagrams (such as data flow diagrams (DFDs), class diagrams, Business Process Diagrams (BPDs), and

---

> **System design.** The phase of the system development life cycle in which a model of the new system and how it will work is formally established.

so forth) necessary to illustrate the new system. To illustrate the input screens and other user interfaces that will be used to input data into the new system, *input designs* (see Figure 12-25) are typically created.

Other factors to be considered when designing a new system include the computers and processing power that will be required, the other systems the new system must interact with, and the type and format of information that will be output. To show the desired format of the output screens and printed reports to be used with the new system, the systems analyst typically creates *output designs* (refer again to Figure 12-25). In addition, the system design should address the security features that will be needed to ensure that data is input accurately and secured against data loss. Other security considerations include restricting physical access to the computers used in the system, adequately securing the networks used with the new system, and the necessary backup and disaster recovery procedures. Network security was covered in Chapter 9; disaster recovery and other computer security issues are discussed in Chapter 15.

INPUT DESIGN
Design for screen used to input data for new customers.

OUTPUT DESIGN
Design for screen used to output customer name and balance once a Customer Number is entered.

FIGURE 12-25
Input and output designs are created during the system design phase.

Cost-Benefit Analysis

Once the new system has been designed, most organizations will perform a *cost-benefit analysis* to help determine whether the expected benefits of implementing the new system are worth its expected cost, in order to determine if the design for the new system should be implemented. The cost of a new system includes the initial investment in hardware, software, and training, as well as ongoing expenses, such as for new personnel and for maintenance. Some benefits can be computed relatively easily by calculating the amount of labor the new system will save, the reduction in paperwork it will allow, and so on. These gains are called *tangible benefits* because they represent quantifiable dollar amounts. Other benefits, such as improvements in customer service or better information supplied to decision makers, are called *intangible benefits* and are significantly more difficult to express as dollar amounts. While the existence of intangible benefits complicates the cost-benefit decision, they are sometimes more important than tangible benefits and so need to be considered. For instance, management must consider both tangible and intangible benefits to evaluate questions such as "Are the new services that we can offer to customers worth the $3 million these services will cost us?"

Documentation: System Design/Specifications

The system design and specifications developed during the system design phase consist of all the documentation necessary to illustrate the new system, including the data dictionary; DFDs, class diagrams, and other diagrams; input and output designs; necessary security controls; and so forth.

System Acquisition

Once a system has been designed and the required types of hardware and software have been specified, the systems analyst must decide where to obtain the necessary components.

This decision lies at the heart of the **system acquisition** phase. While hardware is usually purchased from outside vendors, software can be developed either in-house or obtained from an outside vendor, depending on the needs of the company and whether or not the company has the necessary staff and other resources for in-house development. This decision is referred to as the *make-or-buy decision*.

The Make-or-Buy Decision

One of the first steps in the system acquisition phase is determining whether the software needed for the new system should be created in-house or acquired from a software vendor. If there is a commercial, prewritten software program (either installed software or Web-based) available that meets the specifications for the system, that is often the fastest and least expensive option. This is most likely possible for specific, but general, tasks (such as payroll, accounting, and order entry), as well as for common systems used in specific industries (such as hotel reservation and construction management systems). Although the basic features of a purchased program cannot usually be altered without violating the software license, sometimes the programs allow for some customization, such as adding a company logo to reports or creating custom input screens. The most time-consuming and expensive "buy" option is having the necessary software developed from a company that specializes in creating custom systems.

For example, three options for purchasing a hotel reservation system are shown in Figure 12-26. While the top two alternatives (installed software and Web-based software) allow for some customization (changing the labels on the input screens, adding the company logo and photographs of the hotel, changing the number and type of rooms, and so forth), they will likely not meet system specifications quite as closely as custom software would. Consequently, some compromises might be necessary in order to use these first two alternatives. However, if installed software or Web-based software adequately meets the needs for the new system, it would be a significantly less expensive option compared to purchasing a custom software program.

If an organization decides to develop its own custom application software instead of acquiring software from an outside vendor, it moves into the *program development* process,

FIGURE 12-26
Software purchase options.

INSTALLED SOFTWARE
Installed on the hotel computers; typically allows for a small amount of customization.

WEB-BASED SOFTWARE (SOFTWARE AS A SERVICE)
Accessed via the Internet; typically allows for a small amount of customization.

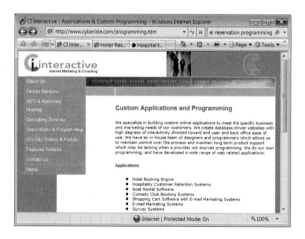

CUSTOM SOFTWARE
Can be created to meet all the specifications for the new system, as time and funding permit.

>**System acquisition.** The phase of the system development life cycle in which hardware, software, and other necessary system components are acquired.

described in detail in Chapter 13. This process uses the system specifications generated in the system design phase of the SDLC and continues through writing, testing, and maintenance of the program. Once the *program development life cycle (PDLC)* has been completed, the system development life cycle continues, just as it would if the software had been purchased.

RFPs and RFQs

Once it has been determined which specific types of hardware and/or software must be purchased for the new system, some organizations may go directly to a strategic partner to purchase the necessary items. Other organizations may choose to or may be required to (as is the case with items over a particular dollar amount that will be purchased with public funds) prepare a *request for proposal (RFP)*. This document contains a list of technical specifications for the equipment, software, and services needed for the new system, as determined during the system design phase, and requests that vendors propose products that meet those specifications. If the organization already knows exactly which hardware, software, and services it needs from vendors and is interested only in a quote on that specific list of items, a *request for quotation (RFQ)*—that names the desired items and asks only for a quote—may be used instead. In either case, the RFP or RFQ document is made available to potential vendors (such as by being mailed to a list of vendors who have participated in the past or by being advertised in a posted document or newspaper notice). Each interested vendor then sends a response (called a *bid*) back to the initiating organization, indicating its recommended solution and price (for an RFP) or just the price (for an RFQ).

Evaluating Bids

Once vendors have submitted their bids in response to an RFP or RFQ, the acquiring organization must decide which one to accept. Organizations typically have procedures in place to evaluate bids fairly in order to identify the bid with the lowest price that meets the necessary criteria. Part of the evaluation may include the use of a **benchmark test** (which is a systematic process for evaluating hardware and software, as discussed in Chapter 2) to evaluate the components proposed by one or more vendors. Benchmark test results for some existing products (such as computers and commercial software programs) are available through independent testing organizations and trade magazines. An organization may also choose to have a benchmark test performed at the vendor's testing center to determine how well the chosen hardware/software configuration will work. If the hardware to be used in the new system is already in place in the organization, another alternative is installing a demo or trial version of the proposed software on that hardware to see how the software performs. Although benchmark tests for the products under consideration may be difficult to find or perform, the results of these tests (when available) can be helpful in evaluating bids for proposed products.

Documentation: RFPs, RFQs, and Vendor Evaluation Materials

The documentation gathered during the system acquisition stage includes the RFP or RFQ sent to potential vendors, the proposals received, and any documentation produced during the evaluation of the bids (such as bid rankings and benchmark test results).

System Implementation

Once the required new hardware has been purchased and the required software has been purchased or developed, the **system implementation** phase can begin. This phase includes

---

>**Benchmark test.** A test used to measure computer system performance under typical usage conditions prior to purchase. >**System implementation.** The phase of the system development life cycle that encompasses activities related to making the system operational.

the tasks necessary to make the system operational, including getting existing data ready to move to the new system (called *data migration*) and installing the new hardware and software. Before data is transferred to the new system, however, the system should be thoroughly tested to ensure it is working properly. Often individual components of the system are tested alone first, and then the complete system is tested. *Test data* that is realistic and includes incorrect data that might accidentally occur during actual use (such as inputting a negative order quantity or leaving a required address field blank) should be developed and used during the preliminary testing process to ensure that input errors are detected by the new system.

Once the system has passed the testing stage, the system conversion process can begin. Typically, system conversion takes place using one or more of the strategies shown in Figure 12-27. With *direct conversion*, the old system is completely deactivated and the new system is immediately implemented—a fast, but extremely risky, strategy. With *parallel conversion*, both systems are operated in tandem until it is determined that the new system is working correctly, and then the old system is deactivated. With *phased conversion*, the system is implemented by module, with each module being implemented with either a

FIGURE 12-27

System conversion.
Converting from an old system to the new one often follows one of these four approaches.

DIRECT CONVERSION
The old system is replaced by the new system all at once.

OLD SYSTEM   NEW SYSTEM

PARALLEL CONVERSION
The old system and new system are both operated until it is determined that the new system is working properly.

OLD SYSTEM
NEW SYSTEM

PHASED CONVERSION
The system is implemented by module (each module can be implemented using either direct or parallel conversion).

MODULE 1
MODULE 2   OLD SYSTEM   NEW SYSTEM
MODULE 3

PILOT CONVERSION
The new system is used at only one location within the organization. After it is determined that the new system is working correctly, it is installed at the other locations.

SITE 1   OLD SYSTEM   NEW SYSTEM
SITE 2   OLD SYSTEM   NEW SYSTEM
SITE 3   OLD SYSTEM   NEW SYSTEM

direct or a parallel conversion. With *pilot conversion*, the new system is used at only one location within the organization. After it is determined that the new system is working correctly, it is installed at the other locations.

After the system is working properly, the final step of the system implementation process is training the end users. The necessary users' manuals and other training materials should be developed and supplied to the users. The training can then take place on the actual system, ideally with a variety of realistic sample data so that users will be exposed to the various situations they will encounter. Training usually occurs in one-on-one or group sessions led by a trainer familiar with the system, although self-paced Web-based training may also be used, if available and appropriate.

Documentation: Implementation Schedule, Test Data and Results, and Training Materials

The implementation schedule, test data and results, and any documentation regarding the type of implementation used should all be saved for future reference. The test data may be needed at a later time; for instance, if modifications are made to the system and it needs to be retested. The data and corresponding results are also useful if a problem occurs in the future in order to determine if the problem is the result of a situation that was not taken into consideration during the system design process or if there is another reason for the new problem. Users' manuals and other training materials should also be saved for future use.

System Maintenance

System maintenance is usually viewed as an ongoing process, beginning when the system is fully implemented and continuing on until the end of the system's life. One of the first activities that often takes place after the system has been implemented is a *post-implementation review*. This is basically a follow-up evaluation that is used to evaluate the new system, including determining whether or not it is meeting its intended goals and identifying any glitches in the new system that need to be corrected.

Common ongoing system maintenance activities include modifying existing software and adding additional software and hardware to the system, as needed, either to update what is already in place or to add new features. It also includes correcting any problems or situations that have arisen since the system was implemented, and ensuring the security of the system remains intact. Maintenance can be costly to an organization, and it is not unusual to spend several dollars in maintenance over time for every dollar that was originally put into developing the system.

A well-designed system should be flexible enough to accommodate changes over a reasonable period of time with minimal disruption. However, if a major change eventually becomes necessary, the organization should consider developing another system to replace the current one. At this point, the system development life cycle—beginning with the preliminary investigation—begins again.

Documentation: Completed Project Folder

After the post-implementation review has been completed, its results are added to the documentation accumulated from the other stages of the SDLC. Since the system is fully implemented at this point, it is a good time to ensure that all documentation has been gathered and organized in some manner, such as inside a *project folder*. This documentation is useful for auditors who may need to assess that proper procedures were followed during

---

>**System maintenance.** The phase of the system development life cycle in which minor adjustments are made to the finished system to keep it operational until the end of the system's life or until the time that the system needs to be redesigned.

the system development process, as well as for systems analysts if the system needs to be modified in the future.

APPROACHES TO SYSTEM DEVELOPMENT

While most system development projects include the six basic SDLC phases, the exact sequence and tasks performed during each phase, and the names and number of the phases, may vary depending on the organization and the type of system being developed. For instance, smaller systems in smaller companies may follow a less formal process of development, such as skipping or condensing some activities. Other development projects may go back and repeat a previous step to refine the process before moving on. Compare this process with an example from everyday life—vacation planning. People do not always design their entire vacation plan as the first step and then execute it, without modification, as the second step. They might design a plan ahead of time, but when the first day of the vacation is over, they might use that day's experiences as a basis for modifying the plan for the second day. Many systems are designed this way as well.

Regardless of the name or order of the phases used during system development, the tasks performed are typically the ones included in the SDLC. Some of the most common approaches to system development are discussed next.

The Traditional Approach

In **traditional system development**, the phases of system development are carried out in a preset order: 1) preliminary investigation, 2) system analysis, 3) system design, 4) system acquisition, 5) system implementation, and 6) system maintenance. Each phase begins only when the one before it has been completed, which is why this approach is sometimes referred to as the *waterfall model* (see Figure 12-28). Although the strict waterfall design has no interactivity between the phases, in practice the adjacent phases often interact, as shown by the dotted lines in Figure 12-28. So, for instance, if a problem is discovered during the system design phase, the systems analyst may decide to go back to the system analysis phase for further study, before returning to the system design phase.

With traditional system development, the entire system is planned and built before anyone gets to test it or use it. As each phase of development is completed, users "sign off" on the recommendations presented to them by the systems analyst, indicating their acceptance. Although this approach allows the system development process to proceed in a logical order, it often is viewed as being too time-consuming. For instance, by the time the new system finally becomes operational, important new needs that were not part of the original plan may have already arisen. Also, the system developed may turn out to be the wrong one since some managers and other users of information systems have difficulty expressing their information needs and it may not be until they begin to use the new system that they discover that it is not really what they need.

These problems notwithstanding, the traditional system development approach is useful when the system being developed is one with which there is a great deal of experience, where user requirements are easy to determine in advance, and where management wants the system completely spelled out before giving its approval. Often, the traditional system development approach is reserved for the development of large transaction processing systems.

> **Traditional system development.** An approach to system development whereby the six phases of the system development life cycle are carried out in a predetermined sequence.

The Iterative Approach

The newer *iterative* (repetitive) *approach* to system development allows the system to be developed incrementally, with a series of development steps being repeated until the system is finalized. This approach allows the developer to take advantage of what was learned during the development of earlier versions of the system. One example of this approach is **prototyping**, in which the focus is on initially developing a small model, or **prototype**, of the system or a portion of the system. The prototype is then tested by users and that feedback is used to modify or redesign the system as needed (refer again to Figure 12-28). As soon as a prototype is refined to the point where management feels confident that a larger version of the system will succeed, either the prototype can be expanded into the final system or the organization can move ahead with the remaining steps of the system development process, using the prototype as a model.

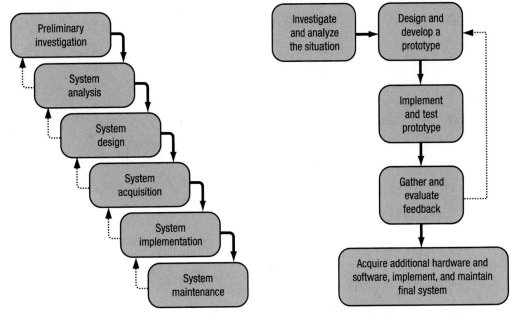

WATERFALL METHOD (TRADITIONAL APPROACH)
Each step in the SDLC is carried out in order, although some interaction typically occurs.

PROTOTYPING (ITERATIVE APPROACH)
An iterative process in which a prototype is designed, developed, and tested, and then an improved prototype is developed and tested, and the process is repeated until the final version is reached.

FIGURE 12-28
Two different approaches to system development.

Prototyping and the traditional system development approach sometimes are combined when building new systems—for instance, by following the traditional approach but using prototyping during the analysis and design phases to clarify user needs.

The End-User Development Approach

With the *end-user development approach*, the user is primarily responsible for the development of the system. This is in contrast to the other types of development discussed here, in which a qualified computer professional (usually the systems analyst) takes charge of the system development process. End-user development is most feasible when the system being developed is relatively small and inexpensive. For instance, an end user might develop a small marketing system designed to send a group of form letters or e-mails to one or more mailing lists. In developing the system, the user might follow a prototyping approach or a condensed version of the traditional system development approach. When end-user development is used in an organization, it is important that measures are taken to ensure that the system is compatible with existing systems and that no new problems are introduced (such as security risks or a system developed that cannot be effectively supported). Nonetheless, when computer professionals within an organization are too overloaded to build small but important systems that users need quickly, end-user development may be the only alternative.

>**Prototyping.** A system development alternative whereby a small model, or **prototype**, of the system is built before the full-scale system development life cycle is undertaken.

SYS

SUMMARY

WHAT IS AN INFORMATION SYSTEM?

Chapter Objective 1:
Understand what information systems are and why they are needed.

A **system** is a collection of elements and procedures that interact to accomplish a goal. An **information system** (**IS**) is a system used to generate information to support users in an organization. **System development** is the process that consists of all activities needed to put a new or modified system into place. System development may be required for many reasons—for example, changes in government regulations, the availability of new computer technology, or a new feature that the company wants to offer customers. A comprehensive framework used to describe and manage an organization's business functions and systems is called **enterprise architecture**. **Business intelligence** (**BI**) is the process of gathering, storing, accessing, and analyzing data about a company in order to make better business decisions. Data about a company and its customers is often stored in a **data warehouse** or **data mart**, and **data mining** can be used to analyze the data in a data warehouse for patterns and relationships.

Chapter Objective 2:
Discuss who uses information systems in a typical organization.

Information systems are most often used by decision makers—typically, managers, such as operational, middle, and executive managers. Managers usually manage the employees who are one level below them on the management pyramid. Managers, nonmanagement workers, and external individuals may all need access to some information systems to make decisions. Information systems used throughout an entire enterprise are called **enterprise systems**. A system that links multiple enterprises, such as a business and its customers, suppliers, and partners, can be referred to as an **inter-enterprise system**.

TYPES OF INFORMATION SYSTEMS

Chapter Objective 3:
Identify several types of information systems commonly found in organizations and describe the purpose of each.

Typically, many types of information systems are used in businesses and other organizations. Systems used to increase productivity and facilitate communications in the office include **office systems**, **document processing systems**, **document management systems** (**DMSs**), **content management systems** (**CMSs**), and **communication systems**. **Transaction processing systems** (**TPSs**) perform tasks that generally involve the tedious recordkeeping that organizations handle regularly; common TPSs include **order entry**, **payroll**, and **accounting systems**. These types of systems are most commonly used by operational managers.

Management information systems (**MISs**) provide decision makers—primarily middle managers—with preselected types of information. A **decision support system** (**DSS**) helps middle and executive managers organize and analyze their own decision making information. *Executive information systems* (*EISs*) are decision support systems customized to meet the special needs of executive managers. A **geographic information system** (**GIS**) is an information system that combines geographic information with other types of data in order to provide a better understanding of the relationships among the data.

Enterprise-wide systems include **electronic data interchange** (**EDI**), **enterprise resource planning** (**ERP**), **inventory management systems**, and **product lifecycle management** (**PLM**) **systems**.

Computers are widely used in industry to improve productivity at both the design stage—through **computer-aided design** (**CAD**)—and the manufacturing stage—via **computer-aided manufacturing** (**CAM**). The ability of some computer systems to perform in ways that would be considered intelligent if observed in humans is referred to as *artificial intelligence* (*AI*). Currently, the four main types of **artificial intelligence** (**AI**) **systems** are **intelligent agents**, **expert systems**, **neural networks**, and **robotics**—the study of **robot** technology. Robots for military, business, and personal use are available today.

RESPONSIBILITY FOR SYSTEM DEVELOPMENT

The *chief information officer* (*CIO*) typically holds primary responsibility for the overall direction of system development. Developing, running, and maintaining the computers and information systems in an organization is usually the responsibility of the **information systems (IS)**—also called **information technology (IT)**—**department**. There are many IS jobs; **systems analysts** are the people involved most closely with the development of systems. When a company lacks the in-house expertise, time, or money to do its own system development, it often turns to **outsourcing**.

Chapter Objective 4:
Explain the individuals responsible for system development.

THE SYSTEM DEVELOPMENT LIFE CYCLE (SDLC)

System development usually proceeds through six phases, which are often referred to collectively as the **system development life cycle** (**SDLC**). The first step is to conduct a **preliminary investigation**. This investigation addresses the nature of the problem under study, the potential scope of the system development effort, the possible solutions, and the costs and benefits of these solutions. By the end of this phase, a *feasibility report* discussing the findings of the preliminary investigation is prepared.

Chapter Objective 5:
Identify and describe the different steps of the system development life cycle (SDLC).

During the **system analysis** phase, the main objectives are to study the application in depth to assess the needs of users and to prepare a list of specific requirements that the new system must meet. These objectives are accomplished through *data collection* and *data analysis*. A number of tools can help with analysis, including *entity-relationship diagrams* (*ERDs*), *data flow diagrams* (*DFDs*), *decision tables, decision trees, class diagrams, use case diagrams*, and *Business Process Modeling Notation* (*BPMN*).

The **system design** phase consists of developing a model of the new system and performing a detailed analysis of benefits and costs. Various tools, such as a *data dictionary* and *input/output diagrams*, can be helpful during this phase. Security procedures to be used with the new system should be included in the system design. Once a system has been designed and the required types of software and hardware have been specified, the **system acquisition** phase begins. The *make-or-buy decision* determines whether the necessary components will be purchased or developed in-house. Many organizations that elect to buy system components use a *request for proposal* (*RFP*) or a *request for quotation* (*RFQ*) to obtain input and *bids* from vendors. Vendors submitting bids are commonly evaluated through a *vendor rating system* and then, possibly, a **benchmark test**.

Once arrangements have been made with one or more vendors for delivery of the necessary hardware and software, the **system implementation** phase begins. This phase includes all the remaining tasks that are necessary to make the system operational, including conversion of data, preparing any equipment to work in the new systems environment, and training. **System maintenance** is an ongoing process that begins when the system is fully implemented and continues until the end of the system's life.

APPROACHES TO SYSTEM DEVELOPMENT

In **traditional system development**, the phases of the SDLC are carried out in the traditional order, sometimes called the *waterfall model*. The focus in **prototyping** is on developing small models, or **prototypes**, of the target system. *End-user development* is a system development approach in which the user is primarily responsible for building the system. This is in contrast to other types of development, in which a qualified computer professional, such as a systems analyst, takes charge of the system development process.

Chapter Objective 6:
Discuss several approaches used to develop systems.

SYS

REVIEW ACTIVITIES

KEY TERM MATCHING

a. benchmark test

b. computer-aided design (CAD)

c. data warehouse

d. geographic information system (GIS)

e. management information system (MIS)

f. neural network

g. robot

h. system development life cycle (SDLC)

i. systems analyst

j. transaction processing system (TPS)

Instructions: Match each key term on the left with the definition on the right that best describes it.

1. _____ A comprehensive collection of data about a company and its customers.

2. _____ A device, controlled by a human operator or a computer, that can move and react to sensory input.

3. _____ A general term applied to the use of computer technology to automate design functions.

4. _____ An expert system in which the human brain's pattern-recognition process is emulated by the computer system.

5. _____ An information system that combines geographic information with other types of data (such as information about customers, sales, and so forth) in order to provide a better understanding of the relationships among the data.

6. _____ A person who studies systems in an organization in order to determine what work needs to be done and how this work may best be achieved.

7. _____ A test used to measure computer system performance under typical usage conditions prior to purchase.

8. _____ A type of information system that processes and records data created by an organization's business transactions.

9. _____ A type of information system that provides decision makers with preselected information that can be used to make middle-management decisions.

10. _____ The process consisting of the six phases of system development: preliminary investigation, system analysis, system design, system acquisition, system implementation, and system maintenance.

SELF-QUIZ

Instructions: Circle **T** if the statement is true, **F** if the statement is false, or write the best answer in the space provided. **Answers for the self-quiz are located in the References and Resources Guide at the end of the book.**

1. **T F** Executive managers tend to make highly unstructured decisions.

2. **T F** A decision support system would most likely be used by a nonmanagement worker.

3. **T F** An expert system is an example of an office system.

4. **T F** Assigning business tasks to an external company is referred to as outsourcing.

5. **T F** Users are only involved in the system development life cycle if the end-user approach is being used.

6. The software program used in an expert system in conjunction with the knowledge base to reach decisions is called the _____.

7. A(n) _____ is the computer professional who holds the primary responsibility for system development within an organization.

8. Benefits that are easy to quantify in dollars are called _____ benefits.

9. A(n) _____ is a model of a system that is built before the full-scale systems development effort is undertaken.

10. Match each term with its description, and write the corresponding number in the blank to the left of each description.

a. _____ Used to store, organize, and retrieve electronic documents.

b. _____ The process of gathering, storing, accessing, and analyzing data about a company to make better business decisions.

c. _____ Used to provide upper managers with the information they need to make decisions.

1. DSS

2. DMS

3. BI

---

1. Match each SDLC phase with its description, and write the corresponding number in the blank to the left of each description.

a. _____ The final phase of the SDLC.

b. _____ The phase that involves studying the system in depth.

c. _____ The phase in which the old system is converted to the new system.

d. _____ The phase that involves RFP or RFQ preparation and benchmark tests.

e. _____ The phase in which a feasibility study is performed.

f. _____ The phase that generates system specifications and a cost-benefit analysis.

1. design

2. preliminary investigation

3. maintenance

4. implementation

5. analysis

6. acquisition

2. Match each activity with its type of information system, and write the corresponding number in the blank to the left of each activity.

a. _____ A robot painting cars in a factory.

b. _____ A manager receiving the same type of report every month.

c. _____ A person buying a software package on the World Wide Web.

d. _____ An architect using a computer system to plan the layout of an office building.

1. TPS

2. CAD

3. MIS

4. AI

3. Indicate what type of employees operational managers typically manage and what type of information systems those employees would most commonly use.

4. Explain the difference between a request for proposal (RFP) and a request for quotation (RFQ).

5. Assume that a company is ready to install a new system at a single location. If it has a reasonable amount of time in which to implement the new system, select the two most appropriate conversion methods for the company to consider and explain under what circumstances it may wish to select one method over the other.

---

1. Some employers today are using a variety of soft benefits (such as free or low-cost on-site child-care, gyms, massages, and restaurants) to recruit and keep talented employees. For instance, Google employees get free lunch and dinner, among other benefits. What are the advantages and disadvantages to both employers and employees of these types of employee benefits? Would these soft benefits make you more inclined to work at that company? Why or why not?

2. Many everyday objects (such as amusement park rides, cars, elevators, and ovens) that you might not normally associate with a computer or information system, in fact, are today. There are obvious benefits, but are there risks as well? For instance, would you feel more or less comfortable riding on a roller coaster that was computer controlled? Do the benefits of computerizing an increasing number of everyday objects outweigh the potential risks? Why or why not?

PROJECTS

1. **Today's Robots** As discussed in the chapter, robots can be used today for a variety of activities in businesses and the military, as well as in the home.

    For this project, select one type of robotic device on the market today—for instance, a robotic toy, vacuum cleaner, or lawn mower; a security or manufacturing robot; a robot used by the military or NASA; or a robotic personal assistant—and research it. Find out what the product does, what it costs, how it is powered and controlled, and if it can be reprogrammed. What are the advantages of the robotics part of the product? Do you think this is a worthwhile or beneficial product? At the conclusion of your research, prepare a one- to two-page summary of your findings and opinions and submit it to your instructor.

2. **Chatterbots** As discussed in the chapter, a chatterbot is a program that attempts to simulate the "chat" of another human.

    For this project, find a chatterbot on a Web page (either Cybelle on the Agentland.com Web site shown in Figure 12-13 or another you find using a search site) and have a conversation with the chatterbot. Form an opinion about how humanlike the exchange was. Do you think the chatterbot responded to your comments in a humanlike fashion? Was it able to answer your questions? If not, what did it do when it could not answer a question? Do you think chatterbots can be a worthwhile addition to a Web site? Would you prefer to chat in real time with a customer service chatterbot if it could answer your questions correctly, or would you rather wait to chat in real time with a human customer service representative? Explain. At the conclusion of your research, prepare a one-page summary of your experience and submit it to your instructor.

3. **Your Decision** The construction of a decision table can be beneficial during the system development process. It can also be used to illustrate personal decisions, such as for your future career plans.

    For this project, select a particular job you may want to pursue upon graduation and construct a "Career Options" decision table that includes various conditions and rules and that could be used to determine if you have completed the necessary actions to obtain that job. On the table, mark your current status for each specified condition and the decision that results from this input in the appropriate location at the bottom of the table. Prepare a short summary of what conditions in your table you have already accomplished and which ones are still to come, and submit your summary to your instructor along with your marked-up decision table.

4. **Smart Robots** Robotics research is continuing to make smarter and more capable robots. For instance, NASA researchers have developed a way to make a crew of robots work together to grasp, lift, and move heavy loads across rough, varied terrain. The software allows the robots to "share a brain" so that each robot knows what the rest are doing. This enables the robots to work together to develop plans, such as how to maneuver around a rock or other obstacle the crew may encounter. What are the ethical repercussions of making continually smarter robots? Can robots get too smart? Is it ethical to continue to replace human laborers with robots? Does it make a difference if the jobs are dangerous? What steps should our society take to ensure that robots cannot become physically dangerous or otherwise pose a risk to humans? If robotics technology evolves to the point where robots can look and act like humans, is it ethical to create robots that might be mistaken for humans?

   For this project, form an opinion about the ethical ramifications of making smarter and more capable robots and be prepared to discuss your position (in class, via an online class discussion group, in a class chat room, or via a class blog, depending on your instructor's directions). You may also be asked to write a short paper expressing your opinion.

ETHICS IN ACTION

5. **Computer Certification** There are a number of certification programs available for computer professionals in a variety of areas, such as application software, computer networking, programming, and system security. Four of the companies or organizations offering the most respected and widely used certification programs are Microsoft, Novell, Cisco Systems, and the Institute for Certification of Computing Professionals (ICCP).

   For this project, select one of the companies or organizations listed in the previous paragraph and research the computer certification programs it currently offers. Select one specific program and determine who the certificate is targeted to, what type of training or testing is required, if you have to have on-the-job work experience to qualify, and what fees and other additional requirements are necessary. Is it an onsite program, or can you complete the program online? Do you think this certification would be useful when looking for a job? Share your findings and opinions with the class in the form of a short presentation. The presentation should not exceed 10 minutes and should make use of one or more presentation aids, such as the chalkboard, handouts, overhead transparencies, or a computer-based slide presentation (your instructor may provide additional requirements). You may also be asked to submit a summary of the presentation to your instructor.

PRESENTATION/ DEMONSTRATION

Instructions: Go to the Chapter 12 page at **www.cengage.com/computerconcepts/np/uc13** to work the following Web Activities.

6. **Interactive Activities** Work the interactive **Crossword Puzzle**, watch the **Video Podcasts** and **Online Videos**, and explore the **Further Exploration** links associated with this chapter.

   If you have a SAM user profile, you may have access to hands-on instruction, practice, and assessment of the skills covered in this chapter. Check with your instructor for instructions and the correct URL/Web site to access those assignments.

7. **Student Edition Labs** Work the following interactive **Student Edition Labs**.
   - ➤ **Project Management**   ➤ **Careers and Technology**

8. **Test Yourself** Review the **Online Study Guide** for this chapter, then test your knowledge of the terms and concepts covered in this chapter by completing the **Key Term Matching** exercise, the **Self-Quiz**, the **Exercises**, and the **Practice Test**.

WEB ACTIVITIES

## chapter 13

Program Development and Programming Languages

After completing this chapter, you will be able to do the following:

1. Understand the differences between structured programming, object-oriented programming (OOP), aspect-oriented programming (AOP), and adaptive software development.

2. Identify and describe the activities involved in the program development life cycle (PDLC).

3. Understand what constitutes good program design and list several tools that can be used by computer professionals when designing a program.

4. Explain the three basic control structures and how they can be used to control program flow during execution.

5. Discuss some of the activities involved with debugging a program and otherwise ensuring it is designed and written properly.

6. List some tools that can be used to speed up or otherwise facilitate program development.

7. Describe several programming languages in use today and explain their key features.

outline

Overview

Approaches to Program Design and Development
Procedural Programming
Object-Oriented Programming (OOP)
Aspect-Oriented Programming (AOP)
Adaptive Software Development

The Program Development Life Cycle (PDLC)
Problem Analysis
Program Design
Program Coding
Program Debugging and Testing
Program Implementation and Maintenance

Tools for Facilitating Program Development
Application Lifecycle Management (ALM) Tools
Application Generators
Device Software Development Tools
Software Development Kits (SDKs) and Application Program Interfaces (APIs)
Rich Internet Application (RIA) Tools

Programming Languages
What Is a Programming Language?
Categories of Programming Languages
Common Programming Languages

admin : boolean

OVERVIEW

If you want to build a house, you would probably begin with some research and planning. You might research current trends and regulations related to home design, draw up some floor plans, estimate the cost of construction, and so on. In other words, you would not start digging a hole and pouring concrete on the first day. Creating successful application programs works the same way—you need to do considerable planning before you jump into coding the application.

When computer professionals need to develop new applications, they use a programming language—a set of rules used to write computer programs. In Chapter 12, we discussed developing complete systems. In this chapter, we look specifically at practices and tools for developing the application programs used within these systems.

The chapter opens with a discussion of the most common approaches to program design and development, followed by a look at the program development life cycle; that is, the phases that occur when a new program needs to be created or an existing program needs to be modified. In this section, topics—such as tools that can be used to design a program, good program design techniques, and types of program errors—are discussed. Next, we turn our attention to tools that can facilitate program development. The chapter closes with a look at some of the most popular programming languages. ■

APPROACHES TO PROGRAM DESIGN AND DEVELOPMENT

There have been various approaches to programming over the years. Two of the most significant approaches are *procedural programming* and *object-oriented programming* (*OOP*). Newer approaches include *aspect-oriented programming* (*AOP*) and *adaptive software development*.

Procedural Programming

Procedural programming focuses on the step-by-step instructions that tell the computer what to do to solve a problem. It is based on the concept of the *procedure call*—locating specific tasks in *procedures* (small sections of program code also called *modules* or *subprograms*) that are called by the main program code when those tasks need to be performed. After a procedure finishes, program control returns to the main program. This approach allows each procedure to be performed as many times as needed and at the appropriate time without requiring multiple copies of the same code, so the overall

SYS

> **Procedural programming.** An approach to program design in which a program is separated into small modules that are called by the main program or another module when needed.

program is smaller and the main program is easier to understand. Reusing code in this manner also allows for faster development time and reduced maintenance costs.

Prior to procedural programming, programs were written as one large set of instructions containing statements that sent control to different parts of the program as needed to perform actions in the proper order. To accomplish this, these programs used statements that jumped from one part of the program code to another, such as a "GOTO 100" statement to send program control to line 100 of the code to execute commands from that point in the program code on, until another GOTO statement was reached. This jumping around continued until the program ended. This type of code is sometimes referred to as *spaghetti code* because it is a disorganized, intertwined, jumble of statements, which makes following the logic of the program as difficult as tracing the path of a single strand of spaghetti in a plate of spaghetti. Procedural programming eliminates this problem by sending control out to a module that performs a specific task whenever it is necessary to perform that task, and then returning to the main program when the task is complete.

Structured programming goes one step further, breaking the program into very small modules of code that perform a single task and prohibiting the use of the GOTO statement. Structured programming embodies a *top-down design* philosophy, in which the overall general tasks that need to be performed by the program are first defined at the highest levels of the hierarchy and then are broken down further at the lower levels until they are represented by the very specific tasks that need to be carried out (see Figure 13-1). Although technically structured programming is a subset of procedural programming, sometimes the terms "structured programming" and "procedural programming" are used interchangeably.

In a computer program, **variables** are named memory locations that are defined for that particular program and are used to store the current value of data items used in the program. In a procedural program, variables can be accessed and their values changed from any module in the program, as appropriate. For instance, a *GrossPay* variable containing an employee's gross pay would be needed in several modules (such as the *Gross Pay, Deductions, Net Pay*, and *Output* modules in the program shown in Figure 13-1). A *StateTaxAmount* variable containing an employee's state tax amount would be assigned the appropriate value in the *Compute state taxes* module, and then used in the *Net Pay* and *Output* modules. In

FIGURE 13-1

Structured programming.

A structured program is divided into individual modules; each module represents a very specific processing task.

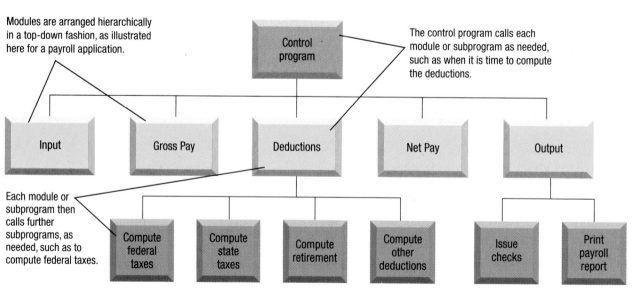

Modules are arranged hierarchically in a top-down fashion, as illustrated here for a payroll application.

The control program calls each module or subprogram as needed, such as when it is time to compute the deductions.

Each module or subprogram then calls further subprograms, as needed, such as to compute federal taxes.

>**Variable.** A named memory location defined in a computer program that is used to store the current value of a data item used in that program.

a computer program, variables are usually designated as *integers* (numeric values that do not have a decimal portion), *real numbers* (numeric values that may have a decimal portion), *character* or *string values* (non-numeric values consisting of the characters on the keyboard), or *Boolean values* (values that represent one of two states—yes (true) or no (false)). Once a variable has been *declared*—that is, given a name and assigned a particular data type—it can be used in program statements, such as to store a value in that variable or use that variable in a formula. When referring to a variable in a program, its assigned name is used; the exact coding of program statements for variable definition and other programming commands varies depending on the programming language being used, as illustrated later in this chapter.

Object-Oriented Programming (OOP)

Instead of focusing on the specific steps and tasks a program must take to solve a problem, **object-oriented programming** (**OOP**) focuses on the things (or *objects*) that make up a program. As described in Chapter 12, an object contains data (usually referred to as *attributes*) that describe the object, as well as the processes (called *methods*) that can be used with that object (see Figure 13-2). A group of objects that share some common properties (attributes and methods) form a *class*; classes may be further divided into *subclasses*. Each specific object in a class (referred to as an *instance*) *inherits*—or automatically possesses— all of the attributes and methods of the class to which it belongs. Just like the variables used in procedural programming, attributes are defined as a particular type of data and the value of each attribute may vary from instance to instance.

The methods used in OOP are similar to the modules used in procedural programming in that they include specific operations that can be performed on an object. For example, the class of objects representing buttons displayed on the screen for a particular program might include one attribute for the color of the button, one attribute for the size of the button's display rectangle, one attribute for the button's location on the screen, and one attribute for the text to appear on the button (refer again to Figure 13-2). The button class would also include methods for any actions that might be taken with the button objects, such as to display, hide, or dim them. When a button object receives a *message* asking it to perform a particular method, the button object executes the specific actions contained in that method. For instance, a button object receiving a message to invoke the *Display* method might result in the button being displayed on the screen; if that button later received a message to invoke the *Hide* method, the button would then be hidden from view.

It is important to realize that each individual object (instance) in a class has the attributes and methods associated with that class, but the values of the attributes may vary from instance to instance. For example, one object in the button class may have a value of *red* for the button color attribute and another may have a value of *blue* for that same attribute. Objects may also have additional attributes and methods that are not common to all members of the class.

The data contained within an object can be in a variety of formats, such as numeric, text, image, video, audio, and so forth. This characteristic, combined with the ability to manipulate different types of objects with the same methods, leads to new applications that were difficult, or impossible, to create with procedural programming languages. For example, the statement

$$c = a + b$$

is a typical statement in most programming languages and is most often used to combine (add) two numbers. In an OOP language, however, the same statement could be

FIGURE 13-2

Button objects.

This class diagram illustrates that each object in the Button class has four attributes to hold data about the current state of the button and three methods to react to messages the object receives.

> **Object-oriented programming (OOP).** An approach to program design in which a program consists of a collection of objects that contain data and methods to be used with that data.

SYS

used to combine two strings of data (contained in the attributes a and b) to display a first and last name next to each other. The same statement could also be used to combine two audio clips, or one video clip and one soundtrack, in order to play them at the same time.

Another advantage of OOP is that objects can be accessed by multiple programs. The program being used to access an object determines which of the object's methods are available to that program. Therefore, objects can be reused without having to alter the code associated with each object, which shortens program development time. For convenience, many object-oriented programming languages have built-in *class libraries* that contain ready to use, predefined classes for common tasks performed when creating an object-oriented program, such as creating a *form* (user interface) or adding a text box or button to a form. When needed, new objects and classes can be created.

Aspect-Oriented Programming (AOP)

Aspect-oriented programming (AOP) is a software development approach that continues the programming trend of breaking a software program into small and more manageable pieces that overlap in functionality as little as possible. Specifically, AOP more clearly separates different functions so that program components can be developed and modified individually from one another and the components can be reused easily. Although both procedural programming and object-oriented programming focus on separating components (by using modules and classes, for example), some common tasks or *programming policies* cannot be separated easily using procedural programming or OOP. Because of this, important programming policies (such as running a security check, performing error-handling procedures, and opening a database connection) may end up being located in hundreds or thousands of places scattered throughout a program's code, making it very difficult to update them when needed. AOP can encapsulate these policies or functions into *aspects*—code segments that can be used as needed without having to repeat the code throughout the program; this helps to reduce redundancy, improve software quality, and lower IT development and maintenance costs. According to IBM, AOP has yielded significant benefits in the quality of the code and the speed with which programmers can write programs. AOP and OOP are currently considered to be complementary, not competing, technologies, although some AOP advocates view AOP as the next evolution in programming.

Adaptive Software Development

Program development methodologies that are designed to make program development faster or more efficient and focus on adapting the program as it is being written are referred to as *adaptive software development*. Adaptive software development typically features *iterative development* (a cyclical approach that allows the repetition of steps and tasks as needed) and/or *incremental development* (developing one piece at a time). One of the most recent adaptive software development approaches is *agile software development* (*ASD*). Like earlier adaptive software development approaches—such as *rapid application development* (*RAD*) and *extreme programming* (*XP*)—the goal of ASD is to create software quickly. However, ASD focuses on building and delivering small functional pieces of applications as the project progresses, instead of delivering one large application at the end of the project. Each piece is typically treated like a separate miniature software project of its own, and the development process is repeated for each piece. ASD emphasizes teams of people (programmers, managers, business experts, customers, and so forth) working

---

>**Aspect-oriented programming (AOP).** An approach to program design in which different functions are clearly separated so program components can be developed and modified individually from one another, and the components can be easily reused with separate, nonrelated objects.

closely together, which provides for continuous learning and adaptation as the project is developed. There are a number of agile development processes with similar approaches. They all focus on adapting quickly to a changing situation and many are based on the *Agile Manifesto*—a definition of agile software development written by the Agile Alliance.

THE PROGRAM DEVELOPMENT LIFE CYCLE (PDLC)

Creating application programs is referred to as *application software development* or **program development**. Program development traditionally takes place during the system acquisition phase of the system development life cycle (SDLC), discussed in Chapter 12, and uses the system specifications that were developed during the system design phase of the SDLC. Once program development has been completed, the SDLC continues. The phases involved in program development are referred to as the **program development life cycle** (**PDLC**) and are illustrated in Figure 13-3.

The activities that take place during each phase of the program development life cycle (PDLC) are discussed in the next few sections. As each development activity takes place, documentation is generated. The types of documentation generated, which consist of details about what the program does and how it works, are summarized in Figure 13-3.

Problem Analysis

As discussed in detail in Chapter 12, the systems analyst develops a set of specifications during the system design phase of the SDLC that indicate exactly what the new system should do and how it should work. These specifications (data flow diagrams, class diagrams, input and output designs, database designs, data dictionary, and so forth) are used during **problem analysis**— the first phase of the PDLC. During this phase, these specifications are reviewed by the systems analyst and the **programmer**—the person who will use a programming language to code the software program according to these specifications. They will determine the programming language to be used, how the new program will need to interact with other programs in the organization, and other important considerations.

FIGURE 13-3

The program development life cycle (PDLC). Each phase of the program development life cycle produces some type of documentation to pass on to the next phase.

Amended program package

1. **Problem analysis**

Program specifications

5. **Program implementation and maintenance**

2. **Program design**

Completed program package

Design specifications

4. **Program debugging and testing**

3. **Program coding**

Documented source code

SYS

> **Program development.** The process of creating application programs. > **Program development life cycle (PDLC).** The process containing the five phases of program development: analyzing, designing, coding, debugging and testing, and implementing and maintaining application software. > **Problem analysis.** The phase of the program development life cycle in which the problem is carefully considered and the program specifications are developed. > **Programmer.** A person whose job it is to write, test, and maintain computer programs.

The systems analyst and the programmer may also meet with the users of the new system to fully understand what features the software program they are creating for the new system must include. Only when the problem is completely understood should the systems analyst and the programmer move on to the next phase of the PDLC—*program design.*

Documentation: Program Specifications

The main result of this first phase in the PDLC is a set of program specifications outlining what the program must do. Typically, there will also be a schedule or a timetable for completing, testing, and implementing the program.

Program Design

In the **program design** phase of the PDLC, the specifications developed during the problem analysis phase are used to develop an *algorithm* for the program; that is, the set of steps that are needed in order for the program to perform all the tasks that it is supposed to do. Only when the program design is complete and tested does the next phase—the actual program coding—begin.

Good program design helps the development process go more smoothly and makes revisions to the software program easier to do when changes to the program are needed in the future. Just as with Web site design (discussed in Chapter 10), careful planning and design of a computer program are extremely important and pay off in the end. Some program design tools and guidelines are discussed next.

Program Design Tools

Program design tools are planning tools. They consist of diagrams, charts, tables, models, and other tools that outline the organization of the program tasks, the steps the program or program component will follow, or the characteristics of objects used by the program. These tools are used to define exactly what the program is to do; once a program has been coded and implemented, the designs generated by program design tools can also provide useful program documentation. Some of the most common program design tools are discussed next. In general, the program design models shown in this textbook are very basic; the program design models used in a real-life program are much more complex.

Structure Charts

Structure charts (sometimes called *hierarchy charts*) depict the overall organization of a structured program. They show the modules used in a program and how the modules relate to one another. Figure 13-1 at the beginning of this chapter contains a structure chart for a payroll application. As shown in Figure 13-1, each box on the chart represents a program module; that is, a set of logically related operations that perform a well-defined task. The modules in the upper rows invoke the modules (subprograms) under them whenever those tasks need to be performed.

Flowcharts

Flowcharts are used to illustrate the step-by-step logic that is to take place within a program, module, or method. The steps in a flowchart are arranged in the same logical sequence as their corresponding program statements in the program. As shown in Figure 13-4, flowcharts use graphical symbols (such as the *decision symbol* to indicate two paths that can be taken

---

>**Program design.** The phase of the program development life cycle in which the program specifications are expanded into a complete design of the new program. >**Flowchart.** A program design tool that shows graphically step-by-step the actions a computer program will take.

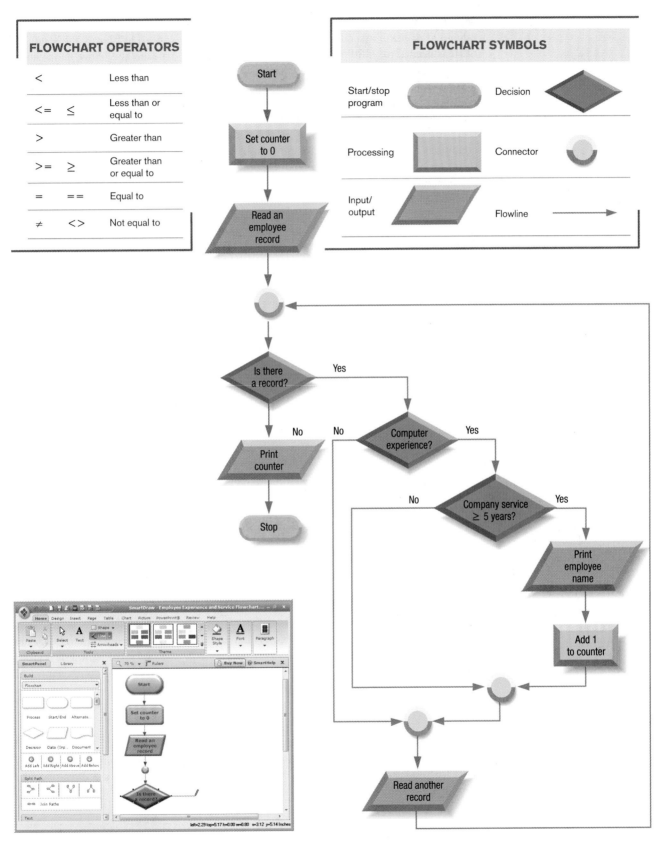

FLOWCHART SOFTWARE
Can be used to create and modify flowcharts.

FIGURE 13-4
A flowchart
example.

depending on whether the result of the condition stated in the decision is true or false) and *relational operators* (such as < for *less than* and = for *equal to*) to portray the sequence of steps needed to fulfill the logic in that program, module, or method. Flowcharts can be drawn by hand, but *flowcharting software* (such as the program shown in Figure 13-4) can make it easier to create and modify flowcharts.

The program illustrated by the flowchart in Figure 13-4 will test all entries in an employee file to determine the employees that have computer experience and at least five years of company service, print the names of the employees who meet these two conditions as they are identified, and then print the total number of employees meeting the criteria when the end of the employee file is reached. To accomplish this, a *looping* operation is needed to repeat some of the steps in the program until the end of the employee file is reached, and a *counter* variable is incremented as needed to keep track of the number of employees meeting both criteria. After the last employee record is read and processed, the value of the counter is printed to complete the printed report, and then the program ends.

Pseudocode

Pseudocode also expresses the steps in a program, module, or method, but uses English-like statements in place of the flowchart's graphical symbols (see Figure 13-5). No formal set of standard rules exists for writing pseudocode; however, the closer the words and phrases used in pseudocode are to the basic computer operations that will occur in the program, the easier it is to move from pseudocode to actual program code. Figure 13-5 shows the pseudocode for the program shown in the flowchart in Figure 13-4 and follows some commonly used conventions. For instance, all words relating to a *control structure* (a decision or loop, as discussed in more detail shortly) are capitalized and the processing steps contained within those structures are indented. Standard words for input and output (*Read* for reading from a file and *Print* for output on paper) are used, variables (such as *counter* and *employee_name*) have meaningful names, the actions the computer will take are written in descriptive natural language, and the keywords *Start* and *Stop* are used to begin and end the pseudocode.

Although it takes longer to model a program or program component using pseudocode, translating a program from pseudocode to a programming language is much faster and more straightforward than from a flowchart to a programming language. Flowcharts, however, are sometimes better than pseudocode for visualizing the logic of a program, and they are usually faster to create. Sometimes a flowchart is first developed to identify the logic of a program or program component, and then the steps of the program are expressed in more detail using pseudocode.

FIGURE 13-5

Pseudocode.

The problem is the same as illustrated in the flowchart in Figure 13-4.

```
Start
counter = 0
Read a record
DO WHILE there are records to process
    IF computer_experience
        IF company_service ≥ 5 years
            Print employee_name
            Increment counter
        ELSE
            Next statement
        END IF
    ELSE
        Next statement
    END IF
    Read another record
END DO
Print counter
Stop
```

Unified Modeling Language (UML) Models

Unified Modeling Language (UML) is a set of standard notations that is widely used for modeling object-oriented programs. The UML standards are developed by the *Object Management Group* (*OMG*). The most current version (*UML 2.2*) has 13

>**Pseudocode.** A program design tool that uses English-like statements to outline the logic of a program. >**Unified Modeling Language (UML).** A set of standard notations for creating business models.

standard diagram types, including diagrams for modeling basic structures (like the *class diagram* shown in Figure 13-6), diagrams for modeling behavior (such as the *use case diagram* shown in Figure 12-24 in Chapter 12), and diagrams for modeling interactions between entities. Similar to flowcharts, UML diagrams can be drawn by hand, though using a software program designed for that purpose makes creating and editing the diagrams easier.

The class diagram shown in Figure 13-6 illustrates the attributes and methods for objects in a Bicycles class, such as might be used in an OOP program to model bicycles controlled by users in a simulation or game. A similar model (without the attributes for current gear and speed and with different methods) could be used in an inventory or order entry program for a sporting goods store. As shown in the figure, the Bicycles class specifies the attributes and methods that all Bicycles objects have in common. Each individual object (instance) in the Bicycles class has a value for each attribute to indicate the overall characteristics of that particular bike (such as type, category, size, color, and number of gears), as well as the current gear and current speed being used. Note that while each instance inherits the attributes and methods of the class, the values for the attributes may or may not be the same for all instances in that class. For example, while the two bike instances shown in Figure 13-6 have the same value (0) for *CurrentSpeed*, the values for all the other attributes are different. The methods included in the Bicycles class express the actions the Bicycles objects can take, such as to change gears and speed, accelerate and brake, stop, and turn.

CLASS
A group of objects that share the same basic properties. A class diagram defines the attributes and methods that all instances in the class possess.

INSTANCES
The specific objects in a class, such as Bike1 and Bike2 in this example.

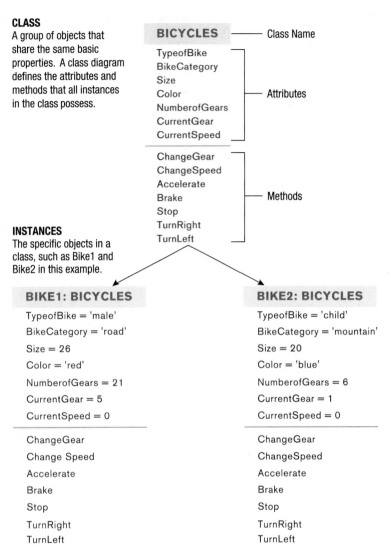

INHERITANCE
All instances of a class inherit all attributes and methods of the class. The values of the attributes for each instance may be different from other instances.

FIGURE 13-6

Class diagrams. This example shows one class and two instances of that class.

Control Structures

A **control structure** is used to illustrate when, how, and in what order the statements in a computer program, module, or method are performed. The three fundamental control structures are *sequence, selection,* and *repetition*; these control structures are illustrated in Figure 13-7 and discussed next.

The Sequence Control Structure

A **sequence control structure** is simply a series of statements that follow one another. After the first statement has been carried out completely, the program control moves to the next statement, and so forth.

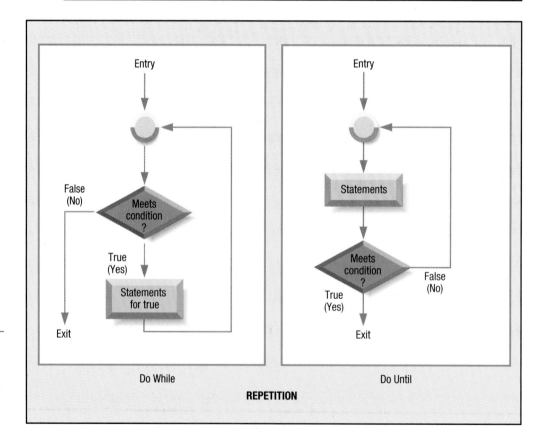

FIGURE 13-7

The three fundamental control structures. Note that each structure has only one entry point and only one exit point.

The Selection Control Structure

With a **selection control structure**, the direction that the program control takes depends on the results of a certain condition. The basic selection control structure is the *if-then-else structure* shown in Figure 13-7, in which the condition can only result in two possibilities—true or false. *If* a certain condition is true, *then* the program follows one path and executes the statements on that path; *else*, if false, the program follows a different path.

An alternate selection control structure can be used when there are more than two possibilities. This structure—known as the *case control structure* and shown in Figure 13-7—allows for as many possible results of the specified condition as needed. For example, the flowchart in Figure 13-4 uses two *nested* if-then-else statements (one statement located inside another) to test for the two conditions "Computer experience?" and "Company service ≥ 5 years?". Since the second condition is only tested if the first condition is true, these two conditions together result in the following three possibilities, or *cases*:

➤ Case 1: No computer experience

➤ Case 2: Computer experience, company service < 5 years

➤ Case 3: Computer experience, company service ≥ 5 years

The case control structure with these three choices could be used in the flowchart in Figure 13-4 instead of the two nested if-then-else statements. The statements for printing the employee's name and incrementing the counter would be listed under Case 3 (the other cases would result in no action being taken), and the next action after exiting the case structure would be to read another record.

The Repetition Control Structure

The **repetition control structure** (also called the *iteration control structure*) is used when one or more statements are to be repeated in a *loop* until a particular condition is reached. There are two forms of this control structure: The *do while structure*, in which the statements in the loop are repeated as long as a certain condition is true ("do *while* true"), and the *do until structure*, in which the statements in the loop are repeated as long as a certain condition is false ("do *until* true"). It is important to realize that if the condition is not true when the program first reaches a do while loop, the statements within the loop will never be executed because the decision test is located at the top of the loop (refer again to Figure 13-7). With a do until loop, the statements in the loop are always executed at least one time, because the decision test is located at the bottom of the loop (refer again to Figure 13-7).

Good Program Design

Good program design is essential. If a program is not well planned before the coding process begins, it usually results in a more time-consuming and, potentially, lower-quality result than if the design process had been carried out properly. In general, time spent planning is time well spent. A few principles that should be kept in mind to help facilitate good program design are discussed next.

>**Selection control structure.** A series of statements in which the results of a decision determine the direction the program takes. >**Repetition control structure.** A series of statements in a loop that are repeated until a particular condition is met.

DIRECTIONS FOR HUMAN	DIRECTIONS FOR COMPUTER
1. Please make me a piece of toast with margarine.	1. Take one slice of bread out of the bag of bread.
	2. Put the bread into the slot on the toaster, narrow edge first with the widest part of the bread fitting into the widest part of the slot.
	3. Push the start lever on the toaster down.
	4. When the toast pops up, remove the toast from the toaster.
	5. Place the toast onto a plate.
	6. Open the silverware drawer, take out a knife, then close the silverware drawer.
	7. Open the refrigerator, remove the margarine, and shut the refrigerator.
	8. Take the lid off the margarine.
	9. Scoop out one teaspoon of margarine with the knife.
	10. Spread the margarine on the top side of the toast, evenly covering that surface of the toast.
	11. Place the lid back on the margarine.
	12. Open the refrigerator, replace the margarine, and shut the refrigerator.

Be Specific

When illustrating the instructions that a computer will follow, *all* things that the computer must do or consider must be specified. Although the instruction "Please make me a piece of toast with margarine" would be a request that another person could follow easily, it is not specific enough for a computer to follow.

To instruct a computer properly, every step the computer must perform and every decision the computer must make has to be stated precisely (see Figure 13-8).

FIGURE 13-8

Writing instructions for a computer versus a person. A computer requires step-by-step instructions.

Follow the One-Entry-Point/One-Exit-Point Rule

An important characteristic of the control structures just discussed is that each permits only one entry point into and one exit point out of any structure (refer again to Figure 13-7). This property is sometimes called the *one-entry-point/one-exit-point rule*. Programs that adhere to this rule are much more readable, their logic is easier to follow, and they are easier to modify in the future.

No Infinite Loops or Logic Errors

An *infinite loop* is a set of instructions that repeats forever. An infinite loop occurs when the condition to exit a loop never occurs, such as when a do while condition never becomes false or a do until condition never becomes true. This can happen when the statement to increment a counter is forgotten, when the wrong operators are used—such as less than (<) instead of greater than (>)—or when a similar error in logic is made. To test for infinite loops and other *logic errors*, it is a good idea to test your finished program design, as discussed next.

Program Design Testing

Once the algorithm for a program or program component has been completed, the design should be tested to locate any errors in the logic of the program. One of the most common ways to test a design is to perform a *desk check*. In a desk check, the programmer "walks" through the program design (such as by following the steps of a finished flowchart), keeping track of the values of any loop counters and other variables in a *tracing table* to ensure the program does what it is intended to do. At the end of the program, the output should be the expected values, based on the test data used. If the output is incorrect, there is an error in the design that needs to be located and corrected before the program moves on to the coding stage. Examples of desk checking a flowchart representing the steps needed to input two numbers and compute their sum (one correct flowchart and one flowchart containing an error) are shown in Figure 13-9.

Documentation: Design Specifications

The documentation resulting from the design phase of the program development life cycle is a set of design specifications that illustrates the program needed to fulfill the program requirements. The design specifications can be expressed using one or more design tools, such as structure charts, flowcharts, pseudocode, and UML models. Any test data and results from desk checking should be included as well.

FURTHER EXPLORATION

Go to the Chapter 13 page at **www.cengage.com/computerconcepts/np/uc13** for links to information about program design.

DESK CHECK RESULTS FOR CORRECT FLOWCHART

Flowchart Stage	Counter	Decision Test Results (Counter < 2)	Number	Sum
Initialization	0	–	–	0
First decision test	0	T	–	0
		(enters loop)		
After first loop	1	–	6	6
Second decision test	1	T	6	6
		(enters loop)		
After second loop	2	–	3	9
Third decision test	2	F	3	9
		(exits loop)		

Test data: 6, 3; Expected results: Sum = 9; Actual results: Sum = 9

DESK CHECK RESULTS FOR INCORRECT FLOWCHART

Flowchart Stage	Counter	Decision Test Results (Counter < 2)	Number	Sum
Initialization	1	–	–	0
First decision test	1	T	–	0
		(enters loop)		
After first loop	2	–	6	6
Second decision test	2	F	6	6
		(exits loop)		

Test data: 6, 3; Expected results: Sum = 9; Actual results: Sum = 6

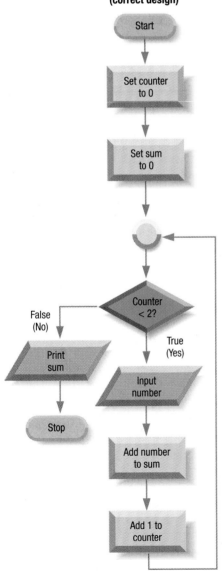

ADDING TWO NUMBERS
(correct design)

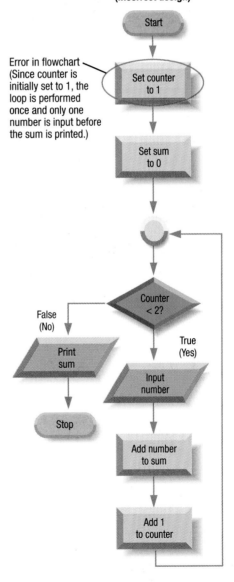

ADDING TWO NUMBERS
(incorrect design)

Error in flowchart (Since counter is initially set to 1, the loop is performed once and only one number is input before the sum is printed.)

SYS

FIGURE 13-9
Desk checking a flowchart.

Program Coding

Once the program design is complete, the next phase is **program coding**—the process of **coding** or writing the actual program steps in the proper format for a particular programming language. Each programming language has its own *syntax*, or rules, regarding how programs can be written, so choosing the programming language to be used is typically the first step. To help produce code rapidly while, at the same time, creating programs that are both easy to maintain and as error-free as possible, many organizations use consistent *coding standards* and *reusable code*. These topics are discussed next.

Choosing a Programming Language

There are a number of different programming languages to choose from when coding a program. These languages are discussed in detail later in this chapter, but several factors that may affect the programming language used are listed next.

- ➤ *Suitability*. Some programming languages are more suited for some applications than others. For instance, an object-oriented programming language (such as *C#* or *Python*) would be used with an object-oriented program and *Java* is a common choice for creating programs to be used on the Web.

- ➤ *Integration*. If the application is going to need to interact with existing programs, it may need to be coded in the same language as those other programs. New trends in programming—such as Microsoft's *.NET framework*, which is a platform designed for building integrated applications from reusable chunks of code that can communicate and share data over the Internet, regardless of the operating system or programming language being used—are helping to bridge different platforms and programming languages.

- ➤ *Standards*. Many information systems departments have standards that dictate using a specific language in a given application environment—such as *COBOL* for transaction processing and Java for Web programming.

- ➤ *Programmer availability*. Both the abilities of current in-house programmers and the skills of new programmers need to be considered. Choosing a widely used language means programmers can be hired more easily.

- ➤ *Portability*. If the application is to run on different platforms—such as Windows, Macintosh, and Linux computers, as well as mobile phones—the ability of a programming language to work with the needed platforms becomes a key factor.

- ➤ *Development speed*. Programs that reuse large chunks of code already in existence or that use a programming language that is easier to code and test can be developed faster.

> **Program coding.** The phase of the program development life cycle in which the program code is written using a programming language.
> **Coding.** The process of writing the programming language statements to create a computer program.

TECHNOLOGY AND YOU

Programming Contests

Think you're an awesome programmer? There are a number of contests available in which programmers can show off their stuff. One example is the *TopCoder Open*, in which college students and professionals compete for bragging rights and their share of the $260,000 prize purse. Individuals select from five competitions (Algorithm, Software Design, Software Development, Marathon Match, and TopCoder Studio) and then compete to advance in the competition. For instance, the Algorithm Competition begins with timed online Qualification Rounds consisting of three phases. In the Coding Phase, contestants have 75 minutes to code solutions for three problems. Solutions must be each contestant's original work and can be coded in Java, C++, C#, or VB.NET. During the Challenge Phase, contestants have 15 minutes to challenge the functionality of other competitors' code. Contestants gain or lose points depending on the outcome of the challenges they make and the challenges made against them. During the System Testing Phase, an automated tester applies a set of inputs to each submitted solution and tests the code to see if the output is correct. Contestants with code deemed to be flawed lose all points previously earned for that code. Ultimately, 48 semifinalists compete on site at the contest. The winners for the 2009 TopCoder Open are shown in the accompanying photograph.

In addition to the TopCoder Open, TopCoder offers competitions online in software design, development, assembly, and testing—including some contests specifically for high-school students. Winning a programming contest is good for your reputation and résumé, and it can also net you some pretty decent bucks.

The 2009 TopCoder Open winners.

The Coding Process
To code a program, the programmer creates it in the selected programming language. Usually this is done by launching the desired programming language application, and then selecting on-screen options and typing code using the proper syntax for the language being used to create the program. Once the program is created, it is saved as a file. This version of the program is called the **source code**. For a look at some programming contests available for both professional and amateur coders alike, see the Technology and You box.

Coding Standards
In the early days of computers, programmers were largely left to code programs in their own styles. The result was often a confusing collection of statements that, while producing correct results, were difficult for anyone except the original programmer to understand.

>**Source code.** A computer program before it is compiled.

SYS

COMMENTS

Comments are usually preceded by a specific symbol (such as *, C, ', #, or //); the symbol used depends on the programming language being used. Anything else in a comment line is ignored by the computer.

Comments at the top of a program should identify the name and author of the program, date written and last modified, purpose of the program, and variables used in the program.

Comments in the main part of a program should indicate what each section of the program is doing. Blank comment lines can also be used to space out the lines of code, as needed for readability.

```
*****************************************************************
* This program inputs two numbers, computes their sum,         *
* and displays the sum.                                        *
*                                                              *
* Written by: Deborah Morley  3/12/10                          *
*****************************************************************
* Variable list                                               *
* SUM: Running sum                                            *
* CNTR: Counter                                               *
* NUM: Number inputted                                        *
*                                                             *
      REAL SUM, CNTR, NUM
*****************************************************************
*
* INITIALIZE VARIABLES
      SUM = 0
      CNTR= 0
*
* INPUT NUMBER, ADD IT TO THE SUM, INCREMENT COUNTER, AND THEN
* REPEAT UNTIL TWO NUMBERS HAVE BEEN ENTERED
      DO 10 CNTR = 1, 2
```

FIGURE 13-10
Program comments.

TIP

It is easier to write comments—particularly comments explaining the logic of a program—at the time the program is coded, instead of trying to add the comments at the end of a project.

To avoid this problem, many organizations today follow a set of *coding standards*—a list of rules designed to standardize programming styles. These coding standards help make programs more universally readable and easier to maintain.

The proper use of *comments* or *remarks* is one of the most important, but often one of the least adhered to, coding standards in organizations. Comments are notes within the actual program code that identify key features and steps of the program but that are written in such a way that the computer knows to ignore them when the program is executed (see Figure 13-10). Usually there is a comment section at the top of the program that identifies the author, the date the program was written or last modified, and the names and descriptions of the variables used in the program. Comments also typically appear at the beginning of each main section of the program to describe the function of that section, such as "Initialize variables," "Compute taxes," and "Calculate net amount due." Comments are also called *internal documentation*—that is, documentation located within the program—and they are especially useful when a program needs to be modified.

Reusable Code

Different programs often perform some of the same basic tasks, such as computing sales tax or displaying product or employee information. If the code for these general tasks is treated as *reusable code*, it enables whole portions of new programs to be created with chunks of pretested, error-free code segments, which greatly reduces development time. Some programming approaches are specifically designed to have reusable components, such as the class libraries that can be used with object-oriented programming.

Documentation: Documented Source Code

The program coding phase results in finished source code; that is, the program written in the desired programming language. The source code should implement the logic illustrated by the program design specifications and include enough internal documentation (comments) to make the source code understandable and easy to update.

INSIDE THE INDUSTRY

The Original Program "Bug"

A program *bug* is an error that causes a program to malfunction. The first official recorded use of the word *bug* in the context of computing is associated with the temporary failure of the Mark II computer, which was in service at the Naval Weapons Center in Dahlgren, Virginia, on September 9, 1945. The problem was traced to a short circuit caused by a moth caught between two contacts in one of the computer's relays. The offending moth was taped into the log book with the notation, "First actual case of a bug being found" (see the accompanying photograph).

Legend has it that *Grace Hopper*, a naval officer and mathematician who is often referred to as the mother of computing, actually discovered the moth. Hopper, who became the first woman to achieve the rank of rear admiral in the United States Navy, led the committee that invented COBOL and is credited with developing the first compiler.

Although some say the wording implies that the term *bug* was already in existence at the time and that this was the first instance of an actual bug being found in a computer, many prefer to believe that this was the origin of the term. Regardless, it is certainly the most widely known "bug" story, and it will likely be repeated for decades to come.

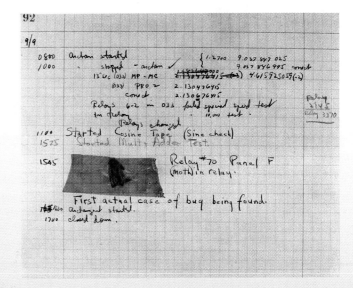

The dead moth that caused the temporary failure of the Mark II computer in 1945, thought to be the origin for the computer term *bug*, was taped into the actual log book for that computer.

Program Debugging and Testing

The **program debugging and testing** phase of the PDLC involves testing the program to ensure is it correct and works as intended. It starts with **debugging**—the process of ensuring that a program is free of errors, or *bugs* (for a look at the origin of the term *bug*, see the Inside the Industry box). Debugging is usually a lengthy process, sometimes amounting to more than 50% of a program's development time. The more careful you are when you are designing a program, testing the logic of the program's design, and writing the actual code, the less debugging time is typically required.

Translating Coded Programs into Executable Code

Before a program can be run—and, therefore, before it can be debugged—it needs to be translated from the source code that a programmer writes into a binary or *machine language* version of the program (called **object code**) that the computer can execute. Code is converted from source code to object code using a **language translator**. Typically, the appropriate language translator is included in a programming application program so the

SYS 13

> **Program debugging and testing.** The phase of the program development life cycle that ensures a program is correct and works as intended.
> **Debugging.** The process of ensuring a program is free of errors. > **Object code.** The machine language version of a computer program generated after the program's source code is compiled. > **Language translator.** A software program that converts program code to machine language.

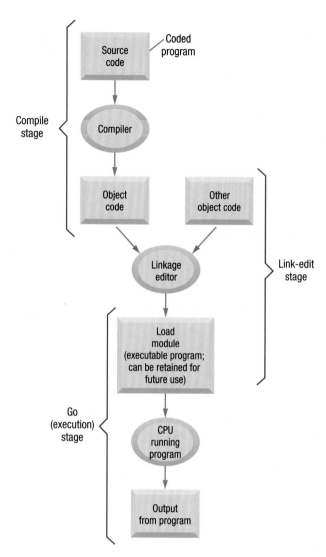

Compiler and linkage editor.
A compiler and a linkage editor convert source code into executable code.

program can be coded, translated, and executed using the same software program. The three most common types of language translators are discussed next.

Compilers

A **compiler** is designed for a specific programming language (such as Java or Python) and translates programs written in that language into machine language so they can be executed. For instance, a program written in the Java programming language needs a Java compiler; Java source code cannot be converted into object code using a Python compiler.

A typical compiling process is shown in Figure 13-11. First, the source code for a program is translated into object code (the *compile stage*), then it is combined with any other modules of object code (either previously written by the programmer or stored in a common library) that the computer needs in order to run the program (the *link-edit stage*). This produces an executable program called a *load module*, which typically has an *.exe* file extension. At this point, the compiling process has reached the *Go* (*execution*) *stage* and the executable load module can be executed, as well as retained for later use.

Interpreters

Interpreters are also language-specific, but they translate source code differently than compilers. Rather than creating object code and an executable program, an interpreter reads, translates, and executes the source code one line at a time as the program is run, every time the program is run. One advantage of using interpreters is that they are relatively easy to use and they help programmers discover program errors more easily because the execution usually stops at the point where an error is encountered. Consequently, interpreters are useful for beginning programmers.

The major disadvantage associated with interpreters is that they work less efficiently than compilers do because they translate each program statement into machine language just before executing it each time the program is run. As a result, interpreted programs run more slowly. This is especially true when the program must repeatedly execute the same statements thousands of times, reinterpreting each one every time. In contrast, a compiler translates each program statement only once—when the object code is created. Compiled programs need to be recompiled only when the source code is modified, such as if an error is discovered and corrected, or the program is updated.

Assemblers

The third type of language translator, an *assembler*, converts *assembly language* statements into machine language. Assembly language, discussed later in this chapter, is used almost exclusively by professional programmers to write efficient code. An assembler works like a compiler, producing object code, but it is used with a specific type of assembly language and, consequently, with a specific computer architecture, such as specific Windows computers, specific Macintosh computers, a particular type of mainframe, a specific supercomputer, or a specific type of mobile device.

Preliminary Debugging

The debugging process begins after the source code is complete and it is ready to be compiled or interpreted. With most programs, compiling or interpreting a program for the first time will result in errors—the preliminary debugging process consists of locating and correcting these errors. The first goal is to eliminate *syntax errors* and other errors that prevent the program from executing; then, any *run time errors* or *logic errors* can be identified and corrected, as discussed next.

Compiler and Syntax Errors

Errors that occur as the program is being interpreted or compiled (often called *compiler errors* since most programs are compiled) prevent the program from running and so need to be corrected before the logic of the program can be tested. These errors are typically **syntax errors**, which occur when the programmer has not followed the proper *syntax* (rules) of the programming language being used. For example, a computer is not able to understand what you are trying to do if you misspell PRINT as PRNT, if you type END OF IF STATEMENT instead of the correct phrase END IF, if you put a required comma or semicolon in the wrong place, or if you try to use the wrong property with an object. As shown in Figure 13-12, when the program is being compiled and a syntax error is reached, an error message is typically displayed. Often this error message indicates the approximate location of the error in the program code (such as by underlining the error with a blue wavy line as in Figure 13-12) to help the programmer locate and correct it.

FIGURE 13-12

Syntax errors. Syntax errors occur when the syntax (grammar rules) for a program is not followed precisely; they become obvious when compiling a program.

1. Clicking the Debug button starts the compilation and debugging process.

2. If a compiler error is encountered, the application typically displays an error message.

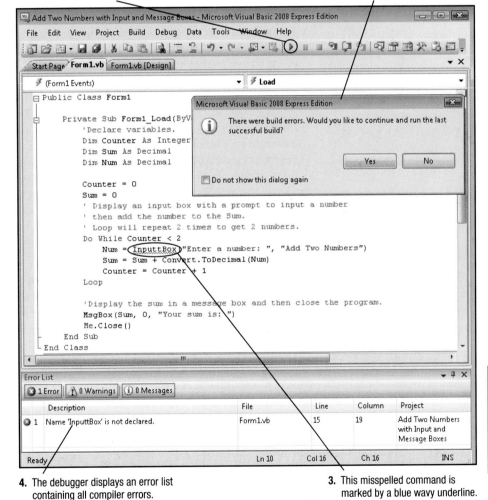

4. The debugger displays an error list containing all compiler errors.

3. This misspelled command is marked by a blue wavy underline.

> **Syntax error.** A programming error that occurs when the programmer has not followed the rules of the programming language.

FURTHER EXPLORATION

Go

Go to the Chapter 13 page at **www.cengage.com/ computerconcepts/np/uc13** for links to information about program debugging and testing.

✓ **TIP**

When using dummy print statements to identify a logic error, be sure to label each statement with the variable name and the location in the program (such as "Just before read loop, counter is" followed by the value of the Counter variable) so you can tell which printed values belong to which variables and when those values change during the program.

Run Time and Logic Errors

Run time errors are errors that occur while the program is running and, consequently, are noticed after all syntax errors are corrected and the program can be executed. Sometimes run time errors occur because the program tries to do something that isn't possible, such as dividing a numeric value by zero. With this type of error, the program typically stops executing and an error message is displayed. However, many run time errors are due to **logic errors**; that is, errors in the logic of the program. Programs containing logic errors typically run—they just produce incorrect results. For instance, logic errors occur when a formula is written incorrectly, when a mistake is made with a decision condition (such as using the wrong relational operator or initializing a counter variable to the wrong value), or when the wrong variable name is used. After a logic error is identified, the programmer corrects it and runs the program again to see if all errors have been removed. This "execute, check, and correct" process is repeated until the program is free of bugs. If a logic error is serious enough, it may involve going back to the program design phase—a costly mistake that emphasizes the importance of good program design.

Most logic errors should be located and corrected during the program design stage if a good desk check procedure is used. However, when logic errors become apparent during preliminary debugging, *dummy print statements*—print statements that are temporarily inserted into the code—can be used to help locate the error. Dummy print statements can be inserted at various locations within the program's code to show how a program is branching (such as printing the text *"Inside loop, counter = "* followed by the current value of the Counter variable) and to output the values of key variables at specific places in the program. Knowing the values of key variables and where program control is branching can help the programmer figure out what the logic error is and where it is located.

For example, running a program to add two numbers based on the logic in the incorrect flowchart in Figure 13-9 would result in an incorrect sum, since only one number is input before the loop terminates. As shown in Figure 13-13, dummy print statements used to show the program control and the values of the counter and sum variables at specific locations in the program reveal that only one number is being input when the program runs; this information can help the programmer determine more quickly that the counter is incorrectly being initialized to 1, instead of to 0.

Testing

At the end of the preliminary debugging process, the program will appear to be correct. At this time, the original programmer—or, preferably, someone else—runs the program with extensive *test data* to try to find any additional errors remaining in the program. Good test data should be the same type of data that will be used with the finished program to subject the program to the conditions it will encounter when it is implemented. Ideally, the test data would be actual data, but to protect the privacy of personal information during testing, test data is usually created that has the same

---

>**Logic error.** A programming error that occurs when running a program produces incorrect results.

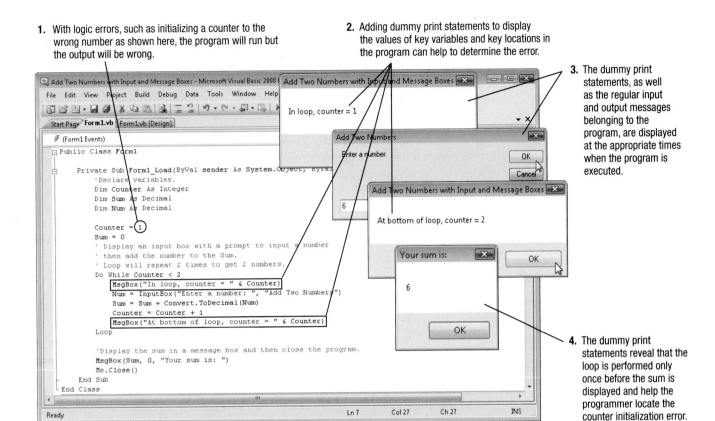

1. With logic errors, such as initializing a counter to the wrong number as shown here, the program will run but the output will be wrong.

2. Adding dummy print statements to display the values of key variables and key locations in the program can help to determine the error.

3. The dummy print statements, as well as the regular input and output messages belonging to the program, are displayed at the appropriate times when the program is executed.

4. The dummy print statements reveal that the loop is performed only once before the sum is displayed and help the programmer locate the counter initialization error.

FIGURE 13-13

Logic errors. Logic errors are more difficult to identify; dummy print statements can help determine the error.

structure as actual data but does not contain any personally identifiable information. The test data should also check for nonstandard situations or possible input errors to make sure the proper corresponding actions are included in the program. For example, will the program issue a check if the amount is $0.00 or will it allow a product quantity of less than 0? Although rigorous testing significantly decreases the chance of an unnoticed error revealing itself after the program is implemented, there is no foolproof guarantee that the completed program will be bug-free. However, proper debugging and testing is vital, because an error that costs only a few dollars to fix at this stage in the development process may cost many thousands of dollars to correct after the program is implemented.

Programs created for mass distribution often have two stages of testing: an internal on-site test (sometimes called an *alpha test*) and one or more rounds of outside tests (called *beta tests*). For instance, companies creating new versions of commercial software programs, such as when Microsoft develops a new version of Microsoft Office, enlist a large number of beta testers to test the versions for bugs and compatibility problems, as well as to provide suggestions for improvement, while the programs are in development. *Beta versions* of freeware and open source software are also often available to the public for testing. Beta testing allows the programs to be tested by a wide variety of individuals using a wide variety of hardware—a much more thorough test than just alpha testing for programs that are to be distributed out of house.

Documentation: Completed Program Package

When the program debugging and testing phase is finished, a copy of the test data, test results, finished program code, and other documentation generated during this phase should be added to the program package. The test data is useful for future program modifications, as well as to see in which situations the program was tested if a problem develops in the future.

So far, virtually all the documents in the collected program documentation could be referred to as *developer documentation*—tools that may be useful when a programmer

SYS

needs to look at or modify the program code in the future. To finish the *program package*, the necessary *user documentation* should also be developed. User documentation normally consists of a user's manual containing instructions for running the program, a description of software commands, and so forth. While the user documentation for a commercial program may be integrated into the program itself, programs for new company systems typically require external user documentation for training and reference purposes.

Program Implementation and Maintenance

Once a program has finished the debugging and testing phase, it is ready to be implemented as part of the SDLC, as discussed in Chapter 12. Once the system containing the program is up and running, the *implementation process* of the **program implementation and maintenance** phase is complete. However, virtually every program requires ongoing maintenance. *Program maintenance* is the process of updating software so it continues to be useful. For instance, if new types of data are added to a company database, program maintenance is necessary so that existing programs can use the new data. Software revisions, new equipment announcements, new legislative mandates, and changes in the way business is conducted also commonly trigger program maintenance.

Program maintenance is costly to organizations. It has been estimated that many organizations spend well over one-half—some estimates put it closer to 80%—of their programming time maintaining existing application programs.

Documentation: Amended Program Package

As program maintenance takes place, the program package should be updated to reflect what new problems or issues occurred and what changes to the program were necessary because of them. If a problem is too serious for routine program maintenance, the program development cycle should begin again.

TOOLS FOR FACILITATING PROGRAM DEVELOPMENT

If you ask most IT managers when they need programs in development to be finished, you will usually get an answer like "yesterday." The sad truth in business today is that programmers are typically under tremendous time pressure to get programs finished as quickly as possible. In extreme cases, getting product into the user's hands is not just a priority—it is *the* priority.

To help programmers create quality systems and programs in a timely manner, many types of *program development tools* are available, as discussed next. The tools can be used in both traditional and adaptive software development approaches.

Application Lifecycle Management (ALM) Tools

Application lifecycle management (**ALM**) is a broad term to describe creating and managing an application throughout its entire life cycle—from design through coding and testing, to maintenance and, eventually, to retirement. ALM software typically has several integrated components that work together for a variety of tasks, such as those that take place during the system design and program development process, and are designed to automate, manage, and simplify the program development process. For instance, many ALM programs include

---

>**Program implementation and maintenance.** The phase of the program development life cycle in which the program is implemented and then maintained, as needed, to remain useful. >**Application lifecycle management (ALM).** A broad term to describe complete systems that can be used to create and manage an application throughout its entire life cycle—from design through retirement.

program design tools—such as those used to create data flow diagrams, structure charts, and the other tools discussed earlier in this chapter and in Chapter 12—and the ability to generate the program code from the finished design to create the application. In a nutshell, an ALM system can help software developers define a solid model of a program first, and then implement that model in whatever programming language—and in as many programming languages—as needed with no additional effort since the ALM program's *code generator* generates much of the code automatically upon demand. Consequently, this saves programming time, as well as makes it possible for companies without a large programming staff to develop applications in-house without having to outsource the coding portion of the program development process. Additional tools that can be included in ALM programs are *requirements management, configuration management*, and *issue tracking*, as discussed next.

Requirements management refers to keeping track of and managing program requirements as they are defined and then modified throughout the program development process. It is important for software requirements to be defined accurately and completely at the beginning of a project because poorly written or inconsistent requirements can lead to costly reworks or even failure of a project. In fact, a recent report by Forrester Research states that defects in requirements are the source of the majority of problems identified during program testing. The *requirements definition* process typically involves real-time collaboration between project members and the use of visual tools to help convey the requirements scenario to all project members, in order to avoid communication problems and to promote additional discussions and questions. Once the requirements are defined, the requirements management process continues throughout the program development process to manage the requirements as they evolve. Since the requirements for a program often change during development—due to technological improvements, competitive pressures, or budget changes, for instance—requirements management software facilitates real-time collaboration between the individuals working on a project to ensure that everyone sees and works with the same version of the current requirements. The overall goal of requirements management is to ensure that the delivered solution actually meets the needs of the business.

Configuration management refers to keeping track of the progress of a program development project, such as documenting revisions, storing each version of the program so it can be recreated if needed, and keeping track of all components used in the final program. Software that supports configuration management may also include security and control features, such as preventing unauthorized access to project files or alerting the appropriate individual whenever a project file is altered.

Issue tracking (see Figure 13-14) involves recording issues (such as bugs or other problems that arise during program development or issues that arise after the system is in place) as they become known, assigning them to a team member, and tracking their status. Software that supports issue tracking can be used during program development, as well as after the system has been implemented.

FIGURE 13-14

Issue tracking software. Allows you to track issues during the development and life of an application.

Application Generators

An *application generator* is a software program that helps programmers develop software. Some application generators (such as the ones included in some ALM programs, as previously discussed) generate source code. Others may generate program components (such as *macros*, reports, or forms) to be used by the end user.

Macros

A *macro* is a sequence of saved actions (such as keystrokes, mouse clicks, and menu selections) that can be replayed whenever needed within the application program in which it was created. Macros are most often used to automate repeated or difficult tasks. Programmers can create predefined macros to be included with a finished program; many programs also allow the end user to create custom macros as needed. For example, the user could create a macro in a word processing program to type a standard closing to a letter or to create a table of a specified size with a certain formatting applied, whenever he or she presses a specific key combination (such as Ctrl+Y).

Programmers typically write macros using a *macro programming language* (such as *Visual Basic for Applications* for Microsoft Office macros). If a program supports custom macros, however, it usually includes a *macro recorder* so the end user can record macros instead of having to write them. To use a macro recorder, the end user starts the macro recorder and then performs the desired tasks—the macro recorder records all of the key-strokes and mouse clicks made until the recorder is turned off. The macro is then saved and assigned a name or keystroke combination; each time the macro is run, the computer performs the recorded keystrokes and mouse clicks in the recorded order. After a macro has been recorded and saved, the code generated by the macro recorder can typically be edited to make minor modifications, as needed.

FIGURE 13-15

Form generators.
The database form generator shown here is used to create input screens for a database application.

ONLINE VIDEO

Go to the Chapter 13 page at www.cengage.com/ computerconcepts/np/uc13 to watch the "Demo of the Android Software Development Kit for Mobile Phones" video clip.

Report and Form Generators

A *report generator* is a tool that prepares reports to be used with a software program quickly and easily. For instance, report generators used in conjunction with database manage-ment systems allow reports to be created simply by declaring which data fields are to be represented as report columns and how the data should be sorted; once defined, a report can be edited as needed, and then generated on demand. Similarly, *form generators* create the forms or input screens used to input data into a program or database (see Figure 13-15). While indi-viduals can use report generators and form generators to create those objects to be used with their personal databases (as dis-cussed in Chapter 14), the forms and reports used in a program being developed for a company system are usually created by the programmer during the program development process.

Device Software Development Tools

Tools to help facilitate the development of software used with computers have been available for quite some time. However, tools for developing programs for devices that use embedded software (such as cars, ATM machines, robots, mobile phones, and other consumer devices)—called *device software development tools*—have not typically been available until recently. Once example of this type of tool is *Wind River Workbench*, which contains a collection of tools designed to accelerate the development of devices that use either Wind River's *VxWorks* operating system or Wind River's version of Linux. It is a complete end-to-end device software development suite used to streamline the design, development, debugging, testing, and management of programs for devices.

Software Development Kits (SDKs) and Application Program Interfaces (APIs)

Another tool that can be used to develop software quickly is the **software development kit (SDK)**. An SDK is a programming package designed for a particular platform (such as the iPhone or Windows Vista computers) that enables programmers to develop applications for

---

> **Software development kit (SDK).** A programming package designed for a particular platform that enables programmers to develop applications for that platform more quickly and easily.

that platform more quickly and easily. SDKs are often released by hardware or software companies to assist developers in creating new applications for their products. For instance, the *iPhone SDK* allows third parties to develop applications for iPhones. SDKs typically contain programming tools, documentation, and at least one *API* (*application program interface*) designed to help applications interface with a particular operating system. As discussed in the Chapter 10 Trend box, APIs are also used in conjunction with Web sites to help build Web applications, such as Google's *Maps API* that allows developers to create *mashup sites* with embedded Google Maps or Google's *OpenSocial API* that is designed to help easily add social networking applications to Web sites.

Rich Internet Application (RIA) Tools

Some tools are designed specifically to create **rich Internet applications** (**RIAs**); that is, Web-based applications that work like installed software programs. Programmers can use

RIA development tools to create RIA applications to be accessible via the company Web site or intranet; increasingly these applications can also be accessed and used as desktop applications when the user is offline.

One new RIA development tool is *Adobe AIR* (*Adobe Integrated Runtime*). Adobe AIR allows software developers to build desktop RIAs using HTML, AJAX, Flash, and other familiar technologies. Desktop RIAs can access local files stored on the computer and be used when no Internet connection is present, although Adobe AIR applications can also be launched from Web pages, if appropriate. Adobe AIR is already being used for many desktop RIAs available today, such as *Yahoo! Live, FedEx Desktop*, and *eBay Desktop*. For a look at the technology behind some offline Web applications—*Google Gears*—see the Trend box. Applications created with Adobe AIR require the user to have Adobe AIR installed (see Figure 13-16)—it can be downloaded for free from the Adobe Web site, if needed.

FIGURE 13-16
Adobe AIR must be installed on a computer in order to run AIR applications.

PROGRAMMING LANGUAGES

As discussed earlier, deciding which programming language will be used is an important program development decision. There are a vast number of programming languages to choose from; however, often the type of application being developed will dictate the type of programming language that should be used.

What Is a Programming Language?

A **programming language** is a set of rules used to write computer programs. To write a computer program, you need an appropriate software program for the programming language you will be using—this software allows you to code the program and convert the finished source code into object code. It may also include a variety of tools that make it easier to develop, debug, edit, maintain, and manage programs. Programming languages are discussed in detail next. Related languages used for Web page development—namely markup languages and scripting languages, such as HTML, JavaScript, and Perl—were discussed in Chapter 10.

>**Rich Internet application (RIA).** A Web-based application that works like an installed software program. >**Programming language.** A set of rules, words, symbols, and codes used to write computer programs.

TREND

Google Gears

Gears is an open source browser plug-in currently being developed by Google that allows software developers to create rich Web applications. One of the most common uses of Gears at the present time is to allow users to access Web applications offline. For instance, Google Docs uses Gears to enable users to access their documents and the Docs interface when they are not connected to the Internet (see the accompanying illustration). While using Google Docs offline, all edits to the user's existing documents are stored on the user's computer; the next time the user connects to the Internet, Gears synchronizes the offline and online documents to bring the online versions of those documents up to date. Currently, in addition to Google Docs, other Web applications (such as *Zoho Writer* and *Remember the Milk*) use Gears to facilitate offline access; more are expected as the Gears project evolves.

Gears allows Google Docs users to work offline.

Categories of Programming Languages

Programming languages can be classified by the types of programs they are designed to create, such as *procedural* (also called *imperative*) *languages* for programs using the procedural approach or *object-oriented languages* for programs using the object-oriented approach. However, they are also often categorized by their level or generation; that is, how evolved the programming language is.

Low-Level Languages

The earliest programming languages—*machine language* and *assembly language*—are referred to as **low-level languages**. This name refers to the fact that the programmers using these languages must write instructions at a very low level (such as just using 0s and 1s) so that the computer's hardware can easily and quickly understand them. In a low-level language, each line of code corresponds to a single action by the computer system and the code is *machine dependent*, which means that it is written for one specific type of computer. For example, a program written in a low-level language for a particular mainframe at one organization cannot be used on a different type of mainframe or on one of the organization's personal computers.

Low-level languages were developed during the *first generation* of programming languages; one example is **machine language**. Machine language programs consist solely of 0s and 1s; consequently, they are the only programs whose source code is understandable to the computer without being translated first. While virtually no one programs in machine language anymore, all programs are converted into machine language by a language translator before they can be executed, as discussed earlier in this chapter.

> **Low-level language.** A class of programming languages that is highly detailed and machine-dependent. > **Machine language.** A low-level programming language in which the program code consists of 0s and 1s.

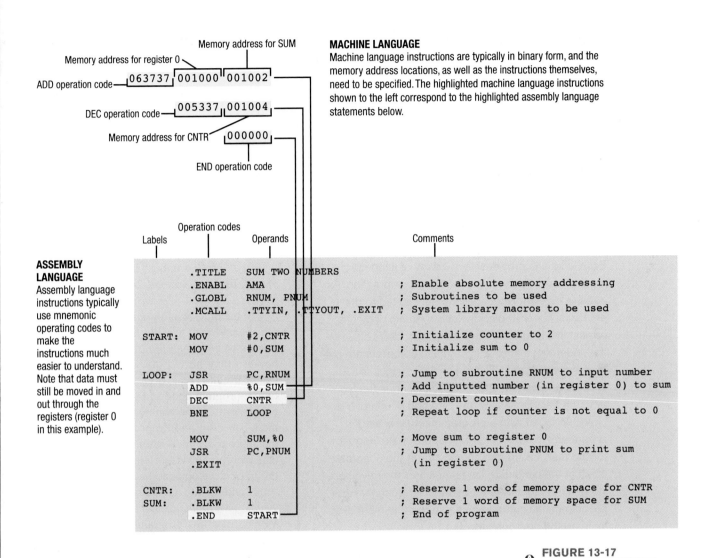

MACHINE LANGUAGE
Machine language instructions are typically in binary form, and the memory address locations, as well as the instructions themselves, need to be specified. The highlighted machine language instructions shown to the left correspond to the highlighted assembly language statements below.

ASSEMBLY LANGUAGE
Assembly language instructions typically use mnemonic operating codes to make the instructions much easier to understand. Note that data must still be moved in and out through the registers (register 0 in this example).

FIGURE 13-17
Assembly and machine language.

Assembly language is another type of low-level language. It was developed during the *second generation* of programming languages to replace some of the 0s and 1s of machine language with names and other symbols that are easier for programmers to understand and remember. The big advantage of assembly language programs is execution efficiency. Unfortunately, assembly language programs take longer to write and maintain than programs written in higher-level languages. However, occasionally a program may be written in assembly language to make it especially efficient.

An example of a program for adding two numbers (the program illustrated by the correct flowchart shown in Figure 13-9) written in assembly language for one type of computer system is shown in Figure 13-17. Also included in that figure are some machine language statements that correspond to the assembly language statements in the program.

High-Level Languages
High-level languages are closer to natural languages than low-level languages and therefore, make programs easier to write. They are also typically *machine independent*,

> **Assembly language.** A low-level programming language that uses names and other symbols to replace some of the 0s and 1s in machine language. > **High-level language.** A class of programming languages that is closer to natural language and easier to work with than a low-level language.

ASK THE EXPERT

Kathleen Fisher, AT&T Research, Chair of the ACM
Special Interest Group on Programming Languages

What is the most important programming language for a college computer student to learn today?

There is no one programming language that is the most important to learn. Rather, it is important for students to understand how programming languages allow people to express precisely what they want computers to do. Each language provides its own way of accomplishing this task by providing a model of computation. As a result, different languages are best suited to different tasks. For example, low-level systems coding is easiest in a language like C, whose model is close to the underlying machine. In contrast, compilers are particularly easy to write in functional languages like ML, Haskell, and Scheme because such languages facilitate tree transformations, the lifeblood of compilers.

When faced with a programming task, astute programmers select the most appropriate language for the task, taking into consideration the characteristics of the candidate languages and their available libraries and tools. As with natural languages, each programming language that a student learns makes learning the next one easier.

which makes programs written in these languages much more flexible since they can be used with more than one computer without alteration. Although a program is normally written for a specific operating system, with a machine independent program the programmer does not need to know the specific details about the hardware that will be used to run the program. Included in this class of languages are what have come to be known as *third-generation programming languages* (*3GLs*). Some examples of procedural 3GLs are *FORTRAN, COBOL, Pascal, BASIC*, and *C*. High-level object-oriented programming languages include *Visual Basic, C++, C#, Java, Python*, and *Ruby*.

Some high-level programming languages are considered *visual programming languages* or *graphical programming languages* because they have a graphical interface that can be used to create programs. So, instead of typing program code and worrying about the proper syntax for commands, the programmers can drag and drop objects to generate the appropriate code automatically. Programs that incorporate visual elements to assist in program development but that still require some coding are sometimes referred to as *visual programming environments* (*VPEs*). VPEs still allow programmers to create the user interface graphically and to create a substantial amount of code simply by dragging and dropping objects and then defining their

FIGURE 13-18

The Scratch graphical programming language.

appearance and behavior. And, when code is typed, the program assists in creating the code by listing options (such as appropriate methods that may be used with the object being used) as soon as the programmer begins to type a line of code, properly indenting and color-coding the code, and so forth. One of the first programming languages to use a visual programming environment was Visual Basic. Since then, visual environments have been created for many programming languages, including C++, Pascal, and Java. These programming languages are all described in the next section.

There are also graphical programming languages designed for educational purposes. For instance, the free *Scratch* programming language shown in Figure 13-18 is designed to enable children to create interactive, animated programs quickly and easily by snapping graphical blocks of commands together. Even though creating complex programs and animations using Scratch is easy because of this building block approach, this program still allows beginning programmers to experiment with and learn basic programming concepts, such as variables and loops.

Fourth-Generation Languages (4GLs)

Fourth-generation languages (**4GLs**) are also sometimes called *very-high-level languages*. Although there is no precise definition of 4GLs, they are even further from machine language than third-generation languages, and, therefore, are much easier to use. One property that makes 4GLs easier to use is that they are *declarative*, rather than *procedural* like third-generation languages. This means that when you program using a 4GL, you tell the computer *what* to do without telling it *how* to do it. Consequently, much of the coding in a *declarative programming language* consists of mouse clicks to select instructions and issue commands to the program. Because 4GLs often allow programmers to create programs while writing very little code, if any, using 4GLs also results in increased productivity. A disadvantage to using 4GLs is that they can result in a greater number of program statements and less efficient object code when they are compiled into machine language.

Fourth-generation languages are commonly used today to access databases. For example, *structured query language (SQL)* is a 4GL commonly used to write *queries* to retrieve information from a database, as discussed in more detail in Chapter 14. Application generators and some of the programs discussed earlier as tools to help facilitate program development are also sometimes considered fourth-generation languages.

Common Programming Languages

There have been a number of programming languages developed over the years. Some, such as *Logo* (which is designed to teach children how to program), *PL/1* (a structured programming language used for business and scientific applications), *Prolog* and *LISP* (used for artificial intelligence applications), and *SmallTalk* (one of the first object-oriented programming languages) are not widely used today. Others, such as COBOL, are in the process of being phased out in many organizations. Some of the most significant programming languages still in use today are discussed and illustrated next.

FORTRAN

FORTRAN (*FORmula TRANslator*), which dates back to 1954, was designed by scientists and is oriented toward manipulating formulas for scientific, mathematical, and engineering applications. FORTRAN is a very efficient language for these types of applications and is still used for high-performance computing tasks, such as forecasting the weather. A related programming language released by Sun Microsystems is *Fortress*. Similar to FORTRAN, Fortress is designed for high-performance computing and some believe it will eventually replace FORTRAN. One advantage of Fortress for today's computers is that it takes advantage of multi-core processors and computers with multiple processors, automatically assigning pieces of a job to different cores or processors and trying to store data where it will be conveniently near the processor that will need it.

A FORTRAN program to add two numbers (as illustrated in the correct flowchart in Figure 13-9) is shown in Figure 13-19. Note the short comments above each main section in the program.

FIGURE 13-19
The adding-two-numbers program written in FORTRAN.

Comments are preceded by an asterisk or a C.

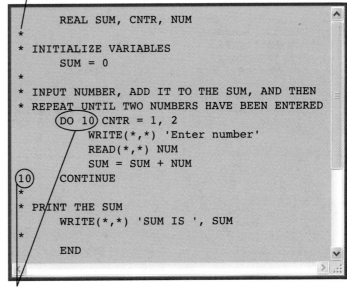

```
      REAL SUM, CNTR, NUM
*
*  INITIALIZE VARIABLES
      SUM = 0
*
*  INPUT NUMBER, ADD IT TO THE SUM, AND THEN
*  REPEAT UNTIL TWO NUMBERS HAVE BEEN ENTERED
      DO 10 CNTR = 1, 2
         WRITE(*,*) 'Enter number'
         READ(*,*) NUM
         SUM = SUM + NUM
10    CONTINUE
*
*  PRINT THE SUM
         WRITE(*,*) 'SUM IS ', SUM
*
      END
```

Program statements can be numbered in order to control loops and other types of branching.

COBOL

COBOL (*COmmon Business-Oriented Language*) is a structured programming language designed for business transaction processing. COBOL programs are typically made up of a collection of modules, as shown in the adding-two-numbers program in Figure 13-20. Its strengths lie in batch processing and its stability—two reasons why so many COBOL programs still exist today, even though some consider the language to be outdated. However, COBOL programs are lengthy and take a long time to write and maintain, and many businesses are migrating from it gradually. To avoid the expense of rewriting all the COBOL code in an organization, as well as possible problems that may arise if the business processes included in those programs are inadvertently altered during translation, some companies are leaving most of their *back-end software* (server software that is not accessed by end users) in COBOL and just moving *front-end software* and new applications (those accessed by end users) to other languages.

While COBOL is not inherently suited to developing interactive applications or Web-based software, it is evolving to support new applications. The language now supports the creation of object-oriented COBOL programs and existing COBOL applications can be converted to *COBOL.NET* so they can better integrate with other .NET applications. However, with a large percentage of business applications still written in COBOL and many original COBOL programmers reaching retirement age, there is still a need for programmers who can program in the conventional COBOL programming language.

Ⓥ **FIGURE 13-20**
The adding-two-numbers program written in COBOL.

Comments are preceded by an asterisk.

Most COBOL programs use a number of modules to break the program into manageable pieces. These submodules are called from the main control module using these statements.

Three submodules are used in this program.

```
ENVIRONMENT DIVISION.
DATA DIVISION.
WORKING-STORAGE SECTION.
01    RESULT          PIC 9(3) VALUE ZERO.
01    CNTR            PIC 9(1) VALUE ZERO.
01    NUM             PIC 9(2) VALUE ZERO.

*******************
PROCEDURE DIVISION.
*******************
      PERFORM InitVariables
      PERFORM GetNumber UNTIL CNTR = 2
      PERFORM PrintSum
      STOP RUN.

*******************
InitVariables.
*******************
*   This module initializes the RESULT and CNTR variables to 0.
      MOVE 0 TO RESULT
      MOVE 0 TO CNTR.
*End of InitVariables

*******************
GetNumber.
*******************
*   This module inputs a number, adds it to the result, and
*   increments the counter.
      DISPLAY "Enter Number: " WITH NO ADVANCING
      ACCEPT NUM
      COMPUTE RESULT = RESULT + NUM
      COMPUTE CNTR = CNTR + 1.

*End of GetNumber module.

*******************
PrintSum.
*******************
*   This module prints the final RESULT.
      DISPLAY "The sum of the numbers you entered is " RESULT.
*End of PrintSum module.
```

> **COBOL.** A high-level programming language developed for transaction processing applications.

Comments are enclosed in { } braces.

The symbol := is used instead of the equal sign.

Semicolons mark the end of command statements.

```
program sum_numbers;

    var
        Num, Sum : real;
        Cntr : integer;

    begin

{ Initialize variables }
        Sum := 0;

{ Input a number, add it to the sum, and repeat }
{ until two numbers have been entered            }
            for Cntr := 1 to 2 do
                begin
                    write('Enter number: ');
                    readln(Num);
                    Sum:= Sum + Num;
                end;

{ Print the sum }
            writeln('The sum of the numbers you entered is ',Sum);
        end.
```

Pascal

Pascal, named after the mathematician Blaise Pascal, was created to fill the need for a teaching tool to encourage structured programming. Pascal typically uses control structures extensively to manipulate program modules in a systematic fashion. Pascal also supports an abundance of data types and is especially appropriate for math and science applications. Figure 13-21 shows the adding-two-numbers program written in Pascal.

FIGURE 13-21
The adding-two-numbers program written in Pascal.

FIGURE 13-22
The adding-two-numbers program written in BASIC.

BASIC and Visual Basic

BASIC (*Beginner's All-purpose Symbolic Instruction Code*) was designed as an easy-to-learn beginner's language that would work in a friendly, nonfrustrating programming environment. Because it is easy to learn and use and because the storage requirements for its language translator are small, BASIC works well on almost all computers and was traditionally one of the most widely used instructional languages for beginners. BASIC is often used for interactive programs, where the programmer writes instructions that pause a program so that the user can take a specific action (such as inputting data, as shown in Figure 13-22, or selecting an option on the screen).

Comments are preceded by a single quotation mark.

Programs typically include input statements that pause the program until the user supplies the appropriate data.

```
'Clear the screen
CLS
'
'Initialize variables
SUM = 0
CNTR = 0
'
'Input number and add it to sum until two numbers have been
'entered.
DO
    INPUT "Enter number: ", NUM
    SUM = SUM + NUM
    CNTR = CNTR + 1
LOOP UNTIL CNTR = 2
'
'When done looping, display Sum on screen
PRINT "The sum of the numbers you entered is "; SUM
END
```

> **Pascal.** A structured, high-level programming language often used to teach structured programming, especially appropriate for use in math and science applications. > **BASIC.** An easy-to-learn, high-level programming language that was developed to be used by beginning programmers.

After the action is taken, the program continues. Figure 13-22 shows the BASIC version of the adding-two-numbers program.

Visual Basic is a version of BASIC that supports object-oriented programming and uses a visual environment to help programmers quickly and easily create programs. It is widely used for creating Windows applications and is part of the *Visual Studio* suite of programming products. The current version of Visual Studio—*Visual Studio 2008*—includes tools to help developers create applications for Windows Vista, Microsoft Office, and the Web. Other programs included in the suite are *Visual C++* and *Visual C#*, discussed shortly. The upcoming *Visual Studio 2010* includes support for parallel processing, application lifecycle management, and cloud development, as well as the ability to integrate with more databases than Visual Studio 2008. Visual Basic code written for the .NET framework is referred to as *VB.NET* code.

When creating a Visual Basic program, the user interface is typically created first by adding objects (such as labels, text boxes, and buttons) to a blank form, and then specifying the appropriate properties (such as name, color, size, and initial value) for each object. Next, the code containing the instructions for what should happen when specific actions are taken (such as the user clicking a command button or entering text in a text box) is added. The Visual Basic code editor helps programmers as they type code, such as suggesting possible methods and properties as soon as the name of an object is typed and by highlighting potential syntax errors. For a closer look at how to create a simple Visual Basic program, see the How It Works box.

C, C++, and C#

C was originally designed as a system programming language and is much closer to assembly language than other high-level languages. This allows for very efficient code, but it can also make programming in C more difficult. However, C has proven to be a powerful and flexible language that is used for a variety of applications.

FIGURE 13-23
The adding-two-numbers program written in C++.

C++ is a newer object-oriented version of C. It includes the basic features of C, making all C++ programs understandable to C compilers, but it has additional features for objects, classes, and other components of an OOP. There are also visual versions of the C++ language, such as *Microsoft Visual C++*. C++ is one of the most popular programming languages for graphical applications. The adding-two-numbers program written in C++ is shown in Figure 13-23.

Comments are preceded by two slashes //.

The instructions in a function or loop are enclosed in { } braces.

```cpp
#include <iostream.h>

void main ()
{

// Declare and initialize variables
     float fSum = 0;
     float fNum;
     int iCntr = 0;

// Input a number, add it to the sum, and repeat
// until two numbers have been entered
     do
        {
        cout << "Enter number: "; // Prompt for input
        cin >> fNum;
        fSum = fSum + fNum;
        iCntr = iCntr + 1;
        }
     while(iCntr < 2);

// Print the sum
     cout << "The sum of the numbers you entered is " << fSum;
}
```

HOW IT WORKS

Visual Basic

Applications created using the Visual Basic program are referred to as *projects*; a project folder contains all of the files that make up the application. The first task when creating a Visual Basic program is to build the user interface, if one will be used with the application being developed. Consequently, when a new project is started, a blank form (initially called "Form1") that can be used for the user interface is displayed. The form can be renamed and resized, and text and images can be added to the form; text boxes and command buttons to be used for input can be added as well. These items are added using the Toolbox; the properties of a selected item can be adjusted using the Properties window. For instance, properties for a form include the form's name, color, and font size (see the first screen below). Common property changes for a text box include changing the box's name (the one that will be used when referring to that box in the program

code), its background color, the text (if any) that should be initially displayed in the box, the font to be used with the box's text, and the border. Properties can also be changed during program execution, when appropriate, such as to disable a command button when it is not appropriate to use it or erasing a text box when a reset button is clicked. These property changes are carried out by statements in the code that perform the desired property changes and are associated with the appropriate action.

To specify what should happen when a form loads or the user performs a specific action or *event* (such as clicking a command button), the appropriate code needs to be associated with that event. Double-clicking any item opens the section of the code associated with that item so the code can be edited. For debugging purposes, the *Build* option tests the code for syntax errors and the *Debug* option runs the program so the logic can be tested. Once all errors have been corrected, the program can be run, as shown in the final screens in the accompanying illustration.

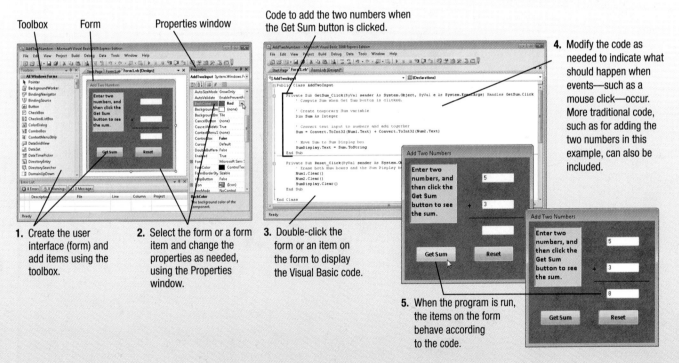

Toolbox   Form   Properties window

Code to add the two numbers when the Get Sum button is clicked.

4. Modify the code as needed to indicate what should happen when events—such as a mouse click—occur. More traditional code, such as for adding the two numbers in this example, can also be included.

1. Create the user interface (form) and add items using the toolbox.

2. Select the form or a form item and change the properties as needed, using the Properties window.

3. Double-click the form or an item on the form to display the Visual Basic code.

5. When the program is run, the items on the form behave according to the code.

The newest version of C is **C#** (pronounced *C sharp*). A hybrid of C and C++, C# is most often used to create Web applications and XML-based Web services and was developed to directly compete with *Java* (discussed next). A version of C used to write programs for Mac OS X computers and iPhones is *Objective-C*.

> **C#.** The newest, object-oriented version of the C programming language.

Java

Java is an object-oriented programming language that is commonly used to write Web applications. It was developed by Sun Microsystems and, in 2007, was released to the public as open-source software. Java programs are compiled into a format called *bytecode*. Bytecode usually has the *.class* extension and can run on any computer that includes *Java Virtual Machine (Java VM)*—the program required to run bytecode programs. Bytecode can also be converted, when needed, into machine language using a *just-in-time (JIT) compiler*. The adding-two-numbers program written in Java is shown in Figure 13-24.

In addition to being used to write complete stand-alone applications, Java can also be used to write *Java applets*—small programs designed to be inserted into a Web page and run using a Java-enabled Web browser. For instance, Java applets can be used to scroll text across a Web page, display a series of banner ads or other images, run a mortgage calculator or game, and so forth. Many Java applets are written using allowable variables (called *parameters*) that enable the applet to be customized when it is used on a Web page, such as to specify the colors to be used, the text or images to scroll, the text size, and so on. To use a Java applet on a Web page, the applet's .class files containing the applet's code must be stored in the Web site's folder. The applet can then be inserted into the Web page, similar to the way an image is added; parameter values are included in the HTML statements used to display the applet on the Web page to specify the desired applet settings. When the Web page is displayed using a Java-compatible browser, the applet is downloaded from the Web server hosting the Web page, and then run on the viewing computer.

⊽ **FIGURE 13-24**
The adding-two-numbers program written in Java.

The java.io package will handle the user input; * indicates all classes will be available.

Comments within the code are preceded by two slashes //.

The attribute *out* and *println* method in the System class of the java.io package is used to output the results.

```java
import java.io.*;
public class AddTwo {
     public static void main(String[] args) throws IOException {
        BufferedReader stdin =
           new BufferedReader ( new InputStreamReader( System.in ) );
        String inData;
        int iSum = 0;
        int iNum = 0;
        int iCntr = 0;
// Input a number, add it to the sum, and repeat
// until two numbers have been entered
     do
       {
       System.out.println("Enter number: ");
       inData = stdin.readLine();              // get number in character form
       iNum = Integer.parseInt( inData );      // convert inData to integer
       iSum = iSum + iNum;
       iCntr = iCntr + 1;
       }
     while (iCntr < 2);

// Print the sum
       System.out.println("The sum of the numbers you entered is " + iSum);
       }
     }
```

>**Java.** A high-level, object-oriented programming language frequently used for Web-based applications.

Java is currently one of the most popular programming languages and has replaced C++ as the programming language used for the computer science Advanced Placement exam taken by high school students to earn college credit. Java is widely used by businesses and is viewed by many as the replacement for both COBOL and C++.

Python

Python is an open-source, dynamic object-oriented programming language. Python can be used to develop a variety of applications, including gaming, scientific, database, and Web applications. Python programs run on computers using the Windows, Linux, UNIX, Mac OS X, or OS/2 operating systems, as well as on Palm and Nokia mobile devices. Although the language was originally developed in the early 1990s, it is just recently gaining a large following. Python is now widely used by many large organizations, including NASA, Google, Honeywell, and the New York Stock Exchange, and some colleges—such as MIT—are replacing other languages with Python for some programming courses. See Figure 13-25 for the Python version of the adding-two-numbers program.

Comments are preceded by a pound symbol #.

```
# Initialize variable
total = 0.0

# Input a number, add it to the total, and repeat
# until two numbers have been entered
for iteration in range(2):
    text = raw_input("Enter number: ")
    total = total + float(text)

# Print the sum
print "The sum of the numbers you entered is", total
```

The indented statements in this For statement will be executed two times.

FIGURE 13-25
The adding-two-numbers program written in Python.

Ruby

Another open-source object-oriented programming language is **Ruby**. Created in 1995, Ruby can be used to create both Web applications and general-purpose programming for Linux, Mac OS X, and Microsoft Windows computers. Similar to Python, Ruby uses a syntax that is relatively easy to read and write. *Ruby on Rails (RoR)* is a framework for developing dynamic Web applications that are written in the Ruby programming language. The primary goal of RoR is to enable developers to create database-driven Web applications easily and quickly. RoR applications run on a variety of types of Web servers and with a variety of databases, and they are growing rapidly in use and popularity. Many popular sites, such as Jobster and Basecamp, are built using RoR.

FURTHER EXPLORATION Go

Go to the Chapter 13 page at **www.cengage.com/ computerconcepts/np/uc13** for links to information about programming languages.

CAUTION CAUTION CAUTION CAUTION CAUTION CAUTION CAUT

Before running code written in any programming language, be sure you know how to interrupt program execution, in case you have a logic error and the program becomes stuck in an endless loop. For instance, to stop the debugging process in VisualBasic, press Ctrl+Break.

> **Python.** A high-level, open-source, dynamic object-oriented programming language that can be used to develop a wide variety of applications.
> **Ruby.** A high-level, open-source, object-oriented programming language that is often used to develop Web applications.

SUMMARY

APPROACHES TO PROGRAM DESIGN AND DEVELOPMENT

Chapter Objective 1:
Understand the differences between structured programming, object-oriented programming (OOP), aspect-oriented programming (AOP), and adaptive software development.

Two common approaches to program design are **procedural programming**, in which programs are written in an organized, modular form, and **object-oriented programming** (**OOP**), in which programs consist of a collection of *objects* that contain data and *methods* to be used with that data. A newer approach is **aspect-oriented programming** (**AOP**), which separates functions more clearly so that program components can be developed and modified individually and so that the components can easily be reused with separate, non-related objects. Other possible approaches are *adaptive software development* approaches that are designed to make program development faster or more efficient, such as *agile software development* (*ASD*). **Variables** (called *attributes* in OOP) are used to store the current value of the data items used in a program.

THE PROGRAM DEVELOPMENT LIFE CYCLE (PDLC)

Chapter Objective 2:
Identify and describe the activities involved in the program development life cycle (PDLC).

Creating application programs is referred to as **program development**. The phases involved with program development are called the **program development life cycle** (**PDLC**). The PDLC begins with **problem analysis**, in which the system specifications are reviewed by the systems analyst and **programmer** to understand what the proposed system—and corresponding new program—must do. In the next phase—**program design**—the program specifications from phase one are refined and expanded into a complete set of design specifications that express the *algorithm* for the program. In the **program coding** phase, the program is written using a programming language. The **program debugging and testing** phase ensures the program works correctly. During the **program implementation and maintenance** phase, the program is put into use and maintained as needed.

Chapter Objective 3:
Understand what constitutes good program design and list several tools that can be used by computer professionals when designing a program.

Good program design is essential. Some key design principles include being very specific, using only one *entry point* into and one *exit point* out of any structure, and ensuring that there are no *infinite loops* in your programs. Many *program design tools* are available to help programmers as they design programs. *Structure charts* depict the overall hierarchical organization of program modules. Program **flowcharts** use graphical symbols and relational operators to provide a graphic display of the sequence of steps involved in a program or program component. **Pseudocode** is a structured technique that uses English-like statements in place of the graphic symbols of the flowchart. **Unified Modeling Language** (**UML**) is a set of standard notations often used when modeling object-oriented programs.

Chapter Objective 4:
Explain the three basic control structures and how they can be used to control program flow during execution.

There are three fundamental **control structures** typically found in programs. A **sequence control structure** is simply a series of procedures that follow one another. The **selection** (or *if-then-else*) **control structure** involves a choice: *If* a certain condition is true, *then* follow one procedure; *else*, if false, follow another. When more than two conditions exist, the *case control structure* can be used. A **repetition control structure** repeats the statements in a loop until a certain condition is met. A loop can take one of two forms: *do while* or *do until*.

Once the program design for an application is finished and the logic is tested (such as by performing a *desk check*), the next phase is to code the program. **Coding**, which is the job of programmers, is the process of writing a program in a particular *programming language* based on a set of design specifications. Among the techniques that have been developed to increase programmer productivity are coding standards and *reusable code*.

Debugging, part of the fourth phase in the PDLC, is the process of making sure that a program is free of errors, or "bugs." Before a program can be run—and, therefore, before it can be debugged—it needs to be translated from the code a programmer writes to the code a computer can execute. A **language translator** converts the application program's **source code** into *machine language* or **object code**. A **compiler** translates the entire program into machine language before executing it. An **interpreter** translates and executes program statements one line at a time. An *assembler* is used to convert an assembly language program into machine language.

Most bugs can be classified as being either **syntax errors** or **logic errors**. While programs with syntax errors will not run, programs with logic errors will run but with erroneous results. Once preliminary debugging is complete, programs will also have to be thoroughly *tested*. Good test data will subject the program to all the conditions it might conceivably encounter when finally implemented. Commercial software programs are also often *beta tested*. After the testing process is complete, the last phase of the PDLC begins and involves first getting the program up and running in the new system, and then updating the software, as needed, so that it continues to be useful.

Chapter Objective 5:
Discuss some of the activities involved with debugging a program and otherwise ensuring it is designed and written properly.

TOOLS FOR FACILITATING PROGRAM DEVELOPMENT

Program development tools can be used to facilitate the program development process. **Application lifecycle management** (**ALM**) tools can be used to create and manage an application throughout its entire life cycle—from design through testing; many include *code generators* to help programmers by generating code based on the design already created with another component of the program. *Application generators*, such as *macros* and *report generators*, enable programmers and end users to code new applications quickly. *Device software development* tools are used for device software development. **Software development kits** (**SDKs**) are programming packages designed for a particular platform that enable programmers to develop applications more quickly and easily. Some tools are designed to create **rich Internet applications** (**RIAs**)—Web-based applications that work like installed software programs.

Chapter Objective 6:
List some tools that can be used to speed up or otherwise facilitate program development.

PROGRAMMING LANGUAGES

An important decision that must be made during the design phase is the selection of a **programming language**. **Low-level languages** include **machine language** and **assembly language**. **High-level languages** include **FORTRAN**, **COBOL**, **Pascal**, **BASIC**, **C**, **C++**, **C#**, and **Java**. *Very-high-level languages*, which are also called **fourth-generation languages** (**4GLs**), are predominantly *declarative languages*, whereas high-level languages are mostly *procedural languages*. Programming languages can also be a *visual language* or *graphical language*, or they can use a *visual programming environment* (*VPE*) like **Visual Basic**. Different programming languages are designed for different purposes. For instance, FORTRAN and Pascal are designed for math and science applications; COBOL is best suited for business transaction processing; C# and Java are designed for Web applications, and Visual Basic is designed to help programmers create sophisticated applications with user interfaces quickly and easily. Java, which can be used to write complete stand-alone applications as well as *Java applets*, is one of the most popular programming languages today. Java programs can be run under any operating system or Web browser that understands *Java bytecode*. Newer open-source object-oriented programming languages include **Python** and **Ruby**.

Chapter Objective 7:
Describe several programming languages in use today and explain their key features.

SYS

REVIEW ACTIVITIES

KEY TERM MATCHING

a. coding

b. compiler

c. debugging

d. flowchart

e. logic error

f. object code

g. object-oriented programming (OOP)

h. source code

i. software development kit (SDK)

j. syntax error

Instructions: Match each key term on the left with the definition on the right that best describes it.

1. _____ A computer program before it is compiled.

2. _____ A language translator that converts an entire program into machine language before executing it.

3. _____ An approach to program design in which a program consists of a collection of objects that contain data and methods to be used with that data.

4. _____ A programming package designed for a particular platform that enables programmers to develop applications for that platform more quickly and easily.

5. _____ A programming error that occurs when running a program produces incorrect results.

6. _____ A programming error that occurs when the programmer has not followed the rules of the programming language.

7. _____ A program design tool that shows graphically step-by-step how a computer program will process data.

8. _____ The machine language version of a computer program generated after the program's source code is compiled.

9. _____ The process of ensuring a program is free of errors.

10. _____ The process of writing the programming language statements to create a computer program.

SELF-QUIZ

Instructions: Circle **T** if the statement is true, **F** if the statement is false, or write the best answer in the space provided. **Answers for the self-quiz are located in the References and Resources Guide at the end of the book.**

1. **T F** A systems analyst is an individual who writes the code for a computer program.

2. **T F** The terms *class* and *inheritance* are associated with the object-oriented programming approach.

3. **T F** With a *do until* structure, the program statements in the loop are always executed at least once.

4. **T F** BASIC is an example of an object-oriented programming language.

5. **T F** Unified Modeling Language (UML) is most often used to model structured programs.

6. A(n) _____ (called an *attribute* in an OOP) in a computer program holds the current value of a data item in that program.

7. A(n) _____ converts the source code of an application program into executable object code (machine language) one line at a time.

8. Using an incorrect formula is an example of a(n) _____ error.

9. A(n) _____ is a programming package designed for a particular platform (such as the iPhone) that enables programmers to develop applications quickly and easily.

10. Indicate the proper order of the phases in the program development life cycle (PDLC) by writing the numbers from 1 to 5 in the blanks to the left of the phases.

a. _____ program coding

b. _____ program design

c. _____ program implementation and maintenance

d. _____ program debugging and testing

e. _____ problem analysis

EXERCISES

1. List at least three types of information that should be included in a program's internal documentation (comments).

2. Match each description with the most appropriate programming language, and write the corresponding number in the blank to the left of each description.

a. _____ A programming language used to write applets for use with Web pages.

b. _____ A low-level programming language.

c. _____ A high-level programming language developed to teach structured programming and used most often for math and science applications.

d. _____ A high-level programming language designed for business transaction processing applications.

1. assembly language
2. Java
3. COBOL
4. Pascal

3. Draw a flowchart for the following situation: Input a person's age. If the person is less than 21 years old, the message "You are under 21." should be displayed. For individuals 21 or older, display the message "You are 21 or older." Be sure to test your flowchart to make sure it illustrates the proper logic.

4. Write pseudocode for the problem described in Exercise #3 above.

5. Trace through the flowchart shown to the right that illustrates the logic of a program that computes the sum of two numbers. Create a tracing table as you go to see if the flowchart does what is intended (use any numbers for your input). If it does not do what it is supposed to do, identify the problem and state how it could be corrected.

Start → Set counter to 0 → Set sum to 0 → Counter < 2? → True (Yes): Input number → Subtract 1 from counter → Add number to sum → (loop back) ; False (No): Print sum → Stop

---

DISCUSSION QUESTIONS

1. When humans and computers are both involved in accomplishing a task and something goes wrong, we tend to blame the computer. There is little question about the existence of software bugs, but can all real-world problems involving computers (such as erroneous bank transactions, military training incidents, or privacy breaches) be attributed to errors in the software program? Today, do you think it is more likely that a computer or a human being would be responsible for a serious system problem? Why?

2. There is a trend in programming to make coding easier and more automatic. Some welcome this trend, but others are concerned about future programmers not learning necessary programming fundamentals if programming is no longer required. For instance, without understanding how looping and variable initializations work, how easily would an individual be able to find a logic error in a looping process? Do you think programmers of the future should still learn programming fundamentals, even if coding is no longer required? Why or why not?

PROJECTS

HOT TOPICS

1. **Open Source Projects** The use of open source software (programs in which the source code is available free of charge to the public to be used and modified) is growing by leaps and bounds. One of the benefits of open source software is that improvements to the program are shared with the open source community. Open source projects provide opportunities for individuals to work on open source programs, and they are often open to anyone who wants to participate.

   For this project, find and investigate two current open source projects and determine who is able to participate and how participants share their improvements with others. Would you be interested in participating in an open source project? What are some advantages for programming students? Any disadvantages? At the conclusion of your research, prepare a one-page summary of your findings and opinions and submit it to your instructor.

SHORT ANSWER/ RESEARCH

2. **New Programming Languages** New programming languages are developed on a continual basis, such as to meet new needs or make programming easier for beginners.

   For this project, identify and research one new or emerging programming language (Scratch, developed by MIT, is one example). Determine why the program was developed, who it is geared for, the cost to use it (if any), and what applications it is designed for. Check online to see if there is a demonstration or a free version available; if so, view the demo or try out the programming language, if possible. Do you think this new program fulfills a need? Why or why not? At the conclusion of your research, prepare a short summary of what you learned and submit it to your instructor.

HANDS ON

3. **Pass or Fail** Flowcharts can be used to model any sequence of actions, in addition to being used to design programs.

   For this project, draw a flowchart that depicts the sequence of steps involved in passing the course for which you are using this textbook. To simplify the diagram, you may assume that you will either pass or fail this class (no grade will be issued) and that there are only three graded components (midterm, final, and projects). The flowchart should print the names of all students on the instructor's roster who have passed the course by achieving a score of at least 70% on each graded component. In addition, you should print the total number of students on the roster, as well as the number that passed the class. Be sure to trace the flowchart to verify your logic, and then write a pseudocode version of this situation. When you have completed this task, submit a copy of the flowchart and pseudocode to your instructor.

ETHICS IN ACTION

4. **Consumer Hacks** There have been many instances where individuals have hacked into consumer products—such as toys, mobile phones, gaming consoles, DVRs, and more—to alter their functionality. Some of these hacks (such as one that required the hacker to break the encryption built into a robot in order to reprogram it to perform other activities) violate the Digital Millennium Copyright Act, which prohibits breaking technological controls placed on any copyrighted work. Do you think hacking into a product you own is ethical? Have you ever considered hacking into a product you own? If so, for what purpose? Do you think consumer hacks should be illegal if the hack requires breaking the product's encryption? If so, should the law apply to those individuals who break through a copy protection scheme for their own use only, or should the law apply just to those individuals who share the circumvention process with others? What about those individuals who try to break a copy protection or security technology just to prove it can be done? Should they be prosecuted, sued, or congratulated for exposing a weakness in the existing technology?

   For this project, form an opinion about the ethical ramifications of consumer hacks and be prepared to discuss your position (in class, via an online class discussion group, in a class chat room, or via a class blog, depending on your instructor's directions). You may also be asked to write a short paper expressing your opinion.

PRESENTATION/ DEMONSTRATION

5. **Bug Hunters** Many security freelance programmers in the software industry (sometimes referred to as *bug hunters*) like to search for security flaws in their spare time and make this information public. The goal is to make unsuspecting users aware of the possible security problems that currently exist and encourage the producer of the software to write security patches to fix these problems.

   For this project, research one recent major security flaw discovered in a widely used software program and present a summary about who found the flaw, how the information was made public, what the security problem was, and how the problem was resolved (or is being resolved). Share your findings and opinions with the class in the form of a short presentation. The presentation should not exceed 10 minutes and should make use of one or more presentation aids, such as the chalkboard, handouts, overhead transparencies, or a computer-based slide presentation (your instructor may provide additional requirements). You may also be asked to submit a summary of the presentation to your instructor.

Instructions: Go to the Chapter 13 page at **www.cengage.com/computerconcepts/np/uc13** to work the following Web Activities.

WEB ACTIVITIES

Student Edition Labs

6. **Interactive Activities** Work the interactive **Crossword Puzzle**, watch the **Video Podcasts** and **Online Videos**, and explore the **Further Exploration** links associated with this chapter.

   If you have a SAM user profile, you may have access to hands-on instruction, practice, and assessment of the skills covered in this chapter. Check with your instructor for instructions and the correct URL/Web site to access those assignments.

7. **Student Edition Labs** Work the following interactive **Student Edition Labs**.
   - ➤ **Visual Programming**   ➤ **Advanced Spreadsheets**

8. **Test Yourself** Review the **Online Study Guide** for this chapter, then test your knowledge of the terms and concepts covered in this chapter by completing the **Key Term Matching** exercise, the **Self-Quiz**, the **Exercises**, and the **Practice Test**.

chapter 14

Databases and Database Management Systems

After completing this chapter, you will be able to do the following:

1. Explain what a database is, including common database terminology, and list some of the advantages and disadvantages of using databases.

2. Discuss some basic concepts and characteristics of data, such as data hierarchy, entity relationships, and data definition.

3. Describe the importance of data integrity, security, and privacy and how they affect database design.

4. Identify some basic database classifications and discuss their differences.

5. List the most common database models and discuss how they are used today.

6. Understand how a relational database is designed, created, used, and maintained.

7. Describe some ways databases are used on the Web.

outline

Overview

What Is a Database?
A Simple Relational Database Example
Individuals Involved with a Database Management System
The Evolution of Databases
Advantages and Disadvantages of the DBMS Approach

Data Concepts and Characteristics
Data Hierarchy
Entities and Entity Relationships
Data Definition
The Data Dictionary
Data Integrity, Security, and Privacy
Data Organization

Database Classifications
Single-User vs. Multiuser Database Systems
Client-Server and N-Tier Database Systems
Centralized vs. Distributed Database Systems
Disk-Based vs. In-Memory Database Systems

Database Models
The Hierarchical and Network Database Models
The Relational Database Model
The Object-Oriented Database Model
Hybrid Database Models
Multidimensional Databases

Databases and the Web
Examples of Web Databases in Use
How Web Databases Work

OVERVIEW

People often need to sort through a large amount of data rapidly to retrieve one piece of information. To do this quickly and easily, a database is often used. Databases can be a variety of sizes, from an address book created and used by an individual, to a companywide database consisting of customer data used by company employees, to a product database used in conjunction with an e-commerce site to enable online shoppers to place real-time orders, to a search engine database consisting of data about billions of Web pages and accessed by individuals around the world.

The focus of this chapter is databases and the software used to create, maintain, and use them. The chapter opens with a look at what a database is, the individuals who use them, and how databases evolved. We then look at some important database concepts and vocabulary, followed by an explanation of database classifications and models, with an extended discussion of the most widely used database model: the relational database. The chapter closes with a discussion of how databases are used on the Web. ■

> **PODCAST**
>
> Go to **www.cengage.com/ computerconcepts/np/uc13** to download or listen to the "Expert Insight on Systems" podcast.

WHAT IS A DATABASE?

As discussed in Chapter 6, a **database** is a collection of related data that is stored and organized in a manner that enables information to be retrieved as needed. *Database software*—more formally called a **database management system** (**DBMS**)—is used to create, maintain, and access a database. A DBMS also controls the organization of the data and protects the *integrity* and *security* of the data so it is entered accurately into the database and then protected against both intentional and accidental damage. While batch processing can be used with databases, most database applications today occur in real time.

A key component of a DBMS is the *database engine*—the part of the program that actually stores and retrieves data. In addition to a database engine, most DBMSs come bundled with a set of tools to perform a variety of necessary tasks, such as creating *forms* (used to input data) and *reports* (used to output data), and interfacing with *query languages* and programming languages for complex applications. Programming languages typically used with databases today include Visual Basic, Java, and C++, although many older *legacy* database systems still use COBOL.

A database typically consists of interrelated **tables** that contain *fields* and *records*. As discussed in Chapter 6, a **field** (also called a **column**) holds a single category of data (such as customer names or employee telephone numbers) that will be stored in a database. A **record** (also called a **row**) is a collection of related fields. The technical difference between the terms *row* and *record* in database terminology is that a row is contained within a single database table, but a record is a collection of fields, which can be either a specific row

> **Database.** A collection of related data that is stored in a manner enabling information to be retrieved as needed; in a relational database, a collection of related tables. > **Database management system (DBMS).** A type of software program used to create, maintain, and access databases. > **Table.** In a relational database, a collection of related records or rows. > **Field.** A single category of data to be stored in a database, such as customer names or employee telephone numbers. Also called a column. > **Column.** A field in a database. > **Record.** A collection of related fields in a database. Also called a row. > **Row.** A collection of related fields located in a single table in a database.

SYS

from a single table or a collection of related fields from multiple tables, such as the records shown in the results of the Order Request screen shown in Figure 14-1 and discussed next. However, in this chapter, as in common usage, the two terms are used interchangeably.

To illustrate these concepts, a simplified example of a possible *relational database*—the type of database most widely used at the present time—is shown in Figure 14-1 and discussed next.

A Simple Relational Database Example

Figure 14-1 illustrates an inventory system for a ski equipment retailer. The tables shown in this figure contain data related to the retailer's products: the Product table (for product descriptions and selling prices), the Inventory table (for current stock levels of products), and the Inventory on Order table (for future shipments of products that have been ordered from suppliers). Each table consists of several fields (columns) and records (rows). The Product table, for example, contains four fields—Product Number, Product Name, Supplier, and Price—and five records—one each for Skis, Boots, Poles, Bindings, and Wax. Each record in the Product table contains data for each of the four fields. The Inventory table contains three fields and five records, and the Inventory on Order table contains four fields and six records. To keep this example simple, the tables containing data about customers and their orders (Customer table and Order table, respectively) are not shown. Real-world databases typically consist of many more tables than are used in this example, each containing thousands of records.

For this example, imagine that you are the sales manager of this company and a customer calls on the phone and wants to order 160 pairs of ski boots. First, you need to find

FIGURE 14-1

Using a relational database in an inventory system.

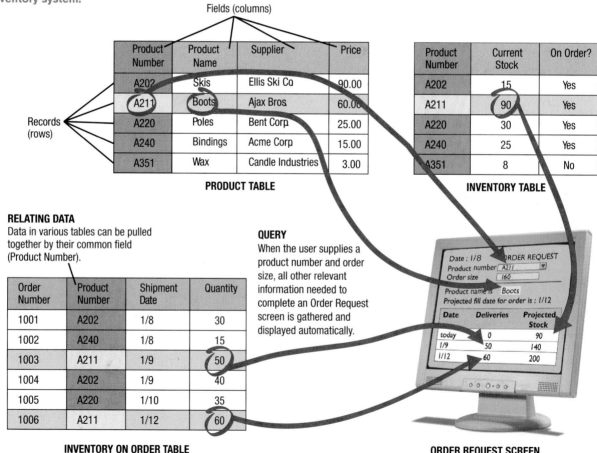

RELATING DATA
Data in various tables can be pulled together by their common field (Product Number).

QUERY
When the user supplies a product number and order size, all other relevant information needed to complete an Order Request screen is gathered and displayed automatically.

out if the order can be filled from stock currently in inventory. If it cannot, you need to know how long it will be before enough stock is available to fill the order. Using your computer, you execute the appropriate command to display an Order Request screen and enter the product number "A211" and the order size "160" as shown in Figure 14-1. The DBMS then displays the name of the product (Boots, in this example), the current level of stock in inventory (90), and as many upcoming shipments of this product (50 and 60) as needed to fill the order. It also provides an estimate as to when the order can be filled: January 12. Within seconds, right in front of you, you have the information you need to respond to the customer's request and close the order.

In a relational database, data from several tables is tied together (*related*) using fields that the tables have in common so that information can be extracted from multiple tables as needed. For instance, in Figure 14-1, data from all three tables was pulled together through a common Product Number field (the green shaded columns) to complete the Order Request screen shown in that figure. Specifically, the Product table was first accessed to locate and display the product name; next, the Inventory table was used to determine and display the number of boots currently in stock; and finally, the Inventory on Order table was used to look up and display the quantities and delivery dates for as many incoming shipments as needed to get a total of at least 160 boots. The end user is typically not aware that multiple tables are being used or of the relationships between tables; instead the user knows only that the information is "somewhere in the database system" and it is retrieved and displayed when requested.

The field in a table that is used to relate that table to other tables is called the **primary key**. A primary key must uniquely identify each record in that table, which means that no two records within a table can have the same value in the primary key field. To ensure the uniqueness of the primary key, it usually consists of an identifying number, such as a student ID number, customer number, or product number. For example, in Figure 14-1, the Product Number field is the primary key field for the Product and Inventory tables and the Order Number field is the primary key field for the Inventory on Order table. When selecting a primary key field, it is important to pick a field that contains unique data that is not likely to change. Consequently, fields containing names, telephone numbers, and addresses are poor choices for a primary key (see Figure 14-2). Although telephone numbers and complete addresses are unique, they may change and will not necessarily always be associated with the original individual.

While most complex database systems will have multiple interrelated tables, you can create a database that does not interrelate tables, or you can create a database that has only a single table, if that's appropriate for your application. DBMSs available for use on personal computers include *Microsoft Access* and *Corel Paradox* (part of the Microsoft Office and WordPerfect Office software suites, respectively). Of these, Access is the most widely used. For more comprehensive enterprise databases, *Oracle Database*, *IBM DB2*, *Microsoft SQL Server*, or another more robust DBMS may be used instead.

Individuals Involved with a Database Management System

To be effective, data in a DBMS must be initially entered into the database, updated as necessary to stay current, and then retrieved in the form of information. Consequently, virtually all DBMSs include a user interface for easy data input, modification, and retrieval. There must also be a way for the database to be backed up and protected against unauthorized access. The individuals most often involved with creating, using, managing, and protecting a DBMS are described next.

The yellow fields will always contain unique data and so are good to use as primary keys.

The blue fields will not always contain unique data and so are not good to use as primary keys.

Product Number	Product Name	Supplier	Price
Student ID Number	Student Name	Address	Phone
Customer Number	Address	Phone	Balance

FIGURE 14-2
Key fields. A key field must contain unique data so it can be used to identify each record in the table.

> **Primary key.** A specific field in a database table that uniquely identifies the records in that table.

Database Designers

As the name suggests, a *database designer* is the individual responsible for designing a database. Because data and databases are so critical in business today, it is essential for databases to be designed appropriately so they can efficiently fulfill the needs of a business. Database designers work with systems analysts and other individuals involved in the system development life cycle (SDLC) to identify the types of data to be collected, the relationships among the data, the types of output required, and other factors that affect the design of the database, and then they design the database accordingly. These individuals are also sometimes called *database architects*, *database engineers*, and *database analysts*.

Database Developers and Programmers

Database developers create the actual database based on the design generated by the database designer and get it ready for data entry. This process includes setting up the database structure and creating the user interface, typically using the tools included with the DBMS. Many databases also require custom programs used to access the database or to tie the database to other applications, such as to a Web site for an e-commerce application. Creating these programs, when needed, is the job of the *database programmer*. Sometimes the user interface is also built using a programming language when very specific requirements exist. In some organizations, one individual may be both the database developer and database programmer; he or she may function as the database designer, as well.

Database Administrators

Database administrators (*DBAs*) are the people responsible for managing the databases within an organization. They perform regular maintenance, assign and monitor user access to the database, monitor the performance of the database system, perform backups, and carry out other necessary maintenance and security duties. Database administrators also work closely with database designers, developers, and programmers to ensure that the *integrity* and *security* of the data will remain intact when a new system is designed or changes are made to an existing system. The DBA also periodically runs reports and checks the data in the database to confirm that the structural integrity of the data is intact. Database integrity and security are discussed later in this chapter.

Users

The *users* are the individuals who enter data, update data, and retrieve information from the database when necessary; that is, the individuals who use the database. Typically, users have no knowledge of how the underlying database is structured, how data is organized, or how data is retrieved. Instead, they interact with the database via a user interface consisting of menus, buttons, and fill-in-the-blank forms (such as the Order Request screen shown in Figure 14-1).

MODEL	FLAT FILES	HIERARCHICAL	NETWORK	RELATIONAL	OBJECT-ORIENTED	MULTI-DIMENSIONAL
YEAR BEGAN	1940s	1960s	1960s	1970s	1980s	1990s
DATA ORGANIZATION	Flat files	Trees	Trees	Tables and relations	Objects	Data cubes, tables and relations, or a combination
DATA ACCESS	Low-level access	Low-level access with a standard navigational language	Low-level access with a standard navigational language	High-level, nonprocedural languages	High-level, nonprocedural, object-oriented languages	OLAP tools or programming languages
SKILL LEVEL REQUIRED TO ACCESS DATA	Programmer	Programmer	Programmer	User	User	User
ENTITY RELATIONSHIPS SUPPORTED	One-to-one	One-to-one, one-to-many	One-to-one, one-to-many, many-to-many	One-to-one, one-to-many, many-to-many	One-to-one, one-to-many, many-to-many	One-to-one, one-to-many, many-to-many
DATA AND PROGRAM INDEPENDENCE	No	No	No	Yes	Yes	Yes

FIGURE 14-3

The evolution of databases. Databases have evolved over the years, becoming more flexible, more capable, and easier to use.

The Evolution of Databases

Databases have evolved dramatically since the early 1960s. This evolution has occurred in response to our increased reliance on information systems; advances in programming languages; the need to store and retrieve a variety of complex data, such as multimedia objects (digital images, video files, audio files, and so forth); and the vast use of databases on the Web. The most significant advances in databases can be summarized primarily in terms of their organization of data and access to data. The organization of data has evolved from a collection of independent *flat files* with tree or branching structures and high levels of data redundancy, to a collection of tables and objects that support multimedia objects with a minimum of data redundancy, to databases that can be viewed from a variety of perspectives or *dimensions*. A summary of this evolution is shown in Figure 14-3; the models and relationships listed in the figure are discussed in more detail later in this chapter. For a look at the *file management systems* used with flat files and how they differ from database management systems, see the Inside the Industry box.

Advantages and Disadvantages of the DBMS Approach

Because a DBMS can pull data out of more than one table at a time (compared to a *file management system* that can only work with one table at a time, as discussed in the Inside the Industry box), there is a very low level of redundancy in the tables in a DBMS database. In fact, often only a single field (the primary key) appears in more than one file. This low level of redundancy has several advantages. For instance, a DBMS database typically has a faster response time and lower storage requirements than a file management system, and it is easier to secure. In addition, data accuracy is increased since updates (such as an address change for a customer) are only made to a single table, cutting down on the possibility of data errors and inconsistencies that can occur when the same update has to be made manually to multiple tables (such as when using a file management system).

One of the most significant potential disadvantages of the DBMS approach is increased vulnerability. Because the data in the database is highly integrated, the potential for data loss (such as if records or tables are accidentally deleted, the system fails, or the database is

SYS

INSIDE THE INDUSTRY

File Management Systems

A *file management system* is a program that allows the creation of individual database tables (often referred to as *flat files*). Each table is stored in its own physical file and is not related to any other file. Consequently, file management systems can work with only one table at a time, and each table has to contain all the data that may need to be accessed or retrieved at one time. As a result, file management systems have a much higher level of redundancy than database management systems. For example, in the accompanying illustration, the Product Name, Supplier, and Price data (the blue-shaded columns) must be entered and stored in all three tables. This redundancy can lead to data entry errors in the database, as well as storage issues since the files contain more data than they would if a DBMS was used. It also requires additional work. For example, the task illustrated in Figure 14-1 would require the sales manager to perform the following steps:

1. Use the product number to look up the product name in the Product table.
2. Use the product number to check the Inventory table to see if the company can fill the order from current stock.
3. If current stock is inadequate, check the Inventory on Order table to see when enough stock will be available to fill the order.
4. Use the Inventory on Order table to determine the date on which the order can be filled.

Because using a file management system with flat files is much slower than using a database management system with related tables, both service to customers and efficiency suffer. As a result, file management systems are rarely used today. They are useful, however, in appreciating the advantages of a DBMS and some of the advances the industry has made over the years.

PRODUCT NUMBER	PRODUCT NAME	SUPPLIER	PRICE
A202	Skis	Ellis Ski Co.	90.00
A211	Boots	Ajax Bros.	60.00
A220	Poles	Bent Corp.	25.00
A240	Bindings	Acme Corp.	15.00
A351	Wax	Candle Industries	3.00

PRODUCT TABLE

PRODUCT NUMBER	PRODUCT NAME	SUPPLIER	PRICE	CURRENT STOCK	ON ORDER?
A202	Skis	Ellis Ski Co.	90.00	15	Yes
A211	Boots	Ajax Bros.	60.00	90	Yes
A220	Poles	Bent Corp.	25.00	30	Yes
A240	Bindings	Acme Corp.	15.00	25	Yes
A351	Wax	Candle Industries	3.00	8	No

INVENTORY TABLE

ORDER NUMBER	PRODUCT NUMBER	SHIPMENT DATE	PRODUCT NAME	SUPPLIER	PRICE	QUANTITY
1001	A202	1/8	Skis	Ellis Ski Co.	90.00	30
1002	A240	1/8	Bindings	Acme Corp.	15.00	15
1003	A211	1/9	Boots	Ajax Bros.	60.00	50
1004	A202	1/9	Skis	Ellis Ski Co.	90.00	40
1005	A220	1/10	Poles	Bent Corp.	25.00	35
1006	A211	1/12	Boots	Ajax Bros.	60.00	60

INVENTORY ON ORDER TABLE

REDUNDANT FIELDS
Instead of just having one field duplicated like in a DBMS (green shaded columns), file management systems require many more fields to be duplicated (green and blue shaded columns). Notice that the blue shaded columns shown here appear only in the Product table in Figure 14-1; when using a DBMS, these fields are not included in the Inventory and Inventory on Order tables.

Since file management systems cannot retrieve data from more than one table at a time, there is a much higher level of redundancy.

breached) is much greater. Consequently, security and backup procedures are an extremely important part of using a DBMS, as discussed in more detail shortly.

DATA CONCEPTS AND CHARACTERISTICS

Data is frequently considered to be one of an organization's most valuable assets. Without it, businesses would find it impossible to perform some of their most basic activities. Data is also the heart of a database. Consequently, its concepts and characteristics need to be understood in order to successfully design, create, and use a database. Some of the most important concepts and characteristics are discussed in the following sections.

Data Hierarchy

Data in a database has a definite hierarchy. At the lowest level, characters are entered into database fields (columns), which hold single pieces of data in the database, such as product names or quantities (refer again to Figure 14-1). At the next level are records (rows)— groups of related fields (such as all the fields for a particular product). At the next level are tables, which are made up of related records. At the top of the hierarchy is the database, which consists of a group of related tables.

> **TIP**
>
> In many DBMSs, including Microsoft Access, the entire database (including all tables) is stored in a single file, which is given an appropriate filename by the user.

Entities and Entity Relationships

An **entity** is something (such as a person, object, or event) of importance to the business or organization. When an entity is something that a business or an organization wants to store data about in a database system, it typically becomes a database table. The characteristics of an entity are called **attributes**. For instance, if a business collects data about customers, then Customer is an entity. Possible Customer attributes are last name, first name, phone number, address, and so forth. Attributes typically become fields in the entity's database table.

A *relationship* describes an association between two or more entities. The three basic *entity relationships* are discussed next.

One-to-One Entity Relationships

One-to-one (1:1) entity relationships exist when one entity is related to only one other entity of a particular type. For example, if a business has multiple store locations and each store has a single manager, the relationship between Store and Manager is a 1:1 relationship. For each store location, you can determine the appropriate manager; for each manager, you can identify his or her store. In this type of relationship, each record in the table belonging to the first entity can have only one matching record in the table belonging to the second entity. This type of relationship is not common, however, because all the data would typically be located in a single table instead of creating a separate table (such as one for stores and one for managers, in this example) for each entity.

One-to-Many Entity Relationships

One-to-many (O:M) entity relationships are the most common and exist when one entity can be related to more than one other entity. For example, if a supplier supplies more than one product to the company, the relationship between Supplier and Products is an O:M relationship and the supplier would have a single entry in the Supplier table but would appear multiple times in the Product table. Consequently, if a specific product number is

---

> **Entity.** Something (such as a person, object, or event) that is important to a business or organization; typically becomes a database table in a database system for that business or organization. > **Attribute.** A characteristic of an entity.

known, its supplier can be determined easily, but if a supplier is known, a single product number cannot be identified.

Many-to-Many Entity Relationships

Many-to-many (M:M) entity relationships exist when one entity can be related to more than one other entity, and those entities can be related to multiple entities of the same type as the original entity. For example, if an order can contain multiple products and one product can appear on many orders, the relationship between Orders and Products is an M:M relationship. If an order number is known, a single corresponding product number cannot be identified, and if a product number is known, a single corresponding order cannot be identified. Consequently, this type of relationship requires a third table—such as an Order Details table used in conjunction with an Orders table and a Products table—to tie the two tables together.

Data Definition

Data definition involves describing the properties of the data that go into each database table, specifically the fields that make up the database. During the data definition process, the following are supplied for each field:

> ➤ *Name* (must be unique within the table).

> ➤ *Data type* (such as *Text*, *Number*, *Currency*, or *Date/Time*); indicates the type of data that will be entered into the field.

> ➤ *Description* (an optional description of the field).

> ➤ *Properties* (such as the *field size* and *format* of the field, any allowable range or required format for the data that will be entered into the field, whether or not the field is required, and/or any initial value to appear in that field when a new record is added).

The properties that can be set for a field depend on the data type being used for that field. For instance, for fields using the Text data type, the field size indicates the number of characters that may be entered for that field. For Number fields, the field size typically indicates how much storage space (in bytes) can be used for each entry and if decimal places are allowed. For instance, the field size *Integer* for Number fields in Microsoft Access can hold any number from -32,768 to 32,767; the *Long Integer* field size can be used for Number fields that will store longer integers. If a field needs to store decimal places, the *Double* or *Decimal* field sizes can be used instead.

The finished specifications for a table (the fields and the properties for those fields) are commonly referred to as the *table structure*. For example, the structure of the Inventory table from Figure 14-1 (shown being created in Microsoft Access in Figure 14-4) consists of three main fields: *Product Number*, *Current Stock*, and *On Order?*. The Product Number field contains text (character-based) data so the Text field type is assigned to the Product Number field. A field size of 4 is specified in this field's properties because product numbers for this business consist of four characters (one letter followed by three numbers). The Current Stock field contains numeric data that must be integers (have no decimal places) because stock is counted in product units; consequently, the Number data type and the Integer field size are assigned to this field. The On Order? field in this table is specified as a *Yes/No* field. Fields using this data type contain a value representing *true* (typically

---

>**Data definition.** The process of describing the properties of data that is to be included in a database table.

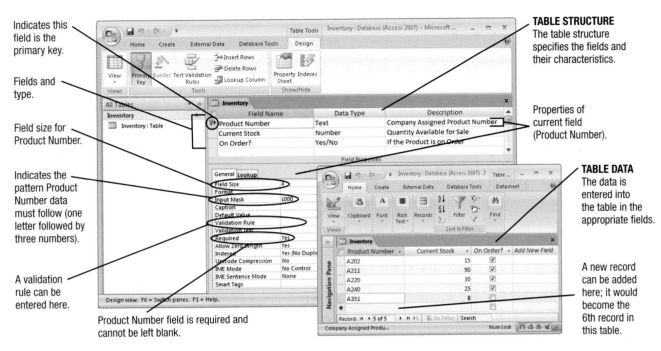

Indicates this field is the primary key.

Fields and type.

Field size for Product Number.

Indicates the pattern Product Number data must follow (one letter followed by three numbers).

A validation rule can be entered here.

Product Number field is required and cannot be left blank.

TABLE STRUCTURE
The table structure specifies the fields and their characteristics.

Properties of current field (Product Number).

TABLE DATA
The data is entered into the table in the appropriate fields.

A new record can be added here; it would become the 6th record in this table.

FIGURE 14-4
Data definition. Each field in a database has a defined data type and properties that can be assigned to that field.

entered by the user as a *T* for *true*, *Y* for *yes*, or a checked box, depending on the program being used), or a value representing *false* (typically entered by the user as an *F* for *false*, *N* for *no*, or an unchecked box). In the Inventory table, a product that is on order is given the value *true*; a product not on order has the value *false*.

Other properties that can be assigned to a field include an *input mask* to specify the format (such as letters, numbers, or symbols) that must be entered into a field, whether or not the field is *required* (if so, it cannot be left blank), and any *validation rules* (specific allowable values for the field, such as a certain range of numeric values for a numeric field or a particular date range for a date field) needed to ensure only valid data is entered into the field. If data typed into a field does not match the data type or the input mask for the field, violates a validation rule, or is blank when the field is required, that record will not be added to the table until the error is corrected, as discussed shortly. The additional properties assigned to the Product Number field in the Inventory table shown in Figure 14-4 include an *input mask* of L000 to ensure that only product numbers that fit this pattern (one letter followed by three numbers) are entered in the Product Number field, and the field is specified as required.

DBMSs designed for use with large computer systems usually include a special language component dedicated to the data definition process. Such languages have generically come to be known as *data definition languages* (*DDLs*). In addition to simply defining data, a major function of the DDL in these large packages is security—protecting the database from unauthorized use. *Data security* is discussed in more detail shortly.

The Data Dictionary

The **data dictionary** contains all data definitions for a database, including table structures (containing the names, types, and properties of each field in a table), security information

>**Data dictionary.** The repository of all data definitions in a database.

(such as the password needed to view or edit a table), relationships between the tables in the database, and so on. Also included in the data dictionary is basic information about each table, such as its current number of records. The data dictionary does not contain any of the data located *in* the database tables, only data (called **metadata**) *about* the database tables. Usually the data dictionary file is created automatically by the DBMS as the structure of each database table is defined and is accessed only by the DBMS, not by the end user.

The data dictionary is used by the DBMS as data is being entered into a table to ensure that the data does not violate any of its assigned properties. For example, the data dictionary would not allow you to enter a seven-character product number in a Product Number field that is defined as four characters long, it would not allow you to type text-based data into a field defined as a Number field, and it would not allow you to leave a required field blank. In addition, without the proper password, the data dictionary would not allow you to view password-protected data. Consequently, these measures can be used to increase *data integrity*, *security*, and *privacy*, discussed next.

Data Integrity, Security, and Privacy

Because data is so essential to organizations, *data integrity* and *data security* are very important issues. Although data integrity and security have always been high-priority database issues, there has been increased attention paid to these issues recently due to the vast number of database security breaches that have occurred in the past few years, as well as the ongoing threat of terrorism. The total destruction of the computer containing a crucial database, as well as the threat of unauthorized access and data alteration of a vital database system, is being viewed as a much more real possibility than just a few years ago. There are also increasing regulations for database security, such as the updated Payment Card Industry (PCI) data security standards that require checks for viruses, spyware, and other types of malicious software on all databases containing credit card data, as well as require companies to ensure that any third parties that they deal with (such as Web hosting providers) have proper controls in place for securing credit card data. Consequently, many businesses and government organizations are evaluating their data integrity and security methods and improving them, if needed. *Database privacy* is also of increasing concern to businesses and many individuals, as database breaches are becoming more frequent and as governments are increasingly implementing new data privacy legislation and regulations.

Data Integrity

Data integrity refers to the accuracy of data. The long-standing computer saying *garbage in, garbage out* is very appropriate for database systems. The quality of the information generated from a database is only as good as the accuracy of the data contained in the database. Although it is possible to generate poor information from quality data (such as by making poor assumptions or using poor data analysis), it is virtually impossible to generate quality information from inaccurate data. Because so many important decisions are based on information generated by information systems (which almost always use some type of database), data integrity is a vital concern for organizations. Responsible, reliable employees at the data entry level, teamed with good *data validation* methods, can increase the accuracy of the data in a database.

Data validation refers to the process of ensuring that the data entered into a database is valid; that is, it matches the specified data type, format, and allowable value for each field. As previously discussed and shown in Figure 14-4, input masks and validation rules can be assigned to a field to ensure that data is entered in the specified format and

---

> **Metadata.** Data about data, such as the data contained in a data dictionary. > **Data integrity.** The accuracy of data. > **Data validation.** The process of ensuring that data entered into a database is valid (matches the data definition).

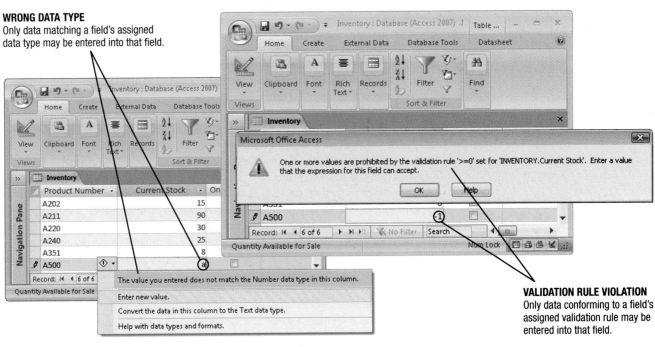

WRONG DATA TYPE
Only data matching a field's assigned data type may be entered into that field.

VALIDATION RULE VIOLATION
Only data conforming to a field's assigned validation rule may be entered into that field.

FIGURE 14-5
Data validation.
Good data validation rules can prevent invalid data from being entered into a database table.

meets the specified criteria. *Record validation rules* can also be assigned to a table, when appropriate; these rules are checked after all fields in a record are completed but before the record is saved. Record validation rules are used when the value of one field in the record needs to be checked against another field in that same record to be sure it is valid, such as to ensure a ship date isn't earlier than the order date. As previously discussed, the data dictionary is responsible for comparing all data entered into a table with the designated requirements and only allows data to be entered into the database table if it follows the specified rules. If invalid data is supplied, a message will usually be displayed on the screen (see Figure 14-5), and the record is not entered into the database table until all fields contain valid data.

In some systems, data integrity is enforced on a *per transaction* basis. This means that if invalid data is supplied and not corrected at some point during the steps necessary to enter a complete transaction into the system, then the entire transaction will fail, not just that one step of the transaction. This ensures that a complete, valid transaction is always entered into the system at one time and that the database is never left with just one piece of a transaction completed. Even if multiple tables will be affected by the transaction, users will not be able to see the changes made due to that transaction until the transaction is *committed*; that is, until all steps in the transaction are deemed valid and the appropriate changes are made to all the affected tables. Once a transaction has been committed, all changes pertaining to the transaction become visible in all corresponding tables at the same time.

Because different users and applications may be trying to change the same data at the same time, it is important that a database be able to temporarily "lock" data that is being accessed so that no other changes can be made to the data until the first user or application is finished. For example, going back to the inventory database scenario shown in Figure 14-1, assume that while the sales manager is working on the order for the 160 boots, using information pulled from the Inventory and Inventory on Order tables, another person in the sales department gets a request for 75 of the same boots. If the database does not lock the pertinent tables while they are being accessed, both of these employees could sell the same 75 in-stock boots to different customers at the same time. This potential problem can be avoided if *database locking* is used. Databases often support various types of locking, such as *row-level locking* (in which an entire table row is locked when any part of that record is being modified), and *column-level locking* (in which the table column involved in the changes is locked until the changes to that field have been completed).

TIP

To increase data integrity, use appropriate properties (such as the proper field type, size, validation rule, and input mask) for each field in a table to ensure it is not possible to enter invalid data into that table.

SYS

Data Security

Because large databases are typically used by numerous people, they are vulnerable to security problems, both from outside hackers and internal users. For example, a hacker may attempt to access a database to steal credit card data, an unscrupulous employee may attempt to alter payroll data, or a careless employee may accidentally delete a record or an entire database file. **Data security** refers to protecting data against destruction and misuse—both intentional and accidental. Data security is a growing challenge for many organizations as they are finding the need to grant increased access to company databases (such as to a larger number of employees than in the past, as well as to outsiders—customers, auditors, contractors, business partners, and so forth).

Data security involves both protecting against unauthorized access to and unauthorized use of the database, as well as preventing data loss. External security measures (such as firewalls and proper access controls, as discussed in Chapter 9) can be used to protect against outside access to a company network and database. In addition to using an access control system (such as usernames and passwords) to limit database access to authorized users, the database administrator may also assign specific access privileges (such as whether the user can only read data, can add data, can modify data, and so forth) to specific individuals or groups of individuals. This access can typically be specified down to the individual column level of a database table. For example, in an airline's passenger reservation database, a regular clerk or agent may not be allowed to rebook a special-rate passenger on an alternate flight, but a high-level supervisor with the appropriate access privileges is able to do so. Similarly, sensitive data, such as salaries, can be hidden from view so that only certain users of the database are able to retrieve them or modify them. As mentioned earlier, these privileges are usually incorporated into the data dictionary and are enforced by the DBMS to ensure only authorized individuals are permitted to view and change data.

One emerging data security risk is the exploitation of known but unpatched vulnerabilities by hackers; that is, hackers breaching a not-yet-patched system through a vulnerability that has been made public via the release of a new database patch. Because many organizations do not install patches immediately—in fact, a 90-day patch cycle is not uncommon—and because code specifically written to exploit new vulnerabilities is now often posted to the Web by hackers within hours of a database patch release, there is often ample time for a criminal to access a database via a known vulnerability before that database is patched. In addition to installing patches as soon as they become available, actively monitoring databases for unusual activity and unauthorized access, as well as adequately locking down data at the database level, can help avoid these types of database breaches. Database vulnerability assessment tools can also be used to detect security weaknesses (such as unpatched vulnerabilities and weak passwords) that an attacker can exploit. For instance, the *database activity monitoring program* shown in Figure 14-6 monitors a database continually to detect and report possible intrusions and other threats in real time; it also updates its knowledge base of known database

FIGURE 14-6

Database security tools. This program monitors database activity and displays alerts for possible problems.

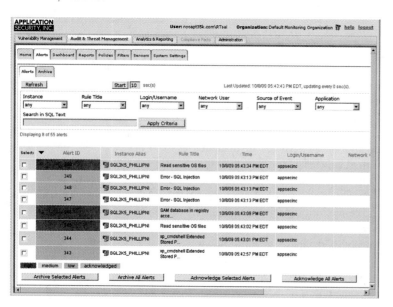

>**Data security.** Protecting the data located in a database against destruction and misuse.

security threats automatically to protect against new threats as they become known. To avoid security problems at the application level, some companies use scanning tools during software development to locate and plug security holes in application software while it is being developed, instead of after it has been deployed. Stronger database encryption tools are also being integrated into DBMS programs, as well as being integrated into stand-alone *database encryption software*.

To protect against data loss caused by a database failure, accidental deletion, or other problem that renders the main copy of a database unusable, stringent backup procedures should be implemented. To protect against data loss due to disasters (such as hard drive failure or the total destruction of the facility due to a fire, flood, or other disaster), appropriate *disaster-recovery procedures* should be used. Possible precautions include keeping a redundant copy of the database on a mirrored drive, backing up the data at very frequent intervals to an offsite location, and having a comprehensive *disaster-recovery plan*. As part of its disaster-recovery plan, some firms maintain a *hot site*—an alternate location equipped with identical hardware and software that can be used (along with the most current data backup) to resume operations quickly in case of a major disaster. Backup procedures were discussed in Chapter 5; disaster-recovery plans are discussed in more detail in Chapter 15.

Data Privacy

A company that stores data about individuals is responsible for protecting the privacy of that data. **Data privacy** is a growing concern because of the vast amounts of personal data stored in databases today and the many data privacy breaches that have occurred in the recent past. With the new laws in many states requiring businesses to notify individuals when their personal data has been lost or exposed to outsiders, data breaches can be costly. In addition to potential loss of customers, costs include printing and postage for notification letters, legal counsel, offers to appease customers (such as free credit monitoring for a period of time), and potential lawsuit settlements. One estimate is a cost of nearly $200 per compromised record, which can run into millions of dollars for a large data breach. To protect the privacy of collected data, companies should first make sure that all the data they are collecting and storing is, in fact, necessary, and then they need to evaluate their data security measures to ensure that the data is adequately protected. Additional privacy issues related to computer use are discussed in Chapter 15.

> **Data privacy.** Protecting the privacy of the data located in a database.

Data Organization

Virtually all databases are organized in some manner to facilitate the retrieval of information. Arranging data for efficient retrieval is called *data organization*. Most methods of data organization use a primary key to identify the locations of records so they can be retrieved when needed. The use of a primary key and a data organization method allows a specific record to be efficiently located, regardless of the actual order the records are stored in the table. The two most common types of data organization used today—*indexed* and *direct*—are discussed next. Both are frequently used with real-time transaction processing, in which records are accessed and updated as transactions occur. An older type of data organization is *sequenced organization*, in which the order of the records is physically based on the content of the key field. Sequenced organization is designed for use with batch processing using a sequential access medium (such as magnetic tape) and so is not frequently used today. For a look at an emerging database organization option—*column databases*—see the How It Works box.

Indexed Organization

FIGURE 14-7
Indexed organization is often used for real-time transaction processing.

With **indexed organization**, an **index** is used to keep track of where data is stored in a database. An index is a small table consisting only of the primary key field and the location information for each record (see Figure 14-7). For example, the Customer table shown in Figure 14-7 uses the Customer Number field as the primary key, so the index for

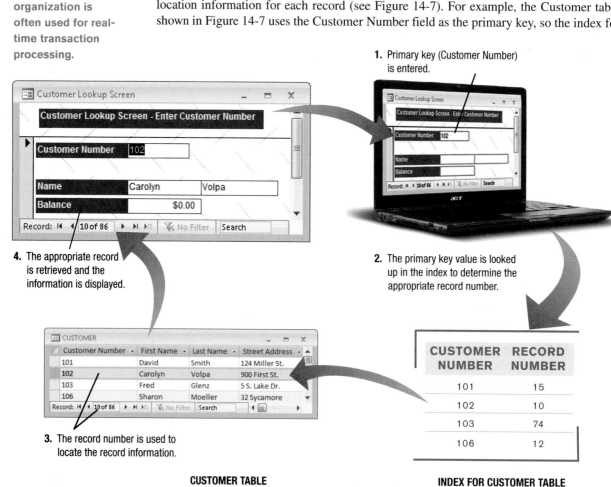

1. Primary key (Customer Number) is entered.

2. The primary key value is looked up in the index to determine the appropriate record number.

3. The record number is used to locate the record information.

4. The appropriate record is retrieved and the information is displayed.

CUSTOMER TABLE

INDEX FOR CUSTOMER TABLE

CUSTOMER NUMBER	RECORD NUMBER
101	15
102	10
103	74
106	12

>**Indexed organization.** A method for organizing data on a storage medium or in a database that uses an index to specify the exact storage location. >**Index.** A small table containing a primary key and the location of the record belonging to that key; used to locate records in a database.

HOW IT WORKS

Column Databases

To increase database performance (particularly with large databases, such as data warehouses) a new option is emerging—storing related data vertically in table columns instead of in rows. While the database tables in a *column database* appear to the user to be organized into rows and columns like a conventional row-oriented database, the way the data is physically stored on the storage medium (by columns instead of by rows) is different than the way it is stored in row-oriented databases (by rows). Because of this physical organization, column database organization minimizes the time needed to read the disk, which improves performance. This is possible because only the columns needed to retrieve the requested information are read from the disk, instead of all data in the table as would be necessary in a typical row-oriented database (see the accompanying illustration). Column orientation also allows for a higher level of data compression because there are often many similar, if not identical, entries in a single column.

Column databases read data via columns instead of rows.

the Customer table (also shown in that figure) includes the Customer Number field, plus the current record number for each record in the Customer table. As shown in the figure, indexes are sorted in order by the primary key field to allow records to be looked up in the index by the primary key field very quickly; the record number is then used to quickly retrieve the requested record from the database. In addition to a record number index, as in Figure 14-7, there can also be indexes to determine the physical location of the record on a storage medium, such as a track or a cylinder number. Indexes are usually viewed only by the program, not by the end user.

Direct Organization

Although indexed files are suitable for many applications, it is potentially more time-consuming than is appropriate for some real-time applications. **Direct organization** was developed to provide faster access. With direct organization, the computer uses each record's primary key field and a mathematical formula called a *hashing algorithm* to determine a unique address that identifies where the record is physically stored in the database file. Several hashing algorithms have been developed. One of the simplest involves dividing the primary key field by a particular prime number. The prime number is determined by the number of records to be stored or the number of storage areas to be used. The *remainder* of this division procedure (see Figure 14-8) becomes the address at which the record is physically stored.

Hashing procedures are difficult to develop, and they pose certain problems. For example, hashing procedures usually result in two or more

FIGURE 14-8
Direct organization is frequently used for faster real-time processing.

HASHING PROCEDURE

1. The key field value (in this case the Customer number) is divided by a prime number.

2. The remainder indicates the location to be used for that record (in this case, 10).

>**Direct organization.** A method of arranging data on a storage medium that uses hashing to specify the exact storage location.

records being assigned the same storage address, an event known as a *collision*. When this occurs, one record is placed in the computed address location and assigned a "pointer" that chains it to the other record. Then the other record typically goes into an available location closest to the hashed address. Good hashing procedures result in an acceptable number of collisions for the table size used—usually a larger table requires the possibility of a larger number of collisions in order to have sufficient speed.

Some systems use a combination of both indexed and direct organization—the key field indicates where the record is located within the table, and a hashing procedure is used to determine where the record is physically stored on the storage medium.

DATABASE CLASSIFICATIONS

A database system can be classified in a variety of ways, including the number of users it supports, the number of *tiers* it has, where the database is located, and so forth. These distinctions are discussed next.

Single-User vs. Multiuser Database Systems

Single-user database systems are located on a single computer and are designed to be accessed by one user. Single-user database systems are widely used for personal applications and very small businesses. Most business database systems today are designed for multiple users, and the database is accessed via a network. Because two or more users in a **multiuser database system** may try to access and modify the same data at the same time, some type of database locking must be used to prevent users from making conflicting changes to the same data at the same time.

Client-Server and N-Tier Database Systems

FIGURE 14-9
Client-server database systems.

Multiuser database systems are typically **client-server database systems**. As discussed in Chapter 7, *client-server networks* consist of servers that supply resources to other computers (such as personal computers), which function as client devices. Similarly, a *client-server database system* is a database system that has both clients and at least one server. In a typical client-server database application, the client is called the *front end*, and the database server is called the *back end*. The back end server contains a DBMS and the database itself, and it processes the commands coming from the front-end client computers. A typical client-server database system scenario is illustrated in Figure 14-9.

While some client-server database systems just have two parts (the clients and the server), others have at least one middle component or *tier* between the

FRONT END (CLIENT COMPUTERS)
The client computers typically utilize a graphical user interface to access the database located on the back-end server.

BACK END (SERVER)
The server contains the database used to fulfill the requests of the client computers.

> **Single-user database system.** A database located on a single computer and designed to be accessed by a single user. > **Multiuser database system.** A database designed to be accessed by multiple users. > **Client-server database system.** A database system where the database is located on a server and accessed by client devices.

client and the server; these systems are referred to as *n-tier database systems*. The additional tiers—such as the middle tier in a *three-tier database system*, shown in Figure 14-10—typically contain software referred to as *middleware*. Middleware usually includes the programs used with the database and the programs needed to connect the client and server components of the database system, as discussed later in this chapter.

One advantage of the n-tier architecture is that it allows the program code used to access the database to be separate from the database, and the code can be divided into any number of logical components. The programs contained in each tier in an n-tier database system can be written in programming languages different from the programming languages used in other tiers, tiers can use different platforms, and tiers can be changed or relocated without affecting the other tiers. Consequently, n-tier database systems provide a great deal of flexibility and scalability, allowing the system to be modified as new needs and opportunities arise. N-tier database systems are most commonly found in e-commerce database applications, as discussed toward the end of this chapter.

2-TIER MODEL
Has just a client and a server.

N-TIER MODEL
Includes middleware, which contains additional programs used to connect the client and server.

FIGURE 14-10
A 2-tier vs. an n-tier database model.

Centralized vs. Distributed Database Systems

With a **centralized database system**, the databases used by the system are all located on a single computer, such as a server or mainframe computer (see Figure 14-11). With a **distributed database system**, the data is divided among several computers connected via a network; for instance, there might be one database stored on a server located at the company headquarters and additional databases stored on computers located at each retail store belonging to that company. With a distributed database system, the database system is logically set up to act as a single database and appears that way to the user. Consequently, the entire database system can be accessed through the network by any authorized user, regardless of which computer the requested data is physically stored on. For example, basic customer data (such as addresses and phone numbers) may be stored at the corporate

FIGURE 14-11
Centralized vs. distributed databases.

■ = database

CENTRALIZED DATABASE
The entire database is stored on a single server.

DISTRIBUTED DATABASE
The data in a database application is stored on more than one server, though it acts as a single database to the users.

>**Centralized database system.** A database system in which all of the data used by the system is located on a single computer. >**Distributed database system.** A database system in which the data used by the system is located on multiple computers that are connected via a network.

headquarters while customer credit histories may be stored in the credit department located in another office across town. However, employees in the credit department can access both the basic customer data and the credit history data as if it were located in a single database stored in a single location.

In determining where to store specific data in a distributed DBMS, factors such as communications cost, response time, storage cost, and security are key considerations. In addition, data is often stored at the site where it is needed most frequently and is best managed, or at the location that makes data retrieval most efficient. For instance, the Digg Web site uses about 20 database servers to store its news stories and its database is broken into pieces, with each piece stored on a different database server. This configuration improves performance by isolating heavy workloads—a practice Google developers coined as *sharding*. The goal of distributing the database in this manner is to get the vast majority of the database system to work very fast. When the user requests information from a distributed DBMS, the user is typically not aware of the steps performed by the DBMS to display the requested information, nor where that data was retrieved from.

Distributed databases that support cloud computing are referred to as *cloud databases* and are becoming more common. For instance, Amazon's *SimpleDB* Web service works with other Amazon cloud services to store, process, and query cloud-based data, and the Oracle 11g DBMS can now be used to run databases using Amazon's Web services, without additional licensing fees. Agreements between Oracle and other cloud computing providers are expected in the near future; other conventional database companies may soon follow suit.

Disk-Based vs. In-Memory Database Systems

While most databases are stored on hard drives (located on personal computers, servers, or mainframes, for instance), **in-memory databases** (**IMDBs**) are designed to hold all data in the main memory of the computer, rather than on disk. The use of in-memory databases is growing because of the lower cost of RAM today and the need for faster processing. IMDBs can perform dramatically faster than disk-based databases; however, backing up data or otherwise periodically storing the data on a nonvolatile medium is extremely important since data in RAM is lost if the computer goes down or if the power goes out. IMDBs are beginning to be used both in high-end systems where performance is crucial (such as in e-commerce applications) and in small-footprint, embedded applications (such as database applications installed on set-top boxes and other smart consumer electronic devices).

DATABASE MODELS

As discussed earlier in this chapter and illustrated in Figure 14-3, databases have evolved significantly since the early 1960s. Two older models are the *hierarchical* and *network database models*; the models more commonly used today include the *relational*, *object-oriented*, and *multidimensional database models*. A newer type of database is the *hybrid XML-relational model*.

The Hierarchical and Network Database Models

In some situations, the types of queries that users need to make are highly predictable and limited. For example, in banking, bank tellers usually only need facts pertaining to

FURTHER EXPLORATION

Go to the Chapter 14 page at **www.cengage.com/ computerconcepts/np/uc13** for links to information about database classifications and models.

>**In-memory database (IMDB).** A database that stores all data in memory instead of on a hard drive.

current customer account balances, deposits, and withdrawals. In such transaction process-ing environments, *hierarchical* and *network database models*—which are designed more for speed and security than flexibility—are sometimes used. A *hierarchical database management system* organizes data in a tree structure (like an organization chart or structure chart). Typically, a one-to-many relationship exists between data entities, so all entries in the second row of the hierarchy are listed under only one top-row entry. If a second-row entry needs to be associated with more than one top-row entry, however, a *network database management system* (which allows both one-to-many and many-to-many relationships) can be used.

Most databases created today do not use the hierarchical or network models, but these models, which are generally used with *legacy* mainframe systems, are still operational and so must be maintained.

The Relational Database Model

The **relational database management system** (**RDBMS**) is the most widely used database model today. As discussed earlier in this chapter, relational databases organize data using tables. Tables are independent, but data can be retrieved from related tables via primary key fields when needed.

Before a relational database can be created, it should be properly designed. Next, the structures for the tables in the database can be created. Finally, the process of entering data into the database or otherwise using the database (such as adding, modifying, or deleting records or retrieving information from the database)—called *data manipulation*—can be carried out. These topics are discussed in the next few sections.

Designing a Relational Database

The steps involved with designing a relational database are summarized in Figure 14-12. As shown in this figure, the first step in designing a relational database is to identify the purpose of the database and the activities that it will be used for (such as to keep track of rental properties, student grades, or customer orders). Then the data (fields) that needs to be included in the database can be determined and the fields can be organized into tables. To determine which fields go in which table, you should group fields that logically belong together—each group of fields will form one table.

After initially placing the necessary fields into tables, it is important to evaluate the proposed table structure to ensure that all fields are represented and in the proper table, and to select the primary key field for each table. If needed, the tables can be restructured to reduce the redundancy of the data. To keep redundancy to a minimum, fields should be included in only one table whenever possible; they should not be placed in multiple tables unless they are needed to relate one table to another. Another consideration when designing and evaluating the basic structure of each table is ensuring the fields are constructed in a manner consistent with the type of information that will need to be extracted from the database. For example, if you want to be able to generate a list of people by just their last name, two separate fields (such as *Last Name* and *First Name*) should be used instead of just a single field called *Name*.

> **TIP**
>
> When you are beginning to design a new database, sketching a diagram of the reports and other desired database output can be helpful in identifying the fields that need to be included in the database.

BASIC DATABASE DESIGN PROCEDURES

1. Identify the purpose of the database.

2. Determine the tables and fields to include in the database.

3. Assign the fields to the appropriate table and restructure as needed to minimize redundancy (normalization).

4. Finalize the structure of each table, listing each field's name, type, size, and so on and selecting a primary key (data definition).

 FIGURE 14-12
Database design steps.

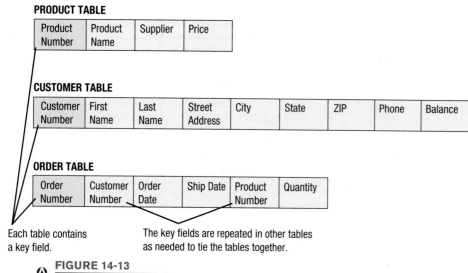

PRODUCT TABLE

Product Number	Product Name	Supplier	Price

CUSTOMER TABLE

Customer Number	First Name	Last Name	Street Address	City	State	ZIP	Phone	Balance

ORDER TABLE

Order Number	Customer Number	Order Date	Ship Date	Product Number	Quantity

Each table contains a key field.

The key fields are repeated in other tables as needed to tie the tables together.

FIGURE 14-13
A preliminary design for three tables in the Inventory database.

A preliminary design for three of the tables in the Inventory database system scenario discussed in this chapter (the Product table shown in Figure 14-1 plus the Customer and Order tables used to store data about customers and their orders) is shown in Figure 14-13. Notice that each table contains a primary key field (shaded in bright yellow in Figure 14-13) and those fields are the only fields that occur in more than one table (see the light yellow fields in Figure 14-13)—and only as needed to tie the tables together.

This process of evaluating and correcting the structures of the tables in a database to minimize data redundancy is called **normalization**. Normalization is usually viewed as a multistep process, adjusting the fields in the tables as needed to move the table structures from *zero normal form* (*ZNF*) to usually *third normal form* (*3NF*), although procedures exist to reach *fifth normal form* (*5NF*). The overall objective of the normalization process is to ensure that redundant fields from table to table are kept to a minimum. A non-normalized table structure is considered to be zero normal form (ZNF). The next three normal forms can be summarized as follows:

> *First normal form* (*1NF*)—the table has unique fields (no *repeating groups*; that is, groups of related entries that belong to one unique person or thing, such as a customer, an order, and so forth) and all fields are dependent on the primary key. Any repeating groups have been placed in a second table and related to the original table via a primary key field (such as customer number or order number). For instance, at this point, the fields relating to the contact information for a customer would only appear in one table, such as a Customer table, and would be related to the other tables by a unique primary key field, such as a Customer Number field.

> *Second normal form* (*2NF*)—the table is in 1NF with no *partial dependencies*; that is, fields in a table that are dependent on part of the primary key (if the table has a composite primary key made up of multiple key fields), and all fields are dependent on a single primary key or on all of the fields in a composite primary key. Any partial dependencies have been removed and these dependent fields (such as those containing product information in an order table) are placed in a separate table and related to the original table via a primary key field (such as a product number field occurring in both tables).

> *Third normal form* (*3NF*)—the table is in 2NF with no *transitive dependencies*; that is, two fields that are not primary keys and are dependent on one another, such as the Supplier Name and Supplier Number fields in a Product table. These dependent fields are placed in a separate table and related to the original table via a primary key field (such as a Supplier Number field occurring in both tables).

Once the fields for each table have been finalized, the name, data type, and other necessary properties should be determined for each field. These properties include field size, any input

> **Normalization.** The process of evaluating and correcting the structure of a database table to minimize data redundancy.

masks or validation rules that should be used to check data as it is entered into the table, and whether or not a field is a required field, as discussed in the Data Definition section earlier in this chapter. Once the design is complete, the database is ready to be created, as discussed next.

Creating a Relational Database

To create a relational database, a new database file (that will contain all tables and other objects included in the database) is first created and named. Next, each table in the database is created, using the table structure developed during the database design process. Once the table structure is complete, data can be entered into the tables and the tables can be related as needed.

Creating the Tables

In Microsoft Access, tables can be created in either *Design view* or *Datasheet view*, as illustrated in Figure 6-20 in Chapter 6 and reviewed in Figure 14-14. To create a table in Design view, you enter each field name and specify the data type and other properties as needed, and then save the table using an appropriate table name. To create a table in Datasheet view, you enter the first record of data into the table to initially create the fields for that table, and then you can change the field names and other properties as needed using the Datasheet tab on the Ribbon in recent versions of Microsoft Access and save the table using an appropriate table name. However, only very basic properties (such as the field name, data type, and whether or not the field is required) can be specified using Datasheet view, so Design view is often still needed to finalize the table structure (such as to change the primary key or add a validation rule or an input mask).

Entering and Editing Data

If a new database is to be used with existing data, the data needs to be transferred from the old files to the new system—a process called *data migration*. If new data is to be used, it is entered into the appropriate database table. Datasheet view can be used to enter data into a table as previously described; however, a **form** (see Figure 14-15) can be created for a table and used instead for easier data entry and a more professional appearance. When a form is created, it automatically includes all of the fields in the table with which the form is associated. If a specific form layout or design is desired, Design view can be used to edit the form, such as to change the form color or the font size used, rearrange the placement of the fields on the form, add a company logo or form heading, and so forth.

The View button is used to select the desired view.

The name of the database file is determined when the database file is created.

DESIGN VIEW
The table structure is created before data is entered.

The user creates all fields and sets the primary key.

Entering data creates appropriate fields; an ID field primary key is created by default.

DATASHEET VIEW
The table structure is created as table data is entered.

FIGURE 14-14
Tables can be created using Design or Datasheet view.

SYS

> **Form.** A formatted way of viewing and editing a table in a database.

1. Click to create a form for the Product table.

2. A form containing all fields in the Product table is created and displayed in Form view.

3. Design view can be used to edit and format the form, including rearranging the fields, adding headings and logos, and so forth.

Current record; can be edited or deleted.

Click to add a new record.

4. The finished form can be used to view and edit the data in the Product table.

FIGURE 14-15
Forms. Forms can be used to view and edit table data.

Either Datasheet view or a form can be used to input, view, and edit data for a table. In either case, records can be added to the table (click the *New (blank) record* button at the bottom of the table or form to display a new blank record), deleted from the table (use the Home tab on the Ribbon in Microsoft Access to delete the current record), or edited (display the appropriate record and then click the field to be edited). Regardless of whether Datasheet view or a form is used to edit the table data, it is the same data that is being edited. So if a new record is added using a form, for example, the new record will be visible when the table is viewed using Datasheet view; and, if an address is edited in Datasheet view, the updated address will be visible when the record is viewed using a form.

Relating Tables

After all the tables in a database application have been created and their primary keys designated, the tables can be *related* to one another via their primary keys so that a primary key for one table can be used to extract data from other tables as needed. For instance, once a Customer table (containing customer data) and an Order table (containing order data) are related via the Customer table's Customer Number primary key field, then that field can be used to extract information from both of these tables, such as to generate an order report or an invoice containing data from the Customer table and the Order table. The process of relating tables in the Inventory database discussed throughout this chapter is shown in Figure 14-16. This figure also illustrates how, once the tables are related, the related data located in other tables can be viewed from inside a single table.

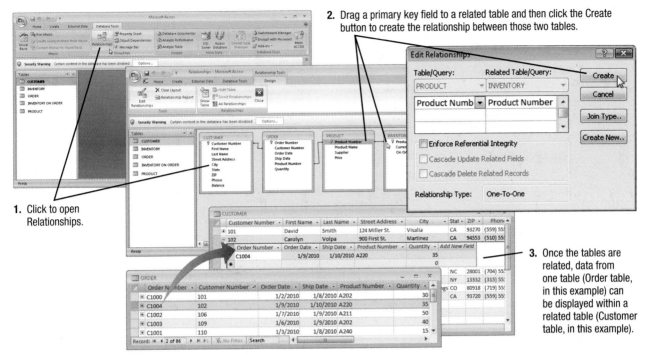

2. Drag a primary key field to a related table and then click the Create button to create the relationship between those two tables.

1. Click to open Relationships.

3. Once the tables are related, data from one table (Order table, in this example) can be displayed within a related table (Customer table, in this example).

FIGURE 14-16
Relating tables.

Retrieving Information from a Relational Database

Database information retrieval can be performed by displaying a single record to answer a specific question about that entity (such as looking up a customer's phone number or current balance by displaying the appropriate record in the Customer table). However, more often information is retrieved from a database using a *query* or a *report*.

A **query** extracts specific information from a database by specifying particular conditions (called *criteria*) about the data you would like to retrieve, such as retrieving all names of customers who live in Tennessee or all products whose inventory level is below 100 units. Every DBMS provides tools users can use to query the database for information. One possibility is using a *query language*, such as **structured query language** (**SQL**)—the standard query language for relational databases. To create a query, users can either type a query using SQL or, more commonly, use the query tools built into the DBMS (such as a query design screen or query wizard) to create a query object. In either case, the query can then be used to extract the data from the table associated with the query that meets the query conditions. An example of creating a query for the Product table using the query design screen in Microsoft Access (along with the SQL version of that query that can be viewed and edited if desired by selecting the *SQL View* option from the View menu on the Home tab) is shown in Figure 14-17. As shown in this figure, the query is created, named, and saved as an object in the database file. Each time a query is run (by opening the appropriate query object), only the records in the Product table meeting the criteria are displayed. In addition to retrieving information from a single table, queries can retrieve information from multiple tables, if the tables are related.

Queries need to be designed to extract the requested information as efficiently as possible. Poorly written queries can impact the overall performance of the system, especially if they are executed frequently—in some systems, queries may be enacted several times

>**Query.** A request to see information from a database that matches specific criteria. >**Structured query language (SQL).** A popular query language standard for information retrieval in relational databases.

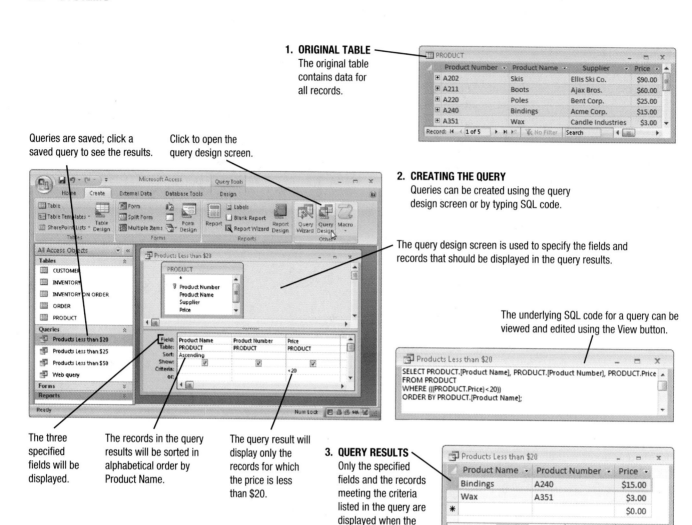

1. ORIGINAL TABLE
The original table contains data for all records.

Queries are saved; click a saved query to see the results.

Click to open the query design screen.

2. CREATING THE QUERY
Queries can be created using the query design screen or by typing SQL code.

The query design screen is used to specify the fields and records that should be displayed in the query results.

The underlying SQL code for a query can be viewed and edited using the View button.

The three specified fields will be displayed.

The records in the query results will be sorted in alphabetical order by Product Name.

The query result will display only the records for which the price is less than $20.

3. QUERY RESULTS
Only the specified fields and the records meeting the criteria listed in the query are displayed when the query is opened.

FIGURE 14-17
Querying a database. This example pulls information from the Product table in the Inventory database.

per second. Even a marginal improvement in performance of frequently used queries can significantly improve the overall performance of the system. Consequently, it is the job of the database administrator to identify regularly used queries that need improvement and to suggest ways in which to make them perform better. Common techniques include alterations to the query itself to improve its performance, adding "hints" to the query to tell the database which tables should be accessed first to speed up performance, and adding additional indexes to heavily used tables.

When more formal or attractive output is needed, a **report** can be used. In essence, a report is a formatted way of looking at some or all of the data contained in a database. The fields to be included in a report are specified when the report is created. A report can be designed to include all the records located in its associated table, or it can be designed to include just the results of a query. Just as with queries, reports in Microsoft Access are saved as objects in the database file, they can pull information from more than one table at a time if the tables are related, and they display the data located in the appropriate tables at the time the report is run. Reports are often created initially using a report wizard (such as the Microsoft Access Report Wizard shown in Figure 14-18) and then their appearance can be modified, as needed, using Design view, similar to a form.

> **Report.** A formatted way of looking at information retrieved from a database table or the results of a query.

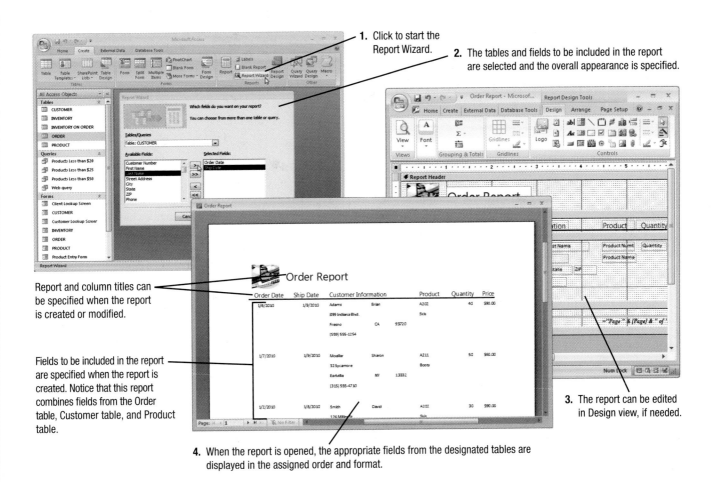

1. Click to start the Report Wizard.

2. The tables and fields to be included in the report are selected and the overall appearance is specified.

Report and column titles can be specified when the report is created or modified.

Fields to be included in the report are specified when the report is created. Notice that this report combines fields from the Order table, Customer table, and Product table.

3. The report can be edited in Design view, if needed.

4. When the report is opened, the appropriate fields from the designated tables are displayed in the assigned order and format.

Maintaining a Relational Database

Although small, personal databases may need little or no maintenance, large enterprise databases frequently require regular maintenance. Maintenance activities are usually performed by the database administrator and include the following tasks:

➤ Modifying the table structure to add new fields or to accommodate values that turned out to be different from those anticipated when the database was designed, such as a customer last name that is longer than the field size specified for the Last Name field.

➤ Adding new indexes, which can be used to speed up queries.

➤ Deleting obsolete data, such as for customers who no longer exist or who have not placed orders for a specified period of time.

➤ Upgrading the database software as needed and installing security patches as they become available.

➤ Repairing or restoring data that has become corrupt, such as the result of a storage media error or a computer virus.

➤ Continually evaluating and improving the security measures used with the database.

FIGURE 14-18
Reports. Reports display table information with a more formal, businesslike appearance.

ASK THE EXPERT

admob **Kevin Scott,** Vice President of Engineering, AdMob; Member-at-Large, ACM Council

What is the hottest IT-oriented job today? What positions do you expect to be in the most demand five years from now?

The explosive growth of networked services and the data that they create is going to continue to create huge demand for Web application developers, distributed systems and network engineers, and analytical engineers experienced in information retrieval, machine learning, natural language processing, data mining, and basic statistical techniques.

CAUTION CAUTION CAUTION CAUTION CAUTION CAUTION CAUT

Because database tables are saved automatically, you cannot undo or undelete deleted rows or columns. Before clicking the Yes button to verify a deletion, make sure the proper row or column is being deleted, and back up your database tables regularly so you can restore any data deleted in error.

The Object-Oriented Database Model

Traditionally, database software has dealt with *structured* types of data; that is, primarily text-based data that can be organized neatly into columns (fields) and rows (records). Structured data is the type you have mostly been reading about in this chapter and probably the type you have been working with on your computer. However, evolving user needs and technologies have changed the types of data in use today. In addition to handling conventional record data (such as text, numbers, and dates), many of today's database applications now need to store a wide variety of types of data, such as documents, digital photographs, video clips, audio clips, RFID and sensor data, and so on. (For a look at an example of the multimedia databases now being used for cancer treatment and research, see the Trend box.) An **object-oriented database management system** (**OODBMS**) is often able to store and retrieve complex, unstructured data better than a relational database management system. Unlike a relational database in which each record has a similar format, little similarity may exist among the data elements that form the objects. An object-oriented database is also a better choice for database applications in which the structure may change frequently.

Similar to object-oriented programming applications (discussed in Chapter 13), an OODBMS stores data in objects. An object contains data along with the methods (actions) that can be taken with that data. Objects in an OODBMS can contain virtually any type of data—a video clip, a photograph with a narrative, text with music, and so on—along with the methods to be used with that data. Objects stored in an OODBMS can be retrieved using queries, such as with an *object query language* (*OQL*)—an object-oriented version of SQL. The objects can also be reused in other applications to develop new applications very quickly. The key characteristics for an OODBMS (including objects, attributes, methods, classes, and inheritance) are similar to the OOP principles discussed in Chapter 13. In fact, OOP languages, such as Java or C++, are often used to manipulate data stored in an object-oriented database. OODBMSs are becoming more common on databases accessed via the Internet. For instance, a Web-based OODBMS containing images and information from the *Sloan Digital Sky Survey* (an astronomical survey that is in the process of mapping one-quarter of the entire sky in detail, including 100 million celestial objects) is shown in Figure 14-19.

ONLINE VIDEO

Go to the Chapter 14 page at **www.cengage.com/ computerconcepts/np/uc13** to watch the "A Look at the Google Sky Map System" video clip.

FIGURE 14-19
Object-oriented databases. The database shown here contains images and information from the Sloan Digital Sky Survey.

VIEWING THE SCHEMA
This Web page is used to view the various tables, views, functions, and constants used with this database; the tables are listed in the current view.

USING THE DATABASE
By entering location parameters using one of the provided forms or by typing a query, images can be retrieved from the database.

> **Object-oriented database management system (OODBMS).** A type of database system in which multiple types of data are stored as objects along with their related code.

TREND

Cancer Research Databases

The *Cancer Biomedical Informatics Grid®* (*caBIG®*) was created by the National Cancer Institute (NCI) to help researchers, physicians, and patients across the U.S. share genetic data, clinical data, and disease information in order to accelerate the discovery of new approaches for the detection, diagnosis, treatment, and prevention of cancer. In a nutshell, caBIG is a collection of open-source interoperable software tools and a grid infrastructure that facilitates the exchange of research and clinical data. To enable this exchange, standardized rules and a common language are used, such as the *Common Data Element* (*CDE*) *Dictionary*—a data dictionary specifying the common vocabulary to be used with caBIG databases and applications, as well as the designated format of that data. caBIG provides access to a number of different databases including the *National Cancer Imaging Archive* (*NCIA*) database (see the accompanying illustration), which stores patients' cancer images along with relevant annotations.

Data sharing systems such as caBIG are viewed as critical to scientific advancements. In fact, components from caBIG form key parts of other health-research areas, such as the National Heart, Lung, and Blood Institute's *CardioVascular Research Grid* and the *Nationwide Health Information Network*.

Hybrid Database Models

Some databases are *hybrid databases*; that is, a combination of two or more database types or models. For instance, a database that combines object and relational database technology can be referred to as an *object-relational database management system* (*ORDBMS*). One emerging type of hybrid database is the **hybrid XML/relational database**—a type of database that can store and retrieve both XML data and relational data. Several vendors have implemented XML data management capabilities into their relational database management systems, but IBM's *DB2* program goes one step further. DB2 9 contains a *hybrid XML/relational database server* which allows XML data to be entered into a database while preserving its structure (the XML data and its properties). This means that nonrelational business data (such as Excel spreadsheets or word processing documents) can be combined with traditional relational data in the same database easily and efficiently. Keeping the XML data structure intact allows queries and other data operations to be much more efficient—IBM claims a performance increase of between two and seven times over competing products by Microsoft and Oracle. Both the relational and XML data stored in the database can be accessed via queries and otherwise manipulated, and they can work together in a single application as needed (see Figure 14-20).

FIGURE 14-20
Hybrid XML/
relational databases.

> **Hybrid XML/relational database.** A type of database system that can store and retrieve both XML data and relational data.

SYS

Multidimensional Databases

The growth and importance of data warehousing (discussed in Chapter 12) has led to another type of database model—the **multidimensional database** (**MDDB**), a type of database optimized for data warehouse applications. Whereas relational databases are appropriate for transactional applications in which data is retrieved or updated typically by rows and object-oriented databases are appropriate when a variety of types of objects need to be stored and retrieved, multidimensional databases are designed to store a collection of summarized data for quick and easy data analysis. The data is typically collected from a variety of enterprise-wide activities (often from existing relational databases) and is then summarized and restructured to enable it to be viewed from multiple perspectives called *dimensions*. For example, sales for a company could be viewed in the dimensions of product model, geography, time, or salesperson, or viewed as a combination of dimensions, such as sales by a particular product model in the southwest United States for Quarter 2 in 2011. The dimensions are predefined, based on what are viewed to be meaningful for that particular database, and the summarized data values are automatically calculated.

One of the most common types of software used in conjunction with a multidimensional database is *Online Analytical Processing* (*OLAP*). According to SAS, a leader in business intelligence and analytics, OLAP used with multi-dimensional databases is typically implemented in one of three ways. With *MOLAP* (*Multidimensional OLAP*), data is stored in a single multidimensional database structure (sometimes called a *data cube*). With *ROLAP* (*Relational OLAP*), the multidimensional information is stored in an existing relational database using tables to store the summary information. With *HOLAP* (*Hybrid OLAP*), a combination of MOLAP and ROLAP technologies is used.

DATABASES AND THE WEB

Databases are extremely common on the Web. Virtually all companies that offer product information, online ordering, research resources, or similar activities via a Web site use a database. For instance, one of the largest databases on the Web belongs to Amazon, which stores data about its customers and their orders, products for sale, and customer reviews of products. In addition, it stores the actual text of many books so they can be searched and viewed online. Web databases are also increasingly used to store user-generated content (that individuals upload to be shared with others), such as content uploaded to Flickr, YouTube, MySpace, and other social networking sites. A few examples of Web databases are discussed next, followed by a look at how Web databases typically work. For a look at one political database application that may be used to influence your vote in an upcoming election—*microtargeting*—see the Technology and You box.

Examples of Web Databases in Use

Web databases today are used for a variety of purposes. One purpose is information retrieval—the Web is, in essence, a huge storehouse of data waiting to be retrieved. Data to be accessed and displayed via a Web page is often stored in a database, and Web site visitors can request and view information upon demand. Search sites are perhaps the

ONLINE VIDEO

Go to the Chapter 14 page at **www.cengage.com/ computerconcepts/np/uc13** to watch the "Real Estate Searching with Google Maps" video clip.

>**Multidimensional database (MDDB).** A type of database designed to be used with data warehousing.

TECHNOLOGY AND YOU

Microtargeting

Microtargeting is the use of analytical tools to identify groups of voters to target during a political campaign. Specifically, it uses public consumer data, demographics, voting histories, and poll results in conjunction with modeling tools to identify patterns that can be used to identify groups of voters throughout a state who are likely to vote a certain way or feel a particular way about certain issues. The individuals are then targeted via campaigning tactics (such as in person, on the phone, or via mail), focusing on the issues that have been identified as important to those individuals. While microtargeting was used to some extent in earlier elections, it was considered an essential tool in the 2008 elections—especially because so many of the races were very close at times. According to Ken Strasmas, president and founder of the data analytics company Strategic Telemetry, microtargeting can make the difference of a couple of percentage points in a close race—perhaps not critical in some races, but essential in others.

While the exact use of microtargeting varies from campaign to campaign, the basic goal is to identify undecided voters and the issues they care about so that campaign funds and other resources can be targeted to those voters, in the hopes of convincing them to vote for the campaign's candidate. Microtargeting firms typically use voter registration lists and

census data along with marketing data and some custom surveying to determine factors like the overall income level, age, occupation, ethnic background, political leanings, and buying habits of individuals in particular geographical areas. They then use statistical modeling software to model various scenarios in an effort to determine which voters should be approached and which issues would appeal to those voters. The campaign can then direct resources (such as customized phone, e-mail, or direct mail messages, or door-to-door campaign volunteers) to those potential supporters.

most obvious Web database application, retrieving and displaying links to Web pages based on the search term supplied by the user. Another common use of databases on the Web is to support and facilitate e-commerce, such as to display product information, pricing, customer information, shopping cart content, order information, and more upon demand. Other information commonly retrieved and displayed from Web databases include product information, press releases, and other documents retrieved from company Web sites; ZIP codes, driving directions, maps, and more retrieved from reference sites (see Figure 14-21); and photos and videos retrieved from photo and video sharing sites.

Web databases allow Web pages to be *dynamic Web pages*; that is, Web pages in which the appearance or content of the pages change based on the user's input or stated preferences instead of just displaying *static* information via the Web pages included on the site. In addition to being used to supply data on demand (such as via a Web site search), Web databases also allow Web sites to display personalized content for each visitor, such as to create a personalized portal page or to display information based on a user's past activities, as is the case with the Amazon.com Web page shown in Figure 14-21.

SYS

REFERENCE SITE
This site stores address information for individuals and businesses in the United States. After the user enters a name or category and a location (in this case, pizza parlors in Pismo Beach, California), the matching information is retrieved from the database.

PERSONALIZED SITE
This site retrieves information from its database to create a personalized page for signed-in viewers, such as recently viewed products and recommendations based on viewed and purchased products.

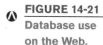

FIGURE 14-21
Database use
on the Web.

FURTHER EXPLORATION

Go to the Chapter 14 page at **www.cengage.com/ computerconcepts/np/uc13** for links to information about Web-based databases.

How Web Databases Work

The request to retrieve information from or store data in a Web database is typically initiated by the Web site visitor. Filling out a Web page form and selecting an option from a menu displayed on a Web page are common ways Web-based database requests are made. The request is received by the Web server, which then converts the request into a database query and passes it on to the database server with the help of *middleware*, discussed in more detail next. The database server retrieves the appropriate information and returns it to the Web server (again, via middleware) where it is displayed on the visitor's screen in the form of a Web page. This process is illustrated in Figure 14-22.

Middleware

Software that connects two otherwise separate applications (such as a Web server and a DBMS to tie a database to a Web site) is referred to as **middleware**. Middleware for Web database applications is commonly written as *scripts*—short sections of code written in a programming or scripting language that are executed by another program. JavaScript and VBScript (discussed in Chapter 10) are two scripting languages often used in conjunction with Web databases. Two other common scripting languages used to connect databases to Web sites are *CGI* and *PHP*. As an alternative to writing scripts from scratch, many Web site authoring programs include capabilities to automatically generate the scripts needed to connect dynamic Web pages to a database when the Web developer selects the appropriate menu options and enters the needed information while that Web site is being created. This capability allows even novice Web developers to include input forms and search capabilities easily on their sites, as well as connect the site and a database, without having to write any scripts directly.

>**Middleware.** Software used to connect two otherwise separate applications, such as a Web server and a database management system.

1. The user fills out the search box and either presses Enter or clicks the Go button, sending the "rocker" data to the Web server.

2. The Web server converts the data entered (rocker) into a database query and sends it to the database server via middleware.

3. The database server performs the query on the database and sends the results back to the Web server via middleware.

USER **WEB SERVER** **DATABASE SERVER**

4. The middleware program converts the query results to HTML, and then the Web server displays the results in the form of a Web page on the user's screen.

FIGURE 14-22
A Web database in action.

CGI Scripts

A *CGI (common gateway interface) script* is a set of instructions written in a programming language (such as C, Perl, Java, or Visual Basic) and designed to accept data from and return data to a Web page visitor. CGI scripts usually reside on the Web server and handle tasks, such as processing input forms and information requests. On very busy sites, CGI can slow down server response time significantly because it processes each request individually.

Active Server Pages (ASPs)

Active Server Pages (ASPs) are dynamic Web pages that have the extension *.asp*. ASPs work similarly to dynamic Web pages utilizing CGI scripts, but the code to tie the database to the Web site is typically written in JavaScript or VBScript.

PHP Scripts

PHP (PHP Hypertext Preprocessor) is a scripting language that is increasingly being used to create dynamic Web pages. It uses code similar to Perl or C++ that is inserted into the HTML code of a Web page using special *PHP tags*. PHP scripts usually reside on the server and are typically used to perform tasks similar to CGI and ASPs, but they have the advantage of high compatibility with many types of databases.

SUMMARY

WHAT IS A DATABASE?

Chapter Objective 1:
Explain what a database is, including common database terminology, and list some of the advantages and disadvantages of using databases.

A **database** is a collection of related data that is stored and organized in a manner that allows information to be retrieved as needed. Most databases consist of one or more **tables**; each table contains a collection of related **records** (**rows**), each of which, in turn, is a collection of related **fields** (**columns**).

A **database management system** (**DBMS**) is a software program used to create database applications—data can be stored in and information can be retrieved from more than one table at a time. A *relational database* is the most common type of computerized database. This type of database relates data in various database tables by using a **primary key**—a field in a table that contains unique data that is unlikely to change and that is used to uniquely identify each record in that table.

The individuals involved with a DBMS include *database designers*, *database developers*, *database programmers*, *database administrators*, and *users*. Over the years, databases have evolved from *flat files* to collections of tables and objects that support interrelated multimedia content with a minimum of data redundancy.

A DBMS offers several advantages over file management systems. Among these advantages are faster response time, lower operating costs, lower data storage requirements, improved data integrity, and better data management. The biggest potential disadvantage is a greater vulnerability to failure.

DATA CONCEPTS AND CHARACTERISTICS

Chapter Objective 2:
Discuss some basic concepts and characteristics of data, such as data hierarchy, entity relationships, and data definition.

Data in a database has a definite hierarchy. Data is entered as characters into fields in the database. Related fields form records, related records form tables, and a group of related tables forms the database.

One task involved with setting up a database is **data definition**—the process of describing data to be entered into a DBMS. The data definitions are used to create a *table structure* for each table. The table structure contains a description of the data to be entered into the table (field name, data type, and other properties). The **data dictionary** contains information (called **metadata**) about all data in the database application. Different types of databases may relate their **entities** differently. Common types of entity relationships include *one-to-one*, *one-to-many*, and *many-to-many*. A characteristic of an entity is called an **attribute**. Entities typically become database tables; attributes typically become table fields.

Chapter Objective 3:
Describe the importance of data integrity, security, and privacy and how they affect database design.

Because data is so vital to an organization, **data integrity**, **data validation**, and **data security** must be maintained to ensure the quality of information retrieved from the database and the safety of the database. Good data validation techniques (such as specifying an allowable range of values or a mandatory format) enforced on a *per transaction* basis and coupled with data *locking* when data is being modified can help ensure data integrity and data validation. Good access control methods can help increase data security. Good backup procedures are essential. **Data privacy** is a growing concern as data breaches become more widespread and as businesses need to comply with regulations related to securing and protecting the data they store in their databases.

Databases typically use **indexes** to more easily locate data when it is requested. In conjunction with or as an alternative to **indexed organization**, **direct organization** can be used. Direct organization uses hashing to provide for rapid direct access. Both indexed and direct organization can be used for *real-time* transaction processing.

DATABASE CLASSIFICATIONS

Database systems can be classified as **single-user** or **multiuser database systems**, depending on how many users need to access the database. **Client-server database systems** are accessed via a network by client computers at the *front end*; the database resides on server computers at the *back end*. In an *n-tier database system*, at least one piece of *middleware* exists between the client and the server.

Many database systems are set up as **distributed database system**. Instead of a single central database located on a central computer (as in a **centralized database system**— the most common practice for storing database data in large companies), the database is divided among several smaller computers or servers that are connected and accessed via a network. **In-memory databases (IMDBs)** hold all data in the main memory of the computer.

Chapter Objective 4:
Identify some basic database classifications and discuss their differences.

DATABASE MODELS

Database models have evolved over time. Traditionally, database systems have conformed to one of three common types: hierarchical, network, and relational, although only the relational model is widely used today. A *hierarchical database management system* stores data in the form of a tree, in which the relationship between data elements is usually one-to-many. In a *network database management system* the relationship between data elements is typically either one-to-many or many-to-many. The **relational database management system (RDBMS)** stores data in tables related by primary keys and is the most widely used database model today. The growing interest in other data types and the need to combine them into multimedia formats for applications have given rise to the **object-oriented database management system (OODBMS)**. These databases use storable entities called *objects*. An object contains both data and relevant code; data can be virtually any type, such as a video clip, photograph, text, or music. A **hybrid XML/relational database** can store both XML data and relational data. Applications such as data warehousing have led to another type of data model—the **multidimensional database (MDDB)**, which allows data to be viewed using multiple dimensions.

To create a relational database, the tables are designed based on the purpose of the database, the fields that need to be included, each field's properties, and the relationships between the tables included in the database. The table structure is then evaluated and modified as needed to minimize redundancy—a process called **normalization**. Next, the structure of each table is created and data is entered into the database. Both the table structure and the data contained in a table can be modified as needed. Table data can be viewed and modified using a **form** for a more formal appearance. Information is usually retrieved using **queries** (to retrieve specific information from a database that matches specified criteria) and **reports**. Queries most often use **structured query language (SQL)**. Once a database has been designed and created, regular maintenance activities are needed.

Chapter Objective 5:
List the most common database models and discuss how they are used today.

Chapter Objective 6:
Understand how a relational database is designed, created, used, and maintained.

DATABASES AND THE WEB

Database applications are plentiful on the Web. When information is retrieved via an input form or other interactive element on a Web page, a database is used. In addition to being used for information retrieval, databases are also used for a variety of e-commerce and *dynamic* Web page activities.

When a request for information is transferred from a Web page to a database, it is converted—using **middleware** software—to a request the database can process. The retrieved information is then passed back to the Web server and displayed in the form of a Web page; dynamic Web pages may be *Active Server Pages (ASPs)*. Middleware for Web database application is commonly written as *scripts*, such as *CGI* or *PHP* scripts.

Chapter Objective 7:
Describe some ways databases are used on the Web.

SYS

REVIEW ACTIVITIES

KEY TERM MATCHING

a. database

b. data dictionary

c. data validation

d. index

e. middleware

f. primary key

g. query

h. record

i. relational database management system (RDBMS)

j. table

Instructions: Match each key term on the left with the definition on the right that best describes it.

1. _____ A collection of related data that is stored in a manner enabling information to be retrieved as needed.

2. _____ A collection of related fields in a database. Also called a row.

3. _____ A request to see information from a database that matches specific criteria.

4. _____ A small table containing a primary key and the location of the record belonging to that key; used to locate records in a database.

5. _____ A specific field in a database table that uniquely identifies the records in that table.

6. _____ A type of database system in which data is stored in tables related by common fields; the most widely used database model today.

7. _____ In a relational database, a collection of related records (rows).

8. _____ Software used to connect two otherwise separate applications, such as a Web server and a database management system.

9. _____ The process of ensuring that data entered into a database matches the data definition.

10. _____ The repository of all data definitions in a database.

SELF-QUIZ

Instructions: Circle **T** if the statement is true, **F** if the statement is false, or write the best answer in the space provided. **Answers for the self-quiz are located in the References and Resources Guide at the end of the book.**

1. **T F** In a relational database, more than one table can be included in a database.

2. **T F** Normalization is used to minimize data redundancy.

3. **T F** Using usernames and passwords is a data validation technique.

4. **T F** The network database model is the most widely used model today.

5. **T F** Dynamic Web pages commonly use databases.

6. In a student information database, *Name* would be considered a(n) _____ in the table, while all of Jennifer Mitchell's information would be a(n) _____.

7. Data _____ refers to the accuracy of data.

8. When _____ organization is used, a hashing procedure determines where data is stored.

9. The terms *front end* and *back end* refer to _____ database systems.

10. Match each term with its example, and write the corresponding number in the blank to the left of the example.

1. Data definition

2. Data integrity

3. Data security

a. _____ When the database does not allow a user to enter a letter in a phone number field.

b. _____ Requiring users to log on to a database system via a fingerprint reader.

c. _____ Assigning a field the property of "required."

1. Would the data type Text, Number, or Yes/No be the most appropriate for a telephone number field that needs to store data in the format (123)555-7890? Explain your answer.

2. Of the following fields, which would be the most appropriate for the primary key in a customer information table? Explain your answer.

   a. Customer Name   **b.** Customer Number   **c.** Phone Number   **d.** Customer Address

3. Refer to the two relational database tables below and answer the following questions:

   a. Which employees work in the Accounting department and make at least $60,000 per year?

   b. Which employees have Hurt as their manager?

   c. In which of the preceding questions did you have to relate data in both tables to get an answer? Through what field(s) did you relate the tables?

   EMPLOYEE TABLE

NAME	LOCATION	DEPARTMENT	SALARY
Doney	Phoenix	Accounting	$58,000
James	San Diego	Sales	$44,000
Giles	San Diego	Accounting	$62,000
Smith	Miami	Accounting	$73,000

   OFFICE TABLE

LOCATION	MANAGER
San Diego	Hurt
Cleveland	Holmes
Miami	Jonas
Phoenix	Alexis

4. Suppose that you need to create a two-table database to record information for a video rental store. The following information needs to be recorded:

   ➤ For all movies: Movie number, title, category, rental rate, and whether or not it is available for rent

   ➤ For all customers: Customer number, name, address, city, state, ZIP, and telephone number

   ➤ For all rented movies: Customer who rented it and due date

   Create a preliminary design (use Figure 14-13 for reference, if needed) for a possible two-table database for this scenario (Movie table and Customer table), locating the fields in the most appropriate tables and having a minimum of redundancy.

5. For Exercise 4 above, is there a field in common in both tables that is appropriate to use as a primary key to relate the two tables? If so, which field? If not, redo Exercise 4 to include an appropriate primary key.

1. It is becoming increasingly common for biometric devices to be used to grant or deny access to facilities, as well as to identify consumers for financial transactions. In order to facilitate this, some data about each participant's biometric features must be stored in a database. How do you feel about your biometric characteristics being stored in a database? Does it depend on whether the system belongs to your bank, employer, school, or the government? Since biometric features cannot be reset, are you at risk using a biometric ID system? Why or why not?

2. There are numerous databases that contain personal, but public, information about individuals. Today much of this data is available online. How do you feel about your personal information being contained in databases that other individuals can access or that might be breached via the Internet? Do you mind that anyone with an Internet connection might be able to find out how much you paid for your house, if you are married, where you live, and other personal information?

PROJECTS

1. **Terrorist Databases** There are a number of databases—such as the FBI's *Combined DNA Index System* (*CODIS*) and *Integrated Automated Fingerprint Identification System* (*IAFIS*), the military's *Biometrics Automated Toolset* (*BAT*), and the Homeland Security Department's *Automated Biometric Identification System* (*IDENT*)—in use today for national security purposes.

   For this project, select one database (either one of the ones listed in the previous paragraph or an alternate database) currently being used for national security purposes. Determine the purpose of the database, who has access to it, and if it has been useful in identifying criminals or terrorists or helpful in other ways. Has there been any movement toward a national database for citizen identification? At the conclusion of your research, prepare a one-page summary of your findings and opinions and submit it to your instructor.

2. **Web Databases** As discussed in the chapter, many Web pages today utilize databases to display information requested by visitors, for customized Web pages, and other dynamic applications.

   For this project, visit one Web site that utilizes a database (such as Switchboard (www.switchboard.com), the Internet Movie Database Web site (imdb.com), Google Maps (maps.google.com), or Amazon.com (www.amazon.com), and request some information from the database. Were you satisfied with the results? Did the database return the correct results in a timely manner? Do you have any suggestions to improve the user interface, such as different directions, additional options, and so forth? At the conclusion of this project, submit a one-page summary of your experience and your recommendations to your instructor.

3. **Designing a Database** While designing a database system for a large enterprise is a highly complex task, designing a small relational database can be a fairly straightforward process.

   For this project, design a relational database to contain data about the students, instructors, and class offerings at your school. The database should consist of three tables (one each for students, classes, and instructors), and each table should have at least four fields. Select an appropriate primary key for each table and determine which of the tables will be related. On paper, design one input screen, one query screen, and one report that might be used with this system; annotate each design with the table and field names for each piece of information to be included. Did any of your three designs utilize data from more than one table? If so, make sure that it is possible to do that, based on your table design and stated relationships. Be sure to include at least one sample record for each table in your design documentation. At the conclusion of this project, submit the completed database design to your instructor.

4. **Multimedia Uploads** There are many Web sites designed to allow individuals to upload photos, videos, and other multimedia content and then visitors can search the site to locate the content they wish to view. In addition, multimedia content is often added to pages located on Facebook or another social networking site. While people certainly have the right to share photos and videos of themselves online if they wish to, many individuals upload multimedia content that also includes their friends or other individuals. Often, photos and videos are taken at social gatherings and other situations where the person being photographed or filmed may not be portrayed at their best. Since there are potential ramifications for any compromising content located online (for instance, many schools monitor social networks for inappropriate behavior and at least 20% of employers check Facebook profiles of job applicants), should individuals get permission for everyone in a photo or video before posting it online? Why or why not? What if the content caused the individual to be reprimanded at school or work, or cost the individual a scholarship or job? Would that change your opinion? How would you feel if you ran across a photo or video of yourself online that you did not upload or give permission to be shared online?

   For this project, form an opinion about the ethical ramifications of uploading photos or videos containing others without their permission and be prepared to discuss your position (in class, via an online class discussion group, in a class chat room, or via a class blog, depending on your instructor's directions). You may also be asked to write a short paper expressing your opinion.

ETHICS IN ACTION

5. **Certifications** There are certification exams available for database skills, such as the certifications offered by Oracle and ICCP.

   For this project, select two database certification programs and research them. Find out who offers them, how long it takes to complete them, how much the programs and exams cost, and how obtaining that certification can benefit you. Try to find job openings that mention one of your selected database certifications. What positions did you find, and what is the starting salary? Do the jobs require experience as well? A college degree? Would you be interested in taking one of these certification programs? Share your findings with the class in the form of a short presentation. The presentation should not exceed 10 minutes and should make use of one or more presentation aids, such as the chalkboard, handouts, overhead transparencies, or a computer-based slide presentation (your instructor may provide additional requirements). You may also be asked to submit a summary of the presentation to your instructor.

PRESENTATION/ DEMONSTRATION

Instructions: Go to the Chapter 14 page at **www.cengage.com/computerconcepts/np/uc13** to work the following Web Activities.

6. **Interactive Activities** Work the interactive **Crossword Puzzle**, watch the **Video Podcasts** and **Online Videos**, and explore the **Further Exploration** links associated with this chapter.

   If you have a SAM user profile, you may have access to hands-on instruction, practice, and assessment of the skills covered in this chapter. Check with your instructor for instructions and the correct URL/Web site to access those assignments.

7. **Student Edition Labs** Work the following interactive **Student Edition Lab**.
   - ➤ **Advanced Databases**

8. **Test Yourself** Review the **Online Study Guide** for this chapter, then test your knowledge of the terms and concepts covered in this chapter by completing the **Key Term Matching** exercise, the **Self-Quiz**, the **Exercises**, and the **Practice Test**.

WEB ACTIVITIES

Student Edition Labs

Systems

A Conversation with **STUART FELDMAN**
Past President of ACM and Vice President, Engineering, Google

" Verification and testing will continue to be essential—lives and jobs frequently depend on systems today. "

My Background . . .

I am one of the original computer brats—I learned to program on a vacuum tube machine in the early 1960s as a kid at a summer course. I was enthralled by computer programming, and the ability to create programs that did new and surprising things.

Throughout my computer career, I've worked as a computer science researcher at Bell Labs, a research manager and software architect at Bellcore, and as Vice President for Computer Science at IBM Research. I am now a Vice President at Google (and responsible for engineering activities at Google's offices in the eastern part of the Americas, as well as some specific products), as well as past President of ACM (Association for Computing Machinery)—the largest computing society in the world. Overall, my career has been spent in research at very high-tech companies, working on the cutting edge of computing. It's fun and exciting.

It's Important to Know . . .

The world of data has shifted radically. I can remember when a megabyte was a lot of information. Today, a gigabyte fits on a thing in your pocket, a terabyte fits on an inexpensive disk, and many large companies manage petabytes—and exabytes are coming soon. The types of information to be managed are also shifting—most information today is visual, audio, or executable (not rows and columns of numbers, as valuable as they are).

Programming languages last a long time. While most programmers write in dynamic languages (such as PERL and Python) today, COBOL and FORTRAN programs are still being written and variants of C are still being born. And even more people do programming without thinking about it (such as creating word processing macros, spreadsheet formulas, and widgets). We will almost certainly see a continuing expansion of the spectrum—a hard core of experts supporting basic systems and tools, and millions (soon billions) of people doing occasional programming and customization.

The impact of systems on society is tremendous. System capabilities have made enormous increases in efficiency possible, and have also opened up new types of business and social activities. Think about how banking has changed in the last decade, and about how you look up information and find people. Also, think about how personal communication and expectations have shifted from sending letters with a stamp, to sending e-mail, to staying in touch with others on a continual basis via mobile phone texting and social networks. Perhaps our attention span has shrunk, but our ability to reach out has increased. Information systems support globalization and rapid business change—sharing of information, shifting of jobs, and the creation of new jobs and whole new types of careers.

How I Use this Technology . . .

I spend a lot of time writing papers and presentations, so I use Google Docs and Microsoft Office applications—both complex systems that maintain data and perform reliably—to create documents and collaborate with others. I use secure, integrated financial systems when I perform online financial transactions. Of course, my favorite system "application" is the World Wide Web, which is a remarkable linkage of data servers, application providers, and communication systems. I use it many times a day for research, communications, personal interactions, shopping, and amusement.

Stuart Feldman is the past President of ACM and currently a Vice President of Engineering at Google. He is a member of the Board of Directors of the AACSB (Association to Advance Collegiate Schools of Business), a Fellow of the IEEE, a Fellow of the ACM, and serves on a number of government advisory committees. He is a recipient of the 2003 ACM Software System Award for creating a seminal piece of software engineering known as Make, a tool for maintaining computer software. Stuart has a Ph.D. in Mathematics from MIT.

What the Future Holds . . .

The cost of computing, measured in cost of instructions executed or information stored or transmitted, will continue to drop. This exponential curve will continue to drive many of the improvements we will see in the future. In addition, the value of information and knowledge that is encapsulated in computer programs will increase—once something is in code, it can be used and replicated at low incremental cost. This will continue to drive our digitization and automation of activities.

There will also be the increasing ability to do massive amounts of computing for enormous numbers of users and to apply computing resources to problems that were too expensive to address just a few years ago. This will be facilitated by the increased use of integration and by using available software and services in innovative ways, as well as by dynamic languages and the increased use of Web standards.

There will be new service computing models, ranging from enterprise integration to service APIs to user-based mashups to entirely new service industries like Google search tools and remote medical advice. For program development, we'll see increasing agility—shifting from waterfall and rigid development methods to more exploratory, prototype-based methods and fast trials and iterations. Verification and testing will continue to be essential—lives and jobs frequently depend on systems today.

Perhaps the biggest shifts will come from our increasing dependence on information and access, the risks when things go wrong, and the possibilities of new applications that can improve our lives. For instance, as information arrives and can be examined more easily, we can do a better job of managing our health, our activities, and our personal interactions.

" . . . the value of information and knowledge that is encapsulated in computer programs will increase—once something is in code, it can be used and replicated at low incremental cost."

My Advice to Students . . .

IT jobs, computer applications, programming languages, approaches to system development, and business needs are always changing. The best preparation for a long and successful career is to understand the fundamentals of computing deeply, and be able to apply them to new situations. You need to become expert in some area—such as a programming language, a methodology, or an environment—but you also must always be prepared to learn new technologies and gain new expertise.

Discussion Question

Stuart Feldman points out how our expectations for the systems we use today have shifted, such as in terms of demands for faster communications and information retrieval. What are your expectations when you send an e-mail message or post an item on a social network? Do you expect an immediate response? Are you disappointed if you don't get immediate feedback? How does instant access to communications, news, personal status, and other timely information affect our society today? Be prepared to discuss your position (in class, via an online class discussion group, in a class chat room, or via a class blog, depending on your instructor's directions). You may also be asked to write a short paper expressing your opinion.

>**For access to Google search tools and applications, visit www.google.com. There are some excellent papers available at research.google.com. For more information about ACM or to access the ACM Digital Library, visit www.acm.org.**

Computers and Society

No study of computers is complete without a look at the growing impact of computers and related technologies on society and our daily lives. As the use of computers continues to become increasingly integrated into our lives at school, on the job, at home, and on the go, the associated risks increase, such as hackers accessing our personal information, computer viruses affecting the performance of our computers, or other potential security or privacy problems. Our networked society also creates new ethical, access, and environmental issues; impacts our physical and mental health; and creates new intellectual property rights issues, such as how intellectual property is used and distributed via the Internet and how it can be protected.

Security risks related to network and Internet use were discussed in Chapter 9. Chapter 15 looks at some of the additional security and privacy issues surrounding computer use today, including a discussion of possible concerns and corresponding safeguards that we can take. Chapter 16 addresses issues related to intellectual property rights, ethics, health, access, and the environment.

Chapter 15
Computer Security and
Privacy 590

Overview 591

Why Be Concerned About Computer
Security? 591

Hardware Loss, Hardware Damage,
and System Failure 591

Software Piracy and Digital Counterfeiting 602

Why Be Concerned About Information
Privacy? 606

Databases, Electronic Profiling, Spam,
and Other Marketing Activities 607

Electronic Surveillance and Monitoring 616

Computer Security and Privacy Legislation 624

Chapter 16
Intellectual Property Rights,
Ethics, Health, Access,
and the Environment 632

Overview 633

Intellectual Property Rights 633

Ethics 638

Computers and Health 652

Access to Technology 661

Environmental Concerns 666

Related Legislation 671

*"Managing your
security and
privacy needs
to be a regular
routine—like
brushing your
teeth."*

For more comments
from Guest Expert **Frank
Molsberry** of Dell Inc., see
the **Expert Insight on . . .
Computers and Society**
feature at the end of the
module.

chapter 15

Computer Security and Privacy

After completing this chapter, you will be able to do the following:

1. Explain why all computer users should be concerned about computer security.

2. List some risks associated with hardware loss, hardware damage, and system failure, and understand ways to safeguard a computer against these risks.

3. Define software piracy and digital counterfeiting, and explain how they may be prevented.

4. Explain what information privacy is and why computer users should be concerned about it.

5. Describe some privacy concerns regarding databases, electronic profiling, spam, and telemarketing, and identify ways individuals can protect their privacy.

6. Discuss several types of electronic surveillance and monitoring, and list ways individuals can protect their privacy.

7. Discuss the status of computer security and privacy legislation.

outline

Overview

Why Be Concerned About Computer Security?

Hardware Loss, Hardware Damage, and System Failure
Hardware Loss
Hardware Damage
System Failure and Other Disasters
Protecting Against Hardware Loss, Hardware Damage, and System Failure

Software Piracy and Digital Counterfeiting
Software Piracy
Digital Counterfeiting
Protecting Against Software Piracy and Digital Counterfeiting

Why Be Concerned About Information Privacy?

Databases, Electronic Profiling, Spam, and Other Marketing Activities
Databases and Electronic Profiling
Spam and Other Marketing Activities
Protecting the Privacy of Personal Information

Electronic Surveillance and Monitoring
Computer Monitoring Software
Video Surveillance
Employee Monitoring
Presence Technology
Protecting Personal and Workplace Privacy

Computer Security and Privacy Legislation

OVERVIEW

The increasing use of computers in our society today has many advantages. It also, however, opens up new possibilities for problems (such as data loss due to a system malfunction or a disaster), as well as new opportunities for computer crime (such as hardware theft, software piracy, and digital counterfeiting). In addition, our networked society has raised a number of privacy concerns. Although we can appreciate that sometimes selected people or organizations have a legitimate need for some types of personal information, whenever information is provided to others there is always the danger that the information will be misused. For instance, facts may be taken out of context and used to draw distorted conclusions, or private information may end up being distributed to others without one's consent or knowledge. And, with the vast amount of information that is contained in databases accessible via the Internet today, privacy is an enormous concern for both individuals and businesses.

Chapter 9 discussed security risks related to network and Internet use. This chapter looks at other types of computer-related security concerns, as well as the computer-related privacy concerns facing us today. First, we explore hardware loss, hardware damage, and system failure, and the safeguards that can help reduce the risk of a problem occurring due to these security concerns. Next, software piracy and digital counterfeiting are discussed, along with the steps that are being taken to prevent these computer crimes. We then turn to privacy topics, including possible risks to personal privacy and precautions that can be taken to safeguard one's privacy. The chapter closes with a summary of legislation related to computer security and privacy. ■

WHY BE CONCERNED ABOUT COMPUTER SECURITY?

Today, there are a number of security concerns surrounding computers and related technology that all individuals should be concerned about, including having your computer stolen, losing a term paper because the storage medium your paper was stored on becomes unreadable, losing your mobile phone containing your entire contact list and calendar, or running the risk of buying pirated or digitally counterfeited products. The most common security risks and computer crimes (including hacking, computer viruses, identity theft, and cyberbullying) that take place via networks and the Internet were discussed in Chapter 9, along with their respective precautions. While these concerns are extremely important today, there are additional computer security issues that are not related specifically to networks and the Internet. These computer security concerns, along with some precautions that users can take to reduce the risks of problems occurring due to these security concerns, are discussed in the next few sections.

HARDWARE LOSS, HARDWARE DAMAGE, AND SYSTEM FAILURE

Hardware loss can occur when a personal computer, USB flash drive, mobile device, or other piece of hardware is stolen or is lost by the owner. Hardware loss, as well as other security issues, can also result from *hardware damage* (both intentional and accidental) and *system failure*.

Hardware Loss

One of the most obvious types of hardware loss is **hardware theft**, which occurs when hardware is stolen from an individual or from a business, school, or other organization. Computers, printers, mobile phones, and other hardware can be stolen during a break-in; portable computers and mobile devices are also frequently stolen from cars, as well as from restaurants, airports, hotels, and other public locations. Although security experts stress that the vast majority of hardware theft is done for the value of the hardware itself, corporate executives and government employees may be targeted for computer theft for the information contained on their computers. In fact, *C-level attacks* (attacks aimed at C-level executives, such as CEOs and CIOs) are rapidly growing as executives are increasingly using e-mail and storing documents on their computers, as well as traveling more with portable computers, mobile phones, and other devices. And even if the data on a device is not the primary reason for a theft, any unencrypted sensitive data stored on the stolen device is at risk of being exposed or used for fraudulent purposes, and this is happening at unprecedented levels today.

Hardware loss also occurs when hardware is being transported in luggage or in a package that is lost by an airline or shipping company, or when an individual misplaces or otherwise loses a piece of hardware. With the vast number of portable devices that individuals carry with them today (such as portable computers, mobile phones, and USB flash drives), this latter type of hardware loss is a growing concern—by one estimate, more than 20 million people per year lose a mobile phone. While lost hardware may be covered by insurance and the data stored on a lost or stolen device may not be used in a fraudulent manner, having to replace the hardware and restore the data—or, worse yet, losing the data entirely if it was not backed up—is still a huge inconvenience. If any sensitive data (such as Social Security numbers, Web site passwords, or credit card data) was contained on the lost hardware, individuals risk identity theft (one study revealed that 80% of users store information that could be used for identity theft on their mobile phones). Businesses hosting sensitive data that is breached have to deal with the numerous issues and potential consequences of that loss, such as notifying customers that their personal information was exposed (as required by more than half of the states in the U.S.), responding to potential lawsuits, and trying to repair damage to the company's reputation.

Hardware Damage

Computer hardware often consists of relatively delicate components that can be damaged easily by power fluctuations, heat, dust, static electricity, water, and abuse. For instance, fans clogged by dust can cause a computer to overheat; dropping a computer will often break it; and spilling a drink on a keyboard or leaving a mobile phone in the pocket of your jeans while they go through the wash will likely cause some damage. In addition to accidental damage, burglars, vandals, disgruntled employees, and other individuals sometimes intentionally damage the computers and other hardware they have access to.

System Failure and Other Disasters

Although many of us may prefer not to think about it, **system failure**—the complete malfunction of a computer system—and other types of computer-related disasters do happen. From accidentally deleting a file to having your computer just stop working, computer problems can be a huge inconvenience, as well as cost you a great deal of time and money. When the system contains your personal documents and data, it is a problem; when it contains the only copy of your company records or controls a vital system—such as a nuclear power plant—it can be a disaster.

> **Hardware theft.** The theft of computer hardware. > **System failure.** The complete malfunction of a computer system.

System failure can occur because of a hardware problem, software problem, or computer virus. It can also occur because of a natural disaster (such as a tornado, fire, flood, or hurricane), sabotage, or a terrorist attack. The terrorist attack on the New York City World Trade Center Twin Towers on September 11, 2001, illustrated this all too clearly. When the Twin Towers collapsed, nearly 3,000 people were killed and hundreds of offices—over 13 million square feet of office space—were completely destroyed; another 7 million square feet of office space was damaged (see Figure 15-1). In addition to the devastating human loss, the offices located in the WTC lost their computer systems—including all the equipment, records, and data stored at that location. The ramifications of these system failures and the corresponding data loss were felt around the world by all the businesses and people connected directly or indirectly to these organizations.

FIGURE 15-1
System destruction. The 9/11 attacks killed nearly 3,000 people and destroyed hundreds of business offices, including critical cables located in this Verizon office adjacent to Ground Zero.

Protecting Against Hardware Loss, Hardware Damage, and System Failure

To protect against hardware loss, hardware damage, and system failure, a number of precautions can be taken, as discussed next.

Door and Computer Equipment Locks

Locked doors and equipment can be simple deterrents to computer theft. For instance, doors to facilities should be secured with door locks, alarm systems, and whatever other access control methods (such as the possessed object and biometric access systems discussed in Chapter 9) are needed to make it difficult to gain access to hardware that might be stolen. In addition, employees should be trained regarding the proper procedures for ensuring visitors only have access to the parts of the facility that they are authorized to access. For a look at a new trend in evaluating security procedures—*social engineering tests* for employees—see the Trend box.

To secure computers and other hardware to a table or other object that is difficult to move, *cable locks* (see Figure 15-2) can be used. Cable locks are frequently used to secure desktop computers in schools and businesses. They can also be used to secure portable computers, external hard drives, and other portable pieces of hardware, and they are increasingly being used by college students and business travelers to secure their portable computers when they are not being used. To facilitate using a computer lock, nearly all computers today come with a *security slot*—a small opening built into the system unit case designed for computer locks. If a security slot is not available, *cable anchors* (which attach to a piece of hardware using industrial strength adhesive and which contain a connector through which the cable lock can be passed—refer again to Figure 15-2) can be used. Computer locks are available in both key and combination versions.

As an additional precaution with portable computers, *laptop alarm software* that emits a very loud alarm noise if the computer is unplugged, if USB devices are removed, or if the computer is shut down

FIGURE 15-2
Cable locks can be used to secure computers and other hardware.

NOTEBOOK COMPUTERS
This combination cable lock connects via a security slot built into the notebook computer.

DESKTOP COMPUTERS AND MONITORS
This keyed cable lock connects via a cable anchor attached to the back of the monitor.

TREND

Social Engineering Tests

With security and privacy breaches occurring on a regular basis today, a growing trend is for businesses to use security firms to perform security audits, also known as *vulnerability assessments*, on themselves. While some of these assessments focus on trying to breach security remotely, *social engineering tests* are designed to test a business's security policies and employees, such as whether or not employees will click a phishing e-mail message or give out sensitive information in response to a phishing telephone call, grant a potential thief physical access to the facility, or plug a USB flash drive found in the office (and potentially containing malware planted by a hacker) into their computers. And the use of these tests is growing. For instance, one security firm that performs social engineering tests—*TraceSecurity Inc.*—estimates that about 70% of its new customers are asking for social engineering tests, up from about 5% three years ago.

To perform a social engineering test, TraceSecurity engineers typically impersonate pest-control workers or fire inspectors in order to gain entry to server rooms and other locations where they can then access sensitive data. They sometimes precede their visit with a spoofed e-mail to office employees, such as announcing an upcoming pest inspection and requesting employees grant the pest control workers full access to check for infestation. Once at the office, TraceSecurity personnel attempt to talk their way into the building and into a room that allows access to the company network. As proof of access, they tag equipment with TraceSecurity stickers (see the accompanying photo), take photographs of the documents and data they were able to access, and sometimes even remove hardware from the building (assuming the business requests this and has granted the appropriate permission). The business receives a report detailing which tests employees passed and failed and, in a follow-up visit, the TraceSecurity employees explain how they were able to infiltrate the business and what

precautions should be taken to prevent this from happening again. Typical recommendations include not using e-mail alone to authorize company visitors; training employees to question any strangers they see in the office and to escort visitors that need access to sensitive areas of the business; and utilizing conventional precautions such as using access devices to secure facilities, using screen savers with passwords to lock computers when employees are away from their desks, not using any unauthorized portable storage devices, and encrypting all sensitive data.

While this type of vulnerability assessment may annoy or embarrass some employees, it tends to have a much greater impact on employees than a receiving a memo or listening to a lecture on security policies. According to TraceSecurity's chief technology officer, "Sometimes you have to get burned to make you really understand."

The red and white sticker shown here marks equipment accessed during a TraceSecurity social engineering test.

without the owner's permission can be used. In addition to physically securing computers, it is also extremely important for businesses to ensure that employees follow security protocols related to portable storage media, such as signing in and out portable hard drives, USB flash drives, and other storage media, if required, and keeping those devices locked up when they are not in use.

Encryption and Self-Encrypting Hard Drives

As discussed in Chapter 9, encryption can be used to prevent a file from being readable if it is intercepted or viewed by an unauthorized individual. To protect the data on an entire computer in case it is lost or stolen, **full disk encryption (FDE)** can be used. FDE systems encrypt everything stored on the drive (the operating system, application programs, data, temporary files, and so forth) automatically without any user interaction, so users don't have to remember to encrypt sensitive documents and the encryption is always enabled. To access a hard drive that uses FDE (often referred to as a **self-encrypting hard drive**), a username and password or biometric characteristic is needed, typically before the computer containing the drive will boot.

While self-encrypting hard drives are used most often with portable computers (in fact, the U.S. federal government is in the process of implementing FDE on all government-owned portable computers and mobile devices), their use is also being expanded to desktop computers and servers. Because FDE requires no user input to enable it and the user has no say in which files are encrypted (since all files are encrypted automatically), these systems provide an easy way to ensure all data is protected, provided strong passwords are used in conjunction with the encryption system so the system cannot be easily hacked. As FDE technology continues to improve to reduce the additional disk access time required by the encryption system, use of self-encrypting hard drives is expected to grow past corporate and government use to individuals' personal computers.

Encryption can also be used to protect the data stored on removable media, such as flash memory cards and USB flash drives; either a strong password or a biometric feature (such as a built-in fingerprint reader, as shown in Figure 15-3) is used to provide access to the data on the drive. Many encrypted devices allow multiple users to be registered as authorized users (by assigning each individual a password or registering his or her fingerprint image, for instance), as well as allow a portion of the device to be designated as unencrypted for nonsensitive documents, if desired. Many businesses today are requiring that all desktop computers, portable computers, portable storage devices, and mobile phones issued to employees be encrypted, in order to protect against a data breach.

Computer Tracking Software and Antitheft Tools

Some software tools are not designed to prevent hardware from being stolen; instead, they are designed to aid in its recovery. This can be beneficial since, according to FBI statistics, the recovery rate of a stolen or lost computer is normally about 2% or 3%. One software tool that can be used to help increase the chances of a stolen or lost computer being recovered is *computer tracking software*. Computer tracking software sends identifying information (such as ownership information and location information determined from nearby Wi-Fi networks) to the computer tracking company on a regular basis, such as once per day if the computer is not reported stolen. When the computer is reported lost

FIGURE 15-3
Encrypted media.
The data on this encrypted USB flash drive cannot be accessed until the user is authenticated via a fingerprint scan.

> **Full disk encryption (FDE).** A technology that encrypts everything stored on a storage medium automatically, without any user interaction.
> **Self-encrypting hard drive.** A hard drive that uses full disk encryption (FDE).

SOC

HOW IT WORKS

Self-Destructing Devices

When a business or an individual is less concerned about recovering a stolen device than about ensuring the data located on the computer is not compromised, devices that self-destruct upon command are a viable option. Available as part of some computer tracking software programs (such as the one shown in the accompanying illustration), as well as stand-alone utilities, *kill switch* capabilities destroy the data on a device (typically by overwriting preselected files multiple times, rendering them unreadable) when instructed. Kill switches built into computer tracking systems are typically activated upon customer request when the device is determined to be lost or stolen. Once the kill switch is activated, all data on the computer is erased whenever it next connects to the Internet or when another predesignated remote trigger is activated (such as a certain number of unsuccessful logon attempts). Kill switch capabilities are also built into some mobile phone applications (such as the *MobileMe* iPhone app) and are typically activated by the owner logging onto an online account or sending the phone a text message containing the proper kill switch password—when the device receives the message, all data stored on the device is erased.

Kill switch technology is also beginning to be built into some USB flash drives and hard drives. For instance, hard drives with EDT's *Dead on Demand* technology contain a small canister filled with a corrosive chemical that completely destroys the drive when the drive is tampered with or when one of up to 17 remote triggers specified by the owner is activated. The self-destruction process does not damage the computer—only the hard drive—and the command to self-destruct can be activated even if the drive is not powered up or if it is removed from the computer. Not quite *Mission Impossible*, but when hardware containing sensitive data is stolen (which could impact an individual's personal privacy or a business's legal liability, reputation, and bottom line), kill switch technology could save the day.

VIDEO PODCAST

Go to the Chapter 15 page at **www.cengage.com/ computerconcepts/np/uc13** to download or listen to the "How To: Track a Stolen Laptop" video podcast.

or stolen, however, the computer tracking software typically increases its contact with the computer tracking software company (such as sending new information every 15 minutes) so current location information can be provided to law enforcement agencies to help them recover the computer. Some software can even take video or photos of the person using the stolen computer (if the computer has a built-in video camera like many portable computers have today) to help identify and prosecute the thief.

Often any sign that computer tracking software is running on the computer or is sending information via the Internet is hidden from the user (this type of tracking software is sometimes called *stealth tracking software*), so the thief is usually not aware that a computer tracking system is installed on the computer. An alternative is tracking software that displays a message on the screen when the computer is lost or stolen. This message might be a plea to return the device for a reward or simply a message like "THIS COMPUTER IS STOLEN" in a big bright banner on the desktop to call attention to the fact that the computer is stolen (the owner can usually specify the message and messages typically reappear every 30 seconds, no matter how many times they are closed by the thief).

Computer tracking systems (the software and the support from the computer tracking company) usually cost between $30 and $50 per year. An alternative for protecting the data on a portable computer if it is stolen is to use a *kill switch*—technology that causes the device to self-destruct, as discussed in the How It Works box.

Another antitheft tool is the use of *asset tags* on hardware and other expensive assets. These labels usually identify the owner of the asset and are designed to be permanently attached to the asset. Some tags are designed to be indestructible; others are *tamper evident labels* that change their appearance if someone (such as a thief) tries to remove them. For instance, some labels have a printed message hidden underneath the label that is etched into the surface of the computer and is exposed when the label is removed. Both of these features alert a potential buyer to the fact that the item is likely stolen.

Additional Precautions for Mobile Users

With an increasing amount of personal data being stored on mobile phones and other mobile devices today, as well as the ability of some mobile phones to be used to make purchases and unlock doors, security features that guard against the unauthorized use of mobile devices are becoming increasingly more important. There is tracking software (similar to the computer tracking systems just discussed) available for mobile phones and other types of devices that are frequently lost or stolen (such as portable digital media players and USB flash drives) to help aid in the recovery of those devices. For instance, *mobile tracking software* can remotely lock down a lost or stolen phone, display a message on the phone containing instructions for returning the device, and/or play a sound to help the owner locate the phone if it is nearby. However, to avoid losing the device in the first place or to prevent someone from accessing the data stored on the device, other precautions should be used.

While on the go, the best antitheft measure is common sense. For example, you should never leave a portable computer or mobile device unattended in a public location (always keep a hand, finger, or other body part in contact with the device so, if you are distracted for a moment and glance away, it cannot be stolen without you noticing). When staying in a hotel, take your computer with you, use a cable lock to secure it to a piece of furniture, or lock it in a hotel safe (many hotel rooms today have room safes large enough to hold a portable computer) when you leave your hotel room for the day. Other sensible precautions include using a plain carrying case to make a portable computer less conspicuous and labeling your portable computer (and other portable hardware that you take with you on the go) with your contact information so a lost or stolen device can be returned to you when it is recovered. One additional possibility for protecting data while on the road is storing all data online or on the company server instead of on the computer you are using while traveling. Businesses can ensure no data is stored on the device by using a thin client portable computer that has no hard drive, such as the *SafeBook* computer. These computers look like ordinary notebook computers, but since all programs and data are stored on the company server and accessed via the Internet through a Wi-Fi, Ethernet, or 3G wireless connection, there is no data stored on the computer. As a result, no data can be compromised if the computer is lost or stolen. In addition, mobile users should disable wireless connections when they are not needed and enable password protection for accessing the device. These precautions are summarized in Figure 15-4.

Proper Hardware Care

Proper care of hardware can help to prevent serious damage to a computer system. The most obvious precaution is to not harm your hardware physically, such as by dropping a portable computer, knocking a piece of hardware off a desk, or jostling a desktop computer's system unit. To help protect portable devices against minor abuse, *protective cases* (see Figure 15-5) can be used. These cases are typically padded or made from protective material to prevent

---

MOBILE COMPUTING PRECAUTIONS

Install and use encryption, antivirus, antispyware, and firewall software.

Secure computers with boot passwords; set your mobile phone to autolock after a short period of time and require a passcode to unlock it.

Use only secure Wi-Fi connections and disable Wi-Fi and Bluetooth when they are not needed.

Never leave usernames, passwords, or other data attached to your computer or inside its carrying case.

Use a plain carrying case to make a portable computer less conspicuous.

Keep an eye on your devices at all times, especially when going through airport security.

Avoid setting your devices on the floor or leaving them in your hotel room; use a cable lock to secure the device to a desk or other object whenever this is unavoidable.

Back up the data stored on the device regularly.

Consider installing tracking or kill switch software.

FIGURE 15-4
Common sense precautions for portable computer and mobile device users.

FIGURE 15-5
Protective cases.

MOBILE PHONE CASES   **NOTEBOOK CASES**

RUGGED PORTABLE COMPUTERS

RUGGED MOBILE DEVICES

RUGGED MOBILE PHONES

FIGURE 15-6
Ruggedized devices.

FIGURE 15-7
Surge suppressors and uninterruptible power supplies (UPSs).

SURGE SUPPRESSOR FOR DESKTOP COMPUTERS

SURGE SUPPRESSOR FOR NOTEBOOK COMPUTERS

UPS FOR HOME COMPUTERS

UPS FOR SERVERS

damage due to occasional bumps and bangs; they also often have a thin protective layer over the device's display to protect against scratches. Some protective cases are water resistant to protect the device from rain or dust damage. There are also neoprene *laptop sleeves* available to protect portable computers from scratches and other damage when they are carried in a conventional briefcase or bag.

For users who need more protection than a protective case can provide, **ruggedized devices** (such as portable computers and mobile phones) are available (see Figure 15-6). These devices are designed to withstand much more physical abuse than conventional devices and range from *semirugged* to *ultrarugged*. For instance, semirugged devices typically have a more durable case and are spill-resistant. Rugged and ultrarugged devices go a few steps further—they are designed to withstand falls from three feet or more onto concrete, extreme temperature ranges, wet conditions, and use while being bounced around over rough terrain in a vehicle. Ruggedized devices are used most often by individuals who work out of the office, such as field workers, construction workers, outdoor technicians, military personnel, police officers, and firefighters.

To protect hardware from damage due to power fluctuations, it is important for all users to use a **surge suppressor** with a computer whenever it is plugged into a power outlet. When electrical power spikes occur, the surge suppressor prevents them from harming your system. For desktop computers, surge suppressors should be used with all of the powered components in the computer system (such as the system unit, monitor, printer, and scanner). Surge suppressors designed for portable computers are typically smaller and designed to connect only one device (see Figure 15-7). There are surge suppressors designed for business and industrial use, as well.

Users who want their desktop computers to remain powered up when the electricity goes off should use an

---

> **Ruggedized device.** A device (such as a portable computer or mobile phone) that is designed to withstand much more physical abuse than a conventional device. > **Surge suppressor.** A device that protects a computer system from damage due to electrical fluctuations.

uninterruptible power supply (UPS), which contains a built-in battery (see Figure 15-7). The length of time that a UPS can power a system depends on the type and number of devices connected to the UPS, the power capacity of the UPS device (typically measured in watts), and the age of the battery (most UPS batteries last only 3 to 5 years before they need to be replaced). Most UPS devices also protect against power fluctuations. UPSs designed for use by individuals usually provide power for a few minutes to keep the system powered up during short power blips, as well as to allow the user to save open documents and shut down the computer properly in case the electricity remains off. Industrial-level UPSs typically run for a significantly longer amount of time (such as a few hours), but not long enough to power a facility during an extended power outage such as those that happen periodically in some parts of the U.S. due to winter storms, summer rotating blackouts, and other factors. To provide longer-term power during extended power outages, as well as to provide continuous power to facilities (such as hospitals, nuclear power plants, and business data centers) that cannot afford to be without power for any period of time, *generators* can be used.

Dust, heat, static electricity, and moisture can also be dangerous to a computer, so be sure not to place your computer equipment in direct sunlight or in a dusty area. Small handheld vacuums made for electrical equipment can be used periodically to remove the dust from the keyboard and from inside the system unit, but be very careful when vacuuming inside the system unit. Also, be sure the system unit has plenty of ventilation, especially around the fan vents. To help reduce the amount of dust that is drawn into the fan vents, raise your desktop computer several inches off the floor. You should also avoid placing a portable computer on a soft surface, such as a couch or blanket, to help prevent overheating (the notebook cooling stands discussed in Chapter 2 can help provide air circulation). To prevent static electricity from damaging the inside of your computer when installing a new expansion card or other internal device, turn off the power to the computer and unplug the power cord from the computer before removing the cover from the system unit. Wearing an antistatic wristband is an additional good precaution. Unless your computer is ruggedized (like the one shown in Figure 15-8), do not get it wet or otherwise expose it to adverse conditions. Be especially careful with mobile phones and other mobile devices when you are near water (such as a swimming pool, lake, or large puddle) so you do not drop them into the water (more than 50% of the phones received by one data recovery firm are water damaged).

Both internal and external magnetic hard drives also need to be protected against jostling or other excess motion that can result in a *head crash*, which occurs when a hard drive's read/write heads actually touch the surface of a hard disk. Unless your portable computer contains a solid-state drive instead of a conventional magnetic hard drive, it is a good idea to turn off the computer, hibernate it, or put it into standby mode before moving it since magnetic hard drives are more vulnerable to damage while they are spinning. In addition, storage media—such as flash memory cards, hard drives, CDs, and DVDs—are all sensitive storage media that work well over time, as long as appropriate care is used. Don't remove a USB storage device (such as a USB flash drive or USB hard drive) when it is being accessed—use the *Safely Remove Hardware* icon in the system tray on a Windows computer to stop the device before unplugging it to avoid data loss and damage to the device. Keep CDs and DVDs in their protective *jewel cases* and handle them carefully to prevent fingerprints and scratches on the data sides of the discs (usually the bottom, unprinted side on a single-sided disc). *Screen protectors* (thin plastic film that covers the display screen of a mobile phone or mobile device) can be used to prevent scratches on the displays of pen-based devices. For more tips on how to protect your computer, see the Technology and You box.

FIGURE 15-8
Proper hardware care. Unless your computer is ruggedized (such as the one shown here), keep it out of the heat, cold, rain, water, and other adverse conditions.

FURTHER EXPLORATION Go

Go to the Chapter 15 page at **www.cengage.com/ computerconcepts/np/uc13** for links to information about protecting your computer from theft or damage.

>**Uninterruptible power supply (UPS).** A device containing a built-in battery that provides continuous power to a computer and other connected components when the electricity goes out.

TECHNOLOGY AND YOU

Protecting Your PC

All computer users should take specific actions to protect their computers. In this world of viruses, worms, hackers, spyware, and "buggy" (error-prone) software, it pays to be cautious. Although safeguards have been covered in detail throughout this book, some specific precautionary steps all computer users should follow are summarized in this box.

Step 1: Protect your hardware.

Be sure to plug all components of your computer system (such as the system unit, monitor, printer, and scanner) into a surge suppressor. Be careful not to bump or move the computer when it is on. Don't spill food or drink onto the keyboard or any other piece of hardware. Store your flash memory cards and CDs properly. If you ever need to work inside the system unit, turn off the computer and unplug it before touching any component inside the system unit. When taking a portable computer on the road, don't ever leave it unattended, and be careful not to drop or lose it.

Step 2: Install and use security software.

Install a good antivirus program and set it up to scan your system on a continual basis, including checking all files and e-mail messages before they are downloaded to your computer. To detect the newest viruses and types of malware, keep your antivirus program up to date (have it automatically check for and install updates) and use a personal two-way firewall program to protect your computer from unauthorized access via the Internet, as well as to detect any attempts by spyware to send data from your computer to another party. For additional protection if you have a home network, enable file sharing only for files and folders that really need to be accessed by other users. Run an antispyware program—such as Ad-Aware or Spybot Search & Destroy—on a regular basis to detect and remove spyware.

Step 3: Back up regularly.

Once you have a new computer set up with all programs installed and the menus and other settings the way you like them, create a full backup so the computer can be restored to that configuration in case of a major problem with your computer or hard drive. Be sure also to back up your data files on a regular basis. Depending on how important your documents are, you may want to back up all of your data every night, or copy each document to a removable storage medium after each major revision. If you use local (instead of Web-based) e-mail, periodically back up the folder containing your e-mail, such as the *Outlook.pst* file used to store Microsoft Outlook mail. To facilitate data backup, keep your data organized using folders (such as storing all data files in a main folder called "Data"). For an even higher level of security, install (and regularly back up) a second hard drive just for data—if your main

hard drive ever becomes unstable and needs to be reformatted or replaced, your data drive will remain untouched. Backups should be stored in a different location than your computer, such as in a different building or in a fire-resistant safe. An easy way to accomplish this is to use an online backup service or upload your backup files to an online storage service.

Step 4: Update your operating system, browser, and e-mail program regularly.

Most companies that produce operating systems, Web browsers, or e-mail programs regularly post updates and patches—small programs that take care of software-specific problems, or bugs, such as security holes—on their Web sites on a regular basis. Some programs include an option within the program to check online for updates; for other programs, you will need to go to each manufacturer's Web site directly to check for any critical or recommended updates. For any programs—such as Windows and most antivirus and firewall programs—that have the option to check for updates automatically, enable that option. Windows users can check their current security settings using the *Windows Security Center* (called the *Action Center* in Windows 7), available through the Control Panel and shown in the accompanying illustration.

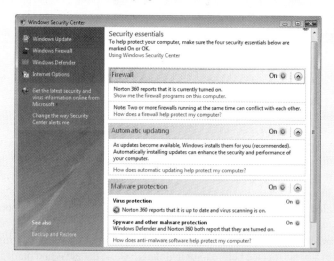

For optimal protection, all security essentials should be enabled.

Step 5: Test your system for vulnerabilities.

There are several free tests available through Web sites to see if your computer's ports are accessible to hackers or if your computer is infected with a virus or spyware. These tests, such as the one on the Symantec Web site shown in Figure 9-10 in Chapter 9 or the ShieldsUP test available on the Gibson Research Web site, should be run to check for any remaining vulnerabilities once you believe your antivirus software, firewall, and any other protective components you are using are set up correctly.

Backups and Disaster Recovery Plans

As discussed and illustrated in Chapter 5, creating a *backup* means making a duplicate copy of important files so that when a problem occurs (such as a hard drive failure or a stolen computer), you can restore those files using the backup copy. Data to be backed up includes company files, personal documents, photos, e-mail messages, and any other files that are important and the owner of the files would miss if they were lost. Backups can be performed for personal computers, servers, mobile phones, and other devices, depending on where the important data is located.

Businesses should make backups of at least all new data on a regular basis (such as once per day); individuals should make backups of important documents as they are created and back up the rest of their data periodically. Businesses and individuals that utilize cloud computing should also back up important data stored online.

After a backup is performed, the backup media used needs to be secured so that it will be intact when it is needed. If stored in-house, backup media should be placed in a fire-resistant safe; however, it is even better to store backup media in a different physical location. For instance, many businesses today use third-party *data storage companies* that store their backup media at a secure remote location; businesses can request their backups be returned whenever they are needed. To secure the data on the backup media while it is in transit and being stored, the data should be encrypted. *Online backup services* perform backups via the Internet so physically transporting backup media to the storage company location is not an issue.

For an even higher level of security than a scheduled backup, *continuous data protection* (*CDP*) can be used. A CDP backup system (most often used with company servers) records data changes on a continual basis so that data can be recovered from any point in time (even just a few minutes ago) with no data loss, and recovery can be as fast as five minutes after a failure. Although expensive, it is one of the best ways to ensure that company data is protected. In addition to business data, CDP is beginning to be used to adhere to the growing requirements for *e-discovery* of electronic business documents. In fact, the size of the e-mail archiving market alone in 2011 is expected to be $1.4 billion, according to research firm IDC.

To supplement backup procedures, businesses and other organizations should have a **disaster recovery plan** (also called a *business continuity* plan)—a plan that spells out what the organization will do to prepare for and recover from a disruptive event, such as a fire,

ASK THE EXPERT

John Christopher, Senior Data Recovery Engineer, DriveSavers, Inc.

Of the hard drives sent to you for recovery, what is the most common type of problem you see and is there a way that problem can be prevented?

We often receive hard drives that have severe media damage. That means that the read/write heads have come in contact with the platters and scraped off portions of the surface and data. This often occurs because the hard drive was left powered on after the problem occurred. The platters inside a drive spin at high speed, so a great deal of damage can occur in a very short period of time as the heads bounce around and create more debris. Eventually the damage becomes too great for even a professional data recovery company to overcome.

The best rule of thumb to prevent the loss of critical data is to back up religiously and to verify that the backup is really backing up the critical files. In addition, if a hard drive exhibits any sign of failure including unusual noises (such as repetitive clicking or grinding) and if the data is irreplaceable and has not been backed up recently, the best solution is to immediately shut down the computer and then seek the assistance of a professional data recovery company like DriveSavers.

VIDEO PODCAST

Go to the Chapter 15 page at **www.cengage.com/ computerconcepts/np/uc13** to download or listen to the "How To: Clone a Hard Drive" video podcast.

> **Disaster recovery plan.** A written plan that describes the steps a company will take following the occurrence of a disaster.

natural disaster, terrorist attack, power outage, or computer failure. Disaster recovery plans should include information about who will be in charge immediately after the disaster has occurred, what alternate facilities and equipment can be used, where backup media is located, the priority of getting each operation back online, disaster insurance coverage information, emergency communications methods, and so forth. If a *hot site*—an alternate location equipped with the computers, cabling, desks, and other equipment necessary to keep a business's operations going—is to be used following a major disaster, it should be set up ahead of time, and information about the hot site should be included in the disaster recovery plan. Businesses that cannot afford to be without e-mail service should also consider making arrangements with an *emergency mail system provider* to act as a temporary mail server if the company mail server is not functioning. Copies of the disaster recovery plan should be located off-site, such as at an appropriate employee's house or at the office of an associated organization located in a different city.

It is important to realize that disaster recovery planning isn't just for large businesses. In fact, disasters such as a fire or computer malfunction can cause a small company to go out of business if its data is not backed up. Measures as straightforward as backing up data daily and storing the backups in a fire-resistant safe at the owner's house with a plan regarding how that data can be quickly reinstated on a new system or otherwise used for business continuity can go a long way in protecting a small business. Companies that are considering using cloud computing services should find out what type of outages are to be expected (such as for regular maintenance) and what type of advance notice will be sent regarding these outages, as well as what type of disaster recovery services (such as switching to alternate servers if the main servers go down) are available.

The importance of a good disaster recovery plan was made obvious following the collapse of the World Trade Center Twin Towers in 2001. Minutes after the first airplane hit the towers, corporate executives, disaster recovery firms, and backup storage companies began arranging for employees and backup data to be moved to alternate sites. Employees at the data storage company Recall Corporation spent the day of the attack gathering backup tapes belonging to clients located in and near the attacks, using barcode scanners to locate the needed 30,000 tapes out of the 2 million in their secure storage facility. Bond trader Cantor Fitzgerald, which lost 700 employees and all the equipment and data located in its WTC offices, relocated to a prearranged hot site where employees received backup tapes the day after the attack, and it was able to begin trading the next morning. Although Cantor Fitzgerald—like the other organizations and businesses located in the WTC—suffered enormous human loss, good disaster recovery planning enabled Cantor Fitzgerald to restore the records containing client accounts and portfolios completely, avoiding an additional economic disaster related to this tragedy.

SOFTWARE PIRACY AND DIGITAL COUNTERFEITING

Instead of stealing an existing computer program, object, or other valuable that belongs to someone else, *software piracy* and *digital counterfeiting* involve creating duplicates of these items, and then selling them or using them as authentic items.

Software Piracy

Software piracy, the unauthorized copying of a computer program, is illegal in the United States and many other—but not all—countries. Because of the ease with which computers can create exact copies of a software program, software piracy is a widespread problem.

> **Software piracy.** The unauthorized copying of a computer program.

According to a 2009 report from the *Business Software Alliance* (*BSA*)—an organization that was formed by a number of the world's leading software developers and that has antipiracy programs in 65 countries worldwide—approximately 41% of all software installed on personal computers globally (and about 20% of all software in the United States) is installed illegally. The report estimates that the annual monetary loss to software vendors as the result of software piracy is more than $50 billion worldwide.

Software piracy can take many forms, including individuals making illegal copies of programs to give to friends, businesses installing software on more computers than permitted in the program's *end-user license agreement* or *EULA* (see Figure 15-9), computer retailers installing unlicensed copies of software on computers sold to consumers, and large-scale operations in which the software and its packaging are illegally duplicated and then sold as supposedly legitimate products. Pirated software—as well as pirated music CDs and movie DVDs—are commonly offered for sale at online auctions; they can also be downloaded from some Web sites and peer-to-peer file sharing services. Creating and distributing pirated copies of any type of *intellectual property* (such as software, music, and movies) is illegal. Intellectual property is discussed in more detail in Chapter 16.

This software can be installed on one primary device and one portable device to be used by a single user.

FIGURE 15-9
An end-user license agreement (EULA).
An EULA specifies the number of computers on which the software can be installed and other restrictions for use.

FIGURE 15-10
Digital counterfeiting.
Documents commonly counterfeited include currency, credit cards, driver's licenses, passports, and checks.

Digital Counterfeiting

The availability of high-quality, full-color imaging products (such as scanners, color printers, and color copiers) has made **digital counterfeiting**—creating counterfeit copies of items (such as currency and other printed resources) using computers and other types of digital equipment—easier and less costly than in the recent past. The U.S. Secret Service estimates that more than 60% of all counterfeit money today is produced digitally—up from 1% in 1996.

With digital counterfeiting, the bill (or other item to be counterfeited) is either color-copied or it is scanned into a computer and then printed. In addition to counterfeiting currency, other items that are digitally counterfeited include fake business checks, credit cards, printed collectibles (such as baseball cards or celebrity autographs), and fake identification papers (such as corporate IDs, driver's licenses, passports, and visas)—see Figure 15-10.

Counterfeiting is illegal in the United States and is taken very seriously. For creating or knowingly circulating counterfeit currency, for instance, offenders can face up to 15 years in prison for each offense. In spite of the risk of prosecution, counterfeiting of U.S. currency and other documents is a growing problem both in the United States and in other countries. Although the majority of counterfeit currency is produced by serious criminals (such as organized crime, gangs, and terrorist organizations), the Secret Service has seen an increase in counterfeiting among high school and college students. This is attributed primarily to the ease of creating counterfeit bills—although not necessarily high-quality counterfeit bills—using digital technology. Because the paper used with real U.S. bills is very expensive and cannot legally be made by paper

>**Digital counterfeiting.** The use of computers or other types of digital equipment to make illegal copies of currency, checks, collectibles, and other items.

mills for any other purpose and because U.S. bills contain a number of other characteristics that are difficult to reproduce accurately, as discussed in more detail shortly, the majority of the counterfeit money made by amateurs is easily detectable.

Protecting Against Software Piracy and Digital Counterfeiting

Software piracy and digital counterfeiting affect individuals, as well as businesses and the government. For instance, some software companies charge higher prices and have less money available for research and development because of the losses from software pirates, which ultimately hurts law-abiding consumers. In addition, individuals and businesses that unknowingly accept counterfeit currency lose the face value of that currency if it is identified as counterfeit while it is in their possession, and they risk legal issues if they knowingly pass the counterfeit bills on to others. Some tools currently being used to curb software piracy and digital counterfeiting are discussed next.

Software Antipiracy Tools

One tool the software industry is using in an attempt to prevent software piracy is education. By educating businesses and consumers about the legal use of software and the possible negative consequences associated with breaking antipiracy laws, the industry hopes to reduce the use of illegal software significantly. To counteract piracy performed because of time or convenience issues, many software companies offer consumers the option of downloading software via the Internet—giving them a legal option for obtaining software that is as fast and convenient as downloading a pirated version. Some software manufacturers have launched extensive public relations campaigns—such as including information on their Web sites, in product information, and in advertisements—to inform consumers what software piracy is, and why they should not commit it or buy pirated software.

Another antipiracy tool is requiring a unique activation code (often called a *registration code* or *product key*) before the software can be installed (for commercial software) or before certain key features of a program are unlocked (for shareware or demo software). Typically the activation code is included in the product packaging (for software purchased on CD or DVD) or is displayed on the screen or sent to the user via e-mail once payment is made (for downloaded software). A related tool is checking the validity of a software installation before upgrades or other resources related to the program can be accessed. For instance, Microsoft checks a user's Windows installation before the user is allowed to download software from Microsoft's Web site (such as templates for Microsoft Office or gadgets for the Windows Vista Sidebar)—if their operating system is identified as invalid, users cannot download the resources. The goal of these techniques is to make pirated software unusable enough so that individuals will buy the licensed software.

Other antipiracy techniques used by software companies include watching online auction sites and requesting the removal of suspicious items, as well as buying pirated copies of software via Web sites and then filing lawsuits against the sellers. The increase in prosecution of consumers for illegally selling or sharing software (and other types of digital content, such as music and movies) may also help reduce some types of piracy and encourage individuals to obtain legal copies of these products. In 2009, for instance, *Operation Fastlink* (a Department of Justice initiative designed to combat online piracy worldwide that is credited with removing more than $50 million worth of illegally copied software, games, movies, and music from illicit distribution channels) resulted in its 60th felony conviction. In another recent instance, a Virginia man pleaded guilty to selling more than $1 million worth of counterfeit software on eBay and he is facing up to 25 years in prison.

One new option for software vendors is incorporating code into their programs that is designed to inform the vendor when pirated copies of its software is being used or when its software is being used in another manner that violates the terms of the software license. For instance, commercial software that contains the newest version of V.i Labs *CodeArmor Intelligence* software is designed to detect and report products in use that

ONLINE VIDEO

Go to the Chapter 15 page at **www.cengage.com/ computerconcepts/np/uc13** to watch the "New Currency Design and Counterfeiting" video clip.

have been tampered with (such as products whose licensing features have been disabled and then resold as legitimate products), as well as products that are being used with more computers than allowed by the software license. Once piracy is detected, information about the infringement is sent to the software vendor's Web-based piracy dashboard. This information includes identifying data about the user of the pirated software (such as the user's domain name or IP address and a link to its location on Google Maps—see Figure 15-11) that can be used to help the vendor identify the user of the pirated software in order to pursue legal actions. It also provides the vendor with useful data about the overall state of piracy of their products, in order to help the company make appropriate business decisions regarding the distribution channels and the safeguards used with its products.

 FIGURE 15-11

Antipiracy software. This software identifies businesses (including their physical locations) using a pirated version of the vendor's software.

Digital Counterfeiting Prevention

To prevent the counterfeiting of U.S. currency, the Treasury Department releases new currency designs every 7 to 10 years. These new designs (such as the new $5 bill released in 2008 and shown in Figure 15-12) contain features (such as *microprinting, watermarks,* and a *security thread*) that make the new currency much more difficult to duplicate than older currency. Because the watermarks and security thread are embedded in the paper, counterfeiters are unable to duplicate those features when creating counterfeit bills either from scratch or by bleaching the ink out of existing lower-denomination bills and reprinting them with higher denominations. Consequently, counterfeit copies of bills using the new designs are easy to detect just by holding them up to the light and looking for the proper watermark or security thread. In addition, digital imaging equipment (such as color copiers and scanners) is equipped with technologies that can be used to track currency and other counterfeit items created with those devices. For example, many color copiers print invisible codes on copied documents, making counterfeit money copied on those machines traceable. This type of technology is also thought to be incorporated into many scanners. In fact, printer and scanner manufacturer Canon has revealed that it has been incorporating anticounterfeiting technologies into its products since 1992, but the company is prohibited by the government from disclosing any information about those technologies.

 FIGURE 15-12

Anticounterfeiting measures used with U.S. currency.

Prevention measures for the counterfeiting of other types of documents—such as checks and identification cards—include using RFID tags, *digital watermarks*, and other difficult-to-reproduce content. As discussed in more detail in Chapter 16, a digital watermark is a subtle alteration that is not noticeable when the work is viewed or played but that can be read using special software to authenticate or identify the owner of the item. Finally, educating consumers about how the appearance of fake products differs from that of authentic products is a vital step in the ongoing battle against counterfeiting.

MICROPRINTING
Extremely small print that is very difficult to reproduce appears in three different locations on the front of the bill (in the left and right borders, at the top of the shield on the Great Seal, and in between the columns of the shield), though it is hard to see without a magnifying glass.

SECURITY THREAD
A plastic security thread embedded in the paper contains the letters "USA" followed by the number "5"; it can be seen when the bill is held up to the light and glows blue when placed in front of an ultraviolet light.

COLORS
Harder to match colors, such as shades of yellow and purple, have been added to some details.

WATERMARKS
Watermark images containing the number "5" located to the right and left of the portrait are incorporated into the paper itself and are visible when the bill is held up to the light (not visible in this photograph).

WHY BE CONCERNED ABOUT INFORMATION PRIVACY?

Privacy is usually defined as the state of being concealed or free from unauthorized intrusion. The term **information privacy** refers to the rights of individuals and companies to control how information about them is collected and used. The problem of how to protect personal privacy—that is, how to keep personal information private—existed long before computers entered the picture. For example, sealing wax and unique signet rings were used centuries ago to seal letters, wills, and other personal documents to guard against their content being revealed to unauthorized individuals, as well as to alert the recipient if such an intrusion occurred while the document was in transit. But today's computers, with their ability to store, duplicate, and manipulate large quantities of data—combined with the fact that databases containing our personal information can be accessed and shared via the Internet—have added a new twist to the issue of personal privacy.

As discussed in Chapters 8 and 9, one concern of many individuals is the privacy of their Web site activities and e-mail messages. Cookies and spyware are possible privacy risks, and e-mail and other documents can be read if intercepted by another individual during transit unless they are encrypted. For businesses and employees, there is the additional issue of whether or not Web activities, e-mail, and instant messages sent through a company network are private. In addition, businesses need to make sure they comply with privacy laws regarding the protection and the security of the private information they store on their servers. Recently, there has been an unprecedented number of high-profile data breaches—some via hacking and other network intrusions discussed in Chapter 9, and others due to lost or stolen hardware, or carelessness with papers or storage media containing Social Security numbers or other sensitive data. Since every data breach occurring today is a risk to information privacy, protecting the data stored in databases today is an important concern for everyone. Other privacy concerns are *spam* and other marketing activities, *electronic surveillance*, and *electronic monitoring*. These concerns, along with precautions that can be taken to safeguard information privacy, are discussed throughout the remainder of this chapter.

ASK THE EXPERT

epic.org **Lillie Coney,** Associate Director, Electronic Privacy Information Center

What is the biggest Internet-related privacy risk for individuals today?

The biggest Internet-related privacy risk for individuals is the rapid consolidation of personal information based on online activity. Today, Web sites often include privacy statements or policies. However, the online experience allows the collection of unlimited amounts of personal information, such as search engine requests and Web sites visited, and the information you choose to share online may be sold to strangers or otherwise shared with others. For instance, in 2007, Facebook introduced the "Beacon" application, which monitored Facebook users who shopped at third-party Web sites and shared users' purchases with their friends via Facebook. The "Beacon" application resulted in a number of lawsuits and Facebook has suspended its use.

The race to monetize Internet activities also leaves the privacy of users in a vulnerable position because of the lack of regulation and government oversight. Furthermore, Internet privacy protection is undermined when online service providers promote anti-privacy proposals as privacy protection.

>**Privacy.** The state of being concealed or free from unauthorized intrusion. >**Information privacy.** The rights of individuals and companies to control how information about them is collected and used.

DATABASES, ELECTRONIC PROFILING, SPAM, AND OTHER MARKETING ACTIVITIES

There are marketing activities that can be considered privacy risks or, at least, a potential invasion of privacy. These include *databases, electronic profiling*, and *spam*.

Databases and Electronic Profiling

Information about individuals can be located in many different databases. For example, most educational institutions have databases containing student information, most organizations use an employee database to hold employee information, and most physicians and health insurance providers maintain databases containing individuals' medical information. If these databases are adequately protected from hackers and other unauthorized individuals and if the data is not transported on a portable computer or other device that may be vulnerable to loss or theft, these databases do not pose a significant privacy concern to consumers because the information can rarely be shared without the individuals' permission. However, the data stored in these types of databases is not always sufficiently protected and has been breached quite often in the past. Consequently, these databases, along with two other types of databases—*marketing databases* and *government databases*—that are typically associated with a higher risk of personal privacy violations and are discussed next, are of growing concern to privacy advocates.

Marketing databases contain marketing and demographic data about people, such as where they live and what products they buy. This information is used for marketing purposes, such as sending advertisements that fit each individual's interests (via regular mail or e-mail) or trying to sign people up over the phone for some type of service. Virtually anytime you provide information about yourself online or offline—for example, when you subscribe to a magazine, fill out a sweepstakes entry or product registration card, or buy a product or service using a credit card—there is a good chance that the information will find its way into a marketing database.

Marketing databases are also used in conjunction with Web activities, such as social network activity and searches performed via some personalized search services. For instance, the data stored on Facebook, MySpace, and other social networking sites can be gathered and used for advertising purposes by marketing companies, and the activities of users of personalized search services (where users log in to use the service) can be tracked and that data can be used for marketing purposes. There has been some objection to several of these possible privacy risks. For instance, Facebook met with significant objection to its *Beacon* advertising service. Beacon, introduced in late 2007, was designed to track members' Web purchases, movie rentals, and other Web activities on more than 40 partner sites and share those purchases and activities with the users' Facebook friends (one user discovered that his Facebook friends had been notified that he had bought an engagement ring before he had even proposed). In response to user complaints, Facebook changed the service to work only on an *opt-in* basis, where it would only be enabled at a member's request. However, it was still ordered to pay $9.5 million in late 2009 to fund a nonprofit privacy organization in response to one class action lawsuit related to the Beacon service. And Google, with its vast array of services that collect enormous amounts of data about individuals, worries many privacy advocates. For instance, Google may have data stored about your search history (Google search site), browsing history (Google Chrome), e-mail (Gmail), appointments (Google Calendar), telephone messages (Google Voice), photos (Picasa Web Albums), reading history (Google Books), and

> **Marketing database.** A collection of data about people that is stored in a large database and used for marketing purposes.

SOC

medical history (Google Health). While Google allows users to *opt out* of collecting some data (such as by not signing into a service) and states that the data stored on separate servers is not combined, the vast amount of collected data is a concern to some.

Information about individuals is also available in **government databases**. Some information, such as Social Security earnings and income tax returns, is confidential and can legally be seen only by authorized individuals. Other information—such as birth records, marriage certificates, and divorce information, as well as property purchases, assessments, liens, and tax values—is available to the public, including to the marketing companies that specialize in creating marketing databases. One emerging government database application is the creation of a *national ID system* that links driver's license databases across the country. Although controversial, this system is mandated by the *Real ID Act* that was passed in 2005, which also requires states to meet new federal standards for driver's licenses and other identification cards (such as the inclusion of a barcode or other machine-readable technology that can be used in conjunction with the ID database). If the proposed *Pass ID Act* that was introduced in 2009 passes, however, the requirement that all state databases be linked will be removed.

In the past, the data about any one individual was stored in a variety of separate locations, such as at different government agencies, individual retail stores, the person's bank and credit card companies, and so forth. Because it would be extremely time consuming to locate all the information about one person from all these different places, there was a fairly high level of information privacy. Today, however, most of an individual's data is stored on computers that can communicate with each other via the Internet, which means accessing personal information about someone is much easier than it used to be. For example, a variety of public information about individuals is available free through the Internet (see Figure 15-13); there are also paid services that can perform online database searches for you. Although often this ability to search online databases

FIGURE 15-13

A variety of searchable databases are available via the Internet.

PROPERTY VALUE SEARCH
Some states permit searches for property located in that state, such as displaying the owner's name, address, and a link to additional information including property value for the supplied owner name.

VITAL RECORDS SEARCH
Some counties and states allow searches for documents related to marriages, divorces, births, legal judgments, deeds, liens, powers of attorney, and so forth.

ADDRESS NUMBER AND PHONE NUMBER SEARCH
Any information listed in a U.S. telephone book can be found using this site. You can search either by name or telephone number to view the available information.

>**Government database.** A collection of data about people that is collected and maintained by the government.

When you make an electronic transaction, information about who you are and what you buy is recorded, usually in a database.

Databases containing the identities of people and what they buy are sold to marketing companies.

The marketing companies add the new data to their marketing databases; they can then reorganize the data in ways that might be valuable to other companies.

The marketing companies create lists of individuals matching the specific needs of companies; the companies buy the lists for their own marketing purposes.

FIGURE 15-14

How electronic profiling might work.

is an advantage—such as checking the background of a potential employee or looking up a misplaced phone number—it does raise privacy concerns. In response to the increased occurrence of identity theft (discussed in detail in Chapter 9), some local governments have removed birth and death information from their available online database records.

Collecting in-depth information about an individual is known as **electronic profiling**. Marketing companies often use data acquired from a variety of sources—such as from product and service purchases that are tied to personally identifiable information, as well as from public information like property values, vehicle registrations, births, marriages, and deaths—to create electronic profiles of individuals for marketing purposes. Electronic profiles are generally designed to provide specific information and can include an individual's name, current and previous addresses, telephone number, marital status, number and age of children, spending habits, and product preferences. The information retrieved from electronic profiles is then sold to companies upon request to be used for marketing purposes (see Figure 15-14). For example, one company might request a list of all individuals in a particular state whose street addresses are considered to be in an affluent area and who buy baby products. Another company might request a list of all SUV owners in a particular

city who have not purchased a car in five years. Still another company may want a list of business travelers who fly to the East Coast frequently.

Most businesses and Web sites that collect personal information have a **privacy policy** (see Figure 15-15) that discloses how the personal information you provide will be used. As long as their actions do not violate their privacy policy, it is legal for businesses to sell the personal data that they collect. There are some problems with privacy policies, however, such as the fact that they are sometimes difficult to decipher and the reality that most people

FIGURE 15-15

Privacy policies. Web site privacy policies explain how your personal information might be used.

This indicates that your personal information may be used to keep you updated on products that might interest you.

This indicates that your personal information may be disclosed to third parties, unless you opt out.

> **Electronic profiling.** Using electronic means to collect a variety of in-depth information about an individual, such as name, address, income, and buying habits. > **Privacy policy.** A policy, commonly posted on a company's Web site, that explains how personal information provided to that company will be used.

SOC

do not take the time to read them before using a site. In addition, many businesses periodically change their privacy policies without warning, requiring consumers to reread privacy policies frequently or risk their personal information being used in a manner that they did not agree to when the information was initially provided. Some companies notify customers by e-mail when their privacy policies change but, more commonly, they expect customers to check the current policy periodically and notify the business if any new actions are objectionable.

Spam and Other Marketing Activities

Spam refers to unsolicited e-mail sent to a large group of individuals at one time. The electronic equivalent of junk mail (see Figure 15-16), spam is most often used to sell products or services to individuals. Spam is also used in phishing schemes and other dot cons and is sent frequently via botnets, as discussed in Chapter 9 (the text message spam shown in Figure 15-16 is an example of a phishing spam message). A great deal of spam involves health-related products (such as medicine or weight loss systems), counterfeit products (such as watches and medicine), pornography, and new—and often fraudulent—business opportunities and stock deals. Spam can also be generated by individuals forwarding e-mail messages they receive (such as jokes, recipes, or notices of possible new privacy or health concerns) to everyone in their address books. In addition to spam, most individuals receive marketing e-mails either from companies they directly provided with their e-mail addresses or from other companies that acquired their e-mail addresses from a third party to whom that information was provided (such as from a partner site or via a purchased mailing list). While these latter types of marketing e-mail messages do not technically fit the definition of spam since they were permission-based, many individuals consider them to be spam. Spam can also be sent via IM (called *spim*); to mobile phones (called *mobile phone spam* or *SMS spam*); to Facebook, MySpace, and Twitter pages and via other social networking communications methods; and to fax machines.

The sheer volume of spam is staggering today. For instance, Symantec's MessageLabs recently estimated that more than 90% of all e-mail messages are now spam. At best, large volumes of spam are an annoyance to recipients and can slow down a mail server's delivery of important messages. At worst, spam can disable a mail network completely, or it can cause recipients to miss or lose important e-mail messages because those messages have been caught in a *spam filter* (discussed shortly) or were accidentally deleted by the recipient while he or she was deleting a large number of spam e-mail messages. Most Internet users spend several minutes each day dealing with spam, making spam very expensive for businesses in terms of lost productivity, consumption of communications bandwidth, and drain of technical support. Spam sent to a mobile phone (either via text message or e-mail) is also expensive for end users that have a limited data or text message allowance.

FIGURE 15-16
Examples of spam.

E-MAIL SPAM

TEXT MESSAGE SPAM

>**Spam.** Unsolicited, bulk e-mail sent over the Internet.

One of the most common ways of getting on a spam mailing list is by having your e-mail address entered into a marketing database, which can happen when you sign up for a free online service or use your e-mail address to register a product or make an online purchase. Spammers also use software to gather e-mail addresses from Web pages, message board posts, and social networking sites. Many individuals view spam as an invasion of privacy because it arrives on computers without permission and costs them time and other resources (bandwidth, mailbox space, and hard drive space, for instance).

Most spam is legal, but there are requirements that must be adhered to in order for it to be legal. For instance, the *CAN-SPAM Act of 2003* established requirements (such as using truthful subject lines and honoring remove requests) for commercial e-mailers, as well as specified penalties for companies and individuals that break the law. While the CAN-SPAM Act has not reduced the amount of spam circulated today, it has increased the number of spammers prosecuted for sending spam. In fact, several spammers have been convicted in recent years. They have either been fined or sent to prison, and more are awaiting trial. For instance, one spammer was recently ordered to pay $230 million to MySpace for spamming MySpace users and another was ordered to pay Facebook a record $873 million for spamming its members.

Protecting the Privacy of Personal Information

There are a number of precautions that can be taken to protect the privacy of personal information. Safeguarding your e-mail address and other personal information is a good start. You can also surf anonymously, *opt out* of some marketing activities, and use filters and other tools to limit your exposure to spam. Businesses also need to take adequate measures to protect the privacy of information stored on their servers and storage media. These precautions are discussed next.

Safeguard Your E-Mail Address

Protecting your e-mail address is one of the best ways to avoid spam. One way to accomplish this is to use one private e-mail address for family, friends, colleagues, and other trusted sources. For online shopping, signing up for free offers, message boards, product registration, and other activities that typically lead to junk e-mail, use a *disposable* or **throw-away e-mail address**—such as a second address obtained from your ISP or a free e-mail address from Yahoo! Mail, AOL Mail, Windows Live Hotmail, or Google's Gmail (see Figure 15-17). Although you will want to check your alternate e-mail address periodically (to check for online shopping receipts or shipping notifications, for instance), this precaution can prevent a great deal of spam from getting to your regular e-mail account.

Another advantage of using a throw-away e-mail address for only noncritical applications is that you can quit using it and obtain a new one if spam begins to get overwhelming or too annoying. To help with this, some ISPs (such as EarthLink) provide disposable anonymous e-mail addresses to their subscribers—e-mail messages sent to a subscriber's anonymous address are forwarded to the subscriber's account until the disposable address is deleted by the subscriber. Consequently, individuals can easily change disposable

FIGURE 15-17
Gmail. Free Web mail services like Gmail can be used for throw-away e-mail addresses, in addition to regular e-mail addresses.

>**Throw-away e-mail address.** An e-mail address used only for nonessential purposes and activities that may result in spam; the address can be disposed of and replaced if spam becomes a problem.

SOC

addresses when they begin to receive too much spam or when the disposable address is not needed any longer. There are also *anonymous e-mail services* (such as the one provided by Anonymizer *Nyms*) that allow users to create and delete anonymous e-mail addresses; messages sent to the anonymous e-mail addresses are forwarded to the user's specified e-mail account. These services typically cost about $20 per year.

To comply with truth-in-advertising laws, an *unsubscribe e-mail address* included in an unsolicited e-mail must be a working address. If you receive a marketing e-mail from a reputable source, you may be able to unsubscribe by clicking the supplied link or otherwise following the unsubscribe instructions. Since spam from less-legitimate sources often has unsubscribe links that do not work or that are present only to verify that your e-mail address is genuine—a very valuable piece of information for future use—many privacy experts recommend never replying to or trying to unsubscribe from any spam.

Be Cautious of Revealing Personal Information

In addition to protecting your real e-mail address, protecting your personal information is a critical step toward safeguarding your privacy. Consequently, it makes sense to be cautious about revealing your private information to anyone. Privacy tips for safeguarding personal information include the following:

> Read a Web site's privacy policy (if one exists) before providing any personal information. Look for a phrase saying that the company will not share your information with other companies under any circumstances. If the Web site reserves the right to share your information if the company is sold or unless you specifically notify them otherwise, it is best to assume that any information you provide will eventually be shared with others—do not use the site if that is unacceptable to you.

> Avoid putting too many personal details about yourself on your Web site or on a social networking site. If you would like to post photographs or other personal documents on a Web site for faraway friends and family members to see, consider using a photo sharing site that allows you to restrict access to your photos (such as *Flickr, Snapfish*, or *Fotki*).

> Beware of Web sites offering prizes or the chance to earn free merchandise in exchange for your personal information. Chances are good that the information will be sold to direct marketers, which will likely result in additional spam. If you choose to sign up for services from these Web sites, use your throw-away e-mail address.

> Consider using privacy software, such as *Anonymous Surfing* (see Figure 15-18) or *Privacy Guardian* to hide your personal information as you browse the Web so it is not revealed and your activities cannot be tracked by marketers.

> Just because a Web site or registration form asks for personal information, that does not mean you have to give it. Supply only the required information (these fields are often marked with an asterisk or are colored differently than nonrequired fields—if not, you can try leaving fields blank and see if the form will still be accepted). If you are asked for more personal information than you are comfortable providing, look for an alternate Web site for the product or information you are seeking. As a rule of thumb, do not provide an e-mail address (or else use a throw-away address) if you do not want to receive offers or other e-mail from that company.

> If you are using a public computer (such as at a school, a library, or an Internet café), be sure to remove any personal information and settings stored on the computer during your session. You can use browser options to delete this data manually from the computer before you leave (use the *Browsing history* option on the General tab of the Internet Options dialog box in Internet Explorer to delete this data). To prevent the deleted data from being recovered, run the Windows Disk Cleanup program on the hard drive, making sure that the options for Temporary

▼ FIGURE 15-18
Anonymous surfing software can be used to protect your privacy online.

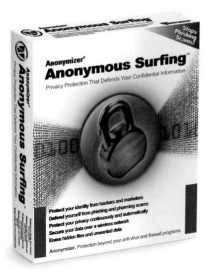

Internet Files and the Recycle Bin are selected during the Disk Cleanup process. An easier option is using the *private browsing* mode offered by some browsers (such as Internet Explorer's *InPrivate* or Chrome's *Incognito* modes (see Figure 15-19) that allow you to browse the Web without leaving any history (such as browsing history, temporary Internet files, form data, cookies, usernames, and passwords) on the computer you are using. In either case, be sure to log out of any Web sites you were using before leaving the computer.

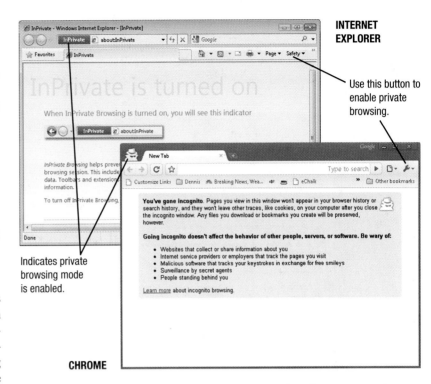

INTERNET EXPLORER

Use this button to enable private browsing.

Indicates private browsing mode is enabled.

CHROME

Use Filters and Opt Out

While keeping your personal information as private as possible can help to reduce spam and other direct marketing activities, *filtering* can also be helpful. Some ISPs automatically block all e-mail messages originating from known or suspected spammers so those e-mail messages never reach the individuals' mailboxes; other ISPs flag suspicious e-mail messages as possible spam, based on their content or subject lines, to warn individuals that those messages may contain spam. To deal with spam that makes it to your computer, you can use an **e-mail filter**—a tool for automatically sorting your incoming e-mail messages. E-mail filters used to capture spam are called **spam filters**. Many e-mail programs have built-in spam filters that identify possible spam and either flag it or move it to a Spam or Junk E-mail folder. Individuals can typically change the spam settings used in their e-mail program to indicate the actions that should be taken with suspected spam. In addition, they can create e-mail filters in their e-mail program, or they can use third-party filtering software to customize their spam filtering further. Many spam filters can also "learn" what each user views as spam based on the user identifying e-mail messages that were classified incorrectly (either spam messages placed in the Inbox or legitimate messages placed in the Spam folder) by the spam filter. The user typically provides this information by clicking a button such as *Report Spam* or *Not Spam* when the message is selected; the spam filter uses this input to classify messages from that sender correctly in the future. Businesses can set up spam filters in-house, but they are increasingly turning to dedicated *antispam appliances* to filter out spam without increasing the load on the company e-mail server.

Custom e-mail filters are used to route messages automatically to particular folders based on stated criteria. For example, you can specify that e-mail messages with keywords frequently used in spam subject lines (such as *free, porn, opportunity, last chance, weight, pharmacy*, and similar terms) be routed into a folder named *Possible Spam*, and you can specify that all e-mail messages from your boss's e-mail address be routed into an *Urgent* folder. Filtering can help you find important messages in your Inbox by preventing it from becoming cluttered with spam. However, you need to be sure to check your Possible Spam or Junk E-mail folder periodically to locate any e-mail messages mistakenly filed

FIGURE 15-19
Private browsing can protect your Web surfing privacy at public computers.

>**E-mail filter.** A tool that automatically sorts your incoming e-mail messages based on specific criteria. >**Spam filter.** An e-mail filter used to redirect spam from a user's Inbox.

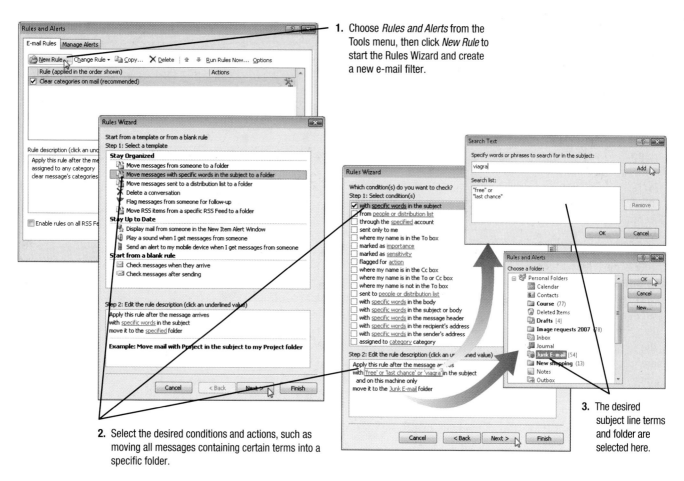

1. Choose *Rules and Alerts* from the Tools menu, then click *New Rule* to start the Rules Wizard and create a new e-mail filter.

2. Select the desired conditions and actions, such as moving all messages containing certain terms into a specific folder.

3. The desired subject line terms and folder are selected here.

FIGURE 15-20
E-mail filtering with Microsoft Outlook.

there—especially before you permanently delete those messages. Creating a new e-mail filter in Microsoft Outlook is shown in Figure 15-20.

Mobile users who receive Web-based e-mail via mobile phones can use the filters available via their Web mail provider to filter out spam. There are also some mobile spam filter applications available for some mobile phones. To block spam sent via text message, most carriers allow you to create an alias for your phone's e-mail address (which typically begins with your mobile phone number) and then block messages sent to that address, in order to prevent receiving text message spam sent by spammers simply guessing your mobile number.

Another alternative for reducing the amount of spam you receive is to **opt out**. *Opting out* refers to following a predesignated procedure to remove yourself from marketing lists, or otherwise preventing your personal information from being obtained by or shared with others. By opting out, you instruct companies you do business with (such as your bank, insurance company, investment company, or an online store) not to share your personal information with third parties. You can also opt out of being contacted by direct and online marketing companies.

To opt out from a particular company or direct marketing association, you can contact them directly—many organizations include opt-out instructions in the privacy policies posted on their Web sites. For Web sites that use registered accounts for repeat visitors,

TIP

Register both your landline and mobile phone numbers with the *National Do Not Call Registry* by going to www.donotcall.gov to prevent telemarketing calls from companies you do not have a business relationship with.

> **Opt out.** To request that you be removed from marketing activities or that your information not be shared with other companies.

opt-out options are sometimes included in your personal settings and can be activated by modifying your personal settings for that site. Opt-out instructions for financial institutions and credit card companies are often included in the disclosure statements that are periodically mailed to customers; they can also often be found on the company's Web site.

To assist consumers with the opt-out process, there are a number of Web sites, such as the *Center for Democracy and Technology* and the *PrivacyRightsNow!* Web sites, which provide opt-out tools for consumers. For example, some sites help visitors create opt-out letters that can be sent to the companies in order to opt out. For online marketing activities, organizations—such as the *Network Advertising Initiative* (*NAI*)—have tools on their Web sites to help consumers opt out of online targeted ads. Typically, this process replaces an advertiser's marketing cookie with an *opt-out cookie*. The opt-out cookie prevents any more marketing cookies belonging to that particular advertiser from being placed on the user's hard drive as long as the opt-out cookie is present (usually until the user deletes the opt-out cookie file, either intentionally or unintentionally).

At the present time, opting-out procedures are confusing and time-consuming, and they do not always work well. Consequently, some privacy groups are pushing to change to an *opt-in* process, in which individuals would need to **opt in** (request participation in) to a particular marketing activity before companies can collect or share any personal data (as is the case in the European Union). In fact, Wal-Mart recently changed its privacy policy to share information with third parties only if customers opt in. However, the general practice in the U.S. business community today is to use your information as allowed for by each privacy policy unless you specifically opt out.

FURTHER EXPLORATION (Go)

Go to the Chapter 15 page at **www.cengage.com/ computerconcepts/np/uc13** for links to information about protecting your privacy online.

Secure Servers and Otherwise Protect Personal Information

Any business that stores personal information about employees, customers, or other individuals must take adequate security measures to protect the privacy of that information. As discussed in Chapter 9, secure servers and encryption can protect the data stored on a server; firewalls and access systems can protect against unauthorized access. To prevent personal information from being sent intentionally or inadvertently via e-mail, organizations can use e-mail encryption systems that automatically encrypt e-mail messages containing certain keywords. For instance, some hospitals use encryption systems that scan all outgoing e-mail messages and attachments and then automatically encrypt all messages that appear to contain patient-identifiable information, such as a Social Security number, medical record number, patient name, or medical term like "cancer." The recipient of an encrypted e-mail message typically receives a link to a secure Web site to log in and view the encrypted e-mail message. Similar systems are used by banks and other businesses. Businesses also need to be very careful with papers, portable hard drives, and other media that contain personal data. For instance, many recent data breaches have occurred because of carelessness, such as papers containing personal information being found in dumpsters, lost in transit, or faxed to the wrong individual.

Ensuring that the private data stored by a business is adequately protected is increasingly the responsibility of a *chief privacy officer* (*CPO*)—a rapidly growing new position in business today. Typically, CPOs are responsible for ensuring privacy laws are complied with, identifying the data in a company that needs to be protected, developing policies to protect that data, and responding to any incidents that occur. Another issue that must

> **Opt in.** To request that you be included in marketing activities or that your information be shared with other companies.

SOC

be dealt with by CPOs is the changing definition of what information is regarded as personal and, therefore, needs to be safeguarded. For instance, the head of the European Union's group of data privacy regulators announced in early 2008 that IP addresses should be regarded as personal information. If that view becomes widespread or integrated into privacy laws, it will have major implications on search sites and other businesses that store the IP address of individuals using online services.

Properly Dispose of Hardware Containing Data

A final consideration for protecting the privacy of personal information for both individuals and businesses is protecting the information located on paper documents and hardware (such as old backup media, used CDs, obsolete computers, and old mobile phones) that are to be disposed of. Papers, CDs, DVDs, and other media containing sensitive data should be shredded (see Figure 15-21), and the hard drives of computers to be disposed of should be *wiped*— overwritten several times using special *disk-wiping* or *disk-erasing* software—before they are sold or recycled. Unlike the data on a drive that has merely been erased or even reformatted (which can still be recovered), data on a properly wiped drive is very difficult or impossible to recover.

Wiping is typically viewed as an acceptable precaution for deleting sensitive data (such as Web site passwords and tax returns) from hard drives and other storage media belonging to individuals, as well as for storage media to be reused within an organization. However, before disposing of storage media containing sensitive data, businesses should consider physically destroying the media, such as by shredding or melting the hardware. To help with this process, *data destruction services* can be used, as discussed in the Inside the Industry box. To ensure that all hardware containing business data is properly disposed of, it is important for all businesses today to develop and implement a policy (often called a *media sanitization* or *data destruction policy*) for destroying data that is no longer needed.

FIGURE 15-21

Media disposal.

When disposing of CDs, DVDs, and other storage media, the media should be shredded to ensure the information on the media is destroyed.

CAUTION CAUTION CAUTION CAUTION CAUTION CAUTION CAUT

When upgrading your mobile phone, be careful not to expose the personal data stored on your old phone to others. Before disposing of or recycling it, be sure to reset your mobile phone to its factory settings to clear all personal data from the phone.

ELECTRONIC SURVEILLANCE AND MONITORING

There are many ways electronic tools can be used to watch individuals, listen in on their conversations, or monitor their activities. Some of these tools—such as devices used by individuals to eavesdrop on wireless telephone conversations—are not legal. Other products and technologies, such as the GPS devices that are built into some cars so they can be located if they are stolen or the monitoring ankle bracelets used for offenders sentenced to house arrest, are used solely for law enforcement purposes. Still other electronic tools, such as *computer monitoring software, video surveillance* equipment, and *presence technology*, discussed next, can often be used legally by individuals, by businesses in conjunction with *employee monitoring*, and by law enforcement agencies.

INSIDE THE INDUSTRY

Data Killers

With the vast amount of sensitive and classified data stored on business computers today, disposing of those devices or removing the data from those devices so they can be reused is an important issue. Business computers typically contain a wide variety of sensitive data that needs to be protected if the hard drive containing that data needs to be disposed of or will be reused by another employee. *Data destruction services* are designed for this purpose.

Data destruction ranges from purging the data (such as wiping the drive clean or degaussing (demagnetizing) the drive so the data cannot be restored) to destroying the drive physically. The level of destruction needed depends on the type of data being deleted and where the hardware will go next. For instance, purging might be appropriate for personal hard drives being sold and for business hard drives that will be reused within the company, but all business hard drives that will no longer be used within the company and that contain sensitive data should be physically destroyed.

While data destruction can be performed in-house, there are data destruction services designed for this purpose. Such services typically can purge, degauss, or shred hard drives and other media, depending on the customer's preference. Once a hard drive has been shredded (see the accompanying photo), it is virtually impossible for any data to be recovered

from the pieces. However, for extra security, drives containing extremely sensitive data can be degaussed and then shredded. To ensure drives are not lost or compromised in transit, most data destruction companies offer secure transportation to the destruction facility using tamper proof locked cases, and will provide signed and dated Certificates of Purging or Certificates of Destruction, when requested. Some even offer destruction on site, if the customer desires. Purged hard drives are returned to the customer; shredded hard drives are typically recycled.

Computer Monitoring Software

Computer monitoring software is used specifically for the purpose of recording keystrokes, logging the programs or Web sites accessed, or otherwise monitoring someone's computer activity. These programs are typically marketed toward parents (to check on their children's online activities), spouses (to determine if a spouse is having an affair, viewing pornography, or participating in other activities that are unacceptable to the other spouse), law enforcement agencies (to collect evidence against suspected criminals), or employers (to ensure employees are using company computers and time only for work-related or otherwise approved activities). Computer monitoring programs can keep a log of all computer keystrokes performed on a computer, record the activities taking place (such as the amount of time spent on and tasks performed via the Web or installed software), take screen shots of the screen at specified intervals, and more (see Figure 15-22). Computer monitoring software designed for businesses also typically provides a summary of the activities (such as the programs used or the Web sites visited) performed by all company computers. In addition, some

> **Computer monitoring software.** Software that can be used to record an individual's computer usage, such as capturing images of the screen, recording the actual keystrokes used, or creating a summary of Web sites and programs accessed.

SOC

Records time spent on Web sites, as well as the actual activities performed via those sites.

Captures the user's screen at specified intervals; can be played back to reenact the user's activities.

Summarizes all Web activity.

FIGURE 15-22
Computer monitoring software.

computer monitoring software can block specific Web sites, as well as notify a designated party (such as the parent or computer administrator) if the individual using the computer being monitored uses specified keywords (such as inappropriate language for children or terms referring to company secrets for employees, for instance) or visits a Web site deemed inappropriate.

Although it is legal to use computer monitoring software on your own computer or on the computers of your employees, installing it on other computers without the owners' knowledge to monitor their computer activity is usually illegal. A growing illegal use of computer monitoring software is the use of a *keystroke logging system* by hackers. A keystroke logging system is typically software-based, but it can also be implemented via a small piece of hardware that is installed between the system unit and the keyboard of a computer. In either case, it is used to record all keystrokes performed on the computer in order to capture usernames, passwords, and other sensitive data entered into the computer via the keyboard. Keystroke logging software can be installed on an individual's computer via malware, or it can be installed on public computers in person if the proper precautions are not taken. For instance, in 2008, a Colombian man pled guilty to installing keystroke logging software on computers located in hotel business centers and Internet cafés around the world; the software collected the personal information he needed to access the bank, payroll, brokerage, and other financial accounts of over 600 individuals. He was sentenced in mid-2009 to nine years in prison and ordered to pay $347,000 in restitution.

In addition to computer monitoring products designed for individuals and businesses, there are also computer monitoring programs available for use only by law enforcement and other government agencies. Like wiretapping, electronic monitoring of computer activity requires a court order or similar authorization to be legal (although the *USA PATRIOT Act* does allow the FBI to conduct a limited form of Internet surveillance first, such as to capture e-mail addresses or IP addresses used with traffic going into or coming from a suspect's computer). With proper authorization and cooperation from a suspect's ISP, law enforcement agencies can use computer monitoring software to intercept files and e-mail messages sent to or from a suspect's computer. If the documents are encrypted, keystroke logging software can be used to record e-mail messages and documents before they are encrypted, as well as to record the private keys to encrypt messages and files.

Video Surveillance

The idea of **video surveillance** is nothing new. Many retail stores, banks, office buildings, and other privately owned facilities that are open to the public routinely use closed circuit security cameras to monitor activities taking place at those facilities for security purposes. In recent years, however, video surveillance has been expanded to a number of additional public locations (such as streets, parks, airports, sporting arenas, subway systems, and so forth) in many cities in the United States and

other countries for law enforcement purposes (worldwide, two of the most monitored cities are London and New York City). These cameras are typically located outside and attached to or built into fixtures, such as lamp posts (see Figure 15-23), or attached to buildings. Video surveillance cameras are also commonly installed in schools in the United States and other countries to enable administrators to monitor both teacher and student activities and to have a record of incidents as they occur. A snapshot of a live video feed from a camera installed inside a computer lab at a university in New York is shown in Figure 15-23.

Public video surveillance systems are often used in conjunction with face recognition technology to try to identify known terrorists and other criminals, to identify criminals when their crimes are caught on tape, and to prevent crimes from occurring. Video surveillance data is proving to be valuable to police for catching terrorists and other types of criminals, and it is routinely used to

FIGURE 15-23

Examples of public video surveillance.

OUTDOOR SURVEILLANCE
Many cameras placed in public locations are designed to blend into their surroundings to be less intrusive, such as the camera inside this light fixture on a Washington, D.C., street.

INDOOR SURVEILLANCE
Many cameras are placed inside businesses, schools, and other locations, such as the ones that broadcast live video from several locations at a university in New York; a snapshot from one of the video cameras is shown here.

>**Video surveillance.** The use of video cameras to monitor activities of individuals, such as employees or individuals in public locations, for work-related or crime-prevention purposes.

identify the individuals and cars used in attacks; this benefit is expected to increase as video surveillance moves to high definition. Some public video surveillance systems are also beginning to be used in conjunction with software to try to identify suspicious behavior (such as an unattended bag or a truck circling a skyscraper) and alert authorities to these possible threats.

Many privacy advocates object to the use of video surveillance and face recognition technology in public locations; their concerns are primarily based on how the video captured by these systems will be used. Privacy advocates also have doubts about the usefulness of these systems in protecting citizens against terrorism. They also object to the fact that, unlike private security video that is typically viewed only after a crime has occurred, the images from many public video cameras are watched all the time. In addition, networks of police video cameras that feed into a central operations center allow the observation of innocent people and activities on a massive scale. However, law enforcement agencies contend that face recognition systems and public video surveillance are no different than the many private video surveillance systems in place today in a wide variety of public locations, such as in retail stores and banks. They view this technology as just one more tool to be used to protect the public, similar to scanning luggage at the airport. Some privacy advocates also fear being under perpetual police surveillance and the eventual expansion of these security surveillance systems, such as using them to look for "deadbeat dads" or for other applications not vital for national security.

An emerging privacy issue related to public video cameras is their use with the display screens used to project advertisements in public places, such as a mall, health club, or retail store. This marketing technique uses tiny video cameras embedded in or on the edge of the screen, in conjunction with software, to identify characteristics of the individual looking at the screen (such as gender and approximate age) in order to display advertising content targeted to each viewer. The video cameras can also be used to determine if the displayed ads are reaching the intended demographic. While still in the infancy stage, this advertising tool is expected to be more prominent in the near future. To alleviate privacy concerns, developers state that no images are ever stored and individuals are not personally identified—only their characteristics. However, the idea of targeted advertisements based on physical appearance is a concern for some privacy advocates.

A related privacy concern is the inclusion of digital camera capabilities in most mobile phones today (see Figure 15-24). Although mobile phone digital cameras are increasingly being used to help law enforcement (such as being used by citizens to take photos of crimes as they are being committed) and camera functions are included for personal enjoyment and convenience, some fear that the ubiquitous nature of mobile phones will lead to increased privacy violations. In fact, some athletic clubs have banned mobile phones entirely to protect the privacy of their members while working out and in the dressing rooms. Many YMCAs, city parks and recreation departments, and other recreational facilities have banned camera phone use in locker rooms and restrooms to protect the privacy of both children and adults. Camera phones are also being banned by some schools to prevent cheating, by many courthouses to prevent witness or jury intimidation, and by many research and production facilities to prevent corporate espionage. Legally speaking, people typically have few rights to privacy in public places, but many believe that new technology—such as camera phones—will require the law to reconsider and redefine

FIGURE 15-24

Camera phones are ubiquitous today.

what is considered to be a public place and where citizens can expect to retain particular aspects of personal privacy.

Employee Monitoring

Employee monitoring refers to companies recording or observing the actions of employees while on the job. With today's technology, employee monitoring is very easy to perform, and much of it can be done through the use of computers. Common employee monitoring activities include screening telephone calls, reviewing e-mail, and tracking computer and Internet usage; with the growing inclusion of video cameras in computers and monitors today, employee monitoring via PC cams may become more prominent in the near future. Although many employees feel that being watched at work is an invasion of their personal privacy, it is legal and very common in the United States. According to the American Management Association (AMA), the vast majority of all U.S. companies use some type of electronic surveillance with their employees, and it is common for employers to discipline employees for misuse of e-mail or the Internet at work. Typically, the primary reason is to monitor Internet usage for legal liability, but monitoring employee productivity is another motivating factor. Many employers are finding that some employees waste large amounts of time on social networking sites and other Web activities. While access to these sites is frequently blocked by employers, many believe a better alternative is identifying employees who abuse their Internet access and then dealing with those employees directly. This can be accomplished using the computer monitoring software discussed in a previous section.

For monitoring the physical locations of employees, video cameras (such as video surveillance cameras or PC video cameras) can be used, but another possibility is the use of smart or RFID-enabled ID cards (sometimes called *proximity cards*). While these cards (such as the one shown in Figure 15-25) are most often used for access control—such as to facilitate access to a building or computer network, to automatically lock an employee's computer when he or she gets a certain distance away from it (to eliminate the problem of nosy coworkers), and to automatically unlock the computer when the employee returns (to eliminate the need for passwords)—they can also be used to track the physical location of employees. Other types of employee monitoring systems designed for tracking an employee's location are GPS-based systems, such as those systems that track an employee via his or her mobile phone or those that notify the employer if the employee's company vehicle exits a prescribed work area. These and other types of GPS monitoring systems were discussed in Chapter 7.

The card is worn by an employee for continuous access and monitoring purposes.

Smart card circuitry

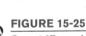

FIGURE 15-25
Smart ID cards. ID cards with smart card or RFID capabilities can be used for facility access, computer access, and employee monitoring.

Although some employees may view workplace monitoring as an invasion of their personal privacy, employers have several valid reasons for monitoring employee activities, such as security concerns, productivity measurement, legal compliance, and legal liability. For example, management has a responsibility to the company (and to its stockholders, for publicly held corporations) to make sure employees do the jobs that they are being paid to do. If any employees are spending too much time away from their desks chatting with other employees, answering their personal e-mail, or placing bids at online auctions, the company has the right to know and the responsibility to stop that misuse of company time and resources. For example, there have been many instances of employees viewing pornography, downloading pirated movies

>**Employee monitoring.** Observing or reviewing employees' actions while they are on the job.

or music, watching live sports video feeds—even running their own businesses—on company time and computers. In addition, the company needs to protect itself against lost business (due to employee incompetence or poor client skills, for example) and lawsuits (such as from employees when offensive e-mail messages are circulated within the office or when an employee includes statements that defame another business or reveal private information in a company blog). In addition, government regulations—such as the *Sarbanes-Oxley Act*, which requires publicly traded companies to keep track of which employees look at sensitive documents—may require it. However, some employees object to being monitored and some privacy advocates feel that some types of employee monitoring cross the line between valid employee monitoring and an invasion of privacy.

Comprehensive employee monitoring systems can be expensive; however, many companies view the cost as insignificant compared to the risk of a potential multimillion-dollar lawsuit. It is becoming increasingly common for U.S. firms to face sexual harassment and/or racial discrimination claims stemming from employee e-mail and Internet use and lawsuits can be costly—Chevron was once ordered to pay female employees $2.2 million to settle a sexual harassment lawsuit stemming from inappropriate e-mails sent by male employees.

To reduce cost and objections from employees, some businesses have found employee training and education to be an effective and cost-efficient alternative to continuous monitoring. Others use statistical-analysis software to detect unusual patterns in data collected about employee computer usage, and then use the reports to investigate only the employees and situations indicated as possible problems. Regardless of the techniques used, it is wise for businesses to inform employees about their monitoring practices (including what activities may be monitored and how long records of that monitoring will be archived), although they are not required by law in the U.S. at the current time to do so. However, bills have been introduced in several states in the United States that would prohibit employee monitoring without employee notification and some countries—such as in the European Union—are much more limiting with respect to the types of employee monitoring that can be performed without active notification. And legislation has been implemented or is being considered in several states to prevent employers from implanting employees with RFID chips without the employee's consent, in order to prevent employers from requiring that chips be implanted into employees for monitoring purposes, security access, or other work-related functions.

Presence Technology

Presence technology refers to the ability of one computing device (a desktop computer, portable computer, or mobile phone, for example) on a network (such as the Internet or a mobile phone network) to identify another device on the same network and determine its status. It can be used to tell when someone on the network is using his or her computer or mobile phone, as well as the individual's availability for communications; that is, whether or not the individual is able and willing to take a call or respond to an IM at the present time. For example, when an employee at a company utilizing presence technology (sometimes called *presence management* in a business context) has a question that needs answering, he or she can check the directory displayed on his or her computer or mobile phone to see which team members are available, regardless of where those team members are physically located. The employee can then call an available team member or send an instant message. Presence technology is expected to be used eventually on company Web

> **Presence technology.** Technology that enables one computing device (such as a computer or mobile phone) to locate and identify the current status of another device on the same network.

pages so that visitors—usually potential or current customers—can see which salespeople, service representatives, or other contacts are currently available. Another possible application is including dynamic presence buttons in e-mail messages—the presence button would display one message (such as "I'm online") if the sender is online at the time the e-mail message is read, and a different message (such as "I'm offline") if the sender is not online at that time.

Presence technology today can be implemented via software, as well as by GPS, RFID, or other technology. For instance, IM software indicates the current status of each buddy on an individual's contact list (based on each buddy's signed-in status). In addition, the presence technology built into many mobile phones today enables individuals to see when a contact is available (see Figure 15-26). The GPS capabilities integrated in many mobile phones today also allow you to keep track of your friends' physical locations, such as by using the Buddy Beacon, GyPSii, or Google Latitude application to view their current locations on a map. The GPS capabilities built into mobile phones can also be used by law enforcement to determine the location of a phone (such as one belonging to a missing individual or a criminal) when needed.

While some aspects of presence technology are useful and intriguing, such as being able to tell that a loved one's flight arrived safely when you notice that his or her mobile phone is on again, knowing if a friend or colleague is available for a telephone call before dialing the number, or identifying the location of your children at any point in time, privacy advocates are concerned about the use of this technology. They are concerned about presence technology being used to target ads and information to individuals based on their current physical location (such as close to a particular restaurant at lunchtime) and other activities that they view as potential privacy violations.

FIGURE 15-26
Presence technology. Presence icons indicate the status of individual contacts.

Protecting Personal and Workplace Privacy

There are not many options for protecting yourself against computer monitoring by your employer or the government, or against video surveillance systems. However, businesses should take the necessary security measures (such as protecting the company network from hackers, monitoring for intrusions, and using security software) to ensure that employee activities are not being monitored by a hacker or other unauthorized individual. Individuals should also secure their home computers to protect against keystroke logging or other computer monitoring software that may be inadvertently installed via an electronic greeting card, game, or other downloaded file, and that is designed to provide a hacker with account numbers, passwords, and other sensitive data that could be used in identity theft or other fraudulent activities. *Antispyware software*, such as the programs discussed in Chapter 9 and the example shown in Figure 15-27, can be used to detect and remove some types of illegal computer monitoring and spyware software.

FIGURE 15-27
Antispyware software. Antispyware software can detect and remove spyware used for computer monitoring purposes.

The Employer's Responsibilities

To protect the personal privacy of their employees and customers, businesses and organizations have a responsibility to keep private information about their employees, the company, and their customers safe. Strong security measures, such as firewalls and access-prevention methods for both computer data and facilities, can help to protect against unauthorized access by hackers. Businesses and organizations should take precautions against both intentional and accidental breaches of privacy by employees. Finally, businesses and organizations have the responsibility to monitor their employees' activities to ensure workers are productive. In general, businesses must maintain a safe and productive workplace environment and protect the privacy of their customers and employees, while at the same time ensure the company is not vulnerable to lawsuits.

All businesses should have an *employee policy* that informs employees about what personal activities (if any) are allowed during company time or on company equipment, as well as about what company communications (such as e-mail messages and blog postings) and what employee activities (such as Web surfing, e-mail, telephone calls, and downloading files to an office computer) may be monitored. Employee policies are usually included in an employee handbook or posted on the company intranet.

The Employees' Responsibilities

Employees have the responsibility to read a company's employee policy when initially hired and to review it periodically to ensure that they understand the policy and do not violate any company rules while working for that organization. In addition, since at-work activities may legally be monitored by an employer, it is wise—from a privacy standpoint—to avoid personal activities at work. From reading the organization's employee policy, an employee can determine if any personal activities are allowed at all (such as checking personal e-mail during the lunch hour), but it is safer to perform personal activities at home, regardless. Be especially careful with any activity, such as sending a joke via e-mail to a coworker, that might be interpreted as harassment. For personal phone calls, employees should use their mobile phones during their lunch hour or a rest break.

COMPUTER SECURITY AND PRIVACY LEGISLATION

The high level of concern regarding computer security and personal privacy has led state and federal legislators to pass a variety of laws since the 1970s. Internet privacy is viewed as one of the top policy issues facing Congress today, and numerous bills have been proposed in the last several years regarding spam, telemarketing, spyware, online profiling, and other very important privacy issues. However, Congress has had difficulty passing new legislation. There are several reasons for this, including that it is difficult for the legal system to keep pace with the rate at which technology changes, and there are jurisdictional issues domestically and internationally, since many computer crimes affect businesses and individuals located in geographic areas other than the one in which the computer criminal is located. In addition, privacy is difficult to define and there is a struggle to balance freedom of speech with the right to privacy.

Another issue is weighing the need to implement legislation versus the use of voluntary methods to protect computer security and personal privacy. For instance, the *Child Online Protection Act (COPA)* has been highly controversial since it was passed in 1998, and, in fact, it has never been implemented. This legislation prohibited making pornography or any other content deemed harmful to minors available to minors via the Internet and carried a $50,000 fine. This law was blocked by the U.S. Supreme Court several times, based on the likelihood that it violates the First Amendment and the possibility that less restrictive alternatives (such as Internet filtering) can be used instead to prevent the access of inappropriate materials by minors. A list of selected federal laws related to computer security and privacy are shown in Figure 15-28.

DATE	LAW AND DESCRIPTION
2006	**U.S. SAFE WEB Act of 2006** Grants additional authority to the FTC to help protect consumers from spam, spyware, and Internet fraud and deception.
2005	**Real ID Act** Establishes national standards for state-issued driver's licenses and identification cards; will be modified if the proposed Pass ID Act of 2009 is passed.
2005	**Junk Fax Prevention Act** Requires unsolicited faxes to have a highly-visible opt-out notice.
2003	**CAN-SPAM Act** Implements regulations for unsolicited e-mail messages and lays the groundwork for a federal Do Not E-Mail Registry.
2003	**Do Not Call Implementation Act** Amends the Telephone Consumer Protection Act to implement the National Do Not Call Registry.
2003	**Health Insurance Portability and Accountability Act (HIPAA)** Includes a Security Rule that sets minimum security standards to protect health information stored electronically.
2002	**Sarbanes-Oxley Act** Requires archiving a variety of electronic records and protecting the integrity of corporate financial data.
2001	**USA PATRIOT Act** Grants federal authorities expanded surveillance and intelligence-gathering powers, such as broadening the ability of federal agents to obtain the real identity of Internet users and intercept e-mail and other types of Internet communications.
1999	**Financial Modernization (Gramm-Leach-Bliley) Act** Extends the ability of banks, securities firms and insurance companies to share consumers' non-public personal information, but requires them to notify consumers and give them the opportunity to opt out before disclosing any information.
1998	**Child Online Protection Act (COPA)** Prohibits online pornography and other content deemed harmful to minors; has been blocked by the Supreme Court.
1998	**Children's Online Privacy Protection Act (COPPA)** Regulates how Web sites can collect information from minors and communicate with them.
1998	**Telephone Anti-Spamming Amendments Act** Applies restrictions to unsolicited, bulk commercial e-mail.
1992	**Cable Act** Extends the Cable Communications Policy Act to include companies that sell wireless services.
1991	**Telephone Consumer Protection Act** Requires telemarketing companies to respect the rights of people who do not want to be called.
1988	**Computer Matching and Privacy Protection Act** Limits the use of government data in determining federal-benefit recipients.
1988	**Video Privacy Protection Act** Limits disclosure of customer information by video-rental companies.
1986	**Electronic Communications Privacy Act** Extends traditional privacy protections governing postal delivery and telephone services to include e-mail, cellular phones, and voice mail.
1984	**Cable Communications Policy Act** Limits disclosure of customer records by cable TV companies.
1974	**Education Privacy Act** Stipulates that, in both public and private schools that receive any federal funding, individuals have the right to keep the schools from releasing such information as grades and evaluations of behavior.
1974	**Privacy Act** Stipulates that the collection of data by federal agencies must have a legitimate purpose.
1970	**Fair Credit Reporting Act** Prevents private organizations from unfairly denying credit and provides individuals the right to inspect their credit records.
1970	**Freedom of Information Act** Gives individuals the right to inspect data concerning them that is stored by the federal government.

FIGURE 15-28
Federal legislation related to computer security and privacy.

SOC

SUMMARY

WHY BE CONCERNED ABOUT COMPUTER SECURITY?

Chapter Objective 1:
Explain why all computer users should be concerned about computer security.

There are a number of important security concerns related to computers, such as having your computer stolen, losing data, and running the risk of buying pirated or digitally counterfeited products online. All computer users should be aware of possible security risks and the safeguards they can implement to prevent security problems since these problems can cost them time and money, as well as be an inconvenience.

HARDWARE LOSS, HARDWARE DAMAGE, AND SYSTEM FAILURE

Chapter Objective 2:
List some risks associated with hardware loss, hardware damage, and system failure, and understand ways to safeguard a computer against these risks.

Hardware loss (perhaps as a result of **hardware theft** or lost hardware), hardware damage (both intentional and unintentional), and **system failure** are important concerns. System failure can occur because of a hardware problem, or it can be the result of a natural or man-made disaster. To protect against hardware theft, door and equipment locks can be used. To protect against accidental hardware damage, **surge suppressors, uninterruptible power supplies** (**UPSs**), proper storage media care, and precautions against excess dust, heat, and static electricity are important. **Ruggedized devices** can be used when necessary. To protect against data loss, backups are essential for both individuals and businesses—most businesses should also develop a **disaster recovery plan** for natural and man-made disasters. Encryption can be used to protect individual files and the content of data stored on a storage medium. **Full disk encryption** (**FDE**) and **self-encrypting hard drives** can be used to encrypt all the content located on a hard drive automatically.

SOFTWARE PIRACY AND DIGITAL COUNTERFEITING

Chapter Objective 3:
Define software piracy and digital counterfeiting, and explain how they may be prevented.

Software piracy (the unauthorized copying of a computer program) and **digital counterfeiting** (creating fake copies of currency and other resources) are illegal in the United States. They cost manufacturers billions of dollars each year, and some of these costs are passed on to law-abiding consumers. Various tools, such as consumer education, holograms, and software activation procedures, can be used to prevent software piracy. Many businesses are also aggressively pursuing software pirates in court in an attempt to reduce piracy. The government has various methods in place to prevent digital counterfeiting of currency, such as using difficult-to-reproduce materials and features like *security threads* and *watermarks*.

WHY BE CONCERNED ABOUT INFORMATION PRIVACY?

Chapter Objective 4:
Explain what information privacy is and why computer users should be concerned about it.

Privacy issues affect the lives of everyone. A number of important **privacy** concerns are related to computers and the Internet. For instance, **information privacy** refers to the rights of individuals and companies to control how information about them is collected and used. Other common concerns include the privacy of Web site activities and e-mail messages, as well as the high number of security breaches on systems that contain personal information. Businesses need to be concerned with protecting the privacy of the personal information they store because data breaches violate the privacy of their customers. In addition, data breaches are costly, and they can result in lawsuits and damaged reputations.

DATABASES, ELECTRONIC PROFILING, SPAM, AND OTHER MARKETING ACTIVITIES

The extensive use of **marketing databases** and **government databases** is of concern to many privacy organizations and individuals. Information in marketing databases is frequently sold to companies and other organizations; information in some government databases is available to the public. Some public information can be retrieved from databases via the Web. **Electronic profiling** is the collection of diverse information about an individual. An organization's **privacy policy** addresses how any personal information submitted to that company will be used. Another privacy issue that individuals need to be concerned about centers on the vast amount of **spam** (unsolicited bulk e-mail) that occurs today.

Protecting your e-mail address is one of the best ways to avoid spam. A **throw-away e-mail address** can be used for any activities that may result in spam; your permanent personal e-mail address can then be reserved for communications that should not result in spam. Before providing any personal information via a Web page, it is a good idea to review the Web site's privacy policy to see if the information will be shared with other organizations. Consider whether or not the Web site is requesting too much personal information, and only provide the required data. Do not provide personal details in chat rooms and personal Web sites. Unless you do not mind spam or are using a throw-away e-mail address, avoid completing online forms, such as to enter sweepstakes.

E-mail filters can be used to manage an individual's e-mail; **spam filters** are used to identify possible spam. To reduce the amount of spam, junk mail, online ads, and telemarketing calls received, an individual can **opt out** of marketing activities. It's possible that more marketing activities in the future will require individuals to **opt in** in order to participate. Individuals and businesses should be cautious when disposing of old hardware, such as hard drives and CDs, that contain sensitive data. Minimally, hard drives to be reused should be *wiped* clean; CDs, DVDs, and other media to be disposed of should be shredded.

ELECTRONIC SURVEILLANCE AND MONITORING

Computer monitoring software that can record an individual's computer use is viewed as a privacy violation by some, as is the increased use of **video surveillance** in public locations. Although it is allowed by law, some employees view **employee monitoring** (such as monitoring computer use, telephone calls, and an individual's location using a smart ID card or video surveillance) as an invasion of their privacy. **Presence technology**—the ability of one computer on a network to know the status of another computer on that network—allows users of computers, mobile phones, and other communications devices to determine the availability of other individuals before contacting them.

To protect the privacy of employees and customers, businesses have a responsibility to keep private information about their employees, the company, and their customers safe. Firewalls, password-protected files, and encryption can help secure this information. Businesses have the responsibility to monitor employee activities in order to ensure that employees are performing the jobs they are being paid to do, are not causing lost business, and are not leaving the company open to lawsuits. To inform employees of allowable activities, an *employee policy* or code of conduct should be developed and distributed to employees. For the highest level of privacy while at the workplace, employees should perform only work-related activities on the job.

COMPUTER SECURITY AND PRIVACY LEGISLATION

Although computer security and privacy are viewed as extremely important issues, legislating these issues is difficult due to ongoing changes in technology, jurisdictional issues, and varying opinions. Some legislation related to computer security has been enacted; new legislation is being considered on a regular basis.

Chapter Objective 5:
Describe some privacy concerns regarding databases, electronic profiling, spam, and telemarketing, and identify ways individuals can protect their privacy.

Chapter Objective 6:
Discuss several types of electronic surveillance and monitoring, and list ways individuals can protect their privacy.

Chapter Objective 7:
Discuss the status of computer security and privacy legislation.

SOC

REVIEW ACTIVITIES

KEY TERM MATCHING

a. digital counterfeiting

b. disaster recovery plan

c. full disk encryption (FDE)

d. information privacy

e. presence technology

f. software piracy

g. spam

h. surge suppressor

i. system failure

j. uninterruptible power supply (UPS)

Instructions: Match each key term on the left with the definition on the right that best describes it.

1. _____ A device containing a built-in battery that provides continuous power to a computer and other connected components when the electricity goes out.

2. _____ A device that protects a computer system from damage due to electrical fluctuations.

3. _____ A written plan that describes the steps a company will take following the occurrence of a disaster.

4. _____ Technology that enables one computing device (such as a computer or mobile phone) to locate and identify the current status of another device on the same network.

5. _____ The complete malfunction of a computer system.

6. _____ The rights of individuals and companies to control how information about them is collected and used.

7. _____ A technology that encrypts everything stored on a storage medium automatically, without any user interaction.

8. _____ The unauthorized copying of a computer program.

9. _____ The use of computers or other types of digital equipment to make illegal copies of currency, checks, collectibles, and other items.

10. _____ Unsolicited, bulk e-mail sent over the Internet.

SELF-QUIZ

Instructions: Circle **T** if the statement is true, **F** if the statement is false, or write the best answer in the space provided. **Answers for the self-quiz are located in the References and Resources Guide at the end of the book.**

1. **T F** As long as a business owns one legal copy of a software program, it can install that program on as many computers as desired without fear of retribution.

2. **T F** Electronic profiling is the act of using electronic means to collect a variety of in-depth information about an individual, such as name, address, income, and buying habits.

3. **T F** Encryption can be used for privacy purposes, in addition to security purposes.

4. **T F** One way of safeguarding your e-mail address is to use a single e-mail address for all online activity, including personal e-mail and online shopping.

5. **T F** Very few major U.S. companies monitor the online activities of their employees.

6. A(n) _____ plan can help a business get operational again following a fire, an act of sabotage, or a similar disaster.

7. Color copying money is an example of _____.

8. An e-mail _____ can be used to route suspected spam automatically into an e-mail folder.

9. If you _____, you are requesting that you be removed from marketing activities or that your information not be shared with other companies; if you _____, you are requesting to participate.

10. Match each precaution with the security risk it is designed to protect against, and write the corresponding number in the blank to the left of each security risk.

a. _____ Digital counterfeiting   **1.** Encryption

b. _____ Hardware theft   **2.** Surge suppressor

c. _____ Privacy breach   **3.** Security thread

d. _____ System damage   **4.** Cable lock

EXERCISES

1. Match each privacy risk with its related term, and write the corresponding number in the blank to the left of each term.

a. _____ Throw-away e-mail address   **1.** Employee monitoring

b. _____ Computer monitoring software   **2.** Video surveillance

c. _____ Riding public transportation   **3.** Spam

2. Supply the missing words to complete the following statements.

a. _____ refers to all content on a storage medium being encrypted automatically.

b. _____ refers to the ability to locate the current status of an individual via a network.

3. List two precautions that can be taken while traveling with a portable computer to guard against its theft.

4. Explain the purpose of an uninterruptible power supply (UPS) and how it differs in function from a surge suppressor.

5. Think of one computer-related security or privacy risk you have encountered recently. Describe the risk and list at least one precaution that could be taken to minimize that risk.

DISCUSSION QUESTIONS

1. Much of the Facebook "Beacon" controversy stemmed from the fact that Facebook members were automatically included instead of having to opt in. Should all online marketing activities be on an opt-in basis? How would you feel if your online activities (such as your online purchases) were shared with others without your consent? Does it make a difference if the activities are linked to your identity or anonymous? Facebook was recently ordered to pay $9.5 million to fund a privacy foundation in response to a Beacon lawsuit—is this justified?

2. Spam is increasingly being filtered by ISPs and e-mail programs, and pop-up blockers can block many Web page advertisements. If this trend continues and these activities are no longer viable marketing activities, what will the long-term effect be? Will free Web content begin to disappear? Is paying Internet users to receive spam or view Web ads a viable option? Just as with television, some amount of advertising is typically necessary in order to support free content. What do you think is the optimal balance for the Web?

PROJECTS

HOT TOPICS

1. **Electronic Health Records** The use of electronic health records (EHRs) is growing rapidly. Proponents view EHRs as a means to deliver better care more efficiently. However, some privacy advocates are concerned about the possible security breaches of servers containing digital private medical information.

   For this project, research the current use of EHRs. What are the benefits? Are EHRs widely used? Are you concerned about your medical history being stored on a computer that, potentially, could be accessed by a hacker or other unauthorized individual? Do you think the risk of a privacy breach is higher with EHRs as compared with the records contained in conventional paper file folders? What about private electronic health systems like Google Health that are designed to help individuals organize their health records and are still stored online? At the conclusion of your research, prepare a one-page summary of your findings and opinions and submit it to your instructor.

SHORT ANSWER/ RESEARCH

2. **E-Voting** E-voting—casting ballots online or via an electronic e-voting machine—has been surrounded by controversy. Concerns include the accuracy and security of e-voting machines, the ability of online voting systems to prevent someone from voting as another individual and to protect the privacy of votes cast electronically, and the ability to perform an accurate recount.

   For this project, research the current status of e-voting. Have universal standards been developed for all e-voting machines used in the United States or is that decision made on a state-by-state basis? What security measures are being used with e-voting and online voting systems to ensure they cannot be hacked and that only the registered voter is permitted to cast his or her vote? Form an opinion about the use of e-voting machines and online voting. Would you be comfortable casting your vote via an e-voting machine? How about online? At some point, do you think online voting will become the norm? If so, how would you suggest handling individuals who have no Internet access available to them on Election Day? At the conclusion of your research, submit your findings and opinions to your instructor in the form of a short paper, no more than two pages in length.

HANDS ON

3. **Browser Privacy Settings** There are a variety of settings in a Web browser that pertain to privacy, such as cookie, cache, and history settings.

   For this project, find a computer (either your own or one in a school computer lab or at your local public library) on which you are permitted to change the Internet options (ask permission first if you are not sure if these actions are allowed) and perform the following tasks:

   a. Open Internet Explorer and use the *Internet Options* option on the Tools menu to check the current settings on the General and Privacy tabs. Using the General tab, delete your browsing history (temporary files, history, cookies, saved passwords, and Web form information).

   b. Visit at least five different Web sites to build a history and cookie list. You may want to go to an e-commerce site and add items to your shopping cart (but don't check out) or personalize a portal page, such as MSNBC.com or iGoogle.com.

   c. Display your history list. Are the Web sites you visited listed? Use the Browsing history Settings button on the Internet Options dialog box to view the temporary files, including your cookie files. Were new cookies added during your session? If so, are they all from the Web sites you visited, or are any of them third-party cookies?

   d. Delete all temporary Internet files, sign out of any personalized pages, and close the browser window. Prepare a short summary of your work to submit to your instructor.

4. **Security Camera Networks** As discussed in the chapter, live surveillance cameras are being used at an increasing number of public locations. Some view this as a valid crime prevention tool; others think it is an invasion of privacy. Is it ethical for businesses to use video cameras to record customers' activities? If so, for what purposes? Does the government have the responsibility to use every means possible to protect the country and its citizens? Or do citizens have the right not to be watched in public? One objection stated about these systems is "It's not the same as a cop on the corner. This is a cop on every corner." What if it were a live police officer at each public video camera location instead of a camera? Would that be more acceptable from a privacy standpoint? If people do not plan to commit criminal acts in public, should they be concerned that law enforcement personnel may see them? Does the risk of being recorded deter some illegal or unethical acts?

   For this project, form an opinion about the ethical ramifications of public video surveillance and be prepared to discuss your position (in class, via an online class discussion group, in a class chat room, or via a class blog, depending on your instructor's directions). You may also be asked to write a short paper expressing your opinion.

ETHICS IN ACTION

5. **Privacy Policy Flip-Flops** Although a company's privacy policy may look acceptable when you read it before submitting personal information to that company, there is no guarantee that the policy will not be changed.

   For this project, locate three different privacy policies on Web sites, analyze them, and compare them. Do the policies specify what personal information might be shared and with whom? Do the organizations reserve the right to change their policies at a later time without notice? If so, will they try to notify consumers? Do any of the policies allow for any sharing of data to third-party organizations? If so, is the data personally identifiable, and can customers opt out? Form an opinion regarding a company's right to change its privacy policy and the impact such a change may have on customer loyalty. Share your findings with the class in the form of a short presentation. The presentation should not exceed 10 minutes and should make use of one or more presentation aids, such as the chalkboard, handouts, overhead transparencies, or a computer-based slide presentation (your instructor may provide additional requirements). You may also be asked to submit a summary of the presentation to your instructor.

PRESENTATION/ DEMONSTRATION

Instructions: Go to the Chapter 15 page at **www.cengage.com/computerconcepts/np/uc13** to work the following Web Activities.

6. **Interactive Activities** Work the interactive **Crossword Puzzle**, watch the **Video Podcasts** and **Online Videos**, and explore the **Further Exploration** links associated with this chapter.

   If you have a SAM user profile, you may have access to hands-on instruction, practice, and assessment of the skills covered in this chapter. Check with your instructor for instructions and the correct URL/Web site to access those assignments.

7. **Student Edition Labs** Work the following interactive **Student Edition Lab**.

   ➤ **Protecting Your Privacy Online**

8. **Test Yourself** Review the **Online Study Guide** for this chapter, then test your knowledge of the terms and concepts covered in this chapter by completing the **Key Term Matching** exercise, the **Self-Quiz**, the **Exercises**, and the **Practice Test**.

WEB ACTIVITIES

Student Edition Labs

SAM

SOC

chapter 16

Intellectual Property Rights, Ethics, Health, Access, and the Environment

After completing this chapter, you will be able to do the following:

1. Understand the different types of intellectual property rights and how they relate to computer use.

2. Explain what is meant by ethics and provide several examples of unethical behavior in computer-related matters.

3. Describe some possible physical and emotional health risks associated with the use of computers.

4. Discuss the impact that factors such as nationality, income, race, education, and physical disabilities may have on computer access and use.

5. Suggest some ways computer users can practice "green computing" and properly dispose of obsolete computer equipment.

6. Discuss the current status of legislation related to intellectual property rights, ethics, access, and the environment in relation to computers.

outline

Overview

Intellectual Property Rights
Copyrights
Trademarks
Patents

Ethics
Ethical Use of Copyrighted Material
Ethical Use of Resources and Information
Computer Hoaxes and Digital Manipulation
Ethical Business Practices and Decision Making

Computers and Health
Physical Health
Emotional Health

Access to Technology
The Digital Divide
Assistive Technology

Environmental Concerns
Green Computing
Recycling and Disposal of Computing Equipment

Related Legislation

OVERVIEW

While computers and related technology add convenience and enjoyment to our daily lives, they also can make it easier to perform some types of illegal or unethical acts, can cause serious health and emotional problems, and can have a negative impact on the environment. In addition, although computer use is becoming almost mandatory in our society, many believe that access to technology is not equally available to all individuals. This chapter continues where Chapter 15 left off by exploring computer-related societal issues that go beyond security and privacy.

The chapter begins with a look at a legal issue that all computer users should be aware of—intellectual property rights. The specific types of intellectual property rights are discussed, along with examples of the types of property that each right protects. Next is a discussion of ethics, including what they are and a variety of ethical issues surrounding computer use by individuals and businesses. Topics include the ethical use of copyrighted material, ethical uses of resources and information, unethical use of digital manipulation, and ethical business practices and decision making. The chapter continues with a look at health-oriented concerns, including the impact computers may have on a user's physical and emotional health, as well as strategies individuals can use to lessen those risks. Next, we turn to the issue of equal access, including a discussion of the digital divide and how other factors—such as gender, age, and physical disabilities—may affect computer access and use. We then look at the potential impact of computers on our environment and some ways of lessening that impact. The chapter closes with a look at legislation related to the issues discussed in this chapter. ■

PODCAST

Go to **www.cengage.com/ computerconcepts/np/uc13** to download or listen to the "Expert Insight on Computers and Society" podcast.

INTELLECTUAL PROPERTY RIGHTS

Intellectual property rights are the legal rights to which the creators of *intellectual property*—original creative works—are entitled. Intellectual property rights indicate who has the right to use, perform, or display a creative work and what can legally be done with that work; how long the creator retains rights to the property; and other related restrictions. Examples of intellectual property include music and movies; paintings, computer graphics, and other works of art; poetry, books, and other types of written works; symbols, names, and designs used in conjunction with a business; architectural drawings; and inventions. The three main types of intellectual property rights are *copyrights, trademarks*, and *patents*. Copyrights, trademarks, and patents are issued by individual countries; U.S. intellectual property rights are discussed in more detail next.

>**Intellectual property rights.** The legal rights to which creators of original creative works (such as artistic or literary works, inventions, corporate logos, and more) are entitled.

SOC

BOOK COPYRIGHT NOTICES

© Red Lobster. All rights reserved.

WEB SITE COPYRIGHT NOTICES

 FIGURE 16-1

Copyright statements.

Statements such as these are often included on books, Web sites, and other original copyrighted works.

FURTHER EXPLORATION

Go to the Chapter 16 page at **www.cengage.com/ computerconcepts/np/uc13** for links to information about intellectual property rights.

Copyrights

A **copyright** is a form of protection available to the creator of an original artistic, musical, or literary work, such as a book, movie, software program, musical composition, or painting. It gives the copyright holder the exclusive right to publish, reproduce, distribute, perform, or display the work. A major revision to U.S. copyright legislation was the *1976 Copyright Act*. This act extended copyright protection to nonpublished works, so, immediately after creating a work in some type of material form (such as on paper, film, videotape, or a digital storage medium), the creator automatically owns the copyright of that work. Consequently, the creator is entitled to copyright protection of that work and has the right to make a statement, such as "Copyright © 2010 John Smith. All rights reserved." Although works created in the United States after March 1, 1989 are not required to display a copyright notice in order to retain their copyright protection, displaying a copyright statement on a published work (see Figure 16-1) reminds others that the work is protected by copyright law and that any use must comply with copyright law. Only the creator of a work (or his or her employer if the work is created as a *work for hire*; that is, within the scope of employment) can rightfully claim copyright. Copyrights can be registered with the *U. S. Copyright Office*. Although registration is not required for copyright protection, it does offer an advantage if the need to prove ownership of a copyright ever arises, such as during a copyright-infringement lawsuit. Most countries offer some copyright protection to works registered in other countries.

Anyone wishing to use copyrighted materials must first obtain permission from the copyright holder and pay any required fee. One exception is the legal concept of *fair use*, which permits limited duplication and use of a portion of copyrighted material for specific purposes, such as criticism, commentary, news reporting, teaching, and research. For example, a teacher may legally read a copyrighted poem for discussion in a poetry class, and a news crew may videotape a small portion of a song at a concert to include in a news report of that concert. Copyrights apply to both published and unpublished works and remain in effect until 70 years after the creator's death. Copyrights for works registered by an organization or as anonymous works last 95 years from the date of publication or 120 years from the date of creation, whichever is shorter.

It is important to realize that purchasing a copyrighted item (such as a book, painting, or movie) does not change the copyright protection afforded to the creator of that item. Although you have purchased the right to use the item, you cannot legally duplicate it or portray it as your own creation. Some of the most widely publicized copyright-infringement issues today center around individuals illegally distributing copyright-protected music and movies via the Internet, as discussed later in this chapter.

To protect their rights, some creators of digital content (such as art, music, photographs, and movies) use **digital watermarks**—a subtle alteration of digital content that is not noticeable when the work is viewed or played but that identifies the copyright holder. For instance, the digital watermark for an image might consist of slight changes to the brightness of a specific pattern of pixels that are imperceptible to people but are easily read by software. Digital watermarks can also be made visible, if desired, such as to add the name of a company or Web site URL to a photo being posted online, or to inform individuals that the photo is copyrighted and should not be used elsewhere.

Digital watermarks can be added to images, music, video, TV shows, and other digital content found online or distributed in digital form to identify their copyright

---

>**Copyright.** The legal right to sell, publish, or distribute an original artistic or literary work; it is held by the creator of a work as soon as it exists in physical form. >**Digital watermark.** A subtle alteration of digital content that is not noticeable when the work is viewed or played, but that identifies the copyright holder.

holders, their authorized distributors, and other important information. They are typically added with software, though digital cameras may soon be available that can add a digital watermark to each photo as it is created. As shown in Figure 16-2, digital watermarks added to photos are invisible until they are read with appropriate software. The purpose of digital watermarking is to give digital content a unique identity that remains intact even if the work is copied, edited, compressed, or otherwise manipulated. For instance, movies sent to movie theaters typically include a digital watermark that can be used to trace a pirated movie back to the theater where the pirated movie was created in order to help authorities locate and prosecute the criminal. Primarily because of the vast amount of copyrighted content distributed via the Internet today, the market for digital watermarking technology is growing rapidly and it is expected to reach nearly $600 million by 2012, according to one study.

Another rights-protection tool used with digital content is **digital rights management (DRM) software**. DRM software is used to control the use of a work. For instance, DRM used in conjunction with business documents (called *enterprise rights management*) can protect a sensitive business document by controlling usage of that document, such as by limiting who can view, print, or copy it. DRM used with digital content (such as movies and music) downloaded via the Internet can control whether or not the downloaded file can be copied to another device, as well as make a video-on-demand movie unviewable after the rental period expires. For a look at a tool used to verify authentic physical intellectual property and prevent counterfeiting of these products, see the Inside the Industry box.

The watermark embedded into this image is not visible.

The information contained in the watermark can be viewed using an image editing program.

FIGURE 16-2
Digital watermarks.

Trademarks

A **trademark** is a word, phrase, symbol, or design (or a combination of words, phrases, symbols, or designs) that identifies and distinguishes one product or service from another. A trademark used to identify a service is also called a *service mark*. Trademarks that are claimed but not registered with the *U. S. Patent and Trademark Office (USPTO)* can use the mark ™; nonregistered service marks can use the symbol ℠. The symbol ® is reserved for registered trademarks and service marks. Trademarks for products usually appear on the product packaging with the appropriate trademark symbol; service marks are typically used in the advertising of a service, since there is no product on which the mark can be printed. Trademarked words and phrases—such as iPod®, Chicken McNuggets®, Windows Vista™, and FedEx 3Day℠ Freight—are widely used today. Trademarked logos (see Figure 16-3) are also common. Trademarks last 10 years, but they can be renewed as many times as desired, as long as they are being used in commerce.

In addition to protecting the actual trademarked words, phrases, or logos, trademark law also protects domain names that match a company's trademark, such as Amazon.com and Lego.com. There have been a number of claims of online trademark infringement in recent years, particularly those involving domain names that contain, or are similar to, a trademark. For instance, several

FIGURE 16-3
Examples of trademarked logos.

i'm lovin' it™

real

ebaY™

Eye-Fi

SOC

INSIDE THE INDUSTRY

High-Tech Anticounterfeiting Systems

With counterfeiters increasingly trying to pass off copies of intellectual property as authentic (the International Anticounterfeiting Coalition estimates that counterfeits now make up 7% of the world's goods), many companies are turning to technology to help fight the fakes. One recent anticounterfeiting system developed by Kodak, called *TRACELESS*, is a new option for goods that are made of paper (like collectible trading cards) or that contain paper labels or product packaging (such as wine, prescription drugs, consumer electronics, apparel, and more). The TRACELESS system uses invisible chemical markers embedded in the product or packaging. The markers can be mixed with various inks, toners, varnishes, and other materials for printing, or they can be mixed into paper pulp, plastics, textiles, and other materials used to create a product or product packaging. The markers can only be detected using secure, handheld TRACELESS readers like the one shown in the accompanying photograph. Being able to determine easily and unequivocally if products are authentic can help retailers ensure they are selling legitimate products; it can also help law enforcement agencies identify counterfeit goods and prosecute counterfeiters. While

high-tech systems such as TRACELESS can help protect consumers and businesses from financial loss, they can also help save lives by preventing patients from ending up with fake prescription drugs masquerading as real drugs.

Invisible markers are embedded into this wine label.

The markers can be detected by this reader.

celebrities—such as Madonna and Jim Carrey—have fought to be given the exclusive right to use what they consider their rightful domain names (Madonna.com and JimCarrey.com, in these examples). Other examples include Microsoft's complaint against another organization using the domain name *microsof.com* and RadioShack's objection to a private individual using *shack.com* for the Web site of his design business.

While businesses and individuals can file lawsuits to recover a disputed domain name, a faster and less expensive option is to file a complaint with a dispute resolution provider, such as the *World Intellectual Property Organization* (*WIPO*). WIPO is a specialized agency of the United Nations and attempts to resolve international commercial disputes about intellectual property between private parties. This includes domain name disputes; in fact, WIPO has resolved more than 16,000 domain name dispute cases since it was formed 10 years ago. During the resolution process, WIPO has the power to award the disputed domain name to the most appropriate party. If the domain name was acquired with the intent to profit from the goodwill of a trademark belonging to someone else (such as by generating revenue from Web site visitors intending to go to the trademark holder's Web site or by trying to sell the domain name to the trademark holder at an inflated price) or to otherwise abuse a trademark, the act of acquiring that domain name is deemed to be **cybersquatting** and the trademark holder generally prevails. If the current domain name holder has a legitimate reason for using that name and does not appear to be a cybersquatter,

> **Cybersquatting.** The act of registering a domain name with the intent to profit from the goodwill of a trademark belonging to someone else.

however, WIPO may allow the holder to continue to use that domain name. For instance, WIPO ruled that microsof.com was confusingly similar to the trademark already owned by Microsoft and that its owner had no legitimate interest in that domain name, so WIPO transferred the disputed domain name to Microsoft Corporation. However, the owner of the design business (whose last name is Shackleton and whose nickname is "Shack") was allowed to keep the shack.com domain name because it was ruled that he had a legitimate interest in that name. The *Anticybersquatting Consumer Protection Act*, which was signed into law in 1999, makes cybersquatting illegal and it allows for penalties up to $100,000 for each willful registration of a domain name that infringes on a trademark.

Many recent cybersquatting cases deal with *typosquatting*—registering a domain name that is similar to a trademark or domain name but that is slightly misspelled in hopes that individuals will accidentally arrive at the site when trying to type the URL of the legitimate site. These sites often contain pay-per-click advertising used to generate revenue for the typosquatter; they can also be phishing sites that use spoofed Web pages to try to obtain sensitive information from visitors, or they can redirect visitors to sites for competing products or services. To prevent typosquatting and to protect their brands and other trademarks, many companies register variations of their domain names proactively. For instance, Verizon has registered more than 10,000 domain names related to its three most visible brands (Verizon, VZ, and FiOS). If a cybersquatter is causing enough damage to warrant it, companies can file a lawsuit against the cybersquatter. For instance, Verizon recently sued a company for unlawfully registering 663 domain names that were either identical or confusingly similar to Verizon trademarks. In late 2008, Verizon was awarded more than $33 million in that case—the largest cybersquatting judgment to date. Another form of cybersquatting involves individuals not affiliated with a company opening social media accounts using the company's brand names or variations of its brand names—typically either to use the account to sell pirated goods posing as the legitimate company, or in hopes the company will pay them to relinquish control of the accounts.

FIGURE 16-4
Patents. The patent shown here is for a new mobile phone.

Patents

Unlike copyrights (which protect artistic and literary works) and trademarks (which protect a company's logo and brand names), a **patent** protects inventions by granting exclusive rights of an invention to its inventor for a period of 20 years. A patented invention is typically a unique product, but it can also be a process or procedure that provides a new way of doing something or that offers a new technical solution to a problem. Like trademarks, U.S. patents are issued by the U.S. Patent and Trademark Office (USPTO). A recent patent issued for a new Nokia mobile phone design is shown in Figure 16-4.

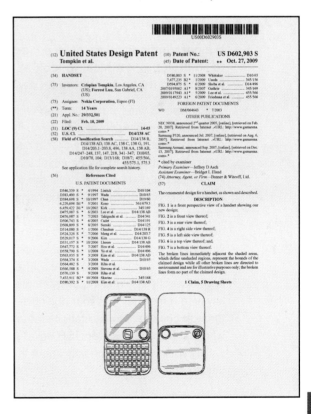

The number of patent applications, particularly those related to computer and Internet products, has skyrocketed in recent years. In the U.S., patents have also been granted for Internet business methods and models, such as Priceline.com's name-your-own-price business model and Amazon.com's one-click purchase procedure. When a product or business model is patented, no other organization can duplicate it without paying a royalty to the patent holder or risking prolonged patent litigation. There have been many

> **Patent.** A form of protection for an invention that can be granted by the government; gives exclusive rights of an invention to its inventor for 20 years.

SOC

objections to some of the Internet business model patents that have been granted and some of these patents, including Amazon's one-click patent, have been challenged. Although several of Amazon's claims to its patent were initially rejected in late 2007 by the USPTO, the final outcome of this patent dispute had not been determined at the time of this writing, and the U.S. Supreme Court agreed in mid-2009 to consider the issue of the use of patents with business methods. There has also been a great deal of patent litigation recently surrounding computer technology. For instance, Apple has been sued in several patent infringement lawsuits related to its iPhone, and Microsoft has claimed that Linux infringed on many of its patents and is, therefore, attempting to collect royalties from vendors that use Linux in commercial products, such as computers and networking hardware.

Patents can be difficult, expensive, and time-consuming to obtain. However, patents can also be very lucrative. For instance, IBM, which has been the top patenting company for close to two decades, was issued over 4,100 patents in 2008 and earns an estimated $2 billion per year from its patents.

ETHICS

The term **ethics** refers to standards of moral conduct. For example, telling the truth is a matter of ethics. An unethical act is not always illegal, although it might be, but an illegal act is usually viewed as unethical by most people. For example, purposely lying to a friend is unethical but usually not illegal, while perjuring oneself in a courtroom as a witness is both illegal and unethical. Whether or not criminal behavior is involved, ethics guide our behavior and play an integral role in our lives.

Much more ambiguous than the law, ethical beliefs can vary widely from one individual to another. Ethical beliefs may also vary based on one's religion, country, race, or culture. In addition, different ethical standards can apply to different areas of one's life. For example, *personal ethics* guide an individual's personal behavior and *business ethics* guide an individual's workplace behavior. Ethics with respect to the use of computers are referred to as **computer ethics**. Computer ethics have taken on more significance in recent years because the proliferation of computers in the home and the workplace provides more opportunities for unethical acts than in the past. The Internet also makes it easy to distribute information that many individuals would view as unethical (such as computer viruses, spam, and spyware), as well as to distribute copies of software, movies, music, and other digital content in an illegal and, therefore, unethical manner.

> **Ethics.** Overall standards of moral conduct. > **Computer ethics.** Standards of moral conduct as they relate to computer use.

TECHNOLOGY AND YOU

Virtual Gold and Income Taxes

While Second Life, World of Warcraft, and other virtual worlds only exist in cyberspace, there is nothing virtual about the money being made via virtual worlds and online multiplayer video games. For instance, in 2006, Ailin Graef (creator of Second Life resident and avatar Anshe Chung) became the first virtual world millionaire. In Second Life, Anshe buys and develops virtual real estate, owns virtual shopping malls, and performs other financial transactions for Graef. Graef announced in late 2006 that her Second Life assets topped $1 million in U.S. dollars (virtual money in Second Life is measured in Linden dollars and has an official market-driven exchange rate, approximately 260 Linden dollars per $1 U.S. at the time of this writing).

While a basic account with Second Life is free, buying land, building homes, and properly outfitting your avatar (see the accompanying illustration) is anything but free. For instance, a pair of new sneakers costs around $0.70 U.S., a plasma TV and leather couch for your avatar's condo costs about $2.15 U.S., a furnished split level retreat costs about $225 U.S., and a private island costs about $1,000 U.S., plus another $295 U.S. per month in maintenance use fees. The amount of real money exchanged in virtual worlds and online multiplayer games like World of Warcraft is staggering—one estimate is more than $1 billion U.S. per year. In addition to buying and selling goods and services within Second Life, World of Warcraft, and other virtual entities, individuals can also buy and sell virtual assets (such as Linden dollars, Second Life islands, World of Warcraft gold, and so on) on eBay and other online marketplaces.

As a result of the amount of money being exchanged within virtual communities, the issue of taxing that money has arisen in the U.S. and other countries. When virtual goods are cashed out for actual cash, it's clear that the profits should be reported as taxable income. But what about taxing virtual profits that never leave the virtual world? This issue is complicated by the fact that goods or services obtained through barter or as prizes are taxable in the U.S. under current law, and the fact that virtual transactions have real-world value. While the IRS has not yet specifically addressed the issue of whether or not virtual income is taxable in the U.S. before it is exchanged for real-life money and/or for goods or services, the issue is being looked into. Some countries have already made that decision, such as Australia, which implemented taxes on virtual income in late 2006, and South Korea, which has a value-added tax on individuals with virtual income over a certain amount. Whether the U.S. and other countries will follow suit remains to be seen.

The vitual money spent for goods and services in Second Life translates into real-world revenue for the sellers when exchanged for U.S. dollars.

Whether at home, at work, or at school, individuals encounter ethical issues every day. For example, you may need to make ethical decisions such as whether or not to accept a relative's offer of a free copy of a downloaded song or movie, whether or not to have a friend help you take an online exam, whether or not to upload a photo of your friend to Facebook without asking permission, whether or not to post a rumor on a campus gossip site, or whether or not to report as taxable income the virtual money you made in Second Life or another virtual world, as discussed in the Technology and You box.

As an employee, you may need to decide whether or not to print your child's birthday party invitations on the office color printer, whether or not to correct your boss if he or she gives you credit for another employee's idea, or whether or not to sneak a look at information that technically you have access to but have no legitimate reason to view. IT employees, in particular, often face this latter ethical dilemma since they typically have both access and the technical ability to retrieve a wide variety of personal and professional information about other employees, such as their salary information, Web surfing history, and personal e-mail.

SOC

Businesses also deal with a variety of ethical issues in the course of normal business activities—from determining how many computers on which a particular software program should be installed, to identifying how customer and employee information should be used, to deciding business practices. **Business ethics** are the standards of conduct that guide a business's policies, decisions, and actions.

Ethical Use of Copyrighted Material

Both businesses and individuals should be very careful when copying, sharing, or otherwise using copyrighted material to ensure that the material is used in both a legal and an ethical manner. Common types of copyrighted material encountered on a regular basis include software, books, Web-based articles, music, and movies. Legal and ethical use of software was discussed in Chapter 6; the rest of these topics are covered next.

Books and Web-Based Articles

Copyright law protects print-based books, newspaper articles, e-books, Web-based articles, and all other types of literary material. Consequently, these materials cannot be reproduced, presented as one's own original material, or otherwise used in an unauthorized manner. Students, researchers, authors, and other writers need to be especially careful when using literary material as a resource for papers, articles, books, and so forth, to ensure the material is used appropriately and is properly credited to the original author. To present someone else's work as your own is **plagiarism**, which is both a violation of copyright law and an unethical act. It can also get you fired, as some reporters have found out the hard way after faking quotes or plagiarizing content from other newspapers. Some examples of acts that would normally be considered or not considered plagiaristic are shown in Figure 16-5.

With the widespread availability of online articles and fee-based online term paper services, some students might be tempted to create their papers by copying and pasting excerpts of online content into their documents to pass off as their original work. But these students should realize that this is plagiarism, and instructors can usually tell when a paper is created in this manner. There are also online sources instructors can use to test the originality of student papers; the results of one such test are shown in Figure 16-6. Most colleges and universities have strict consequences for plagiarism, such as automatically failing the assignment or course, or being expelled from the institution. As Internet-based plagiarism continues to expand to younger and younger students, many middle schools and high schools are developing strict plagiarism policies as well.

TIP

For a review of how to cite online material properly, refer to Figure 8-16 in Chapter 8.

 FIGURE 16-5

Examples of what is and what is not normally considered plagiarism.

PLAGIARISM	NOT PLAGIARISM
A student including a few sentences or a few paragraphs written by another author in his term paper without crediting the original author.	A student including a few sentences or a few paragraphs written by another author in his term paper, either indenting the quotation or placing it inside quotation marks, and crediting the original author with a citation in the text or with a footnote or endnote.
A newspaper reporter changing a few words in a sentence or paragraph written by another author and including the revised text in an article without crediting the original author.	A newspaper reporter paraphrasing a few sentences or paragraphs written by another author without changing the meaning of the text, including the revised text in an article, and crediting the original author with a proper citation.
A student copying and pasting information from various online documents to create her research paper without crediting the original authors.	A student copying and pasting information from various online documents and using those quotes in her research paper either indented or enclosed in quotation marks with the proper citations for each author.
A teacher sharing a poem with a class, leading the class to believe the poem was his original work.	A teacher sharing a poem with a class, clearly identifying the poet.

>**Business ethics.** Standards of moral conduct that guide a business's policies, decisions, and actions. >**Plagiarism.** Presenting someone else's work as your own.

Instructor submits electronic versions of student papers; the results are usually available online almost immediately.

The black text was correctly identified as being original.

The red text was correctly identified as being taken from a HowStuffWorks.com online article.

The green text was correctly identified as being taken from a Webopedia.com definition.

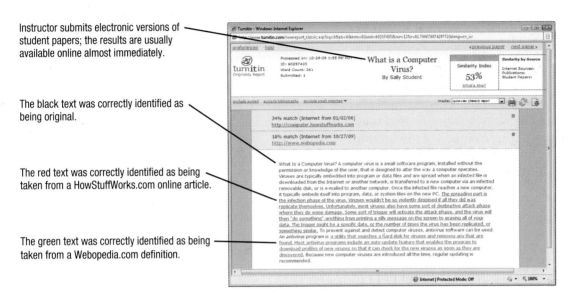

FIGURE 16-6

Results of an online originality test on an essay that contained plagiarized content.

Music

There have been many issues regarding the legal and ethical use of music over the past few years. The controversy started with the emergence and widespread use of *Napster* (the first P2P music sharing site that facilitated the exchange of music files from one Napster user's computer to another). Many exchanges via the original Napster service violated copyright law and a flood of lawsuits from the music industry eventually shut down Napster and other P2P sites that were being used to exchange copyright-protected content illegally. Additional issues arose with the introduction of recordable and rewritable CD and DVD drives, portable digital media players, and other technology that can be used to duplicate digital music. Some issues regarding the legal and ethical use of digital music have been resolved. For instance, downloading a music file from a P2P site without compensating the artist and record label is a violation of copyright law and an unethical act; so is transferring legally obtained songs to a storage medium to sell or give to others. To give individuals a legal alternative for obtaining digital music quickly and easily, music can be purchased and downloaded via a number of online music stores and services today. However, illegal music exchanges are still taking place and law enforcement agencies, as well as the Recording Industry Association of America (RIAA), are pursuing individuals who violate music copyrights. For instance, the RIAA won its first lawsuit against an individual in late 2007 when a young woman was found guilty of sharing music online and was ordered to pay a total of $222,000 to record companies. At a new trial in 2009, the verdict was the same but the award was increased to $1.92 million—$80,000 per downloaded song.

Once an MP3 file or audio CD has been obtained legally, however, most experts agree that it falls within the fair use concept for an individual to transfer those songs to a CD, computer, or portable digital media player, as long as it is for personal, noncommercial use and does not violate a user agreement. In the past, songs downloaded from some online music stores included DRM controls, which prevented the songs from being copied to other devices. While this helped prevent the illegal copying of downloaded songs from one user to another, it also prevented users from transferring legally downloaded music from one of their devices to another. In response to user protests, most music stores today (such as the one shown in Figure 16-7) offer their songs in the universal (and DRM-free) MP3 format, so they can be played on a wide range of devices.

VIDEO PODCAST

Go to the Chapter 16 page at **www.cengage.com/ computerconcepts/np/uc13** to download or listen to the "How To: Restore Your Computer's Music Library from Your iPod" video podcast.

FIGURE 16-7

Many music stores today offer DRM-free song downloads.

• DRM-free MP3s play on your iPod, Zune, mobile phone, computer, or any MP3 player

Cecily Mak, Associate General Counsel and Director of Music Licensing, RealNetworks, Inc.

How can an individual know that music available for download via the Internet is legal to download?

Distribution of copyrighted works (including music) without permission from the copyright owners is illegal. The best way to determine whether music available for download is authorized is to evaluate the source—is the Web site from which you want to download the music legitimate? If the Web site has a license from the copyright owner to distribute the musical content, the copyright owner is likely being paid and the download is legal. A good test to consider is whether you have to pay for the music or view advertisements as a condition of getting the music. If the Web site is not authorized to distribute the music (often indicated by a "too good to be true" free MP3 catalog), the download is not legal and you could be held personally liable for copyright infringement. Furthermore, it is never legal to download unauthorized music from peer-to-peer (P2P) systems or pirate sites.

One long-standing controversy related to digital music is the issue of royalties. While conventional radio stations pay licensing fees to air music, they have been battling record companies for years over whether or not the broadcasters should pay a royalty each time a song is aired. At the time of this writing, the *Performance Rights Act* was being considered—if it passes, broadcasters would have to pay a performance fee for all music played over the air. A similar issue that arose in 2009 was whether or not a mobile phone ringtone playing in public can be considered a performance and, therefore, should subject mobile phone providers to a royalty fee each time a customer's ringtone is played. In late 2009, however, a judge ruled that mobile phone providers are only responsible for the transmission of the song to the phone and ringtones do not constitute a performance, so performance royalties do not apply.

Movies

Since 1984, when Disney and Universal sued Sony to stop production of the *Betamax* (the first personal VCR), concern about movie piracy has increased dramatically. The lawsuit was eventually decided in Sony's favor—the Supreme Court upheld the consumers' rights to record shows for convenience (called *time shifting*), as long as it was for personal use. As a result of this decision, VCR use became commonplace. Interestingly, in direct contrast to the views held by the entertainment industry in 1984, videos have been credited with boosting Hollywood's revenues tremendously over the years. Nevertheless, the entertainment industry continues to be concerned about the ability of consumers to make copies of movies—especially today, since digital content can be duplicated an unlimited number of times without losing quality. The Motion Picture Association of America (MPAA) estimates that losses due to movie piracy worldwide exceed $18 billion per year.

To prevent individuals from making unauthorized copies of feature films purchased on DVDs or downloaded via the Internet, many of these items contain copy protection or some other form of DRM. Movie pirates, however, can often circumvent copy protection with software and other tools in order to duplicate the movies and create illegal copies. Pirated copies of movies are also often created today by videotaping them with a camcorder during a prerelease screening or on the opening day of a movie. This practice has resulted in a vast number of movies becoming illegally available on DVDs and via the Internet at about the same time they arrive in theaters. As a result, Congress passed the *Family Entertainment and Copyright Act of 2005*, which makes transmitting or recording a movie during a performance at a U.S. movie theater illegal. To help identify and prosecute a "cammer," most movie studios now embed invisible digital watermarks in each print released to a theater, as discussed earlier in this chapter. The information contained in these watermarks can be used to identify the location where the movie was recorded once a bootleg copy of a movie is discovered.

The access to both authorized and unauthorized copies of movies via the Internet, as well as the widespread use of digital video recorders (DVRs) and DVD players that support recordable and rewritable DVDs today, create new legal and ethical dilemmas for individuals. If one individual records a television show and then shares it with a friend via the Internet or a DVD disc, does that go beyond the concept of fair use? If you run across a Web site from which you can download a copy of a movie not yet out on DVD, are you legally at risk if you make the download? What if you watch the movie once and then delete it—are you still in the wrong? What if you download a video-on-demand movie and then share it with a friend? Is that any different, legally or ethically, from sharing a movie rented from a brick-and-mortar video store with a friend before you return it? What about the place shifting products on the market, such as the Slingbox discussed in Chapter 7? If you use such a product to transfer a movie or TV show obtained through your cable or satellite TV connection to another location, are you rebroadcasting that content or simply place shifting it? What if you send the content to another individual to watch via his or her computer—is that legal?

While the answers to these questions have yet to be unequivocally decided, distributing bootleg copies of movies via the Internet is both illegal and unethical. There have been many local, state, and federal operations in the U.S. and other countries in recent years focused on targeting online piracy of copyrighted software, movies, music, and games. To help remind individuals that piracy is illegal, the FBI introduced the *FBI Anti-Piracy Warning Seal* (see Figure 16-8) designed to be used in conjunction with movie DVDs, music CDs, and other intellectual properties that are commonly pirated. Today, this seal is often printed on product packaging and it is displayed with additional piracy warnings when many DVD movies are played.

FIGURE 16-8
The FBI Anti-Piracy Warning seal.

The MPAA also recently began pursuing civil litigation against movie pirates. The organization is concentrating mainly on the individuals who create illegal DVDs, but prosecution of individuals who upload movies to be shared via the Internet is also occurring. To catch people who are sharing movies illegally on the Internet, the MPAA uses special software that monitors file sharing networks to find copyrighted movies and then identifies the responsible individual by using the IP address of the computer being used to share the movie. Members of the movie industry also hire special firms, such as BayTSP, that specialize in monitoring P2P networks, Web sites, and other Internet resources in order to identify their clients' copyrighted material (such as documents, graphics, music, or movie files) that is being misused on the Internet. These firms typically use automated programs to scan the Web in order to find intellectual property that the firm is charged with protecting. When a firm finds a client's file that is being shared illegally, the firm can issue an infringement notice to the violator via his or her ISP. The firm also typically collects any data that might be needed in case the client (the copyright holder) decides to pursue legal action.

To prevent the sharing of movies that have been downloaded legally (such as video-on-demand movie rentals and movies purchased in downloadable form), many downloaded movies include DRM controls. For instance, DRM controls can be used to prevent the movie from being copied to another medium or they can allow the movie to be used only for a specified period of time (such as a 24-hour period beginning when the movie first starts to play). Consumers have some objections to the current movie DRM systems, similar to the objections they have with music DRM systems. In response, some services (such as TiVo) have changed their systems to allow consumers to transfer video content to other devices (such as a portable computer or a portable digital media player) for convenience. For a look at *Digital Copy*—a new option for taking your legally purchased movies with you on your computer or portable digital media player—see the How It Works box.

Ethical Use of Resources and Information

A variety of resources (such as school computers, company computers, and equipment) and types of information (such as customer or employee information) can be used in an unethical manner. For example, some employees use company computers for personal use,

HOW IT WORKS

Digital Copy Movies

Did you ever want to take a copy of a DVD movie you own with you on your portable digital media player, but didn't want to pay to download a second digital copy of the movie? Well, now you can, with *Digital Copy*.

A new trend in movie delivery available from most major movie studios (including Twentieth Century Fox, Warner Brothers, Sony Pictures, and Disney), Digital Copy allows individuals who purchase a DVD or Blu-Ray Disc movie that supports Digital Copy to copy the movie to a computer and a portable device, such as a portable digital media player. The DVD package typically includes two discs—a conventional DVD disc containing the movie that can be played in a computer DVD drive or a DVD player as usual, and a Digital Copy disc that can be used to install the movie on a computer and portable device.

The general procedure for installing a Digital Copy movie is shown in the accompanying illustration. While the process varies some from studio to studio, you typically follow these steps: First, insert the Digital Copy disc into your computer's DVD drive. Next, use the menus (supplying the activation code contained inside the movie case when prompted) to copy the movie to the iTunes or Windows Media Player library on your computer. (Which library you use depends on the type of portable device the movie will be copied to, as discussed shortly, and iTunes users will need to log in to their account in order to activate the movie.) After the movie is installed in the library on your computer, the Digital Copy disc is no longer needed to play the movie from the library on your computer, and you can use the sync process to transfer the movie to one portable device.

At the present time, iTunes users can transfer Digital Copy movies only to an iPod or an iPhone, and Windows Media Player users can transfer Digital Copy movies only to *Certified for Windows Vista* (previously called *PlaysForSure*) devices that support DRM Windows Media .wmv files (such as a Sony Walkman or Creative Zen). While these compatibility issues limit the use of Digital Copy movies for some users and only time will tell if Digital Copy is a viable solution for the issue of legally playing purchased movies on more than one device, for users with devices that work seamlessly with the Digital Copy process, Digital Copy is an interesting option for taking your DVD movies with you while on the go.

1. The movie includes a Digital Copy disc—insert it into your computer.

2. Use the menus to activate your Digital Copy and transfer the movie to your computer.

3. The movie is installed in (and can be played from) your library—use the sync process to transfer it to your portable device.

4. The movie can be played on your portable device.

some students perform dishonest acts while completing assignments or taking exams, and some job applicants provide erroneous or misleading information during the application or interview process.

Ethical Use of School or Company Resources

What is considered proper and ethical use of school or company resources may vary from school to school or company to company. To explain what is allowed, many schools and businesses have policies that specify which activities are allowed and which are forbidden. Often, these policies are available as a written document—frequently called a **code of conduct**—included in a student or employee handbook. They are also often available online via an organization's intranet or Web site (a code of conduct was shown in Figure 9-1 in Chapter 9). Policies can vary from organization to organization; for example, one school may allow the use of school computers to download software programs and another school may not, and one business may allow limited use of the office photocopier or printer for personal use while another may forbid that activity. As a result, all students and employees should make it a point to find out what is considered ethical use of resources at their school or place of business, including what types of computer and Internet activities are considered acceptable, and what personal use (if any) of resources, such as computers, printers, photocopiers, telephones, and fax machines, is allowed. To enforce its policies, businesses may use employee monitoring, which was discussed in Chapter 15.

Another common type of code widely used by various industries and organizations is a **code of ethics**. Codes of ethics, such as the one shown in Figure 16-9, summarize the moral guidelines adopted by a particular organization (frequently a professional society). They typically address such issues as honesty, integrity, fairness, responsibility to others, proper use of intellectual property, confidentiality, and accountability. So, while codes of conduct usually address specific activities that can and cannot be performed, codes of ethics cover broader ethical standards of conduct.

Although employees are typically forbidden from revealing confidential or proprietary information to outsiders, a dilemma exists when that information is related to an illegal, an unethical, or a dangerous activity involving the business. Employees who reveal wrongdoing within an organization to the public or to authorities are referred to as *whistle-blowers*. These individuals have varying degrees of protection from retaliation (such as being fired) for whistle-blowing. The type and extent of protection depends on the kind of wrongdoing and the organization involved, as well as the state in which the company and employee are located. The *Sarbanes-Oxley Act* (also called the *Corporate Responsibility Act* and signed into law in mid-2002) provides federal protection for whistle-blowers who report alleged violations of Securities and Exchange Commission rules or any federal law relating to shareholder fraud.

FIGURE 16-9
A sample code
of ethics.

Ethical Use of Employee and Customer Information

While a business may be legally bound by such restrictions as employee confidentiality laws, union contracts, and its customer privacy policy, there are gray areas inside which ethical decisions need to be made. For example, should an ISP comply with a request from a foreign government for customer e-mail records or the identity of a customer matching an IP address? Or should a business share or sell customer information, even if it is legal to do so? This latter decision is one that many businesses have struggled with, especially in challenging economic times when a quick source of revenue gained from selling customer data is tempting. Although some businesses have succumbed to

> **Code of conduct.** A policy, often for a school or business, that specifies allowable use of resources, such as computers and other equipment.
> **Code of ethics.** A policy, often for an organization or industry, that specifies overall moral guidelines adopted by that organization or industry.

this temptation and have sold their customer lists, others believe that any short-term gains achieved through ethically questionable acts will adversely affect customer loyalty and will ultimately hurt the business in the long run.

To prepare future employees for these types of decisions, most business schools incorporate business ethics into their curriculum. However, there is the ongoing question of how effective the training is. In fact, AACSB International (an accrediting agency for business schools in the United States) recently reported that business schools have not done enough to raise the ethical awareness of MBA students. Ethics training is also becoming mandatory at some businesses. This may be even more important given the recent economic uncertainty because the Ethics Resource Center reports that workplace misconduct tends to increase by at least 11% during times of turmoil, such as layoffs and budget cuts. In addition, a recent survey of executives found that nearly one-half expected fraud levels within their companies to increase in the coming year.

Cheating and Falsifying Information

Just as computers and the Internet make it easier for individuals to plagiarize documents, computers and the Internet also make it easier for individuals to cheat on assignments or online exams, or to perform other similar unethical acts.

Unfortunately, cheating by students at both the high school level and the college level is rampant today. Cheating today is often performed via the Internet and mobile phones, such as creating a paper from material plagiarized from Web sites, storing notes on a mobile phone to view during a test, texting answers to another student during a test, or taking photos of an exam to pass on to a student taking the test later in the day. While technology does make it easier to cheat, it also may make it feel less like cheating. During one recent study of middle and high school students, for instance, about 25% of the students didn't think storing notes on a mobile phone or texting during an exam constituted cheating.

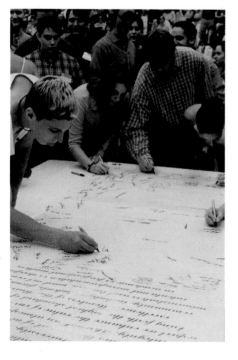

⊘ FIGURE 16-10

Academic honor codes. The honor code at the University of Denver is signed by virtually all incoming students.

Traditionally, it was typically weaker students who cheated to prevent failing a course or an exam. Today, however, studies have shown that honor students and others with higher GPAs are more likely to cheat. For college students, MBA students tend to cheat more often than other graduate students—according to Donald McCabe of Rutgers University, this might be because the students are emulating behaviors they believe are necessary to succeed in the corporate world. But whether they realize it or not, students who choose to cheat are cheating themselves of an education. They are also being unfair to honest students by possibly altering the grading curve. Widespread cheating can also have a negative impact on society, such as if underprepared employees enter the workforce.

To explain to students what behavior is expected of them, many schools are developing *academic honor codes*. These codes are usually published in the student handbook and on the school Web site; they may also be included in course syllabi. Research has shown that having an academic honor code effectively reduces cheating. For example, one McCabe study found that cheating on tests on campuses with honor codes is typically one-third to one-half less than on campuses that do not have honor codes, and the level of cheating on written assignments is one-quarter to one-third lower. To bring attention to their honor codes, some schools encourage incoming students to sign their honor codes upon admission. For instance, all incoming University of Denver students are asked to sign the school's honor code publicly (see Figure 16-10). Regardless of whether or not students choose to sign the honor code, they are required to abide by it.

Like academic cheating, lying on a job application or résumé is more common than most of us may think it is. The practice of providing false information in an attempt to look more qualified for a job, sometimes referred to as *résumé padding*, is both dishonest and unethical. It is also widespread. Recent research conducted by the *New York Times* found that almost half of hiring managers and 84% of job seekers believe that résumé padding is done by a significant number of candidates. In addition to being unethical, providing false information to a potential employer can have grave consequences. The majority of the companies surveyed in the *New York Times* study have a policy that lists termination as the appropriate action for employees who were hired based on falsified résumés or applications. Being blacklisted from an industry or being sued for breach of contract are also possibilities. Résumé writers should remember that background checks are easily available on the Web, which means credentials are easy to check and verify. Even if individuals believe they will not be caught, applicants should not embellish their résumés or job applications to any extent because it is an unethical thing to do. Another recent ethical issue surrounding IT employees is cheating on IT certification exams. Copies of certification questions and entire certification exams are available for purchase online, and some Web sites offer the services of "gunmen" (usually located in Asia) who take certification tests for individuals at a cost of up to several thousand dollars each. In response, companies that offer IT certifications are looking at the security of their testing processes to try to put a stop to this new type of cheating.

There are also situations in personal life that tempt some individuals to provide inaccurate personal information, such as when writing personal advertisements, when participating in chat rooms, and when individuals may otherwise wish to appear to be someone different from the person they really are. There are differing opinions about how ethical these actions are—some individuals believe that it is a person's right to portray himself or herself in any way desired; others feel that any type of dishonesty is unethical.

Computer Hoaxes and Digital Manipulation

Most people realize that information in print media can, at times, be misleading and that photos can be manipulated. Information found on the Internet may also be inaccurate, misleading, or biased. Some of this type of information is published on Web pages; other information is passed on via e-mail. Two types of computer-oriented misinformation include computer hoaxes and digital manipulation.

Computer Hoaxes

A **computer hoax** is an inaccurate statement or story—such as the "fact" that flesh-eating bacteria have been found in banana shipments or that Applebee's will send you a gift certificate for forwarding on an e-mail—spread through the use of computers. These hoaxes are sometimes published on Web pages, but they are more commonly spread via e-mail. Common computer hoax subjects include nonexistent computer viruses, serious health risks, impending terrorist attacks, chain letters, and free prizes or giveaways. Inaccurate information posted on a Web site or wiki just to be misleading can also be considered a computer hoax. E-mail hoaxes are written with the purpose of being circulated to as many people as possible. Some are started as experiments to see how fast and how far information can travel via the Internet; others originate from a joke or the desire to frighten people. Similar to spam, e-mail hoaxes can be annoying, waste people's time, bog down e-mail systems, and clog users' Inboxes. Because computer hoaxes are so common, it is a good idea to double-check any warning you receive by e-mail or read on a Web site before passing that warning on to another person, regardless of how realistic or frightening the information appears to be (sites like the one shown in Figure 16-11 can help you research potential hoaxes).

FIGURE 16-11
Hoax-Slayer. This is one site that can be used to research possible computer hoaxes.

>**Computer hoax.** An inaccurate statement or story spread through the use of computers.

Digital Manipulation

Computers make it very easy to copy or modify text, images, photographs, music, and other digital content. In addition to being a copyright concern, **digital manipulation** (digitally altering digital content) can be used to misquote individuals, repeat comments out of context, retouch photographs—even create false or misleading photographs—and so is an ethical concern, as well. While there are some beneficial, ethical, noncontroversial applications of digital manipulation (such as aging photos of missing children to show what they may look like at the present time, or altering photos of wanted criminals or suspects to show possible alternate appearances for law enforcement purposes), the matter of altering photos for publication purposes is the subject of debate. Some publications and photographers see no harm in altering photographs to remove an offending item (such as a telephone pole behind someone's head), to make someone look a little more attractive, to illustrate a point, or to increase circulation; others view any change in content as unethical and a great disservice to both the public and our history. For example, fifty years from now, will anyone know that a staged or altered photograph of a historical event was not an actual depiction of the event?

Although manipulation of photographs has occurred for quite some time in tabloids and other publications not known as being reputable news sources, there have been several incidents of more reputable news publications using digitally altered photographs in recent years. Many of these became known because the unaltered photograph was used in another publication at about the same time. One of the most widely publicized cases occurred in 1994, just following the arrest of O. J. Simpson. While *Newsweek* ran Simpson's mug shot unaltered, *TIME* magazine darkened the photograph, creating a more sinister look and making Simpson's skin color appear darker than it actually is. This photo drew harsh criticism from Simpson supporters who felt the photograph made him appear guilty, the African-American community who viewed the alteration as an act of racial insensitivity, and news photographers who felt that the action damaged the credibility not only of that particular magazine, but also of all journalists.

A more recent example is the case of a one-time Pulitzer Prize finalist who resigned from a Toledo, Ohio, newspaper after it was discovered that he had submitted for publication nearly 80 doctored photos in just the 14 weeks prior to his resignation, including one sports photo of a basketball game with a digitally-added basketball placed in mid-air. Other recent instances of digitally manipulated images being printed in news media include a photo released by the U.S. Army of a U.S. soldier killed in action, whose picture was later discovered to be a composite of the soldier's head on another soldier's body; a photo printed in an Israeli newspaper of the Prime Minister, President, and members of the Cabinet of that country that the newspaper edited to replace the two female Cabinet members with male members; and a photo of an Iranian missile test that appeared in many newspapers but that contained a digitally added missile to replace one that did not fire during the test (see Figure 16-12).

Perhaps the most disturbing thing about known alterations such as these is that some may never have been noticed, and may consequently have been accepted as true representations. Adding to the problem of unethical digital manipulation is the use of digital cameras today, which eliminate the photo negatives that could be used with film cameras to show what photographs actually looked like at the time they were taken. Although some

FIGURE 16-12

Digital manipulation. The digitally manipulated photo (left) added an additional missile launching to the real photo (right) and appeared on the front page of many major newspapers.

DIGITALLY ALTERED PHOTO   ORIGINAL PHOTO

>**Digital manipulation.** The alteration of digital content, usually text or photographs.

publications allow the use of "photo illustrations," others have strict rules about digital manipulation—especially for news photojournalists. For instance, the *LA Times* fired a staff photographer covering the war in Iraq when he combined two of his photographs into one to convey a point better.

Ethical Business Practices and Decision Making

Most businesses must make a variety of ethics-related business decisions, such as whether or not to sell a product or service that some may find offensive or objectionable, whether or not to install video cameras in the workplace for monitoring purposes, whether or not to release potentially misleading information, or whether or not to perform controversial research. In addition, corporate integrity, as it relates to accounting practices and proper disclosure, is a business ethics topic that has come to the forefront because of the many recent incidents involving corporate scandals and bankruptcies.

Fraudulent Reporting and Other Scandalous Activities

Following the large number of corporate scandals occurring since 2002, business ethics have moved into the public eye. The scandals, such as the ones surrounding executives at Enron, Tyco International, and WorldCom, involved lies, fraud, deception, and other illegal and unethical behavior. This behavior forced both Enron and WorldCom into bankruptcy proceedings. When asked to comment on the scandals, 3Com Chief Executive Officer Bruce Claflin said on CNBC, "I would argue we do not have an accounting problem—we have an ethics problem."

In reaction to the scandals, Congress passed the *Sarbanes-Oxley Act of 2002*. This law includes provisions to improve the quality of financial reporting, independent audits, and accounting services for public companies; to increase penalties for corporate wrong-doing; to protect the objectivity and independence of securities analysts; and to require CEOs and CFOs to vouch personally for the truth and fairness of their company's disclosures. Businesses need to keep current laws in mind, as well as the businesses' ethical standards, when preparing financial reports, press releases, and other important documents that represent a company's position.

Ethically Questionable Products or Services

One ethical issue a business may run into is whether or not to sell products or services that some people find objectionable. For example, the eBay Web site states that it prohibits the sale of some controversial or sensitive items, in addition to illegal items. For instance, it will not allow items that promote or glorify hated; violence; or racial, sexual, or religious intolerance. Consequently, it bans Nazi propaganda materials, Ku Klux Klan (KKK) memorabilia, crime scene and morgue photographs, and letters and belongings of notorious criminals, even though sellers may legally be able to sell such items elsewhere.

Another ethical decision for businesses that allow individuals to upload content to their Web sites (such as wikis, classified ad sites, message boards, and photo or video sharing sites) is how (if at all) they should monitor the content posted on their sites. For instance, YouTube relies on the user community to flag videos that might be inappropriate for some viewers (such as the Saddam Hussein execution video posted on YouTube shortly after that execution took place). All flagged videos are viewed by YouTube staff members and they are either removed or flagged as age-restricted; flagged videos first display a warning screen and viewers need to verify that they are over 18 by logging in to their YouTube account. In another example, the popular online classified ad site Craigslist has been under fire recently for numerous crimes (including rape, murder, prostitution, and attempted baby-selling) that have occurred via ads posted on its site. While not agreeing to censor ads or eliminate its adult-oriented categories, Craigslist did recently agree to crack down on ads for prostitution by requiring those who post "exotic services" ads to provide a working telephone number where they can be reached and to pay a fee using a credit card in order to post the ad.

Companies that do business in more than one country also have global considerations to address. For instance, a Brazilian court ordered YouTube in 2007 to shut down access to a racy video clip of a Brazilian celebrity and her boyfriend on the beach, even though YouTube is a U.S. company. Cultural issues such as these are discussed in more detail shortly.

Another decision is the need for age verification. To protect children from predators, many states are pushing social networking sites, such as MySpace and Facebook, to implement age verification systems. Age verification procedures also benefit the adults who use these sites so they know they are acting appropriately with other members. Businesses that offer products or services that are inappropriate for children (such as alcohol, tobacco, adult movies and video games, pornography, online gambling, and so forth) also need to make decisions regarding access; for example, the number and types of safeguards they need to provide to ensure that children do not have access to these products and services. They also need to determine if the company is required legally, or just ethically, to provide these safeguards. This is especially significant for businesses with an e-commerce presence. In a conventional store, individuals can be asked to show an ID to prove they are of the required age before they are allowed to buy tobacco products, alcohol, pornographic materials, and other products that cannot legally be sold to minors. But, during an online transaction, it is much more difficult to verify that a buyer is the required age.

To comply with state and federal laws, as well as to protect themselves from potential litigation, Web sites selling or providing adult products and services should implement adequate age-verification procedures. Some sites require visitors to click a statement declaring they are the required age or to enter a valid credit card number before accessing or purchasing adult-only content or products. However, these precautions can be bypassed by underage visitors easily. Requiring proof of age at delivery (see Figure 16-13) is a safer precaution for physical goods purchased online and is required by law in some states for certain types of shipments.

The decisions about which products or services to offer online and offline are important—and sometimes difficult—ethical decisions for businesses to make. Typically, these decisions are based on the company's overall corporate mission and desired public image. Consequently, some businesses may choose not to sell adult-only content at all. Others may decide to sell it via the Internet only in conjunction with a third-party age verification system, or to sell those products or services online but require an adult to sign for the items when they are delivered. Still other businesses may feel that a warning statement or similar precaution on their Web sites is all that is needed, and that it is the parents' responsibility to make sure their children do not purchase illegal or inappropriate items or view adult-only content via the Internet.

FIGURE 16-13

Ethical e-commerce.

Businesses selling products or services that are inappropriate or illegal for minors should require proof of age at delivery.

> Due to the alcoholic content of this gift, an adult signature is required upon delivery.

Vaporware

Vaporware is a term used to designate software and hardware products that have been announced and advertised, but are not yet—and may never be—available. Sometimes a premature announcement is not intentional, such as when a delay in production or other last-minute problem results in a late introduction. At other times, it may be an intentional act, designed to convince customers to wait for the company's upcoming product instead of buying an existing competitive product—an act some consumers are likely to view as an unethical business practice.

Workplace Monitoring

As discussed in Chapter 15, the majority of businesses in the U.S. today monitor employees to some extent. Although businesses have the right and responsibility to ensure that employees are productive and that company resources are not being abused, many believe that businesses also have an ethical responsibility to inform employees of any monitoring that takes place. This is especially true in countries other than the U.S., such as in the European Union where companies are much more limited in what types of monitoring they can legally do without notifying employees.

Cultural Considerations

With today's global economy, businesses also need to be sensitive to the ethical differences that may exist between different businesses located in the same country, as well as between businesses located in different countries. Ethics are fundamentally based on values, so when beliefs, laws, customs, and traditions vary among businesses, the ethics associated with those businesses will likely differ as well. One example is the concept of *human cloning*. There are widely differing beliefs within the United States about the ethics of human cloning—some disabled Americans look to cloning as a means of finding a medical cure to their disabilities, while other citizens and groups oppose cloning for religious or ethical reasons.

FIGURE 16-14

Cultural considerations. In some countries, bootleg copies of music CDs and movie DVDs are sold openly, such as this DVD seen recently at a store in China.

Ethical decisions need to be made whenever a business practice or product is legal or socially acceptable in one country, but not in another. One example is copyright law. While the United States and many other countries have copyright laws, some countries do not have copyright laws or, if they do, those laws are not strongly enforced. Although an individual may be able to purchase a bootleg copy of a software program, music CD, or movie in some countries (see Figure 16-14), import restrictions prevent these items from being brought legally into the United States to be sold. With the Internet, however, U.S. citizens now have the capability of buying unauthorized copies of copyrighted materials from countries in which those copies are legal or copyright law is not strongly enforced. This raises the question of ethical responsibility. Is it the individual's responsibility not to make these types of unethical purchases, even if technology makes it possible? What role should the government play in preventing citizens from buying products from other countries that are illegal in its country? What legal and ethical responsibility do businesses have to ensure that customers do not have access to products or services that are illegal in their customers' locations?

In addition to legal issues, organizations conducting business in other countries should also take into consideration the ethical standards prevalent in the countries with which they do business. Factors such as gender roles, religious beliefs, and cultural customs should be considered and respected when corresponding, negotiating, and otherwise interacting with businesses located in other countries. For example, some cultures may require a handshake or other ritual that is impossible to carry out online in order to close a deal. In this case, while the terms of the deal may be carried out online, the deal itself would need to be closed in person. Some cultures also move at a different pace than others. And, while private e-mail messages in the United States are often respected as private and not forwarded to others, group-focused cultures may feel obligated to share personal e-mails with the entire team—a potential embarrassment for individuals if they are not aware of that custom while working with businesses in those countries. Businesses should also be careful not to offend individuals from other countries or other cultures that they do business with. Some straightforward questions acceptable in the United States—such as a request to verify certain numbers or double-check a source—may be viewed as an insult in some cultures.

To prepare students properly to succeed in our global economy, some business schools include diversity and cross-cultural training in their curriculum. Similarly, in order to avoid offending their international business partners or clients, some international organizations arrange for their employees to have such training prior to traveling out of the country. Other companies are modifying products and services to appeal to a more global customer base. For example, several mobile phone models today are geared

TIP

When exchanging e-mails with individuals in other countries, especially business e-mails, avoid trying to add humor to your messages. Humor can be difficult to translate to other languages and cultures, and it can be misinterpreted if read at a later time, such as during an audit or legal proceeding.

toward Muslims and include Islamic features, such as reminder alarms at prayer times, automatically switching to vibration mode during prayer times, and an automatic Qibla direction finder (showing the direction toward Mecca from the user's current position anywhere in the world).

CAUTION CAUTION CAUTION CAUTION CAUTION CAUTION CAUT

When purchasing goods from another country, it is important to realize that the laws regarding the sale of products, as well as the laws regarding the privacy of personal information supplied to a vendor during a transaction, vary from one country to another. Avoid purchasing questionable goods online and avoid providing personal information to any Web site in a country that may have lax privacy laws—as a minimum, be sure to read the privacy statements for any Web site carefully before you provide them with any personal information you do not wish to be shared with others.

COMPUTERS AND HEALTH

Despite their many benefits, computers can pose a threat to a user's physical and mental well-being. *Repetitive stress injuries* and other injuries related to the workplace environment are estimated to account for one-third of all serious workplace injuries and cost employees, employers, and insurance companies in lost wages, healthcare expenses, legal costs, and worker's compensation claims. Other physical dangers (such as heat burns and hearing loss) can be associated with computers and related technology, and there are some concerns about the long-term effect of using computers and other related devices. *Stress, burnout, computer/Internet addiction*, and other emotional health problems are more difficult to quantify, although many experts believe computer-related emotional health problems are on the rise. While researchers are continuing to investigate the physical and emotional risks of computer use and while researchers are working to develop strategies for minimizing those risks, all computer users should be aware of the possible effects of computers on their health, and what they can do today to stay healthy while using a computer both for personal use and while on the job.

Physical Health

Common physical conditions caused by computer use include eyestrain, blurred vision, fatigue, headaches, backaches, and wrist and finger pain. Some conditions are classified as **repetitive stress injuries** (**RSIs**), in which hand, wrist, shoulder, or neck pain is caused by performing the same physical movements over and over again. For instance, extensive keyboard and mouse use has been associated with RSIs, although RSIs can be caused by non-computer-related activities, as well. One RSI related to the repetitive finger movements made when using a keyboard is **carpal tunnel syndrome** (**CTS**)—a painful and crippling condition affecting the hands and wrists. CTS occurs when the nerve in the *carpal tunnel* located on the underside of the wrist is compressed. An RSI associated with typing on the tiny keyboards and thumbpads commonly found on mobile phones and mobile devices is **DeQuervain's tendonitis**—a condition in which the tendons on the thumb side of the wrists are swollen and irritated. Another physical condition is *computer vision syndrome* (*CVS*)—a collection of eye and vision problems associated with computer use. The most common symptoms are eyestrain or eye fatigue, dry eyes,

> **Repetitive stress injury (RSI).** A type of injury, such as carpal tunnel syndrome, that is caused by performing the same physical movements over and over again. > **Carpal tunnel syndrome (CTS).** A painful and crippling condition affecting the hands and wrists that can be caused by computer use. > **DeQuervain's tendonitis.** A condition in which the tendons on the thumb side of the wrist are swollen and irritated.

burning eyes, light sensitivity, blurred vision, headaches, and pain in the shoulders, neck, or back. Eyestrain and CVS are growing more common as individuals are increasingly reading content on the small displays commonly built into mobile phones and mobile devices.

Some recent physical health concerns center around heat. For instance, one study measured the peak temperature on the underside of a typical notebook computer at over 139° Fahrenheit—this means that some notebook computers are now hot enough to burn a person's legs when operated on the user's lap. Consequently, many portable computer manufacturers now warn against letting any part of the computer touch your body, and a variety of notebook cooling stands (such as the one shown in Figure 2-13 in Chapter 2) are available to place between the computer and your lap for those occasions when a better work surface is not available.

Another growing physical health concern is noise-induced hearing loss, mainly due to portable digital media players whose volume can be turned up very high without audio distortion and to the earbud headsets typically used with these devices that deliver sound directly into the ear. In addition, people often listen to the music stored on these devices while they are on the go; as a result, they may increase the volume in an attempt to drown out outside noise, further posing a risk to their hearing. To protect against hearing loss, experts suggest a 60/60 rule, which means using earbuds for only about 60 minutes per day with the volume less than 60% of the device's maximum volume. For extended use, *noise reduction headphones* that help block out external noise to allow listeners to hear music better at lower volumes can help, as can using over-the-ear-headphones instead of earbuds and using an external speaker whenever possible.

A new danger that came into the forefront recently is text messaging while driving. There have been many cases of texting-related car accidents, including many fatalities. A recent nationwide insurance study found that one in seven drivers admits sending text messages while driving—among drivers 18 to 24 year old, it is a staggering 50%. Currently, 13 states in the United States have laws against texting while driving and 5 have laws against talking on a mobile phone while driving (drivers must place calls or send text messages using hands-free devices, such as via a Bluetooth headset or a speakerphone instead). While some feel these laws are a step in the right direction, studies have found that using a mobile phone with a hands-free device still distracts drivers. One possible solution is using a service, such as *DriveAssist* (see Figure 16-15), that automatically switches your phone to "driving mode" when the car you are in is in motion. In driving mode, all incoming voice calls are greeted with a message stating the subscriber is driving and the call is routed to voice mail, all incoming text messages are stored until the car stops moving, and all outgoing calls are blocked (except for 911 calls and calls by passengers if the passenger override option is selected).

An additional health concern is the possible risks due to the radiation emitted from wireless devices, such as mobile phones, Wi-Fi and Bluetooth devices, wireless peripherals, and so forth. Mobile phones, in particular, have been studied for several decades because of their close proximity to the user's head. The results of the studies have been conflicting, with many experts believing that the possible health risks (such as cancer and brain tumors) due to wireless technology have been exaggerated, and others believing the risks are very real. A new possible health risk identified in a recent study is the particles emitted from some laser printers. While more research is needed to link laser printers with health risks definitively, it is possible that the small particles released from these printers could be inhaled and cause lung problems. Until more research is performed, health experts recommend that rooms with laser printers be well ventilated.

FURTHER EXPLORATION Go

Go to the Chapter 16 page at **www.cengage.com/ computerconcepts/np/uc13** for links to information about computer use injuries and how they can be prevented.

FIGURE 16-15
DriveAssist. This product deactivates a mobile phone when the car is in motion.

What Is Ergonomics?

Ergonomics is the science of fitting a work environment to the people who work there. It typically focuses on making products and workspaces more comfortable and safe to use. With respect to computer use, it involves designing a safe and effective workspace, which includes properly adjusting furniture and hardware and using *ergonomic hardware* when needed. A proper work environment—used in conjunction with good user habits and procedures—can prevent many physical problems caused by computer use. A proper work environment is important for anyone who works on a computer, including employees using a computer on the job, individuals using a computer at home, and children doing computer activities at home or at school.

Workspace Design

The design of a safe and an effective computer workspace—whether it is located at work, home, or school—includes the placement and adjustment of all the furniture and equipment involved, such as the user's desk, chair, keyboard, and monitor. Workspace lighting or glare from the sun also needs to be taken into consideration. Proper workspace design can result in fewer injuries, headaches, and general aches and pains for computer users. Businesses can reap economic benefits from proper workspace design, such as fewer absences taken by employees, higher productivity, and lower insurance costs. For example, when one government department in New Jersey installed ergonomically correct workstations in its offices, computer-related health complaints fell by 40% and doctor visits dropped by 25% in less than one year.

Proper placement and adjustment of furniture is a good place to start when evaluating a workspace from an ergonomic perspective (see Figure 16-16). The desk should be placed where the sun and other sources of light cannot shine directly onto the screen or into the user's eyes. The monitor should be placed directly in front of the user about an arm's length away, and the top of the screen should be no more than 3 inches above the user's eyes once the user's chair is adjusted. The desk chair should be adjusted so that the keyboard is at, or slightly below, the height at which the user's forearms are horizontal to the floor (there are also special *ergonomic chairs* that can be used, when desired). A footrest should be used, if needed, to keep the user's feet flat on the floor once the chair height has been set. The monitor settings should be adjusted to make the screen brightness match the brightness

FIGURE 16-16

Workspace design.
Shown here are some guidelines for designing an ergonomic workspace.

TILT-AND-SWIVEL MONITOR
Adjusts for a comfortable viewing angle; top of screen should be no higher than 3 inches above the user's eyes.

DOCUMENT HOLDER
Keeps documents close to the monitor so the user does not have to turn his or her head.

PROPER USER POSITION
Sit straight with shoulders back, about 24 inches away from the monitor; keep forearms, wrists, and hands straight; keep forearms and thighs parallel to the floor.

ADJUSTABLE TABLE/DESK
Optimal height is between 25 and 29 inches tall. Keyboard and mouse should be at or just below elbow height; use a keyboard drawer if needed.

FOOTREST
Can be used, if needed, to keep legs properly positioned.

ADJUSTABLE CHAIR
Height is adjustable and has support for the lower back.

> **Ergonomics.** The science of fitting a work environment to the people who work there.

of the room and to have a high amount of contrast; the screen should also be periodically wiped clean of dust. Some setups allow the user to raise the workspace in order to work while standing, when desired.

When designing or evaluating a computer workspace, the type of computer work to be performed should be considered. For example, people who refer to written documents while working on their computers should use *document holders* to keep their documents close to their monitors. Document holders help users avoid the repetitive motion of looking between the document and the monitor—an action that can create or aggravate neck problems. These users should also place their keyboards directly in front of them for easy access. Users who do a great deal of Web surfing or other computer activities (such as computer-aided design or graphics design) that require a great deal of mouse work should give placement of the mouse for comfortable access a high priority.

The workspace design principles just discussed and illustrated in Figure 16-16 apply to users of both desktop and portable computers. However, an ergonomic workspace is more difficult to obtain when using a portable computer. To create a safer and more comfortable work environment, portable computer users should attach and use a separate keyboard and mouse whenever possible (*travel mice* and *travel keyboards*, which are smaller and lighter than conventional models, can make this easier), both at home and while traveling. In addition to being able to position the keyboard and mouse at more comfortable positions, using a separate keyboard and mouse enables the user to elevate the screen of the portable computer to a better viewing angle. To help with this and with connecting peripheral devices to a portable computer, *docking stations* and *notebook stands* can also be used.

While a keyboard, mouse, monitor, and printer can be connected to a portable computer directly, a **docking station** is a device designed to connect a portable computer to peripheral devices more easily. As shown in Figure 16-17, the computer connects to the docking station, and then the ports on the docking station can be used with that computer. Docking stations are often used in homes and offices when a notebook computer is used as a primary computer—typically, the peripheral devices remain connected to the docking station and the computer is just connected and disconnected as needed. A **notebook stand** (shown in Figure 16-17) can also be used to connect peripheral devices to a portable computer, but is designed primarily to elevate the display screen of a notebook or tablet computer to the proper height (some notebook stands also allow a second display screen to be connected at that height for a more productive workspace). If the notebook stand has built-in USB ports (such as in Figure 16-17), USB peripheral devices can be connected to the computer; if not, any peripheral devices (such as a keyboard and mouse) to be used with the computer while it is inserted into the notebook stand need to be connected directly to the computer. Smaller, lightweight portable notebook stands can be used to elevate a notebook's display while traveling. In addition to helping with screen placement

TIP

If your notebook computer has a monitor port, you can connect an external monitor to be used in place of, or in addition to, the built-in display, when desired.

FIGURE 16-17
Docking stations and notebook stands.

Docking station   Ports

DOCKING STATIONS
Contain a variety of ports; when the portable computer is connected to the docking station, the devices attached to these ports can be used.

Notebook stand   USB ports

NOTEBOOK STANDS
Elevate a notebook's display screen; if the notebook stand contains USB ports, devices attached to these ports can be used with the notebook while it is in the notebook stand.

> **Docking station.** A device designed to easily connect a portable computer to conventional hardware, such as a keyboard, mouse, monitor, and printer. > **Notebook stand.** A device that elevates the display of a notebook or tablet computer to a better viewing height; can contain USB ports to connect additional hardware.

OCCASIONAL USERS	FULL-TIME USERS
Sit with the computer on a table and position it for comfortable wrist posture. If no table is available, use a notebook cooling stand to protect your legs from the computer's heat.	Sit with the computer on a desk or table and position it for comfortable wrist posture if you won't be using a separate keyboard and mouse.
Adjust the screen to a comfortable position, so you can see the screen as straight on as possible. If you have a portable notebook stand, use it to elevate the display screen for easier viewing.	Elevate the computer so the screen is at the proper height, or connect the computer to a stand-alone monitor instead of using the computer's built-in display; consider using a docking station or notebook stand.
Bring a travel keyboard and mouse to use with the computer, whenever possible.	Use a separate keyboard and mouse, either attached directly to the computer or to a docking station or notebook stand.
When purchasing a portable computer, pay close attention to the total weight of the system (computer, power supply, additional hardware, etc.) if you will be using the computer primarily while traveling; purchase a lightweight system to avoid neck and shoulder injuries when carrying the computer from one location to another.	When purchasing a portable computer, pay close attention to the size and clarity of the monitor, unless you will be using a separate stand-alone monitor, and pay close attention to the keyboard design, unless you will be using a separate keyboard.

and connectivity, notebook stands also allow air to circulate around the bottom of the computer. For additional cooling, some notebook stands have a built-in cooling fan that is powered (via a USB port) by the computer. Some additional ergonomic tips for portable computer users are included in Figure 16-18.

Ergonomic Hardware

In addition to the workspace devices (adjustable chairs and tables, footrests, docking stations, notebook stands, laptop desks, and so on) already discussed, **ergonomic hardware** can be used to help users avoid physical problems due to extensive computer use or to help alleviate the discomfort associated with an already existing condition. Some of the most common types of ergonomic hardware are shown in Figure 16-19 and discussed next.

FIGURE 16-18
Ergonomic tips for occasional and full-time portable computer users.

➤ *Ergonomic keyboards* use a shape and key arrangement designed to lessen the strain on the hands and wrists. The keyboard shown in Figure 16-19 can be used flat, on an incline, or vertically, as needed.

➤ *Trackballs* are essentially upside-down mice that can be more comfortable to use than a conventional mouse.

FIGURE 16-19
Ergonomic devices.

ERGONOMIC KEYBOARDS

TRACKBALLS

DOCUMENT HOLDERS

ANTIGLARE SCREENS

KEYBOARD DRAWERS

WRIST SUPPORTS

COMPUTER GLOVES

>**Ergonomic hardware.** Hardware, typically an input or output device, that is designed to be more ergonomically correct than its nonergonomic counterpart.

➤ *Document holders*—sometimes called *copy holders*—can be used to keep documents close to the monitor, enabling the user to see both the document and the monitor without turning his or her head. Document holders are available for both desktop and portable computers.

➤ *Antiglare screens*—sometimes called *privacy filters*—cover the monitor screen and can be used to lessen glare and resulting eyestrain. Many antiglare screens double as privacy screens, preventing others sitting next to you (such as on an airplane) from reading what is displayed on your computer screen.

➤ *Keyboard drawers* lower the keyboard, enabling the user to keep his or her forearms parallel to the floor more easily.

➤ *Wrist supports* are designed to be placed next to the mouse or keyboard and can be used to help keep wrists straight while those devices are being used, as well as to provide support for the wrists and forearms when the devices are not being used.

➤ *Computer gloves* support the wrist and thumb while allowing the full use of the hands. They are designed to prevent and relieve wrist pain, including carpal tunnel syndrome, tendonitis, and other RSIs.

 FIGURE 16-20

Good user habits. These preventative measures can help avoid discomfort while working on a computer.

Good User Habits and Precautions

In addition to establishing an ergonomic workspace, computer users can follow a number of preventive measures while working at their computers (see Figure 16-20) to help avoid physical problems. Finger and wrist exercises, as well as frequent breaks in typing, are good precautions for helping to prevent repetitive hand and finger stress injuries. Using good posture and periodically taking a break to relax or stretch the body can help reduce or prevent back and neck strain. Rotating tasks—such as alternating between computer work, telephone work, and paperwork every 15 minutes or so—is also a good idea. For locations where some glare from a nearby window is unavoidable at certain times of the day, closing the curtains or blinds can help to prevent eyestrain. All computer users should refocus their eyes on an object in the distance for a minute or so, on a regular basis, and mobile phone and mobile device users should increase font size and light level when viewing text on a small display screen. Eyeglass wearers should discuss any eye fatigue or blurriness during computer use with their eye doctors—sometimes a different lens prescription or special *computer glasses* can be used to reduce eyestrain while working on a computer. Computer glasses are optimized for viewing in the

CONDITION	PREVENTION
Wrist/arm/hand soreness and injury	➤ Use a light touch on the keyboard. ➤ Rest and gently stretch your fingers and arms every 15 minutes or so. ➤ Keep your wrists and arms relaxed and parallel to the floor when using the keyboard. ➤ When using a device with a small keyboard, type short messages, take frequent breaks, and use a separate keyboard whenever possible. ➤ Use an ergonomic keyboard, ergonomic mouse, computer gloves, and other ergonomic devices if you begin to notice wrist or hand soreness.
Eyestrain	➤ Cover windows or adjust lighting to eliminate glare. ➤ Concentrate on blinking your eyes more often. ➤ Rest your eyes every 15 minutes or so by focusing on an object in the distance (at least 20 feet away) for one minute and then closing your eyes for an additional minute. ➤ Make sure your monitor's brightness and contrast settings are at an appropriate level. ➤ Use a larger text size or lower screen resolution, if needed. You should be able to read what is displayed on your monitor from three times the distance at which you normally sit.
Sore or stiff neck	➤ Use good posture. ➤ Place the monitor and any documents you need to refer to while using your computer directly in front of you. Use a document holder if possible. ➤ Adjust your monitor to a comfortable viewing angle with the top of the screen no higher than 3 inches above your eyes. ➤ Use a telephone headset if you spend a significant amount of time each day on the telephone.
Backache; general fatigue	➤ Use good posture and adjust your chair to support your lower back; use an ergonomic chair, if needed. ➤ Use a footrest, if needed, to keep your feet flat on the floor. ➤ Walk around or stretch briefly at least once every hour. ➤ Alternate activities frequently. ➤ When traveling with a computer, bring a lightweight notebook or netbook computer and carry only the essentials with you.
Ringing in the ears; hearing loss	➤ Turn down the volume when using headphones (you should be able to hear other people's voices). ➤ Wear over-the-ear-headphones instead of earbuds. ➤ Limit the amount of time you use headphones or earbuds. ➤ Use external speakers instead of headphones when possible.
Leg discomfort or burns	➤ Use a laptop desk or other barrier between a portable computer and your legs when using a computer on your lap.

SOC

intermediate zone of vision where a computer monitor usually falls; that is, closer than glasses designed for driving and farther away than glasses designed for reading.

Emotional Health

The extensive use of computers and related technology in the home and office in recent years has raised new concerns about emotional health. Factors such as financial worries, feelings of being overworked, being unable to relax, and information overload often produce emotional stress. Decades of research have linked stress to a variety of health concerns, such as heart attacks, stroke, diabetes, and weakened immune systems. Workers who report feeling stressed incur more healthcare costs—according to the American Institute of Stress, stress costs U.S. employers more than $300 billion each year in healthcare, missed work, and stress-reduction services provided to employees.

For many individuals, computer use or computer-related events are the cause of, or at least partially contribute to, the stress that they experience. Another emotional health concern related to computer use is addiction to the Internet or another technology.

RESTAURANT SERVERS

SERVICE TECHNICIANS

FIGURE 16-21
Computer-related jobs. Many jobs that did not require computer use in the past require computer use today.

Stress of Ever-Changing Technology

When computers were first introduced into the workplace, workers needed to learn the appropriate computer skills if their jobs required computer use. Airline agents, for example, had to learn to use computer databases. Secretaries and other office employees needed to learn to use word processing and other office-related software, and customer service representatives needed to learn how to use e-mail. Today, many people entering the workforce are aware of the computer skills they will need to perform the tasks associated with their chosen professions. However, as computers have become continually more integrated into our society, jobs that did not require the use of a computer in the recent past may very well require it today (see Figure 16-21). And, at the rapid pace that technology keeps changing, many workers must regularly learn new skills to keep up to date. For example, they may need to upgrade to a new version of a software program, learn how to use a new software program, or learn how to use a new piece of hardware. Although some find this exciting, the ongoing battle to stay current with changing technology creates stress for many individuals.

POLICE OFFICERS

PHYSICIANS

Impact of Our 24/7 Society

One benefit of our communications-oriented society is that one never has to be out of touch. With the use of mobile phones, mobile devices, and portable computers, as well as the ability to access e-mail and company networks from virtually anywhere, individuals can be available around the clock, if needed (see Figure 16-22). Although the ability to be in touch constantly is an advantage for some people under certain conditions, it can also be a source of great stress. For example, employees who feel that they are "on call" 24/7 and cannot ever get away from work may find it difficult to relax during their downtime. Others who are used to being in touch constantly may not be able to relax when they are on vacation and supposed to be unavailable because they are afraid of missing something important that may affect their careers. In either case, these individuals may lose the distinction between personal time and work time, and so they may end up being always "on the job." This can affect their personal lives, emotional health, and overall well-being. Finding a balance between work time and personal time is important for good emotional health.

Information Overload

Although the amount of information available through the Internet is a great asset, it can also be overwhelming at times. When you combine Internet information with TV and radio news broadcasts; newspaper, journal, and magazine articles; and telephone calls, voice mail messages, and faxes; some Americans are practically drowning in information. The amount of e-mail received each day by some individuals and organizations is almost unfathomable. For example, the U.S. Senate receives millions of e-mail messages each day, and it is estimated that workers in the United States spend an average of two hours per day dealing with e-mail messages. Several strategies can be used to avoid becoming completely overwhelmed by information overload.

For efficiently extracting the information you need from the vast amount of information available over the Internet, good search techniques are essential. Perhaps the most important thing to keep in mind when dealing with information overload is that you cannot possibly read everything ever written on a particular subject. At some point in time when performing Internet research, the value of additional information decreases and, eventually, it is not worth your time to continue the search. Knowing when to quit a search or when to try another research approach is an important skill in avoiding information overload.

Efficiently managing your incoming e-mail is another way to avoid information overload. Tools for managing e-mail can help alleviate the stress of an overflowing Inbox, as well as cut down the amount of time you spend dealing with your online correspondence. As discussed in Chapter 15, e-mail filters can be used to route messages automatically into specific folders (such as suspected spam into a Spam folder) based on criteria you set. This allows you to concentrate on the messages most important to you first and leave the others—such as the possible spam—to be sorted through and dealt with at your convenience. If you need to follow up on a message at a later time, flag it so you don't have to worry about forgetting to follow up at the appropriate time.

Many e-mail programs, such as Microsoft Outlook shown in Figure 16-23, allow you to flag messages with a specific follow-up time (such as tomorrow or next week), as well as to add a reminder alarm so you will be reminded automatically when it is time to follow up. Some productivity training companies advise treating e-mail like physical mail and opening e-mail only a limited number of times per day. Because it can take up to 25 minutes after an interruption to concentrate fully again on a task, these companies have found that employees who avoid continually jumping back and forth between e-mail and other activities usually

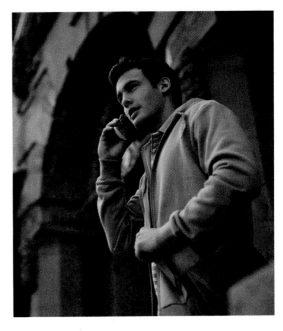

FIGURE 16-22
Our 24/7 society.
With mobile phones and portable computers, many individuals are available 24/7.

TIP
For a review of how to perform efficient and effective Internet searches, refer again to Chapter 8.

FIGURE 16-23
Outlook reminder flags can help you organize your Inbox.

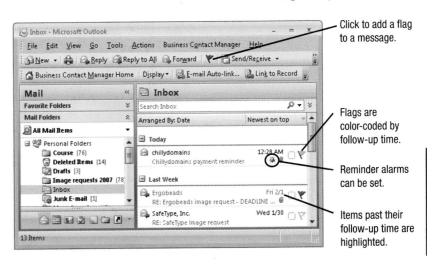

Click to add a flag to a message.

Flags are color-coded by follow-up time.

Reminder alarms can be set.

Items past their follow-up time are highlighted.

increase productivity and decrease stress significantly. To help avoid the temptation of checking e-mail more frequently, close your e-mail program, turn off your new e-mail alert notifier, or mute your speakers so you do not hear new messages arrive.

Burnout

Our heavy use of computers, combined with information overload and 24/7 accessibility via technology, can lead to **burnout**—a state of fatigue or frustration brought about by overwork. Burnout is often born from good intentions—when, for example, hardworking people try to reach goals that, for one reason or another, become unrealistic. Early signs of burnout include a feeling of emotional and physical exhaustion, no longer caring about a project that used to be interesting or exciting, irritability, feelings of resentment about the amount of work that needs to be done, and feeling pulled in many directions at once.

When you begin to notice the symptoms of burnout, experts recommend reevaluating your schedule, priorities, and lifestyle. Sometimes, just admitting that you are feeling overwhelmed is a good start to solving the problem. Taking a break or getting away for a day can help put the situation in perspective. Saying no to additional commitments and making sure that you eat properly, exercise regularly, and otherwise take good care of yourself are also important strategies for coping with and alleviating both stress and burnout.

Internet and Technology Addiction

When an individual overuses, or is unable to stop using, the Internet, it becomes a problem and is referred to as **Internet addiction** (also called *Internet addiction disorder (IAD), cyberaddiction, computer addiction disorder (CAD)*, and *technology addiction*, depending on the technology being used). According to Dr. Kimberly Young, an expert on Internet addiction and the director of the Center for Internet Addiction Recovery in Pennsylvania, Internet addiction is an established psychological condition. And it is growing; in fact, researchers at Stanford University Medical School estimate that 1 in 8 Americans suffer from at least one sign of problematic Internet use. Internet addiction is considered a serious disorder and is being considered for inclusion as a new diagnosis in the upcoming revision of the *Diagnostic and Statistical Manual of Mental Disorders (DSM-V)*.

Originally, Internet addiction sufferers were stereotyped as younger, introverted, socially awkward, computer-oriented males. However, with the increased access to computers and the Internet today, this stereotype is no longer accurate. Internet addiction can affect anyone of any age, race, or social class and can take a variety of forms. Some individuals become addicted to e-mailing or text messaging. Others become compulsive online shoppers or online gamblers, or become addicted to social networking activities. Still others are addicted to cybersex, cyberporn, or online gaming, or struggle with real-world relationships because of virtual relationships. Currently, the most common forms of addictive behaviors include multiuser online role-playing games, instant messaging, online chatting, online pornography, and social networking. See Figure 16-24 for Dr. Young's list of Internet addiction symptoms.

TIP

View your Inbox as a temporary location only; after reading an e-mail message, immediately delete it, flag it, or file it in an e-mail folder to keep your Inbox clean.

FIGURE 16-24

Signs of Internet addiction. You may be addicted to the Internet if you answer "yes" to at least five of these questions.

Do you feel preoccupied with the Internet (think about previous online activity or anticipate next online session)?

Do you feel the need to use the Internet with increasing amounts of time in order to achieve satisfaction?

Have you repeatedly made unsuccessful efforts to control, cut back, or stop Internet use?

Do you feel restless, moody, depressed, or irritable when attempting to cut down or stop Internet use?

Do you stay online longer than originally intended?

Have you jeopardized or risked the loss of a significant relationship, job, educational, or career opportunity because of the Internet?

Have you lied to family members, a therapist, or others to conceal the extent of involvement with the Internet?

Do you use the Internet as a way of escaping from problems or of relieving a dysphoric mood (e.g., feelings of helplessness, guilt, anxiety, depression)?

> **Burnout.** A state of fatigue or frustration usually brought on by overwork. > **Internet addiction.** The problem of overusing, or being unable to stop using, the Internet.

Like other addictions, addiction to using a computer, the Internet, or other technology may have significant consequences, such as relationship problems, job loss, academic failure, health problems, financial consequences, loss of custody of children, and even suicide. There is also growing concern about the impact of constant use of technology among teenagers. In addition to texting via mobile phones and posting to Facebook via portable computers during the day, teens are taking these devices to bed with them, raising concerns about sleep deprivation and its consequences, such as concentration problems, anxiety and depression, and unsafe driving. In fact, one recent Belgian study found that late-night texting is affecting the sleep cycles of 44% of that country's 16-year-olds, with 12% of the youths studied waking up every night or every other night to text. Internet addiction is also increasingly being tied to crime and even death in countries (such as China and South Korea) that have high levels of broadband Internet access. For instance, Internet addiction is blamed for much of the juvenile crime in China, a number of suicides, and several deaths from exhaustion by players unable to tear themselves' away from marathon gaming sessions.

Internet addiction is viewed as a growing problem worldwide. Both China and South Korea have implemented military-style boot camps to treat young people identified as having Internet addiction, and the growing number of Internet-addicted youth prompted the Chinese government to ban minors from Internet cafés. In the U.S., there are a number of inpatient treatment centers that treat Internet addiction, such as the Illinois Institute for Addiction Recovery and the reSTART program in Washington, which recently opened as the first intensive 45-day residential program specially designed to treat Internet addiction.

Many experts believe that while Internet addiction is a growing problem, it can be treated, similar to other addictions, with therapy, support groups, and medication. Research to investigate its impact, risk factors, and treatment possibilities, as well as investigate treatment differences among the various types of technology abuse, is ongoing. New studies are also looking at the overall impact of technology and how its overuse or abuse may also impact people's lives, in order to identify other potential problems and possible solutions.

ACCESS TO TECHNOLOGY

For many, a major concern about the increased integration of computers and technology into our society is whether or not technology is accessible to all individuals. Some believe there is a distinct line dividing those who have access and those who do not. Factors such as age, gender, race, income, education, and physical abilities can all impact one's access to technology and how one uses it.

The Digital Divide

The term **digital divide** refers to the gap between those who have access to information and communications technology and those who do not—often referred to as the "haves" and "have nots." Typically, the digital divide is thought to be based on physical access to computers, the Internet, and related technology. Some individuals, however, believe that the definition of the digital divide goes deeper than just access. For example, they classify those individuals who have physical access to technology but who do not understand how to use it or are discouraged from using it in the "have not" category. Groups and individuals trying to eliminate the digital divide are working toward providing real

> **Digital divide.** The gap between those who have access to technology and those who do not.

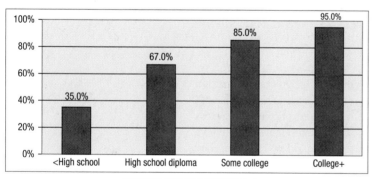

access to technology (including access to up-to-date hardware, software, Internet, and training) so that it can be used to improve people's lives. In addition to access to computers and the Internet, digital divides related to other technologies may exist as well. For instance, one recent study revealed a digital divide in electronic health records (EHRs) at hospitals in the United States. The study found that hospitals that primarily serve low-income patients are less likely to have adopted EHRs and other safety-related technologies (such as clinical decision supports, electronic medication lists, and computerized discharge summaries) than hospitals with more affluent patients.

The digital divide can refer to the differences between individuals within a particular country, as well as to the differences between countries. Within a country, use of computers and related technology can vary based on such factors as age, race, education, and income.

The U.S. Digital Divide

Although there is disagreement among experts about the current status of the digital divide within the United States, there is an indication that it is continuing to shrink. While the digital divide involves more than just Internet use—it involves the use of any type of technology necessary to succeed in our society— the growing amount of Internet use is an encouraging sign. As discussed in Chapter 8, nearly 75% of the United States population are Internet users, using the Internet at work, home, school, or another location. Free Internet access at libraries, school, and other public locations, as well as the availability of low-cost computers and low-cost or free Internet access in many areas today, has helped Internet use begin to approach the popularity and widespread use of telephones and TVs, and has helped it become more feasible for low-income families today than in the past. In general, however, according to recent reports by the Pew Internet & American Life Project, individuals with a higher level of income or a higher level of education are more likely to go online, and younger individuals are more likely to be online than older Americans. Some overall demographic data about Internet use in the United States is shown in Figure 16-25.

Because the United States is such a technologically advanced society, reducing—and trying to eliminate—the digital divide is extremely important

FIGURE 16-25

Key U.S. Internet use statistics. Shows the percent of individuals in each category who use the Internet.

to ensure that all citizens have an equal chance to be successful in this country. Although there has been lots of progress in that direction, more work still remains. For instance, the Navajo Nation (a sovereign tribal nation with more than 250,000 citizens living across 27,000 square miles in New Mexico, Arizona, and Utah) has lagged significantly behind the rest of the U.S. in terms of technology. Many schools lack computers and Internet access, many residents (63%, according to the 2000 Census) have no telephone, and even some government entities within the Navajo Nation have dial-up or no Internet access. However, this is slowly changing as a result of the *Internet to the Hogan* project—a project to build an integrated wired and wireless network infrastructure to enable communications for government entities, as well as for individuals (via connections at community-based chapter houses) within the Navajo Nation. Once the basic infrastructure is in place, the goal is to expand to schools, medical clinics, hospitals, firehouses, and homes within a 15 to 30 mile radius of each chapter house, in order to provide additional services (such as telemedicine and distance learning) and to open up new job opportunities (such as personal Web-based businesses or telecommuting) that are not possible without high-speed Internet connectivity.

Many individuals view computers and the Internet as essential for all Americans today. For instance, students need access to technology and Internet resources to stay informed and be prepared for further education and careers. As already discussed, most jobs in the U.S. require some sort of computer or Internet use. And the Internet is becoming an increasingly important resource for older Americans, particularly for forming decisions about health and healthcare options. However, it is important to realize that not all individuals want to use computers or go online. Just as some people choose not to have televisions, mobile phones, or other technologies, some people—rich or poor—choose not to have a computer or go online. Sometimes this is a religious decision; at other times, it is simply a lifestyle choice.

The Global Digital Divide

While the digital divide within a country is about some individuals within that country having access to technology and others not having the same access, the global digital divide is about some countries having access to technology and others not having the same level of access. It is becoming increasingly important for all countries to have access to information and communications technology in order to be able to compete successfully in our global economy. The global digital divide is perhaps more dramatic than the U.S. digital divide. According to InternetWorldStats.com, about 1.6 billion people globally are online—only about 24% of the world's population. With nearly 74% of its population online, North America is the leading world region in Internet users; with less than 7% of its population online, Africa has one of the lowest percentages of Internet users.

For some, it is difficult to imagine how computers and the Internet would benefit the world's hungry or all of the billion people in the world without access to reliable electricity. Others view technology as a means to bridge the global digital divide. For instance, mobile phones and computers with solar-rechargeable batteries can be used in developing countries for education and telemedicine. New wireless Internet projects, such as the *Wildnet* technology that is being used to extend Wi-Fi in remote areas in order to connect areas up to 60 miles apart, are also helping to bridge the gap. Currently deployed in several countries, Wildnets are already being used to provide Internet access to rural schools in Ghana and the Philippines, and to connect doctors in a main hospital in India with technicians in remote eye-care clinics in remote villages.

For personal computer use, new products are emerging that could help lessen the global digital divide. Perhaps the most widely known project in this area is the *One Laptop Per Child (OLPC)* project. The goal of OLPC is to ensure that every child in the world between the ages of 6 and 12 has immediate access to a personal laptop computer by 2015, in order to provide them with access to new channels of learning, sharing, and self-expression. The current model of the *XO laptop* developed by OLPC is shown in Figure 16-26.

ONLINE VIDEO

Go to the Chapter 16 page at **www.cengage.com/computerconcepts/np/uc13** to watch the "Intel World Ahead Program" video clip.

FIGURE 16-26
The OLPC XO laptop.

The XO laptop is made of thick plastic for durability with a display that can be viewed in direct sunlight. The rubber keyboard is sealed to keep out dirt and water, and the XO is very energy-efficient, consuming just a fraction of the energy required for a standard notebook computer. It can be charged via an electrical outlet, as well as from a car battery, foot pedal, or pull string. The XO is relatively small and light, has a 7.5-inch display, and is designed to be power efficient. It is Linux-based; contains a variety of communications and connectivity capabilities, including a Wi-Fi adapter, USB ports, a flash memory slot, and a built-in video camera and microphone; and uses 1 GB of flash memory for storage. The XO is currently being sold to governments of developing countries to be distributed to school-aged children—more than 1.5 million units have been deployed across the world in countries such as Peru, Uruguay, Rwanda, Ethiopia, Iran, Mongolia, and Afghanistan. The cost is currently $188 per computer, but the goal is to decrease the cost to $75 per computer eventually. According to OLPC, making it possible for students in developing countries to have a laptop will greatly impact their education, as well as society as a whole. They believe that by empowering children to educate themselves, a new generation will ultimately be better prepared to tackle the other serious problems (poverty, malnutrition, disease) facing their societies.

Assistive Technology

Research has found that people with disabilities tend to use computers and the Internet at rates below the average for a given population. Part of the reason may be that some physical conditions—such as visual impairment or limited dexterity—make it difficult to use a conventional computer system. That is where **assistive technology**—hardware and software specially designed for use by individuals with physical disabilities—fits in. While assistive technology is not currently available to help with all types of computer content (primarily streaming video and other multimedia content increasingly found on Web pages), there has been much improvement in assistive technology in recent years. In addition, researchers are continuing to develop additional types of assistive technology, such as *multimedia accessibility tools* to help individuals with visual impairments better control and experience Web-based multimedia. This growth in assistive technology is due in part to demands by disabled individuals and disability organizations for equal access to computers and Web content, as well as the *Americans with Disabilities Act (ADA)*. The ADA requires companies with 15 or more employees to make reasonable accommodations for known physical or mental limitations of otherwise qualified individuals, unless doing so results in undue hardship for the company. Some states have additional accessibility laws and there has been an increase in accessibility lawsuits recently. For instance, blind visitors to the Target Web site sued Target for its lack of accessibility. Target recently settled the suit for $6 million to be distributed to the plaintiffs and agreed to make the Target.com site fully accessible to blind visitors.

To help provide individuals with physical disabilities equal access to technology, assistive input and output devices—such as *Braille keyboards*, specialized pointing devices, large monitors, and *screen readers*—are available for personal computers, as well as some mobile phones and mobile devices.

Assistive Input Systems

Assistive input devices allow for input in a nontraditional manner (see Figure 16-27). For example, *Braille keyboards*, large-key keyboards, or conventional keyboards with Braille or large-print key overlays are available for visually impaired computer users. *Keyguards*—metal or plastic plates that fit over conventional keyboards—enable users with limited hand

> **Assistive technology.** Hardware and software specifically designed for use by individuals with physical disabilities.

BRAILLE KEYBOARDS
The keys on this keyboard contain Braille overlays.

ONE-HANDED KEYBOARDS
Each key on this half keyboard contains two letters (one for the right half and one for the left) so all keys can be reached with one hand.

EYE TRACKING SYSTEMS
Cameras track the user's eye movements, which are used to select icons and other objects on the screen.

FIGURE 16-27
Assistive input devices.

mobility to press the keys on a keyboard (using his or her fingers or a special device) without accidentally pressing other keys. *One-handed keyboards* are available for users who have the use of only one hand, and speech recognition systems can be used to input data and commands to the computer hands-free, as discussed in Chapter 4. *Switches*—hardware devices that can be activated with hand, foot, finger, or face movement, or with sips and puffs of air—can be used to input data and commands into a computer. Some conventional input devices can also be used for assistive purposes, such as scanners, which—if they have optical character recognition (OCR) capabilities—can input printed documents as editable text.

For mouse alternatives, there are assistive pointing devices that can be used—sometimes in conjunction with a switch—to move and select items with an on-screen pointer; they can also be used to enter text-based data when used in conjunction with an on-screen keyboard. For example, *foot-controlled mice* are controlled by the feet, *head pointing systems* control the on-screen pointer using head movement, and *eye tracking systems* allow users to select items on-screen using only their gaze.

In addition to its use by disabled computer users, assistive hardware can also be used by the general population. For example, one-handed keyboards are sometimes used by people who wish to keep one hand on the mouse and one hand on the keyboard at all times; voice input systems are used by individuals who would prefer to speak input instead of type it; and head pointing systems are available for gaming and virtual reality (VR) applications.

Assistive Output Systems

Once data has been input into the computer, a variety of *assistive output devices* can be used. For instance, some examples of assistive output devices that can be used by blind and other visually impaired individuals are shown in Figure 16-28. A *screen reader* is a software

FIGURE 16-28
Assistive output devices.

SCREEN READER SOFTWARE

BRAILLE DISPLAYS

BRAILLE PRINTERS

program that reads aloud all text information available via the computer screen, such as instructions, menu options, documents, and Web pages. *Braille displays* are devices that can be attached to conventional computers (or built into portable computers and mobile devices designed for visually impaired individuals) and that continuously convert screen output into Braille form. *Braille printers* print embossed output in Braille format on paper instead of, or in addition to, conventional ink output.

Some operating systems also include accessibility features. For instance, recent versions of Windows and Mac OS include a screen reader, on-screen keyboard, speech recognition capabilities, and settings that can be used to magnify the screen, change text size and color, convert audio cues into written text, and otherwise make the computer more accessible.

ENVIRONMENTAL CONCERNS

The increasing use of computers in our society has created a variety of environmental concerns. The amount of energy used to power personal computers, servers, and computer components, as well as the heat generated by computing equipment, is one concern. Another is our extensive use of paper, CDs, and other disposables, and how much of it ends up as trash in landfills. The hazardous materials contained in computer equipment or generated by the production of computers and related technology, as well as the disposal of used computing products, are additional concerns.

FIGURE 16-29
Eco-labels.

UNITED STATES

EUROPEAN UNION

KOREA

BRAZIL

GERMANY

Green Computing

The term **green computing** refers to the use of computers in an environmentally friendly manner. Minimizing the use of natural resources, such as energy and paper, is one aspect of green computing. To encourage the development of energy-saving devices, the U.S. Department of Energy and the Environmental Protection Agency (EPA) developed the **ENERGY STAR** program. Hardware that is ENERGY STAR compliant exceeds the minimum federal standards for reduced energy consumption and can display the ENERGY STAR label shown in Figure 16-29. The most recent ENERGY STAR requirements for computers (version 5.0) focus on efficiency while the devices are being used, as well as power management features that can put the devices into sleep or hibernation mode after a designated period of inactivity. **Eco-labels**—environmental performance certifications—are also used in other countries; Figure 16-29 show some examples.

Energy Consumption and Conservation

With the high cost of electricity today and the recent increase in data center energy usage, power consumption and heat generation by computers are key concerns for businesses today. Today's faster and more powerful computers tend to use more energy and run hotter than computers from just a few years ago, which leads to greater cooling costs. Servers, in particular, are power-hungry, so consolidating servers (such as by the use of virtualization) is a common energy saving tactic used by businesses today. But energy use is still growing. In fact, a recent Environmental Protection Agency (EPA) study showed that servers and data centers use more than 1.5% of all electricity generated in the U.S. and that number is expected to double in the next five years. To help IT managers compare energy consumption in their facilities with other

---

> **Green computing.** The use of computers in an environmentally friendly manner. > **ENERGY STAR.** A program developed by the U.S. Department of Energy and the Environmental Protection Agency to encourage the development of energy-saving devices. > **Eco-label.** A certification, usually by a government agency, that identifies a device as meeting minimal environmental performance specifications.

data centers, in order to help them improve data center efficiency, the EPA is in the process of developing an energy performance rating system for data centers. The EPA estimates that even a 10% reduction in energy consumption by U.S. data centers would save enough energy to power up to 1 million homes per year and save U.S. businesses $740 million annually.

In response to the growing emphasis on green computing today, hardware manufacturers are working to develop more energy efficient personal computers, servers, microprocessors, storage systems, and other computer components. Some energy-saving features found on computer hardware today include devices (such as computers and printers) that can go into very low-power sleep mode when not in use, low-power-consumptive chips and boards, high-efficiency power supplies, energy-efficient flat-panel displays, liquid cooling systems, and CPUs that power up and down on demand. The energy savings by using more energy-efficient hardware can be significant. For instance, moving to an LED flat-panel display instead of a conventional LCD display saves around 12% in energy consumption.

While ENERGY STAR 5.0-compliant computers are more efficient in standby and sleep mode than in the past, computers can still draw quite a bit of power when they are in these modes—particularly with a screen saver enabled. Because of this, businesses and schools are also increasingly using software to shut down computers automatically when they are not in use to save power. Mobile phone manufacturers are also working to reduce the environmental impact of their products, such as displaying reminders on mobile phones to unplug them from their chargers when they are fully charged because chargers can draw up to five watts per hour even if nothing is plugged into them. Other devices that draw power when they are turned off (sometimes called *energy vampires*) include computers, home electronics, and home appliances. In fact, it is estimated that the average U.S. household spends $100 per year powering devices that are turned off or in stand-by mode. To determine how much power a device is using, you can use a special device like the *Kill a Watt EZ* shown in Figure 16-30. This device displays the amount of power (in kilowatts or dollar value) any device plugged into it is currently using. To save on vampire power costs, unplug your devices when you are not using them (you can connect your electronic devices to a power strip and just switch off the power at the power strip to make this process easier). However, don't cut the power to any device (such as a wireless router, DVR, or cable box) that will need to be active to perform a needed function. A *smart power strip* that turn off outlets on the strip when it senses those devices aren't being used, is another alternative.

Alternate Power

In addition to more energy-efficient hardware, other possibilities for greener computing are being developed, such as alternate power sources for computers and mobile devices. For instance, *solar power* is a growing alternative for powering electronic devices, including mobile phones and portable computers. With solar power, *solar panels* convert sunlight into direct current (DC) electricity, which is then stored in a battery.

Although it has been expensive to implement in the past, improvements in solar technology are making its use more feasible for a greater number of individuals. Solar technology is now considered to be in its third generation, with *thin-film solar panels* being created by printing nanoparticles onto rolls of thin, flexible panels to create the panels at a fraction of the cost of earlier generations. As a result, solar panels are becoming available for an increasing number of applications. For instance, solar panels to be built into the covers of notebook computers are being designed and both solar-powered and hand-powered chargers (see Figure 16-31) are available for use with portable computers, mobile phones, and other small portable devices. These devices can be used wherever dependable electricity is not available, such as in developing countries and while outdoors. In addition, there are solar panels that are designed to be placed on the roof of the Toyota Prius, in order to add an additional 2 miles to the gallon, and the U.S. Army is testing prototypes of emergency

FIGURE 16-30
Energy usage monitors. This monitor displays in real time the amount of electricity (in kilowatt-hours or approximate cost) a connected device is using.

Solar panels are built into the bag.

SOLAR COMPUTER BAGS

Solar panels

SOLAR-POWERED CHARGERS

HAND-POWERED CHARGERS

 FIGURE 16-31

Alternate power.
Solar and hand power can be used to power mobile phones, portable digital media players, GPS devices, portable computers, and other devices.

tents with built-in solar panels to power radios, heaters, and other critical devices. The messenger bag shown in Figure 16-31 includes enough solar panels to fully charge a typical notebook computer, and, as an added environmental plus, the bag uses fabrics made from recycled plastics like soda bottles. For a look at another emerging option for powering your devices—*portable fuel cell chargers*—see the Trend box.

Solar power can be also used to power more permanent computer setups, as well. For instance, some Web hosting companies in the U.S. (including Solar Energy Host and AISO.Net) are now 100% solar powered and the solar panels that cover most of the rooftops at Google's Mountain View, California, headquarters power 30% of the energy needs for that complex. Solar power plants are also being developed, and some experts predict that many buildings in the future will be *solar buildings* with solar cells integrated into the rooftop, walls, and windows of the building to generate electricity.

Green Components

In addition to being more energy-efficient, computers today are being built to run quieter and cooler, and they are using more recyclable hardware and packaging. Many computer manufacturers are also reducing the amount of toxic chemicals being used in personal computers. For instance, Dell bans the use of some hazardous chemicals, such as cadmium and mercury; has reduced the amount of lead used in several desktop computers; and meets the European Union requirement of being completely lead-free for all electronics shipped to the EU. Some mobile phones are also going green, being made out of recycled plastics, including solar panels to charge the phone's battery, and including a pedometer and other applications to calculate the volume of CO_2 emissions you have avoided by not driving.

Recycling and Disposal of Computing Equipment

Another environmental concern is the amount of trash—and sometimes toxic trash—generated by computer use. One concern is paper waste. It now appears that the so-called *paperless office* that many visionaries predicted would arrive is largely a myth. Instead, research indicates that global paper use has grown more than six-fold since 1950, and one-fifth of all wood harvested in the world today ends up as paper. The estimated number of pages generated by computer printers worldwide is almost one-half billion a year—an amount that would stack more than 25,000 miles high. One possible solution for the future (electronic paper) was discussed in the Inside the Industry box in Chapter 4. There are also utilities, such as the free *GreenPrint World* and *PrintWhatYouLike.com* services, designed to reduce paper consumption. These utilities eliminate images, blank pages, and other non-critical content located on documents and/or Web pages, in order to print just the necessary content on the least number of pages possible.

In addition to paper-based trash, computing refuse includes used toner cartridges, obsolete or broken hardware, and discarded CDs, DVDs, and other storage media. Mobile phones that are discarded when individuals switch providers—as well as new disposable consumer products, such as disposable digital cameras—also add to the amount of **e-trash** (also called *electronic trash* and *e-waste*) generated today. A surge in discarded televisions is also expected as prices of plasma TVs continue to decrease and many consumers replace their older TVs with flat-screen displays and TVs that support digital TV.

>**E-trash.** Electronic trash or waste, such as discarded computer components.

Compounding the problem of the amount of e-trash generated today is the fact that computers, mobile phones, and related hardware contain a variety of toxic and hazardous materials. For instance, the average CRT monitor alone contains about eight pounds of lead, and a single desktop computer may contain up to 700 different chemical elements and compounds, many of which (such as arsenic, lead, mercury, and cadmium) are hazardous and expensive to dispose of properly.

A global concern regarding e-trash is where it all eventually ends up. The majority of all discarded computer equipment (at least 70%, according to most estimates) ends up in landfills and in countries, such as China, India, and Nigeria, with lower recycling costs, cheaper labor, and more lax environmental standards than found in the United States. Much of the e-trash exported to these countries is simply dumped into fields and other informal dumping areas. Unaware of the potential danger of these components, rural villagers often sort through and dismantle discarded electronics parts looking for precious metals and other sources of revenue (see Figure 16-32)—potentially endangering their health as well as polluting nearby rivers, ponds, and other water sources. Compounding the problem, the remaining waste is often burned, generating huge clouds of potentially toxic smoke. Activists believe unchecked dumping by the United States and other countries—such as England, Japan, Australia, and Singapore—has been going on for at least 10 years. The primary reason for exporting e-trash is expense—proper disposal of a computer in the United States normally costs between $5 and $10, compared to $1 or less in third-world countries. Another reason is that some states in the United States are beginning to ban the most dangerous computing equipment—such as CRT monitors—from landfills.

While it is difficult—or, perhaps, impossible—to correct the damage that has already occurred from e-trash, many organizations are working to develop ways to protect people and the environment from future contamination. For instance, the *Climate Savers Computing Initiative* is an industry group started by Google and Intel in 2007 that is dedicated to reducing greenhouse-gas emissions, and the *Green Grid Alliance* is a global consortium dedicated to advancing energy efficiency in data centers and business computing. There are also some environmental regulations (such as California's *Electronic Waste Recycling Act* and Europe's *Restrictions on Hazardous Substances Directive*) that prohibit throwing away some types of computer components. For instance, California does not allow computer monitors to be thrown out as trash and has implemented mandatory fees of $8 to $25 on all TV and computer monitor purchases; these fees are used to fund the collection, recycling, and proper disposal of discarded electronic components. In the United States, computer manufacturers are beginning to produce more environmentally friendly components, such as system units made from recyclable plastic, nontoxic flame-retardant coatings, and lead-free solder on the motherboard.

Even though recycling computer equipment is difficult because of the materials currently being used, proper disposal is essential to avoid pollution and health hazards. Some recycling centers will accept computer equipment, but many charge a fee for this service. Many computer manufacturers have recycling programs that will accept obsolete or broken computer equipment from consumers, typically for a fee of about $15 to $30 per unit. Expired toner cartridges and ink cartridges can sometimes be returned to the manufacturer (using the supplied shipping label included with some cartridges) or exchanged when ordering new cartridges; the cartridges are then *recharged* (refilled) and resold. Cartridges that cannot be refilled can be sent to a recycling facility. In addition to helping to reduce e-trash in landfills, using recharged printer cartridges saves the consumer money since they are less expensive than new cartridges. Other computer components—such as CDs, DVDs, USB flash drives, and hard drives—can also be recycled through some organizations, such

FIGURE 16-32

E-trash. The vast majority of the 40 million or so computers that become obsolete each year end up as e-trash in landfills.

ONLINE VIDEO

Go to the Chapter 16 page at **www.cengage.com/ computerconcepts/np/uc13** to watch the "Climate Savers Computing Initiative" video clip.

FURTHER EXPLORATION   Go

Go to the Chapter 16 page at **www.cengage.com/ computerconcepts/np/uc13** for links to further information about green computing.

SOC

TREND

Portable Fuel Cell Chargers

Tired of your mobile phone or laptop battery running out of power at inopportune times? Well, *portable fuel cells* just might be the solution. Unlike conventional batteries, which need to be recharged with electricity when they run out of electrons, fuel cells produce electricity using a chemical reaction between a fuel (originally hydrogen, but also sometimes methanol or butane today) and air. When more electricity is needed, more fuel is added to the fuel cell device.

While fuel cells may eventually be economical enough to power computers directly, the initial application today is powering mobile phones and other mobile devices on the go. One of the first consumer products on the market, released in Japan in late 2009, is *Dynario*, a methanol-based fuel cell charger developed by Toshiba. This palm-sized product (see the accompanying illustration) is connected to a mobile device via a USB cable to provide nearly instant power to the mobile device (the charger is refilled using dedicated methanol solution cartridges; one refill can charge a typical mobile phone two times).

In addition to their consumer applications, fuel cells are viewed as a possible option for powering devices used by U.S. soldiers on missions in order to reduce the number of batteries they have to carry. Currently, soldiers may carry up to 35 pounds of batteries with them for a 72-hour mission—the military would like to reduce that to 12 pounds. The goal is to develop efficient power sources that are lighter than current batteries, but are safe to carry and use in the field. Fuel cells, possibly in conjunction with other technologies like solar power, might help obtain this goal.

The Dynario portable fuel cell charger powers mobile devices with methanol.

Ⓥ **FIGURE 16-33**

Operation Homelink. Computers donated to this organization are used to help soldiers (such as this soldier in Iraq) communicate with their loved ones.

as *GreenDisk*. GreenDisk accepts shipments of all types of storage media (plus printer cartridges, mobile phones, mobile devices, notebook computers, power cords, and more) for a modest charge (such as $6.95 for 20 pounds of items if you ship them yourself); it reuses salvageable items and recycles the rest. There are also a number of recycling programs specifically designed for discarded mobile phones. These programs typically refurbish and sell the phones; many organizations donate a portion of the proceeds to nonprofit organizations.

In lieu of recycling, older equipment that is still functioning can be used for alternate purposes (such as for a child's computer, a personal Web server, or a DVR), or it can be donated to schools and nonprofit groups. Some organizations accept and repair donated equipment and then distribute it to disadvantaged groups or other individuals in need of the hardware. In the United States, for instance, Operation Homelink refurbishes donated computers and sends them free of charge to families of U.S. military personnel deployed overseas, who then use the computers to communicate with the soldiers via e-mail and videoconferences (see Figure 16-33).

For security and privacy purposes, data stored on all computing equipment should be completely removed before disposing of that equipment so that someone else cannot recover the data stored on that device. As discussed in Chapter 15, hard drives should be wiped clean (not just erased) using special software that overwrites the data on the drive several times to ensure it is completely destroyed; storage media that cannot be wiped (such as rewritable DVDs) or that contain very sensitive data (such as business hard drives being discarded) should be shredded. The shredded media is then typically recycled.

Consumers and companies alike are recognizing the need for green computing. A growing number of computing equipment manufacturers are announcing that they are committed to environmental responsibility. Support for a nationwide recycling program is growing, and new classifications from the EPA are expected to encourage recycling of an even greater number of computer components. So, even though computer manufacturing and recycling have a long way to go before computing equipment stops being an environmental and health hazard, it is encouraging that the trend is moving toward creating a safer and less wasteful environment.

RELATED LEGISLATION

There have been several new laws over the past decade or so attempting to revise intellectual property laws to reflect digital content and the Internet. For instance, the *Family Entertainment and Copyright Act of 2005* makes it illegal to transmit or record a movie being shown at a movie theater; the *U.S. Anticybersquatting Consumer Protection Act of 1999* makes domain name cybersquatting illegal; and the *Digital Millennium Copyright Act (DMCA)* makes it illegal to circumvent antipiracy measures built into digital media and devices. Other laws, such as ones to increase the penalties for illegally sharing music and movies via the Internet, are proposed on a regular basis.

Legislation regarding ethics has been more difficult to pass—or to keep as law once it has passed. For example, as discussed in Chapter 8, the *Communications Decency Act* that was signed into law in 1996 and made it a criminal offense to distribute patently indecent or offensive material online was eventually declared unconstitutional on the basis of free speech. The courts so far have had difficulty defining what is "patently offensive" and "indecent," as well as finding a fair balance between protection and censorship. Consequently, very few ethically oriented laws have been passed in recent years. The most significant recent legislation regarding accessibility has been the 1998 amendment to *Section 508* of the *Rehabilitation Act* requiring federal agencies to make their electronic and information technology accessible to people with disabilities. This act applies to all federal Web sites, as well, creating a trend of Web sites that are Section 508 compliant. While there are currently no federal computer recycling laws in the U.S., federal agencies are required to purchase energy-efficient electronic products. In addition, some federal laws (such as the Sarbanes-Oxley Act and HIPAA) have established privacy and data protection standards for companies disposing of computer hardware that contained specific types of data and some states have implemented laws related to electronic waste.

ASK THE EXPERT

Lauren Ornelas, Campaign Director, Silicon Valley Toxics Coalition

What impact does U.S. e-waste have on other countries?

According to the California Department of Toxic Substances Control report that was released in 2007, roughly 20 million pounds of e-waste were shipped out of California alone in 2006 to places such as Brazil, China, India, South Korea, Malaysia, Mexico, and Vietnam. For some countries, we have some idea of the impact. When we visited India, for instance, we saw workers (including children) dismantling electronics without adequate protection for themselves or the environment. Consequently, the workers and those around them are exposed to lead and other hazardous substances. These toxic substances also get into the soil, water, and air. In some areas, the water is so polluted that they can no longer drink from local water sources and water has to be shipped in from other towns. Nigeria has become a place where our e-waste is essentially just dumped with the pretense of it being recycled. While many electronic products are shipped to Nigeria under the guise of reuse, up to 75% of what is being shipped cannot be repaired or recycled.

TIP

When donating old computers and equipment to nonprofit organizations, be sure to verify the organizations are actually nonprofit—some scammers pose as nonprofit organizations to obtain equipment for free that they then resell for a profit.

VIDEO PODCAST

Go to the Chapter 16 page at **www.cengage.com/computerconcepts/np/uc13** to download or listen to the "How To: Make a DVR from an Old Computer" video podcast.

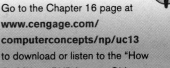

SUMMARY

INTELLECTUAL PROPERTY RIGHTS

Intellectual property rights specify how *intellectual property*, such as original music compositions, drawings, essays, software programs, symbols, and designs, may be lawfully used. **Copyrights** protect the creators of original artistic or literary works and are granted automatically once a work exists in a physical medium. A copyright can be registered, which provides additional protection should infringement occur. The copyright symbol © can be used to remind others that content is copyrighted; **digital watermarks** can be incorporated into digital content so that the copyright information can be viewed, even if the work is altered. **Digital rights management (DRM) software** can be used to protect the rights of creators and to manage digital content, such as art, music, photographs, and movies. **Trademarks** are words, phrases, symbols, or designs that identify an organization's goods or services and can be either claimed (and use the symbol ™ or ˢᴹ) or registered (and use the symbol ®). Registering a domain name with the intent to profit from someone else's trademark is called **cybersquatting**. **Patents** grant an exclusive right to an invention for 20 years. In addition to products, processes and procedures may be patented as well.

ETHICS

Ethics are standards of moral conduct. *Personal ethics* guide one's personal life; **business ethics** provide the standards of conduct guiding business decisions, and **computer ethics** provide the standards of conduct with respect to computers and computer use. Computer ethics have taken on more significance in recent years because the increased use of computers in the home, in the workplace, and at school provides more opportunities for unethical behavior than in the past.

Today one of the most important ethical concerns regarding computers is using someone else's property in an improper way. Books, music, movies, and other types of intellectual property are protected by copyright law, but are still often used in an illegal or unethical manner. Presenting someone else's work as your own is referred to as **plagiarism**, which is illegal and unethical. It is becoming increasingly common for businesses and schools to establish **codes of conduct** to address what behavior is considered ethical and unethical at that particular organization. Some organizations and industries publish **codes of ethics** listing overall standards of conduct, such as honesty, fairness, confidentiality, and more.

A **computer hoax** is an inaccurate statement or story spread through the use of computers, often by e-mail. It is a good idea to make sure questionable information is not a computer hoax before passing the information on to others. **Digital manipulation** is the use of computers to modify something in digital form, usually text or a photograph. Ethics are highly intertwined with determining business practices and making business decisions. Decisions, such as which financial information to publicize, which products or services to provide, which safeguards (if any) to establish with products or services that are illegal for minors or objectionable to some individuals, and whether or not to promote potential *vaporware* products, all require ethical consideration.

Because ethics are fundamentally based on values, different types of businesses may have different ethics. Ethics and moral standards may vary from country to country and from culture to culture. In addition to legal considerations, businesses with global connections should consider the prevailing ethical standards of all countries involved when making business decisions.

COMPUTERS AND HEALTH

Since the entry of computers into the workplace and their increased use in our society, they have been blamed for a variety of physical ailments. **Carpal tunnel syndrome (CTS)**, **DeQuervain's tendonitis**, and other types of **repetitive stress injuries (RSIs)** are common physical ailments related to computer use; *computer vision syndrome* (*CVS*), eyestrain, fatigue, backaches, and headaches are additional possible physical risks.

Ergonomics is the science of how to make a computer workspace, hardware, and environment fit the individual using it. Using an ergonomically correct workspace and **ergonomic hardware** can help avoid or lessen the pain associated with some RSIs. In addition, all users should use good posture, take rest breaks, alternate tasks, and take other common-sense precautions. For portable computers, **docking stations** and **notebook stands** can be used to create more ergonomically-correct workspaces.

The *stress* of keeping up with ever-changing technology, layoffs, always being in touch, fear of being out of touch, information overload, **burnout**, and **Internet addiction** are all possible emotional problems related to computer use.

Chapter Objective 3:
Describe some possible physical and emotional health risks associated with the use of computers.

ACCESS TO TECHNOLOGY

The **digital divide** refers to the gap between those who have access to computers and communications technology and those who do not. There can be a digital divide within a country or between countries. Globally, the digital divide separates countries with access to technology from those without access to technology.

Research suggests that people with disabilities tend to use computers and the Internet at rates lower than the average population. Part of the reason may be because some types of conventional hardware—such as keyboards and monitors—are difficult to use with some types of physical conditions. **Assistive technology** includes hardware and software that makes conventional computer systems easier for users with disabilities to use.

Chapter Objective 4:
Discuss the impact that factors such as nationality, income, race, education, and physical disabilities may have on computer access and use.

ENVIRONMENTAL CONCERNS

Green computing refers to using computers in an environmentally friendly manner. It can include using environmentally friendly hardware (such as devices approved by an **eco-label** system like the **ENERGY STAR** certification used in the United States), as well as using procedures (such as consolidating servers and using power management features to place devices into standby or sleep mode when not in use) to reduce energy consumption. Environmentally friendly computers are just starting to come on the market, and alternate-powered hardware is beginning to become available.

In addition to practicing green computing when buying and using computer equipment, discarded equipment should be reused whenever possible. Computer equipment that is still functioning may be able to be donated and refurbished for additional use, and toner and ink cartridges can often be refilled and reused. Hardware that cannot be reused should be recycled if possible, or properly disposed of if not recyclable so that it does not end up as hazardous **e-trash** in landfills. Storage media containing personal or sensitive data should be disposed of properly, such as wiped or shredded before being reused or recycled.

Chapter Objective 5:
Suggest some ways computer users can practice "green computing" and properly dispose of obsolete computer equipment.

RELATED LEGISLATION

There are numerous laws in place to protect intellectual property. Because moral and ethical standards are more difficult to agree on, ethical legislation is slower in coming. However, some laws have been implemented. The most significant legislation regarding accessibility is the 1998 amendment to the *Rehabilitation Act* requiring federal agencies to make their electronic and information technology accessible to people with disabilities. In the U.S., some federal regulations and state laws impact the disposal of computer hardware.

Chapter Objective 6:
Discuss the current status of legislation related to intellectual property rights, ethics, access, and the environment in relation to computers.

REVIEW ACTIVITIES

KEY TERM MATCHING

a. assistive technology

b. computer ethics

c. copyright

d. digital divide

e. ergonomic hardware

f. intellectual property rights

g. Internet addiction

h. patent

i. plagiarism

j. trademark

Instructions: Match each key term on the left with the definition on the right that best describes it.

1. _____ A form of protection for an invention that can be granted by the government; gives exclusive rights of an invention to its inventor for 20 years.

2. _____ A word, phrase, symbol, or design that identifies goods or services.

3. _____ Hardware and software specifically designed for use by individuals with physical disabilities.

4. _____ Hardware, typically an input or output device, that is designed to be more ergonomically correct than its nonergonomic counterpart.

5. _____ Presenting someone else's work as your own.

6. _____ Standards of moral conduct as they relate to computer use.

7. _____ The gap between those who have access to technology and those who do not.

8. _____ The legal right to sell, publish, or distribute an original artistic or literary work; it is held by the creator of a work as soon as it exists in physical form.

9. _____ The problem of overusing, or being unable to stop using, the Internet.

10. _____ The rights to which creators of original creative works (such as artistic or literary works, inventions, corporate logos, and more) are entitled.

SELF-QUIZ

Instructions: Circle **T** if the statement is true, **F** if the statement is false, or write the best answer in the space provided. **Answers for the self-quiz are located in the References and Resources Guide at the end of the book.**

1. **T   F**   All unethical acts are illegal.

2. **T   F**   Changing the background behind a television newscaster to make it appear that he or she is reporting on location instead of from inside the television studio would be an example of digital manipulation.

3. **T   F**   Carpal tunnel syndrome can be caused by using a computer keyboard.

4. **T   F**   As computer use has become more common, the potential for stress related to computer use has decreased.

5. **T   F**   Assistive technology is hardware and software designed to help all beginning computer users learn how to use a computer.

6. A software program would be protected by _____ law, while a corporate logo would be protected by _____ law.

7. Turning in a copy of a poem you found on a Web site as your original composition for a poetry class assignment is an example of _____.

8. Registering the domain name microsft.com to profit from it would be an act of _____.

9. The _____ can be used to describe discrepancies in access to technology by individuals within a country, as well as to compare access from country to country.

10. Match each term to its description or example, and write the corresponding number in the blank to the left of each description or example.

a. _____ What the symbol © stands for.

b. _____ Can vary from another's depending on his or her values, culture, and so forth.

c. _____ A warning about a nonexistent virus spread via e-mail.

d. _____ A subtle alteration of digital content that identifies the copyright holder.

1. Computer hoax

2. Copyright

3. Digital watermark

4. Ethics

---

1. For each of the following situations, write the appropriate letter—E (ethical) or U (unethical)—in the blank to the right of the situation to indicate how most individuals would view the act.

Situation

Type of Situation

a. A teenager rips a new CD she just bought and e-mails the MP3 files to all her friends.

_____

b. A photographer combines two of his photographs to create a new composite artistic piece.

_____

c. A physician incorporates another doctor's research into her journal article submission, including the researcher's name and article in her submission.

_____

2. Match each term with its related example, and write the corresponding number in the blank to the left of each example.

a. _____ Assistive hardware.

b. _____ Server consolidation.

c. _____ Docking stations.

1. Green computing

2. Ergonomics

3. Digital divide

3. Assume that you have created a Web site to display your favorite original photographs. Is the site and/or your photographs protected by copyright law? Why or why not?

4. List three possible negative physical effects that can result from computer use and describe one way to lessen each effect.

5. List three possible negative effects on the environment that can result from computer use and describe one way to lessen each effect.

---

1. There are research services available online that can be used by students preparing term papers. Is the use of these services ethical? Is the use of programs to detect plagiarism by instructors ethical? How can the problem of plagiarism and other forms of cheating at schools today be resolved? Whose responsibility is it to ensure students do not cheat themselves out of a proper education?

2. While the Web contains a vast amount of extremely useful information, some content can be harmful. Think about suicide Web sites that explain in detail how to kill oneself, Web sites that broadcast the beheadings by terrorists, and Web sites that explain how to build bombs. If a Web site instructs visitors how to perform an illegal act, should the site's creators be criminally liable if a visitor carries out those instructions? Who, if anyone, is responsible for preventing potentially harmful information from being shared via the Web? Is there any Internet content that you believe a government has the right or obligation to censor? If so, what? Where should the line between freedom of speech and national or personal safety be drawn?

SOC

PROJECTS

HOT TOPICS

1. **Ethics and Virtual Worlds** As discussed in the chapter, there are a number of ethical issues surrounding virtual worlds, such as Second Life.

   For this project, consider some of the issues discussed in the chapter, such as reporting income from virtual world activities to the IRS, using online age verification systems to enable visitors to access age-restricted areas, and the ability to portray oneself differently than you really are. Select one issue and research it to find out its current status and to form an opinion on that issue, including what you think is the ethical thing to do with respect to this issue, what you think the majority of individuals do with respect to this issue, the potential ramifications of this issue, and any changes you think are needed in the future. At the end of your research, prepare a one-page summary of your findings and opinions and submit it to your instructor.

SHORT ANSWER/ RESEARCH

2. **Copyright Registration** Think of an original creation (paper, poem, photograph, or song) to which you believe you are entitled copyright protection and assume that you would like to register a copyright for your creation.

   For this project, research how you would obtain a copyright for your chosen creation. Visit the U.S. Copyright Office Web site (search for it using a search site) and determine the necessary procedure for registration, the required paperwork, and the necessary fee. Use the information located on the site to make sure your creation is entitled to copyright protection, then find the appropriate online registration form (if one is available online). If possible, open and print just one page of the form. From the site, also determine what notice you will receive once your copyright claim has been recorded and how long it will take to receive it. Prepare a short summary of your findings to submit to your instructor, stapled to the single page of the appropriate application if you were able to print it.

HANDS ON

3. **Ergonomic Workspaces** Some aspects of an ergonomic workspace, such as a comfortable chair and nonglaring light, may feel good right from the beginning. Others, such as using an ergonomic keyboard or wrist rest, may take a little getting used to.

   For this project, find at least one local store that has some type of ergonomic equipment—such as adjustable office chairs, desks with keyboard drawers, ergonomic keyboards, or notebook stands—on display that you can try out. Test each piece, adjusting it as needed, and evaluate how comfortable it seems. Next, evaluate your usual computer workspace. Are there any adjustments you should make or any new equipment you would need to acquire to make your workspace setup more comfortable? Make a note of any changes you could make for free, as well as a list of items you would need to purchase and the estimated cost. Prepare a short summary of your findings to submit to your instructor. If you made any adjustments to your regular workspace during this project, be sure to include a comment regarding whether or not you think it increased your comfort.

4. **Toxic PCs** As discussed in the chapter, computer hardware can contain a variety of toxic and hazardous materials. Is it ethical for computer manufacturers to continue to use hazardous materials in their products? What if a restriction on these compounds severely limited the types of computer equipment that could be manufactured or significantly increased the price? Is it ethical for consumers to buy products that are made of hazardous materials or are not recyclable? What efforts should be made to recycle e-trash in the U.S. and who is ethically responsible for the cost—the manufacturers, the consumers, or the government? Should the government require the recycling of e-trash? Should it ban the exportation of e-trash?

   For this project, form an opinion about the ethical ramifications of toxic PCs and e-trash and be prepared to discuss your position (in class, via an online class discussion group, in a class chat room, or via a class blog, depending on your instructor's directions). You may also be asked to write a short paper expressing your opinion.

ETHICS IN ACTION

5. **Recycle or Trash?** As mentioned in the chapter, a great deal of obsolete computer equipment eventually ends up in a landfill, even though there may be alternative actions that could be taken instead.

   For this project, research what options would be available to discard the following: (1) a 10-year-old computer that is no longer functioning, (2) a 4-year-old computer that still works but is too slow for your needs, and (3) a used-up toner cartridge for a laser printer. Check with your local schools and charitable organizations to see if they would accept any of these items. Check with at least one computer manufacturer and one recycling company to see if they would accept the computers, and, if so, what the procedure and cost would be. Check with at least one vendor selling recharged toner cartridges to see if it buys old cartridges or requires a trade-in with an order. Share your findings with the class in the form of a short presentation. Be sure to include any costs associated with the disposal options you found, as well as your recommendation for each disposal situation. The presentation should not exceed 10 minutes and should make use of one or more presentation aids, such as the chalkboard, handouts, overhead transparencies, or a computer-based slide presentation (your instructor may provide additional requirements). You may also be asked to submit a summary of the presentation to your instructor.

PRESENTATION/ DEMONSTRATION

Instructions: Go to the Chapter 16 page at **www.cengage.com/computerconcepts/np/uc13** to work the following Web Activities.

6. **Interactive Activities** Work the interactive **Crossword Puzzle**, watch the **Video Podcasts** and **Online Videos**, and explore the **Further Exploration** links associated with this chapter.

   If you have a SAM user profile, you may have access to hands-on instruction, practice, and assessment of the skills covered in this chapter. Check with your instructor for instructions and the correct URL/Web site to access those assignments.

7. **Student Edition Labs** Work the following interactive **Student Edition Labs**.
   > **Installing and Uninstalling Software**   > **Computer Ethics**

8. **Test Yourself** Review the **Online Study Guide** for this chapter, then test your knowledge of the terms and concepts covered in this chapter by completing the **Key Term Matching** exercise, the **Self-Quiz**, the **Exercises**, and the **Practice Test**.

WEB ACTIVITIES

Student Edition Labs

SOC

Computers and Society

DELL

Frank Molsberry is a Technologist in Dell's Office of the CTO. Prior to his current position, he helped found Dell's Workstation Architecture and Development team and, more recently, the Enterprise Architecture and Technology Group. In all, he has over 25 years of management and engineering experience in advanced system software development and PC system architectures. Frank has a Bachelor's degree in Computer Science and has several patents in the area of computer security. He does regular customer briefings on security and emerging technology trends.

A conversation with FRANK MOLSBERRY
Technologist for Dell Inc.

"Security is a mindset. In the same way you look at the features, usability, and performance of a solution, you need to specifically look at the security characteristics, as well."

My Background ...

I've been in the field of computer software and hardware development for over 25 years. I joined Dell in 1998 after working at IBM for 15 years. I am currently a Technologist in the Office of the CTO. My focus area is on Security Architecture and Technology. In that role, I support the current engineering efforts for incorporating security hardware and software into Dell products, work with the various security technology companies to evaluate and influence current and planned offerings, and participate with standards organizations, such as the Trusted Computing Group (TCG), in the definition of future security standards.

In many cases the subjects we focus on now (such as security) are not about stand-alone systems anymore, but instead involve an entire ecosystem of hardware devices, software applications, and the infrastructure connecting them. Because this can entail a great deal of breadth and depth of knowledge, I've found that it is important to have a "big-picture" vision and the ability to rapidly drill into the details as needed, but only to the level needed to answer the questions in front of you.

It's Important to Know ...

The recommendations presented in these chapters are not one time things. Managing your security and privacy needs to be a regular routine—like brushing your teeth.

Technology is a double-edged sword and can always have a dark side. As you develop new and innovative hardware or software applications, you must always look at the threats that can be brought against it and, more importantly, how the technology could be misused beyond its intended purpose. By stepping back and identifying these issues up front, the developers and users of the technology can be better prepared to combat it. Security is a mindset. In the same way you look at the features, usability, and performance of a solution, you need to specifically look at the security characteristics, as well.

We now have a global economy. The products and services you provide must consider a global culture and have the flexibility to satisfy the varying customs, rules, and requirements of a global economy.

How I Use this Technology ...

I use all the standard precautions on my personal computer—such as antivirus software, antispyware software, and backing up my data—to avoid data loss. I keep my systems on a UPS/surge protector and use power management features to save electricity. When traveling, I use a privacy screen to prevent others from viewing my work and I use encryption software to protect the data on my computer and portable media, such as USB flash drives.

What the Future Holds . . .

The next big thing is not usually a revolution as much as it is a continued progression that, when looked at over a long window of a time, shows up as a major change in technology or use model. So the trends of faster, smaller, cheaper will continue for the next decade.

The impact of security and privacy technology on society is huge. One of the biggest issues is identity theft and the tremendous effort it takes to recover from it. Tasks like shredding papers and monitoring your credit report activity can help prevent identity theft or alert you to suspicious activity. Social media and cloud-based services are seeing explosive growth, but little consideration is given to the use, security, and privacy of the personal information stored via these services, or to what happens when one of these entities is purchased or goes out of business. One must ask, "Can the collection of information I provide about myself online be used to compromise my identity?"

Methods to protect the environment from the impact of technology on the environment will continue to expand. Major manufacturers like Dell have implemented initiatives to reduce or eliminate hazardous materials like lead from their systems, and there are major programs for computer recycling and for returning consumables, such as printer cartridges. A possible development for the future is using more modular architectures, allowing the average user to easily change or upgrade the capabilities of a computer, TV, or printer without having to purchase an entirely new system.

It's important to realize that the digital divide is not new. It occurs when each new method of information communication is developed, such as with the introduction of radio and television. The continued decreases in the cost of computing, new categories of devices like netbooks, and improvements in wireless connectivity will help to close the current divide, but there may be new digital divides in the future. However, we must not lose sight of where information and communications fit in the hierarchy of needs. For those populations where the basic needs of food, clothing, and shelter are not being met, solutions to those problems may need to be reached before focusing on access to computing resources. Another key is connectivity—it does little good to have a computer today without Internet access. Advancements in 4G wireless communications like WiMAX and LTE are crucial.

" Social media and cloud-based services are seeing explosive growth, but little consideration is given to the use, security, and privacy of the personal information stored via these services. . ."

My Advice to Students . . .

Computers and the ever changing technology they are based on are just tools. It is important not to just focus on the "coolness" of something new, but the problem it is trying to solve, the user experience, and the barriers to adoption.

Discussion Question

Frank Molsberry believes that developers must look at how new products could be misused. Think about a few recent new technologies or products. Have they been used in an illegal or unethical manner? What responsibility, if any, does a developer have if its product is used inappropriately? Be prepared to discuss your position (in class, via an online class discussion group, in a class chat room, or via a class blog, depending on your instructor's directions). You may also be asked to write a short paper expressing your opinion.

> **For more information on Dell, visit www.dell.com and www.dell.com/innovation. For security information, visit www.trustedcomputinggroup.org and searchsecurity.techtarget.com. For a summary of many online tech news sites, visit www.dailyrotation.com.**

REFERENCES AND RESOURCES
GUIDE

INTRODUCTION

When working on a computer or taking a computer course, you often need to look up information related to computers. For instance, you may need to find out when the IBM PC was first invented, you may want tips about what to consider when buying a computer, or you may want to find out more about how numbering systems work. To help you with the tasks just mentioned and more, this References and Resources Guide brings together in one convenient location a collection of computer-related references and resources. These resources plus additional resources (such as a variety of interactive activities and study tools) are located on this textbook's Web site, at www.cengage.com/computerconcepts/np/uc13.

OUTLINE

Computer History Timeline R-2

Guide to Buying a PC R-8

A Look at Numbering Systems R-11

Coding Charts R-15

Answers to Self-Quiz R-17

COMPUTER HISTORY TIMELINE

The earliest recorded calculating device, the abacus, is believed to have been invented by the Babylonians sometime between 500 B.C. and 100 B.C. It and similar types of counting boards were used solely for counting.

Blaise Pascal invented the first mechanical calculator, called the Pascaline Arithmetic Machine. It had the capacity for eight digits and could add and subtract.

Dr. John V. Atanasoff and Clifford Berry designed and built ABC (for Atanasoff-Berry Computer), the world's first electronic computer.

500 B.C.

1642

1937

Precomputers and Early Computers

1621

1804

1944

French silk weaver Joseph-Marie Jacquard built a loom that read holes punched on a series of small sheets of hardwood to control the weave of the pattern. This automated machine introduced the use of punch cards and showed that they could be used to convey a series of instructions.

The Mark I, considered to be the first digital computer, was introduced by IBM. It was developed in cooperation with Harvard University, was more than 50 feet long, weighed almost five tons, and used electromechanical relays to solve addition problems in less than a second; multiplication and division took about 6 and 12 seconds, respectively.

The slide rule, a precursor to the electronic calculator, was invented. Used primarily to perform multiplication, division, square roots, and the calculation of logarithms, its wide-spread use continued until the 1970s.

Precomputers and Early Computers (before approximately 1945)

Most precomputers and early computers were mechanical machines that worked with gears and levers. Electromechanical devices (using both electricity and gears and levers) were developed toward the end of this era.

First Generation (approximately 1946–1957)

Powered by vacuum tubes, these computers were faster than electromechanical machines, but they were large and bulky, generated excessive heat, and had to be physically wired and reset to run programs. Input was primarily on punch cards; output was on punch cards or paper. Machine and assembly languages were used to program these computers.

The UNIVAC 1, the first computer to be mass produced for general use, was introduced by Remington Rand. In 1952, it was used to analyze votes in the U.S. presidential election and correctly predicted that Dwight D. Eisenhower would be the victor only 45 minutes after the polls closed, though the results were not aired immediately because they weren't trusted.

The COBOL programming language was developed by a committee headed by Dr. Grace Hopper.

The first floppy disk (8 inches in diameter) was introduced.

UNIX was developed at AT&T's Bell Laboratories; Advanced Micro Devices (AMD) was formed; and ARPANET (the predecessor of today's Internet) was established.

REF

IBM unbundled some of its hardware and software and began selling them separately, allowing other software companies to emerge.

1951   1960   1967   1969

| First Generation | Second Generation | Third Generation |

1947   1957   1964   1968

The FORTRAN programming language was introduced.

Robert Noyce and Gordon Moore founded the Intel Corporation.

John Bardeen, Walter Brattain, and William Shockley invented the transistor, which had the same capabilities as a vacuum tube but was faster, broke less often, used less power, and created less heat. They won a Nobel Prize for their invention in 1956 and computers began to be built with transistors shortly afterwards.

The first mouse was invented by Doug Engelbart.

The IBM System/360 computer was introduced. Unlike previous computers, System/360 contained a full line of compatible computers, making upgrading easier.

Second Generation (approximately 1958–1963)
Second-generation computers used transistors instead of vacuum tubes. They allowed the computer to be physically smaller, more powerful, more reliable, and faster than before. Input was primarily on punch cards and magnetic tape; output was on punch cards and paper; and magnetic tape and disks were used for storage. High-level programming languages were used with these computers.

Third Generation (approximately 1964–1970)
The third generation of computers evolved when integrated circuits (IC)—computer chips—began being used instead of conventional transistors. Computers became even smaller and more reliable. Keyboards and monitors were introduced for input and output; magnetic disks were used for storage. The emergence of the operating system meant that operators no longer had to manually reset relays and wiring.

R-3

The first microprocessor, the Intel 4004, was designed by Ted Hoff. The single processor contained 2,250 transistors and could execute 60,000 operations per second.

Bill Gates and Paul Allen wrote a version of BASIC for the Altair, the first computer programming language designed for a personal computer. Bill Gates dropped out of Harvard to form Microsoft with Paul Allen.

Software Arts Inc's Visi-Calc, the first electronic spreadsheet and business program for personal computers, was released. This program is seen as one of the reasons personal computers first became widely accepted in the business world.

IBM introduced the IBM PC. This DOS-based PC used a 4.77 MHz 8088 CPU with 64 KB of RAM and quickly became the standard for business personal computers.

1971   1975   1979   1981

Fourth Generation

1972   1976   1980

The C programming language was developed by Dennis Ritchie at Bell Labs.

Seymour Cray, called the "father of supercomputing," founded Cray Research, which would go on to build some of the fastest computers in the world.

Steve Wozniak and Steve Jobs' founded Apple computer and released the Apple I (a single-board computer), followed by the Apple II (a complete personal computer that became an instant success in 1977). They originally ran the company out of Jobs' garage.

Sony Electronics introduced the 3.5-inch floppy disk and drive.

Seagate Technology announced the first Winchester 5.25-inch hard disk drive, revolutionizing computer storage.

IBM chose Microsoft to develop the operating system for its upcoming personal computer. That operating system was PC-DOS.

Fourth Generation (approximately 1971–present)

The fourth generation of computers began with large-scale integration (LSI), which resulted in chips that could contain thousands of transistors. Very large-scale integration (VLSI) resulted in the microprocessor and the resulting microcomputers. The keyboard and mouse are predominant input devices, though many other types of input devices are now available; monitors and printers provide output; storage is obtained with magnetic disks, optical discs, and memory chips.

The first general-interest CD-ROM product (*Grolier's Electronic Encyclopedia*) was released, and computer and electronics companies worked together to develop a universal CD-ROM standard.

Intel introduced the Intel386 CPU.

Compaq Corporation released the first IBM-compatible personal computer that ran the same software as the IBM PC, marking the beginning of the huge PC-compatible industry.

The first version of Microsoft Windows, a graphical environment, was released.

Tim Berners-Lee of CERN invented the World Wide Web.

Linus Torvalds created Linux, which launched the open source revolution. The penguin logo/mascot soon followed.

Intel introduced the Intel486 chip, the world's first million transistor CPU.

1983   1985   1989   1994

1982   1984   1986   1993

Intel introduced the 80286 CPU.

The Apple Macintosh debuted. It featured a simple, graphical user interface, used an 8 MHz, 32-bit Motorola 68000 CPU, and had a built-in 9-inch black and white screen.

Intel introduced the Pentium CPU.

NCSA released the Mosaic Web browser, developed by students at the University of Illinois. Mosaic was one of the first browsers to support graphics, and it was the first to support both Windows and Macintosh computers. Three million people were connected to the Internet.

Apple's Steve Jobs founded Pixar.

TIME magazine named the computer its "Machine of the Year" for 1982, emphasizing the importance the computer had already reached in our society at that time.

Microsoft was listed on the New York Stock Exchange and began to sell shares to the public; Bill Gates became one of the world's youngest billionaires.

The first DVD players used for playing movies stored on DVD discs were sold.

Shawn Fanning, 19, wrote the software to drive his Napster P2P service and began the debate about P2P filesharing and online music.

Apple introduced the iPod personal music player.

Intel's first 64-bit CPU, the Itanium, was introduced.

Palm released the Palm VII, its first handheld computer with wireless Internet access.

After winning 2 of 6 games in their first contest in 1996, the IBM computer Deep Blue beat chess master Garry Kasparov in a chess match.

Microsoft released its XP line of products, including Windows XP and Office XP.

The Intel Pentium III CPU was introduced.

The number of Internet users worldwide surpassed 100 million.

1997

1999

2001

1995

1998

2000

2003

Windows 95 was released and sold more than 1 million copies in 4 days.

Microsoft shipped Windows 98.

The first USB flash drives were released.

AMD released the 64-bit Opteron server CPU and the Athlon 64, the first 64-bit CPU designed for desktop computer use.

Microsoft shipped the Office 2003 editions of its Microsoft Office System.

Both eBay and Amazon.com were founded.

Apple released the iMac, a modernized version of the Macintosh computer. Its futuristic design helped to make this computer immensely popular.

Digital camera sales in the United States exceeded 14 million, surpassing film camera sales for the first time.

Sun Microsystems released Java, which is still one of the most popular Web programming languages.

Intel introduced its Pentium 4 CPU chip. A popular advertising campaign, launched in 2001, featured the Blue Man Group.

The Internet and wireless networks enabled people to work and communicate with others while on the go.

Spyware became a major problem; some studies indicated that over 80% of computers had spyware installed.

2004

Delivery of TV shows and other media to mobile phones became more common.

New Internet-enabled gaming consoles, like the Wii shown here, were released.

Blu-ray Disc and HD-DVD movies, discs, and players became available in the U.S.

Use of the Internet for online shopping, as well as downloads of music, movies, games, and television shows, continued to grow.

Broadband Internet access approached the norm and improvements to wireless networking (such as WiMAX) continued to be developed.

2006

Netbooks were introduced.

facebook

Google introduced the Chrome operating system.

Use of social networking sites exploded; Facebook announced it had more than 100 million users.

The HD-DVD format was discontinued, leaving Blu-ray Disc the HD format winner.

2008

2005

Phishing and identity theft became household words as an increasing number of individuals fell victim to these Internet scams.

The capabilities of mobile devices continued to grow; Palm's LifeDrive came with a 4 GB hard drive and built-in Wi-Fi and Bluetooth support.

Portable media players, such as the iPod, were common; digital music capabilities were built into a growing number of objects and devices.

Intel and AMD their first dual-core CPUs both released

2007

The Twitter microblogging service was launched.

Apple released the revolutionary iPhone.

Microsoft released Windows Vista and Office 2007.

Windows Vista

Quad-core CPUs were released by both Intel and AMD.

2009

Geobrowsing applications became more prominent; 4G phones became available.

Cloud computing entered the main-stream for both individuals and businesses.

Google apps

Microsoft released Windows 7.

Windows 7

GUIDE TO BUYING A PC

Before buying a new computer, it is important to give some thought to what your needs are, including what software programs you wish to run, any other computers with which you need to be compatible, how you might want to connect to the Internet, and how much portability is needed. This section of the References and Resources Guide explores topics related to buying a new personal computer. ∎

Analyzing Needs

When referring to a computer system, a need refers to a functional requirement that the computer system must be able to meet. For example, at a video rental store, a computer system must be able to enter barcodes automatically from videos or DVDs being checked in and out, identify customers with overdue movies, manage movie inventories, and do routine accounting operations. Portability is another example of a possible need. For example, if you need to take your computer with you as you travel or work out of the office, you will need a portable computer instead of a desktop computer.

Selecting a computer for home or business use must begin with the all-important question "What do I want the system to do?" Once you have determined what tasks the system will be used for and the amount of portability that is needed, you can choose among the software and hardware alternatives available. Making a list of your needs in the areas discussed in the next few sections can help you get a picture of what type of system you are shopping for. If you are not really sure what you want a system to do, you should think twice about buying one yet—you can easily make expensive mistakes if you are uncertain about what you want a system to do. Some common decision categories are discussed next; Figure R-1 provides a list of questions that can help you define the type of computer that will meet your needs.

ⓥ FIGURE R-1
Questions to consider when getting ready to buy a personal computer.

POSSIBLE QUESTIONS

What tasks will I be using the computer for (writing papers, accessing the Internet, watching TV, making telephone calls, composing music, playing games, etc.)?

Do I prefer a Mac or a PC-compatible? Are there any other computers I need my documents and storage media to be compatible with?

How fast do I need the system to be?

Do I need portability? If so, do I need a powerful desktop replacement or will a netbook or UMPC suffice?

What size screen do I need? Do I need two monitors?

What removable storage media will I need to use (such as DVDs, flash memory cards, or USB flash drives)?

What types of Internet access will I be using (such as conventional dial-up, DSL, cable, satellite, or mobile wireless)?

Do I need to be able to connect the computer to a network? If so, is it a wired or wireless network and what type of network adapter is needed to connect to that network?

What additional hardware do I need (scanner, printer, TV tuner/antenna, wireless router, or digital camera, for example)?

What brand(s) do I prefer? When do I need the computer?

Do I want to pay extra for a better warranty (such as a longer time period, more comprehensive coverage, or on-site service)?

Application Software Decisions

Determining what functions you want the system to perform will also help you decide which application software is needed. Most users start with an application suite containing a word processor, spreadsheet, and other programs. In addition, specialty programs, such as tax preparation, drawing, home publishing, reference software, games, and more, may be needed or desired.

Not all software is available for all operating systems. Consequently, if a specific piece of software is needed, that choice may determine which operating system you need to use. In addition, your operating system and application software decisions may already be made for you if your documents need to be compatible with those of another computer (such as other office computers or between a home and an office computer).

Platforms and Configuration Options

If your operating system has already been determined, that is a good start in deciding the overall platform you will be looking for—most users will choose between the PC-compatible and Apple Macintosh platform. PC-compatible computers usually run either Windows or Linux; Apple computers almost always use Mac OS.

Configuration decisions initially involve determining the size of the machine desired (see Figure R-2). For nonportable systems, you have the choice between tower, desktop, or all-in-one configurations; in addition, the monitor size needs to be determined. Fully functioning personal computers can be notebook or tablet computers. For tablet computers, you need to decide if you will require keyboard use on a regular basis; if so, a convertible tablet computer would be the best choice. If a powerful fully functioning computer is not required, you may decide to go with a more portable option, such as a netbook or UMPC.

You should also consider any other specifications that are important to you, such as the size of the hard drive, types of other storage devices needed, amount of memory required, and so forth. As discussed in the next section, these decisions often require reconciling the features you want with the amount of money you are willing to spend.

DESKTOPS

Power vs. Budget Requirements

As part of the needs analysis, you should look closely at your need for a powerful system versus your budgetary constraints. Most users do not need a state-of-the-art system. Those who do should expect to pay more than the average user. A computer that was top of the line six months or a year ago is usually reasonably priced and more than adequate for most users' needs. Individuals who want a computer only for basic tasks, such as using the Internet and word processing, can likely get by with an inexpensive computer designed for home use.

When determining your requirements, be sure to identify the features and functions that are absolutely essential for your primary computing tasks (such as a large hard drive and lots of memory for multimedia applications, a fast video card for gaming, a fast Internet connection, a TV tuner card for individuals who wish to use the computer as a TV set, and so forth). After you have the minimum configuration determined, you can add optional or desirable components, as your budget allows.

NOTEBOOKS

NETBOOKS

Listing Alternatives

After you consider your needs and the questions mentioned in Figure R-1, you should have a pretty good idea of the hardware and software you will need. You will also know what purchasing options are available to you, depending on your time frame (while some retail stores have systems that can be purchased and brought home the same day, special orders or some systems purchased online will take longer). The next step is to get enough information from possible vendors to compare and contrast a few alternative systems that satisfy your stated needs. Most often, these vendors are local stores (such as computer stores, warehouse clubs, and electronic stores) and/or online stores (such as manufacturer Web sites and e-tailers). To compare prices and specifications for possible computer systems, find at least three systems that meet or exceed your needs by looking through newspaper advertisements, configuring systems online via manufacturer and e-tailer Web sites, or calling or visiting local stores. A comparison sheet listing your criteria and the systems you are considering, such as the one in Figure R-3, can help you summarize your options. Although it is sometimes very difficult to compare the prices of systems since they typically have somewhat different configurations and some components (such as CPUs) are difficult to compare, you can assign an approximate dollar value to each extra feature a system has (such as $50 for an included printer or a larger hard drive). Be sure to also include any sales tax and shipping charges when you compare the prices of each total system.

If your budget is limited, you will have to balance the system you need with extra features you may want. But do not skimp on memory or hard drive space because sufficient memory can help your programs to run faster and with fewer problems and hard

ULTRA-MOBILE PCS (UMPCs)

FIGURE R-2
Types of personal computers.

COMPONENT	EXAMPLE OF DESIRED SPECIFICATIONS	SYSTEM #1 VENDOR:	SYSTEM #2 VENDOR:	SYSTEM #3 VENDOR:
Operating system	Windows 7 Home Premium			
Manufacturer	HP or Dell			
Style	Notebook			
CPU	Intel dual core			
RAM	2 GB or higher			
Hard drive	500 GB or higher			
Removable storage	8-in-1 and flash memory card reader			
Optical drive	DVD-RW			
Monitor	Widescreen 15.4" minimum			
Video card and video RAM	Prefer dedicated video RAM			
Keyboard/mouse	Portable USB mouse with scroll wheel			
Sound card/speakers	No preference			
Modem	None			
Network card	Wi-Fi (802.11n)			
Printer	Ink-jet if get deal on price with complete system			
Included software	Microsoft Office			
Warranty	3 years min. (1 year onsite if not a local store)			
Other features	3 USB ports minimum, TV tuner, ExpressCard module			
Price				
Tax				
Shipping				
TOTAL COST				

Ⓐ **FIGURE R-3**

Comparing computer alternatives. A checklist such as this one can help to organize your desired criteria and evaluate possible systems.

drive space is consumed quickly. Often for just a few extra dollars, you can get additional memory, a faster CPU, or a larger hard drive—significantly cheaper than trying to upgrade any of those features later. A good rule of thumb is to try to buy a little more computer than you think you need. On the other hand, do not buy a top-of-the-line system unless you fall into the power user category and really need it. Generally, the second or third system down from the top of the line is a very good system for a much more reasonable price. Some guidelines for minimum requirements for most home users are as follows:

➤ A relatively fast multi-core CPU (generally, any multi-core CPU currently being sold today is fast enough for most users).

➤ 3 GB of RAM for desktop and notebook users.

➤ 320 GB or more hard drive space.

➤ Recordable or rewritable DVD drive.

➤ Network adapter or modem for the desired type(s) of Internet access.

➤ Sound card and speakers.

➤ At least 3 USB ports.

➤ A built-in flash memory media reader.

A LOOK AT NUMBERING SYSTEMS

As discussed in Chapter 2 of this text, a numbering system is a way of representing numbers. People generally use the *decimal numbering system* explained in Chapter 2 and reviewed next; computers process data using the *binary numbering system*. Another numbering system related to computer use is the *hexadecimal numbering system*, which can be used to represent long strings of binary numbers in a manner more understandable to people than the binary numbering system. Following a discussion of these three numbering systems, we take a look at conversions between numbering systems and principles of computer arithmetic, and then close with a look at how to perform conversions using a scientific calculator. ■

The Decimal and Binary Numbering System

The *decimal (base 10)* numbering system uses 10 symbols—the digits 0, 1, 2, 3, 4, 5, 6, 7, 8, and 9—to represent all possible numbers and is the numbering system people use most often. The *binary (base 2)* numbering system is used extensively by computers to represent numbers and other characters. This system uses only two digits—0 and 1. As illustrated in Figure 2-3 in Chapter 2, the place values (columns) in the binary numbering system are different from those used in the decimal system.

The Hexadecimal Numbering System

Computers often output diagnostic and memory-management messages and identify network adapters and other hardware in *hexadecimal (hex)* notation. Hexadecimal notation is a shorthand method for representing the binary digits stored in a computer. Because large binary numbers—for example, 1101010001001101—can easily be misread by people, hexadecimal notation groups binary digits into units of four, which, in turn, are represented by other symbols.

The hexadecimal numbering system is also called the *base 16 numbering system* because it uses 16 different symbols. Since there are only 10 possible numeric digits, hexadecimal uses letters instead of numbers for the additional 6 symbols. The 16 hexadecimal symbols and their decimal and binary counterparts are shown in Figure R-4.

The hexadecimal numbering system has a special relationship to the 8-bit bytes of ASCII and EBCDIC that makes it ideal for displaying addresses and other data quickly. As you can see in Figure R-4, each hex character has a 4-bit binary counterpart, so any combination of 8 bits can be represented by exactly two hexadecimal characters. For example, the letter N (represented in ASCII by 01001110) has a hex representation of *4E* (see the Binary Equivalent columns for the hexadecimal characters *4* and *E* in Figure R-4).

FIGURE R-4
Hexadecimal characters and their decimal and binary equivalents.

HEXADECIMAL CHARACTER	DECIMAL EQUIVALENT	BINARY EQUIVALENT
0	0	0000
1	1	0001
2	2	0010
3	3	0011
4	4	0100
5	5	0101
6	6	0110
7	7	0111
8	8	1000
9	9	1001
A	10	1010
B	11	1011
C	12	1100
D	13	1101
E	14	1110
F	15	1111

Converting Between Numbering Systems

In Figure 2-3 in Chapter 2, we illustrated how to convert from binary to decimal. Three other types of conversions are discussed next.

Hexadecimal to Decimal

As shown in Figure R-5, the process for converting a hexadecimal number to its decimal equivalent is similar to converting a binary number to its decimal equivalent, except the base number is 16 instead of 2. To determine the decimal equivalent of a hexadecimal number (such as 4F6A, as shown in Figure R-5), multiply the decimal equivalent of each individual hex character (determined by using the table in Figure R-4) by the appropriate power of 16 and then add the results to obtain the decimal equivalent of that hex number.

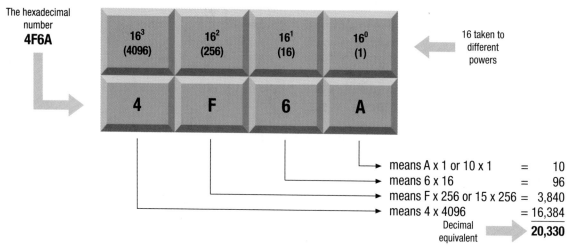

Hexadecimal to Binary and Binary to Hexadecimal

To convert from hexadecimal to binary, we convert each hexadecimal digit separately to 4 binary digits (using the table in Figure R-4). For example, to convert F6A9 to binary, we get

F	6	A	9
1111	0110	1010	1001

or 1111011010101001 in binary representation. To convert from binary to hexadecimal, we go through the reverse process. If the number of digits in the binary number is not divisible by 4, we add leading zeros to the binary number to force an even division. For example, to convert the binary number 1101101010011 to hexadecimal, we get

0001	1011	0101	0011
1	B	5	3

or 1B53 in hexadecimal representation. Note that three leading zeros were added to change the initial 1 to 0001 before making the conversion.

Decimal to Binary and Decimal to Hexadecimal

To convert from decimal to either binary or hexadecimal, we can use the *remainder method*. To use the remainder method, the decimal number is divided by 2 (to convert to a binary number) or 16 (to convert to a hexadecimal number). The *remainder* of the division operation is recorded and the division process is repeated using the *quotient* as the next dividend, until the quotient becomes 0. At that point, the collective remainders (written backwards) represent the equivalent binary or hexadecimal number (see Figure R-6).

Consider the decimal number **79**

BINARY

Dividends Quotients Remainder

1. **Divide the decimal number by 2.**
   - 79 ÷ 2 = 39 R 1
   - 39 ÷ 2 = 19 R 1
   - 19 ÷ 2 = 9 R 1
   - 9 ÷ 2 = 4 R 1
   - 4 ÷ 2 = 2 R 0
   - 2 ÷ 2 = 1 R 0
   - 1 ÷ 2 = 0 R 1

2. **Repeat the process using the quotient from the previous division until the quotient is 0.**

   Stop at 0

   1001111

3. **Collect the remainders backwards to get the binary number 1001111.**

HEXADECIMAL

Dividends Quotients Remainder

- 79 ÷ 16 = 4 R 15 or F
- 4 ÷ 16 = 0 R 4

Stop at 0

4F

1. **Divide the decimal number by 16.**

2. **Repeat the process using the quotient from the previous division until the quotient is 0.**

3. **Collect the remainders backwards to get the hexadecimal number 4F.**

🅐 **FIGURE R-6**
The remainder method. The remainder method can be used to convert decimal numbers to binary or hex format.

A table summarizing all the numbering system conversion procedures covered in this text is provided in Figure R-7.

🅖 **FIGURE R-7**
Summary of conversions.

| | **TO BASE** | | |
FROM BASE	**2**	**10**	**16**
2		Starting at the right-most digit, multiply binary digits by 2^0, 2^1, 2^2, etc., respectively, and then add products.	Starting at the right-most digit, convert each group of four binary digits to a hex digit.
10	Divide repeatedly by 2 using each quotient as the next dividend until the quotient becomes 0, and then collect the remainders in reverse order.		Divide repeatedly by 16 using each quotient as the next dividend until the quotient becomes 0, and then collect the remainders in reverse order.
16	Convert each hex digit to four binary digits.	Starting at the right-most digit, multiply hex digits by 16^0, 16^1, 16^2, etc., respectively, and then add products.	

🅥 **FIGURE R-8**
Adding and subtracting with the decimal, binary, and hexadecimal numbering systems.

Computer Arithmetic

To most people, decimal arithmetic is second nature. Addition and subtraction of binary and hexadecimal numbers is not much different than the process used with decimal numbers—just the number of symbols used in each system varies. For instance, the digits in each column are added or subtracted and you carry to and borrow from the column to the left as needed as you move from right to left. Instead of carrying or borrowing 10, however—as you would in the decimal system—you carry or borrow 2 (binary) or 16 (hexadecimal).

Figure R-8 provides an example of addition and subtraction with decimal, binary, and hexadecimal numbers.

	DECIMAL	**BINARY**	**HEXADECIMAL**
	1	1 1 1	1
	144	100101	8E
	+ 27	+ 10011	+ 2F
Addition	171	111000	BD
	3	0 0	7 1
	144	100101	8E
	- 27	- 10011	- 2F
Subtraction	117	10010	5F

Using a Scientific Calculator

A scientific calculator can be used to convert numbers between numbering systems, or to check conversions performed by hand. Many conventional calculators have different numbering system options; scientific calculator programs can be used for this purpose, as well. For example, Figure R-9 shows how to use the Windows Calculator program to double-check the hand calculations performed in Figure R-6 (the Scientific option must be selected using the View menu to display the options shown in the figure). Arithmetic can also be performed in any numbering system on a calculator, once that numbering system is selected on the calculator. Notice that, depending on which numbering system is currently selected, not all numbers on the calculator are available—only the possible numbers are displayed, such as only 0 and 1 when the binary numbering system is selected, as in the bottom screen in the figure.

FIGURE R-9

Using a scientific calculator. A physical calculator or calculator program can be used to convert between numbering systems, as well as to perform arithmetic in different numbering systems.

WINDOWS CALCULATOR
The Calculator program is typically located under Accessories on the Windows Start menu; select the *Scientific* option using the Calculator's View menu.

1. After entering a number (such as the decimal number 79 with the decimal numbering system selected shown here), select the numbering system to which the number should be converted (hex in this example).

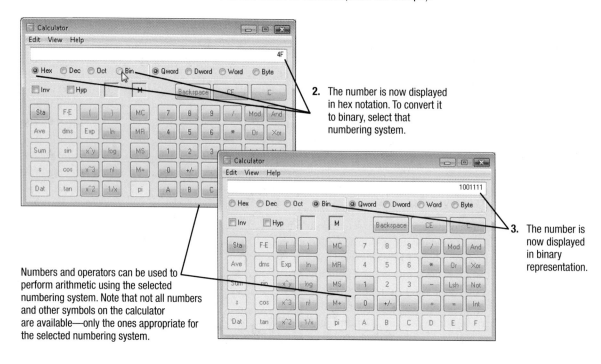

2. The number is now displayed in hex notation. To convert it to binary, select that numbering system.

3. The number is now displayed in binary representation.

Numbers and operators can be used to perform arithmetic using the selected numbering system. Note that not all numbers and other symbols on the calculator are available—only the ones appropriate for the selected numbering system.

CODING CHARTS

As discussed in Chapter 2 of this text, coding systems for text-based data include ASCII, EBCDIC, and Unicode. ∎

ASCII and EBCDIC

Figure R-10 provides a chart listing the 8-digit ASCII and EBCDIC representations (in binary) for most of the symbols found on a typical keyboard.

FIGURE R-10
ASCII and EBCDIC binary codes for typical keyboard symbols.

SYMBOL	ASCII	EBCDIC	SYMBOL	ASCII	EBCDIC	SYMBOL	ASCII	EBCDIC
A	0100 0001	1100 0001	e	0110 0101	1000 0101	8	0011 1000	1111 1000
B	0100 0010	1100 0010	f	0110 0110	1000 0110	9	0011 1001	1111 1001
C	0100 0011	1100 0011	g	0110 0111	1000 0111	(	0010 1000	0100 1101
D	0100 0100	1100 0100	h	0110 1000	1000 1000	)	0010 1001	0101 1101
E	0100 0101	1100 0101	i	0110 1001	1000 1001	/	0010 1111	0110 0001
F	0100 0110	1100 0110	j	0110 1010	1001 0001	-	0010 1101	0110 0000
G	0100 0111	1100 0111	k	0110 1011	1001 0010	*	0010 1010	0101 1100
H	0100 1000	1100 1000	l	0110 1100	1001 0011	+	0010 1011	0100 1110
I	0100 1001	1100 1001	m	0110 1101	1001 0100	,	0010 1100	0110 1011
J	0100 1010	1101 0001	n	0110 1110	1001 0101	.	0010 1110	0100 1011
K	0100 1011	1101 0010	o	0110 1111	1001 0110	:	0011 1010	0111 1010
L	0100 1100	1101 0011	p	0111 0000	1001 0111	;	0011 1011	0101 1110
M	0100 1101	1101 0100	q	0111 0001	1001 1000	&	0010 0110	0101 0000
N	0100 1110	1101 0101	r	0111 0010	1001 1001	\	0101 1100	1110 0000
O	0100 1111	1101 0110	s	0111 0011	1010 0010	$	0010 0100	0101 1011
P	0101 0000	1101 0111	t	0111 0100	1010 0011	%	0010 0101	0110 1100
Q	0101 0001	1101 1000	u	0111 0101	1010 0100	=	0011 1101	0111 1110
R	0101 0010	1101 1001	v	0111 0110	1010 0101	>	0011 1110	0110 1110
S	0101 0011	1110 0010	w	0111 0111	1010 0110	<	0011 1100	0100 1100
T	0101 0100	1110 0011	x	0111 1000	1010 0111	!	0010 0001	0101 1010
U	0101 0101	1110 0100	y	0111 1001	1010 1000	|	0111 1100	0110 1010
V	0101 0110	1110 0101	z	0111 1010	1010 1001	?	0011 1111	0110 1111
W	0101 0111	1110 0110	0	0011 0000	1111 0000	@	0100 0000	0111 1100
X	0101 1000	1110 0111	1	0011 0001	1111 0001	_	0101 1111	0110 1101
Y	0101 1001	1110 1000	2	0011 0010	1111 0010	'	0110 0000	1011 1001
Z	0101 1010	1110 1001	3	0011 0011	1111 0011	{	0111 1011	1100 0000
a	0110 0001	1000 0001	4	0011 0100	1111 0100	}	0111 1101	1101 0000
b	0110 0010	1000 0010	5	0011 0101	1111 0101	~	0111 1110	1010 0001
c	0110 0011	1000 0011	6	0011 0110	1111 0110	[	0101 1011	0100 1010
d	0110 0100	1000 0100	7	0011 0111	1111 0111	]	0101 1101	0101 1010

A 0041	N 004E	a 0061	n 006E	0 0030	{ 007B	* 002A	■ 25A0	অ 0985
B 0042	O 004F	b 0062	o 006F	1 0031	| 007C	+ 002B	□ 25A1	গ 0997
C 0043	P 0050	c 0063	p 0070	2 0032	} 007D	, 002C	▲ 25B2	ে 09C7
D 0044	Q 0051	d 0064	q 0071	3 0033	~ 007E	- 002D	% 2105	৶ 09F6
E 0045	R 0052	e 0065	r 0072	4 0034	! 0021	. 002E	℞ 211E	ȅ 0685
F 0046	S 0053	f 0066	s 0073	5 0035	" 0022	/ 002F	⅓ 2153	ڴ 06B4
G 0047	T 0054	g 0067	t 0074	6 0036	# 0023	£ 20A4	⅔ 2154	ڪ 06AA
H 0048	U 0055	h 0068	u 0075	7 0037	$ 0024	Σ 2211	♛ 2655	α 03B1
I 0049	V 0056	i 0069	v 0076	8 0038	% 0025	∅ 2205	☂ 2602	β 03B2
J 004A	W 0057	j 006A	w 0077	9 0039	& 0026	√ 221A	❏ 2750	Δ 0394
K 004B	X 0058	k 006B	x 0078	[005B	' 0027	∞ 221E	☀ 2742	φ 03A6
L 004C	Y 0059	l 006C	y 0079	\ 005C	(0028	≤ 2264	➲ 27B2	Ω 03A9
M 004D	Z 005A	m 006D	z 007A	] 005D	) 0029	≥ 2265	♥ 2665	Ÿ 03AB

FIGURE R-11
Selected Unicode codes.

FIGURE R-12
Using Unicode.

Unicode

Since consistent worldwide representation of symbols is increasingly needed today, use of Unicode is growing rapidly. Unicode can be used to represent every written language, as well as a variety of other symbols. Unicode codes are typically listed in hexadecimal notation—a sampling of Unicode is shown in Figure R-11.

The capability to display characters and other symbols using Unicode coding is incorporated into many programs. For instance, when the Symbol dialog box is opened using the Insert menu in Microsoft Office Word, the Unicode representation (as well as the corresponding ASCII code in either decimal or hexadecimal representation) can be viewed (see Figure R-12). Some programs allow you to enter a Unicode symbol using its Unicode hexadecimal value. For instance, in Microsoft Office programs you can use the Alt+X command when the insertion point is just to the right of a Unicode hex value to convert that hex value into the corresponding symbol. For example, the keystrokes

2264Alt+X

result in the symbol corresponding to the Unicode code 2264 (the less than or equal sign ≤) being inserted into the document; entering 03A3 and then pressing Alt+X inserts the symbol shown in the Word screen in Figure R-12.

Unicode representation for Greek capital letter sigma Σ symbol.

1. Type code, and then press Alt+X.

2. The corresponding symbol appears.

UNICODE REPRESENTATION
The Symbol dialog box shown here lists the Unicode representation of each symbol as it is selected. If preferred, the ASCII representation can be displayed.

INSERTING SYMBOLS USING UNICODE
In Microsoft Office programs, typing the hexadecimal Unicode code for a symbol and then pressing Alt+X displays the corresponding symbol.

Chapter 1
1. T 2. F 3. F 4. F 5. T 6. Input 7. tablet 8. Virtualization 9. electronic mail or e-mail 10. a. 4 b. 2 c. 1 d. 3

Chapter 2
1. T 2. F 3. T 4. T 5. F 6. 13 7. quad-core 8. port 9. multiprocessing 10. a. 6 b. 2 c. 4 d. 9 e. 7 f. 1 g. 8 h. 5 i. 3

Chapter 3
1. F 2. T 3. F 4. T 5. F 6. C 7. volatile 8. 650 MB 9. smart card 10. flash memory

Chapter 4
1. F 2. T 3. T 4. T 5. F 6. handwriting recognition 7. scanner, optical scanner, flatbed scanner, or portable scanner
8. pixel 9. flat-panel or LCD; cathode-ray tube or CRT 10. a. 2 b. 5 c. 1 d. 4 e. 3

Chapter 5
1. T 2. F 3. T 4. F 5. F 6. Multitasking 7. Linux 8. file compression 9. back up 10. a. 3 b. 4 c. 2 d. 1

Chapter 6
1. T 2. T 3. F 4. F 5. T 6. open source 7. insertion point or cursor 8. function 9. table 10. a. 2 b. 3 c. 1

Chapter 7
1. F 2. T 3. F 4. T 5. F 6. bus 7. dual-mode 8. personal area network or PAN 9. virtual private network or VPN
10. a. 3 b. 4 c. 1 d. 5 e. 2

Chapter 8
1. F 2. F 3. T 4. T 5. F 6. Digital Subscriber Line or DSL 7. keyword; directory 8. social networking site
9. online auction 10. a. 2 b. 4 c. 1 d. 3

Chapter 9
1. F 2. T 3. F 4. T 5. F 6. war driving 7. Biometric 8. virtual private network or VPN 9. digital signature
10. a. 3 b. 4 c. 1 d. 2

Chapter 10
1. F 2. T 3. F 4. T 5. F 6. Streaming 7. intended audience; objectives 8. Web site authoring 9. page layout
10. a. 1 b. 3 c. 2

Chapter 11
1. T 2. F 3. T 4. F 5. T 6. brokerage 7. digital wallet 8. banner ad 9. Search site optimization or SSO 10. a. 1 b. 3 c. 2

Chapter 12
1. T 2. F 3. F 4. T 5. F 6. inference engine 7. systems analyst 8. tangible 9. prototype 10. a. 2 b. 3 c. 1

Chapter 13
1. F 2. T 3. T 4. F 5. F 6. variable 7. interpreter 8. logic 9. software development kit or SDK 10. a. 3 b. 2 c. 5
d. 4 e. 1

Chapter 14
1. T 2. T 3. F 4. F 5. T 6. field or column; record or row 7. integrity 8. direct 9. client-server 10. a. 2 b. 3 c. 1

Chapter 15
1. F 2. T 3. T 4. F 5. F 6. disaster recovery 7. digital counterfeiting 8. filter 9. opt out; opt in 10. a. 3 b. 4 c. 1 d. 2

Chapter 16
1. F 2. T 3. T 4. F 5. F 6. copyright; trademark 7. plagiarism 8. cybersquatting 9. digital divide 10. a. 2 b. 4
c. 1 d. 3

Throughout the modules: Screen shots of Microsoft Access®, Excel®, Paint®, PowerPoint®, Visual Basic®, Word®, and Windows® reprinted with permission from Microsoft Corporation. Copyright © Microsoft Explorer® reprinted with permission from Microsoft Corporation.

Chapter 1

Figure 1-1a, Photo courtesy of Nokia; **Figure 1-1b**, Courtesy Microsoft Corporation; **Figure 1-2a**, Courtesy Dell Inc.; **Figure 1-2b**, Courtesy Epson America; **Figure 1-2c**, Courtesy of Nintendo; **Figure 1-3a**, Courtesy Intel Corporation; **Figure 1-3b**, Courtesy General Dynamics Itronix; **Figure 1-3c**, Courtesy U.S. Army; **Figure 1-4a**, Courtesy of iStockphoto © Steve Cole; **Figure 1-4b**, Courtesy General Dynamics Itronix; **Figure 1-4c**, BlackBerry®, RIM®, Research In Motion®, SureType®, SurePress™ and related trademarks, names and logos are the property of Research In Motion Limited and are registered and/or used in the U.S. and countries around the world.; **Figure 1-4d**, Courtesy Ingersoll Rand Security Technologies; **You box**, Courtesy Abilene Christian University; **Figure 1-5a**, Courtesy Bluetooth SIG; **Figure 1-5b**, Courtesy 3M Touch Systems; **Figure 1-5c**, Courtesy MasterCard Worldwide; **Figure 1-5d**, Courtesy Ingersoll Rand Security Technologies; **Figure 1-7acde**, Courtesy IBM Corporate Archives; **Figure 1-7b**, Courtesy U.S. Army; **Figure 1-9a**, Courtesy of Gateway, Inc.; **Figure 1-9b**, Courtesy, Hewlett-Packard Company; **Figure 1-9c**, ©2009 Logitech. All rights reserved. Images/materials on page 15 used with permission from Logitech.; **Figure 1-9d**, Courtesy D-Link Systems, Inc.; **Figure 1-9e**, Courtesy Kingston Technology Company, Inc.; **Figure 1-11c**, Courtesy RedLobster.com; **Trend box a**, Courtesy of HTC; **Trend box b**, Courtesy Acer America Corporation; **Trend box c**, Courtesy Microsoft Corporation; **Trend box d**, Courtesy Dell Inc.; **Figure 1-12**, Courtesy Volvo Cars of North America; **Figure 1-13**, Courtesy of HTC; **Figure 1-14a**, Courtesy, Hewlett-Packard Company; **Figure 1-14b**, Courtesy Dell Inc.; **Inside box**, Courtesy of iStockphoto © Carsten Madsen; **Figure 1-15a**, Courtesy Belkin International, Inc.; **Figure 1-15b**, Courtesy Fujitsu America; **Figure 1-15c**, Courtesy MSI Computer Corporation; **Figure 1-15d**, Courtesy General Dynamics Itronix; **Figure 1-16a**, Photo by Dom Miguel Photography for Seaport; **Figure 1-16b**, Courtesy Chumby Industries. Chumby and the Chumby Logo are the registered trademarks of Chumby Industries, Inc.; **Figure 1-16c**, Courtesy of Nintendo; **Figure 1-17a**, Courtesy Ergotron Inc.; **Figure 1-17b**, Courtesy Dell Inc.; **Figure 1-18**, Courtesy of IBM; **Figure 1-19**, Courtesy of IBM; **Figure 1-20acd**, Courtesy of Gateway, Inc.; **Figure 1-20b**, Courtesy Dell Inc.; **Figure 1-20e**, Courtesy, Hewlett-Packard Company; **Figure 1-21a**, Image ©2009 by Kelty; **Figure 1-21b**, Google screenshot © Google Inc. and used with permission.; **Figure 1-21c**, Used by Permission of Clear Channel Radio.; **Figure 1-21e**, Courtesy Classmates.com; **Figure 1-21f**, Courtesy CastTV; **Figure 1-23a**, Courtesy of Gateway, Inc.; **How box**, Courtesy e2Campus by Omnilert, LLC; **Figure 1-25**, Courtesy of Stanford University; **Figure 1-26**, Google Chrome screenshot © Google Inc. and used with permission.; **Figure 1-27ac**, Courtesy of Gateway, Inc.; **Figure 1-27b**, Courtesy Dell Inc.; **Figure 1-28**, The Survivor: Tocantins Logo is a registered trademark of Survivor Productions, LLC. CSB.com website contents © CBS Broadcasting Inc. Used by permission. CBS and the CBS Eye are registered trademarks of CBS Broadcasting Inc.; **Figure 1-29**, Courtesy of Symantec Corp; **Figure 1-31**, Courtesy www.snopes.com; **Ask the Expert 2**, Courtesy Jack in the Box Inc.; **Ask the Expert 3**, Courtesy TabletKiosk; **Expert Insight**, Courtesy D-Link Systems, Inc.

Chapter 2

Figure 2-8ad, Courtesy of Intel Corporation; **Figure 2-8bc**, (C) 2003, 2005, 2006 2007 Advanced Micro Devices, Inc., Reprinted with permission. AMD, the AMD Arrow logo, AMD Opteron, AMD Turion and combinations thereof as well as certain other marks listed at http://www.amd.com/legal/trademarks.html are trademarks of Advanced Micro Devices, Inc.; **How box**, Courtesy of IBM; **Figure 2-11**, Courtesy Kingston Technology Company, Inc.; **Figure 2-13a**, Courtesy of ABS Computer Technologies Inc. All rights reserved.; **Figure 2-13b**, Courtesy Belkin International, Inc.; **Figure 2-14a**, Courtesy D-Link Systems, Inc.; **Figure 2-16a**, Courtesy Dell Inc.; **Figure 2-16b-f**, Courtesy of Belkin International, Inc.; **Figure 2-16g**, Courtesy Cables To Go; **Figure 2-17**, Courtesy D-Link Systems, Inc.; **Figure 2-18a**, Courtesy Fujitsu America; **Figure 2-18b**, Courtesy Socket Mobile, Inc.; **Figure 2-18c**, Courtesy Kingston Technology Company, Inc.; **Inside box**, Courtesy Intel Corporation; **Trend box**, Courtesy TAEUS International Corporation; **Figure 2-21**, © 2009 Micron Technology, Inc. All Rights Reserved. Used with permission.; **Figure 2-23**, Copyright IMEC; **You box**, Photo courtesy of Nokia; **Figure 2-25**, Courtesy BMC Cycling; **Figure 2-26**, Image reproduced by permission of IBM Research, Almaden Research Center. Unauthorized use not permitted.; **Figure 2-27**, Courtesy Intel Corporation; **Figure 2-28**, Courtesy of IBM; **Ask the Expert 1**, Courtesy Unicode Inc.; **Ask the Expert 2**, Courtesy Tom's Hardware; **Ask the Expert 3**, Courtesy Kingston Technology Company, Inc.

Chapter 3

Figure 3-1, Courtesy of Gateway, Inc.; **Figure 3-4a**, Courtesy of Hitachi Global Storage Technologies; **Figure 3-4b**, Courtesy Western Digital; **Inside box**, Courtesy of DriveSavers, Inc. www.drivesavers.com; **Figure 3-6**, SanDisk is a trademark of SanDisk Corporation, registered in the United States and other countries. Other brand names mentioned herein are for identification purposes only and may be the trademarks of their respective holder(s).; **Figure 3-7ab**, Copyright © Iomega Corporation. All Rights Reserved. Iomega, the stylized "i" logo and all product images are property

of Iomega Corporation in the United States and/or other countries.; **Figure 3-7cd**, Courtesy Transcend Information USA; **Figure 3-8**, Courtesy of Seagate Technology LLC; **Figure 3-11**, Copyright © Iomega Corporation. All Rights Reserved. Iomega, the stylized "i" logo and all product images are property of Iomega Corporation in the United States and/or other countries.; **Figure 3-12ab**, Courtesy Verbatim America LLC; **Figure 3-12c**, Courtesy CD Digital Card www.cddigitalcard.com; **Figure 3-13**, © 2006 Danjaq, LLC, United Artists Corporation and Columbia Pictures Industries, Inc. All Rights Reserved.; **Figure 3-14a**, Courtesy Verbatim America LLC; **Figure 3-14b**, Courtesy Memorex Products, Inc.; **Figure 3-14c**, Courtesy of Sony Electronics Inc.; **Trend box**, Courtesy IronKey; **Figure 3-15a**, Courtesy of Sony Electronics Inc.; **Figure 3-15c**, © 2009 Micron Technology, Inc. All Rights Reserved. Used with permission.; **Figure 3-16adfg**, SanDisk, the SanDisk logo, SanDisk Extreme and ImageMate are trademarks of SanDisk Corporation, registered in the United States and other countries. SD and SDHC are trademarks. SanDisk is an authorized licensee of the xD trademark. Other brand names mentioned herein are for identification purposes only and may be the trademarks of their respective holder(s).; **Figure 3-16b**, Courtesy Kingston Technology Company, Inc.; **Figure 3-16c**, Courtesy of Sony Electronics Inc.; **Figure 3-16e**, © 2009 Micron Technology, Inc. All Rights Reserved. Used with permission.; **Figure 3-17a**, Courtesy Kingston Technology Company, Inc.; **Figure 3-17bc**, Courtesy CustomUSB.com; **You box a**, Courtesy Kingston Technology Company, Inc.; **You box b**, Courtesy PortableApps.com; **Figure 3-18b**, Copyright © Iomega Corporation. All Rights Reserved. Iomega, the stylized "i" logo and all product images are property of Iomega Corporation in the United States and/or other countries.; **Figure 3-20**, Photo by HID Global Corporation; **Figure 3-21**, Courtesy InPhase Technologies; **Figure 3-22**, Courtesy 3PARdata, Inc.; **Figure 3-24**, Courtesy Data Robotics; **Figure 3-25**, Courtesy Imation; **Ask the Expert 1**, Courtesy of Seagate Technology LLC; **Ask the Expert 2**, Courtesy Kingston Technology Company, Inc.; **Ask the Expert 3**, Copyright © Iomega Corporation. All Rights Reserved. Iomega, the stylized "i" logo and all product images are property of Iomega Corporation in the United States and/or other countries.

Chapter 4

Figure 4-1, ©2009 Logitech. All rights reserved. Images/materials on page 130 used with permission from Logitech.; **Figure 4-2a**, Photo courtesy of Nokia; **Figure 4-2b**, Courtesy of HTC; **Figure 4-2c**, Courtesy Verizon Wireless; **Figure 4-3a**, ©2009 Logitech. All rights reserved. Images/materials on page 131 used with permission from Logitech.; **Figure 4-3b**, Courtesy 3Dconnexion; **Figure 4-4b**, Courtesy Kensington; **Trend box**, Courtesy GestureTek; **Figure 4-5a**, Courtesy Intermec Technologies; **Figure 4-5b**, Courtesy Motion Computing; **Figure 4-5c**, Courtesy Wacom Technology Corp.; **Figure 4-6**, Courtesy of Mi-Co; **Figure 4-7a**, Courtesy Livescribe; **Figure 4-7b**, Courtesy Wacom Technology Corp.; **Figure 4-7c**, Courtesy of NCR Corporation; **Figure 4-8a**, Courtesy Dell Inc.; **Figure 4-8b**, Courtesy of Sony Electronics Inc.; **Figure 4-8c**, Courtesy Microsoft Corporation; **Figure 4-8d**, Courtesy of NCR Corporation; **Figure 4-9a**, ©2009 Logitech. All rights reserved. Images/materials on page 137 used with permission from Logitech.; **Figure 4-9b**, SanDisk is a trademark of SanDisk Corporation, registered in the United States and other countries. Other brand names mentioned herein are for identification purposes only and may be the trademarks of their respective holder(s).; **Figure 4-9c**, © Fujitsu Siemens Computers; **How box**, Courtesy 3M Touch Systems; **Figure 4-10a**, Courtesy General Dynamics Itronix; **Figure 4-10b**, Courtesy of Motorola; **Figure 4-11a**, Courtesy, Hewlett-Packard Company; **Figure 4-11b**, Courtesy WizCom Technologies; **Figure 4-11c**, Courtesy of NCR Corporation; **Figure 4-13abe**, Courtesy of Motorola; **Figure 4-14a**, Courtesy of NCR Corporation; **Figure 4-14b**, Courtesy of Motorola; **Figure 4-14c**, Photo courtesy of Nokia; **Figure 4-15**, Courtesy Intermec Technologies; **Figure 4-16a**, Courtesy Intermec Technologies; **Figure 4-16b**, Courtesy of teamaxess.com; **Figure 4-16c**, Courtesy MasterCard Worldwide; **Figure 4-16d**, © AP Images/Denis Poroy; **Figure 4-17**, Courtesy Scantron Corporation®; **Figure 4-18**, Courtesy of NV Energy; **You box**, Courtesy of Mitek Systems; **Figure 4-19**, Courtesy of NCR Corporation; **Figure 4-20a**, Courtesy of UPEK, Inc.; **Figure 4-20b**, Courtesy LaCie Ltd.; **Figure 4-21a**, Courtesy Canon USA; **Figure 4-21b**, Courtesy Kingston Technology Company, Inc.; **Figure 4-21c**, Courtesy of Sony Electronics Inc.; **Figure 4-21d**, BlackBerry®, RIM®, Research In Motion®, SureType®, SurePress™ and related trademarks, names and logos are the property of Research In Motion Limited and are registered and/or used in the U.S. and countries around the world.; **Figure 4-22a**, Courtesy of Sony Electronics Inc.; **Figure 4-22b**, Courtesy of iStockphoto; **Figure 4-23a**, Courtesy David Shopper and Nuance Communications, Inc.; **Figure 4-23b**, Courtesy Dell Inc.; **Figure 4-24**, Courtesy Ergotron Inc.; **Figure 4-25a**, Courtesy of Gateway, Inc.; **Figure 4-25b**, Courtesy Bluetooth SIG; **Figure 4-25cce**, Courtesy of Sony Electronics Inc.; **Figure 4-25d**, Courtesy of HTC; **Figure 4-25f**, Courtesy of Clear Channel Spectacolor; **Figure 4-26**, Courtesy CineMassive Displays; **Figure 4-27a**, Courtesy Acer America Corporation; **Figure 4-28**, Courtesy ZOTAC; **Figure 4-29**, Courtesy Kensington; **Figure 4-30**, Courtesy Lumus Ltd.; **Inside box a**, Courtesy of Sony Electronics Inc.; **Inside box b**, Courtesy E Ink Corporation; **Figure 4-31a**, Courtesy of Sony Electronics Inc.; **Figure 4-32**, Courtesy of Universal Display Corporation; **Figure 4-33**, Courtesy of QUALCOMM MEMS Technologies, Inc.; **Figure 4-34a**, Courtesy of ViewSonic Corporation; **Figure 4-34b**, Courtesy Microvision, Inc.; **Figure 4-34c**, Courtesy Laser Magic Productions, Inc.; **Figure 4-35**, Courtesy InfoPrint Solutions Company; **Figure 4-36**, Courtesy, Hewlett-Packard Company; **Figure 4-37**, Courtesy Epson America; **Figure 4-39b**, Courtesy, Hewlett-Packard Company; **Figure 4-40a**, Courtesy, Hewlett-Packard Company; **Figure 4-40b**, Courtesy of Intermec Technologies; **Figure 4-40c**, Courtesy ZINK Imaging; **Figure 4-40d**, Courtesy Canon USA; **Figure 4-40e**, Courtesy Stratasys Inc.; **Figure 4-41a**, Courtesy of Altec Lansing; **Figure 4-41b**, Courtesy NordicTrack; **Figure 4-41c**, Courtesy Plantronics; **Ask the Expert 1**, Courtesy TabletKiosk; **Ask the Expert 2**, Courtesy GestureTek; **Ask the**

Expert 3, SanDisk is a trademark of SanDisk Corporation, registered in the United States and other countries. Other brand names mentioned herein are for identification purposes only and may be the trademark of their respective holder(s).; **Expert Insight,** Courtesy Acer America Corporation.

Chapter 5

Figure 5-1a, Courtesy Bluetooth SIG; **Figure 5-8a,** Courtesy Kingston Technology Company, Inc.; **Figure 5-8b,** Courtesy Western Digital; **Figure 5-11a,** Courtesy Dell Inc.; **Figure 5-11b,** Courtesy of Gateway, Inc.; **Figure 5-11c,** Courtesy InfoPrint Solutions Company; **Trend box a,** Courtesy ASUS Computer International (ACI); **Trend box b,** Courtesy Mini-Box.com; **Figure 5-16,** Courtesy Novell, Inc.; **Inside box,** Courtesy, Volvo Cars of North America, LLC; **Figure 5-17a,** Courtesy of HTC; **Figure 5-17b,** Courtesy T-Mobile USA; **Figure 5-17c,** Courtesy Belkin International, Inc.; **Figure 5-17d,** BlackBerry®, RIM®, Research In Motion®, SureType®, SurePress™ and related trademarks, names and logos are the property of Research In Motion Limited and are registered and/or used in the U.S. and countries around the world.; **Figure 5-18,** Courtesy of Symantec; **How box,** WinZip is a registered trademark of WinZip International LLC. All rights reserved.; **Figure 5-21,** WinZip is a registered trademark of WinZip International LLC. All rights reserved.; **Figure 5-22b,** Courtesy of Mozy; **You box,** Google Docs screenshot (c) Google Inc. and used with permission.; **Ask the Expert 1,** Courtesy Strike Fighter Weapons School Pacific, NAS Lemoore; **Ask the Expert 2,** Courtesy The Linux Foundation; **Ask the Expert 3,** Courtesy of DriveSavers, Inc. www.drivesavers.com.

Chapter 6

Figure 6-1a, Courtesy of Symantec Corp; **Figure 6-1b,** Courtesy Holersoft; **Inside box,** Courtesy OpenOffice.org; **Figure 6-3,** Courtesy of Tucows; **Figure 6-4a,** Courtesy DataViz, Inc.; **Figure 6-4b,** Courtesy Microsoft Corporation; **Figure 6-4cd,** Courtesy Ilium Software; **Figure 6-4e,** Courtesy T-Mobile USA; **Figure 6-5,** Courtesy of Symantec Corp.; **Figure 6-6a,** Courtesy Zoho; **Figure 6-6b,** Courtesy Zillow; **Figure 6-6c,** Courtesy Soonr; **You box,** Courtesy Yahoo! Inc.; **Figure 6-7a,** Courtesy Microsoft Corporation; **Figure 6-7b,** Box shot reprinted with permission of Corel Corporation; **6-7c,** Courtesy of Apple Inc.; **Trend box,** Courtesy Microsoft Corporation; **Figure 6-26b,** Courtesy Corel Corporation; **Figure 6-26c,** Google Picassa screenshot (c) Google Inc. and used with permission. Courtesy Nick Morley; **Figure 6-27,** Courtesy of Sony Creative Software Inc. Sony Sound Forge Audio Studio 9.0 is a trademark/registered trademark of Madison Media Software, Inc. All rights reserved.; **Figure 6-28,** © Serif (Europe) Limited 2009 - www.serif.com; **Figure 6-29,** © 1995-2009 RealNetworks, Inc. All rights reserved. RealNetworks, Real.com, RealAudio, RealVideo, RealSystem, RealPlayer, RealJukebox and RealMedia are trademarks or registered trademarks of RealNetworks, Inc.; **Figure 6-30,** © Serif (Europe) Limited 2009 - www.serif.com; **Figure 6-31,** Courtesy Circus Ponies Software, Inc. All Rights Reserved.; **Figure 6-32,** Courtesy The Application Cubby LLC and Courtesy Belkin International; **Figure 6-33,** Courtesy YouSendIt; **Ask the Expert 1,** Courtesy of Tucows; **Ask the Expert 2,** Courtesy OpenOffice.org; **Ask the Expert 3,** Courtesy Bark Animation Co.; **Expert Insight,** Courtesy Microsoft, Inc.

Chapter 7

Inside box, © 2009 Fulton Innovation LLC. All Rights Reserved. Used with Permission.; **Figure 7-2a,** Courtesy of Motorola; **Figure 7-2b,** T-Mobile USA; **Figure 7-2c,** Courtesy Iridium; **Figure 7-3a,** Courtesy Magellan; **Figure 7-3b,** Courtesy Volvo Cars of North America; **Figure 7-3c,** Courtesy Garmin International; **Figure 7-4,** Courtesy LiveViewGPS Inc. www.liveviewgps.com; **Figure 7-5,** Courtesy Intel Corporation; **Figure 7-6,** Courtesy Sling Media; **Figure 7-7,** Courtesy Cisco Systems, Inc.; **Figure 7-8a,** Courtesy InTouch Health, Inc.; **Figure 7-8b,** Courtesy, University of Rochester; **Figure 7-8c,** Photo made available by St. Joseph's Healthcare Hamilton; **Figure 7-9a,** Courtesy, Hewlett-Packard Company; **Figure 7-9b,** Courtesy of Cisco Systems Inc.; **Figure 7-9c,** Courtesy InfoPrint Solutions Company; **Figure 7-10a,** Courtesy, Hewlett-Packard Company; **Figure 7-10b,** Courtesy of Linksys; **Figure 7-10c,** Courtesy InfoPrint Solutions Company; **Figure 7-11a,** Courtesy, Hewlett-Packard Company; **Figure 7-11b,** Courtesy of Cisco Systems Inc.; **Figure 7-11c,** Courtesy InfoPrint Solutions Company; **Figure 7-12,** Courtesy Intel Corporation; **Figure 7-13,** Courtesy City of Riverside; **Figure 7-16a,** Courtesy, Hewlett-Packard Company; **Figure 7-18abcf,** Courtesy of Black Box Corporation; **Figure 7-18de,** Courtesy Belkin International, Inc.; **Figure 7-21abde,** Photo(s) courtesy of Hughes Network Systems, LLC.; **Figure 7-21c,** Courtesy, Hewlett-Packard Company; **Figure 7-22a,** Courtesy of Gateway, Inc.; **Figure 7-22c,** Courtesy Acer America; **Figure 7-24,** Courtesy D-Link Systems, Inc.; **Figure 7-25a,** Courtesy Dell Inc.; **Figure 7-25b,** Courtesy Verizon Wireless; **Figure 7-25c,** Courtesy of Sony Electronics Inc.; **Figure 7-25d,** Courtesy ARCHOS; **Figure 7-25e,** Courtesy of Nintendo; **You box,** Courtesy Eye-Fi; **Figure 7-27,** Courtesy Wi-Fi Alliance. The Wi-Fi CERTIFIED logo is a registered trademark of the Wi-Fi Alliance.; **Figure 7-29,** Courtesy Sprint Nextel; **Figure 7-30,** Courtesy Bluetooth SIG; **Figure 7-32af,** Courtesy D-Link Systems, Inc.; **Figure 7-32bcd,** Courtesy Belkin International, Inc.; **Figure 7-32e,** Courtesy Cricket Wireless; **Figure 7-33,** Courtesy D-Link Systems, Inc.; **Figure 7-34a,** Courtesy, Hewlett-Packard Company; **Figure 7-34b,** Courtesy D-Link Systems, Inc.; **Figure 7-34c,** Courtesy of Cisco Systems Inc.; **Figure 7-34d,** Courtesy of Nintendo; **Figure 7-34e,** Courtesy of Gateway, Inc.;

Figure 7-34f, Courtesy Data Comm for Business Inc.; **Figure 7-34g,** Courtesy Dell Inc.; **Figure 7-34h,** Photo courtesy of Nokia; **Figure 7-34i,** Courtesy of Apple Inc.; **Trend box,** Courtesy Verizon Wireless; **Ask the Expert 1,** Courtesy of Google Inc.; **Ask the Expert 2,** Courtesy of Symantec; **Ask the Expert 3,** Courtesy McDonald's Corporation.

Chapter 8

Figure 8-1a, Courtesy of Gateway, Inc.; **Figure 8-1b,** The Survivor: Tocantins Logo is a registered trademark of Survivor Productions, LLC. CSB.com website contents © CBS Broadcasting Inc. Used by permission. CBS and the CBS Eye are registered trademarks of CBS Broadcasting Inc.; **Figure 8-2a,** Use of the AT&T logo is granted under permission by AT&T Intellectual Property.; **Figure 8-2b,** Courtesy of Verizon Communications; **Figure 8-2c,** Courtesy Comcast; **Figure 8-2d,** Photo(s) courtesy of Hughes Network Systems, LLC; **Figure 8-2e,** Courtesy EarthLink, Inc.; **Figure 8-2f,** Courtesy Clearwire; **Figure 8-4,** Courtesy CinemaNow; **Inside box,** Courtesy U.S. Air Force; **Figure 8-5a,** Courtesy of Gateway, Inc.; **Figure 8-5b,** Courtesy of HTC; **Figure 8-5c,** Courtesy of Yahoo!; **Figure 8-8,** Courtesy Tranzeo Wireless USA; **Figure 8-9a,** Courtesy of iStockphoto © Sean Locke; **Figure 8-9b,** Courtesy Fujitsu America; **Figure 8-9c,** Courtesy Abilene Christian University; **Figure 8-11ab,** Google screenshot (c) Google Inc. and used with permission.; **Figure 8-13b,** Google screenshot (c) Google Inc. and used with permission.; **Figure 8-17,** Courtesy Microsoft Corporation; **Trend box,** Courtesy of Helio By Virgin Mobile USA; **Figure 8-18a,** Courtesy of Yahoo!; **Figure 8-18b,** Courtesy Microsoft Corporation; **Figure 8-19b,** Courtesy Vonage; **Figure 8-19c,** Courtesy D-Link Systems, Inc.; **Figure 8-20,** Courtesy of Intel Corporation; **Figure 8-21a,** Courtesy Facebook, Inc.; **Figure 8-21b,** Courtesy LinkedIn; **You box,** Courtesy Yoono; **Figure 8-24a,** Courtesy MobiTV; **Figure 8-24b,** Courtesy CastTV; **Figure 8-24c,** Courtesy Roku, Inc.; **Figure 8-25b,** MapQuest and the MapQuest logo are registered trademarks of MapQuest, Inc. Map content (c) 2009 by MapQuest, Inc. and its respective copyright holders. Used with permission.; **Figure 8-26,** iGoogle screenshot (c) Google Inc. and used with permission.; **How box a,** "Audacity" is a trademark of Dominic Mazzoni; **Figure 8-27,** Courtesy FactCheck.org; **Figure 8-29,** Courtesy Software Secure, Inc.; **Figure 8-30,** Courtesy of Zach Sunderland www.zacsunderland.com; **Ask the Expert 1,** Courtesy McDonald's Corporation; **Ask the Expert 2,** Courtesy Throw the Fight www.myspace.com/throwthefight, www. throwthefight.com.; **Ask the Expert 3,** Courtesy of IDPI.

Chapter 9

Figure 9-2, Courtesy JiWire, Inc.; **Figure 9-6a,** Courtesy ActivIdentity; **Figure 9-6b,** Joseph Mehling, Dartmouth College; **Figure 9-7a,** Courtesy Fujitsu America; **Figure 9-7b,** Courtesy Ingersoll Rand Security Technologies; **Figure 9-7c,** Courtesy L-1 Identity Solutions; **Figure 9-7d,** DoD photo by Staff Sgt. Jonathan C. Knauth, U.S. Marine Corps.; **How box,** Courtesy D-Link Systems, Inc.; **Figure 9-10,** Courtesy of Symantec; **Trend box,** Courtesy WiTopia and Viscosity; **Figure 9-13,** Courtesy Centennial Software Limited; **Figure 9-14ad,** Courtesy of Gateway, Inc.; **Figure 9-14bcf,** Courtesy Acer America Corporation; **Figure 9-14e,** Courtesy Kingston Technology Company, Inc.; **Figure 9-15,** Courtesy BleepingComputer.com; **Figure 9-16ac,** Courtesy, Hewlett-Packard Company; **Figure 9-16b,** Courtesy Dell Inc.; **Figure 9-17a,** Courtesy of Symantec; **Figure 9-17b,** Courtesy Lavasoft AB; **Inside box,** Google screenshot (c) Google Inc. and used with permission.; **You box,** Courtesy Mint. com; **Ask the Expert 1,** Courtesy ACM; **Ask the Expert 2,** Courtesy of Symantec; **Ask the Expert 3,** Courtesy of Symantec; **Expert Insight,** Courtesy of Symantec.

Chapter 10

Figure 10-1c, Courtesy CastTV; **Figure 10-d,** Second Life is a trademark of Linden Research, Inc.; **Figure 10-2a,** Google screenshot (c) Google Inc. and used with permission.; **Inside box,** Image and the Crowne Plaza® Hotels and Resorts name appear courtesy of InterContinental Hotels Group.; **Figure 10-4b,** Courtesy of iStockphoto. com; **Figure 10-7,** Courtesy of Jim McNew and Photoholic.com; **Figure 10-9a,** Courtesy of PBS and Thirteen/WNET New York © 2009; **Figure 10-9b,** ARTHUR Web site (c) 2009 WGBH; underlying ARTHUR TM/(c) Marc Brown.; **You box,** Courtesy Qik, Inc.; **10-10,** Adobe product screen shot(s) reprinted with permission from Adobe Systems Incorporated.; **Figure 10-11b,** Brought to you by SCORE "Counselors to America's Small Business" at www.score.org.; **Figure 10-11c,** ARTHUR Web site (c) 2009 WGBH; underlying ARTHUR TM/(c) Marc Brown.; **Figure 10-13a,** Google screenshot © Google Inc. and used with permission.; **Figure 10-14ab,** Courtesy MySpace; **Figure 10-14c,** Courtesy of Gateway, Inc.; **Figure 10-15,** Courtesy of Stanford University; **Figure 10-16a,** Courtesy Theorem Creations; **Figure 10-16b,** Adobe product screen shot(s) reprinted with permission from Adobe Systems Incorporated.; **Trend box,** Google screenshot (c) Google Inc. and used with permission.; **Ask the Expert 1,** Courtesy Throw the Fight www.myspace.com/throwthefight, www. throwthefight.com; **Ask the Expert 2,** Courtesy WGBH Interactive; **Ask the Expert 3,** Courtesy ACM.

Chapter 11

You box, Photo courtesy of Nokia; **Figure 11-3,** Courtesy Pricegrabber.com Inc.; **How box,** Courtesy Zazzle.com; **Figure 11-4a,** © 2009 Dell Inc. All Rights Reserved.; **Figure 11-4b,** Courtesy InfoPrint Solutions Company; **Figure 11-4c,** Courtesy CRAIGSLIST; **Figure 11-6,** These materials have been reproduced with the permission

* (asterisk), 316
@ (at sign), 31, 32
= (equal sign), 231
/ (forward slash), 32
. (period), 31, 32, 37
_ (underscore), 31
802.11. *See* Wi-Fi (802.11)
802.3. *See* Ethernet (802.3)

A

<A> tag, 415
AAC format, 405
abacus, 12
absolute cell referencing, 232–233
academic cheating, 646–647
access
    control systems, 351
    to technology, 661–666
Access (Microsoft), 235, 551, 557, 569,
    570, 572, 573
accessibility issues, 412, 413. *See also*
    assistive technology; Braille
accounting software, 245
accounting system A type of transaction
    system that deals with the financial
    transactions and financial record-
    keeping for an organization. **473**
Acrobat (Adobe), 359
acronyms, 38
ActiveX (Microsoft), 420–421
ACU (Abilene Christian University), 9
ad retargeting services, 454
ADA (Americans with Disabilities Act),
    413, 664
adaptive software development, 510–511
Address bar, 33
AdMob (company), 573
Adobe Acrobat, 359
Adobe After Effects, 414
Adobe Director, 414
Adobe Dreamweaver, 408, 421, 422
Adobe Flash A popular program for
    creating Web animations and
    interactive Web-based multimedia
    applications. 405, 414, 418
    authoring tools and, 421
    described, **404**
    RIAs and, 531

Adobe Illustrator, 241
Adobe Integrated Runtime (AIR), 531
Adobe Photoshop, 241
adware, 338, 339
Aero interface, 190, 191
After Effects (Adobe), 414
Agile Alliance, 511
Agile Manifesto, 511
AI See artificial intelligence (AI) system
AIFF format, 405
AIR (Adobe Integrated Runtime), 531
AJAX A set of Web standards designed
    to better handle Web page
    interactivity by downloading only
    new data from the Web server,
    instead of re-downloading the entire
    Web page. **419**, 420–421, 531
algorithms, 512, 518
**ALM (application lifecycle
    management)** A broad term to
    describe complete systems that can
    be used to create and manage an
    application throughout its entire
    life cycle from design through
    retirement. **528**, 529
alpha tests, 527
alternative power sources, 667–668
alternative text A text description for a
    Web page image; is displayed when
    the image is pointed to and can be
    read by assistive technology. **413**
ALU (arithmetic/logic unit) The part of
    a CPU core that performs logical
    operations and integer arithmetic.
    73, 80
AMA (American Management
    System), 621
Amazon.com, 19, 116, 156, 420,
    637–638, 566, 577–578
American National Standards Institute.
    See ANSI (American National
    Standards Institute)
American Standard Code for Information
    Interchange. *See* ASCII (American
    Standard Code for Information
    Interchange)
analog signal A type of signal where the
    data is represented by continuous
    waves. **271**

AND operators, 315
Android A Linux-based operating system
    designed for mobile phones and
    developed by a group of companies
    that includes Google. **196**, 197,
    218, 520
Android Market, 218
Angelini, Chris, 61
animated GIF A group of GIF images
    saved as an animated GIF file that
    is inserted in a Web page; the
    individual images are displayed
    one after another to simulate
    movement. **404**
animation The process by which a series
    of graphical images are displayed
    one after the other to simulate
    movement. 239, **404**
anonymity factor, 39
ANSI (American National Standards
    Institute), 278
antenna A device used for receiving or
    sending radio signals; often used
    to increase the range of a network.
    290, 291
anticounterfeiting systems, 636
Anticybersquatting Consumer Protection
    Act, 450, 637, 671
antispyware programs, 204, 369, 623.
    See also spyware
antitheft tools, 595–597
antivirus software Software used to
    detect and eliminate computer
    viruses and other types of malware.
    16, 37, 78, 204, 366, **369**, 600.
    See also viruses
AOP (aspect-oriented programming)
    An approach to program design
    in which different functions are
    clearly separated so program
    components can be developed and
    modified individually from one
    another, and the components can
    be easily reused with separate,
    non-related objects. **510**
APD (Avalanche Photodetector) silicon
    light sensor, 84–85
API (application programming interface),
    420, 530–531

Apple iPhone OS The operating system designed for Apple mobile phones and mobile devices. 133, 135, 194, 217
described, **197**
Digital Copy and, 644
intellectual property and, 638
program development and, 520, 531, 539
SDK, 531
security and, 596
Apple iPod, 21, 158–159, 644. *See also* digital media players
Apple Keynote, 238
Apple Macintosh, 14, 21–22, 186, 201. *See also* Mac OS; Mac OS X
Apple Numbers, 230
application assistants, 479
application generators, 529
Application Security (company), 561
application service provider. *See* ASP (application service provider)
application software Programs that enable users to perform specific tasks on a computer, such as writing a letter or playing a game. *See also specific software*
described, **17**
overview, 177, 212–253
arguments, 231
arithmetic/logic unit. *See* ALU (arithmetic/logic unit)
Army (United States), 13
ARPANET The predecessor of the Internet, named after the Advanced Research Projects Agency (ARPA), which sponsored its development. 290, **300**
artificial intelligence (AI) system A system in which a computer performs actions that are characteristic of human intelligence. 14, **479**
ASCII (American Standard Code for Information Interchange) A fixed-length, binary coding system used to represent text-based data for computer processing on many types of computers. 53, **54**, R-15
ASD (agile software development), 510–511
aspect-oriented programming. *See* AOP (aspect-oriented programming)
aspect ratio, 152
ASP (application service provider) A company that manages and distributes software-based services over the Internet. 218, **303**
ASPs (Active Server Pages), 579
assemblers, 524–525

assembly language A low-level programming language that uses names and other symbols to replace some of the 0s and 1s in machine language. 524–525, 532, **533**
asset tags, 596
assistive technology Hardware and software specifically designed for use by individuals with physical disabilities. technology, 413, **664**, 665–666
asterisk (*), 316
at sign (@), 31, 32
AT&T (American Telephone & Telegraph), 193, 304, 306, 310, 534
ATMs (automatic teller machines), 9, 196, 352, 354, 372, 530
attribute A characteristic of an entity. Java and, 540
described, **555**
OOP and, 509
audio Sound, such as music, spoken voice, and/or sound effects. *See also* music
capture software, 241–242
coding systems for, 55
described, **404**
editing software, 241–242
file formats, 404–405
input, 148–150
output, 165–166
overview, 404–405
ports, 70, 71
samples, 55
augmented VR (augmented virtual reality), 397
authentication, 8, 10, 352–353, 370
described, **351**
e-commerce and, 444, 455
automatic bidding systems, 439
avatars, 398, 639
AVI format, 405

B

<B> tag, 415
B2B (business-to-business) model An e-commerce model in which a business provides goods or services to other businesses. 426, **437**, 441, 446–447
B2C (business-to-consumer) model An e-commerce model in which a business provides goods or services to consumers. 426, **437**, 441
B2G (business-to-government) model An e-commerce model in which a business provides

goods and services to government organizations. 426, **437–438**
back end
software, 536
use of the term, 564
backbone, 27, 301
backup A duplicate copy of data or other computer content in case the original version is destroyed.
described, **203**
importance of, 600
midrange servers and, 25
overview, 203, 601–602
utility programs, 203–204
Baker, Paul, 12
bandwidth The amount of data that can be transferred in a given period of time; also referred to as throughput.
described, **62**
multimedia and, 409
overview, 270–271
banner ad exchanges, 453
banner ads, 453, 454
banner images, 409
barcode A machine-readable code that represents data as a set of bars. **140**
barcode printer An output device that prints barcoded documents. 141
barcode reader An input device that reads barcodes. 11, 72, 140, **141**, 142
Bardens, Ben, 241
Bark Animation Company, 241
Barnard, David, 520
Barquin, Ramon C., 638
base numbers, 53
BASIC An easy-to-learn, high-level programming language that was developed to be used by beginning programmers. 17, 534, 537–538
Baustert, Ryan, 321, 397
BD (Blu-ray Disc) A high-capacity (typically 25 MB or 50 MB) that is often used to deliver high-definition movies, as well as to store user data. **106**
BD-R disc A recordable Blu-ray Disc. **109**
BD-RE disc A rewritable Blu-ray Disc. **109**
BD-ROM disc A Blu-ray Disc that can be read from, but not written to, by the user. **108**
behavioral ads, 454
benchmark test A test used to measure computer system performance under typical usage conditions prior to purchase. 60, 61, **495**
Berners-Lee, Tim, 300
beta tests, 527
Beta versions, 527

BI (business intelligence) The process of gathering, storing, accessing, and analyzing data about a company in order to make better business decisions. **469**

binary numbering system The numbering system that represents all numbers using just two symbols (0 and 1). **52**, 53, R-11

biometric access system An access control system that uses one unique physical characteristic of an individual (such as a fingerprint, face, or voice) to authenticate that individual. 114, 129, 353, **354**, 355

biometric reader A device used to input biometric data, such as an individual's fingerprint or voice. **146**

BIOS (basic input/output system), 65

bit The smallest unit of data a digital computer can recognize; represented by a 0 or a 1. 51, **52**

bit depth, 153

bit rates, **55**

bitmap images, 54–55, 401. *See also* graphics; images

BitTorrent, 306

BlackBerry OS The operating system designed for BlackBerry devices. 22, **197**, 218

blade servers, 25

blade workstations, 25

bloatware, 179

blog A Web page that contains short, frequently updated entries in chronological order, typically by just one individual. 302, 334
described, **333**
e-commerce and, 450

Bluetooth A networking standard for very short-range wireless connections; the devices are automatically connected once they get within the allowable range. 57, 71, 275

Blu-Ray Disc (BD). *See* BD (Blu-Ray Disc)
described, **285**
health issues and, 653
I/O and, 154
overview, 284–287
security and, 351, 597

<BODY> tag, 415

BoF (broadband over fiber) Internet access Very fast, direct Internet access via fiber-optic networks; also referred to as fiber-to-the-premises (FTTP) Internet access. **310**

Bookmarks menu, 34

Boolean operators, 315

Boolean values, 509

boot To start up a computer. **16**, 179

bot A computer that is controlled by a hacker or other computer criminal. **364**

botnet A group of bots that are controlled by one individual. **364**

BPDs (Business Process Diagrams), 492

BPL (Broadband over Powerline) standard, 280–281, 308

BPMN (Business Process Modeling Notation), 490–491

 tag, 415

Braille, 36, 413, 664, 665, 666

brick-and-mortar store A conventional store with a physical presence. **431**, 434

broadband Internet, 79, 289, 306, 307, 327

Broadband Internet Fairness Act, 306

broadband over fiber. *See* BoF (broadband over fiber) Internet access

broadband routers, 289

broadband-enabled TVs, 307, 327

broadcasting, 272–273

brokerage site A type of Web site that brings buyers and sellers together to facilitate transactions between them; the site earns revenue in the form of commissions on sales made via the site. **438**

Brown, Michelle, 373

browser A program used to view Web pages. 18, 308
ActiveX and, 420–421
cookies and, 337–338
described, **28**
design principles and, 408–409
direct connections and, 308
filtering options, 335–336
history of, 6, 300–301
Java and, 540
privacy issues and, 336–337, 612–613
searches with, 312–317
sniffing, 408–409
system software and, 205
updating, 600
using, 33–34, 312–317

BSA (Business Software Alliance), 603

buffer An area in RAM or on the hard drive designated to hold input and output on their way in and out of the system. **184**, 185

bug, use of the term, 523

Bureau of Labor Statistics (United States), 484

burnout A state of fatigue or frustration usually brought on by overwork. **660**

bus An electronic path on the motherboard or within the CPU or other computer component along which data is transferred.
architecture, 69
described, **68**
frontside (FSB), 68, **69**
overview, 68–69
speed, 60, 62
width, 60, 62

bus interface unit The part of a CPU core that allows it to communicate with other CPU components. **73**

bus network A network consisting of a central cable to which all network devices are attached. **267**

business-to-business. *See* B2B (business-to-business (B2B) model)

business-to-consumer. *See* B2C (business-to-consumer (B2C) model)

business-to-government. *See* B2G (business-to-government (B2G) model)

business ethics Standards of moral conduct that guide a business's policies, decisions, and actions. 638, **640**, 648

business intelligence. *See* BI (business intelligence)

byte A group of 8 bits. **52**

bytecode, 540

C

C A high-level structured programming language that has the execution efficiency of an assembly language. 534, **538**, 539

C++ A newer, object-oriented version of the C programming language. 17, 521, 534
C# and, relationship of, 539
databases and, 549, 574, 579
described, **538**
Java and, 541

C# The newest, object-oriented version of the C programming language. 520, 521, 534
C and, relationship of, 539
described, **539**

C2C (consumer-to-consumer) model An e-commerce model in which a consumer provides goods or services to other consumers. 426, **437**, 439

cable anchors, 593

cable Internet access Fast, direct Internet access via cable TV lines. 78, 273–278, **309**

cable locks, 593

cables, types of, 273–278

cache memory A group of fast memory circuitry located on or near the CPU to help speed up processing. 60, **61**, 62

CAD (computer-aided design) A general term applied to the use of computer technology to automate design functions. 244–245, **477**, 478

call centers, 487

CAM (computer-aided manufacturing) A general term applied to the use of computer technology to automate manufacturing functions. **477**, 478

campus emergency notification systems, 32

CAN-SPAM Act, 377, 383, 611, 625

Cantor Fitzgerald (company), 602

carbon nanotubes Tiny, hollow tubes made of carbon atoms. 64, 80, **82**, 83

CareerBuilder.com, 486

carpal tunnel syndrome. *See* CTS (carpal tunnel syndrome)

Carterfone Decision, 304

Cartfly, 450

Cascading Style Sheet. *See* CSS (Cascading Style Sheet)

case control structure, 517

CD (compact disc) A low capacity (typically 650 MB) optical disc that is often used to deliver music and software, as well as to store user data. 15, 55, 93–94, **106**, 107–110, 203–204

burning, 406

intellectual property rights and, 641–642

CD-R disc A recordable CD. **108**, 109

CD-ROM disc A CD that can be read from, but not written to, by the user. **108**

CD-RW disc A rewritable CD. **109**

CDP (continuous data protection), 601

cell(s) The location at the intersection of a row and column on a worksheet into which data can be typed.

active, 230, 231

addresses, 230

described, **230**

entering data in, 230–231

formatting, 231

height/width, 231

pointers, 230

referencing, 232–233

cellular phone A mobile phone that communicates via a cellular network; also called a cell phone. *See also* mobile phone

described, **259**

overview, 259–260

standards, 276–277, 283–284

cellular radio A form of broadcast radio designed for use with cellular telephones that broadcasts using antennas located inside honeycomb-shaped cells. **276–277**

central processing unit. *See* CPU (central processing unit)

censorship, 334–339

Census (United States), 12, 13

<CENTER> tag, 415

centralized database system A database system in which all of the data used by the system is located on a single computer. **565**, 566

Certificate Authorities, 359, 379–381

Certificates, digital A group of electronic data that can be used to verify the identity of a person or organization; includes a key pair that can be used for encryption and digital signatures. **379**, 380

CGI (common gateway interface), 578, 579

character (string) values, 509

charts, 233

chatterbots, 479

cheating, academic, 646–647

Check 21 Law, 145

checkout pages, 441, 447

chess matches, 478–479

Chevron, 622

Christopher, John, 202, 601

Chrome, 188, 205, 312, 338, 613

Chuang, Tanya, 147

Chumby device, 24, 25

CIPA (Children's Internet Protection Act), 335

circuit boards, 25. *See also* motherboards

circuit switching, 272–273

citations, 317

Claflin, Bruce, 648

clamshell design, 23

class(es)

diagrams, 492, 515

libraries, 510

overview, 509

sub-, 509

UML and, 515

cleaning computers, 78

cleanup utilities, 202

C-level attacks, 592

click fraud, 453, 455

clickstream data, 469

client(s). *See also* client-server database system

-server networks, 267

thin, **24**

client-server database system A database system where the database is located on a server and accessed by client devices. **564**, 565

clip art, 227, 229, 400–401

cloud databases, 566

cloud storage. *See* online storage

cloudware. *See* Web-based software

cluster One or more sectors; the smallest addressable area of a disk. **99**

CMS (content management system) A document management system that includes images, multimedia files, and other content in addition to conventional documents. **472**

coaxial cable A networking cable consisting of a center wire inside a grounded, cylindrical shield, capable of sending data at high speeds. **273–274**

COBOL A high-level programming language developed for transaction processing applications. 13, 17, 520, 523, 534, 535, 549

described, **536**

overview, 536–537

COBOL.NET, 536

code. *See also* code of conduct; code of ethics; coding; source code

executable, translating coded programs into, 523–525

generators, 529

machine dependent, 532

reusable, 522

spaghetti, 508

code of conduct A policy, often for a school or business, that specifies allowable use of resources, such as computers and other equipment. **645**

code of ethics A policy, often for an organization or industry, that specifies overall moral guidelines adopted by that organization or industry. **645**. *See also* ethics

CodeArmor Intelligence, 604–605

coding The process of writing the programming language statements to create a computer program. 51, 53–56. *See also* code

color-, 55

described, **520**
overview, 521
program, **520**
standards, 520, 521–522
collaborative computing, 263
collaboration software, 245
collision, 564
color
16-bit, 55
24-bit, 55
coding systems and, 55
printers, 160
column In a database, a field. 549, 563
described, **234**
-level locking, 559
column In a spreadsheet program, a vertical group of cells on a worksheet. **230**
Comcast, 306
command line interface A user interface that requires the user to communicate instructions to the computer via typed commands. **185**, 188
comments, 522, 541
COBOL and, 536
Java, 540
Pascal and, 537
commercial software Copyrighted software that is developed, usually by a commercial company, for sale to others. **214**, 215–216
commodity brokers, 440
commodity exchanges, 440
communication system A system that allows employees to communicate with each other, as well as with business partners and customers. **472**
communications The transmission of data from one device to another. **11**, 16
Communications Decency Act, 335, 382, 671
comparison shopping, 433, 434
compiler A language translator that converts an entire program into machine language before executing it.
C++ and, 538
described, **524**
errors, 525
just-in-time, 540
compression
of audio, 55
of images, 55, 148, 402, 403
programs, **203**
computer A programmable, electronic device that accepts data input, performs processing operations

on that data, and outputs and stores the results.
described, **10**
end users, overview, 17–19
equipment locks, 593–594
fifth-generation, 14
first-generation, 12–13
to fit every need, 19–27
fourth-generation, 13–14
guide to buying, R-8
history of, 12–14, R-2
operations personnel, 18
overview, 4–47
professionals, overview, 17–18
reasons to learn about, 5–6
second-generation, 13
setting up, for Internet access, 311–312
society and, relationship between, 36–39
tasks performed by, 10–19
third-generation, 13
tracking software, 595–597
upgrades, 6
in your life, 5–10
computer-aided design. *See* CAD (computer-aided design)
computer-aided manufacturing. *See* CAM (computer-aided manufacturing)
computer crime Any illegal act involving a computer. **347**, 348
computer ethics Standards of moral conduct as they relate to computer use. **638**, 639–652
computer hoax An inaccurate statement or story spread through the use of computers. **647**
computer literacy The knowledge and understanding of basic computer fundamentals. **6**
computer sabotage An act of malicious destruction to a computer or computer resource. **364**, 365–370
computer monitoring software Software that can be used to record an individual's computer usage, such as capturing images of the screen, recording the actual keystrokes used, or creating a summary of Web sites and programs accessed. **617**, 618–619
computer software engineers, 484, 485
computer worm A malicious program designed to spread rapidly to a large number of computers by sending copies of itself to other computers. **366**, 367
concentrators, 291

Coney, Lillie, 606
configuration management, 529
connectors, 70–72
constant value A numerical entry in a worksheet cell. **231**
Constitution (United States), 335, 624
consumer brokerage sites, 440
consumer kiosks, 9, 135, 154
consumer-to-consumer. *See* C2C (consumer-to-consumer (C2C) model)
content management system. *See* CMS (content management system)
contests, programming, 521
Control Panel, 77, 153, 600
control structure A pattern for controlling the flow of logic in a computer program, module, or method. 514, **515**, 516–517
control unit The part of a CPU core that coordinates its operations. **73**
conventional dial-up Internet access Dial-up Internet access via standard telephone lines. 307, 308, **309**
convertible tablets, 23
cookie A small file stored on a user's hard drive by a Web server; commonly used to identify personal preferences and settings for that user. 338, 454, 606
described, **337**
opt-out, 615
cooling systems, 85
COPA (Child Online Protection Act), 624, 625
copyright The legal right to sell, publish, or distribute an original artistic or literary work; it is held by the creator of a work as soon as it exists in physical form. 215, 217, 243, 268
described, **634–635**
ethics and, 640–652
Copyright Act, 634
Corel Painter, 241
Corel Presentations, 238
Corel Quattro Pro, 230
Corel WordPerfect, 221, 227, 551
CorelDRAW, 241
cost
-benefit analysis, 493
per click (CPC), 453
counterfeiting, digital The use of computers or other types of digital equipment to make illegal

copies of currency, checks, collectibles, and other items. **603**, 604–605
coupon codes, 444, 445
CPC (cost per click), 453
CPO (chief privacy officer), 615–616
CPU (central processing unit) The chip located on the motherboard of a computer that performs the processing for a computer. Also called the processor.
   application software and, 215
   architecture, 79
   buses and, 68–69
   described, **58**
   dual-core, **58**
   energy conservation and, 667
   how they work, 72–76
   improved materials for, 79–80
   motherboard and, 56–57
   multi-core, **58**, 59
   multitasking and, 182
   optical computers and, 84
   overview, 14–15
   quad-core, **58**, 59
   registers and, 65
   single-core, 59
   storage and, 103
   supercomputers and, 27
   system clock, 60–61, **75**, 76
   system software and, 182, 183, 184, 186–187
   triple-core, 59
Craigslist, 437, 649
crashes, 33
Cray supercomputers, 198
credit card(s)
   numbers, virtual, 435, 442
   prepaid, 443
   processing, 442–443
CRM (customer relationship management), 447. *See also* eCRM (electronic customer relationship management)
crossbar latch, 84
crowdsourcing, 487
crowdSPRING, 487
CRT monitor A type of display device that projects images onto a display screen using a technology similar to the one used with conventional TVs. **151**, 152, 157
CSMA (Carrier Sense Multiple Access/ Collision Detection), 280
CSS (Cascading Style Sheet) A tool used to specify and apply the styles used for a Web site. **418**, 421

CTS (carpal tunnel syndrome) A painful and crippling condition affecting the hands and wrist that can be caused by computer use. **652**
cultural differences, 651–652
customer(s). *See also* users
   advantages of e-commerce for, 433–434
   information, ethical use of, 645–646
   profiling, 469
   relationship management (CRM), 447
CVS (computer vision syndrome), 652–653
cyberbullying Children or teenagers bullying other children or teenagers via the Internet. **381**, 382–383
Cyberchase Web site, 418–419
cybersquatting The act of registering a domain name with the intent to profit from the goodwill of a trademark belonging to someone else. 450, 451, **636**, 637
cyberstalking Repeated threats or harassing behavior between adults carried out via e-mail or another Internet communications method. **381**, 382–383
cyberterrorism, 349. *See also* terrorism
cylinder The collection of tracks located in the same location on a set of hard disk surfaces. **99**

D

DARPA (Defense Advanced Research Projects Agency), 482
data
   alteration, 368
   analysis, 490
   centers, 26
   collection, 490
   concepts/characteristics, 555–557
   described, **11**
   destruction services, 616, 617
   entering/editing, 569–570
   hierarchy, 555
   information versus, 11–12
   -leakage prevention, 363
   migration, 496
   organization, 562–564
   recovery, 101
   test, 496
   theft, 371–372
data definition The process of describing the properties of data that is to be included in a database table. **556**, 557
data dictionary The repository of all data definitions in a database. **557–558**

data integrity The accuracy of data. **558**, 559
data mart A collection of data related to a particular subject or department in a company. **469**
data mining The process of using intelligent software to analyze data warehouses for patterns and relationships. **469**
data privacy Protecting the privacy of the data located in a database. **561**
data projector A display device that projects all computer output to a wall or projection screen. 15, **158**, 159
data security Protecting the data located in a database against destruction and misuse. **560**, 561
data validation The process of ensuring that data entered into a database is valid (matches the data definition). **558–559**
data warehouse A comprehensive collection of data about a company and its customers. **469**, 576
database A collection of related data that is stored in a manner enabling information to be retrieved as needed; in a relational database, a collection of related tables. 219, 221, 235–237. *See also* DBMS (database management system)
   activity monitoring programs, 560–561
   administrators (DBAs), 552, 560
   classifications, 564–566
   described, **549**
   designers, 552
   developers, 552
   encryption software, 561
   engines, **549**
   evolution of, 553
   hierarchical, 566–567
   locking, 559
   management system, 549
   models, 566–576
   network, 566–567
   overview, 235–237, 545–587
   privacy and, 607–610
   program development and, 541
   programmers, 552
   the Web and, 576–578
database software Application software that allows the creation and manipulation of an electronic database. **234**
Datasheet view, 235, 236, 569, 570
Davis, Mark, 55
DBAs (database administrators), 552, 560

DBMS (database management system) A type of software program used to create, maintain, and access databases. *See also* databases
advantages/disadvantages of, 553–555
data dictionaries and, 558
described, **549**
distributed, 566
individuals involved with, 551
middleware and, 578
PCs and, 551
queries and, 571
security and, 561
DDLs (data definition languages), 557
DDoS (distributed denial of service attack), 368
DDR (double-data rate), 63
De Heer, Walter, 80
dead spots, 289
Dead on Demand technology, 596
debit card(s)
numbers, virtual, 444
processing, 442–443
debugging The process of ensuring a program is free of errors. 526, 539
described, **523**
preliminary, 525–526
DEC (Digital Equipment Corporation), 75
decimal numbering system The numbering system that represents all numbers using ten symbols. **52,** 53, R-11
decision making
ethics and, 649–650
support systems, 473–475
decision support system. *See* DSS (decision support system)
decision tables, 490, 491
decision trees, 490
declaration statements, 417
decode unit The part of a CPU core that translates instructions into a form that can be processed by the ALU and FPU. **73**
Defense Department (United States), 260, 300
Dell Computer, 678–679
demo (trial) versions, 215
demographics, 577
denial of service attack. *See* DoS (denial of service attack)
DeQuervain's tendonitis A condition in which the tendons on the thumb side of the wrist are swollen and irritated. **652**
Design view, 569, 572, 573
desk checks, 519

desktop computer A personal computer designed to fit on or next to a desk.
cases, 21
cleaning, 78
CPUs and, 58, 60
described, **21**
I/O and, 133, 135
overview, 21–22
software, mobile software versus, 217
desktop publishing software, 243–244
device driver A program that enables an operating system to communicate with a specific hardware device; often referred to simply as a driver. **180**
device software development tools, 530
DFDs (data flow diagrams), 490, 491, 492
Dhariwal, Kewal, 552
diagnostic programs, 202
dial-up connection A type of Internet connection in which the computer or other device must dial up and connect to a service provider's computer via telephone lines before being connected to the Internet. 29, 78
conventional, 307, 308, **309**
described, 308
dialog boxes, 17
Digg Web site, 566
digital billboards, 150, 151
digital camera An input device that takes pictures and records them as digital images. 138–139, **146,** 147–148
digital cash, 441
digital certificates A group of electronic data that can be used to verify the identity of a person or organization; includes a key pair that can be used for encryption and digital signatures. **379,** 380
Digital Copy, 644
digital coupons, 444, 445
digital counterfeiting The use of computers or other types of digital equipment to make illegal copies of currency, checks, collectibles, and other items. **603,** 604–605
digital dashboards, 469, 470
digital divide The gap between those who have access to technology and those who do not. **661,** 662–664
digital gift certificates, 444
digital manipulation The alteration of digital content, usually text or photographs. **648,** 649
digital media players, 137, 196, 243, 597. *See also* iPod (Apple)

digital photo frames, 150, 151
digital rights management. *See* DRM (digital rights management) software
digital signage, 150, 151
digital signal A type of signal where the data is represented by 0s and 1s. **271**
digital signature A unique digital code that can be attached to a file or an e-mail message to verify the identity of the sender and guarantee the file or message has not been changed since it was signed. **380**
Digital Subscriber Line. *See* DSL (Digital Subscriber Line)
digital video cameras, 148. *See also* digital camera
digital wallet A program or online service that holds a buyer's information (such as electronic payment, billing, and shipping information) that can be used to speed up online purchase transactions. **444–445**
digital wallet programs, 445
digital watermark A subtle alteration of digital content that is not noticeable when the work is viewed or played, but that identifies the copyright holder. **634,** 635
digital writing systems, 134
dimension, use of the term, 576
DIMMs (dual-inline memory modules), 63
direct connection A type of Internet connection in which the computer or other device is connected to the Internet continually. 29, **308**
direct organization A method of arranging data on a storage medium that uses hashing to specify the exact storage location. **563,** 564
Director (Adobe), 414
directories. *See* folders
directory search A type of Internet search in which categories are selected to locate information on the Internet. 312, **313**
disabilities. *See* accessibility issues
disaster recovery plan A written plan that describes the steps a company will take following the occurrence of a disaster. 561, **601–602**
disk
defragmentation, 202
management programs, 202
mirroring, 119–120
striping, 119–120
use of the term, 96
-wiping software, 616

disk access time The time it takes to locate and read data from (or position and write data to) a storage medium. **103**, 104

disk cache Memory used in conjunction with a magnetic hard drive to improve system performance. **103**, 104

Disk Operating System. *See* DOS (Disk Operating System)

display device An output device that contains a viewing screen.
2D versus 3D, 154
aspect ratio, 152
color versus monochrome, 151
described, **150**
flat-panel, 155
overview, 150–159
size of, 152
wired versus wireless, 154

display screen A display device built into a notebook computer, netbook, UMPC, or other device. **150**

distance learning A learning environment in which the student is physically located away from the instructor and other students; commonly, instruction and communications take place via the Web. 7–8, **332**

distributed database system A database system in which the data used by the system is located on multiple computers that are connected via a network. **565**, 566

DMCA (Digital Millennium Copyright Act), 671

DMS (document management system) A type of system used to store, organize, and retrieve documents once they have been created in or converted to an electronic format. **472**

DNS (domain name system) servers, 30, 375

do until structure, 517

do while structure, 517

docking station A device designed to easily connect a portable computer to conventional hardware, such as a keyboard, mouse, monitor, and printer. 24, **655**

document management system. *See* DMS (document management system)

document processing system A type of system used to create electronic documents. 471, **472**

documentation. *See also* document processing system

information systems and, 489, 492, 493, 495, 497
internal, 522
program development and, 512, 519, 522, 527–528
user, 528

domain name A text-based Internet address used to uniquely identify a computer on the Internet. 29, **30**, 33
e-commerce and, 450–451
registering, 450
top-level (TLD), 451
trademarks and, 636

doors, locking, 593–594

DoS (denial of service) attack An act of sabotage that attempts to flood a network server or a Web server with so much activity that it is unable to function. **367**, 368, 370

DOS (Disk Operating System) The operating system designed for and widely used on early IBM and IBM-compatible PCs. 185, **188**

dot con A fraud or scam carried out through the Internet. **370**, 377–381, 610

dot-com An Internet-only store with no physical presence. **431**

dot-matrix printers, 159

downloading
programs, 199
use of the term, 267

dpi (dots per inch), 140, 160

Dreamweaver (Adobe), 408, 421, 422

drive bays, 57, 58

driver. *See* device driver

DRM (digital rights management) software Software used to protect and manage the rights of creators of digital content, such as art, music, photographs, and movies. **635**, 641–644

DSL (Digital Subscriber Line) Internet access Fast, direct Internet access via standard telephone lines. 78, **309**

DSS (decision support system) A type of information system typically used by upper management that provides people with the tools and capabilities to organize and analyze their decision-making information. **474**

dual-core CPU A CPU that contains two separate processing cores. **58**

dual-mode phone A mobile phone that can be used with more than one communications network, such as with both a cellular and Wi-Fi network. **259**, 260

dumb terminals, 24

DVD disc A medium capacity (typically 4.7 MB or 8.5 MB) optical disc that is often used to deliver software and movies, as well as to store user data. 15, 57, 58
authoring software, 242–243
backups and, 203
burning, 242–243
coding systems and, 56
described, **106**
intellectual property rights and, 642–643
types of, 107–110

DVD-R/DVD+R discs Recordable DVDs. **109**

DVD-ROM disc A DVD that can be read from, but not written to, by the user. **108**

DVD-RW/DVD+RW discs Rewritable DVDs. **109**

DVRs (digital video recorders), 7

dynamic pricing site, 439

E

EAI (enterprise application integration), 476

EB. *See* exabyte (EB)

eBay, 420, 439, 531

EBCDIC (Extended Binary-Coded Decimal Interchange Code), 53, 54, R-15

e-book readers, 150, 156

eco-label A certification, usually by a government agency, that identifies a device as meeting minimal environmental performance specifications. 666

e-commerce The act of doing business transactions over the Internet or similar technology. *See also* e-commerce business model
advantages of, 432–433
databases and, 577
described, **431**
disadvantages of, 435
implementing, 440–455
merchant accounts, 442
multimedia and, 397
overview, 430–463
sales/marketing strategies, 449–450
tax collection, 451
Web site design for, 447–449

e-commerce business model A description of how an e-commerce company does business, such as the types of buyers and sellers involved. **436**, 437–438, 441 eCRM (electronic customer relationship management), 433, 441, 451. *See also* CRM (customer relationship management)

EDI (electronic data interchange) The transfer of data between different companies using the Internet or another network. **475**

editing Changing the content of a document, such as inserting or deleting words. **223**, 224

EFT (electronic funds transfers), 431

electromagnetic spectrum, 275–276

Electronic Privacy Information Center (EPIC), 606, 619

electronic profiling Using electronic means to collect a variety of in-depth information about an individual, such as name, address, income, and buying habits. 607–608, **609**, 610

electronic slide show A group of electronic slides that are displayed one after the other on a computer monitor or other display device. **238**

electronic surveillance, 616–624

e-mail (electronic mail) Electronic messages sent from one user to another over the Internet or other network. *See also* e-mail address; e-mail filter; spam
anonymity and, 39
convergence and, 6
cultural differences and, 651
described, **34**
emergency systems for, 602
offline e-mail services, 35
overview, 34–35
privacy, 339, 610–612
productive handling of, 659–660
security and, 339, 350, 351, 359–360, 366, 370, 594, 600, 602, 606, 610–615
software, 18, 35, 600
Web-based, 35

e-mail address An Internet address consisting of a username and computer domain name that uniquely identifies a person on the Internet. 29, 32, 33. *See also* spam
described, **31**
protecting, 611–612
throw-away, 611

e-mail filter A tool that automatically sorts your incoming e-mail messages based on specific criteria. **613**, 614–615

e-marketplaces, 440

embedded computer A tiny computer embedded in a product and designed to perform specific tasks or functions for that product. 19, **20**

embedded Linux A version of Linux designed for mobile devices. 198. *See also* Linux

embedded operating system A type of operating system embedded into devices, such as cars and consumer devices. **186**

emoticons, 38

employee(s). *See also* employee monitoring
disgruntled, 361–362
information, ethical use of, 645–646
policies, 624
privacy and, 621–624
responsibilities of, 623–624

employee monitoring Observing or reviewing employees' actions while they are on the job. **621**, 622, 650–651

encryption A method of scrambling the contents of an e-mail message or a file to make it unreadable if an unauthorized user intercepts it. 84, 203, 351
databases and, 561
described, **358**
e-mail and, 339, 359–360, 615
hardware loss and, 592
keystroke logging and, 619
overview, 358–360, 594–595
private-key, **359**
public-key, **359**
Wi-Fi and, 355–356

energy consumption, 26, 666–667

Energy Department (United States), 27, 666

ENERGY STAR A program developed by the U.S. Department of Energy and the Environmental Protection Agency to encourage the development of energy-saving devices. **666**

Enron, 648

enterprise architecture A comprehensive framework used to describe and manage an organization's business functions and systems. **468**, 469

enterprise resource planning. *See* ERP (enterprise resource planning)

enterprise rights-management software, 363

enterprise system A system that is used throughout an entire enterprise

(business, organization, government agency, and so on). **469**

entertainment
bots, 479
overview, 398
software, 244

entity Something (such as a person, object, or event) that is important to a business or organization; typically becomes a database table in a database system for that business or organization.
described, **555**
relationships between, 555–556

environmental concerns, 666–671

EPA (Environmental Protection Agency), 666, 667, 671

e-paper, 155, 156

e-portfolio A collection of an individual's work accessible via the Web. **334**

equal sign (=), 231

ERDs (entity-relationship diagrams), 490

ergonomic hardware Hardware, typically an input or output device, that is designed to be more ergonomically correct than its non-ergonomic counterpart. **656**, 657

ergonomics The science of fitting a work environment to the people who work there. 24, **654**

ERP (enterprise resource planning) A large integrated system that ties together all of a business's activities. 447, **475–476**

errors. *See also* debugging
compiler, 525
logic, **526**, 527
program development and, 522, 525, 526
syntax, **525**

eSATA (external SATA) ports, 71, 72

e-stamps, 164

e-tailer An online retailer. 438

Ethernet (802.3) A widely used wired LAN networking standard. 161, 279–280, 287–289

ethics Overall standards of moral conduct.
business, 638, **640**, 648
copyrights and, 640–652
cultural considerations for, 651–652
customer information and, 645–646
decision making and, 649–650
employee information and, 645–646

information use and, 643–644
personal, 638
use of resources and, 643–645
e-trash Electronic trash or waste, such as discarded computer components. 58, **668**, 669
EULA (end-user license agreement), 603
exabyte (EB) Approximately 1,000 petabytes. **52**
Excel (Microsoft), 230, 233, 575. *See also* spreadsheets
executable code, translating coded programs into, 523–525
executable files, 203
expansion bus A bus on the motherboard used to connects peripheral devices. **68**, 69
expansion card A circuit board that can be inserted into an expansion slot location on a computer's motherboard to add additional functionality or to connect a peripheral device to that computer. 57, **66**, 67–69
expansion slot A location on the motherboard into which expansion cards are inserted. 57, **66**, 67
expert system A computer system that provides the type of advice that would be expected from a human expert. **480**, 481
ExpressCard module A module that can be inserted into a computer's ExpressCard slot to add additional functionality or to connect a peripheral device to that computer; commonly used with notebook computers. **67**, 102
Expression Web (Microsoft), 421
Extensible Hypertext Markup Language *See* XHTML (Extensible Hypertext Markup Language)
Extensible Markup Language *See* XML (Extensible Markup Language)
extranet An intranet that is at least partially accessible to authorized outsiders. **270**

F

Facebook, 10, 19, 21, 28, 321, 322
e-commerce and, 450
emergency notification systems and, 32
job hunting and, 486
lifestreaming and, 407
multimedia and, 407, 409

netiquette and, 38
security and, 606, 607
storage and, 115
Web Slices and, 34
FACTA (Fair and Accurate Credit Transactions Act), 378, 383
Family Entertainment and Copyright Act, 642, 671
fans, 57, 65–66, 65
FAQs (Frequently Asked Questions), 451
FAT file system, 104
FAT32 file system, 104
fault tolerance, 119
Favorites feature, 33, 34
FBI (Federal Bureau of Investigation), 347, 364, 370, 595, 619, 643
FCC (Federal Communications Commission), 275, 304
feasibility reports, 489
FedEx
Desktop, 531
Kinko's, 434
Feldman, Stuart, 586–587
fiber-optic cable A networking cable that utilizes hundreds of thin transparent fibers over which lasers transmit data as light. **274**, 275
fiber-to-the-premises (FTTP) Internet access *See* broadband over fiber (BoF) Internet access
field A single category of data to be stored in a database, such as a person's last name or telephone number. Also called a column. 236, 549
data definition and, 556–557
described, **234**
redundant, 554
fifth normal form (5NF), 568
file(s) Something stored on a storage medium, such as a program, a document, or an image.
copying, 200
deleting, 201
described, **95**
moving, 200
overview, 181
file compression program A program that reduces the size of files, typically to be stored or transmitted more efficiently. **203**. *See also* compression
file management program A utility program that enables the user to perform file management tasks, such as copying and deleting files. 180–181, **198**, 199
file management systems, 553, 554
file servers, 267

filename(s) A name given to a file by the user; it is used to retrieve the file at a later time.
changing, 200
conventions, 181–182
described, **95**
extensions, 31, 37, 181–182, 235, 415, 524, 540
search tools and, 201
word processing and, 227
financial brokerage sites, 440
fingerprint readers, 146
FiOS (fiber-optic service), 309
firewall A collection of hardware and/or software intended to protect a computer or computer network from unauthorized access. 182, 204, 308, **356**, 357–358, 600
FireWire A high-speed bus standard often used to connect digital video cameras and other multimedia hardware to a computer. **69**, 70–72, 180
firmware, 288
First Amendment, 335, 624
first normal form (INF), 568
Fisher, Kathleen, 534
fixed wireless Internet access Fast, direct Internet access available in some areas via the airwaves. **309–310**
Flash (Adobe) A popular program for creating Web animations and interactive Web-based multimedia applications. 405, 414, 418
authoring tools and, 421
described, **404**
RIAs and, 531
flash memory Nonvolatile memory chips that can be used for storage by the computer or user; can be built into a computer or a storage medium. 62, 64, 65, 67, 71. *See also* flash memory card
described, **110**
disc caches, 103
overview, 98, 110–114
flash memory card A small, rectangular flash memory medium, such as a CompactFlash (CF) or Secure Digital (SD) card; often used with digital cameras and other portable devices. 15, **110**, 111–112, 147. *See also* flash memory; flash memory card readers
flash memory card readers, 15, 57, 58, 93–94, 111–112
flat-panel display A slim type of display device that uses electronically

charged chemicals or gases instead of an electron gun to display images. 151, **152**

flatbed scanner An input device that scans flat objects one at a time. **139**, 140

Flickr, 115, 321, 323, 407, 420
databases and, 576
privacy and, 612

floating point unit. *See* FPU (floating point unit)

flowchart (program design) A program design tool that shows graphically step-by-step the actions a computer program will take. **512**, 513–515, 519, 526

flowchart (Web design) A tool that can be used during the Web design process to illustrate how the pages in a Web site relate to one another. **410**

flowcharting software, 513, 514

folder A named place on a storage medium into which files can be stored to keep the files stored on that medium organized.
copying, 200
deleting, 201
described, **95**
moving, 200
naming, 200
overview, 181
storage and, 95, 116
viewing, 200

fonts, 224, 227, 228
HTML and, 415
multimedia and, 400, 415
types of, 400

form A formatted way of viewing and editing a table in a database.
creating, 510, 569–570
databases and, 549, 569–570, 578
described, **569**
generators, 530
Visual Basic and, 539

formatting Changing the appearance of a document, such as changing the margins or font size.
characters, 228
documents, **224**
paragraphs, 228

formula An entry in a worksheet cell that performs computations on worksheet data and displays the results. 230, **231**, 232

FORTRAN A high-level programming language used for mathematical, scientific, and engineering applications. 13, 534, **535**

Fortress, 535

forward slash (/), 32

fourth normal form (4NF), 568

fourth-generation language (4GL) A class of programming languages that is closer to natural language and easier to work with than a high-level language. **535**

FPU (floating-point unit) The part of a CPU core that performs decimal arithmetic. **73**, 74, 80

fraudulent reporting, 648

freeware Copyrighted software that may be used free of charge. 214, **216**, 217

front end
software, 536
use of the term, 564

frontside bus (FSB) The bus that connects the CPU (via the I/O bridge) to the rest of the bus architecture. 68, **69**

FTC (Federal Trade Commission), 373

FTP (File Transfer Protocol), 31, 305, 423

FTTP (fiber-to-the-premises) Internet. *See* BoF (broadband over fiber) Internet access

full disk encryption (FDE) A technology that encrypts everything stored on a storage medium automatically, without any user interaction. **594**

function A named formula that can be entered into a worksheet cell to perform some type of calculation or to extract information from other cells in the worksheet. **231**

G

gadgets, 190, 191, 327, 329

Gaidano, Scott, 101

game(s), 136–137, 151, 154, 307
artificial intelligence and, 478–479
consoles, 7, 24–25
described, **327**
ports, 71

GB. *See* gigabyte (GB)

Gelsinger, Patrick, 84

geobrowsing, 220, 318, 319

Germany, Julie B., 331

gesture input, 133, 136, 154–155

Gesturetek, 133, 136, 154–155

G.hn standard, 280–281

GIF (Graphics Interchange Format) An image format that supports 256 colors and is commonly used for Web page

line art images. 403, 421. *See also* graphics; images
animated, **404**
described, **402**
interlaced, 402
transparent, 402

gift cards, 444

gigabyte (GB) Approximately 1 billion bytes. **52**

GIS (geographic information system) An information system that combines geographic information with other types of data (such as information about customers, sales, and so forth) in order to provide a better understanding of the relationships among the data. **474–475**

Go (execution) phase, 524

Google, 263, 312–314, 482, 586–587
Apps, 9, 19
Checkout, 445
Chrome, 188, 205, 312, 338, 613
click fraud and, 455
coding systems and, 55
databases and, 566
desktop search tools, 201
Docs, 115, 218, 205, 220, 532
Gears, 531, 532
Gmail, 611
Maps, 22, 531, 420, 605
overview, 34
Python and, 541
security and, 350, 371, 380, 605, 607–608, 611, 613
solar power and, 668
Web site promotion through, 452, 453, 454

GOTO statement, 508

government database A collection of data about people that is collected and maintained by the government. 607, **608**

government Web sites, 331

GPS (global positioning system) A system that uses satellites and a receiver to determine the exact geographic location of the receiver. 10, 32, 220, 275, 277, 397
described, **260**
monitoring systems and, 261–262, 621
overview, 260–261
presence technology and, 623
system software and, 194, 195, 196

Graef, Ailin, 639

graphene chips, 80

graphical information system. *See* GIS (graphical information system)

graphical programming languages, 534

graphical user interface. *See* GUI (graphical user interface)

graphics. *See also* images
coding systems and, 54–55
described, **400**
formats, choosing, 403
storing, on external hard drives, 77
word processing and, 229

graphics software Application software used to create or modify images. **240**, 241

graphics tablet A flat, rectangular input device that is used in conjunction with a stylus to transfer drawings, sketches, and anything written on the device to a computer. 134, **135**

green components, 668

green computing The use of computers in an environmentally friendly manner. 26, **666**

grid computing, 19

GUIs (graphical user interface) A graphically based interface that allows a user to communicate instructions to the computer easily. **185**, 301

H

<H1...H6> tags, 415

hacking Using a computer to break into another computer system. 18, 368
described, **348–349**
privacy and, 606

handheld computers. *See* UMPC (ultra-mobile PC)

handwriting recognition The ability of a device to identify handwritten characters. 133, 134

Hansen, Bill, 115

hard drive The primary storage system for most computers; used to store most programs and data used with a computer.
buying a larger or second, 78
defragmenting, 77
described, **96**
external, 96, 102–103, 599
history of computers and, 13, 14
hybrid, **103**, 104
interface standards, 105
internal, 102–103, 599
magnetic, 96, **97**, 120, 121, 599
overview, 96–105
partitions, 104
portable, 102
read/write heads, 97, 103
removing/wiping data from, 670–671

self-encrypting, 594, **595**
speed, 103–104
system unit and, 57

hardware The physical parts of a computer system, such as the keyboard, monitor, printer, and so forth. *See also specific hardware*
damage, 591–602
described, **14**
energy conservation and, 667
external components, 14
finding new, 180
internal components, 14
Internet-related, 303–306
loss, 591–602
networks and, 287–288
overview, 14–16
proper care of, 597–600
properly disposing of, 616
recycling, 668–671
security and, 591–602

hardware theft The theft of computer hardware. **582**

hashing procedures, 563–564

<HEAD> tag, 415

headers and footers, 227, 228

headphone A personal audio output device used by an individual so only he or she can hear the sound; headphones with a built-in microphone are typically referred to as headsets.
described, **165**
noise reduction, 653

headset. *See* headphones

health issues. *See also* ergonomics
emotional, 658–661
overview, 652–666

heat sinks, 65–66

help, accessing, 224–225

hexidecimal numbering system, R-11

Hide method, 509

high-level language A class of programming languages that is closer to natural language and easier to work with than a low-level language. **533–534**. *See also specific programming languages*

Higher Education Opportunity Act, 32

HIPPA (Health Insurance Portability and Accountability Act), 119, 468, 625, 671

hiring, 361

History lists, 34

HOLAP (Hybrid OLAP), 576

Hollerith, Herman, 12

holographic storage An emerging type of storage technology that uses

multiple blue laser beams to store data in three dimensions. 100, **117**, 118

HomePNA 3.0, 280–281

homes, "smart", 7

Hopper, Grace, 523

horizontal hubs, 437

hot sites, 561, 602

hotspots, 8, 265, 266, 270. *See also* Wi-Fi hotspots
described, **310–311**
personal, 291

hot-swappable devices, 71–72

<HR> tag, 415

HTML (HyperText Markup Language) A markup language widely used for creating Web pages. 31, 263
AJAX and, 419
authoring tools and, 421, 422
databases and, 579
described, **415**
Java and, 540
meta tags and, 452
RIAs and, 531
XHTML and, comparison of, 416, 417
version 5, 417–418

<HTML> tag, 415

HTTP (HyperText Transfer Protocol), 31

Huffman coding, 406

Hurricane Katrina, 475

hybrid hard drive A hard drive that contains both a large amount of flash memory and magnetic hard disks. **103**, 104

hybrid XML/relational database A type of database system that can store and retrieve both XML data and relational data. **575**

hybrid XML/relational database server, 575

hyperlinks, 17, 33–34, 313
assistive technology and, 413
broken, 421
checking, 423

HyperText Markup Language. *See* HTML (HyperText Markup Language)

I

<I> tag, 415

Iannucci, Bob, 82

IBM (International Business Machines), 12, 14, 59, 198, 367
AOP and, 510
cooling systems, 85
DB2, 235, 551, 575
Deep Blue computer, 478–479
EBDCIC and, 54
intellectual property and, 638

Linux and, 194
mainframes, 26
PCs, 21–22, 188
quantum computing and, 83
Second Life Grid and, 399
supercomputers and, 26, 27, 81, 479
z/OS, 198
IC3 (Internet Crime Complaint Center), 370, 376
ICANN (Internet Corporation for Assigned Names and Numbers), 304
icons, desktop, 16, 17
ICs (integrated circuits), 13, 56–57
identity theft Using someone else's identity to purchase goods or services, obtain new credit cards or bank loans, or otherwise illegally masquerade as that individual. 37, 204, 371, **372**, 373
if-then-else structure, 516, 517
Illustrator (Adobe), 241
IM (instant messaging) A way of exchanging real-time typed messages with other individuals. 16, 28, 31, 317, **318**, 319–320
presence technology and, 623
privacy and, 610
image A digital representation of a photograph, drawing, chart, or other visual image; also called a graphic. *See also* graphics
authoring tools and, 421
compression, 55, 148, 402, 403
described, **400**
multimedia and, 400–402
optimizing, 401
thumbnail, **403**
image maps, 409
IMDB (in-memory database) A database that stores all data in memory instead of on a hard drive. **566**
<IMG> tag, 415
IMOD (interferometric modulator) displays, 157–158
implementation process, 528
income taxes, 639
index A small table containing a primary key and the location of the record belonging to that key; used to locate records in a database. **562**, 563
indexed organization A method for organizing data on a storage medium or in a database that uses an index to specify the exact storage location. **562**, 563
information Data that has been processed into a meaningful form. *See also* information system (IS)

data versus, 11–12
delivery, 396–397
described, **11**
integrity, 39
overload, 659–660
privacy, **606**
theft, 371–372
information system (IS) A system used to generate information to support users in an organization.
described, **467**
overview, 466–505
types of, 471–483
users, 469–471
information systems (IS) department The department in an organization responsible for that organization's computers, systems, and other technology; also called the information technology (IT) department. **484**
infotainment systems, 195
infrared (IR) transmissions A wireless networking medium that sends data as infrared light rays. **278**
ink-jet printer An output device that sprays droplets of ink to produce images on paper. 162, 163
in-memory database. *See* IMDB (in-memory database)
input The process of entering data into a computer; can also refer to the data itself.
described, **10–11**
overview, 14–15
input masks, 557, 558–559
insertion point An on-screen character that looks like a blinking vertical line; indicates the current location in a document, which is where the next change will be made. **223**
installed software Software that must be installed on a computer in order to be used.
described, **218**
Web-based software versus, 217
installing programs, 199
instant messaging. *See* IM (instant messaging)
Institute of Electrical and Electronics Engineers (IEEE), 278, 280, 282–283
instruction sets, 75
integers, 509
Intel, 84–85
intellectual property rights The legal rights to which creators of original creative works (such as artistic or

literary works, inventions, corporate logos, and more) are entitled. *See also* copyright; patent; trademark
described, **633**
overview, 633–638
intelligent agent A program that performs specific tasks to help make a user's work environment more efficient or entertaining and that typically modifies its behavior based on the user's actions. **479**, 480
inter-enterprise system A system that links multiple enterprises, such as a business and its suppliers and strategic partners. **469**
interface engine, 480
intermediary hubs, 437
Internet The largest and most well-known computer network, linking millions of computers all over the world.
accessing, 29
addiction, 327
citing resources from, 317
connection types, 307–308
convergence and, 6
described, **27**
evolution of, 6, 299–305
merchant accounts, 442
myths about, 304–305
overview, 258, 298–345
searching, 312–317
setup, 305–312
upgrading connections to, 78–79
Internet addiction The problem of overusing, or being unable to stop using, the Internet. **660**, 661
Internet address An address that identifies a computer, person, or Web page on the Internet, such as an IP address, domain name, or e-mail address. **29**
Internet appliance A specialized network computer designed primarily for Internet access and/or e-mail exchange. **24**
Internet content provider A person or an organization that provides Internet content. **302–303**
Internet Explorer (Microsoft). *See also* browser
Content Advisor, 336
overview, 33–34
searching with, 312
Internet filtering Using a software program or browser option to block access to particular Web pages or types of Web pages. **335**, 336

Internet service provider. *See* ISP (Internet service provider)

Internet telephony, 320. *See also* VoIP (Voice over Internet Protocol)

Internet2, 290, 301–302

InternetWorldStats.com, 663

interpreter A language translator that converts program statements line-by-line into machine language, immediately executing each one. **524**

intranet A private network that is set up similar to the Internet and is accessed via a Web browser. **269**, 270

inventory management system A system used to track and manage inventory. **476**, 477

Iomega Corporation, 115

IP (Internet Protocol), 30, 32–33

IP address A numeric Internet address used to uniquely identify a computer on the Internet. 29, 32–33

described, **30**

overview, 605

security and, 605, 616

IPC (instructions per cycle), 76

iPhone OS (Apple) The operating system designed for Apple mobile phones and mobile devices. 133, 135, 194, 217

described, **197**

Digital Copy and, 644

intellectual property and, 638

program development and, 520, 531, 539

SDK, 531

security and, 596

iPod (Apple), 21, 158–159, 644. *See also* digital media players

IR. *See* infrared (IR) transmissions

IS. *See* information system (IS)

ISOC (Internet Society), 304

isochronous transmission, 271–272

ISP (Internet service provider) A business or other organization that provides Internet access to others, typically for a fee. 27, 29, 30, 33, 35, 308

anonymity and, 39

bandwidth limits and, 306

concentrators and, 291

described, **302**

fees, 304–305

privacy and, 611

security and, 339, 350, 351, 370, 619

selecting, 311–312

VoIP and, 320

issue tracking, 529

IT (information technology) department, **484**, 485–488

iterative approach, 499

iTunes, 397

J

Jack in the Box (company), 22, 595

Java A high-level, object-oriented programming language frequently used for Web-based applications. 17, 54, 520, 521, 534

compilers and, 524

databases and, 549, 574

described, **540**

Development Kit (JDK), 540

overview, 540–541

Virtual Machine (JVM), 540

Java applet A small program inserted into a Web page that performs a specific task, such as changing the values in a stock portfolio or scrolling text across the screen. 404, 540

java.io package, 540

JavaScript A scripting language widely used to add dynamic content to Web pages. 263, 405, 414, 418

authoring tools and, 421

databases and, 578, 579

described, **418**

JDK (Java Development Kit), 540

Jensen, Debra, 22, 595

Jeopardy! (television show), 58, 59, 479

JIT (just-in-time) strategy, 476, 540

job

hunting, 486

managing/monitoring, 180

JPEG (Joint Photographic Experts Group) format An image format that supports true color and is commonly used for Web page photographs. 55, 401, **402–403**. *See also* graphics; images

Jupiter Research, 321, 453

just-in-time (JIT) compiler, 540

Justice Department (United States), 604

JVM (Java Virtual Machine), 540

K

Kaine, Sean, 451

Kaspersky Lab, 371

KB See kilobyte (KB)

kernel The essential portion, or core, of an operating system. 179

keyboard An input device containing numerous keys that can be used to input letters, numbers, and other symbols. 13, 14, 15, 71

buffers, 184

controllers, 150

described, 129

overview, 129–130

keyboard shortcut A combination of keyboard keys that are pressed in unison to issue a specific software command. 221, **222**, 223

keystroke logging systems, 618, 619

keyword A word typed in a search box on a search site or other Web page to locate information related to that keyword. 34, 312, 313, 315–316

described, **514**

HTML and, 415

security and, 618

kill switches, 596

kilobyte (KB) Approximately one thousand bytes (1,024 bytes to be precise). **52**

kinesthetic learners, 398

Kingston Technology, 64, 114

kiosks, 9, 135, 154

knowledge base, 480

Kodak, 636

KPI (key performance indicator), 470

Kramnik, Vladimir, 478

Krintz, Chandra, 419

L

label A text-based entry in a worksheet cell that identifies data on the worksheet. **231**

landscape orientation, 228

language translator A software program that converts program code to machine language. **523**, 524, 532

LAN (local area network) A network that connects devices located in a small geographical area, such as within a building. **269**, 272, 279–280, 289

laptop computer. *See* notebook computer

laser printer An output device that uses toner powder and technology similar to that of a photocopier to produce images on paper. 159, **161**, 162

Lawrence Livermore National Laboratory, 27

LCD (liquid crystal display) A type of flat-panel display that uses charged liquid crystals to display images. **155**, 158, 157, 667

LEDs (light emitting diodes), 155–158

legacy
    ports, 70
    systems, 567
Level 1 (L1) cache, 62
Level 2 (L2) cache, 62
Level 3 (L3) cache, 62
license tokens, 215–216
lifecasting, 407
lifestreaming, 407
line art, 403
LinkedIn, 322, 409
link-edit stage, 524
links. *See* hyperlinks
Linux An open source operating system
    that is available without charge over
    the Internet and is increasingly being
    used with mobile devices, personal
    computers, servers, mainframes, and
    supercomputers. 16, 185, 186, 194,
    196–198
    described, **193**
    intellectual property and, 638
    program development and, 530, 541
    XO laptop and, 664
Linux Foundation, 526
liquid crystal display. *See* LCD (liquid
    crystal display)
LISP, 535
lithography, 79
load module, 524
local area network. *See* LAN (local area
    network)
Loebner Prize, 478
logic error A programming error that
    occurs when running a program
    produces incorrect results. 518, 525,
    526, 527
logical representation, 95
Logo (programming language), 535
loop(s)
    debugging and, 526
    infinite, 518
    program development and, 514, 518, 526
Los Alamos National Lab, 27
lossless file compression, 402
low-level language A class of
    programming languages that is
    highly detailed and machine-
    dependent. **532**, 533

M
MAC (Media Access Control) address
    filtering, 357
Mac OS The operating system used on
    Apple computers; the most recent
    version as of this printing is Mac OS

X Snow Leopard. 16, 54, **192**, 193,
    358, 666
Mac OS X The current version of Mac
    OS as of this printing. 16, **192**, 193,
    539, 541
Mac OS X Server The version of Mac
    OS X designed for server use. **193**
MacDougall, Francis, 154–155
machine cycle The series of operations
    involved in the execution of a a
    single machine level instruction. **76**
machine language A binary-based lan-
    guage for representing computer pro-
    grams that the computer can execute
    directly. **56**, 524–525, 532–533
Macintosh (Apple), 14, 21–22, 186, 201.
    See also Mac OS; Mac OS X
macros
    overview, 529–530
    programming languages, 530
    recorders, 530
magnetic hard drive A hard drive
    consisting of one or more metal
    magnetic disks permanently sealed,
    with an access mechanism and read/
    write heads, inside its drive. 96, **97**,
    120, 121, 599
magnetic tape Storage media consisting
    of plastic tape with a magnetizable
    surface that stores data as a series of
    magnetic spots; typically comes as a
    cartridge. 13, **120**, 121
mail servers, 31, 35, 267
mainframe computer A computer
    used in large organizations
    (such as hospitals, large businesses,
    and colleges) that need to manage
    large amounts of centralized
    data and run multiple programs
    simultaneously. 20, 25, **26**, 198, 567
maintenance
    database, 573–574
    program, 528
    system, 77–78, **497**
Mak, Cecily, 642
make-or-buy decision, 494–495
malware Any type of malicious software.
    37, **364**, 365–367, 371
management information system. *See* MIS
    (management information system)
management pyramids, 470
MAN (metropolitan area network)
    A network designed to service a
    metropolitan area. **269**
manufacturer Web sites, 331
many-to-many (M:M) relationship, 556
Mark II computer, 523

market exchange sites, 440
marketing database A collection of data
    about people that is stored in a large
    database and used for marketing
    purposes. **607**, 608–610
markup language A language that uses
    symbols or tags to describe what
    a document should look like when
    it is displayed in a Web browser.
    414, 415. *See also specific markup
    languages*
mashup sites, 420
MB. *See* megabyte (MB)
McCabe, Donald, 646
McCarthy, John, 478
McCreesh, John, 224
McDonald's Corporation, 284, 301, 476
m-commerce E-commerce carried out
    via mobile phones and other mobile
    devices. **421–432**
MDDB (multidimensional database) A
    type of database designed to be used
    with data warehousing. **576**
mechanical calculator, 12
megabyte (MB) Approximately one
    million bytes. **52**
Melfi, Joe, 46–47
Melissa computer virus, 361
memory Chip-based storage.
    adding more, 77
    addressing, 64
    architecture, 63
    booting and, 179
    controllers, 72
    described, **62**
    history of computers and, 14
    management, 183–184
    modules, 63
    registers, 64
    slots, 57
    system software and, 179
    system unit and, 56, 60
    volatile, **62**
menu(s)
    bar, 17, 222
    overview, 221–223
Merritt, Marian, 270, 364, 373
mesh network A network in which there
    are multiple connections between
    the devices on the network so that
    messages can take any of several
    possible paths. **267**
message board A Web page that enables
    individuals to post messages on a
    particular topic for others to read and
    respond to; also called a discussion
    group or online forum. 39, **320**

meta tag A special HTML or XHTML tag containing information about a Web page that is added by the person creating the Web page and is used primarily by search sites. 415, **452**

metadata Data about data, such as the data contained in a data dictionary. **558**

metropolitan area network. *See* MAN (metropolitan area network)

MFD (multifunction device) A device that offers multiple functions (such as printing, scanning, and faxing) in a single unit. **161**

MICR (magnetic ink character recognition) readers, 144–145

microarchitecture, 72

microblogging. *See* twittering

microbrowsers, 418

microcode, 75

microcomputer(s), 6, **21**. *See also* PC (personal computer)

microphones, 15

microprinting, 605

microprocessor A central processing unit (CPU) for a personal computer. 14, **58**. *See also* CPU (central processing unit)

Microsoft Corporation. *See also specific products*
   intellectual property and, 638
   trademarks and, 636–637

Microsoft .NET framework, 520, 536, 538

microtargeting, 576, 577

microwave station An earth-based device that sends and receives high-frequency, high-speed radio signals. **277**

middleware Software used to connect two otherwise separate applications, such as a Web server and a database management system. 565, **578**

MIDI (Musical Instrument Digital Interface), 71, 130, 150, 404

midrange server A medium-sized computer used to host programs and data for a small network. 20, **25**, 26

military computing, 134

MIS (management information system) A type of information system that provides decision makers with preselected information that can be used to make middle-management decisions. **473–474**

MIT (Massachusetts Institute of Technology), 541

Mitek Systems, 145

MMX (Multimedia Extensions), 79

mobile device A very small communications device that has built-in computing or Internet capability. 10, 19, **20–21**, 72, 133, 135, 151

mobile phone A phone, such as a cellular or satellite phone, that uses a wireless network. *See also* cellular phone
   banking and with, 145
   convergence and, 6
   described, **259**
   digital cameras integrated with, 147
   dual-mode, 7
   energy conservation and, 667
   Internet usage and, 306–307
   privacy and, 614
   program development and, 530
   protective cases for, 598–599
   used while driving, 653
   uses of, on the job, 22
   Web site design and, 412

mobile operating system A type of operating system used with mobile phones and other mobile devices. **186**, 194–198

mobile tracking software, 597

mobile wireless Internet access Internet access via a mobile phone network. **310**

Mobile WiMAX A version of WiMAX designed to be used with mobile phones. **283**

modem A device that enables a computer to communicate over analog networking media, such as connecting to the Internet via telephone lines. 15, 16, 71, **287**

modules. *See* procedures

MOLAP (Multidimensional OLAP), 576

Molsberry, Frank, 678–679

monitor A display device for a desktop computer. 13, 15, 70, 72, 150

monitoring systems, 261–262, 616–624. *See also* employee monitoring

Monster.com, 486

Moore's Law, 72, 73

Morph concept, 82

Mosaic Web browser, 300–301. *See also* browsers

motherboard The main circuit board of a computer, located inside the system unit, to which all computer system components connect. 56, **57**

mouse A common pointing device that the user slides along a flat surface to move a pointer around the screen and clicks its buttons to make selections. 14, 15, 71, **131**, 132

MP3 format, 55, 404, 406

MPEG (Motion Pictures Expert Group) format, 55, 405

msconfig, 179

multi-core CPU A CPU that contains the processing components or core of more than one processor in a single CPU. **58**, 59

multidimensional database. *See* MDDB (multidimensional database)

multifunction device. *See* MFD (multifunction device)

multimedia The integration of a variety of media, such as text, images, video, animation, and sound. *See also* audio; graphics; video; Web-based multimedia
   concepts, 240–241
   described, **395**
   future of, 423
   networks and, 262
   overview, 394–429
   Web site design, 407–413

multiplexers, 291

multiprocessing The capability to use multiple processors or multiple processing cores in a single computer, usually to process multiple jobs at one time faster than could be performed with a single processor. 80, **81**, 183

multitasking The capability of an operating system to run more than one program at one time. **182**

multithreading, 182

multiuser database system A database designed to be accessed by multiple users. **564**

music. *See also* audio; MIDI (Musical Instrument Digital Interface)
   copyrights and, 243
   impact of the Internet on, 397
   input systems, 150
   intellectual property rights and, 641–642
   online, 325, 326

mySimon.com, 434

MySpace, 28, 321, 322, 323, 407, 607
   databases and, 576
   e-commerce and, 450

N

nanogenerators, 82

nanoparticles, 83

nanosensors, 83

nanotechnology The science of creating tiny computers and components by working at the individual atomic and molecular levels. 14, 79, **81**, 82–83

Napster, 397, 641

NAS (network attached storage) A high-performance storage device individually connected to a network to provide storage for computers on that network. **114**, 115, 119

national ID system, 608

National White Collar Crime Center, 370

Navajo Nation, 662–663

Naval Weapons Center, 523

NCI (National Cancer Institute), 575

NCIA (National Cancer Imaging Archive), 575

nested statements, 517

net neutrality issue, 306

netbook A very small notebook computer. **23**, 58, 60

Netflix, 438

netiquette, **38**

network A collection of computers and other hardware devices that are connected together to share hardware, software, and data, as well as to communicate electronically with one another.
  accessing, 29
  applications for, 258–265
  architectures, 267
  characteristics, 265–270
  coverage areas, 268
  data transmission characteristics, 270–273
  databases and, 566–567
  described, **27**
  hardware, 287–288
  history of computers and, 14
  licenses, 214
  media, 273–278
  overview, 27, 256–297
  ports, 70, 72
  printers, 160–161
  protocols, 278–287
  security overview, 346–391
  servers, 24, 267
  size, 268
  storage and, 114–116
  topologies, 266–267

network adapter A network interface, such as an expansion card or external network adapter. 16, **287**

network attached storage. *See* NAS (network attached storage)

network interface card. *See* NIC (network interface card)

Network Solutions, 450, 451

networked economy, 36

neural network An expert system in which the human brain's pattern-recognition process is emulated by the computer system. **481**

news sites, 328

NFC (near Field Communications), 432

NIC (network interface card) An expansion card through which a computer can connect to a network. **287**

Nigerian letter fraud scheme, 376

Nokia, 82, 541

nonvolatile A characteristic of memory or storage in which data is retained even when the power to the computer is turned off. **62**, 64

normalization The process of evaluating and correcting the structure of a database table to minimize data redundancy. **568**

NOT operator, 315

note taking software, 244

notebook computer A fully functioning portable computer that opens to reveal a screen and keyboard; also called a laptop computer.
  cleaning, 78
  CPUs and, 59–60
  described, **23**
  I/O and, 151, 152
  ports, 72
  protective cases for, 597–598
  security and, 593–594
  storage and, 97

notebook stand A device that elevates the display of a notebook or tablet computer to a better viewing height; can contain USB ports to connect additional hardware. **66**, 653, 655

Novell, 194

n-tier database systems, 564, **565**

numbering systems, 52–53

O

Obama, Barack, 22, 349

object code The machine language version of a computer program generated after the program's source code is compiled. **523**

object-oriented database. *See* OODBMS (object-oriented database management system)

object-oriented programming. *See* OOP (object-oriented programming)

Objective-C, 520, 539

OCR (optical character recognition) The ability of a computer to recognize scanned text characters and convert them to electronic form as text, not images. 139, **144**, 665

Office (Microsoft) One of the most widely used office software suites. 21, 196, 217, 218, 333. *See also specific applications*
  2010 version, 223
  coding systems and, 54
  collaboration and, 229
  databases and, 551
  described, **221**
  macros, 530
  Picture Manager, 140, 241
  security and, 359, 604

office system A type of system in which hardware, software, and other resources are used to facilitate communications and enhance productivity. **471**, 472

OLAP (Online Analytical Processing), 576

OLE (object linking and embedding), 420

OLED (organic light emitting diode) display A type of flat-panel display that uses emissive organic material to display brighter and sharper images. **155**, 156–158

OLPC (One Laptop Per Child) project, 663–664

OMG (Object Management Group), 514

Omnilert, 32

OMRs (optical mark readers), **144**

one-entry-point/one-exit-point rule, 518

one-to-many (1:M) relationship, 555–556

one-to-one (1:1) relationship, 555

online auction An online activity for which bids are placed for items, and the highest bidder purchases the item. 18, 325, 375–376, 380–381
  described, **324**
  C2C model and, 437
  Web sites, 439, 440

online banking Performing banking activities via the Web. 145, **245**, 325

online classified ads, 437

online digital wallets, 445

online education, 331–332

online fraud, 370–381

online gaming Playing games via the Web. **327**. *See also* games

online investing Buying and selling stocks or other types of investments via the Web. **324**, 325, 430–463. *See also* e-commerce

online movies Feature films available via the Web. **326**, 327, 642–643, 644. *See also* video

online music Music played or obtained via the Web. **325**, 326. *See also* music

online payment service A type of payment service accessed via the Internet and used to make electronic payments to others, such as via deposited funds, a bank account, or a credit card. **443**, 444

online portfolio management software, 245

online shopping. *See* shopping, online

online storage Remote storage devices accessed via the Internet; also called cloud storage. **115**, 116

online testing, 332–333

online theft, 370–381

online TV Live or recorded TV shows available via the Web. **326**, 327

online video Video watched or downloaded via the Web. **326**, 327. *See also* video

Onorati, Tony, 189

OODBMS (object-oriented database management system) A type of database system in which multiple types of data are stored as objects along with their related code. **574**, 575

OOP (object-oriented programming) An approach to program design in which a program consists of a collection of objects that contain data and methods to be used with that data.
  databases and, 574
  described, **509–510**
  UML and, 515
  Visual Basic and, 538

open source software Software programs whose source code is made available to the public. **214**, 215, 526

OpenOffice.org, 215, 221, 224

operating system The main component of system software that enables the computer to manage its activities and the resources under its control, run application programs, and interface with the user. *See also* system software
  described, **178**
  functions of, 178–179
  future of, 205
  for larger computers, 198
  types of, 185–187

opt in To request that you be included in marketing activities or that your information be shared with other companies. 607

opt out To request that you be removed from marketing activities or that your information not be shared with other companies. 608, 613, **614**, 615

optical character recognition. *See* OCR (optical character recognition)

optical computer A computer that uses light, such as from laser beams or infrared beams, to perform digital computations. 14, **84**

optical disc A type of storage medium read from and written to using a laser beam. 14, **105**, 106–110

optical drive A drive used with optical discs, such as CD or DVD discs. **106**, 107

optimizing ads, 453–454

OQL (object query language), 574

OR operator, 315

Oracle, 235, 526, 551, 566, 575

ORDBMS (object-relational database management system), 575

order entry system A type of transaction system that records and manages order processing. **473**

order-fulfillment (e-fulfillment) companies, 447

organic light emitting diode display. *See* OLED (organic light emitting diode) display

Ornelas, Lauren, 671

OTP (one-time password), 435, 442, 443, 444

Outlook (Microsoft), 35, 303

output The process of presenting the results of processing; can also refer to the results themselves. **10–11**

outsourcing Turning over specific business tasks to an outside vendor; increasingly, the vendor is located in a different country with lower labor costs. 399, 447
  described, **485**
  information systems and, 485–488
  overview, 485–488

ownership rights, 213–216

P

<P> tag, 415, 417

P2P (peer-to-peer) networks, 267–278, 306, 363, 365, 641

packet(s)
  overview, 272
  sniffing, 351
  switching, 272–273, 284

page files, 184

page layout A sketch of a Web page often developed during the Web design process to illustrate the basic layouts of the home page and the rest of the pages on a Web site. **410**, 411

Palm OS The original operating system designed for Palm devices. **197**, 541

Palm webOS The newest operating system designed for Palm devices. **197**

Palomar Pomerado Health, 399

PAN (personal area network) A network that connects an individual's personal devices that are located close together. **268–269**, 284–285

parallel processing A processing technique that uses multiple processors or multiple processing cores simultaneously, usually to process a single job as fast as possible. 80, **81**, 183

parallel transmission A type of data transmission in which bytes of data are transmitted at one time, with the bits in each byte taking a separate path. **271**, 272

parameters, 540

parental controls, 336

Pass ID Act, 608

Pascal A structured, high-level programming language often used to teach structured programming, especially appropriate for use in math and science applications. **527**, 534

password A secret combination of characters used to gain access to a computer, computer network, or other resource. 29, 353–354, 561
  described, **352**
  protecting, 597

patent A form of protection for an invention that can be granted by the government; gives exclusive rights of an invention to its inventor for 20 years. **637**, 638

PayPal, 443–444, 450

payroll system A type of transaction system that generates employee payroll amounts and reports. **473**

PB. *See* petabyte (PB)

PC (personal computer) A type of computer based on a microprocessor and designed to be used by one person at a time; also called a microcomputer. 14, 19
  databases and, 551

described, **21**
Internet usage and, 306
overview, 6, 21–24
security and, 600
PCI Express (PCIe) bus One of the buses most commonly used to connect peripheral devices. 68, **69**
PCI (Peripheral Component Interconnect), 67, 68–69, 153, 288
PDAs (personal digital assistants), 20–21
PDLC (program development life cycle) The process containing the five phases of program development: analyzing, designing, coding, debugging and testing, and implementing and maintaining application software. 495, **511**, 512–528
pen(s)
-based computers, 132–134
overview of, 132
Performance Rights Act, 642
period (.), 31, 32, 37
Perl, 418, 419, 579
personal area network. *See* PAN (personal area network)
personal finance software, 245
personal operating system A type of operating system designed to be installed on a single personal computer. **185**
personal publishing software, 243–244
petabyte (PB) Approximately 1,000 terabytes. **52**
Pew Internet & American Life Project, 302, 319, 662
PGP (Pretty Good Privacy), 359
pharming The use of spoofed domain names to obtain personal information to be used in fraudulent activities. **375**, 377–378
phishing The use of spoofed e-mail messages to gain credit card numbers and other personal data to be used for fraudulent purposes. 37, 347, **373**, 374–375, 377–379, 610
Phoneline standard, 280–281
photo printer An output device designed for printing digital photographs. **163**, 164
photos, digital, 7, 55, 163, 164, 400–401. *See also* graphics; images
Photoshop (Adobe), 241
PHP (PHP Hypertext Preprocessor), 520, 578, 579
phrase searching, 314–315
PINs (personal identification numbers), 352, 442–443

pipelining The capability of a CPU to begin processing a new instruction as soon as the previous instruction completes the first stage of the machine cycle. **80**
pixel The smallest colorable area in an electronic image, such as a scanned image, a digital photograph, or an image displayed on a display screen. 54–55, **151**, 153, 155, 157, 241
PL/1 (programming language), 535
plagiarism Presenting someone else's work as your own. **640**
plasma display A type of flat-panel display that uses layers of gas to display images; most often used on large displays. **158**
PLM (product lifecycle management) system A system designed to manage a product as it moves through the various stages of its life cycle, from design to retirement. **477**
Plug and Play, 71, 180
plug-ins, 401, 409
PNG An image format designed specifically for use with Web page images. 401, **402**, 403
podcast A recorded audio or video file that can be played or downloaded via the Web. **32**, 241, 330
pointing device An input device that moves an on-screen pointer, such as an arrow, to allow the user to select objects on the screen. **131**, 132
pornography, 382
port A connector on the exterior of a computer to which a device may be attached. 57, **70**, 71–72, 153–154
portability, 520
portable computer A small personal computer, such as a notebook, tablet, netbook, or ultra-mobile PC (UMPC), designed to be carried around easily. 10, 19, **23**, 24
portable fuel cell chargers, 670
portable printer A small, lightweight printer designed to be used while on the go. 163, 164
portable scanner A scanner designed to capture input while on the go. 139, **140**
portal Web page A Web page designed to be designated as a browser home page; typically can be customized to display personalized content. **329**
portrait orientation, 228

POS (point-of-sale) systems, 9–10, 141–142, 473, 595
possessed knowledge access system An access control system that uses information only the individual should know to identify that individual. **352**
possessed object access system An access control system that uses a physical object an individual has in his or her possession to identify that individual. **353**, 354
POST (power-on self-test), 65
power supplies, 57–58
Powerline standard, 280–281
PowerPoint (Microsoft), 238. *See also* presentation graphics software
ppm (pages per minute), 160
PRAM (phase change random access memory), 64
prefetch unit The part of a CPU core that attempts to retrieve data and instructions before they are needed for processing in order to avoid delays. **73**, 74
preliminary investigation The phase of the system development life cycle in which a brief feasibility study is performed to assess whether or not a full-scale project should be undertaken. **488**, 489
presence technology Technology that enables one computing device (such as a computer or mobile phone) to locate and identify the current status of another device on the same network. 318, **622**, 623
presentation graphic An image, such as a graph or text chart, designed to visually enhance a presentation. 237
presentation graphics software Application software used to create presentation graphics and electronic slide shows. 221, 237, **238**, 239–240
PriceGrabber.com, 434
Priceline.com, 439, 637
primary key A specific field in a database table that uniquely identifies the records in that table.
composite, 551
described, **551**
principle of least privilege, 561
print
buffers, 184
queues, 184, 186
servers, 267
statements, 526, 527

printer An output device that produces output on paper. 34, 184, 186
 3D (three-dimensional), 163, **164**, 165
 barcode, 163, 164
 described, **159**
 dot-matrix, 159
 ink-jet, 159, **162**, 163
 laser, 159, **161**, 162
 overview, 159–165
 photo, **163**, 164
 portable/integrated, 163, **164**
 speed, 160
 wide-format, 163
privacy The state of being concealed or free from unauthorized intrusion. 37–39, 334–339
 databases and, 561
 described, **606**
 e-commerce and, 451–452
 legislation, 624
 overview, 606–616
 protecting, 623
 seals, 452
 video surveillance and, 620–621
 workplace, 621–623
privacy policy A policy, commonly posted on a company's Web site, that explains how personal information provided to that company will be used. 451–452, **609**, 610, 612
private-key encryption A type of encryption that uses a single key to encrypt and decrypt the file or message. **359**
problem analysis The phase of the program development life cycle in which the problem is carefully considered and the program specifications are developed. **511**, 512
procedural programming An approach to program design in which a program is separated into small modules that are called by the main program or another module when needed. **507**, 508–509
procedure calls, 507
processing Performing operations on data that has been input into a computer to convert that input to output. **10–11**, 14–15
processors. *See also* CPUs (central processing units)
 32-bit, 61
 64-bit, 61
 described, **58**
product(s)

ethically questionable, 649–650
 keys, 604
program(s). *See also* software
 representation, overview of, 51–56
 unauthorized alteration of, 368
 uninstalling, 77
program coding The phase of the program development life cycle in which the program code is written using a programming language. **520**
program debugging and testing The phase of the program development life cycle that ensures a program is correct and works as intended. **523**
program design The phase of the program development life cycle in which the program specifications are expanded into a complete design of the new program. 512–519
program development The process of creating application programs.
 described, **511**
 life cycle, 511
 overview, 506–547
 tools for facilitating, 528–531
program implementation and maintenance The phase of the program development life cycle in which the program is implemented and then maintained, as needed, to remain useful. **528**
programmer A person whose job it is to write, test, and maintain computer programs. 18, **511**, 520, 552
programming language A set of rules, words, symbols, and codes used to write computer programs. *See also specific programming languages*
 categories of, 532–535
 choosing, 520–521
 common, 535–541
 databases and, 549
 described, **531**
 first-generation, 532
 fourth-generation, **535**
 overview, 506–547
 second-generation, 533
 third-generation, 534
project
 folders, 497
 management software, 245
Prolog, 535
protective cases, for hardware, 597–598
protocols, 278–287

prototypes, **499**
prototyping A system development alternative whereby a small model, or prototype, of the system is built before the full-scale system development life cycle is undertaken. **499**
proximity cards, 621
pseudocode A program design tool that uses English-like statements to outline the logic of a program. **514**
public domain software Software that is not copyrighted and may be used without restriction. 214, **217**
public-key encryption A type of encryption that uses key pairs to encrypt and decrypt the file or message. **359**
punch cards, 12
Python A high-level, open-source, dynamic object-oriented programming language that can be used to develop a wide variety of applications. 17, 54, 520, 534, **541**

Q

quad-core CPU A CPU that contains four separate processing cores. **58**, 59
quantum computing A technology that applies the principles of quantum physics and quantum mechanics to computers to direct atoms or nuclei to work together as quantum bits (qubits), which function simultaneously as the computer's processor and memory. **83**, 84
query A request to see information from a database that matches specific criteria. 236–237, 535
 described, **571**
 design, 571–572
query languages, 549, 571
Quick Access toolbar, 223
Quick Launch toolbar, 181
QuickTime file format, 405
QWERTY keyboard, 130

R

Radicati Group, 35
RAID (redundant arrays of independent disks) A storage method that uses several hard drives working together, typically to increase performance and/or fault-tolerance. **119**, 120

radio frequency identification. *See* RFID (radio frequency identification)

radio networks, 260, 275–277

RAM (random access memory) Chips connected to the motherboard that provide a temporary location for the computer to hold data and program instructions while they are needed, 57, 79, 103
- adding more, 77
- CPUs and, 60, 61, 76
- databases and, 566
- described, **62**
- I/O and, 153
- memory management and, 183–184
- overview, 62–64

range extender A repeater for a wireless network. **289**

ranges, 230

RATs (Remote-Access Trojans), 367

RDBM (relational database management system) A type of database system in which data is stored in tables related by common fields; the most widely used database model today.
- described, **567**
- overview, 567–574

read-only memory. *See* ROM (read-only memory)

readers, 138–139

real numbers, 509

Real ID Act, 608, 625

real-time search engines, 312–313

Really Simple Syndication. *See* RSS (Really Simple Syndication)

RealNetworks, 642

Recall Corporation, 602

record A collection of related fields in a database. Also called a row.
- *See also* rows
- deleting, 570
- described, **234**
- overview, 549
- validation rules, 559

recovery utility programs, 101, 203–204

Recycle Bin, 77

recycling, 668–671

redundant arrays of independent disks. *See* RAID (redundant arrays of independent disks)

reference
- software, 244
- sites, 34, 328

regional networks, 27

register High-speed memory built into the CPU that temporarily stores data during processing. **65**, 73

Register.com, 450

registration codes, 604

registry, 179

Rehabilitation Act, 413

relational databases, 234, 235. *See also* databases
- creating, 569–571
- designing, 567–569
- examples of, 550–551
- maintaining, 573–574
- overview, 567–574
- retrieving information from, 571–572

relative cell referencing, 232–233

remote access software, 245

remote storage A storage device that is not directly connected to the computer being used, such as one accessed through a local network or the Internet. **114**, 115–116

repeater A device on a network that amplifies signals. **289**

repetition control structure A series of statements in a loop that are repeated until a particular condition is met. 516, **517**

repetitive stress injury. *See* RSI (repetitive stress injury)

report A formatted way of looking at information retrieved from a database table or the results of a query. 236–237, 549, 572
- described, **572**
- generators, 530

Report Wizard, 572, 573

requirements
- definition, 529
- management, 529

resolution
- of display devices, 152–153
- of images, 401
- of printers, 160
- of scanners, 140

resources, managing/monitoring, 180

résumés, falsified, 646–647

retailer Web sites, 331

reusable code, 522

RFID (radio frequency identification) A technology used to store and transmit data located in RFID tags. **142**, 143, 164, 261–262, 353. *See also* RFID tag

RFID tag A device containing a tiny chip and a radio antenna that is attached to an object so it can be identified using RFID technology. 142, 143, 164, 261–262, 353. *See also* RFID (radio frequency identification)

databases and, 574
- described, **605**
- e-commerce and, 432
- employee monitoring and, 621, 622
- presence technology and, 623

RFP (request for proposal), 495

RFQ (request for quotation), 495

Ribbon A feature found in recent versions of Microsoft Office that uses tabs to organize groups of related commands. 17, 221, **222**, 223, 227–229, 231, 235, 570

Rice University, 349

rich Internet application (RIA) A Web-based application that works like an installed software program. **531**

rich media ads, 453, 454

ripping software, 241–242

Roadrunner supercomputer, 27, 81

robot A device, controlled by a human operator or a computer, that can move and react to sensory input.
- business/industrial, 482–483
- described, **481**
- military, 481–482, 483
- personal/service, 483
- program development and, 530

robotics The study of robot technology. **481**, 482–483

Roker, Al, 136

ROLAP (Relational OLAP), 576

ROM (read-only memory) Nonvolatile chips located on the motherboard into which data or programs have been permanently stored. 62, **65**

root directory, 181

rootkits, 349

RoR (Ruby on Rails), 541

router A device that connects multiple networks together; routes packets to their next location in order to efficiently reach their destination. 265, 287–288, **289**, 357

row (database) A collection of related fields located in a single table in a database. **234**, 549

row (spreadsheet) A horizontal group of cells on a worksheet. **230**

RSI (repetitive stress injury) A type of injury, such as carpal tunnel syndrome, that is caused by performing the same physical movements over and over again. **652**, 653–658

RSS (Really Simple Syndication) A tool used to deliver selected Web content to subscribers as the content is published to a Web site. **329**, 330

Ruby A high-level, open-source, object-oriented programming language that is often used to develop Web applications. 534, **541**

ruggedized device A device (such as a portable computer or mobile phone) that is designed to withstand much more physical abuse than a conventional device. **598**

run time errors, 525, 526

S

SaaS (Software as a Service), 16, **218**, 219, 303

salami shaving, 371

sales tax, 451

SanDisk, 147

SAN (storage area network) A network of hard drives or other storage devices that provide storage for another network of computers. **114**, 115–116, 119

Sarbanes-Oxley Act, 119, 363, 383, 468, 622, 625, 645, 648, 671

SAS (company), 576

satellite An earth-orbiting device that relays communications signals over long distances. **277–278**

satellite Internet access Fast, direct Internet access via the airwaves and a satellite dish. 78, 309

satellite phone A mobile phone that communicates via satellite technology. 259, 260

scalability, 19

scandals, 648

scanner An input device that reads printed text and graphics and transfers them to a computer in digital form. 138, **139**, 140

scheduling routines, 180

SCM (supply chain management), 476

Scott, Kevin, 484, 573

Scratch (programming language), 534

screen readers, 413, 664, 665–666

scripting languages, 415, **418–420**

scripts, 418–420, 578

SCSI (Small Computer Systems Interface), 71, 105, 117

SDIO (Secure Digital Input/Output) standard, 72

SDK (software development kit) A programming package designed for a particular platform that enables programmers to develop applications for that platform more quickly and easily. **530–531**

SDLC (system development life cycle) The process consisting of the six phases of system development: preliminary investigation, system analysis, system design, system acquisition, system implementation, and system maintenance.
approaches to, 498–499
databases and, 552
described, **488**
overview, 488–498

SDRAM (synchronous dynamic RAM), 63, 64

search engine A software program used by a search site to retrieve matching Web pages from a search database. **312**

search site A Web site designed to help users search for Web pages that match specified keywords or selected categories. 34, **312**, 314–316

search site optimization. *See* SSO (search site optimization)

search tool A utility program designed to search for files on the user's hard drive. **201**, 202

second normal form (2NF), 568

Second Life, 639

sector A small piece of a track. **99**, 105

secure Web page A Web page that uses encryption to protect information transmitted via that Web page. **358**

security. *See also specific topics*
browsers and, 33
data, **560**, 561
databases and, 560–561, 573
e-commerce and, 451–452, 455
flash drives and, 110
mobile phones and, 22
overview, 37, 182, 346–391, 592–631
patches, 182
people-driven, 370, 371
policies, 362–362
seals, 452
slots, 593
specialists, 18
threads, 605

security software Software, typically a suite of programs, used to protect your computer against a variety of threats. 204, **369**, 370

SEDs (surface-conduction electron-emitter displays), 158

selection control structure A series of statements in which the results of a decision determine the direction the program takes. 516, **517**

self-checkout systems, 10

self-destructing devices, 596

self-encrypting hard drive A hard drive that uses full disk encryption (FDE). **594**

Semantic Web, 480

sensor networks, 262

sequence control structure A series of statements that follow one another. **515**, 516

sequential access, 94

sequential processing, 183

serial transmission A type of data transmission in which the bits in a byte travel down the same path one after the other. **271**, 272

serif typefaces, 400

server(s). *See also* Web server
cloud computing and, 19
CPUs and, 58, 59, 60
databases and, 564–565
domain name system (DNS), 30, 375
file, 267
high-end (enterprise-class), 26
mail, 31, 35, 267
midrange, 20, **25**, 26
networks and, 27, 30, 245, 375
print, 267
remote access software and, 245
security and, 615–616
storage and, 102
virtualization, 26

server operating system A type of operating system designed to be installed on a network server. **185**, 186, 188–194

services, ethically questionable, 649–650

sharding, 566

shareware Copyrighted software that is distributed on the honor system; consumers should either pay for it or uninstall it after the trial period. 214, **216**

Shaul, Josh, 561

Sheth, Rajen, 263, 482

Shockwave, 404, 414, 421

Shockwave Player, 414

shopping, online Buying products or services over the Internet. 324, 325, 430–463. *See also* e-commerce

shopping bots, 434, 479

shopping cart
abandonment, 449
databases and, 577

shopping cart software E-commerce software designed to add ordering capabilities to an existing Web site. **449**

Shribman, Bill, 401, 447

signature, digital A unique digital code that can be attached to a file or an e-mail message to verify the identity of the sender and guarantee the file or message has not been changed since it was signed. **380**

signature capture devices, 134, 135

silicon photonics, 84–85

Silicon Valley Toxics Coalition, 671

Silverlight A technology used to create and display Web animations and interactive Web-based multimedia applications. 404, 414, 418

Simpson, O. J., 648

single-user database system A database located on a single computer and designed to be accessed by a single user. **564**

single-user licenses, 214

site
  licenses, 214
  -specific digital wallets, 445
  submission services, 452

slate tablets, 23

slide A one-page presentation graphic that can be displayed in a group with others to form an electronic slide show. **237**, 238

slide rule, 12

Slingbox, 245, 262

Sloan Digital Sky Survey, 574

SmallTalk, 535

smart card A credit card-sized piece of plastic containing a chip and other circuitry that can store data. **116**, 117, 195, 442

smart power strips, 667

smartphone A mobile device based on a mobile phone. **20–21**

Smekal, Martin, 24, 135

Smith, David, 361

SMS (Short Message Service), 35, 318

Snapfish, 434

social engineering tests, 594

social networking site A site that enables a community of individuals to communicate and share information. 10, 28, 29. *See also specific sites*
  databases and, 576
  described, **321**
  ethics and, 649, 650
  overview, 321–324
  security and, 381–382, 607, 610, 611

software The instructions, also called computer programs, that are used to

tell a computer what it should do. *See also* programs
  commands, common, 221–223
  described, **16**
  installed versus Web-based, 217
  Internet, 303–304

Software as a Service (SaaS). *See* Software as a Service (SaaS)

software development kit. *See* SDK (software development kit)

software license An agreement, either included in a software package or displayed on the screen during installation, that specifies the conditions under which a buyer of the program can use it. **213**, 214–217

software piracy The unauthorized copying of a computer program.
  described, **602**
  overview, 602–605

software suite A collection of software programs bundled together and sold as a single software package. **220**, 221

solar power, 667–668

solid state drive (SSD). *See* SSD

sound. *See* audio

source code A computer program before it is compiled.
  described, **521**
  documented, 522

spaghetti code, 508

spam Unsolicited, bulk e-mail sent over the Internet. 36–37, 606, **610**, 611, 613

spam filter An e-mail filter used to redirect spam from a user's Inbox. 610, **613**

speakers Output devices connected to computers that provide audio output. 15, **165**

spear phishing A personalized phishing scheme targeted at an individual. 373, **374**, 375

speech recognition system A system, consisting of appropriate hardware and software, used to recognize voice input, such as dictation or audio computer commands. 36, 148, **149**, 190, 228

spim Spam sent via IM. 610

sponsored links, 453

spooling The process of placing items in a buffer so the appropriate device (such as a printer) can retrieve them when needed. **184**, 185

spreadsheet A document containing a group of values and other data

organized into rows and columns; also called a worksheet in a spreadsheet program. **230**, 231–233, 237

spreadsheet software Application software used to create spreadsheets, which typically contain a great deal of numbers and mathematical computations organized into rows and columns. 221, **230**, 232–233

spyware A software program that is installed without the user's permission and that secretly gathers information to be sent to others. 78, **338**, 339

SQL (structured query language) A popular query language standard for information retrieval in relational databases. 452, 535, 571, 574. *See also* query

SQL Server (Microsoft), 551

SSD (solid-state drive) A hard drive that uses flash memory media instead of metal magnetic hard disks. 96–97, **100**, 101–103

SSL (Secure Sockets Layer), 358

SSO (search site optimization) The process of evaluating a Web site and making changes as needed to improve search site results. **453**

SSTP (Streamlined Sales Tax Project), 451

star network A network that uses a host device connected directly to several other devices. **266**, 279

Start button, 17

status bar, 33

status updates, 319

stealth tracking software, 596

storage The operation of saving data, programs, or output for future use.
  alternatives, evaluating, 121
  described, **10–11**
  external, 93–94
  history of computers and, 13
  internal, 93–94
  for large computer systems, 118–119
  network, 114–116
  overview, 93–127

storage area network. *See* SAN (storage area network)

storage device A piece of hardware, such as a DVD drive, into which a storage medium is inserted to be read from or written to. 15, **93**, 94

storage medium The part of a storage system where data is stored, such as a DVD disc. **93**, 94

storage server A storage device designed for large computer systems and that typically contains multiple high-speed hard drives. **119**

storefront software E-commerce software that facilitates the creation of an online store. 447, **448**, 449

storyboard An ordered series of sketches that can be developed during the design process of an animated sequence or other multimedia component of a Web site that illustrates what each page or screen will look like. 410, **411**

Stoudt, Christiaan, 454

streaming video, 406. *See also* video

stress, dealing with, 658–661

structure charts, 512

structured programming, 508

structured query language. *See* SQL (structured query language)

stylus An input device that is used to write electronically on the display screen. **132**

subscription site A site that sells access to its online content. **438**

Sun Microsystems, 535, 540

supercomputer The fastest, most expensive, and most powerful type of computer. 20, **26**, 27, 479

supercomputing cluster A supercomputer comprised of numerous smaller computers connected together to act as a single computer. **27**

Supreme Court, 451, 624, 638

surface computing, 136

surge suppressor A device that protects a computer system from damage due to electrical fluctuations. **598**

swap files, 184

switch A device used to connect multiple devices on a single (typically wired) network; forwards packets to only the intended recipient. **288**, 289

Symantec, 364, 371, 373

Symbian OS An operating system widely used with mobile phones; primarily used outside North America. **197**

synonyms, 315–316

syntax error A programming error that occurs when the programmer has not followed the rules of the programming language. **525**

system A collection of elements and procedures that interact to accomplish a goal. **467**

system analysis The phase of the system development life cycle in which

a problem area is thoroughly examined to determine what should be done. **489–491**

system acquisition The phase of the system development life cycle in which hardware, software, and other necessary system components are acquired. 493, **494**

system clock The timing mechanism within the computer system that synchronizes the computer's operations. 60–61, **75**, 76

system conversion, 496–497

system design The phase of the system development life cycle in which a model of the new system and how it will work is formally established. **492**, 493

system development The process of designing and implementing a new or modified system.
approaches to, 498–499
described, **468**
life cycle, 488
need for, 468
overview, 466–505
responsibility for, 484–488

system failure The complete malfunction of a computer system. 591, **592**

system implementation The phase of the system development life cycle that encompasses activities related to making the system operational. **495–496**, 497

system maintenance The phase of the system development life cycle in which minor adjustments are made to the finished system to keep it oper-ational until the end of the system's life or until the time that the system needs to be redesigned. 77–78, **497**

system software Programs, such as the operating system, that control the operation of a computer and its devices, as well as enable application software to run on the computer.
described, **177–178**
overview, 16–17, 178–188
for PCs, 188–194

system tray, 17, 179

system unit The main box of a computer that houses the CPU, motherboard, memory, and other devices. 14, 15, **56**, 57–72

systems analyst A person who studies systems in an organization in order to determine what work needs to be done and how this work may best be achieved. **484**, 485

T

tabbed browsing, 33

table In a relational database, a collection of related records or rows. 227, 229
creating, 569
data definition and, 556–557
described, **235**
overview, 549
relating, 570

tablet computer A portable computer about the size of a notebook that is designed to be used with an electronic pen. **23**, 133

TabletKiosk, 24, 135

TAEUS International, 75

tamper evident labels, 596–597

Task Manager, 179

taskbar
buttons, 17
toolbar, 17

taxes, collecting, 451

TB. *See* terabyte (TB)

TCP/IP (Transmission Control Protocol/Internet Protocol) A networking protocol that uses packet switching to facilitate the transmission of messages; the protocol used with the Internet. **278**, 279, 284

Tekunoff, Mark, 64, 114

Telecommunications Act, 304

telecommuting The use of computers and networking technology to enable an individual to work from a remote location. 263, **264**

telemedicine The use of networking technology to provide medical information and services. **264**, 265

telephone service, 259–260

telepresence video conferencing, 263

telesurgery A form of robot-assisted surgery in which the doctor's physical location is different from the patient's physical location and the doctor controls the robot remotely over the Internet or another network. **264**, 265

television, 260, 262, 275, 277
broadband-enabled, 307, 327
Internet usage and, 307

temporary files, 77

terabyte (TB) Approximately one trillion bytes. **52**

terrorism, 349, 593, 602, 620

testing, 496, 518, 523
program development and, 526–527
security and, 600

text Alphanumeric characters kept in a text, not graphic, format. *See also* fonts
alternate, **413**
described, **400**

text messaging A way of exchanging real-time typed messages with other individuals via a cellular network and, typically, cell phones. 20, 32, 35, **318**

thin client A personal computer designed to access a network for processing and data storage, instead of performing those tasks locally; also called a network computer (NC). **24**

third normal form (3NF), 568

3D applications, 26

3D chips, 85

3D display devices, 154

3D printer An output device designed to print three-dimensional objects, such as product prototypes. 163, **164**, 165

3D virtual worlds, 39, 84–85, 398, 399

three-tier database system, 565

throughput, 62. *See also* bandwidth

throw-away e-mail address An e-mail address used only for nonessential purposes and activities that may result in spam; the address can be disposed of and replaced if spam becomes a problem. **611**

thumb wheel, 137

thumbnail image A small image on a Web page that is linked to a larger, higher-resolution image. **403**

TIFF (Tagged Information File Format) files, 401

time on page statistics, 422

Tinker, John, 100

<TITLE> tag, 415

toolbars, 17, 33, 34, 221–223

top-down design, 508

Toshiba, 670

touch pad A small rectangular-shaped input device, often found on notebook computers, that is touched with the finger or thumb to control an on-screen pointer and make selections. **137**

touch screen A display device that is touched with the finger to issue commands or otherwise provide input to the connected device. 133, **135**, 138, 154–155

TPS (transaction processing system) A type of information system that processes and records data created by an organization's business transactions. **472**, 473

TRACELESS systems, 636

track A concentric path on a disk where data is recorded. **99**, 105, 106

trackballs, 137

trademark A word, phrase, symbol, or design that identifies goods or services. 30, 450–451, **635**, 636–637

traditional system development An approach to system development whereby the six phases of the system development life cycle are carried out in a predetermined sequence. **498**

tranceivers, 57

TransferJet A networking standard for very short-range wireless connections between devices; devices need to touch in order to communicate. **286**

transistors, 13, 57, 72

translation, 482

transportation management system. *See* TMS (transportation management system)

Treasury Department (United States), 605

Trojan horse A malicious program that masquerades as something else. **366**, 367

TRUSTe trustmark, 452

Tucows, 216

Turing Test, 478

twisted-pair cable A networking cable consisting of wire strands twisted in sets of two and bound into a cable. **273**

Twitter, 22, 32, 318–319, 321–323, 368

twittering Sending short status updates about your current activities via the Twitter service. **318–319**

two-factor authentication Using two different methods to authenticate a user. **353**

Tyco International (company), 648

typosquatting, 637

U

ubiquitous computing, 5–6

Ultra Wideband. *See* UWB (Ultra Wideband)

UML (Unified Modeling Language) A set of standard notations for creating business models.
described, **514**
versions of, 514–515

UMPC (ultra-mobile PC) A portable personal computer that is small enough to fit in one hand; also called a handheld computer. 21, **23**, 67, 72, 130, 132, 194–198

unauthorized access Gaining access to a computer, network, file, or other resource without permission. **348**, 351–363

unauthorized use Using a computer resource for unapproved activities. **348**, 351–363

underscore (_), 31

Unicode An international coding system that can be used to represent text-based data in any written language. 53, **54**, 55, R-16

Unified Modeling Language. *See* UML (Unified Modeling Language)

uninstall utilities, 202

UNIVAC, 13

Universal Display Corporation, 157

UNIX An operating system developed in the late 1960s for midrange servers and mainframes; many variations of this operating system are in use today. 185, **193**

uploading, use of the term, 267

UPS (uninterruptible power supply) A device containing a built-in battery that provides continuous power to a computer and other connected components when the electricity goes out. 598, **599**

URL (Uniform Resource Locator) An Internet address (usually beginning with http://) that uniquely identifies a Web page. 29–31, 33–34
described, **30–31**
e-commerce and, 431, 450–455
promoting, 452–455
publishing Web sites and, 423
RSS and, 329
search engines and, 312
security and, 371, 377–379
trademarks and, 637
Web site design and, 412

USA PATRIOT Act, 619, 625

USB (Universal Serial Bus) A universal bus used to connect up to 127 peripheral devices to a computer without requiring the use of additional expansion cards.
described, **69**
display adapters, 153–154
drivers and, 180
hubs, 71
security tokens, 353–354
wireless, 285, **286**

USB flash drive A small storage device that plugs into a USB port and contains flash memory media. 15, 156, 203, 285, 286, 288
described, **112**

cost of, 121

overview, 112–114

security and, 110, 362–363, 366, 369, 592, 595, 596, 597

USB ports, 15, 57, 67, 121, 153, 154

overview, 70, 71

printers and, 160

use case diagrams, 492

user(s)

of computers, overview of, 17–19

databases and, 552–553

documentation and, 528

information system, 469–471

interfacing with, 179

of the Internet, 302

productivity support systems, 471–472

username A name that uniquely identifies a user on a specific computer network. 29, **31**, 597

utility program A type of software that performs a specific task, usually related to managing or maintaining the computer system.

described, **198**

downloading, 199

installing, 199

overview, 198–205

UWB (Ultra Wideband) A networking standard for very short-range wireless connections among multimedia devices. 284–285, **286**, 287

V

vacuum tubes, 12

vaporware, 650

Vardi, Moshe, 349

variable A named memory location defined in a computer program that is used to store the current value of a data item used in that program.

debugging and, 526

declaring, 509

described, **508**

Java and, 540

loops and, 514

VB.NET (Microsoft), 521

VBScript (Microsoft), 418, **419**, 578, 579

vehicle monitoring systems, 261

vendors, evaluating, 495

Verizon, 291, 310, 637

vertical hubs, 437

video A continuous stream of visual information broken into separate images or frames to be displayed one after the other to simulate the original visual event. See also video surveillance; videoconferencing

cards, 67, 79, 153–154

coding systems and, 56

described, **405**

editing software, 242–243

formats, 405–406

memory, 79

overview, 405–407

storing, on external hard drives, 77

streaming, 406

video-on-demand. See VOD (video-on-demand)

video surveillance The use of video cameras to monitor activities of individuals, such as employees or individuals in public locations, for work-related or crime-prevention purposes. **619**, 620–621

videoconferencing The use of computers, video cameras, microphones, and networking technologies to conduct face-to-face meetings over a network. **263**, 264

Vincent, Vincent John, 136

Virginia Tech shootings, 32

virtual account numbers, 442

virtual credit card numbers, 435, 442

virtual goods, 639

virtual memory A memory-management technique that uses hard drive space as additional RAM. **183**

virtual models, 397

virtual private network. See VPN (virtual private network)

virtual reality (VR) See VR (virtual reality)

virtualization Creating virtual (rather than actual) versions of a computing resource, such as several separate environments that are located on a single server but act like different servers. **25**, 26, 187

virus A software program installed without the user's knowledge and designed to alter the way a computer operates or to cause harm to the computer system. 37, 347, 361

described, **365**

drivers and, 180

flash drives and, 362–363

Visual Basic (Microsoft) A version of the BASIC programming language that is visual and supports object-oriented programming. 17, 534, **538**, 539, 549

Visual Basic for Applications (Microsoft), 530

visual learners, 398

visual programming languages, 534

Visual Studio (Microsoft), 538

VOD (video-on-demand) The process of downloading movies and television shows, on demand, via the Web. **327**, 438

voice input, 148–149

VoIP (Voice over Internet Protocol) The process of placing telephone calls via the Internet. 7, 148, 318

described, **320**

security and, 351, 360

volatile A characteristic of memory or storage in which data is not retained when the power to the computer is turned off. 64, 94

VPEs (visual programming environments), 534

VPN (virtual private network) A private, secure path over the Internet that provides authorized users a secure means of accessing a private network via the Internet. **270**, 360, 361

VR (virtual reality) The use of a computer to create three-dimensional environments that look like they do in the real world. 39, 84–85, **397**, 398, 399, 421

VRML (Virtual Reality Modeling Language), 421

vulnerability assessments, 594

W

W3C (World Wide Web Consortium), 304, 413, 417–418

wallet, digital A program or online service that holds a buyer's information (such as electronic payment, billing, and shipping information) that can be used to speed up online purchase transactions. **444–445**

Wal-Mart, 444, 615

Walt Disney Imagineering, 12

WAN (wide area network) A network that connects devices located in a large geographical area. **269**, 272, 289

war driving Driving around an area with a Wi-Fi-enabled computer or mobile device to find a Wi-Fi network to access and use without authorization. **350**, 351 waterfall model, 498, 499

watermark, digital A subtle alteration of digital content that is not noticeable when the work is viewed or played, but that identifies the copyright holder. **634**, 635

Watson, Graham, 175, 252–253

WBT (Web-based training) Instruction delivered on an individual basis via the Web. **332**, 397

Web analytic tools, 453

Web conference A face-to-face meeting taking place via the Web; typically uses video cameras and microphones to enable participants to see and hear each other. 320, **321**

Web logs. *See* blogs

Web mail Web-based e-mail. 35

Web page A document, typically containing hyperlinks to other documents, located on a Web server and available through the World Wide Web.

described, **28**

dynamic, 577

education and, 7, 9

printing, 34

secure, 358

Web server A computer that is continually connected to the Internet and hosts Web pages that are accessible through the Internet. 267, 447. *See also* servers

described, **28**

publishing Web sites to, 422–423

scripting languages and, 419

Web service A self-contained business application that operates over the Internet. 303

Web Slices, 33, 34

Web site A collection of related Web pages usually belonging to an organization or individual.

access, considerations, 412

audiences, determining, 409–410

described, **28**

design, **407–408**

e-commerce and, 447–449

maintaining, 422–423

multimedia and, 407–413

navigation, 411–412

principles, 408–409

promoting, 452–455

publishing, 422–423

testing, 422–423

unauthorized alteration of, 368

Web site authoring software A type of application program used to create

Web pages and entire Web sites. **421**, 422

Web site development The process of creating, testing, publishing, and maintaining a Web site. **414**, 415–423

Web-based multimedia Multimedia located on Web pages. *See also* multimedia

advantages/disadvantages of, 398–399

applications, 396–398

described, **395**

reasons to learn about, 395–396

Web-based software Software that is delivered on demand via the Web; also referred to as Software as a Service (SaaS) and cloudware. 16, 217, **218**, 219–220

Webinar A seminar presented via the Web. 320, **321**

Weick, Dave, 284, 301, 476

Weir, Greg, 216

WEP (Wired Equivalent Privacy), 356

WGBH Interactive, 401, 447

what-if analysis, 230, 233

whitelisting, 370, 371

wide area network. *See* WAN (wide area network)

Wi-Fi (802.11) A widely used networking standard for medium-range wireless networks. 7, 147, 259, 288, 291. *See also* Wi-Fi hotspots

adapters, 266

described, **281**

health issues and, 653

I/O and, 154, 156, 158–161

MANs and, 269

printers and, 160, 161

routers and, 289

SD cards, 282–283

security and, 349–351, 355–356, 360–362, 597

standard, 281–282

wireless spectrums and, 275–276

Wi-Fi hotspot A location that provides wireless Internet access to the public. 265, 266, 270, 291, 309. *See also* hotspots

described, **310–311**

security and, 350–351, 361, 362

Wi-Fi piggybacking Accessing an unsecured Wi-Fi network from your current location without authorization. **350**, 351

widgets, 327

Wiki A collaborative Web page that is designed to be edited and

republished by a variety of individuals. **334**

Wikipedia, 55, 334

wildcard characters, 315–316

WiMAX An emerging wireless networking standard that is faster and has a greater range than Wi-Fi. **283**, 287, 288, 309

Wind River VxWorks, 530

Wind River Workbench, 530

Windows (Microsoft) The primary personal computer operating system developed by Microsoft Corporation; the most recent version is Windows 7. *See also specific versions*

accessibility features, 666

coding systems and, 54

CPUs and, 186

described, **188**

Disk Cleanup, 77

launching programs with, 17

Live, 19, 35, 611

Media Center, 187, 190, 262

Media Player, 243

memory and, 63, 64

overview, 16, 188

program development and, 541

registry, 77–78

search tools and, 201

security and, 358, 600, 604, 611

versions of, 188–189

Windows 7 (Microsoft) The current version of Windows.

described, **190**

overview, 190–191

Windows desktop The background work area displayed on the screen in Microsoft Windows. **16**, 17

Windows Embedded A family of operating systems based on Windows that is designed for non-personal computer devices, such as cash registers and consumer electronic devices. 194–195, **196**, 197

Windows Explorer The file management program built into the Windows operating systems. 95

described, **198**

file management and, 182

overview, 198–202

storage and, 104

Windows Home Server (Microsoft), 192

Windows Mobile (Microsoft) The version of Windows designed for mobile phones. 194–195, **196**

Windows Server (Microsoft) The version of Windows designed for server use; the current version is Windows Server 2008 R2. **192**

Windows Vista (Microsoft)
Digital Copy and, 644
overview, 189–191
security and, 604
speech recognition and, 226

Windows XP (Microsoft), 189

WinZip, 203

WIPO (World Intellectual Property Organization), 636, 637

wired network A network in which computers and other devices are connected to the network via physical cables. **265**, 266

wireless access point A device on a wireless network that connects wireless devices to that network. **289**

wireless network A network in which computers and other devices are connected to the network without physical cables; data is typically sent via radio waves. *See also* Wi-Fi (802.11)
described, **265**
history of computers and, 14
overview, 265–266
standards, 281–287
transmission media for, 275–278

wireless power transmission, 258

wireless router A router with a built-in wireless access point; most often used to connect wireless devices to a network and an Internet connection and often contains a built-in switch. **289**

wireless spectrum, 275–276

Wireless USB A wireless version of USB designed to connect peripheral devices. 285, **286**

wireless Web, 307

WirelessHD (WiHD) An emerging wireless networking specification designed for connecting home consumer devices. **286**

WISPs (wireless ISPs), 302

WML (Wireless Markup Language) A language used to display Web pages on WAP-enabled devices, such as some mobile phones. **418**

WMV (Windows Media Video) format, 405

Word (Microsoft), 225, 226, 227, 359. *See also* word processing

word processing Using a computer and word processing software to create, edit, save, and print written documents, such as letters, contracts, and manuscripts.
concepts, 224–229
described, **225**
documents, creating, 227–228
templates, 229

word processing software Application software used to create, edit, save, and print written documents. 18

word size, 61

word wrap The feature in a word processing progra m that automatically returns the insertion point to the next line when the end of the screen line is reached. 227, 228

workbook A collection of worksheets saved in a single spreadsheet file. **230**

worksheet A single spreadsheet document in a spreadsheet program. **230**, 231

workstations, 22, 25, 58, 59, 60

World Wide Web (WWW) The collection of Web pages available through the Internet. *See also* browser; Web page; Web site
databases and, 576–578
described, **28**
history of, 6
overview, 27–28, 298–345
surfing, 33

WorldCom, 648

worm A malicious program designed to spread rapidly to a large number of computers by sending copies of itself to other computers. **366**, 367

WWW. *See* World Wide Web (WWW)

WYSIWYG editing, 422

XHTML (Extensible Hypertext Markup Language) A newer, stricter version of HTML that is based on XML.
AJAX and, 419
authoring tools and, 421, 422
described, **416**
meta tags and, 452
overview, 416–418
tags, 416–418
validators, 422, 423

XML (Extensible Markup Language) A set of rules used for exchanging data over the Web; addresses only the content, not the formatting of the data, and the content displays in an appropriate format based on the device being used.
databases and, 575
described, **416**
overview, 416–418
intelligent agents and, 480
tags, 416–418

Y

Yahoo!, 55, 201, 220, 315, 380
click fraud and, 455
Mail, 611
program development and, 531
Web site promotion through, 452

yottabyte (YB) Approximately 1,000 zettabytes. **52**

Young, Kimberly, 660

YouTube, 7, 19, 321, 322
databases and, 576
ethics and, 649, 650
mashups and, 420
multimedia and, 406, 420

Z

Zazzle, 434

Zemlin, Jom, 194, 526

zero normal form (ZNF), 568

zettabyte (ZB) Approximately 1,000 exabytes. **52**

ZigBee, 286, 287

Preface

The Shelly Cashman Series® offers the finest textbooks in computer education. We are proud that since Mircosoft Office 4.3, our series of Microsoft Office textbooks have been the most widely used books in education. With each new edition of our Office books, we make significant improvements based on the software and comments made by instructors and students. For this Microsoft Office 2010 text, the Shelly Cashman Series development team carefully reviewed our pedagogy and analyzed its effectiveness in teaching today's Office student. Students today read less, but need to retain more. They need not only to be able to perform skills, but to retain those skills and know how to apply them to different settings. Today's students need to be continually engaged and challenged to retain what they're learning.

With this Microsoft Office 2010 text, we continue our commitment to focusing on the user and how they learn best.

Objectives of This Textbook

Microsoft Office 2010: Essential is intended for a course that includes an essential introduction to Office 2010. No experience with a computer is assumed, and no mathematics beyond the high school freshman level is required. The objectives of this book are:

- To teach the fundamentals of, Microsoft Word 2010, Microsoft PowerPoint 2010, Microsoft Excel 2010, Microsoft Access 2010, and Microsoft Windows 7

- To expose students to practical examples of the computer as a useful tool

- To acquaint students with the proper procedures to create documents, worksheets, databases, and presentations suitable for coursework, professional purposes, and personal use

- To help students discover the underlying functionality of Office 2010 so they can become more productive

- To develop an exercise-oriented approach that allows learning by doing

New to This Edition

Microsoft Office 2010: Essential offers a number of new features and approaches, which improve student understanding, retention, transference, and skill in using Office 2010 programs. The following enhancements will enrich the learning experience:

- Office 2010 and Windows 7: Essential Concepts and Skills chapter prevents repetitive coverage of basic skills in the application chapters.

- Streamlined first chapters for each application allow the ability to cover more advanced skills earlier.

- Chapter topic redistribution offers concise chapters that ensure complete skill coverage.

- Expanded coverage of PowerPoint gives exposure to the numerous enhancements made to this application.

- New pedagogical elements enrich material creating an accessible and user-friendly approach.

  - Break Points, a new boxed element, identify logical stopping points and give students instructions regarding what they should do before taking a break.

  - Within step instructions, Tab | Group Identifiers, such as (Home tab | Bold button), help students more easily locate elements in the groups and on the tabs on the Ribbon.

  - Modified step-by-step instructions tell the student what to do and provide the generic reason why they are completing a specific task, which helps students easily transfer given skills to different settings.

The Shelly Cashman Approach

A Proven Pedagogy with an Emphasis on Project Planning

Each chapter presents a practical problem to be solved, within a project planning framework. The project orientation is strengthened by the use of Plan Ahead boxes, which encourage critical thinking about how to proceed at various points in the project. Step-by-step instructions with supporting screens guide students through the steps. Instructional steps are supported by the Q&A, Experimental Step, and BTW features.

A Visually Engaging Book that Maintains Student Interest

The step-by-step tasks, with supporting figures, provide a rich visual experience for the student. Call-outs on the screens that present both explanatory and navigational information provide students with information they need when they need to know it.

Supporting Reference Materials (Appendices, Quick Reference)

The appendices provide additional information about the Application at hand and include such topics and project planning guidelines and certification. With the Quick Reference, students can quickly look up information about a single task, such as keyboard shortcuts, and find page references of where in the book the task is illustrated.

Integration of the World Wide Web
The World Wide Web is integrated into the Office 2010 learning experience by (1) BTW annotations; (2) BTW, Q&A, and Quick Reference Summary Web pages; and (3) the Learn It Online section for each chapter.

End-of-Chapter Student Activities
Extensive end-of-chapter activities provide a variety of reinforcement opportunities for students where they can apply and expand their skills.

Instructor Resources

The Instructor Resources include both teaching and testing aids and can be accessed via CD-ROM or at www.cengage.com/login.

Instructor's Manual Includes lecture notes summarizing the chapter sections, figures and boxed elements found in every chapter, teacher tips, classroom activities, lab activities, and quick quizzes in Microsoft Word files.

Syllabus Easily customizable sample syllabi that cover policies, assignments, exams, and other course information.

Figure Files Illustrations for every figure in the textbook in electronic form.

PowerPoint Presentations A multimedia lecture presentation system that provides slides for each chapter. Presentations are based on chapter objectives.

Solutions to Exercises Includes solutions for all end-of-chapter and chapter reinforcement exercises.

Test Bank & Test Engine Test Banks include 112 questions for every chapter, featuring objective-based and critical thinking question types, and including page number references and figure references, when appropriate. Also included is the test engine, ExamView, the ultimate tool for your objective-based testing needs.

Data Files for Students Includes all the files that are required by students to complete the exercises.

Additional Activities for Students Consists of Chapter Reinforcement Exercises, which are true/false, multiple-choice, and short answer questions that help students gain confidence in the material learned.

SAM: Skills Assessment Manager

SAM 2010 is designed to help bring students from the classroom to the real world. It allows students to train on and test important computer skills in an active, hands-on environment.

SAM's easy-to-use system includes powerful interactive exams, training, and projects on the most commonly used Microsoft Office applications. SAM simulates the Microsoft Office 2010 application environment, allowing students to demonstrate their knowledge and think through the skills by performing real-world tasks such as bolding word text or setting up slide transitions. Add in live-in-the-application projects, and students are on their way to truly learning and applying skills to business-centric documents.

Designed to be used with the Shelly Cashman Series, SAM includes handy page references so that students can print helpful study guides that match the Shelly Cashman textbooks used in class. For instructors, SAM also includes robust scheduling and reporting features.

Content for Online Learning

Course Technology has partnered with the leading distance learning solution providers and class-management platforms today. To access this material, instructors will visit our password-protected instructor resources available at www.cengage.com/coursetechnology. Instructor resources include the following: additional case projects, sample syllabi, PowerPoint presentations per chapter, and more. For additional information or for an instructor user name and password, please contact your sales representative. For students to access this material, they must have purchased a WebTutor PIN-code specific to this title and your campus platform. The resources for students may include (based on instructor preferences), but are not limited to: topic   review, review questions, and practice tests.

CourseNotes

Course Technology's CourseNotes are six-panel quick reference cards that reinforce the most important and widely used features of a software application in a visual and user-friendly format. CourseNotes serve as a great reference tool during and after the student completes the

course. CourseNotes are available for software applications such as Microsoft Office 2010, Word 2010, PowerPoint 2010, Excel 2010, Access 2010, and Windows 7. Topic-based CourseNotes are available for Best Practices in Social Networking, Hot Topics in Technology, and Web 2.0. Visit www.cengage.com/ct/coursenotes to learn more!

A Guided Tour

Add excitement and interactivity to your classroom with "*A Guided Tour*" product line. Play one of the brief mini-movies to spice up your lecture and spark classroom discussion. Or, assign a movie for homework and ask students to complete the correlated assignment that accompanies each topic. "*A Guided Tour*" product line takes the prep work out of providing your students with information about new technologies and applications and helps keep students engaged with content relevant to their lives; all in under an hour!

About Our Covers

The Shelly Cashman Series is continually updating our approach and content to reflect the way today's students learn and experience new technology. This focus on student success is reflected on our covers, which feature real students from Bentley University using the Shelly Cashman Series in their courses, and reflect the varied ages and backgrounds of the students learning with our books. When you use the Shelly Cashman Series, you can be assured that you are learning computer skills using the most effective courseware available.

Textbook Walk-Through

The Shelly Cashman Series Pedagogy: Project-Based — Step-by-Step — Variety of Assessments

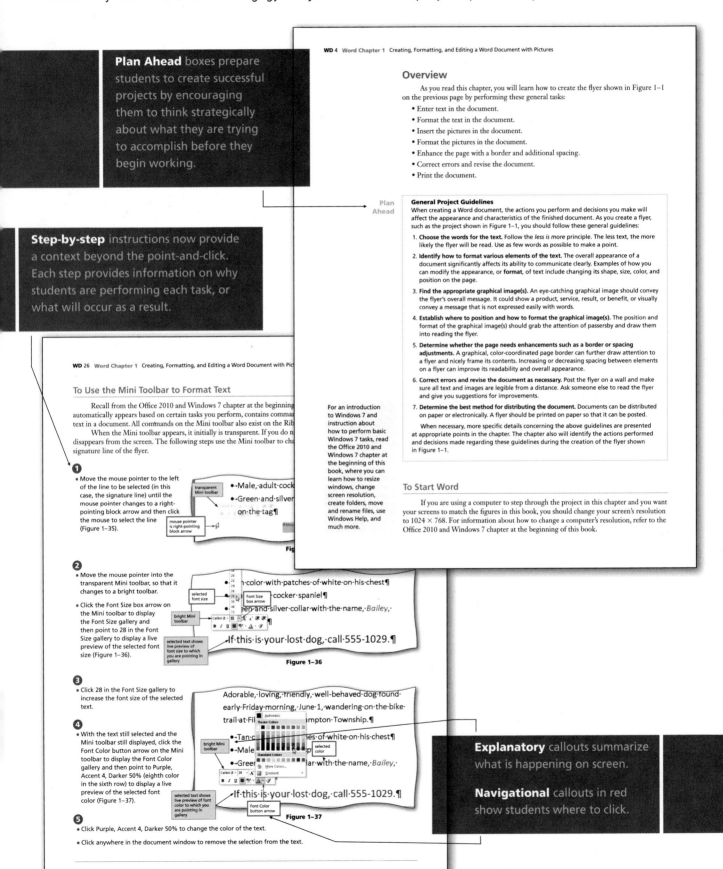

Plan Ahead boxes prepare students to create successful projects by encouraging them to think strategically about what they are trying to accomplish before they begin working.

Step-by-step instructions now provide a context beyond the point-and-click. Each step provides information on why students are performing each task, or what will occur as a result.

Overview

As you read this chapter, you will learn how to create the flyer shown in Figure 1–1 on the previous page by performing these general tasks:

- Enter text in the document.
- Format the text in the document.
- Insert the pictures in the document.
- Format the pictures in the document.
- Enhance the page with a border and additional spacing.
- Correct errors and revise the document.
- Print the document.

Plan Ahead

General Project Guidelines

When creating a Word document, the actions you perform and decisions you make will affect the appearance and characteristics of the finished document. As you create a flyer, such as the project shown in Figure 1–1, you should follow these general guidelines:

1. **Choose the words for the text.** Follow the *less is more* principle. The less text, the more likely the flyer will be read. Use as few words as possible to make a point.

2. **Identify how to format various elements of the text.** The overall appearance of a document significantly affects its ability to communicate clearly. Examples of how you can modify the appearance, or **format**, of text include changing its shape, size, color, and position on the page.

3. **Find the appropriate graphical image(s).** An eye-catching graphical image should convey the flyer's overall message. It could show a product, service, result, or benefit, or visually convey a message that is not expressed easily with words.

4. **Establish where to position and how to format the graphical image(s).** The position and format of the graphical image(s) should grab the attention of passersby and draw them into reading the flyer.

5. **Determine whether the page needs enhancements such as a border or spacing adjustments.** A graphical, color-coordinated page border can further draw attention to a flyer and nicely frame its contents. Increasing or decreasing spacing between elements on a flyer can improve its readability and overall appearance.

6. **Correct errors and revise the document as necessary.** Post the flyer on a wall and make sure all text and images are legible from a distance. Ask someone else to read the flyer and give you suggestions for improvements.

7. **Determine the best method for distributing the document.** Documents can be distributed on paper or electronically. A flyer should be printed on paper so that it can be posted.

When necessary, more specific details concerning the above guidelines are presented at appropriate points in the chapter. The chapter also will identify the actions performed and decisions made regarding these guidelines during the creation of the flyer shown in Figure 1–1.

For an introduction to Windows 7 and instruction about how to perform basic Windows 7 tasks, read the Office 2010 and Windows 7 chapter at the beginning of this book, where you can learn how to resize windows, change screen resolution, create folders, move and rename files, use Windows Help, and much more.

To Start Word

If you are using a computer to step through the project in this chapter and you want your screens to match the figures in this book, you should change your screen's resolution to 1024 × 768. For information about how to change a computer's resolution, refer to the Office 2010 and Windows 7 chapter at the beginning of this book.

To Use the Mini Toolbar to Format Text

Recall from the Office 2010 and Windows 7 chapter at the beginning automatically appears based on certain tasks you perform, contains commar text in a document. All commands on the Mini toolbar also exist on the Rib

When the Mini toolbar appears, it initially is transparent. If you do n disappears from the screen. The following steps use the Mini toolbar to cha signature line of the flyer.

1
- Move the mouse pointer to the left of the line to be selected (in this case, the signature line) until the mouse pointer changes to a right-pointing block arrow and then click the mouse to select the line (Figure 1–35).

transparent Mini toolbar

mouse pointer is right-pointing block arrow

• Male, adult cock
• Green and silver
on the tag¶

Fig

2
- Move the mouse pointer into the transparent Mini toolbar, so that it changes to a bright toolbar.
- Click the Font Size box arrow on the Mini toolbar to display the Font Size gallery and then point to 28 in the Font Size gallery to display a live preview of the selected font size (Figure 1–36).

selected font size

Font Size box arrow

bright Mini toolbar

selected text shows live preview of font size to which you are pointing in gallery

n color with patches of white on his chest¶

cocker spaniel¶

een and silver collar with the name, *Bailey,*

If this is your lost dog, call 555-1029.¶

Figure 1–36

3
- Click 28 in the Font Size gallery to increase the font size of the selected text.

4
- With the text still selected and the Mini toolbar still displayed, click the Font Color button arrow on the Mini toolbar to display the Font Color gallery and then point to Purple, Accent 4, Darker 50% (eighth color in the sixth row) to display a live preview of the selected font color (Figure 1–37).

Adorable, loving, friendly, well-behaved dog found early Friday morning, June 1, wandering on the bike trail at Fil   mpton Township.¶

bright Mini toolbar

selected color

Tan c   es of white on his chest¶
Male
Gree   ar with the name, *Bailey,*

selected text shows live preview of font color to which you are pointing in gallery

If this is your lost dog, call 555-1029.¶

Font Color button arrow

Figure 1–37

5
- Click Purple, Accent 4, Darker 50% to change the color of the text.
- Click anywhere in the document window to remove the selection from the text.

Explanatory callouts summarize what is happening on screen.

Navigational callouts in red show students where to click.

Q&A boxes offer questions students may have when working through the steps and provide additional information about what they are doing right where they need it.

Experiment Steps within our step-by-step instructions, encourage students to explore, experiment, and take advantage of the features of the Office 2010 user interface. These steps are not necessary to complete the projects, but are designed to increase the confidence with the software and build problem-solving skills.

1
- With the shape still selected, click the More button (shown in Figure 3–6) in the Shape Styles gallery (Drawing Tools Format tab | Shape Styles group) to expand the gallery.

Q&A What if my shape is no longer selected?

Click the shape to select it.

- Point to Intense Effect - Brown, Accent 4 in the Shape Styles gallery to display a live preview of that style applied to the shape in the document (Figure 3–7).

Experiment
- Point to various styles in the Shape Styles gallery and watch the style of the shape change in the document.

2
- Click Intense Effect - Brown, Accent 4 in the Shape Styles gallery to apply the selected style to the shape.

Figure 3–7

Other Ways		
1. Click Format Shape Dialog Box Launcher (Drawing Tools Format tab | Shape Styles group), click Picture Color in left pane	(Format Shape dialog box), select desired colors, click Close button	shortcut menu, click Picture Color in left pane (Format Shape dialog box), select desired colors, click Close button
	2. Right-click shape, click Format Shape on	

Selecting Text

In many of the previous steps, you have selected text. Table 1–3 summarizes the techniques used to select various items.

Table 1–3 Techniques for Selecting Text		
Item to Select	**Mouse**	**Keyboard (where applicable)**
Block of text	Click at beginning of selection, scroll to end of selection, position mouse pointer at end of selection, hold down SHIFT key and then click; or drag through the text.	
Character(s)	Drag through character(s).	SHIFT+RIGHT ARROW or SHIFT+LEFT ARROW
Document	Move mouse to left of text until mouse pointer changes to a right-pointing block arrow and then triple-click.	CTRL+A
Graphic	Click the graphic.	
Line	Move mouse to left of line until mouse pointer changes to a right-pointing block arrow and then click.	HOME, then SHIFT+END or END, then SHIFT+HOME
Lines	Move mouse to left of first line until mouse pointer changes to a right-pointing block arrow and then drag up or down.	HOME, then SHIFT+DOWN ARROW or END, then SHIFT+UP ARROW
Paragraph	Triple-click paragraph; or move mouse to left of paragraph until mouse pointer changes to a right-pointing block arrow and then double-click.	CTRL+SHIFT+DOWN ARROW or CTRL+SHIFT+UP ARROW
Paragraphs	Move mouse to left of paragraph until mouse pointer changes to a right-pointing block arrow, double-click, and then drag up or down.	CTRL+SHIFT+DOWN ARROW or CTRL+SHIFT+UP ARROW repeatedly
Sentence	Press and hold down CTRL key and then click sentence.	
Word	Double-click the word.	CTRL+SHIFT+RIGHT ARROW or CTRL+SHIFT+LEFT ARROW
Words	Drag through words.	CTRL+SHIFT+RIGHT ARROW or CTRL+SHIFT+LEFT ARROW repeatedly

To Save an Existing Document with the Same File Name

You have made several modifications to the document since you last saved it. Thus, you should save it again. The following step saves the document again. For an example of the step listed below, refer to the Office 2010 and Windows 7 chapter at the beginning of this book.

1 Click the Save button on the Quick Access Toolbar to overwrite the previously saved file.

Break Point: If you wish to take a break, this is a good place to do so. You can quit Word now (refer to page WD 44 for instructions). To resume at a later time, start Word (refer to pages WD 4 and WD 5 for instructions), open the file called Found Dog Flyer (refer to page WD 45 for instructions), and continue following the steps from this location forward.

Inserting and Formatting Pictures in a Word Document

With the text formatted in the flyer, the next step is to insert digital pictures in the flyer and format the pictures. Flyers usually contain graphical images, such as a picture, to attract the attention of passersby. In the following pages, you will perform these tasks:

1. Insert the first digital picture into the flyer and then reduce its size.
2. Insert the second digital picture into the flyer and then reduce its size.
3. Change the look of the first picture and then the second picture.

...on name to the shape. The following steps add text to a shape.

Figure 3–8

Break Points identify logical breaks in the chapter if students need to stop before completing the project.

Textbook Walk-Through

Chapter Summary A concluding paragraph, followed by a listing of the tasks completed within a chapter together with the pages on which the step-by-step, screen-by-screen explanations appear.

To Quit Word

The project now is complete. Thus, the following steps quit Word. For an example of the step listed below, refer to the Office 2010 and Windows 7 chapter at the beginning of this book.

1. If you have one Word document open, click the Close button on the right side of the title bar to close the document and quit Word; or if you have multiple Word documents open, click File on the Ribbon to open the Backstage view and then click Exit in the Backstage view to close all open documents and quit Word.

2. If a Microsoft Word dialog box appears, click the Save button to save any changes made to the document since the last save.

BTW
Printed Borders
If one or more of your borders do not print, click the Page Borders button (Page Layout tab | Page Background group), click the Options button (Borders and Shading dialog box), click the Measure from box arrow and click Text, change the four text boxes to 15 pt, and then click the OK button in each dialog box. Try printing the document again. If the borders still do not print, adjust the text boxes in the dialog box to a number smaller than 15 point.

Chapter Summary

In this chapter, you have learned how to enter text in a document, format text, insert a picture, format a picture, add a page border, and print a document. The items listed below include all the new Word skills you have learned in this chapter.

1. Start Word (WD 4)
2. Type Text (WD 6)
3. Display Formatting Marks (WD 7)
4. Insert a Blank Line (WD 7)
5. Wordwrap Text as You Type (WD 8)
6. Check Spelling and Grammar as You Type (WD 9)
7. Save a Document (WD 12)
8. Center a Paragraph (WD 14)
9. Select a Line (WD 15)
10. Change the Font Size of Selected Text (WD 16)
11. Change the Font of Selected Text (WD 17)
12. Change the Case of Selected Text (WD 18)
13. Apply a Text Effect to Selected Text (WD 19)

23. Bold Text (WD 28)
24. Change Theme Colors (WD 28)
25. Save an Existing Document with the Same File Name (WD 30)
26. Insert a Picture (WD 31)
27. Zoom the Document (WD 33)
28. Resize a Graphic (WD 34)
29. Resize a Graphic by Entering Exact Measurements (WD 36)
30. Apply a Picture Style (WD 37)
31. Apply Picture Effects (WD 38)
32. View One Page (WD 40)
33. Add a Page Border (WD 41)
34. Change Spacing before and after a Paragraph (WD 44)
35. Quit Word (WD 44)
36. Open a Document from Word (WD 45)
37. Insert Text in an Existing Document (WD 46)
38. Delete Text (WD 47)
39. Move Text (WD 47)
40. Change Document Properties (WD 49)
41. Print a Document (WD 51)

... (WD 26)

... profile, your instructor may have assigned an autogradable ... o, log into the SAM 2010 Web site at www.cengage.com/sam2010 ... nd start files.

BTW
Quick Reference
For a table that lists how to complete the tasks covered in this book using the mouse, Ribbon, shortcut menu, and keyboard, see the Quick Reference Summary at the back of this book, or visit the Word 2010 Quick Reference Web page (scsite.com/wd2010/qr).

STUDENT ASSIGNMENTS

Learn It Online

Test your knowledge of chapter content and key terms.

Instructions: To complete the Learn It Online exercises, start your browser, click the Address bar, and then enter the Web address **scsite.com/wd2010/learn**. When the Word 2010 Learn It Online page is displayed, click the link for the exercise you want to complete and then read the instructions.

Chapter Reinforcement TF, MC, and SA
A series of true/false, multiple choice, and short answer questions that test your knowledge of the chapter content.

Who Wants To Be a Computer Genius?
An interactive game that challenges your knowledge of chapter content in the style of a television quiz show.

Flash Cards
An interactive learning environment where you identify chapter key terms associated with displayed definitions.

Wheel of Terms
An interactive game that challenges your knowledge of chapter key terms in the style of the television show *Wheel of Fortune*.

Practice Test
A series of multiple choice questions that test your knowledge of chapter content and key terms.

Crossword Puzzle Challenge
A crossword puzzle that challenges your knowledge of key terms presented in the chapter.

Apply Your Knowledge

Reinforce the skills and apply the concepts you learned in this chapter.

Modifying Text and Formatting a Document
Note: To complete this assignment, you will be required to use the Data Files for Students. See the inside back cover of this book for instructions on downloading the Data Files for Students, or contact your instructor for information about accessing the required files.

Instructions: Start Word. Open the document, Apply 1-1 Buffalo Photo Shoot Flyer Unformatted, from the Data Files for Students. The document you open is an unformatted flyer. You are to modify text, format paragraphs and characters, and insert a picture in the flyer.

Perform the following tasks:
1. Delete the word, single, in the sentence of body copy below the headline.
2. Insert the word, Creeks, between the words, Twin Buffalo, in the sentence of body copy below the headline.
3. At the end of the signature line, change the period to an exclamation point.
4. Center the headline and the signature line.
5. Change the theme colors to the Aspect color scheme.
6. Change the font and font size of the headline to 48-point Impact, or a similar font. Change the case of the headline text to all capital letters. Apply the text effect called Gradient Fill – Orange, Accent 1, Outline – White to the headline.
7. Change the font size of body copy between the headline and the signature line to 20 point.
8. Use the Mini toolbar to change the font size of the signature line to 26 point.
9. Select the words, hundreds of buffalo, in the paragraph below the headline and underline them.

Learn It Online Every chapter features a Learn It Online section that is comprised of six exercises. These exercises include True/False, Multiple Choice, Short Answer, Flash Cards, Practice Test, and Learning Games.

Apply Your Knowledge This exercise usually requires students to open and manipulate a file from the Data Files that parallels the activities learned in the chapter. To obtain a copy of the Data Files for Students, follow the instructions on the inside back cover of this text.

Extend Your Knowledge

Extend the skills you learned in this chapter and experiment with new skills. You may need to use Help to complete the assignment.

Modifying Text and Picture Formats and Adding Page Borders

Note: To complete this assignment, you will be required to use the Data Files for Students. See the inside back cover of this book for instructions on downloading the Data Files for Students, or contact your instructor for information about accessing the required files.

Instructions: Start Word. Open the document, Extend 1-1 TVC Cruises Flyer, from the Data Files for Students. You will enhance the look of the flyer shown in Figure 1–76. *Hint:* Remember, if you make a mistake while formatting the picture, you can reset it by clicking the Reset Picture button or Reset Picture button arrow (Picture Tools Format tab | Adjust group).

Perform the following tasks:

1. Use Help to learn about the following formats: remove bullets, grow font, shrink font, art page borders, decorative underline(s), picture bullets, picture border shading, shadow picture effects, and color saturation and tone.

2. Remove the bullet from the paragraph below the picture.

3. Select the text, 10 percent, and use the Grow Font button to increase its font size.

4. Add an art page border to the flyer. If the border is not in color, add color to it.

5. Change the solid underline below the word, cruises, to a decorative underline. Change

---

add art page border

NEED AN ESCAPE?

change border color and add shadow effect; change color saturation and color tone

remove bullet → • **Tango Vacation Club members receiv**
a 10 percent discount for cruises
booked during May. Select from a
variety of destinations.

use Grow Font button to increase font size

      An experience of a lifetime awaits you

change to picture bullets →
- **Ultimate relaxation**
- **Endless fun and entertainment**
- **Breathtaking scenery**
- **Friendly, attentive staff**
- **Clean facilities**

Interested? Call TVC at 555-1029

Figure 1–76

Extend Your Knowledge projects at the end of each chapter allow students to extend and expand on the skills learned within the chapter. Students use critical thinking to experiment with new skills to complete each project.

Make It Right

Analyze a document and correct all errors and/or improve the design.

Correcting Spelling and Grammar Errors

Note: To complete this assignment, you will be required to use the Data Files for Students. See the inside back cover of this book for instructions on downloading the Data Files for Students, or contact your instructor for information about accessing the required files.

Instructions: Start Word. Open the document, Make It Right 1-1 Karate Academy Flyer Unchecked, from the Data Files for Students. The document is a flyer that contains spelling and grammar errors, as shown in Figure 1–77. You are to correct each spelling (red wavy underline) and grammar error (green and blue wavy underlines) by right-clicking the flagged text and then clicking the appropriate correction on the shortcut menu.

If your screen does not display the wavy underlines, click File on the Ribbon and then click Options in the Backstage view. When the Word Options dialog box is displayed, click Proofing in the left pane, be sure the 'Hide spelling errors in this document only' and 'Hide grammar errors in this document only' check boxes do not contain check marks, and then click the OK button. If your screen still does not display the wavy underlines, redisplay the Word Options dialog box, click Proofing, and then click the Recheck Document button.

Change the document properties, including keywords, as specified by your instructor. Save the revised document with the name, Make It Right 1-1 Karate Academy Flyer, and then submit it in the format specified by your instructor.

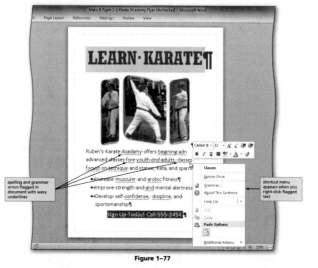

spelling and grammar errors flagged in document with wavy underlines

shortcut menu appears when you right-click flagged text

Figure 1–77

Make It Right projects call on students to analyze a file, discover errors in it, and fix them using the skills they learned in the chapter.

Textbook Walk-Through

In the Lab

Design and/or create a document using the guidelines, concepts, and skills presented in this chapter. Labs are listed in order of increasing difficulty.

Lab 1: Creating a Flyer with a Picture

Problem: As a part-time employee in the Student Services Center at school, you have been asked to prepare a flyer that advertises study habits classes. First, you prepare the unformatted flyer shown in Figure 1–78a, and then you format it so it looks like Figure 1–78b. *Hint:* Remember, if you make a mistake while formatting the flyer, you can click the Undo button on the Quick Access Toolbar to undo your last action.

Note: To complete this assignment, you will be required to use the Data Files for Students. See the inside back cover of this book for instructions on downloading the Data Files for Students, or contact your instructor for information about accessing the required files.

Instructions: Perform the following tasks:

1. Start Word. Display formatting marks on the screen.
2. Type the flyer text, unformatted, as shown in Figure 1–78a, inserting a blank line between the headline and the body copy. If Word flags any misspelled words as you type, check their spelling and correct them.
3. Save the document using the file name, Lab 1-1 Study Habits Flyer.
4. Center the headline and the signature line.
5. Change the theme colors to Concourse.
6. Change the font size of the headline to 36 point and the font to Ravie, or a similar font. Apply the text effect called Gradient Fill – Dark Red, Accent 6, Inner Shadow.
7. Change the font size of body copy between the headline and the signature line to 20 point.
8. Change the font size of the signature line to 22 point. Bold the text in the signature line.

In the Lab Three all new in-depth assignments per chapter require students to utilize the chapter concepts and techniques to solve problems on a computer.

Studying All Night?

blank line →

Let us help you! Our expert instructors teach effective stud
energy-building techniques.

Classes are $15.00 per session

Sessions last four weeks

Classes meet in the Student Services Center twice a week

Call 555-2838 or stop by to sign up today!

Figure 1–78 (a) Unforma

---

create a building block for Fair Grove Elementary School and insert the building block whenever you have to enter the school name. Resize table columns to fit contents. Check the spelling of the letter. Change the document properties, as specified by your instructor. Save the letter with Lab 3-3 Education Board Letter as the file name.

Cases and Places

Apply your creative thinking and problem solving skills to design and implement a solution.

Note: To complete these assignments, you may be required to use the Data Files for Students. See the inside back cover of this book for instructions on downloading the Data Files for Students, or contact your instructor for information about accessing the required files.

1: Create a Letter to a Potential Employer

Academic

As a student about to graduate, you are actively seeking employment in your field and have located an advertisement for a job in which you are interested. You decide to write a letter to the potential employer: Ms. Janice Tremont at Home Health Associates, 554 Mountain View Lane, Blue Dust, MO 64319.

The draft wording for the letter is as follows: I am responding to your advertisement for the nursing position in the *Blue Dust Press*. I have tailored my activities and education for a career in geriatric medicine. This month, I will graduate with concentrations in Geriatric Medicine (24 hours), Osteopathic Medicine (12 hours), and Holistic Nursing (9 hours). In addition to receiving my bachelor degree in nursing, I have enhanced my education by participating in the following activities: volunteered at Blue Dust's free health care clinic; attended several continuing education and career-specific seminars, including An Aging Populace, Care of the Homebound, and Special Needs of the Elderly; completed one-semester internship at Blue Dust Community Hospital in spring semester of 2012; completed Certified Nursing Assistant (CNA) program at Blue Dust Community College; and worked as nurse's aide for two years during college. I look forward to an interview so that we can discuss the position you offer and my qualifications. With my background and education, I am confident that I will make a positive contribution to Home Health Associates.

The letter should contain a letterhead that uses a shape and clip art, a table (use a table to present the areas of concentration), and a bulleted list (use a bulleted list to present the activities). Insert nonbreaking spaces in the newspaper name. Use the concepts and techniques presented in this chapter to create and format a letter according to the modified block style, creating appropriate paragraph breaks and rewording the draft as necessary. Use your personal information for contact information in the letter. Be sure to check the spelling and grammar of the finished letter. Submit your assignment in the format specified by your instructor.

2: Create a Letter Requesting Donations

Personal

As an alumnus of your historic high school, you are concerned that the building is being considered for demolition. You decide to write a letter to another graduate: Mr. Jim Lemon, 87 Travis Parkway, Vigil, CT 06802.

The draft wording for the letter is as follows: As a member of the class of 1988, you, like many others, probably have many fond memories of our alma mater, Vigil East High School. I recently learned that the building is being considered for demolition because of its age and structural integrity.

Cases & Places exercises call on students to create open-ended projects that reflect academic, personal, and business settings.

Continued >

Office 2010 and Windows 7: Essential Concepts and Skills

Objectives

You will have mastered the material in this chapter when you can:

- Perform basic mouse operations
- Start Windows and log on to the computer
- Identify the objects on the Windows 7 desktop
- Identify the programs in and versions of Microsoft Office
- Start a program
- Identify the components of the Microsoft Office Ribbon

- Create folders
- Save files
- Change screen resolution
- Perform basic tasks in Microsoft Office programs
- Manage files
- Use Microsoft Office Help and Windows Help

Office 2010 and Windows 7: Essential Concepts and Skills

Office 2010 and Windows 7

This introductory chapter covers features and functions common to Office 2010 programs, as well as the basics of Windows 7.

Overview

As you read this chapter, you will learn how to perform basic tasks in Windows and Office programs by performing these general activities:

- Start programs using Windows.
- Use features common across Office programs.
- Organize files and folders.
- Change screen resolution.
- Quit Office programs.

Introduction to the Windows 7 Operating System

Windows 7 is the newest version of Microsoft Windows, which is the most popular and widely used operating system. An **operating system** is a computer program (set of computer instructions) that coordinates all the activities of computer hardware such as memory, storage devices, and printers, and provides the capability for you to communicate with the computer.

The Windows 7 operating system simplifies the process of working with documents and programs by organizing the manner in which you interact with the computer. Windows 7 is used to run **application software**, which consists of programs designed to make users more productive and/or assist them with personal tasks, such as word processing.

Windows 7 has two interface variations, Windows 7 Basic and Windows 7 Aero. Computers with up to 1 GB of RAM display the Windows 7 Basic interface (Figure 1a). Computers with more than 1 GB of RAM also can display the Windows Aero interface (Figure 1b), which provides an enhanced visual appearance. The Windows 7 Professional, Windows 7 Enterprise, Windows 7 Home Premium, and Windows 7 Ultimate editions have the capability to use Windows Aero.

Using a Mouse

Windows users work with a mouse that has at least two buttons. For a right-handed user, the left button usually is the primary mouse button, and the right mouse button is the secondary mouse button. Left-handed people, however, can reverse the function of these buttons.

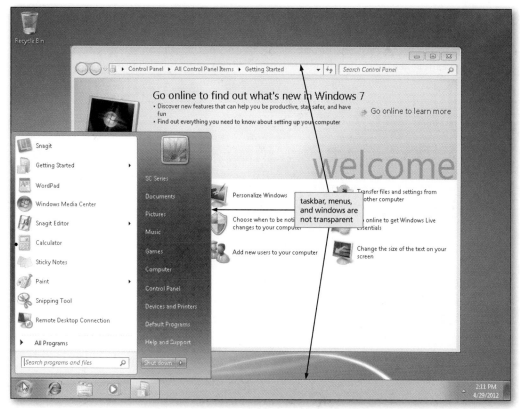

Figure 1 (a) Windows 7 Basic interface

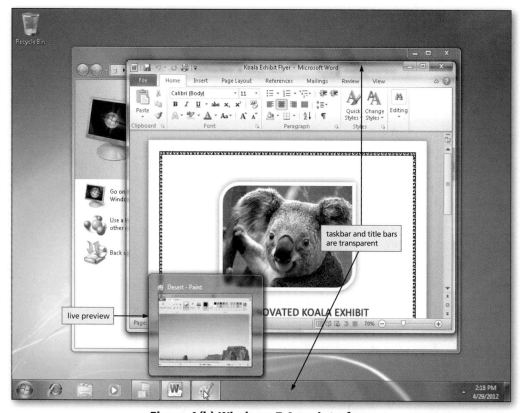

Figure 1 (b) Windows 7 Aero interface

Table 1 explains how to perform a variety of mouse operations. Some programs also use keys in combination with the mouse to perform certain actions. For example, when you hold down the CTRL key while rolling the mouse wheel, text on the screen becomes larger or smaller based on the direction you roll the wheel. The function of the mouse buttons and the wheel varies depending on the program.

Table 1 Mouse Operations		
Operation	**Mouse Action**	**Example***
Point	Move the mouse until the pointer on the desktop is positioned on the item of choice.	Position the pointer on the screen.
Click	Press and release the primary mouse button, which usually is the left mouse button.	Select or deselect items on the screen or start a program or program feature.
Right-click	Press and release the secondary mouse button, which usually is the right mouse button.	Display a shortcut menu.
Double-click	Quickly press and release the left mouse button twice without moving the mouse.	Start a program or program feature.
Triple-click	Quickly press and release the left mouse button three times without moving the mouse.	Select a paragraph.
Drag	Point to an item, hold down the left mouse button, move the item to the desired location on the screen, and then release the left mouse button.	Move an object from one location to another or draw pictures.
Right-drag	Point to an item, hold down the right mouse button, move the item to the desired location on the screen, and then release the right mouse button.	Display a shortcut menu after moving an object from one location to another.
Rotate wheel	Roll the wheel forward or backward.	Scroll vertically (up and down).
Free-spin wheel	Whirl the wheel forward or backward so that it spins freely on its own.	Scroll through many pages in seconds.
Press wheel	Press the wheel button while moving the mouse.	Scroll continuously.
Tilt wheel	Press the wheel toward the right or left.	Scroll horizontally (left and right).
Press thumb button	Press the button on the side of the mouse with your thumb.	Move forward or backward through Web pages and/or control media, games, etc.

*Note: the examples presented in this column are discussed as they are demonstrated in this chapter.

Scrolling

A **scroll bar** is a horizontal or vertical bar that appears when the contents of an area may not be visible completely on the screen (Figure 2). A scroll bar contains **scroll arrows** and a **scroll box** that enable you to view areas that currently cannot be seen. Clicking the up and down scroll arrows moves the screen content up or down one line. You also can click above or below the scroll box to move up or down a section, or drag the scroll box up or down to move up or down to move to a specific location.

Shortcut Keys

In many cases, you can use the keyboard instead of the mouse to accomplish a task. To perform tasks using the keyboard, you press one or more keyboard keys, sometimes identified as

Figure 2

a **shortcut key** or **keyboard shortcut**. Some shortcut keys consist of a single key, such as the F1 key. For example, to obtain help about Windows 7, you can press the F1 key. Other shortcut keys consist of multiple keys, in which case a plus sign separates the key names, such as CTRL+ESC. This notation means to press and hold down the first key listed, press one or more additional keys, and then release all keys. For example, to display the Start menu, press CTRL+ESC, that is, hold down the CTRL key, press the ESC key, and then release both keys.

Starting Windows 7

It is not unusual for multiple people to use the same computer in a work, educational, recreational, or home setting. Windows 7 enables each user to establish a **user account**, which identifies to Windows 7 the resources, such as programs and storage locations, a user can access when working with a computer.

Each user account has a user name and may have a password and an icon, as well. A **user name** is a unique combination of letters or numbers that identifies a specific user to Windows 7. A **password** is a private combination of letters, numbers, and special characters associated with the user name that allows access to a user's account resources. A **user icon** is a picture associated with a user name.

When you turn on a computer, an introductory screen consisting of the Windows logo and copyright messages is displayed. The Windows logo is animated and glows as the Windows 7 operating system is loaded. After the Windows logo appears, depending on your computer's settings, you may or may not be required to log on to the computer. **Logging on** to a computer opens your user account and makes the computer available for use. If you are required to log on to the computer, the **Welcome screen** is displayed, which shows the user names of users on the computer (Figure 3). Clicking the user name or picture begins the process of logging on to the computer.

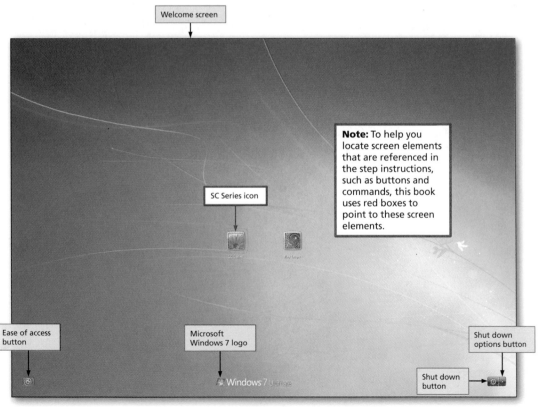

Note: To help you locate screen elements that are referenced in the step instructions, such as buttons and commands, this book uses red boxes to point to these screen elements.

Welcome screen

SC Series icon

Ease of access button

Microsoft Windows 7 logo

Shut down options button

Shut down button

Figure 3

At the bottom of the Welcome screen is the 'Ease of access' button, Windows 7 logo, a Shut down button, and a 'Shut down options' button. The following list identifies the functions of the buttons and commands that typically appear on the Welcome screen:

- Clicking the 'Ease of access' button displays the Ease of Access Center, which provides tools to optimize your computer to accommodate the needs of the mobility, hearing, and vision impaired users.
- Clicking the Shut down button shuts down Windows 7 and the computer.
- Clicking the 'Shut down options' button, located to the right of the Shut down button, provides access to a menu containing commands that perform actions such as restarting the computer, putting the computer in a low-powered state, and shutting down the computer. The commands available on your computer may differ.

  - The **Restart command** closes open programs, shuts down Windows 7, and then restarts Windows 7 and displays the Welcome screen.
  - The **Sleep command** waits for Windows 7 to save your work and then turns off the computer fans and hard disk. To wake the computer from the Sleep state, press the power button or lift a notebook computer's cover, and log on to the computer.
  - The **Shut down command** shuts down and turns off the computer.

To Log On to the Computer

After starting Windows 7, you might need to log on to the computer. The following steps log on to the computer based on a typical installation. You may need to ask your instructor how to log on to your computer. This set of steps uses SC Series as the user name. The list of user names on your computer will be different.

1

- Click the user icon (SC Series, in this case) on the Welcome screen (shown in Figure 3 on the previous page); depending on settings, this either will display a password text box (Figure 4) or will log on to the computer and display the Windows 7 desktop.

Q&A Why do I not see a user icon?

Your computer may require you to type a user name instead of clicking an icon.

Q&A What is a text box?

A text box is a rectangular box in which you type text.

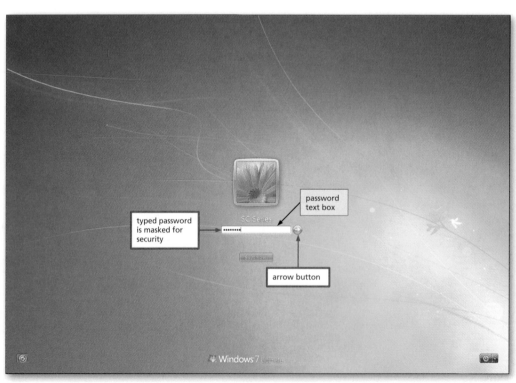

Figure 4

Q&A Why does my screen not show a password text box?

Your account does not require a password.

2

- If Windows 7 displays a password text box, type your password in the text box and then click the arrow button to log on to the computer and display the Windows 7 desktop (Figure 5).

Q&A

Why does my desktop look different from the one in Figure 5?

The Windows 7 desktop is customizable, and your school or employer may have modified the desktop to meet its needs. Also, your screen resolution, which affects the size of the elements on the screen, may differ from the screen resolution used in this book. Later in this chapter, you learn how to change screen resolution.

Figure 5

The Windows 7 Desktop

The Windows 7 desktop (Figure 5) and the objects on the desktop emulate a work area in an office. Think of the Windows desktop as an electronic version of the top of your desk. You can perform tasks such as placing objects on the desktop, moving the objects around the desktop, and removing items from the desktop.

When you start a program in Windows 7, it appears on the desktop. Some icons also may be displayed on the desktop. For instance, the icon for the **Recycle Bin**, the location of files that have been deleted, appears on the desktop by default. A **file** is a named unit of storage. Files can contain text, images, audio, and video. You can customize your desktop so that icons representing programs and files you use often appear on your desktop.

Introduction to Microsoft Office 2010

Microsoft Office 2010 is the newest version of Microsoft Office, offering features that provide users with better functionality and easier ways to work with the various files they create. These features include enhanced design tools, such as improved picture formatting tools and new themes, shared notebooks for working in groups, mobile versions of Office programs, broadcast presentation for the Web, and a digital notebook for managing and sharing multimedia information.

Microsoft Office 2010 Programs

Microsoft Office 2010 includes a wide variety of programs such as Word, PowerPoint, Excel, Access, Outlook, Publisher, OneNote, InfoPath, SharePoint Workspace, Communicator, and Web Apps:

- **Microsoft Word 2010**, or Word, is a full-featured word processing program that allows you to create professional-looking documents and revise them easily.
- **Microsoft PowerPoint 2010**, or PowerPoint, is a complete presentation program that allows you to produce professional-looking presentations.
- **Microsoft Excel 2010**, or Excel, is a powerful spreadsheet program that allows you to organize data, complete calculations, make decisions, graph data, develop professional-looking reports, publish organized data to the Web, and access real-time data from Web sites.
- **Microsoft Access 2010**, or Access, is a database management system that allows you to create a database; add, change, and delete data in the database; ask questions concerning the data in the database; and create forms and reports using the data in the database.
- **Microsoft Outlook 2010**, or Outlook, is a communications and scheduling program that allows you to manage e-mail accounts, calendars, contacts, and access to other Internet content.
- **Microsoft Publisher 2010**, or Publisher, is a desktop publishing program that helps you create professional-quality publications and marketing materials that can be shared easily.
- **Microsoft OneNote 2010**, or OneNote, is a note taking program that allows you to store and share information in notebooks with other people.
- **Microsoft InfoPath 2010**, or InfoPath, is a form development program that helps you create forms for use on the Web and gather data from these forms.
- **Microsoft SharePoint Workspace 2010**, or SharePoint, is collaboration software that allows you access and revise files stored on your computer from other locations.
- **Microsoft Communicator** is communications software that allows you to use different modes of communications such as instant messaging, video conferencing, and sharing files and programs.
- **Microsoft Web Apps** is a Web application that allows you to edit and share files on the Web using the familiar Office interface.

Microsoft Office 2010 Suites

A **suite** is a collection of individual programs available together as a unit. Microsoft offers a variety of Office suites. Table 2 lists the Office 2010 suites and their components.

Programs in a suite, such as Microsoft Office, typically use a similar interface and share features. In addition, Microsoft Office programs use **common dialog boxes** for performing actions such as opening and saving files. Once you are comfortable working with these elements and this interface and performing tasks in one program, the similarity can help you apply the knowledge and skills you have learned to another Office program(s). For example, the process for saving a file in Word is the same in PowerPoint, Excel, and the other Office programs. While briefly showing how to use several Office programs, this chapter illustrates some of the common functions across the programs and also identifies the characteristics unique to these programs.

Table 2 Microsoft Office 2010 Suites	Microsoft Office Professional Plus 2010	Microsoft Office Professional 2010	Microsoft Office Home and Business 2010	Microsoft Office Standard 2010	Microsoft Office Home and Student 2010
Microsoft Word 2010	✓	✓	✓	✓	✓
Microsoft PowerPoint 2010	✓	✓	✓	✓	✓
Microsoft Excel 2010	✓	✓	✓	✓	✓
Microsoft Access 2010	✓	✓	✗	✗	✗
Microsoft Outlook 2010	✓	✓	✓	✓	✗
Microsoft Publisher 2010	✓	✓	✗	✓	✗
Microsoft OneNote 2010	✓	✓	✓	✓	✓
Microsoft InfoPath 2010	✓	✗	✗	✗	✗
Microsoft SharePoint Workspace 2010	✓	✗	✗	✗	✗
Microsoft Communicator	✓	✗	✗	✗	✗

Starting and Using a Program

To use a program, you must instruct the operating system to start the program.
Windows 7 provides many different ways to start a program, one of which is presented
in this section (other ways to start a program are presented throughout this chapter).
After starting a program, you can use it to perform a variety of tasks. The following pages
use Word to discuss some elements of the Office interface and to perform tasks that are
common to other Office programs.

Word

Word is a full-featured word processing program that allows you to create many
types of personal and business documents, including flyers, letters, memos, resumes,
reports, fax cover sheets, mailing labels, and newsletters. Word also provides tools that
enable you to create Web pages and save these Web pages directly on a Web server. Word
has many features designed to simplify the production of documents and add visual
appeal. Using Word, you easily can change the shape, size, and color of text. You also can
include borders, shading, tables, images, pictures, charts, and Web addresses in documents.

To Start a Program Using the Start Menu

Across the bottom of the Windows 7 desktop is the taskbar. The taskbar contains the **Start button**, which you use to access programs, files, folders, and settings on a computer. A **folder** is a named location on a storage medium that usually contains related documents. The taskbar also displays a button for each program currently running on a computer.

Clicking the Start button displays the Start menu. The **Start menu** allows you to access programs, folders, and files on the computer and contains commands that allow you to start programs, store and search for documents, customize the computer, and obtain help about thousands of topics. A **menu** is a list of related items, including folders, programs, and commands. Each **command** on a menu performs a specific action, such as saving a file or obtaining help.

The following steps, which assume Windows 7 is running, use the Start menu to start an Office program based on a typical installation. You may need to ask your instructor how to start Office programs for your computer. Although the steps illustrate starting the Word program, the steps to start any Office program are similar.

❶

- Click the Start button on the Windows 7 taskbar to display the Start menu (Figure 6).

Q&A Why does my Start menu look different?

It may look different depending on your computer's configuration. The Start menu may be customized for several reasons, such as usage requirements or security restrictions.

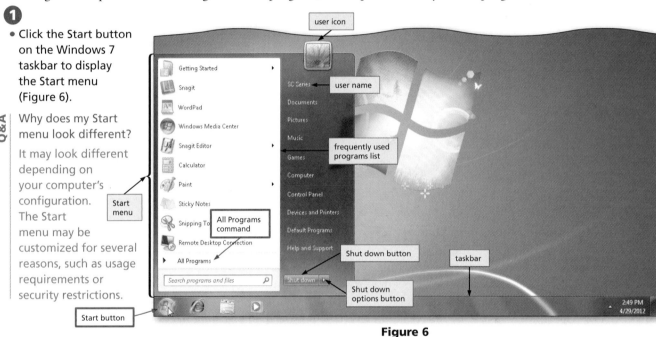

Figure 6

❷

- Click All Programs at the bottom of the left pane on the Start menu to display the All Programs list (Figure 7).

Q&A What is a pane?

A **pane** is an area of a window that displays related content. For example, the left pane on the Start menu contains a list of frequently used programs, as well as the All Programs command.

Q&A Why might my All Programs list look different?

Most likely, the programs installed on your computer will differ from those shown in Figure 7. Your All Programs list will show the programs that are installed on your computer.

Figure 7

3

- If the program you wish to start is located in a folder, click or scroll to and then click the folder (Microsoft Office, in this case) in the All Programs list to display a list of the folder's contents (Figure 8).

Q&A Why is the Microsoft Office folder on my computer?

During installation of Microsoft Office 2010, the Microsoft Office folder was added to the All Programs list.

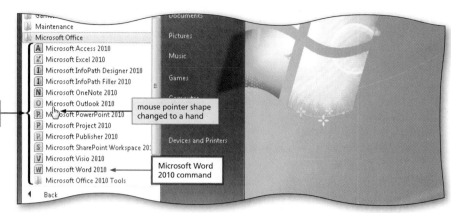

Figure 8

4

- Click, or scroll to and then click, the program name (Microsoft Word 2010, in this case) in the list to start the selected program (Figure 9).

Q&A What happens when you start a program?

Many programs initially display a blank document in a program window, as shown in the Word window in Figure 9; others provide a means for you to create a blank document. A **window** is a rectangular area that displays data and information. The top of a window has a **title bar**, which is a horizontal space that contains the window's name.

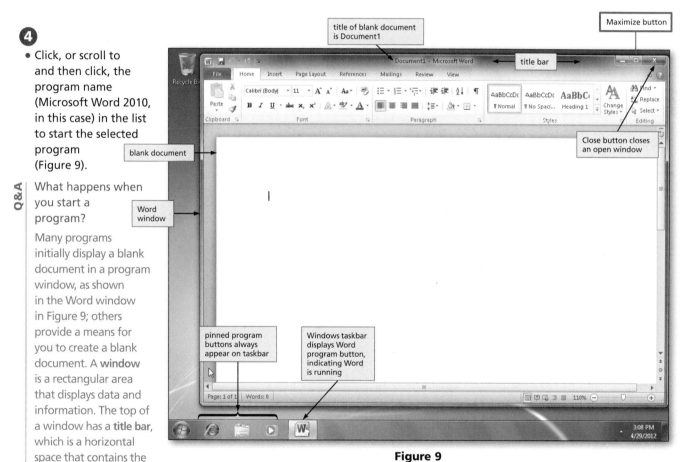

Figure 9

Q&A Why is my program window a different size?

The Word window shown in Figure 9 is not maximized. Your Word window already may be maximized. The next steps maximize a window.

Other Ways
1. Double-click program icon on desktop, if one is present
2. Click program name in left pane of Start menu, if present
3. Display Start menu, type program name in search box, click program name
4. Double-click file created using program you want to start

To Maximize a Window

Sometimes content is not visible completely in a window. One method of displaying the entire contents of a window is to **maximize** it, or enlarge the window so that it fills the entire screen. The following step maximizes the Word window; however, any Office program's window can be maximized using this step.

1

- If the program window is not maximized already, click the Maximize button (shown in Figure 9 on the previous page) next to the Close button on the window's title bar (the Word window title bar, in this case) to maximize the window (Figure 10).

Q&A What happened to the Maximize button?

It changed to a Restore Down button, which you can use to return a window to its size and location before you maximized it.

Q&A How do I know whether a window is maximized?

A window is maximized if it fills the entire display area and the Restore Down button is displayed on the title bar.

Figure 10

Other Ways

1. Double-click title bar
2. Drag title bar to top of screen

The Word Document Window, Ribbon, and Elements Common to Office Programs

The Word window consists of a variety of components to make your work more efficient and documents more professional. These include the document window, Ribbon, Mini toolbar, shortcut menus, and Quick Access Toolbar. Most of these components are common to other Microsoft Office 2010 programs; others are unique to Word.

You view a portion of a document on the screen through a **document window** (Figure 11). The default (preset) view is **Print Layout view**, which shows the document on a mock sheet of paper in the document window.

Scroll Bars You use a scroll bar to display different portions of a document in the document window. At the right edge of the document window is a vertical scroll bar. If a document is too wide to fit in the document window, a horizontal scroll bar also appears at the bottom of the document window. On a scroll bar, the position of the scroll box reflects the location of the portion of the document that is displayed in the document window.

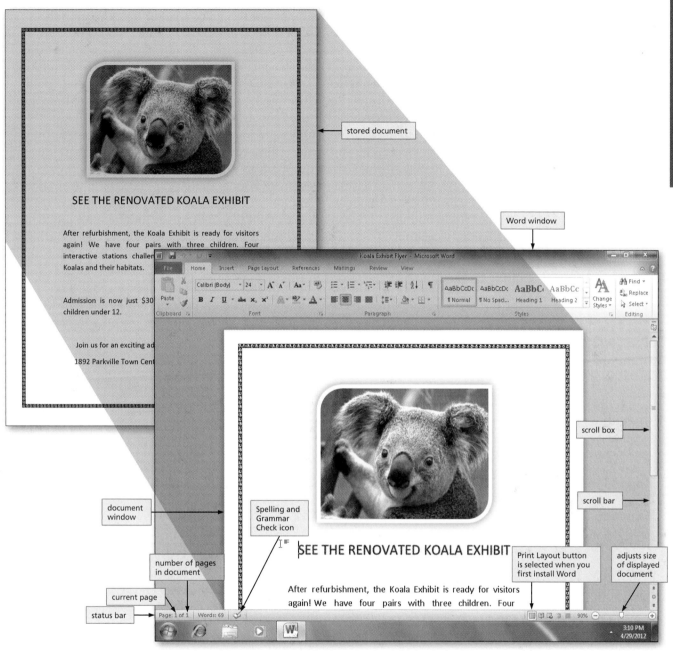

Figure 11

Status Bar The **status bar**, located at the bottom of the document window above the Windows 7 taskbar, presents information about the document, the progress of current tasks, and the status of certain commands and keys; it also provides controls for viewing the document. As you type text or perform certain tasks, various indicators and buttons may appear on the status bar.

The left side of the status bar in Figure 11 shows the current page followed by the total number of pages in the document, the number of words in the document, and an icon to check spelling and grammar. The right side of the status bar includes buttons and controls you can use to change the view of a document and adjust the size of the displayed document.

Ribbon   The Ribbon, located near the top of the window below the title bar, is the control center in Word and other Office programs (Figure 12). The Ribbon provides easy, central access to the tasks you perform while creating a document. The Ribbon consists of tabs, groups, and commands. Each **tab** contains a collection of groups, and each **group** contains related functions. When you start an Office program, such as Word, it initially displays several main tabs, also called default tabs. All Office programs have a **Home tab**, which contains the more frequently used commands.

In addition to the main tabs, Office programs display **tool tabs**, also called contextual tabs (Figure 13), when you perform certain tasks or work with objects such as pictures or tables. If you insert a picture in a Word document, for example, the Picture Tools tab and its related subordinate Format tab appear, collectively referred to as the Picture Tools Format tab. When you are finished working with the picture, the Picture Tools Format tab disappears from the Ribbon. Word and other Office programs determine when tool tabs should appear and disappear based on tasks you perform. Some tool tabs, such as the Table Tools tab, have more than one related subordinate tab.

Items on the Ribbon include buttons, boxes (text boxes, check boxes, etc.), and galleries (Figure 12). A **gallery** is a set of choices, often graphical, arranged in a grid or in a list. You can scroll through choices in an in-Ribbon gallery by clicking the gallery's scroll arrows. Or, you can click a gallery's More button to view more gallery options on the screen at a time.

Figure 12

Some buttons and boxes have arrows that, when clicked, also display a gallery; others always cause a gallery to be displayed when clicked. Most galleries support **live preview**, which is a feature that allows you to point to a gallery choice and see its effect in the document — without actually selecting the choice (Figure 13).

Figure 13

Some commands on the Ribbon display an image to help you remember their function. When you point to a command on the Ribbon, all or part of the command glows in shades of yellow and orange, and an Enhanced ScreenTip appears on the screen. An **Enhanced ScreenTip** is an on-screen note that provides the name of the command, available keyboard shortcut(s), a description of the command, and sometimes instructions for how to obtain help about the command (Figure 14). Enhanced ScreenTips are more detailed than a typical ScreenTip, which usually displays only the name of the command.

Some groups on the Ribbon have a small arrow in the lower-right corner, called a **Dialog Box Launcher**, that when clicked, displays a dialog box or a task pane with additional options for the group (Figure 15). When presented with a dialog box, you make selections and must close the dialog box before returning to the document. A **task pane**, in contrast to a dialog box, is a window that can remain open and visible while you work in the document.

Figure 14

Mini Toolbar The **Mini toolbar**, which appears automatically based on tasks you perform, contains commands related to changing the appearance of text in a document. All commands on the Mini toolbar also exist on the Ribbon. The purpose of the Mini toolbar is to minimize mouse movement.

When the Mini toolbar appears, it initially is transparent (Figure 16a). If you do not use the transparent Mini toolbar, it disappears from the screen. To use the Mini toolbar, move the mouse pointer into the toolbar, which causes the Mini toolbar to change

Figure 15

from a transparent to bright appearance (Figure 16b). If you right-click an item in the document window, Word displays both the Mini toolbar and a shortcut menu, which is discussed in a later section in this chapter.

(a) transparent Mini toolbar

(b) bright Mini toolbar

Quick Access Toolbar   The **Quick Access Toolbar**, located initially (by default) above the Ribbon at the left edge of the title bar, provides convenient, one-click access to frequently used commands (Figure 14 on the previous page). The commands on the Quick Access Toolbar always are available, regardless of the task you are performing. The Quick Access Toolbar is discussed in more depth later in the chapter.

KeyTips   If you prefer using the keyboard instead of the mouse, you can press the ALT key on the keyboard to display **KeyTips**, or keyboard code icons, for certain commands (Figure 17). To select a command using the keyboard, press the letter or number displayed in the KeyTip, which may cause additional KeyTips related to the selected command to appear. To remove KeyTips from the screen, press the ALT key or the ESC key until all KeyTips disappear, or click the mouse anywhere in the program window.

Figure 17

To Display a Different Tab on the Ribbon

When you start Word, the Ribbon displays eight main tabs: File, Home, Insert, Page Layout, References, Mailings, Review, and View. The tab currently displayed is called the **active tab**.

The following step displays the Insert tab, that is, makes it the active tab.

- Click Insert on the Ribbon to display the Insert tab (Figure 18).

 Experiment

- Click the other tabs on the Ribbon to view their contents. When you are finished, click the Insert tab to redisplay the Insert tab.

Q&A
If I am working in a different Office program, such as PowerPoint or Access, how do I display a different tab on the Ribbon?

Follow this same procedure; that is, click the desired tab on the Ribbon.

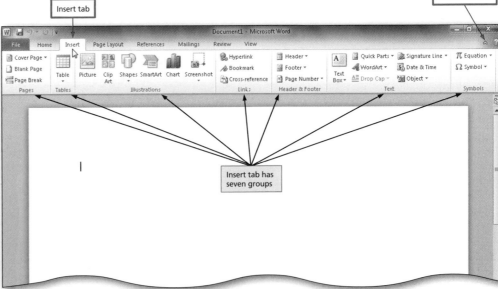

Figure 18

To Minimize, Display, and Restore the Ribbon

To display more of a document or other item in the window of an Office program, some users prefer to minimize the Ribbon, which hides the groups on the Ribbon and displays only the main tabs. Each time you start an Office program, the Ribbon appears the same way it did the last time you used that Office program. The chapters in this book, however, begin with the Ribbon appearing as it did at the initial installation of the software.

The following steps minimize, display, and restore the Ribbon in an Office program.

1

- Click the Minimize the Ribbon button on the Ribbon (shown in Figure 18) to minimize the Ribbon (Figure 19).

Q&A What happened to the groups on the Ribbon?

When you minimize the Ribbon, the groups disappear so that the Ribbon does not take up as much space on the screen.

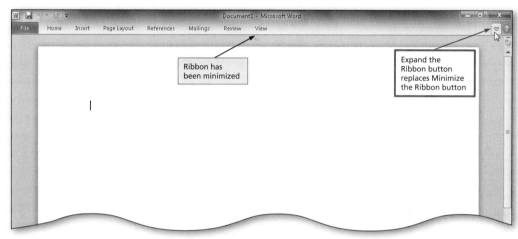

Figure 19

Q&A What happened to the Minimize the Ribbon button?

The Expand the Ribbon button replaces the Minimize the Ribbon button when the Ribbon is minimized.

2

- Click Home on the Ribbon to display the Home tab (Figure 20).

Q&A Why would I click the Home tab?

If you want to use a command on a minimized Ribbon, click the main tab to display the groups for that tab. After you select a command on the Ribbon, the groups will be hidden once again. If you decide not to use a command on the Ribbon, you can hide the groups by clicking the same main tab or clicking in the program window.

Figure 20

3

- Click Home on the Ribbon to hide the groups again (shown in Figure 19).

- Click the Expand the Ribbon button on the Ribbon (shown in Figure 19) to restore the Ribbon.

Other Ways
1. Double-click Home on the Ribbon
2. Press CTRL+F1

To Display and Use a Shortcut Menu

When you right-click certain areas of the Word and other program windows, a shortcut menu will appear. A **shortcut menu** is a list of frequently used commands that relate to the right-clicked object. When you right-click a scroll bar, for example, a shortcut menu appears with commands related to the scroll bar. When you right-click the Quick Access Toolbar, a shortcut menu appears with commands related to the Quick Access Toolbar. You can use shortcut menus to access common commands quickly. The following steps use a shortcut menu to move the Quick Access Toolbar, which by default is located on the title bar.

- Right-click the Quick Access Toolbar to display a shortcut menu that presents a list of commands related to the Quick Access Toolbar (Figure 21).

Figure 21

- Click Show Quick Access Toolbar Below the Ribbon on the shortcut menu to display the Quick Access Toolbar below the Ribbon (Figure 22).

Figure 22

- Right-click the Quick Access Toolbar to display a shortcut menu (Figure 23).

- Click Show Quick Access Toolbar Above the Ribbon on the shortcut menu to return the Quick Access Toolbar to its original position (shown in Figure 21).

Figure 23

To Customize the Quick Access Toolbar

The Quick Access Toolbar provides easy access to some of the more frequently used commands in Office programs. By default, the Quick Access Toolbar contains buttons for the Save, Undo, and Redo commands. You can customize the Quick Access Toolbar by changing its location in the window, as shown in the previous steps, and by adding more buttons to reflect commands you would like to access easily. The following steps add the Quick Print button to the Quick Access Toolbar.

1

• Click the Customize Quick Access Toolbar button to display the Customize Quick Access Toolbar menu (Figure 24).

Q&A Which commands are listed on the Customize Quick Access Toolbar menu?

It lists commands that commonly are added to the Quick Access Toolbar.

Q&A What do the check marks next to some commands signify?

Check marks appear next to commands that already are on the Quick Access Toolbar. When you add a button to the Quick Access Toolbar, a check mark will be displayed next to its command name.

Figure 24

2

• Click Quick Print on the Customize Quick Access Toolbar menu to add the Quick Print button to the Quick Access Toolbar (Figure 25).

Q&A How would I remove a button from the Quick Access Toolbar?

You would right-click the button you wish to remove and then click Remove from Quick Access Toolbar on the shortcut menu.

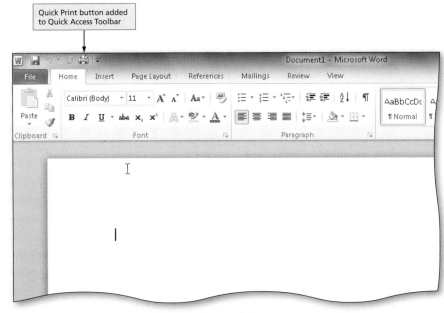

Figure 25

To Enter Text in a Document

The first step in creating a document is to enter its text by typing on the keyboard. By default, Word positions text at the left margin as you type. To begin creating a flyer, for example, you type the headline in the document window. The following steps type this first line of text, a headline, in a document.

- Type **SEE THE RENOVATED KOALA EXHIBIT** as the text (Figure 26).

Q&A What is the blinking vertical bar to the right of the text?

The insertion point. It indicates where text, graphics, and other items will be inserted in the document. As you type, the insertion point moves to the right, and when you reach the end of a line, it moves downward to the beginning of the next line.

Q&A What if I make an error while typing?

You can press the BACKSPACE key until you have deleted the text in error and then retype the text correctly.

Figure 26

- Press the ENTER key to move the insertion point to the beginning of the next line (Figure 27).

Q&A Why did blank space appear between the entered text and the insertion point?

Each time you press the ENTER key, Word creates a new paragraph and inserts blank space between the two paragraphs.

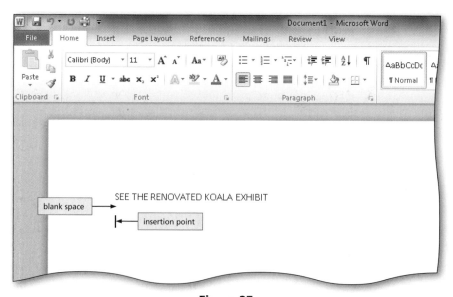

Figure 27

Saving and Organizing Files

While you are creating a document, the computer stores it in memory. When you save a document, the computer places it on a storage medium such as a hard disk, USB flash drive, or optical disc. A saved document is referred to as a file. A **file name** is the name assigned to a file when it is saved. It is important to save a document frequently for the following reasons:

- The document in memory might be lost if the computer is turned off or you lose electrical power while a program is running.

- If you run out of time before completing a project, you may finish it at a future time without starting over.

When saving files, you should organize them so that you easily can find them later. Windows 7 provides tools to help you organize files.

BTW

File Type
Depending on your Windows 7 settings, the file type .docx may be displayed immediately to the right of the file name after you save the file. The file type .docx is a Word 2010 document.

Organizing Files and Folders

A file contains data. This data can range from a research paper to an accounting spreadsheet to an electronic math quiz. You should organize and store these files in folders to avoid misplacing a file and to help you find a file quickly.

If you are a freshman taking an introductory computer class (CIS 101, for example), you may want to design a series of folders for the different subjects covered in the class. To accomplish this, you can arrange the folders in a hierarchy for the class, as shown in Figure 28.

Figure 28

The hierarchy contains three levels. The first level contains the storage device, in this case a USB flash drive. Windows 7 identifies the storage device with a letter, and, in some cases, a name. In Figure 28, the USB flash drive is identified as REMOVABLE (E:). The second level contains the class folder (CIS 101, in this case), and the third level contains seven folders, one each for a different Office program that will be covered in the class (Word, PowerPoint, Excel, Access, Outlook, Publisher, and OneNote).

When the hierarchy in Figure 28 is created, the USB flash drive is said to contain the CIS 101 folder, and the CIS 101 folder is said to contain the separate Office folders (i.e., Word, PowerPoint, Excel, etc.). In addition, this hierarchy easily can be expanded to include folders from other classes taken during additional semesters.

The vertical and horizontal lines in Figure 28 form a pathway that allows you to navigate to a drive or folder on a computer or network. A **path** consists of a drive letter (preceded by a drive name when necessary) and colon, to identify the storage device, and one or more folder names. Each drive or folder in the hierarchy has a corresponding path.

BTW

Saving Online
Instead of saving files on a USB flash drive, some people prefer to save them online so that they can access the files from any computer with an Internet connection. For more information, read Appendix C.

Table 3 shows examples of paths and their corresponding drives and folders.

Table 3 Paths and Corresponding Drives and Folders	
Path	**Drive and Folder**
Computer ▶ REMOVABLE (E:)	Drive E (REMOVABLE (E:))
Computer ▶ REMOVABLE (E:) ▶ CIS 101	CIS 101 folder on drive E
Computer ▶ REMOVABLE (E:) ▶ CIS 101 ▶ Word	Word folder in CIS 101 folder on drive E

The following pages illustrate the steps to organize the folders for this class and save a file in one of those folders:

1. Create the folder identifying your class.
2. Create the Word folder in the folder identifying your class.
3. Create the remaining folders in the folder identifying your class (one each for PowerPoint, Excel, Access, Outlook, Publisher, and OneNote).
4. Save a file in the Word folder.
5. Verify the location of the saved file.

To Create a Folder

When you create a folder, such as the CIS 101 folder shown in Figure 28 on the previous page, you must name the folder. A folder name should describe the folder and its contents. A folder name can contain spaces and any uppercase or lowercase characters, except a backslash (\), slash (/), colon (:), asterisk (*), question mark (?), quotation marks ("), less than symbol (<), greater than symbol (>), or vertical bar (|). Folder names cannot be CON, AUX, COM1, COM2, COM3, COM4, LPT1, LPT2, LPT3, PRN, or NUL. The same rules for naming folders also apply to naming files.

To store files and folders on a USB flash drive, you must connect the USB flash drive to an available USB port on a computer. The following steps create your class folder (CIS 101, in this case) on a USB flash drive.

- Connect the USB flash drive to an available USB port on the computer to open the AutoPlay window (Figure 29).

Q&A Why does the AutoPlay window not open?

Some computers are not configured to open an AutoPlay window. Instead, they might display the contents of the USB flash drive automatically, or you might need to access contents of the USB flash drive using the Computer window. To use the Computer window to display the USB flash drive's contents, click the Start button, click Computer on the Start menu, and then click the icon representing the USB flash drive.

Figure 29

Q&A Why does the AutoPlay window look different from the one in Figure 29?

The AutoPlay window that opens on your computer might display different options. The type of USB flash drive, its contents, and the next available drive letter on your computer all will determine which options are displayed in the AutoPlay window.

- Click the 'Open folder to view files' link in the AutoPlay window to open the USB flash drive window (Figure 30).

Q&A

Why does Figure 30 show REMOVABLE (E:) for the USB flash drive?

REMOVABLE is the name of the USB flash drive used to illustrate these steps. The (E:) refers to the drive letter assigned by Windows 7 to the USB flash drive. The name and drive letter of your USB flash drive probably will be different.

Figure 30

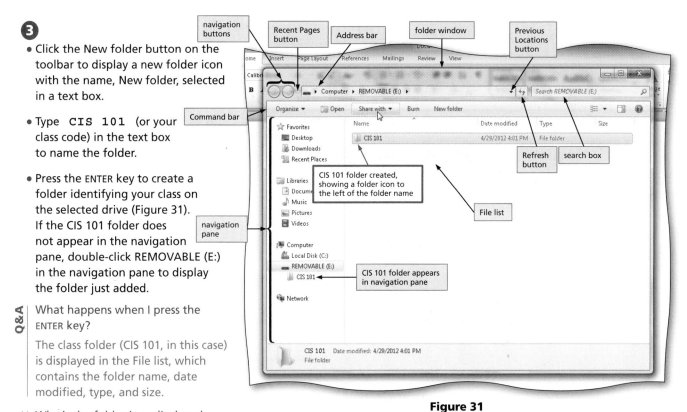

- Click the New folder button on the toolbar to display a new folder icon with the name, New folder, selected in a text box.

- Type **CIS 101** (or your class code) in the text box to name the folder.

- Press the ENTER key to create a folder identifying your class on the selected drive (Figure 31). If the CIS 101 folder does not appear in the navigation pane, double-click REMOVABLE (E:) in the navigation pane to display the folder just added.

Q&A

What happens when I press the ENTER key?

The class folder (CIS 101, in this case) is displayed in the File list, which contains the folder name, date modified, type, and size.

Q&A

Why is the folder icon displayed differently on my computer?

Windows might be configured to display contents differently on your computer.

Figure 31

Folder Windows

The USB flash drive window (shown in Figure 31 on the previous page) is called a folder window. Recall that a folder is a specific named location on a storage medium that contains related files. Most users rely on **folder windows** for finding, viewing, and managing information on their computer. Folder windows have common design elements, including the following (Figure 31).

- The **Address bar** provides quick navigation options. The arrows on the Address bar allow you to visit different locations on the computer.
- The buttons to the left of the Address bar allow you to navigate the contents of the left pane and view recent pages. Other buttons allow you to specify the size of the window.
- The **Previous Locations button** saves the locations you have visited and displays the locations when clicked.
- The **Refresh button** on the right side of the Address bar refreshes the contents of the right pane of the folder window.
- The **search box** to the right of the Address bar contains the dimmed word, Search. You can type a term in the search box for a list of files, folders, shortcuts, and elements containing that term within the location you are searching. A **shortcut** is an icon on the desktop that provides a user with immediate access to a program or file.
- The **Command bar** contains five buttons used to accomplish various tasks on the computer related to organizing and managing the contents of the open window.
- The **navigation pane** on the left contains the Favorites area, Libraries area, Computer area, and Network area.
- The **Favorites area** contains links to your favorite locations. By default, this list contains only links to your Desktop, Downloads, and Recent Places.
- The **Libraries area** shows links to files and folders that have been included in a library.

A **library** helps you manage multiple folders and files stored in various locations on a computer. It does not store the files and folders; rather, it displays links to them so that you can access them quickly. For example, you can save pictures from a digital camera in any folder on any storage location on a computer. Normally, this would make organizing the different folders difficult; however, if you add the folders to a library, you can access all the pictures from one location regardless of where they are stored.

To Create a Folder within a Folder

With the class folder created, you can create folders that will store the files you create using each Office program. The following steps create a Word folder in the CIS 101 folder (or the folder identifying your class).

- Double-click the icon or folder name for the CIS 101 folder (or the folder identifying your class) in the File list to open the folder (Figure 32).

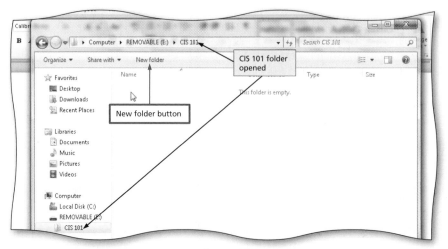

Figure 32

2

- Click the New folder button on the toolbar to display a new folder icon and text box for the folder.

- Type **Word** in the text box to name the folder.

- Press the ENTER key to create the folder (Figure 33).

Figure 33

To Create the Remaining Folders

The following steps create the remaining folders in the folder identifying your class (in this case, CIS 101).

1 Click the New folder button on the toolbar to display a new folder icon and text box.

2 Type **PowerPoint** in the text box to name the folder.

3 Repeat Steps 1 and 2 to create each of the remaining folders, using the names Excel, Access, Outlook, Publisher, and OneNote as the folder names (Figure 34).

Figure 34

To Expand a Folder, Scroll through Folder Contents, and Collapse a Folder

Folder windows display the hierarchy of items and the contents of drives and folders in the right pane. You might want to expand a drive in the navigation pane to view its contents, scroll through its contents, and collapse it when you are finished viewing its contents. When a folder is expanded, it lists all the folders it contains. By contrast, a collapsed folder does not list the folders it contains. The following steps expand, scroll through, and then collapse the folder identifying your class (CIS 101, in this case).

- Double-click the folder identifying your class (CIS 101, in this case), which expands the folder to display its contents and displays a black arrow to the left of the folder icon (Figure 35).

Q&A Why are the subject folders indented below the CIS 101 folder in the navigation pane?

It shows that the folders are contained within the CIS 101 folder.

Q&A Why did a scroll bar appear in the navigation pane?

When all contents cannot fit in a window or pane, a scroll bar appears. As described earlier, you can view areas currently not visible by (1) clicking the scroll arrows, (2) clicking above or below the scroll bar, and (3) dragging the scroll box.

Figure 35

Experiment

- Click the down scroll arrow on the vertical scroll bar to display additional folders at the bottom of the navigation pane.

- Click the scroll bar above the scroll box to move the scroll box to the top of the navigation pane.

- Drag the scroll box down the scroll bar until the scroll box is halfway down the scroll bar.

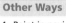

- Double-click the folder identifying your class (CIS 101, in this case) to collapse the folder (Figure 36).

Other Ways

1. Point in navigation pane to display arrows, click white arrow to expand or click black arrow to collapse

2. Select folder to expand or collapse using arrow keys, press RIGHT ARROW to expand; press LEFT ARROW to collapse.

Figure 36

To Switch from One Program to Another

The next step is to save the Word file containing the headline you typed earlier. Word, however, currently is not the active window. You can use the program button on the taskbar and live preview to switch to Word and then save the document in the Word document window.

If Windows Aero is active on your computer, Windows displays a live preview window whenever you move your mouse on a button or click a button on the taskbar. If Aero is not supported or enabled on your computer, you will see a window title instead of a live preview. The steps below use the Word program; however, the steps are the same for any active Office program currently displayed as a program button on the taskbar.

The following steps switch to the Word window.

- Point to the Word program button on the taskbar to see a live preview of the open document(s) or the window title(s) of the open document(s), depending on your computer's configuration (Figure 37).

- Click the program button or the live preview to make the program associated with the program button the active window (shown in Figure 27 on page OFF 20).

Figure 37

Q&A What if multiple documents are open in a program?

If Aero is enabled on your computer, click the desired live preview. If Aero is not supported or not enabled, click the window title.

To Save a File in a Folder

Now that you have created the folders for storing files, you can save the Word document. The following steps save a file on a USB flash drive in the Word folder contained in your class folder (CIS 101, in this case) using the file name, Koala Exhibit.

- With a USB flash drive connected to one of the computer's USB ports, click the Save button on the Quick Access Toolbar to display the Save As dialog box (Figure 38).

Q&A Why does a file name already appear in the File name text box?

Word automatically suggests a file name the first time you save a document. The file name normally consists of the first few words contained in the document. Because the suggested file name is selected, you do not need to delete it; as soon as you begin typing, the new file name replaces the selected text.

2

- Type **Koala Exhibit** in the File name text box (Save As dialog box) to change the file name. Do not press the ENTER key after typing the file name because you do not want to close the dialog box at this time (Figure 39).

What characters can I use in a file name?

The only invalid characters are the backslash (\), slash (/), colon (:), asterisk (*), question mark (?), quotation mark ("), less than symbol (<), greater than symbol (>), and vertical bar (|).

Figure 39

3

- Navigate to the desired save location (in this case, the Word folder in the CIS 101 folder [or your class folder] on the USB flash drive) by performing the tasks in Steps 3a, 3b, and 3c.

3a

- If the navigation pane is not displayed in the dialog box, click the Browse Folders button to expand the dialog box.

- If Computer is not displayed in the navigation pane, drag the navigation pane scroll bar until Computer appears.

- If Computer is not expanded in the navigation pane, double-click Computer to display a list of available storage devices in the navigation pane.

- If necessary, scroll through the dialog box until your USB flash drive appears in the list of available storage devices in the navigation pane (Figure 40).

Figure 40

3b

• If your USB flash drive is not expanded, double-click the USB flash drive in the list of available storage devices in the navigation pane to select that drive as the new save location and display its contents in the right pane.

3c

• If your class folder (CIS 101, in this case) is not expanded, double-click the CIS 101 folder to select the folder and display its contents in the right pane.

Q&A What if I do not want to save in a folder?

Although storing files in folders is an effective technique for organizing files, some users prefer not to store files in folders. If you prefer not to save this file in a folder, skip all instructions in Step 3c and proceed to Step 4.

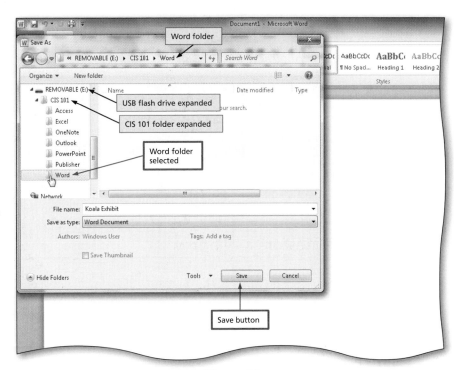

Figure 41

• Click the Word folder to select the folder and display its contents in the right pane (Figure 41).

4

• Click the Save button (Save As dialog box) to save the document in the selected folder on the selected drive with the entered file name (Figure 42).

Q&A How do I know that the file is saved?

While an Office program is saving a file, it briefly displays a message on the status bar indicating the amount of the file saved. In addition, the USB flash drive may have a light that flashes during the save process.

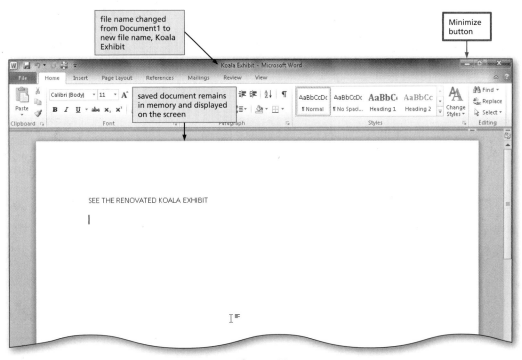

Figure 42

Other Ways
1. Click File on Ribbon, click Save, type file name, navigate to desired save location, click Save button   2. Press CTRL+S or press SHIFT+F12, type file name, navigate to desired save location, click Save button

Navigating in Dialog Boxes

Navigating is the process of finding a location on a storage device. While saving the Koala Exhibit file, for example, Steps 3a – 3c in the previous set of steps navigated to the Word folder located in the CIS 101 folder. When performing certain functions in Windows programs, such as saving a file, opening a file, or inserting a picture in an existing document, you most likely will have to navigate to the location where you want to save the file or to the folder containing the file you want to open or insert. Most dialog boxes in Windows programs requiring navigation follow a similar procedure; that is, the way you navigate to a folder in one dialog box, such as the Save As dialog box, is similar to how you might navigate in another dialog box, such as the Open dialog box. If you chose to navigate to a specific location in a dialog box, you would follow the instructions in Steps 3a – 3c on pages OFF 28 and OFF 29.

To Minimize and Restore a Window

Before continuing, you can verify that the Word file was saved properly. To do this, you will minimize the Word window and then open the USB flash drive window so that you can verify the file is stored on the USB flash drive. A **minimized window** is an open window hidden from view but that can be displayed quickly by clicking the window's program button on the taskbar.

In the following example, Word is used to illustrate minimizing and restoring windows; however, you would follow the same steps regardless of the Office program you are using.

The following steps minimize the Word window, verify that the file is saved, and then restore the minimized window.

- Click the Minimize button on the program's title bar (shown in Figure 42 on the previous page) to minimize the window (Figure 43).

Is the minimized window still available?

The minimized window, Word in this case, remains available but no longer is the active window. It is minimized as a program button on the taskbar.

- If necessary, click the Windows Explorer program button on the taskbar to open the USB flash drive window.

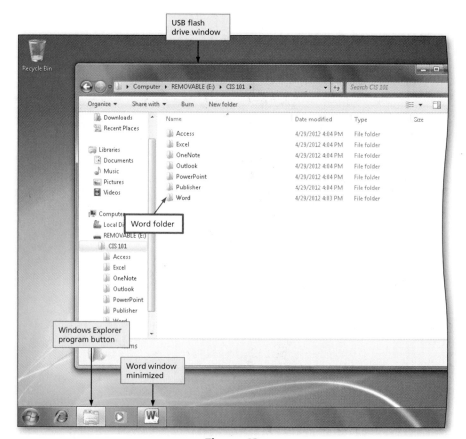

Figure 43

2

- Double-click the Word folder to select the folder and display its contents (Figure 44).

Figure 44

Q&A

Why does the Windows Explorer button on the taskbar change?

The button changes to reflect the status of the folder window (in this case, the USB flash drive window). A selected button indicates that the folder window is active on the screen. When the button is not selected, the window is open but not active.

3

- After viewing the contents of the selected folder, click the Word program button on the taskbar to restore the minimized window (as shown in Figure 42 on page OFF 29).

Other Ways
1. Right-click title bar, click Minimize on shortcut menu, click taskbar button in taskbar button area   2. Press WINDOWS+M, press WINDOWS+SHIFT+M

Screen Resolution

Screen resolution indicates the number of pixels (dots) that the computer uses to display the letters, numbers, graphics, and background you see on the screen. When you increase the screen resolution, Windows displays more information on the screen, but the information decreases in size. The reverse also is true: as you decrease the screen resolution, Windows displays less information on the screen, but the information increases in size.

Screen resolution usually is stated as the product of two numbers, such as 1024 × 768 (pronounced "ten twenty-four by seven sixty-eight"). A 1024 × 768 screen resolution results in a display of 1,024 distinct pixels on each of 768 lines, or about

786,432 pixels. Changing the screen resolution affects how the Ribbon appears in Office programs. Figure 45 shows the Word Ribbon at screen resolutions of 1024 × 768 and 1280 × 800. All of the same commands are available regardless of screen resolution. Word, however, makes changes to the groups and the buttons within the groups to accommodate the various screen resolutions. The result is that certain commands may need to be accessed differently depending on the resolution chosen. A command that is visible on the Ribbon and available by clicking a button at one resolution may not be visible and may need to be accessed using its Dialog Box Launcher at a different resolution.

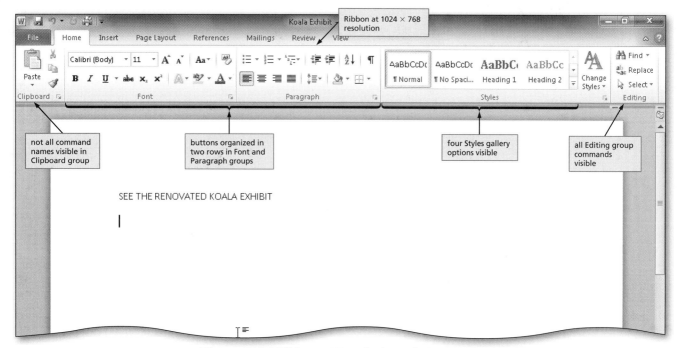

Figure 45 (a) Ribbon at Resolution of 1024 x 768

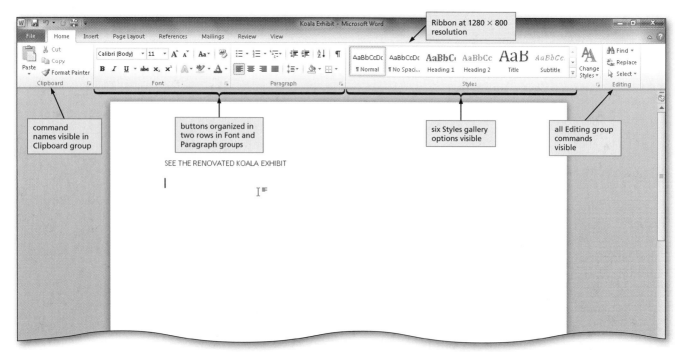

Figure 45 (b) Ribbon at Resolution of 1280 x 800

Comparing the two Ribbons in Figure 45, notice the changes in content and layout of the groups and galleries. In some cases, the content of a group is the same in each resolution, but the layout of the group differs. For example, the same gallery and buttons appear in the Styles groups in the two resolutions, but the layouts differ. In other cases, the content and layout are the same across the resolution, but the level of detail differs with the resolution. In the Clipboard group, when the resolution increases to 1280×800, the names of all the buttons in the group appear in addition to the buttons themselves. At the lower resolution, only the buttons appear.

To Change the Screen Resolution

If you are using a computer to step through the chapters in this book and you want your screen to match the figures, you may need to change your screen's resolution. The figures in this book use a screen resolution of 1024×768. The following steps change the screen resolution to 1024×768. Your computer already may be set to 1024×768 or some other resolution. Keep in mind that many computer labs prevent users from changing the screen resolution; in that case, read the following steps for illustration purposes.

1

- Click the Show desktop button on the taskbar to display the Windows 7 desktop.

- Right-click an empty area on the Windows 7 desktop to display a shortcut menu that displays a list of commands related to the desktop (Figure 46).

Why does my shortcut menu display different commands?

Depending on your computer's hardware and configuration, different commands might appear on the shortcut menu.

Figure 46

• Click Screen resolution on the shortcut menu to open the Screen Resolution window (Figure 47).

Figure 47

• Click the Resolution button in the Screen Resolution window to display the resolution slider.

Q&A What is a slider?

A **slider** is an object that allows users to choose from multiple predetermined options. In most cases, these options represent some type of numeric value. In most cases, one end of the slider (usually the left or bottom) represents the lowest of available values, and the opposite end (usually the right or top) represents the highest available value.

• If necessary, drag the resolution slider until the desired screen resolution (in this case, 1024 × 768) is selected (Figure 48).

Q&A What if my computer does not support the 1024 × 768 resolution?

Some computers do not support the 1024 × 768 resolution. In this case, select a resolution that is close to the 1024 × 768 resolution.

Figure 48

5

- Click an empty area of the Screen Resolution window to close the resolution slider.

- Click the OK button to change the screen resolution and display the Display Settings dialog box (Figure 49).

- Click the Keep changes button (Display Settings dialog box) to accept the new screen resolution.

Q&A Why does a message display stating that the image quality can be improved?

Some computer monitors are designed to display contents better at a certain screen resolution, sometimes referred to as an optimal resolution.

Figure 49

To Quit an Office Program with One Document Open

When you quit an Office program, such as Word, if you have made changes to a file since the last time the file was saved, the Office program displays a dialog box asking if you want save the changes you made to the file before it closes the program window. The dialog box contains three buttons with these resulting actions: the Save button saves the changes and then quits the Office program, the Don't Save button quits the Office program without saving changes, and the Cancel button closes the dialog box and redisplays the file without saving the changes.

If no changes have been made to an open document since the last time the file was saved, the Office program will close the window without displaying a dialog box.

The following steps quit an Office program. In the following example, Word is used to illustrate quitting an Office program; however, you would follow the same steps regardless of the Office program you were using.

1

- If necessary, click the Word program button on the taskbar to display the Word window on the desktop.

- Point to the Close button on the right side of the program's title bar, Word in this case (Figure 50).

Figure 50

2

- Click the Close button to close the document and quit Word.

Q&A What if I have more than one document open in an Office program?

You would click the Close button for each open document. When you click the last open document's Close button, the Office program also quits. As an alternative, you could click File on the Ribbon to open the Backstage view and then click Exit in the Backstage view to close all open documents and quit the Office program.

Q&A What is the Backstage view?

The **Backstage view** contains a set of commands that enable you to manage documents and data about the documents. The Backstage view is discussed in more depth later in this chapter.

3

- If a Microsoft Word dialog box appears, click the Save button to save any changes made to the document since the last save.

Other Ways

1. Right-click the Office program button on Windows 7 taskbar, click Close window or 'Close all windows' on shortcut menu

2. Press ALT + F4

Break Point: If you wish to take a break, this is a good place to do so. To resume at a later time, continue to follow the steps from this location forward.

Additional Microsoft Office Programs

The previous section used Word to illustrate common features of Office and some basic elements unique to Word. The following sections present elements unique to PowerPoint, Excel, and Access, as well as illustrate additional common features of Office.

In the following pages, you will learn how to do the following:

1. Start an Office program (PowerPoint) using the search box.
2. Create two small documents in the same Office program (PowerPoint).
3. Close one of the documents.
4. Reopen the document just closed.
5. Create a document in a different Office program (Excel).
6. Save the document with a new file name.
7. Create a file in a different Office program (Access).
8. Close the file and then open the file.

PowerPoint

PowerPoint is a complete presentation program that allows you to produce professional-looking presentations (Figure 51). A PowerPoint **presentation** also is called a **slide show**. PowerPoint contains several features to simplify creating a slide show. To make presentations more impressive, you can add diagrams, tables, pictures, video, sound, and animation effects. Additional PowerPoint features include the following:

- **Word processing** — Create bulleted lists, combine words and images, find and replace text, and use multiple fonts and font sizes.
- **Outlining** — Develop a presentation using an outline format. You also can import outlines from Microsoft Word or other word processing programs, including single-level and multilevel lists.
- **Charting** — Create and insert charts into presentations and then add effects and chart elements.
- **Drawing** — Create and modify diagrams using shapes such as arcs, arrows, cubes, rectangles, stars, and triangles. Then, customize and add effects to the diagrams, and arrange these objects by sizing, scaling, and rotating them.
- **Inserting multimedia** — Insert artwork and multimedia effects into a slide show. The Microsoft Clip Organizer, included with Office programs, contains hundreds of media files, including pictures, sounds, and movies.
- **Saving to the Web** — Save presentations or parts of a presentation so that they can be viewed in a Web browser. You can publish your slide show to the Internet or to an intranet.
- **E-mailing** — Send an entire slide show as an attachment to an e-mail message.
- **Collaborating** — Share a presentation with friends and coworkers. Ask them to review the slides and then insert comments that offer suggestions to enhance the presentation.
- **Preparing delivery** — Rehearse integrating PowerPoint slides into your speech by setting timings, using presentation tools, showing only selected slides in a presentation, and packaging the presentation for an optical disc.

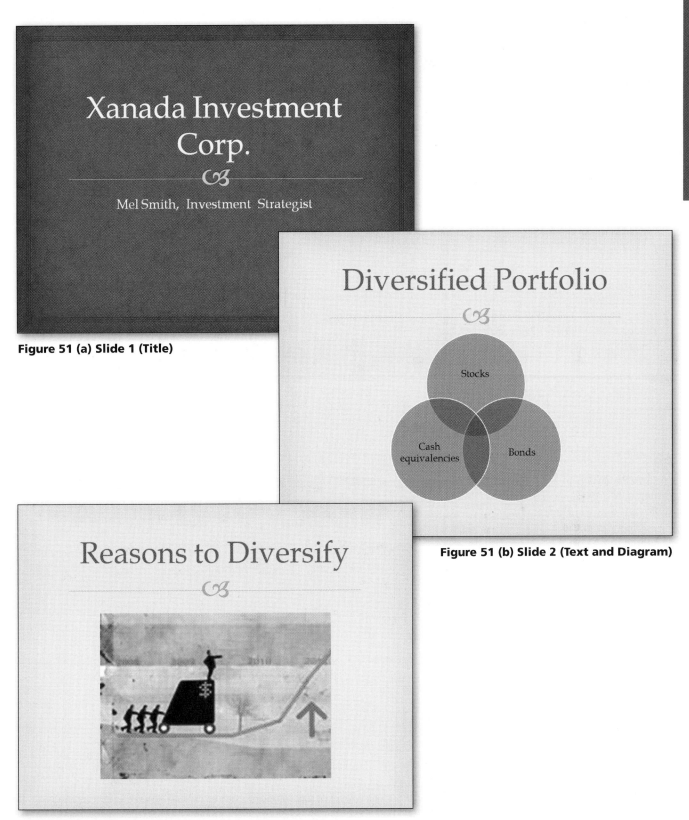

Figure 51 (a) Slide 1 (Title)

Figure 51 (b) Slide 2 (Text and Diagram)

Figure 51 (c) Slide 3 (Text and Picture)

To Start a Program Using the Search Box

The steps on the next page, which assume Windows 7 is running, use the search box to start the PowerPoint Office program based on a typical installation; however, you would follow similar steps to start any Office program. You may need to ask your instructor how to start programs for your computer.

• Click the Start button on the Windows 7 taskbar to display the Start menu.

• Type **Microsoft PowerPoint** as the search text in the 'Search programs and files' text box and watch the search results appear on the Start menu (Figure 52).

Q&A

Do I need to type the complete program name or correct capitalization?

No, just enough of it for the program name to appear on the Start menu. For example, you may be able to type PowerPoint or powerpoint, instead of Microsoft PowerPoint.

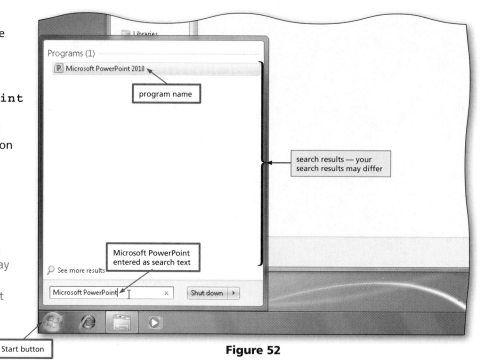

Figure 52

---

❸

• Click the program name, Microsoft PowerPoint 2010 in this case, in the search results on the Start menu to start PowerPoint and display a new blank presentation in the PowerPoint window.

• If the program window is not maximized, click the Maximize button on its title bar to maximize the window (Figure 53).

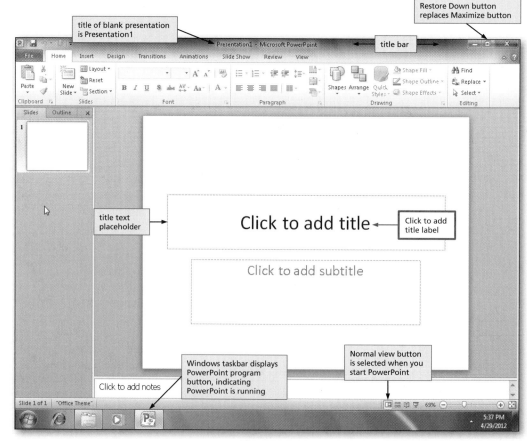

Figure 53

The PowerPoint Window and Ribbon

The PowerPoint window consists of a variety of components to make your work more efficient and documents more professional: the window, Ribbon, Mini toolbar, shortcut menus, and Quick Access Toolbar. Many of these components are common to other Office programs and have been discussed earlier in this chapter. Other components, discussed in the following paragraphs and later in subsequent chapters, are unique to PowerPoint.

The basic unit of a PowerPoint presentation is a **slide**. A slide may contain text and objects, such as graphics, tables, charts, and drawings. **Layouts** are used to position this content on the slide. When you create a new presentation, the default **Title Slide** layout appears (Figure 54). The purpose of this layout is to introduce the presentation to the audience. PowerPoint includes eight other built-in standard layouts.

The default slide layouts are set up in **landscape orientation**, where the slide width is greater than its height. In landscape orientation, the slide size is preset to 10 inches wide and 7.5 inches high when printed on a standard sheet of paper measuring 11 inches wide and 8.5 inches high.

BTW

Portrait Orientation
If your slide content is dominantly vertical, such as a skyscraper or a person, consider changing the slide layout to a portrait orientation. To change the orientation to portrait, click the Slide Orientation button (Design tab | Page Setup group) and then click Portrait. You can use both landscape and portrait orientation in the same slide show.

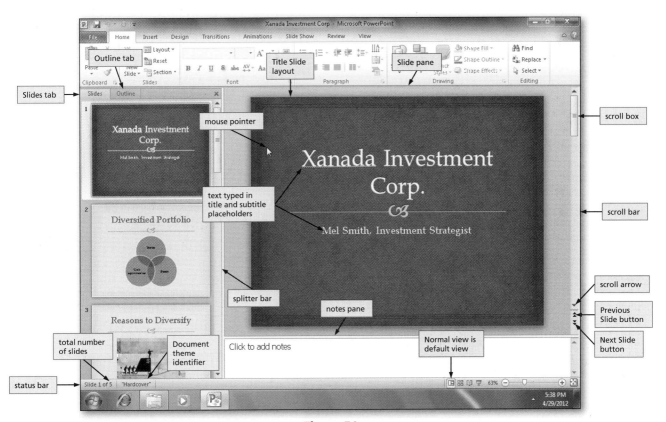

Figure 54

Placeholders **Placeholders** are boxes with dotted or hatch-marked borders that are displayed when you create a new slide. All layouts except the Blank slide layout contain placeholders. Depending on the particular slide layout selected, title and subtitle placeholders are displayed for the slide title and subtitle; a content text placeholder is displayed for text, art, or a table, chart, picture, graphic, or movie. The title slide in Figure 53 has two text placeholders for the main heading, or title, of a new slide and the subtitle.

Ribbon   The Ribbon in PowerPoint is similar to the one in Word and the other Microsoft Office programs. When you start PowerPoint, the Ribbon displays nine main tabs: File, Home, Insert, Design, Transitions, Animations, Slide Show, Review, and View.

To Enter Content in a Title Slide

With the exception of a blank slide and a slide with a picture and caption, PowerPoint assumes every new slide has a title. Many of PowerPoint's layouts have both a title text placeholder and at least one content placeholder. To make creating a presentation easier, any text you type after a new slide appears becomes title text in the title text placeholder. As you begin typing text in the title text placeholder, the title text also is displayed in the Slide 1 thumbnail in the Slides tab. The presentation title for this presentation is Xanada Investments. The following steps enter a presentation title on the title slide.

- Click the label 'Click to add title' located inside the title text placeholder (shown in Figure 53 on page OFF 38) to select the placeholder (Figure 55).

Figure 55

- Type **Xanada Investments** in the title text placeholder. Do not press the ENTER key because you do not want to create a new line of text (Figure 56).

What are the white squares and circles that appear around the title text placeholder as I type the presentation title?

The white squares and circles are sizing handles, which you can drag to change the size of the title text placeholder. Sizing handles also can be found around other placeholders and objects within a presentation.

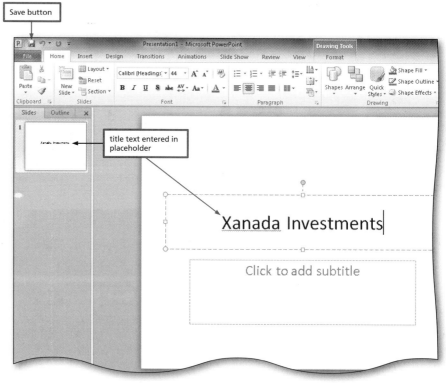

Figure 56

To Save a File in a Folder

The following steps save the presentation in the PowerPoint folder in the class folder (CIS 101, in this case) on a USB flash drive using the file name, Xanada Investments.

1 With a USB flash drive connected to one of the computer's USB ports, click the Save button on the Quick Access Toolbar to display the Save As dialog box.

2 If necessary, type **Xanada Investments** in the File name text box to change the file name. Do not press the ENTER key after typing the file name because you do not want to close the dialog box at this time.

3 Navigate to the desired save location (in this case, the PowerPoint folder in the CIS 101 folder [or your class folder] on the USB flash drive). For specific instructions, perform the tasks in Steps 3a through 3g.

3a If a navigation pane is not displayed in the Save As dialog box, click the Browse Folders button to expand the dialog box.

3b If Computer is not displayed in the navigation pane, drag the navigation pane scroll bar (Save As dialog box) until Computer appears.

3c If Computer is not expanded in the navigation pane, double-click Computer to display a list of available storage devices in the navigation pane.

3d If necessary, scroll through the Save As dialog box until your USB flash drive appears in the list of available storage devices in the navigation pane.

3e If your USB flash drive is not expanded, double-click the USB flash drive in the list of available storage devices in the navigation pane to select that drive as the new save location and display its contents in the right pane.

3f If your class folder (CIS 101, in this case) is not expanded, double-click the CIS 101 folder to select the folder and display its contents.

3g Click the PowerPoint folder to select it as the new save location and display its contents in the right pane.

4 Click the Save button (Save As dialog box) to save the presentation in the selected folder on the selected drive with the entered file name.

To Create a New Office Document from the Backstage View

As discussed earlier, the Backstage view contains a set of commands that enable you to manage documents and data about the documents. From the Backstage view in PowerPoint, for example, you can create, open, print, and save presentations. You also can share documents, manage versions, set permissions, and modify document properties. In other Office 2010 programs, the Backstage view may contain features specific to those programs. The steps on the following pages create a file, a blank presentation in this case, from the Backstage view.

1

• Click File on the Ribbon to open the Backstage view (Figure 57).

Q&A

What is the purpose of the File tab?

The **File** tab is used to display the Backstage view for each Office program.

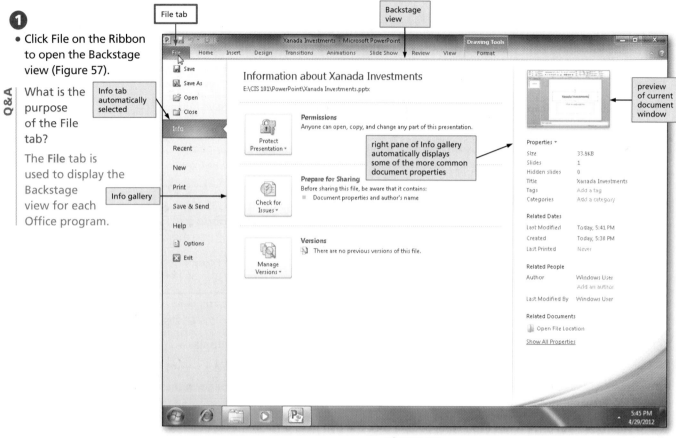

Figure 57

2

• Click the New tab in the Backstage view to display the New gallery (Figure 58).

Q&A

Can I create documents through the Backstage view in other Office programs?

Yes. If the Office program has a New tab in the Backstage view, the New gallery displays various options for creating a new file.

Figure 58

- Click the Create button in the New gallery to create a new presentation (Figure 59).

Figure 59

Other Ways

1. Press CTRL+N

To Enter Content in a Title Slide of a Second PowerPoint Presentation

The presentation title for this presentation is Koala Exhibit Gala. The following steps enter a presentation title on the title slide.

1 Click the title text placeholder (shown in Figure 59) to select it.

2 Type **Koala Exhibit Gala** in the title text placeholder. Do not press the ENTER key (Figure 60).

Figure 60

To Save a File in a Folder

The following steps save the second presentation in the PowerPoint folder in the class folder (CIS 101, in this case) on a USB flash drive using the file name, Koala Exhibit Gala.

1 With a USB flash drive connected to one of the computer's USB ports, click the Save button on the Quick Access Toolbar to display the Save As dialog box.

2 If necessary, type **Koala Exhibit Gala** in the File name text box to change the file name. Do not press the ENTER key after typing the file name because you do not want to close the dialog box at this time.

3 If necessary, navigate to the desired save location (in this case, the PowerPoint folder in the CIS 101 folder [or your class folder] on the USB flash drive).

4 Click the Save button (Save As dialog box) to save the presentation in the selected folder on the selected drive with the entered file name.

To Close an Office File Using the Backstage View

Sometimes, you may want to close an Office file, such as a PowerPoint presentation, entirely and start over with a new file. You also may want to close a file when you are finished working with it so that you can begin a new file. The following steps close the current active Office file, that is, the Koala Exhibit Gala presentation, without quitting the active program (PowerPoint in this case).

1
- Click File on the Ribbon to open the Backstage view (Figure 61).

2
- Click Close in the Backstage view to close the open file (Koala Exhibit Gala, in this case) without quitting the active program.

 What if the Office program displays a dialog box about saving?

Click the Save button if you want to save the changes, click the Don't Save button if you want to ignore the changes since the last time you saved, and click the Cancel button if you do not want to close the document.

Can I use the Backstage view to close an open file in other Office programs, such as Word and Excel?

Yes.

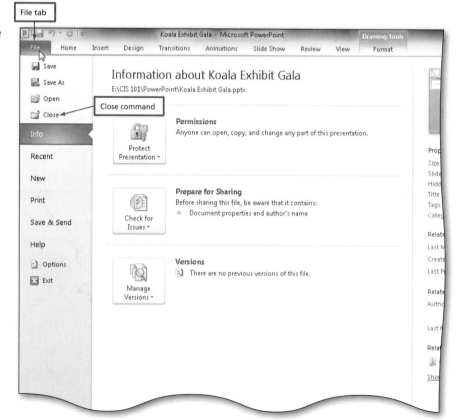

Figure 61

To Open a Recent Office File Using the Backstage View

You sometimes need to open a file that you recently modified. You may have more changes to make such as adding more content or correcting errors. The Backstage view allows you to access recent files easily. The following steps reopen the Koala Exhibit Gala file just closed.

1

- Click File on the Ribbon to open the Backstage view.

- Click the Recent tab in the Backstage view to display the Recent gallery (Figure 62).

2

- Click the desired file name in the Recent gallery, Koala Exhibit Gala in this case, to open the file (shown in Figure 60 on page OFF 43).

Q&A

Can I use the Backstage view to open a recent file in other Office programs, such as Word and Excel?

Yes, as long as the file name appears in the list of recent files in the Recent gallery.

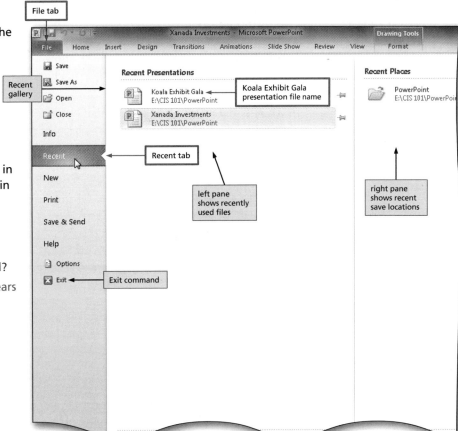

Figure 62

Other Ways

1. Click Start button, point to program name, click file name on submenu

2. Click File on Ribbon, click Open in Backstage view, navigate to file (Open dialog box), click Open button

To Quit an Office Program

You are finished using PowerPoint. Thus, you should quit this Office program. The following steps quit PowerPoint.

1 If you have one Office document open, click the Close button on the right side of the title bar to close the document and quit the Office program; or if you have multiple Office documents open, click File on the Ribbon to open the Backstage view and then click Exit in the Backstage view to close all open documents and quit the Office program.

2 If a dialog box appears, click the Save button to save any changes made to the document since the last save.

Excel

Excel is a powerful spreadsheet program that allows users to organize data, complete calculations, make decisions, graph data, develop professional-looking reports (Figure 63), publish organized data to the Web, and access real-time data from Web sites. The four major parts of Excel are:

• **Workbooks and Worksheets** - A **workbook** is like a notebook. Inside the workbook are sheets, each of which is called a **worksheet**. In other words, a workbook is a collection of worksheets. Worksheets allow users to enter, calculate, manipulate, and analyze data such as numbers and text. The terms worksheet and spreadsheet are interchangeable.

• **Charts** - Excel can draw a variety of charts.

• **Tables** - Tables organize and store data within worksheets. For example, once a user enters data into a worksheet, an Excel table can sort the data, search for specific data, and select data that satisfies defined criteria.

• **Web Support -** Web support allows users to save Excel worksheets or parts of a worksheet in HTML format, so that a user can view and manipulate the worksheet using a browser. Excel Web support also provides access to real-time data, such as stock quotes, using Web queries.

Figure 63

To Create a New Blank Office Document from Windows Explorer

Windows Explorer provides a means to create a blank Office document without ever starting an Office program. The following steps use Windows Explorer to create a blank Excel document.

- If necessary, click the Windows Explorer program button on the taskbar to make the folder window the active window in Windows Explorer.

- Double-click your class folder (CIS 101, in this case) in the navigation pane to display the contents of the selected folder.

- Double-click the Excel folder to display its contents in the right pane.

- With the Excel folder selected, right-click an open area in the right pane to display a shortcut menu.

- Point to New on the shortcut menu to display the New submenu (Figure 64).

Figure 64

- Click Microsoft Excel Worksheet on the New submenu to display an icon and text box for a new file in the current folder window (Figure 65).

Figure 65

3

- Type **Brain Busters** in the text box and then press the ENTER key to assign a name to the new file in the current folder (Figure 66).

Figure 66

To Start a Program from Windows Explorer and Open a File

Previously, you learned how to start an Office program using the Start menu and the search box. Another way start an Office program is to open an existing file from Windows Explorer, which causes the program in which the file was created to start and then open the selected file. The following steps, which assume Windows 7 is running, use Windows Explorer to start the Excel Office program based on a typical installation. You may need to ask your instructor how to start Office programs for your computer.

- If necessary, display the file to open in the folder window in Windows Explorer (shown in Figure 66 on the previous page).

- Right-click the file icon or file name (Brain Busters, in this case) to display a shortcut menu (Figure 67).

Figure 67

2

- Click Open on the shortcut menu to open the selected file in the program used to create the file, Microsoft Excel in this case (Figure 68).

- If the program window is not maximized, click the Maximize button on the title bar to maximize the window.

- For Excel users, if the worksheet window in Excel is not maximized, click the worksheet window Maximize button to maximize the worksheet window within Excel.

Figure 68

Instead of using Windows Explorer, can I start Excel using the same method shown previously for Word and PowerPoint?

Yes, you can use any method of starting an Office program to start Excel.

Unique Features of Excel

The Excel window consists of a variety of components to make your work more efficient and worksheets more professional. These include the document window, Ribbon, Mini toolbar and shortcut menus, Quick Access Toolbar, and the Backstage view. Some of these components are common to other Microsoft Office 2010 programs; others are unique to Excel.

Excel opens a new workbook with three worksheets. If necessary, you can add additional worksheets as long as your computer has enough memory to accommodate them.

Each worksheet has a sheet name that appears on a **sheet tab** at the bottom of the workbook. For example, Sheet1 is the name of the active worksheet displayed in the Brain Busters workbook. If you click the sheet tab labeled Sheet2, Excel displays the Sheet2 worksheet.

The Worksheet   The worksheet is organized into a rectangular grid containing vertical columns and horizontal rows. A column letter above the grid, also called the **column heading**, identifies each column. A row number on the left side of the grid, also called the **row heading**, identifies each row. With the screen resolution set to 1024 × 768 and the Excel window maximized, Excel displays 15 columns (A through O) and 25 rows (1 through 25) of the worksheet on the screen, as shown in Figure 68.

The intersection of each column and row is a cell. A **cell** is the basic unit of a worksheet into which you enter data. Each worksheet in a workbook has 16,384 columns and 1,048,576 rows for a total of 17,179,869,180 cells. Only a small fraction of the active worksheet appears on the screen at one time.

A cell is referred to by its unique address, or **cell reference**, which is the coordinates of the intersection of a column and a row. To identify a cell, specify the column letter first, followed by the row number. For example, cell reference E2 refers to the cell located at the intersection of column E and row 2 (Figure 68).

One cell on the worksheet, designated the **active cell**, is the one into which you can enter data. The active cell in Figure 68 is A1. The active cell is identified in three ways. First, a heavy border surrounds the cell; second, the active cell reference shows immediately above column A in the Name box; and third, the column heading A and row heading 1 are highlighted so it is easy to see which cell is active (Figure 68).

The horizontal and vertical lines on the worksheet itself are called **gridlines**. Gridlines make it easier to see and identify each cell in the worksheet. If desired, you can turn the gridlines off so that they do not show on the worksheet, but it is recommended that you leave them on for now.

The mouse pointer in Figure 68 has the shape of a block plus sign. The mouse pointer appears as a block plus sign whenever it is located in a cell on the worksheet. Another common shape of the mouse pointer is the block arrow. The mouse pointer turns into the block arrow when you move it outside the worksheet or when you drag cell contents between rows or columns. The other mouse pointer shapes are described when they appear on the screen.

Ribbon   When you start Excel, the Ribbon displays eight main tabs: File, Home, Insert, Page Layout, Formulas, Data, Review, and View. The Formulas and Data tabs are specific to Excel. The Formulas tab allows you to work with Excel formulas, and the Data tab allows you to work with data processing features such as importing and sorting data.

BTW **The Worksheet Size and Window**
The 16,384 columns and 1,048,576 rows in Excel make for a huge worksheet that – if you could imagine – takes up the entire side of a building to display in its entirety. Your computer screen, by comparison, is a small window that allows you to view only a minute area of the worksheet at one time. While you cannot see the entire worksheet, you can move the window over the worksheet to view any part of it.

BTW **Customizing the Ribbon**
In addition to customizing the Quick Access Toolbar, you can add items to and remove items from the Ribbon. To customize the Ribbon, click File on the Ribbon to open the Backstage view, click Options in the Backstage view, and then click Customize Ribbon in the left pane of the Options dialog box. More information about customizing the Ribbon is presented in a later chapter.

Formula Bar The formula bar appears below the Ribbon (Figure 69). As you type, Excel displays the entry in the **formula bar**. You can make the formula bar larger by dragging the sizing handle at the bottom of the formula bar or clicking the expand button to the right of the formula bar. Excel also displays the active cell reference in the **Name box** on the left side of the formula bar.

Figure 69

To Enter a Worksheet Title

To enter data into a cell, you first must select it. The easiest way to select a cell (make it active) is to use the mouse to move the block plus sign mouse pointer to the cell and then click. An alternative method is to use the arrow keys that are located just to the right of the typewriter keys on the keyboard. An arrow key selects the cell adjacent to the active cell in the direction of the arrow on the key.

In Excel, any set of characters containing a letter, hyphen (as in a telephone number), or space is considered text. **Text** is used to place titles, such as worksheet titles, column titles, and row titles, on the worksheet. The following steps enter the worksheet title in cell A1.

• If it is not already the active cell, click cell A1 to make it the active cell (Figure 70).

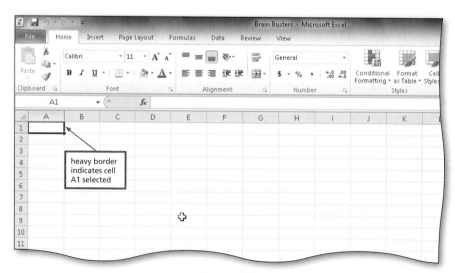

Figure 70

②

- Type **Brain Buster Book Rentals** in cell A1 (Figure 71).

Why did the appearance of the formula bar change?

Excel displays the title in the formula bar and in cell A1. When you begin typing a cell entry, Excel displays two additional boxes in the formula bar: the Cancel box and the Enter box. Clicking the Enter box completes an entry. Clicking the Cancel box cancels an entry.

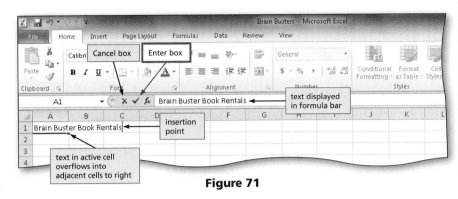

Figure 71

③

- Click the Enter box to complete the entry and enter the worksheet title in cell A1 (Figure 72).

Figure 72

Other Ways		
1. To complete entry, click any cell other than active cell	2. To complete entry, press ENTER, HOME, PAGE UP, PAGE DOWN, END,	UP, DOWN, LEFT ARROW, or RIGHT ARROW

To Save an Existing Office Document with the Same File Name

Saving frequently cannot be overemphasized. You have made modifications to the file (spreadsheet) since you created it. Thus, you should save again. Similarly, you should continue saving files frequently so that you do not lose your changes since the time you last saved the file. You can use the same file name, such as Brain Busters, to save the changes made to the document. The following step saves a file again.

①

- Click the Save button on the Quick Access Toolbar to overwrite the previously saved file (Brain Busters, in this case) on the USB flash drive (Figure 73).

Why did the Save As dialog box not appear?

Office programs, including Excel, overwrite the document using the setting specified the first time you saved the document.

Figure 73

Other Ways
1. Press CTRL+S or press SHIFT+F12

To Use Save As to Change the Name of a File

You might want to save a file with a different name and even to a different location. For example, you might start a homework assignment with a data file and then save it with a final file name for submitting to your instructor, saving it to a location designated by your instructor. The following steps save a file with a different file name.

1 With your USB flash drive connected to one of the computer's USB ports, click File on the Ribbon to open the Backstage view.

2 Click Save As in the Backstage view to display the Save As dialog box.

3 Type **Brain Busters Rental Summary** in the File name text box (Save As dialog box) to change the file name. Do not press the ENTER key after typing the file name because you do not want to close the dialog box at this time.

4 Navigate to the desired save location (the Excel folder in the CIS 101 folder [or your class folder] on the USB flash drive, in this case). For specific instructions, perform the tasks in steps 4a through 4g.

4a If a navigation pane is not displayed in the Save As dialog box, click the Browse Folders button to expand the dialog box.

4b If Computer is not displayed in the navigation pane, drag the navigation pane scroll bar (Save As dialog box) until Computer appears.

4c If Computer is not expanded in the navigation pane, double-click Computer to display a list of available storage devices in the navigation pane.

4d If necessary, scroll through the Save As dialog box until your USB flash drive appears in the list of available storage devices in the navigation pane.

4e If your USB flash drive is not expanded, double-click the USB flash drive in the list of available storage devices in the navigation pane to select that drive as the new save location and display its contents in the right pane.

4f If your class folder (CIS 101, in this case) is not expanded, double-click the CIS 101 folder to select the folder and display its contents.

4g Double-click the Excel folder to select it and display its contents in the right pane.

5 Click the Save button (Save As dialog box) to save the file in the selected folder on the selected drive with the new file name.

To Quit an Office Program

You are finished using Excel. The following steps quit Excel.

1 If you have one Office document open, click the Close button on the right side of the title bar to close the document and quit the Office program; or if you have multiple Office documents open, click File on the Ribbon to open the Backstage view and then click Exit in the Backstage view to close all open documents and quit the Office program.

2 If a dialog box appears, click the Save button to save any changes made to the file since the last save.

Access

The term **database** describes a collection of data organized in a manner that allows access, retrieval, and use of that data. **Microsoft Access 2010**, usually referred to as simply **Access,** is a database management system. A **database management system** is software that allows you to use a computer to create a database; add, change, and delete data in the database; create queries that allow you to ask questions concerning the data in the database; and create forms and reports using the data in the database.

To Start a Program

The following steps, which assume Windows 7 is running, start the Access program based on a typical installation. You may need to ask your instructor how to start programs for your computer.

1 Click the Start button on the Windows 7 taskbar to display the Start menu.

2 Type the name of the program, **Microsoft Access** in this case, as the search text in the 'Search programs and files' text box and watch the search results appear on the Start menu.

3 Click the name of the program, Microsoft Access 2010 in this case, in the search results on the Start menu to start Access.

4 If the program window is not maximized, click the Maximize button on its title bar to maximize the window (Figure 74).

Q&A   Do I have to start Access using these steps?

No. You can use any previously discussed method of starting an Office program to start Access.

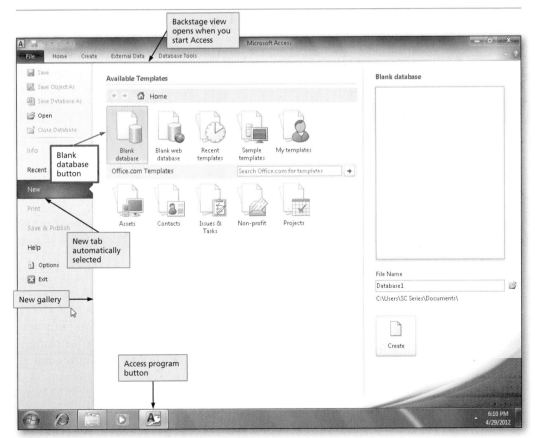

Figure 74

Unique Elements in Access

You work on objects such as tables, forms, and reports in the **Access work area**. In Figure 74, the Access window contains no open objects. Figure 75 shows a work area with multiple objects open. **Object tabs** for the open objects appear at the top of the work area. You select an open object by clicking its tab. In the figure, the Suppliers Split Form is the selected object. To the left of the work area is the Navigation Pane, which contains a list of all the objects in the database. You use this pane to open an object. You also can customize the way objects are displayed in the Navigation Pane.

Because the Navigation Pane can take up space in the window, you may not have as much open space for working as you would with Word or Excel. You can use the Shutter Bar Open/Close button to minimize the Navigation Pane when you are not using it, which allows more space to work with tables, forms, reports, and other database elements.

Figure 75

Ribbon When you start Access, the Ribbon displays five main tabs: File, Home, Create, External Data, and Database Tools. Access has unique groupings such as Sort & Filter and Records that are designed specifically for working with databases. Many of the formatting options are reserved for the tool tabs that appear when you are working with forms and reports.

To Create an Access Database

Unlike the other Office programs, Access saves a database when you first create it. When working in Access, you will add data to an Access database. As you add data to a database, Access automatically saves your changes rather than waiting until you manually save the database or quit Access. Recall that in Word and Excel, you entered the data first and then saved it.

Because Access automatically saves the database as you add and change data, you do not have to always click the Save button. In fact, the Save button in Access is used for saving the objects (including tables, queries, forms, reports, and other database objects) a database contains. You can use either the Blank Database option or a template to create a new database. If you already know the organization of your database, you would use the Blank Database option. If not, you can use a template. Templates can guide you by suggesting some commonly used database organizations.

The following steps use the Blank Database option to create a database named Charmed Excursions in the Access folder in the class folder (CIS 101, in this case) on a USB flash drive.

1

- If necessary, click the Blank database button in the New gallery (shown in Figure 74 on page OFF 53) in the Backstage view to select the template type.

- Click the File Name text box to select the default database name.

- Type **Charmed Excursions** in the File Name text box to enter the new file name. Do not press the ENTER key after typing the file name because you do not want to create the database at this time (Figure 76).

Figure 76

Q&A Why is the Backstage view automatically open when you start Access?

Unlike other Office programs, you first must save a database before adding any data. For this reason, the Backstage view opens automatically when you start Access.

2

- Click the 'Browse for a location to put your database' button to display the File New Database dialog box.

- Navigate to the location for the database, that is, the USB flash drive, then to the folder identifying your class (CIS 101, in this case), and then to the Access folder (Figure 77). For detailed steps about navigating, see Steps 3a – 3c on pages OFF 28 and OFF 29.

Q&A Why does the 'Save as type' box say Microsoft Access 2007 Databases?

Microsoft Access database formats change with some new versions of Microsoft Access. The most recent format is the Microsoft Access 2007 Databases format, which was released with Access 2007.

Figure 77

3

• Click the OK button (File New Database dialog box) to select the Access folder as the location for the database and close the dialog box (Figure 78).

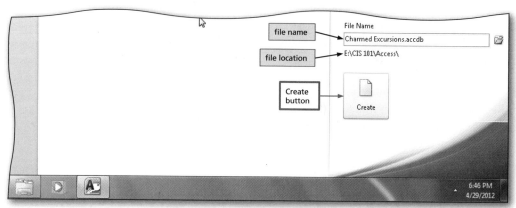

Figure 78

4

• Click the Create button in the Backstage view to create the database on the selected drive in the selected folder with the file name, Charmed Excursions. If necessary, click the Enable Content button (Figure 79).

Q&A How do I know that the Charmed Excursions database is created?

The name of the database appears on the title bar.

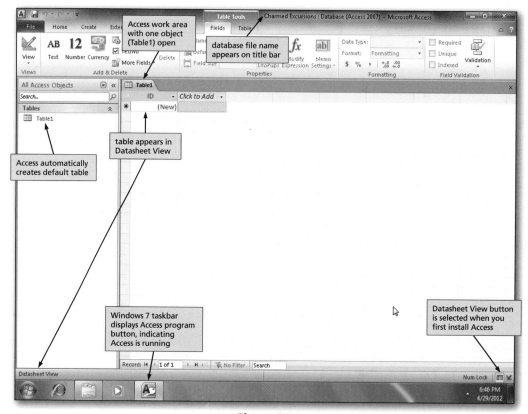

Figure 79

To Close an Office File

Assume you need to close the Access database and return to it later. The following step closes an Office file.

1 Click File on the Ribbon to open the Backstage view and then click Close Database in the Backstage view to close the open file (Charmed Excursions, in this case) without quitting the active program.

Q&A Why is Access still on the screen?

When you close a database, the program remains open.

To Open an Existing Office File

Assume you wish to continue working on an existing file, that is, a file you previously saved. Earlier in this chapter, you learned how to open a recently used file through the Backstage view. The following steps open a database, specifically the Charmed Excursions database, from the USB flash drive.

- With your USB flash drive connected to one of the computer's USB ports, if necessary, click File on the Ribbon to open the Backstage view.

- Click Open in the Backstage view to display the Open dialog box (Figure 80).

- Navigate to the location of the file to be opened (in this case, the USB flash drive, then to the CIS 101 folder [or your class folder], and then to the Access folder). For detailed steps about navigating, see Steps 3a – 3c on pages OFF 28 and OFF 29.

Q&A

What if I did not save my file in a folder?

If you did not save your file in a folder, the file you wish to open should be displayed in the Open dialog box before navigating to any folders.

Figure 80

- Click the file to be opened, Charmed Excursions in this case, to select the file (Figure 81).

- Click the Open button (Open dialog box) to open the selected file and display the opened file in the current program window (shown in Figure 79).

Other Ways

1. Click File on the Ribbon, click Recent in Backstage view, double-click file
2. Press CTRL+O
3. Navigate to file in Windows Explorer, double-click file

Figure 81

To Quit an Office Program

You are finished using Access. The following step quits Access.

 Click the Close button on the right side of the title bar to close the file and quit the Office program.

Other Office Programs

In addition to the Office programs discussed thus far, three other programs are useful when collaborating and communicating with others: Outlook, Publisher, and OneNote.

Outlook

Outlook is a powerful communications and scheduling program that helps you communicate with others, keep track of contacts, and organize your calendar. Personal information manager (PIM) programs such as Outlook provide a way for individuals and workgroups to organize, find, view, and share information easily. Outlook allows you to send and receive electronic mail (e-mail) and permits you to engage in real-time messaging with family, friends, or coworkers using instant messaging. Outlook also provides a means to organize contacts. Users can track e-mail messages, meetings, and notes related to a particular contact. Outlook's Calendar, Contacts, Tasks, and Notes components aid in this organization. Contact information readily is available from the Outlook Calendar, Mail, Contacts, and Task components by accessing the Find a Contact feature.

Electronic mail (e-mail) is the transmission of messages and files over a computer network. E-mail has become an important means of exchanging information and files between business associates, classmates and instructors, friends, and family. Businesses find that using e-mail to send documents electronically saves both time and money. Parents with students away at college or relatives who live across the country find that communicating by e-mail is an inexpensive and easy way to stay in touch with their family members. Exchanging e-mail messages is one of the more widely used features of the Internet.

The Outlook Window Figure 82 shows an Outlook window, which is divided into six panes: the Favorites folder pane, Mail folder pane, and Navigation Pane on the left side of the window, the Inbox message pane to the left of center, the Reading Pane to the right of center, and the People Pane just below the Reading Pane.

When an e-mail message is open in Outlook, it is displayed in a Message window (Figure 83). When you open a message, the Message window Ribbon displays the Message tab, which contains the more frequently used commands.

Figure 82

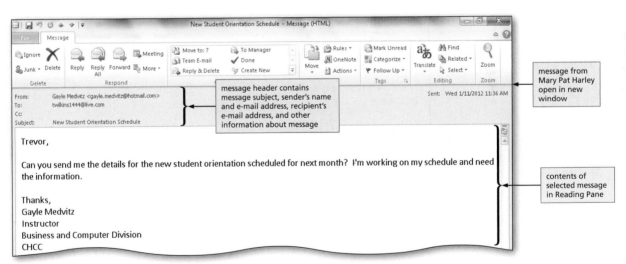

Figure 83

Publisher

Publisher is a powerful desktop publishing (DTP) program that assists you in designing and producing professional-quality documents that combine text, graphics, illustrations, and photos. DTP software provides additional tools beyond those typically found in word processing programs, including design templates, graphic manipulation tools, color schemes or libraries, advanced layout and printing tools, and Web components. For large jobs, businesses use DTP software to design publications that are camera ready, which means the files are suitable for outside commercial printing. In addition, DTP software can be used to create Web pages and interactive Web forms.

Publisher is used by people who regularly produce high-quality color publications, such as newsletters, brochures, flyers, logos, signs, catalogs, cards, and business forms. Saving publications as Web pages or complete Web sites is a powerful component of Publisher. All publications can be saved in a format that easily is viewed and manipulated using a browser.

Publisher has many features designed to simplify production and make publications visually appealing. Using Publisher, you easily can change the shape, size, and color of text and graphics. You can include many kinds of graphical objects, including mastheads, borders, tables, images, pictures, charts, and Web objects in publications, as well as integrate spreadsheets and databases.

The Publisher Window   On the right side of the Backstage view, Publisher displays the New template gallery, which includes a list of publication types. **Publication types** are typical publications used by desktop publishers. The more popular types are displayed in the center of the window. Each publication type is a link to display various templates and blank publications from which you may choose.

Once you select a publication type, the window changes to allow you to select a specific template (Figure 84). Some templates are installed with Publisher, and others are available online. Clicking a publication type causes template previews to be displayed in the center of the window. The templates are organized by purpose (for example, Sales) and then alphabetically by design type. On the right, Publisher will display a larger preview of the selected template, along with some customization options if the template is installed or a download option if the template is online. In Figure 84, the installed Arrows template is selected so that the customize options appear.

Figure 84

When you click the Create button, Publisher creates the document and sets it up for you to edit. Figure 85 shows the Arrows document that Publisher creates when default options are selected.

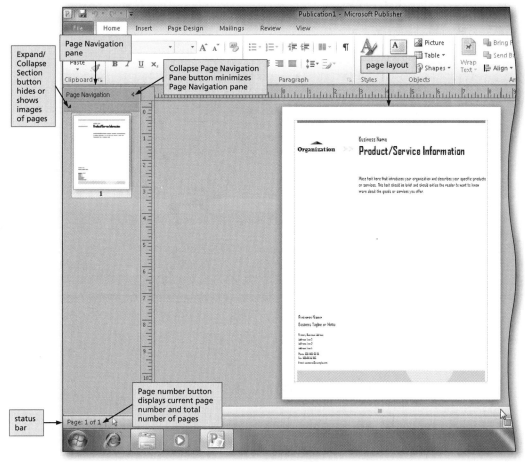

Figure 85

OneNote

OneNote is a note taking program that assists you in entering, saving, organizing, searching, and using notes. It enables you to create pages, which are organized in sections, just as in a physical notebook. In OneNote, you can type notes anywhere on a page and then easily move the notes around on the page. You can create lists and outlines, use handwriting to enter notes, and create drawings. If you use a Tablet PC to add handwritten notes to a document, OneNote can convert the handwriting to text. It also can perform searches on the handwritten entries. Pictures and data from other programs easily are incorporated in your notes.

In addition to typing and handwriting, you can take audio notes. For example, you could record conversations during a meeting or lecture. As you record, you can take additional notes. When you play back the audio notes, you can synchronize the additional notes you took; that is, OneNote will show you during playback the exact points at which you added the notes. A variety of note flags, which are symbols that call your attention to notes on a page, enable you to flag notes as being important. You then can use the Note Flags summary to view the flagged notes, which can be sorted in a variety of ways.

OneNote includes tools to assist you with organizing a notebook and navigating its contents. It also includes a search facility, making it easy to find the specific notes in which you are interested. For short notes that you always want to have available readily, you can use Side Notes, which are used much like the sticky notes that you might use in a physical notebook.

OneNote Window All activity in OneNote takes place in the **notebook** (Figure 86). Like a physical notebook, the OneNote notebook consists of notes that are placed on **pages**. The pages are grouped into **sections**, which can be further grouped into **folders**. (No folders are shown in the notebook in the figure.) You can use the Search All Notebooks box to search for specific text in your notes.

You can add pages to the notebook using the New Page button in the Page Tabs pane. If Page Tabs are displayed, then you can switch to a page by clicking its tab. Figure 86 shows the Top Uses page being displayed for the General notebook.

Figure 86

Break Point: If you wish to take a break, this is a good place to do so. To resume at a later time, continue to follow the steps from this location forward.

Moving, Renaming, and Deleting Files

Earlier in this chapter, you learned how to organize files in folders, which is part of a process known as **file management**. The following sections cover additional file management topics including renaming, moving, and deleting files.

To Rename a File

In some circumstances, you may want to change the name of, or rename, a file or a folder. For example, you may want to distinguish a file in one folder or drive from a copy of a similar file, or you may decide to rename a file to better identify its contents. The Word folder shown in Figure 87 contains the Word document, Koala Exhibit. The following steps change the name of the Koala Exhibit file in the Word folder to Koala Exhibit Flyer.

1

- If necessary, click the Windows Explorer program button on the taskbar to display the folder window in Windows Explorer.

- Navigate to the location of the file to be renamed (in this case, the Word folder in the CIS 101 [or your class folder] folder on the USB flash drive) to display the file(s) it contains in the right pane.

- Right-click the Koala Exhibit icon or file name in the right pane to select the Koala Exhibit file and display a shortcut menu that presents a list of commands related to files (Figure 87).

Figure 87

2

- Click Rename on the shortcut menu to place the current file name in a text box.

- Type **Koala Exhibit Flyer** in the text box and then press the ENTER key (Figure 88).

Are any risks involved in renaming files that are located on a hard disk?

If you inadvertently rename a file that is associated with certain programs, the programs may not be able to find the file and, therefore, may not execute properly. Always use caution when renaming files.

Can I rename a file when it is open?

No, a file must be closed to change the file name.

Figure 88

Other Ways

1. Select file, press F2, type new file name, press ENTER

To Move a File

At some time, you may want to move a file from one folder, called the source folder, to another, called the destination. When you move a file, it no longer appears in the original folder. If the destination and the source folders are on the same disk drive, you can move a file by dragging it. If the folders are on different disk drives, then you will need to right-drag the file. The following step moves the Brain Busters Rental Summary file from the Excel folder to the OneNote folder.

- In Windows Explorer, navigate to the location of the file to be moved (in this case, the Excel folder in the CIS 101 folder [or your class folder] on the USB flash drive).

- Click the Excel folder in the navigation pane to display the files it contains in the right pane (Figure 89).

- Drag the Brain Busters Rental Summary file in the right pane to the OneNote folder in the navigation pane.

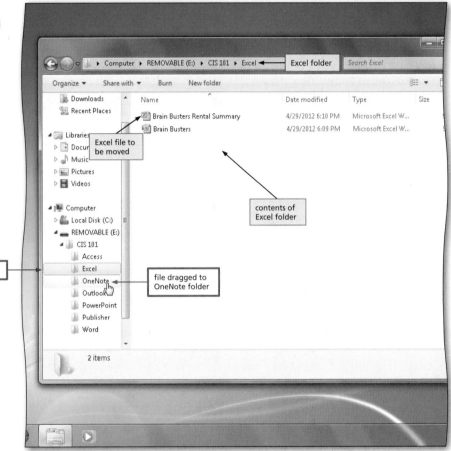

Figure 89

Other Ways

1. Right-click file, drag file to destination folder, click Move here
2. Right-click file to copy, click Cut on shortcut menu, right-click destination folder, click Paste on shortcut menu
3. Select file to copy, press CTRL+X, select destination folder, press CTRL+V

To Delete a File

A final task you may want to perform is to delete a file. Exercise extreme caution when deleting a file or files. When you delete a file from a hard disk, the deleted file is stored in the Recycle Bin where you can recover it until you empty the Recycle Bin. If you delete a file from removable media, such as a USB flash drive, the file is deleted permanently. The next steps delete the Koala Exhibit Gala file from the PowerPoint folder.

1

- In Windows Explorer, navigate to the location of the file to be deleted (in this case, the PowerPoint folder in the CIS 101 folder [or your class folder] on the USB flash drive).

- Click the PowerPoint folder in the navigation pane to display the files it contains in the right pane.

- Right-click the Koala Exhibit Gala icon or file name in the right pane to select the file and display a shortcut menu (Figure 90).

Figure 90

2

- Click Delete on the shortcut menu to display the Delete File dialog box (Figure 91).

- Click the Yes button (Delete File dialog box) to delete the selected file.

 Can I use this same technique to delete a folder?

Yes. Right-click the folder and then click Delete on the shortcut menu. When you delete a folder, all of the files and folders contained in the folder you are deleting, together with any files and folders on lower hierarchical levels, are deleted as well.

Figure 91

Other Ways
1. Select icon, press DELETE

Microsoft Office and Windows Help

At any time while you are using one of the Microsoft Office 2010 programs, you can use Office Help to display information about all topics associated with the program. To illustrate the use of Office Help, this section uses Word. Help in other Office 2010 programs operates in a similar fashion.

In Office 2010, Help is presented in a window that has Web-browser-style navigation buttons. Each Office 2010 program has its own Help home page, which is the starting Help page that is displayed in the Help window. If your computer is connected to the Internet, the contents of the Help page reflect both the local help files installed on the computer and material from Microsoft's Web site.

To Open the Help Window in an Office Program

The following step opens the Word Help window.

- Start an Office program, in this case Word.

- Click the Office program's Help button near the upper-right corner of the program window (the Microsoft Word Help button, in this case) to open the program's Help window (Figure 92).

Figure 92

Other Ways
1. Press F1

Moving and Resizing Windows

Up to this point, this chapter has used minimized and maximized windows. At times, however, it is useful, or even necessary, to have more than one window open and visible on the screen at the same time. You can resize and move these open windows so that you can view different areas of and elements in the window. In the case of the Help window, for example, it could be covering document text in the Word window that you need to see.

To Move a Window by Dragging

You can move any open window that is not maximized to another location on the desktop by dragging the title bar of the window. The following step drags the Word Help window to the top left of the desktop.

- Drag the window title bar (the Word Help window title bar, in this case) so that the window moves to the top left of the desktop, as shown in Figure 93.

Figure 93

Other Ways

1. Right-click title bar, click Move on shortcut menu, drag window

To Resize a Window by Dragging

Sometimes, information is not visible completely in a window. A method used to change the size of the window is to drag the window borders. The following step changes the size of the Word Help window by dragging its borders.

- Point to the lower-right corner of the window (the Word Help window, in this case) until the mouse pointer changes to a two-headed arrow.

- Drag the bottom border downward to display more of the active window (Figure 94).

Q&A

Can I drag other borders on the window to enlarge or shrink the window?

Yes, you can drag the left, right, and top borders and any window corner to resize a window.

Q&A

Will Windows 7 remember the new size of the window after I close it?

Yes. When you reopen the window, Windows 7 will display it at the same size it was when you closed it.

Figure 94

Using Office Help

Once an Office program's Help window is open, several methods exist for navigating Help. You can search for help by using any of the three following methods from the Help window:

1. Enter search text in the 'Type words to search for' text box
2. Click the links in the Help window
3. Use the Table of Contents

To Obtain Help Using the 'Type words to search for' Text Box

Assume for the following example that you want to know more about the Backstage view. The following steps use the 'Type words to search for' text box to obtain useful information about the Backstage view by entering the word, Backstage, as search text.

1

• Type **Backstage** in the 'Type words to search for' text box at the top of the Word Help window to enter the search text.

• Click the Search button arrow to display the Search menu (Figure 95).

• If it is not selected already, click All Word on the Search menu, so that Help performs the most complete search of the current program (Word, in this case). If All Word already is selected, click the Search button arrow again to close the Search menu.

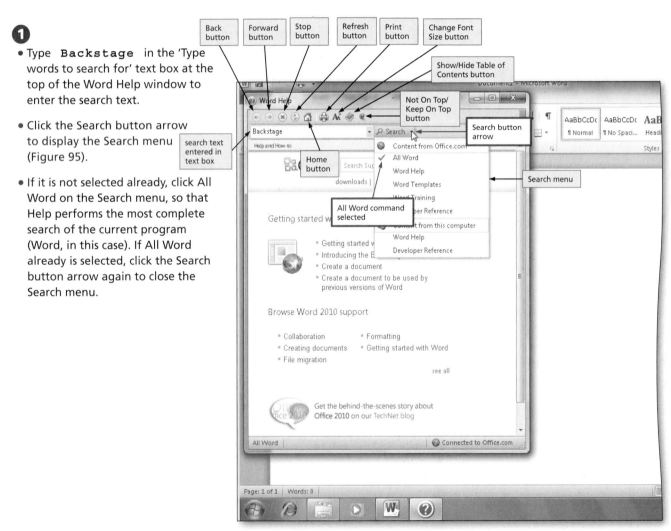

Figure 95

Q&A

Why select All Word on the Search menu?

Selecting All Word on the Search menu ensures that Word Help will search all possible sources for information about your search term. It will produce the most complete search results.

2
- Click the Search button to display the search results (Figure 96).

 Why do my search results differ?

If you do not have an Internet connection, your results will reflect only the content of the Help files on your computer. When searching for help online, results also can change as material is added, deleted, and updated on the online Help Web pages maintained by Microsoft.

 Why were my search results not very helpful?

When initiating a search, be sure to check the spelling of the search text; also, keep your search specific, with fewer than seven words, to return the most accurate results.

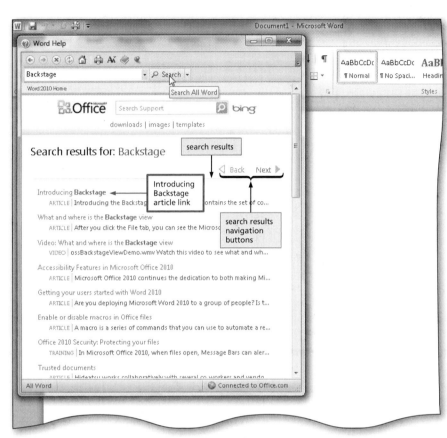

Figure 96

3
- Click the Introducing Backstage link to open the Help document associated with the selected topic (Figure 97).

Figure 97

• Click the Home button on the
toolbar to clear the search results
and redisplay the Help home page
(Figure 98).

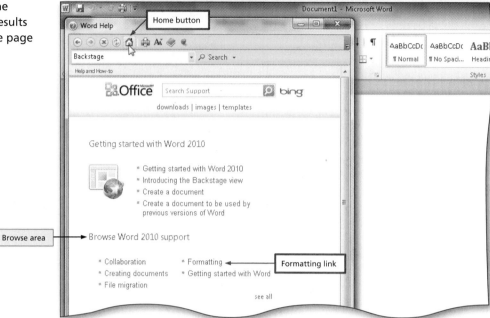

Figure 98

To Obtain Help Using the Help Links

If your topic of interest is listed in the Browse area of the Help window, you can click the link to begin
browsing the Help categories instead of entering search text. You browse Help just as you would browse a Web site.
If you know which category contains your Help information, you may wish to use these links. The following step
finds the Formatting Help information using the category links from the Word Help home page.

• Click the Formatting link on
the Help home page (shown in
Figure 98) to display the Formatting
page (Figure 99).

Figure 99

To Obtain Help Using the Help Table of Contents

A third way to find Help in Office programs is through the Help Table of Contents. You can browse through the Table of Contents to display information about a particular topic or to familiarize yourself with an Office program. The following steps access the Help information about themes by browsing through the Table of Contents.

1

- Click the Home button on the toolbar to display the Help home page.

- Click the Show Table of Contents button on the toolbar to display the Table of Contents pane on the left side of the Help window. If necessary, click the Maximize button on the Help title bar to maximize the window (Figure 100).

Why does the appearance of the Show Table of Contents button change?

When the Table of Contents is displayed in the Help window, the Hide Table of Contents button replaces the Show Table of Contents button.

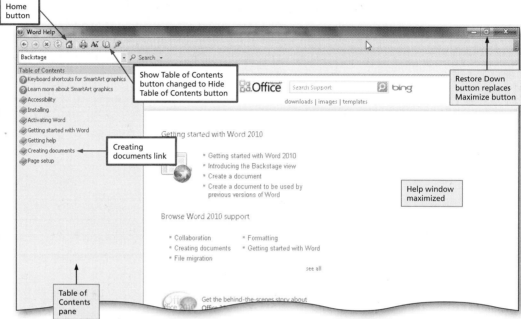

Figure 100

2

- Click the Creating documents link in the Table of Contents pane to view a list of Help subtopics.

- Click the Apply themes to Word documents link in the Table of Contents pane to view the selected Help document in the right pane (Figure 101).

- After reviewing the page, click the Close button to quit Help.

- Click the Office program's Close button (Word, in this case) to quit the Office program.

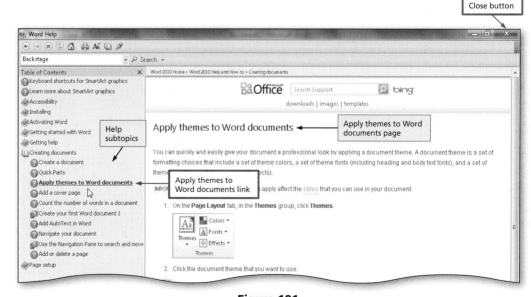

Figure 101

How do I remove the Table of Contents pane when I am finished with it?

The Show Table of Contents button acts as a toggle. When the Table of Contents pane is visible, the button changes to Hide Table of Contents. Clicking it hides the Table of Contents pane and changes the button to Show Table of Contents.

Obtaining Help while Working in an Office Program

Help in the Office programs provides you with the ability to obtain help directly, without the need to open the Help window and initiate a search. For example, you may be unsure about how a particular command works, or you may be presented with a dialog box that you are not sure how to use.

Figure 102 shows one option for obtaining help while working in Word. If you want to learn more about a command, point to the command button and wait for the Enhanced ScreenTip to appear. If the Help icon appears in the Enhanced ScreenTip, press the F1 key while pointing to the command to open the Help window associated with that command.

Figure 102

Figure 103 shows a dialog box that contains a Help button. Pressing the F1 key while the dialog box is displayed opens a Help window. The Help window contains help about that dialog box, if available. If no help file is available for that particular dialog box, then the main Help window opens.

Figure 103

Using Windows Help and Support

One of the more powerful Windows 7 features is Windows Help and Support. **Windows Help and Support** is available when using Windows 7 or when using any Microsoft program running under Windows 7. This feature is designed to assist you in using Windows 7 or the various programs. Table 4 describes the content found in the Help and Support Center. The same methods used for searching Microsoft Office Help can be used in Windows Help and Support. The difference is that Windows Help and Support displays help for Windows 7, instead of for Microsoft Office.

Table 4 Windows Help and Support Center Content Areas	
Area	**Function**
Find an answer quickly	This area contains instructions about how to do a quick search using the search box.
Not sure where to start?	This area displays three topics to help guide a user: How to get started with your computer, Learn about Windows Basics, and Browse Help topics. Clicking one of the options navigates to corresponding Help and Support pages.
More on the Windows Website	This area contains links to online content from the Windows Web site. Clicking the links navigates to the corresponding Web pages on the Web site.

To Start Windows Help and Support

The following steps start Windows Help and Support and display the Windows Help and Support window, containing links to more information about Windows 7.

1

- Click the Start button on the taskbar to display the Start menu (Figure 104).

Q&A

Why are the programs that are displayed on the Start menu different?

Windows adds the programs you have used recently to the left pane on the Start menu. You have started several programs while performing the steps in this chapter, so those programs now are displayed on the Start menu.

Figure 104

2

- Click Help and Support on the Start menu to open the Windows Help and Support window (Figure 105).

- After reviewing the Windows Help and Support window, click the Close button to quit Windows Help and Support.

Figure 105

Other Ways

1. Press CTRL+ESC, press RIGHT ARROW, press UP ARROW, press ENTER

2. Press WINDOWS+F1

Chapter Summary

In this chapter, you learned about the Windows 7 interface. You started Windows 7, were introduced to the components of the desktop, and learned several mouse operations. You opened, closed, moved, resized, minimized, maximized, and scrolled a window. You used folder windows to expand and collapse drives and folders, display drive and folder contents, create folders, and rename and then delete a file.

You also learned some basic features of some Microsoft Office 2010 programs, including Word, PowerPoint, Excel, and Access. As part of this learning process, you discovered the common elements that exist among these different Office programs. You now can save basic document, presentation, spreadsheet, and database files. Additional Office programs, including Outlook, Publisher, and OneNote also were discussed.

Microsoft Office Help was demonstrated, and you learned how to use the Office Help window. You were introduced to the Windows 7 Help and Support Center and learned how to use it to obtain more information about Windows 7.

The items listed below include all of the new Windows 7 and Office 2010 skills you have learned in this chapter.

1. Log On to the Computer (OFF 6)
2. Start a Program Using the Start Menu (OFF 10)
3. Maximize a Window (OFF 12)
4. Display a Different Tab on the Ribbon (OFF 16)
5. Minimize, Display, and Restore the Ribbon (OFF 17)
6. Display and Use a Shortcut Menu (OFF 18)
7. Customize the Quick Access Toolbar (OFF 19)
8. Enter Text in a Document (OFF 20)
9. Create a Folder (OFF 22)
10. Create a Folder within a Folder (OFF 24)
11. Expand a Folder, Scroll through Folder Contents, and Collapse a Folder (OFF 26)
12. Switch from One Program to Another (OFF 27)
13. Save a File in a Folder (OFF 27)
14. Minimize and Restore a Window (OFF 30)
15. Change the Screen Resolution (OFF 33)

16. Quit an Office Program with One Document Open (OFF 35)
17. Start a Program Using the Search Box (OFF 37)
18. Enter Content in a Title Slide (OFF 40)
19. Create a New Office Document from the Backstage View (OFF 41)
20. Close an Office File Using the Backstage View (OFF 44)
21. Open a Recent Office File Using the Backstage View (OFF 45)
22. Create a New Blank Office Document from Windows Explorer (OFF 47)
23. Start a Program from Windows Explorer and Open a File (OFF 48)
24. Enter a Worksheet Title (OFF 50)
25. Save an Existing Document with the Same File Name (OFF 51)

26. Create an Access Database (OFF 55)
27. Open an Existing Office File (OFF 57)
28. Rename a File (OFF 63)
29. Move a File (OFF 64)
30. Delete a File (OFF 64)
31. Open the Help Window in an Office Program (OFF 66)
32. Move a Window by Dragging (OFF 66)
33. Resize a Window by Dragging (OFF 67)
34. Obtain Help Using the 'Type words to search for' Text Box (OFF 68)
35. Obtain Help Using the Help Links (OFF 70)
36. Obtain Help Using the Help Table of Contents (OFF 71)
37. Start Windows Help and Support (OFF 73)

If you have a SAM 2010 user profile, your instructor may have assigned an autogradable version of this assignment. If so, log into the SAM 2010 Web site at www.cengage.com/sam2010 to download the instruction and start files.

Learn It Online

Test your knowledge of chapter content and key terms.

Instructions: To complete the Learn It Online exercises, start your browser, click the Address bar, and then enter the Web address **scsite.com/office2010/learn**. When the Office 2010 Learn It Online page is displayed, click the link for the exercise you want to complete and then read the instructions.

Chapter Reinforcement TF, MC, and SA
A series of true/false, multiple choice, and short answer questions that test your knowledge of the chapter content.

Flash Cards
An interactive learning environment where you identify chapter key terms associated with displayed definitions.

Practice Test
A series of multiple choice questions that test your knowledge of chapter content and key terms.

Who Wants To Be a Computer Genius?
An interactive game that challenges your knowledge of chapter content in the style of a television quiz show.

Wheel of Terms
An interactive game that challenges your knowledge of chapter key terms in the style of the television show *Wheel of Fortune*.

Crossword Puzzle Challenge
A crossword puzzle that challenges your knowledge of key terms presented in the chapter.

Apply Your Knowledge

Reinforce the skills and apply the concepts you learned in this chapter.

Creating a Folder and a Document

Instructions: You will create a Word folder and then create a Word document and save it in the folder.

Perform the following tasks:

1. Connect a USB flash drive to an available USB port and then open the USB flash drive window.

2. Click the New folder button on the toolbar to display a new folder icon and text box for the folder name.

3. Type `Word` in the text box to name the folder. Press the ENTER key to create the folder on the USB flash drive.

4. Start Word.

5. Enter the text shown in Figure 106.

6. Click the Save button on the Quick Access Toolbar. Navigate to the Word folder on the USB flash drive and then save the document using the file name, Apply 1 Class List.

7. If your Quick Access Toolbar does not show the Quick Print button, add the Quick Print button to the Quick Access Toolbar. Print the document using the Quick Print button on the Quick Access Toolbar. When you are finished printing, remove the Quick Print button from the Quick Access Toolbar.

8. Submit the printout to your instructor.

9. Quit Word.

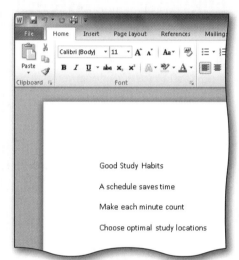

Figure 106

Extend Your Knowledge

Extend the skills you learned in this chapter and experiment with new skills. You will use Help to complete the assignment.

Using Help

Instructions: Use Office Help to perform the following tasks.

Perform the following tasks:

1. Start Word.

2. Click the Microsoft Word Help button to open the Word Help window (Figure 107).

3. Search Word Help to answer the following questions.

   a. What are the steps to add a new group to the Ribbon?

   b. What are Quick Parts?

4. With the Word program still running, start PowerPoint.

Figure 107

5. Click the Microsoft PowerPoint Help button on the title bar to open the PowerPoint Help window.

6. Search PowerPoint Help to answer the following questions.

   a. What is a slide master?

   b. How do you copy slides from another presentation into the existing presentation?

7. Quit PowerPoint.

8. Start Excel.

9. Click the Microsoft Excel Help button to open the Excel Help window.

10. Search Excel Help to answer the following questions.

   a. What are three different functions available in Excel?

   b. What are sparklines?

11. Quit Excel.

12. Start Access.

13. Click the Microsoft Access Help button to open the Access Help window.

14. Search Access Help to answer the following questions.

   a. What is SQL?

   b. What is a data macro?

15. Quit Access.

16. Type the answers from your searches in the Word document. Save the document with a new file name and then submit it in the format specified by your instructor.

17. Quit Word.

Make It Right

Analyze a file structure and correct all errors and/or improve the design.

Organizing Vacation Photos

Instructions: See the inside back cover of this book for instructions on downloading the Data Files for Students, or contact your instructor for information on accessing the required files.

     Traditionally, you have stored photos from past vacations together in one folder. The photos are becoming difficult to manage, and you now want to store them in appropriate folders. You will create the folder structure shown in Figure 108. You then will move the photos to the folders so that they will be organized properly.

1. Connect a USB flash drive to an available USB port to open the USB flash drive window.

2. Using the techniques presented in the chapter, create the hierarchical folder structure shown in Figure 108.

3. Using the techniques presented in the chapter, move the vacation photos to their appropriate folders.

4. Submit your work in the format specified by your instructor.

Figure 108

In the Lab

Use the guidelines, concepts, and skills presented in this chapter to increase your knowledge of Windows 7 and Office 2010. Labs are listed in order of increasing difficulty.

Lab 1: Using Windows Help and Support

Problem: You have a few questions about using Windows 7 and would like to answer these questions using Windows Help and Support.

Instructions: Use Windows Help and Support to perform the following tasks:

1. Display the Start menu and then click Help and Support to start Windows Help and Support.

2. Use the Help and Support Content page to answer the following questions.

   a. How do you reduce computer screen flicker?

   b. Which dialog box do you use to change the appearance of the mouse pointer?

   c. How do you minimize all windows?

   d. What is a VPN?

3. Use the Search Help text box in Windows Help and Support to answer the following questions.

   a. How can you minimize all open windows on the desktop?

   b. How do you start a program using the Run command?

   c. What are the steps to add a toolbar to the taskbar?

   d. What wizard do you use to remove unwanted desktop icons?

4. The tools to solve a problem while using Windows 7 are called **troubleshooters**. Use Windows Help and Support to find the list of troubleshooters (Figure 109), and answer the following questions.

   a. What problems does the HomeGroup troubleshooter allow you to resolve?

   b. List five Windows 7 troubleshooters that are not listed in Figure 109.

5. Use Windows Help and Support to obtain information about software licensing and product activation, and answer the following questions.

   a. What is genuine Windows?

   b. What is activation?

   c. What steps are required to activate Windows?

   d. What steps are required to read the Microsoft Software License Terms?

   e. Can you legally make a second copy of Windows 7 for use at home, work, or on a mobile computer or device?

   f. What is registration?

6. Close the Windows Help and Support window.

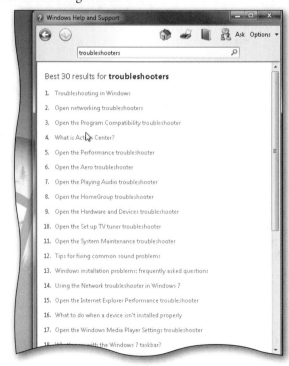

Figure 109

In the Lab

Lab 2: Creating Folders for a Pet Supply Store

Problem: Your friend works for Pete's Pet Supplies. He would like to organize his files in relation to the types of pets available in the store. He has five main categories: dogs, cats, fish, birds, and exotic. You are to create a folder structure similar to Figure 110.

Instructions: Perform the following tasks:

1. Connect a USB flash drive to an available USB port and then open the USB flash drive window.

2. Create the main folder for Pete's Pet Supplies.

3. Navigate to the Pete's Pet Supplies folder.

4. Within the Pete's Pet Supplies folder, create a folder for each of the following: Dogs, Cats, Fish, Birds, and Exotic.

5. Within the Exotic folder, create two additional folders, one for Primates and the second for Reptiles.

6. Submit the assignment in the format specified by your instructor.

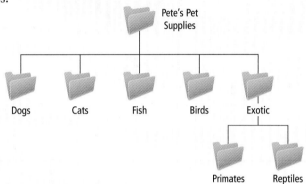

Figure 110

In the Lab

Lab 3: Creating Office Documents

Problem: You are taking a class that requires you to create a Word, PowerPoint, Excel, and Access file. You will save these files to folders named for four different Office programs (Figure 111).

Instructions: Create the folders shown in Figure 111. Then, using the respective Office program, create a small file to save in each folder (i.e., create a Word document to save in the Word folder, a PowerPoint presentation to save in the PowerPoint folder, and so on).

Figure 111

1. Connect a USB flash drive to an available USB port and then open the USB flash drive window.

2. Create the folder structure shown in Figure 111.

3. Navigate to the Word folder.

4. Create a Word document containing the text, My First Word Document, and then save it in the Word folder.

5. Navigate to the PowerPoint folder.

6. Create a PowerPoint presentation containing the title text, My First PowerPoint Presentation, and then save it in the PowerPoint folder.

7. Navigate to the Excel folder.

Continued >

In the Lab *continued*

8. Create an Excel spreadsheet containing the text, My First Excel Spreadsheet, in cell A1 and then save it in the Excel folder.

9. Navigate to the Access folder.

10. Save an Access database named, My First Database, in the Access folder.

11. Close all open Office programs.

12. Submit the assignment in the format specified by your instructor.

Cases and Places

Apply your creative thinking and problem solving skills to design and implement a solution.

Note: To complete these assignments, you may be required to use the Data Files for Students. See the inside back cover of this book for instructions on downloading the Data Files for Students, or contact your instructor for information about accessing the required files.

1: Creating Beginning Files for Classes

Academic

You are taking the following classes: Introduction to Engineering, Beginning Psychology, Introduction to Biology, and Accounting. Create folders for each of the classes. Use the following folder names: Engineering, Psychology, Biology, and Accounting, when creating the folder structure. In the Engineering folder, use Word to create a Word document with the name of the class and the class meeting location and time (MW 10:30 – 11:45, Room 317). In the Psychology folder, use PowerPoint to create your first lab presentation. It should begin with a title slide containing the text, Behavioral Observations. In the Biology folder, save a database named Research in the Biology folder. In the Accounting folder, create an Excel spreadsheet with the text, Tax Information, in cell A1. Use the concepts and techniques presented in this chapter to create the folders and files.

2: Using Help

Personal

Your parents enjoy working and playing games on their home computers. Your mother uses a notebook computer downstairs, and your father uses a desktop computer upstairs. They expressed interest in sharing files between their computers and sharing a single printer, so you offered to research various home networking options. Start Windows Help and Support, and search Help using the keywords, home networking. Use the link for installing a printer on a home network. Start Word and then type the main steps for installing a printer. Use the link for setting up a HomeGroup and then type the main steps for creating a HomeGroup in the Word document. Use the concepts and techniques presented in this chapter to use Help and create the Word document.

3: Creating Folders

Professional

Your boss at the bookstore where you work part-time has asked for help with organizing her files. After looking through the files, you decided upon a file structure for her to use, including the following folders: books, magazines, tapes, DVDs, and general merchandise. Within the books folder, create folders for hardback and paperback books. Within magazines, create folders for special issues and periodicals. In the tapes folder, create folders for celebrity and major release. In the DVDs folder, create a folder for book to DVD. In the general merchandise folder, create folders for novelties, posters, and games. Use the concepts and techniques presented in this chapter to create the folders.

1 Creating, Formatting, and Editing a Word Document with Pictures

Objectives

You will have mastered the material in this chapter when you can:

- Enter text in a Word document
- Check spelling as you type
- Format paragraphs
- Format text
- Undo and redo commands or actions
- Change theme colors
- Insert digital pictures in a Word document
- Format pictures
- Add a page border
- Correct errors and revise a document
- Change document properties
- Print a document

1 | Creating, Formatting, and Editing a Word Document with Pictures

Introduction

To advertise a sale, promote a business, publicize an event, or convey a message to the community, you may want to create a flyer and hand it out in person or post it in a public location. Libraries, schools, religious organizations, grocery stores, coffee shops, and other places often provide bulletin boards or windows for flyers. These flyers announce personal items for sale or rent (car, boat, apartment); garage or block sales; services being offered (animal care, housecleaning, lessons); membership, sponsorship, or donation requests (club, religious organization, charity); and other messages such as a lost or found pet.

Project Planning Guidelines

> The process of developing a document that communicates specific information requires careful analysis and planning. As a starting point, establish why the document is needed. Once the purpose is determined, analyze the intended readers of the document and their unique needs. Then, gather information about the topic and decide what to include in the document. Finally, determine the document design and style that will be most successful at delivering the message. Details of these guidelines are provided in Appendix A. In addition, each project in this book provides practical applications of these planning considerations.

Project — Flyer with Pictures

Individuals and businesses create flyers to gain public attention. Flyers, which usually are a single page in length, are an inexpensive means of reaching the community. Many flyers, however, go unnoticed because they are designed poorly.

The project in this chapter follows general guidelines and uses Word to create the flyer shown in Figure 1–1. This colorful, eye-catching flyer announces that a dog has been found. The pictures of the dog, taken with a camera phone, entice passersby to stop and look at the flyer. The headline on the flyer is large and colorful to draw attention into the text. The body copy below the pictures briefly describes where and when the dog was found, along with a bulleted list that concisely highlights important identifying information. The signature line of the flyer calls attention to the contact phone number. The dog's name, Bailey, and signature line are in a different color so that they stand apart from the rest of the text on the flyer. Finally, the graphical page border nicely frames and complements the contents of the flyer.

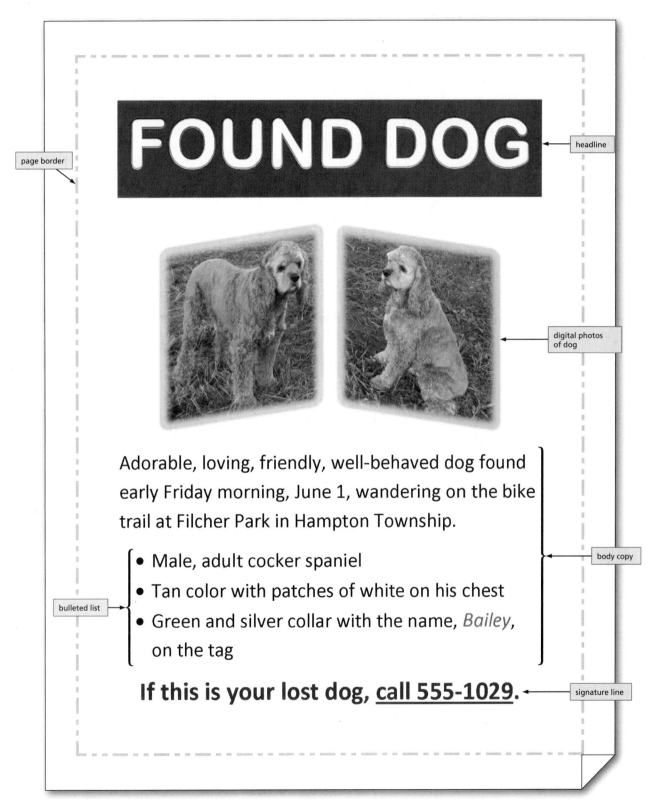

Figure 1–1

Overview

As you read this chapter, you will learn how to create the flyer shown in Figure 1–1 on the previous page by performing these general tasks:

- Enter text in the document.
- Format the text in the document.
- Insert the pictures in the document.
- Format the pictures in the document.
- Enhance the page with a border and additional spacing.
- Correct errors and revise the document.
- Print the document.

Plan
Ahead

General Project Guidelines

When creating a Word document, the actions you perform and decisions you make will affect the appearance and characteristics of the finished document. As you create a flyer, such as the project shown in Figure 1–1, you should follow these general guidelines:

1. **Choose the words for the text.** Follow the *less is more* principle. The less text, the more likely the flyer will be read. Use as few words as possible to make a point.

2. **Identify how to format various elements of the text.** The overall appearance of a document significantly affects its ability to communicate clearly. Examples of how you can modify the appearance, or **format**, of text include changing its shape, size, color, and position on the page.

3. **Find the appropriate graphical image(s).** An eye-catching graphical image should convey the flyer's overall message. It could show a product, service, result, or benefit, or visually convey a message that is not expressed easily with words.

4. **Establish where to position and how to format the graphical image(s).** The position and format of the graphical image(s) should grab the attention of passersby and draw them into reading the flyer.

5. **Determine whether the page needs enhancements such as a border or spacing adjustments.** A graphical, color-coordinated page border can further draw attention to a flyer and nicely frame its contents. Increasing or decreasing spacing between elements on a flyer can improve its readability and overall appearance.

6. **Correct errors and revise the document as necessary.** Post the flyer on a wall and make sure all text and images are legible from a distance. Ask someone else to read the flyer and give you suggestions for improvements.

7. **Determine the best method for distributing the document.** Documents can be distributed on paper or electronically. A flyer should be printed on paper so that it can be posted.

When necessary, more specific details concerning the above guidelines are presented at appropriate points in the chapter. The chapter also will identify the actions performed and decisions made regarding these guidelines during the creation of the flyer shown in Figure 1–1.

For an introduction to Windows 7 and instruction about how to perform basic Windows 7 tasks, read the Office 2010 and Windows 7 chapter at the beginning of this book, where you can learn how to resize windows, change screen resolution, create folders, move and rename files, use Windows Help, and much more.

To Start Word

If you are using a computer to step through the project in this chapter and you want your screens to match the figures in this book, you should change your screen's resolution to 1024×768. For information about how to change a computer's resolution, refer to the Office 2010 and Windows 7 chapter at the beginning of this book.

The following steps, which assume Windows 7 is running, start Word based on a typical installation. You may need to ask your instructor how to start Word for your computer. For a detailed example of the procedure summarized below, refer to the Office 2010 and Windows 7 chapter.

1 Click the Start button on the Windows 7 taskbar to display the Start menu.

2 Type **Microsoft Word** as the search text in the 'Search programs and files' text box and watch the search results appear on the Start menu.

3 Click Microsoft Word 2010 in the search results on the Start menu to start Word and display a new blank document in the Word window.

4 If the Word window is not maximized, click the Maximize button next to the Close button on its title bar to maximize the window.

5 If the Print Layout button on the status bar is not selected (shown in Figure 1–2 on the next page), click it so that your screen is in Print Layout view.

Q&A What is Print Layout view?

The default (preset) view in Word is **Print Layout view**, which shows the document on a mock sheet of paper in the document window.

6 If Normal (Home tab | Styles group) is not selected in the Quick Style gallery (shown in Figure 1–2), click it so that your document uses the Normal style.

Q&A What is the Normal style?

When you create a document, Word formats the text using a particular style. The default style in Word is called the **Normal style**, which is discussed later in this book.

Q&A What if rulers appear on my screen?

Click the View Ruler button above the vertical scroll bar to hide the rulers, or click View on the Ribbon to display the View tab and then place a check mark in the Ruler check box.

BTW
For an introduction to Office 2010 and instruction about how to perform basic tasks in Office 2010 programs, read the Office 2010 and Windows 7 chapter at the beginning of this book, where you can learn how to start a program, use the Ribbon, save a file, open a file, quit a program, use Help, and much more.

BTW
The Word Window
The chapters in this book begin with the Word window appearing as it did at the initial installation of the software. Your Word window may look different depending on your screen resolution and other Word settings.

Entering Text

The first step in creating a document is to enter its text. With the projects in this book, you enter text by typing on the keyboard. By default, Word positions text you type at the left margin. In a later section of this chapter, you will learn how to format, or change the appearance of, the entered text.

Plan Ahead

Choose the words for the text.
The text in a flyer is organized into three areas: headline, body copy, and signature line.

- The **headline** is the first line of text on the flyer. It conveys the product or service being offered, such as a car for sale or personal lessons, or the benefit that will be gained, such as a convenience, better performance, greater security, higher earnings, or more comfort; or it can contain a message such as a lost or found pet.

- The **body copy** consists of all text between the headline and the signature line. This text highlights the key points of the message in as few words as possible. It should be easy to read and follow. While emphasizing the positive, the body copy must be realistic, truthful, and believable.

- The **signature line**, which is the last line of text on the flyer, contains contact information or identifies a call to action.

BTW
Zooming
If text is too small for you to read on the screen, you can zoom the document by dragging the Zoom slider on the status bar or clicking the Zoom Out or Zoom In buttons on the status bar. Changing the zoom has no effect on the printed document.

To Type Text

To begin creating the flyer in this chapter, type the headline in the document window. The following steps type this first line of text in the document.

- Type **Found Dog** as the headline (Figure 1–2).

Q&A What if I make an error while typing?

You can press the BACKSPACE key until you have deleted the text in error and then retype the text correctly.

Q&A Why did the Spelling and Grammar Check icon appear on the status bar?

When you begin typing text, the **Spelling and Grammar Check icon** appears on the status bar with an animated pencil writing on paper to indicate that Word is checking for spelling and grammar errors. When you stop typing, the pencil changes to a blue check mark (no errors) or a red X (potential errors found). Word flags potential errors in the document with a red, green, or blue wavy underline. Later in this chapter, you will learn how to fix flagged errors.

Figure 1–2

- Press the ENTER key to move the insertion point to the beginning of the next line (Figure 1–3).

Q&A Why did blank space appear between the headline and the insertion point?

Each time you press the ENTER key, Word creates a new paragraph and inserts blank space between the two paragraphs. Later in this chapter, you will learn how to adjust the spacing between paragraphs.

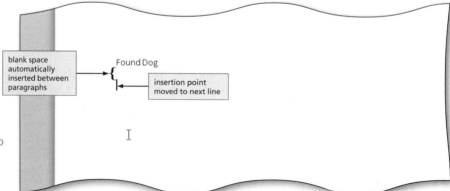

Figure 1–3

To Display Formatting Marks

To indicate where in a document you press the ENTER key or SPACEBAR, you may find it helpful to display formatting marks. A **formatting mark**, sometimes called a **nonprinting character**, is a character that Word displays on the screen but is not visible on a printed document. For example, the paragraph mark (¶) is a formatting mark that indicates where you press the ENTER key. A raised dot (·) shows where you press the SPACEBAR. Other formatting marks are discussed as they appear on the screen.

Depending on settings made during previous Word sessions, your Word screen already may display formatting marks (Figure 1–4). The following step displays formatting marks, if they do not show already on the screen.

1

- If the Home tab is not the active tab, click Home on the Ribbon to display the Home tab.

- If it is not selected already, click the Show/Hide ¶ button (Home tab | Paragraph group) to display formatting marks on the screen (Figure 1–4).

Q&A

What if I do not want formatting marks to show on the screen?

You can hide them by clicking the Show/Hide ¶ button (Home tab | Paragraph group) again. It is recommended that you display formatting marks so that you visually can identify when you press the ENTER key, SPACEBAR, and other keys associated with nonprinting characters; therefore, most of the document windows presented in this book show formatting marks.

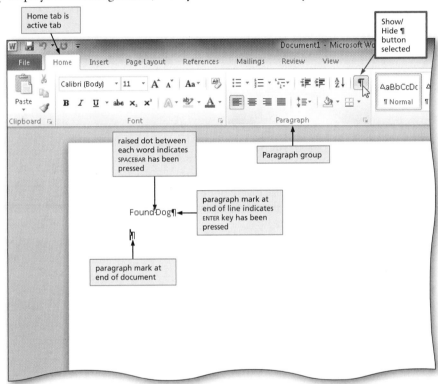

Figure 1–4

Other Ways
1. Press CTRL+SHIFT+*

To Insert a Blank Line

In the flyer, the digital pictures of the dog appear between the headline and body copy. You will not insert these pictures, however, until after you enter and format all text. Thus, you leave a blank line in the document as a placeholder for the pictures. To enter a blank line in a document, press the ENTER key without typing any text on the line. The following step inserts one blank line below the headline.

1

- Press the ENTER key to insert a blank line in the document (Figure 1–5).

Figure 1–5

Wordwrap

Wordwrap allows you to type words in a paragraph continually without pressing the ENTER key at the end of each line. As you type, if a word extends beyond the right margin, Word also automatically positions that word on the next line along with the insertion point.

Word creates a new paragraph each time you press the ENTER key. Thus, as you type text in the document window, do not press the ENTER key when the insertion point reaches the right margin. Instead, press the ENTER key only in these circumstances:

1. To insert a blank line(s) in a document (as shown in the steps on the previous page)
2. To begin a new paragraph
3. To terminate a short line of text and advance to the next line
4. To respond to questions or prompts in Word dialog boxes, task panes, and other on-screen objects

To Wordwrap Text as You Type

The next step in creating the flyer is to type the body copy. The following step illustrates how the body copy text wordwraps as you enter it in the document.

1

- Type the first sentence of the body copy: `Adorable, loving, friendly, well-behaved dog found early Friday morning, June 1, wandering on the bike trail at Filcher Park in Hampton Township.`

Why does my document wrap on different words?

The printer connected to a computer is one factor that can control where wordwrap occurs for each line in a document. Thus, it is possible that the same document could wordwrap differently if printed on different printers.

- Press the ENTER key to position the insertion point on the next line in the document (Figure 1–6).

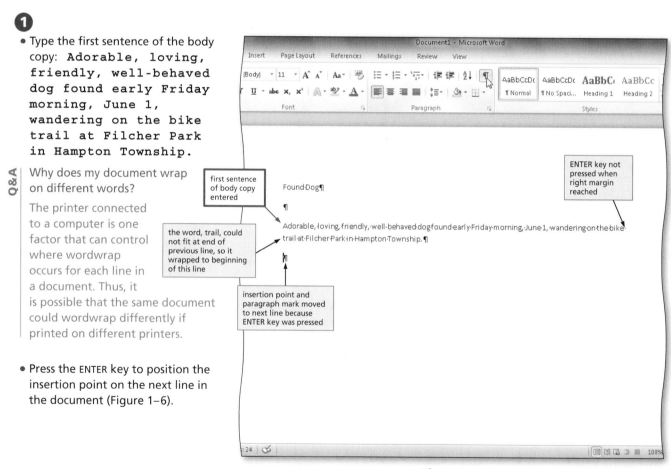

Figure 1–6

Spelling and Grammar Check

As you type text in a document, Word checks your typing for possible spelling and grammar errors. If all of the words you have typed are in Word's dictionary and your grammar is correct, as mentioned earlier, the Spelling and Grammar Check icon on the status bar displays a blue check mark. Otherwise, the icon shows a red X. In this case, Word flags the potential error in the document window with a red, green, or blue wavy underline. A red wavy underline means the flagged text is not in Word's dictionary (because it is a proper name or misspelled). A green wavy underline indicates the text may be incorrect grammatically. A blue wavy underline indicates the text may contain a contextual spelling error such as the misuse of homophones (words that are pronounced the same but that have different spellings or meanings, such as one and won). Although you can check the entire document for spelling and grammar errors at once, you also can check flagged errors as they appear on the screen.

A flagged word is not necessarily misspelled. For example, many names, abbreviations, and specialized terms are not in Word's main dictionary. In these cases, you can instruct Word to ignore the flagged word. As you type, Word also detects duplicate words while checking for spelling errors. For example, if your document contains the phrase, to the the store, Word places a red wavy underline below the second occurrence of the word, the.

BTW

Automatic Spelling Correction
As you type, Word automatically corrects some misspelled words. For example, if you type recieve, Word automatically corrects the misspelling and displays the word, receive, when you press the SPACEBAR or type a punctuation mark. To see a complete list of automatically corrected words, click File on the Ribbon to open the Backstage view, click Options in the Backstage view, click Proofing in the left pane (Word Options dialog box), click the AutoCorrect Options button, and then scroll through the list near the bottom of the dialog box.

To Check Spelling and Grammar as You Type

In the following steps, the word, patches, has been misspelled intentionally as paches to illustrate Word's check spelling as you type feature. If you are doing this project on a computer, your flyer may contain different misspelled words, depending on the accuracy of your typing.

1

- Type **Tan color with paches** and then press the SPACEBAR so that a red wavy line appears below the misspelled word (Figure 1–7).

Q&A

What if Word does not flag my spelling and grammar errors with wavy underlines?

To verify that the check spelling and grammar as you type features are enabled, click File on the Ribbon to open the Backstage view and then click Options in the Backstage view. When the Word Options dialog box is displayed, click Proofing in the left pane, and then ensure the 'Check spelling as you type' and 'Mark grammar errors as you type' check boxes contain check marks. Also ensure the 'Hide spelling errors in this document only' and 'Hide grammar errors in this document only' check boxes do not have check marks. Click the OK button.

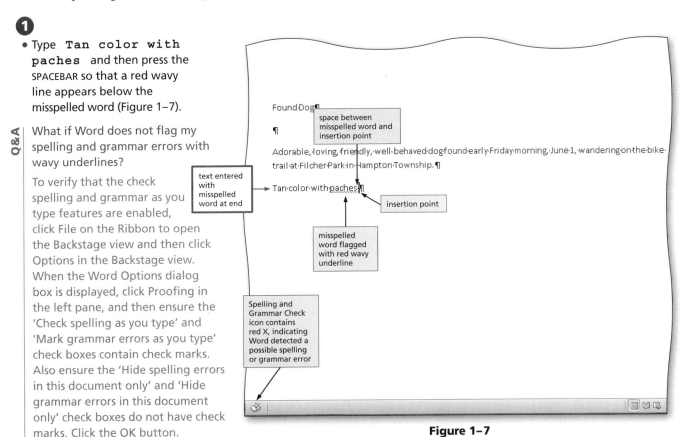

Figure 1–7

2

- Right-click the flagged word (paches, in this case) to display a shortcut menu that presents a list of suggested spelling corrections for the flagged word (Figure 1–8).

Q&A

What if, when I right-click the misspelled word, my desired correction is not in the list on the shortcut menu?

You can click outside the shortcut menu to close the shortcut menu and then retype the correct word, or you can click Spelling on the shortcut menu to display the Spelling dialog box. Chapter 2 discusses the Spelling dialog box.

Q&A

What if a flagged word actually is, for example, a proper name and spelled correctly?

Right-click it and then click Ignore All on the shortcut menu to instruct Word not to flag future occurrences of the same word in this document.

Figure 1–8

3

- Click patches on the shortcut menu to replace the misspelled word in the document with a correctly spelled word (Figure 1–9).

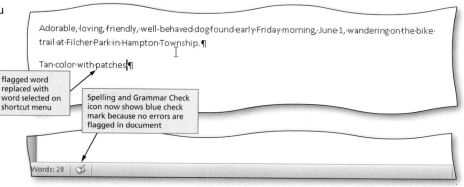

Figure 1–9

Other Ways

1. Click Spelling and Grammar Check icon on status bar, click desired word on shortcut menu

BTW

Character Widths
Many word processing documents use variable character fonts, where some characters are wider than others; for example, the letter w is wider than the letter i.

To Enter More Text

In the flyer, the text yet to be entered includes the remainder of the body copy, which will be formatted as a bulleted list, and the signature line. The next steps enter the remainder of text in the flyer.

① Press the END key to move the insertion point to the end of the current line.

② Type `of white on his chest` and then press the ENTER key.

③ Type `Male, adult cocker spaniel` and then press the ENTER key.

④ Type `Green and silver collar with the name, Bailey, on the tag` and then press the ENTER key.

⑤ Type the signature line in the flyer (Figure 1–10):
`If this is your lost dog, call 555-1029.`

three paragraphs of body copy entered, which will be formatted as a bulleted list

Tan·color·with·patches·of·white·on·his·chest¶

Male,·adult·cocker·spaniel¶

Green·and·silver·collar·with·the·name,·Bailey,·on·the·tag¶

signature line entered

If·this·is·your·lost·dog,·call·555-1029.¶

Figure 1–10

Navigating a Document

You view only a portion of a document on the screen through the document window. At some point when you type text or insert graphics, Word probably will **scroll** the top or bottom portion of the document off the screen. Although you cannot see the text and graphics once they scroll off the screen, they remain in the document.

You can use either the keyboard or the mouse to scroll to a different location in a document and/or move the insertion point around a document. When you use the keyboard, the insertion point automatically moves when you press the desired keys. For example, the previous steps used the END key to move the insertion point to the end of the current line. Table 1–1 outlines various techniques to navigate a document using the keyboard.

With the mouse, you can use the scroll arrows or the scroll box on the scroll bar to display a different portion of the document in the document window and then click the mouse to move the insertion point to that location. Table 1–2 explains various techniques for using the scroll bar to scroll vertically with the mouse.

BTW

Minimize Wrist Injury
Computer users frequently switch between the keyboard and the mouse during a word processing session; such switching strains the wrist. To help prevent wrist injury, minimize switching. For instance, if your fingers already are on the keyboard, use keyboard keys to scroll. If your hand already is on the mouse, use the mouse to scroll.

Table 1–1 Moving the Insertion Point with the Keyboard

Insertion Point Direction	Key(s) to Press	Insertion Point Direction	Key(s) to Press
Left one character	LEFT ARROW	Up one paragraph	CTRL+UP ARROW
Right one character	RIGHT ARROW	Down one paragraph	CTRL+DOWN ARROW
Left one word	CTRL+LEFT ARROW	Up one screen	PAGE UP
Right one word	CTRL+RIGHT ARROW	Down one screen	PAGE DOWN
Up one line	UP ARROW	To top of document window	ALT+CTRL+PAGE UP
Down one line	DOWN ARROW	To bottom of document window	ALT+CTRL+PAGE DOWN
To end of line	END	To beginning of document	CTRL+HOME
To beginning of line	HOME	To end of document	CTRL+END

Table 1–2 Using the Scroll Bar to Scroll Vertically with the Mouse

Scroll Direction	Mouse Action	Scroll Direction	Mouse Action
Up	Drag the scroll box upward.	Down one screen	Click anywhere below the scroll box on the vertical scroll bar.
Down	Drag the scroll box downward.	Up one line	Click the scroll arrow at the top of the vertical scroll bar.
Up one screen	Click anywhere above the scroll box on the vertical scroll bar.	Down one line	Click the scroll arrow at the bottom of the vertical scroll bar.

BTW

Organizing Files and Folders
You should organize and store files in folders so that you easily can find the files later. For example, if you are taking an introductory computer class called CIS 101, a good practice would be to save all Word files in a Word folder in a CIS 101 folder. For a discussion of folders and detailed examples of creating folders, refer to the Office 2010 and Windows 7 chapter at the beginning of this book.

To Save a Document

You have performed many tasks while creating this flyer and do not want to risk losing work completed thus far. Accordingly, you should save the document.

The following steps assume you already have created folders for storing your files, for example, a CIS 101 folder (for your class) that contains a Word folder (for your assignments). Thus, these steps save the document in the Word folder in the CIS 101 folder on a USB flash drive using the file name, Found Dog Flyer. For a detailed example of the procedure summarized below, refer to the Office 2010 and Windows 7 chapter at the beginning of this book.

1 With a USB flash drive connected to one of the computer's USB ports, click the Save button on the Quick Access Toolbar to display the Save As dialog box.

2 Type **Found Dog Flyer** in the File name text box to change the file name. Do not press the ENTER key after typing the file name because you do not want to close the dialog box at this time.

3 Navigate to the desired save location (in this case, the Word folder in the CIS 101 folder [or your class folder] on the USB flash drive).

4 Click the Save button (Save As dialog box) to save the document in the selected folder on the selected drive with the entered file name.

Formatting Paragraphs and Characters

With the text for the flyer entered, the next step is to **format**, or change the appearance of, its text. A paragraph encompasses the text from the first character in the paragraph up to and including its paragraph mark (¶). **Paragraph formatting** is the process of changing the appearance of a paragraph. For example, you can center or add bullets to a paragraph. Characters include letters, numbers, punctuation marks, and symbols. **Character formatting** is the process of changing the way characters appear on the screen and in print. You use character formatting to emphasize certain words and improve readability of a document. For example, you can color or underline characters. Often, you apply both paragraph and character formatting to the same text. For example, you may center a paragraph (paragraph formatting) and underline some of the characters in the same paragraph (character formatting).

Although you can format paragraphs and characters before you type, many Word users enter text first and then format the existing text. Figure 1–11a shows the flyer in this chapter before formatting its paragraphs and characters. Figure 1–11b shows the flyer after formatting. As you can see from the two figures, a document that is formatted is easier to read and looks more professional. The following pages discuss how to format the flyer so that it looks like Figure 1–11b.

Characters that appear on the screen are a specific shape and size. The **font**, or typeface, defines the appearance and shape of the letters, numbers, and special characters. In Word, the default font usually is Calibri (shown in Figure 1–12 on page WD 14). You can leave characters in the default font or change them to a different font. **Font size** specifies the size of the characters and is determined by a measurement system called points. A single **point** is about 1/72 of one inch in height. The default font size in Word typically is 11 (Figure 1–12). Thus, a character with a font size of 11 is about 11/72 or a little less than 1/6 of one inch in height. You can increase or decrease the font size of characters in a document.

A document **theme** is a set of unified formats for fonts, colors, and graphics. Word includes a variety of document themes to assist you with coordinating these visual elements in a document. The default theme fonts are Cambria for headings and Calibri for body text. By changing the document theme, you quickly can give your document a new look. You also can define your own document themes.

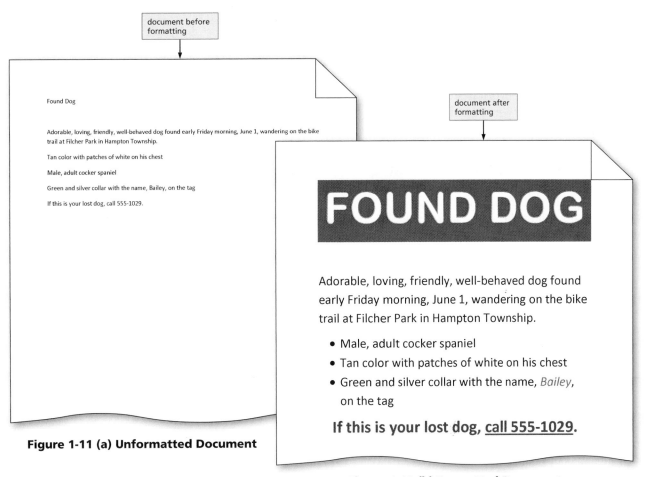

document before formatting

document after formatting

Found Dog

Adorable, loving, friendly, well-behaved dog found early Friday morning, June 1, wandering on the bike trail at Filcher Park in Hampton Township.

Tan color with patches of white on his chest

Male, adult cocker spaniel

Green and silver collar with the name, Bailey, on the tag

If this is your lost dog, call 555-1029.

FOUND DOG

Adorable, loving, friendly, well-behaved dog found early Friday morning, June 1, wandering on the bike trail at Filcher Park in Hampton Township.

- Male, adult cocker spaniel
- Tan color with patches of white on his chest
- Green and silver collar with the name, *Bailey*, on the tag

If this is your lost dog, call 555-1029.

Figure 1-11 (a) Unformatted Document

Figure 1-11 (b) Formatted Document

Identify how to format various elements of the text.

By formatting the characters and paragraphs in a document, you can improve its overall appearance. In a flyer, consider the following formatting suggestions.

Plan Ahead

- **Increase the font size of characters.** Flyers usually are posted on a bulletin board or in a window. Thus, the font size should be as large as possible so that passersby easily can read the flyer. To give the headline more impact, its font size should be larger than the font size of the text in the body copy. If possible, make the font size of the signature line larger than the body copy but smaller than the headline.

- **Change the font of characters.** Use fonts that are easy to read. Try to use only two different fonts in a flyer, for example, one for the headline and the other for all other text. Too many fonts can make the flyer visually confusing.

- **Change paragraph alignment.** The default alignment for paragraphs in a document is **left-aligned**, that is, flush at the left margin of the document with uneven right edges. Consider changing the alignment of some of the paragraphs to add interest and variety to the flyer.

- **Highlight key paragraphs with bullets.** A bulleted paragraph is a paragraph that begins with a dot or other symbol. Use bulleted paragraphs to highlight important points in a flyer.

- **Emphasize important words.** To call attention to certain words or lines, you can underline them, italicize them, or bold them. Use these formats sparingly, however, because overuse will minimize their effect and make the flyer look too busy.

- **Use color.** Use colors that complement each other and convey the meaning of the flyer. Vary colors in terms of hue and brightness. Headline colors, for example, can be bold and bright. Signature lines should stand out more than body copy but less than headlines. Keep in mind that too many colors can detract from the flyer and make it difficult to read.

To Center a Paragraph

The headline in the flyer currently is left-aligned (Figure 1–12). You want the headline to be **centered**, that is, positioned horizontally between the left and right margins on the page. Recall that Word considers a single short line of text, such as the two-word headline, a paragraph. Thus, you will center the paragraph containing the headline. The following steps center a paragraph.

- Click somewhere in the paragraph to be centered (in this case, the headline) to position the insertion point in the paragraph to be formatted (Figure 1–12).

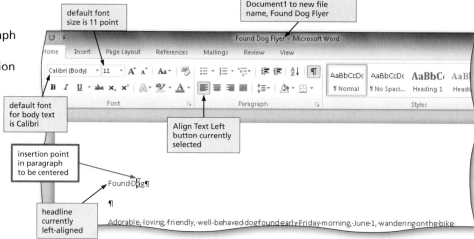

Figure 1–12

2

- Click the Center button (Home tab | Paragraph group) to center the paragraph containing the insertion point (Figure 1–13).

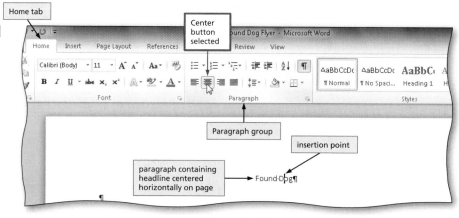

Q&A

What if I want to return the paragraph to left-aligned?

You would click the Center button again or click the Align Text Left button (Home tab | Paragraph group).

Figure 1–13

Other Ways

1. Right-click paragraph, click Center button on Mini toolbar
2. Right-click paragraph, click Paragraph on shortcut menu, click Indents and Spacing tab
3. Click Paragraph Dialog Box Launcher (Home tab or Page Layout tab | Paragraph group), click Indents and Spacing tab (Paragraph dialog box), click Alignment box arrow, click Centered, click OK button
   (Paragraph dialog box), click Alignment box arrow, click Centered, click OK button
4. Press CTRL+E

BTW

File Type
Depending on your Windows settings, the file type .docx may be displayed on the title bar immediately to the right of the file name after you save the file. The file type .docx is a Word 2010 document.

To Center Another Paragraph

In the flyer, the signature line is to be centered to match the paragraph alignment of the headline. The following steps center the signature line.

1 Click somewhere in the paragraph to be centered (in this case, the signature line) to position the insertion point in the paragraph to be formatted.

2 Click the Center button (Home tab | Paragraph group) to center the paragraph containing the insertion point (shown in Figure 1–14).

Formatting Single versus Multiple Paragraphs and Characters

As shown on the previous pages, to format a single paragraph, simply move the insertion point in the paragraph, to make it the current paragraph, and then format the paragraph. Similarly, to format a single word, position the insertion point in the word, to make it the current word, and then format the word.

To format multiple paragraphs or words, however, you first must select the paragraphs or words you want to format and then format the selection. If your screen normally displays dark letters on a light background, which is the default setting in Word, then selected text displays light letters on a dark background.

To Select a Line

The default font size of 11 point is too small for a headline in a flyer. To increase the font size of the characters in the headline, you first must select the line of text containing the headline. The following steps select a line.

1

- Move the mouse pointer to the left of the line to be selected (in this case, the headline) until the mouse pointer changes to a right-pointing block arrow (Figure 1–14).

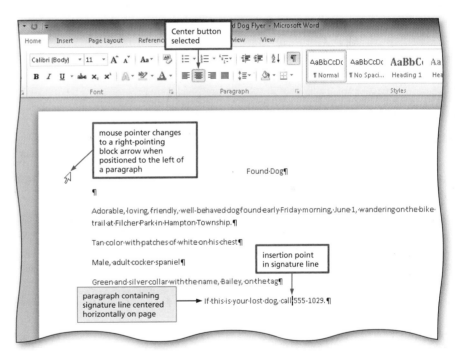

Figure 1–14

2

- While the mouse pointer is a right-pointing block arrow, click the mouse to select the entire line to the right of the mouse pointer (Figure 1–15).

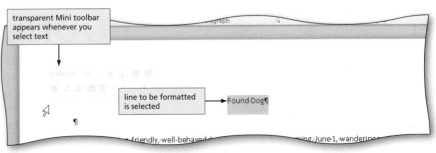

Figure 1–15

Other Ways	
1. Drag mouse through line	2. With insertion point at beginning of desired line, press SHIFT+DOWN ARROW

To Change the Font Size of Selected Text

The next step is to increase the font size of the characters in the selected headline. You would like the headline to be as large as possible and still fit on a single line, which in this case is 72 point. The following steps increase the font size of the headline from 11 to 72 point.

- With the text selected, click the Font Size box arrow (Home tab | Font group) to display the Font Size gallery (Figure 1–16).

Q&A Why are the font sizes in my Font Size gallery different from those in Figure 1–16?

Font sizes may vary depending on the current font and your printer driver.

Q&A What happened to the Mini toolbar?

The Mini toolbar disappears if you do not use it. These steps use the Font Size box arrow on the Home tab instead of the Font Size box arrow on the Mini toolbar.

Figure 1–16

- Point to 72 in the Font Size gallery to display a live preview of the selected text at the selected point size (Figure 1–17).

Experiment

- Point to various font sizes in the Font Size gallery and watch the font size of the selected text change in the document window.

- Click 72 in the Font Size gallery to increase the font size of the selected text.

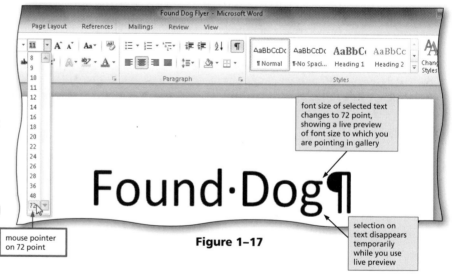

Figure 1–17

Other Ways

1. Click Font Size box arrow on Mini toolbar, click desired font size in Font Size gallery

2. Right-click selected text, click Font on shortcut menu, click Font tab (Font dialog box), select font size in Size list, click OK button

3. Click Font Dialog Box Launcher, click Font tab (Font dialog box), select desired font size in Size list, click OK button

4. Press CTRL+D, click Font tab (Font dialog box), select desired font size in Size list, click OK button

To Change the Font of Selected Text

The default theme font for headings is Cambria and for all other text, called body text in Word, is Calibri. Many other fonts are available, however, so that you can add variety to documents.

To draw more attention to the headline, you change its font so that it differs from the font of other text in the flyer. The following steps change the font of the headline from Calibri to Arial Rounded MT Bold.

1

- With the text selected, click the Font box arrow (Home tab | Font group) to display the Font gallery (Figure 1–18).

Q&A

Will the fonts in my Font gallery be the same as those in Figure 1–18?

Your list of available fonts may differ, depending on the type of printer you are using and other settings.

Q&A

What if the text is no longer selected?

Follow the steps on page WD 15 to select a line.

Figure 1–18

2

- Scroll through the Font gallery, if necessary, and then point to Arial Rounded MT Bold (or a similar font) to display a live preview of the selected text in the selected font (Figure 1–19).

Experiment

- Point to various fonts in the Font gallery and watch the font of the selected text change in the document window.

3

- Click Arial Rounded MT Bold (or a similar font) to change the font of the selected text.

Figure 1–19

Other Ways

1. Click Font box arrow on Mini toolbar, click desired font in Font gallery

2. Right-click selected text, click Font on shortcut menu, click Font tab (Font dialog box), select desired font in Font list, click OK button

3. Click Font Dialog Box Launcher (Home tab | Font group), click Font tab (Font dialog box), select desired font in Font list, click OK button

4. Press CTRL+D, click Font tab (Font dialog box), select desired font in the Font list, click OK button

To Change the Case of Selected Text

The headline currently shows the first letter in each word capitalized, which sometimes is referred to as initial cap. To draw more attention to the headline, you would like the entire line of text to be capitalized, or in uppercase letters. The following steps change the headline to uppercase.

1
- With the text selected, click the Change Case button (Home tab | Font group) to display the Change Case gallery (Figure 1–20).

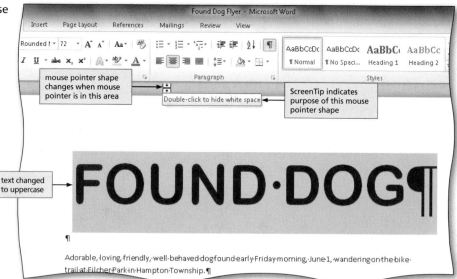

Figure 1–20

2
- Click UPPERCASE in the Change Case gallery to change the case of the selected text (Figure 1–21).

Q&A

What if a ruler appears on the screen or the mouse pointer shape changes?

Depending on the position of your mouse pointer and locations you click on the screen, a ruler may automatically appear or the mouse pointer shape may change. Simply move the mouse and the ruler should disappear and/or the mouse pointer shape will change.

Figure 1–21

Other Ways

1. Right-click selected text, click Font on shortcut menu, click Font tab (Font dialog box), select All caps in Effects area, click OK button

2. Click Font Dialog Box Launcher (Home tab | Font group), click Font tab (Font dialog box), select All caps in Effects area, click OK button

3. Press SHIFT+F3 repeatedly until text is desired case

To Apply a Text Effect to Selected Text

You would like the text in the headline to be even more noticeable. Word provides many text effects to add interest and variety to text. The following steps apply a text effect to the headline.

- With the text selected, click the Text Effects button (Home tab | Font group) to display the Text Effects gallery (Figure 1–22).

Figure 1–22

- Point to Fill – White, Gradient Outline – Accent 1 (first text effect in third row) to display a live preview of the selected text in the selected text effect (Figure 1–23).

🔍 **Experiment**

- Point to various text effects in the Text Effects gallery and watch the text effects of the selected text change in the document window.

- Click Fill – White, Gradient Outline – Accent 1 to change the text effect of the selected text.

Figure 1–23

- Click anywhere in the document window to remove the selection from the selected text.

Other Ways

1. Right-click selected text, click Font on shortcut menu, click Font tab (Font dialog box), click Text Effects button, select desired text effects (Format Text Effects dialog box), click Close button, click OK button

2. Click Font Dialog Box Launcher (Home tab | Font group), click Font tab (Font dialog box), click Text Effects button, select desired text effects (Format Text Effects dialog box), click Close button, click OK button

To Shade a Paragraph

To make the headline of the flyer more eye-catching, you would like to shade it. When you **shade** text, Word colors the rectangular area behind any text or graphics. If the text to shade is a paragraph, Word shades the area from the left margin to the right margin of the current paragraph. To shade a paragraph, place the insertion point in the paragraph. To shade any other text, you must first select the text to be shaded. This flyer uses brown as the shading color for the headline. The following steps shade a paragraph.

- Click somewhere in the paragraph to be shaded (in this case, the headline) to position the insertion point in the paragraph to be formatted.

- Click the Shading button arrow (Home tab | Paragraph group) to display the Shading gallery (Figure 1–24).

Q&A

What if I click the Shading button by mistake?

Click the Shading button arrow and proceed with Step 2.

Figure 1–24

- Point to Orange, Accent 6, Darker 50% (rightmost color in the sixth row) to display a live preview of the selected shading color (Figure 1–25).

Experiment

- Point to various colors in the Shading gallery and watch the shading color of the current paragraph change.

Figure 1–25

- Click Orange, Accent 6, Darker 50% to shade the current paragraph.

Q&A

What if I apply a dark shading color to dark text?

When the font color of text is Automatic, it usually is black. If you select a dark shading color, Word automatically may change the text color to white so that the shaded text is easier to read.

Other Ways
1. Click Border button arrow (Home tab | Paragraph group), click Borders and Shading, click Shading   tab (Borders and Shading dialog box), click Fill box arrow, select desired color, click OK button

To Select Multiple Lines

The next formatting step for the flyer is to increase the font size of the characters between the headline and the signature line so that they are easier to read from a distance. To change the font size of the characters in multiple lines, you first must select all the lines to be formatted. The following steps select multiple lines.

- Move the mouse pointer to the left of the first paragraph to be selected until the mouse pointer changes to a right-pointing block arrow (Figure 1–26).

Figure 1–26

- Drag downward to select all lines that will be formatted (Figure 1–27).

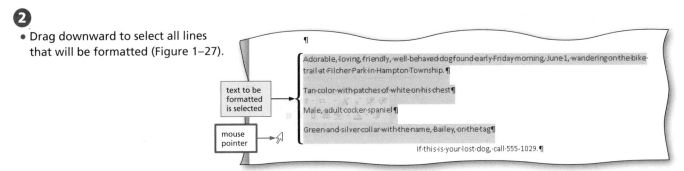

Figure 1–27

Other Ways

1. With insertion point at beginning of desired line, press SHIFT+DOWN ARROW repeatedly until all lines are selected

To Change the Font Size of Selected Text

The characters between the headline and the signature line in the flyer currently are 11 point. To make them easier to read from a distance, this flyer uses 22 point for these characters. The steps on the next page change the font size of the selected text.

1 With the text selected, click the Font Size box arrow (Home tab | Font group) to display the Font Size gallery.

2 Click 22 in the Font Size gallery to increase the font size of the selected text.

3 Click anywhere in the document window to remove the selection from the text.

4 If necessary, scroll so that you can see all the text on the screen (Figure 1–28).

Figure 1–28

To Bullet a List of Paragraphs

The next step is to format as a bulleted list the three paragraphs of identifying information that are above the signature line in the flyer. A **bulleted list** is a series of paragraphs, each beginning with a bullet character.

To format a list of paragraphs with bullets, you first must select all the lines in the paragraphs. The following steps bullet a list of paragraphs.

1
- Move the mouse pointer to the left of the first paragraph to be selected until the mouse pointer changes to a right-pointing block arrow.

- Drag downward until all paragraphs that will be formatted with a bullet character are selected (Figure 1–29).

Figure 1–29

- Click the Bullets button (Home tab | Paragraph group) to place a bullet character at the beginning of each selected paragraph (Figure 1–30).

Q&A How do I remove bullets from a list or paragraph?

Select the list or paragraph and then click the Bullets button again.

Q&A What if I accidentally click the Bullets button arrow?

Press the ESCAPE key to remove the Bullets gallery from the screen and then repeat Step 2.

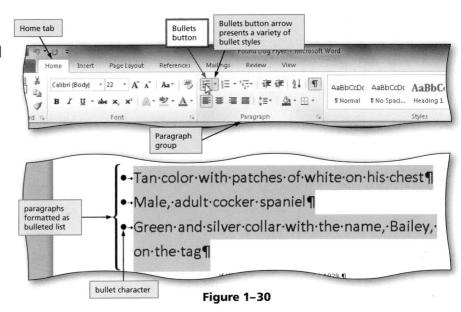

Figure 1–30

To Undo and Redo an Action

Word provides a means of canceling your recent command(s) or action(s). For example, if you format text incorrectly, you can undo the format and try it again. When you point to the Undo button, Word displays the action you can undo as part of a ScreenTip.

If, after you undo an action, you decide you did not want to perform the undo, you can redo the undone action. Word does not allow you to undo or redo some actions, such as saving or printing a document. The next steps undo the bullet format just applied and then redo the bullet format.

- Click the Undo button on the Quick Access Toolbar to reverse your most recent action (in this case, remove the bullets from the paragraphs) (Figure 1–31).

- Click the Redo button on the Quick Access Toolbar to reverse your most recent undo (in this case, place a bullet character on the paragraphs again) (shown in Figure 1–30).

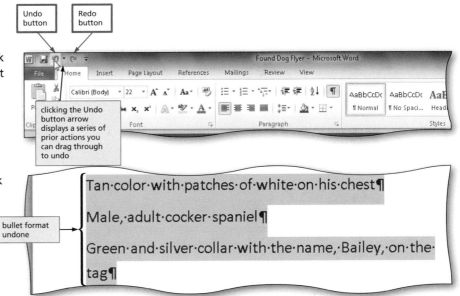

Figure 1–31

To Italicize Text

The next step is to italicize the dog's name, Bailey, in the flyer to further emphasize it. **Italicized** text has a slanted appearance. As with a single paragraph, if you want to format a single word, you do not need to select it. Simply position the insertion point somewhere in the word and apply the desired format. The following step formats a word in italics.

- Click somewhere in the word to be italicized (Bailey, in this case) to position the insertion point in the word to be formatted.

- Click the Italic button (Home tab | Font group) to italicize the word containing the insertion point (Figure 1–32).

Q&A How would I remove an italic format?

You would click the Italic button a second time, or you immediately could click the Undo button on the Quick Access Toolbar or press CTRL+Z.

Q&A How can I tell what formatting has been applied to text?

The selected buttons and boxes on the Home tab show formatting characteristics of the location of the insertion point. With the insertion point in the word, Bailey, the Home tab shows these formats: 22-point Calibri italic font, bulleted paragraph.

Figure 1–32

Other Ways

1. Click Italic button on Mini toolbar
2. Right-click selected text, click Font on shortcut menu, click Font tab

(Font dialog box), click Italic in Font style list, click OK button

3. Click Font Dialog Box Launcher (Home tab |

Font group), click Font tab (Font dialog box), click Italic in Font style list, click OK button

4. Press CTRL+I

Plan Ahead

Use color.
When choosing color, associate the meaning of color to your message:

- Red expresses danger, power, or energy, and often is associated with sports or physical exertion.

- Brown represents simplicity, honesty, and dependability.

- Orange denotes success, victory, creativity, and enthusiasm.

- Yellow suggests sunshine, happiness, hope, liveliness, and intelligence.

- Green symbolizes growth, healthiness, harmony, blooming, and healing, and often is associated with safety or money.

- Blue indicates integrity, trust, importance, confidence, and stability.

- Purple represents wealth, power, comfort, extravagance, magic, mystery, and spirituality.

- White stands for purity, goodness, cleanliness, precision, and perfection.

- Black suggests authority, strength, elegance, power, and prestige.

- Gray conveys neutrality and thus often is found in backgrounds and other effects.

BTW

Q&As
For a complete list of the Q&As found in many of the step-by-step sequences in this book, visit the Word 2010 Q&A Web page (scsite.com/wd2010/qa).

To Color Text

To emphasize the dog's name even more, its color is changed to a shade of blue. The following steps change the color of the word, Bailey.

- With the insertion point in the word to format, click the Font Color button arrow (Home tab | Font group) to display the Font Color gallery (Figure 1–33).

Q&A
What if I click the Font Color button by mistake?

Click the Font Color button arrow and then proceed with Step 2.

- Point to Blue, Accent 1, Darker 25% (fifth color in the fifth row) to display a live preview of the selected font color.

Experiment

- Point to various colors in the Font Color gallery and watch the color of the current word change.

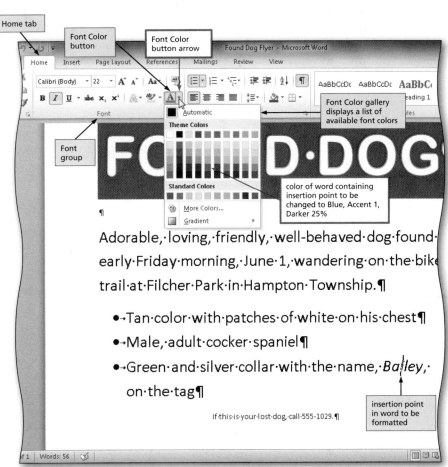

Figure 1–33

- Click Blue, Accent 1, Darker 25% to change the color of the text (Figure 1–34).

Q&A
How would I change the text color back to black?

You would position the insertion point in the word or select the text, click the Font Color button arrow (Home tab | Font group) again, and then click Automatic in the Font Color gallery.

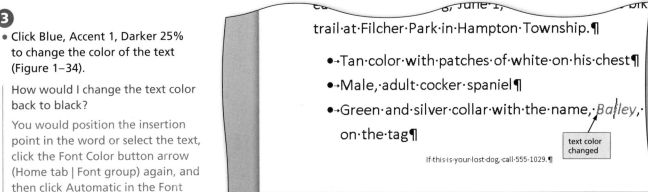

Figure 1–34

Other Ways

1. Click Font Color button arrow on Mini toolbar, click desired color

2. Right-click selected text, click Font on shortcut menu, click Font tab

   (Font dialog box), click Font color box arrow, click desired color, click OK button

3. Click Font Dialog Box Launcher (Home tab |

   Font group), click Font tab (Font dialog box), click Font color box arrow, click desired color, click OK button

To Use the Mini Toolbar to Format Text

Recall from the Office 2010 and Windows 7 chapter at the beginning of this book that the Mini toolbar, which automatically appears based on certain tasks you perform, contains commands related to changing the appearance of text in a document. All commands on the Mini toolbar also exist on the Ribbon.

When the Mini toolbar appears, it initially is transparent. If you do not use the transparent Mini toolbar, it disappears from the screen. The following steps use the Mini toolbar to change the color and font size of text in the signature line of the flyer.

- Move the mouse pointer to the left of the line to be selected (in this case, the signature line) until the mouse pointer changes to a right-pointing block arrow and then click the mouse to select the line (Figure 1–35).

Figure 1–35

- Move the mouse pointer into the transparent Mini toolbar, so that it changes to a bright toolbar.

- Click the Font Size box arrow on the Mini toolbar to display the Font Size gallery and then point to 28 in the Font Size gallery to display a live preview of the selected font size (Figure 1–36).

Figure 1–36

- Click 28 in the Font Size gallery to increase the font size of the selected text.

- With the text still selected and the Mini toolbar still displayed, click the Font Color button arrow on the Mini toolbar to display the Font Color gallery and then point to Purple, Accent 4, Darker 50% (eighth color in the sixth row) to display a live preview of the selected font color (Figure 1–37).

Figure 1–37

- Click Purple, Accent 4, Darker 50% to change the color of the text.

- Click anywhere in the document window to remove the selection from the text.

To Select a Group of Words

To emphasize the contact information (call 555-1029), these words are underlined in the flyer. To format a group of words, you first must select them. The following steps select a group of words.

- Position the mouse pointer immediately to the left of the first character of the text to be selected, in this case, the c in call (Figure 1–38).

Q&A Why did the shape of the mouse pointer change?

The mouse pointer's shape is an I-beam when positioned in unselected text in the document window.

Figure 1–38

- Drag the mouse pointer through the last character of the text to be selected, in this case, the 9 in the phone number (Figure 1–39).

Q&A Why did the mouse pointer shape change again?

When the mouse pointer is positioned in selected text, its shape is a left-pointing block arrow.

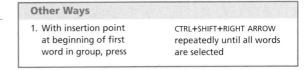

Figure 1–39

Other Ways	
1. With insertion point at beginning of first word in group, press	CTRL+SHIFT+RIGHT ARROW repeatedly until all words are selected

To Underline Text

Underlines are used to emphasize or draw attention to specific text. **Underlined** text prints with an underscore (_) below each character. In the flyer, the contact information, call 555-1029, in the signature line is emphasized with an underline. The following step formats selected text with an underline.

- With the text selected, click the Underline button (Home tab | Font group) to underline the selected text (Figure 1–40).

Q&A How would I remove an underline?

You would click the Underline button a second time, or you immediately could click the Undo button on the Quick Access Toolbar.

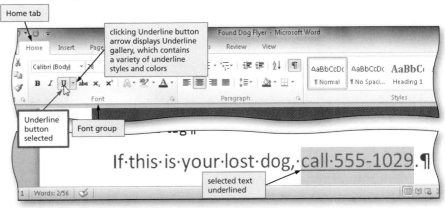

Figure 1–40

Other Ways		
1. Right-click text, click Font on shortcut menu, click Font tab (Font dialog box), click Underline style box arrow, click desired	underline style, click OK button	(Font dialog box), click Underline style box arrow, click desired underline style, click OK button
	2. Click Font Dialog Box Launcher (Home tab | Font group), click Font tab	3. Press CTRL+U

To Bold Text

Bold characters appear somewhat thicker and darker than those that are not bold. To further emphasize the signature line, it is bold in the flyer. To format the line, as you have learned previously, you select the line first. The following steps format the signature line bold.

- Move the mouse pointer to the left of the line to be selected (in this case, the signature line) until the mouse pointer changes to a right-pointing block arrow and then click the mouse to select the text to be formatted.

- With the text selected, click the Bold button (Home tab | Font group) to bold the selected text (Figure 1–41).

Q&A

How would I remove a bold format?

You would click the Bold button a second time, or you immediately could click the Undo button on the Quick Access Toolbar.

- Click anywhere in the document window to remove the selection from the screen.

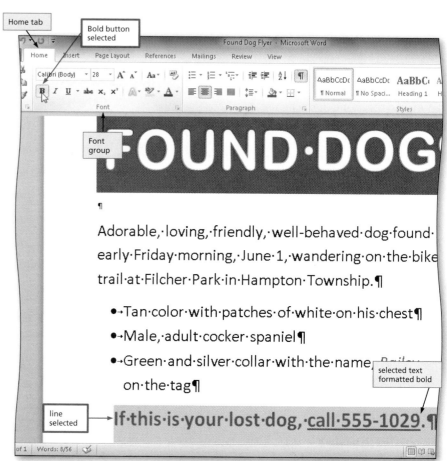

Figure 1–41

Other Ways

1. Click Bold button on Mini toolbar

2. Right-click selected text, click Font on shortcut menu, click Font tab (Font dialog box), click Bold in Font style list, click OK button

3. Click Font Dialog Box Launcher (Home tab | Font group), click Font tab (Font dialog box), click Bold in Font style list, click OK button

4. Press CTRL+B

To Change Theme Colors

A **color scheme** in Word is a document theme that identifies 12 complementary colors for text, background, accents, and links in a document. With more than 20 predefined color schemes, Word provides a simple way to select colors that work well together.

In the flyer, you want all the colors to convey honesty, dependability, and healing, that is, shades of browns and greens. In Word, the Aspect color scheme uses these colors. Thus, you will change the color scheme from the default, Office, to Aspect. The next steps change theme colors.

1

- Click the Change Styles button (Home tab | Styles group) to display the Change Styles menu.

- Point to Colors on the Change Styles menu to display the Colors gallery (Figure 1–42).

Experiment

- Point to various color schemes in the Colors gallery and watch the colors change in the document window.

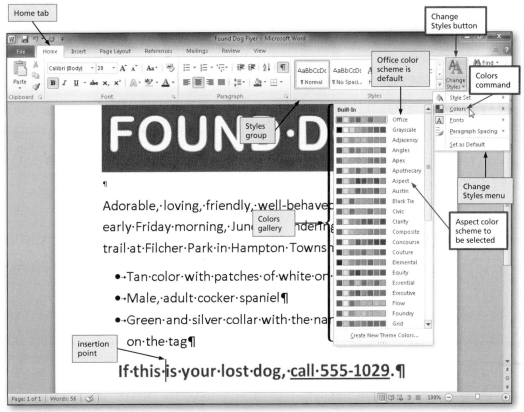

Figure 1–42

2

- Click Aspect in the Colors gallery to change the document theme colors (Figure 1–43).

Q&A

What if I want to return to the original color scheme?

You would click the Change Styles button again, click Colors on the Change Styles menu, and then click Office in the Colors gallery.

Figure 1–43

Other Ways
1. Click Theme Colors button (Page Layout tab | Themes group), select desired color scheme

Selecting Text

In many of the previous steps, you have selected text. Table 1–3 summarizes the techniques used to select various items.

Table 1–3 Techniques for Selecting Text		
Item to Select	**Mouse**	**Keyboard (where applicable)**
Block of text	Click at beginning of selection, scroll to end of selection, position mouse pointer at end of selection, hold down SHIFT key and then click; or drag through the text.	
Character(s)	Drag through character(s).	SHIFT+RIGHT ARROW or SHIFT+LEFT ARROW
Document	Move mouse to left of text until mouse pointer changes to a right-pointing block arrow and then triple-click.	CTRL+A
Graphic	Click the graphic.	
Line	Move mouse to left of line until mouse pointer changes to a right-pointing block arrow and then click.	HOME, then SHIFT+END or END, then SHIFT+HOME
Lines	Move mouse to left of first line until mouse pointer changes to a right-pointing block arrow and then drag up or down.	HOME, then SHIFT+DOWN ARROW or END, then SHIFT+UP ARROW
Paragraph	Triple-click paragraph; or move mouse to left of paragraph until mouse pointer changes to a right-pointing block arrow and then double-click.	CTRL+SHIFT+DOWN ARROW or CTRL+SHIFT+UP ARROW
Paragraphs	Move mouse to left of paragraph until mouse pointer changes to a right-pointing block arrow, double-click, and then drag up or down.	CTRL+SHIFT+DOWN ARROW or CTRL+SHIFT+UP ARROW repeatedly
Sentence	Press and hold down CTRL key and then click sentence.	
Word	Double-click the word.	CTRL+SHIFT+RIGHT ARROW or CTRL+SHIFT+LEFT ARROW
Words	Drag through words.	CTRL+SHIFT+RIGHT ARROW or CTRL+SHIFT+LEFT ARROW repeatedly

To Save an Existing Document with the Same File Name

You have made several modifications to the document since you last saved it. Thus, you should save it again. The following step saves the document again. For an example of the step listed below, refer to the Office 2010 and Windows 7 chapter at the beginning of this book.

 Click the Save button on the Quick Access Toolbar to overwrite the previously saved file.

Break Point: If you wish to take a break, this is a good place to do so. You can quit Word now (refer to page WD 44 for instructions). To resume at a later time, start Word (refer to pages WD 4 and WD 5 for instructions), open the file called Found Dog Flyer (refer to page WD 45 for instructions), and continue following the steps from this location forward.

Inserting and Formatting Pictures in a Word Document

With the text formatted in the flyer, the next step is to insert digital pictures in the flyer and format the pictures. Flyers usually contain graphical images, such as a picture, to attract the attention of passersby. In the following pages, you will perform these tasks:

1. Insert the first digital picture into the flyer and then reduce its size.
2. Insert the second digital picture into the flyer and then reduce its size.
3. Change the look of the first picture and then the second picture.

Plan
Ahead

Find the appropriate graphical image.
To use a graphical image, also called a graphic, in a Word document, the image must be stored digitally in a file. Files containing graphical images are available from a variety of sources:

- Word includes a collection of predefined graphical images that you can insert in a document.

- Microsoft has free digital images on the Web for use in a document. Other Web sites also have images available, some of which are free, while others require a fee.

- You can take a picture with a digital camera or camera phone and **download** it, which is the process of copying the digital picture from the camera or phone to your computer.

- With a scanner, you can convert a printed picture, drawing, or diagram to a digital file.

  If you receive a picture from a source other than yourself, do not use the file until you are certain it does not contain a virus. A **virus** is a computer program that can damage files and programs on your computer. Use an antivirus program to verify that any files you use are virus free.

Plan
Ahead

Establish where to position and how to format the graphical image.
The content, size, shape, position, and format of a graphic should capture the interest of passersby, enticing them to stop and read the flyer. Often, the graphic is the center of attraction and visually the largest element on a flyer. If you use colors in the graphical image, be sure they are part of the document's color scheme.

To Insert a Picture

The next step in creating the flyer is to insert one of the digital pictures of the dog so that it is centered on the blank line below the headline. The picture, which was taken with a camera phone, is available on the Data Files for Students. See the inside back cover of this book for instructions on downloading the Data Files for Students, or contact your instructor for information about accessing the required files.

The following steps insert a centered picture, which, in this example, is located in the Chapter 01 folder in the Word folder in the Data Files for Students folder on a USB flash drive.

1
- Position the insertion point on the blank line below the headline, which is the location where you want to insert the picture.

- Click the Center button (Home tab | Paragraph group) to center the paragraph that will contain the picture.

- Click Insert on the Ribbon to display the Insert tab (Figure 1–44).

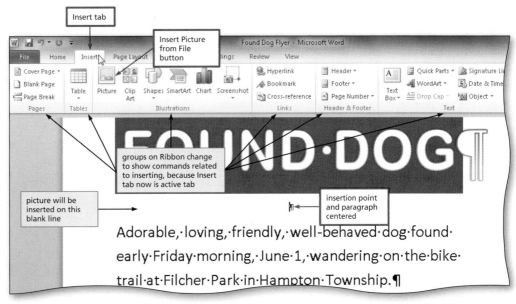

Figure 1–44

2
- With your USB flash drive connected to one of the computer's USB ports, click the Insert Picture from File button (Insert tab | Illustrations group) (shown in Figure 1-44) to display the Insert Picture dialog box (shown in Figure 1-45 on the next page).

3

- Navigate to the picture location (in this case, the Chapter 01 folder in the Word folder in the Data Files for Students folder on a USB flash drive). For a detailed example of this procedure, refer to Steps 3a – 3c in the To Save a File in a Folder section in the Office 2010 and Windows 7 chapter at the beginning of this book.

- Click Dog Picture 1 to select the file (Figure 1–45).

Q&A

What if the picture is not on a USB flash drive?

Use the same process, but select the storage location containing the picture.

Figure 1–45

4

- Click the Insert button (Insert Picture dialog box) to insert the picture at the location of the insertion point in the document (Figure 1–46).

Q&A

What are the symbols around the picture?

A selected graphic appears surrounded by a **selection rectangle**, which has small squares and circles, called **sizing handles**, at each corner and middle location.

Figure 1–46

To Zoom the Document

The next step is to reduce the size of the picture so that both pictures will fit side-by-side on the same line. With the current picture size, the flyer now has expanded to two pages. The final flyer, however, should fit on a single page. In Word, you can change the zoom so that you can see the entire document (that is, both pages) on the screen at once. Seeing the entire document at once helps you determine the appropriate size for the picture. The following step zooms the document.

1

Experiment

- Repeatedly click the Zoom Out and Zoom In buttons on the status bar and watch the size of the document change in the document window.

- Click the Zoom Out or Zoom In button as many times as necessary until the Zoom button on the status bar displays 50% on its face (Figure 1–47).

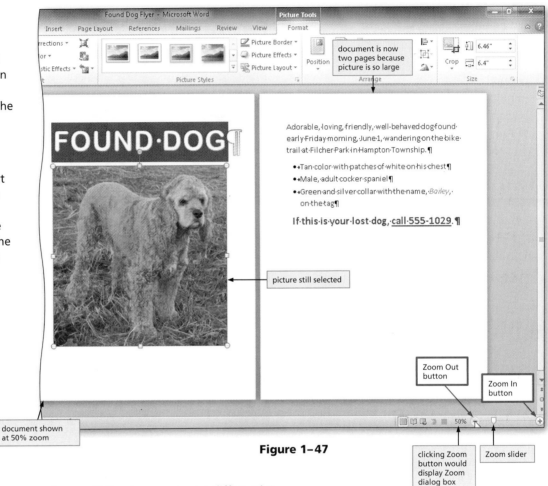

Figure 1–47

Q&A | If I change the zoom percentage, will the document print differently?

Changing the zoom has no effect on the printed document.

Q&A | Are there predefined zoom options?

Yes. Through the View tab | Zoom group or the Zoom dialog box, you can zoom to one page, two pages, many pages, page width, text width, and a variety of set percentages. Page width zoom places the edges of the page at the edges of the Word window, whereas Text width zoom places the contents of the page at the edges of the Word window.

Other Ways
1. Drag Zoom slider on status bar
2. Click Zoom button on status bar, select desired zoom percent or type (Zoom dialog box), click OK button
3. Click Zoom button (View tab | Zoom group), select desired zoom percent or type (Zoom dialog box), click OK button

To Resize a Graphic

The next step is to resize the picture so that both pictures will fit side-by-side on the same line below the headline. **Resizing** includes both enlarging and reducing the size of a graphic. In this flyer, you will reduce the size of the picture. With the entire document displayed in the document window, you will be able to see how the resized graphic will look on the entire page. The following steps resize a selected graphic.

- With the graphic still selected, point to the upper-right corner sizing handle on the picture so that the mouse pointer shape changes to a two-headed arrow (Figure 1–48).

Q&A

What if my graphic (picture) is not selected?

To select a graphic, click it.

Figure 1–48

- Drag the sizing handle diagonally inward until the crosshair mouse pointer is positioned approximately as shown in Figure 1–49.

- Release the mouse button to resize the graphic, which in this case should have a height of about 2.74" and a width of about 2.73".

Q&A

How can I see the height and width measurements?

Look in the Size group on the Picture Tools Format tab to see the height and width measurements of the currently selected graphic (shown in Figure 1–46 on page WD 32).

Q&A

What if the graphic is the wrong size?

Repeat Steps 1, 2, and 3; or enter the desired height and width values in the Shape Height and Shape Width boxes (Picture Tools Format tab | Size group).

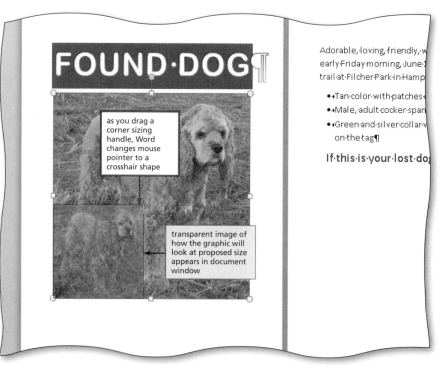

Figure 1–49

4

- Click to the right of the graphic to deselect it (Figure 1–50).

Q&A What happened to the Picture Tools Format tab?

When you click outside of a graphic or press a key to scroll through a document, Word deselects the graphic and removes the Picture Tools Format tab from the screen.

Q&A What if I want to return a graphic to its original size and start again?

With the graphic selected, click the Size Dialog Box Launcher (Picture Tools Format tab | Size group), click the Size tab (Layout dialog box), click the Reset button, and then click the OK button.

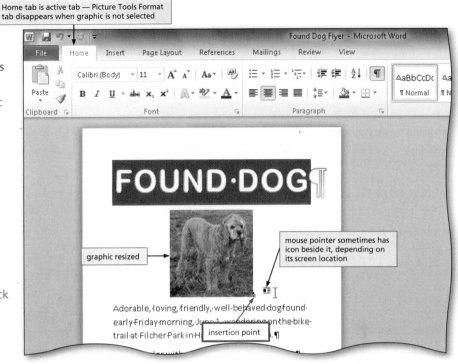

Figure 1–50

Other Ways

1. Enter height and width of graphic in Shape Height and Shape Width boxes (Picture Tools Format tab | Size group)

2. Click Size Dialog Box Launcher (Picture Tools Format tab | Size group), click Size tab (Layout dialog box), enter desired height and width values in boxes, click OK button

To Insert Another Picture

The next step is to insert the other digital picture of the dog immediately to the right of the current picture. This second picture also is available on the Data Files for Students. See the inside back cover of this book for instructions on downloading the Data Files for Students, or contact your instructor for information about accessing the required files.

The following steps insert another picture immediately to the right of the current picture.

1 With the insertion point positioned as shown in Figure 1–50, click Insert on the Ribbon to display the Insert tab.

2 With your USB flash drive connected to one of the computer's USB ports, click the Insert Picture from File button (Insert tab | Illustrations group) to display the Insert Picture dialog box.

3 If necessary, navigate to the picture location (in this case, the Word folder in the CIS 101 folder [or your class folder] on the USB flash drive). For a detailed example of this procedure, refer to Steps 3a – 3c in the To Save a File in a Folder section in the Office 2010 and Windows 7 chapter at the beginning of this book.

4 Click Dog Picture 2 to select the file.

5 Click the Insert button (Insert Picture dialog box) to insert the picture at the location of the insertion point in the document.

BTW

Word Help
At any time while using Word, you can find answers to questions and display information about various topics through Word Help. Used properly, this form of assistance can increase your productivity and reduce your frustrations by minimizing the time you spend learning how to use Word. For instruction about Word Help and exercises that will help you gain confidence in using it, read the Office 2010 and Windows 7 chapter at the beginning of this book.

To Resize a Graphic by Entering Exact Measurements

The next step is to resize the second picture so that it is the exact same size as the first picture. The height and width measurements of the first graphic are approximately 2.74" and 2.73", respectively. When a graphic is selected, its height and width measurements show in the Size group of the Picture Tools Format tab. The following steps resize a selected graphic by entering its desired exact measurements.

1

- With the second graphic still selected, click the Shape Height box (Picture Tools Format tab | Size group) to select the contents in the box and then type **2.74** as the height.

Q&A What if the Picture Tools Format tab no longer is displayed on my Ribbon?

Double-click the picture to display the Picture Tools Format tab.

Q&A What if the contents of the Shape Height box are not selected?

Triple-click the Shape Height box.

2

- Click the Shape Width box to select the contents in the box, type **2.73** as the width, and then click the picture to apply the settings.

- If necessary, scroll up to display the entire document in the window (Figure 1–51).

Q&A Why did my measurements change slightly?

Depending on relative measurements, the height and width values entered may change slightly.

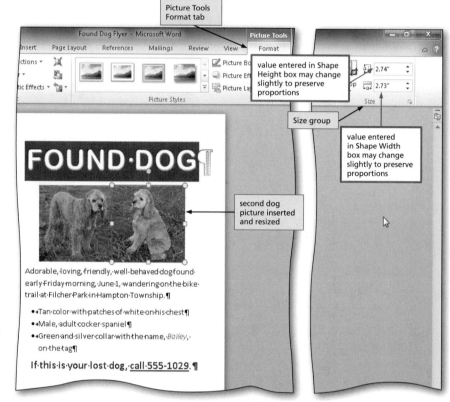

Figure 1–51

Other Ways

1. Right-click picture, enter shape height and width values in boxes on shortcut menu	2. Right-click picture, click Size and Position on shortcut menu, click Size tab (Layout dialog box),	enter shape height and width values in boxes, click OK button

To Zoom the Document

You are finished resizing the graphics and no longer need to view the entire page in the document window. Thus, the following step changes the zoom back to 100 percent.

1 Click the Zoom In button on the status bar as many times as necessary until the Zoom button displays 100% on its face (shown in Figure 1–52).

To Apply a Picture Style

A **style** is a named group of formatting characteristics. Word provides more than 25 picture styles that enable you easily to change a picture's look to a more visually appealing style, including a variety of shapes, angles, borders, and reflections. The flyer in this chapter uses a style that applies soft edges to the picture. The following steps apply a picture style to a picture.

1

- Click the leftmost dog picture to select it (Figure 1–52).

Q&A

What is the green circle attached to the selected graphic?

It is called a rotate handle. When you drag a graphic's rotate handle, the graphic moves in either a clockwise or counterclockwise direction.

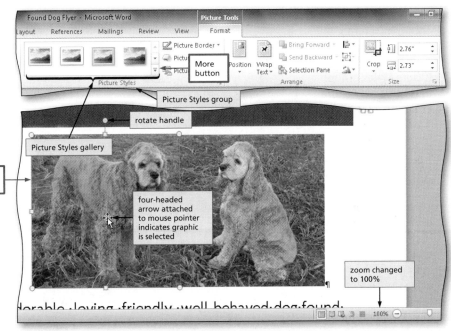

Figure 1–52

2

- Click the More button in the Picture Styles gallery (Picture Tools Format tab | Picture Styles group) (shown in Figure 1–52) to expand the gallery.

- Point to Soft Edge Rectangle in the Picture Styles gallery to display a live preview of that style applied to the picture in the document (Figure 1–53).

Experiment

- Point to various picture styles in the Picture Styles gallery and watch the style of the picture change in the document window.

3

- Click Soft Edge Rectangle in the Picture Styles gallery to apply the style to the selected picture.

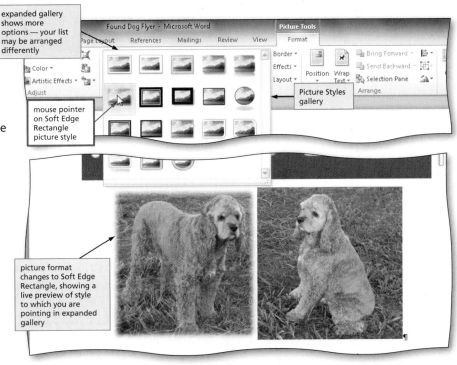

Figure 1–53

To Apply Picture Effects

Word provides a variety of picture effects so that you can further customize a picture. Effects include shadows, reflections, glow, soft edges, bevel, and 3-D rotation. The difference between the effects and the styles is that each effect has several options, providing you with more control over the exact look of the image.

In this flyer, the leftmost dog picture has a slight tan glow effect and is turned inward toward the center of the page. The following steps apply picture effects to the selected picture.

- Click the Picture Effects button (Picture Tools Format tab | Picture Styles group) to display the Picture Effects menu.

- Point to Glow on the Picture Effects menu to display the Glow gallery.

- Point to Tan, 5 pt glow, Accent color 6 in the Glow Variations area (rightmost glow in first row) to display a live preview of the selected glow effect applied to the picture in the document window (Figure 1–54).

Figure 1–54

Experiment

- Point to various glow effects in the Glow gallery and watch the picture change in the document window.

- Click Tan, 5 pt glow, Accent color 6 in the Glow gallery to apply the selected picture effect.

Q&A What if I wanted to discard formatting applied to a picture?

You would click the Reset Picture button (Picture Tools Format tab | Adjust group). To reset formatting and size, you would click the Reset Picture button arrow (Picture Tools Format tab | Adjust group) and then click Reset Picture & Size on the Reset Picture menu.

3

- Click the Picture Effects button (Picture Tools Format tab | Picture Styles group) to display the Picture Effects menu again.

- Point to 3-D Rotation on the Picture Effects menu to display the 3-D Rotation gallery.

- Point to Off Axis 1 Right in the Parallel area (second rotation in second row) to display a live preview of the selected 3-D effect applied to the picture in the document window (Figure 1–55).

Experiment

- Point to various 3-D rotation effects in the 3-D Rotation gallery and watch the picture change in the document window.

4

- Click Off Axis 1 Right in the 3-D Rotation gallery to apply the selected picture effect.

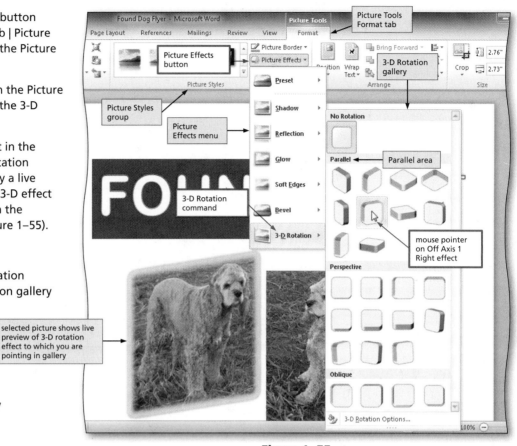

Figure 1–55

Other Ways

1. Right-click picture, click Format Picture on shortcut menu, select desired options (Format Picture dialog box), click Close button

2. Click Format Shape Dialog Box Launcher (Picture Tools Format tab | Picture Styles group), select desired options (Format Picture dialog box), click Close button

To Apply a Picture Style and Effects to Another Picture

In this flyer, the rightmost dog picture also uses the soft edge picture style, has a slight tan glow effect, and is turned inward toward the center of the page. The following steps apply the picture style and picture effects to the picture.

1 Click the rightmost dog picture to select it.

2 Click the More button in the Picture Styles gallery (Picture Tools Format tab | Picture Styles group) to expand the gallery and then click Soft Edge Rectangle in the Picture Styles gallery to apply the selected style to the picture.

3 Click the Picture Effects button (Picture Tools Format tab | Picture Styles group) to display the Picture Effects menu and then point to Glow on the Picture Effects menu to display the Glow gallery.

4 Click Tan, 5 pt glow, Accent color 6 (rightmost glow in first row) in the Glow gallery to apply the picture effect to the picture.

5 Click the Picture Effects button (Picture Tools Format tab | Picture Styles group) to display the Picture Effects menu again and then point to 3-D Rotation on the Picture Effects menu to display the 3-D Rotation gallery.

6 Click Off Axis 2 Left (rightmost rotation in second row) in the Parallel area in the 3-D Rotation gallery to apply the picture effect to the selected picture.

7 Click to the right of the picture to deselect it (Figure 1–56).

picture style and picture effects applied to picture

Figure 1–56

Enhancing the Page

With the text and graphics entered and formatted, the next step is to look at the page as a whole and determine if it looks finished in its current state. As you review the page, answer these questions:

- Does it need a page border to frame its contents, or would a page border make it look too busy?
- Is the spacing between paragraphs and graphics on the page adequate? Do any sections of text or graphics look as if they are positioned too closely to the items above or below them?

You determine that a graphical, color-coordinated border would enhance the flyer. You also notice that the flyer would look more proportionate if it had a little more space above and below the pictures. The following pages make these enhancements to the flyer.

To View One Page

Earlier in this chapter, you changed the zoom using the Zoom Out and Zoom In buttons on the status bar. If you want to display an entire page as large as possible in the document window, Word can compute the correct zoom percentage for you. The next steps display a single page in its entirety in the document window as large as possible.

1

- Click View on the Ribbon to display the View tab.

2

- Click the One Page button (View tab | Zoom group) to display the entire page in the document window as large as possible (Figure 1–57).

Figure 1–57

To Add a Page Border

In Word, you can add a border around the perimeter of an entire page. The flyer in this chapter has a light green dashed border. The following steps add a page border.

1

- Click Page Layout on the Ribbon to display the Page Layout tab.

- Click the Page Borders button (Page Layout tab | Page Background group) to display the Borders and Shading dialog box (Figure 1–58).

Figure 1–58

2

- Scroll through the Style list (Borders and Shading dialog box) and select the style shown in Figure 1–59.

- Click the Color box arrow to display a Color palette (Figure 1–59).

Figure 1–59

3

- Click Dark Green, Accent 4, Lighter 60% (eighth color in third row) in the Color palette to select the color for the page border.

- Click the Width box arrow and then click 3 pt to select the thickness of the page border (Figure 1–60).

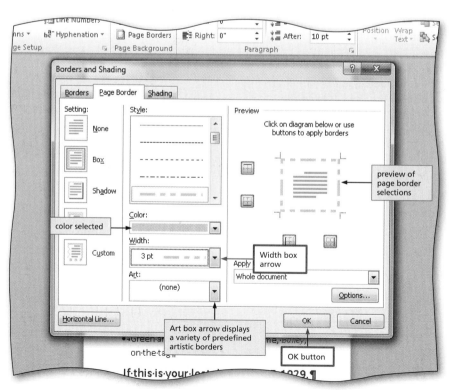

Figure 1–60

4

- Click the OK button to add the border to the page (Figure 1–61).

 Q&A

What if I wanted to remove the border?

You would click None in the Setting list in the Borders and Shading dialog box.

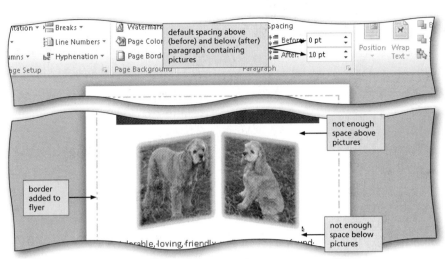

Figure 1–61

To Change Spacing before and after a Paragraph

The default spacing above (before) a paragraph in Word is 0 points and below (after) is 10 points. In the flyer, you want to increase the spacing above and below the paragraph containing the pictures. The following steps change the spacing above and below a paragraph.

1

- Position the insertion point in the paragraph to be adjusted, in this case, the paragraph containing the pictures.

- Click the Spacing Before box up arrow (Page Layout tab | Paragraph group) as many times as necessary until 24 pt is displayed in the Spacing Before box to increase the space above the current paragraph.

2

- Click the Spacing After box up arrow (Page Layout tab | Paragraph group) so that 12 pt is displayed in the Spacing After box to increase the space below the current paragraph (Figure 1–62).

- If the text flows to two pages, reduce the spacing above and below paragraphs as necessary.

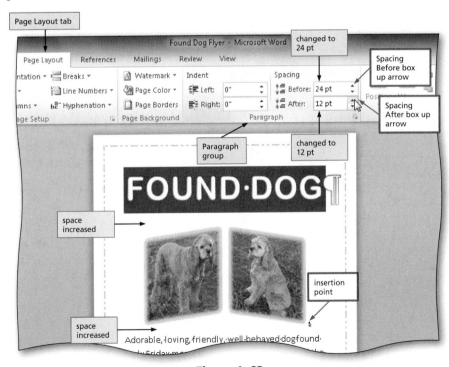

Figure 1–62

Other Ways

1. Right-click paragraph, click Paragraph on shortcut menu, click Indents and Spacing tab (Paragraph dialog box), enter spacing before and after values, click OK button

2. Click Paragraph Dialog Box Launcher (Home tab or Page Layout tab | Paragraph group), click Indents and Spacing tab (Paragraph dialog box), enter spacing before and after values, click OK button

To Save an Existing Document with the Same File Name

You have made several modifications to the document since you last saved it. Thus, you should save it again. The following step saves the document again. For an example of the step listed below, refer to the Office 2010 and Windows 7 chapter at the beginning of this book.

1 Click the Save button on the Quick Access Toolbar to overwrite the previously saved file.

To Quit Word

Certification
The Microsoft Office Specialist (MOS) program provides an opportunity for you to obtain a valuable industry credential — proof that you have the Word 2010 skills required by employers. For more information, visit the Word 2010 Certification Web page (scsite.com/ wd2010/cert).

Although you still need to make some edits to this document, you want to quit Word and resume working on the project at a later time. Thus, the following steps quit Word. For a detailed example of the procedure summarized below, refer to the Office 2010 and Windows 7 chapter at the beginning of this book.

1 If you have one Word document open, click the Close button on the right side of the title bar to close the document and quit Word; or if you have multiple Word documents open, click File on the Ribbon to open the Backstage view and then click Exit in the Backstage view to close all open documents and quit Word.

2 If a Microsoft Word dialog box appears, click the Save button to save any changes made to the document since the last save.

Break Point: If you wish to take a break, this is a good place to do so. To resume at a later time, continue following the steps from this location forward.

Correcting Errors and Revising a Document

After creating a document, you may need to change it. For example, the document may contain an error, or new circumstances may require you to add text to the document.

Types of Changes Made to Documents

The types of changes made to documents normally fall into one of the three following categories: additions, deletions, or modifications.

Additions Additional words, sentences, or paragraphs may be required in a document. Additions occur when you omit text from a document and want to insert it later. For example, you may want to add your e-mail address to the flyer.

Deletions Sometimes, text in a document is incorrect or is no longer needed. For example, you may discover the dog's collar is just green. In this case, you would delete the words, and silver, from the flyer.

Modifications If an error is made in a document or changes take place that affect the document, you might have to revise a word(s) in the text. For example, the dog may have been found in Hampton Village instead of Hampton Township.

To Start Word

Once you have created and saved a document, you may need to retrieve it from your storage medium. For example, you might want to revise the document or print it. The following steps, which assume Windows 7 is running, start Word so that you can open and modify the flyer. You may need to ask your instructor how to start Word for your computer. For a detailed example of the procedure summarized below, refer to the Office 2010 and Windows 7 chapter at the beginning of this book.

1 Click the Start button on the Windows 7 taskbar to display the Start menu.

2 Type `Microsoft Word` as the search text in the 'Search programs and files' text box and watch the search results appear on the Start menu.

3 Click Microsoft Word 2010 in the search results on the Start menu to start Word and display a new blank document in the Word window.

4 If the Word window is not maximized, click the Maximize button next to the Close button on its title bar to maximize the window.

To Open a Document from Word

Earlier in this chapter, you saved your project on a USB flash drive using the file name, Found Dog Flyer. The following steps open the Found Dog Flyer file from the Word folder in the CIS 101 folder on the USB flash drive. For a detailed example of the procedure summarized below, refer to the Office 2010 and Windows 7 chapter at the beginning of this book.

1 With your USB flash drive connected to one of the computer's USB ports, click File on the Ribbon to open the Backstage view.

2 Click Open in the Backstage view to display the Open dialog box.

3 Navigate to the location of the file to be opened (in this case, the Word folder in the CIS 101 folder [or your class folder] on the USB flash drive). For a detailed example of this procedure, refer to Steps 3a – 3c in the To Save a File in a Folder section in the Office 2010 and Windows 7 chapter at the beginning of this book.

4 Click Found Dog Flyer to select the file to be opened.

5 Click the Open button (Open dialog box) to open the selected file and display the opened document in the Word window.

Q&A Could I have clicked the Recent tab to open the file?

Yes. Because the file was recently closed, it should appear in the Recent Documents list.

To Zoom the Document

While modifying the document, you prefer the document at 100 percent so that it is easier to read. Thus, the following step changes the zoom back to 100 percent.

1 If necessary, click the Zoom In button on the status bar as many times as necessary until the Zoom button displays 100% on its face (shown in Figure 1–63 on the next page).

To Insert Text in an Existing Document

Word inserts text to the left of the insertion point. The text to the right of the insertion point moves to the right and downward to fit the new text. The following steps insert the word, very, to the left of the word, early, in the flyer.

1

• Scroll through the document and then click to the left of the location of text to be inserted (in this case, the e in early) to position the insertion point where text should be inserted (Figure 1–63).

Figure 1–63

2

• Type **very** and then press the SPACEBAR to insert the word to the left of the insertion point (Figure 1–64).

 Q&A

Why did the text move to the right as I typed?

In Word, the default typing mode is **insert mode**, which means as you type a character, Word moves all the characters to the right of the typed character one position to the right.

Figure 1–64

Deleting Text from a Document

It is not unusual to type incorrect characters or words in a document. As discussed earlier in this chapter, you can click the Undo button on the Quick Access Toolbar to undo a command or action immediately — this includes typing. Word also provides other methods of correcting typing errors.

To delete an incorrect character in a document, simply click next to the incorrect character and then press the BACKSPACE key to erase to the left of the insertion point, or press the DELETE key to erase to the right of the insertion point.

To Delete Text

To delete a word or phrase, you first must select the word or phrase. The following steps select the word, very, that was just added in the previous steps and then delete the selection.

- Position the mouse pointer somewhere in the word to be selected (in this case, very) and then double-click to select the word (Figure 1–65).

> Adorable, loving, friendly, well-behaved dog found very early Friday morning, June 1, wandering on the bike trail at Filcher Park in Hampton Township.¶

text to be deleted is selected

mouse pointer

Figure 1–65

2

- With the text selected, press the DELETE key to delete the selected text (shown in Figure 1–63).

To Move Text

While proofreading the flyer, you realize that the body copy would read better if the first two bulleted paragraphs were reversed. An efficient way to move text a short distance, such as reversing two paragraphs, is drag-and-drop editing. With **drag-and-drop editing**, you select the text to be moved and then drag the selected item to the new location and then *drop*, or insert, it there. Another technique for moving text is the cut-and-paste technique, which is discussed in the next chapter. The following steps use drag-and-drop editing to move text.

1

- Position the mouse pointer in the paragraph to be moved (in this case, the second bulleted item) and then triple-click to select the paragraph.

- With the mouse pointer in the selected text, press and hold down the mouse button, which displays a dotted insertion point and a small dotted box with the mouse pointer (Figure 1–66).

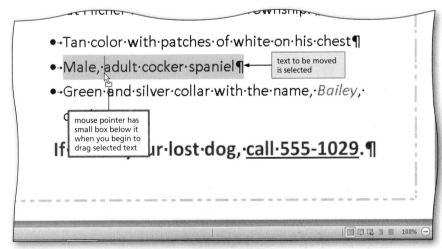

- Tan color with patches of white on his chest¶
- Male, adult cocker spaniel¶

text to be moved is selected

- Green and silver collar with the name, *Bailey,*

mouse pointer has small box below it when you begin to drag selected text

If ... ur lost dog, call 555-1029.¶

100%

Figure 1–66

2

● Drag the dotted insertion point to the location where the selected text is to be moved, as shown in Figure 1–67.

selected text to be dropped at location of dotted insertion point

Adorable,·loving,·friendly,·well-behaved·dog·found· early·Friday·morning,·June·1,·wandering·on·the·bike· trail·at·Filcher·Park·in·Hampton·Township.¶

●→Tan·color·with·patches·of·white·on·his·chest¶

●→Male,·adult·cocker·spaniel¶

●→Green·and·silver·collar·with·the·name,·*Bailey*,· on·the·tag¶

If·this·is·your·lost·dog,·call·555-1029.¶

Figure 1–67

3

● Release the mouse button to move the selected text to the location of the dotted insertion point (Figure 1–68).

Q&A What if I accidentally drag text to the wrong location?

Click the Undo button on the Quick Access Toolbar and try again.

Q&A Can I use drag-and-drop editing to move any selected item?

Yes, you can select words, sentences, phrases, and graphics and then use drag-and-drop editing to move them.

Q&A What is the purpose of the Paste Options button?

If you click the Paste Options button, a menu appears that allows you to change the format of the item that was moved. The next chapter discusses the Paste Options menu.

● Click anywhere in the document window to remove the selection from the bulleted item.

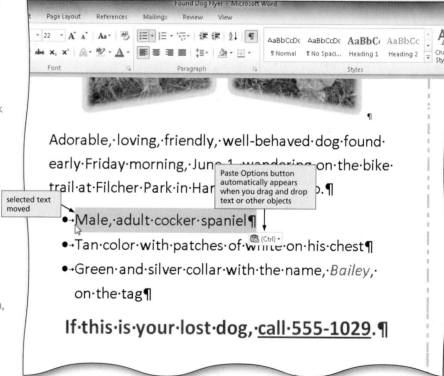

selected text moved

Paste Options button automatically appears when you drag and drop text or other objects

Figure 1–68

Other Ways

1. Click Cut button (Home tab | Clipboard group), click where text or object is to be pasted, click Paste button (Home tab | Clipboard group)

2. Right-click selected text, click Cut on shortcut menu, right-click where text or object is to be pasted, click Keep Source Formatting on shortcut menu

3. Press CTRL+X, position insertion point where text or object is to be pasted, press CTRL+V

Changing Document Properties

Word helps you organize and identify your files by using **document properties**, which are the details about a file. Document properties, also known as **metadata**, can include information such as the project author, title, subject, and keywords. A **keyword** is a word or phrase that further describes the document. For example, a class name or document topic can describe the file's purpose or content.

Document properties are valuable for a variety of reasons:

- Users can save time locating a particular file because they can view a document's properties without opening the document.

- By creating consistent properties for files having similar content, users can better organize their documents.

- Some organizations require Word users to add document properties so that other employees can view details about these files.

Five different types of document properties exist, but the more common ones used in this book are standard and automatically updated properties. **Standard properties** are associated with all Microsoft Office documents and include author, title, and subject. **Automatically updated properties** include file system properties, such as the date you create or change a file, and statistics, such as the file size.

BTW

Printing Document Properties
To print document properties, click File on the Ribbon to open the Backstage view, click the Print tab in the Backstage view to display the Print gallery, click the first button in the Settings area to display a list of options specifying what you can print, click Document Properties in the list to specify you want to print the document properties instead of the actual document, and then click the Print button in the Print gallery to print the document properties on the currently selected printer.

To Change Document Properties

The **Document Information Panel** contains areas where you can view and enter document properties. You can view and change information in this panel at any time while you are creating a document. Before saving the flyer again, you want to add your name and course information as document properties. The following steps use the Document Information Panel to change document properties.

1

- Click File on the Ribbon to open the Backstage view.

- If necessary, click the Info tab to display the Info gallery (Figure 1–69).

Q&A

How do I close the Backstage view?

Click File on the Ribbon or click the preview of the document in the Info gallery to return to the Word document window.

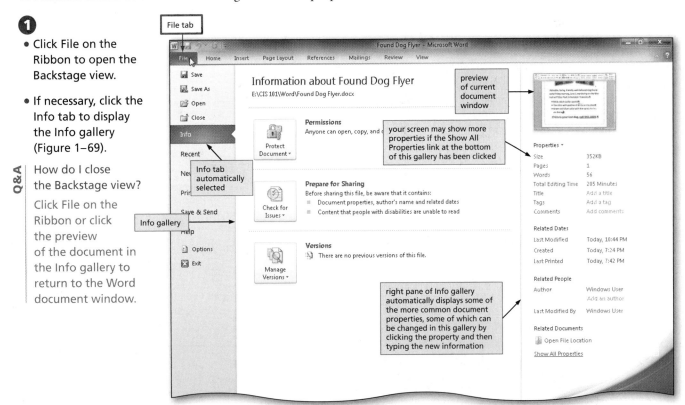

Figure 1–69

2

- Click the Properties button in the right pane of the Info gallery to display the Properties menu (Figure 1–70).

Figure 1–70

3

- Click Show Document Panel on the Properties menu to close the Backstage view and display the Document Information Panel in the Word document window (Figure 1–71).

 Why are some of the document properties in my Document Information Panel already filled in?

The person who installed Microsoft Office 2010 on your computer or network may have set or customized the properties.

Figure 1–71

4

- Click the Author text box, if necessary, and then type your name as the Author property. If a name already is displayed in the Author text box, delete it before typing your name.

- Click the Subject text box, if necessary delete any existing text, and then type your course and section as the Subject property.

- If an AutoComplete dialog box appears, click its Yes button.

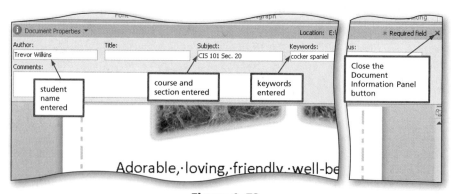

Figure 1–72

- Click the Keywords text box, if necessary delete any existing text, and then type **cocker spaniel** as the Keywords property (Figure 1–72).

Q&A What types of document properties does Word collect automatically?

Word records details such as time spent editing a document, the number of times a document has been revised, and the fonts and themes used in a document.

5

- Click the Close the Document Information Panel button so that the Document Information Panel no longer is displayed.

Other Ways

1. Click File on Ribbon, click Info in Backstage view, if necessary click Show All Properties link in Info gallery, click property to change and then type new information, close Backstage view

To Save an Existing Document with the Same File Name

You are finished editing the flyer. Thus, you should save it again. The following step saves the document again. For an example of the step listed below, refer to the Office 2010 and Windows 7 chapter at the beginning of this book.

 Click the Save button on the Quick Access Toolbar to overwrite the previously saved file.

Printing a Document

After creating a document, you may want to print it. Printing a document enables you to distribute the document to others in a form that can be read or viewed but typically not edited. It is a good practice to save a document before printing it, in the event you experience difficulties printing.

Determine the best method for distributing the document.
The traditional method of distributing a document uses a printer to produce a hard copy. A **hardcopy** or **printout** is information that exists on a physical medium such as paper. For users that can receive fax documents, you can elect to print a hard copy on a remote fax machine. Hard copies can be useful for the following reasons:

- Many people prefer proofreading a hard copy of a document rather than viewing it on the screen to check for errors and readability.

- Hard copies can serve as reference material if your storage medium is lost or becomes corrupted and you need to recreate the document.

  Instead of distributing a hard copy of a document, users can choose to distribute the document as an electronic image that mirrors the original document's appearance. The electronic image of the document can be e-mailed, posted on a Web site, or copied to a portable storage medium such as a USB flash drive. Two popular electronic image formats, sometimes called fixed formats, are PDF by Adobe Systems and XPS by Microsoft. In Word, you can create electronic image files through the Print tab in the Backstage view, the Send & Save tab in the Backstage view, and the Save As dialog box. Electronic images of documents, such as PDF and XPS, can be useful for the following reasons:

- Users can view electronic images of documents without the software that created the original document (e.g., Word). Specifically, to view a PDF file, you use a program called Acrobat Reader, which can be downloaded free from Adobe's Web site. Similarly, to view an XPS file, you use a program called an XPS Viewer, which is included in the latest versions of Windows and Internet Explorer.

- Sending electronic documents saves paper and printer supplies. Society encourages users to contribute to **green computing**, which involves reducing the environmental waste generated when using a computer.

Plan Ahead

BTW

Conserving Ink and Toner
If you want to conserve ink or toner, you can instruct Word to print draft quality documents by clicking File on the Ribbon to open the Backstage view, clicking Options in the Backstage view to display the Word Options dialog box, clicking Advanced in the left pane (Word Options dialog box), scrolling to the Print area in the right pane, placing a check mark in the 'Use draft quality' check box, and then clicking the OK button. Then, use the Backstage view to print the document as usual.

To Print a Document

With the completed document saved, you may want to print it. Because this flyer is being posted, you will print a hard copy on a printer. The steps on the next page print a hard copy of the contents of the saved Found Dog Flyer document.

1

- Click File on the Ribbon to open the Backstage view.

- Click the Print tab in the Backstage view to display the Print gallery (Figure 1–73).

Q&A How can I print multiple copies of my document?

Increase the number in the Copies box in the Print gallery.

Q&A What if I decide not to print the document at this time?

Click File on the Ribbon to close the Backstage view and return to the Word document window.

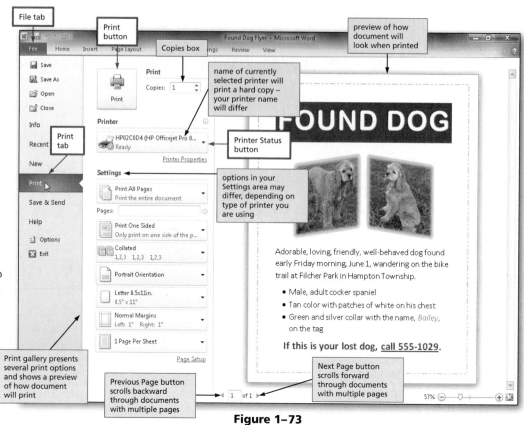

Figure 1–73

2

- Verify the printer name that appears on the Printer Status button will print a hard copy of the document. If necessary, click the Printer Status button to display a list of available printer options and then click the desired printer to change the currently selected printer.

3

- Click the Print button in the Print gallery to print the document on the currently selected printer.

- When the printer stops, retrieve the hard copy (Figure 1–74).

Q&A Do I have to wait until my document is complete to print it?

No, you can follow these steps to print a document at any time while you are creating it.

Q&A What if I want to print an electronic image of a document instead of a hard copy?

You would click the Printer Status button in the Print gallery and then select the desired electronic image option such as a Microsoft XPS Document Writer, which would create an XPS file.

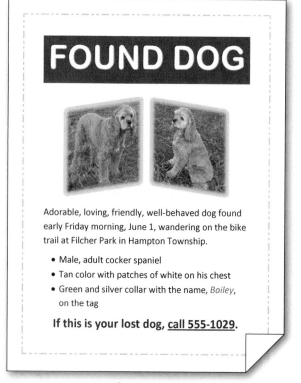

Figure 1–74

Other Ways

1. Press CTRL+P, press ENTER

To Quit Word

The project now is complete. Thus, the following steps quit Word. For an example of the step listed below, refer to the Office 2010 and Windows 7 chapter at the beginning of this book.

1 If you have one Word document open, click the Close button on the right side of the title bar to close the document and quit Word; or if you have multiple Word documents open, click File on the Ribbon to open the Backstage view and then click Exit in the Backstage view to close all open documents and quit Word.

2 If a Microsoft Word dialog box appears, click the Save button to save any changes made to the document since the last save.

BTW

Printed Borders

If one or more of your borders do not print, click the Page Borders button (Page Layout tab | Page Background group), click the Options button (Borders and Shading dialog box), click the Measure from box arrow and click Text, change the four text boxes to 15 pt, and then click the OK button in each dialog box. Try printing the document again. If the borders still do not print, adjust the text boxes in the dialog box to a number smaller than 15 point.

Chapter Summary

In this chapter, you have learned how to enter text in a document, format text, insert a picture, format a picture, add a page border, and print a document. The items listed below include all the new Word skills you have learned in this chapter.

1. Start Word (WD 4)
2. Type Text (WD 6)
3. Display Formatting Marks (WD 7)
4. Insert a Blank Line (WD 7)
5. Wordwrap Text as You Type (WD 8)
6. Check Spelling and Grammar as You Type (WD 9)
7. Save a Document (WD 12)
8. Center a Paragraph (WD 14)
9. Select a Line (WD 15)
10. Change the Font Size of Selected Text (WD 16)
11. Change the Font of Selected Text (WD 17)
12. Change the Case of Selected Text (WD 18)
13. Apply a Text Effect to Selected Text (WD 19)
14. Shade a Paragraph (WD 20)
15. Select Multiple Lines (WD 21)
16. Bullet a List of Paragraphs (WD 22)
17. Undo and Redo an Action (WD 23)
18. Italicize Text (WD 24)
19. Color Text (WD 25)
20. Use the Mini Toolbar to Format Text (WD 26)
21. Select a Group of Words (WD 27)
22. Underline Text (WD 27)
23. Bold Text (WD 28)
24. Change Theme Colors (WD 28)
25. Save an Existing Document with the Same File Name (WD 30)
26. Insert a Picture (WD 31)
27. Zoom the Document (WD 33)
28. Resize a Graphic (WD 34)
29. Resize a Graphic by Entering Exact Measurements (WD 36)
30. Apply a Picture Style (WD 37)
31. Apply Picture Effects (WD 38)
32. View One Page (WD 40)
33. Add a Page Border (WD 41)
34. Change Spacing before and after a Paragraph (WD 44)
35. Quit Word (WD 44)
36. Open a Document from Word (WD 45)
37. Insert Text in an Existing Document (WD 46)
38. Delete Text (WD 47)
39. Move Text (WD 47)
40. Change Document Properties (WD 49)
41. Print a Document (WD 51)

 If you have a SAM 2010 user profile, your instructor may have assigned an autogradable version of this assignment. If so, log into the SAM 2010 Web site at www.cengage.com/sam2010 to download the instruction and start files.

BTW

Quick Reference

For a table that lists how to complete the tasks covered in this book using the mouse, Ribbon, shortcut menu, and keyboard, see the Quick Reference Summary at the back of this book, or visit the Word 2010 Quick Reference Web page (scsite.com/wd2010/qr).

Learn It Online

Test your knowledge of chapter content and key terms.

Instructions: To complete the Learn It Online exercises, start your browser, click the Address bar, and then enter the Web address **scsite.com/wd2010/learn**. When the Word 2010 Learn It Online page is displayed, click the link for the exercise you want to complete and then read the instructions.

Chapter Reinforcement TF, MC, and SA
A series of true/false, multiple choice, and short answer questions that test your knowledge of the chapter content.

Flash Cards
An interactive learning environment where you identify chapter key terms associated with displayed definitions.

Practice Test
A series of multiple choice questions that test your knowledge of chapter content and key terms.

Who Wants To Be a Computer Genius?
An interactive game that challenges your knowledge of chapter content in the style of a television quiz show.

Wheel of Terms
An interactive game that challenges your knowledge of chapter key terms in the style of the television show *Wheel of Fortune*.

Crossword Puzzle Challenge
A crossword puzzle that challenges your knowledge of key terms presented in the chapter.

Apply Your Knowledge

Reinforce the skills and apply the concepts you learned in this chapter.

Modifying Text and Formatting a Document
Note: To complete this assignment, you will be required to use the Data Files for Students. See the inside back cover of this book for instructions on downloading the Data Files for Students, or contact your instructor for information about accessing the required files.

Instructions: Start Word. Open the document, Apply 1-1 Buffalo Photo Shoot Flyer Unformatted, from the Data Files for Students. The document you open is an unformatted flyer. You are to modify text, format paragraphs and characters, and insert a picture in the flyer.

Perform the following tasks:
1. Delete the word, single, in the sentence of body copy below the headline.
2. Insert the word, Creeks, between the words, Twin Buffalo, in the sentence of body copy below the headline.
3. At the end of the signature line, change the period to an exclamation point.
4. Center the headline and the signature line.
5. Change the theme colors to the Aspect color scheme.
6. Change the font and font size of the headline to 48-point Impact, or a similar font. Change the case of the headline text to all capital letters. Apply the text effect called Gradient Fill – Orange, Accent 1, Outline – White to the headline.
7. Change the font size of body copy between the headline and the signature line to 20 point.
8. Use the Mini toolbar to change the font size of the signature line to 26 point.
9. Select the words, hundreds of buffalo, in the paragraph below the headline and underline them.

10. Italicize the word, every, in the paragraph below the headline. Undo this change and then redo the change.

11. Select the three lines (paragraphs) of text above the signature line and add bullets to the selected paragraphs.

12. Switch the last two bulleted paragraphs. That is, select the Questions bullet and move it so that it is the last bulleted paragraph.

13. Bold the first word of each bulleted paragraph. Change the font color of these same three words to Dark Green, Accent 4, Darker 50%.

14. Bold the text in the signature line. Shade the signature line Dark Green, Accent 4, Darker 50%. If the font color does not automatically change to a lighter color, change it to a shade of white.

15. Change the zoom so that the entire page is visible in the document window.

16. Insert the picture of the buffalo centered on the blank line below the headline. The picture is called Buffalo and is available on the Data Files for Students. Apply the Snip Diagonal Corner, White picture style to the inserted picture. Apply the glow called Dark Green, 5 pt glow, Accent color 4 to the picture.

17. Change the spacing after the headline paragraph to 6 point.

18. The entire flyer now should fit on a single page. If it flows to two pages, resize the picture or decrease spacing before and after paragraphs until the entire flyer text fits on a single page.

19. Change the zoom to text width, then page width, then 100% and notice the differences.

20. Enter the text, Twin Creeks, as the keywords in the document properties. Change the other document properties, as specified by your instructor.

21. Click File on the Ribbon and then click Save As. Save the document using the file name, Apply 1-1 Buffalo Photo Shoot Flyer Formatted.

22. Print the document. Submit the revised document, shown in Figure 1–75, in the format specified by your instructor.

23. Quit Word.

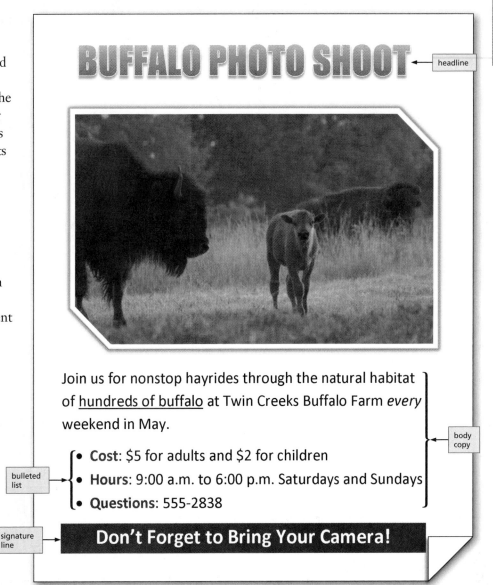

Figure 1–75

Extend Your Knowledge

Extend the skills you learned in this chapter and experiment with new skills. You may need to use Help to complete the assignment.

Modifying Text and Picture Formats and Adding Page Borders

Note: To complete this assignment, you will be required to use the Data Files for Students. See the inside back cover of this book for instructions on downloading the Data Files for Students, or contact your instructor for information about accessing the required files.

Instructions: Start Word. Open the document, Extend 1-1 TVC Cruises Flyer, from the Data Files for Students. You will enhance the look of the flyer shown in Figure 1–76. *Hint:* Remember, if you make a mistake while formatting the picture, you can reset it by clicking the Reset Picture button or Reset Picture button arrow (Picture Tools Format tab | Adjust group).

Perform the following tasks:
1. Use Help to learn about the following formats: remove bullets, grow font, shrink font, art page borders, decorative underline(s), picture bullets, picture border shading, shadow picture effects, and color saturation and tone.
2. Remove the bullet from the paragraph below the picture.

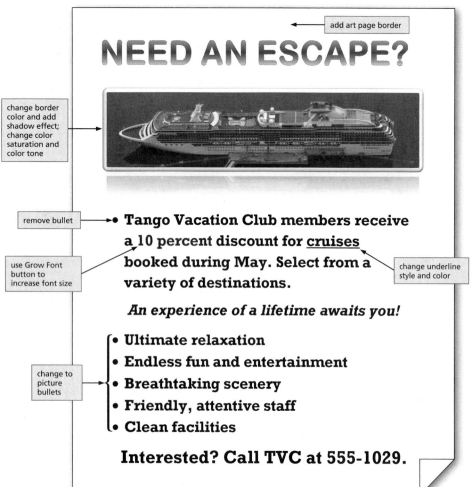

3. Select the text, 10 percent, and use the Grow Font button to increase its font size.

4. Add an art page border to the flyer. If the border is not in color, add color to it.

5. Change the solid underline below the word, cruises, to a decorative underline. Change the color of the underline.

6. Change the style of the bullets to picture bullet(s).

7. Change the color of the picture border. Add a shadow picture effect to the picture.

8. Change the color saturation and color tone of the picture.

9. Change the document properties, including keywords, as specified by your instructor. Save the revised document with a new file name and then submit it in the format specified by your instructor.

Figure 1–76

Make It Right

Analyze a document and correct all errors and/or improve the design.

Correcting Spelling and Grammar Errors

Note: To complete this assignment, you will be required to use the Data Files for Students. See the inside back cover of this book for instructions on downloading the Data Files for Students, or contact your instructor for information about accessing the required files.

Instructions: Start Word. Open the document, Make It Right 1-1 Karate Academy Flyer Unchecked, from the Data Files for Students. The document is a flyer that contains spelling and grammar errors, as shown in Figure 1–77. You are to correct each spelling (red wavy underline) and grammar error (green and blue wavy underlines) by right-clicking the flagged text and then clicking the appropriate correction on the shortcut menu.

If your screen does not display the wavy underlines, click File on the Ribbon and then click Options in the Backstage view. When the Word Options dialog box is displayed, click Proofing in the left pane, be sure the 'Hide spelling errors in this document only' and 'Hide grammar errors in this document only' check boxes do not contain check marks, and then click the OK button. If your screen still does not display the wavy underlines, redisplay the Word Options dialog box, click Proofing, and then click the Recheck Document button.

Change the document properties, including keywords, as specified by your instructor. Save the revised document with the name, Make It Right 1-1 Karate Academy Flyer, and then submit it in the format specified by your instructor.

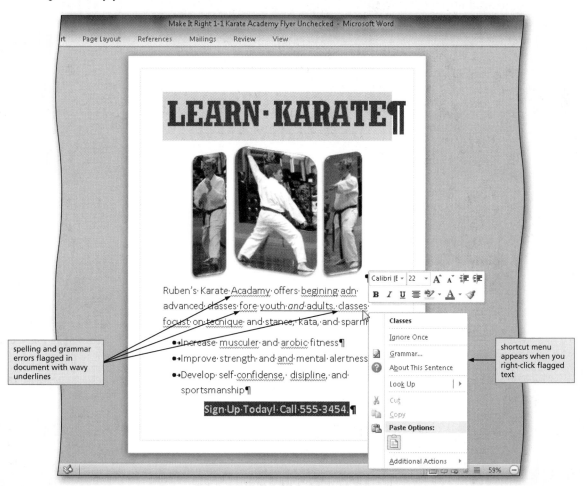

Figure 1–77

In the Lab

Design and/or create a document using the guidelines, concepts, and skills presented in this chapter. Labs are listed in order of increasing difficulty.

Lab 1: Creating a Flyer with a Picture

Problem: As a part-time employee in the Student Services Center at school, you have been asked to prepare a flyer that advertises study habits classes. First, you prepare the unformatted flyer shown in Figure 1–78a, and then you format it so that it looks like Figure 1–78b. *Hint:* Remember, if you make a mistake while formatting the flyer, you can click the Undo button on the Quick Access Toolbar to undo your last action.

Note: To complete this assignment, you will be required to use the Data Files for Students. See the inside back cover of this book for instructions on downloading the Data Files for Students, or contact your instructor for information about accessing the required files.

Instructions: Perform the following tasks:

1. Start Word. Display formatting marks on the screen.
2. Type the flyer text, unformatted, as shown in Figure 1–78a, inserting a blank line between the headline and the body copy. If Word flags any misspelled words as you type, check their spelling and correct them.
3. Save the document using the file name, Lab 1-1 Study Habits Flyer.
4. Center the headline and the signature line.
5. Change the theme colors to Concourse.
6. Change the font size of the headline to 36 point and the font to Ravie, or a similar font. Apply the text effect called Gradient Fill – Dark Red, Accent 6, Inner Shadow.
7. Change the font size of body copy between the headline and the signature line to 20 point.
8. Change the font size of the signature line to 22 point. Bold the text in the signature line.

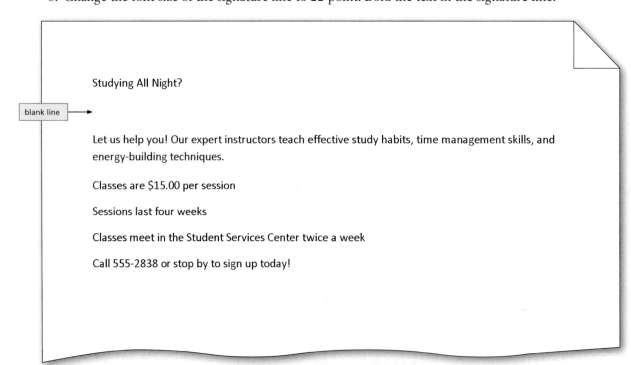

Figure 1–78 (a) Unformatted Flyer

9. Change the font of the body copy and signature line to Rockwell, and change the color of the signature line to Dark Red, Accent 6.

10. Bullet the three lines (paragraphs) of text above the signature line.

11. Bold and capitalize the text, Let us help you!, and change its color to Dark Red, Accent 6.

12. Italicize the word, or, in the signature line.

13. Underline the text, Student Services Center, in the third bulleted paragraph.

14. Change the zoom so that the entire page is visible in the document window.

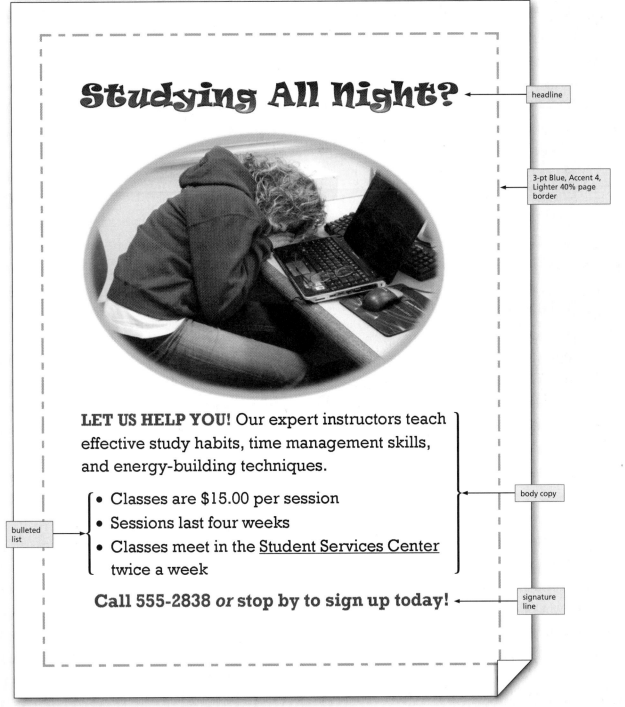

Figure 1–78 (b) Formatted Flyer

Continued >

In the Lab *continued*

15. Insert the picture centered on a blank line below the headline. The picture is called Sleeping and is available on the Data Files for Students.

16. Apply the Soft Edge Oval picture style to the inserted picture. Apply the glow effect called Blue, 5 pt glow, Accent color 4 to the picture.

17. The entire flyer should fit on a single page. If it flows to two pages, resize the picture or decrease spacing before and after paragraphs until the entire flyer text fits on a single page.

18. Add the page border shown in Figure 1–78b on the previous page.

19. Change the document properties, including keywords, as specified by your instructor. Save the flyer again with the same file name. Submit the document, shown in Figure 1–78b, in the format specified by your instructor.

In the Lab

Lab 2: Creating a Flyer with a Resized Picture

Problem: Your boss at Granger Camera House has asked you to prepare a flyer that announces the upcoming photography contest. You prepare the flyer shown in Figure 1–79. *Hint:* Remember, if you make a mistake while formatting the flyer, you can click the Undo button on the Quick Access Toolbar to undo your last action.

Note: To complete this assignment, you will be required to use the Data Files for Students. See the inside back cover of this book for instructions on downloading the Data Files for Students, or contact your instructor for information about accessing the required files.

Instructions: Perform the following tasks:

1. Start Word. Type the flyer text, unformatted. If Word flags any misspelled words as you type, check their spelling and correct them.

2. Save the document using the file name, Lab 1-2 Photography Contest Flyer.

3. Change the theme colors to the Apex color scheme.

4. Center the headline, the line that says RULES, and the signature line.

5. Change the font size of the headline to 36 point and the font to Stencil, or a similar font. Shade the headline paragraph Lavender, Background 2, Darker 50%. Apply the text effect called Fill – Lavender, Accent 6, Outline – Accent 6, Glow – Accent 6.

6. Change the font size of body copy between the headline and the signature line to 18 point.

7. Change the font size of the signature line to 24 point and the font to Stencil. Bold the text in the signature line. Change the font color of the text in the signature line to Gray-50%, Text 2.

8. Bullet the three paragraphs of text above the signature line.

9. Italicize the word, not.

10. Bold the word, landscape.

11. Underline the text, August 31.

12. Shade the line that says RULES to the Gray-50%, Text 2 color. If the font color does not automatically change to a lighter color, change it to White, Background 1.

13. Change the zoom so that the entire page is visible in the document window.

14. Insert the picture on a blank line below the headline. The picture is called Wind Power and is available on the Data Files for Students.

15. Resize the picture so that it is approximately 3.5" × 5.25". Apply the Rotated, White picture style to the inserted picture. Apply the glow effect called Lavender, 5 pt glow, Accent color 6 to the picture.

16. The entire flyer should fit on a single page. If it flows to two pages, resize the picture or decrease spacing before and after paragraphs until the entire flyer text fits on a single page.

17. Add the page border shown in Figure 1–79.

18. Change the document properties, including keywords, as specified by your instructor. Save the flyer again with the same file name. Submit the document, shown in Figure 1–79, in the format specified by your instructor.

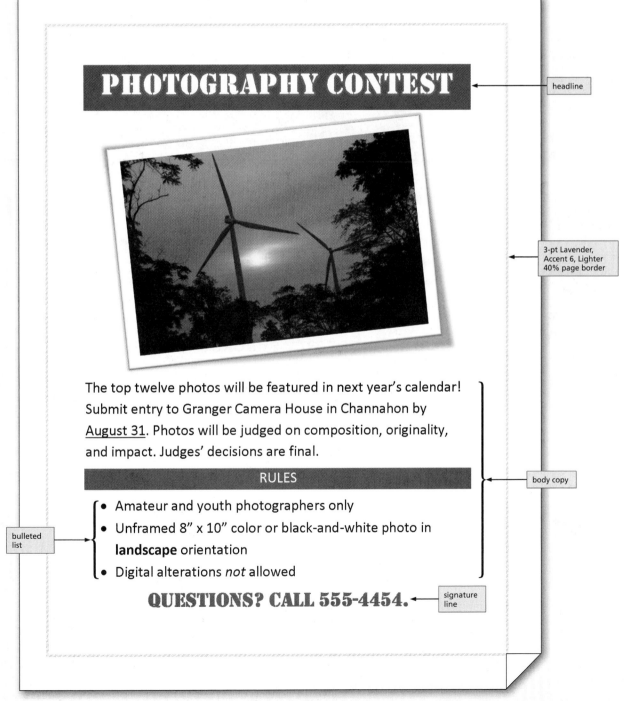

Figure 1–79

In the Lab

Lab 3: Creating a Flyer with Pictures

Problem: Your boss at Warner Depot has asked you to prepare a flyer that advertises its scenic train ride. You prepare the flyer shown in Figure 1–80.

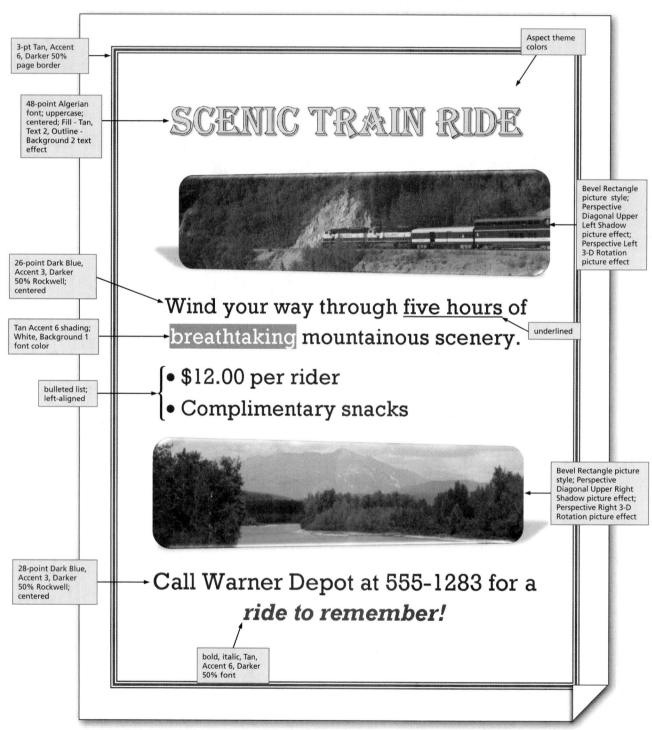

3-pt Tan, Accent 6, Darker 50% page border

48-point Algerian font; uppercase; centered; Fill - Tan, Text 2, Outline - Background 2 text effect

Aspect theme colors

Bevel Rectangle picture style; Perspective Diagonal Upper Left Shadow picture effect; Perspective Left 3-D Rotation picture effect

26-point Dark Blue, Accent 3, Darker 50% Rockwell; centered

Tan Accent 6 shading; White, Background 1 font color

underlined

bulleted list; left-aligned

Bevel Rectangle picture style; Perspective Diagonal Upper Right Shadow picture effect; Perspective Right 3-D Rotation picture effect

28-point Dark Blue, Accent 3, Darker 50% Rockwell; centered

bold, italic, Tan, Accent 6, Darker 50% font

Figure 1–80

Note: To complete this assignment, you will be required to use the Data Files for Students. See the inside back cover of this book for instructions on downloading the Data Files for Students, or contact your instructor for information about accessing the required files.

Instructions: Start Word. Enter the text in the flyer, checking spelling as you type, and then format it as shown in Figure 1–80. The pictures to be inserted are called Train and Scenery and are available on the Data Files for Students. Adjust spacing before and after paragraphs and resize pictures as necessary so that the flyer fits on a single page.

Change the document properties, including keywords, as specified by your instructor. Save the document using the file name, Lab 1-3 Train Ride Flyer. Submit the document, shown in Figure 1–80, in the format specified by your instructor.

Cases and Places

Apply your creative thinking and problem solving skills to design and implement a solution.

Note: To complete these assignments, you may be required to use the Data Files for Students. See the inside back cover of this book for instructions on downloading the Data Files for Students, or contact your instructor for information about accessing the required files.

1: Design and Create a Spring Break Flyer

Academic

As secretary of your school's Student Government Association, you are responsible for creating and distributing flyers for spring break group outings. This year, you have planned a trip to Settlers Resort. The flyer should contain two digital pictures appropriately resized; the Data Files for Students contains two pictures called Cabin 1 and Cabin 2, or you can use your own digital pictures if they are appropriate for the topic of the flyer. The flyer should contain the headline, Feeling Adventurous?, and this signature line: Call Lyn at 555-9901 to sign up. The body copy consists of the following, in any order: Spring Break – Blast to the Past. Settlers Resort is like a page right out of a history textbook! Spend five days living in the 1800s. The bulleted list in the body copy is as follows: One-room cabins with potbelly stoves, Campfire dining with authentic meals, and Horseback riding and much more.

Use the concepts and techniques presented in this chapter to create and format this flyer. Be sure to check spelling and grammar. Submit your assignment in the format specified by your instructor.

2: Design and Create a Yard Sale Flyer

Personal

You are planning a yard sale and would like to create and post flyers around town advertising the upcoming sale. The flyer should contain two digital pictures appropriately resized; the Data Files for Students contains two pictures called Yard Sale 1 and Yard Sale 2, or you can use your own digital pictures if they are appropriate for the topic of the flyer. The flyer should contain the headline, Yard Sale!, and this signature line: Questions? Call 555-9820. The body copy consists of the following, in any order: Hundreds of items for sale. After 20 years, we are moving to a smaller house and are selling anything that won't fit. Everything for sale must go! The bulleted list in the body copy is as follows: When: August 7, 8, 9 from 9:00 a.m. to 7:00 p.m.; Where: 139 Ravel Boulevard; and What: something for everyone – from clothing to collectibles.

Use the concepts and techniques presented in this chapter to create and format this flyer. Be sure to check spelling and grammar. Submit your assignment in the format specified by your instructor.

Continued >

Cases and Places *continued*

3: Design and Create a Village Fireworks Flyer

Professional

As a part-time employee at the Village of Crestwood, your boss has asked you to create and distribute flyers for the upcoming fireworks extravaganza. The flyer should contain two digital pictures appropriately resized; the Data Files for Students contains two pictures called Fireworks 1 and Fireworks 2, or you can use your own digital pictures if they are appropriate for the topic of the flyer. The flyer should contain the headline, Light Up The Sky, and this signature line: Call 555-2983 with questions. The body copy consists of the following, in any order: Join Us! The Village of Crestwood will present its tenth annual Light Up The Sky fireworks extravaganza on August 8 at 9:00 p.m. during the end of summer celebration in Douglas Park. The bulleted list in the body copy is as follows: Pork chop dinners will be sold for $3.00 beginning at 6:00 p.m., Bring chairs and blankets, and Admission is free.

Use the concepts and techniques presented in this chapter to create and format this flyer. Be sure to check spelling and grammar. Submit your assignment in the format specified by your instructor.

1 | Creating and Editing a Presentation with Clip Art

Objectives

You will have mastered the material in this chapter when you can:

- Select a document theme
- Create a title slide and a text slide with a multi-level bulleted list
- Add new slides and change slide layouts
- Insert clips and pictures into a slide with and without a content placeholder
- Move and size clip art

- Change font size and color
- Bold and italicize text
- Duplicate a slide
- Arrange slides
- Select slide transitions
- View a presentation in Slide Show view
- Print a presentation

1 | Creating and Editing a Presentation with Clip Art

Introduction

A PowerPoint **presentation,** also called a **slide show**, can help you deliver a dynamic, professional-looking message to an audience. PowerPoint allows you to produce slides to use in an academic, business, or other environment. One of the more common uses of these slides is to enhance an oral presentation. A speaker may desire to convey information, such as urging students to volunteer at a fund-raising event, explaining changes in employee compensation packages, or describing a new laboratory procedure. The PowerPoint slides should reinforce the speaker's message and help the audience retain the information presented. Custom slides can fit your specific needs and contain diagrams, charts, tables, pictures, shapes, video, sound, and animation effects to make your presentation more effective. An accompanying handout gives audience members reference notes and review material for your presentation.

Project Planning Guidelines

The process of developing a presentation that communicates specific information requires careful analysis and planning. As a starting point, establish why the presentation is needed. Next, analyze the intended audience for the presentation and its unique needs. Then, gather information about the topic and decide what to include in the presentation. Finally, determine the presentation design and style that will be most successful at delivering the message. Details of these guidelines are provided in Appendix A. In addition, each project in this book provides practical applications of these planning considerations.

BTW

Energy-Saving Information
The U.S. Department of Energy's Web site has myriad information available on the topics of energy efficiency and renewable energy. These features can provide news and product research that you can share with audiences with the help of a PowerPoint presentation.

Project — Presentation with Bulleted Lists and Clip Art

In this chapter's project, you will follow proper design guidelines and learn to use PowerPoint to create, save, and print the slides shown in Figures 1–1a through 1–1e. The objective is to produce a presentation, called It Is Easy Being Green, to help consumers understand basic steps they can take to save energy in their homes. This slide show has a variety of clip art and visual elements to add interest and illustrate energy-cutting measures. Some of the text has formatting and color enhancements. Transitions help one slide flow gracefully into the next during a slide show. In addition, you will print a handout of your slides to distribute to audience members.

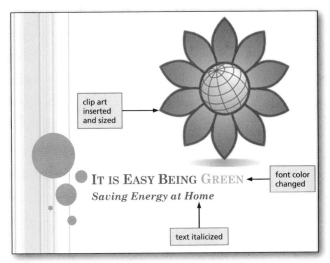

(a) Slide 1 (Title Slide with Clip Art)

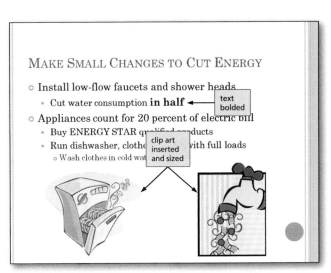

(b) Slide 2 (Multi-Level Bulleted List with Clip Art)

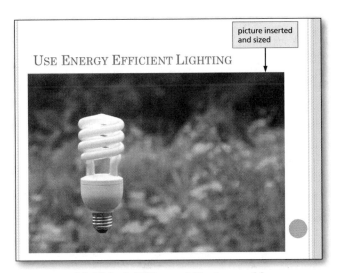

(c) Slide 3 (Title and Photograph)

(d) Slide 4 (Comparison Layout and Clip Art)

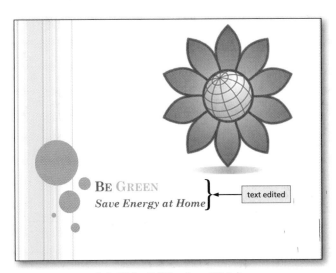

(e) Slide 5 (Closing Slide)

Figure 1–1

Overview

BTW

BTWs
For a complete list of the BTWs found in the margins of this book, visit the PowerPoint 2010 BTW Web page (scsite.com/ppt2010/btw).

As you read this chapter, you will learn how to create the presentation shown in Figure 1–1 on the previous page by performing these general tasks:

- Select an appropriate document theme.
- Enter titles and text on slides.
- Change the size, color, and style of text.
- Insert clips and a photograph.
- Add a transition to each slide.
- View the presentation on your computer.
- Print your slides.

Plan Ahead

> **General Project Guidelines**
>
> When creating a PowerPoint document, the actions you perform and decisions you make will affect the appearance and characteristics of the finished document. As you create a presentation such as the project shown in Figure 1–1, you should follow these general guidelines:
>
> 1. **Find the appropriate theme.** The overall appearance of a presentation significantly affects its capability to communicate information clearly. The slides' graphical appearance should support the presentation's overall message. Colors, fonts, and layouts affect how audience members perceive and react to the slide content.
>
> 2. **Choose words for each slide.** Use the less is more principle. The less text, the more likely the slides will enhance your speech. Use the fewest words possible to make a point.
>
> 3. **Format specific elements of the text.** Examples of how you can modify the appearance, or **format**, of text include changing its shape, size, color, and position on the slide.
>
> 4. **Determine where to save the presentation.** You can store a document permanently, or **save** it, on a variety of storage media, including a hard disk, USB flash drive, or CD. You also can indicate a specific location on the storage media for saving the document.
>
> 5. **Determine the best method for distributing the presentation.** Presentations can be distributed on paper or electronically. You can print a hard copy of the presentation slides for proofing or reference, or you can distribute an electronic image in various formats.
>
> When necessary, more specific details concerning the above guidelines are presented at appropriate points in the chapter. The chapter also will identify the actions performed and decisions made regarding these guidelines during the creation of the slides shown in Figure 1–1.

For an introduction to Windows 7 and instruction about how to perform basic Windows 7 tasks, read the Office 2010 and Windows 7 chapter at the beginning of this book, where you can learn how to resize windows, change screen resolution, create folders, move and rename files, use Windows Help, and much more.

To Start PowerPoint

If you are using a computer to step through the project in this chapter and you want your screens to match the figures in this book, you should change your screen's resolution to 1024×768. For information about how to change a computer's resolution, refer to the Office 2010 and Windows 7 chapter at the beginning of this book.

The following steps, which assume Windows 7 is running, start PowerPoint based on a typical installation. You may need to ask your instructor how to start PowerPoint for your computer. For a detailed example of the procedure summarized below, refer to the Office 2010 and Windows 7 chapter.

1 Click the Start button on the Windows 7 taskbar to display the Start menu.

2 Type `Microsoft PowerPoint` as the search text in the 'Search programs and files' text box and watch the search results appear on the Start menu.

③ Click Microsoft PowerPoint 2010 in the search results on the Start menu to start PowerPoint and display a new blank document in the PowerPoint window.

④ If the PowerPoint window is not maximized, click the Maximize button next to the Close button on its title bar to maximize the window.

Choosing a Document Theme

You can give a presentation a professional and integrated appearance easily by using a document theme. A **document theme** provides consistency in design and color throughout the entire presentation by setting the color scheme, font set, and layout of a presentation. This collection of formatting choices includes a set of colors (the Theme Colors group), a set of heading and content text fonts (the Theme Fonts group), and a set of lines and fill effects (the Theme Effects group). These groups allow you to choose and change the appearance of all the slides or individual slides in your presentation. The left edge of the status bar in Figure 1–2 shows the current slide number followed by the total number of slides in the document and a document theme identifier.

Find the appropriate theme.
In the initial steps of this project, you will select a document theme by locating a particular built-in theme in the Themes group. You could, however, apply a theme at any time while creating the presentation. Some PowerPoint slide show designers create presentations using the default Office Theme. This blank design allows them to concentrate on the words being used to convey the message and does not distract them with colors and various text attributes. Once the text is entered, the designers then select an appropriate document theme.

To Choose a Document Theme

The document theme identifier shows the theme currently used in the slide show. PowerPoint initially uses the **Office Theme** until you select a different theme. The following steps change the theme for this presentation from the Office Theme to the Oriel document theme.

①

• Click Design on the Ribbon to display the Design tab (Figure 1–2).

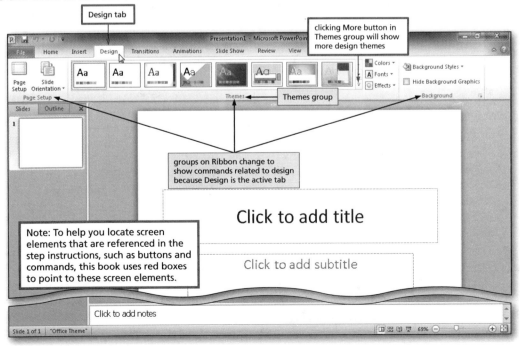

Figure 1–2

2

- Click the More button (Design tab | Themes group) to expand the gallery, which shows more Built-In theme gallery options (Figure 1–3).

🔍 **Experiment**

- Point to various document themes in the Themes gallery and watch the colors and fonts change on the title slide.

Q&A | Are the themes displayed in a specific order?

Yes. They are arranged in alphabetical order running from left to right. If you point to a theme, a ScreenTip with the theme's name appears on the screen.

Figure 1–3

Q&A | What if I change my mind and do not want to select a new theme?

Click anywhere outside the All Themes gallery to close the gallery.

3

- Click the Oriel theme to apply this theme to Slide 1 (Figure 1–4).

Q&A | If I decide at some future time that this design does not fit the theme of my presentation, can I apply a different design?

Yes. You can repeat these steps at any time while creating your presentation.

Figure 1–4

Creating a Title Slide

When you open a new presentation, the default **Title Slide** layout appears. The purpose of this layout is to introduce the presentation to the audience. PowerPoint includes eight other built-in standard layouts. The default (preset) slide layouts are set up in **landscape orientation**, where the slide width is greater than its height. In landscape orientation, the slide size is preset to 10 inches wide and 7.5 inches high when printed on a standard sheet of paper measuring 11 inches wide and 8.5 inches high.

Placeholders are boxes with dotted or hatch-marked borders that are displayed when you create a new slide. Most layouts have both a title text placeholder and at least one content placeholder. Depending on the particular slide layout selected, title and sub-title placeholders are displayed for the slide title and subtitle; a content text placeholder is displayed for text, art, or a table, chart, picture, graphic, or movie. The title slide has two text placeholders where you can type the main heading, or title, of a new slide and the subtitle.

With the exception of a blank slide, PowerPoint assumes every new slide has a title. To make creating a presentation easier, any text you type after a new slide appears becomes title text in the title text placeholder. The following steps create the title slide for this presentation.

Choose the words for the slide.

No doubt you have heard the phrase, "You get only one chance to make a first impression." The same philosophy holds true for a PowerPoint presentation. The title slide gives your audience an initial sense of what they are about to see and hear. It is, therefore, extremely important to choose the text for this slide carefully. Avoid stating the obvious in the title. Instead, create interest and curiosity using key ideas from the presentation.

Some PowerPoint users create the title slide as their last step in the design process so that it reflects the tone of the presentation. They begin by planning the final slide in the presentation so that they know where and how they want to end the slide show. All the slides in the presentation should work toward meeting this final slide.

Plan Ahead

To Enter the Presentation Title

The presentation title for Project 1 is It Is Easy Being Green. This title creates interest by introducing the concept of simple energy conservation tasks. The following step creates the slide show's title.

- Click the label, Click to add title, located inside the title text placeholder to select the placeholder (Figure 1–5).

Figure 1–5

Type `It Is Easy Being Green` **in the title text placeholder. Do not press the ENTER key (Figure 1–6).**

Q&A

Why does the text display with capital letters despite the fact I am typing uppercase and lowercase letters?

The Oriel theme uses the Small Caps effect for the title text. This effect converts lowercase letters to uppercase and reduces their size.

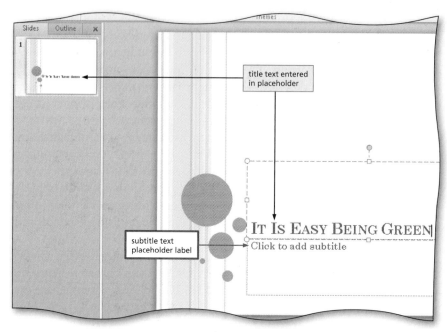

Figure 1–6

Correcting a Mistake When Typing

If you type the wrong letter, press the BACKSPACE key to erase all the characters back to and including the one that is incorrect. If you mistakenly press the ENTER key after typing the title and the insertion point is on the new line, simply press the BACKSPACE key to return the insertion point to the right of the letter n in the word, Green.

When you install PowerPoint, the default setting allows you to reverse up to the last 20 changes by clicking the Undo button on the Quick Access Toolbar. The ScreenTip that appears when you point to the Undo button changes to indicate the type of change just made. For example, if you type text in the title text placeholder and then point to the Undo button, the ScreenTip that appears is Undo Typing. For clarity, when referencing the Undo button in this project, the name displaying in the ScreenTip is referenced. You can reapply a change that you reversed with the Undo button by clicking the Redo button on the Quick Access Toolbar. Clicking the Redo button reverses the last undo action. The ScreenTip name reflects the type of reversal last performed.

For an introduction to Office 2010 and instruction about how to perform basic tasks in Office 2010 programs, read the Office 2010 and Windows 7 chapter at the beginning of this book, where you can learn how to start a program, use the Ribbon, save a file, open a file, quit a program, use Help, and much more.

Paragraphs

Text in the subtitle text placeholder supports the title text. It can appear on one or more lines in the placeholder. To create more than one subtitle line, you press the ENTER key after typing some words. PowerPoint creates a new line, which is the second paragraph in the placeholder. A **paragraph** is a segment of text with the same format that begins when you press the ENTER key and ends when you press the ENTER key again. This new paragraph is the same level as the previous paragraph. A **level** is a position within a structure, such as an outline, that indicates the magnitude of importance. PowerPoint allows for five paragraph levels.

To Enter the Presentation Subtitle Paragraph

The first subtitle paragraph links to the title by giving further detail that the presentation will focus on energy-saving measures at home. The following steps enter the presentation subtitle.

1
- Click the label, Click to add subtitle, located inside the subtitle text placeholder to select the placeholder (Figure 1–7).

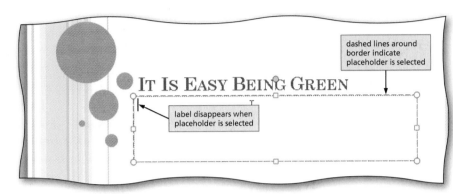

Figure 1–7

2
- Type **Saving Energy at Home** but do not press the ENTER key (Figure 1–8).

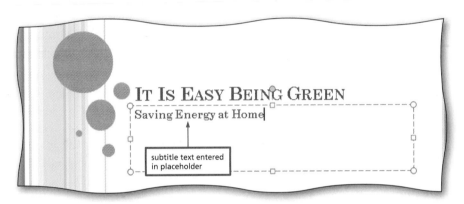

Figure 1–8

Identify how to format specific elements of the text.
Most of the time, you use the document theme's text attributes, color scheme, and layout. Occasionally, you may want to change the way a presentation looks, however, and still keep a particular document theme. PowerPoint gives you that flexibility.

Graphic designers use several rules when formatting text.

- Avoid all capital letters, if possible. Audiences have difficulty comprehending sentences typed in all capital letters, especially when the lines exceed seven words. All capital letters leaves no room for emphasis or inflection, so readers get confused about what material deserves particular attention. Some document themes, however, have a default title text style of all capital letters.

- Avoid text with a font size less than 30 point. Audience members generally will sit a maximum of 50 feet from a screen, and at this distance 30-point type is the smallest size text they can read comfortably without straining.

- Make careful color choices. Color evokes emotions, and a careless color choice may elicit the incorrect psychological response. PowerPoint provides a color gallery with hundreds of colors. The built-in document themes use complementary colors that work well together. If you stray from these themes and add your own color choices, without a good reason to make the changes, your presentation is apt to become ineffective.

Plan Ahead

Formatting Characters in a Presentation

Recall that each document theme determines the color scheme, font set, and layout of a presentation. You can use a specific document theme and then change the characters' formats any time before, during, or after you type the text.

BTW

Q&As
For a complete list of the Q&As found in many of the step-by-step sequences in this book, visit the PowerPoint 2010 Q&A Web page (scsite.com/ppt2010/qa).

Fonts and Font Styles

Characters that appear on the screen are a specific shape and size. Examples of how you can modify the appearance, or **format**, of these typed characters on the screen and in print include changing the font, style, size, and color. The **font**, or typeface, defines the appearance and shape of the letters, numbers, punctuation marks, and symbols. **Style** indicates how the characters are formatted. PowerPoint's text font styles include regular, italic, bold, and bold italic. **Size** specifies the height of the characters and is gauged by a measurement system that uses points. A **point** is 1/72 of an inch in height. Thus, a character with a font size of 36 is 36/72 (or 1/2) of an inch in height. **Color** defines the hue of the characters.

This presentation uses the Oriel document theme, which uses particular font styles and font sizes. The Oriel document theme default title text font is named Century Schoolbook. It has a bold style with no special effects, and its size is 30 point. The Oriel document theme default subtitle text font also is Century Schoolbook with a font size of 18 point.

To Select a Paragraph

You can use many techniques to format characters. When you want to apply the same formats to multiple words or paragraphs, it is efficient to select the desired text and then make the desired changes to all the characters simultaneously. The first formatting change you will make will apply to the title slide subtitle. The following step selects this paragraph.

- Triple-click the paragraph, Saving Energy at Home, in the subtitle text placeholder to select the paragraph (Figure 1–9).

Q&A

Can I select the paragraph using a technique other than triple-clicking?

Yes. You can move your mouse pointer to the left of the first paragraph and then drag to the end of the line.

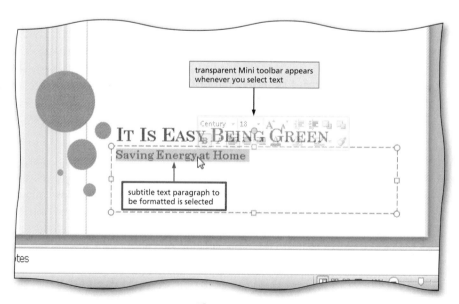

Figure 1–9

To Italicize Text

Different font styles often are used on slides to make them more appealing to the reader and to emphasize particular text. **Italicized** text has a slanted appearance. Used sparingly, it draws the readers' eyes to these characters. The following step adds emphasis to the second line of the subtitle text by changing regular text to italic text.

- With the subtitle text still selected, click the Italic button on the Mini toolbar to italicize that text on the slide (Figure 1–10).

If I change my mind and decide not to italicize the text, how can I remove this style?

Click the Italic button a second time or immediately click the Undo button on the Quick Access Toolbar or press CTRL+Z.

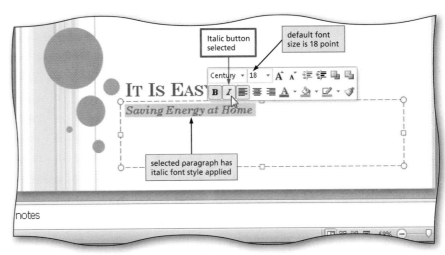

Figure 1–10

Other Ways
1. Right-click selected text, click Font on shortcut menu, click Font tab (Font dialog box), click Italic in Font style list, click OK button   2. Select text, click Italic button (Home tab | Font group)   3. Click Font Dialog Box Launcher (Home tab | Font group), click Font tab (Font dialog box), click Italic in Font style list, click OK button   4. Select text, press CTRL+I

To Increase Font Size

To add emphasis, you increase the font size for the subtitle text. The Increase Font Size button on the Mini toolbar increases the font size in preset increments. The following step uses this button to increase the font size.

- Click the Increase Font Size button on the Mini toolbar twice to increase the font size of the selected text from 18 to 24 point (Figure 1–11).

Figure 1–11

Other Ways
1. Click Font Size box arrow on Mini toolbar, click desired font size in Font Size gallery   2. Click Increase Font Size button (Home tab | Font group)   3. Click Font Size box arrow (Home tab | Font group), click desired font size in Font Size gallery   4. Press CTRL+SHIFT+>

To Select a Word

PowerPoint designers use many techniques to emphasize words and characters on a slide. To add emphasis to the energy-saving concept of your slide show, you want to increase the font size and change the font color to green for the word, Green, in the title text. You could perform these actions separately, but it is more efficient to select the word and then change the font attributes. The following steps select a word.

- Position the mouse pointer somewhere in the word to be selected (in this case, in the word, Green) (Figure 1–12).

Figure 1–12

- Double-click the word to select it (Figure 1–13).

Figure 1–13

Other Ways

1. Position mouse pointer before first character, press CTRL+SHIFT+RIGHT ARROW

Plan Ahead

Format text colors.

When selecting text colors, try to limit using red. This color often is associated with dangerous or alarming situations. In addition, at least 15 percent of men have difficulty distinguishing varying shades of green or red. They also often see the color purple as blue and the color brown as green. This problem is more pronounced when the colors appear in small areas, such as slide paragraphs or line chart bars.

To Change the Text Color

PowerPoint allows you to use one or more text colors in a presentation. To add more emphasis to the word, Green, in the title slide text, you decide to change the color. The following steps add emphasis to this word by changing the font color from black to green.

- With the word, Green, selected, click the Font Color arrow on the Mini toolbar to display the gallery of Theme Colors and Standard Colors (Figure 1–14).

Q&A If the Mini toolbar disappears from the screen, how can I display it once again?

Right-click the text, and the Mini toolbar should appear.

Experiment

- Point to various colors in the gallery and watch the word's font color change.

Figure 1–14

- Click the Green button in the Standard Colors row on the Mini toolbar (sixth color) to change the font color to green (Figure 1–15).

Q&A Why did I select the color Green?

Green is one of the 10 standard colors associated with every document theme, and it is a universal color to represent respecting natural resources. The color will emphasize the fact that the presentation focuses on green conservation measures.

Figure 1–15

Q&A What is the difference between the colors shown in the Theme Colors area and the Standard Colors?

The 10 colors in the top row of the Theme Colors area are two text, two background, and six accent colors in the Oriel theme; the five colors in each column under the top row display different transparencies. These colors are available in every document theme.

- Click outside the selected area to deselect the word.

Other Ways
1. Right-click selected text, click Font on shortcut menu, click Font Color button, click Green in Standard Colors row   2. Click Font Color arrow (Home tab | Font group), click Green in Standard Colors row

Organizing Files and Folders
You should organize and store files in folders so that you easily can find the files later. For example, if you are taking an introductory computer class called CIS 101, a good practice would be to save all PowerPoint files in a PowerPoint folder in a CIS 101 folder. For a discussion of folders and detailed examples of creating folders, refer to the Office 2010 and Windows 7 chapter at the beginning of this book.

To Save a Presentation

You have performed many tasks while creating this slide and do not want to risk losing work completed thus far. Accordingly, you should save the document.

The following steps assume you already have created folders for storing your files, for example, a CIS 101 folder (for your class) that contains a PowerPoint folder (for your assignments). Thus, these steps save the document in the PowerPoint folder in the CIS 101 folder on a USB flash drive using the file name, Saving Energy. For a detailed example of the procedure summarized below, refer to the Office 2010 and Windows 7 chapter at the beginning of this book.

1 With a USB flash drive connected to one of the computer's USB ports, click the Save button on the Quick Access Toolbar to display the Save As dialog box.

2 Type **Saving Energy** in the File name text box to change the file name. Do not press the ENTER key after typing the file name because you do not want to close the dialog box at this time.

3 Navigate to the desired save location (in this case, the PowerPoint folder in the CIS 101 folder [or your class folder] on the USB flash drive).

4 Click the Save button (Save As dialog box) to save the document in the selected folder on the selected drive with the entered file name.

Adding a New Slide to a Presentation

With the text for the title slide for the presentation created, the next step is to add the first text slide immediately after the title slide. Usually, when you create a presentation, you add slides with text, clip art, graphics, or charts. Some placeholders allow you to double-click the place-holder and then access other objects, such as media clips, charts, diagrams, and organization charts. You can change the layout for a slide at any time during the creation of a presentation.

To Add a New Text Slide with a Bulleted List

When you add a new slide, PowerPoint uses the Title and Content slide layout. This layout provides a title placeholder and a content area for text, art, charts, and other graphics. A vertical scroll bar appears in the Slide pane when you add the second slide so that you can move from slide to slide easily. A thumbnail of this slide also appears in the Slides tab. The following steps add a new slide with the Title and Content slide layout.

1

• Click Home on the Ribbon to display the Home tab (Figure 1–16).

Figure 1–16

2

- Click the New Slide button (Home tab | Slides group) to insert a new slide with the Title and Content layout (Figure 1–17).

Q&A
Why does the bullet character display an orange circle?

The Oriel document theme determines the bullet characters. Each paragraph level has an associated bullet character.

Q&A
I clicked the New Slide arrow instead of the New Slide button. What should I do?

Click the Title and Content slide thumbnail in the layout gallery.

Figure 1–17

Other Ways
1. Press CTRL+M

Choose the words for the slide.
All presentations should follow the 7 × 7 rule, which states that each slide should have a maximum of seven lines, and each line should have a maximum of seven words. PowerPoint designers must choose their words carefully and, in turn, help viewers read the slides easily.
Avoid line wraps. Your audience's eyes want to stop at the end of a line. Thus, you must plan your words carefully or adjust the font size so that each point displays on only one line.

Plan Ahead

Creating a Text Slide with a Multi-Level Bulleted List

The information in the Slide 2 text placeholder is presented in a bulleted list with three levels. A **bulleted list** is a list of paragraphs, each of which is preceded by a bullet. A slide that consists of more than one level of bulleted text is called a **multi-level bulleted list slide**. In a multi-level bulleted list, a lower-level paragraph is a subset of a higher-level paragraph. It usually contains information that supports the topic in the paragraph immediately above it.

Two of the Slide 2 bullets appear at the same paragraph level, called the first level: Install low-flow faucets and shower heads, and Appliances count for 20 percent of electric bill. Beginning with the second level, each paragraph indents to the right of the preceding level and is pushed down to a lower level. For example, if you increase the indent of a first-level paragraph, it becomes a second-level paragraph. The second, fourth, and fifth paragraphs on Slide 2 are second-level paragraphs. The last paragraph, Wash clothes in cold water, is a third-level paragraph.

BTW

The Ribbon and Screen Resolution
PowerPoint may change how the groups and buttons within the groups appear on the Ribbon, depending on the computer's screen resolution. Thus, your Ribbon may look different from the ones in this book if you are using a screen resolution other than 1024 x 768.

Creating a text slide with a multi-level bulleted list requires several steps. Initially, you enter a slide title in the title text placeholder. Next, you select the content text placeholder. Then, you type the text for the multi-level bulleted list, increasing and decreasing the indents as needed. The next several sections add a slide with a multi-level bulleted list.

To Enter a Slide Title

PowerPoint assumes every new slide has a title. The title for Slide 2 is Make Small Changes to Cut Energy. The following step enters this title.

- Click the label, Click to add title, to select it and then type **Make Small Changes to Cut Energy** in the placeholder. Do not press the ENTER key (Figure 1–18).

Q&A

What are those six icons grouped in the middle of the slide?

You can click one of the icons to insert a specific type of content: table, chart, SmartArt graphic, picture, clip art, or media clip.

Figure 1–18

To Select a Text Placeholder

Before you can type text into the text placeholder, you first must select it. The following step selects the text placeholder on Slide 2.

- Click the label, Click to add text, to select the text placeholder (Figure 1–19).

Q&A

Why does my mouse pointer have a different shape?

If you move the mouse pointer away from the bullet, it will change shape.

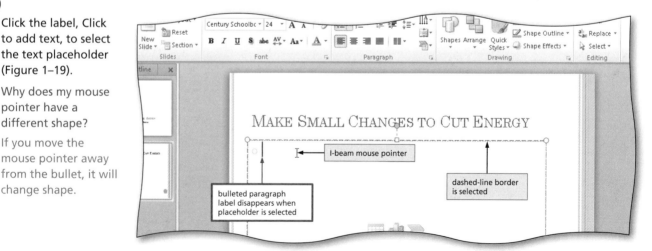

Figure 1–19

Other Ways
1. Press CTRL+ENTER

To Type a Multi-Level Bulleted List

The content placeholder provides an area for the text characters. When you click inside a placeholder, you then can type or paste text. As discussed previously, a bulleted list is a list of paragraphs, each of which is preceded by a bullet. A paragraph is a segment of text ended by pressing the ENTER key.

The content text placeholder is selected, so the next step is to type the multi-level bulleted list that consists of six paragraphs, as shown in Figure 1–1b on page PPT 3. Creating a lower-level paragraph is called **demoting** text; creating a higher-level paragraph is called **promoting** text. The following steps create a multi-level bulleted list consisting of three levels.

1

- Type **Install low-flow faucets and shower heads** and then press the ENTER key (Figure 1–20).

Figure 1–20

2

- Click the Increase List Level button (Home tab | Paragraph group) to indent the second paragraph below the first and create a second-level paragraph (Figure 1–21).

Q&A

Why does the bullet for this paragraph have a different size and color?

A different bullet is assigned to each paragraph level.

Figure 1–21

3

- Type **Cut water consumption in half** and then press the ENTER key (Figure 1–22).

Figure 1–22

4

• Click the Decrease List Level button (Home tab | Paragraph group) so that the second-level paragraph becomes a first-level paragraph (Figure 1–23).

Q&A

Can I delete bullets on a slide?

Yes. If you do not want bullets to display in a particular paragraph, click the Bullets button (Home tab | Paragraph group) or right-click the paragraph and then click the Bullets button on the shortcut menu.

Other Ways

1. Press TAB to promote paragraph; press SHIFT+TAB to demote paragraph

Figure 1–23

To Type the Remaining Text for Slide 2

The following steps complete the text for Slide 2.

1 Type `Appliances count for 20 percent of electric bill` and then press the ENTER key.

2 Click the Increase List Level button (Home tab | Paragraph group) to demote the paragraph to the second level.

3 Type `Buy ENERGY STAR qualified products` and then press the ENTER key to add a new paragraph at the same level as the previous paragraph.

4 Type `Run dishwasher, clothes washer with full loads` and then press the ENTER key.

5 Click the Increase List Level button (Home tab | Paragraph group) to demote the paragraph to the third level.

6 Type `Wash clothes in cold water` but do not press the ENTER key (Figure 1–24).

Q&A

I pressed the ENTER key in error, and now a new bullet appears after the last entry on this slide. How can I remove this extra bullet?

Press the BACKSPACE key twice.

Figure 1–24

To Select a Group of Words

PowerPoint designers use many techniques to emphasize words and characters on a slide. To add emphasis to your slide show's concept of saving natural resources, you want to bold and increase the font size of the words, in half, in the body text. You could perform these actions separately, but it is more efficient to select the words and then change the font attributes. The following steps select two words.

- Position the mouse pointer immediately to the left of the first character of the text to be selected (in this case, the i in the word, in) (Figure 1–25).

Figure 1–25

- Drag the mouse pointer through the last character of the text to be selected (in this case, the f in half) (Figure 1–26).

Figure 1–26

Other Ways
1. Press CTRL+SHIFT+RIGHT ARROW

To Bold Text

Bold characters display somewhat thicker and darker than those that display in a regular font style. Clicking the Bold button on the Mini toolbar is an efficient method of bolding text. To add more emphasis to the amount of water savings that can occur by installing low-flow faucets and shower heads, you want to bold the words, in half. The following step bolds this text.

1

- With the words, in half, selected, click the Bold button on the Mini toolbar to bold the two words (Figure 1–27).

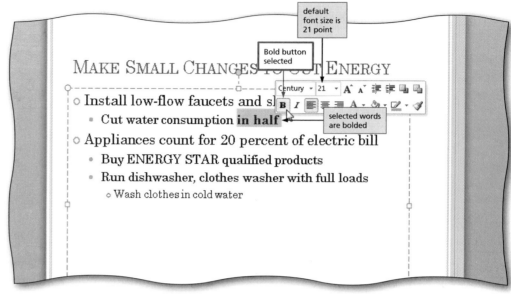

Figure 1–27

Other Ways

1. Click Bold button (Home tab | Font group)
2. Press CTRL+B

Formatting Words
To format one word, position the insertion point anywhere in the word. Then make the formatting changes you desire. The entire word does not need to be selected for the change to occur.

To Increase Font Size

To add emphasis, you increase the font size for the words, in half. The following step increases the font size from 21 to 24 point.

1 With the words, in half, still selected, click the Increase Font Size button on the Mini toolbar once (Figure 1–28).

Figure 1–28

Adding New Slides and Changing the Slide Layouts

Slide 3 in Figure 1–1c on page PPT 3 contains a photograph and does not contain a bulleted list. When you add a new slide, PowerPoint applies the Title and Content layout. This layout along with the Title Slide layout for Slide 1 are the default styles. A **layout** specifies the arrangement of placeholders on a slide. These placeholders are arranged in various configurations and can contain text, such as the slide title or a bulleted list, or they can contain content, such as SmartArt graphics, pictures, charts, tables, shapes, and clip art. The placement of the text, in relationship to content, depends on the slide layout. You can specify a particular slide layout when you add a new slide to a presentation or after you have created the slide.

Using the **Layout gallery**, you can choose a slide layout. The nine layouts in this gallery have a variety of placeholders to define text and content positioning and formatting. Three layouts are for text: Title Slide, Section Header, and Title Only. Five are for text and content: Title and Content, Two Content, Comparison, Content with Caption, and Picture with Caption. The Blank layout has no placeholders. If none of these standard layouts meets your design needs, you can create a **custom layout**. A custom layout specifies the number, size, and location of placeholders, background content, and optional slide and placeholder-level properties.

When you change the layout of a slide, PowerPoint retains the text and objects and repositions them into the appropriate placeholders. Using slide layouts eliminates the need to resize objects and the font size because PowerPoint automatically sizes the objects and text to fit the placeholders.

BTW

Experimenting with Normal View
As you learn to use PowerPoint's features, experiment with using the Outline tab and with closing the Tabs pane to maximize the slide area. To close the Tabs pane, click the x to the right of the Outline tab. To redisplay the Tabs pane, click the View tab on the Ribbon and then click Normal in the Presentation Views group.

To Add a Slide with the Title Only Layout

The following steps add Slide 3 to the presentation with the Title Only slide layout style.

1

• If necessary, click Home on the Ribbon to display the Home tab.

• Click the New Slide arrow (Home tab | Slides group) to display the Layout gallery (Figure 1–29).

Figure 1–29

2
- Click Title Only to add a new slide and apply that layout to Slide 3 (Figure 1–30).

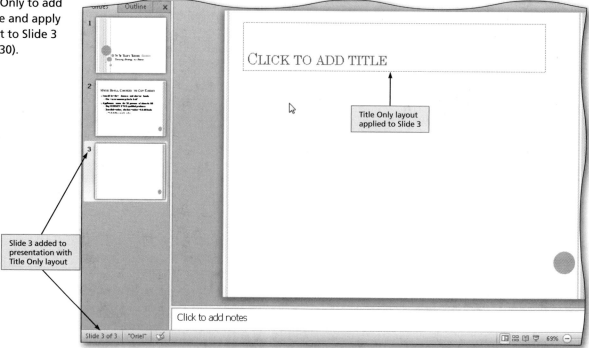

Figure 1–30

To Enter a Slide Title

The only text on Slide 3 is the title. The following step enters the title text for this slide.

1 Type **Use Energy Efficient Lighting** as the title text but do not press the ENTER key (Figure 1–31).

BTW

Portrait Page Orientation
If your slide content is dominantly vertical, such as a skyscraper or a person, consider changing the slide layout to a portrait page orientation. To change the orientation, click the Slide Orientation button (Design tab | Page Setup group) and then click the desired orientation.

Figure 1–31

To Add a New Slide and Enter a Slide Title and Headings

The text on Slide 4 in Figure 1–1d on page PPT 3 consists of a title and two headings. The appropriate layout for this slide is named Comparison. The following steps add Slide 4 to the presentation with the Comparison layout and then enter the title and heading text for this slide.

1
- Click the New Slide arrow in the Slides group to display the Layout gallery (Figure 1–32).

Figure 1–32

2
- Click Comparison to add Slide 4 and apply that layout.

- Type **Adjust Your Thermostats** in the title text placeholder but do not press the ENTER key.

- Click the left orange heading placeholder with the label, Click to add text, to select this placeholder (Figure 1–33).

Figure 1–33

3

- Type **Furnace: 68 degrees** but do not press the ENTER key.

- Click the right orange heading placeholder and then type **Water heater: 120 degrees** but do not press the ENTER key (Figure 1–34).

Figure 1–34

Break Point: If you wish to take a break, this is a good place to do so. You can quit PowerPoint now (refer to page PPT 50 for instructions). To resume at a later time, start PowerPoint (refer to pages PPT 4 and PPT 5 for instructions), open the file called Saving Energy (refer to pages PPT 50 and PPT 51 for instructions), and continue following the steps from this location forward.

PowerPoint Views

The PowerPoint window display varies depending on the view. A **view** is the mode in which the presentation appears on the screen. PowerPoint has four main views: Normal, Slide Sorter, Reading, and Slide Show. It also has another view, called Notes Page view, used for entering information about a slide.

The default view is **Normal view**, which is composed of three working areas that allow you to work on various aspects of a presentation simultaneously. The left side of the screen has a Tabs pane that consists of a **Slides tab** and an **Outline tab**. These tabs alternate between views of the presentation in a thumbnail, or miniature, view of the slides and an outline of the slide text. You can type the text of the presentation on the Outline tab and easily rearrange bulleted lists, paragraphs, and individual slides. As you type, you can view this text in the **Slide pane**, which shows a large view of the current slide on the right side of the window. You also can enter text, graphics, animations, and hyperlinks directly in the Slide pane. The **Notes pane** at the bottom of the window is an area where you can type notes and additional information. This text can consist of notes to yourself or remarks to share with your audience. If you want to work with your notes in full page format, you can display them in **Notes Page view**.

In Normal view, you can adjust the width of the Slide pane by dragging the **splitter bar** and the height of the Notes pane by dragging the pane borders. After you have created at least two slides, a scroll bar containing **scroll arrows** and **scroll boxes** will appear on the right edge of the window.

To Move to Another Slide in Normal View

When creating or editing a presentation in Normal view (the view you are currently using), you often want to display a slide other than the current one. Before continuing with developing this project, you want to display the title slide by dragging the scroll box on the vertical scroll bar. When you drag the scroll box, the **slide indicator** shows the number and title of the slide you are about to display. Releasing the mouse button shows the slide. The following steps move from Slide 4 to Slide 1 using the scroll box on the Slide pane.

- Position the mouse pointer on the scroll box.

- Press and hold down the mouse button so that Slide: 4 of 4 Adjust Your Thermostats appears in the slide indicator (Figure 1–35).

Figure 1–35

2

- Drag the scroll box up the vertical scroll bar until Slide: 1 of 4 It Is Easy Being Green appears in the slide indicator (Figure 1–36).

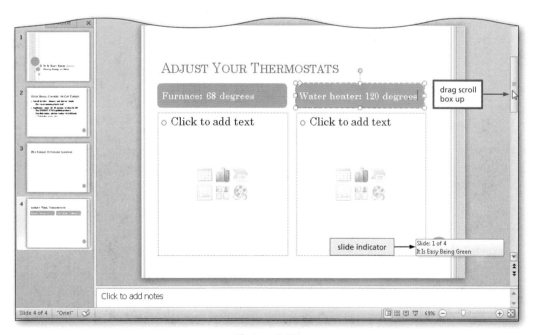

Figure 1–36

3

- Release the mouse button so that Slide 1 appears in the Slide pane and the Slide 1 thumbnail has an orange border in the Slides tab (Figure 1–37).

Figure 1–37

Other Ways

1. Click Next Slide button or Previous Slide button to move forward or back one slide

2. Click slide thumbnail on Slides tab

3. Press PAGE DOWN or PAGE UP to move forward or back one slide

BTW

Today's Clip
Each day, Microsoft features "today's clip," which reflects events or themes specific to this time. For example, the pictures, illustrations, and clip art have back-to-school images, winter scenes, and holiday characters.

Inserting Clip Art and Photographs into Slides

A **clip** is a single media file that can include art, sound, animation, or movies. Adding a clip can help increase the visual appeal of many slides and can offer a quick way to add professional-looking graphic images and sounds to a presentation without creating these files yourself. This art is contained in the **Microsoft Clip Organizer**, a collection of drawings, photographs, sounds, videos, and other media files shared among Microsoft Office applications. The **Office Collections** contains all these media files included with Microsoft Office.

You also can add your own clips to slides. You can insert these files directly from a storage medium, such as a USB flash drive. In addition, you can add them to the other files in the Clip Organizer so that you can search for and reuse these images, sounds, animations, and movies. When you create these media files, they are stored on your hard disk in **My Collections**. The Clip Organizer will find these files and create a new collection with these files. Two other locations for clips are Shared Collections and Web Collections. Files in the **Shared Collections** typically reside on a shared network file server and are accessible to multiple users. The **Web Collections** clips reside on the Microsoft Clip Art and Media Home page on the Microsoft Office Online Web site. They are available only if you have an active Internet connection.

The Clip Art Task Pane

You can add clips to your presentation in two ways. One way is by selecting one of the slide layouts that includes a content placeholder with a Clip Art button. A second method is by clicking the Clip Art button in the Images area on the Insert tab. Clicking the Clip Art button opens the Clip Art task pane. The **Clip Art task pane** allows you to search for clips by using descriptive keywords, file names, media file formats, and clip collections. Specific file formats could be for clip art, photographs, movies, and sounds.

Clips are organized in hierarchical **clip collections** that combine topic-related clips into categories, such as Academic, Business, and Technology.

Clips have one or more keywords associated with various entities, activities, labels, and emotions. In most instances, the keywords give the name of the clip and related categories. For example, an image of a cow in the Animals category has the keywords animals, cattle, cows, dairies, farms, and Holsteins. You can enter these keywords in the Search for text box to find clips when you know one of the words associated with the image. Otherwise, you might find it necessary to scroll through several categories to find an appropriate clip.

Depending on the installation of the Microsoft Clip Organizer on your computer, you might not have the clip art used in this chapter. Contact your instructor if you are missing clips used in the following steps. If you have an active connection to the Internet, clips from the Microsoft Office Online Web site will display automatically as the result of your search results.

<table>
<tr><td>

Adhere to copyright regulations.

You have permission to use the clips from the Microsoft Clip Organizer. If you want to use a clip from another source, be certain you have the legal right to insert this file in your presentation. Read the copyright notices that may accompany the clip and may be posted on the Web site where you obtained the clip. The owners of these images and files often ask you to give them credit for using their work, which may be satisfied by stating where you obtained the images.

</td><td>

Plan Ahead

</td></tr>
</table>

To Insert a Clip from the Clip Organizer into the Title Slide

Slide 1 uses the Title Slide layout, which has two placeholders for text but none for graphical content. You desire to place a graphic on Slide 1, so you will locate a clip art image of a green globe and flower and then insert it in this slide. Later in this chapter, you will size and position it in an appropriate location. The following steps add a clip to Slide 1.

- Click Insert on the Ribbon to display the Insert tab.

- Click the Clip Art button (Insert tab | Images group) to display the Clip Art task pane.

- Click the Search for text box in the Clip Art task pane, if necessary delete any letters that are present, and then type **green globe** in the Search for text box.

- If necessary, click the 'Include Office.com content' check box to select it (Figure 1–38).

Figure 1–38

2

- Click the Go button so that the Microsoft Clip Organizer will search for and display all clips having the keywords, green globe.

- If necessary, click the Yes button if a Microsoft Clip Organizer dialog box appears asking if you want to include additional clip art images from Office.com.

- If necessary, scroll down the list to display the globe clip shown in Figure 1–39.

- Click the clip to insert it into the slide (Figure 1–39).

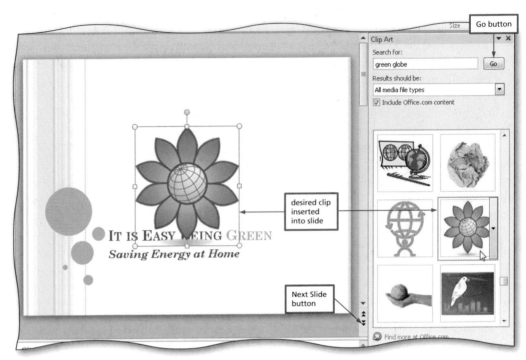

Figure 1–39

Q&A | What if the globe image displayed in Figure 1–39 is not shown in my Clip Art task pane?

Select a similar clip. Your clips may be different depending on the clips installed on your computer and if you have an active connection to the Internet.

Q&A | What is the yellow star image that displays in the lower-right corner of some clips in the Clip Art task pane?

The star indicates the image is animated and will move when the slide containing this clip is displayed during a slide show.

Q&A | Why is this globe clip displayed in this location on the slide?

The slide layout does not have a content placeholder, so PowerPoint inserts the clip in the center of the slide.

To Insert a Clip from the Clip Organizer into a Slide without a Content Placeholder

The next step is to add two clips to Slide 2. Slide 2 has a bulleted list in the text placeholder, so the icon group does not display in the center of the placeholder. Later in this chapter, you will resize the inserted clips. The Clip Art task pane is displayed and will remain open until you close it. The following steps add one clip to Slide 2.

1 Click the Next Slide button to display Slide 2.

2 Click the Search for text box in the Clip Art task pane and then delete the letters in the Search for text box.

3 Type `faucets` and then click the Go button.

4 If necessary, scroll down the list to display the faucet clip shown in Figure 1–40 and then click the clip to insert it into Slide 2 (Figure 1–40).

Figure 1–40

To Insert a Second Clip from the Clip Organizer into a Slide without a Content Placeholder

The following steps add a second clip to Slide 2. PowerPoint inserts this clip on top of the faucet clip in the center of the slide. Both clips will be moved and resized later in this project.

1 Click the Search for text box in the Clip Art task pane and then delete the letters in the text box.

2 Type **dishwasher**, click the Go button, locate the clip shown in Figure 1–41, and then click the clip to insert it into Slide 2 (Figure 1–41).

BTW

Clip Properties
Each clip has properties that identify its characteristics. When you right-click a clip in the Microsoft Clip Organizer, you will see details of the clip's name, file type, size, dimensions, keywords, and creation date. You also can preview the clip and edit its assigned keywords.

Figure 1–41

To Insert a Clip from the Clip Organizer into a Content Placeholder

Slide 4 uses the Comparison layout, which has a content placeholder below each of the two headings. You desire to insert clip art into both content placeholders to reinforce the concept that consumers should adjust the heating temperatures of their furnace and water heater. The following steps insert clip art of a furnace into the left content placeholder and a water heater into the right content placeholder on Slide 4.

- Click the Close button in the Clip Art task pane so that it no longer is displayed.

- Click the Next Slide button twice to display Slide 4.

- Click the Clip Art button in the left content placeholder to select that placeholder and to open the Clip Art task pane (Figure 1–42).

Q&A

Do I need to close the Clip Art task pane when I am finished inserting the two clips into Slide 2?

No. You can leave the Clip Art task pane open and then display Slide 4. It is often more convenient, however, to open this pane when you are working with a layout that has a content placeholder so that the clip is inserted in the desired location.

Figure 1–42

- Click the Search for text box in the Clip Art task pane, delete any letters that are present, type **furnace** in the Search for text box, and then click the Go button to search for and display all pictures having the keyword, furnace.

- If necessary, scroll down the list to display the furnace clip shown in Figure 1–43.

- Click the clip to insert it into the left content placeholder (Figure 1–43).

Figure 1–43

❸

- Click anywhere in the right placeholder except one of the six icons to select the placeholder.

Q&A I clicked the Clip Art icon by mistake, which closed the Clip Art task pane. How do I open it?

Click the Clip Art icon.

❹

- Click the Search for text box in the Clip Art task pane, delete any letters that are present, type **water heater** in the Search for text box, and then click the Go button.

- If necessary, scroll down the list to display the water heater clip shown in Figure 1–44 and then click the clip to insert it into the right content placeholder (Figure 1–44).

Figure 1–44

Photographs and the Clip Organizer

In addition to clip art, you can insert pictures into a presentation. These may include scanned photographs, line art, and artwork from storage media, such as USB flash drives, hard disks, optical discs, and memory cards. To insert a picture into a presentation, the picture must be saved in a format that PowerPoint can recognize. Table 1–1 identifies some of the formats PowerPoint recognizes.

Table 1–1 Primary File Formats PowerPoint Recognizes	
Format	**File Extension**
Computer Graphics Metafile	.cgm
CorelDRAW	.cdr, .cdt, .cmx, and .pat
Encapsulated PostScript	.eps
Enhanced Metafile	.emf
FlashPix	.fpx
Graphics Interchange Format	.gif
Hanako	.jsh, .jah, and .jbh
Joint Photographic Experts Group (JPEG)	.jpg
Kodak PhotoCD	.pcd
Macintosh PICT	.pct
PC Paintbrush	.pcx
Portable Network Graphics	.png
Tagged Image File Format	.tif
Windows Bitmap	.bmp, .rle, .dib
Microsoft Windows Metafile	.wmf
WordPerfect Graphics	.wpg

BTW

Compressing File Size
When you add a picture to a presentation, PowerPoint automatically compresses this image. Even with this compression applied, a presentation that contains pictures usually has a large file size. To reduce this size, you can compress a picture further without affecting the quality of how it displays on the slide. To compress a picture, select the picture and then click the Compress Pictures button (Picture Tools Format tab | Adjust group). You can restore the picture's original settings by clicking the Reset Picture button (Picture Tools Format tab | Adjust group).

BTW

Wrapping Text around a Picture
PowerPoint 2010 does not allow you to wrap text around a picture or other graphics, such as tables, shapes, charts, or graphics. This feature, however, is available in Word 2010.

You can import files saved with the .emf, .gif, .jpg, .png, .bmp, .rle, .dib, and .wmf formats directly into PowerPoint presentations. All other file formats require separate filters that are shipped with the PowerPoint installation software and must be installed separately. You can download additional filters from the Microsoft Office Online Web site.

To Insert a Photograph from the Clip Organizer into a Slide without a Content Placeholder

Next, you will add a photograph to Slide 3. You will not insert this picture into a content placeholder, so it will display in the center of the slide. Later in this chapter, you will resize this picture. To start the process of locating this photograph, you do not need to click the Clip Art button in the content placeholder because the Clip Art task pane already is displayed. The following steps add a photograph to Slide 3.

1 Click the Previous Slide button to display Slide 3.

2 Click the Search for text box in the Clip Art task pane, delete the letters in the text box, type **CFL**, and then click the Go button.

3 If necessary, scroll down the list to display the picture of a light bulb shown in Figure 1–45, and then click the photograph to insert it into Slide 2 (Figure 1–45).

Q&A Why is my photograph a different size from the one shown in Figure 1–1c on page PPT 3?
The photograph was inserted into the slide and not into a content placeholder. You will resize the picture later in this chapter.

Figure 1–45

Break Point: If you wish to take a break, this is a good place to do so. You can quit PowerPoint now (refer to page PPT 50 for instructions). To resume at a later time, start PowerPoint (refer to pages PPT 4 and PPT 5 for instructions), open the file called Saving Energy (refer to pages PPT 50 and PPT 51 for instructions), and continue following the steps from this location forward.

Resizing Clip Art and Photographs

Sometimes it is necessary to change the size of clip art. **Resizing** includes enlarging or reducing the size of a clip art graphic. You can resize clip art using a variety of techniques. One method involves changing the size of a clip by specifying exact dimensions in a dialog box. Another method involves dragging one of the graphic's sizing handles to the desired location. A selected graphic appears surrounded by a **selection rectangle**, which has small squares and circles, called **sizing handles** or move handles, at each corner and middle location.

To Resize Clip Art

On Slides 1, 2, and 4, much space appears around the clips, so you can increase their sizes. Likewise, the photograph on Slide 3 can be enlarged to fill more of the space below the slide title. To change the size, drag the corner sizing handles to view how the clip will look on the slide. Using these corner handles maintains the graphic's original proportions. Dragging the square sizing handles alters the proportions so that the graphic's height and width become larger or smaller. The following steps increase the size of the Slide 1 clip using a corner sizing handle.

- Click the Close button in the Clip Art task pane so that it no longer is displayed.

- Click the Previous Slide button two times to display Slide 1.

- Click the globe clip to select it and display the selection rectangle.

- Point to the lower-left corner sizing handle on the clip so that the mouse pointer changes to a two-headed arrow (Figure 1–46).

Figure 1–46

- Drag the sizing handle diagonally toward the lower-left corner of the slide until the mouse pointer is positioned approximately as shown in Figure 1–47.

Q&A What if the clip is not the same size as the one shown in Figure 1–47?

Repeat Steps 1 and 2.

Figure 1–47

- Release the mouse button to resize the clip.
- Click outside the clip to deselect it (Figure 1–48).

Q&A What happened to the Picture Tools Format tab?

When you click outside the clip, PowerPoint deselects the clip and removes the Picture Tools Format tab from the screen.

Q&A What if I want to return the clip to its original size and start again?

With the graphic selected, click the Reset Picture button (Picture Tools Format tab | Adjust group).

Figure 1–48

To Resize Clips on Slide 4

The two clip art images on Slide 4 also can be enlarged to fill much of the white space below the headings. You will reposition the clips in a later step. The following steps resize these clips using a sizing handle.

1 Click the Next Slide button three times to display Slide 4.

2 Click the furnace clip to select it.

3 Drag the lower-left corner sizing handle on the clip diagonally outward until the clip is resized approximately as shown in Figure 1–49.

4 Click the water heater clip to select it.

5 Drag the lower-right corner sizing handle on the clip diagonally outward until the clip is resized approximately as shown in Figure 1–49.

Figure 1–49

To Resize a Photograph

The light bulb picture in Slide 3 can be enlarged slightly to fill much of the space below the slide title. You resize a photograph in the same manner that you resize clip art. The following steps resize this photograph using a sizing handle.

1 Click the Previous Slide button to display Slide 3.

2 Click the light bulb photograph to select it.

BTW

Minimalist Design
Resist the urge to fill your slides with clips from the Microsoft Clip Organizer. Minimalist style reduces clutter and allows the slide content to display prominently. This simple, yet effective design helps audience members with short attention spans to focus on the message.

3 Drag the lower-left corner sizing handle on the photograph diagonally outward until the photograph is resized approximately as shown in Figure 1–50.

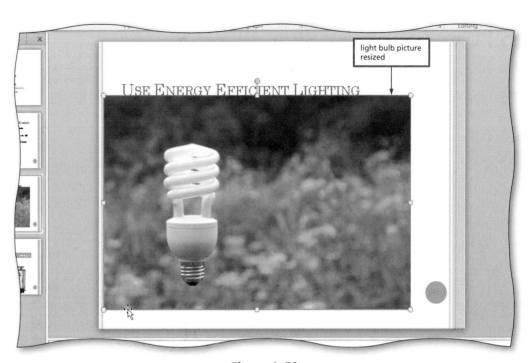

light bulb picture resized

Figure 1–50

To Move Clips

After you insert clip art or a photograph on a slide, you might want to reposition it. The light bulb photograph on Slide 3 could be centered in the space between the slide title and the left and right edges of the slide. The clip on Slide 1 could be positioned in the upper-right corner of the slide. On Slide 4, the furnace and water heater clips could be centered under each heading. The following steps move these graphics.

1

- If necessary, click the light bulb photograph on Slide 3 to select it.

- Press and hold down the mouse button and then drag the photograph diagonally downward below the title text (Figure 1–51).

- If necessary, select the photograph and then use the ARROW keys to position it precisely as shown in Figure 1–51.

 The photograph still is not located exactly where I want it to display. What can I do to align the photograph?

Press the CTRL key while you press the ARROW keys. This key combination moves the clip in smaller increments than when you press only an ARROW key.

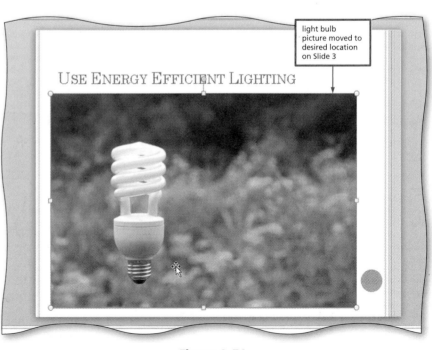

light bulb picture moved to desired location on Slide 3

Figure 1–51

2

- Click the Next Slide button to display Slide 4.

- Click the furnace clip to select it, press and hold down the mouse button, and then drag the clip to center it under the furnace heading.

- Click the water heater clip and then drag the clip to center it under the water heater heading (Figure 1–52).

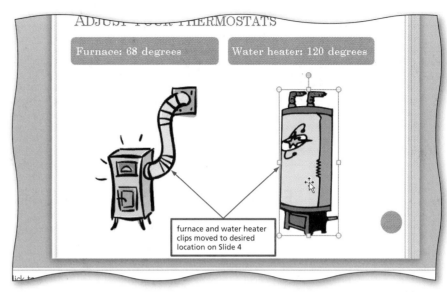

Figure 1–52

3

- Click the Previous Slide button twice to display Slide 2.

- Click the dishwasher clip, which is on top of the faucet clip, and then drag the clip to center it under the last bulleted paragraph, Wash clothes in cold water.

- Click the faucet clip and then drag the clip so that the faucet handle is centered under the words, full loads.

- Drag a corner sizing handle on the faucet clip diagonally outward until the clip is resized approximately as shown in Figure 1–53. You may need to drag the clip to position it in the desired location.

- Select the dishwasher clip and then resize and move it so that the clip displays approximately as shown in Figure 1–53.

Figure 1–53

4

- Click the Previous Slide button to display Slide 1.

- Click the globe clip and then drag it to the upper-right corner of the slide. You may want to adjust its size by selecting it and then dragging the corner sizing handles.

- Click outside the clip to deselect it (Figure 1–54).

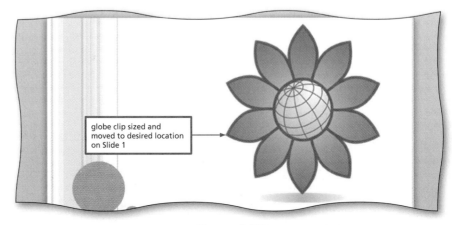

Figure 1–54

Plan
Ahead

Choose a closing slide.

After the last slide appears during a slide show, the default PowerPoint setting is to end the presentation with a **black slide**. This black slide appears only when the slide show is running and concludes the slide show, so your audience never sees the PowerPoint window. It is a good idea, however, to end the presentation with a final closing slide to display at the end of the presentation. This slide ends the presentation gracefully and should be an exact copy, or a very similar copy, of your title slide. The audience will recognize that the presentation is drawing to a close when this slide appears. It can remain on the screen when the audience asks questions, approaches the speaker for further information, or exits the room.

Ending a Slide Show with a Closing Slide

All the text for the slides in the Saving Energy slide show has been entered. This presentation thus far consists of a title slide, one text slide with a multi-level bulleted list, a third slide for a photograph, and a fourth slide with a Comparison layout. A closing slide that resembles the title slide is the final slide to create.

To Duplicate a Slide

When two slides contain similar information and have the same format, duplicating one slide and then making minor modifications to the new slide saves time and increases consistency.

Slide 5 will have the same layout and design as Slide 1. The most expedient method of creating this slide is to copy Slide 1 and then make minor modifications to the new slide. The following steps duplicate the title slide.

- With Slide 1 selected, click the New Slide arrow (Home tab | Slides group) to display the Oriel layout gallery (Figure 1–55).

Figure 1–55

- Click Duplicate Selected Slides in the Oriel layout gallery to create a new Slide 2, which is a duplicate of Slide 1 (Figure 1–56).

Figure 1–56

Break Point: If you wish to take a break, this is a good place to do so. You can quit PowerPoint now (refer to page PPT 50 for instructions). To resume at a later time, start PowerPoint (refer to pages PPT 4 and PPT 5 for instructions), open the file called Saving Energy (refer to pages PPT 50 and PPT 51 for instructions), and continue following the steps from this location forward.

To Arrange a Slide

The new Slide 2 was inserted directly below Slide 1 because Slide 1 was the selected slide. This duplicate slide needs to display at the end of the presentation directly after the final title and content slide.

Changing slide order is an easy process and is best performed in the Slides pane. When you click the slide thumbnail and begin to drag it to a new location, a line indicates the new location of the selected slide. When you release the mouse button, the slide drops into the desired location. Hence, this process of dragging and then dropping the thumbnail in a new location is called **drag and drop**. You can use the drag-and-drop method to move any selected item, including text and graphics. The following step moves the new Slide 2 to the end of the presentation so that it becomes a closing slide.

1

- With Slide 2 selected, drag the Slide 2 slide thumbnail in the Slides pane below the last slide thumbnail (Figure 1–57).

Q&A

The Slide 2 thumbnail is not visible in the Slides pane when I am dragging the thumbnail downward. How do I know it will be positioned in the desired location?

A blue horizontal bar indicates where the slide will move.

cursor shape indicates drag-and-drop method

bar indicates new location of slide

Figure 1–57

Other Ways

1. Click slide icon on Outline tab, drag icon to new location
2. Click Slide Sorter (View tab | Presentation Views group), click slide thumbnail, drag thumbnail to new location

Making Changes to Slide Text Content

After creating slides in a presentation, you may find that you want to make changes to the text. Changes may be required because a slide contains an error, the scope of the presentation shifts, or the style is inconsistent. This section explains the types of changes that commonly occur when creating a presentation.

You generally make three types of changes to text in a presentation: additions, replacements, and deletions.

- Additions are necessary when you omit text from a slide and need to add it later. You may need to insert text in the form of a sentence, word, or single character. For example, you may want to add the presenter's middle name on the title slide.

- Replacements are needed when you want to revise the text in a presentation. For example, you may want to substitute the word *their* for the word *there*.

- Deletions are required when text on a slide is incorrect or no longer is relevant to the presentation. For example, a slide may look cluttered. Therefore, you may want to remove one of the bulleted paragraphs to add more space.

Editing text in PowerPoint basically is the same as editing text in a word processing program. The following sections illustrate the most common changes made to text in a presentation.

BTW

Checking Spelling
As you review your slides, you should examine the text for spelling errors. In Chapter 3, you will learn to use PowerPoint's built-in spelling checker to help you perform this task.

Replacing Text in an Existing Slide

When you need to correct a word or phrase, you can replace the text by selecting the text to be replaced and then typing the new text. As soon as you press any key on the keyboard, the selected text is deleted and the new text is displayed.

PowerPoint inserts text to the left of the insertion point. The text to the right of the insertion point moves to the right (and shifts downward if necessary) to accommodate the added text.

Deleting Text

You can delete text using one of three methods. One is to use the BACKSPACE key to remove text just typed. The second is to position the insertion point to the left of the text you want to delete and then press the DELETE key. The third method is to drag through the text you want to delete and then press the DELETE or BACKSPACE key. Use the third method when deleting large sections of text.

To Delete Text in a Placeholder

To keep the ending slide clean and simple, you want to delete a few words in the slide show title and subtitle text. The following steps change It Is Easy Being Green to Be Green and then change Saving Energy at Home to Save Energy.

1

- With Slide 5 selected, position the mouse pointer immediately to the left of the first character of the text to be selected (in this case, the I in the word, It).

- Drag the mouse pointer through the last character of the text to be selected (in this case, the space after the y in Easy) (Figure 1–58).

Figure 1–58

- Click the Cut button (Home tab | Clipboard group) to delete all the selected text (Figure 1–59).

Figure 1–59

- Select the letters, ing, in the word, Being.
- Click the Cut button (Figure 1–60).

Figure 1–60

- Select the letters, ing, in the word, Saving, and then click the Cut button.

- Type e to change the word to Save (Figure 1–61).

Other Ways

1. Right-click selected text, click Cut on shortcut menu

2. Select text, press DELETE or BACKSPACE key

3. Select text, press CTRL+X

Figure 1–61

Adding a Transition

PowerPoint provides many animation effects to add interest and make a slide show presentation look professional. **Animation** includes special visual and sound effects applied to text or content. A **slide transition** is a special animation effect used to progress from one slide to the next in a slide show. You can control the speed of the transition effect and add a sound.

PowerPoint provides a variety of transitions arranged into three categories that describe the types of effects: Subtle, Exciting, and Dynamic Content.

To Add a Transition between Slides

In this presentation, you apply the Doors transition in the Exciting category to all slides and change the transition speed from 1.40 seconds to 2 seconds. The following steps apply this transition to the presentation.

1

- Click the Transitions tab on the Ribbon and then point to the More button (Transitions tab | Transition to This Slide group) (Figure 1–62).

Q&A
Is a transition applied now?

No. The first slide icon in the Transitions group has an orange border, which indicates no transition has been applied.

Figure 1–62

2

- Click the More button to expand the Transitions gallery.

- Point to the Doors transition in the Exciting category in the Transitions gallery (Figure 1–63).

Q&A
Can I add a sound to play during this transition?

Yes. Click the Sound arrow (Transitions tab | Timing group) to display the Sound list and then select a sound from this list. You also can use your own sound if you select Other Sound in the list, select the desired sound (Add Audio dialog box), and then click the OK button

Figure 1–63

3

- Click Doors in the Exciting category in the Transitions gallery to apply this transition to the closing slide.

Q&A Why does a star appear next to Slide 5 in the Slides tab?

The star indicates that a transition animation effect is applied to that slide.

- Click the Duration up arrow (Transitions tab | Timing group) three times to change the transition speed from 01.40 seconds to 02.00 seconds (Figure 1–64).

Q&A Why did the time change?

Each transition has a default duration time. The Doors transition time is 1:40 seconds.

Figure 1–64

4

- Click the Preview Transitions button (Transitions tab | Preview area) to view the transition and the new transition time (Figure 1–65).

Q&A Can I adjust the duration time I just set?

Yes. Click the Duration up or down arrows or type a speed in the Duration text box and preview the transition until you find the time that best fits your presentation.

Figure 1–65

- Click the Apply To All button (Transitions tab | Timing group) to apply the Doors transition and the increased transition time to Slides 1 through 4 in the presentation (Figure 1–66).

Q&A

What if I want to apply a different transition and duration to each slide in the presentation?

Repeat Steps 2 and 3 for each slide individually.

Figure 1–66

Changing Document Properties

PowerPoint helps you organize and identify your files by using **document properties**, which are the details about a file. Document properties, also known as **metadata**, can include information such as the project author, title, subject, and keywords. A **keyword** is a word or phrase that further describes the document. For example, a class name or document topic can describe the file's purpose or content.

Document properties are valuable for a variety of reasons:

- Users can save time locating a particular file because they can view a document's properties without opening the document.
- By creating consistent properties for files having similar content, users can better organize their documents.
- Some organizations require PowerPoint users to add document properties so that other employees can view details about these files.

Five different types of document properties exist, but the more common ones used in this book are standard and automatically updated properties. **Standard properties** are associated with all Microsoft Office documents and include author, title, and subject. **Automatically updated properties** include file system properties, such as the date you create or change a file, and statistics, such as the file size.

To Change Document Properties

The **Document Information Panel** contains areas where you can view and enter document properties. You can view and change information in this panel at any time while you are creating a document. Before saving the presentation again, you want to add your name and course information as document properties. The following steps use the Document Information Panel to change document properties.

- Click File on the Ribbon to open the Backstage view.

- If necessary, click the Info tab in the Backstage view to display the Info gallery (Figure 1–67).

Q&A

How do I close the Backstage view?

Click File on the Ribbon or click the preview of the document in the Info gallery to return to the PowerPoint document window.

Figure 1–67

- Click the Properties button in the right pane of the Info gallery to display the Properties menu (Figure 1–68).

Figure 1–68

- Click Show Document Panel on the Properties menu to close the Backstage view and display the Document Information Panel in the PowerPoint document window (Figure 1–69).

Figure 1–69

Q&A

Why are some of the document properties in my Document Information Panel already filled in?

The person who installed Microsoft Office 2010 on your computer or network may have set or customized the properties.

- Click the Author text box, if necessary, and then type your name as the Author property. If a name already is displayed in the Author text box, delete it before typing your name.

Figure 1–70

- Click the Subject text box, if necessary delete any existing text, and then type your course and section as the Subject property.

- If an AutoComplete dialog box appears, click its Yes button.

- Click the Keywords text box, if necessary delete any existing text, and then type `energy savings` as the Keywords property (Figure 1–70).

Q&A What types of document properties does PowerPoint collect automatically?

PowerPoint records details such as time spent editing a document, the number of times a document has been revised, and the fonts and themes used in a document.

- Click the Close the Document Information Panel button so that the Document Information Panel no longer is displayed.

Other Ways

1. Click File on Ribbon, click Info in Backstage view, if necessary click Show All Properties link in Info gallery, click property to change and type new information, close Backstage view

To Save an Existing Presentation with the Same File Name

You have made several modifications to the presentation since you last saved it. Thus, you should save it again. The following step saves the document again. For an example of the step listed below, refer to the Office 2010 and Windows 7 chapter at the beginning of this book.

 Click the Save button on the Quick Access Toolbar to overwrite the previously saved file.

BTW **Saving in a Previous PowerPoint Format** To ensure that your presentation will open in PowerPoint 2003 or older versions of this software, you must save your file in PowerPoint 97-2003 format. These files will have the .ppt extension.

Viewing the Presentation in Slide Show View

The Slide Show button, located in the lower-right corner of the PowerPoint window above the status bar, allows you to show a presentation using a computer. The computer acts like a slide projector, displaying each slide on a full screen. The full-screen slide hides the toolbars, menus, and other PowerPoint window elements.

To Start Slide Show View

When making a presentation, you use **Slide Show view**. You can start Slide Show view from Normal view or Slide Sorter view. Slide Show view begins when you click the Slide Show button on the lower-right corner of the status bar. PowerPoint then shows the current slide on the full screen without any of the PowerPoint window objects, such as the menu bar or toolbars. The following steps start Slide Show view.

1

- Click the Slide 1 thumbnail in the Slides pane to select and display Slide 1.

- Point to the Slide Show button in the lower-right corner of the PowerPoint window on the status bar (Figure 1–71).

Q&A

Why did I need to select Slide 1?

When you run a slide show, PowerPoint begins the show with the currently displayed slide. If you had not selected Slide 1, then only Slide 5 would have displayed in the slide show.

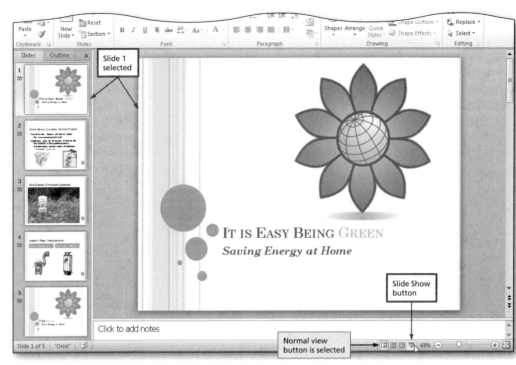

Figure 1–71

2

- Click the Slide Show button to display the title slide (Figure 1–72).

Q&A

Where is the PowerPoint window?

When you run a slide show, the PowerPoint window is hidden. It will reappear once you end your slide show.

Other Ways

1. Click Slide Show From Beginning button (Slide Show tab | Start Slide Show group)

2. Press F5

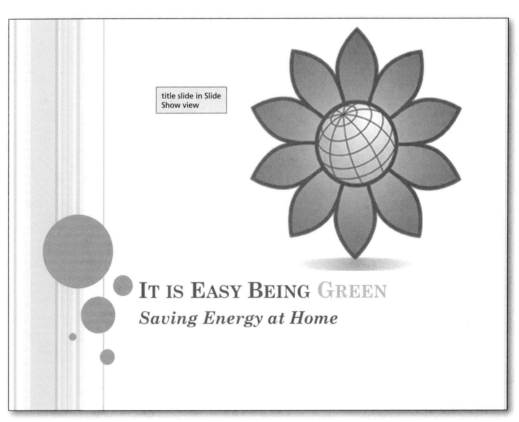

Figure 1–72

To Move Manually through Slides in a Slide Show

After you begin Slide Show view, you can move forward or backward through the slides. PowerPoint allows you to advance through the slides manually or automatically. During a slide show, each slide in the presentation shows on the screen, one slide at a time. Each time you click the mouse button, the next slide appears. The following steps move manually through the slides.

- Click each slide until Slide 5 (Be Green) is displayed (Figure 1–73).

Q&A

I see a small toolbar in the lower-left corner of my slide. What is this toolbar?

The Slide Show toolbar appears when you begin running a slide show and then move the mouse pointer. The buttons on this toolbar allow you to navigate to the next slide, the previous slide, to mark up the current slide, or to change the current display.

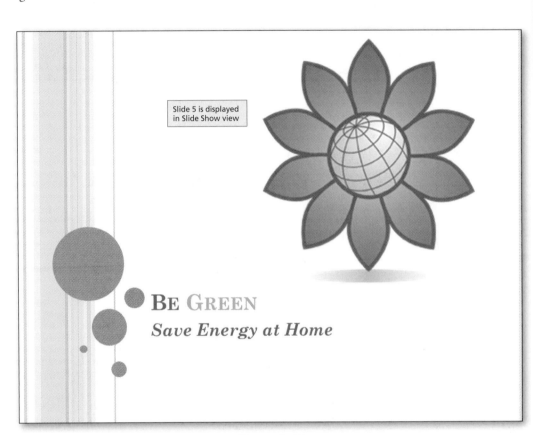

Slide 5 is displayed in Slide Show view

BE GREEN
Save Energy at Home

Figure 1–73

- Click Slide 5 so that the black slide appears with a message announcing the end of the slide show (Figure 1–74).

Q&A

How can I end the presentation at this point?

Click the black slide to return to Normal view in the PowerPoint window or press the ESC key.

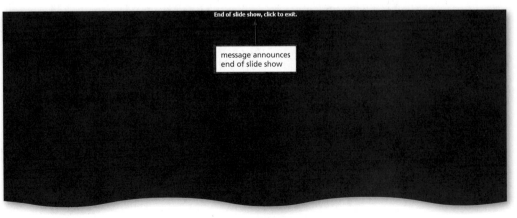

End of slide show, click to exit.

message announces end of slide show

Figure 1–74

Other Ways
1. Press PAGE DOWN to advance one slide at a time, or press PAGE UP to go back one slide at a time   2. Press RIGHT ARROW or DOWN ARROW to advance one slide at a time, or press LEFT ARROW or UP ARROW to go back one slide at a time   3. If Slide Show toolbar is displayed, click Next Slide or Previous Slide button on toolbar

BTW

Eliminating the Black Slide
By default, a black slide is displayed at the end of a slide show. If you do not want this slide to appear, click the File tab, click Options, and then click the Advanced link. In the Slide Show group, click 'End with black slide' to uncheck it.

To Quit PowerPoint

This project now is complete. The following steps quit PowerPoint. For a detailed example of the procedure summarized below, refer to the Office 2010 and Windows 7 chapter at the beginning of this book.

1 If you have one PowerPoint presentation open, click the Close button on the right side of the title bar to close the document and quit PowerPoint; or if you have multiple PowerPoint presentations open, click File on the Ribbon to open the Backstage view and then click Exit in the Backstage view to close all open documents and quit PowerPoint.

2 If a Microsoft PowerPoint dialog box appears, click the Save button to save any changes made to the document since the last save.

BTW

Certification
The Microsoft Office Specialist (MOS) program provides an opportunity for you to obtain a valuable industry credential — proof that you have the PowerPoint 2010 skills required by employers. For more information, visit the PowerPoint 2010 Certification Web page (scsite.com/ppt2010/cert).

To Start PowerPoint

Once you have created and saved a document, you may need to retrieve it from your storage medium. For example, you might want to revise the presentation or print it. The following steps, which assume Windows 7 is running, start PowerPoint so that you can open and modify the presentation. You may need to ask your instructor how to start PowerPoint for your computer. For a detailed example of the procedure summarized below, refer to the Office 2010 and Windows 7 chapter at the beginning of this book.

1 Click the Start button on the Windows 7 taskbar to display the Start menu.

2 Type `Microsoft PowerPoint` as the search text in the 'Search programs and files' text box and watch the search results appear on the Start menu.

3 Click Microsoft PowerPoint 2010 in the search results on the Start menu to start PowerPoint and display a new blank document in the PowerPoint window.

4 If the PowerPoint window is not maximized, click the Maximize button next to the Close button on its title bar to maximize the window.

To Open a Document from PowerPoint

Earlier in this chapter you saved your project on a USB flash drive using the file name, Saving Energy. The following steps open the Saving Energy file from the PowerPoint folder in the CIS 101 folder on the USB flash drive. For a detailed example of the procedure summarized below, refer to the Office 2010 and Windows 7 chapter at the beginning of this book.

1 With your USB flash drive connected to one of the computer's USB ports, click File on the Ribbon to open the Backstage view.

2 Click Open in the Backstage view to display the Open dialog box.

3 Navigate to the location of the file to be opened (in this case, the USB flash drive, then to the CIS 101 folder [or your class folder], and then to the PowerPoint folder).

4 Click Saving Energy to select the file to be opened.

5 Click the Open button (Open dialog box) to open the selected file and display the opened document in the PowerPoint window.

Printing a Presentation

After creating a presentation, you may want to print the slides. Printing a presentation enables you to distribute the document to others in a form that can be read or viewed but typically not edited. It is a good practice to save a presentation before printing it, in the event you experience difficulties printing.

Plan
Ahead

Determine the best method for distributing the presentation.
The traditional method of distributing a presentation uses a printer to produce a hard copy. A **hardcopy** or **printout** is information that exists on a physical medium such as paper. For users who can receive fax documents, you can elect to print a hard copy on a remote fax machine. Hard copies can be useful for the following reasons:

- Many people prefer proofreading a hard copy of a document rather than viewing it on the screen to check for errors and readability.

- Hard copies can serve as reference material if your storage medium is lost or becomes corrupted and you need to recreate the document.

    Instead of distributing a hard copy of a presentation slides, users can choose to distribute the presentation as an electronic image that mirrors the original document's appearance. The electronic image of the document can be e-mailed, posted on a Web site, or copied to a portable storage medium such as a USB flash drive. Two popular electronic image formats, sometimes called fixed formats, are PDF by Adobe Systems and XPS by Microsoft. In PowerPoint, you can create electronic image files through the Print tab in the Backstage view, the Save & Send tab in the Backstage view, and the Save As dialog box. Electronic images of documents, such as PDF and XPS, can be useful for the following reasons.

- Users can view electronic images of documents without the software that created the original document (e.g., PowerPoint). Specifically, to view a PDF file, you use a program called Acrobat Reader, which can be downloaded free from Adobe's Web site. Similarly, to view an XPS file, you use a program called an XPS Viewer, which is included in the latest versions of Windows and Internet Explorer.

- Sending electronic documents saves paper and printer supplies. Society encourages users to contribute to **green computing**, which involves reducing the environmental waste generated when using a computer.

To Print a Presentation

With the completed presentation saved, you may want to print it. If copies of the presentation are being distributed to audience members, you will print a hard copy of each individual slide on a printer. The following steps print a hard copy of the contents of the saved Saving Energy presentation.

1

- Click File on the Ribbon to open the Backstage view.

- Click the Print tab in the Backstage view to display the Print gallery (Figure 1–75).

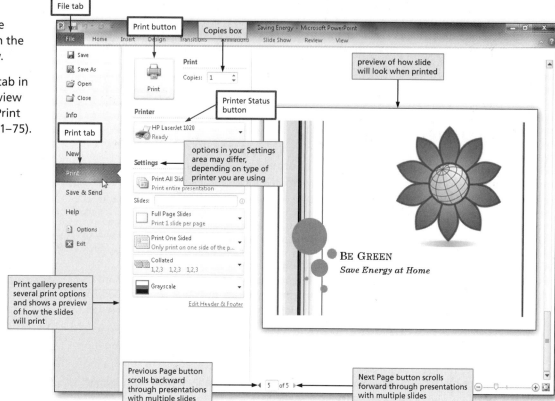

Figure 1–75

Q&A How do I preview Slides 2 through 5?

Click the Next Page button in the Print gallery to scroll forward through pages in the document; similarly, click the Previous Page button to scroll backward through pages.

Q&A How can I print multiple copies of my slides?

Increase the number in the Copies box in the Print gallery.

Q&A What if I decide not to print the document at this time?

Click File on the Ribbon to close the Backstage view and return to the PowerPoint document window.

2

- Verify the printer name that appears on the Printer box Status button will print a hard copy of the document. If necessary, click the Printer Status button to display a list of available printer options and then click the desired printer to change the currently selected printer.

BTW

Quick Reference
For a table that lists how to complete the tasks covered in this book using the mouse, Ribbon, shortcut menu, and keyboard, see the Quick Reference Summary at the back of this book, or visit the PowerPoint 2010 Quick Reference Web page (scsite.com/ppt2010/qr).

3

- Click the Print button in the Print gallery to print the document on the currently selected printer.

- When the printer stops, retrieve the hard copy (Figure 1–76).

Q&A

Do I have to wait until my document is complete to print it?

No, you can follow these steps to print a document at any time while you are creating it.

Q&A

What if I want to print an electronic image of a document instead of a hard copy?

You would click the Printer Status button in the Print gallery and then select the desired electronic image option such as a Microsoft XPS Document Writer, which would create an XPS file.

(a) Slide 1

(b) Slide 2

(c) Slide 3

(d) Slide 4

(e) Slide 5

Figure 1–76

Other Ways
1. Press CTRL+P, press ENTER

To Quit PowerPoint

The project now is complete. The following steps quit PowerPoint. For a detailed example of the procedure summarized below, refer to the Office 2010 and Windows 7 chapter at the beginning of this book.

1 If you have one PowerPoint document open, click the Close button on the right side of the title bar to close the document and quit PowerPoint; or if you have multiple PowerPoint documents open, click File on the Ribbon to open the Backstage view and then click Exit in the Backstage view to close all open documents and quit PowerPoint.

2 If a Microsoft Office PowerPoint dialog box appears, click the Save button to save any changes made to the document since the last save.

Chapter Summary

In this chapter you have learned how to apply a document theme, create a title slide and text slides with a bulleted list, clip art, and a photograph, size and move clip art and a photograph, format and edit text, add a slide transition, view the presentation in Slide Show view, and print slides as handouts. The items listed below include all the new PowerPoint skills you have learned in this chapter.

1. Start PowerPoint (PPT 4)
2. Choose a Document Theme (PPT 5)
3. Enter the Presentation Title (PPT 7)
4. Enter the Presentation Subtitle Paragraph (PPT 9)
5. Select a Paragraph (PPT 10)
6. Italicize Text (PPT 11)
7. Increase Font Size (PPT 11)
8. Select a Word (PPT 12)
9. Change the Text Color (PPT 13)
10. Save a Presentation (PPT 14)
11. Add a New Text Slide with a Bulleted List (PPT 14)
12. Enter a Slide Title (PPT 16)
13. Select a Text Placeholder (PPT 16)
14. Type a Multi-Level Bulleted List (PPT 17)
15. Select a Group of Words (PPT 19)
16. Bold Text (PPT 19)
17. Add a Slide with the Title Only Layout (PPT 21)
18. Add a New Slide and Enter a Slide Title and Headings (PPT 23)
19. Move to Another Slide in Normal View (PPT 25)
20. Insert a Clip from the Clip Organizer into the Title Slide (PPT 27)
21. Insert a Clip from the Clip Organizer into a Content Placeholder (PPT 30)
22. Insert a Photograph from the Clip Organizer into a Slide without a Content Placeholder (PPT 32)
23. Resize Clip Art (PPT 33)
24. Move Clips (PPT 36)
25. Duplicate a Slide (PPT 38)
26. Arrange a Slide (PPT 39)
27. Delete Text in a Placeholder (PPT 41)
28. Add a Transition between Slides (PPT 43)
29. Change Document Properties (PPT 46)
30. Save an Existing Presentation with the Same File Name (PPT 47)
31. Start Slide Show View (PPT 47)
32. Move Manually through Slides in a Slide Show (PPT 49)
33. Quit PowerPoint (PPT 50)
34. Open a Document from PowerPoint (PPT 50)
35. Print a Presentation (PPT 51)

 If you have a SAM 2010 user profile, your instructor may have assigned an autogradable version of this assignment. If so, log into the SAM 2010 Web site at www.cengage.com/sam2010 to download the instruction and start files.

Learn It Online

Test your knowledge of chapter content and key terms.

Instructions: To complete the Learn It Online exercises, start your browser, click the Address bar, and then enter the Web address **scsite.com/ppt2010/learn**.   When the PowerPoint 2010 Learn It Online page is displayed, click the link for the exercise you want to complete and then read the instructions.

Chapter Reinforcement TF, MC, and SA

A series of true/false, multiple choice, and short answer questions that test your knowledge of the chapter content.

Flash Cards

An interactive learning environment where you identify chapter key terms associated with displayed definitions.

Practice Test

A series of multiple choice questions that test your knowledge of chapter content and key terms.

Who Wants To Be a Computer Genius?

An interactive game that challenges your knowledge of chapter content in the style of a television quiz show.

Wheel of Terms

An interactive game that challenges your knowledge of chapter key terms in the style of the television show *Wheel of Fortune*.

Crossword Puzzle Challenge

A crossword puzzle that challenges your knowledge of key terms presented in the chapter.

Apply Your Knowledge

Reinforce the skills and apply the concepts you learned in this chapter.

Modifying Character Formats and Paragraph Levels and Moving a Clip

Note: To complete this assignment, you will be required to use the Data Files for Students. See the inside back cover of this book for instructions on downloading the Data Files for Students, or contact your instructor for information about accessing the required files.

Instructions: Start PowerPoint. Open the presentation, Apply 1-1 Flu Season, from the Data Files for Students.

The two slides in the presentation discuss ways to avoid getting or spreading the flu. The document you open is an unformatted presentation. You are to modify the document theme, indent the paragraphs, resize and move the clip art, and format the text so the slides look like Figure 1–77 on the next page.

Continued >

Apply Your Knowledge *continued*

Perform the following tasks:

1. Change the document theme to Urban. On the title slide, use your name in place of Student Name and bold and italicize your name. Increase the title text font size to 60 point. Resize and position the clip as shown in Figure 1–77a.

2. On Slide 2, increase the indent of the second, third, and fifth paragraphs (Cover mouth and nose with a tissue; No tissue? Use your elbow or sleeve; Use soap, warm water for 20 seconds) to second-level paragraphs. Then combine paragraphs six and seven (Drink fluids; Get plenty of rest) to read, Drink fluids and get plenty of rest, as shown in Figure 1–77b.

3. Change the document properties, as specified by your instructor. Save the presentation using the file name, Apply 1–1 Avoid the Flu. Submit the revised document in the format specified by your instructor.

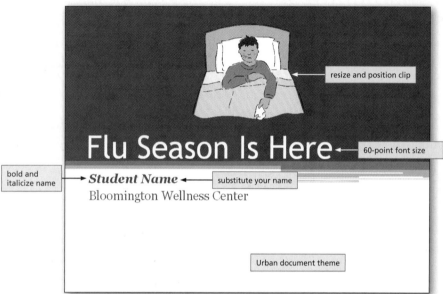

(a) Slide 1 (Title Slide with Clip Art)

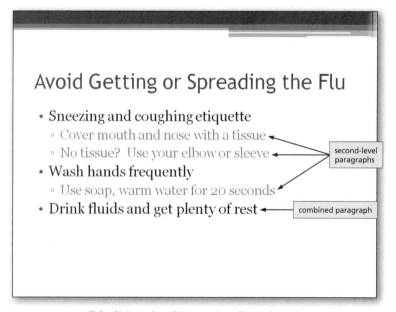

(b) Slide 2 (Multi-Level Bulleted List)

Figure 1–77

Extend Your Knowledge

Extend the skills you learned in this chapter and experiment with new skills. You may need to use Help to complete the assignment.

Changing Slide Theme, Layout, and Text

Note: To complete this assignment, you will be required to use the Data Files for Students. See the inside back cover of this book for instructions on downloading the Data Files for Students, or contact your instructor for information about accessing the required files.

Instructions: Start PowerPoint. Open the presentation that you are going to prepare for your dental hygiene class, Extend 1–1 Winning Smile, from the Data Files for Students.

You will choose a theme, format slides, and create a closing slide.

Perform the following tasks:
1. Apply an appropriate document theme.
2. On Slide 1, use your name in place of Student Name. Format the text on this slide using techniques you learned in this chapter, such as changing the font size and color and also bolding and italicizing words.
3. On Slide 2, change the slide layout and adjust the paragraph levels so that the lines of text are arranged under two headings: Discount Dental and Dental Insurance (Figure 1–78).
4. On Slide 3, create paragraphs and adjust the paragraph levels to create a bulleted list. Edit the text so that the slide meets the 7×7 rule, which states that each line should have a maximum of seven words, and each slide should have a maximum of seven lines.
5. Create an appropriate closing slide using the title slide as a guide.
6. The slides contain a variety of clips downloaded from the Microsoft Clip Organizer. Size and move them when necessary.
7. Apply an appropriate transition to all slides.
8. Change the document properties, as specified by your instructor. Save the presentation using the file name, Extend 1–1 Dental Plans.
9. Submit the revised document in the format specified by your instructor.

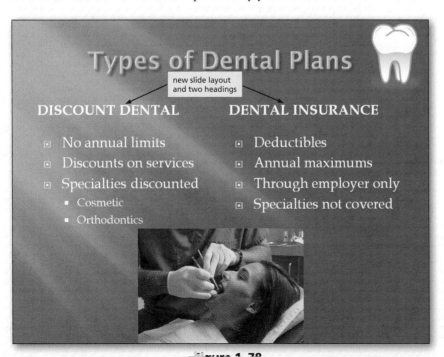

Figure 1–78

Make It Right

Analyze a presentation and correct all errors and/or improve the design.

Correcting Formatting and List Levels

Note: To complete this assignment, you will be required to use the Data Files for Students. See the inside back cover of this book for instructions on downloading the Data Files for Students, or contact your instructor for information about accessing the required files.

Instructions: Start PowerPoint. Open the presentation, Make It Right 1–1 Air Ducts, from the Data Files for Students.

Members of your homeowners' association are having their semiannual meeting, and each member of the board is required to give a short presentation on the subject of energy savings. You have decided to discuss the energy-saving benefits of maintaining the air ducts in your home. Correct the formatting problems and errors in the presentation while keeping in mind the guidelines presented in this chapter.

Perform the following tasks:

1. Change the document theme from Origin, shown in Figure 1–79, to Module.
2. On Slide 1, replace the words, Student Name, with your name. Format your name so that it displays prominently on the slide.
3. Increase the size of the clip on Slide 1 and move it to the upper-right corner.
4. Move Slide 2 to the end of the presentation so that it becomes the new Slide 3.
5. On Slide 2, correct the spelling errors and then increase the font size of the Slide 2 title text, Check Hidden Air Ducts, to 54 point. Increase the size of the clip and move it up to fill the white space on the right of the bulleted list.
6. On Slide 3, correct the spelling errors and then change the font size of the title text, Energy Savings, to 54 point. Increase the indent levels for paragraphs 2 and 4. Increase the size of the clips. Center the furnace clip at the bottom of the slide.
7. Change the document properties, as specified by your instructor. Save the presentation using the file name, Make It Right 1–1 Ducts Presentation.
8. Apply the same transition and duration to all slides.
9. Submit the revised document in the format specified by your instructor.

Figure 1–79

In the Lab

Design and/or create a presentation using the guidelines, concepts, and skills presented in this chapter. Labs 1, 2, and 3 are listed in order of increasing difficulty.

Lab1: Creating a Presentation with Bulleted Lists, a Closing Slide, and Clips

Problem: You are working with upper-level students to host a freshmen orientation seminar. When you attended this seminar, you received some helpful tips on studying for exams. Your contribution to this year's seminar is to prepare a short presentation on study skills. You develop the outline shown in Figure 1–80 and then prepare the PowerPoint presentation shown in Figures 1–81a through 1–81d.

Hit the Books
Studying for an Exam
Sarah Jones

Prepare in Advance
   Location
      Quiet, well-lit
   Timing
      15-minute breaks every hour
   Material
      Quiz yourself

Exam Time
   Day of Exam
      Rest properly
      Eat a good meal
      Wear comfy clothes
      Be early
      Be confident

Figure 1–80

Perform the following tasks:

1. Create a new presentation using the Aspect document theme.

2. Using the typed notes illustrated in Figure 1–80, create the title slide shown in Figure 1–81a, using your name in place of Sarah Jones. Italicize your name and increase the font size to 24 point. Increase the font size of the title text paragraph, Hit the Books, to 48 point. Increase the font size of the first paragraph of the subtitle text, Studying for an Exam, to 28 point.

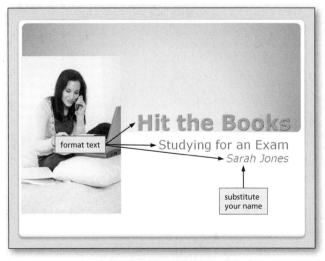

(a) Slide 1 (Title Slide)
Figure 1–81

Continued >

STUDENT ASSIGNMENTS

In the Lab *continued*

3. Using the typed notes in Figure 1–80, create the two text slides with bulleted lists and find and insert clips from the Microsoft Clip Organizer, as shown in Figures 1–81b and 1–81c.

4. Create a closing slide by duplicating Slide 1, deleting your name, replacing the photograph with the photograph shown in Figure 1–81d, and moving the slide to the end of the presentation.

5. On Slide 3, change the font color of the words, Be confident, to Yellow (fourth color in the Standard Colors row) and then bold this text.

6. Apply the Uncover transition in the Subtle category to all slides. Change the duration to 1.25 seconds.

7. Drag the scroll box to display Slide 1. Click the Slide Show button to start Slide Show view. Then click to display each slide.

8. Change the document properties, as specified by your instructor. Save the presentation using the file name, Lab 1–1 Study Skills.

9. Submit the document in the format specified by your instructor.

(b) Slide 2

(c) Slide 3

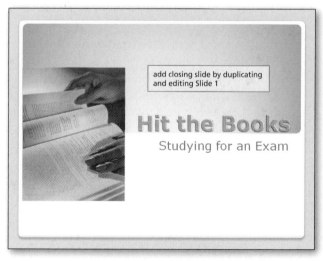

(d) Slide 4 (Closing Slide)

Figure 1–81 (continued)

In the Lab

Lab 2: Creating a Presentation with Bulleted Lists and Clips

Problem: Your health class instructor has assigned every student a different vitamin to research. She hands you the outline shown in Figure 1–82 and asks you to create the presentation about Vitamin D shown in Figures 1–83a through 1–83d on pages PPT 62 and PPT 63.

Vitamin D

The Sunshine Vitamin
Are You D-ficient?
Presented by Jim Warner

Why Is Vitamin D Important?
　　We need Vitamin D
　　　　Vital to our bodies
　　　　　　Promotes absorption of calcium and magnesium
　　　　　　　　For healthy teeth and bones
　　　　　　Maintains calcium and phosphorus in blood

　　Daily Requirements
　　　　How much do we need?
　　　　　　Child: 5 mcg (200 IU)
　　　　　　Adult: 10-20 mcg (400-600 IU)

Vitamin D Sources
　　Sunshine
　　　　Is our primary source
　　　　　　Vitamin manufactured by our body after exposure
　　　　　　　　Three times a week
　　　　　　　　For 10-15 minutes
　　Foods and Supplements
　　　　Contained in few foods
　　　　　　Some fish liver oils
　　　　　　Flesh of fatty fish
　　　　Fortified products
　　　　　　Milk and cereals
　　　　Available as supplement

Vitamin D History
　　Research began in 1924
　　　　Found to prevent rickets
　　United States and Canada
　　　　Instituted policy of fortifying foods with Vitamin D
　　　　　　Milk – food of choice
　　Other countries
　　　　Fortified cereal, bread, margarine

Figure 1–82

Continued >

In the Lab *continued*

Perform the following tasks:

1. Create a new presentation using the Solstice document theme.

2. Using the typed notes illustrated in Figure 1–82, create the title slide shown in Figure 1–83a, using your name in place of Jim Warner. Italicize the title, The Sunshine Vitamin, and increase the font size to 48 point. Change the font size of the first line of the subtitle text, Are You D-ficient?, to 36 point. Change the font color of the title text to Orange (third color in the Standard Colors row) and both lines of the subtitle text to Light Blue (seventh color in the Standard Colors row).

3. Using the typed notes in Figure 1–82, create the three text slides with bulleted lists shown in Figures 1–83b through 1–83d. Change the color of the title text on all slides and the text above the bulleted lists on Slides 2 and 3 to Orange.

4. Add the photographs and clip art shown in Figures 1–83a through 1–83d from the Microsoft Clip Organizer. Adjust the clip sizes when necessary.

5. Apply the Ripple transition in the Exciting category to all slides. Change the duration to 2.00 seconds.

6. Drag the scroll box to display Slide 1. Click the Slide Show button to start Slide Show view. Then click to display each slide.

(a) Slide 1 (Title Slide)

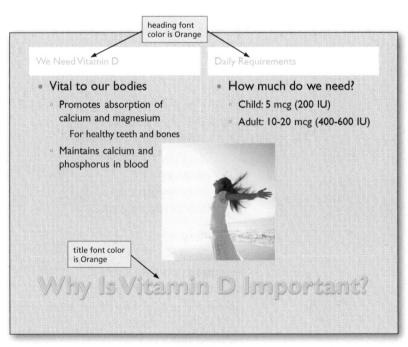

(b) Slide 2

Figure 1–83

7. Change the document properties, as specified by your instructor. Save the presentation using the file name, Lab 1–2 Vitamin D.

8. Submit the revised document in the format specified by your instructor.

(c) Slide 3

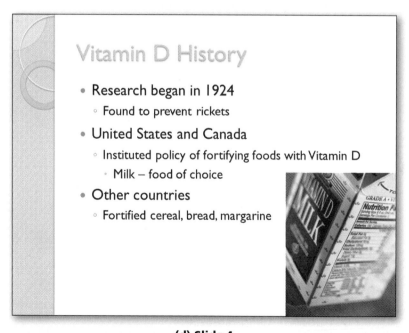

(d) Slide 4

Figure 1–83 (continued)

In the Lab

Lab 3: Creating and Updating Presentations with Clip Art

Problem: You are employed part time at your health club, and the Child Care Center director has asked you to put together a presentation for her to use at the next open house. The club has a large playroom that is perfect for children's parties.

Instructions Part 1:   Using the outline in Figure 1–84, create the presentation shown in Figure 1–85. Use the Office Theme document theme. On the title slide shown in Figure 1–85a, increase the font size of the title paragraph, Make It a Party!, to 48, change the font color to Red, and change the text font style to italic. Decrease the font size of the entire subtitle paragraph to 28, and change the font color to Blue.

Make It a Party!
Host Your Child's
Next Birthday Party
at the Oaks Health Club

We Do the Work
You Enjoy the Moment
Two-hour party
Two chaperones
Lunch & cake provided
Game or craft activity available
Decorations

Two Party Packages
Package No. 1 - $8/child
Lunch
Hot Dogs
Pizza
Package No. 2 - $12/child
Lunch including beverage
Hot Dogs
Pizza
Game
Craft (age appropriate)

Reserve Your Party Date
Reserve 2 weeks in advance
Deposit required
Party room can hold 20 children
Sign up in the Child Care Center

Figure 1–84

Create the three text slides with multi-level bulleted lists, photographs, and clip art shown in Figures 1–85b through 1–85d on the next page. Adjust the clip sizes when necessary. Apply the Vortex transition in the Exciting category to all slides and decrease the duration to 3.00 seconds. Change the document properties, as specified by your instructor. Save the presentation using the file name, Lab 1–3 Part One Child Party.

(a) Slide 1 (Title Slide)

(b) Slide 2
Figure 1–85

Continued >

In the Lab *continued*

Two Party Packages

Package No. 1 - $8/child

- Lunch
  - Hot Dogs
  - Pizza

Package No. 2 - $12/child

- Lunch including beverage
  - Hot Dogs
  - Pizza
- Game
- Craft (age appropriate)

(c) Slide 3

Reserve Your Party Date

- Reserve 2 weeks in advance
- Deposit required
- Party room can hold 20 children
- Sign up in the Child Care Center

(d) Slide 4
Figure 1–85 (continued)

Instructions Part 2: The children's parties have proved to be a great perk for members of the health club. A large group of older adults work out at the club and also meet socially once a month. These members have asked about renting the playroom to hold a retirement party for some of their friends. You decide to modify the children's party presentation to promote retirement parties. Use the outline in Figure 1–86 to modify the presentation created in Part 1 to create the presentation shown in Figure 1–87 on the next page. Required changes are indicated by a yellow highlight.

To begin, save the current presentation with the new file name, Lab 1–3 Part Two Retirement Party. Change the document theme to Flow. On Slide 3, change the pianist's name from Ms. Winn to your name. Apply the Fade transition in the Subtle category to all slides and change the duration speed to 2.25 seconds. View the slide show. Change the document properties, as specified by your instructor. Submit both Part One and Part Two documents in the format specified by your instructor.

Make It a Party!
    Host Your
    Retirement Party
    at the Oaks Health Club

We Do the Work
You Enjoy the Moment
    Two-hour party

    Lunch & cake provided

    Decorations
    Music

Two Party Packages
    Package No. 1 - $9/person
        Lunch
            Lasagna
            Salad & bread
    Package No. 2 - $20/person
        Lunch including beverage
            Lasagna
            Salad & bread
    Ms. Winn on piano
    Photo booth

Reserve Your Party Date
    Reserve 2 weeks in advance
    Deposit required
    Party room can hold 15 adults
    Sign up at the main desk

Figure 1–86

Continued >

In the Lab continued

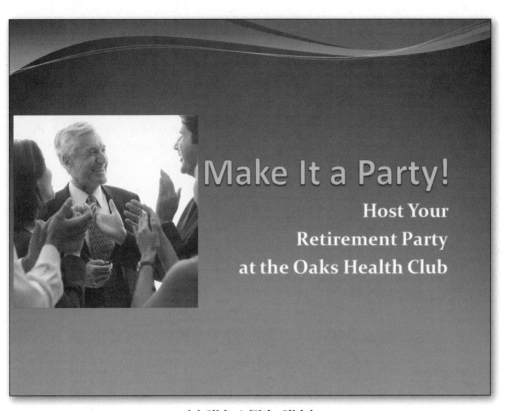

(a) Slide 1 (Title Slide)

(b) Slide 2
Figure 1–87

(c) Slide 3

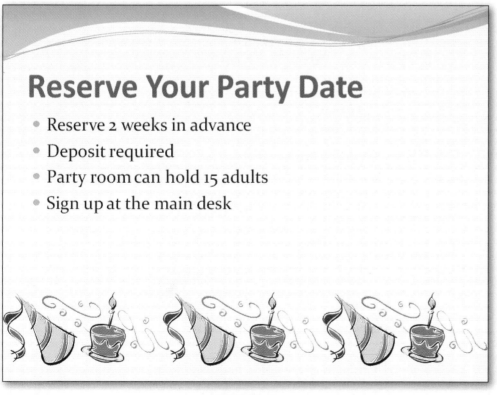

(d) Slide 4
Figure 1–87 (continued)

Cases and Places

Apply your creative thinking and problem-solving skills to design and implement a solution.

Note: To complete these assignments, you may be required to use the Data Files for Students. See the inside back cover of this book for instructions on downloading the Data Files for Students, or contact your instructor for information about accessing the required files.

As you design the presentations, remember to use the 7 × 7 rule: a maximum of seven words on a line and a maximum of seven lines on one slide.

1: Design and Create a Presentation about Galileo

Academic

Italian-born Galileo is said to be the father of modern science. After the invention of the telescope by a Dutch eyeglass maker named Hans Lippershey, Galileo made his own telescope and made many discoveries. You decide to prepare a PowerPoint presentation to accompany a speech that is required in your Astronomy class. You create the outline shown in Figure 1–88 about Galileo. Use this outline, along with the concepts and techniques presented in this chapter, to develop and format a slide show with a title slide and three text slides with bulleted lists. Add photographs and clip art from the Microsoft Clip Organizer and apply a transition. Submit your assignment in the format specified by your instructor.

Galileo Galilei
  Father of Modern Science
  Astronomy 201
  Sandy Wendt

Major Role in Scientific Revolution
February 15, 1564 – January 8, 1642
  Physicist
  Mathematician
  Astronomer
  Philosopher

Galileo's Research Years
  1581 - Studied medicine
  1589-1592 - Studied math and physics
  1592-1607 - Padua University
    Developed Law of Inertia
  1609 - Built telescope
    Earth's moon
    Jupiter's moons

Galileo's Later Years
  Dialogue - Two Chief World Systems
    Controversy develops
  1633 - Rome
    Heresy trial
    Imprisoned
  1642 - Dies

Figure 1–88

2: Design and Create a Presentation Promoting Hiking for Family Fitness

Personal

A great way for the entire family to get exercise is by participating in a hiking adventure. Employees at the local forest preserve district near your home have remodeled the nature center, and you have volunteered to give a presentation at the open house to help families plan their hikes. Use the outline shown in Figure 1–89 and then create an accompanying PowerPoint presentation. Use the concepts and techniques presented in this chapter to develop and format this slide show with a title slide, three text slides with bulleted lists, and clip art. Add photographs and clip art from the Microsoft Clip Organizer and apply a transition. Submit your assignment in the format specified by your instructor.

Take a Hike
    An Adventure with Kids
    Presented by Joshua Lind
    Pines Nature Center

Planning the Adventure
    Trail length — varies by child's age
        Ages 2 to 4: 1 to 2 miles
        Ages 5 to 7: 3 to 4 miles
        Ages 8 to 12: 5 to 7 miles
    Backpack — limit to 20 percent of child's weight

Packing Supplies
    Snacks and Drinks
        Child's favorite healthy foods
            Fruit and nuts
        Water
    Miscellaneous
        Sunscreen
        Insect repellent
        First-aid kit

Wearing the Right Clothes
    Dress in layers
        Children get cold quicker than adults
    Wear long pants and long-sleeved shirt
        Protect against insects and cuts
    Wear a hat and comfortable shoes
        Keep body warm

Figure 1–89

Continued >

Cases and Places *continued*

3: Design and Create a Landscaping Service Presentation

Professional

The home and garden center where you work is hosting weekend clinics for customers. The owner asks you to give a presentation about the center's new landscaping division and hands you the outline shown in Figure 1–90. Use the concepts and techniques presented in this chapter to develop and format a PowerPoint presentation with a title slide, three text slides with bulleted lists, and clip art. Add photographs and clip art from the Microsoft Clip Organizer and apply a transition. Submit your assignment in the format specified by your instructor.

Barry's Landscaping Service
Bensenville, Indiana

Full-Service Landscaping
        Initial design
        Installation
        Maintenance

Scope of Services
        Landscape design
        Irrigation
        Lighting
        Lawn-care programs
        Tree/shrub maintenance
        Masonry, carpentry
        Water features

Our Promise to You
        Deliver on-time service
        Provide highest level of workmanship
        Give maximum value for your dollar
        Install high-quality plants and materials
        Respond quickly to your needs

Figure 1–90

1 | Creating a Worksheet and an Embedded Chart

Objectives

You will have mastered the material in this chapter when you can:

- Describe the Excel worksheet
- Enter text and numbers
- Use the Sum button to sum a range of cells
- Copy the contents of a cell to a range of cells using the fill handle
- Apply cell styles
- Format cells in a worksheet

- Create a Clustered Cylinder chart
- Change a worksheet name and worksheet tab color
- Change document properties
- Preview and print a worksheet
- Use the AutoCalculate area to display statistics
- Correct errors on a worksheet

1 | Creating a Worksheet and an Embedded Chart

Introduction

Almost any organization collects vast amounts of data. Often, data is consolidated into a summary so that people in the organization better understand the meaning of the data. An Excel worksheet allows data easily to be summarized and charted. A chart conveys a visual representation of data. In this chapter, you will create a worksheet that includes a chart. The data in the worksheet and chart includes data for donations made to a not-for-profit organization that operates in several cities.

Project Planning Guidelines

> The process of developing a worksheet that communicates specific information requires careful analysis and planning. As a starting point, establish why the worksheet is needed. Once the purpose is determined, analyze the intended users of the worksheet and their unique needs. Then, gather information about the topic and decide what to include in the worksheet. Finally, determine the worksheet design and style that will be most successful at delivering the message. Details of these guidelines are provided in Appendix A. In addition, each project developed in this book provides practical applications of these planning considerations.

Project — Worksheet with an Embedded Chart

The project in this chapter follows proper design guidelines and uses Excel to create the worksheet shown in Figure 1–1. The worksheet contains fundraising data for the Save Sable River Foundation. The Save Sable River Foundation raises funds to care for the environment and preserve the usability of a river that flows through six cities. The foundation raises funds by using five different fundraising activities. Through a concentrated marketing campaign and providing visible results to the communities, the Save Sable River Foundation quickly became a popular local institution. After several years of successful fundraising, senior management requested an easy-to-read worksheet that shows lifetime fundraising amounts for each fundraising technique by city. In addition, they asked for a chart showing lifetime fundraising amounts because the president of the foundation likes to have a graphical representation that allows him quickly to identify stronger and weaker fundraising activities by city.

Figure 1–1

The first step in creating an effective worksheet is to make sure you understand what is required. The person or persons requesting the worksheet should supply their requirements in a requirements document. A **requirements document** includes a needs statement, a source of data, a summary of calculations, and any other special requirements for the worksheet, such as charting and Web support. Figure 1–2 on the following page shows the requirements document for the new workbook to be created in this chapter.

Excel 2010 Features

With its what-if analysis tools, research capabilities, collaboration tools, streamlined user interface, smart tags, charting features, Web capabilities, hundreds of functions, and enhanced formatting capabilities, Excel 2010 is one of the easier and more powerful spreadsheet programs available. Its dynamic analytical features make it possible to answer complicated what-if questions and its Web capabilities allow you to create, publish, view, share, and analyze data on an intranet or the World Wide Web.

requirements document →

Worksheet Development Cycle

Spreadsheet specialists do not sit down and start entering text, formulas, and data into a blank Excel worksheet as soon as they have a spreadsheet assignment. Instead, they follow an organized plan, or methodology, that breaks the development cycle into a series of tasks. The recommended methodology for creating worksheets includes: (1) analyze requirements (supplied in a requirements document); (2) design solution; (3) validate design; (4) implement design; (5) test solution; and (6) document solution.

REQUEST FOR NEW WORKBOOK	
Date Submitted:	March 22, 2012
Submitted By:	Kevin Li
Worksheet Title:	Save Sable River Foundation Lifetime Fundraising Summary
Needs:	An easy-to-read worksheet that shows a summary of the Save Sable River Foundation's lifetime fundraising efforts for each city in which we operate (Allentown, Chamber City, Pattonsville, Sable Village, Strongville, and the Town of Cary). The worksheet also should include total funds raised for each city, total funds raised for each fundraising activity, and total lifetime funds raised.
Source of Data:	The data for the worksheet is available from the chief financial officer (CFO) of the Save Sable River Foundation.
Calculations:	The following calculations must be made for the worksheet: (a) total lifetime funds raised for each of the six cities; (b) total lifetime funds raised for each of the five fundraising activities; and (c) total lifetime funds raised for the organization.
Chart Requirements:	Below the data in the worksheet, construct a Clustered Cylinder chart that compares the total funds raised for each city within each type of fundraising activity.

Approvals

Approval Status:	X	Approved
		Rejected
Approved By:	Marsha Davis	
Date:	March 29, 2012	
Assigned To:	J. Quasney, Spreadsheet Specialist	

Figure 1–2

Overview

As you read this chapter, you will learn how to create the worksheet shown in Figure 1–1 on the previous page by performing these general tasks:

- Enter text in the worksheet
- Total data in the worksheet
- Format the text in the worksheet
- Insert a chart into the worksheet
- Identify the worksheet with a worksheet name
- Preview and print the worksheet

BTWs

For a complete list of the BTWs found in the margins of this book, visit the Excel 2010 BTW Web page (scsite.com/ex2010/btw).

General Project Guidelines

While creating an Excel worksheet, you need to make several decisions that will determine the appearance and characteristics of the finished worksheet. As you create the worksheet shown in Figure 1–1, you should follow these general guidelines:

1. **Select titles and subtitles for the worksheet.** Follow the *less is more* guideline. The less text in the titles and subtitles, the more impact the titles and subtitles will have. Use the fewest words possible to specify the information presented in the worksheet to the intended audience.

(continued)

(continued)

2. **Determine the contents for rows and columns.** Rows typically contain information that is analogous to items in a list, such as the fundraising techniques used by an organization. Columns typically contain descriptive information about items in rows or contain information that helps to group the data in the worksheet, such as the locations in which the organization operates. Row headings and column headings are usually placed in alphabetical sequence, unless an alternative order is recommended in the requirements document.

3. **Determine the calculations that are needed.** You can decide to total data in a variety of ways, such as across rows or in columns. You also can include a grand total.

4. **Determine where to save the workbook.** You can store a workbook permanently, or **save** it, on a variety of storage media including a hard disk, USB flash drive, CD, or DVD. You also can indicate a specific location on the storage media for saving the workbook.

5. **Identify how to format various elements of the worksheet.** The overall appearance of a worksheet significantly affects its ability to communicate clearly. Examples of how you can modify the appearance, or format, of text include changing its shape, size, color, and position on the worksheet.

6. **Decide on the type of chart needed.** Excel can create many different types of charts, such as cylinder charts and pie charts. Each type of chart relays a different message about the data in the worksheet. Choose a type of chart that relays the message that you want to convey.

7. **Establish where to position and how to format the chart.** The position and format of the chart should command the attention of the intended audience. If possible, position the chart so that it prints with the worksheet data on a single page.

8. **Choose a name for the worksheet.** Each worksheet in a workbook should be named to clarify its purpose. A good worksheet name is succinct, unique to the workbook, and meaningful to any user of the workbook.

9. **Determine the best method for distributing the workbook.** Workbooks and worksheets can be distributed on paper or electronically. The decision regarding how to distribute workbooks and worksheets greatly depends on your intended audience. For example, a worksheet may be printed for inclusion in a report, or a workbook may be distributed using e-mail if the recipient intends to update the workbook.

   When necessary, more specific details concerning the above guidelines are presented at appropriate points in the chapter. The chapter also will identify the actions performed and decisions made regarding these guidelines during the creation of the worksheet shown in Figure 1–1 on page EX 3.

BTW

Worksheet Development
The key to developing a useful worksheet is careful planning. Careful planning can reduce your effort significantly and result in a worksheet that is accurate, easy to read, flexible, and useful. When analyzing a problem and designing a worksheet solution, you should follow these steps: (1) define the problem, including need, source of data, calculations, charting, and Web or special requirements; (2) design the worksheet; (3) enter the data and formulas; and (4) test the worksheet.

   After carefully reviewing the requirements document (Figure 1–2) and making the necessary decisions, the next step is to design a solution or draw a sketch of the worksheet based on the requirements, including titles, column and row headings, the location of data values, and the Clustered Cylinder chart, as shown in Figure 1–3 on the following page. The dollar signs, 9s, and commas that you see in the sketch of the worksheet indicate formatted numeric values.

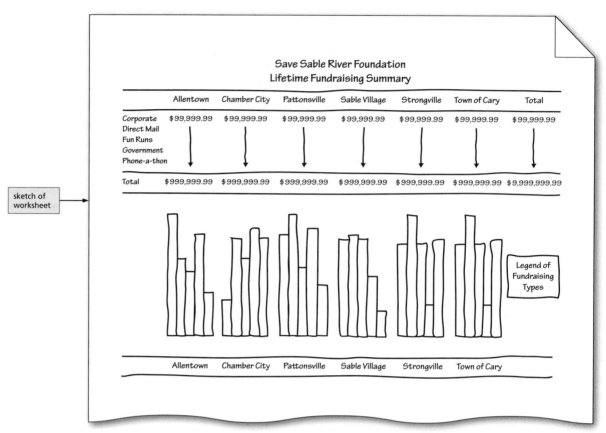

Figure 1–3

For an introduction to Windows 7 and instruction about how to perform basic Windows 7 tasks, read the Office 2010 and Windows 7 chapter at the beginning of this book, where you can learn how to resize windows, change screen resolution, create folders, move and rename files, use Windows Help, and much more.

With a good understanding of the requirements document, an understanding of the necessary decisions, and a sketch of the worksheet, the next step is to use Excel to create the worksheet and chart.

To Start Excel

If you are using a computer to step through the project in this chapter and you want your screens to match the figures in this book, you should change your screen's resolution to 1024×768. For information about how to change a computer's resolution, refer to the Office 2010 and Windows 7 chapter at the beginning of this book.

The following steps, which assume Windows 7 is running, start Excel based on a typical installation. You may need to ask your instructor how to start Excel for your computer. For a detailed example of the procedure summarized below, refer to the Office 2010 and Windows 7 chapter.

1 Click the Start button on the Windows 7 taskbar to display the Start menu.

2 Type **Microsoft Excel** as the search text in the 'Search programs and files' text box and watch the search results appear on the Start menu.

3 Click Microsoft Excel 2010 in the search results on the Start menu to start Excel and display a new blank workbook in the Excel window.

4 If the Excel window is not maximized, click the Maximize button next to the Close button on its title bar to maximize the window.

BTW

The Ribbon and Screen Resolution
Excel may change how the groups and buttons within the groups appear on the Ribbon, depending on the computer's screen resolution. Thus, your Ribbon may look different from the ones in this book if you are using a screen resolution other than 1024×768.

Selecting a Cell

To enter data into a cell, you first must select it. The easiest way **to select a cell** (make it active) is to use the mouse to move the block plus sign mouse pointer to the cell and then click.

An alternative method is to use the arrow keys that are located just to the right of the alphanumeric keys on a standard keyboard. An arrow key selects the cell adjacent to the active cell in the direction of the arrow on the key.

You know a cell is selected, or active, when a heavy border surrounds the cell and the active cell reference appears in the Name box on the left side of the formula bar. Excel also changes the active cell's column heading and row heading to a gold color.

Entering Text

In Excel, any set of characters containing a letter, hyphen (as in a telephone number), or space is considered text. **Text** is used to place titles, such as worksheet titles, column titles, and row titles, on the worksheet.

Select titles and subtitles for the worksheet.
Worksheet titles and subtitles should be as brief and meaningful as possible. A worksheet title could include the name of the organization, department, or a description of the content of the worksheet. A worksheet subtitle, if included, could include a more detailed description of the content of the worksheet. Examples of worksheet titles are December 2010 Payroll and Year 2011 Projected Budget, and examples of subtitles are Marketing Department and Rent and Utilities, respectively.

Plan Ahead

Determine the contents of rows and columns.
As shown in Figure 1–4, data in a worksheet often is identified by row and column titles so that the user of a worksheet easily can identify the meaning of the data. Rows typically contain information that is similar to items in a list. Columns typically contain descriptive information about items in rows or contain information that helps to group the data in the worksheet. Examples of row titles are Product and Total, and examples of column titles are Name and Address.

Plan Ahead

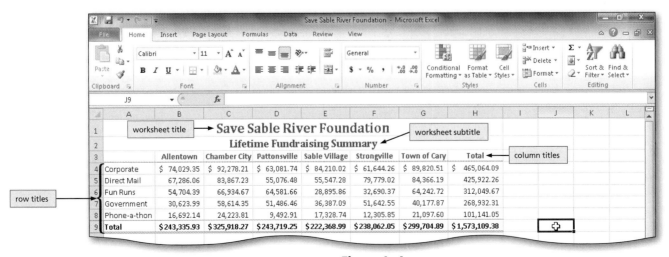

Figure 1–4

To Enter the Worksheet Titles

As shown in Figure 1–4 on the previous page, the worksheet title, Save Sable River Foundation, identifies the organization for which the worksheet is being created in Chapter 1. The worksheet subtitle, Lifetime Fundraising Summary, identifies the type of report.

The following steps enter the worksheet titles in cells A1 and A2. Later in this chapter, the worksheet titles will be formatted so they appear as shown in Figure 1–4.

- If necessary, click cell A1 to make cell A1 the active cell (Figure 1–5).

Q&A What if I make a mistake while typing?

If you type the wrong letter and notice the error before clicking the Enter box or pressing the ENTER key, use the BACKSPACE key to delete all the characters back to and including the incorrect letter. To cancel the entire entry before entering it into the cell, click the Cancel box in the formula bar or press the ESC key. If you see an error in a cell after entering the text, select the cell and retype the entry.

Figure 1–5

- Type `Save Sable River Foundation` in cell A1 and then point to the Enter box in the formula bar to prepare to enter text in the active cell (Figure 1–6).

Q&A Why did the appearance of the formula bar change?

Excel displays the title in the formula bar and in cell A1. When you begin typing a cell entry, Excel displays two additional boxes in the formula bar:

Note: To help you locate screen elements that are referenced in the step instructions, such as buttons and commands, this book uses red boxes to point to these screen elements.

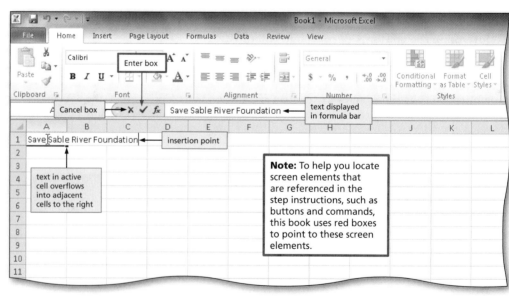

Figure 1–6

the Cancel box and the Enter box. Clicking the **Enter box** completes an entry. Clicking the **Cancel box** cancels an entry.

Q&A What is the vertical line in cell A1?

The text in cell A1 is followed by the insertion point. The **insertion point** is a blinking vertical line that indicates where the next typed character will appear.

3

- Click the Enter box to complete the entry and enter a worksheet title (Figure 1–7).

Q&A Why does the entered text appear in three cells?

When the text is longer than the width of a column, Excel displays the overflow characters in adjacent cells to the right as long as those adjacent cells contain no data. If the adjacent cells contain data, Excel would hide the overflow characters. Excel displays the overflow characters in the formula bar whenever that cell is the active cell.

Figure 1–7

4

- Click cell A2 to select it.

- Type `Lifetime Fundraising Summary` as the cell entry.

- Click the Enter box to complete the entry and enter a worksheet subtitle (Figure 1–8).

Q&A What happens when I click the Enter box?

When you complete an entry by clicking the Enter box, the insertion point disappears and the cell in which the text is entered remains the active cell.

Figure 1–8

Other Ways		
1. To complete entry, click any cell other than active cell	3. To complete entry, press HOME, PAGE UP, PAGE DOWN, or END	LEFT ARROW, or RIGHT ARROW.
2. To complete entry, press ENTER	4. To complete entry, press UP ARROW, DOWN ARROW,	

AutoCorrect

The **AutoCorrect feature** of Excel works behind the scenes, correcting common mistakes when you complete a text entry in a cell. AutoCorrect makes three types of corrections for you:

1. Corrects two initial capital letters by changing the second letter to lowercase.

2. Capitalizes the first letter in the names of days.

3. Replaces commonly misspelled words with their correct spelling. For example, it will change the misspelled word *recieve* to *receive* when you complete the entry. AutoCorrect will correct the spelling of hundreds of commonly misspelled words automatically.

BTW

Q&As
For a complete list of the Q&As found in many of the step-by-step sequences in this book, visit the Excel 2010 Q&A Web page (scsite.com/ex2010/qa).

To Enter Column Titles

The column titles in row 3 (Allentown, Chamber City, Pattonsville, Sable Village, Strongville, Town of Cary, and Total) identify the numbers in each column. In the case of the Save the Sable River Foundation data, the cities identify the funds raised using each fundraising type. The cities, therefore, are placed in columns. To enter the column titles in row 3, select the appropriate cell and then enter the text. The following steps enter the column titles in row 3.

- Click cell B3 to make it the active cell (Figure 1–9).

Figure 1–9

- Type **Allentown** to begin entry of a column title in the active cell (Figure 1–10).

Figure 1–10

3

- Press the RIGHT ARROW key to enter a column title and make the cell to the right the active cell (Figure 1–11).

Q&A

Why is the RIGHT ARROW key used to complete the entry in the cell?

If the next entry you want to enter is in an adjacent cell, use the arrow keys to complete the entry in a cell. When you press an arrow key to complete an entry, the adjacent cell in the direction of the arrow (up, down, left, or right) becomes the active cell. If the next entry is in a nonadjacent cell, complete the current entry by clicking the next cell in which you plan to enter data. You also can click the Enter box or press the ENTER key and then click the appropriate cell for the next entry.

Figure 1–11

4

- Repeat Steps 2 and 3 to enter the remaining column titles; that is, enter **Chamber City** in cell C3, **Pattonsville** in cell D3, **Sable Village** in cell E3, **Strongville** in cell F3, **Town of Cary** in cell G3, and **Total** in cell H3 (complete the last entry in cell H3 by clicking the Enter box in the formula bar) (Figure 1–12).

Figure 1–12

To Enter Row Titles

The next step in developing the worksheet for this project is to enter the row titles in column A. For the Save Sable River Foundation data, the list of fundraising activities meets the criterion that information that identifies columns be in a list. It is more likely that in the future, the organization will add more fundraising activities as opposed to more cities. Each fundraising activity, therefore, should be placed in its own row. The row titles in column A (Corporate, Direct Mail, Fun Runs, Government, Phone-a-thon, and Total) identify the numbers in each row.

This process for entering row titles is similar to the process for entering column titles. The following steps enter the row titles in the worksheet.

1

- Click cell A4 to select it.

- Type **Corporate** and then press the DOWN ARROW key to enter a row title and to make the cell below the current cell the active cell (Figure 1–13).

Figure 1–13

2

- Repeat Step 1 to enter the remaining row titles in column A; that is, enter **Direct Mail** in cell A5, **Fun Runs** in cell A6, **Government** in cell A7, **Phone-a-thon** in cell A8, and **Total** in cell A9 (Figure 1–14).

Q&A

Why is the text left-aligned in the cells?

When you enter text, Excel automatically left-aligns the text in the cell. Excel treats any combination of numbers, spaces, and nonnumeric characters as text. For example, Excel recognizes the following entries as text:

401AX21, 921–231, 619 321, 883XTY

You can change the text alignment in a cell by realigning it. Other alignment techniques are discussed later in this chapter.

Figure 1–14

Entering Numbers

In Excel, you can enter numbers into cells to represent amounts. A **number** can contain only the following characters:

0 1 2 3 4 5 6 7 8 9 + - ( ) , / . $ % E e

If a cell entry contains any other keyboard character (including spaces), Excel interprets the entry as text and treats it accordingly. The use of the special characters is explained when they are used in this book.

BTW

Numeric Limitations
In Excel, a number can be between approximately –1 × 10308 and 1 × 10308. This means it can be between a negative 1 followed by 308 zeros and a positive 1 followed by 308 zeros. To enter a number such as 6,000,000,000,000,000, you can type 6,000,000,000,000,000, or you can type 6E15, which translates to 6 × 1015.

To Enter Numbers

The Save Sable River Foundation Lifetime Fundraising Summary numbers used in Chapter 1 are summarized in Table 1–1. These numbers, which represent lifetime fundraising amounts for each of the fundraising activities and cities, must be entered in rows 4, 5, 6, 7, and 8.

Table 1–1 Save Sable River Foundation Lifetime Fundraising Summary						
	Allentown	**Chamber City**	**Pattonsville**	**Sable Village**	**Strongville**	**Town of Cary**
Corporate	74029.35	92278.21	63081.74	84210.02	61644.26	89820.51
Direct Mail	67286.06	83867.23	55076.48	55547.28	79779.02	84366.19
Fun Runs	54704.39	66934.67	64581.66	28895.86	32690.37	64242.72
Government	30623.99	58614.35	51486.46	36387.09	51642.55	40177.87
Phone-a-thon	16692.14	24223.81	9492.91	17328.74	12305.85	21097.60

The following steps enter the numbers in Table 1–1 one row at a time.

- Click cell B4 to select it.

- Type **74029.35** and then press the RIGHT ARROW key to enter the data in the selected cell and make the cell to the right the active cell (Figure 1–15).

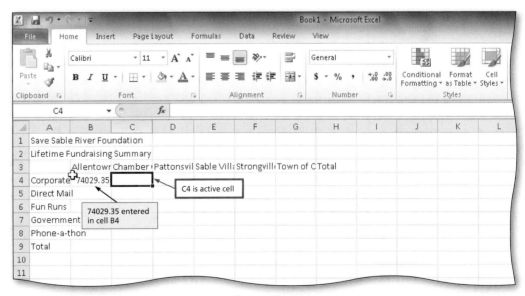

Figure 1–15

Q&A

Do I need to enter dollar signs, commas, or trailing zeros for the fundraising summary amounts?

You are not required to type dollar signs, commas, or trailing zeros. When you enter a dollar value that has cents, however, you must add the decimal point and the numbers representing the cents. Later in this chapter, the numbers will be formatted to use dollar signs, commas, and trailing zeros to improve the appearance and readability of the numbers.

2

- Enter 92278.21 in cell C4, 63081.74 in cell D4, 84210.02 in cell E4, 61644.26 in cell F4, and 89820.51 in cell G4 to complete the first row of numbers in the worksheet (Figure 1–16).

Q&A Why are the numbers right-aligned?

When you enter numeric data in a cell, Excel recognizes the values as numbers and right-aligns the values in order to properly vertically align decimal and integer values. For example, values entered below those entered in this step automatically will be right-aligned as well so that the decimals of the values properly align.

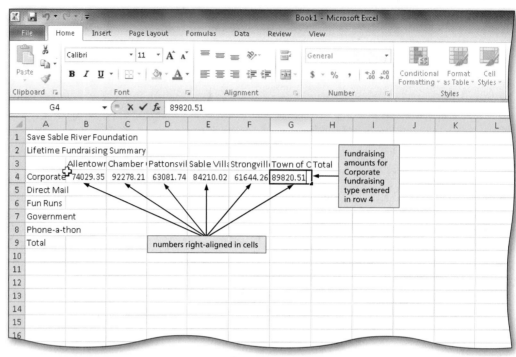

Figure 1–16

3

- Click cell B5 to select it and complete the entry in the previously selected cell.

- Enter the remaining lifetime fundraising summary numbers provided in Table 1–1 on page EX 13 for each of the four remaining fundraising activities in rows 5, 6, 7, and 8 to finish entering numbers in the worksheet (Figure 1–17).

Q&A Why did clicking cell B5 complete the entry in cell G4?

Selecting another cell completes the entry in the previously selected cell in the same way as pressing the ENTER key, pressing an arrow key, or clicking the Enter box on the formula bar. In the next set of steps, the entry of the number in cell G4 will be completed by selecting another cell.

Figure 1–17

Calculating a Sum

The next step in creating the worksheet is to perform any necessary calculations, such as calculating the column and row totals.

To Sum a Column of Numbers

As stated in the requirements document in Figure 1–2 on page EX 4, totals are required for each city, each fundraising activity, and the organization. The first calculation is to determine the fundraising total for the fundraising activities in the city of Allentown in column B. To calculate this value in cell B9, Excel must add, or sum, the numbers in cells B4, B5, B6, B7, and B8. Excel's **SUM function**, which adds all of the numbers in a range of cells, provides a convenient means to accomplish this task.

A **range** is a series of two or more adjacent cells in a column or row or a rectangular group of cells. For example, the group of adjacent cells B4, B5, B6, B7, and B8 is called a range. Many Excel operations, such as summing numbers, take place on a range of cells.

After the total lifetime fundraising amount for the fundraising activities in the city of Allentown in column B is determined, the totals for the remaining cities and totals for each fundraising activity will be determined. The following steps sum the numbers in column B.

1
- Click cell B9 to make it the active cell and complete the entry in the previously selected cell.

- Click the Sum button (Home tab | Editing group) to display a formula in the formula bar and in the active cell (Figure 1–18).

Figure 1–18

Q&A How does Excel know which cells to sum?

When you enter the SUM function using the Sum button, Excel automatically selects what it considers to be your choice of the range to sum. When proposing the range to sum, Excel first looks for a range of cells with numbers above the active cell and then to the left. If Excel proposes the wrong range, you can correct it by dragging through the correct range before pressing the ENTER key. You also can enter the correct range by typing the beginning cell reference, a colon (:), and the ending cell reference.

BTW **Calculating Sums**
Excel calculates sums for a variety of data types. For example, Boolean values, such as TRUE and FALSE, can be summed. Excel treats the value of TRUE as 1 and the value of FALSE as 0. Times also can be summed. For example, Excel treats the sum of 1:15 and 2:45 as 4:00.

2

- Click the Enter box in the formula bar to enter a sum in the active cell (Figure 1–19).

Q&A

What is the purpose of the Sum button arrow?

If you click the Sum button arrow on the right side of the Sum button (Home tab | Editing group) (Figure 1–19), Excel displays a list of often used functions from which you can choose. The list includes functions

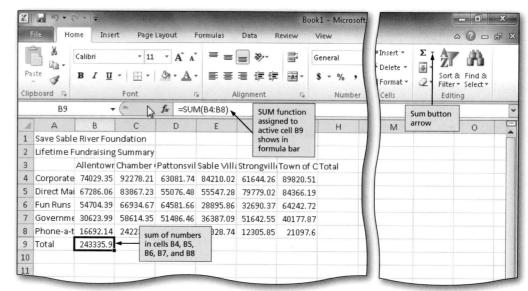

Figure 1–19

that allow you to determine the average, the number of items in the selected range, the maximum value, or the minimum value of a range of numbers.

Other Ways

1. Click Insert Function button in the formula bar, select SUM in Select a function list, click OK button, select range, click OK button

2. Click Sum button arrow (Home tab | Editing group), click More Functions, select SUM (Insert Function dialog box), click OK button, select range, click OK button

3. Type = s in cell, select SUM from list, select range

4. Press ALT + EQUAL SIGN (=) twice

BTW

Entering Numbers as Text
Sometimes, you will want Excel to treat numbers, such as postal codes and telephone numbers, as text. To enter a number as text, start the entry with an apostrophe (').

Using the Fill Handle to Copy a Cell to Adjacent Cells

Excel also must calculate the totals for Chamber City in cell C9, Pattonsville in cell D9, Sable Village in cell E9, Strongville in cell F9, and the Town of Cary in cell G9. Table 1–2 illustrates the similarities between the entry in cell B9 and the entries required to sum the totals in cells C9, D9, E9, F9 and G9.

Table 1–2 Sum Function Entries in Row 9		
Cell	**Sum Function Entries**	**Remark**
B9	=SUM(B4:B8)	Sums cells B4, B5, B6, B7, and B8
C9	=SUM(C4:C8)	Sums cells C4, C5, C6, C7, and C8
D9	=SUM(D4:D8)	Sums cells D4, D5, D6, D7, and D8
E9	=SUM(E4:E8)	Sums cells E4, E5, E6, E7, and E8
F9	=SUM(F4:F8)	Sums cells F4, F5, F6, F7, and F8
G9	=SUM(G4:G8)	Sums cells G4, G5, G6, G7, and G8

To place the SUM functions in cells C9, D9, E9, F9, and G9, you could follow the same steps shown previously in Figures 1–18 on page EX 15 and 1–19. A second, more efficient method, however, is to copy the SUM function from cell B9 to the range C9:G9. The cell being copied is called the **source area** or **copy area**. The range of cells receiving the copy is called the **destination area** or **paste area**.

Although the SUM function entries in Table 1–2 are similar, they are not exact copies. The range in each SUM function entry uses cell references that are one column to the right of the previous column. When you copy formulas that include cell references, Excel automatically adjusts them for each new position, resulting in the SUM function entries illustrated in Table 1–2. Each adjusted cell reference is called a **relative reference**.

To Copy a Cell to Adjacent Cells in a Row

The easiest way to copy the SUM formula from cell B9 to cells C9, D9, E9, F9, and G9 is to use the fill handle. The **fill handle** is the small black square located in the lower-right corner of the heavy border around the active cell. The following steps use the fill handle to copy cell B9 to the adjacent cells C9:G9.

1

- With cell B9 active, point to the fill handle to activate it (Figure 1–20).

Figure 1–20

2

- Drag the fill handle to select the destination area, range C9:G9, to display a shaded border around the source area and the destination area (Figure 1–21). Do not release the mouse button.

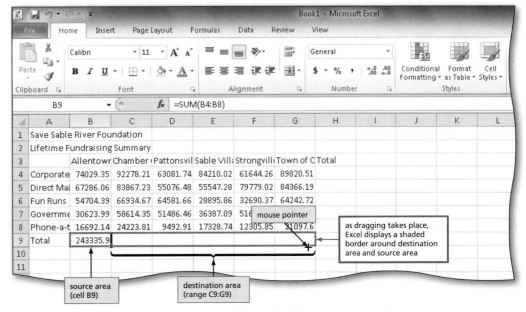

Figure 1–21

3

• Release the mouse button to copy the SUM function from the active cell to the destination area and calculate the sums (Figure 1–22).

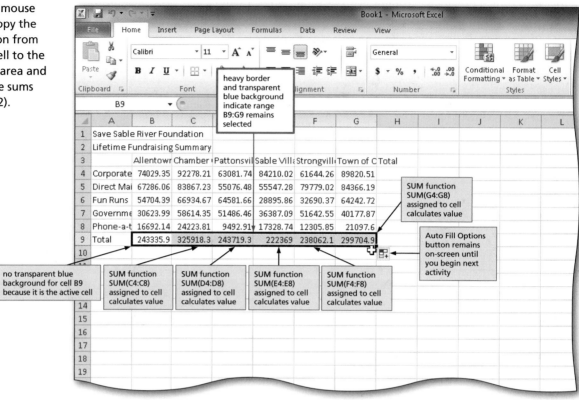

Figure 1–22

Q&A

What is the purpose of the Auto Fill Options button?

When you copy one range to another, Excel displays an Auto Fill Options button (Figure 1–22). The Auto Fill Options button allows you to choose whether you want to copy the values from the source area to the destination area with formatting, do so without formatting, or copy only the format. To view the available fill options, click the Auto Fill Options button. The Auto Fill Options button disappears when you begin another activity in Excel, such as typing data in another cell or applying formatting to a cell or range of cells.

Other Ways
1. Select source area, click Copy button (Home tab | Clipboard group), select destination area, click Paste button (Home tab | Clipboard group)	2. Right-click source area, click Copy on shortcut menu, right-click destination area, click Paste on shortcut menu	3. Select source area and then point to border of range; while holding down CTRL, drag source area to destination area

To Determine Multiple Totals at the Same Time

The next step in building the worksheet is to determine the lifetime fundraising totals for each fundraising activity and total lifetime fundraising for the organization in column H. To calculate these totals, you can use the SUM function much as it was used to total the lifetime fundraising amounts by city in row 9. In this example, however, Excel will determine totals for all of the rows at the same time. The following steps sum multiple totals at once.

1

- Click cell H4 to make it the active cell (Figure 1–23).

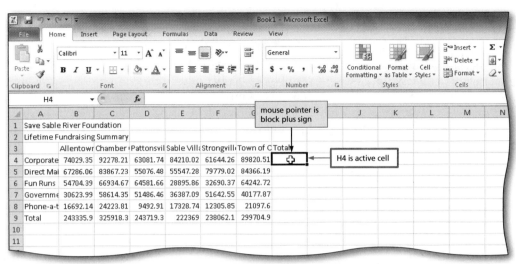

Figure 1–23

2

- With the mouse pointer in cell H4 and in the shape of a block plus sign, drag the mouse pointer down to cell H9 to highlight the range with a transparent view (Figure 1–24).

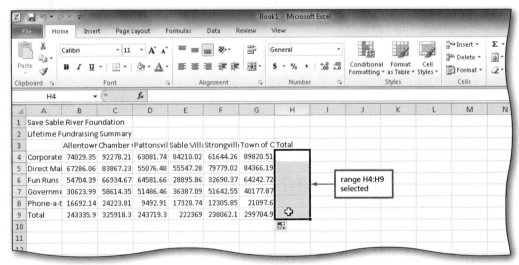

Figure 1–24

3

- Click the Sum button (Home tab | Editing group) to calculate and display the sums of the corresponding rows (Figure 1–25).

- Select cell A10 to deselect the selected range.

Q&A

How does Excel create unique totals for each row?

If each cell in a selected range is next to a row of numbers, Excel assigns the SUM function to each cell when you click the Sum button.

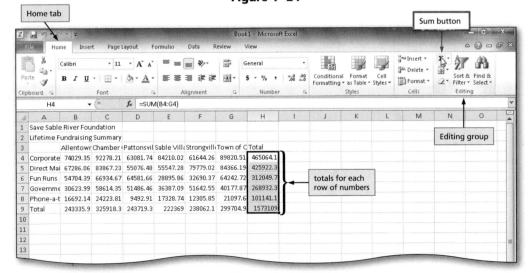

Figure 1–25

BTW

Organizing Files and Folders

You should organize and store files in folders so that you easily can find the files later. For example, if you are taking an introductory computer class called CIS 101, a good practice would be to save all Excel files in an Excel folder in a CIS 101 folder. For a discussion of folders and detailed examples of creating folders, refer to the Office 2010 and Windows 7 chapter at the beginning of this book.

To Save a Workbook

You have performed many tasks while creating this workbook and do not want to risk losing work completed thus far. Accordingly, you should save the workbook.

The following steps assume you already have created folders for storing your files, for example, a CIS 101 folder (for your class) that contains an Excel folder (for your assignments). Thus, these steps save the workbook in the Excel folder in the CIS 101 folder on a USB flash drive using the file name, Save Sable River Foundation. For a detailed example of the procedure summarized below, refer to the Office 2010 and Windows 7 chapter at the beginning of this book.

1 With a USB flash drive connected to one of the computer's USB ports, click the Save button on the Quick Access Toolbar to display the Save As dialog box.

2 Type `Save Sable River Foundation` in the File name text box to change the file name. Do not press the ENTER key after typing the file name because you do not want to close the dialog box at this time.

3 Navigate to the desired save location (in this case, the Excel folder in the CIS 101 folder [or your class folder] on the USB flash drive).

4 Click the Save button (Save As dialog box) to save the document in the selected folder on the selected drive with the entered file name.

Break Point: If you wish to take a break, this is a good place to do so. You can quit Excel. To resume at a later time, start Excel, open the file called Save Sable River Foundation, and continue following the steps from this location forward.

AutoRecover

The AutoRecover feature of Excel, sometimes called AutoSave, allows you to specify how often and where Excel automatically saves workbooks. If your computer loses power, becomes unusable while you are interacting with a workbook, or you forget to save a workbook before closing it, Excel notifies you if there are workbooks that were automatically saved when one of these events occurred. You view and change AutoRecover options by clicking the Options button in the Backstage view and then clicking Save in the left panel of the Excel Options dialog box.

Plan Ahead

Formatting the Worksheet

The text, numeric entries, and functions for the worksheet now are complete. The next step is to format the worksheet. You **format** a worksheet to emphasize certain entries and make the worksheet easier to read and understand.

Figure 1–26a shows the worksheet before formatting. Figure 1–26b shows the worksheet after formatting. As you can see from the two figures, a worksheet that is formatted not only is easier to read but also looks more professional.

Identify how to format various elements of the worksheet.
By formatting the contents of the worksheet, you can improve its overall appearance. When formatting a worksheet, consider the following formatting suggestions:

- **Increase the font size of cells.** An increased font size gives more impact to the text in a cell. In order to indicate their relative importance, worksheet titles should have the largest font size, followed by worksheet subtitles, and then column and row headings.

- **Change the font color of cells.** Different cell colors help the reader of a worksheet quickly differentiate between the sections of a worksheet. Worksheet titles and subtitles easily should be identifiable from column and row headings. The overuse of too many colors, however, may be distracting to the reader of a worksheet.

- **Center the worksheet titles, subtitles, and column headings.** Centering text in worksheet titles and subtitles over the portion of the worksheet that they represent helps the reader of a worksheet quickly to identify the information that is of interest to them.

(continued)

(continued)

- **Modify column widths to best fit text in cells.** Make certain that text in a cell does not overflow into another cell. A column's width should be adjusted to accommodate the largest amount of text used in a cell in the column. Columns that contain data that is similar in nature to other columns should share the same column width.

- **Change the font style of cells.** Use a bold font style to make worksheet titles, worksheet subtitles, column headings, row heading, and totals stand out. Use italics and underline font styles judiciously, as specific rules of grammar apply to their use.

Plan Ahead

Figure 1–26 (a) Before Formatting

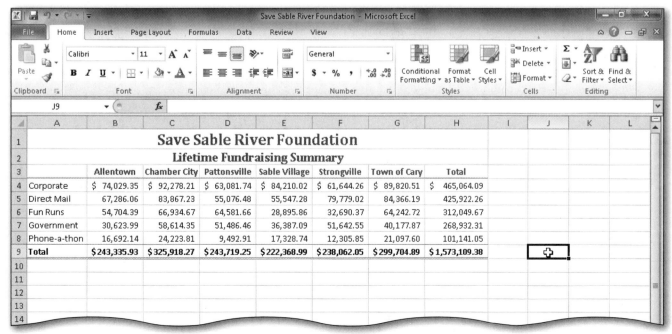

Figure 1–26 (b) After Formatting

To change the unformatted worksheet in Figure 1–26a on the previous page to the formatted worksheet in Figure 1–26b on the previous page, the following tasks must be completed:

1. Change the font, change the font style to bold, increase the font size, and change the font color of the worksheet titles in cells A1 and A2.

2. Center the worksheet titles in cells A1 and A2 across columns A through H.

3. Format the body of the worksheet. The body of the worksheet, range A3:H9, includes the column titles, row titles, and numbers. Formatting the body of the worksheet changes the numbers to use a dollars-and-cents format, with dollar signs in the first row (row 4) and the total row (row 9); adds underlining that emphasizes portions of the worksheet; and modifies the column widths to fit the text in the columns and make the text and numbers readable.

The remainder of this section explains the process required to format the worksheet. Although the formatting procedures are explained in the order described above, you should be aware that you could make these format changes in any order. Modifying the column widths, however, usually is done last because other formatting changes may affect the size of data in the cells in the column.

Font, Style, Size, and Color

The characters that Excel displays on the screen are a specific font, style, size, and color. The **font**, or font face, defines the appearance and shape of the letters, numbers, and special characters. Examples of fonts include Calibri, Cambria, Times New Roman, Arial, and Courier. **Font style** indicates how the characters are emphasized. Common font styles include regular, bold, underline, and italic. The **font size** specifies the size of the characters on the screen. Font size is gauged by a measurement system called points. A single point is about 1/72 of one inch in height. Thus, a character with a **point size** of 10 is about 10/72 of one inch in height. The **font color** defines the color of the characters. Excel can display characters in a wide variety of colors, including black, red, orange, and blue.

When Excel begins, the preset font for the entire workbook is Calibri, with a font size, font style, and font color of 11–point regular black. Excel allows you to change the font characteristics in a single cell, a range of cells, the entire worksheet, or the entire workbook.

To Change a Cell Style

Excel includes the capability of changing several characteristics of a cell, such the font, font size, and font color, all at once by assigning a predefined cell style to a cell. Using the predefined styles that Excel includes provides a consistent appearance to common portions of your worksheets, such as worksheet titles, worksheet subtitles, column headings, and total rows. The following steps assign the Title cell style to the worksheet title in cell A1.

1

- Click cell A1 to make cell A1 the active cell.

- Click the Cell Styles button (Home tab | Styles group) to display the Cell Styles gallery (Figure 1–27).

Figure 1–27

2

- Point to the Title cell style in the Titles and Headings area of the Cell Styles gallery to see a live preview of the cell style in the active cell (Figure 1–28).

Experiment

- Point to several other cell styles in the Cell Styles gallery to see a live preview of other cell styles in cell A1.

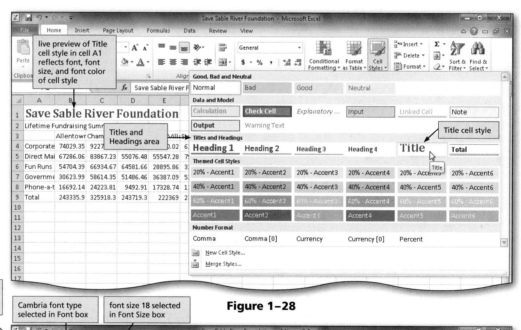

Figure 1–28

3

- Click the Title cell style to apply the cell style to the active cell (Figure 1–29).

Q&A

Why do several items in the Font group on the Ribbon change?

The changes to the Font box, Bold button, and Font Size box indicate the font changes applied to the active cell, cell A1, as a result of applying the Title cell style.

Figure 1–29

To Change the Font

Different fonts often are used in a worksheet to make it more appealing to the reader and to relate or distinguish data in the worksheet. The following steps change the worksheet subtitle's fonts from Calibri to Cambria.

1

- Click cell A2 to make it the active cell.

- Click the Font box arrow (Home tab | Font group) to display the Font gallery (Figure 1–30).

Q&A

Which fonts are displayed in the Font gallery?

Because many programs supply additional fonts beyond what comes with the Windows 7 operating system, the number of fonts available on your computer will depend on the programs installed. This book uses only fonts that come with the Windows 7 operating system and Microsoft Office 2010.

Figure 1–30

2

- Point to Cambria in the Theme Fonts area of the Font gallery to see a live preview of the selected font in the active cell (Figure 1–31).

Experiment

- Point to several other fonts in the Font gallery to see a live preview of other fonts in the selected cell.

Q&A

What is the Theme Fonts area?

Excel applies the same default theme to any new workbook that you start. A **theme** is a collection of cell styles and other styles that have common characteristics, such as a color scheme and font. The default theme for an Excel workbook is the Office theme. The Theme Fonts area of the Font gallery includes the fonts included in the default Office theme. Cambria is recommended for headings and Calibri is recommended by Microsoft for cells in the body of the worksheet (Figure 1–31).

Figure 1–31

❸

- Click Cambria in the Theme Fonts area to change the font of the worksheet subtitle to Cambria (Figure 1–32).

Figure 1–32

To Bold a Cell

You **bold** an entry in a cell to emphasize it or make it stand out from the rest of the worksheet. The following step bolds the worksheet subtitle in cell A2.

❶

- With cell A2 active, click the Bold button (Home tab | Font group) to change the font style of the active cell to bold (Figure 1–33).

Q&A What if a cell already includes a bold style?

If the active cell is already bold, then Excel displays the Bold button with a transparent orange background.

Q&A How do I remove the bold style from a cell?

Clicking the Bold button (Home tab | Font group) a second time removes the bold font style.

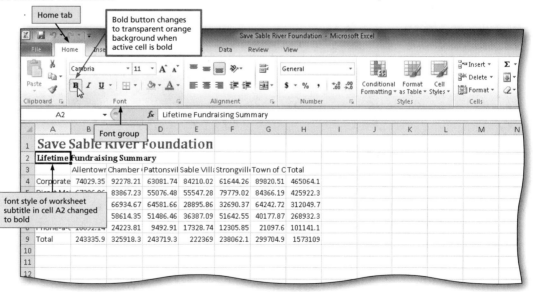

Figure 1–33

To Increase the Font Size of a Cell Entry

Increasing the font size is the next step in formatting the worksheet subtitle. You increase the font size of a cell so that the entry stands out and is easier to read. The following steps increase the font size of the worksheet subtitle in cell A2.

1

- With cell A2 selected, click the Font Size box arrow (Home tab | Font group) to display the Font Size list.

- Point to 14 in the Font Size list to see a live preview of the active cell with the selected font size (Figure 1–34).

 Experiment

- Point to several other font sizes in the Font Size list to see a live preview of other font sizes in the selected cell.

Figure 1–34

2

- Click 14 in the Font Size list to change the font size in the active cell (Figure 1–35).

 Can I assign a font size that is not in the Font Size list?

Yes. An alternative to clicking a font size in the Font Size list is to click the Font Size box (Home tab | Font group), type the font size, and then press the ENTER key. This procedure allows you to assign a font size not available in the Font Size list to a selected cell entry.

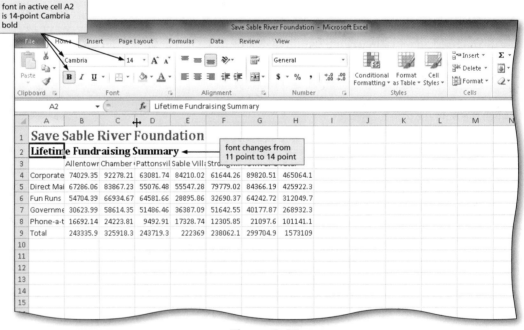

Figure 1–35

Other Ways

1. Click Increase Font Size button (Home tab | Font group) or Decrease Font Size button (Home tab | Font group)

2. Click Font Size box arrow on Mini toolbar, click desired font size in Font Size gallery

3. Right-click cell, click Format Cells on shortcut menu, click Font tab (Format Cells dialog box), select font size in Size box, click OK button

Excel Chapter 1

To Change the Font Color of a Cell Entry

The next step is to change the color of the font in cell A2 from black to dark blue. The following steps change the font color of a cell entry.

- With cell A2 selected, click the Font Color button arrow (Home tab | Font group) to display the Font Color gallery.

- Point to Dark Blue, Text 2 (dark blue color in column 4, row 1) in the Theme Colors area of the Font Color gallery to see a live preview of the font color in the active cell (Figure 1–36).

Experiment

- Point to several other colors in the Font Color gallery to see a live preview of other font colors in the active cell.

Q&A
Which colors does Excel make available on the Font Color gallery?

You can choose from more than 60 different font colors on the Font Color gallery (Figure 1–36). Your Font Color gallery may have more or fewer colors, depending on color settings of your operating system. The Theme Colors area includes colors that are included in the current workbook's theme.

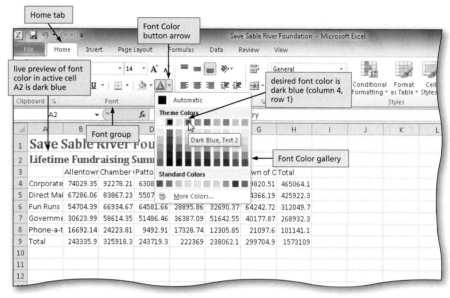

Figure 1–36

2

- Click Dark Blue, Text 2 (column 4, row 1) on the Font Color gallery to change the font of the worksheet subtitle in the active cell (Figure 1–37).

Q&A
Why does the Font Color button change after I select the new font color?

When you choose a color on the Font Color gallery, Excel changes the Font Color button (Home tab | Font group) to the chosen color. Thus, to change the font color of the cell entry in another cell to the same color, you need only to select the cell and then click the Font Color button (Home tab | Font group).

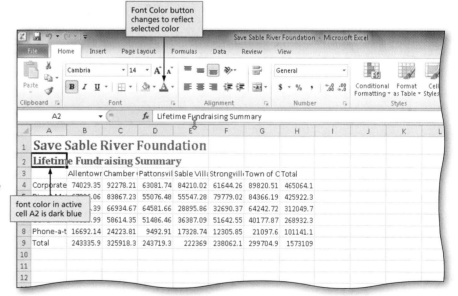

Figure 1–37

Other Ways

1. Click Font Color box arrow on Mini toolbar, click desired font color in the Font Color gallery

2. Right-click cell, click Format Cells on shortcut menu, click Font tab (Format Cells dialog box), select color in Font Color gallery, click OK button

To Center Cell Entries Across Columns by Merging Cells

The final step in formatting the worksheet title and subtitle is to center them across columns A through H. Centering a title across the columns used in the body of the worksheet improves the worksheet's appearance. To do this, the eight cells in the range A1:H1 are combined, or merged, into a single cell that is the width of the columns in the body of the worksheet. The eight cells in the range A2:H2 are merged in a similar manner. **Merging cells** involves creating a single cell by combining two or more selected cells. The following steps center the worksheet title and subtitle across columns by merging cells.

1

• Select cell A1 and then drag to cell H1 to highlight the range to be merged and centered (Figure 1–38).

Q&A

What if a cell in the range B1:H1 contains data?

For the Merge & Center button (Home tab | Alignment group) to work properly, all the cells except the leftmost cell in the selected range must be empty.

Figure 1–38

2

• Click the Merge & Center button (Home tab | Alignment group) to merge cells A1 through H1 and center the contents of the leftmost cell across the selected columns (Figure 1–39).

Q&A

What happened to cells B1 through H1?

After the merge, cells B1 through H1 no longer exist. The new cell A1 now extends across columns A through H.

Figure 1–39

3

- Repeat Steps 1 and 2 to merge and center the worksheet subtitle across cells A2 through H2 (Figure 1–40).

Q&A

Are cells B1 through H1 and B2 through H2 lost forever?

No. The opposite of merging cells is **splitting a merged cell**. After you have merged multiple cells to create one merged cell, you can unmerge, or split, the merged cell to display the original cells on the

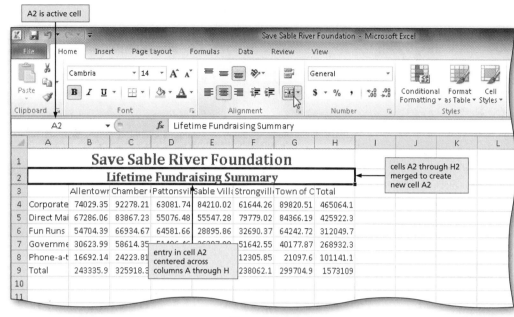

Figure 1–40

worksheet. You split a merged cell by selecting it and clicking the Merge & Center button. For example, if you click the Merge & Center button a second time in Step 2, it will split the merged cell A1 into cells A1, B1, C1, D1, E1, F1, G1, and H1.

Other Ways

1. Right-click selection, click Merge & Center button on Mini toolbar

2. Right-click selection, click Format Cells on shortcut menu, click Alignment tab (Format Cells dialog box), select Center Across Selection in Horizontal list, click OK button

---

To Format Column Titles and the Total Row

The next step to format the worksheet is to format the column titles in row 3 and the total values in row 9. Column titles and the total row should be formatted so anyone who views the worksheet quickly can distinguish the column titles and total row from the data in the body of the worksheet. The following steps format the column titles and total row using cell styles in the default worksheet theme.

1

- Click cell A3 and then drag the mouse pointer to cell H3 to select a range (Figure 1–41).

Q&A

Why is cell A3 selected in the range for the column headings?

The style to be applied to the column headings includes an underline that will help to distinguish the column headings from the rest of the worksheet. Including cell A3 in the range ensures that the cell will include the underline, which is visually

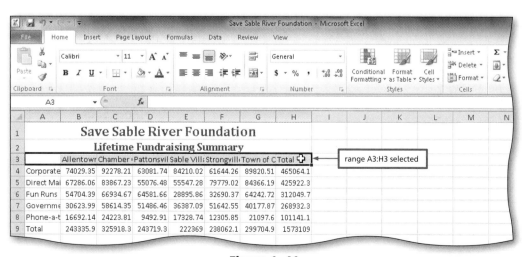

Figure 1–41

appealing and further helps to separate the data in the worksheet.

2

- Click the Cell Styles button (Home tab | Styles group) to display the Cell Styles gallery.

- Point to the Heading 3 cell style in the Titles and Headings area of the Cell Styles gallery to see a live preview of the cell style in the selected range (Figure 1–42).

Figure 1–42

- Point to other cell styles in the Titles and Headings area of the Cell Styles gallery to see a live preview of other cell styles in the selected range, A3:H3.

3

- Click the Heading 3 cell style to apply the cell style to the selected range.

- Click the Center button (Home tab | Alignment group) to center the column headings in the selected range.

- Click cell A9 and then drag the mouse pointer to cell H9 to select a range (Figure 1–43).

Figure 1–43

Q&A Why should I choose Heading 3 instead of another heading cell style?

Excel includes many types of headings, such as Heading 1 and Heading 2, because worksheets often include many levels of headings above columns. In the case of the worksheet created for this project, the Heading 3 title includes formatting that makes the column titles' font size smaller than the title and subtitle and makes the column titles stand out from the data in the body of the worksheet.

4

- Click the Cell Styles button (Home tab | Styles group) to display the Cell Styles gallery and then click the Total cell style in the Titles and Headings area to apply the selected cell style to the cells in the selected range.

- Click cell A11 to select it (Figure 1–44).

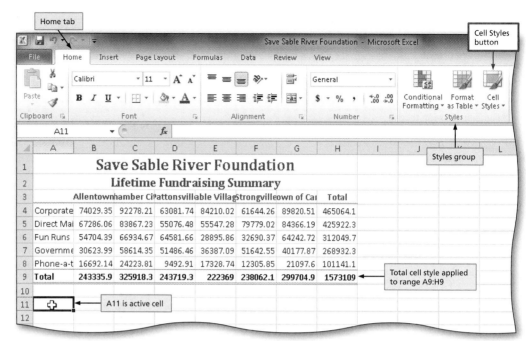

Figure 1–44

To Format Numbers in the Worksheet

As previously noted, the numbers in the worksheet should be formatted to use a dollar-and-cents format, with dollar signs in the first row (row 4) and the total row (row 9). Excel allows you to format numbers in a variety of ways, and these methods are discussed in other chapters in this book. The following steps use buttons on the Ribbon to format the numbers in the worksheet.

1

- Select cell B4 and drag the mouse pointer to cell H4 to select a range (Figure 1–45).

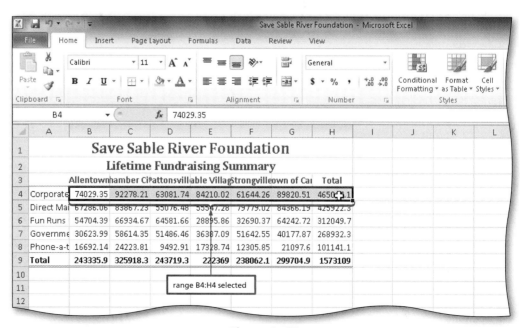

Figure 1–45

2

- Click the Accounting Number Format button (Home tab | Number group) to apply the Accounting Number format to the cells in the selected range.

- Select the range B5:H8 (Figure 1–46).

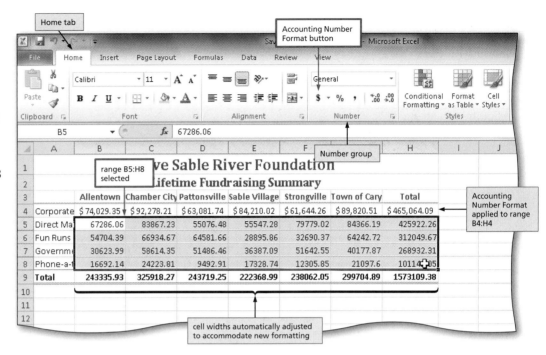

Figure 1–46

Q&A | What effect does the Accounting Number format have on the selected cells?

The Accounting Number format causes the cells to be displayed with two decimal places so that decimal places in cells below the selected cells align vertically. Cell widths are adjusted automatically to accommodate the new formatting.

3

- Click the Comma Style button (Home tab | Number group) to apply the Comma Style format to the selected range.

- Select the range B9:H9 to make it the active range (Figure 1–47).

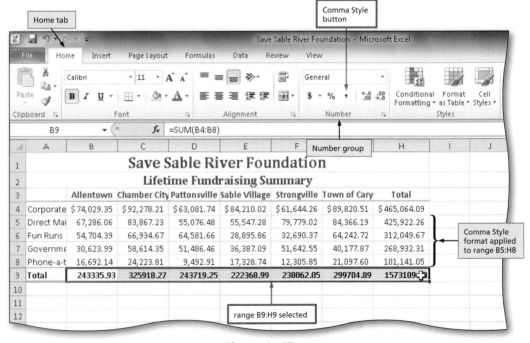

Figure 1–47

Q&A | What effect does the Comma Style format have on the selected cells?

The Comma Style format causes the cells to be displayed with two decimal places and commas as thousands separators.

4

- Click the Accounting Number Format button (Home tab | Number group) to apply the Accounting Number format to the cells in the selected range.

- Select cell A11 (Figure 1–48).

Q&A

Why did the column widths automatically adjust again?

Because the total row contains larger numbers, the Accounting Number format again causes the cell widths automatically to adjust to accommodate the new formatting just as occurred in Step 2.

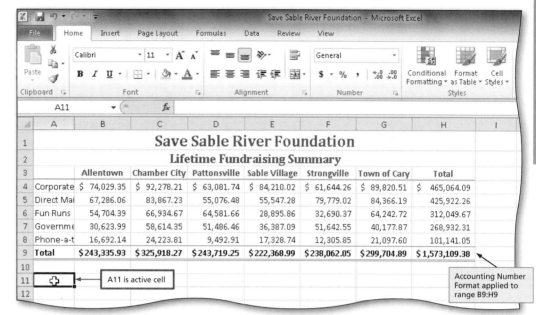

Figure 1–48

Other Ways

1. Click Accounting Number Format or Comma Style button on Mini toolbar

2. Right-click selection, click Format Cells on the shortcut menu, click

Number tab (Format Cells dialog box), select Accounting in Category list or select Number and click Use 1000 Separator, click OK button

---

To Adjust the Column Width

The last step in formatting the worksheet is to adjust the width of column A so that the word Phone-a-thon in cell A8 is shown in its entirety in the cell. Excel includes several methods for adjusting cell widths and row heights, and these methods are discussed later in this book. The following steps adjust the width of column A so that the contents of cell A8 are displayed in the cell.

1

- Point to the boundary on the right side of the column A heading above row 1 to change the mouse pointer to a split double arrow (Figure 1–49).

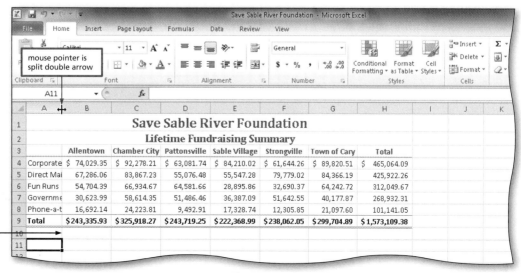

Figure 1–49

2

- Double-click on the boundary to adjust the width of the column to the width of the largest item in the column (Figure 1–50).

Q&A

What if none of the items in column A extends through the entire width of the column?

If all of the items in column A were shorter in length than the width of the column when you double-click the right side of the column A heading, then Excel still would adjust the column width to the largest item in the column. That is, Excel would reduce the width of the column to the largest item.

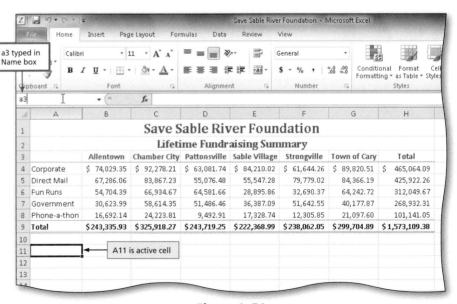

Figure 1–50

Using the Name Box to Select a Cell

The next step is to chart the lifetime fundraising amounts for the five fundraising activities used by the organization. To create the chart, you first must select the cell in the upper-left corner of the range to chart (cell A3). Rather than clicking cell A3 to select it, the next section describes how to use the Name box to select the cell.

To Use the Name Box to Select a Cell

The Name box is located on the left side of the formula bar. To select any cell, click the Name box and enter the cell reference of the cell you want to select. The following steps select cell A3 using the Name box.

1

- Click the Name box in the formula bar and then type **a3** as the cell you wish to select (Figure 1–51).

Q&A

Why is cell A11 still selected?

Even though cell A11 is the active cell, Excel displays the typed cell reference a3 in the Name box until you press the ENTER key.

Figure 1–51

2

- Press the ENTER key to change the active cell in the Name box (Figure 1–52).

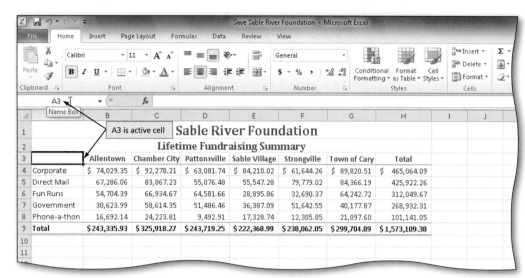

Figure 1–52

Other Ways to Select Cells

As you will see in later chapters, in addition to using the Name box to select any cell in a worksheet, you also can use it to assign names to a cell or range of cells. Excel supports several additional ways to select a cell, as summarized in Table 1–3.

Table 1–3 Selecting Cells in Excel	
Key, Box, or Command	**Function**
ALT+PAGE DOWN	Selects the cell one worksheet window to the right and moves the worksheet window accordingly.
ALT+PAGE UP	Selects the cell one worksheet window to the left and moves the worksheet window accordingly.
ARROW	Selects the adjacent cell in the direction of the arrow on the key.
CTRL+ARROW	Selects the border cell of the worksheet in combination with the arrow keys and moves the worksheet window accordingly. For example, to select the rightmost cell in the row that contains the active cell, press CTRL+RIGHT ARROW. You also can press the END key, release it, and then press the appropriate arrow key to accomplish the same task.
CTRL+HOME	Selects cell A1 or the cell one column and one row below and to the right of frozen titles and moves the worksheet window accordingly.
Find command on Find and Select menu or SHIFT+F5	Finds and selects a cell that contains specific contents that you enter in the Find and Replace dialog box. If necessary, Excel moves the worksheet window to display the cell. You also can press CTRL+F to display the Find dialog box.
Go To command on Find and Select menu or F5	Selects the cell that corresponds to the cell reference you enter in the Go To dialog box and moves the worksheet window accordingly. You also can press CTRL+G to display the Go To dialog box.
HOME	Selects the cell at the beginning of the row that contains the active cell and moves the worksheet window accordingly.
Name box	Selects the cell in the workbook that corresponds to the cell reference you enter in the Name box.
PAGE DOWN	Selects the cell down one worksheet window from the active cell and moves the worksheet window accordingly.
PAGE UP	Selects the cell up one worksheet window from the active cell and moves the worksheet window accordingly.

Break Point: If you wish to take a break, this is a good place to do so. Be sure to save the Save Sable River Foundation file again and then you can quit Excel. To resume at a later time, start Excel, open the file called Save Sable River Foundation, and continue following the steps from this location forward.

Adding a Clustered Cylinder Chart to the Worksheet

As outlined in the requirements document in Figure 1–2 on page EX 4, the worksheet should include a Clustered Cylinder chart to graphically represent the lifetime fundraising for each fundraising activity in which the organization engages. The Clustered Cylinder chart shown in Figure 1–53 is called an **embedded chart** because it is drawn on the same worksheet as the data.

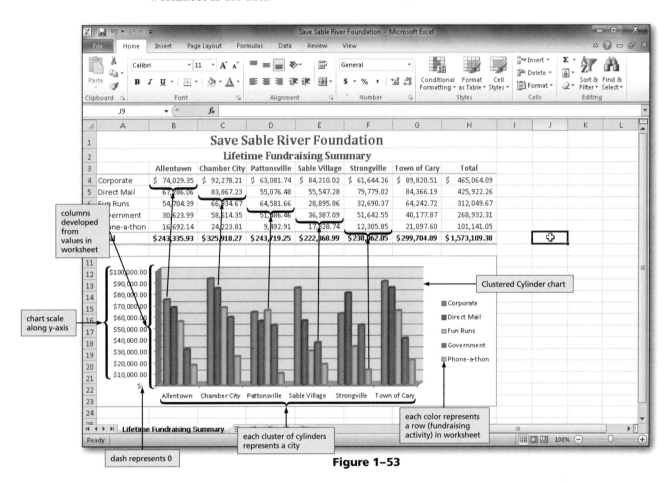

Figure 1–53

Plan Ahead

Decide on the type of chart needed.

Excel includes 11 chart types from which you can choose, including column, line, pie, bar, area, X Y (scatter), stock, surface, doughnut, bubble, and radar. The type of chart you choose depends on the type of data that you have, how much data you have, and the message you want to convey.

A line chart often is used to illustrate changes in data over time. Pie charts show the contribution of each piece of data to the whole, or total, of the data. Area charts, like line charts, illustrate changes over time, but often are used to compare more than one set of data and the area under the lines is filled in with a different color for each set of data. An X Y (scatter) chart is used much line a line chart, but each piece of data is represented by a dot and is not connected with a line. A stock chart provides a number of methods commonly

(continued)

(continued)

used in the financial industry to show stock market data. A surface chart compares data from three columns and/or rows in a three-dimensional manner. A doughnut chart is much like a pie chart, but a doughnut chart allows for comparing more than one set of data, resulting in a chart that looks like a doughnut, with each subsequent set of data surrounding the previous set. A bubble chart is much like an X Y (scatter) chart, but a third set of data results indicates how large each individual dot, or bubble, is on the chart. A radar chart can compare several sets of data in a manner that resembles a radar screen, with each set of data represented by a different color. A column or cylinder chart is a good way to compare values side by side. A Clustered Cylinder chart can go even further in comparing values across categories.

Establish where to position and how to format the chart.

- When possible, try to position charts so that both the data and chart appear on the screen on the worksheet together and so that the data and chart can be printed in the most readable manner possible.

- When choosing/selecting colors for a chart, consider the color scheme of the rest of the worksheet. The chart should not present colors that are in stark contrast to the rest of the worksheet. If the chart will be printed in color, minimize the amount of dark colors on the chart so that the chart both prints quickly and conserves ink.

Plan Ahead

BTW

Cell Values and Charting
When you change a cell value on which a chart is dependent, Excel redraws the chart instantaneously, unless automatic recalculation is disabled. If automatic recalculation is disabled, then you must press the F9 key to redraw the chart. To enable or disable automatic recalculation, click the Calculations Options button (Formulas tab | Calculation group).

In the case of the Save Sable River Foundation Lifetime Fundraising Summary, comparisons of fundraising activities within each city can be made side by side with a Clustered Cylinder chart. The chart uses differently colored cylinders to represent amounts raised for different fundraising activities. Each city uses the same color scheme for identifying fundraising activities, which allows for easy identification and comparison.

- For the city of Allentown, for example, the dark blue cylinder representing Corporate donations shows lifetime donations of $74,029.35

- For Chamber City, the maroon cylinder representing Direct Mail donations shows lifetime donations of $83,867.23

- For the city of Pattonsville, the lime green cylinder representing donations for Fun Runs shows lifetime donations of $64,581.66

- For Sable Village, the purple cylinder representing Government donations shows lifetime donations of $36,387.09

- For the city of Strongville, the light blue cylinder representing Phone-a-thon donations shows lifetime donations of $12,305.85

Because the same color scheme is used in each city to represent the five fundraising activities, you easily can compare funds raised by each fundraising activity among the cities. The totals from the worksheet are not represented, because the totals are not in the range specified for charting.

Excel derives the chart scale based on the values in the worksheet and then displays the scale along the vertical axis (also called the **y-axis** or **value axis**) of the chart. For example, no value in the range B4:G8 is less than 0 or greater than $100,000.00, so the scale ranges from 0 to $100,000.00. Excel also determines the $10,000.00 increments of the scale automatically. For the numbers along the y-axis, Excel uses a format that includes representing the 0 value with a dash (Figure 1–53).

BTW

Using Dual Axes on a Chart
Figure 1–53 shows a chart with a y-axis along the left side of the chart. If you have additional data to chart for each city, you can overlay a second chart with a different y-axis on top of the first chart. The second y-axis is displayed on the right side of the chart. In this case, the chart is said to have dual axes. Additionally, a different type of chart usually is laid over the first chart. For example, if a second y-axis were added to the chart shown in Figure 1–53, a good choice for the second chart would be a line chart. To add a second y-axis to a chart, click the data series to plot on the new axis, click Format Selection (Chart Tools Format tab | Current Selection group), click the Secondary Axis option button (Format Data Series dialog box), and then click the Close button.

To Add a Clustered Cylinder Chart to the Worksheet

The area on the worksheet where the chart appears is called the chart location. As shown in Figure 1–53 on page EX 36, the chart location in this worksheet is the range A11:G23; this range is immediately below the worksheet data. Placing the chart below the data on the Save Sable River Foundation Lifetime Fundraising Summary worksheet makes it easier to read the chart along with the data, and the chart and data easily can be printed on one sheet of paper.

The following steps draw a Clustered Cylinder chart that compares the funds raised by fundraising activity for the six cities.

1

• Click cell A3 and then drag the mouse pointer to cell G8 to select the range to be charted (Figure 1–54).

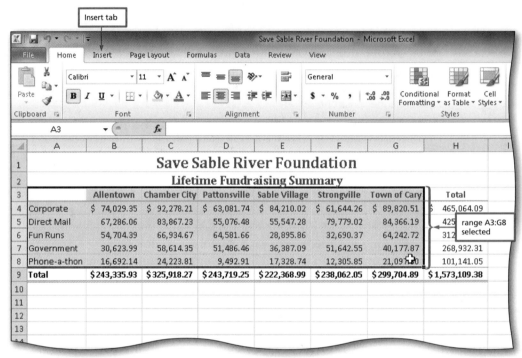

Figure 1–54

2

• Click Insert on the Ribbon to display the Insert tab (Figure 1–55).

Q&A What tasks can I perform with the Insert tab?

The Insert tab includes commands that allow you to insert various objects, such as shapes, tables, illustrations, and charts, into a worksheet. These objects will be discussed as they are used throughout this book.

Figure 1–55

3

- Click the Column button (Insert tab | Charts group) to display the Column gallery (Figure 1–56).

Figure 1–56

4

- Click the Clustered Cylinder chart type in the Cylinder area of the Column gallery to add the selected chart type to the middle of the worksheet in a selection rectangle.

- Press and hold down the mouse button while pointing to the upper-right edge of the selection rectangle to change the mouse pointer to a double two-headed arrow (Figure 1–57).

Q&A Why is a new tab displayed on the Ribbon?

When you select objects such as shapes or charts, Excel displays contextual tabs that include special commands that are used to work

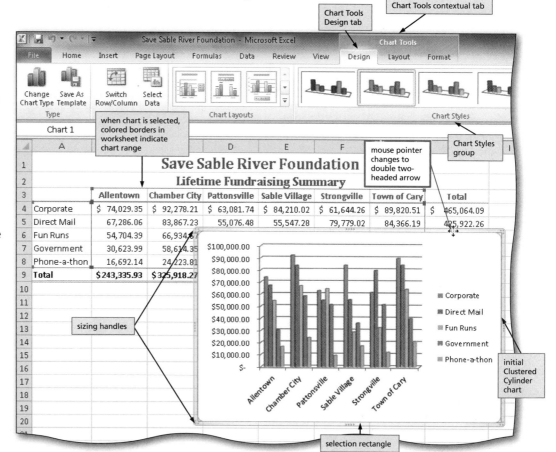

Figure 1–57

with the type of object selected. Because a chart is selected, Excel displays the Chart Tools contextual tab. The three tabs below the Chart Tools contextual tab, Design, Layout, and Format, are tabs that include commands to work with charts.

5

• Drag the chart down and to the left to position the upper-left corner of the dotted line rectangle over the upper-left corner of cell A11.

• Press and hold down the mouse button while pointing to the middle sizing handle on the right edge of the chart (Figure 1–58).

Q&A

How does Excel know which data to use to create the chart?

Excel automatically selects the entries in the topmost row of the chart range (row 3) as the titles for the horizontal axis (also called the **x-axis** or **category axis**) and draws a column for each of the 30 cells in the range containing numbers.

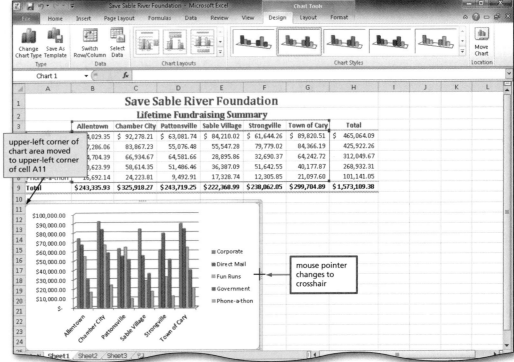

Figure 1–58

6

• While continuing to hold down the mouse button, press the ALT key and drag the right edge of the chart to the right edge of column H and then release the mouse button to resize the chart.

• Press and hold down the mouse button while pointing to the middle sizing handle on the bottom edge of the selection rectangle and do not release the mouse button (Figure 1–59).

Q&A

Why should I hold the ALT key down while I resize a chart?

Holding down the ALT key while you drag a chart **snaps** (aligns) the edge of the chart area to the worksheet gridlines. If you do not hold down the ALT key, then you can place an edge of a chart in the middle of a column or row.

Figure 1–59

- While continuing to hold down the mouse button, press the ALT key and drag the bottom edge of the chart up to the bottom edge of row 23 and then release the mouse button to resize the chart.

- If necessary, scroll the worksheet so that row 1 displays at the top of the worksheet.

- Click the More button in the Chart Styles gallery (Chart Tools Design tab | Chart Styles group) to expand the gallery (Figure 1–60).

Figure 1–60

- Click Style 34 in the Chart Styles gallery (column 2, row 5) to apply the chart style to the chart.

- Click cell J9 to deselect the chart and complete the worksheet (Figure 1–61).

Q&A

What is the purpose of the items on the right side of the chart?

The items to the right of the column chart in Figure 1–61 are the **legend**, which identifies the colors assigned to each bar in the chart. Excel automatically selects the entries in the leftmost column of the chart range (column A) as titles within the legend.

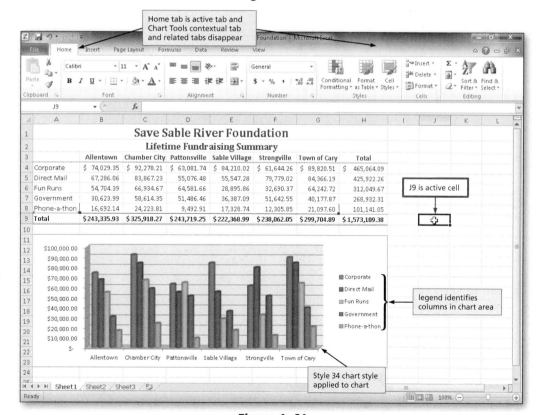

Figure 1–61

Changing the Worksheet Names

The sheet tabs at the bottom of the window allow you to view any worksheet in the workbook. You click the sheet tab of the worksheet you want to view in the Excel window. By default, Excel presets the names of the worksheets to Sheet1, Sheet2, and so on. The worksheet names become increasingly important as you move toward more sophisticated workbooks, especially workbooks in which you reference cells between worksheets.

Plan Ahead

> **Choose a name for the worksheet.**
> Use simple, meaningful names for each worksheet. Worksheet names often match the worksheet title. If a worksheet includes multiple titles in multiple sections of the worksheet, use a name that encompasses the meaning of all of the sections.

To Change the Worksheet Names

Lifetime Fundraising Summary is a meaningful name for the Save Sable River Foundation Lifetime Fundraising Summary worksheet. The following steps rename worksheets by double-clicking the sheet tabs.

1

- Double-click the sheet tab labeled Sheet1 in the lower-left corner of the window.

- Type **Lifetime Fundraising Summary** as the worksheet name and then press the ENTER key to display the new worksheet name on the sheet tab (Figure 1–62).

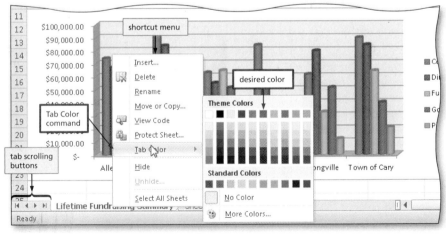

Figure 1–62

What is the maximum length for a worksheet tab?

Worksheet names can be up to 31 characters (including spaces) in length. Longer worksheet names, however, mean that fewer sheet tabs will show. To view more sheet tabs, you can drag the tab split box (Figure 1–62) to the right. This will reduce the size of the scroll bar at the bottom of the screen. Double-click the tab split box to reset it to its normal position.

2

- Right-click the sheet tab labeled Lifetime Fundraising Summary in the lower-left corner of the window to display a shortcut menu.

- Point to Tab Color on the shortcut menu to display the color gallery (Figure 1–63).

How can I quickly move between worksheet tabs?

You can use the tab scrolling buttons to the left of the sheet tabs (Figure 1–63) to move between worksheets. The leftmost and rightmost scroll buttons move to the first or last worksheet in the workbook. The two middle scroll buttons move one worksheet to the left or right.

Figure 1–63

3

- Click Red, Accent 2 (column 6, row 1) in the Theme Colors area to change the color of the tab (Figure 1–64)

4

- If necessary, click Home on the Ribbon to display the Home tab.

Figure 1–64

Changing Document Properties

Excel helps you organize and identify your files by using **document properties**, which are the details about a file. Document properties, also known as **metadata**, can include information such as the project author, title, subject, and keywords. A **keyword** is a word or phrase that further describes the document. For example, a class name or document topic can describe the file's purpose or content.

Document properties are valuable for a variety of reasons:

- Users can save time locating a particular file because they can view a document's properties without opening the document.

- By creating consistent properties for files having similar content, users can better organize their documents.

- Some organizations require Excel users to add document properties so that other employees can view details about these files.

Five different types of document properties exist, but the more common ones used in this book are standard and automatically updated properties. **Standard properties** are associated with all Microsoft Office documents and include author, title, and subject. **Automatically updated properties** include file system properties, such as the date you create or change a file, and statistics, such as the file size.

To Change Document Properties

The **Document Information Panel** contains areas where you can view and enter document properties. You can view and change information in this panel at any time while you are creating a workbook. Before saving the workbook again, you want to add your name and course information as document properties. The following steps use the Document Information Panel to change document properties.

1

- Click File on the Ribbon to open the Backstage view. If necessary, click the Info tab in the Backstage view to display the Info gallery (Figure 1–65).

Q&A

How do I close the Backstage view?

Click File on the Ribbon or click the preview of the document in the Info gallery to return to the Excel document window.

Figure 1–65

- Click the Properties button in the right pane of the Info gallery to display the Properties menu (Figure 1–66).

Figure 1–66

- Click Show Document Panel on the Properties menu to close the Backstage view and display the Document Information Panel in the Excel workbook window (Figure 1–67).

Q&A Why are some of the document properties in my Document Information Panel already filled in?

The person who installed Microsoft Office 2010 on your computer or network may have set or customized the properties.

Figure 1–67

4

- Click the Author text box, if necessary, and then type your name as the Author property. If a name already is displayed in the Author text box, delete it before typing your name.

- Click the Subject text box, if necessary delete any existing text, and then type your course and section as the Subject property.

- If an AutoComplete dialog box appears, click its Yes button.

- Click the Keywords text box, if necessary delete any existing text, and then type **Lifetime Fundraising Summary** as the Keywords property (Figure 1–68).

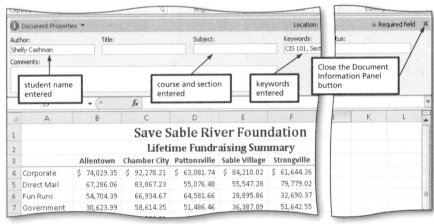

Figure 1–68

Q&A What types of document properties does Excel collect automatically?

Excel records details such as time spent editing a workbook, the number of times a workbook has been revised, and the fonts and themes used in a workbook.

- Click the Close the Document Information Panel button so that the Document Information Panel no longer is displayed. If a dialog box is displayed, click the No button to close it.

Other Ways

1. Click File on Ribbon, click Info in the Backstage view, if necessary click Show All Properties link in Info gallery, click property to change and type new information, close the Backstage view

To Save an Existing Workbook with the Same File Name

You have made several modifications to the workbook since you last saved it. Thus, you should save it again. The following step saves the workbook again. For an example of the step listed below, refer to the Introduction to Office 2010 and Windows 7 chapter at the beginning of this book.

 Click the Save button on the Quick Access Toolbar to overwrite the previously saved file.

Previewing and Printing a Worksheet

After creating a worksheet, you may want to print it. Printing a worksheet enables you to distribute the worksheet to others in a form that can be read or viewed but typically not edited. It is a good practice to save a workbook before printing a worksheet, in the event you experience difficulties printing.

Determine the best method for distributing the worksheet.

The traditional method of distributing a worksheet uses a printer to produce a hard copy. A **hardcopy or printout** is information that exists on a physical medium such as paper. For users that can receive fax documents, you can elect to print a hard copy on a remote fax machine. Hard copies can be useful for the following reasons:

- Many people prefer proofreading a hard copy of a worksheet rather than viewing it on the screen to check for errors and readability.

- Hard copies can serve as reference material if your storage medium is lost or becomes corrupted and you need to re-create the worksheet.

Instead of distributing a hard copy of a worksheet, users can choose to distribute the worksheet as an electronic image that mirrors the original worksheet's appearance. The electronic image of the worksheet can be e-mailed, posted on a Web site, or copied to a portable storage medium such as a USB flash drive. Two popular electronic image formats, sometimes called fixed formats, are PDF by Adobe Systems and XPS by Microsoft. In Excel, you can create electronic image files through the Print tab in the Backstage view, the Save & Send tab in the Backstage view, and the Save As dialog box. Electronic images of worksheets, such as PDF and XPS, can be useful for the following reasons:

- Users can view electronic images of worksheets without the software that created the original worksheet (e.g., Excel). Specifically, to view a PDF file, you use a program called Acrobat Reader, which can be downloaded free from Adobe's Web site. Similarly, to view an XPS file, you use a program called an XPS Viewer, which is included in the latest versions of Windows and Internet Explorer.

- Sending electronic documents saves paper and printer supplies. Society encourages users to contribute to **green computing**, which involves reducing the environmental waste generated when using a computer.

**Plan
Ahead**

BTW

Printing Document Properties
To print document properties, click File on the Ribbon to open the Backstage view, click the Print tab in the Backstage view to display the Print gallery, click the first button in the Settings area to display a list of options specifying what you can print, click Document Properties in the list to specify you want to print the document properties instead of the actual document, and then click the Print button in the Print gallery to print the document properties on the currently selected printer.

BTW

Conserving Ink and Toner
If you want to conserve ink or toner, you can instruct Excel to print draft quality documents by clicking File on the Ribbon to open the Backstage view, clicking Options in the Backstage view to display the Excel Options dialog box, clicking Advanced in the left pane (Excel Options dialog box), scrolling to the Print area in the right pane, placing a check mark in the 'Use draft quality' check box, and then clicking the OK button. Then, use the Backstage view to print the document as usual.

To Preview and Print a Worksheet in Landscape Orientation

With the completed workbook saved, you may want to print it. Because the worksheet is included in a report, you will print a hard copy on a printer. The following steps print a hard copy of the contents of the Save Sable River Foundation Lifetime Fundraising Summary worksheet.

- Click File on the Ribbon to open the Backstage view.

- Click the Print tab in the Backstage view to display the Print gallery (Figure 1–69).

Q&A How can I print multiple copies of my worksheet?

Increase the number in the Copies box in the Print gallery.

Q&A What if I decide not to print the worksheet at this time?

Click File on the Ribbon to close the Backstage view and return to the Excel workbook window.

Figure 1–69

- Verify the printer name that appears on the Printer Status button will print a hard copy of the document. If necessary, click the Printer Status button to display a list of available printer options and then click the desired printer to change the currently selected printer.

- Click the Portrait Orientation button in the Settings area and then select Landscape Orientation to change the orientation of the page to landscape and view the entire worksheet on one page (Figure 1–70).

Figure 1–70

4

- Click the Print button in the Print gallery to print the worksheet in landscape orientation on the currently selected printer.

- When the printer stops, retrieve the hard copy (Figure 1–71).

Q&A
Do I have to wait until my worksheet is complete to print it?

No, you can follow these steps to print a document at any time while you are creating it.

Q&A
What if I want to print an electronic image of a worksheet instead of a hard copy?

You would click the Printer Status button in the Print gallery and then select the desired electronic image option such as a Microsoft XPS Document Writer, which would create an XPS file.

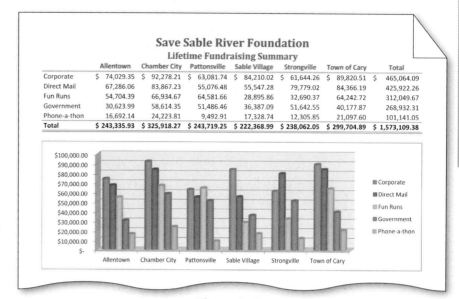

Figure 1–71

Other Ways
1. Press CTRL+P, press ENTER

To Quit Excel

This Save Sable River Foundation workbook now is complete. The following steps quit Excel if only one workbook is open. For a detailed example of the procedure summarized below, refer to the Office 2010 and Windows 7 chapter at the beginning of this book.

1 If you have one Excel workbook open, click the Close button on the right side of the title bar to close the document and quit Excel; or if you have multiple Excel workbooks open, click File on the Ribbon to open the Backstage view and then click the Exit button to close all open workbooks and quit Excel.

2 If a Microsoft Office Excel dialog box appears, click the Save button to save any changes made to the workbook since the last save.

Starting Excel and Opening a Workbook

Once you have created and saved a workbook, you may need to retrieve it from your storage medium. For example, you might want to revise a worksheet or reprint it. Opening a workbook requires that Excel is running on your computer.

To Start Excel

1 Click the Start button on the Windows 7 taskbar to display the Start menu.

2 Type **Microsoft Excel** as the search text in the 'Search programs and files' text box and watch the search results appear on the Start menu.

3 Click Microsoft Excel 2010 in the search results on the Start menu to start Excel and display a new blank workbook in the Excel window.

4 If the Excel window is not maximized, click the Maximize button next to the Close button on its title bar to maximize the window.

Managing Versions
Excel automatically saves your work, even when you have not saved a file. If you inadvertently close a file without saving it, you can recover your work by clicking Info in the Backstage view and then clicking the Manage Versions button. On the Manage Versions list, click Recover Unsaved Workbooks to display the Open dialog box. Select the file you want to recover and then click the Open button (Open dialog box) to display the file. You also can click the file to recover in the Versions list next to the Manage Versions button. To delete recent copies of unsaved files, click Delete All Unsaved Workbooks on the Manage Versions list.

To Open a Workbook from Excel

Earlier in this chapter you saved your project on a USB flash drive using the file name, Save Sable River Foundation. The following steps open the Save Sable River Foundation file from the Excel folder in the CIS 101 folder on the USB flash drive. For a detailed example of the procedure summarized below, refer to page OFF 57 in the Office 2010 and Windows 7 chapter at the beginning of this book.

1 With your USB flash drive connected to one of the computer's USB ports, click File on the Ribbon to open the Backstage view.

2 Click Open in the Backstage view to display the Open dialog box.

3 Navigate to the location of the file to be opened (in this case, the USB flash drive, then to the CIS 101 folder [or your class folder], and then to the Excel folder).

4 Click Save Sable River Foundation to select the file to be opened.

5 Click the Open button (Open dialog box) to open the selected file and display the opened workbook in the Excel window.

AutoCalculate

AutoCalculate
Use the AutoCalculate area on the status bar to check your work as you enter data in a worksheet. If you enter large amounts of data, you select a range of data and then check the AutoCalculate area to provide insight into statistics about the data you entered. Often, you will have an intuitive feel for whether the numbers are accurate or if you may have made a mistake while entering the data.

You easily can obtain a total, an average, or other information about the numbers in a range by using the **AutoCalculate area** on the status bar. First, select the range of cells containing the numbers you want to check. Next, right-click the AutoCalculate area to display the Status Bar Configuration shortcut menu (Figure 1–72). The check mark to the left of the active functions (Average, Count, and Sum) indicates that the sum, count, and average of the selected range are displayed in the AutoCalculate area on the status bar. The functions of the AutoCalculate commands on the Status Bar Configuration shortcut menu are described in Table 1–4.

Table 1–4 AutoCalculate Shortcut Menu Commands	
Command	**Function**
Average	AutoCalculate area displays the average of the numbers in the selected range
Count	AutoCalculate area displays the number of nonblank cells in the selected range
Numerical Count	AutoCalculate area displays the number of cells containing numbers in the selected range
Minimum	AutoCalculate area displays the lowest value in the selected range
Maximum	AutoCalculate area displays the highest value in the selected range
Sum	AutoCalculate area displays the sum of the numbers in the selected range

To Use the AutoCalculate Area to Determine a Maximum

The following steps display the largest amounts of funds raised for any city for the Fun Runs fundraising activity.

1

- Select the range B6:G6 and then right-click the AutoCalculate area on the status bar to display the Customize Status Bar shortcut menu (Figure 1–72).

 Q&A

What is displayed on the Customize Status Bar shortcut menu?

This shortcut menu includes several commands that allow you to control the items displayed on the Customize Status Bar shortcut menu. The AutoCalculate area includes six commands as well as the result of the associated calculation on the right side of the menu.

Figure 1–72

2

- Click Maximum on the shortcut menu to display the Maximum value in the range B6:G6 in the AutoCalculate area of the status bar.

Figure 1–73

- Click anywhere on the worksheet to cause the shortcut menu to disappear (Figure 1–73).

3

- Right-click the AutoCalculate area and then click Maximum on the shortcut menu to cause the Maximum value to no longer appear in the AutoCalculate area.

- Click anywhere on the worksheet to cause the shortcut menu to disappear.

Correcting Errors

You can correct errors on a worksheet using one of several methods. The method you choose will depend on the extent of the error and whether you notice it while typing the data or after you have entered the incorrect data into the cell.

Correcting Errors While You Are Typing Data into a Cell

If you notice an error while you are typing data into a cell, press the BACKSPACE key to erase the incorrect characters and then type the correct characters. If the error is a major one, click the Cancel box in the formula bar or press the ESC key to erase the entire entry and then reenter the data from the beginning.

Correcting Errors After Entering Data into a Cell

If you find an error in the worksheet after entering the data, you can correct the error in one of two ways:

1. If the entry is short, select the cell, retype the entry correctly, and then click the Enter box or press the ENTER key. The new entry will replace the old entry.

2. If the entry in the cell is long and the errors are minor, using Edit mode may be a better choice than retyping the cell entry. Use the Edit mode as described below.

   a. Double-click the cell containing the error to switch Excel to Edit mode. In **Edit mode**, Excel displays the active cell entry in the formula bar and a flashing insertion point in the active cell (Figure 1–74). With Excel in Edit mode, you can edit the contents directly in the cell — a procedure called **in-cell editing**.

   b. Make changes using in-cell editing, as indicated below.

     (1) To insert new characters between two characters, place the insertion point between the two characters and begin typing. Excel inserts the new characters at the location of the insertion point.

     (2) To delete a character in the cell, move the insertion point to the left of the character you want to delete and then press the DELETE key or place the insertion point to the right of the character you want to delete and then press the BACKSPACE key. You also can use the mouse to drag through the character or adjacent characters you want to delete and then press the DELETE key or click the Cut button (Home tab | Clipboard group).

     (3) When you are finished editing an entry, click the Enter box or press the ENTER key.

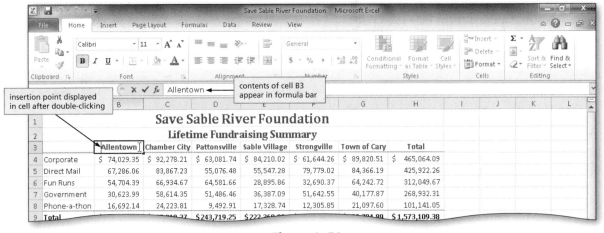

Figure 1–74

When Excel enters the Edit mode, the keyboard usually is in Insert mode. In **Insert mode**, as you type a character, Excel inserts the character and moves all characters to the right of the typed character one position to the right. You can change to Overtype mode by pressing the INSERT key. In **Overtype mode**, Excel overtypes, or replaces, the character to the right of the insertion point. The INSERT key toggles the keyboard between Insert mode and Overtype mode.

While in Edit mode, you may have reason to move the insertion point to various points in the cell, select portions of the data in the cell, or switch from inserting characters to overtyping characters. Table 1–5 summarizes the more common tasks performed during in-cell editing.

Table 1–5 Summary of In-Cell Editing Tasks

	Task	Mouse	Keyboard
1	Move the insertion point to the beginning of data in a cell.	Point to the left of the first character and click.	Press HOME
2	Move the insertion point to the end of data in a cell.	Point to the right of the last character and click.	Press END
3	Move the insertion point anywhere in a cell.	Point to the appropriate position and click the character.	Press RIGHT ARROW or LEFT ARROW
4	Highlight one or more adjacent characters.	Drag the mouse pointer through adjacent characters.	Press SHIFT+RIGHT ARROW or SHIFT+LEFT ARROW
5	Select all data in a cell.	Double-click the cell with the insertion point in the cell if there are no spaces in the data in the cell.	
6	Delete selected characters.	Click the Cut button (Home tab | Clipboard group)	Press DELETE
7	Delete characters to the left of the insertion point.		Press BACKSPACE
8	Delete characters to the right of the insertion point.		Press DELETE
9	Toggle between Insert and Overtype modes.		Press INSERT

BTW

Excel Help
At any time while using Excel, you can find answers to questions and display information about various topics through Excel Help. Used properly, this form of assistance can increase your productivity and reduce your frustrations by minimizing the time you spend learning how to use Excel. For instruction about Excel Help and exercises that will help you gain confidence in using it, read the Office 2010 and Windows 7 chapter at the beginning of this book.

Undoing the Last Cell Entry

Excel provides the Undo command on the Quick Access Toolbar (Figure 1–75), which allows you to erase recent cell entries. Thus, if you enter incorrect data in a cell and notice it immediately, click the Undo button and Excel changes the cell entry to what it was prior to the incorrect data entry.

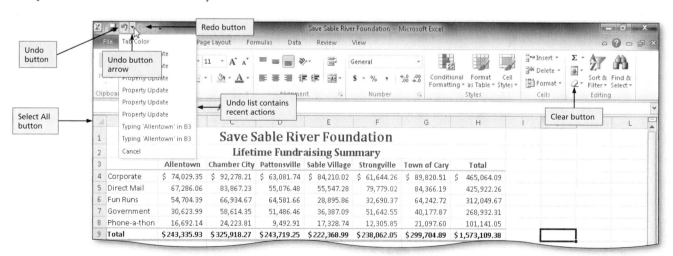

Figure 1–75

Excel remembers the last 100 actions you have completed. Thus, you can undo up to 100 previous actions by clicking the Undo button arrow to display the Undo list and then clicking the action to be undone (Figure 1–75). You can drag through several actions in the Undo list to undo all of them at once. If no actions are available for Excel to undo, then the Undo button is dimmed and inoperative.

The Redo button, next to the Undo button on the Quick Access Toolbar, allows you to repeat previous actions.

Clearing a Cell or Range of Cells

If you enter data into the wrong cell or range of cells, you can erase, or clear, the data using one of the first four methods listed below. The fifth method clears the formatting from the selected cells.

To Clear Cell Entries Using the Fill Handle

1. Select the cell or range of cells and then point to the fill handle so the mouse pointer changes to a crosshair.
2. Drag the fill handle back into the selected cell or range until a shadow covers the cell or cells you want to erase. Release the mouse button.

To Clear Cell Entries Using the Shortcut Menu

1. Select the cell or range of cells to be cleared.
2. Right-click the selection.
3. Click Clear Contents on the shortcut menu.

To Clear Cell Entries Using the delete Key

1. Select the cell or range of cells to be cleared.
2. Press the DELETE key.

To Clear Cell Entries and Formatting Using the Clear Button

1. Select the cell or range of cells to be cleared.
2. Click the Clear button (Home tab | Editing group) (Figure 1–75 on the previous page).
3. Click Clear Contents on the menu.

To Clear Formatting Using the Cell Styles Button

1. Select the cell or range of cells from which you want to remove the formatting.
2. Click the Cell Styles button (Home tab | Styles group) and point to Normal.
3. Click Normal in the Cell Styles Gallery.

The Clear button (Home tab | Editing group) is the only command that clears both the cell entry and the cell formatting. As you are clearing cell entries, always remember that you should *never press the* SPACEBAR *to clear a cell*. Pressing the SPACEBAR enters a blank character. A blank character is text and is different from an empty cell, even though the cell may appear empty.

Clearing the Entire Worksheet

If the required worksheet edits are extremely extensive, you may want to clear the entire worksheet and start over. To clear the worksheet or delete an embedded chart, you would use the following steps.

To Clear the Entire Worksheet

1. Click the Select All button on the worksheet (Figure 1–75).
2. Click the Clear button (Home tab | Editing group) and then click Clear All on the Clear menu to delete both the entries and formats.

The Select All button selects the entire worksheet. Instead of clicking the Select All button, you can press CTRL+A. To clear an unsaved workbook, click the workbook's Close Window button or click the Close button in the Backstage view. Click the No button if the Microsoft Excel dialog box asks if you want to save changes. To start a new, blank workbook, click the New button in the Backstage view.

BTW

Getting Back to Normal
If you accidentally assign unwanted formats to a range of cells, you can use the Normal cell style selection in the Cell Styles gallery. Click Cell Styles (Home tab | Styles group) and then click Normal in the Cell Styles gallery. Doing so changes the format to Normal style. To view the characteristics of the Normal style, right-click the style in the Cell Styles gallery and then click Modify or press ALT+APOSTROPHE (').

BTW

Certification
The Microsoft Office Specialist (MOS) program provides an opportunity for you to obtain a valuable industry credential — proof that you have the Excel 2010 skills required by employers. For more information, visit the Excel 2010 Certification Web page (scsite.com/ex2010/cert).

To delete an embedded chart, you would complete the following steps.

TO DELETE AN EMBEDDED CHART

1. Click the chart to select it.
2. Press the DELETE key.

To Quit Excel

The project now is complete. The following steps quit Excel. For a detailed example of the procedure summarized below, refer to the Office 2010 and Windows 7 chapter at the beginning of this book.

1 If you have one Excel workbook open, click the Close button on the right side of the title bar to close the document and quit Excel; or if you have multiple Excel workbooks open, click File on the Ribbon to open the Backstage view and then click Exit in the Backstage view to close all open workbooks and quit Excel.

2 If a Microsoft Office Excel dialog box appears, click the Save button to save any changes made to the document since the last save.

BTW

Quitting Excel
Do not forget to remove your USB flash drive from the USB port after quitting Excel, especially if you are working in a laboratory environment. Nothing can be more frustrating than leaving all of your hard work behind on a USB flash drive for the next user.

Chapter Summary

In this chapter you have learned how to enter text and numbers to create a worksheet, how to select a range, how to use the Sum button, format cells, insert a chart, and preview and print a worksheet. The items listed below include all the new Excel skills you have learned in this chapter.

1. To Start Excel (EX 6)
2. Enter the Worksheet Titles (EX 8)
3. Enter Column Titles (EX 10)
4. Enter Row Titles (EX 12)
5. Enter Numbers (EX 13)
6. Sum a Column of Numbers (EX 15)
7. Copy a Cell to Adjacent Cells in a Row (EX 17)
8. Determine Multiple Totals at the Same Time (EX 18)
9. Save a Workbook (EX 20)
10. Change a Cell Style (EX 22)
11. Change the Font (EX 24)
12. Bold a Cell (EX 25)
13. Increase the Font Size of a Cell Entry (EX 26)
14. Change the Font Color of a Cell Entry (EX 27)
15. Center Cell Entries Across Columns by Merging Cells (EX 28)
16. Format Column Titles and the Total Row (EX 29)
17. Format Numbers in the Worksheet (EX 31)
18. Adjust the Column Width (EX 33)
19. Use the Name Box to Select a Cell (EX 34)
20. Add a Clustered Cylinder Chart to the Worksheet (EX 38)
21. Change the Worksheet Names (EX 42)
22. Change Document Properties (EX 43)
23. Save an Existing Workbook with the Same File Name (EX 45)
24. Preview and Print a Worksheet in Landscape Orientation (EX 46)
25. Quit Excel (EX 47)
26. Start Excel (EX 47)
27. Open a Workbook from Excel (EX 48)
28. Use the AutoCalculate Area to Determine a Maximum (EX 49)
29. Clear Cell Entries Using the Fill Handle (EX 52)
30. Clear Cell Entries Using the Shortcut Menu (EX 52)
31. Clear Cell Entries Using the DELETE Key (EX 52)
32. Clear Cell Entries and Formatting Using the Clear Button (EX 52)
33. Clear Formatting Using the Cell Styles Button (EX 52)
34. Clear the Entire Worksheet (EX 52)
35. Delete an Embedded Chart (EX 53)

If you have a SAM 2010 user profile, your instructor may have assigned an autogradable version of this assignment. If so, log into the SAM 2010 Web site at www.cengage.com/sam2010 to download the instruction and start files.

Learn It Online

Test your knowledge of chapter content and key terms.

Instructions: To complete the Learn It Online exercises, start your browser, click the Address bar, and then enter the Web address **scsite.com/ex2010/learn**. When the Excel 2010 Learn It Online page is displayed, click the link for the exercise you want to complete and then read the instructions.

Chapter Reinforcement TF, MC, and SA
A series of true/false, multiple choice, and short answer questions that test your knowledge of the chapter content.

Flash Cards
An interactive learning environment where you identify chapter key terms associated with displayed definitions.

Practice Test
A series of multiple choice questions that test your knowledge of chapter content and key terms.

Who Wants To Be a Computer Genius?
An interactive game that challenges your knowledge of chapter content in the style of a television quiz show.

Wheel of Terms
An interactive game that challenges your knowledge of chapter key terms in the style of the television show *Wheel of Fortune*.

Crossword Puzzle Challenge
A crossword puzzle that challenges your knowledge of key terms presented in the chapter.

Apply Your Knowledge

Reinforce the skills and apply the concepts you learned in this chapter.

Changing the Values in a Worksheet
Instructions: Start Excel. Open the workbook Apply 1–1 Clothes Campus Third Quarter Expenses (Figure 1–76a). See the inside back cover of this book for instructions for downloading the Data Files for Students, or see your instructor for information on accessing the files required in this book.

1. Make the changes to the worksheet described in Table 1–6 so that the worksheet appears as shown in Figure 1–76b. As you edit the values in the cells containing numeric data, watch the totals in row 7, the totals in column F, and the chart change.

2. Change the worksheet title in cell A1 to the Title cell style and then merge and center it across columns A through F. Use buttons in the Font group on the Home tab on the Ribbon to change the worksheet subtitle in cell A2 to 16-point Cambria red, bold font and then center it across columns A through F. Use the Red, Accent 2 theme color (column 6, row 1 on the Font gallery) for the red font color.

3. Apply the worksheet name, Third Quarter Expenses, to the sheet tab and apply the Red, Accent 2 theme color to the sheet tab.

4. Change the document properties as specified by your instructor. Save the workbook using the file name, Apply 1–1 Clothed for Campus Third Quarter Expenses. Submit the revised workbook as specified by your instructor.

Table 1–6 New Worksheet Data	
Cell	**Change Cell Contents To**
A1	Clothed for Campus
B4	7829.50
C4	19057.83
D5	24217.92
E5	25859.62
E6	35140.84

(a) Before

(b) After

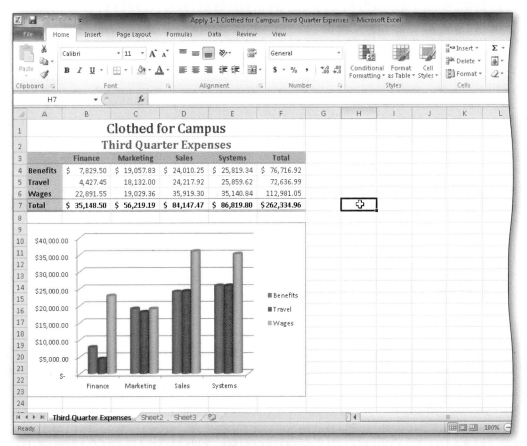

Figure 1–76

Extend Your Knowledge

Extend the skills you learned in this chapter and experiment with new skills. You may need to use Help to complete the assignment.

Formatting a Worksheet and Adding Additional Charts

Instructions: Start Excel. Open the workbook Extend 1–1 Pack Right Moving Supplies. See the inside back cover of this book for instructions for downloading the Data Files for Students, or see your instructor for information on accessing the files required in this book. Perform the following tasks to format cells in the worksheet and to add two charts to the worksheet.

1. Use the commands in the Font group on the Home tab on the Ribbon to change the font of the title in cell A1 to 22-point Arial Black, green, bold, and the subtitle of the worksheet to 14-point Arial, red, bold.

2. Select the range A3:G8, click the Insert tab on the Ribbon, and then click the Dialog Box Launcher in the Charts group on the Ribbon to open the Insert Chart dialog box. If necessary, drag the lower-right corner of the Insert Chart dialog box to expand it (Figure 1–77).

Figure 1–77

3. Insert a Stacked Area in 3-D chart by clicking the Stacked Area in 3-D chart in the gallery and then clicking the OK button. You may need to use the scroll box on the right side of the Insert Chart dialog box to view the Area charts in the gallery. Move the chart either below or to the right of the data in the worksheet. Click the Design tab and apply a chart style of your choice to the chart.

4. Deselect the chart and reselect the range A3:G8, and then follow Step 3 above to insert a Clustered Horizontal Cone chart in the worksheet. Move the chart either below or to the right of the data so that each chart does not overlap the Stacked Area in 3-D chart. Make sure to make the values on the horizontal axis readable by expanding the size of the chart. Choose a different chart style for this chart than the one you selected for the Stacked Area in 3-D chart.

5. Resize each chart so that each snaps to the worksheet gridlines. You may need to scroll the worksheet to resize and view the charts. Preview the worksheet.

6. Apply a worksheet name to the sheet tab and apply a color of your choice to the sheet tab.

7. Change the document properties as specified by your instructor. Save the workbook using the file name, Extend 1–1 Pack Right Moving Supplies Charts. Submit the revised workbook as specified by your instructor.

Make It Right

Analyze a workbook and correct all errors and/or improve the design.

Fixing Formatting Problems and Data Errors in a Worksheet

Instructions: Start Excel. Open the workbook Make It Right 1–1 Pets. See the inside back cover of this book for instructions for downloading the Data Files for Students, or see your instructor for information on accessing the files required for this book. Correct the following formatting problems and data errors (Figure 1–78) in the worksheet, while keeping in mind the guidelines presented in this chapter.

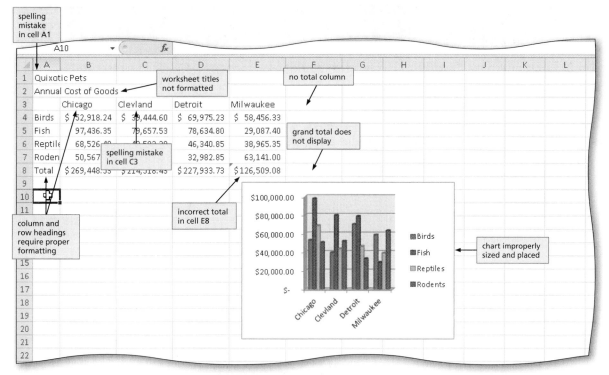

Figure 1–78

1. Merge and center the worksheet title and subtitle appropriately.

2. Format the worksheet title with a cell style appropriate for a worksheet title.

3. Format the subtitle using commands in the Font group on the Home tab on the Ribbon and apply the Red, Accent 2 color to the subtitle.

4. Correct the spelling mistake in cell A1 by changing Quixotic to Exotic. Correct the spelling mistake in cell C3 by changing Clevland to Cleveland.

Continued >

Make It Right *continued*

5. Add a column header for totals in column F and create the necessary totals in row 8.

6. Apply proper formatting to the column headers and total row, including centering the column headers.

7. Adjust the column sizes so that all data in each column is visible.

8. Create the grand total for the annual cost of goods.

9. The SUM function in cell E8 does not sum all of the numbers in the column. Correct this error by editing the range for the SUM function in the cell.

10. Resize and move the chart so that it is below the worksheet data and does not extend past the right edge of the worksheet data. Be certain to snap the chart to the worksheet gridlines by holding down the ALT key as you resize the chart to the right edge of column F and the bottom of row 22.

11. Apply a worksheet name to the sheet tab and apply the Aqua, Accent 5 color to the sheet tab.

12. Change the document properties as specified by your instructor. Save the workbook using the file name, Make It Right 1–1 Exotic Pets Annual Cost of Goods. Submit the revised workbook as specified by your instructor.

In the Lab

Design and/or create a workbook using the guidelines, concepts, and skills presented in this chapter. Labs 1, 2, and 3 are listed in order of increasing difficulty.

Lab 1: Annual Revenue Analysis Worksheet

Problem: You work as a spreadsheet specialist for A Healthy Body Shop, a high-end total fitness center franchise. Your manager has asked you to develop an annual revenue analysis worksheet similar to the one shown in Figure 1–79.

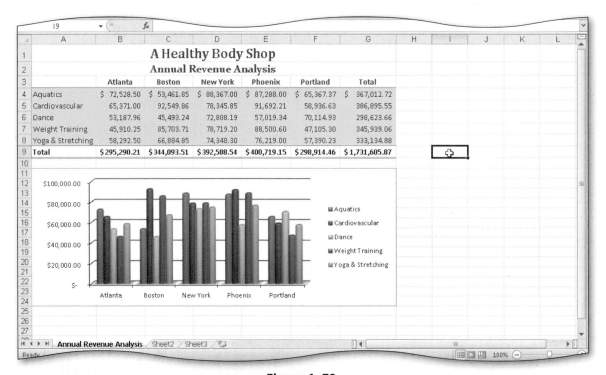

Figure 1–79

Instructions: Perform the following tasks.

1. Start Excel. Enter the worksheet title, A Healthy Body Shop, in cell A1 and the worksheet subtitle, Annual Revenue Analysis, in cell A2. Beginning in row 3, enter the franchise locations, fitness activities, and annual revenues shown in Table 1–7.

Table 1–7 A Healthy Body Shop Annual Revenues					
	Atlanta	Boston	New York	Phoenix	Portland
Aquatics	72528.50	53461.85	88367.00	87288.00	65367.37
Cardiovascular	65371.00	92549.86	78345.85	91692.21	58936.63
Dance	53187.96	45493.24	72808.19	57019.34	70114.93
Weight Training	45910.25	85703.71	78719.20	88500.60	47105.30
Yoga & Stretching	58292.50	66884.85	74348.30	76219.00	57390.23

2. Create totals for each franchise location, fitness activity, and company grand total.

3. Format the worksheet title with the Title cell style. Center the title across columns A through G. Do not be concerned if the edges of the worksheet title are not displayed.

4. Format the worksheet subtitle to 14-point Constantia dark blue, bold font, and center it across columns A through G.

5. Use Cell Styles to format the range A3:G3 with the Heading 3 cell style, the range A4:G8 with the 40% - Accent 6 cell style, and the range A9:G9 with the Total cell style. Center the column headers in row 3. Apply the Accounting Number format to the range B4:G4 and the range B9:G9. Apply the Comma Style to the range B5:G8. Adjust any column widths to the widest text entry in each column.

6. Select the range A3:F8 and then insert a Clustered Cylinder chart. Apply the Style 26 chart style to the chart. Move and resize the chart so that it appears in the range A11:G24. If the labels along the horizontal axis (x-axis) do not appear as shown in Figure 1–79, then drag the right side of the chart so that it is displayed in the range A11:G24.

7. Apply the worksheet name, Annual Revenue Analysis, to the sheet tab and apply the Orange, Accent 6, Darker 25% color to the sheet tab. Change the document properties, as specified by your instructor.

8. Save the workbook using the file name Lab 1-1 A Healthy Body Shop Annual Revenue Analysis.

9. Preview and print the worksheet in landscape orientation.

10. Make the following two corrections to the sales amounts: 62,675.45 for New York Weight Training (cell D7), 67,238.56 for Portland Cardiovascular (cell F5). After you enter the corrections, the company totals in cell G8 should equal $1,723,864.05.

11. Preview and print the revised worksheet in landscape orientation. Close the workbook without saving the changes.

12. Submit the assignment as specified by your instructor.

In the Lab

Lab 2: Semiannual Sales Analysis Worksheet

Problem: As the chief accountant for Play 'em Again, a reseller of cell phones, DVDs, electronic games, MP3 players, and accessories, you have been asked by the vice president to create a worksheet to analyze the semiannual sales for the company by products across sales channels (Figure 1–80 on the following page). The sales channels and corresponding revenue by product for the year are shown in Table 1–8.

Continued >

In the Lab *continued*

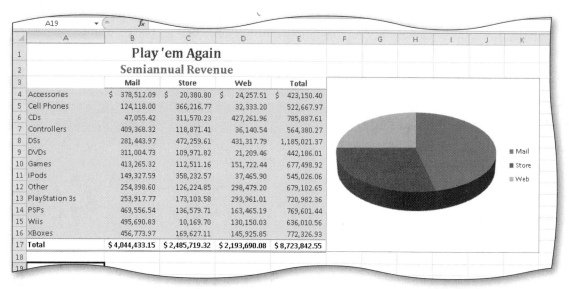

Figure 1–80

Instructions: Perform the following tasks.

1. Create the worksheet shown in Figure 1–80 using the data in Table 1–8.

2. Use the SUM function to determine total revenue for the three sales channels, the totals for each product, and the company total. Add column and row headings for the totals row and totals column, as appropriate.

Table 1–8 Play 'em Again Semiannual Revenue			
	Mail	**Store**	**Web**
Accessories	378512.09	20380.80	24257.51
Cell Phones	124118.00	366216.77	32333.20
CDs	47055.42	311570.23	427261.96
Controllers	409368.32	118871.41	36140.54
DSs	281443.97	472259.61	431317.79
DVDs	311004.73	109971.82	21209.46
Games	413265.32	112511.16	151722.44
iPods	149327.59	358232.57	37465.90
Other	254398.60	126224.85	298479.20
PlayStation 3s	253917.77	173103.58	293961.01
PSPs	469556.54	136579.71	163465.19
Wiis	495690.83	10169.70	130150.03
XBoxes	456773.97	169627.11	145925.85

3. Format the worksheet title with the Title cell style and center it across columns A through E. Use the Font group on the Ribbon to format the worksheet subtitle to 16-point Cambria red, bold font. Center the title across columns A through E.

4. Format the range B3:E3 with the Heading 3 cell style and center the text in the cells. Format the range A4:E16 with the 20% - Accent 4 cell style, and the range A17:E17 with the Total cell style. Format cells B4:E4 and B17:E17 with the Accounting Number Format and cells B5:E16 with the Comma Style numeric format.

5. Create a pie chart that shows the revenue contributions of each sales channel. Chart the sales channel names (B3:D3) and corresponding totals (B17:D17). That is, select the range B3:D3, and then while holding down the CTRL key, select the range B17:D17. Insert the Pie in 3-D chart, as shown in Figure 1–80, by using the Pie button (Insert tab | Charts group). Use the chart location F3: K17.

6. Apply the worksheet name, Semiannual Revenue, to the sheet tab and apply the Purple, Accent 4, Lighter 80% color to the sheet tab. Change the document properties, as specified by your instructor.

7. Save the workbook using the file name, Lab 1-2 Play 'em Again Semiannual Revenue. Print the worksheet in landscape orientation.

8. Two corrections to the figures were sent in from the accounting department. The correct revenue is $118,124.45 for Cell Phones sold through the mail (cell B5) and $43,573.67 for iPods sold over the Web (cell D11). After you enter the two corrections, the company total in cell E17 should equal $8,723,956.77. Print the revised worksheet in landscape orientation.

9. Use the Undo button to change the worksheet back to the original numbers in Table 1–8. Use the Redo button to change the worksheet back to the revised state.

10. Close Excel without saving the latest changes. Start Excel and open the workbook saved in Step 7. Double-click cell E6 and use in-cell editing to change the PSPs revenue (cell C14) to $128,857.32. Write the company total in cell E17 at the top of the first printout. Click the Undo button.

11. Click cell A1 and then click the Merge & Center button on the Home tab on the Ribbon to split cell A1 into cells A1, B1, C1, D1, and E1. To merge the cells into one again, select the range A1:E1 and then click the Merge & Center button.

12. Close the workbook without saving the changes. Submit the assignment as specified by your instructor.

In the Lab

Lab 3: Projected College Cash Flow Analysis Worksheet

Problem: Attending college is an expensive proposition and your resources are limited. To plan for your four-year college career, you have decided to organize your anticipated resources and expenses in a worksheet. The data required to prepare your worksheet is shown in Table 1–9.

Table 1–9 College Cost and Resources				
Resources	**Freshman**	**Sophomore**	**Junior**	**Senior**
529 Plans	2700.00	2889.00	3091.23	3307.62
Financial Aid	5250.00	5617.50	6010.73	6431.48
Job	3100.00	3317.00	3549.19	3797.63
Parents	3700.00	3959.00	4236.13	4532.66
Savings	4250.00	4547.50	4865.83	5206.43
Other	1100.00	1177.00	1259.39	1347.55
Expenses	**Freshman**	**Sophomore**	**Junior**	**Senior**
Activities Fee	500.00	535.00	572.45	612.52
Books	650.00	695.50	744.19	796.28
Clothes	750.00	802.50	858.68	918.78
Entertainment	1650.00	1765.50	1889.09	2021.32
Room & Board	7200.00	7704.00	8243.28	8820.31
Tuition	8250.00	8827.50	9445.43	10106.60
Miscellaneous	1100.00	1177.00	1259.39	1347.55

Continued >

In the Lab *continued*

Instructions Part 1: Using the numbers in Table 1–9, create the worksheet shown in columns A through F in Figure 1–81. Format the worksheet title as Calibri 24-point bold purple. Merge and center the worksheet title in cell A1 across columns A through F. Format the worksheet subtitles in cells A2 and A11 as Calibri 16-point bold red. Format the ranges A3:F3 and A12:F12 with the Heading 2 cell style and center the text in the cells. Format the ranges A4:F9 and A13:F19 with the 20% - Accent 2 cell style, and the ranges A10:F10 and A20:F20 with the Total cell style.

Change the name of the sheet tab and apply the Purple color from the Standard Colors area to the sheet tab. Update the document properties, including the addition of at least one keyword to the properties, and save the workbook using the file name, Lab 1-3 Part 1 College Resources and Expenses. Print the worksheet. Submit the assignment as specified by your instructor.

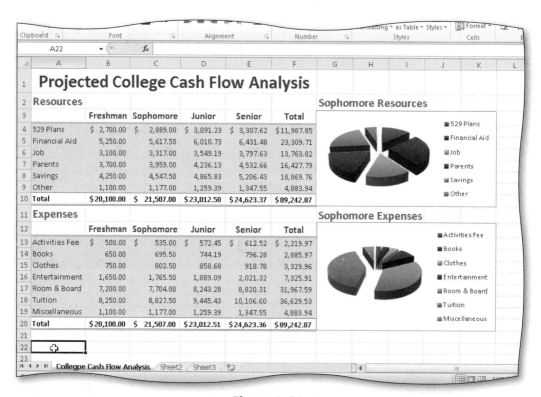

Figure 1–81

After reviewing the numbers, you realize you need to increase manually each of the Sophomore-year expenses in column C by $400, except for the Activities Fee. Change the Sophomore-year expenses to reflect this change. Manually change the Parents resources for the Sophomore year by the amount required to cover the increase in costs. The totals in cells F10 and F20 should equal $91,642.87. Print the worksheet. Close the workbook without saving changes.

Instructions Part 2: Open the workbook Lab 1-3 Part 1 College Resources and Expenses and then save the workbook using the file name, Lab 1-3 Part 2 College Resources and Expenses. Insert an Exploded pie in 3-D chart in the range G3:K10 to show the contribution of each category of resources for the Freshman year. Chart the range A4:B9 and apply the Style 26 chart style to the chart. Add the Pie chart title as shown in cell G2 in Figure 1–81. Insert an Exploded pie in 3-D chart in the range G12:K20 to show the contribution of each category of expenses for the Freshman year. Chart the range A13:B19 and apply the Style 26 chart style to the chart. Add the Pie chart title shown in cell G11 in Figure 1–81. Save the workbook. Print the worksheet in landscape orientation. Submit the assignment as specified by your instructor.

Instructions Part 3: Open the workbook Lab 1-3 Part 2 College Resources and Expenses and then save the workbook using the file name, Lab 1-3 Part 3 College Resources and Expenses. A close inspection of Table 1–9 shows that both cost and financial support figures increase 7% each year. Use Excel Help to learn how to enter the data for the last three years using a formula and the Copy and Paste buttons (Home tab | Clipboard group). For example, the formula to enter in cell C4 is =B4*1.07. Enter formulas to replace all the numbers in the range C4:E9 and C13:E19. If necessary, reformat the tables, as described in Part 1. The worksheet should appear as shown in Figure 1–81, except that some of the totals will be off by approximately 0.01 due to rounding errors. Save the workbook. Submit the assignment as specified by your instructor. Close the workbook without saving changes.

Cases and Places

Apply your creative thinking and problem solving skills to design and implement a solution.

1: Analyzing Quarterly Expenses

Academic

To estimate the funds needed by your school's Travel Club to make it through the upcoming quarter, you decide to create a report for the club itemizing the expected quarterly expenses. The anticipated expenses are listed in Table 1–10. Use the concepts and techniques presented in this chapter to create the worksheet and an embedded Clustered Cylinder chart. Be sure to use an appropriate chart style that compares the quarterly cost of each expense. Total each expense item and each quarter. Include a grand total for all of the expenses. Use the AutoCalculate area to determine the average amount spent per quarter on each expense. Manually insert the averages with appropriate titles in an appropriate area on the worksheet.

Table 1–10 Travel Club Quarterly Expenses				
	1st Quarter	**2nd Quarter**	**3rd Quarter**	**4th Quarter**
Copies and Supplies	75	50	80	150
Meeting Room Rent	400	425	400	425
Miscellaneous	150	100	175	70
Refreshments	130	155	150	225
Speaker Fees	200	200	400	500
Travel	450	375	500	375

2: Create an Exploded Pie in 3-D Chart to Summarize Property Values

Personal

Your wealthy Aunt Nicole owns several properties of varying value. She would like to see the values of the properties in a worksheet and chart that helps her to better understand her investments. She has asked you to develop a worksheet totaling the values of the properties and also to include other relevant statistics. The property values are: Property 1, $56,671.99; Property 2, $82,276.58; Property 3, $60,135.45; Property 4, $107,373.39; and Property 5, $87,512.82. Create an Exploded pie in 3-D chart to illustrate the relative property values. Use the AutoCalculate area to find the average, maximum, and minimum property values and manually enter them and their corresponding identifiers in an appropriate area of the worksheet. Use the Sum button to total the property values.

Continued >

Cases and Places *continued*

3: Analyzing Historical Yearly Sales

Business

You are working part-time for Noble's Mobile Services. Your manager has asked you to prepare a worksheet to help her analyze historical yearly sales by type of product (Table 1–11). Use the concepts and techniques presented in this chapter to create the worksheet and an embedded 3-D Clustered Column chart that includes proper numerical formatting, totaling, and formatting of the worksheet.

Table 1–11 Noble's Mobile Services Historical Yearly Sales				
	2008	2009	2010	2011
Camera Phones	92598	10487	136791	176785
Headsets	9035	8909	4886	6512
Music Phones	57942	44923	54590	67696
Other Accessories	27604	38793	24483	33095
Satellite Radios	17161	19293	30763	44367
Standard Mobile Phones	8549	9264	7600	6048
Wireless PDAs	57963	68059	103025	87367

1 Databases and Database Objects: An Introduction

Objectives

You will have mastered the material in this chapter when you can:

- Design a database to satisfy a collection of requirements
- Describe the features of the Access window
- Create a database
- Create tables in Datasheet and Design views
- Add records to a table

- Close a database
- Open a database
- Print the contents of a table
- Create and use a query
- Create and use a form
- Create and print custom reports
- Modify a report in Layout view

1 | Databases and Database Objects: An Introduction

Introduction

The term **database** describes a collection of data organized in a manner that allows access, retrieval, and use of that data. Microsoft Access 2010, usually referred to as simply Access, is a database management system. A **database management system**, such as Access, is software that allows you to use a computer to create a database; add, change, and delete data in the database; ask and answer questions concerning the data in the database; and create forms and reports using the data in the database.

Project Planning Guidelines

> The process of developing a database that communicates specific information requires careful analysis and planning. As a starting point, establish why the database is needed. Once the purpose is determined, analyze the intended users of the database and their unique needs. Then, gather information about the topic and decide what to include in the database. Finally, determine the database design and style that will be most successful at delivering the message. Details of these guidelines are provided in Appendix A. In addition, each project in this book provides practical applications of these planning considerations.

Project — Database Creation

Camashaly Design Group is a small company that provides custom marketing solutions for the service, nonprofit, and retail sectors. Alyssa Morgan, Camden Scott, and Ashton James started the business after they graduated from a local university. The three owners, all computer graphics design majors and business minors, worked on a service learning project during college that produced a Web site for a nonprofit organization. Alyssa, Camden, and Ashton worked well together. Upon researching the local area for competing businesses, they decided to form their own company. The company specializes in designing and maintaining Web sites and using social networking Web sites for online marketing. They also conduct market research and develop printed media. Camashaly already has received one award for its design work. Camashaly is also recognized for its efforts in providing work opportunities to individuals who want flexible schedules and to student interns.

BTW

BTWs
For a complete list of the BTWs found in the margins of this book, visit the Access 2010 BTW Web page (scsite.com/ac2010/btw).

Camashaly uses business analysts to work collaboratively with clients. Business analysts are employees who translate business requirements into marketing specifications and serve as the interface between clients and Camashaly. Business analysts are paid a base salary and can earn incentive pay for maintaining and expanding client relationships.

Camashaly charges a one-time fee for Web site development. Clients can pay for Web site maintenance by contracting for a specified number of hours or can pay for maintenance on an hour-by-hour basis. Other fees vary depending on the specific scope of work.

To ensure that operations run smoothly, Camashaly organizes data on its clients and business analysts in a database managed by Access. In this way, Camashaly keeps its data current and accurate while the owners can analyze the data for trends and produce a variety of useful reports. In this chapter, you will create the Camashaly database.

In a **relational database** such as those maintained by Access, a database consists of a collection of tables, each of which contains information on a specific subject. Figure 1–1 shows the database for Camashaly Design. It consists of two tables: the Client table (Figure 1–1a) contains information about the clients to whom Camashaly provides services, and the Business Analyst table (Figure 1–1b) contains information about the business analysts to whom these clients are assigned.

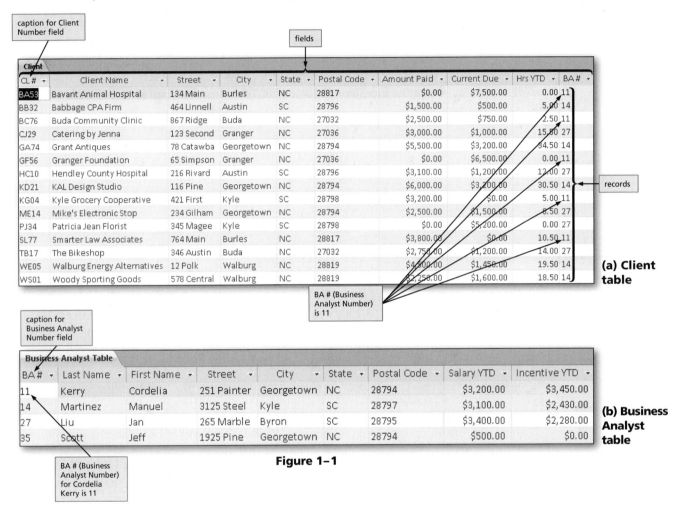

Figure 1–1

The rows in the tables are called **records**. A record contains information about a given person, product, or event. A row in the Client table, for example, contains information about a specific client, such as the client's name, address information, and other data.

The columns in the tables are called fields. A **field** contains a specific piece of information within a record. In the Client table, for example, the fourth field, City, contains the name of the city where the client is located.

The first field in the Client table is CL #, which is an abbreviation for Client Number. Camashaly Design assigns each client a client number. As is common to the way in which many organizations format client numbers, Camashaly Design calls it a number, although it actually contains letters. The Camashaly client numbers consist of two uppercase letters followed by a two-digit number.

The client numbers are unique; that is, no two clients are assigned the same number. Such a field can be used as a **unique identifier**. A unique identifier, as its name suggests, is a way of uniquely identifying each record in the database. A given client number will appear only in a single record in the table. Only one record exists, for example, in which the client number is BB32. A unique identifier also is called a **primary key**. Thus, the Client Number field is the primary key for the Client table.

The next eight fields in the Client table are Client Name, Street, City, State, Postal Code, Amount Paid, Current Due, and Hrs YTD, which is an abbreviation for Contract Hours YTD. YTD is an abbreviation for year to date. The Amount Paid column contains the amount that the client has paid Camashaly Design YTD prior to the current period. The Current Due column contains the amount due to Camashaly for the current period. The Hrs YTD column contains the number of hours the client has contracted for Web site maintenance so far this year. For example, client BB32 is Babbage CPA Firm. The address is 464 Linnell in Austin, South Carolina. The postal code is 28796. The client has paid $1,500.00 for services so far this year. The amount due for the current period is $500.00. The client has contracted for 5.00 hours of Web site maintenance.

Camashaly assigns a single business analyst to work with each client. The last column in the Client table, BA #, which is an abbreviation for Business Analyst Number, gives the number of the client's business analyst.

The first field in the Business Analyst table is also BA #, an abbreviation for Business Analyst Number. The business analyst numbers are unique, so the Business Analyst Number field is the primary key of the Business Analyst table.

The other fields in the Business Analyst table are Last Name, First Name, Street, City, State, Postal Code, Salary YTD, and Incentive YTD. The Salary YTD field gives the salary paid to the analyst thus far this year. The Incentive YTD gives the incentive for which the analyst qualified thus far this year. For example, business analyst 14 is Manuel Martinez. His address is 3125 Steel in Kyle, South Carolina. The Postal Code is 28797. So far this year, he has been paid $3,100.00 in salary. He has earned $2,430.00 in incentive pay.

The business analyst number appears in both the Client table and the Business Analyst table, and relates clients and business analysts. For example, in the Client table, you see that the business analyst number for client Babbage CPA Firm is 14. To find the name of this business analyst, look for the row in the Business Analyst table that contains 14 in the BA # column. After you have found it, you know the client is assigned to Manuel Martinez. To find all the clients assigned to Cordelia Kerry, you would first look in the Business Analyst table to find that her number is 11. You would then look through the Client table for all the clients that contain 11 in the BA # column. Her clients are BA53 (Bavant Animal Hospital), BC76 (Buda Community Clinic), GF56 (Granger Foundation), KG04 (Kyle Grocery Cooperative), and SL77 (Smarter Law Associates).

The last business analyst in the Business Analyst table, Jeff Scott, has not been assigned any clients yet; therefore, his business analyst number, 35, does not appear on any row in the Client table.

Overview

As you read this chapter, you will learn how to create the database shown in Figure 1–1 by performing these general tasks:

- Design the database.
- Create a new blank database.
- Create a table and add the records.
- Preview and print the contents of a table.
- Create a second table and import the records.
- Create a simple query.
- Create a simple form.
- Create and modify a report.

Database Design Guidelines

Plan
Ahead

Database design refers to the arrangement of data into tables and fields. In the example in this chapter, the design is specified, but in many cases, you will have to determine the design based on what you want the system to accomplish.

When designing a database to satisfy a given set of requirements, the actions you take and the decisions you make will determine the tables and fields that will be included in the database. As you create a database, such as the one shown in Figure 1–1 on page AC 3, you should follow these general guidelines:

1. **Identify the tables.** Examine the requirements for the database to identify the main objects that are involved. There will be a table for each object you identify.

   In one database, for example, the main objects might be departments and employees. Thus, there would be two tables: one for departments and the other for employees. In another database, the main objects might be clients and business analysts. In this case, there also would be two tables: one for clients and the other for business analysts. In still another database, the main objects might be books, publishers, and authors. This database would require three tables: one for books, a second for publishers, and a third for authors.

2. **Determine the primary keys.** Recall that the primary key is the unique identifier for records in the table. For each table, determine the unique identifier. In a Department table, for example, the unique identifier might be the Department Code. For a Book table, the unique identifier might be the ISBN.

3. **Determine the additional fields.** The primary key will be a field or combination of fields in a table. A table typically will contain many additional fields, each of which contains a type of data. Examine the project requirements to determine these additional fields. For example, in an Employee table, the additional fields might include such fields as Employee Name, Street Address, City, State, Postal Code, Date Hired, Salary, and so on.

4. **Determine relationships between the tables.** Examine the list of tables you have created to see which tables are related. When you determine that two tables are related, include matching fields in the two tables. For example, in a database containing employees and departments, there is a relationship between the two tables because one department can have many employees assigned to it. Department Code could be the matching field in the two tables.

5. **Determine data types for the fields.** For each field, determine the type of data the field can contain. One field, for example, might contain only numbers. Another field might contain currency amounts, while a third field might contain only dates. Some fields contain text data, meaning any combination of letters, numbers, and special characters (!, ;, ', &, and so on). For example, in an Employee table, the Date Hired field would contain dates, the Salary field would contain currency amounts, and the Hours Worked field would contain numbers. The other fields in the Employee table would contain text data, such as Employee Name and Department Code.

6. **Identify and remove any unwanted redundancy.** Redundancy is the storing of a piece of data in more than one place. Redundancy usually, but not always, causes problems, such as wasted space, difficulties with update, and possible data inconsistency. Examine each table you have created to see if it contains redundancy and, if so, determine whether the redundancy causes the problems described. If it does, remove the redundancy by splitting the table into two tables. For example, you might have a single table of employees. In addition to typical employee data (name, address, earnings, and so on), the table might contain Department Number and Department Name. If so, the Department Name could repeat multiple times. Every employee whose department number is 12, for example, would have the same department name. It would be better to split the table into two tables: one for Employees and one for Department. In the Department table, the Department Name is stored only once.

7. **Determine a storage location for the database.** The database you have designed will be stored in a single file. You need to determine a location in which to store the file.

8. **Determine additional properties for fields.** Before creating the database, determine any other properties you should specify for the fields. These could include a field size, which is

(continued)

Plan
Ahead

(continued)

the maximum number of characters that can be stored in the field. If you want something other than the field name to appear at the top of a column (such as an abbreviation), you can change the caption to the desired heading. You also can add a description, which is a message that appears on the screen concerning a field whenever the field is selected.

9. **Determine the best method for distributing the database objects.** The traditional method of distributing database objects uses a printer to produce a hard copy of a table or report on paper. You also can distribute the table as an electronic image that mirrors the original table's appearance.

When necessary, more specific details concerning the above guidelines are presented at appropriate points in the chapter. The chapter also will identify the actions performed and decisions made regarding these guidelines during the creation of the database shown in Figure 1–1 on page AC 3.

Designing a Database

This section illustrates the database design process by showing how you would design the database for Camashaly Design from a set of requirements. In this section, you will use commonly accepted shorthand to represent the tables and fields that make up the database as well as the primary keys for the tables. For each table, you give the name of the table followed by a set of parentheses. Within the parentheses is a list of the fields in the table separated by columns. You underline the primary key. For example,

BTW

Determining Database Requirements
The determination of database requirements is part of a process known as systems analysis. A systems analyst examines existing and proposed documents, and examines organizational policies to determine exactly the type of data needs the database must support.

Product (<u>Product Code</u>, Description, On Hand, Price)

represents a table called Product. The Product table contains four fields: Product Code, Description, On Hand, and Price. The Product Code field is the primary key.

Database Requirements

The Camashaly Design database must maintain information on both clients and business analysts. The business currently keeps this data in two Word tables and two Excel workbooks, as shown in Figure 1–2. They use Word tables for address information and Excel workbooks for financial information.

Client Number	Client Name	Street	City	State	Postal Code
BA53	Bavant Animal Hospital	134 Main	Burles	NC	28817
BB32	Babbage CPA Firm	464 Linnell	Austin	SC	28796
BC76	Buda Community Clinic	867 Ridge	Buda	NC	27032
CJ29	Catering by Jenna	123 Second	Granger	NC	27036
GA74	Grant Antiques	78 Catawba	Georgetown	NC	28794
GF56	Granger Foundation	65 Simpson	Granger	NC	27036
HC10	Hendley County Hospital	216 Rivard	Austin	SC	28796
KD21	KAL Design Studio	116 Pine	Georgetown	NC	28794
KG04	Kyle Grocery Cooperative	421 First	Kyle	SC	28798
ME14	Mike's Electronic Stop	234 Gilham	Georgetown	NC	28794
PJ34	Patricia Jean Florist	345 Magee	Kyle	SC	28798
SL77	Smarter Law Associates	764 Main	Burles	NC	28817
TB17	The Bikeshop	346 Austin	Buda	NC	27032
WE05	Walburg Energy Alternatives	12 Polk	Walburg	NC	28819
WS01	Woody Sporting Goods	578 Central	Walburg	NC	28819

Figure 1–2   (a) Client Address Information (Word Table)

	A	B	C	D	E	F	G	H
1	Client Number	Client Name	Amount Paid	Current Due	Contract Hours YTD			
2	BA53	Bavant Animal Hospital	0.00	7,500.00	0			
3	BB32	Babbage CPA Firm	1,500.00	500.00	5			
4	BC76	Buda Community Clinic	2,500.00	750.00	2.5			
5	CJ29	Catering by Jenna	3,000.00	1,000.00	15.5			
6	GA74	Grant Antiques	5,500.00	3,200.00	34.5			
7	GF56	Granger Foundation	0.00	6,500.00	0			
8	HC10	Hendley County Hospital	3,100.00	1,200.00	12			
9	KD21	KAL Design Studio	6,000.00	3,200.00	30.5			
10	KG04	Kyle Grocery Cooperative	3,200.00	0.00	5			
11	ME14	Mike's Electronic Stop	2,500.00	1,500.00	8.5			
12	PJ34	Patricia Jean Florist	0.00	5,200.00	0			
13	SL77	Smarter Law Associates	3,800.00	0.00	10.5			
14	TB17	The Bikeshop	2,750.00	1,200.00	14			
15	WE05	Walburg Energy Alternatives	4,500.00	1,450.00	19.5			
16	WS01	Woody Sporting Goods	2,250.00	1,600.00	18.5			

Figure 1–2   (b) Client Financial Information (Excel Worksheet)

Business Analyst Number	Last Name	First Name	Street	City	State	Postal Code
11	Kerry	Cordelia	251 Painter	Georgetown	NC	28794
14	Martinez	Manuel	3125 Steel	Kyle	SC	28797
27	Liu	Jan	265 Marble	Byron	SC	28795
35	Scott	Jeff	1925 Pine	Georgetown	NC	28794

Figure 1–2   (c) Business Analyst Address Information (Word Table)

	A	B	C	D	E	F	G	H	I
1	Business Analyst Number	Last Name	First Name	Salary YTD	Incentive YTD				
2	11	Kerry	Cordelia	3,200.00	3,450.00				
3	14	Martinez	Manuel	3,100.00	2,430.00				
4	27	Liu	Jan	3,400.00	2,280.00				
5	35	Scott	Jeff	500.00	0.00				

Figure 1–2   (d) Business Analyst Financial Information (Excel Worksheet)

For clients, Camashaly needs to maintain address data. It currently keeps this address data in a Word table (Figure 1–2a). It also maintains financial data for each client. This includes the amount paid, current amount due, and contract hours YTD for the client. It keeps these amounts, along with the client name and number, in the Excel workbook shown in Figure 1–2b.

Camashaly keeps business analyst address data in a Word table, as shown in Figure 1–2c. Just as with clients, it keeps financial data for business analysts, including their salary YTD and incentive YTD, in a separate Excel workbook, as shown in Figure 1–2d.

Finally, it keeps track of which clients are assigned to which business analysts. Each client is assigned to a single business analyst, but each business analyst might be assigned many clients. Currently, for example, clients BA53 (Bavant Animal Hospital), BC76 (Buda Community Clinic), GF56 (Granger Foundation), KG04 (Kyle Grocery Cooperative), and SL77 (Smarter Law Associates) are assigned to business analyst 11 (Cordelia Kerry). Clients BB32 (Babbage CPA Firm), GA74 (Grant Antiques), KD21 (KAL Design Studio), WE05 (Walburg Energy Alternatives), and WS01 (Woody Sporting Goods) are assigned to business analyst 14 (Manuel Martinez). Clients CJ29 (Catering by Jenna), HC10 (Hendley County Hospital), ME14 (Mike's Electronic Stop), PJ34 (Patricia Jean Florist), and TB17 (The Bikeshop) are assigned to business analyst 27 (Jan Liu). Camashaly has an additional business analyst, Jeff Scott, whose number has been assigned as 35, but who has not yet been assigned any clients.

BTW

Additional Data for Camashaly
There are many other types of data that Camashaly could include in a database. For example, they might keep all employee information in a database as well as information on client contracts and an inventory of hardware and software.

Naming Tables and Fields

BTW

Naming Files
The following characters cannot be used in a file name: question mark (?), quotation mark ("), slash (/), backslash (\ ), colon (:), asterisk (*), vertical bar (|), greater than symbol (>), and less than symbol (<).

In designing your database, you must name the tables and fields. Thus, before beginning the design process, you must understand the rules Access applies to table and field names. These rules are:

1. Names can be up to 64 characters in length.
2. Names can contain letters, digits, and spaces, as well as most of the punctuation symbols.
3. Names cannot contain periods (.), exclamation points (!), accent graves (`), or square brackets ([ ]).
4. The same name cannot be used for two different fields in the same table.

The approach to naming tables and fields used in this text is to begin the names with an uppercase letter and to use lowercase for the other letters. In multiple-word names, each word begins with an uppercase letter, and there is a space between words (for example, Client Number). You should know that other approaches exist, all of which are acceptable in Access. Some people omit the space (ClientNumber). Still others use an underscore in place of the space (Client_Number). Finally, some use an underscore in place of a space, but use the same case for all letters (CLIENT_NUMBER or client_number).

Identifying the Tables

BTW

Naming Fields
Access 2010 has a number of reserved words, words that have a special meaning to Access. You cannot use these reserved words as field names. For example, Name is a reserved word and could not be used in the Client table to describe a client's name. For a complete list of reserved words in Access 2010, consult Access Help.

Now that you know the rules for naming tables and fields, you are ready to begin the design process. The first step is to identify the main objects involved in the requirements. For the Camashaly Design database, the main objects are clients and business analysts. This leads to two tables, which you must name. Reasonable names for these two tables are:

Client

Business Analyst

Determining the Primary Keys

The next step is to identify the fields that will be the unique identifiers, or primary keys. Client numbers uniquely identify clients, and business analyst numbers uniquely identify business analysts. Thus, the primary key for the Client table is the client number, and the primary key for the Business Analyst table is the business analyst number. Reasonable names for these fields would be Client Number and Business Analyst Number, respectively. Adding these primary keys to the tables gives:

Client (<u>Client Number</u>)
Business Analyst (<u>Business Analyst Number</u>)

Determining Additional Fields

After identifying the primary keys, you need to determine and name the additional fields. In addition to the client number, the Client Address Information shown in Figure 1–2a on page AC 6 contains the client name, street, city, state, and postal code. These would be fields in the Client table. The Client Financial Information shown in Figure 1–2b also contains the client number and client name, which are already included in the Client table. The financial information also contains the amount paid, current due, and contract hours YTD. Adding the amount paid, current due, and contract hours YTD fields to those already identified in the Client table and assigning reasonable names gives:

Client (<u>Client Number</u>, Client Name, Street, City, State, Postal Code,
    Amount Paid, Current Due, Contract Hours YTD)

Similarly, examining the Business Analyst Address Information in Figure 1–2c adds the last name, first name, street, city, state, and postal code fields to the Business Analyst table. In addition to the business analyst number, last name, and first name, the Business Analyst Financial Information in Figure 1–2d would add the salary YTD and Incentive YTD. Adding these fields to the Business Analyst table and assigning reasonable names gives:

> Business Analyst (<u>Business Analyst Number</u>, Last Name, First Name, Street, City, State, Postal Code, Salary YTD, Incentive YTD)

Determining and Implementing Relationships Between the Tables

Plan
Ahead

Determine relationships between the tables.
The most common type of relationship you will encounter between tables is the **one-to-many relationship**. This means that each row in the first table may be associated with many rows in the second table, but each row in the second table is associated with only one row in the first. The first table is called the "one" table and the second is called the "many" table. For example, there may be a relationship between departments and employees, in which each department can have many employees, but each employee is assigned to only one department. In this relationship, there would be two tables, Department and Employee. The Department table would be the "one" table in the relationship. The Employee table would be the "many" table.

> To determine relationships between tables, you can follow these general guidelines:

- Identify the "one" table.
- Identify the "many" table.
- Include the primary key from the "one" table as a field in the "many" table.

According to the requirements, each client has one business analyst, but each business analyst can have many clients. Thus, the Business Analyst table is the "one" table, and the Client table is the "many" table. To implement this one-to-many relationship between business analysts and clients, add the Business Analyst Number field (the primary key of the Business Analyst table) to the Client table. This produces:

> Client (<u>Client Number</u>, Client Name, Street, City, State, Postal Code, Amount Paid, Current Due, Contract Hours YTD, Business Analyst Number)
> Business Analyst (<u>Business Analyst Number</u>, Last Name, First Name, Street, City, State, Postal Code, Salary YTD, Incentive YTD)

BTW

Database Design Language (DBDL)
DBDL is a commonly accepted shorthand representation for showing the structure of a relational database. You write the name of the table and then within parentheses you list all the columns in the table. If the columns continue beyond one line, indent the subsequent lines.

Determining Data Types for the Fields

Each field has a **data type**. This indicates the type of data that can be stored in the field. Three of the most commonly used data types are:

1. **Text** — The field can contain any characters. A maximum number of 255 characters is allowed in a field whose data type is Text.

2. **Number** — The field can contain only numbers. The numbers either can be positive or negative. Fields are assigned this type so they can be used in arithmetic operations. Fields that contain numbers but will not be used for arithmetic operations (such as postal codes) usually are assigned a data type of Text.

3. **Currency** — The field can contain only monetary data. The values will appear with currency symbols, such as dollar signs, commas, and decimal points, and with two digits following the decimal point. Like numeric fields, you can use currency fields in arithmetic operations. Access assigns a size to currency fields automatically.

Table 1–1 shows the other data types that are available in Access.

BTW

Data Types
Different database
management systems have
different available data
types. Even data types that
are essentially the same
can have different names.
The Currency data type
in Access, for example, is
referred to as Money in
SQL Server.

Table 1–1 Additional Data Types

Data Type	Description
Memo	Field can store a variable amount of text or combinations of text and numbers where the total number of characters may exceed 255.
Date/Time	Field can store dates and times.
AutoNumber	Field can store a unique sequential number that Access assigns to a record. Access will increment the number by 1 as each new record is added.
Yes/No	Field can store only one of two values. The choices are Yes/No, True/False, or On/Off.
OLE Object	Field can store an OLE object, which is an object linked to or embedded in the table.
Hyperlink	Field can store text that can be used as a hyperlink address.
Attachment	Field can contain an attached file. Images, spreadsheets, documents, charts, and so on can be attached to this field in a record in the database. You can view and edit the attached file.
Calculated	Field specified as a calculation based on other fields. The value is not actually stored.

In the Client table, because the Client Number, Client Name, Street, City, and State can all contain letters, their data types should be Text. The data type for Postal Code is Text instead of Number because postal codes are not used in arithmetic operations; you do not add postal codes or find an average postal code, for example. The Amount Paid and Current Due fields both contain monetary data, so their data types should be Currency. The Contract Hours YTD field contains a number that is not a currency amount, so its data type should be Number.

Similarly, in the Business Analyst table, the data type for the Business Analyst Number, Last Name, First Name, Street, City, State, and Postal Code fields all should be Text. The Salary YTD and Incentive YTD fields both contain monetary amounts, so their data types should be Currency.

Fields whose data type is Number often require you to change the field size, which is the storage space assigned to the field by Access. Table 1–2 shows the possible field sizes for Number fields. If the size were Byte, Integer, or Long Integer, for example, only integers could be stored. If you try to store a value that has decimal places, such as 2.50, the portion to the right of the decimal point would be removed, giving a result of 2. To address this problem, you would change to a size such as Single.

Table 1–2 Field Sizes for Number Fields

Field Size	Description
Byte	Integer value in the range of 0 to 255
Integer	Integer value in the range of –32,768 to 32,767
Long Integer	Integer value in the range of –2,147,483,648 to 2,147,483,647
Single	Numeric values with decimal places to seven significant digits — requires 4 bytes of storage
Double	Numeric values with decimal places to more accuracy than Single — requires 8 bytes of storage
Replication ID	Special identifier required for replication
Decimal	Numeric values with decimal places to more accuracy than Single or Double — requires 12 bytes of storage.

Identifying and Removing Redundancy

Redundancy means storing the same fact in more than one place. It usually results from placing too many fields in a table — fields that really belong in separate tables — and often causes serious problems. If you had not realized there were two objects, clients and business analysts, for example, you might have placed all the data in a single Client table. Figure 1–3 shows an example of a table that includes both client and business analyst information. Notice that the data for a given business analyst (number, name, address, and so on) occurs on more than one record. The data for analyst 11, Cordelia Kerry, is repeated in the figure.

Client Table

Client Number	Client Name	Street	...	Business Analyst Number	Last Name	First Name	...
BA53	Bavant Animal Hospital	134 Main	...	11	Kerry	Cordelia	...
BB32	Babbage CPA Firm	464 Linnell	...	14	Martinez	Manuel	...
BC76	Buda Community Clinic	867 Ridge	...	11	Kerry	Cordelia	...
...	...	...	...	...	...	...	...

business analyst numbers are 11

name of business analyst 11 appears more than once

Figure 1–3

Storing this data on multiple records is an example of redundancy, which causes several problems, including:

1. Wasted storage space. The name of business analyst 11, Cordelia Kerry, for example, should be stored only once. Storing this fact several times is wasteful.

2. More difficult database updates. If, for example, Cordelia Kerry's name is spelled wrong and needs to be changed in the database, her name would need to be changed in several different places.

3. A possibility of inconsistent data. Nothing prohibits the business analyst's last name from being Kerry on client BA53's record and Bronson on client BC76's record. The data would be inconsistent. In both cases, the business analyst number is 11, but the last names are different.

The solution to the problem is to place the redundant data in a separate table, one in which the data no longer will be redundant. If, for example, you place the data for business analysts in a separate table (Figure 1–4), the data for each business analyst will appear only once.

Client Table

Client Number	Client Name	Street	...	Business Analyst Number
BA53	Bavant Animal Hospital	134 Main	...	11
BB32	Babbage CPA Firm	464 Linnell	...	14
BC76	Buda Community Clinic	867 Ridge	...	11
...	...	...		

business analyst numbers are 11

Business Analyst Table

Business Analyst Number	Last Name	First Name	...
11	Kerry	Cordelia	...
14	Martinez	Manuel	...
...	...		...

name of business analyst 11 appears only once

Figure 1–4

BTW

Postal Codes
Some organizations with customers throughout the country have a separate table of postal codes, cities, and states. When placing an order, you typically are asked for your postal code (or ZIP code), rather than city, state, and postal code. You then are asked to confirm that the city and state correspond to that postal code.

Notice that you need to have the business analyst number in both tables. Without it, there would be no way to tell which business analyst is associated with which client. The remaining business analyst data, however, was removed from the Client table and placed in the Business Analyst table. This new arrangement corrects the problems of redundancy in the following ways:

1. Because the data for each business analyst is stored only once, space is not wasted.

2. Changing the name of a business analyst is easy. You have only to change one row in the Business Analyst table.

3. Because the data for a business analyst is stored only once, inconsistent data cannot occur. Designing to omit redundancy will help you to produce good and valid database designs.

You should always examine your design to see if it contains redundancy. If it does, you should decide whether you need to remove the redundancy by creating a separate table.

If you examine your design, you'll see that there is one area of redundancy (see the data in Figure 1–1 on page AC 3). Cities and states are both repeated. Every client whose postal code is 28794, for example, has Georgetown as the city and NC as the state. To remove this redundancy, you would create a table whose primary key is Postal Code and that contains City and State as additional fields. City and State would be removed from the Client table. Having City, State, and Postal Code in a table is very common, however, and usually you would not take such action. No other redundancy exists in your tables.

For an introduction to Windows 7 and instruction about how to perform basic Windows 7 tasks, read the Office 2010 and Windows 7 chapter at the beginning of this book, where you can learn how to resize windows, change screen resolution, create folders, move and rename files, use Windows Help, and much more.

To Start Access

If you are using a computer to step through the project in this chapter and you want your screens to match the figures in this book, you should change your screen's resolution to 1024×768. For information about how to change a computer's resolution, refer to the Office 2010 and Windows 7 chapter at the beginning of this book.

The following steps, which assume Windows 7 is running, start Access based on a typical installation. You may need to ask your instructor how to start Access for your computer. For a detailed example of the procedure summarized below, refer to the Office 2010 and Windows 7 chapter.

1 Click the Start button on the Windows 7 taskbar to display the Start menu.

2 Type **Microsoft Access** as the search text in the 'Search programs and files' text box and watch the search results appear on the Start menu.

3 Click Microsoft Access 2010 in the search results on the Start menu to start Access and display the Backstage view for Access.

4 If the Access window is not maximized, click the Maximize button next to the Close button on its title bar to maximize the window.

Creating a Database

In Access, all the tables, reports, forms, and queries that you create are stored in a single file called a database. Thus, you first must create the database to hold the tables, reports, forms, and queries. You can use either the Blank database option or a template to create a new database. If you already know the tables and fields you want in your database, you would use the Blank database option. If not, you can use a template. Templates can guide you by suggesting some commonly used databases.

Determine a storage location for the database.
When creating a database, you must decide which storage medium to use.

If you always work on the same computer and have no need to transport your database to a different location, then your computer's hard drive will suffice as a storage location. It is a good idea, however, to save a backup copy of your database on a separate medium in case the file becomes corrupted or the computer's hard drive fails.

If you plan to work on your database in various locations or on multiple computers, then you can consider saving your projects on a portable medium, such as a USB flash drive or CD. The projects in this book are stored on a USB flash drive, which saves files quickly and reliably and can be reused. CDs are easily portable and serve as good backups for the final versions of projects because they generally can save files only one time.

**Plan
Ahead**

For an introduction to Office 2010 and instruction about how to perform basic tasks in Office 2010 programs, read the Office 2010 and Windows 7 chapter at the beginning of this book, where you can learn how to start a program, use the Ribbon, save a file, open a file, quit a program, use Help, and much more.

To Create a Database

Because you already know the tables and fields you want in the Camashaly Design database, you would use the Blank database option rather than using a template. The following steps assume you already have created folders for storing your files, for example, a CIS 101 folder (for your class) that contains an Access folder (for your assignments). Thus, these steps save the document in the Access folder in the CIS 101 folder on a USB flash drive using the file name, Camashaly Design. For a detailed example of the procedure summarized below, refer to the Office 2010 and Windows 7 chapter at the beginning of this book.

① With a USB flash drive connected to one of the computer's USB ports, ensure the New tab is selected in the Backstage view and that Blank database is selected in the New gallery.

② Click the Browse button in the right pane of the New gallery to display the File New Database dialog box.

③ Type `Camashaly Design` in the File New Database dialog box to change the file name. Do not press the ENTER key after typing the file name.

④ Navigate to the desired save location (in this case, the Access folder in the CIS 101 folder [or your class folder] on the USB flash drive).

⑤ Click the OK button, which returns you to the New gallery. (Your screen may show Camashaly Design.accdb.)

⑥ Click the Create button in the right pane of the New gallery to create the database on the selected drive with the entered file name (Figure 1–5).

BTW

Q&As
For a complete list of the Q&As found in many of the step-by-step sequences in this book, visit the Access 2010 Q&A Web page (scsite.com/ac2010/qa).

Q&A

The title bar for my Navigation Pane contains All Tables rather than All Access Objects, as in the figure. Is that a problem?

It is not a problem. The title bar indicates how the Navigation Pane is organized. You can carry out the steps in the text with either organization. To make your screens match the ones in the text, click the Navigation Pane arrow and then click Object Type.

Q&A

I do not have the Search bar that appears on the figure. Is that a problem?

It is not a problem. If your Navigation Pane does not display a Search bar and you want your screens to match the ones in the text, right-click the Navigation Pane title bar arrow to display a shortcut menu, and then click Search Bar.

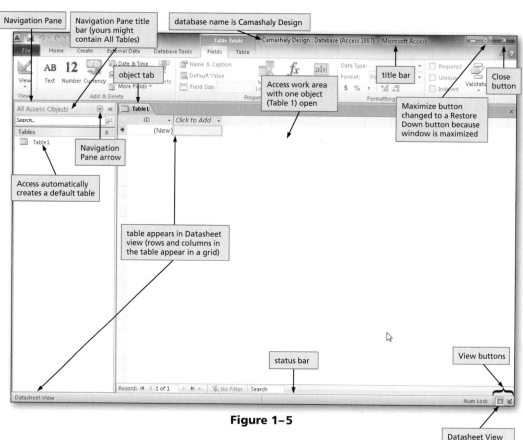

Figure 1–5

To Create a Database Using a Template

BTW

Available Templates
The Blank web database button on the New tab in the Backstage view allows you to create a database that you can publish to a SharePoint server running Access Services. Access 2010 also includes five Web-based templates. To display previously used templates, click the My templates button.

Ideally, you will design your own database, create a blank database, and then create the tables you have determined that your database should contain. If you are not sure what database design you will need, you could use a template. Templates can guide you by suggesting some commonly used databases. To create a database using a template, you would use the following steps.

1. After starting Access, be sure the Backstage view is open. If it is not, click File on the Ribbon to open it.

2. Click the New tab if it is not already selected.

3. Click Sample templates to display a list of templates stored locally or search Microsoft Office online for additional templates.

4. Click the template you want to use.

5. Enter a file name (or accept the suggested file name) and select a location for the database.

6. Click the Create button to create the database or the Download button to download the database and create the database, if necessary.

The Access Window

The Access window consists of a variety of components to make your work more efficient and documents more professional. These include the Navigation Pane, Access work area, Ribbon, shortcut menus, and Quick Access Toolbar. Some of these components are common to other Microsoft Office 2010 programs; others are unique to Access.

Navigation Pane and Access Work Area

You work on objects such as tables, forms, and reports in the **Access work area**. In the work area in Figure 1–5, a single table, Table1, is open in the work area. **Object tabs** for the open objects appear at the top of the work area. If you have multiple objects open at the same time, you can select one of the open objects by clicking its tab. To the left of the work area is the Navigation Pane. The **Navigation Pane** contains a list of all the objects in the database. You use this pane to open an object. You also can customize the way objects are displayed in the Navigation Pane.

The **status bar**, located at the bottom of the Access window, presents information about the database object, the progress of current tasks, and the status of certain commands and keys; it also provides controls for viewing the object. As you type text or perform certain commands, various indicators may appear on the status bar. The left edge of the status bar in Figure 1–5 shows that the table object is open in Datasheet view. Toward the right edge are View buttons, which you can use to change the view that currently is displayed.

Creating a Table

To create a table, you must describe the structure of the table to Access. That is, you must describe all the fields that make up the table and their characteristics. You must also indicate the primary key.

In Access, you can use two different views to create a table: Datasheet view and Design view. In **Datasheet view**, the data in the table is presented in rows and columns, similar to a spreadsheet. Although the main reason to use Datasheet view is to add or update records in a table, you can also use it to create a table or to later modify its structure. The other view, **Design view**, is only used to create a table or to modify the structure of the table.

As you might expect, Design view has more functionality for creating a table than Datasheet view. That is, there are certain actions that can only be performed in Design view. If creating your table requires such actions, you must use Design view. If not, you can choose either view. In this chapter, you will create the first table, the Business Analyst table, in Datasheet view. You will create the second table, the Client table, in Design view.

Whichever view you choose to use, before creating the table, you need to determine the names and data types of the fields that will make up the table. You already have determined the types for the Camashaly fields. You also need to determine additional properties for the fields.

BTW

The Ribbon and Screen Resolution
Access may change how the groups and buttons within the groups appear on the Ribbon, depending on the computer's screen resolution. Thus, your Ribbon may look different from the ones in this book if you are using a screen resolution other than 1024 × 768.

> **Determine additional properties for fields.**
>
> • **Determine if a special caption is warranted.** Normally, the field name will appear as the label for a field on a form or report and as the column name in Datasheet view. If you would rather have a different name appear, you can change the field's caption to the desired name. One common use of captions is to shorten the column heading. If the data in a column is considerably shorter than the column heading, you could change the caption to a shorter heading. This would enable you to reduce the width of the column and yet still be able to see the entire column heading.
>
> • **Determine if a special description is warranted.** Determine whether to include a description that would appear in the status bar whenever the field is selected.
>
> • **Determine field sizes.** For Text fields, determine the field size; that is, the maximum number of characters that can be entered in the field. Users will be prohibited from entering a value that has more characters than the field size.
>
> • **Determine formats.** Determine whether the data in the field should be formatted in any particular way. You could, for example, specify that a number field is to be formatted with precisely two decimal places.

BTW

Naming Tables
Database users typically have their own guidelines for naming tables. Some use the singular version of the object being described while others use the prefix tbl with a table name. This book uses the singular version of the object (Client, Business Analyst) but adds the word Table to the name for the Business Analyst table to illustrate another possible approach. Including the word Table can assist visually impaired users when viewing the Navigation Pane.

The results of these decisions for the fields in the Business Analyst table are shown in Table 1–3. The table also shows the data types and field sizes of the fields as well as any special properties that need to be changed. The Business Analyst Number field has a caption of BA #, enabling the width of the Business Analyst Number column to be reduced in the datasheet.

Table 1–3 Structure of Business Analyst Table

Field Name	Data Type	Field Size	Description
Business Analyst Number	Text	2	**Primary Key** **Description:** Business Analyst Number **Caption:** BA #
Last Name	Text	15	
First Name	Text	15	
Street	Text	15	
City	Text	15	
State	Text	2	
Postal Code	Text	5	
Salary YTD	Currency		
Incentive YTD	Currency		

To Modify the Primary Key

When you first create your database, Access automatically creates a table for you. You can immediately begin defining the fields. If, for any reason, you do not have this table or inadvertently delete it, you can create the table by clicking Create on the Ribbon and then clicking the Table button (Create tab | Tables group). In either case, you are ready to define the fields.

The following steps define the first field, the Business Analyst Number field, which is the primary key. Access has already created a primary key field, which it has named ID. Thus, the steps will change the name, data type, and other properties of this field to match the Business Analyst field in Table 1–3.

1

- Right-click the column heading for the ID field to display a shortcut menu (Figure 1–6).

Why does my shortcut menu look different?

You right-clicked within the column instead of right-clicking the column heading.

Figure 1–6

2

- Click Rename Field on the shortcut menu to highlight the current name.

- Type **Business Analyst Number** to assign a name to the new field.

- Click the white space immediately below the field name to complete the addition of the field (Figure 1–7).

Figure 1–7

Why does the name not appear in its entirety?

The default column size is not large enough for Business Analyst Number to appear in its entirety. You will address this issue in later steps.

- Because the data type needs to be changed from AutoNumber to Text, click the Data Type box arrow (Table Tools Fields tab | Formatting group) to display a menu of available data types (Figure 1–8).

Figure 1–8

- Click Text to select the data type for the field (Figure 1–9).

Figure 1–9

- Click the Field Size text box (Table Tools Fields tab | Properties group) to select the current field size, use either the DELETE or BACKSPACE keys to erase the current field size, and then type 2 as the new field size.

- Click the Name & Caption button (Table Tools Fields tab | Properties group) to display the Enter Field Properties dialog box.

- Click the Caption text box (Enter Field Properties dialog box), and then type **BA #** as the caption.

- Click the Description text box, and then type **Unique identifier of business analyst** as the description (Figure 1–10).

Figure 1–10

- Click the OK button (Enter Field Properties dialog box) to change the caption and description (Figure 1–11).

Figure 1–11

To Define the Remaining Fields in a Table

To define an additional field, you click the Click to Add column heading, select the data type, and then type the field name. This is different from the process you used to modify the ID field, which was an existing field. The following steps define the remaining fields shown in Table 1–3 on page AC 16.

1

- Click the Click to Add column heading to display a menu of available data types (Figure 1–12).

Q&A Why did I follow a different process when I renamed this field?

The ID field was an existing field, created automatically by Access. For a new field, you need to click the Click to Add heading.

Figure 1–12

2

- Click Text in the menu of available data types to select the Text data type.

- Type Last Name to enter a field name.

- Click the white space below the field name to complete the change of the name. Click the white space a second time to select the field (Figure 1–13).

Q&A I realized after I entered the field name that I selected the wrong data type. How can I correct it?

Click the Data Type box arrow and then select the correct type.

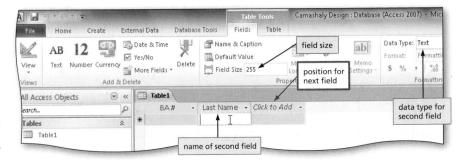

Figure 1–13

Q&A I inadvertently clicked the white space before entering the field name. How can I correct the name?

Right-click the field name, click Rename Field on the shortcut menu, and then type the new name.

3

- Change the field size to 15 just as you changed the field size of the Business Analyst Number field.

- Using the same technique, add the remaining fields in the Business Analyst table. For the First Name, Street, City, State, and Postal Code fields, the Text data type is correct, but you will need to change the field size to match Table 1–3. For the Salary YTD and Incentive YTD fields, you need to change the data type to Currency. Before defining the Incentive YTD field, you may need to click the right scroll arrow to bring the column for the field to the screen (Figure 1–14).

Figure 1–14

Q&A Why does Currency appear twice?

The second Currency is the format, which indicates how the data will be displayed. For the Currency data type, Access automatically sets the format to Currency, which is usually what you would want. You could change it to something else, if desired, by clicking the arrow and selecting the desired format.

Q&A I have an extra row between the row containing the field names and the row that begins with the asterisk. What happened? Is this a problem? If so, how do I fix it?

You inadvertently added a record to the table by pressing some key. Even pressing the SPACEBAR would add a record. You now have a record you do not want. To fix it, you need to delete the record, which you will do in Step 4.

- If you have an additional record between the field names and the asterisk, press the ESC key to delete the record.

Making Changes to the Structure

BTW

Currency Symbols
To show the symbol for the Euro (€) instead of the dollar sign, change the Format property for the field whose data type is currency. To change the default symbols for currency, change the settings in the operating system using the control panel.

When creating a table, check the entries carefully to ensure they are correct. If you discover a mistake while still typing the entry, you can correct the error by repeatedly pressing the BACKSPACE key until the incorrect characters are removed. Then, type the correct characters. If you do not discover a mistake until later, you can use the following techniques to make the necessary changes to the structure:

- To undo your most recent change, click the Undo button on the Quick Access Toolbar. If there is nothing that Access can undo, this button will be dim, and clicking it will have no effect.
- To delete a field, right-click the column heading for the field (the position containing the field name), and then click Delete Field on the shortcut menu.
- To change the name of a field, right-click the column heading for the field, click Rename Field on the shortcut menu, and then type the desired field name.
- To insert a field as the last field, click the Click to Add column heading, click the appropriate data type on the menu of available data types, type the desired field name, and, if necessary, change the field size.
- To insert a field between existing fields, right-click the column heading for the field that will follow the new field, and then click Insert Field on the shortcut menu. Right-click the column heading for the field, click Rename Field on the shortcut menu, and then type the desired field name.
- To move a field, click the column heading for the field to be moved to select the field, and then drag the field to the desired position.

As an alternative to these steps, you may want to start over. To do so, click the Close button for the table, and then click the No button in the Microsoft Access dialog box. Click Create on the Ribbon and then click the Table button to create a table. You then can repeat the process you used earlier to define the fields in the table.

To Save a Table

The Business Analyst table structure now is complete. The final step is to save the table within the database. As part of the process, you will give the table a name. The following steps save the table, giving it the name, Business Analyst Table.

1
- Click the Save button on the Quick Access Toolbar to display the Save As dialog box (Figure 1–15).

Figure 1–15

2
- Type **Business Analyst Table** to change the name to be assigned to the table.

- Click the OK button (Save As dialog box) to save the table (Figure 1–16).

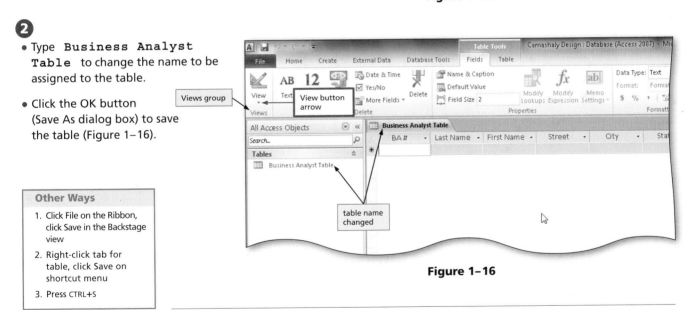

Figure 1–16

Other Ways

1. Click File on the Ribbon, click Save in the Backstage view

2. Right-click tab for table, click Save on shortcut menu

3. Press CTRL+S

To View the Table in Design View

Even when creating a table in Datasheet view, Design view can be helpful. You should view the fields, data types, and properties to ensure you have entered them correctly. This viewing is easier to do in Design view. It is also easier to determine the primary key in Design view. The following steps view the structure of the Business Analyst Table in Design view so that you can verify the design is correct.

- Click the View button arrow (Table Tools Fields tab | Views group) to display the View button menu (Figure 1–17).

Q&A

Could I just click the View button rather than the arrow?

Yes. Clicking the button is equivalent to clicking the command represented by the icon currently appearing on the button. Because the icon on the button in Figure 1–17 is the icon for Design view, clicking the button would display the table in Design view. If you are uncertain, you can always click the arrow and select from the menu.

Figure 1–17

2

- Click Design View on the View button menu to view the table in Design view (Figure 1–18).

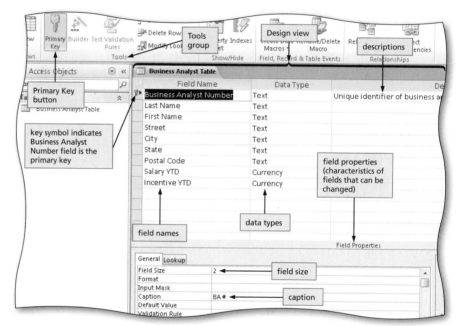

Figure 1–18

Other Ways

1. Click Design View button on status bar

Checking the Structure in Design View

You should use Design view to carefully check the entries you have made. In Figure 1–18, for example, you can see that the Business Analyst Number field is the primary key of the Business Analyst Table by the key symbol in front of the field name. If your table does not have a key symbol, you can click the Primary Key button (Table Tools Design tab | Tools group) to designate the field as the primary key. You also can check that the data type, the description, the field size, and the caption are all correct.

For the other fields, you can see the field name, data type, and description without taking any special action. To see the field size and/or caption for a field, click the field's **row selector**, the small box that precedes the field. Clicking the row selector for the Last Name field, for example, displays the field properties for the field (Figure 1–19). You then can check to see that the field size is correct. In addition, if the field has a caption, you can check to see if that is correct as well. If you find any mistakes, you can make the necessary corrections on this screen. When you have finished, you would click the Save button to save your changes.

To Close the Table

Once you are sure that your entries are correct and you have saved your changes, you can close the table. The following step closes the table.

- Click the Close button for the Business Analyst Table to close the table (Figure 1–19).

Figure 1–19

Other Ways
1. Right-click tab for table, click Close on shortcut menu

To Add Records to a Table

Creating a table by building the structure and saving the table is the first step in a two-step process. The second step is to add records to the table. To add records to a table, the table must be open. When making changes to tables, you work in Datasheet view. In Datasheet view, the table is represented as a collection of rows and columns called a **datasheet**.

You often add records in phases. For example, you might not have enough time to add all the records in one session. The following steps open the Business Analyst Table in Datasheet view and then add the first two records in the Business Analyst Table (Figure 1–20).

Business Analyst Table								
BA # ▾	Last Name ▾	First Name ▾	Street ▾	City ▾	State ▾	Postal Code ▾	Salary YTD ▾	Incentive YTD ▾
11	Kerry	Cordelia	251 Painter	Georgetown	NC	28794	$3,200.00	$3,450.00
14	Martinez	Manuel	3125 Steel	Kyle	SC	28797	$3,100.00	$2,430.00

Figure 1–20

- Right-click the Business Analyst Table in the Navigation Pane to display the shortcut menu (Figure 1–21).

Figure 1–21

2

- Click Open on the shortcut menu to open the table in Datasheet view.

Q&A

What if I want to return to Design view?

You can open Design view by clicking Design View on the shortcut menu.

- Click the Shutter Bar Open/Close Button to close the Navigation Pane (Figure 1–22).

Figure 1–22

3

- Click the BA # field if necessary to display an insertion point, and type 11 to enter the first business analyst number (Figure 1–23).

Figure 1–23

4

- Press the TAB key to move to the next field.

- Enter the last name, first name, street, city, state, and postal code by typing the following entries, pressing the TAB key after each one: **Kerry** as the last name, **Cordelia** as the first name, **251 Painter** as the street, **Georgetown** as the city, **NC** as the state, and **28794** as the postal code.

- Type **3200** in the Salary YTD field (Figure 1–24).

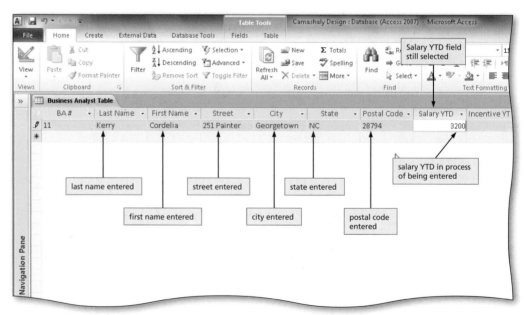

Figure 1–24

Do I need to type a dollar sign?

You do not need to type dollar signs or commas. In addition, because the digits to the right of the decimal point are both zeros, you do not need to type either the decimal point or the zeros.

5

- Press the TAB key to complete the entry for the field.

- Type 3450 in the Incentive YTD field, and then press the TAB key to complete the entry of the first record (Figure 1–25).

How and when do I save the record?

As soon as you have entered or modified a record and moved to another record, the original record is saved. This is different from other applications. The rows entered in an Excel worksheet, for example, are not saved until the entire worksheet is saved.

Figure 1–25

6

- Use the techniques shown in Steps 3 through 5 to enter the data for the second record (Figure 1–26).

Experiment

- Click the Salary YTD field on either of the records. Be sure the Table Tools Fields tab is selected. Click the Format box arrow and then click each of the formats in the Format box menu to see the effect on the values in the Salary YTD field. When finished, click Currency in the Format box menu.

Figure 1–26

Making Changes to the Data

As you enter data, check your entries carefully to ensure they are correct. If you make a mistake and discover it before you press the TAB key, correct it by pressing the BACKSPACE key until the incorrect characters are removed, and then type the correct characters. If you do not discover a mistake until later, you can use the following techniques to make the necessary corrections to the data:

- To undo your most recent change, click the Undo button on the Quick Access Toolbar. If there is nothing that Access can undo, this button will be dimmed, and clicking it will have no effect.

- To add a record, click the New (blank) record button, click the position for the Business Analyst Number field on the first open record, and then add the record. Do not worry about it being in the correct position in the table. Access will reposition the record based on the primary key, in this case, the Business Analyst Number.

BTW

Adding Records
You can add records in any order. When you close a table and reopen it, the records will be in order by primary key.

- To delete a record, click the record selector, shown in Figure 1–26, for the record to be deleted. Then press the DELETE key to delete the record, and click the Yes button when Access asks you to verify that you do indeed want to delete the record.

- To change the contents of one or more fields in a record, the record must be on the screen. If it is not, use any appropriate technique, such as the UP ARROW and DOWN ARROW keys or the vertical scroll bar, to move to it. If the field you want to correct is not visible on the screen, use the horizontal scroll bar along the bottom of the screen to shift all the fields until the one you want appears. If the value in the field is currently highlighted, you can simply type the new value. If you would rather edit the existing value, you must have an insertion point in the field. You can place the insertion point by clicking in the field or by pressing F2. You then can use the arrow keys, the DELETE key, and the BACKSPACE key for making the correction. You also can use the INSERT key to switch between Insert and Overtype mode. When you have made the change, press the TAB key to move to the next field.

If you cannot determine how to correct the data, you may find that you are "stuck" on the record, in which case Access neither allows you to move to another record nor allows you to close the table until you have made the correction. If you encounter this situation, simply press the ESC key. Pressing the ESC key will remove from the screen the record you are trying to add. You then can move to any other record, close the table, or take any other action you desire.

To Close a Table

Now that you have created and saved the Business Analyst Table, you can close it. The following step closes the table.

1 Click the Close button for the Business Analyst Table, shown in Figure 1–26, to close the table (Figure 1–27).

Figure 1–27

To Quit Access

The following steps quit Access. For a detailed example of the procedure summarized below, refer to the Office 2010 and Windows 7 chapter at the beginning of this book.

1 Click the Close button on the right side of the title bar to quit Access.

2 If a Microsoft Access dialog box appears, click the Save button to save any changes made to the object since the last save.

Break Point: If you wish to take a break, this is a good place to do so. To resume at a later time, continue following the steps from this location forward.

Starting Access and Opening a Database

Once you have created and later closed a database, you will need to open it in the future in order to use it. Opening a database requires that Access is running on your computer.

To Start Access

1 Click the Start button on the Windows 7 taskbar to display the Start menu.

2 Type `Microsoft Access` as the search text in the 'Search programs and files' text box and watch the search results appear on the Start menu.

3 Click Microsoft Access 2010 in the search results on the Start menu to start Access.

To Open a Database from Access

Earlier in this chapter, you saved your database on a USB flash drive using the file name, Camashaly Design. The following steps open the Camashaly Design database from the Access folder in the CIS 101 folder on the USB flash drive. For a detailed example of the procedure summarized below, refer to the Office 2010 and Windows 7 chapter at the beginning of this book.

1 With your USB flash drive connected to one of the computer's USB ports, click File on the Ribbon to open the Backstage view, if necessary.

2 Click Open in the Backstage view to display the Open dialog box.

3 Navigate to the location of the file to be opened (in this case, the USB flash drive, then to the CIS 101 folder [or your class folder], and then to the Access folder).

4 Click Camashaly Design to select the file to be opened.

5 Click the Open button (Open dialog box) to open the selected file and display the opened database in the Access window.

6 If a Security Warning appears, click the Enable Content button (Figure 1–28).

BTW
Organizing Files and Folders
You should organize and store files in folders so that you easily can find the files later. For a discussion of folders and detailed examples of creating folders, refer to the Office 2010 and Windows 7 chapter at the beginning of this book.

Q&A
When would I not want to enable the content?

You would want to disable the content if you suspected that your database might contain harmful content or damaging macros. Because you are the one who created the database and no one else has used it, you should have no such suspicions.

Figure 1–28

Other Ways
1. Click File on the Ribbon, click Recent in the Backstage view, click file name

To Add Additional Records to a Table

You can add records to a table that already contains data using a process almost identical to that used to add records to an empty table. The only difference is that you place the insertion point after the last record before you enter the additional data. To do so, use the **Navigation buttons**, which are buttons used to move within a table, found near the lower-left corner of the screen when a table is open. The purpose of each of the Navigation buttons is described in Table 1–4.

Table 1–4 Navigation Buttons in Datasheet View	
Button	**Purpose**
First record	Moves to the first record in the table
Previous record	Moves to the previous record
Next record	Moves to the next record
Last record	Moves to the last record in the table
New (blank) record	Moves to the end of the table to a position for entering a new record

The following steps add the remaining records (Figure 1–29) to the Business Analyst table.

Figure 1–29

- If the Navigation Pane is closed, click the Shutter Bar Open/Close Button, shown in Figure 1–27, to open the Navigation Pane (Figure 1–30).

Figure 1–30

- Right-click the Business Analyst Table in the Navigation Pane to display a shortcut menu.

- Click Open on the shortcut menu to open the table in Datasheet view.

- Close the Navigation Pane by clicking the Shutter Bar Open/Close Button (Figure 1–31).

Figure 1–31

3

- Click the New (blank) record button to move to a position to enter a new record (Figure 1–32).

Q&A

Could you just click the Business Analyst Number (BA #) on the first open record and then add the record?

Yes, but it is a good habit to use the New (blank) Record button. Once a table contains more records than will fit on the screen, it is easier to click the New (blank) record button.

Figure 1–32

4

- Add the records shown in Figure 1–29, using the same techniques you used to add the first two records (Figure 1–33).

Figure 1–33

Other Ways

1. Click New button (Home tab | Records group)
2. Press CTRL+PLUS SIGN (+)

To Resize Columns in a Datasheet

Access assigns default column sizes, which do not always allow all the data in the field to appear. In some cases, the data might appear but not the entire field name. You can correct this problem by **resizing** the column (changing its size) in the datasheet. In some instances, you may want to reduce the size of a column. The State field, for example, is short enough that it does not require all the space on the screen that is allotted to it. Changing a column width changes the **layout**, or design, of a table.

The following steps resize the columns in the Business Analyst table and save the changes to the layout.

1

- Point to the right boundary of the field selector for the Business Analyst (BA #) field (Figure 1–34) so that the mouse pointer becomes a two-headed arrow.

Figure 1–34

2

- Double-click the right boundary of the field selector to resize the field so that it best fits the data.

- Use the same technique to resize all the other fields to best fit the data (Figure 1–35).

3

- Save the changes to the layout by clicking the Save button on the Quick Access Toolbar (Figure 1–35).

- Click the table's Close button (shown in Figure 1–33) to close the table.

Figure 1–35

Q&A

What if I closed the table without saving the layout changes?

You would be asked if you want to save the changes.

Other Ways

1. Right-click field name, click Field Width

Plan Ahead

Determine the best method for distributing the database objects.

The traditional method of distributing database objects uses a printer to produce a hard copy of a table. A **hard copy** or **printout** is information that exists on a physical medium such as paper. For users who can receive fax documents, you can elect to print a hard copy on a remote fax machine. Hard copies can be useful for the following reasons:

- Many people prefer proofreading a hard copy of a document rather than viewing it on the screen to check for errors and readability.

- Hard copies can serve as reference material if your storage medium is lost or becomes corrupted and you need to re-create the document.

Instead of distributing a hard copy, users can choose to distribute the document as an electronic image that mirrors the original document's appearance. The electronic image of the document can be e-mailed, posted on a Web site, or copied to a portable medium such as a USB flash drive. Two popular electronic image formats, sometimes called fixed formats, are PDF by Adobe Systems and XPS by Microsoft. In Access, you can create PDF and XPS files through the External Data tab on the Ribbon. Electronic images of documents, such as PDF and XPS, can be useful for the following reasons.

- Users can view electronic images of documents without the software that created the original document (i.e., Access). Specifically, to view a PDF file, you use a program called Acrobat Reader, which can be downloaded free from Adobe's Web site. Similarly, to view an XPS file, you use a program called an XPS Viewer, which is included in the latest versions of Windows and Internet Explorer.

- Sending electronic documents saves paper and printer supplies. Society encourages users to contribute to **green computing**, which involves reducing the environmental waste generated when using a computer.

BTW

Changing Printers
To change the default printer that appears in the Print dialog box, click File on the Ribbon, click the Print tab in the Backstage view, click Print in the Print gallery, then click the Name box arrow and select the desired printer.

Previewing and Printing the Contents of a Table

When working with a database, you often will need to print a copy of the table contents. Figure 1–36 shows a printed copy of the contents of the Business Analyst table. (Yours may look slightly different, depending on your printer.) Because the Business Analyst table is substantially wider than the screen, it also will be wider than the normal printed page in portrait orientation. **Portrait orientation** means the printout is across the width of the page. **Landscape orientation** means the printout is across the height of the page. Thus, to print the wide database table, you might prefer to use landscape orientation. A convenient way to change to landscape orientation is to preview what the printed copy will look like by using Print Preview. This allows you to determine whether landscape orientation is necessary and, if it is, to change the orientation easily to landscape. In addition, you also can use Print Preview to determine whether any adjustments are necessary to the page margins.

Business Analyst Table								4/12/2012

BA #	Last Name	First Name	Street	City	State	Postal Code	Salary YTD	Incentive YTD
11	Kerry	Cordelia	251 Painter	Georgetown	NC	28794	$3,200.00	$3,450.00
14	Martinez	Manuel	3125 Steel	Kyle	SC	28797	$3,100.00	$2,430.00
27	Liu	Jan	265 Marble	Byron	SC	28795	$3,400.00	$2,280.00
35	Scott	Jeff	1925 Pine	Georgetown	NC	28794	$500.00	$0.00

Figure 1–36

To Preview and Print the Contents of a Table

The following steps use Print Preview to preview and then print the contents of the Business Analyst table.

1

- If the Navigation Pane is closed, open the Navigation Pane by clicking the Shutter Bar Open/Close Button.

- Be sure the Business Analyst table is selected.

Q&A

Why do I have to be sure the Business Analyst table is selected? It is the only object in the database.

When the database contains only one object, you do not have to worry about selecting the object. Ensuring that the correct object is selected is a good habit to form, however, to make sure that the object you print is the one you want.

- Click File on the Ribbon to open the Backstage view.

Figure 1–37

- Click the Print tab in the Backstage view to display the Print gallery (Figure 1–37).

2

- Click the Print Preview button in the Print gallery to display a preview of what the table will look like when printed.

- Close the Navigation Pane to free up more of the screen for the preview (Figure 1–38).

Q&A

I cannot read the table. Can I magnify a portion of the table?

Yes. Point the mouse pointer, whose shape will change to a magnifying glass, at the portion of the table that you want to magnify, and then click. You can return the view of the table to the one shown in the figure by clicking a second time

Figure 1–38

3

- Click the mouse pointer in the position shown in Figure 1–38 to magnify the upper-right section of the table (Figure 1–39).

Q&A

My table was already magnified in a different area. How can I see the area shown in the figure?

One way is to use the scroll bars to move to the desired portion of the table. You also can click the mouse pointer anywhere in the table to produce a screen like the one in Figure 1–38, and then click in the location shown in the figure.

Figure 1–39

4

- Click the Landscape button to change to landscape orientation (Figure 1–40).

- Click the Print button (Print Preview tab | Print group) to display the Print dialog box.

- Click the OK button (Print dialog box) to print the table.

- When the printer stops, retrieve the hard copy of the Business Analyst Table.

- Click the Close Print Preview button (Print Preview tab | Close Preview group) to close the Print Preview window.

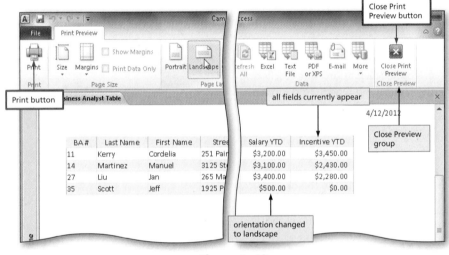

Figure 1–40

Other Ways

1. Press CTRL+P, click OK button (Print dialog box)

Creating Additional Tables

The Camashaly Design database contains two tables, the Business Analyst table and the Client table. You still need to create the Client table and add records to it. You created the Business Analyst table in Datasheet view. You will create the Client table in Design view.

Recall that the fields for the Client table are Client Number, Client Name, Street, City, State, Postal Code, Amount Paid, Current Due, Contract Hours YTD, and Business Analyst Number. The details that must be entered for these fields are shown in Table 1–5. The Client Number is the primary key. The Client Number field and the Business Analyst Number fields have both descriptions and captions. The Contract Hours YTD field has a caption.

Because the values in the Contract Hours YTD field have decimal places, only Single, Double, or Decimal would be possible field size choices. (See Table 1–2 on Page AC 10 for a description of the possible field sizes for Number fields.) The difference between these choices concerns the amount of accuracy. Double is more accurate than Single, for example, but requires more storage space. Because the rates are only two decimal places, Single is a perfectly acceptable choice.

In addition to changing the field size for the Contract Hours YTD, you will also change the format to Fixed (a fixed number of decimal places) and the number of decimal places to 2.

Table 1–5 Structure of Client Table

Field Name	Data Type	Field Size	Notes
Client Number	Text	4	**Primary Key** **Description:** Client Number (two uppercase letters followed by 2-digit number) **Caption:** CL #
Client Name	Text	30	
Street	Text	15	
City	Text	15	
State	Text	2	
Postal Code	Text	5	
Amount Paid	Currency		
Current Due	Currency		
Contract Hours YTD	Number	Single	**Caption:** Hrs YTD **Format:** Fixed **Decimal Places:** 2
Business Analyst Number	Text	2	**Caption:** BA # **Description:** Business Analyst Number (number of business analyst for client)

To Create a Table in Design View

The next step in creating the table is to define the fields by specifying the required details in Design view. You will make entries in the Field Name, Data Type, and Description columns and enter additional information in the Field Properties box in the lower portion of the Table window. As you define the fields, the row selector (Figure 1–19 on page AC 23) indicates the field you currently are describing. Clicking the row selector selects the entire row. It is positioned on the first field, indicating Access is ready for you to enter the name of the first field in the Field Name column.

The following steps use Design view to define the fields in the table.

• Open the Navigation Pane.

• Click Create on the Ribbon to display the Create tab (Figure 1–41).

Figure 1–41

2

- Click the Table Design button (Create tab | Tables group) to create a new table in Design view (Figure 1–42).

Q&A

Could I save the table now so I can assign it the name I want, rather than Table1?

You certainly could. Be aware, however, that you will still need to save it again once you have added all your fields.

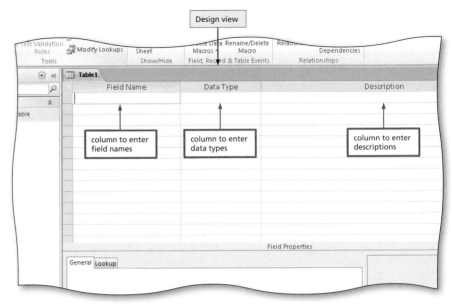

Figure 1–42

3

- Type **Client Number** (the name of the first field) in the Field Name column and then press the TAB key to accept the field name and move to the Data Type column (Figure 1–43).

Figure 1–43

4

- Because the Client Number field is the primary key, click the Primary Key button (Table Tools Design tab | Tools group) to designate the Client Number field as the primary key (Figure 1–44).

Figure 1–44

- Press the TAB key to move to the Description column, and then type **Client Number (two uppercase letters followed by a two-digit number)** as the description.

- Click the Field Size text box in the Field Properties pane to produce an insertion point, use either the BACKSPACE or DELETE key as necessary to erase the current entry (255), and then type **4** to change the field size.

- Click the Caption text box to produce an insertion point, and then type **CL #** to enter a caption (Figure 1–45).

Figure 1–45

- Click the Field Name column on the second row to produce an insertion point and then make the entries for the Client Name field.

- Use the techniques illustrated in Steps 1 through 5 to make the entries for the remaining fields in the Client table structure, shown in Table 1–5 on page AC 33, up through and including the name of the Amount Paid field.

- Click the Data Type box arrow to display a menu of available data types (Figure 1–46).

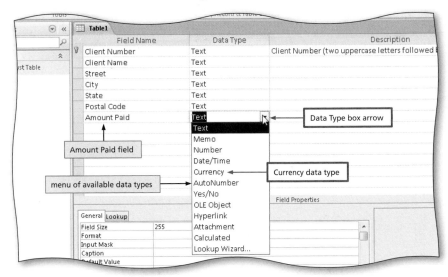

Figure 1–46

- Click Currency to select the data type.

- Enter the Current Due field and select the Currency data type.

- Enter the Contract Hours YTD field and select the Number data type (Figure 1–47).

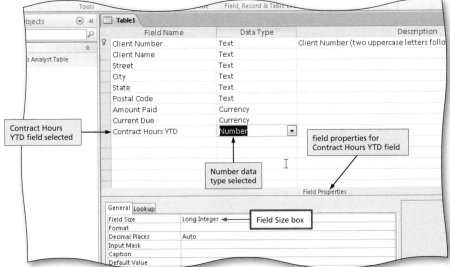

Figure 1–47

8

- Click the Field Size box to display the Field Size box arrow.

- Click the Field Size box arrow to display the Field Size box menu (Figure 1–48).

Q&A

What would happen if I left the field size set to Integer?

If the field size is Integer, no decimal places can be stored. Thus a value of 2.50 would be stored as 2. If you enter your hours and none of the values have decimal places, probably you did not change the field size.

Figure 1–48

9

- Click Single to select single precision as the field size.

- Click the Format box to display the Format box arrow.

- Click the Format box arrow to display the Format box menu (Figure 1–49).

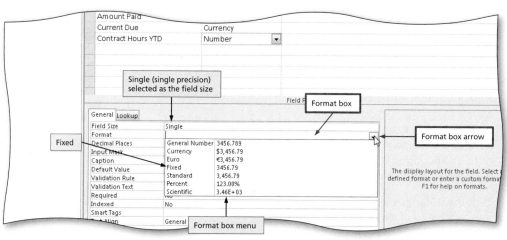

Figure 1–49

10

- Click Fixed to select fixed as the format.

- Click the Decimal Places box to display the Decimal Places box arrow.

- Click the Decimal Places box arrow to enter the number of decimal places.

- Click 2 to select 2 as the number of decimal places.

- Click the Caption text box to produce an insertion point, and then type **Hrs YTD** to enter a caption (Figure 1–50).

Figure 1–50

11

- Enter the Business Analyst Number field from Table 1–5. Be sure to change the description, field size, and caption to the ones shown in the table.

- Click the Save button on the Quick Access Toolbar to display the Save As dialog box, type Client as the name of the table, and then click the OK button (Save As dialog box) to save the table (Figure 1–51).

Figure 1–51

Other Ways

1. Press F6 to move between the upper pane and the lower pane in the Table Design window

Correcting Errors in the Structure

When creating a table, check the entries carefully to ensure they are correct. If you make a mistake and discover it before you press the TAB key, you can correct the error by repeatedly pressing the BACKSPACE key until the incorrect characters are removed. Then, type the correct characters. If you do not discover a mistake until later, you can click the entry, type the correct value, and then press the ENTER key. You can use the following techniques to make changes to the structure:

- If you accidentally add an extra field to the structure, select the field by clicking the row selector (the leftmost column on the row that contains the field to be deleted). Once you have selected the field, press the DELETE key. This will remove the field from the structure.

- If you forget to include a field, select the field that will follow the field you want to add by clicking the row selector, and then press the INSERT key. The remaining fields move down one row, making room for the missing field. Make the entries for the new field in the usual manner.

- If you made the wrong field a primary key field, click the correct primary key entry for the field and then click the Primary Key button (Table Tools Design tab | Tools group).

- To move a field, click the row selector for the field to be moved to select the field, and then drag the field to the desired position.

As an alternative to these steps, you may want to start over. To do so, click the Close button for the window containing the table, and then click the No button in the Microsoft Access dialog box. Click Create on the Ribbon and then click the Table Design button to create a table. You then can repeat the process you used earlier to define the fields in the table.

BTW

AutoCorrect Feature
The AutoCorrect feature of Access corrects common mistakes when entering text in a cell. AutoCorrect corrects two capital letters by changing the second letter to lowercase and capitalizes the first letter in the names of days. It also corrects more than 400 commonly misspelled words.

BTW

Other AutoCorrect Options
Using the Office AutoCorrect feature, you can create entries that will replace abbreviations with spelled-out names and phrases automatically. To specify AutoCorrect rules, click File on the Ribbon to open the Backstage view, click Options, and then click Proofing in the Access Options dialog box.

To Close the Table

Now that you have completed and saved the Client table, you can close it. The following step closes the table.

 Click the Close button for the Client table (see Figure 1–51) to close the table.

Importing Data from Other Applications to Access

Now that you have created the Client table, you could add the records to it just as you did with the Business Analyst table. Access provides an alternative, however, that is available because Camashaly Design has already stored the necessary data in an Excel workbook (Figure 1–52). The data is stored in the form of an Excel **list**; that is, the first row contains column headings describing the data in each of the columns, and the remaining rows contain the data. Camashaly can **import** the data, which means to make a copy of the data in a table in the Access database.

When importing data, you have two choices. You can create a new table, in which case the column headings in the worksheet become the field names in the table. Access will attempt to assign appropriate data types. You would need to review the data types, adjust field sizes, captions, descriptions, and formats after the data was imported. The other option is to add the records to an existing table. This method is appropriate if you have already created the table, provided the column headings in the worksheet match the field names in the table, as they do in the case of the Client table.

	A	B	C	D	E	F	G	H	I	J	K
1	Client Number	Client Name	Street	City	State	Postal Code	Amount Paid	Current Due	Contract Hours YTD	Business Analyst Number	
2	BA53	Bavant Animal Hospital	134 Main	Burles	NC	28817	$0.00	$7,500.00	0.00	11	
3	BB32	Babbage CPA Firm	464 Linnell	Austin	SC	28796	$1,500.00	$500.00	5.00	14	
4	BC76	Buda Community Clinic	867 Ridge	Buda	NC	27032	$2,500.00	$750.00	2.50	11	
5	CJ29	Catering by Jenna	123 Second	Granger	NC	27036	$3,000.00	$1,000.00	15.50	27	
6	GA74	Grant Antiques	78 Catawba	Georgetown	NC	28794	$5,500.00	$3,200.00	34.50	14	
7	GF56	Granger Foundation	65 Simpson	Granger	NC	27036	$0.00	$6,500.00	0.00	11	
8	HC10	Hendley County Hospital	216 Rivard	Austin	SC	28796	$3,100.00	$1,200.00	12.00	27	
9	KD21	KAL Design Studio	116 Pine	Georgetown	NC	28794	$6,000.00	$3,200.00	30.50	14	
10	KG04	Kyle Grocery Cooperative	421 First	Kyle	SC	28798	$3,200.00	$0.00	5.00	11	
11	ME14	Mike's Electronic Stop	234 Gilham	Georgetown	NC	28794	$2,500.00	$1,500.00	8.50	27	
12	PJ34	Patricia Jean Florist	345 Magee	Kyle	SC	28798	$0.00	$5,200.00	0.00	27	
13	SL77	Smarter Law Associates	764 Main	Burles	NC	28817	$3,800.00	$0.00	10.50	11	
14	TB17	The Bikeshop	346 Austin	Buda	NC	27032	$2,750.00	$1,200.00	14.00	27	
15	WE05	Walburg Energy Alternatives	12 Polk	Walburg	NC	28819	$4,500.00	$1,450.00	19.50	14	
16	WS01	Woody Sporting Goods	578 Central	Walburg	NC	28819	$2,250.00	$1,600.00	18.50	14	
17											

Figure 1–52

The process of importing into an Access database uses a wizard. Specifically, if the data is imported from an Excel worksheet, the process will use the Import Spreadsheet Wizard. The wizard takes you through some basic steps, asking a few simple questions. After you have answered the questions, the wizard will import or link the data.

To Import an Excel Worksheet

To import the data in the Camashaly Client Data workbook, you use the Import Spreadsheet Wizard to place the rows from an Excel worksheet into an existing table. The following steps import the Camashaly Client Data Excel workbook, which is provided as a data file. See the inside back cover of this book for instructions on downloading the Data Files for Students, or contact your instructor for more information about accessing the required files.

• Click External Data on the Ribbon to display the External Data tab (Figure 1–53).

Figure 1–53

2

• Click the Excel button (External Data tab | Import & Link group) to display the Get External Data – Excel Spreadsheet dialog box.

• Click the Browse button (Get External Data – Excel Spreadsheet dialog box) to display the File Open dialog box.

• Navigate to the USB flash drive (or the location of your data files).

• Double-click your USB flash drive, and then click Camashaly Client Data to select the file to be opened.

• Click the Open button (File Open dialog box), which will return you to the Get External Data dialog box with the Camashaly Client Data workbook selected.

3

• Click the option button to append a copy of records to a table (Figure 1–54).

What happens if I select the option button to import records into a new table?

Instead of the records being added to an existing table, they will be placed in a new table. Access will assign all the data types. You would then need to ensure they are correct. You also would need to change any field sizes, descriptions, captions, formats, or number of decimal places to the ones you want.

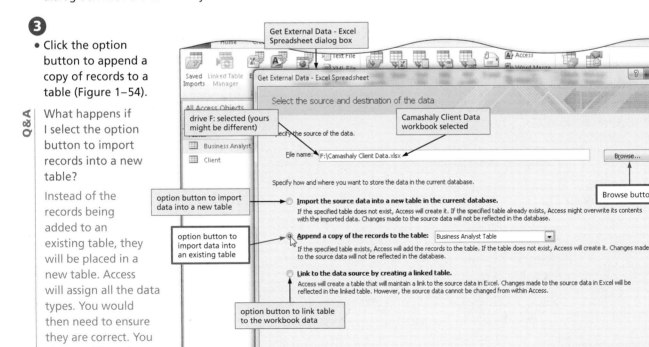

Figure 1–54

4

- Click the arrow to produce a menu of available tables.

- Click the Client table to select the table to which a copy of the records will be appended (Figure 1–55).

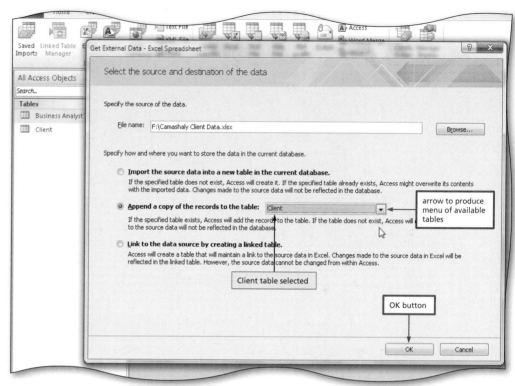

Figure 1–55

5

- Click the OK button to move to the next Import Spreadsheet Wizard screen (Figure 1–56).

The First Row Contains Column Headings check box is checked, but it is dimmed. What if I want to remove the check mark?

When you are appending records to an existing table, the first row must contain column headings. If instead you were creating a new table, the first row might not contain column headings. In that case, you would have control over this check box.

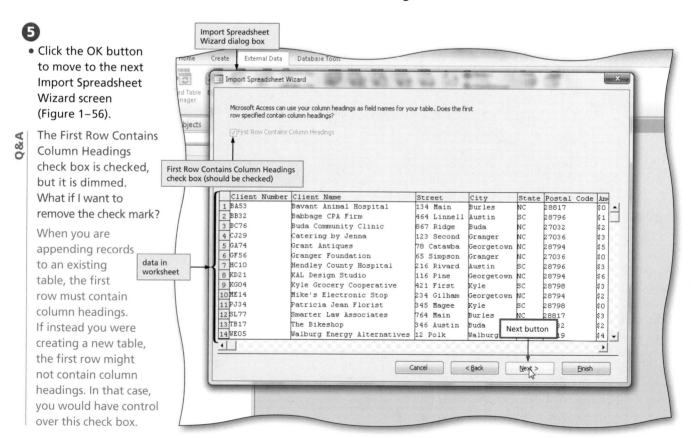

Figure 1–56

6

- Click the Next button to move to the next Import Spreadsheet Wizard screen (Figure 1–57).

Q&A

What happens if I later realize I have selected the wrong table?

If you have not yet clicked the Finish button, you can click the Back button to return to the screen where you selected the table, and then select the correct table.

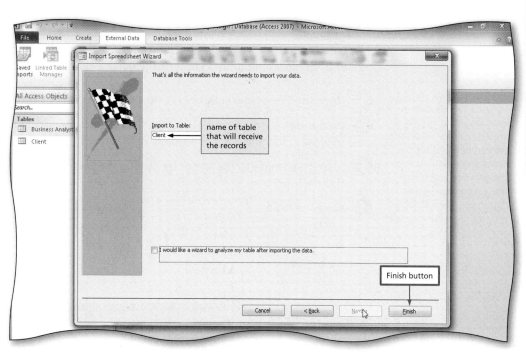

Figure 1–57

7

- Because the table name is correct, click the Finish button to import the data (Figure 1–58).

Q&A

I got an error message that stated that a particular field did not exist in the Client table. What did I do wrong? How do I fix it?

When you created the table, you did not name that particular field correctly. Open the table in Design view and change the field name to the correct name. Check other field names as well. When you are done, save and close the table. Then, repeat the import process.

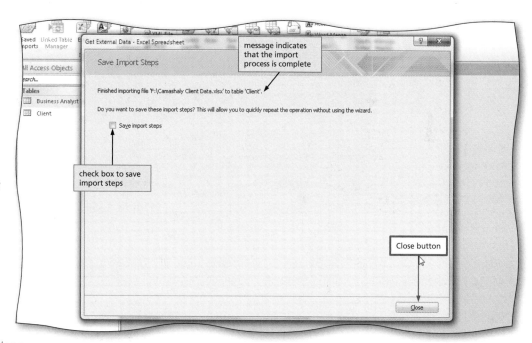

Figure 1–58

8

- Because you will not save the import steps, click the Close button.

Q&A

When would I save the import steps?

If you think you might need to repeat these steps in the future, you can save time by saving the steps.

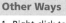

Other Ways

1. Right-click table in Navigation Pane, click Import on shortcut menu

To Resize Columns in a Datasheet

You can resize the columns in the datasheet for the Client table just as you resized the columns in the datasheet for the Business Analyst table. The following steps resize the columns in the Client table to best fit the data.

BTW

Resizing Columns
To resize all columns in a datasheet to best fit simultaneously, select the column heading for the first column, hold down the SHIFT key and select the last column in the datasheet. Then, double-click the right boundary of any field selector.

1 Open the Client table in Datasheet view and then close the Navigation Pane.

2 Double-click the right boundary of the field selectors of each of the fields to resize the columns so that they best fit the data.

3 Save the changes to the layout by clicking the Save button on the Quick Access Toolbar (Figure 1–59).

4 Close the table.

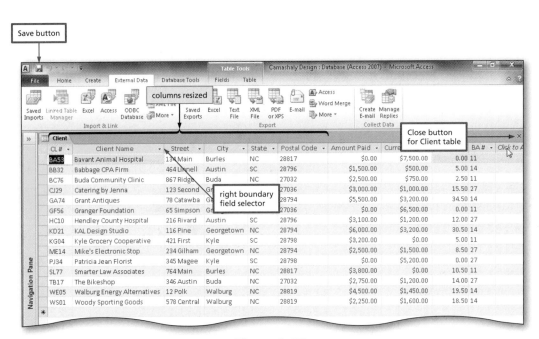

Figure 1–59

Break Point: If you wish to take a break, this is a good place to do so. You can quit Access now. To resume at a later time, start Access, open the database called Camashaly Design, and continue following the steps from this location forward.

Additional Database Objects

A computerized database such as Access contains many types of objects. Tables are the objects you use to store and manipulate data. Access supports other important types of objects as well; each of these objects has a specific purpose that assists in maximizing the benefits of a database. Through queries (questions), Access makes it possible to ask complex questions concerning the data in the database and then receive instant answers. Access also allows the user to produce attractive and useful forms for viewing and updating data. Additionally, Access includes report creation tools that make it easy to produce sophisticated reports for presenting data.

To Use the Simple Query Wizard to Create a Query

Queries are simply questions, the answers to which are in the database. Access contains a powerful query feature that helps you find the answers to a wide variety of questions. Once you have examined the question you want to ask to determine the fields involved in the question, you can begin creating the query. If there are no restrictions involved in the query, nor any special order or calculations, you can use the Simple Query Wizard.

The following steps use the Simple Query Wizard to create a query that Camashaly Design might use to obtain financial information on its clients. The query displays the number, name, amount paid, current due, contract hours YTD, and business analyst number of all clients.

1

- If the Navigation Pane is closed, click the Shutter Bar Open/Close Button to open the Navigation Pane.

- Be sure the Client table is selected.

- Click Create on the Ribbon to display the Create tab.

- Click the Query Wizard button (Create tab | Queries group) to display the New Query dialog box (Figure 1–60).

Figure 1–60

2

- Be sure Simple Query Wizard is selected, and then click the OK button (New Query dialog box) to display the Simple Query Wizard dialog box (Figure 1–61).

Q&A What would happen if the Business Analyst Table were selected instead of the Client table?

The list of available fields would contain fields from the Business Analyst Table rather than the Client table.

Q&A If the list contained Business Analyst Table fields, how could I make it contain Client table fields?

Click the arrow in the Tables/Queries box and then click the Client table in the list that appears.

- With the Client Number field selected, click the Add Field button to add the field to the query.

- With the Client Name field selected, click the Add Field button a second time to add the field.

- Click the Amount Paid field, and then click the Add Field button to add the field.

- In a similar fashion, add the Current Due, Contract Hours YTD, and Business Analyst Number fields (Figure 1–62).

Figure 1–62

- Click the Next button to move to the next screen.

- Ensure that the Detail (shows every field of every record) option button is selected (Figure 1–63).

Q&A What is the difference between Detail and Summary?

Detail shows all the records and fields. Summary only shows computations (for example, the total amount paid).

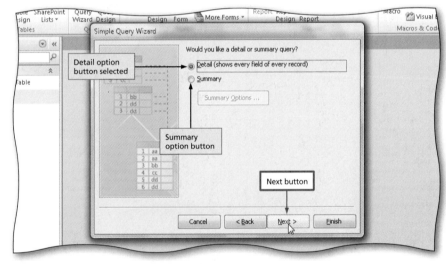

Figure 1–63

- Click the Next button to move to the next screen.

- Ensure the title of the query is Client Query (Figure 1–64).

Figure 1–64

6

• Click the Finish button to create the query (Figure 1–65).

• Click the Close button for the Client Query to remove the query results from the screen.

Q&A

If I want to use this query in the future, do I need to save the query?

Normally you would. The one exception is a query created by the wizard. The wizard automatically saves the query it creates.

Figure 1–65

Using Queries

After you have created and saved a query, Access stores it as a database object and makes it available for use in a variety of ways:

• To view the results of the query, open it by right-clicking the query in the Navigation Pane and clicking Open on the shortcut menu.

• To print the results with the query open, click File on the Ribbon, click the Print tab, and then click either Print or Quick Print.

• If you want to change the design of the query, right-click the query in the Navigation Pane and then click Design View on the shortcut menu to open the query in Design view.

• To print the query without first opening it, be sure the query is selected in the Navigation Pane and click File on the Ribbon, click the Print tab, and then click either Print or Quick Print.

You can switch between views of a query using the View button (Home tab | Views group). Clicking the arrow in the bottom of the button produces the View button menu. You then click the desired view in the menu. The two query views you will use in this chapter are Datasheet view (see the results) and Design view (change the design). You also can click the top part of the View button, in which case, you will switch to the view identified by the icon on the button. In the figure, the button contains the icon for Design view, so clicking the button would change to Design view. For the most part, the icon on the button represents the view you want, so you can usually simply click the button.

To Use a Criterion in a Query

After you have determined the fields to be included in a query, you will determine whether there are any restrictions on the records that are to be included. For example, you might only want to include those clients whose business analyst number is 14. In such a case, you need to enter the 14 as a **criterion**, which is a condition that the records to be included must satisfy. To do so, you will open the query in Design view, enter the criterion below the appropriate field, and then view the results of the query. The following steps enter a criterion to include only the clients of business analyst 14 and then view the query results.

1
- Right-click the Client Query in the Navigation Pane to produce a shortcut menu (Figure 1–66).

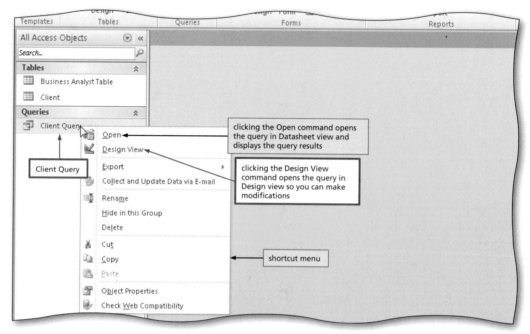

Figure 1–66

2
- Click Design View on the shortcut menu to open the query in Design view (Figure 1–67).

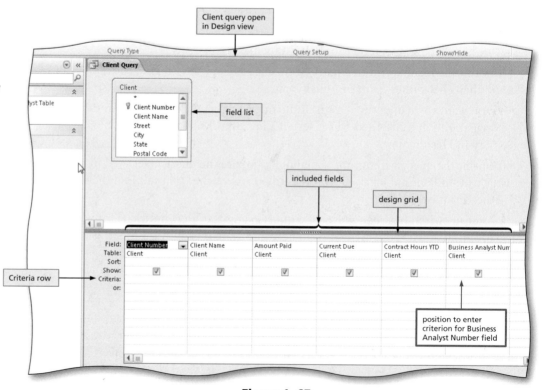

Figure 1–67

3

- Click the Criteria row in the Business Analyst Number column of the grid, and then type 14 as the criterion (Figure 1–68).

Q&A The Business Analyst Number field is a text field. Do I need to enclose the value for a text field in quotation marks?

You could, but it is not necessary, because Access inserts the quotation marks for you automatically.

Figure 1–68

4

- Click the View button to display the query results in Datasheet view (Figure 1–69).

Q&A Could I click the View button arrow and then click Datasheet view?

Yes, if the icon representing the view you want appears on the View button; however, it is easier just to click the button.

Figure 1–69

5

- Click the Close button for the Client Query to close the query.

- When asked if you want to save your changes, click the No button.

Q&A If I saved the query, what would happen the next time I ran the query?

You would see only clients of business analyst 14.

Q&A Could I save the query with another name?

Yes. To save the query with another name, click File on the Ribbon, click Save Object As, enter a new file name in the Save As dialog box and click the OK button (Save As dialog box).

Other Ways

1. Click Run button (Query Tools Design tab | Results group)

2. Click Datasheet View button on status bar

To Print the Results of a Query

The following steps print the results of a saved query.

1 With the Client Query selected in the Navigation Pane, click File on the Ribbon to open the Backstage view.

2 Click the Print tab in the Backstage view to display the Print gallery.

3 Click the Quick Print button to print the query.

Creating and Using Forms

In Datasheet view, you can view many records at once. If there are many fields, however, only some of the fields in each record might be visible at a time. In **Form view**, where data is displayed in a form on the screen, you usually can see all the fields, but only for one record.

To Create a Form

Like a paper form, a **form** in a database is a formatted document with fields that contain data. Forms allow you to view and maintain data. Forms also can be used to print data, but reports are more commonly used for that purpose. The simplest type of form in Access is one that includes all the fields in a table stacked one above the other. The following steps create a form, use the form to view records, and then save the form.

1

• Select the Client table in the Navigation Pane.

• If necessary, click Create on the Ribbon to display the Create tab (Figure 1–70).

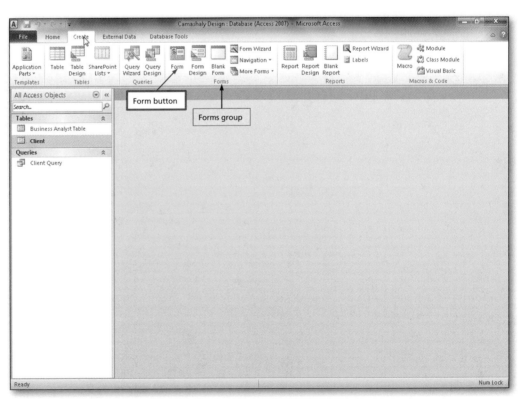

Figure 1–70

2

- Click the Form button (Create tab | Forms group) to create a simple form (Figure 1–71).

A Field list appeared on my screen. What should I do?

Click the Add Existing Fields button (Form Layout Tools Design tab | Tools group) to remove the Field list from the screen.

Figure 1–71

3

- If the form appears in Layout view, click the Form View button on the Access status bar to display the form in Form view.

How can I recognize Layout view?

Access identifies Layout view in three ways. The left side of the status bar will contain the words Layout View; there will be shading around the outside of the selected field in the form; and the Layout View button will be selected on the right side of the status bar.

- Click the Next Record button three times to move to record 4 (Figure 1–72).

Figure 1–72

4

- Click the Save button on the Quick Access Toolbar to display the Save As dialog box (Figure 1–73).

Figure 1–73

Q&A

Did I have to click the Next Record button before saving?

No. The only reason you were asked to click the button was so that you could experience navigation within the form.

5

- Type **Client Form** as the form name, and then click the OK button to save the form.

- Click the Close button for the form to close the form.

Other Ways

1. Click View button (Form Layout Tools Design tab | Views group)

Using a Form

After you have saved a form, you can use it at anytime by right-clicking the form in the Navigation Pane and then clicking Open in the shortcut menu. In addition to viewing data in the form, you can also use it to enter or update data, a process that is very similar to updating data using a datasheet. If you plan to use the form to enter or revise data, you must ensure you are viewing the form in Form view.

Break Point: If you wish to take a break, this is a good place to do so. You can quit Access now. To resume at a later time, start Access, open the database called Camashaly Design, and continue following the steps from this location forward.

Creating and Printing Reports

Camashaly Design wants to create the Client Financial Report shown in Figure 1–74. Just as you can create a form containing all fields by clicking a single button, you can click a button to create a report containing all the fields. Doing so will not match the report shown in Figure 1–74, however, which does not contain all the fields. Some of the column headings are different. In addition, some of the headings in the report in Figure 1–74 are split over multiple lines, whereas the ones in the report created by clicking the button will not be split. Fortunately, you can later modify the report design to make it precisely match the figure. To do so, you use Layout view for the report.

| | Client Financial Report | | | | Thursday, April 12, 2012 |
| | | | | | 5:17:00 PM |
Client Number	Client Name	Amount Paid	Current Due	Hrs YTD	Business Analyst Number
BA53	Bavant Animal Hospital	$0.00	$7,500.00	0.00	11
BB32	Babbage CPA Firm	$1,500.00	$500.00	5.00	14
BC76	Buda Community Clinic	$2,500.00	$750.00	2.50	11
CJ29	Catering by Jenna	$3,000.00	$1,000.00	15.50	27
GA74	Grant Antiques	$5,500.00	$3,200.00	34.50	14
GF56	Granger Foundation	$0.00	$6,500.00	0.00	11
HC10	Hendley County Hospital	$3,100.00	$1,200.00	12.00	27
KD21	KAL Design Studio	$6,000.00	$3,200.00	30.50	14
KG04	Kyle Grocery Cooperative	$3,200.00	$0.00	5.00	11
ME14	Mike's Electronic Stop	$2,500.00	$1,500.00	8.50	27
PJ34	Patricia Jean Florist	$0.00	$5,200.00	0.00	27
SL77	Smarter Law Associates	$3,800.00	$0.00	10.50	11
TB17	The Bikeshop	$2,750.00	$1,200.00	14.00	27
WE05	Walburg Energy Alternatives	$4,500.00	$1,450.00	19.50	14
WS01	Woody Sporting Goods	$2,250.00	$1,600.00	18.50	14
		$40,600.00	$34,800.00	176.00	

Figure 1–74

To Create a Report

You will first create a report containing all fields. The following steps create and save the initial report. They also modify the report title.

- • Be sure the Client table is selected in the Navigation Pane.

- • Click Create on the Ribbon to display the Create tab (Figure 1–75).

Q&A

Why do I need to select the Client table prior to clicking Create on the Ribbon?

You do not need to select it at that point. You do need to select it prior to clicking the Report button at the next step because Access will include all the fields in whichever table or query is currently selected.

Figure 1–75

2

- • Click the Report button (Create tab | Reports group) to create the report (Figure 1–76).

Q&A

Why is the report title Client?

Access automatically assigns the name of the table or query as the title. It also automatically includes the date. You can change either of these later.

Figure 1–76

3

- Click the Save button on the Quick Access Toolbar to display the Save As dialog box and then type **Client Financial Report** as the name of the report (Figure 1–77).

Figure 1–77

4
- Click the OK button (Save As dialog box) to save the report (Figure 1–78).

The name of the report changed. Why did the report title not change too?

The report title just happens to begin with the same name as the report. If you change the name of the report, Access will not change the report title. You can change it at any time to any title you like.

Figure 1–78

5
- Close the report by clicking its Close button.

Using Layout View in a Report

When working with a report in Access, there are four different ways to view the report. They are Report view, Print Preview, Layout view, and Design view. Report view shows the report on the screen. Print Preview shows the report as it will appear when printed. Layout view is similar to Report view in that it shows the report on the screen, but it also allows you to make changes to the report. It is usually the easiest way to make such changes. Design view also allows you to make changes, but it does not show you the actual report. It is most useful when the changes you need to make are especially complex. In this chapter, you will use Layout view to modify the report.

To Modify Column Headings and Resize Columns

To make the report match the one in Figure 1–74, you need to change the title, remove some columns, modify the column headings, and also resize the columns. The following steps use Layout view to make the necessary modifications to the report.

- Right-click Client Financial Report in the Navigation Pane, and then click Layout View on the shortcut menu to open the report in Layout view.

- If a Field list appears, click the Add Existing Fields button (Report Layout Tools Design tab | Tools group) to remove the Field list from the screen.

- Close the Navigation Pane.

- Click the report title once to select it.

- Click the report title a second time to produce an insertion point (Figure 1–79).

Figure 1–79

Q&A
I clicked at a different position in the title and my insertion point is in the middle of Client. How do I produce an insertion point at the position shown in the figure?

You can use the RIGHT ARROW key to move the insertion point to the position in the figure or you can click the desired position.

2

- Press the SPACEBAR to insert a space and then type **Financial Report** to complete the title.

- Click the column heading for the Street field to select it.

- Hold the SHIFT key down and then click the column headings for the City field, the State field, and the Postal Code fields to select multiple column headings.

Q&A
What happens if I do not hold down the SHIFT key?

As soon as you click the column heading, it will be the only one that is selected. To select multiple objects, you need to hold the SHIFT key down for every object after the first one.

Figure 1–80

Q&A I selected the wrong collection of objects. What should I do?

You can click somewhere else on the report so that the objects you want are not selected, and then begin the process again. Alternatively, you can repeatedly click the Undo button on the Quick Access Toolbar to undo your selections. Once you have done so, you can select the objects you want.

- Click Arrange on the Ribbon to display the Arrange tab (Figure 1–80).

- Click the Select Column button (Report Layout Tools Arrange tab | Rows & Columns group) to select the entire columns corresponding to the column headings you selected in the previous step.

- Press the DELETE key to delete the columns.

- Click the column heading for the Client Number field twice, once to select it and the second time to produce an insertion point (Figure 1–81).

Q&A I inadvertently selected the wrong field. What should I do?

Click somewhere outside the various fields to deselect the one you have selected. Then, click the Client Number field twice.

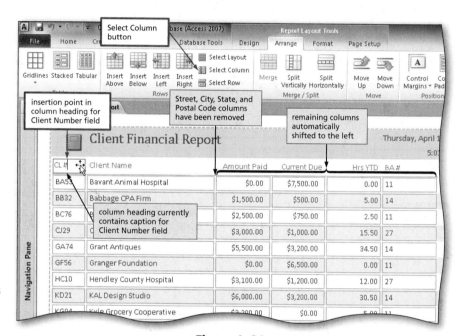

Figure 1–81

- Use the DELETE or BACKSPACE keys as necessary to erase the current entry and then type `Client Number` as the new entry.

- Click the heading for the Business Analyst Number field twice, erase the current entry, and then type `Business Analyst Number` as the new entry.

- Click the Client Number field heading to select it, point to the lower boundary of the heading for the Client Number field so that the mouse pointer changes to a two-headed arrow and then drag the lower boundary to the approximate position shown in Figure 1–82 to expand the column headings.

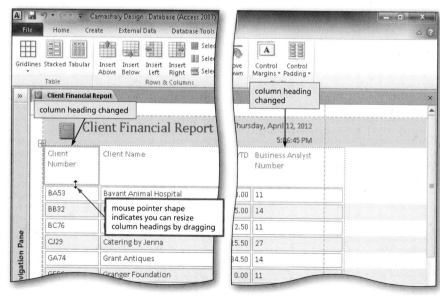

Figure 1–82

Q&A Do I have to be exact?

No. If you are in a slightly different position, your report would look a little different from the one in the figure, but the difference would not be significant.

• Point to the right boundary of the heading for the Client Number field so that the mouse pointer changes to a two-headed arrow and then drag the right boundary to the approximate position shown in Figure 1–83 to reduce the width of the column.

Do I have to be exact?

No. Again, if you are in a slightly different position, the difference between your report and the one in the figure would not be significant.

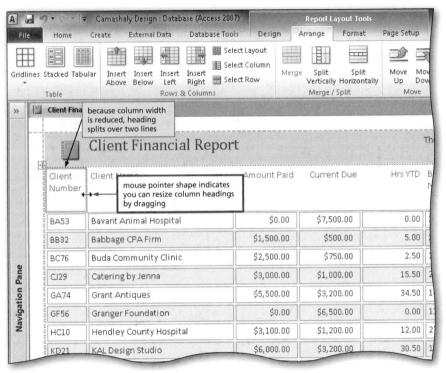

Figure 1–83

• Using the same technique, resize the other columns to the sizes shown in Figure 1–84.

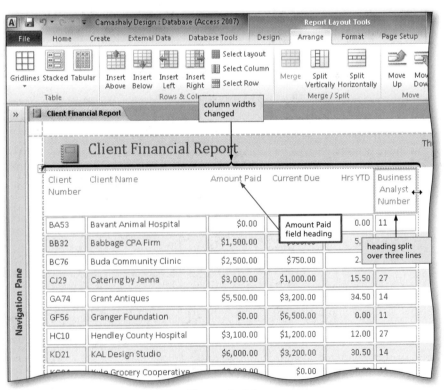

Figure 1–84

To Add Totals to a Report

The report in Figure 1–74 contains totals for the Amount Paid, Current Due, and Hrs YTD columns. You can use Layout view to add these totals. The following steps use Layout view to include totals for these three columns.

1

- Click the Amount Paid field heading (shown in Figure 1–84) to select the field.

Q&A

Do I have to click the heading? Could I click the field on one of the records?

You do not have to click the heading. You also could click the Amount Paid field on any record.

- Click Design on the Ribbon to display the Design tab.

- Click the Totals button (Report Layout Tools Design tab | Grouping & Totals group) to display the list of available calculations (Figure 1–85).

Figure 1–85

2

- Click Sum to calculate the sum of the amount of paid values.

Q&A

Is Sum the same as Total?

Yes.

- Using the same technique, add totals for the Current Due and Hrs YTD columns.

- Scroll down to the bottom of the report to verify that the totals are included. If necessary, expand the size of the total controls so they appear completely.

- Click the Page number to select it and then drag it to the approximate position shown in Figure 1–86.

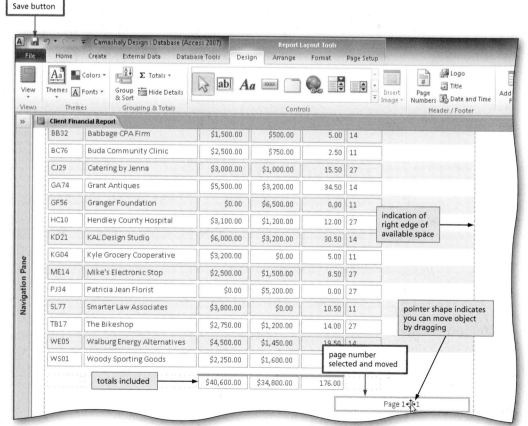

Figure 1–86

Q&A

Why did I need to move the page number?

The dotted line near the right-hand edge of the screen indicates the right-hand border of the available space on the printed page, based on whatever margins and orientation are currently selected. A portion of the page number extends beyond this border. By moving the page number, it no longer extends beyond the border.

- Click the Save button on the Quick Access Toolbar to save your changes to the report layout.

- Close the report.

To Print a Report

The following steps print the report.

1 With the Client Financial Report selected in the Navigation Pane, click File on the Ribbon to open the Backstage view.

2 Click the Print tab in the Backstage view to display the Print gallery.

3 Click the Quick Print button to print the report.

Q&A

How can I print multiple copies of my report?

Click File on the Ribbon to open the Backstage view. Click the Print tab, click Print in the Print gallery to display the Print dialog box, increase the number in the Number of Copies box, and then click the OK button (Print dialog box).

Q&A

How can I print a range of pages rather than printing the whole report?

Click File on the Ribbon to open the Backstage view. Click the Print tab, click Print in the Print gallery to display the Print dialog box, click the Pages option button in the Print Range area, enter the desired page range, and then click the OK button (Print dialog box).

BTW

Tabbed Documents Versus Overlapping Windows
By default, Access 2010 displays database objects in tabbed documents instead of overlapping windows. If your database is in overlapping windows mode, click File on the Ribbon, click Options in the Backstage view, click Current Database in the Access Options dialog box, and select the Display Document Tabs check box and the Tabbed Documents option button.

Database Properties

Access helps you organize and identify your databases by using **database properties**, which are the details about a file. Database properties, also known as **metadata**, can include such information as the file's author, title, or subject. **Keywords** are words or phrases that further describe the database. For example, a class name or database topic can describe the file's purpose or content.

Five different types of document properties exist, but the more common ones used in this book are standard and automatically updated properties. **Standard properties** are associated with all Microsoft Office documents and include author, title, and subject. **Automatically updated properties** include file system properties, such as the date you create or change a file, and statistics, such as the file size.

To Change Database Properties

The Database Properties dialog box contains areas where you can view and enter database properties. You can view and change information in this dialog box at anytime while you are working on your database. It is a good idea to add your name and class name as database properties. You also can add keywords that further describe your database. The following steps use the Properties dialog box to change database properties.

1

- Click File on the Ribbon to open the Backstage view.

- If necessary, click the Info tab in the Backstage view to display the Info gallery (Figure 1–87).

Q&A How do I close the Backstage view?

Click File on the Ribbon or click the preview of the document in the Info gallery to return to the Access database window.

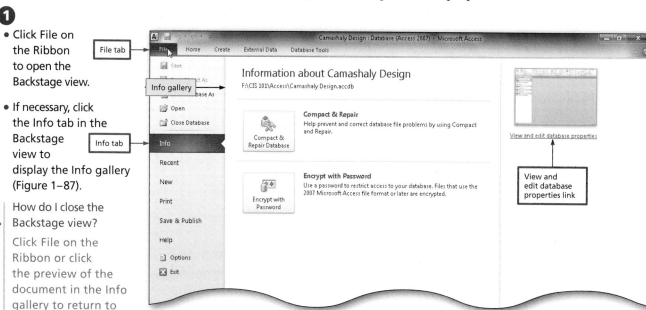

Figure 1–87

2

- Click the 'View and edit database properties' link in the right pane of the Info gallery to display the Camashaly Design.accdb Properties dialog box (Figure 1–88).

Q&A Why are some of the database properties in my Properties dialog box already filled in?

The person who installed Microsoft Office 2010 on your computer or network may have set or customized the properties.

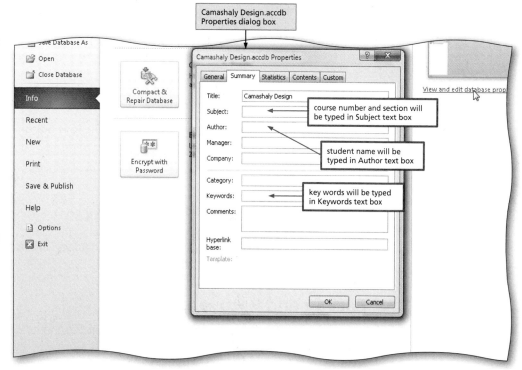

Figure 1–88

3

- If necessary, click the Summary tab.

- Click the Subject text box, if necessary delete any existing text, and then type `CIS 101, Section 20` as the Subject property.

- Click the Author text box and then type `Trevor Wilkins` as the Author property. If a name already is displayed in the Author text box, delete it before typing the new name.

- Click the Keywords text box, if necessary delete any existing text, and then type `online marketing, Web site design` as the Keywords property (Figure 1–89).

What types of properties does Access collect automatically?

Access records such details as when the database was created, when it was last modified, total editing time, and the various objects contained in the database.

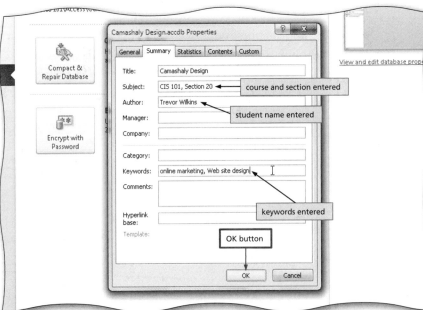

Figure 1–89

4

- Click the OK button to save your changes and remove the Camashaly Design.accdb Properties dialog box from the screen.

To Quit Access

The following steps quit Access.

1 Click the Close button on the right side of the title bar to quit Access.

2 If a Microsoft Access dialog box appears, click the Save button to save any changes made to the object since the last save.

Special Database Operations

The special operations involved in maintaining a database are backup, recovery, compacting a database, and repairing a database.

Backup and Recovery

It is possible to damage or destroy a database. Users can enter data that is incorrect; programs that are updating the database can end abnormally during an update; a hardware problem can occur; and so on. After any such event has occurred, the database may contain invalid data. It even might be totally destroyed.

Obviously, you cannot allow a situation in which data has been damaged or destroyed to go uncorrected. You must somehow return the database to a correct state. This process is called recovery; that is, you **recover** the database.

The simplest approach to recovery involves periodically making a copy of the database (called a **backup copy** or a **save copy**). This is referred to as **backing up** the database. If a problem occurs, you correct the problem by copying this backup copy over the actual database, often referred to as the **live database**.

To back up the database that is currently open, you use the Back Up Database command on the Save & Publish tab in the Backstage view. In the process, Access suggests a name that is a combination of the database name and the current date. For example, if you back up the Camashaly Design database on April 20, 2012, Access will suggest the name, Camashaly Design_2012-04-20. You can change this name if you desire, although it is a good idea to use this name. By doing so, it will be easy to distinguish between all the backup copies you have made to determine which is the most recent. In addition, if you discover that a critical problem occurred on April 18, 2012, you may want to go back to the most recent backup before April 18. If, for example, the database was not backed up on April 17 but was backed up on April 16, you would use Camashaly Design_2012-04-16.

TO BACK UP A DATABASE

You would use the following steps to back up a database to a file on a hard disk or high-capacity removable disk.

1. Open the database to be backed up.
2. Click File on the Ribbon to open the Backstage view, and then click the Save & Publish tab.
3. With Save Database As selected in the File Types area, click Back Up Database in the Save Database As area, and then click the Save As button.
4. Selected the desired location in the Save As box. If you do not want the name Access has suggested, enter the desired name in the File name text box.
5. Click the Save button to back up the database.

Access creates a backup copy with the desired name in the desired location. Should you ever need to recover the database using this backup copy, you can simply copy it over the live version.

Compacting and Repairing a Database

As you add more data to a database, it naturally grows larger. When you delete an object (records, tables, forms, or queries), the space previously occupied by the object does not become available for additional objects. Instead, the additional objects are given new space; that is, space that was not already allocated. To remove this wasted space from the database, you must **compact** the database. The same option that compacts the database also repairs problems that might have occurred in the database.

TO COMPACT AND REPAIR A DATABASE

You would use the following steps to compact and repair a database.

1. Open the database to be compacted.
2. Click File on the Ribbon to open the Backstage view, and then, if necessary, select the Info tab.
3. Click the Compact & Repair Database button in the Info gallery to compact and repair the database.

The database now is the compacted form of the original.

BTW

Access Help
At any time while using Access, you can find answers to questions and display information about various topics through Help. Used properly, this form of assistance can increase your productivity and reduce your frustrations by minimizing the time you spend learning how to use Access. For instruction about Access Help and exercises that will help you gain confidence in using it, read the Office 2010 and Windows 7 chapter at the beginning of this book.

Additional Operations

Additional special operations include opening another database, closing a database without quitting Access, and saving a database with another name. They also include deleting a table (or other object) as well as renaming an object. Finally, you can change properties of a table or other object, such as the object's description.

When you open another database, Access will automatically close the database that previously was open. Before deleting or renaming an object, you should ensure that the object has no dependent objects; that is, other objects that depend on the object you want to delete.

TO OPEN ANOTHER DATABASE

To open another database, you would use the following steps.

1. Click File on the Ribbon to open the Backstage view.
2. Click Open.
3. Select the database to be opened.
4. Click the Open button.

TO CLOSE A DATABASE WITHOUT QUITTING ACCESS

You would use the following steps to close a database without quitting Access.

1. Click File on the Ribbon to open the Backstage view.
2. Click Close Database.

BTW

Certification
The Microsoft Office Specialist (MOS) program provides an opportunity for you to obtain a valuable industry credential — proof that you have the Access 2010 skills required by employers. For more information, visit the Access 2010 Certification Web page (scsite.com/ac2010/cert).

TO SAVE A DATABASE WITH ANOTHER NAME

To save a database with another name, you would use the following steps.

1. Click File on the Ribbon to open the Backstage view, and then select the Save & Publish tab.
2. With Save Database As selected in the File Types area and Access Database selected in the Save Database As area, click the Save As button.
3. Enter a name and select a location for the new version.
4. Click the Save button.

TO DELETE A TABLE OR OTHER OBJECT IN THE DATABASE

You would use the following steps to delete a database object.

1. Right-click the object in the Navigation Pane.
2. Click Delete on the shortcut menu.
3. Click the Yes button in the Microsoft Access dialog box.

BTW

Quick Reference
For a table that lists how to complete the tasks covered in this book using the mouse, Ribbon, shortcut menu, and keyboard, see the Quick Reference Summary at the back of this book, or visit the Access 2010 Quick Reference Web page (scsite.com/ac2010/qr).

TO RENAME AN OBJECT IN THE DATABASE

You would use the following steps to rename a database object.

1. Right-click the object in the Navigation Pane.
2. Click Rename on the shortcut menu.
3. Type the new name and press the ENTER key.

Chapter Summary

In this chapter you have learned to design a database, create an Access database, create tables and add records to them, print the contents of tables, create queries, create forms, and create reports. You also have learned how to change database properties. The items listed below include all the new Access skills you have learned in this chapter.

1. Start Access (AC 12)
2. Create a Database (AC 13)
3. Create a Database Using a Template (AC 14)
4. Modify the Primary Key (AC 16)
5. Define the Remaining Fields in a Table (AC 19)
6. Save a Table (AC 21)
7. View the Table in Design View (AC 21)
8. Close the Table (AC 23)
9. Add Records to a Table (AC 23)
10. Quit Access (AC 26)
11. Open a Database from Access (AC 27)
12. Add Additional Records to a Table (AC 28)
13. Resize Columns in a Datasheet (AC 29)
14. Preview and Print the Contents of a Table (AC 31)
15. Create a Table in Design View (AC 33)
16. Import an Excel Worksheet (AC 38)
17. Use the Simple Query Wizard to Create a Query (AC 43)
18. Use a Criterion in a Query (AC 46)
19. Print the Results of a Query (AC 48)
20. Create a Form (AC 48)
21. Create a Report (AC 52)
22. Modify Column Headings and Resize Columns (AC 54)
23. Add Totals to a Report (AC 57)
24. Change Database Properties (AC 59)
25. Back Up a Database (AC 61)
26. Compact and Repair a Database (AC 61)
27. Open Another Database (AC 62)
28. Close a Database without Quitting Access (AC 62)
29. Save a Database with Another Name (AC 62)
30. Delete a Table or Other Object in the Database (AC 62)
31. Rename an Object in the Database (AC 62)

 If you have a SAM 2010 user profile, your instructor may have assigned an autogradable version of this assignment. If so, log into the SAM 2010 Web site at www.cengage.com/sam2010 to download the instruction and start files.

Learn It Online

Test your knowledge of chapter content and key terms.

Instructions: To complete the Learn It Online exercises, start your browser, click the Address bar, and then enter the Web address **scsite.com/ac2010/learn**. When the Access 2010 Learn It Online page is displayed, click the link for the exercise you want to complete and then read the instructions.

Chapter Reinforcement TF, MC, and SA
A series of true/false, multiple choice, and short answer questions that test your knowledge of the chapter content.

Flash Cards
An interactive learning environment where you identify chapter key terms associated with displayed definitions.

Practice Test
A series of multiple choice questions that test your knowledge of chapter content and key terms.

Who Wants To Be a Computer Genius?
An interactive game that challenges your knowledge of chapter content in the style of a television quiz show.

Wheel of Terms
An interactive game that challenges your knowledge of chapter key terms in the style of the television show *Wheel of Fortune*.

Crossword Puzzle Challenge
A crossword puzzle that challenges your knowledge of key terms presented in the chapter.

Apply Your Knowledge

Reinforce the skills and apply the concepts you learned in this chapter.

Adding a Caption, Creating a Query, Creating a Form, and Creating a Report

Instructions: Start Access. Open the Babbage CPA Firm database. See the inside back cover of this book for instructions for downloading the Data Files for Students, or see your instructor for information on accessing the files required in this book.

The Babbage CPA Firm employs bookkeepers who maintain the books for those clients who need bookkeeping services. The Babbage CPA Firm has a database that keeps track of its bookkeepers and clients. Each client is assigned to a single bookkeeper, but each bookkeeper may be assigned many clients. The database has two tables. The Client table contains data on the clients who use the bookkeeping services of the Babbage CPA Firm. The Bookkeeper table contains data on the bookkeepers employed by Babbage CPA Firm.

Perform the following tasks:

1. Open the Bookkeeper table in Design view and add BKR # as the caption for Bookkeeper Number. Save the changes to the table.

2. Open the Bookkeeper table in Datasheet view and resize all columns to best fit the data. Save the changes to the layout of the table.

3. Use the Simple Query Wizard to create a query for the Client table that contains the Client Number, Client Name, Amount Paid, and Balance Due. Use the name, Client Query, for the query.

4. Create a simple form for the Bookkeeper table. Use the name, Bookkeeper, for the form.

5. Close the Bookkeeper form.

6. Create the report shown in Figure 1–90 for the Client table. The report includes totals for both the Amount Paid and Balance Due fields. Be sure the totals appear completely. You might need to expand the size of the controls. Move the page number so that it is within the margins.

7. Compact the database.

8. Back up the database.

9. Change the database properties, as specified by your instructor. Submit the revised database in the format specified by your instructor.

Client Financial Report Thursday, April 12, 2012 8:38:16 PM

Client Number	Client Name	Amount Paid	Balance Due	Bookkeeper Number
A54	Afton Mills	$575.00	$315.00	22
A62	Atlas Suppliers	$250.00	$175.00	24
B26	Blake-Scripps	$875.00	$250.00	24
D76	Dege Grocery	$1,015.00	$325.00	22
G56	Grand Cleaners	$485.00	$165.00	24
H21	Hill Shoes	$0.00	$285.00	34
J77	Jones Plumbing	$685.00	$0.00	22
M26	Mohr Crafts	$125.00	$185.00	24
S56	SeeSaw Industries	$1,200.00	$645.00	22
T45	Tate Repair	$345.00	$200.00	34
W24	Woody Sporting Goods	$975.00	$0.00	34
C29	Catering by Jenna	$0.00	$250.00	34
		$6,530.00	$2,795.00	

Figure 1–90

Extend Your Knowledge

Extend the skills you learned in this chapter and experiment with new skills. You may need to use Help to complete the assignment.

Using a Database Template to Create a Students Database

Instructions: Access includes a number of templates that you can use to create a beginning database that can be modified to meet your specific needs. You will create a Students database using the Students template. The database includes sample tables, queries, forms, and reports. You will change the database and create the Student Birthdays Query, shown in Figure 1–91.

Figure 1–91

Perform the following tasks:

1. Start Access.

2. With a USB flash drive connected to one of the computer's USB ports, ensure the New tab is selected in the Backstage view and select Sample templates in the New gallery.

3. Select the Students template and create a new database on your USB drive with the file name, Students.

4. Close the Student List form and change the organization of the Navigation Pane to Tables and Related Views .

5. Delete the Student Details form.

6. Use the Query Wizard to create the query shown in Figure 1–91. Save the query as Student Birthdays Query.

7. Open the Student Phone List in Layout view and use the tools on the Format tab to make the Student Phone List title bold and change the font size to 24. Delete the control containing the time.

8. Save your changes to the report.

9. Compact the database.

10. Change the database properties, as specified by your instructor. Submit the revised database in the format specified by your instructor.

Make It Right

Analyze a database and correct all errors and/or improve the design.

Correcting Errors in the Table Structure

Instructions: Start Access. Open the Beach Rentals database. See the inside back cover of this book for instructions for downloading the Data Files for Students, or see your instructor for information on accessing the files required in this book.

Beach Rentals is a database containing information on rental properties available at a beach resort. The Rentals table shown in Figure 1–92 contains a number of errors in the table structure. You are to correct these errors before any additional records can be added to the table. The Rental Code field is a Text field that contains a maximum of three characters. The field Address was omitted from the table. The Address field is a Text field with a maximum of 20 characters. It should appear after Rental Code. Only whole numbers should be allowed in the Bedrooms and Bathrooms fields. The column heading Weakly Rental is misspelled, and the field should contain monetary values. The Distance field represents the walking distance from the beach; the field should display two decimal places. The table name should be Rental Units, not Rentals.

Change the database properties, as specified by your instructor. Submit the revised database in the format specified by your instructor.

Figure 1–92

In the Lab

Design, create, modify, and/or use a database using the guidelines, concepts, and skills presented in this chapter. Labs are listed in order of increasing difficulty.

Lab 1: Creating Objects for the ECO Clothesline Database

Problem: ECO Clothesline is a local company that designs and manufactures eco-friendly casual wear, yoga clothing, and fitness apparel. All clothes are made from earth-friendly fabrics, such as bamboo, hemp, organic cotton, and natural silk. The company recently decided to store its customer and sales rep data in a database. Each customer is assigned to a single sales rep, but each sales rep may be assigned many customers. The database and the Customer table have been created, but there is no data in the Customer table. The Sales Rep table has not been created. The company plans to import the Customer data from an Excel workbook, shown in Figure 1–93a. The other Excel workbook (Figure 1–93b) contains information on the sales representatives that ECO employs. ECO would like to finish storing this data in a database and has asked for your help.

Instructions: Perform the following tasks: Start Access and open the ECO Clothesline database. See the inside back cover of this book for instructions for downloading the Data Files for Students, or see your instructor for information on accessing the files required in this book.

1. Import the Lab 1-1 Customer Data workbook into the Customer table.

2. Add the captions Cust # to the Customer Number field and SR # to the Sales Rep Number field in the Customer table and save the changes.

3. Open the Customer table in Datasheet view and resize the columns to best fit the data. Save the changes to the layout of the table.

4. Use Datasheet view to create a table in which to store the data related to sales reps. Use the name Sales Rep for the table. The fields and the data for the Sales Rep table are shown in Figure 1–93b.

(a) Customer Data (Excel Workbook)

	A	B	C	D	E	F	G	H	I	J	K
1	Customer Number	Customer Name	Street	City	State	Postal Code	Balance	Amount Paid	Sales Rep Number		
2	AM23	Amy's Store	223 Johnson	Oxford	TN	37021	195.00	1,695.00	44		
3	BF34	Barbara's Fashions	1939 Jackson	Lowton	TN	37084	150.00	0.00	51		
4	BL15	Blondie's on Main	3294 Main	Oxford	TN	37021	555.00	1,350.00	49		
5	CM09	Casual by Marie	3140 Halsted	Ashton	VA	20123	295.00	1,080.00	51		
6	CY12	Curlin Yoga Studio	1632 Clark	Georgetown	NC	28794	145.00	710.00	49		
7	DG14	Della's Designs	312 Gilham	Granger	NC	27036	340.00	850.00	44		
8	EC07	Environmentally Casual	1805 Broadway	Pineville	VA	22503	0.00	1,700.00	44		
9	FN19	Fitness Counts	675 Main	Oxford	TN	37021	345.00	1,950.00	51		
10	JN34	Just Natural	2200 Lawrence	Ashton	VA	20123	360.00	700.00	49		
11	LB20	Le Beauty	13 Devon	Lowton	TN	37084	200.00	1,250.00	49		
12	NC25	Nancy's Place	1027 Wells	Walburg	NC	28819	240.00	550.00	44		
13	RD03	Rose's Day Spa	787 Monroe	Pineville	VA	22503	0.00	975.00	51		
14	TT21	Tan and Tone	1939 Congress	Ashton	VA	20123	160.00	725.00	44		
15	TW56	The Workout Place	34 Gilham	Granger	NC	27036	680.00	125.00	51		
16	WS34	Woody's Sporting Goods	578 Central	Walburg	NC	28819	1,235.00	0.00	49		
17											

(b) Sales Rep Data (Excel Workbook)

	A	B	C	D	E	F	G	H	I	J
1	Sales Rep Number	Last Name	First Name	Street	City	State	Postal Code	Base Pay YTD	Comm Rate	
2	44	Jones	Pat	43 Third	Oxford	TN	37021	13,000.00	0.05	
3	49	Gupta	Pinn	678 Hillcrest	Georgetown	NC	28794	15,000.00	0.06	
4	51	Ortiz	Gabe	982 Victoria	Ashton	VA	20123	12,500.00	0.05	
5	55	Sinson	Terry	45 Elm	Walburg	NC	28819	500.00	0.04	
6										

Figure 1–93

The primary key for the Sales Rep table is Sales Rep Number. Assign the caption SR # to the Sales Rep Number field. Comm Rate is a Number field, and Base Pay YTD is a Currency data type. The field size for Sales Rep Number is 2. The State field size is 2, and the Postal Code field size is 5. All other text fields have a field size of 15.

5. Open the Sales Rep table in Design view and change the field size for the Comm Rate field to Single, the format to Fixed, and the Decimal Places to 2.

6. Add the data shown in Figure 1–93b to the Sales Rep table. Resize the columns to best fit the data. Save the changes to the layout of the table.

7. Create a query using the Simple Query Wizard for the Customer table that displays the Customer Number, Customer Name, Balance, Amount Paid, and Sales Rep Number fields. Use the name Customer Query.

8. Create and save the report shown in Figure 1–94 for the Customer table. The report should include Customer Number, Customer Name, Balance, and Sales Rep Number fields. Include a total for the Balance field.

9. Change the database properties, as specified by your instructor. Submit the revised database in the format specified by your instructor.

Customer Balance Report			Thursday, April 12, 2012
			8:55:32 PM
Customer Number	Customer Name	Balance	Sales Rep Number
AM23	Amy's Store	$195.00	44
BF34	Barbara's Fashions	$150.00	51
BL15	Blondie's on Main	$555.00	49
CM09	Casual by Marie	$295.00	51
CY12	Curlin Yoga Studio	$145.00	49
DG14	Della's Designs	$340.00	44
EC07	Environmentally Casual	$0.00	44
FN19	Fitness Counts	$345.00	51
JN34	Just Natural	$360.00	49
LB20	Le Beauty	$200.00	49
NC25	Nancy's Place	$240.00	44
RD03	Rose's Day Spa	$0.00	51
TT21	Tan and Tone	$160.00	44
TW56	The Workout Place	$680.00	51
WS34	Woody's Sporting Goods	$1,235.00	49
		$4,900.00	

Figure 1–94

In the Lab

Lab 2: Creating the Walburg Energy Alternatives Database

Problem: Walburg Energy Alternatives is a nonprofit organization that promotes the use of energy alternatives such as solar power and wind power. The organization provides a variety of services and funds itself through donations. Recently, the organization decided to sell a small number of items in its education center to help fund programs. The store purchases the items from vendors that deal in energy-saving products. Currently, the information about the items and vendors is stored in the Excel workbook shown in Figure 1–95. Each item is assigned to a single vendor, but each vendor may be assigned many items. You volunteer part-time at the store, and the store manager has asked you to create a database that will store the item and vendor information. You have already determined that you need two tables in which to store the information: an Item table and a Vendor table.

Instructions: Perform the following tasks:

1. Design a new database in which to store all the objects related to the items for sale. Call the database Walburg Energy Alternatives.

2. Use the information shown in the Excel workbook in Figure 1–95 to determine the primary keys and determine additional fields. Then, determine the relationships between tables, the data types, and the field sizes.

3. Create the Item table using the information shown in Figure 1–95.

4. Create the Vendor table using the information shown in Figure 1–95. Be sure that the field size for the Vendor Code in the Item table is identical to the field size for the Vendor Code in the Vendor table. Add the caption, Phone, for the Telephone Number field.

Figure 1–95

5. Add the appropriate data to the Item table. Resize the columns to best fit the data and save the changes to the layout.

6. Add the appropriate data to the Vendor table. Resize the columns to best fit the data and save the changes to the layout.

7. Create a query for the Item table. Include the Item Number, Description, Cost, Selling Price, and Vendor Code in the query. Save the query as Item Query.

8. Open the Item Query and add a criterion to limit retrieval to those items supplied by Scryps Distributors. Save the query as Item-Scryps Query.

9. Create a simple form for the Item table. Use the name, Item, for the form.

10. Create the report shown in Figure 1–96 for the Item table. Do not add any totals.

11. Change the database properties, as specified by your instructor. Submit the database in the format specified by your instructor.

Inventory Status Report

Thursday, April 12, 2012
8:56:19 PM

Item Number	Description	On Hand	Cost
3663	Air Deflector	8	$5.45
3673	Energy Booklet	25	$2.70
4553	Energy Saving Kit	7	$42.75
4573	Faucet Aerator	20	$0.89
4583	Fluorescent Light Bulb	18	$4.50
5923	Low Flow Shower Head	11	$8.75
6185	Luminescent Night Light	12	$3.75
6234	Programmable Thermostat	3	$34.25
6345	Rain Gauge	16	$2.89
7123	Retractable Clothesline	10	$13.25
7934	Shower Timer	15	$2.45
8136	Smoke Detector	10	$6.10
8344	Toilet Tank Water Saver	18	$3.35
8590	Water Conservation Kit	8	$13.45
9458	Windows Insulator Kit	10	$4.95

Figure 1–96

In the Lab

Lab 3: Creating the Philamar Training Database

Problem: Philamar Training provides business processes and information technology training to various companies and organizations. Philamar employs trainers who work with individual companies to determine training needs and then conduct the training. Currently, Philamar keeps data on clients and trainers in two Word documents and two Excel workbooks. Philamar also keeps track of which clients are assigned to which trainers. Each client is assigned to a single trainer, but each trainer might be assigned many clients. Currently, clients BS27, FI28, and MC28 are assigned to trainer 42, Belinda Perry. Clients CE16, CP27, FL93, HN83, and TE26 are assigned to trainer 48, Michael Stevens. Clients EU28 and PS82 are assigned to trainer 53, Manuel Gonzalez. Philamar has an additional trainer, Marty Danville, who has been assigned trainer number 67, but who has not yet been assigned any clients.

Instructions: Using the data shown in Figure 1 – 97 and the information in the previous paragraph, design the Philamar Training database. The data shown in Figure 1–97 is included in the Data Files for Students in the following files: Lab 1-3a.docx, Lab 1-3b.docx, Lab 1-3c.xlsx, and Lab 1-3d.xlsx. Use the database design guidelines in this chapter to help you in the design process.

Client Number	Client Name	Address	City	State	Postal Code
BS27	Blant and Sons	4806 Park	Kingston	TX	76653
CE16	Center Services	725 Mitchell	San Rita	TX	78364
CP27	Calder Plastics	7300 Cedar	Kingston	TX	76653
EU28	Elba's Furniture	1445 Hubert	Tallmadge	TX	77231
FI28	Farrow-Idsen	829 Wooster	Cedar Ridge	TX	79342
FL93	Fairland Lawn	143 Pangborn	Kingston	TX	76653
HN83	Hurley National	3827 Burgess	Tallmadge	TX	77231
MC28	Morgan-Alyssa	923 Williams	Crumville	TX	76745
PS82	PRIM Staffing	72 Crestview	San Rita	TX	78364
TE26	Telton-Edwards	5672 Anderson	Dunston	TX	77893

(a) Client Address Information (Word Table)

	A	B	C	D	E
1	Client Number	Client Name	Amount Paid	Current Due	
2	BS27	Blant and Sons	$11,876.00	$892.50	
3	CE16	Center Services	$12,512.00	$1,672.00	
4	CP27	Calder Plastics	$5,725.00	$0.00	
5	EU28	Elba's Furniture	$3,245.00	$202.00	
6	FI28	Farrow-Idsen	$8,287.50	$925.50	
7	FL93	Fairland Lawn	$976.00	$0.00	
8	HN83	Hurley National	$0.00	$0.00	
9	MC28	Morgan-Alyssa	$3,456.00	$572.00	
10	PS82	PRIM Staffing	$7,500.00	$485.00	
11	TE26	Telton-Edwards	$6,775.00	$0.00	
12					

(c) Client Financial Information (Excel Workbook)

Trainer Number	Last Name	First Name	Address	City	State	Postal Code
42	Perry	Belinda	261 Porter	Burdett	TX	76734
48	Stevens	Michael	3135 Gill	Rockwood	TX	78884
53	Gonzalez	Manuel	265 Maxwell	Camino	TX	76574
67	Danville	Marty	1827 Maple	Dunston	TX	77893

(b) Trainer Address Information (Word Table)

	A	B	C	D	E
1	Trainer Number	Last Name	First Name	Hourly Rate	YTD Earnings
2	42	Perry	Belinda	$23.00	$17,620.00
3	48	Stevens	Michael	$21.00	$13,567.50
4	53	Gonzalez	Manuel	$24.00	$19,885.00
5	67	Danville	Marty	$20.00	$0.00
6					

(d) Trainer Financial Information (Excel Workbook)

Figure 1–97

When you have completed the database design, create the database, create the tables, and add the data to the appropriate tables. Be sure to determine the correct data types and field sizes.

Finally, prepare the Client Query shown in Figure 1–98 and the Client Status Report shown in Figure 1–99. The report does not include totals. Change the database properties, as specified by your instructor. Submit the database in the format specified by your instructor.

Figure 1–98

Client Status Report

Thursday, April 12, 2012
8:57:10 PM

Client Number	Client Name	Amount Paid	Current Due	Trainer Number
BS27	Blant and Sons	$11,876.00	$892.50	42
CE16	Center Services	$12,512.00	$1,672.00	48
CP27	Calder Plastics	$5,725.00	$0.00	48
EU28	Elba's Furniture	$3,245.00	$202.00	53
FI28	Farrow-Idsen	$8,287.50	$925.50	42
FL93	Fairland Lawn	$976.00	$0.00	48
HN83	Hurley National	$0.00	$0.00	48
MC28	Morgan-Alyssa	$3,456.00	$572.00	42
PS82	PRIM Staffing	$7,500.00	$485.00	53
TE26	Telton-Edwards	$6,775.00	$0.00	48

Figure 1–99

Cases and Places

Apply your creative thinking and problem solving skills to design and implement a solution.

See the inside back cover of this book for instructions for downloading the Data Files for Students, or see your instructor for information on accessing the files required in this book.

1: Design and Create an Advertising Database

Academic

You are a Marketing major currently doing an internship with the Chamber of Commerce in a local city. The Chamber publishes a Newcomer's Guide that contains advertisements from local businesses. Ad reps contact the businesses to arrange for advertising. Each advertiser is assigned to a single ad rep, but each ad rep may be assigned many advertisers. The Chamber would like your help in creating a database of advertisers and advertising representatives.

Based on the information in the Case 1-1 Chamber of Commerce workbook, use the concepts and techniques presented in this chapter to design and create a database to store the data that the Chamber needs. Submit your assignment in the format specified by your instructor.

2: Design and Create a Consignment Database

Personal

You are involved in a volunteer organization that provides clothing and school supplies to needy children. Recently, the Board of Directors decided to open a consignment shop as a way to raise additional funds. In a consignment shop, individuals bring in unwanted items, and the shop sells the items. Proceeds are split between the seller and the shop. The database must keep track of the items for sale in the shop as well as maintain data on the sellers. Each item is assigned to a single seller, but each seller may be assigned many items. The Board has asked you to create a database to store information about the consignment items.

Use the concepts and techniques presented in this chapter to design and create a database to store the consignment data. Then create the necessary tables and enter the data from the Case 1-2 Consignment workbook. Create an Available Items Report that lists the item number, description, price, and seller code. Submit your assignment in the format specified by your instructor.

3: Design and Create a Senior Care Database

Professional

You are co-owner of a company, Senior Care, that provides nonmedical services to older adults who need assistance with daily living. Helpers will drive individuals to appointments, do the grocery shopping, fill prescriptions, help with personal care, and provide companionship. Each client is assigned to a single helper, but each helper may be assigned many clients. The other owners have asked you to create a database of clients and helpers. Use the concepts and techniques presented in this chapter to design and create a database to meet Senior Care needs. Then create the necessary tables and enter the data from the Case 1-3 Senior Care workbook. Create a Client Report that lists each client's client number, client last name, client first name, balance, and helper number. Submit your assignment in the format specified by your instructor.

NOTES

NOTES

NOTES

NOTES

Appendix A

Project Planning Guidelines

Using Project Planning Guidelines

The process of communicating specific information to others is a learned, rational skill. Computers and software, especially Microsoft Office 2010, can help you develop ideas and present detailed information to a particular audience.

Using Microsoft Office 2010, you can create projects such as Word documents, PowerPoint presentations, Excel spreadsheets, and Access databases. Productivity software such as Microsoft Office 2010 minimizes much of the laborious work of drafting and revising projects. Some communicators handwrite ideas in notebooks, others compose directly on the computer, and others have developed unique strategies that work for their own particular thinking and writing styles.

No matter what method you use to plan a project, follow specific guidelines to arrive at a final product that presents information correctly and effectively (Figure A–1). Use some aspects of these guidelines every time you undertake a project, and others as needed in specific instances. For example, in determining content for a project, you may decide that a chart communicates trends more effectively than a paragraph of text. If so, you would create this graphical element and insert it in an Excel spreadsheet, a Word document, or a PowerPoint slide.

Determine the Project's Purpose

Begin by clearly defining why you are undertaking this assignment. For example, you may want to track monetary donations collected for your club's fund-raising drive. Alternatively, you may be urging students to vote for a particular candidate in the next election. Once you clearly understand the purpose of your task, begin to draft ideas of how best to communicate this information.

Analyze Your Audience

Learn about the people who will read, analyze, or view your work. Where are they employed? What are their educational backgrounds? What are their expectations? What questions do they have?

PROJECT PLANNING GUIDELINES

1. DETERMINE THE PROJECT'S PURPOSE
Why are you undertaking the project?

2. ANALYZE YOUR AUDIENCE
Who are the people who will use your work?

3. GATHER POSSIBLE CONTENT
What information exists, and in what forms?

4. DETERMINE WHAT CONTENT TO PRESENT TO YOUR AUDIENCE
What information will best communicate the project's purpose to your audience?

Figure A–1

Design experts suggest drawing a mental picture of these people or finding photos of people who fit this profile so that you can develop a project with the audience in mind.

By knowing your audience members, you can tailor a project to meet their interests and needs. You will not present them with information they already possess, and you will not omit the information they need to know.

Example: Your assignment is to raise the profile of your college's nursing program in the community. How much do they know about your college and the nursing curriculum? What are the admission requirements? How many of the applicants admitted complete the program? What percent pass the state board exams?

Gather Possible Content

Rarely are you in a position to develop all the material for a project. Typically, you would begin by gathering existing information that may reside in spreadsheets or databases. Web sites, pamphlets, magazine and newspaper articles, and books could provide insights of how others have approached your topic. Personal interviews often provide perspectives not available by any other means. Consider video and audio clips as potential sources for material that might complement or support the factual data you uncover.

Determine What Content to Present to Your Audience

Experienced designers recommend writing three or four major ideas you want an audience member to remember after reading or viewing your project. It also is helpful to envision your project's endpoint, the key fact you wish to emphasize. All project elements should lead to this ending point.

As you make content decisions, you also need to think about other factors. Presentation of the project content is an important consideration. For example, will your brochure be printed on thick, colored paper or posted on the Web? Will your PowerPoint presentation be viewed in a classroom with excellent lighting and a bright projector, or will it be viewed on a notebook computer monitor? Determine relevant time factors, such as the length of time to develop the project, how long readers will spend reviewing your project, or the amount of time allocated for your speaking engagement. Your project will need to accommodate all of these constraints.

Decide whether a graph, photo, or artistic element can express or emphasize a particular concept. The right hemisphere of the brain processes images by attaching an emotion to them, so audience members are more apt to recall these graphics long term rather than just reading text.

As you select content, be mindful of the order in which you plan to present information. Readers and audience members generally remember the first and last pieces of information they see and hear, so you should place the most important information at the top or bottom of the page.

Summary

When creating a project, it is beneficial to follow some basic guidelines from the outset. By taking some time at the beginning of the process to determine the project's purpose, analyze the audience, gather possible content, and determine what content to present to the audience, you can produce a project that is informative, relevant, and effective.

Appendix B

Publishing Office 2010 Web Pages Online

With Office 2010 programs, you use the Save As command in the Backstage view to save a Web page to a Web site, network location, or FTP site. **File Transfer Protocol (FTP)** is an Internet standard that allows computers to exchange files with other computers on the Internet.

You should contact your network system administrator or technical support staff at your Internet access provider to determine if their Web server supports Web folders, FTP, or both, and to obtain necessary permissions to access the Web server.

Using an Office Program to Publish Office 2010 Web Pages

When publishing online, someone first must assign the necessary permissions for you to publish the Web page. If you are granted access to publish online, you must obtain the Web address of the Web server, a user name, and possibly a password that allows you to connect to the Web server. The steps in this appendix assume that you have access to an online location to which you can publish a Web page.

To CONNECT TO AN ONLINE LOCATION

To publish a Web page online, you first must connect to the online location. To connect to an online location using Windows 7, you would perform the following steps.

1. Click the Start button on the Windows 7 taskbar to display the Start menu.

2. Click Computer in the right pane of the Start menu to open the Computer window.

3. Click the 'Map network drive' button on the toolbar to display the Map Network Drive dialog box. (If the 'Map network drive' button is not visible on the toolbar, click the 'Display additional commands' button on the toolbar and then click 'Map network drive' in the list to display the Map Network Drive dialog box.)

4. Click the 'Connect to a Web site that you can use to store your documents and pictures' link (Map Network Drive dialog box) to start the Add Network Location wizard.

5. Click the Next button (Add Network Location dialog box).

6. Click 'Choose a custom network location' and then click the Next button.

7. Type the Internet or network address specified by your network or system administrator in the text box and then click the Next button.

8. Click 'Log on anonymously' to deselect the check box, type your user name in the User name text box, and then click the Next button.

9. If necessary, enter the name you want to assign to this online location and then click the Next button.

10. Click to deselect the Open this network location when I click Finish check box, and then click the Finish button.

11. Click the Cancel button to close the Map Network Drive dialog box.

12. Close the Computer window.

To Save a Web Page to an Online Location

The online location now can be accessed easily from Windows programs, including Microsoft Office programs. After creating a Microsoft Office file you wish to save as a Web page, you must save the file to the online location to which you connected in the previous steps. To save a Microsoft Word document as a Web page, for example, and publish it to the online location, you would perform the following steps.

1. Click File on the Ribbon to display the Backstage view and then click Save As in the Backstage view to display the Save As dialog box.

2. Type the Web page file name in the File name text box (Save As dialog box). Do not press the ENTER key because you do not want to close the dialog box at this time.

3. Click the 'Save as type' box arrow and then click Web Page to select the Web Page format.

4. If necessary, scroll to display the name of the online location in the navigation pane.

5. Double-click the online location name in the navigation pane to select that location as the new save location and display its contents in the right pane.

6. If a dialog box appears prompting you for a user name and password, type the user name and password in the respective text boxes and then click the Log On button.

7. Click the Save button (Save As dialog box).

The Web page now has been published online. To view the Web page using a Web browser, contact your network or system administrator for the Web address you should use to connect to the Web page.

Appendix C

Saving to the Web Using Windows Live SkyDrive

Introduction

Windows Live SkyDrive, also referred to as **SkyDrive**, is a free service that allows users to save files to the Web, such as documents, presentations, spreadsheets, databases, videos, and photos. Using SkyDrive, you also can save files in folders, providing for greater organization. You then can retrieve those files from any computer connected to the Internet. Some Office 2010 programs including Word, PowerPoint, and Excel can save files directly to an Internet location such as SkyDrive. SkyDrive also facilitates collaboration by allowing users to share files with other SkyDrive users (Figure C–1).

Figure C–1

Note: An Internet connection is required to perform the steps in this appendix.

To Save a File to Windows Live SkyDrive

You can save files directly to SkyDrive from within Word, PowerPoint, and Excel using the Backstage view. The following steps save an open Word document (Koala Exhibit Flyer, in this case) to SkyDrive. These steps require you to have a Windows Live account. Contact your instructor if you do not have a Windows Live account.

1
- Start Word and then open a document you want to save to the Web (in this case, the Koala Exhibit Flyer).
- Click File on the Ribbon to display the Backstage view (Figure C–2).

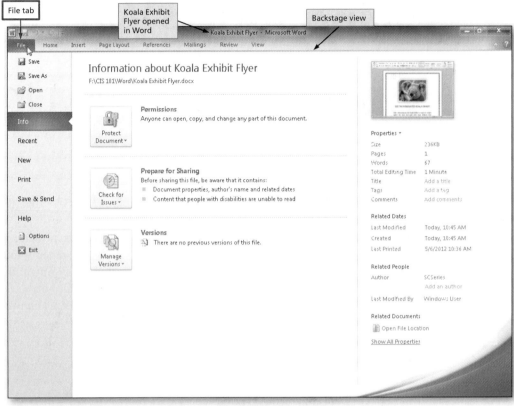

Figure C–2

2
- Click the Save & Send tab to display the Save & Send gallery (Figure C–3).

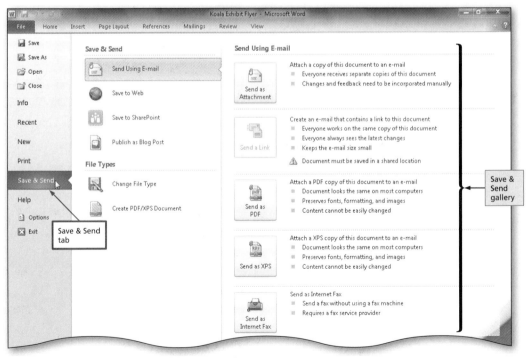

Figure C–3

3

- Click Save to Web in the Save & Send gallery to display information about saving a file to the Web (Figure C–4).

Figure C–4

4

- Click the Sign In button to display a Windows Live login dialog box that requests your e-mail address and password (Figure C–5).

What if the Sign In button does not appear?

If you already are signed into Windows Live, the Sign In button will not be displayed. Instead, the contents of your Windows Live SkyDrive will be displayed. If you already are signed into Windows Live, proceed to Step 6.

Figure C–5

5

- Enter your Windows Live e-mail address in the E-mail address box (Windows Live login dialog box).

- Enter your Windows Live password in the Password text box.

- Click the OK button to sign into Windows Live and display the contents of your Windows Live SkyDrive in the right pane of the Save & Send gallery.

- If necessary, click the My Documents folder to set the save location for the document (Figure C–6).

What if the My Documents folder does not exist?

Click another folder to select it as the save location. Record the name of this folder so that you can locate and retrieve the file later in this appendix.

Figure C–6

My SkyDrive shows personal and shared folders. What is the difference?

Personal folders are private and are not shared with anyone. Shared folders can be viewed by SkyDrive users to whom you have assigned the necessary permissions.

6

- Click the Save As button in the right pane of the Save & Send gallery to contact the SkyDrive server (which may take some time, depending on the speed of your Internet connection) and then display the Save As dialog box (Figure C–7).

Figure C–7

7

- Type **Koala Exhibit Web** in the File name text box to enter the file name and then click the Save button (Save As dialog box) to save the file to Windows Live SkyDrive (Figure C–8).

Figure C–8

Q&A

Is it necessary to rename the file?

It is good practice to rename the file. If you download the file from SkyDrive to your computer, having a different file name will preserve the original file.

8

- If you have one Word document open, click the Close button on the right side of the title bar to close the document and quit Word; or if you have multiple Word documents open, click File on the Ribbon to open the Backstage view and then click Exit in the Backstage view to close all open documents and quit Word.

Web Apps

Microsoft has created a scaled-down, Web-based version of its Microsoft Office suite, called **Microsoft Office Web Apps,** or **Web Apps**. Web Apps contains Web-based versions of Word, PowerPoint, Excel, and OneNote that can be used to view and edit files that are saved to SkyDrive. Web Apps allows users to continue working with their files even while they are not using a computer with Microsoft Office installed. In addition to working with files located on SkyDrive, Web Apps also enables users to create new Word documents, PowerPoint presentations, Excel spreadsheets, and OneNote notebooks. After returning to a computer with the Microsoft Office suite, some users choose to download files from SkyDrive and edit them using the associated Microsoft Office program.

Note: As with all Web applications, SkyDrive and Office Web Apps are subject to change. Consequently, the steps required to perform the actions in this appendix might be different from those shown.

To Download a File from Windows Live SkyDrive

Files saved to SkyDrive can be downloaded from a Web browser using any computer with an Internet connection. The following steps download the Koala Exhibit Web file using a Web browser.

1

- Click the Internet Explorer program button pinned on the Windows 7 taskbar to start Internet Explorer.

- Type **skydrive.live.com** in the Address bar and then press the ENTER key to display a SkyDrive Web page requesting you sign in to your Windows Live account (Figure C–9). (If the contents of your SkyDrive are displayed instead, you already are signed in and can proceed to Step 3 on the next page.)

Q&A Why does the Web address change after I enter it in the Address bar?

The Web address changes because you are being redirected to sign into Windows Live before you can access SkyDrive.

Q&A Can I open the file from Microsoft Word instead of using the Web browser?

If you are opening the file on the same computer from which you saved it to the SkyDrive, click File on the Ribbon to open the Backstage view. Click the Recent tab and then click the desired file name (Koala Exhibit Web, in this case) in the Recent Documents list, or click Open and then navigate to the location of the saved file (for a detailed example of this procedure, refer to the Office 2010 and Windows 7 chapter at the beginning of this book).

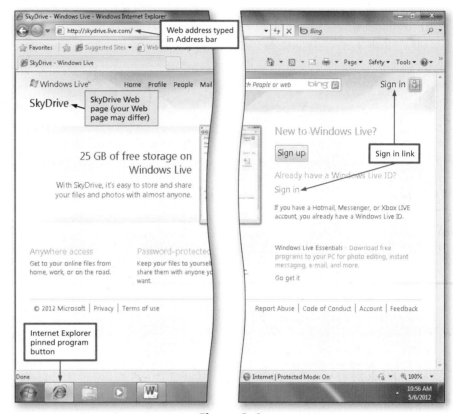

Figure C–9

2

- Click the Sign in link to display the Windows Live ID and Password text boxes (Figure C–10).

Q&A Why can I not locate the Sign in link?

If your computer remembers your Windows Live sign in credentials from a previous session, your e-mail address already may be displayed on the SkyDrive Web page. In this case, point to your e-mail address to display the Sign in button, click the Sign in button, and then proceed to Step 3. If you cannot locate your e-mail address or Sign in link, click the Sign in with a different Windows Live ID link and then proceed to Step 3.

Figure C–10

• If necessary, enter your Windows Live ID and password in the appropriate text boxes and then click the Sign in button to sign into Windows Live and display the contents of your SkyDrive (Figure C–11).

Q&A

What if my screen shows the contents of a particular folder, instead of all folders?

To display all folders on your SkyDrive, point to Windows Live in the upper-left corner of the window and then click SkyDrive on the Windows Live menu.

Figure C–11

• Click the My Documents folder, or the link corresponding to the folder containing the file you wish to open, to select the folder and display its contents (Figure C–12).

Figure C–12

5

- Point to the Koala Exhibit Web file to select the file and display commands associated with the file.

- Click the More link to display the More menu (Figure C–13).

Figure C–13

6

- Click Download on the More menu to display the File Download dialog box (Figure C–14).

Figure C–14

7

- Click the Save button (File Download dialog box) to display the Save As dialog box (Figure C–15).

- Navigate to the desired save location.

- Click the Save button to save the file on your computer's hard disk or other storage device connected to the computer.

Figure C–15

Collaboration

In today's workplace, it is common to work with others on projects. Collaborating with the members of your team often requires sharing files. It also can involve multiple people editing and working with a certain set of files simultaneously. Placing files on SkyDrive in a public or shared folder enables others to view or modify the files. The members of the team then can view and edit the files simultaneously using Web Apps, enabling the team to work from one set of files (Figure C–16). Collaboration using Web Apps not only enables multiple people to work together, it also can reduce the amount of time required to complete a project.

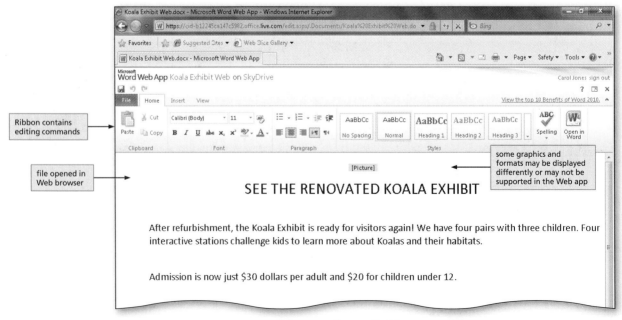

Figure C–16

Index

A

Access, **OFF 53**
  See also databases
  features and operations, OFF 54–56
  Help, AC 62
  importing data from other
    applications to, AC 38–42
  overview of, OFF 53–56
  quitting, OFF 58, AC 26, AC 60
  starting, OFF 53, AC 12, AC 27
  window, Navigation Pane, work
    area, AC 15
Access work area, **AC 15**, **OFF 54**
Accounting Number format,
  EX 32–33
Acrobat Reader, EX 45
actions, undoing and redoing,
  WD 23
active cell (Excel), **OFF 49**
active tabs, **OFF 16**
adding
  content to Title Slide, OFF 40,
    OFF 43
  page borders, WD 41–43
  records to tables, AC 23–25,
    AC 28–29
  slides to presentations, PPT 14–20,
    PPT 21–24
  text to documents, OFF 20
  text to slides, PPT 40–42
  totals to reports, AC 56
  transitions between slides,
    PPT 43
Address bar, **OFF 24**
Aero, OFF 2–3, OFF 27
aligning
  numbers, EX 14
  paragraphs, WD 13
  photographs, PPT 36–38
  snapping charts, EX 40
  text, EX 12
All Programs list, OFF 10
animations, adding slide transitions,
  PPT 43–45
apostrophes (')
  entering numbers as text, EX 16
  viewing style characteristics,
    EX 52
application software, **OFF 2**
applications, importing data to
  Access from, AC 38–42
area charts, EX 36

B

backing up (database), **AC 61**
backslash (\) and file, folder names,
  OFF 22, OFF 28
BACKSPACE key, to correct errors,
  EX 49
Backstage view, **OFF 35**
  closing, EX 43, WD 49, AC 59
  closing Office files using, OFF 44
  creating new Office documents
    from, OFF 41–43
  opening recent Office files using,
    OFF 45
  saving files to SkyDrive, APP 5–8
backup copy, **AC 61**
Basic, Windows 7, OFF 2–3
Blank Database option, OFF 55
Blank layout, PPT 21
blank lines, inserting, WD 7
body copy, **WD 5**
bold, **EX 25**
  cell entries, EX 25
  making text, WD 28, PPT 19–20
borders
  adding page, WD 41–43
  printing, WD 53
BTW Web page, PPT 4
bubble charts, EX 37
bulleted lists, **WD 22–23**,
  PPT 14–15
bullets
  removing, WD 23
  using, WD 13
buttons, removing from Quick
  Access Toolbar, OFF 19

arranging slides, PPT 39–40
arrow keys, completing entry in
  adjacent cells, EX 11
asterisk (*) and file, folder names,
  OFF 22, OFF 28
audience, analyzing, APP 1–2
Auto Fill options, EX 18
AutoCalculate, using, EX 48–49
AutoCalculate area, **EX 48**
AutoCorrect feature, **EX 9**
AutoCorrect options, AC 37
automatically updated properties,
  WD 49, PPT 45, EX 43, AC 58
AutoPlay window, opening,
  OFF 22

C

calculating
  with AutoCalculate, EX 48, EX 49
  sums, EX 15–16
Cancel box, formula bar, **EX 8**
Cancel button, OFF 35
capitalization, WD 18, EX 9
category axis, **EX 40**
cell reference (Excel), **OFF 49**
Cell Styles button EX 52
cells
  active, OFF 49
  bolding entries, EX 25
  calculating sums, EX 15–16
  centering entries across columns,
    EX 28–29
  changing font colors of entries,
    EX 27
  changing styles, EX 22–23
  clearing, EX 52
  completing entry in previously
    selected cells, EX 14
  completing entry with arrow keys,
    EX 11
  copying to adjacent cells, EX 16–18
  correcting errors while you type,
    EX 49–51
  editing contents of, EX 50
  increasing font size of entries,
    EX 26
  merging, EX 28–29
  selecting, EX 6, EX 34–35
  splitting merged, EX 29
  undoing last entry, EX 51
  values and charting, EX 37
centered, **WD 14**
centering
  cell entries across columns,
    EX 28–29
  page contents vertically, WD 40
  paragraphs, WD 14
certification, Microsoft Office
  Specialist (MOS), WD 44,
    EX 52, AC 62
certifications, PPT 50
changing
  data in tables, AC 25–26
  database properties, AC 59–60
  document properties, WD 49–50,
    PPT 45–47, EX 43–44
  file names, OFF 52
  font colors of cell entries, EX 27

fonts in worksheets, EX 24–25
screen resolution, OFF 33–34,
    WD 4, PPT 4, EX 5
table structure, AC 20–22
text color, PPT 13
text fonts, case, WD 17–18
worksheets names, EX 42–43
character formatting, **WD 12**
characters
  deleting, WD 47
  formatting, WD 12–30, PPT 12–14
  nonprinting, WD 7
  variable character fonts, WD 10
charting
  Excel feature, **OFF 46**
  PowerPoint feature, OFF 36
charts
  cell values and charting, EX 37
  embedded, **EX 36**
  legends, **EX 41**
  resizing, EX 40
  types of, EX 36–37
clearing cells, ranges, worksheets,
    EX 52–53
clip art
  inserting into slides, PPT 26–33
  resizing, PPT 33–36
Clip Art task pane, **PPT 26–31**
clips, **PPT 26**
  copyright regulations, PPT 27
  inserting into slides, PPT 27–31
  moving, PPT 36–38
  properties, PPT 29
Close button, OFF 35
closing
  Backstage view, WD 49, PPT 46,
    EX 43, AC 59
  databases, AC 62
  Office files, OFF 44, OFF 56
  programs, OFF 35
  tables, AC 26
closing slide, ending slide shows
    with, PPT 38–40
Clustered Cylinder charts, EX 37–42
collaboration using SkyDrive,
    APP 12
collapsing folders, OFF 26
collections, PPT 26
colon (:) and file, folder names,
    OFF 22, OFF 28
color themes, **WD 28–29**
colors
  of bullets, PPT 17
  cell entry font, EX 27
  font, **PPT 10, EX 22**

shading, WD 20
text, WD 24–25, PPT 12–13
using in flyer, WD 13
using in presentations, PPT 9
column charts, EX 37
column heading (Excel), **OFF 49**
columns, EX 5
  adjusting widths, EX 33–34
  centering cell entries across,
    EX 28–29
  entering titles, EX 10–11
  formatting titles, EX 29–31
  resizing, AC 54–56
  resizing datasheet, AC 29–30,
    AC 42
Comma Style format, EX 32
Command bar, **OFF 24**
commands, **OFF 10**
  See also specific command
  adding to Quick Access Toolbar,
    OFF 19
  AutoCalculate shortcut menu
    (table), EX 48
  cell selection, EX 35
  on Ribbon, OFF 14–15
comments, adding to presentations,
    PPT 24
common dialog boxes, **OFF 8**
compact (database), **AC 61**
Comparison slide layout, PPT 21,
    PPT 23
compressing file size, PPT 31
computers
  changing screen resolution,
    OFF 31–34
  logging on to, OFF 6–7
connecting to online location,
    APP 3–4
conserving ink, toner, WD 51
content
  changing slide text, PPT 40–42
  standard layouts for, PPT 21
contextual tabs, EX 39
copy area, **EX 17**
copying
  cells to adjacent cells, EX 16–18
  slides, PPT 38–39
copyright regulations, PPT 27
creating
  bulleted lists, PPT 14–15
  databases, OFF 55–56, AC 13
  documents, OFF 20
  folders, OFF 22–25
  forms, AC 48–50
  new paragraphs, OFF 20, WD 6

Office documents, OFF 41–43,
    OFF 47
Publisher documents,
    OFF 60–61
reports, AC 51–58
tables, AC 15–20, AC 32–37
title slides, PPT 7–8
criterion, using in queries,
    AC 46–47
Currency data type, **AC 9**, AC 20
currency symbols, AC 20
custom layouts, **PPT 21**
customizing
  Quick Access Toolbar, OFF 19
  Ribbon, OFF 49
cylinder charts, EX 37

D

data types, **AC 9**
  available in Access (table), AC 10
  determining, AC 5
database design, **AC 5**
database management systems
    (DBMSs), **OFF 53**, AC 2
database properties, changing,
    AC 58–60
databases, **AC 2**, **OFF 53**
  backup and recovery, AC 60–62
  closing, AC 62
  compacting, AC 61
  creating, OFF 55–56, AC 13
  creating using templates, AC 14
  design guidelines, AC 5–6
  opening, OFF 57, AC 27, AC 62
  overview, components of,
    AC 2–12
  relational, **AC 3**
  tables. *See* tables
Datasheet view, **AC 15**, AC 48
datasheets
  described, **AC 23**
  resizing columns in, AC 29–30,
    AC 42
DELETE key, clearing cell entries,
    EX 52
deleting
  bullets from slides, PPT 18
  databases, database objects,
    AC 62
  embedded charts, EX 53
  files, folders, OFF 64–65
  records, AC 20, AC 26
  text from documents, WD 47
  text from slides, PPT 40–42

demoting (text), **PPT 17**
Design view, **AC 15**, AC 21–22
 creating tables in, AC 33–37
 opening, AC 24
 for reports, AC 53
designing databases, AC 5–12
desktop, Windows, OFF 7
desktop publishing. *See* Publisher
destination area, **EX 17**
Dialog Box Launcher, **OFF 15**
dialog boxes
 common, described, **OFF 8**
 navigating, OFF 30
displaying
 formatting marks, WD 7
 hidden windows, OFF 67
 Mini toolbar, PPT 13
 PowerPoint window, PPT 48
 Ribbon, OFF 17
 Ribbon tabs, OFF 16
 Start menu, OFF 10–11
 user icons, OFF 6
Document Information Panel,
  WD 49, EX 43
 changing document properties
  using, EX 43–44
 using, PPT 46–47
document properties, **WD 49,
  PPT 45, EX 43**
 changing, WD 49–50, PPT 45–47,
  EX 43–44
 printing, WD 49, EX 45
document themes, **PPT 5–6**
document window components,
  OFF 12–16
documents
 choosing themes, PPT 5–6
 correcting errors, WD 44
 creating from Backstage view,
  OFF 41–43
 creating new, OFF 20
 creating Publisher, OFF 60–61
 deleting text from, WD 47
 formatting generally, WD 12–13
 inserting pictures in, WD 30–32,
  WD 35
 inserting text, WD 46
 navigating, WD 11
 opening from PowerPoint,
  PPT 50–51
 planning, WD 4
 printing, WD 51–52, PPT 53
 quitting Office program with open,
  OFF 35
 saving, WD 12

saving, organizing, OFF 21–30
saving Office, OFF 51–52
 tabbed, AC 58
 zooming, WD 33, WD 45
.docx files, OFF 21, WD 14
dollar sign ($), entering, EX 13
doughnut charts, EX 37
download described, **WD 30**
drag and drop
 to delete text, PPT 41–42
 method described, **PPT 39**
 moving items using, PPT 39–40
drag-and-drop editing, **WD 47**
dragging
 to move windows, OFF 66–67
 to resize windows, OFF 67
drawing (PowerPoint feature),
  OFF 36
drives, organizing files and
  folders on, OFF 21–30
duplicating. *See* copying

E

Ease of Access Center, OFF 6
Edit mode, **EX 50**
editing
 drag-and-drop, WD 47
 in-cell, EX 50
effects
 applying picture, WD 38–39
 applying text, WD 19–20
electronic mail, **OFF 58**
e-mail
 See also Outlook
 described, **OFF 58**
e-mailing PowerPoint presentations,
  OFF 36
embedded charts, **EX 36**, EX 53
energy-saving information, PPT 2
Enhanced ScreenTips, **OFF 15**
Enter box, formula bar, **EX 8**
ENTER key, WD 8
ergonomics, preventing wrist
  injuries, OFF 4
errors
 See also mistakes
 correcting in documents, WD 44
 correcting text input, OFF 20
 methods of correcting,
  EX 49–53
Excel, **OFF 46**
 See also workbooks, worksheets
 creating documents from Windows
  Explorer, OFF 47

features and operations, OFF 49–52
 importing worksheets into Access,
  AC 38–42
Excel 2010
 Help, EX 51
 new features, EX 4
 opening workbook from, EX 47–48
 quitting, EX 47
 starting, EX 5
 window, OFF 49–50
expanding folders, OFF 26

F

Favorites area, **OFF 24**
fields, **AC 3**
 determining special properties for,
  AC 16
 naming, AC 8
 renaming, AC 19
 selecting, deselecting, AC 55
file formats
 .docx files, OFF 21
 for importing, PPT 32
 recognized by PowerPoint (table),
  PPT 31
file management
 described, **OFF 62**
 moving, renaming, deleting files,
  OFF 63–65
file names
 changing, OFF 52
 described, **OFF 21**
File Transfer Protocol (FTP),
  APP 3
files, **OFF 7**
 See also specific file type
 closing, OFF 56
 collaboration using SkyDrive,
  APP 12
 compressing size of, PPT 31
 creating through Backstage view,
  OFF 42
 deleting, OFF 64–65
 document properties, using,
  PPT 45
 moving, OFF 64
 opening existing Office, OFF 57
 opening from SkyDrive,
  APP 9–12
 opening recent Office, using
  Backstage view, OFF 45
 organizing, WD 12, EX 20
 PDFs, EX 45
 renaming, OFF 63, APP 8

saving, organizing, OFF 21–30
saving in folders, OFF 27–28
saving presentation, OFF 41,
   PPT 47
saving to SkyDrive, APP 5–8
fill handles, **EX 17**
   clearing cell entries, EX 52
   copying cells to adjacent cells using,
      EX 16–18
folder windows, **OFF 24**
folders, **OFF 10**
   creating, OFF 22–23
   creating within folders,
      OFF 24–25
   deleting, OFF 65
   expanding, collapsing, navigating,
      OFF 26
   Microsoft Office, OFF 11
   organizing, WD 12, PPT 14,
      EX 20
   personal vs. shared, APP 7
   private, APP 10
   saving, organizing files in,
      OFF 21–30, OFF 41, OFF 44
folders (OneNote), **OFF 62**
font color, **EX 22**
Font gallery, EX 24
font size, **WD 12, EX 22**
   changing, WD 16, WD 21–22
   increasing cell entry, EX 26
font style, **EX 22**
fonts, **WD 12, PPT 10, EX 22**
   changing, WD 13, WD 17,
      EX 24–25
   coloring, WD 24–25
   increasing size, PPT 11,
      PPT 20
   size, in presentations, PPT 9
   variable character, WD 10
Form view, **AC 48**, AC 50
format described, **WD 12,
   PPT 10, EX 22**
formatting
   charts, EX 37
   paragraphs, WD 12–15,
      WD 22–23
   text in presentations, PPT 9
   using Mini toolbar, WD 26
   words, PPT 20
   worksheets, EX 22–34
formatting marks, displaying,
   WD 7
forms, creating, using, **AC 48–50**
formula bar, **OFF 50**, OFF 51,
   EX 8

G
galleries, **OFF 14**
grammar and spelling check,
   WD 9–11
graphics, resizing, WD 34–35,
   WD 36
greater than symbol (>) and file,
   folder names, OFF 22, OFF 28
green computing, **EX 45, AC 30**
gridlines (Excel), **OFF 49**
groups on Ribbon, OFF 17
guidelines, project planning,
   APP 1–2

H
hard copy, **AC 30**
hardcopies, **EX 45**
headings
   levels of, EX 30
   report columns, changing,
      AC 54–56
   row and column, OFF 49, EX 5
headlines, **WD 5**
health, preventing wrist injuries,
   OFF 4, WD 11
Help, WD 35, EX 51, AC 62
   obtaining for Windows 7, OFF 5
   obtaining using links, OFF 70
   PowerPoint, PPT 45
   searching for, OFF 68–70
   Table of Contents, OFF 71
   Windows Help and Support,
      OFF 73–74
   Word, OFF 66
hiding
   Mini toolbar, OFF 15
   ruler, WD 5
   spelling errors, WD 9
Home tab
   described, **OFF 14**
   displaying, using, OFF 17

I
icons
   See also specific icon
   content-insertion, PPT 16
   folder, OFF 22
images
   clips. See clips
   copyright regulations, PPT 27
Import Spreadsheet Wizard,
   AC 38–42

importing, **AC 38**
   data from other applications to
      Access, AC 38–42
   file types, PPT 32
in-cell editing, **EX 50**, EX 51
increasing font size, PPT 20
ink, conserving, WD 51
Insert mode, **EX 50**
Insert tab, EX 36
inserting
   See also adding
   blank lines, WD 7
   clip art, photographs into slides,
      PPT 26–33
   photographs into presentations,
      PPT 31–32
   pictures in documents, WD 30–32,
      WD 35
   text into documents, WD 46
insertion point, OFF 20, WD 11,
   EX 8
italicized text, **WD 24, PPT 13**
italicizing text, WD 24

K
keyboard
   document navigation with, WD 11
   KeyTips, **OFF 16**
keyboard shortcuts, **OFF 4–5**,
   EX 35
keywords, **PPT 45, EX 43, AC 58**

L
landscape orientation, **OFF 39,
   PPT 7**, EX 46, **AC 30**
Layout gallery, **PPT 21**
Layout view, AC 49, AC 53–58
layouts, **OFF 39, PPT 21, AC 29**
   changing slide, PPT 21–24
   custom, **PPT 21**
left-aligned text, WD 14
legends, chart, **EX 41**
less than symbol (<) and file, folder
   names, OFF 22, OFF 28
levels (paragraph), **PPT 8**
libraries, **OFF 24**
Libraries area, **OFF 24**
line charts, EX 36
lines
   inserting blank, WD 7
   selecting, WD 15, WD 21
links, Help, OFF 70
lists (Excel), **AC 38**

lists, creating bulleted, PPT 14–15
live database, **AC 61**
live preview, **OFF 14**, OFF 27
lock icon, APP 10
logging on to computers, **OFF 5–7**

M

magnifying text. *See* zooming
maximizing windows, **OFF 12**
maximums, calculating using
    AutoCalculate, EX 49
menus, **OFF 10**
    See also specific menu
    using shortcut, OFF 18
Merge & Center button, Home tab,
    EX 28
merging cells, **EX 28–29**
metadata, **EX 43**, **PPT 45**, **AC 58**
Microsoft Access 2010
    See also Access
    described, **OFF 8**, **OFF 53**
Microsoft Certified Application
    Specialist (MCAS), PPT 50
Microsoft Clip Organizer, **PPT 26**,
    PPT 27–31
Microsoft Communicator, **OFF 8**
Microsoft Excel 2010
    See also Excel
    described, **OFF 8**
Microsoft InfoPath 2010, **OFF 8**
Microsoft Office 2010, **OFF 7**
    introduction to, PPT 8
    publishing Web pages online,
        APP 3–4
    programs, OFF 8
Microsoft Office folder, OFF 11
Microsoft Office Specialist (MOS),
    WD 44, EX 52, AC 62
Microsoft Office suites, OFF 8–9
Microsoft Office Web Apps,
    APP 8
Microsoft OneNote 2010, **OFF 8**
Microsoft Outlook 2010, **OFF 8**
Microsoft PowerPoint 2010
    See also PowerPoint
    described, **OFF 8**
Microsoft Publisher 2010, **OFF 8**,
    OFF 59–61
Microsoft SharePoint Workspace
    2010, **OFF 8**
Microsoft Web Apps, **OFF 8**
Microsoft Word 2010
    See also Word
    described, **OFF 8**

Mini toolbar
    described, using, **OFF 15**, WD 16,
        WD 26
    displaying, PPT 13
minimalist style, PPT 35
minimized windows, **OFF 30**
minimizing
    Ribbon, OFF 17
    windows, OFF 30–31
mistakes
    AutoCorrect feature, **EX 9**
    automatic spelling correction,
        WD 9
    correcting errors in documents,
        WD 44
    correcting table structure errors,
        AC 37
    correcting typing, WD 6,
        PPT 8–9
    methods of correcting errors,
        EX 49–53
    undoing, EX 8, AC 20
    using AutoCalculate to avoid,
        EX 48
mouse
    document navigation with,
        WD 11
    operations (table), OFF 4
    using, OFF 2
    using in Excel, OFF 49
moving
    clips, PPT 36–38
    files, OFF 64
    manually through slides in slide
        shows, PPT 49
    text, WD 47–48
    windows, OFF 66–67
multi-level bulleted list slides,
    adding, **PPT 15–18**
multimedia, using in PowerPoint
    presentations, OFF 36
My Collections, **PPT 26**

N

Name box
    formula bar, **OFF 50**
    selecting cell using, EX 34–35
names
    fields, AC 8
    file, **OFF 21**, OFF 27–28, OFF 52
    folder, OFF 22–23
    tables, AC 8
    user, **OFF 5**
    worksheets, EX 42–43

navigating
    described, **OFF 30**
    dialog boxes, OFF 30
    documents, WD 11
    using mouse, OFF 2–4
Navigation Pane, **OFF 24**, OFF 54,
    AC 14, **AC 15**
nonprinting characters, displaying,
    WD 7
Normal cell style, EX 52
Normal style, WD 5
Normal view, PPT 21, **PPT 24**,
    PPT 25
notebooks (OneNote), **OFF 62**
Notes Page view, **PPT 24**
Notes pane, **PPT 24**
note-taking program (OneNote),
    OFF 61–62
Number data type, **AC 9**
numbers
    alignment in cells, EX 14
    entering, EX 13–14
    entering as text, EX 16
    formatting in worksheets,
        EX 31–33
    numeric limitations of Excel,
        EX 13
    summing columns of, EX 15–16

O

Object tabs (Access), **AC 15**,
    OFF 54
Office 2010, **OFF 7**, PPT 8,
    APP 3–4
Office Collections, **PPT 26**
Office programs, suites, OFF 8–9
    See also specific program
    obtaining Help, OFF 68–72
    starting from Windows Explorer,
        OFF 48
    Windows Help and Support,
        OFF 73–74
Office Theme, **PPT 5**
OneNote, OFF 61–62
one-to-many relationship, **AC 9**
opening
    AutoPlay window, OFF 22
    Backstage view, OFF 42
    Clip Art task pane, PPT 31
    databases, AC 27, AC 62
    Design view, AC 24
    documents from PowerPoint,
        PPT 50–51
    documents from Word, WD 45

existing files, OFF 57
files from SkyDrive, APP 9–12
forms, AC 50
operating systems, **OFF 2**
organizing files and folders,
OFF 21–30, WD 12, PPT 14,
EX 20
orientation
landscape, **PPT 7**
portrait page, PPT 22
Outline tab, PPT 21, **PPT 24**
outlining (PowerPoint feature),
OFF 36
Outlook, **OFF 58**
Outlook window, OFF 58–59
overlapping windows vs. tabbed
documents, AC 58
Overtype mode, **EX 50**

P

pages
See also documents
centering contents vertically,
WD 40–41
OneNote, **OFF 62**
viewing single, WD 40–41
panes, **OFF 10**
navigation, OFF 24
task, **OFF 15**
paragraph formatting, **WD 12**
paragraphs, **PPT 8**
centering, WD 14
creating new, OFF 20, WD 6
formatting, WD 12–30
formatting mark (¶), WD 7
selecting, PPT 12
shading, WD 20
spacing before, after, WD 43
using in presentations,
PPT 8–9
password text box, OFF 6–7
passwords
described, **OFF 5**
and user accounts, OFF 6–7
paste area, **EX 17**
Paste Options, WD 48
paths, **OFF 21**
paths and corresponding drives,
folders, **OFF 21–22**
PDF files
described, **AC 30**
viewing, EX 45
people icon, APP 10

personal folders vs. shared folders,
APP 7
photographs
inserting into presentations,
PPT 31–32
inserting into slides, PPT 26–33
resizing, PPT 35–36
picture effects, applying, WD 38–39
picture styles, WD 37
Picture Tools Format tab, OFF 14
pictures. *See also* graphics, images,
photographs
inserting in documents, WD 30–32,
WD 35
wrapping text around, PPT 32
pie charts, EX 36
pixels, screen resolution,
OFF 31–32
placeholders, **OFF 39, PPT 7**
deleting text in, PPT 41–42
selecting text, PPT 16
using with slides, PPT 7
planning
databases, AC 2
distribution of worksheets, EX 45
printing of documents, WD 51
projects, WD 2, PPT 2, PPT 4
projects, guidelines, APP 1–2
use of color, WD 24
Word documents, WD 4
worksheets, EX 2
worksheets formatting, EX 22–23
plus sign (+) and shortcut keys,
OFF 5
point size, **EX 22**
points (font), **PPT 10**
portrait orientation, **AC 30**,
OFF 39, EX 46
portrait page orientation, PPT 22
positioning charts, EX 37
postal codes, AC 12
PowerPoint, **OFF 36–38**
BTW Web page, PPT 4
file formats recognized (table),
PPT 31
Help, PPT 45
Office suites (table), **OFF 9**
opening documents from,
PPT 50–51
quitting, PPT 50
presentations, overview of,
PPT 2–4
Ribbon, OFF 39–40
saving files in folders, OFF 41

starting, OFF 37–38, PPT 4–5,
PPT 50
views, using, PPT 24–25
window, OFF 39–40, PPT 48
presentations, **OFF 36–37, PPT 2**
See also slide shows
adding slides to, PPT 14–20
creating title for, PPT 7–8
inserting photographs into,
PPT 31–32
printing, PPT 51–53
saving, PPT 14, PPT 47
preview, live, OFF 14
previewing
and printing worksheets,
EX 45–47
slide shows, PPT 52
tables, AC 30–32
Previous Locations button,
OFF 24
primary keys, **AC 3–4**
determining, AC 5, AC 8–9
modifying, AC 16–17
Print Layout view, **OFF 12**,
WD 5
Print Preview, AC 53
printing
document properties, WD 49,
EX 45
documents, WD 51–52
presentations, PPT 51–53
tables, AC 30–32
worksheets, EX 45–47
printouts, **AC 30, EX 45**
private folders, APP 10
programs
See also specific program
Help, obtaining, OFF 72
Office suites, **OFF 8**
panes, OFF 10
quitting, OFF 35, OFF 45, OFF 52
starting and using, OFF 9–11,
OFF 37–38
switching between, OFF 27
tabs in, OFF 14
project planning guidelines,
APP 1–2
projects
database creation, AC 2–12
flyer with pictures, WD 2–4
presentation with bulleted lists,
clip art, PPT 2–4
worksheet with embedded chart,
EX 2–4

promoting (text), **PPT 17**
properties
See also specific property
clip, PPT 29
document, and standard, **EX 43**
standard, automatically updated,
WD 49, **PPT 45**
publication types, **OFF 60**
Publisher
creating documents, OFF 60–61
described, **OFF 59–60**
publishing Office 2010 Web pages
online, APP 3–4

Q

queries, **AC 42–43**
creating, AC 43–45
saving, AC 47
using, AC 45–48
using criterion in, AC 46–47
question mark (?) and file, folder
names, OFF 22, OFF 28
Quick Access Toolbar, **OFF 16**
customizing, OFF 19
using shortcut menus, OFF 18
Quick Reference Web page, PPT 52
quitting
Access, AC 26, AC 60
Excel, EX 47
Office program with open
document, OFF 35
Office programs, OFF 45, OFF 52
PowerPoint, PPT 50
Word, WD 53
quotation marks (')
and file, folder names, OFF 22,
OFF 28
and text fields, AC 47

R

radar charts, EX 37
ranges, **EX 15**
clearing, EX 52
copying one to another, EX 18
records, **AC 3**
adding to tables, AC 23–25,
AC 28–29
deleting, AC 20, AC 26
recover (database), **AC 61**
Recycle Bin, **OFF 7**
Redo command, OFF 19, EX 51
redoing actions, WD 23

redundancy, identifying and
removing, AC 5, AC 10–12
Refresh button, **OFF 24**
relational databases, **AC 3**
relationships, determining,
implementing between tables,
AC 9
relative references, **EX 17**
removing
See also deleting
bold styles from cells, EX 25
bullets, WD 23
KeyTips from screen, OFF 16
redundancy, AC 10–12
styles, PPT 11
renaming
database objects, AC 62
fields, AC 19
files, APP 8, OFF 63
repairing databases, AC 61
replacing slide text content,
PPT 40–42
Report view, AC 53
reports
adding totals to, AC 56
creating, AC 51–53
Layout view, using in, AC 53–58
repositioning
clips, PPT 36–38
slides, PPT 39–40
requirements document, **EX 3**
resizing, **PPT 33**, **WD 34**
charts, EX 40
clip art, photographs, PPT 33–36
datasheet columns, **AC 29–30**,
AC 42
graphics, WD 34–36
report columns, AC 54–56
windows, OFF 66–67
resolution, screen. *See* screen
resolution
Restart command, **OFF 6**
restoring
Ribbon, OFF 17
windows, OFF 30–31
reversing changes, undoing mistakes,
PPT 8
Ribbon, **OFF 14–15**
Access, OFF 54
appearance of, PPT 15
customizing, OFF 49
displaying tabs, minimizing,
restoring, OFF 16–17
Excel, OFF 49

PowerPoint, **OFF 40**
screen resolution and, WD 8
at various screen resolutions,
OFF 32–33
rotate handles, WD 37
row heading (Excel), **OFF 49**
row selector, **AC 22**
rows
copying cells to adjacent cells,
EX 17–18
determining contents for, EX 5
entering titles, EX 12
rulers, showing or hiding, WD 5

S

Save & Send gallery, APP 5–8
Save As command, APP 3
Save As dialog box, OFF 51–52
Save command, OFF 19
save copy, **AC 61**
saving
backup and recovery operations,
AC 60–62
databases, OFF 55, AC 62
documents, WD 12
existing document with same
name, WD 30
files in folders, OFF 27–29,
OFF 41
files in Office programs,
OFF 8
files to SkyDrive, APP 5–8
import steps, AC 41
Office documents with same file
name, OFF 51
and organizing files, OFF 21–30
presentations, PPT 14, PPT 47
queries, AC 47
records, AC 25
tables, AC 21
Web pages to online location,
APP 3–4
workbooks, EX 20, EX 45
screen resolution
changing, OFF 33–34, WD 4,
EX 5
described, **OFF 31–32**, PPT 4
ScreenTips, Enhanced, **OFF 15**
scroll arrows, **OFF 4**
scroll bars, **OFF 4**, OFF 12–13
scroll box, **OFF 4**
scrolling through folder contents,
OFF 26

search box
 described, **OFF 24**
 starting programs using,
  OFF 37–38
searching for Help topics,
  OFF 68–70
Section Header slide layout,
  PPT 21
sections (OneNote), **OFF 62**
selecting
 cells, EX 6, EX 34–35
 lines, WD 15, WD 21
 paragraphs, PPT 10
 text placeholders, PPT 16
 words, WD 27–28, PPT 12,
  PPT 19
selection rectangles, **WD 32,
 PPT 33**
shade, applying, **WD 20**
Shared Collections, **PPT 26**
shared folders vs. personal folders,
  APP 7
sheet tab (Excel), **OFF 49**
shortcut keys, **OFF 4–5**
shortcut menus, using, **OFF 18,**
  OFF 33–34
Shut down command, **OFF 6**
Shutter Bar Open/Close button,
  OFF 54
shutting down Windows 7,
  OFF 6
signature lines, **WD 5**
signing in to Windows Live, APP 7,
  APP 9–10
Simple Query Wizard, AC 43–45
size, font, **EX 22**
sizing
 See also resizing
 charts, EX 40
 font size, **WD 12,** WD 13
 fonts, WD 16
sizing handles, OFF 40,
  PPT 33
SkyDrive, **APP 5**
 collaboration using, APP 12
 opening files from, APP 9–12
 saving files to, APP 5–8
 Web Apps, APP 8
slash (/) and file names, OFF 28
Sleep command, **OFF 6**
slide indicator, **PPT 25**
Slide pane, **PPT 24**
Slide Show toolbar, PPT 49
Slide Show view, **PPT 47–50**

slide shows, **OFF 36–37, PPT 2**
 See also presentations
 ending with closing slide,
  PPT 38–40
 Title Slide, OFF 39–40
slide transitions, **PPT 43**
sliders, using, OFF 34
slides, **OFF 39**
 adding to presentations,
  PPT 14–20, PPT 21–24
 changing layouts, PPT 21–24
 changing text content,
  PPT 40–42
 closing, PPT 38–40
 copying, PPT 38–39
 creating title, PPT 7–8
 editing text in, PPT 40–42
 emphasis, adding, PPT 12
 inserting clip art, photographs into,
  PPT 26–33
 moving to another, in Normal view,
  PPT 24
 multi-level bulleted list,
  PPT 15–18
 in presentations generally, PPT 2
 spell-checking, PPT 40
Slides tab, **PPT 24**
snaps described, **EX 40**
software. *See specific program*
source area, **EX 17**
spacing before, after paragraphs,
  WD 43
spelling check, WD 9–11, PPT 40,
  EX 9
splitting merged cells, EX 29
spreadsheets. *See* worksheets
Standard Colors, PPT 13
standard properties, **WD 49,
 PPT 45, EX 43, AC 58**
Start button, **OFF 10**
Start menu, starting programs using,
  OFF 10–11
starting
 Access, AC 12, AC 27
 Excel, OFF 48, EX 5, EX 47
 PowerPoint, PPT 4–5, PPT 50
 programs, OFF 9–11, OFF 37–38
 Publisher, OFF 60
 slide shows, PPT 47–48
 Windows 7, OFF 5–7
 Windows Help and Support,
  OFF 73–74
 Word, WD 4–5, WD 45
Status bar, **OFF 13, AC 15**

Status Bar Configuration shortcut
  menu, EX 48–49
stock charts, EX 36–37
storage for databases, AC 13
styles, **WD 37**
 See also specific style
 applying picture, WD 37
 changing cell, EX 22–23
 font, PPT 12–14, **EX 22**
 minimalist, PPT 35
 Normal, WD 5
subtitles, worksheet, EX 7
suites, **OFF 8**
SUM function, **EX 15–16**
sums
 calculating, EX 15–16, AC 56
 determining multiple totals at same
  time, EX 18–19
surface charts, EX 37
switching between programs,
  OFF 27

T

tabbed documents, AC 58
tables, **OFF 46**
 See also databases
 adding records to, AC 23–25,
  AC 28–29
 changing structure of, AC 20–22,
  AC 37
 checking structure in Design view,
  AC 22
 closing, AC 23, AC 26
 creating, AC 15–20, AC 32–37
 determining relationships between,
  AC 9
 identifying, AC 5
 naming, AC 8
 previewing, printing, AC 30–32
 saving, AC 21
tabs
 changing Ribbon, OFF 16–17,
  OFF 49
 contextual, EX 39
 on Ribbon, **OFF 14**
Tabs pane, PPT 21
task panes, **OFF 15**
templates
 creating databases using, AC 14
 publication types, OFF 60
text, **EX 7**
 applying text effects, WD 20
 changing font, WD 17

changing font size, WD 21–22
changing slide content, PPT 40–42
choosing for slides, PPT 7
colored, PPT 12–13
correcting errors in documents,
    WD 44
deleting from documents, WD 47
elements of, WD 13
entering, WD 5–8, EX 12
entering in documents, OFF 20
entering numbers as, EX 16
in Excel, **OFF 50**
inserting into documents, WD 46
italicizing, WD 24, PPT 13
making bold, WD 28, PPT 19–20
moving, WD 47–48
selecting, WD 27–28
spelling and grammar check,
    WD 9–11
standard layouts for, PPT 21
underlining, WD 27
wordwrap, WD 8
wrapping around pictures, PPT 32
text boxes, OFF 6
Text data type, **AC 9**
text effects, applying, WD 19–20
text placeholders, selecting, PPT 16
text slides, creating with multi-level
    bulleted list, PPT 15–18
Theme Colors, PPT 13
themes, **WD 12**, EX 22, **EX 24**
  color, **WD 28–29**
  document, **PPT 5–6**
title bars, **OFF 11**
Title Only slide layout, PPT 21–22
Title Slides
  creating, PPT 7–8
  entering content in, OFF 40,
    OFF 43
  layout, **OFF 39**, PPT 21
titles
  entering column, EX 10–11
  entering row, EX 12
  entering worksheet, OFF 50–51,
    EX 8
  formatting column, EX 29–31
  report, AC 52–53
  worksheet, EX 7
toner, conserving, WD 51
tool tabs, **OFF 14**
toolbars
  Mini toolbar, **OFF 15**
  Quick Access Toolbar, **OFF 16**
  Slide Show, PPT 49

totals
  adding to reports, AC 56
  determining multiple at same time,
    EX 18–19
transitions, adding slide, **PPT 43**

U

underlining
  spelling, grammar errors, WD 9
  text, WD 27
Undo command, OFF 19, EX 51
undoing
  actions, WD 23
  changes in tables, AC 25
  input mistakes, AC 20
  last cell entry, EX 51
  mistakes, EX 8, PPT 8, PPT 34
  picture formatting, WD 38
  typing mistakes, WD 6
unique identifiers, **AC 3–4**
USB flash drives
  saving files on, OFF 21–22,
    OFF 27–29, OFF 44
  storing databases on, AC 13
  storing files, folders on, OFF 22–23
user accounts, **OFF 5**
user icons, **OFF 5**, OFF 6
user names, **OFF 5**

V

value axis, **EX 37**
verifying saved files, OFF 30
vertical bar (|) and file, folder names,
    OFF 28
viewing
  presentations in Slide Show view,
    PPT 47–50
  single page, WD 40–41
views
  See also specific view
  Access, AC 15
  PowerPoint, PPT 24–25
  for reports, AC 53
  switching between query, AC 45

W

Web, Excel support, OFF 46
Web Apps, **APP 8**
Web Collections, **PPT 26**
Web pages, publishing Office 2010
    online, APP 3–4

Web-based templates, AC 14
Welcome screen, **OFF 5–6**
windows, **OFF 11**
  Access, AC 15
  Excel, OFF 49–50
  folder, OFF 24–25
  maximizing, **OFF 12**
  minimizing, restoring,
    OFF 30–31
  moving, OFF 66–67
  OneNote, OFF 62
  Outlook, OFF 58–59
  overlapping, vs. tabbed documents,
    AC 58
  PowerPoint, OFF 39–40
  Publisher, OFF 60
  resizing, OFF 66–67
  Word, WD 5
  Windows 7, **OFF 2**
  starting, logging on, OFF 5–7
  Windows Help and Support,
    OFF 73–74
  Windows 7 Aero, OFF 2–3
  Windows 7 Basic, OFF 2–3
  Windows desktop, OFF 7
  Windows Explorer
    creating Office document from,
      OFF 47
    moving, renaming, deleting files,
      OFF 62–65
    starting Office program using,
      OFF 48
  Windows Help and Support,
    OFF 73–74
  Windows Live SkyDrive
    See also SkyDrive
    described, **APP 5**
  Word, OFF 9
    Help, OFF 66, OFF 68–72,
      WD 35
    Office suites (table), **OFF 9**
    opening documents from,
      WD 45
    quitting, WD 44, WD 53
    saving files to SkyDrive, APP 5–8
    starting, WD 4–5, WD 45
  word processing
    PowerPoint feature, OFF 36
    Word. *See* Word
  Word window, OFF 12–16, WD 5
  words
    formatting, PPT 20
    selecting, PPT 12, PPT 19
  wordwrap, **WD 8**

workbooks, **OFF 46**
  opening from Excel, EX 48
  saving, EX 20
worksheets, **OFF 46**
  See also cells, columns, rows
  adding Clustered Cylinder chart to,
    EX 38–42
  adjusting column widths,
    EX 33–34
  changing fonts, EX 24–25
  changing names, EX 42–43
  clearing, EX 52–53
  components, navigation of,
    OFF 49
  development cycle, EX 4

entering titles, EX 8–9, OFF 50–51
formatting, EX 22–34
formatting in worksheets, EX 31–33
importing into Access, AC 38–42
planning, EX 2–6
printing, EX 45–47
titles, subtitles, EX 7
wrapping text around pictures,
    PPT 32
wrist injuries, minimizing, WD 11

X

X Y (scatter) charts, EX 36
x-axis, **EX 40**

XPS files, **AC 30**, EX 47
XPS Viewer, EX 45

Y

y-axis, **EX 37**

Z

zooming
  described, WD 5
  documents, WD 33, WD 45

Quick Reference Summary

Table 1: Microsoft Word 2010 Quick Reference Summary

Task	Page Number	Mouse	Ribbon	Shortcut Menu	Keyboard Shortcut
Bold	WD 28	Bold button on Mini toolbar	Bold button (Home tab | Font group)	Font, Font tab (Font dialog box)	CTRL+B
Bullets, Apply	WD 22		Bullets button (Home tab | Paragraph group)	Bullets	* (ASTERISK), SPACEBAR
Center	WD 14	Center button on Mini toolbar	Center button (Home tab | Paragraph group)	Paragraph, Indents and Spacing tab (Paragraph dialog box)	CTRL+E
Change Case	WD 18		Change Case button (Home tab | Font group)	Font, Font tab (Font dialog box)	SHIFT+F3
Change Spacing before or after Paragraph	WD 43		Spacing Before or Spacing After box arrow (Page Layout tab | Paragraph group)	Paragraph, Indents and Spacing tab (Paragraph dialog box)	
Color Text	WD 25	Font Color button on Mini toolbar	Font Color button arrow (Home tab | Font group)		
Document Properties, Change	WD 49		Properties button (File tab | Info tab)		
Font Size, Change	WD 16	Font Size box arrow on Mini toolbar	Font Size box arrow (Home tab | Font group)	Font, Font tab (Font dialog box)	CTRL+D
Font, Change	WD 17	Font box arrow on Mini toolbar	Font box arrow (Home tab | Font group)	Font, Font tab (Font dialog box)	CTRL+D
Formatting Marks	WD 7		Show/Hide ¶ button (Home tab | Paragraph group)		CTRL+SHIFT+*
Graphic, Resize	WD 34	Drag sizing handle	Shape Height and Shape Width text boxes (Picture Tools Format tab | Size group)	Size and Position, Size tab (Layout dialog box)	
Insertion Point, Move Down/Up One Line	WD 11				DOWN ARROW/ UP ARROW
Insertion Point, Move Down/Up One Paragraph	WD 11				CTRL+DOWN ARROW/ CTRL+UP ARROW

Table 1: Microsoft Word 2010 Quick Reference Summary *(continued)*

Task	Page Number	Mouse	Ribbon	Shortcut Menu	Keyboard Shortcut
Insertion Point, Move Down/Up One Screen	WD 11				PAGE DOWN/ PAGE UP
Insertion Point, Move Left/ Right One Character	WD 11				LEFT ARROW/ RIGHT ARROW
Insertion Point, Move Left/ Right One Word	WD 11				CTRL+LEFT ARROW/ CTRL+RIGHT ARROW
Insertion Point, Move to Beginning/End of Document	WD 11				CTRL+HOME/ CTRL+END
Insertion Point, Move to Beginning/End of Line	WD 11				HOME/ END
Insertion Point, Move to Bottom of Document Window	WD 11				ALT+CTRL+PAGE DOWN/ ALT+CTRL+PAGE UP
Italicize	WD 24	Italic button on Mini toolbar	Italic button (Home tab | Font group)	Font, Font tab (Font dialog box)	CTRL+I
Move Text	WD 47	Drag and drop selected text	Cut button (Home tab | Clipboard group); Paste button (Home tab | Clipboard group)	Cut; Paste	CTRL+X; CTRL+V
Open a Document	WD 45		Open (File tab)		CTRL+O
Page Border, Add	WD 41		Page Borders button (Page Layout tab | Page Background group)		
Picture Style, Apply	WD 37		More button in Picture Styles gallery (Picture Tools Format tab | Picture Styles group)		
Picture Effects, Apply	WD 38		Picture Effects button (Picture Tools Format tab | Picture Styles group)	Format Picture	
Picture, Insert	WD 31		Insert Picture from File button (Insert tab | Illustrations group)		
Print Document	WD 51		Print button (File tab | Print tab)		CTRL+P
Quit Word	WD 44	Close button on title bar	Exit (File tab)		ALT+F4
Redo	WD 23	Redo button on Quick Access Toolbar			CTRL+Y
Save New Document	WD 12	Save button on Quick Access Toolbar	Save or Save As (File tab)		F12
Save Document, Same File Name	WD 30	Save button on Quick Access toolbar	Save (File tab)		CTRL+S
Scroll, Up/Down One Line	WD 11	Click scroll arrow at top/bottom of vertical scroll bar			
Scroll, Up/Down One Screen	WD 11	Click above/below scroll box on vertical scroll bar			
Select Block of Text	WD 30	Click beginning, SHIFT-click end			
Select Character(s)	WD 30	Drag through characters			SHIFT+RIGHT ARROW or SHIFT+LEFT ARROW

Table 1: Microsoft Word 2010 Quick Reference Summary (continued)

Task	Page Number	Mouse	Ribbon	Shortcut Menu	Keyboard Shortcut
Select Entire Document	WD 30	In left margin, triple-click	Select button arrow (Home tab | Editing group)		CTRL+A
Select Graphic	WD 30	Click graphic			
Select Group of Words	WD 27	Drag mouse pointer through words			CTRL+SHIFT+RIGHT ARROW
Select Line	WD 15	Click in left margin			SHIFT+DOWN ARROW
Select Multiple Lines	WD 21	Drag mouse pointer in left margin			SHIFT+DOWN ARROW
Select Nonadjacent Items	WD 15	Select first item, hold down CTRL key while selecting item(s)			
Select Paragraph	WD 30	Triple-click paragraph			CTRL+SHIFT+DOWN ARROW or CTRL+SHIFT+UP ARROW
Select Sentence	WD 30	CTRL-click			
Select Word	WD 30	Double-click word			CTRL+SHIFT+RIGHT ARROW or CTRL+SHIFT+LEFT ARROW
Shade Paragraph	WD 20		Shading button arrow (Home tab | Paragraph group)		
Spelling, Check as You Type	WD 9	Click word, Spelling and Grammar Check icon on status bar		Right-click error, click correct word on shortcut menu	
Text Effect, Apply	WD 19		Text Effects button (Home tab | Font group)		
Theme Colors, Change	WD 28		Change Styles button (Home tab | Styles group)		
Underline	WD 27	Underline button on Mini toolbar	Underline button (Home tab | Font group)	Font, Font tab (Font dialog box)	CTRL+U
Undo	WD 23	Undo button on Quick Access Toolbar			CTRL+Z
Zoom Document	WD 33	Zoom Out or Zoom In button on status bar	Zoom button (View tab | Zoom group)		
Zoom One Page	WD 41		One Page button (View tab | Zoom group)		

Table 2: Microsoft PowerPoint 2010 Quick Reference Summary

Task	Page Number	Mouse	Ribbon	Shortcut Menu	Keyboard Shortcut
Clip Art, Insert	PPT 27	Clip Art icon in slide	Clip Art button (Insert tab | Images group)		
Clip Art, Photo, or Shape, Move	PPT 36	Drag			ARROW KEYS move selected image in small increments
Document Properties, Change	PPT 46		Properties button (File tab | Info tab)		
Document Theme, Choose	PPT 5		More button (Design tab | Themes group)		

Table 2: Microsoft PowerPoint 2010 Quick Reference Summary *(continued)*

Task	Page Number	Mouse	Ribbon	Shortcut Menu	Keyboard Shortcut
Font Size, Increase	PPT 11	Increase Font Size button or Font Size box arrow on Mini toolbar	Increase Font Size button or Font Size box arrow (Home tab | Font group)		CTRL+SHIFT+>
Font, Change Color	PPT 13	Font Color button or Font Color button arrow on Mini toolbar	Font Color button or Font Color button arrow (Home tab | Font group)	Font, Font tab (Font dialog box)	CTRL+SHIFT+F
List Level, Increase	PPT 17	Increase List Level button on Mini toolbar	Increase List Level button (Home tab | Paragraph group)		TAB or ALT+SHIFT+RIGHT ARROW
List Level, Decrease	PPT 18	Decrease List Level button on Mini toolbar	Decrease List Level button (Home tab | Paragraph group)		SHIFT+TAB or ALT+SHIFT+LEFT ARROW
Next Slide	PPT 25	Next Slide button on vertical scroll bar or next slide thumbnail on Slides tab			PAGE DOWN
Open Presentation	PPT 50		Open (File tab)		CTRL+O
Photo, Insert	PPT 32	Insert Picture from File icon on slide or Insert Clip Art icon on slide	Picture button or Clip Art button (Insert tab | Images group)		
Previous Slide	PPT 26	Previous Slide button on vertical scroll bar or click previous slide thumbnail on Slides tab			PAGE UP
Print a Presentation	PPT 51		Print button (File tab | Print tab)		CTRL+P
Quit PowerPoint	PPT 50	Close button on title bar	Exit (File tab)	Right-click Microsoft PowerPoint button on taskbar, click Close window	ALT+F4
Resize	PPT 33	Drag sizing handles	Enter height and width values (Picture Tools Format tab | Size group or Drawing Tools Format tab | Size group)	Format Picture or Format Shape, Size tab; or enter height and width in Shape Height and Shape Width boxes	
Save a Presentation	PPT 14	Save button on Quick Access Toolbar	Save or Save As (File tab)		CTRL+S or F12
Slide, Add	PPT 14		New Slide button (Home tab | Slides group)		CTRL+M
Slide, Arrange	PPT 39	Drag slide in Slides tab or Outline tab to new position, or in Slide Sorter view drag to new position			
Slide, Duplicate	PPT 38		New Slide arrow (Home tab | Slides group), Duplicate Selected Slides		

Table 2: Microsoft PowerPoint 2010 Quick Reference Summary *(continued)*

Task	Page Number	Mouse	Ribbon	Shortcut Menu	Keyboard Shortcut
Slide, Select Layout	PPT 21		Layout button or New Slide arrow (Home tab | Slides group)		
Slide Show View	PPT 47	Slide Show button at lower-right PowerPoint window	Slide Show button (Slide Show tab | Start Slide Show group)		F5
Slide Show, End	PPT 49	Click black ending slide		End Show	ESC or HYPHEN
Text, Bold	PPT 20	Bold button on Mini toolbar	Bold button (Home tab | Font group)	Font, Font tab (Font dialog box)	CTRL+B
Text, Change Color	PPT 13	Font Color button or Font Color button arrow on Mini toolbar	Font Color button or Font Color button arrow (Home tab | Font group)	Font, Font tab (Font dialog box)	
Text, Delete	PPT 41		Cut button (Home tab | Clipboard group)	Cut	DELETE or CTRL+X or BACKSPACE
Text, Italicize	PPT 11	Italic button on Mini toolbar	Italic button (Home tab | Font group)	Font, Font tab (Font dialog box)	CTRL+I
Text, Select Paragraph	PPT 10	Triple-click paragraph			SHIFT+DOWN ARROW or SHIFT+UP ARROW
Text, Select Word	PPT 12	Double-click word			CTRL+SHIFT+RIGHT ARROW or CTRL+SHIFT+LEFT ARROW
Transition, Add	PPT 43		Transitions tab | Transition to This Slide group		ALT+A , T

Table 3: Microsoft Excel 2010 Quick Reference Summary

Task	Page Number	Mouse	Ribbon	Shortcut Menu	Keyboard Shortcut
All data in a cell, Select	EX 51	Double-click if there are no spaces in data			
Auto Fill	EX 18	Drag fill handle	Auto Fill Options button (Home tab | Editing group)		
AutoCalculate	EX 48	Select range | right-click AutoCalculate area | click calculation			
Bold	EX 25	Bold button on Mini toolbar	Bold button (Home tab | Font group)	Format Cells on shortcut menu | Font tab | Bold	CTRL+B
Cell Entries, Clear Selected	EX 52	Drag fill handle from empty cell through cells with entries	Clear button (Home tab | Editing group) | Clear Contents	Clear Contents on shortcut menu	DELETE
Cell Style, Change	EX 52		Cell Styles button (Home tab | Styles group)		
Cell, Highlight	EX 19	Drag mouse pointer			

Table 3: Microsoft Excel 2010 Quick Reference Summary (continued)

Task	Page Number	Mouse	Ribbon	Shortcut Menu	Keyboard Shortcut
Cell, Select	EX 34	Click cell or click Name box, type cell reference, press ENTER			Use arrow keys
Cells, Merge and Center	EX 28	Merge & Center button on Mini toolbar	Merge & Center button (Home tab | Alignment group)	Format Cells on shortcut menu | Alignment tab	
Characters to left of insertion point, Delete	EX 50				BACKSPACE
Characters to right of insertion point, Delete	EX 50				DELETE
Characters, Highlight	EX 51	Drag through adjacent characters			SHIFT+RIGHT ARROW or SHIFT+LEFT ARROW
Chart, Add	EX 38		Charts group | Insert tab		
Color Text	EX 27	Font Color button on Mini toolbar	Font Color button arrow (Home tab | Font group)		
Column Width	EX 33	Drag column heading boundary		Column Width on shortcut menu	
Complete an Entry	EX 8	Click Enter box			Press ENTER
Document Properties, Change	EX 43		Properties button (File tab | Info tab)		
Document Properties, Print	EX 45		File tab | Print tab, first box arrow (Settings area)		
Document Properties, Set or View	EX 43		File | Info tab		
Entry, Complete	EX 8	Click Enter box			Press ENTER
Font Color	EX 27	Font Color box arrow on Mini toolbar	Font Color button arrow (Home tab | Font group)	Format Cells on shortcut menu | Font tab	
Font Size, Decrease	EX 26	Font Size box arrow on Mini toolbar	Decrease Font Size button (Home tab | Font group)	Format Cells on shortcut menu | Font tab	
Font Size, Increase	EX 26	Font Size box arrow on Mini toolbar	Increase Font Size button (Home tab | Font group)	Format Cells | Font Tab	
Font Type	EX 24	Font box arrow on Mini toolbar	Font box (Home tab | Font group)	Format Cells | Font tab	
Font, Change	EX 24	Font Size box arrow on Mini toolbar	Font box arrow (Home tab | Font group)	Format Cells | Font tab	
light Cells	EX 18	Drag mouse pointer			SHIFT+ARROW KEY
diting	EX 50	Double-click cell			F2
es, Toggle	EX 50				INSERT
	EX 8	Click			Use arrow keys
	EX 51	Point to left of first character and click			HOME
	EX 51	Point to right of last character and click			END

Table 3: Microsoft Excel 2010 Quick Reference Summary *(continued)*

Task	Page Number	Mouse	Ribbon	Shortcut Menu	Keyboard Shortcut
Numbers, Format	EX 31	Accounting Number Format, Percent Style, or Comma Style button on Mini toolbar	Cell Styles button (Home tab | Styles group) or Accounting Number Format, Percent Style, or Comma Style button (Home tab | Number group), or Format Cells: Number dialog box launcher | Accounting, or Percentage or Number Format list arrow | Accounting or Percentage		
Open a Workbook	EX 48		Open or Recent (File tab)		CTRL+O
Print Worksheet	EX 46		File tab | Print tab		CTRL+P
Quit Excel	EX 47	Close button on right side of title bar	Exit (File tab)		
Range, Deselect	EX 18	Click outside range			
Range, Select	EX 28	Drag fill handle through range			
Redo	EX 51	Redo button on Quick Access Toolbar			CTRL+Y
Save Workbook	EX 20	Save button on Quick Access Toolbar	Save (File tab | Save button)		CTRL+S
Save Workbook, New Name	EX 20	Save button on Quick Access Toolbar			
Save Workbook, Same Name	EX 20	Save button on Quick Access Toolbar	Save (File tab | Save button)		CTRL+S
Select Cell	EX 7	Click cell or click Name box, type cell reference, press ENTER			Use arrow keys
Select Entire Worksheet	EX 52	Click Select All button			CTRL+A
Selected characters, Delete	EX 50		Cut button (Home tab | Clipboard group)		DELETE
Selected Chart, Delete	EX 53				DELETE
Sheet Name, Change	EX 42	Double-click type name		Rename on shortcut menu	
Sum	EX 15	Click Insert Function button in formula bar | SUM in Select a function list | OK | range | OK	Sum button (Home tab | Editing group)		ALT+EQUAL SIGN (=) twice
Text, Delete after typing but before pressing the ENTER key	EX 8	Click Cancel box in formula bar			Press ESC
Text, Delete while typing	EX 8				Press BACKSPACE
Undo	EX 51	Undo button on Quick Access Toolbar			CTRL+Z
Worksheet Name, Change	EX 42	Double-click sheet tab, type name		Rename on shortcut menu	
Worksheet, Clear	EX 52		Select All button | Clear button (Home tab | Editing group)		CTRL A, pre
Worksheet, Preview	EX 46		File tab | Print tab		CTRL+P

Table 4: Microsoft Access 2010 Quick Reference Summary

Task	Page Number	Mouse	Ribbon	Shortcut Menu	Keyboard Shortcut
Close Object	AC 23	Close button for object		Right-click item, Close	
Column Headings, Modify	AC 54			Right-click field name, Rename Field	
Column, Resize	AC 54, AC 55	Double-click right boundary of field selector in datasheet		Right-click field name, Field Width	
Criterion, Use	AC 46	Right-click query, Design View, Criteria row			
Data, Import	AC 38		Button for imported data format (External Data tab | Import & Link group)	Right-click object, click selected format on Import menu	
Database Properties, Change	AC 59		View and edit database properties link (File tab | Info tab)		
Database, Create	AC 13		Blank database button (File tab | New tab)		
Form, Create	AC 48		Form button (Create tab | Forms group)		
Open Database	AC 27		Open button (File tab)		
Open Table	AC 24	Double-click table in Navigation Pane		Right-click table in Navigation Pane, click Open in shortcut menu	
Preview or Print Object	AC 31		Print or Print Preview button (File tab | Print tab)		CTRL+P, ENTER
Query, Create using Simple Query Wizard	AC 43		Query Wizard button (Create tab | Queries group)		
Record, Add	AC 28	New (blank) record button in Navigation buttons	New button (Home tab | Records Group)		CTRL+PLUS SIGN (+)
Remaining Fields in Table, Define	AC 19	In Datasheet view, click Click to Add field (Fields tab)			
Report, Create	AC 52		Report button (Create tab | Reports group)		
....e Object	AC 21	Save button on Quick Access Toolbar	File tab, Save		CTRL+S
...ate in Design View	AC 33		Table Design button (Create tab | Tables group)		
....esign View	AC 21		View button arrow (Table Tools Fields tab | Views group), Design View		
	AC 57		Totals button (Report Layout Tools Design tab | Grouping & Totals group)		